# Public Productivity Handbook

# PUBLIC ADMINISTRATION AND PUBLIC POLICY

## A Comprehensive Publication Program

*Executive Editor*

**JACK RABIN**
Professor of Public Administration and Public Policy
School of Public Affairs
The Capital College
The Pennsylvania State University—Harrisburg
Middletown, Pennsylvania

# Public Productivity Handbook

Second Edition, Revised and Expanded

**edited by**

## Marc Holzer

*Rutgers, The State of University of New Jersey*
*Newark, New Jersey, U.S.A.*

## Seok-Hwan Lee

*The Catholic University of Korea*
*Songsim Campus, South Korea*

MARCEL DEKKER, INC.          NEW YORK · BASEL

The previous edition was published as the *Public Productivity Handbook* edited by Marc Holzer.

**Library of Congress Cataloging-in-Publication Data**
A catalog record for this book is available from the Library of Congress.

**ISBN: 0-8247-4721-6**
This book is printed on acid-free paper.

**Headquarters**
Marcel Dekker, Inc., 270 Madison Avenue, New York, NY 10016, U.S.A.
tel: 212-696-9000; fax: 212-685-4540

**Distribution and Customer Service**
Marcel Dekker, Inc., Cimarron Road, Monticello, New York 12701, U.S.A.
tel: 800-228-1160; fax: 845-796-1772

**Eastern Hemisphere Distribution**
Marcel Dekker AG, Hutgasse 4, Postfach 812, CH-4001 Basel, Switzerland
tel: 41-61-260-6300; fax: 41-61-260-6333

**World Wide Web**
http://www.dekker.com

The publisher offers discounts on this book when ordered in bulk quantities. For more information, write to Special Sales/Professional Marketing at the headquarters address above.

# Preface

This handbook is primarily directed to public administration professionals who are seeking insights into improving productivity and performance in the context of efficiency, effectiveness, quality, and outcomes. There is no simple definition of this group. Virtually all public servants in professional, managerial, and supervisory positions are responsible for improving productivity, and thus could utilize parts of this volume.

The rationale for this handbook is that the field of public administration is in need of a systematic, detailed approach to the concepts of productivity and performance improvement. Although the term "productivity" has been utilized for many years, it is often simplified, misinterpreted, and misapplied. The term "performance" may represent a more attractive conceptual path toward improvement. But both concepts are underlying premises of public administration and the core of an ongoing effort (or steady movement) that persists because it addresses a fundamental linkage: a productive society is dependent upon high-performing government. If productivity and performance improvement is not a formal movement, in part for lack of a consistent designation, it is increasingly recognized as a legitimate expectation, as a rational and lasting emphasis that is a central assumption of federal, state, or municipal administration, and the underlying premise of a relatively loosely coordinated series of efforts to date.

Improved government is a concept that is comprehensive and complicated, and incorporates many elements. The objective of this book, therefore, is to define the emerging field of productivity and performance improvement as an umbrella covering a range of subjects and strategies. In the process, we hope to dispel fears and myths, such as "common sense" assumptions that outputs and outcomes of public agencies cannot be measured; that managerial risks outweigh rewards; that work will be accelerated and safety standards neglected; that labor, fearing unfair treatment and loss of jobs, will refuse to cooperate; that improved performance is a normal expectation that does not require specific efforts; or even that the private sector model and privatization are the only paths to productive government.

In pursuit of more efficient and effective utilization of scarce resources, both sectors have complemented good intentions with good insights, technical approaches used by other organizations, enlightened leadership grounded in the social and psychological realities of groups and individuals, and comprehensive management systems. But only the public sector has drawn lessons from both public and private sector organizations; the private sector remains chauvinistic and myopic.

A quarter of a century ago the federal government sponsored the *Productivity Improvement Handbook for State and Local Government* (George Washnis, Editor. New York: Wiley, 1980), a thorough compilation of some 1492 pages. Now out of print, both its worth and its absence helped motivate this project, beginning with the first edition of the *Public Productivity Handbook*. One function of this volume is to serve as a synopsis of a rapidly growing literature of books, reports, and articles. It may be especially timely, as the first decade of the twenty-first century is likely to be an era of relative austerity in the public sector, a period in which productive alternatives will be eagerly pursued and the field of productivity and performance improvement will be increasingly relevant.

This project is the product of many labors. Although the authors represented herein are the most obvious contributors, other members of the team include:

Jack Rabin, editor of the Public Administration and Public Policy Series, who encouraged and supported this compendium from proposal to publication.

Paige Force and other members of the production staff at Marcel Dekker, Inc., who have been exceedingly patient and professional in all respects;

Arwiphawee Srithongrung at the University of Illinois at Springfield,

Sung-Ryul Ahn at Kookmin University, South Korea,

Joon-Yeon Park at Korea University, South Korea who helped construct the index;

This volume is dedicated to our family members—Madeleine Holzer and our sons, Ben and Matt and his wife Wendy; Kyung-Yeon, and our son, Joshua (Dong-Joon)—who patiently tolerated our compulsive attention to this effort.

*Marc Holzer*
*Seok-Hwan Lee*

# Contents

# Contributors

**Mohamad G. Alkadry** is an Assistant Professor of Public Administration at West Virginia University, Morgantown, West Virginia, U.S.A., where he teaches citizen participation and research methods. He is the author of several publications in the area of public management and citizen participation. His current research focuses on public participation, organizational behavior, and theories of democracy in an age of globalization. He received his Ph.D. from Florida Atlantic University. He finished his other graduate and undergraduate education at the American University of Beirut (Lebanon), Carleton University (Canada), and Concordia University (Quebec). He is co-editor (with Hugh Miller) of *These Things Happen: Stories from the Public Sector*.

**David N. Ammons** is a Professor of Public Administration and Government and Director of the Master of Public Administration Program at the University of North Carolina, Chapel Hill, North Carolina, U.S.A. His works include *Municipal Benchmarks: Assessing Local Performance and Establishing Community Standards* (Sage Publications, 2001), *Tools for Decision Making: A Practical Guide for Local Government* (CQ Press, 2002), and other books on local government management. He consults with public sector units on organizational and management concerns, including performance measurement, benchmarking, and productivity improvement.

**Maria P. Aristigueta** is an Associate Professor and Associate Policy Scientist with the Institute of Public Administration at the School of Urban Affairs and Public Policy, University of Delaware, Newark, Delaware, U.S.A. Her teaching and research interests are primarily in the areas of public sector management and include topics around the issues of performance measurement, strategic planning, public engagement, and organizational behavior. She has a doctorate in public administration from the University of Southern California.

**Deborah A. Auger** is on the faculty of the School of Urban Affairs and Public Policy at the University of Delaware, Newark, Delaware, U.S.A., where she directs the MPA MidCareer Program and teaches courses both on public administration and on nonprofit leadership and management. Her current research is in the area of government-nonprofit relations in the human services. She received her Master's degree from the Maxwell School at Syracuse University and her Ph.D. from the Massachusetts Institute of Technology. She also holds an appointment as Associate Scholar in the Center on Nonprofits and Philanthropy at the Urban Institute in Washington, D.C.

**Evan M. Berman**, Ph.D., is an Associate Professor in the Department of Public Administration, University of Central Florida, Orlando, Florida, U.S.A. He has over 75 publications in the areas of productivity, local government, ethics and human resource management. He is active in the American Society for Public Administration and is past chair of the Section of Personnel and Labor Relations. He is the 2001 winner of the Public Administration Review Editor's Choice award. He has served as a policy analyst for the National Science Foundation and as a consultant to the National Academy of Sciences and U.S. Congress. He is the author of *Essential Statistics for Public Managers and Policy Analysts* (CQ Press, 2002), Human *Resource Management in Public Service* (Sage, 2001, with Bowman, West and Van Wart) and *Third Sector Management* (Georgetown University Press, 2001, with Werther).

**James S. Bowman** is Professor of Public Administration at the Askew School of Public Administration and Policy at Florida State University, Tallahassee, Florida, U.S.A. His primary research area is human resource management. Noted for his work in ethics and quality management, he also has done research in environmental administration. He is the author of nearly 100 journal articles and book chapters, as well as the editor of five anthologies. Bowman's latest co-authored work is *Human Resource Management in Public Service: Paradoxes, Problems, and Processes* (Sage, 2001). He is editor-in-chief of *Public Integrity*, a journal sponsored by four professional associations; he also serves on the editorial boards of three other professional journals. A past National Association of Schools of Public Affairs and Administration Fellow as well as a Kellogg Fellow, he has experience in both the military and civil service in addition to business.

**Willa Bruce** is a professor in the DPA program at the University of Illinois, Springfield, Illinois, U.S.A., and formerly Kayser Professor at the University of Nebraska at Omaha. She is an advocate for a government service in which citizens receive courteous and equitable assistance delivered by employees who are able to use their own strengths and talents in a work place where they are appreciated and empowered. Her 6 books, 7 book chapters, 36 refereed journal articles, and 64 conference presentations address the areas of administrative ethics, spirituality of work, job performance and satisfaction, and dual career couples. Her three entries in the *International Encyclopedia of Public Administration* are on ethics. She is currently working on a book titled *Private Morality: Public Service*.

**Kathe Callahan** (M.P.A., Ph.D. Rutgers University) is an assistant professor of public administration at Rutgers, The State University of New Jersey, Newark, New Jersey, U.S.A., and an Associate Director of the National Center for Public Productivity. Prof. Callahan publishes on the topics of citizen participation, public sector productivity improvement, and performance measurement. Her most recent publications include "Citizen Participation in Budgeting" co-edited with Jerry Miller, a symposium in the journal of the *Public Budgeting, Accounting and Financial Management*; and "The Utilization and Effectiveness of Citizen Advisory Committees in the Budget Process of Local Governments" in the *Public Budgeting, Accounting and Financial Management*.

**Beverly A. Cigler**, Professor of Public Policy and Administration, Pennsylvania State University, Harrisburg, Pennsylvania, U.S.A., was a Visiting Scholar in the Pennsylvania legislature during 2000–2002 and is a former NASPAA-FEMA Fellow. She specializes in state-local relations, focusing on fiscal issues, alternative service delivery, multi-community and intermunicipal collaboration, and hazards and growth management. Cigler has presented more than 140 invited speeches and testimony nationwide, and dozens of professional papers. She has published approximately 145 academic articles and book chapters and is the co-author/co-editor of 7 completed and 2 forthcoming books. Cigler has received several national and state awards for her research and professional services, including the Donald Stone Intergovernmental Research Award from ASPA's intergovernmental section, PSH's research award, a Distinguished Alumni Award from Thiel College, and the "Friend of County Government" award from the County Commissioners Association of Pennsylvania (CCAP).

**Ali Farazmand** is a Professor in the School of Public Administration at Florida Atlantic University, Fort Lauderdale, Florida, U.S.A., where he teaches administrative theory, organization theory and behavior, human resources management, ethics, and public management. He is the author and editor of over 18 books and handbooks, and has published over 70 journal articles and book chapters. He is also the founding Editor-in-chief of *Public Organization Review: a Global Journal*. His current research areas include organization theory (elite theory, chaos and transformation theories, and institutional theory), ethics and accountability, strategic management, privatization, governance, globalization and the state, political economy, and crisis management. He is currently working on the following books, *Globalization, Governance, and Administration*; and *Building Human Capital for the 21st Century*; and *Global Management of Crises*.

**Gerald T. Gabris** is a Professor in the Division of Public Administration at Northern Illinois University, DeKalb, Illinois, U.S.A. He is a former managing editor of the *Public Administration Review* and his research focuses primarily in the area of leadership, organization development, and human resources management.

**Gerasimos A. Gianakis** is currently an associate professor of public management in the Sawyer School of Management at Suffolk University, Boston, Massachusetts, U.S.A. where he teaches courses in organizational behavior, budgeting and quantitative analysis. He received his Ph.D. in public administration from the Florida State University in 1992. His research has been published in a wide range of journals, and he is co-author of *Local Government Budgeting: A Managerial Approach*.

**Ray Gonzales** is the Research Director at a United Way in northern New Jersey and a Ph.D., candidate in Public Administration at Rutgers, The State University of New Jersey, Newark, New Jersey, U.S.A. His dissertation looks at managerial perceptions of outcome assessment system utility in the provision of human services. He holds a bachelor's degree in Political Science from California State University, Los Angeles, and a master's degree in Communication Studies from West Virginia University. His other academic interests include research methods, municipal finance, and emergency management. He enjoys teaching statistics and consults with human service organizations and universities in the name of developing assessment capacity.

**Mary E. Guy** holds the Jerry Collins Eminent Scholar Chair in Public Administration in the Reubin O'D. Askew School of Public Administration & Policy, Florida State University, Tallahassee, Florida, U.S.A. She has published numerous books and articles on public management, focusing on the human resource dimension to productivity. She is a Fellow of the National Academy of Public Administration, past president of the American Society for Public Administration and Editor-in-Chief of the *Review of Public Personnel Administration*.

**Arie Halachmi** is Professor of Public Management at Tennessee State University, Nashville, Tennessee, U.S.A. He has a research appointment at the National Center For Public Administration, Zhongshan University, Guangdong, Guangzhou, China, and is a Visiting Professor at the University of Twente (The Netherlands). He is the author/editor of many books and hundreds of articles. He has been a productivity consultant to governments all over the world.

**Gary Helfand** is Professor of Public Administration and head of the Justice Administration Program at the University of Hawaii—West Oahu, Pearl City, Hawaii, U.S.A. He received his Ph.D. in Public Administration from New York University and his MPA from Baruch College in New York. He has also taught at the graduate level at John Jay College of Criminal Justice and Public Affairs in New York, and has published numerous articles and four books in public administration and criminal justice. He has also done extensive management consulting in these fields for federal, state, and local agencies.

**Marc Holzer** is Chair and Professor of Public Administration at Rutgers, The State University of New Jersey, Newark, New Jersey, U.S.A. Dr. Holzer also serves as Director of the Ph.D. Program in Public Administration and as Executive Director of the National Center for Public Productivity. His primary research emphasis has been in public sector productivity, a field he helped establish and develop. He is the founder and Editor-in-Chief of the *Public Performance and Management Review* (formerly *Public Productivity and Management Review*). He is the author or editor of fourteen books, most recently *Classics of Public Service* (Westview, 2000), *Government at Work* (Sage, 1998) and the *International Encyclopedia of Public Policy and Administration* (Associate Editor) (Westview, 1998). Dr. Holzer is widely published in numerous professional journals, compendia and symposia. Dr. Holzer is the Past President of the American Society for Public Administration (2000-2001), and is a recipient of several national awards in the field: the Charles H. Levine Memorial Award for Demonstrated Excellence in Teaching, Research and Service to the Community, 2000; the Donald Stone National ASPA Achievement Award, 1994; and the National Association of Schools of Public Affairs and Administration Excellence in Teaching Award, Oct. 1998. Dr. Holzer holds the Ph.D. in Political Science and the Master of Public Administration degrees, both from the University of Michigan.

**Douglas M. Ihrke** is an Associate Professor in the Department of Political Science at the University of Wisconsin, Milwaukee, Wisconsin, U.S.A. He is the Director of the Public Administration program and his research focuses on local government, human resources management, and organizational change.

**George Julnes** is Assistant Professor of Psychology and Director of the Center for Policy and Program Evaluation (www.usu.edu/eval) at Utah State University, Logan, Utah, U.S.A. He is an author of numerous articles in the major journals in the field of evaluation, including *Evaluation Review*, *Evaluation*, and the *American Journal of Evaluation*. In addition, he has been an editor of two volumes of *New Directions for Evaluation*, the most recent being a volume on the "Outcomes of Welfare Reform for Families Leaving TANF." An acknowledged scholar in the area of integrating quantitative and qualitative methods in the study of policy problems, he co-authored the 2000 book, *Evaluation: An Integrated Framework For Understanding, Guiding, and Improving Policies and Programs* (San Francisco: Jossey-Bass).

**Patria de Lancer Julnes**, Ph.D. is Assistant Professor in the Department of Political Science and coordinator of the Master of Social Science in Public Administration at Utah State University, Logan, Utah, U.S.A. Her research focuses on public productivity—measurement and management, comparative public administration reform, and policy analysis. She teaches graduate and undergraduate courses in public policy, public administration, and research methods. She serves as a member of the Board of Directors of ASPA's Center for Accountability and Performance (CAP) and in NASPAA's International Network for Public Administration Education.

**Hwang-Sun Kang** is an Assistant Professor of Public Administration at the KonKuk University, Seoul, South Korea where he teaches public management and performance management. He has published in the areas of governance, knowledge management, and performance measurement. He has published several journal articles in these areas and has coauthored several books: *Performance Measurement Initiatives, Transparent Bureaucracy, Citizen-Driven Performance Measurement,* and *Building Good Governance*. Kang is a former Research Fellow of Seoul Development Institute, as well as a Senior Research Fellow of National Center for Public Productivity. He has also worked with many Korean government agencies on establishing and refining performance management systems.

**Seok-Hwan Lee** is an Assistant Professor of Public Administration, The Catholic University of Korea, Songsim Campus, South Korea. Prior to joining the faculty at the university, he was also an Assistant Professor in the Doctor of Public Administration (DPA) program and appointed faculty in the Abraham Lincoln Presidential Center for Governmental Studies at the University of Illinois, Springfield. His research interests include productivity improvement in the public sector, organization theory and behavior, and human resource management. He previously served as the Assistant Editor of the *Public Performance and Management Review* (formerly the *Public Productivity and Management Review*) from 1998–2000. He is the author/coauthor of a variety of scholarly journals, book chapters and professional publications, including the *Public Administration Review, Review of Public Personnel Administration, Public Productivity & Management Review, International Journal of Organizational Analysis,* and the *International Review of Public Administration*. He also serves on editorial boards of *Public Performance & Management Review, Review of Public Personnel Administration, Public Voices,* and the *International Review of Public Administration*. Dr. Lee received the MPA degree from Korea University, South Korea and the Ph.D. degree in Public Administration from Rutgers, the State University of New Jersey.

**Helisse Levine** is a Ph.D. student in the Graduate Department of Public Administration at Rutgers, The State University of New Jersey, Newark, New Jersey, U.S.A. Her research interests include public management and finance.

**Richard A. Loverd**, currently retired in Acton, Massachusetts, U.S.A., was a professor at the University of Connecticut, the University of Pittsburgh, Villanova University and Northeastern University. He has published in such journals as the *Public Productivity and Management Review*, *Public Administration Review*, *Policy Studies Journal* and the *Presidential Studies Quarterly*. In 1997, he wrote a book entitled, *Leadership for the Public Service*, published by Prentice Hall. He holds MPA and PhD Degrees from the Syracuse University Maxwell School and an MBA from Columbia.

**James Melitski** is now with Marist College, Poughkeepsie, New York, U.S.A. and previously served as director of the E-governance Institute at Rutgers, The State University of New Jersey, Newark, New Jersey, U.S.A. in the Graduate Department of Public Administration. His Ph.D. dissertation on Information Technology (IT) in the public sector examined how state governments have successfully used the Internet to communicate, enhance participation, and deliver services. His research interests include e-government, state science and technology policies, citizen participation, performance measurement and nonprofit management. Prior to his work at Rutgers University, James Melitski was a financial manager for a nonprofit organization in Washington, DC where he worked with the U.S. Environmental Protection Agency's Environmental Education Division.

**Gerald J. Miller** is Professor of Public Administration, Rutgers, The State University of New Jersey, Newark, New Jersey, U.S.A. The author of over fifty research articles, his work has been published in numerous journals in the United States and abroad, including the *Public Administration Review*, *Policy Studies Journal*, *Public Productivity and Management Review*, *International Journal of Public Administration* and the *Public Administration Quarterly*. Having published over twenty books, he is the author of *Government Financial Management Theory* (Marcel Dekker) and co-author of the *Public Budgeting Laboratory* (Vinson Insitute of Government, University of Georgia). He is the editor of the *Handbook of Debt Management* and coeditor of the *Handbook of Research Methods in Public Administration* (with Marcia Whicker), the *Handbook of Strategic Management* (with Jack Rabin and W. Bartley Hildreth), the *Handbook of Public Administration* (with Jack Rabin and W. Bartley Hildreth), the *Handbook of Public Personnel Administration and Labor Relations*, and the *Handbook of Public Sector Labor Relations* (both with Jack Rabin, Thomas Vocino and W. Bartley Hildreth) (all titles, Marcel Dekker, Inc.). In addition, he has published *Managerial Behavior and Organization Demands* (ed. with Robert T. Golembiewski and Frank K. Gibson published by F. E. Peacock), *Budget Management, and Budgeting: Formulation and Execution* (both edited with Jack Rabin and W. Bartley Hildreth, published by the Vinson Institute of Government, University of Georgia). He is an editorial board member of eight journals. He serves as a book review editor for the *Public Administration Quarterly*. As a former investment banker with the firm of Rauscher, Pierce, Refsnes, Inc. (Phoenix, Arizona, now RBC Dain Rauscher, Inc.), Dr. Miller continues an active consulting practice in the United States, Canada and Western Europe with clients including national, state, and local government organizations in legislative, executive and judicial branches of government, as well as private businesses and business and public sector associations such as the Chartered Institute of Public Finance and Accountancy (England and Wales), the Government Finance Officers Association of the U.S. and Canada and the International City and County Management Association. His research seeks understanding and asserts the dominance of resource allocation in the control of public organizations; his work has received continuous and substantial support from government and private donors in the United States, Canada, England and Wales, and the European Union. Dr. Miller received the B. S. Degree in economics and M.P.A. degree from Auburn University. He received the Ph. D. Degree in political science from the University of Georgia.

**Meredith A. Newman** is an Associate Professor and Chair of the Department of Public Administration, University of Illinois at Springfield, Springfield, Illinois, U.S.A. and holds a Ph.D. from Deakin University, Australia. Professor Newman has written widely on the subjects of public management, and gender and workplace issues. Prior to her current career in academia, she served with the Australian Foreign Service and later with the U.S. Department of State. Professor Newman is the recipient of several awards, including the Distinguished Research Award of the American Society for Public Administration, Section for Women in Public Administration; the Research Excellence Award, Washington State University Vancouver; and the Editors' Choice Award, Public Administration Review. Newman is a past-National Council Representative of ASPA.

**Dorothy Olshfski** is an Associate Professor in the Graduate Department of Public Administration at Rutgers, The State University of New Jersey, Newark, New Jersey, U.S.A. For six years she served as managing editor of the *Public Performance and Management Review* and she is presently the case editor for that publication. Her research examines executive behavior, organizational commitment, and executive and middle level managers as they operate in the policy making process.

**Theodore H. Poister** is Professor of Public Administration at Georgia State University, Atlanta, Georgia, U.S.A. where he specializes in public management and applied research methods. Much of his research focuses on strategic planning and management, performance measurement, and quality and productivity improvement in government, and he has published widely on these topics in the major public administration journals. Poister has a particular interest in transportation policy and management, and he recently completed a review of innovative strategic management practices in state transportation departments.

**Byron E. Price** is an Assistant Professor at the Department of Public Administration, Rutgers, The State University of New Jersey, Newark, New Jersey, U.S.A. He received his Ph.D. in Public Policy and Administration from Mississippi State University in 2002. He taught program evaluation, public administration, American political systems, and public policy at the University of Dayton for and year and a half, and joined the Department of Public Administration at Rutgers in 2003. He has co-authored two book chapters on Mississippi politics and contributed three entries to the Malcolm X Encyclopedia. His current research agenda includes constitutional implications of public and private arrangements, prison privatization, and education reform. While at Mississippi State, he won an American Society of Engineering Science (ASEE) Summer Faculty Fellowship with the NASA Stennis Space Center.

**Ross Prizzia** is the Chair of the Professional Studies Division (Public and Business Administration) and a Professor of Public Administration at the University of

Hawaii—West Oahu, Pearl City, Hawaii, U.S.A. He received his Ph.D. at the University of Hawaii and M.A. at the State University of New York. He consults with public, private, and non-profit organizations, and has published various reports, articles, study guides, and two books in the areas of human resources, labor-relations, privatization, and environmental regulation in an international perspective.

**Jeffrey A. Raffel** is the Charles P. Messick Professor of Public Administration and the Director of the School of Urban Affairs and Public Policy at the University of Delaware, Newark, Delaware, U.S.A. Dr. Raffel has conducted research on state and local management as well as educational policy issues. His articles have appeared in a range of journals including the *Public Productivity and Management Review*, *Educational Evaluation and Policy Analysis*, and the *Journal of Urban Affairs*. His books include *Selling Cities* and the *Historical Dictionary of School Segregation and Desegregation*. Dr. Raffel received his Ph.D. in Political Science from M.I.T. and his A.B. in Political Science from the University of Rochester.

**Donijo Robbins** is an Assistant Professor for the School of Public & Nonprofit Administration at Grand Valley State University in Grand Rapids, Michigan, U.S.A. where she teaches courses in public budgeting, financial management, and research methods. Her research has appeared in the *Journal of Labor Research*, *Journal of Public Budgeting, Accounting, & Financial Management*, and the *Handbook of Research Methods in Public Administration* and it focuses on public economics, local economic development and budgeting issues. Professor Robbins received the B.S. degree (1994) in economics and political science from Central Michigan University, the M.A. degree (1995) in economics and the Ph.D. degree (1998) in public administration from Rutgers, The State University Of New Jersey in Newark.

**Roe Ann Roberts** is now the program coordinator of the Masters in Public Administration Program at Midwestern State University, Wichita Falls, Texas, U.S.A. She earned her Ph.D. in Public Administration (1989) and her Master's in Public Administration (1986) from Florida International University. In 1998, she was tenured at Eastern Washington University. At Eastern she was awarded the College of Business and Public Administration's "Outstanding Teacher of the Year" (1998) and the "Outstanding Research Award" (2002). She has also been listed in Who's Who's Among American Teachers in 1998 and 2002. During 2001–2002, she published an article on the impacts of communication on mammography rates in preventive medicine, had two papers and a poster accepted for the American Public Health Association's Annual Meeting for the fall 2002. The papers explore the use of alternative medicine by cystic fibrosis patients and health communication issues facing aging gay, lesbian, bisexual and transgendered individuals. The poster discusses the health effects of EPA's PM2.5 policy as applied to agriculture burning.

**Hindy Lauer Schachter** is a Professor in the School of Management at New Jersey Institute of Technology, Newark, New Jersey, U.S.A. She is the author of *Reinventing Government or Reinventing Ourselves: The Role of Citizen Owners in Making a Better Government* (SUNY Press, 1997), *Frederick Taylor and the Public Administration Community: A Reevaluation* (SUNY Press, 1989), and *Public Agency Communication: Theory and Practice* (Nelson Hall, 1983). Her articles have appeared in the *Public Administration Review*, *Administration and Society*, *Journal of Management History* and other journals.

**Montgomery Van Wart** is Professor of Public Administration at the University of Central Florida, Orlando, Florida, U.S.A. In the past he served as the Director of the Center for Public Service at Texas Tech University, the MPA Director at Iowa State University, and the Director of the Advanced Public Executive Program at Arizona State University. In addition to traditional faculty duties, he has specialized in providing executive and management training on both a national and regional basis. His books include *Handbook of Training and Development for the Public Sector* (Jossey-Bass), *Changing Public Sector Values* (Garland), and *Human Resource Management in Public Service* (with Berman, Bowman, and West; Sage). He has published extensively in *Public Performance and Management Review* and *Public Administration Review*, among others.

**Russell L. Williams** is a an Assistant Professor at the Department of Political Science and Public Administration, University of North Florida, Jacksonville, Florida, U.S.A. His research interests include human resource management, public administration ethics, organization theory, and leadership. He is the assistant editor of the *Review of Public Personnel Administration*. His work has appeared in *Public Administration Review*, *Public Integrity*, and *Public Productivity and Management Review*.

**Mengzhong Zhang** is the Associate Director and a Senior Research Fellow at the National Center for Public Productivity (NCPP) at Rutgers, The State University of New Jersey, Newark, New Jersey, U.S.A. He is the Associate Director of US/China Public Administration Secretariat (affiliated to ASPA, American Society for Public Administration). He is the Managing Editor of the *Chinese Public Administration Review*, Editorial Board member of *Public Performance and Management Review*, *Public Voices*, and an adjunct professor at more than ten universities in China. Mr. Zhang has a number of articles published in China, UK and USA. He is editor-in-Chief (with Marc Holzer) of the book *Chinese Public Administration in Exploration*. Mr. Zhang is the translator (and principal translator) of a number of books (from English to Chinese) and also translated articles from Chinese to English.

# Introduction

## Organization of the Handbook

Public sector productivity and performance are complex concepts, including top management leadership, committed people at all levels, performance measurement systems, effective teamwork, cooperative partnerships, employee training, reward structures, community involvement, technological innovations, feedback mechanisms, and budget management decisions. It is one thing for an organization to hope to see high levels of productivity and performance. It is another for that organization to see those high levels in reality. What this means is that productivity and performance improvement requires detailed, systematic approaches, and effective internal and external interconnections.

The impetus for this second edition is a demand from the field that the principles of improving public sector productivity and performance, which have evolved rapidly, now require more detailed, systematic approaches.

Accordingly, this handbook is structured in terms of four major parts.

Part I emphasizes that productivity and performance improvement must be systematically managed for improvement.

In the first chapter, "Mastering Public Productivity and Performance Improvement from a Productive Management Perspective," Marc Holzer and Seok-Hwan Lee begin by defining the terms productivity and performance in the public sector, recognizing that the use of the term productivity has been comingled with the term performance. They view the term productivity as a broad concept that includes the term performance. While admitting that productivity and performance improvements are not easy, particularly in the public sector, Holzer and Lee emphasize that well-constructed and well-managed public sector productivity programs will benefit all interested parties in a win-win relationship and that productive management is a function of intangible as well as tangible supports. Furthermore, from a productive management point of view, they suggest a productivity and performance improvement model that includes understandings of the role of leadership, multiple dimensions of employee commitment, maintaining psychologically balanced relationships between people, and multiple employee–organization relationships. Those concepts are woven into a ten-step capacity building model.

Hindy Lauer Schachter, in "Public Productivity in the Classical Age of Public Administration," points out that public administration stretches from Frederick Taylor's work on scientific management through the municipal reform literature into the principles work of the 1920s, 1930s, and early 1940s. In particular, this chapter explores the influence of scientific management on the public productivity literature. Schachter examines Taylor's work on factory productivity and its impact on the New York Bureau of Municipal Research, as well as Cooke's efforts and the principles literature. The chapter concludes with Simon's critique of the classical approach to public productivity.

Kathe Callahan's chapter, "Performance Measurement and Citizen Participation," explores the relationship between performance measurement and citizen participation. The value of involving citizens in the measurement of state and local government performance is discussed, as are the challenges associated with developing and sustaining meaningful participation techniques. Questions addressed in this chapter include: How do public administrators develop indicators of performance that are meaningful to citizens *and* public managers? How can public managers effectively communicate measures of performance to the public so that citizens can hold government accountable for results? How can public administrators develop appropriate participation techniques to foster and sustain citizen involvement? Citizen-driven performance measurement involves the use of measures or indicators that are socially relevant to citizens—they are easy to understand and have practical value. When citizens are involved in measuring performance, or when public administrators ensure the performance data they collect and report is meaningful to citizens, the data collected enables citizens to hold government officials accountable for performance and enables them to answer the question "Am I getting value for my tax dollar?" Models of success, primarily projects supported by the Alfred P. Sloan Foundation, are discussed throughout the chapter.

Gerasimos A. Gianakis' "Decision Making and Managerial Capacity in the Public Sector" points out that various views of public sector decision making are examined from the perspective of what is described as the elemental problem in public sector management: the public's desire to employ professional expertise and its need to control the managerial discretion necessary to apply that expertise effectively. This issue is operationalized as managerial capacity, or the ability to act responsibly and responsively in the identification and delivery of public services. Responsible action refers to how expertise is applied, and raises the question of "efficiency for what?" Responsive action recognizes the political environment of public management, and raises the question of "responsive to whom?" The failure of the discipline to develop realistic theories of public management decision-making has made the field vulnerable to irrelevant and potentially damaging market model approaches manifested by the New Public Management. The chapter concludes that managerial capacity in the public sector can be enhanced by focusing on the core responsibilities of individual areas of expertise, and on the necessity for the public organization to engage the public as a community of experts rather than as a collection of individual experts responding to particular constituencies.

Montgomery Van Wart's "Public Sector Values and Productivity" argues that public sector values determine the instruments of democratic accountability and responsibility, the structures, cultures, and processes of organizations, the way employees are treated, and even the definition of the concept of "publicness." Yet the challenges of understanding public sector values are manifold because they are numerous, often competing, and changing. Additionally, values are often poorly defined and inconsistently acted upon. Therefore, values have more than a passing importance to public administrators in general, and to their pursuit of productivity. First, values determine the very definition of productivity, as well as the definition of an appropriate organizational culture, structure, process, etc. Second, when values shift, definitions of productivity also shift. Third, and most important, confusion about values inevitably reduces productivity. For these reasons, public administrators must be able to discern the important value issues, articulate them dispassionately, and facilitate values discussions. The purpose of this chapter is to assist administrators in values clarification skills by discussing the nature of values, by identifying some important value clusters at both the macro and mid levels, and by relating some of the more difficult value shifts (and clashes) currently occurring in public administration.

"Privatization," by Marc Holzer, Byron E. Price, and Hwang-Sun Kang argues that despite government's "businesslike" innovations in quality, human resources and technology, the rush to privatize government has seemingly gained unstoppable momentum. Touted regularly by politicians and emphasized by the media, it is now virtually an unquestioned assumption. Privatization, however, is only one form of competition. An equally productive alternative is an expanded form of competition in which public organizations are competitive bidders. While competition is certainly an important assumption, it is not the only paradigm. The flip side of competition—cooperation—is also an essential productivity enhancement strategy, and one that is very often overlooked in the shadow of pressures for privatization. Yet joint public-private initiatives are options to which innovative public officials often turn, and cooperative arrangements for service provision are increasingly evident as the public sector seeks creative ways to stretch resources. They conclude that in contrast to privatization, these new relationships are joint problem-solving efforts, or partnerships, which may be initiated by either side. They are frequently recognized as working alliances between the work force and management; between levels of government and between neighboring local governments; and between government and citizens, government and corporations, government and not-for-profits. These innovations have proven to be effective arrangements aimed at improving government services and cutting costs. Because they represent the ability to think and act outside the rigid but familiar "bureaucratic box," they can be essential for pooling resources and improving productivity in an increasingly resource-scarce atmosphere.

In Deborah A. Auger and Jeffrey A. Raffel's chapter, "Public Management of Privatization and Contracting," the authors maintain that Americans believe that the private sector is inherently dynamic, productive, and dependable, and that private institutions are intrinsically superior to public institutions for the delivery of goods and services. This chapter attempts to get past the rhetoric both for, and against, privatization to determine where and under what circumstances there is compelling evidence that shifting the provision of goods and services from public to private or nonprofit sector actors will enhance productivity. Proponents of privatization are convinced that the private sector typically does a more efficient job than the public sector in delivering services; opponents are sure that privatization is associated with corruption and a reduction or loss in service to the poor. While this would seem to be an ideal subject on which research could shed light, even the more formal, as opposed to anecdotal, research has methodological problems. There is general agreement that privatization can lead to improved service and lower costs in areas that are measurable, monitorable, and technical in nature such as solid waste collection. Both the unique characteristics of human services delivery and the mutually-dependent nature of government's relationship with nonprofit sector entities pose special productivity challenges for government managers seeking to effectively privatize in this area. A number of privatization alternatives have been suggested to solve America's educational crisis, but despite the rhetoric there exists little objective research that privatization increases student achievement. Their review discusses four principal questions for the public manager: (1) What programmatic activities are the best candidates for privatization? (2) Is privatization is feasible for these? (3) How do the costs of public and private provision compare? (4) How can accountability be ensured? Privatization approaches may be useful in informing and reforming the work of the public sector (e.g. the use of choice and competition and the attention to measuring services quantitatively). Sophisticated public managers should also be aware that when it comes to privatization and contracting, the devil is in the details.

In David N. Ammons' chapter, "Productivity Barriers in the Public Sector," he describes a host of barriers that can threaten productivity initiatives. Some of these barriers are associated with characteristics common to the public sector environment; some are related to characteristics of particular organizations; and others are associated with the personal traits, attitudes, and behavior of individual administrators. Although the sheer number of potential impediments is great, it is the particular combination of barriers that are relevant in a given organizational setting that frames the nature and magnitude of the challenge facing officials who strive to improve performance. As Ammons notes, some administrators have proven to be especially adept at spotting relevant barriers in advance and developing strategies to cope with them in order to achieve desired results.

Evan M. Berman, in "The Implementation Game," discusses processes of implementing productivity improvement efforts, examining how, rather than what, is improved. Two organizations may achieve vastly different outcomes due to different starting conditions. The effectiveness of productivity improvement efforts is increased when the following conditions are in place: (1) higher officials' support, (2) a widely felt need for change, (3) a critical mass of people, (4) a specific initial project, and (5) organizational trust. This chapter also discusses strategies for small and large scale change. Small unit change often involves the following steps: (1) getting a mandate to start the project; (2) stating a clear reason for the project; (3) explaining the goals and target dates; (4) stating the belief that goals and target dates can be achieved, and giving some examples of how this can be done; (5) completing initial first steps and, if appropriate, a pilot project; (6) empowering people to operationalize the plan; (7) monitoring implementation: keeping the project on track, interfering to keep it moving forward, and being available for crisis intervention. Processes for productivity improvement in large organizations are also discussed.

Beverly A. Cigler's chapter, "Government Reinvention," argues that over the past two decades governments worldwide have accomplished extraordinary changes in how their bureaucracies operate internally and in delivering services to their "customers. " In some cases, the changes have been accompanied by a dramatic transformation of the role of government in society, especially government's relationship to citizens and the non-profit and private sectors. Government's role as a relationship builder—a facilitator, broker, and manager of the complex networks that operate within the seemingly self-steering capacity of society—is part of the new governance that includes co-production of services, co-regulation, co-guidance, and co-steering of societal thinking and practice. The chapter defines government reinvention and the new governance as two parts of the broad reform movement. It then identifies the underlying principles and assumptions that are reshaping public sector bureaucracies and government's roles within the broader governance system; describes and categorizes the general patterns of administrative change that define government reinvention within public bureaucracies and the role of government within the larger context of civil society and its governance system; suggests explanations for these unprecedented efforts toward change; and assesses progress and the likely next steps in government reform.

James S. Bowman and Russell L. Williams' chapter, "Productivity and Ethics: The Leadership Challenge," posits that productivity (doing things right) and ethics (doing right things) are reciprocally integral to success: together they mean doing right things right. Technical expertise—knowing how to do one's job—is critical. Indeed, the temptation is to define a professional as simply one who is technically proficient. It also makes it easy to equate public administration with corporate management. However, being ethically sound—knowing why one does one's job—is at least as important as being technically capable. Moreover, along with being as technically competent as their business counterparts, public administrators are charged with a concern for, and devotion to, the greater good. Governmental managers, in short, have an obligation not only to work productively, but also to wisely husband public assets. To address this challenge, this chapter first briefly defines productivity and ethics, and presents a decision-making framework to integrate them. Agency internal and external relations are examined and illustrated by a recent case study showing how productivity and ethics intersect. An approach to building an effective and practical workplace code of ethics that supports productivity is presented. The discussion concludes by arguing that authentic public service requires attention to productivity and ethics—but not necessarily in that order.

Marc Holzer and Mengzhong Zhang's chapter, "Trust, Performance, and the Pressures for Productivity in the Public Sector," examines the theme of trust and performance in the context of the intellectual history of public administration. Then the chapter discusses the concepts of trust, social capital, civil society, and how these concepts are associated with organizational development. The author re-examines the topic of trust and performance in the private sector as Fukuyama's hypotheses are only applicable within organizational level and cannot be extrapolated to the societal dimension. That is, the level of social trust cannot explain a country's success in economic terms. The main focus of the article, however, is testing the hypothesis that "the higher the government performance, the higher the public trust," and vice versa. Using empirical evidence, the article analyzes the relationship between public performance and public trust. Given multiple factors influencing the public's confidence in the government, and also multiple forces that impact on government performance, the hypotheses are only partially confirmed. Nonetheless, the article reveals a complicated relationship between trust and performance.

Part II, Measurement and Analysis, argues that productivity and performance improvement in the public sector are only possible with well-defined measurement systems in which democratic values and a process management philosophy are reflected on a continuing basis.

Theodore H. Poister, in his chapter on "Monitoring Quality and Productivity in the Public Sector," points out that with the passage of the Government Performance and Results Act (GPRA) of 1993 at the federal level, and similar legislation or executive mandates in most states, there has been a tremendous renewal of interest in performance measurement at all levels of government over the past several years. And, there are a number of resources that make performance measurement tools and approaches accessible to public managers for practical application in public agencies. Particularly with the passage of GPRA and similar state and local government mandates, attention focuses now more than ever on measuring *outcomes*, the end results or real impacts produced by public programs. This is obviously a very positive development, because it is impossible to know whether programs are effective, whether they are really making a difference or not, if outcomes are not being measured. Such measures of outcomes or effectiveness are, or at least should be, the "bottom line" in assessing a public agency's performance. However, there are a number of other criteria of program or agency performance that are also important to monitor although they are subordinate to effectiveness, precisely because they are linked to producing desired outcomes. From this perspective, Poister presents the kinds of performance measures used most frequently to monitor productivity and service quality in public agencies, and illustrates how they are used with a variety of examples. Finally he concludes that rather than linking to overall program goals, policy objectives, or substantive strategic initiatives, tracking quality and productivity measures tends to focus more on the "nuts and bolts" of service delivery systems and ongoing operations.

In "Evaluation Research and Performance Measurement: Dealing with Issues of Purpose and Perspective," Arie Halachmi points out that evaluation research can provide managers with a basis for informed decisions for starting, modifying, or terminating a program. Managers may emphasize results or the process for getting them as a prime consideration. Therefore the evaluation should be designed with the decision-maker's needs in mind. This chapter offers a conceptual framework to help managers and evaluators relate the purpose of an evaluation to the perspective the decision-maker prefers. The political context of public agencies may not be conducive to productivity improvement through evaluation research; but the chapter suggests that the proposed framework can help increase the productivity of the evaluation itself.

In George Julnes' chapter, "Program Evaluation: Pragmatic Support for Better Government," he maintains that the public productivity paradigm presumes that information can be used to improve the effectiveness of public sector policies and programs. The practice and profession of evaluation is focused on providing such information. After years of debates within the field about the types of methodologies that are best suited for providing this information to appropriate stakeholders, a consensus is beginning to emerge around a pragmatic approach to evaluation that incorporates insights from different traditions. Quantitative methods can be balanced with qualitative ones, and an emphasis on performance measurement can be combined with the social science emphasis on internal validity. This chapter summarizes the development of this pragmatic view of evaluation and details some of the implications of this approach for guiding the major decisions that need to be made in designing and implementing an evaluation—focusing on context-specific evaluation purposes, selecting and combining methods to address the identified major purposes, and managing the value-related issues required for informing judgments in political contexts.

In "Balanced Measurement in the Public Sector: Stakeholder-Driven Measurement," Marc Holzer and Hwang-Sun Kang discuss balanced measurement of the public sector from two perspectives. From an intra-organizational perspective, this chapter deals with the balanced scorecard as an example of balanced measurement. It discusses the rationale of balanced scorecard and examples in the public sector. Applauding its usefulness as a multidimensional approach to government performance, the authors point out that balanced performance measurement has multiple uses, not only for performance improvement, but also for a strategic channel of democratic communication between government and its many stakeholders, such as citizens and business groups. Integrating two perspectives, the general rationale and practice of stakeholder-driven measurement are discussed. Stakeholder-driven performance measurement, in particular, is very important in the public sector where so many conflicting stakeholders compete for resources and services. It values mutual collaboration between those stakeholders in developing measurement indicators and implementing the entire process of measurement activity.

In "Measurement as Accountability," Mohamad G. Alkadry and Ali Farazmand argue that theories of governance (including New Public Management, Good Government (UN), Managerialism, Reinvention, and Performance Government) advocate a form of measurement or performance accountability that shuts out political accountability in favor of a form of economic accountability that seems neutral but is in fact ideologically loaded. A number of conditions contribute to the pervasiveness of performance government. These conditions include the rise in the New Right Movements in most of the influential Western world, the resurgence of Managerialism as a guiding ideological force in the reform movement, calls for reinventing government, and the rise of the new ideological and intellectual ethos of Public Management (or New Public Management) based on globalization of capital and the re-emerging of the New Right. The result of these conditions is a form of Public Management that places more value on small and efficient government than it places on political accountability.

In "The Measurement of Human Services," Ray Gonzales argues that human service, social intervention, or impact programs exist with the explicit intent of ameliorating the effect of a social ill. The nature of these services makes measurement efforts more difficult in comparison to other public services. Consequently, this chapter aims to provide the reader with an understanding of performance measurement as it operates in these organizations, paying special attention to the role of nonprofits, from academic and applied points of view. The chapter maintains that measurement in human services is grounded in evaluation because of the importance of causal reasoning in effectiveness arguments. Because this is the case, emphasis should be placed on the evaluation literature when addressing the mechanics of outcome assessment systems. A number of recommendations for research and practice are made.

Arie Halachmi, in his chapter on "Performance Measurements, Accountability, and Improving Performance," points out that if performance measurement is just another ball in the political football game, one must wonder whether the cost of performance measurement can always be justified. He raises a question about the extent to which the instruments that foster *accountability* (e.g., by establishing whether a planned action was carried out as promised) can be as useful for enhancing *performance* or *productivity* (e.g., by generating new ideas, innovations, and experimentation for the purpose of assuming a proactive posture or improving performance). From this perspective, Halachmi asserts that performance measurement may have some serious dysfunctions that should be considered when organizations review existing performance measurement schemes or decide to introduce them in the first place. This chapter starts by discussing the problematic nature of the need to assess the benefit and cost of performance measurement. He argues that though we may seem to agree on the desirability of performance measurements, in principle, we know little about their economic (vs. political or symbolic) benefits and opportunity costs from societal and systemic points of view. This chapter concludes that certain performance measurements can facilitate better accountability but when it comes to improving performance, such measurements can hinder progress, innovation, and experimentation, slowing down adjustment to changing circumstances and adaptations to new situations.

Patria de Lancer Julnes, in her chapter on "The Utilization of Performance Measurement Information: Adopting, Implementing, and Sustaining," presents the argument that the utilization of performance measurement is a special case of knowledge utilization and proceeds to understand the apparent lack of use of such information from a knowledge utilization framework. This framework was developed in a way that reconciles past controversies of what knowledge utilization means, and allows us the systematic assessment in one study of many factors often addressed in isolation. The author presents a model of performance measures utilization developed from survey data, and then further elaborates and verifies the model using data from telephone interviews. At least three stages of the utilization process are recognized— the initial adoption of a performance measurement system, the subsequent implementation or actual use of the system, and the accommodation and sustained use of the system.

Gerald J. Miller and Donijo Robbins, in their chapter on "Performance, Productivity, and Budgeting," outline purposes attached to budget systems and their implications for achieving greater productivity in government organizations. The chapter begins by describing large-scale budget reform structures in terms of their relationship to productivity, asking: What budget methods have governments used traditionally, and how do they address performance and productivity issues? A succeeding portion of this chapter discusses the budget methods in some detail: first, the line-item budget as a rudimentary way of assessing expenditures and means; early performance budgeting as a method of going one step beyond the line-item budget by classifying items by function and determining the efficiency of the budgeted expenditures; program budgeting, as a means of combining planning, budgeting, and economic analysis of allocation choices; and budgeting to decentralize decision-making and reorient budgets among old and new programs through zero base budgeting. The chapter then goes beyond budget reforms as they have appeared up to and through zero base budgeting to investigate productivity-friendly budgeting practices, including measurement and incentives. Finally the chapter describes other budget systems that have come into being in the late 20th century for the specific purpose of pursuing government productivity and performance, for example expenditure control budgets, target based budgets, and performance based budgets.

In a related chapter, "Benefit–Cost Analysis," Gerald J. Miller and Donijo Robbins look at the rationale and methods of benefit–cost analysis (BCA) and critique its use in achieving productivity. This chapter introduces the fiscal allocation role of government in society and briefly explains how government fulfills that role by coping with market failure. The chapter then discusses the decision-making process used to determine the appropriate amounts and types of public goods that should be produced by governments according to welfare economists. Here the chapter describes micro- and macro-levels of analysis and some practical ways the two levels may complement each other. To test the assumption that one particular technique will provide the best guide for project selection, research involving seasoned state government executives is presented. The final section of the chapter places benefit–cost analysis within the even larger body of literature characterizing economic reasoning in government.

Maria P. Aristigueta's chapter, "Indicators of Living Conditions: Challenges and Opportunities for Accountability and Governance," points out that government reform and devolution serve as the impetus for accountability both to the funding source and to the public. The current reforms have at least two measurement models associated with them—social indicators, sometimes called benchmarks or milestones, and performance measures. In this regard, this chapter provides an overview of the history of social indicators, discusses the differences between social indicators and performance measures, and offers criteria for developing the indicators. Aristigueta also discusses the uses and misuses of the social indicators, and lessons learned from practice and from the literature. Social indicators are important for governance, and critical in times of increased accountability, particularly in terms of performance requirements on personal and community well being that are coupled with reduced social benefits. From a management perspective, social indicators provide an umbrella for political and organizational priorities, and for alignment to agency performance measures.

Part III, Managing Human Resources, sheds light on the importance of utilizing human resources for productivity and performance improvement in public organizations. Although a quick path to productivity enhancement might be to mechanize processes and systems, the more difficult, but more promising means to enhancement over the long term might well be to maximize people's willingness to enhance productivity. The chapters in Part III address this issue.

Mary E. Guy, in "The Human Side of Productive Work Environments," argues that technology cannot substitute for, nor can money buy, the intangible commitment that causes employees to perform at their best. The desire to achieve is generated by the relationship between management and workers, pride in workmanship, and commitment to mission. Intangible but essential are rapport, commitment, and conscientiousness among staff amid an atmosphere conducive to productivity, all within a context that maximizes quality and quantity. How to achieve this? This chapter attempts to answer this question by, first, differentiating between the external and internal environments, for each influences workers differently. Next, the discussion calls attention to variables that management can control, which include coaching, goal setting, and contingency strategies. The elements of each are explained and a case study demonstrates their application. The bottom line to productive work environments is that they require harnessing those elements that are healthy and productive, and reinforcing them. This means keeping the lines of communication open and placing the right people at the right place at the right time, where they can build on their strengths and do what they do best.

Willa Bruce and Dorothy Olshfski, in their chapter on "The New American Workplace," argue that efforts to increase productivity by tightening internal operating efficiencies of the personnel process should proceed with the recognition that the issues and assumptions that guided thinking about personnel have changed. What workers do, how they do it, and who they are is different than it was even 15 years ago. They go on to argue that productivity issues are not the only reasons for concern and that quality of life issues have surfaced as the old assumptions about motivational incentives, the nature of family life, and the availability of a support network break down. From this perspective, Bruce and Olshfski examine some topics that are emerging as major issues in public personnel administration. Two large trends are examined and discussed: changes in the nature of work and organization, and changes in the nature of the work force. Both of these are examined with respect to the public sector.

Meredith A. Newman's chapter on "Broadening Workplace Participation" sketches out the changing nature of the workforce and the persistence of lingering discrimination. The chapter addresses the issue of diversity and broadening workplace participation by going beyond the numbers. That is, diversity in the public workplace is examined both in terms of a demographically diverse workforce and also in terms of diversifying the work itself. The central premise is that it is necessary but insufficient to examine workplace participation by strict attention to the numbers—either in the aggregate or at various levels within organizations. Rather, the more appropriate approach to diversity is to stress the importance of integration by explicitly linking diverse workers to diverse approaches to the work itself, including the way work is organized, performed, and evaluated, as well as what the organization does in service to its mission. The chapter proceeds with an examination of the demographic composition of the current and projected workforce. The representativeness of the workforce is discussed by reference to employee categories of sex, race, ethnicity, age, and disability. The challenges to broadening workplace participation are identified, and managerial strategies available to expand employment opportunities, especially for nontraditional employees, are presented in turn. The chapter concludes with a discussion of the importance of diversity, broadly construed, for our increasingly entrepreneurial public workplaces.

In Gerald T. Gabris and Douglas M. Ihrke's chapter, "Merit Pay and Employee Performance," the authors point out that merit pay remains an important component of the human resources management (HRM) process for most public organizations. Ironically, it also remains one of the least popular HRM techniques from the perspective of both managers and employees. More often than not, managers and employees feel merit pay does not increase individual performance. This chapter attempts to highlight the more common reasons why merit pay does not motivate employees or improve individual performance. It also provides recommendations for how public organizations can make existing merit pay systems more effective. Merit pay is presented as a public sector reality that is unlikely to diminish in significance even though the development and implementation of merit pay plans often cause problems. Therefore, it is incumbent upon professional public administrators to learn how to utilize and maximize the positive aspects of these systems to the highest degree possible. This chapter, while not resolving all the issues involved with merit pay, addresses the larger concerns that public administrators are likely to face on a routine basis.

In "Nonmonetary Incentives for Productivity Enhancement," Roe Ann Roberts discusses several nonmonetary approaches to productivity enhancement in the workplace. They are broken out into two general groups of approaches aimed at retaining and motivating employees. The first group provides managers with four different approaches that can be used to proactively change the present work environment by reevaluating the job tasks and the work environment. These include a system wide, or departmental, analysis, the use of organizational ombudsmen, quality circles, and job description analysis and redesign. The second group focuses on the restructuring of the work environment in order to increase worker satisfaction and to encourage strong social ties in the work place. These approaches include job teams, flexible job time and telecommuting, employee merit/recognition systems, employee education programs, and child day care and elder care. A decline in productivity is not only a labor problem, but also a failure of management. The key to improving productivity is a radically improved attitude toward human resource management. Human resource management must be an integral part of every organization's planning. A systematic management approach which uses feedback and positive reinforcement must be developed which arises from a sincere desire by management to create a partnership with the workers. Organizations must focus on long-term prosperity rather than quick dividends. That is, management must become future oriented.

Montgomery Van Wart, in his chapter on "Training and Development for Productivity," argues that contemporary public sector organizations that want to use training and development for greater productivity face four challenges. First, training and development must be used more strategically, which in turn, will mean a strategic overhaul of most training systems themselves. What should occur in a robust organization bent on producing routine operational quality and flexibility and innovation in operations and programs? Second, because almost all of the reform initiatives being undertaken require more decentralization, empowerment, job expansion, and power sharing, more broadly trained employees are necessary. Technical skills are no less important, but management and quasi-management skills will require a greater emphasis. Third, the more strategic use and design of training systems, and a broader training agenda, cannot detract from a renewed emphasis on training basics. Untutored trainers, more often than not, are poor trainers. Finally, there needs to be a reemphasis on curriculum and instructional design as training programs and systems are rebuilt. This is particularly true with new emphases on self-training, certification systems and higher levels of accountability, as well as immense changes in technology that are often poorly understood and thus badly used. This chapter addresses each of these issues in the context of a review of organizational learning needs, organizational competency clusters, individual learning needs, and individual training methods.

"Rewarding and Punishing for Productive Performance," by Richard A. Loverd, presents a means for promoting more productive behavior, the different needs of employees and the intrinsic and extrinsic factors available in the workplace to meet those needs. Then, a number of different methods for encouraging desirable behavior and discouraging undesirable behavior through reinforcement techniques are explored, followed by an examination of the promise and challenge of expectancy theory as a vehicle for building relationships between performance and rewards, while making good use of needs and reinforcement theories. After having investigated these different types of reward and punishment approaches, their relevance to the public sector context is considered. In many ways, it is suggested that such a context provides as much challenge as the technologies of reward and punishment methods themselves. That is, if productivity is to be improved, constructive changes in the nature of that context, starting with the merit system and reaching out to the larger public, will need to be developed.

Seok-Hwan Lee and Marc Holzer, in their chapter on "Labor–Management Partnerships: Direct Paths to Productivity Improvement," maintain that the labor–management partnership is a backdrop for virtually everything that is going on in government at all levels. Even though there are many success stories in labor–management cooperation in the public sector, those stories have not been widely and sufficiently disseminated so as to provide useful insights to public sector scholars and practitioners. While it has been said that adversarial perceptions between the two have prevailed in the workplace, which, in turn, has hindered both sides from working together, many scholars and practitioners in the public sector agree that a harmonious relationship between management and workforce is the key to enhancing productivity in any organization. It is necessary, therefore, to identify successful factors affecting a harmonious labor–management relationship in the public sector from a comprehensive perspective. Based on success stories identified in the public sector, this chapter provides a "big picture" as to what should be emphasized in order to establish labor–management cooperation for productivity improvement. The authors conclude that when labor and management work together in a harmonious work environment, that situation leads the way to improvement.

Ross Prizzia and Gary Helfand, in "Reducing Workplace Stress: Prevention and Mitigation Strategies for Increased Productivity," examine the various factors that contribute to work-related stress within organizations, including lack of participation in decision-making, poor communication, role confusion, inequitable reward systems, new technology, chronic overwork, a negative physical and/or social work environment, and others. They then proceed to look at ways in which workplace stress can be reduced with the help of such tools as an occupational stress audit and a stress-related organizational diagnosis. They then explain how this would lead to the development of a comprehensive plan for stress reduction and prevention, which would include such elements as training and retraining, the utilization of team-based group work, increased work schedule flexibility, counseling and conflict management sessions, job redesign, and other strategies. The concluding section focuses on occupational stress as a collective bargaining issue and emphasizes the importance of joint labor–management strategies to reduce and prevent stress. As an added dimension, the impact of privatization on occupational stress is also explored within the context of public sector collective bargaining. Finally, Prizzia and Helfand contend that a present and future challenge for the public sector is to develop stress prevention and reduction models that are customized for different types of government agencies and the specific kinds of workers they employ.

Part IV, New Organizational Technologies, presents emerging management techniques and advanced approaches to organizational improvement. Successful organizations are the ones that are able to respond to a rapidly changing environment as quickly as possible using a variety of innovative management technologies and resources. In this regard, this Part provides us with important information on what strategies ought to be considered, as well as productivity improvement resources in print and on the web.

In "Organizational Change and Innovation," Dorothy Olshfski and Helisse Levine argue that organizational change may be intended or unexpected, may be positive or disruptive, radical or incremental. People may react with acceptance, resistance, or sabotage. As a byproduct of globalization and our advanced technology, both government bureaucracies and private companies are continually being challenged by change. In the private sector, pioneering new technologies, processes, and applications are increasingly recognized as central to a firm's long-term viability. In the public sector, the emphasis on change has not been as strident as it has been in the private sector. After all, government is not as threatened by change, and will not go out of business. (Or will it?) Despite opinions to the contrary, government bureaucracies change and innovate. The reinventing and reengineering movements, and the emphasis on privatization and contracting out, have refocused government activity and changed the size and scope of government. In a fast changing world, dealing successfully with change is how the government maintains its fit and ensures its legitimacy. This chapter examines theoretical models of organizational change and types of change as they present themselves to public and private organizations, and suggests recommendations for both research and practice in dealing with change.

In Arie Halachmi's chapter on "Strategic Management and Productivity," the author begins by addressing the issue of public sector productivity. He points out that a statement about productivity conveys judgment rather than an objective value. Thus, what may seem to be right and prudent in the short run may prove to be much less than that in the long run. The chapter suggests that productivity is a mediating variable between the organization and the environment, and that it can be studied as a dependent or an independent variable. The discussion of strategizing in the public sector includes observations on who defines missions and key operational parameters in the public sector, on the difference between the public and private sectors when it comes to perceived threats and opportunities, and on how each sector deals with an apparent threat. Halachmi goes on to define some of the reasons strategizing in the public sector may not be cost effective. This chapter concludes by suggesting that when strategic management is not cost-effective or feasible, management initiatives to enhance productivity at the subsystem level might be a way to obtain strategic gains (i.e., to develop desired strengths and eliminate or reduce certain weaknesses).

Seok-Hwan Lee and Marc Holzer, in their chapter on "Total Quality Management and Customer Focus: Linking Philosophy of TQM to Responsive Public Agencies," posit that experience with TQM in the public sector has also produced mixed results. Some agencies report success in adopting and implementing TQM, while some other agencies believe TQM has not contributed to improving productivity. Perhaps this is partly attributable to the misunderstanding of TQM's management philosophy among managers and employees. The foremost and the first emphasis in TQM is customer focus. If this focus were applied to the public sector, though the definition of customer is a matter of debate, the implication would then be to enhance responsiveness of public agencies to the public. From this perspective, Lee and Holzer argue that many factors that are believed to hinder either responsiveness of public agencies or successful implementation of TQM are the ones that TQM originally intended to improve. Although TQM was originally invented to solve existing management problems, little has been discussed about what problems TQM can actually solve, particularly in terms of organizational responsiveness. From this perspective, they identify major assumptions of TQM and examine factors that are believed to hinder organizational responsiveness in the public sector. Assuming that top management support and leadership is a necessary first step in transformation of any organization, Lee and Holzer suggest how TQM's philosophy helps solve those problems relating to responsiveness to the public in the public sector.

In James Melitski's chapter on "E-Government and Information Technology in the Public Sector: Definitions, Distinctions, and Organizational Capacity," the author discusses the adoption and implementation of e-government in public organizations. He proposes a model of e-government implementation based on the information technology (IT) capacity of public organizations. This chapter defines seven key information technology capacity factors: strategic planning for information technology; knowledge management; information technology decision making; integration; performance measurement; staffing; and security. After discussing each of the IT capacity factors, this research examines the influence of the factors on agency e-government performance. The two-part analysis examines in depth interviews conducted with public sector information technology managers and experts in the state of New Jersey. First, Melitski conducts a case analysis of four departments in New Jersey state government that were early adopters of innovative e-government programs. Following the case analysis, this chapter presents a content analysis examining the relationship between IT capacity factors and e-government performance. Based on that analysis, Melitski suggests that there are several means public organizations can undertake to enhance the performance of e-government initiatives.

Arie Halachmi, in "Information Technology and Productivity: Selected Issues and Considerations," emphasizes the proper use of information technology for productivity improvement. The best way for managers to receive the benefits of IT without experiencing much of its possible dysfunctional implications is to take a proactive stand. In that regard, this chapter goes beyond the issue of whether or not investment in IT is justified. There are several other issues public managers must consider in order to gain better understanding of the role of IT and its productivity consequences in government agencies, which are part of the service sector. He points out that government agencies have no choice in whether or not to use IT. Regulatory agencies stand little chance of being able to carry out their mission without effective use of IT, since regulated entities use IT to avoid conforming to government regulations. Similarly, the public expects government service providers to use IT to facilitate access to information and services; lack of evident, intensive use of IT is likely to be perceived as substandard service. Thus, this chapter aims to highlight a few important points that may help managers to enhance productivity by counteracting possible dysfunctional outcomes of IT, while taking advantage of what it can offer for transforming employees into knowledgeable workers. This chapter consists of two major components. The first explores some of the ways in which IT influences the interface of government organizations with their environment. The second touches briefly on the various ways in which IT modifies organizational behavior by changing the interface of individual employees with co-workers, their behavior as group members, and the formation and functioning of groups and their dealings with other groups. Halachmi concludes that organizations need to take a proactive stand to compensate for the absence of regular interpersonal interactions in order to retain employees' loyalty and commitment to the organization.

Finally, Marc Holzer and Seok-Hwan Lee, in their chapter on "Productivity Improvement Resources: In Print and on the Web," argue that although productivity improvement is comprehensive in scope and requires multiple approaches, it is often difficult for public sector scholars and practitioners to find appropriately helpful information to apply to specific organizational contexts. Public sector productivity improvement resources are widely scattered in print or on the web. It is useful, therefore, to build a database integrating all information relevant to productivity improvement in the public sector. Although it is impossible to list all publications and reports due to limited space, this chapter introduces selected collections, including textbooks, handbooks, recent journal articles, government reports, professional association-related publications, and other comprehensive resources on the web.

Productivity and performance improvements in the public sector are not simple. They require detailed and systematic approaches. The chapters in this handbook highlight the importance of using a comprehensive approach in which well-managed and well-constructed public productivity programs promise to benefit all interested parties in a win-win relationship.

# 1

# Mastering Public Productivity and Performance Improvement from a Productive Management Perspective

**MARC HOLZER**
*Rutgers, The State University of New Jersey, Newark, New Jersey, U.S.A.*

**SEOK-HWAN LEE**
*The Catholic University of Korea, Songsim Campus, South Korea*

## I. UNDERSTANDING PRODUCTIVITY AND PERFORMANCE IN THE PUBLIC SECTOR

Although the issue of productivity and performance enhancement in the public sector is nothing new, for decades scholars and practitioners have worked to identify what makes government productive and effective.

In fact, the use of the term "productivity" has been intermingled with the term "performance." Various researchers have defined each term in different ways. But there appears to have been consensus on both terms. Whether productivity is dollar input (both direct and indirect; Vough, 1979), output per employee hour, quality considered (Sutermeister, 1977), or producing more with the same amount of human effort (Glaser, 1976), the concept itself implies the effective and efficient use of resources that are available in an organization to achieve a given goal (Berman and West, 1998). Likewise, the term performance also has multiple meanings. It is almost impossible to define it clearly. However, high performance organizations are certainly productive ones, and performance and productivity are often used interchangeably.

Performance is usually divided into three levels: individual, group, and organizational. This assumes that each level of performance can contribute to overall organizational productivity. We prefer to view productivity as a broad concept that includes the term performance.

In an era of limited resources, there is extensive discussion of teamwork-based organization, balanced performance measurement, and performance-based management and budgeting. But there still do not appear to be simple direct paths to productivity and performance in public organizations given that public organizations are different from private ones in many respects, including organizational environment, structure, and motivational bases. As has been discussed in the literature concerning public–private distinctions (Rainey et al., 1975, 1976; Rainey, 1983; Buchanan, 1974a, 1974b), compared to the private sector, public sector goals are more complex, and therefore progress is more difficult to measure; motivational bases of public employees are different; layers of rules and regulations often prevent public employees from improving the general public welfare in a timely manner. Of course, those rules and regulations are necessary to protect fundamental rights such as life, liberty, and property of the general public in a democratic society—goals that are certainly paramount and that must take precedence.

## II.   PRODUCTIVITY IMPROVEMENT AS A COMPREHENSIVE CONCEPT

The means of enhancing productivity and performance must be comprehensive in scope, and applicable to specific situations. Broad prescriptions, such as "businesslike government," are simplistic, skewed, and inadequate "solutions" for delivering important services with limited resources. Productivity and performance improvement is a function of many factors, ranging from top management support to feedback from citizens, and all of these factors are equally important.

The literature argues that productivity improvement is a function of a variety of factors, including top management support, committed people at all levels, a performance measurement system, employee training, reward structures, community involvement, and feedback and correction on budget-management decisions (Greiner, 1986; Buntz, 1981; McGowan, 1984; Holzer and Callahan, 1998; Halachmi and Holzer, 1986; Werther et al., 1986). It is important, therefore, to build such capacities for productivity improvement.

Productivity improvement—production of more and/or better services for each tax dollar and staff hour invested—has been an especially attractive strategy for the many governments facing tight or shrinking resources (Greiner, 1986, p.81). Halachmi and Holzer (1986, pp. 5–6) view productivity improvement as an open system. As they state,

> Organizations obtain inputs (e.g., mission requirements as defined by law or public policy; demands for existing services, products or procedures; resources, including materials, budgets and personnel), plans, and schedules from their environment and transform them (using processes or procedures) into outputs (e.g., products or services for individuals and other organizations) that are released back into the environment. Those outputs, in turn, generate feedback regarding performance-feedback that may affect subsequent inputs, processes and procedures. Productivity improvement can, therefore, be perceived as a desired relationship among the components of a given system, one that improves the survivability of the system as such.

Buntz argues that because productivity is a function of technology, staff ability, and motivation and environmental factors such as public attitudes, policy shifts, and client characteristics, improvement should focus on these factors (Buntz, 1981, p. 308). Holzer and Callahan (1998) suggest a comprehensive public sector productivity improvement model. According to this model, managing for quality, developing human resources, adapting technologies, building partnerships, and measuring performance combine to improve productivity in the public sector (see Figure 1).

McGowan (1984) argues that in order to improve productivity in the public sector, we have to consider the environmental domain (public/private partnership,

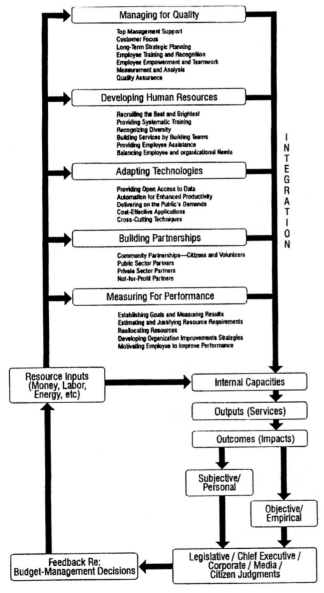

**Figure 1** Comprehensive public sector productivity improvement. (From Holzer and Callahan 1998).

marketing of public service delivery, etc.), the organizational domain (e.g., structural changes, labor–management relations, computer technology, etc.), and the individual domain (e.g., performance incentives, professionalism, and management development and training). Among those three domains, McGowan sees the individual domain as the core factor for productivity improvement. In other words, innovation, whether in management or any discipline, springs from the individual (McGowan, 1984, p. 178). He holds that the "bottom line" for productivity improvement is the workers' commitment.

In this regard, Holzer and Zalk's (see Holzer, 1992, pp. 7–8) capacity building model of 10 steps provides a very useful guideline for productivity improvement. They suggest obtaining top management support, locating models, identifying promising areas, building a team, planning the project, collecting program data, modifying project plans, expecting problems, implementing improvement actions, and evaluating and publicizing results. The step-by-step process is as follows.

*Step One. Clarifying Goals and Obtaining Support.* Productivity programs must agree upon, and have commitments to, reasonable goals and objectives, adequate staff and resource support, and organizational visibility. The full cooperation of top management and elected officials is a prerequisite to success.

*Step Two. Locating Models.* Because productivity is an increasing priority of government, existing projects can suggest both successful paths and ways to avoid potential mistakes. Models are available on the Internet, the professional literature, at conferences, and so on.

*Step Three. Identifying Promising Areas.* As a means of building a successful track record, new productivity programs might select as targets those functions continually faced with large backlogs, slipping deadlines, high turnover, or many complaints. Because personnel costs are the largest expenditure for most public agencies, improved morale, training, or working conditions might offer a high payoff. Organizations might also target functions in which new techniques, procedures, or emerging technologies seem to offer promising paybacks.

*Step Four. Building a Team.* Productivity programs are much more likely to succeed as bottom-up, rather than top-down or externally directed, entities. Productivity project teams should include middle management, supervisors, employees, and union representatives. They should also include citizens, clients, and representatives of advocacy groups. If employees and citizens are involved in looking for opportunities, then they are likely to suggest which barriers or obstacles need to be overcome; what tasks can be done more efficiently, dropped, or simplified; and which workloads are unrealistically high or low.

*Step Five. Planning the Project.* Team members should agree on a specific statement of scope, objectives, tasks, responsibilities, and time frames. This agreement should be detailed as a project management plan, which should then be updated and discussed on a regular basis.

*Step Six. Collecting Program Data.* Potentially relevant information should be defined broadly and might include reviews of existing databases, interviews, budgets, and studies by consultants or client groups. A measurement system should be developed to collect data on a regular basis, and all data should be supplied to the team for periodic analysis. The validity and usefulness of such information must be constantly monitored.

*Step Seven. Modifying Project Plans.* Realistic decisions, based on continuing team discussions of alternative approaches and data, must be made about program problems, opportunities, modifications, and priorities. For instance, would a problem best be solved through the more intensive use of technology, improved training, better supervision, or improved incentives?

*Step Eight. Expecting Problems.* Projects are more likely to succeed if potential misunderstandings, misconceptions, slippages, resource shortages, client and employee resistance, and so on are openly confronted and discussed. Any such problem, if unaddressed, can cause a project to fail.

*Step Nine. Implementing Improvement Actions.* Implementation should be phased in on a modest basis and without great fanfare. Projects that are highly touted, but then do not deliver as expected, are more likely to embarrass top management (and political supporters). Projects that adopt a low profile are less likely to threaten key actors, especially middle management and labor.

*Step Ten. Evaluating and Publicizing Results.* Measurable success, rather than vague claims, is important. Elected officials, the press, and citizen groups are more likely to accept claims of success if they are backed up by hard data. "Softer" feedback can then support such claims. Particularly important in providing evidence of progress are timely data that reflect cost savings, additional services, independent evaluations of service levels, citizen satisfaction, and reductions in waiting or processing times.

Of course, this model does not always fit any situation without modification. As Holzer and Callahan (1998, p. 145) point out in discussing the 10-step model above, or indeed any other such model:

> As with any other "generic recipe," this model should be modified and adapted to specific organizational contexts. Real cases will always be slightly different than the model; in some cases one or two steps might be missing because of the organizational and cultural assumptions of the situation; in other cases, several steps can be combined into one. Still because the steps of model are analytically distinguishable, the model is useful for analyzing real organizations and programs to highlight the strengths and illuminate the weaknesses of cases under discussion.

## III. FOCUSING MORE ON INTANGIBLE FACTORS: PRODUCTIVITY IMPROVEMENT THROUGH PEOPLE

Although public sector productivity improvement incorporates many elements, Holzer and Callahan (1998, p. 164) maintain that "in an era of semi-permanent fiscal stress, commitment, professionalism, and intangible support are relatively more important than fiscal resources, either as budgetary pressures or as slack resources."

In fact, recognizing a crisis in public service, many scholars suggest that employee commitment, along with top management, is the key to achieving public sector innovation and increasing productivity (Holzer and Callahan, 1998; Werther et al., 1986; Usilaner, 1981; Ammons, 1985; Balfour and Wechsler, 1991, 1996; Steinhaus and Perry, 1996; Tang and Lane, 1996; Lee, 2000).

Productive organizations are a function of the development of their people, who ultimately determine the level of productivity (Werther et al., 1986). Any approach to improving organizational productivity must include an examination of personnel issues, inasmuch as it is the people who do the work of the organization. Ban et al. (1992, p. 401) also point out, "most of the work on personnel or human resources management and productivity has focused primarily on how to motivate employees to increase their productivity." Guy (1992a, 1992b) also maintains that productivity improvement requires people's commitment at all levels in an organization.

According to Buntz (1981, p. 312), "since productivity is a function of motivation, among other things, low levels of motivation can seriously impede improvement." Usilaner (1981, p. 246) argues that "with top-level management's support and commitment, from the legislative and executive branches, productivity improvement efforts can and should succeed." Ammons (1985) also emphasizes the fact that, despite all of the barriers, many local government managers have been successful in improving productivity, not because the path was easy but because they were determined to overcome the barriers to change.

Holzer (1984, p. 75) argues that "pressured public administration now recognizes that a prerequisite to productivity improvement, and a counterforce to negative and misleading assumptions, is cooperation between the organization's policy makers and the work force." This argument also supports the importance of people in public organizations.

Greiner (1986, p. 82) also points out the importance of people in productivity improvement in government:

> A variety of productivity improvement strategies are available to state and local governments. Most of them fall into five broad categories: (1) introduction of new or improved technology, (2) improvement of operational procedures, (3) revision of organizational structures, (4) enhancement of the skills of management and line employees, and (5) improvement of employee motivation. However, from accepting new technologies to responding to employee incentives, public employees represent a critical element in the productivity improvement equation.

Holzer and Olshfski (1990–1996) began an empirical exploration of innovation through a survey and interviews of EXSL (Exemplary State and Local Award) winners. According to their research, having committed personnel along with having support from top agency executives were the most important factors for innovation (Holzer and Olshfski, 1990–1996, quoted in Holzer and Callahan, 1998). In addition, "to do the right thing" turns out to be the first motivational factor for innovation. Furthermore, Holzer (1984, p. 83) maintains that the focus on public employees is the key to innovation in the public sector:

> If public administrators receive enlightened political support, if they are treated as administrative professionals on a par with their private sector colleagues, if they are relieved of artificial constraints on financial rewards for performance and management prerogatives, and if they are allowed to become less bureaucratic, then innovative, clearly focused programs and initiatives will be more rapidly and widely developed and implemented. And this will occur in spite of, as well as because of budget cuts and limited resources.

Synthesizing the approaches above, Figure 2 provides critical elements for productivity and performance improvement from a productive management point of view, and shows how it could be achieved.

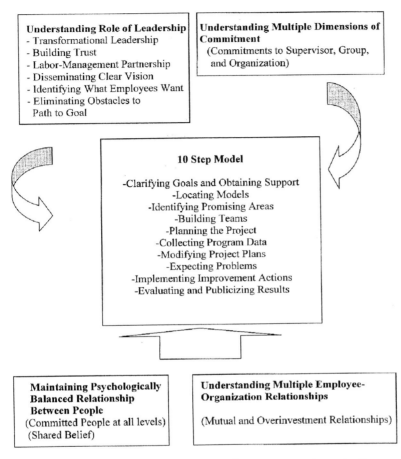

**Figure 2**  Productivity and performance improvement: A productive management perspective.

## A.  Understanding the Role of Leadership

Without top management support and leadership, no productivity and performance improvements are possible. Gabris and colleagues (2000) point out that leadership credibility is positively associated with perceived success of managerial innovation and that dysfunctional governing board behavior is negatively associated with perceived success of innovation among public employees. As such, leadership plays a critical role in improving productivity in any organization. Leadership also affects culture change, thereby contributing to a higher level of productivity (Hennessey 1998).

As productivity improvement is also directly related to successful organizational transformation that must be led by excellent leaders, the following points may help effective leaders transform their organizations, thereby enhancing productivity.

### 1.  Transformational Leadership and Employee Motivation

In recent years, transformational leadership has received much attention from both scholars and practitioners (Rainey, 1997; Burns, 1978). Although transactional leaders place much emphasis on motivating employees by recognizing their needs and providing rewards to fulfill those needs in exchange for their performance and support, transformational leaders try to link employees' goals to higher visions (Rainey, 1997). Exchange relationships between leaders and employees cannot promise a long-term relationship and may not be strong enough to fully motivate followers to work harder or smarter. Excellent leaders must be able to persuade followers to accept an organization's vision by using effective communication, and establishing trust among employees. The role of effective leaders is to set the goals and to thank employees. Leaders must create an atmosphere where everyone feels appreciated and feels there is always possibility for growth. Saying "thank you for the job well done" is simple, without monetary cost, and effective.

Because transformational leaders consider individuals' self-actualizations, focus on personal, staff, and team development; and inspire others through charisma to accept their vision as their own, they are interested in knowing what their followers really want from their jobs. Jurkiewicz and colleagues (1998), in an empirical study that examined public sector motivation, point out that disparity between "wants" and "gets" may create serious problems in motivating employees. According to their study, what public employees want is job security, however, what they are getting from their jobs turns out to be a chance to learn something important.

Given that employees have performance-outcome as well as effort-performance expectancies, it may be hard to expect a high level of productivity from those who feel outcomes are unattractive. Therefore, before considering motivational strategies, transformational leaders should be aware of what employees really want from their jobs. Then financial reward systems and other forms of compensation should be consistent with those desires.

## 2. Building Trust

Public sector innovation requires risk-taking behaviors from employees, therefore unless employees trust their organizations it is almost impossible for any organization to be creative and productive. Productive employees should be able to feel free to express new ideas whenever necessary. Trust is defined as "reliance upon the behavior of a person in order to achieve a desired but uncertain objective in a risky situation (Griffin, 1967, p. 105)." Therefore, employees should believe that supervisors or the organization will back them up in a pinch and that they can tell their supervisor anything about the job. Without such a belief, even if employees are unhappy with current situations and have a strong willingness to innovate, they are unlikely to suggest new ideas or support productivity improvement strategies. As Nyhan (2000) suggests, empowerment, frequent feedback from supervisors, and increased participation in decision making will contribute to increasing organizational trust. In order for any organization to be productive, effective leaders, therefore, should pay attention to how to increase the level of trust from employees. It is the leader's role to create a culture of no fear. Employees should be able to express themselves professionally and to tell the truth without having to worry about hidden agendas or conflicting interests.

## 3. Disseminating a Clear Vision and Eliminating Obstacles

Commitment of top management is a necessary first step in disseminating quality improvement values throughout the organization. Leaders must be committed to achieving excellence (Holzer and Callahan, 1998). In particular, a harmonious labor–management relationship, which is a backdrop for productivity, is a function of top management support and leadership. One of the characteristics of effective leaders is the ability to overcome natural resistance to change by creating visions of the future that evoke confidence in and mastery of new behaviors and practices (Grace and Holzer, 1992).

The case of the City of Charlotte illustrates how the success of the employee involvement approach is possible. In other words, top management was willing to delegate power and authority. Management showed faith in the abilities of firefighters' committees empowering them to speak directly to the City Council (U.S. Department of Labor, 1996).

Leadership communicates a vision of the organization's mission or role in society. The vision becomes the "socially integrating myth" which, if it can appeal to a broad enough base of believers, provides energy and helps to link the differentiated parts of the organization together in achieving the vision (Wilkins, 1983). Excellent leaders create and communicate a clear vision of where they intend to lead an organization in the near future. By sharing this vision, leaders provide each employee with a sense of purpose, clarity, meaning, and security—all of which are critical to maximizing productivity (David, 2001).

Successful leaders should be able to identify and eliminate various obstacles that might make an employee hesitate to take an action. As Kotter (1995, p. 62) points out, "an employee understands the new vision and wants to help make it happen. But something appears to be blocking the path. Worst of all are bosses who refuse to change and who make demands that are inconsistent with the overall effort."

Employees typically have a strong willingness to achieve specific goals. But if they believe that required procedures are rigid, the possibility of cooperation is low, there is no time available for problem solving, and a rigid, bureaucratic organizational culture exists, they are far less likely to work toward those goals.

## B.  Understanding Multiple Dimensions of Employee Commitment

In order to improve productivity in the public sector, another important factor is public employees' commitments. Commitment is defined as the psychological attachment of workers to their workplaces (Becker et al., 1996; Allen and Meyer, 1990; O'Reilly and Chatman, 1986). In fact, higher levels of commitment are likely to be related to higher levels of performance and productivity. Committed employees are less likely to leave the organization and more likely to make extra efforts on its behalf than other, less committed, employees (Balfour and Wechsler, 1991). These commitments are directly related to willingness to support productivity strategies in the public sector.

A conventional view has exclusively focused on commitment to organization. In contrast to this conventional view, a number of researchers have begun to view employee commitment as having multiple foci and bases (Becker et al., 1995; Reichers, 1985, 1986; Becker, 1992; Gordon et al., 1980; Meyer et al., 1993). Those subtle distinctions have not been made in the more conventional views of commitment (Becker et al., 1995).

In response to deficiencies of organizational commitment, O'Reilly and Chatman (1986) have proposed an alternative approach in which commitment is defined as the psychological attachment felt by the person for the organization, reflecting the degree to which the person internalizes or adopts the characteristics or perspectives of that organization. They also suggested three bases of commitment to an organization: compliance, identification, and internalization commitments. Here, compliance occurs when people adopt attitudes and behaviors in order to obtain specific rewards or to avoid specific punishments. Identification occurs when people adopt attitudes and behaviors in order to be associated with a satisfying, self-defining relationship with another person or group. Internalization occurs when people adopt attitudes and behaviors because their content is congruent with the individuals' value systems (Kelman, 1958). Using these three dimensions of commitment, Balfour and Wechsler (1991) examined two aspects of organizational commitment as they relate to public organizations: identification of the antecedents of compliance, identification, and internalization commitment; and determination of the effects of these dimensions on three hypothesized outcome measures—desire to remain with the organization, extra-role behaviors, and in-role behaviors. According to their findings, increased commitment among public employees showed a strong relation to their desire to remain with the organization, but did not increase their willingness to make extra efforts on behalf of the organization. They argue that increased commitment, therefore, may produce valuable results, such as reducing turnover, but may not increase productivity and performance.

As Reichers (1985) argues, the theory underlying the multiple commitments literature holds that an employee's commitment to the workplace cannot be adequately explained by commitment to the organization alone, because the coalitional nature of organizations leads employee commitment to be multidimensional.

Becker et al. (1995) examined the relative ability of the multidimensional view of commitment and theory of reasoned action to explain employee intentions and predict work behavior. In their study, they found that the commitment variables explain significant variance in each of the intentions and behaviors, controlling for the demographic variables.

In a study that employed a multiple constituency framework to examine the correlates of organizational commitment among a sample of 124 mental health professionals, Reichers (1986) found that only commitment to top management's goals was positively associated with commitment to the organization.

In addition to this growing evidence that the attitudinal commitment of employees to the workplace is multidimensional, it has been found that the foci and bases of commitment can improve the prediction of employee intentions and behaviors (Reichers, 1985; Becker et al., 1995). Foci of commitment are the individuals and groups to whom an employee is attached (Reichers, 1985). Employees can be committed to such foci as professions (Morrow, 1983; Gouldner, 1958) and unions (Angle and Perry, 1986; Gordon et al., 1984), as well as having a commitment to organizations (Mowday et al., 1982). Recent research suggests that workers can also be differentially committed to occupations, top management, supervisors, coworkers, and customers (Becker, 1992; Meyer et al., 1993; Reichers, 1986).

Becker et al. (1996) pointed out that previous research has found that employee commitment and job performance are largely unrelated because prior work has not distinguished among individual foci (targets) and bases (motives) of commitment. Drawing on their empirical findings, they argued that commitment to supervisors was positively related to performance and was more strongly associated with performance than was commitment to organization.

Becker (1992, p. 232) also discovered that:

Commitment to top management, supervisor, and work group were important determinants of job satisfaction, intent to quit, and prosocial organizational behaviors over
and above commitment to an organization. Commitment to foci other than an employing organization, specifically to top management, supervisors, and work groups,
were negatively related to intent to quit and positively related to satisfaction and
prosocial organizational behaviors, and explained variance in these dependent variables
over and above that explained by commitment to organization.

In a study comparing American public managers' commitment with Korean
public managers' commitment, Lee (2000b) divided employee commitment into three
types: commitment to supervisor, commitment to group, and commitment to organization. In his research, in the United States, the major factor affecting extra-role behavior was the commitment to supervisor due to an individualistic-oriented organizational culture, whereas in Korea the strongest factor was commitment to work group
owing to an elite group-based organizational culture. Furthermore, willingness to
support productivity strategies was a function of commitment to supervisor, whereas
commitment to group was a motivational base for willingness. Given that productive
organization often requires extra-role behavior from employees (Bass, 1985), and
productivity improvement is impossible without employees' commitments, these
findings suggest that effective public managers should pay special attention to foci
of employee commitment and should realize that employees' motivational bases could
also vary with organizational culture.

Top management should also realize that different dimensions of employee
commitment could be differentially associated with different dimensions of productivity improvement strategies. As Table 1 shows, productivity improvement strategies
can be divided into three types: organization-wide performance strategies, group
performance-driven strategies, and individual performance-driven strategies. It is
assumed that these three dimensions of performance improvement strategies will
contribute to productivity enhancement at the organizational level. As noted above,
commitment to supervisor is more likely to be related to willingness for individual
performance-driven strategies than the other two dimensions of commitment, and
commitment to group is more likely to affect willingness for group performance-driven
strategies. Although real impacts of productivity improvement strategies below are
arguable, linking different motivational bases to different dimensions of strategies can
provide valuable information to top management who are considering effective ways
to enhance productivity in any organization.

In addition, Lee (2000b) also found that American public managers showed
proactive attitudes toward group-based performance-driven strategies, and particularly preferred Total Quality Management (TQM) to any other strategies, thus placing
an emphasis on "teamwork" spirit. Considering that teamwork or group-based activities are receiving greater attention in American public administration, the high level
of preference of group performance-driven strategies suggests a bright future for
productive workplaces.

## C. Maintaining a Psychologically Balanced Relationship Between People

Although a multidimensional view of commitment is important in understanding
employees' motivational bases, increasing employee commitment does not necessarily

**Table 1**  Productivity Improvement Strategies

Organization-wide performance strategies
  Public–private partnerships at the organizational level
  Community-based partnerships
  Public–public partnerships
  Labor–management partnerships
  Performance measurements
  Based on citizen/customer curveys
  Budget allocations based on outcomes at the organizational level
  Organization performance evaluation by external consultants
  Benchmarking
Group performance-driven strategies
  Total quality management
  Interdepartmental teamwork
  Multiunit teamwork
  Pay-for-group performance
  Public–private partnerships at group level
  Budget allocations based on outcomes at group level
Individual performance-driven strategies
  Empowerment to lower levels
  Management by objectives
  Pay-for-individual performance
  360-Degree feedback

*Source*: Lee 2000b.

guarantee a high level of productivity. Lee (2000b) points out that the three dimensions of employee commitment are not automatically connected to employees' willingness to support productivity improvement strategies. Only when an employee believes that his or her supervisor, managerial-level group, or organization is committed to productivity improvement is a connection found. In particular, in the United States, commitment to supervisor was the major factor affecting overall willingness to support productivity improvement strategies, whereas commitment to managerial-level group was the major factor in Korea.

Even if employees are highly committed to their supervisor, group, or organization, they will not dare to support a specific productivity improvement strategy as long as they believe that any of the three is uncomfortable with the strategy. In other words, employees are not expected to support their preferred strategies against supervisor, group, or organization. This means that top management support and committed people at all levels are the most important prerequisites for productivity improvement. Employee commitment and willingness to support productivity strategies, will not occur unless employees believe that each focus of employee commitment is committed to productivity improvement. In a productive organization, everyone must feel comfortable with either expressing new ideas or supporting preferred productivity strategies.

## D.  Understanding Multiple Employee–Organization Relationships

Productivity and performance improvement is also a function of productive employee–organization relationships. Tsui et al. (1997) identified four different relationships between employer and employees: mutual investment relationship (social exchange relationship), quasi-spot contract relationship (economic exchange relationship), overinvestment relationship, and underinvestment relationship. Their study surveyed 976 employees in the private sector, and they found that employees showed higher levels of performance and more favorable attitudes toward their workplaces when they worked in either an overinvestment relationship or a mutual investment relationship. Many organizations, under fiscal pressure, may prefer either a quasi-spot contract relationship or underinvestment relationship to the other two. It should be noted, however, that an employee's performance will remain high in the long term only with overinvestment and mutual investment relationships.

## IV. CONCLUSION: IMPORTANCE OF INTANGIBLE FACTORS

In recent years, interest in the Balanced Scorecard, as a new performance measurement technique, has burgeoned. The Balanced Scorecard (BSC) is a framework and management methodology developed as a result of research performed by Kaplan and Norton (1992). The concept underlying BSC is that traditional performance measurement systems (those relying primarily on financial measures) hinder organizational growth and progress, and that four perspectives must be considered simultaneously for balanced performance measurement: customer, financial, internal process, and learning and growth perspectives. The City of Charlotte's corporate scorecard is one of the successful applications of the balanced score card in the public sector. As a result, the city highlights improvements in management across diverse agencies and departments. Success is a function of top management leadership and employees' commitments to productivity improvement. However, the city also holds that developing a balanced scorecard is hard work, and the process necessarily takes time and commitment because of resistance from employees and agencies that feel uncomfortable with change. No matter what productivity improvement strategies and plans are considered, unless there are commitment, professionalism, and intangible supports, it is hard to expect real outcomes (City of Charlotte, 2000).

Productivity and performance improvements are not easily accomplished in any sector—public, for-profit, or not-for-profit. However, well-constructed and well-managed public sector productivity programs will benefit all interested parties in a win–win relationship.

## REFERENCES

Allen, N. J., Meyer, J. P. (1990). The measurement and antecedents of affective, continuance and normative commitment to the organization. *J. Occupational Psychol.* 63:1–18.

Ammons, D. N. (1985). Common barriers to productivity improvement in local government. *Public Product. Manage. Rev.* 9:293–310.

Angle, H. L., Perry, J. L. (1986). Dual commitment and labor-management relationship climates. *Acad. Manage. J.* 29:31–50.

Balfour, D. L., Wechsler, B. (1991). Commitment, performance, and productivity in public organizations. *Public Product. Manage. Rev.* 14:355–368.

Balfour, D. L., Wechsler, B. (1996). Organizational commitment: Antecedents and outcomes in public organizations. *Public Product. Manage. Rev.* 19:256–277.

Ban, C., Faerman, S. R., Riccucci, N. M. (1992). Productivity and personnel process. In: Holzer, M., ed. *Public Productivity Handbook*. New York: Marcel Dekker, pp. 401–424.

Bass, M. D. (1985). Leadership and performance beyond expectations. New York: Free Press.

Becker, T. E. (1992). Foci and bases of commitment: Are they distinctions worth making? *Acad. Manage. J.* 35:232–244.

Becker, T. E., Billings, R. S., Eveleth, D. M., Gilbert, N. L. (1996). Foci and bases of employee commitment: Implications for job performance. *Acad. Manage. J.* 39:464–482.

Becker, T. E., Randall, D. M., Riegel, C. D. (1995). The multidimensional view of commitment and the theory of reasoned action: A comparative evaluation. *J. Manage.* 21:617–638.

Berman, E. M., West, J. P. (1998). Productivity enhancement efforts in public and nonprofit organizations. *Public Product. Manage. Rev.* 22:207–219.

Buchanan, B. (1974a). Building organizational commitment: The socialization of managers in work organizations. *Admin. Sci. Quart.* 19:533–546.

Buchanan, B. (1974b). Government managers, business executives, and organizational commitment. *Public Admin. Rev.* 34:339–347.

Buntz, C. G. (1981). Problems and issues in human service productivity improvement. *Public Product. Manage. Rev.* 5:299–320.

Burns, J. M. (1978). *Leadership*. New York: HarperCollins.

City of Charlotte (2000). *Balanced Score Card*. Charlotte, NC: City of Charlotte (On-Line) (Available at *http://www.ci.charlotte.nc.us/cibudget/workarea/FY2000/bscchp.pdf*).

David, M. (2001). Motivation secrets. *Exec. Excell.* 20:20.

Gabris, G. T., Grenell, K., Ihrke, D. M., Kaatz, J. (2000). Managerial innovation at the local level: Some effects of administrative leadership and governing board behavior. *Public Product. Manage. Rev.* 23:486–494.

Glaser, E. M. (1976). Productivity gains through worklife improvement. New York: Harcourt.

Gordon, M. E., Beauvais, L. L., Ladd, R. T. (1984). The job satisfaction and union commitment of unionized engineers. *Indust. Labor Relations Rev.* 37:359–370.

Gordon, M. E., Philpot, J. W., Burt, R. E., Thompson, C. A., Spiller, W. E. (1980). Commitment to union: Development of a measure and an examination of its correlates. *J. Appl. Psychol.* 65:479–499.

Gouldner, A. W. (1958). Cosmopolitans and locals: Toward an analysis of latent social roles. *Admin. Sci. Quart.* 2:444–480.

Grace, S. L., Holzer, M. (1992). Labor-management cooperation: An opportunity for change. In: Holzer, M., ed. *Public Productivity Handbook*. New York: Marcel Dekker, pp. 307–320.

Greiner, J. M. (1986). Motivational programs and productivity improvements in times of limited resources. *Public Product. Manage. Rev.* 10:81–101.

Griffin, K. (1967). The contribution of studies of source credibility to a theory of interpersonal trust in the communication process. *Psychol. Bull.* 68:104–120.

Guy, M. E. (1992a). Managing people. In: Holzer, M., ed. *Public Productivity Handbook*. New York: Marcel Dekker, pp. 307–320.

Guy, M. E. (1992b). Productive work environment. In: Holzer, M., ed. *Public Productivity Handbook*. New York: Marcel Dekker, pp. 321–334.

Halachmi, A., Holzer, M. (1986). Introduction: Toward strategic perspectives on public productivity. In: Halachmi, A., Holzer, M., eds. *Strategic Issues in Public Sector Productivity: The Best of Public Productivity Review, 1975–1985*. San Francisco, CA: Jossey-Bass, pp. 5–16.

Hennessey, J. T. (1998). Reinventing government: Does leadership make a difference? *Public Admin. Rev.* 58:522–532.

Holzer, M. (1984). Public administration under pressure. In: Holzer, M., Nagel, S. S., eds. *Productivity and Public Policy*. Thousand Oaks, CA: Sage, pp. 71–86.

Holzer, M. (1992). Mastering public productivity improvement. In: Holzer, M., ed. *Public Productivity Handbook*. New York: Marcel Dekker, pp. 1–11.

Holzer, M. (1995). Building capacity for productivity improvement. In: Halachmi, A., Holzer,

M., eds. *Competent Government: Theory and Practices: The Best of Public Productivity and Management Review, 1985–1993.* Burke, VA: Chatelaine Press, pp. 456–457.

Holzer, M., Callahan, K. (1998). *Government at Work: Best Practices and Model Programs.* Thousand Oaks, CA: Sage.

Holzer, M., Lee, S.-H. (1999). Labor-management tension and partnership: Where are we? What should we do? *Int. Rev. Public Admin.* 4:33–44.

Jurkiewicz, C. L., Massey, T. K. Jr., Brown, R. G. (1998). Motivation in public and private organizations: A comparative study. *Public Product. Manage. Rev.* 21:230–250.

Kaplan, R. S., Norton, D. P. (1992). The balanced scorecard: Measures that drive performance. *Harvard Bus. Rev.* January–February, 71–79.

Kelman, H. C. (1958). Compliance, identification, and internalization: Three processes of attitude change. *J. Conflict Resolution* 2:51–60.

Kotter, J. P. (1995). Leading change: Why transformation efforts fail. *Harvard Bus. Rev.* 73:59–67.

Lee, S.-H. (2000a). Understanding productivity improvement in a turbulent environment: A symposium introduction. *Public Product. Manage. Rev.* 23:423–427.

Lee, S.-H. (2000b). A multidimensional view of public sector employee commitment and willingness to support productivity improvement strategies: A comparative study of public employees at managerial level between the United States and South Korea. PhD dissertation, Rutgers University, Newark, NJ.

McGowan, R. P. (1984). Improving efficiency in public management: The torment of Sisyphus. *Public Product. Manage. Rev.* 8:162–178.

Meyer, J. P., Allen, N. J., Smith, C. A. (1993). Commitment to organizations and occupations: Extension and test of a three-component conceptualization. *J. Appl. Psychol.* 78:538–551.

Morrow, P. C. (1983). Concept redundancy in organizational research: The case of work commitment. *Acad. Manage. Rev.* 8:486–500.

Mowday, R. T., Porter, L. W., Steers, R. M. (1982). *Employee–Organization Linkages: The Psychology of Commitment, Absenteeism, and Turnover.* New York: Academic.

Nyhan, R. C. (2000). Changing the paradigm: Trust and its role in public sector organizations. *Am. Rev. Public Admin.* 30:87–109.

O'Reilly, C. A., Chatman, J. (1986). Organizational commitment and psychological attachment: The effects of compliance, identification, and internalization on prosocial behavior. *J. Appl. Psychol.* 71:492–499.

Rainey, H. G. (1983). Public agencies and private firms: Incentive structures, goals, and individual roles. *Admin. Soc.* 15:207–242.

Rainey, H. G. (1997). *Understanding and Managing Public Organizations.* 2nd ed. San Francisco: Jossey Bass.

Rainey, H. G., Pandey, S., Bozeman, B. (1975). Research note: Public and private managers' perceptions of red tape. *Public Admin. Rev.* 55:567–574.

Rainey, H. G., Backoff, R. W., Levine, C. L. (1976). Comparing public and private organizations. *Public Admin. Rev.* 36:233–246.

Reichers, A. E. (1985). A review and reconceptualization of organizational commitment. *Acad. Manage. Rev.* 10:476–485.

Reichers, A. E. (1986). Conflict and organizational commitments. *J. Appl. Psychol.* 71:508–514.

Robertson, P. J., Tang, S. (1995). The role of commitment in collective action: Comparing the organizational behavior and rational choice perspectives. *Public Admin. Rev.* 55:67–80.

Steinhaus, C. S., Perry, J. (1996). Organizational commitment: Does sector matter? *Public Product. Manage. Rev.* 19:278–289.

Sutermeister, R. A. (1977). *People and Productivity.* 3rd ed. New York: McGraw-Hill.

Tang, S.-Y., Robertson, P. J., Lane, C. E. (1996). Organizational types, commitment, and managerial actions. *Public Product. Manage. Rev.* 19:289–312.

Tsui, A., Pearce, J., Porter, L., Tripoli, A. (1997). Alternative approaches to the employee–organization relationship: Does investment in employees pay off? *Acad. Manage. J.* 40:1089–1121.

U.S. Department of Labor (1996). *Working Together for Public Service*. Washington, DC: Government Printing Office.

Usilaner, B. L. (1981). Can we expect productivity improvement in the federal government? *Public Product. Manage. Rev.* 5:237–246.

Vough, C. F. (1979). *Productivity: A Practical Program for Improving Efficiency*. New York: Amacon.

Werther, W. B., Ruch, W. A., McClure, L. (1986). *Productivity Through People*. New York: West.

Wilkins, A. L. (1983). Organizational stories as symbols which control the organization. In: Pondy, L. R., ed. *Organizational Symbolism*. Greenwich: JAI, pp. 81–92.

# 2

# Public Productivity in the Classical Age of Public Administration

**HINDY LAUER SCHACHTER**
*New Jersey Institute of Technology, Newark, New Jersey, U.S.A.*

Some modern public administration textbooks (Gordon, 1986, p. 45; Rosenbloom, 1989, pp. 15–16) identify a classical era in the field which begins with Frederick Winslow Taylor's (1895, 1947a, 1947b) work on scientific management, and encompasses the municipal reform movement and the literature up until the early 1940s. In this period, productivity, discussed under the rubric of efficiency or optimizing output/input, emerged as an important criterion in assessing public and private organizations. This chapter explores scientific management's impact on the classical era's public productivity literature. The first two sections examine the contribution of Frederick Taylor to the study of factory productivity and how his insights were used by the New York Bureau of Municipal Research (BMR) and Taylor disciple, Morris Cooke, to increase public sector efficiency. The subsequent two sections discuss Taylor's influence on the principles literature, a key part of public administration scholarship in the 1920s though the early 1940s. The final section describes Herbert Simon's critique of the classical approach to productivity.

## I. FREDERICK WINSLOW TAYLOR

When Frederick Taylor gave a presentation on piece rate systems at the American Society of Mechanical Engineers (ASME) meeting in 1895, the society had already been discussing productivity for at least nine years. At the 1886 meeting Captain Henry Metcalfe (1886) of the United States Army Ordnance had delivered a paper on expediting the flow of organizational communication. Between 1887 and 1891, papers by Halsey (1891), Partridge (1887), and Towne (1888) dealt with the promise of wage incentives. Taylor's contribution was to argue that organizations could increase productivity by creating a work science applicable to even the most routine tasks. His paper critiques the earlier wage-incentive proposals because they use actual output to set base rates. The earlier papers assume that the practice of their time approximates a fair day's work, whereas Taylor argues that researchers have to break jobs into constituent activities and experiment to learn how much time it takes to complete each operation under different circumstances. Managers have to investigate different work technologies and train workers in the best techniques before they can set a base wage. Thus, right from the start, Taylor argues that increasing productivity puts new responsibilities on managers.

In *The Principles of Scientific Management*, Taylor (1947b, pp. 36–37) elaborates on the duties of productive managers. They develop a work science to replace the old rule-of-thumb methods. They use this science to select, train, and develop workers, cooperating with the workers to see that activities proceed in accordance with the principles of the work science. They take on new responsibilities so that there is almost an equal division of labor between managers and their subordinates. Managers use the technique of time study to learn more efficient operating methods. They train workers in these methods, making certain to give employees ample feedback on their performance. When scientific management succeeds, a mental revolution takes place; bosses and workers substitute "hearty brotherly cooperation for contention and strife" (Taylor, 1947c, p. 30). Managers and employees stop worrying about dividing the surplus and cooperate to make it bigger. To see how this is done, let us examine the concepts of time study and feedback.

## A. Time Study

As a machine-shop supervisor at the Midvale Steel Company in the 1880s, Taylor realized that low productivity stemmed from the company's inability to define a fair day's time for each task. Managers required an empirical way to ascertain the time a worker needed to complete a specific job. Researchers could then perform workplace experiments to see whether changes in equipment or tools affected times. At Midvale, Taylor (1895) experimented on the proper cutting speed of tools and what happens to worker times when you vary tool shape, duration of cut, quality and hardness of the metal being cut, or cut depth and thickness of feed.

Time study requires deconstructing a job into elementary actions and timing each with a stopwatch. (For more details see Wren, 1979, pp. 125–140.) The number of elementary actions changes with the task. Taylor (1947a, p. 48) identifies five separate elements for the relatively simple task of loading pig-iron on railroad cars: picking up the pig from the ground, walking with it on level ground, walking with it up an incline, throwing the pig down, and walking back empty to get a new load. He lists 77 elements for the more complex job of preparing to do machine work on lathes.

Time study is done by specialists in a separate planning department rather than by line supervisors. These central-office researchers identify elements, select a skilled worker, and time and record each of his or her movements. The researchers then try to improve times by changing tools, machines, and layouts. Line workers can move into the planning department if they have good suggestions on how to improve production (e.g., Gilbreth, 1973, p. 51). At the Tabor Manufacturing Company, line workers moved into the planning department after the introduction of time study (Evidence Taken by the Interstate Commerce Commission, 1911, p. 2674).

Taylor (1947b, p. 64) found that people loading pig iron were most productive if they had specific rest periods during the day. When his experiments showed that people shoveling material were most productive with a load of 21 pounds on their shovels, he suggested that the Bethlehem Company stop telling workers to bring tools from home. The more productive strategy was for the company to issue shovels that held 21 pounds of whatever a given worker lifted, a smaller one for coal and a larger one for ashes. Labor historian Daniel Nelson (1992, p. 7) considers time study Taylor's "signature contribution to industrial management."

## B.  Feedback

Taylor believed that managers needed more information to increase productivity. He also argued that productive workers needed feedback on their performance. Inasmuch as workers "require a great deal of information that they have not got" (Taylor, 1947a, p. 195), therefore, "the most important object of both the workmen and the management should be the training and development of each individual" (Taylor, 1947b, p. 12). Taylor (1947a, p. 52) gave each worker at Midvale a slip of paper every morning listing that individual's productivity and pay on the previous day. This information allowed the worker to measure performance against earnings.

Many of Taylor's experiments concerned work that is conventionally labeled unskilled. Under scientific management, however, no work is considered so routine that productivity can not rise after training. Even immigrant workers who can not read or write English are trained with translators, bilingual assignment cards, and pictures (Gilbreth, 1973, p. 16).

Some of Taylor's contemporaries objected to the place of training in his system. Old-line business managers asserted that only lazy workers needed training or pay incentives to increase productivity (e.g., Hawkins, 1903). Frank Halsey (1895), another speaker at the ASME conferences, wondered why employees deserved higher pay if increased productivity resulted from management-initiated time study and training. Compare this point of view with Upton Sinclair's contention that a 61% wage increase is too small if Taylorism brings a 362% productivity increase to a plant (cited in Copley, 1923, vol. II, pp. 50–51).

Organized labor also objected to time study. Some machinists argued that training eliminated scope for their initiative. They predicted that time study and training would depress wages by allowing companies to develop unskilled laborers to take their jobs (e.g., Hudson, 1911). Braverman (1974) is a modern author who subscribes to the machinist's condemnation of Taylorism as a scheme to degrade skilled craft.

Taylor's early twentieth-century supporters specifically praise the feedback and training the system provides. Farnham (1916) cites education as one benefit workers get from scientific management. Thompson (1974) praises Taylor both for his use of bulletin boards to keep workers posted on their progress and for the one-on-one instruction his use of multiple functional supervisors provides. Lillian Gilbreth (1914) praises the emphasis on training because such emphasis shows that the system's objective is to develop each worker's skills and special abilities. Nyland (1989) and Schachter (1989) are modern authors who defend Taylor's approach.

## II. TAYLORISM OUTSIDE THE FACTORY

Although Taylor (1910b) conceived his books primarily for people who were "doing the manufacturing and construction work of our country, both employers and employees," his ideas have implications for nonprofit and government productivity as well. Larson (1977, p. 141) argues that in the first two decades of the twentieth century, Taylor's ideas were actually more attuned to the Progressive agenda for the public sector than to the interests of business executives who often did not want to share control with researchers. At this time, political science journals featured articles applying Taylor's theories to public sector activities (e.g., Dunaway, 1916; Leiserson, 1914).

Some of the most important public sector applications of Taylorism were made by the New York Bureau of Municipal Research, the first organization to use shop-management to increase urban productivity, and Morris Cooke, the Taylor disciple most involved in nonprofit and government work. We examine each of these applications in turn.

### A. New York Bureau of Municipal Research

The BMR was incorporated in 1907 as an organization for the scientific study of government, the successor to a one-year trial organization called the Bureau of City Betterment. It had a three-person directorate: William Allen, Henry Bruere, and Frederick Cleveland. [Histories of the BMR appear in Dahlberg (1966); Kahn (1977); and Schachter (1997).]

Taylor's primary insight for the BMR was the idea that productivity questions are researchable, that knowledge gained from experiments can lead to training and development which alters production possibilities. In a report on public safety, the BMR (1913) argues that much police work is inefficient because no one knows the best methods of investigating crimes. To start, the police commissioner needs information on the present, for example, number of complaints, how each is investigated, and so on. The department uses this information as a basis to experiment with different investigative methods and sees the results of each and which are most efficient. Successful strategies are then taught police recruits in academies staffed by experienced officers. Similar plans work in the fire function. Experiments are done on efficient hose size, how to connect a nozzle or how to empty a burning building. Fire recruits learn the best strategies in a three-week school.

In Taylor's system factory workers can contribute suggestions to the planning department. Bruere (1914) argues that patrolmen should also contribute suggestions for improving productivity on their sections or beats. Some old-line managers objected that this was an inappropriate activity for a patrolman (Bolton, 1914). Bruere (1914, p. 544) counters that scientific management will "develop and utilize" the patrol officer's latent power.

From its inception until 1914, the BMR tackled the political implications of shop management by introducing an external actor into the information-gathering stage. To maximize efficient government, citizens as well as administrators must spend time collecting and analyzing data. As part of the citizen's obligation to oversee administrative efforts, Bruere (1912, pp. 288–290) suggests that citizens prepare precinct maps. They should then list regulations police are supposed to enforce and examine police records to see what has been done about violations. They should trace 200 to 500 cases through the courts, make unannounced visits to police precincts to see how posts are being covered, and analyze complaints made to the precinct. To prepare citizens for these responsibilities, schools must teach children how to read and interpret city data, and municipal agencies must assemble their reports in easily accessible form.

For the BMR, optimum productivity requires citizen action. Cleveland (1913) argues that citizens should organize to determine their needs and help people know what the government should do to promote welfare. They should enforce requirements that records be kept. They must instruct politicians and bureaucrats on what citizens want and remonstrate with them when they do not seem to respond. They must protect agency employees who are doing a good job from false accusations and misinformation. Cleveland (1909, p. 352) notes, "it is the duty of the citizen quite as much as the . . . officer to assume responsibility for the constructive side of government."

## B. Morris Cooke

Morris Cooke, a mechanical engineer (Lehigh University, 1895) by training, became interested in Taylor's ideas in about 1903. He wanted to apply them in the publishing industry where he was a manager. In 1909 the Carnegie Foundation for the Advancement of Teaching asked Taylor to suggest a person to prepare an efficiency study of colleges; Taylor suggested Cooke.

As Taylor's disciple, Cooke saw this consulting assignment as a chance to increase production. Because Cooke considered education (rather than research or scholarship) to be a college's mission, he wanted to increase effective teaching through motivation and training. After surveying physics departments at Columbia University, Harvard University, Haverford College, the Massachusetts Institute of Technology, Princeton University, the University of Toronto, the University of Wisconsin, and Williams College, Cooke urged departments to hire additional faculty members to develop standard lecture notes and laboratory/recitation exercises. All physics teachers would consult these documents and augment them so that "the value of this part of the departmental equipment was constantly appreciating" (Cooke, 1910a, p. 25). He advocated training in pedagogical techniques for assistants who taught most of the large introductory sections. He suggested that the university should reward the best teachers with highly paid chairs and distinguished professorships. These suggestions translate into a university setting Taylor's concept of hiring staff workers to develop improved materials (i.e., lecture notes and exercises). The report puts the onus on management to offer entry-level line employees, such as teaching assistants, training that can lead to greater pay.

Although Cooke (1909) states that "any improvements suggested by this report . . . will be made by the professors themselves," he expected to startle his audience with his novel viewpoint. After all, many machinists disliked time study and central planning. Physics professors objected that the report showed little appreciation of the way faculty members actually educate undergraduates, with particularly scant regard for the role of research and scholarship in education (Savage, 1953, p. 108). University chief executives were split; President A. Lawrence Lowell of Harvard thought highly of the report whereas President Woodrow Wilson of Princeton was less sanguine (Cooke, 1910b).

From 1911 to 1915 Cooke was director of Philadelphia's department of public works, a position which Taylor (1911) said he took, "with the distinct idea of being able to introduce our methods." Cooke's (1914, 1918) publications from this period and slightly afterwards advocate conducting municipal experiments on the most productive way to accomplish relatively routine tasks such as removing snow or paving streets. Cooke emphasizes the need to explain experiments to the citizenry in clear language and allow voters to decide which innovations the city should implement. He notes (1918, pp. 119–120) that although some people consider standardization in areas such as paving inimical to worker initiative, he sees standardization as the beginning of initiative. Employees using the best planning department methods can suggest improvements that will move city work even further forward.

Layton (1971, p. 160) argues that because Cooke was unable to give wage incentives in Philadelphia, he was not really using the Taylor system. Yet Cooke (1912) communicated with Taylor and requested his advice throughout the public works appointment and it is clear that both men saw him as applying Taylorism to city government. Taylor's (1912) acceptance of Cooke's work shows that the use of wage incentives was actually an optional motivation technique in shop management rather than central to it. The central feature in Taylor's system was manager–employee cooperation in learning about production. With this feature in place, Cooke (1918) felt free to concentrate on social and esteem motivators such as a mayor's reception for city employees or a plan for workers to sign their own reports.

## III. TAYLORISM AND ADMINISTRATIVE PRINCIPLES

Perhaps one of the most influential statements in Shop Management is Taylor's (1947a, p. 63) admonition that in his system, "Management . . . will rest upon well recognized, clearly defined and fixed principles instead of depending on more or less hazy ideas received from a limited observation of the few organizations with which the individual may have come in contact." This admonition took shop management away from dissecting discrete tasks to forming generic rules. Beginning in the teens with the work of Emerson (1912a, 1912b) in America and later with Fayol (1949) in France, writers proposed lists of administrative rules or principles designed to guide all organizations, public or private, to greater productivity. Codification of principles became a central management-scholarship trend in the late 1920s and 1930s [e.g., Gulick (1937), and Urwick (1933, 1938, 1944)].

The principles literature moves from Taylor's concern to find the most efficient tools, materials, or layouts to an attempt to design the most efficient overall organizational structure, particularly in regard to division of labor and coordination through hierarchy. A major assumption of the authors is that structure influences performance; form creates optimal functioning. Specialization, unity of command, authority commensurate with responsibility, and tight span of control are important to productivity.

The goal is efficiency, a concept Emerson (1912a, p. 373) defines as "waste elimination." Managers can bring a whole plant up to the highest efficiency if they apply the right principles. Certain structures are good because they enhance efficiency. Thus Gulick (1937, pp. 9–10) advocates specialization because, "[T]he efficiency of a group working together is directly related to the homogeneity of the work they are performing."

Much of this literature ignores distinctions between public and private management. The authors are relatively unconcerned with an organization's environment or social function including the political aspects of public administration and citizen roles. Emerson (1912a, p. 373) says, "The mere purpose for which waste is to be eliminated is not important." Urwick (1937, p. 49) writes that the principles, "can be studied as a technical question, irrespective of the purpose of the enterprise, the personnel composing it, or any constitutional, political or social theory underlying its creation." Only Gulick notes that public managers have to consider not simply efficiency but the values of politics and the social order as well.

Authors in this literature cite Taylor as an authority [e.g., Fayol (1949, p. 69) or Gulick (1937)], but Taylor put his imprimatur on almost none of this work, even on those articles or books completed before his death in March, 1915. At least from 1912 on Taylor is explicit that the objective of his system is cooperation between employers and employees. Such cooperation is the overarching aim; all efficiency techniques must lead to this goal. Some of Taylor's fiercest barbs fall on Harrington Emerson, one of the earliest writers in the principles genre, because his work seems to regard efficiency rather than cooperation as the ultimate goal. Among Emerson's (1912a, 1912b) principles are the use of staff experts, common sense, careful selection of workers, fair wages, reliable records, and standardized operations and schedules, all pieces of advice that relate to Taylor's Midvale work or ASME pronouncements. Yet Taylor (1910a) deplores the shortcuts Emerson takes as a time-study consultant at the American Locomotive Company and tells Cooke that the problem with Emerson's project is, "the use of time study as a club, not as a means of harmonizing the interests of employers and employees, as we use it . . . we cannot afford to let Harrington Emerson's name be associated with our work."

## A.  Style of the Principles Literature

The principles literature is very fond of lists. Some lists are prescriptive such as Fayol's (1949) principles of management:

1.  Division of labor
2.  Authority and responsibility
3.  Discipline
4.  Unity of command
5.  Unity of direction
6.  Subordinating the individual's interest to the general interest
7.  Fair remuneration of personnel
8.  Centralization
9.  Scalar chain followed for communications
10.  Order
11.  Equity
12.  Stability of tenure of personnel
13.  Initiative
14.  Esprit de corps

Other lists are presented as descriptive or as analytic aids such as Gulick's (1937) functions of the chief executive, also known by the acronym POSDCORB:

1.  Planning—working out the things that the organization needs to get done
2.  Organizing—establishing formal structures of authority
3.  Staffing—establishing and maintaining the personnel function
4.  Directing—making decisions and leading

5. Coordinating—relating the parts of the work
6. Reporting—informing those to whom the executive is responsible
7. Budgeting—planning fiscal matters, accounting, and control

Some authors in the principles literature present their lists as if they were analogous to the Ten Commandments; Emerson (1912a, p. 380) says that if you implement his list of principles, you know with "absolute certainty" that you will hit the right standards. Urwick (1944, p. 9) says that going against the principles is an antisocial act in the same category as forgery or murder.

But how are these lists created? Rarely do they emanate from experimentation. The principles literature contains no experiments to test whether its structural preferences are, in fact, efficient. A hallmark of scientific management is its insistence on experimenting to find better ways of increasing productivity. Taylor spent three years at Bethlehem Steel comparing the loads workers could handle with different shovels. In sequence, he provided implements that held 38 pounds of a given material and then 34 pounds and then 30 pounds, and compared output over a day. If the lists' authors were true to this aspect of Taylor's oeuvre, they would design variant structures for a series of organizations in a single field and see how efficient each setup really is. They would, for example, switch a manager from an eight- to a four-person span of control and see which consequences follow. Such empirical evidence is never collected. The need to follow the principles is stated rather than shown. Readers must take on faith that the prescriptions really do improve productivity.

Harmon and Mayer (1986, p. 129) call this literature, "a kind of intellectualized Scientific Management." This definition is apt only if intellectual activity is conceived as pure ratiocination rather than theorizing grounded in empirical evidence and experiments.

## IV. PUBLIC ADMINISTRATION AND THE PRINCIPLES

Shortly after the end of World War I, political scientist W. F. Willoughby (1919) asserted that the task of public administration research was to look for the proper principles of organization to improve efficiency. This task plays a key role in public administration scholarship of the twenties through the early forties. The author of the field's first textbook of generic public administration, rather than municipal or state administration, White (1926) states in a separate article that no student of public administration would neglect the field's principles (White, 1936). Willoughby, author of the field's second textbook, writes in his preface that "in administration, there are certain fundamental principles of general application analogous to those characterizing any science which must be observed if the end of administrative efficiency in operation, is to be secured" (Willoughby, 1927, p. ix). Both textbooks focus on structural reform as the key to productivity (White, 1926; Willoughby, 1927).

### A. Brownlow Committee Report

In 1937 the President's Committee on Administrative Management with Louis Brownlow, chair, and Luther Gulick and Charles Merriam, members, reported on how to improve efficiency in the federal government. Although the committee is generally known as the "Brownlow Committee" after its chair, Gulick is widely credited as the report's author (e.g., Stillman, 1991, p. 117). The committee's prescriptions are compatible with the principles literature and with Gulick's POSDCORB formula for executive functions.

The Brownlow report maintains that the canons of efficiency require a responsible chief executive with expanded staff and managerial aids. The government needs planning and a revised fiscal system. The hundred-plus agencies, authorities, boards, and commissions of the period should be reorganized into a few large executive departments. One advantage of this reorganization is promoting unity of command by placing independent commissions under the president. Another advantage is giving the president a reasonable span of control.

The report admits that the "efficiency of government rests upon two factors: the consent of the governed and good management," but the author gives different weight to each of these prerequisites (President's Committee on Administrative Management, 1937, p. 3). He assumes that "[I]n a democracy consent may be achieved readily .... Efficient management ... is a factor of peculiar significance" (President's Committee on Administrative Management, 1937, p. 3). The emphasis, therefore, is on how to structure for efficiency rather than on how to be more responsive to citizens. The report accepts structure as the key to enhancing productivity.

Although the structural approach dominates public administration in the interwar years, the field is also heir to the BMR's concern with the political nature of public management and the role of citizens in maximizing efficiency. Some early urban administration texts do promote a role for citizens in productivity enhancement.

## B. Citizenship and Productivity

Munro's (1915, p. 3) urban administration textbook argues that "[T]he first essential of efficient administration is intelligent citizenship. In most discussions of municipal reform this is put last on the list, as if it were merely a by-product of charter overhauling .... That is getting at things from the wrong angle altogether." The average citizen wants to participate when he or she has an opportunity to learn about street, fire, or garbage services. Cities have to inform voters about these services and make them interested in administration if municipalities are to become effective agents of social betterment.

Capes' (1922) urban government text asserts that citizen interest is needed for efficiency. Such interest only emerges when residents have information about the urban condition. Capes (1922, p. 2) argues that "[I]n our effort to improve municipal services, we have been emphasizing too much the responsibility of the public official, and thinking too little about the responsibility of the citizen." He believes that "[G]ood city government can be as severely handicapped through indifferent citizenship as through apathetic administration" (Capes, 1922, p. 14). Both Munro (1915, p. 14) and Capes (1922, pp. 3–25) cite the work of the Bureau of Municipal Research's executives when they stress the need to have an informed citizenry to increase productive management.

## C. Synthesis and Tension

Elements of an apolitical, structurally oriented approach mingle with a more specifically public orientation in many authors of the 1930s and early 1940s. Dimock (1945, p. 5), for example, is in step with the principles literature when he writes that executives in business and government have much in common and that the "requirements of successful management are everywhere the same." He departs from Emerson or Fayol when he says that productive public management entails more than correct organization and appropriate methods of management; it also must take into account laws and sociological, economic, and political conditions from which administration grows (Dimock, 1936, p. 9). In his view, if public administration separates management techniques from the content of governmental problems, the field will become detached and unreal. Scholars must search for what is distinctive and fundamental about state activity (Dimock, 1937).

Dimock (1936) argues against overgeneralizing. His review of the principles literature cautions public administration scholars to "beware that in the name of scientific method . . . we do not place certainty above understanding" (Dimock, 1938, p. 288).

Writings such as Dimock's hint at a tension between an apolitical road to efficiency and a concern that public productivity requires a path attuned to political realities. One way of releasing this tension might have been to resolve the two approaches and focus on developing a theory of what is and is not distinctive about public sector production. During the classical period, such resolution did not occur— nor does the field have consensus today on the contours of such a theory. Instead, the field received a jolt when Herbert Simon, fresh from the doctoral program at the University of Chicago, demolished any scientific authority the principles literature had ever had.

## V. SIMON'S CRITIQUE OF THE PRINCIPLES LITERATURE

In the immediate post-World War II era Herbert Simon (1947) began an auspicious career by proposing that the principles had fatal defects as guides to managerial action. The principles of Gulick or Urwick praise specialization but they are silent on the question of what kind of specialization promotes efficiency, whether, for example, a public health manager should have nurses specialize by function or district. The principles laud unity of command but they do not explain when this dictum must give way to the need for specialization. They do not tell you when it promotes efficiency for a line officer to follow the orders of the finance department, rather than the line hierarchy, on a financial matter. The principles praise narrow spans of control but they are silent on the problem of excessively tall hierarchies that result when each manager can only directly supervise a few people. Rather than being effective guides to conduct, the principles prove ambiguous when put to empirical tests.

By themselves the lists of principles cannot tell a manager how to act. In fact, too much of a given principle may harm efficiency. A certain amount of specialization aids productivity. Too much leads a unit to forget the goals of the entire organization. Overspecialization can foster a lack of talk among divisions, resulting in narrow frames of reference and ultimate stagnation. The principles are simply criteria for describing organizational situations. Managers have to weigh one criterion against another.

By pointing out that the principles are ambiguous, Simon is not adding anything absolutely new to the discussion. It caricatures the earlier literature to suggest that its primary spokespeople believed a manager could always apply prescriptions mechanically; these writers do occasionally note that the rules offer different advantages and disadvantages in different situations. Although Emerson (1912a, p. 380) says that the principles bring standards with "absolute certainty," he also cautions that this guarantee only applies when "a valiant and competent man" implements them. This caveat suggests that correct use requires experience and intelligence. Gulick (1937) insists that we need more scientific study to determine the best span of control in a given situation. This caution suggests that different spans of control may work best in different functions or industries.

Simon's contribution lies in shifting the discussion's focus. What had been a throwaway clause or aside in the prewar literature becomes a central analytical point. Simon (1947) declares the discipline not ripe for principles. Students of administration need operational concepts first. Only when they have concrete terms to describe administrative situations can they undertake experiments to learn the effect of different criteria on organizational functioning. Such experiments must isolate one factor from others that may be operating on the organization at the same time. Theory will direct experiments and empirical evidence in turn will provide a test and correction for theory. The field will escape reliance on slogans and proceed to analyze organizational realities.

Researchers will use this analysis in two ways. They will create a sociology of administration that describes how human beings actually behave in organizations. They will also create a practical science of administration that will show how people in organizations should behave if they want to maximize goal attainment with scarce means.

For Simon structure remains important. His public administration textbook stresses the role of internal organization in fostering efficiency. (See Simon et al., 1950.) The difference between him and the principles authors is that he wants to offer no "best" way without empirical evidence; he stresses that the ideal structure will vary according to the situation.

Simon's attack is generally seen as the start of public administration's post- or neoclassical period. Henceforth, Taylor, the BMR, Gulick, and Urwick are relegated to the history section in textbooks. New standardbearers appropriate intellectual center field.

## REFERENCES

Bolton, R. (1914). Discussion. *Am. Soc. Mech. Eng. Trans.* 36:547.

Braverman, H. (1974). *Labor and Monopoly Capitalism: The Degradation of Work in the Twentieth Century*. New York: Monthly Review Press.

Bruere, H. (1912). *The New City Government*. New York: Appleton.

Bruere, H. (1914). The future of the police arm from an engineering standpoint. *Am. Soc. Mech. Eng. Trans.* 36:535–547.

Bureau of Municipal Research. (1913). *Report on a Survey of the Department of Public Safety, Pittsburgh*. New York: Bureau of Municipal Research.

Capes, W. (1922). *The Modern City and Its Government*. New York: Dutton.

Cleveland, F. (1909). *Chapters on Municipal Administration and Accounting*. New York: Longmans, Green.

Cleveland, F. (1913). *Organized Democracy*. New York: Longmans, Green.

Cooke, M. (1909, Oct. 12). *Personal letter to Frederick Taylor. Available in the Taylor Collection*. Hoboken, NJ: Stevens Institute of Technology.

Cooke, M. (1910a). *Academic and Industrial Efficiency*. New York: Carnegie Foundation for the Advancement of Teaching.

Cooke, M. (1910b, Feb. 24). *Personal letter to Frederick Taylor. Available in the Taylor Collection*. Hoboken, NJ: Stevens Institute of Technology.

Cooke, M. (1912, June 27). *Personal letter to Frederick Taylor. Available in the Taylor Collection*. Hoboken, NJ: Stevens Institute of Technology.

Cooke, M. (1914). Some factors in municipal engineering. *Am. Soc. Mech. Eng. Trans.* 36:605–618.

Cooke, M. (1918). *Our Cities Awake*. New York: Doubleday, Page.

Copley, F. (1923). *Frederick Taylor*. New York: Harper and Brothers.

Dahlberg, J. (1966). *The New York Bureau of Municipal Research*. New York: New York University Press.

Dimock, M. (1936). The meaning and scope of public administration. In: Gaus, J., White, L., Dimock, M., eds. *The Frontiers of Public Administration*. Chicago: University of Chicago Press, pp. 1–12.

Dimock, M. (1937). The study of administration. *Am. Poli. Sci. Rev.,* 1:28–40.

Dimock, M. (1938). Administration as a science. *Nat. Muni. Rev., XXVII* 4:265–266, 288.

Dimock, M. (1945). *The Executive in Action*. New York: Harper and Brothers.

Dunaway, J. (1916). Standardization and inspection. *Am. Poli. Sci. Rev.* 10(2):315–319.

Emerson, H. (1912a). *Efficiency as a Basis for Operations and Wages*. New York: Engineering Magazine Press.

Emerson, H. (1912b). *Twelve Principles of Efficiency*. New York: Engineering Magazine Press.

*Evidence Taken by the Interstate Commerce Commission in the Matter of Proposed Advances in Freight Rates by Carriers*. (1911). Vol. IV, U.S. Senate Document 725, 61st Congress, 3rd Sess. Washington DC: U.S. Government Printing Office.

Farnham, D. (1916, April). The brief for scientific management. Paper presented at the Efficiency Society Meeting. Available in the Taylor Collection. Stevens Institute of Technology.

Fayol, H. (1949). *General and Industrial Management (transl. C. Storrs)*. London: Sir Isaac Pitman.

Gilbreth, F. (1973). *Primer of Scientific Management*. Easton, PA: Hive.

Gilbreth, L. (1914). *The Psychology of Management: The Function of the Mind in Determining, Teaching and Installing Methods of Least Waste*. New York: Sturgis and Walton.

Gordon, G. (1986). *Public Administration in America*. 3rd ed. New York: St. Martin's.

Gulick, L. (1937). Notes on the theory of organization. In: Gulick, L., Urwick, L., eds. *Papers on the Science of Administration*. New York: Institute of Public Administration, pp. 1–46.

Halsey, F. (1891). Premium plan of paying for labor. *Am. Soc. Mech. Eng. Trans.* 12:755–764.

Halsey, F. (1895). Discussion. *Am. Soc. Mech. Eng. Trans.* 16:885.

Harmon, M., Mayer, R. (1986). *Organization Theory for Public Administration*. Boston: Little, Brown.

Hawkins, J. (1903). Discussion. *Am. Soc. Mech. Eng. Trans.* 24:1460–1461.

Hudson, F. (1911, April 27). The machinist's side of Taylorism. *Am. Machinist* 773.

Kahn, J. (1977). *Budgeting Democracy: State Building and Citizenship in America, 1890–1928*. Ithaca, NY: Cornell University Press.

Larson, M. S. (1977). *The Rise of Professionalism*. Berkeley, CA: University of California Press.

Layton, E. Jr. (1971). *The Revolt of the Engineers: Social Responsibility and the American Engineering Profession.* Cleveland, OH: Case Western Reserve University Press.

Leiserson, W. (1914). The theory of public employment offices and the principles of their practical administration. *Poli. Sci. Quart.* 29(1):28–46.

Metcalfe, H. (1886). The shop order system of accounts. *Am. Soc. Mech. Eng. Trans.* 7:440–448.

Munro, W. B. (1915). *Principles and Methods of Municipal Administration.* New York: Macmillan.

Nelson, D. (1992). Scientific management in retrospect. In: Nelson, D., ed. *A Mental Revolution: Scientific Management since Taylor.* Columbus, OH: Ohio State University Press, pp. 5–39.

Nyland, C. (1989). *Reduced Worktime and the Management of Production.* Cambridge, UK: Cambridge University Press.

Partridge, W. (1887). Capital's need for high-priced labor. *Am. Soc. Mech. Eng. Trans.* 8:269–275.

President's Committee on Administrative Management. (1937). *Report of the Committee with Studies of Administrative Management in the Federal Government.* Washington, DC: U.S. Government Printing Office.

Rosenbloom, D. (1989). *Public Administration: Understanding Management, Politics and Law in the Public Sector.* 2nd ed. New York: Random House.

Savage, H. (1953). *Fruit of an Impulse: The Carnegie Foundation, 1905–1950.* New York: Harcourt Brace.

Schachter, H. L. (1989). *Frederick Taylor and the Public Administration Community: A Reevaluation.* Albany, NY: State University of New York Press.

Schachter, H. L. (1997). *Reinventing Government or Reinventing Ourselves: The Role of Citizen Owners in Making A Better Government.* Albany, NY: State University of New York Press.

Simon, H. (1947). *Administrative Behavior.* New York: Free Press.

Simon, H., Smithberg, D., Thompson, V. (1950). *Public Administration.* New York: Knopf.

Stillman, R. (1991). *Preface to Public Administration: A Search for Themes and Direction.* New York: St. Martin's.

Taylor, F. (1895). A piece rate system being a step towards partial solution of the labor problem. *Am. Soc. Mech. Eng. Trans.* 16:856–883.

Taylor, F. (1910a, Jan. 13). Personal letter to Morris Cooke. Available in the Taylor Collection. Hoboken, NJ: Stevens Institute of Technology.

Taylor, F. (1910b, Dec. 10). Personal letter to Morris Cooke. Available in the Taylor Collection. Hoboken, NJ: Stevens Institute of Technology.

Taylor, F. (1911, Nov. 27). Personal letter to Morris Cooke. Available in the Taylor Collection. Hoboken, NJ: Stevens Institute of Technology.

Taylor, F. (1912, July 2). Personal letter to Morris Cooke. Available in the Taylor Collection. Hoboken, NJ: Stevens Institute of Technology.

Taylor, F. (1947a). *Shop Management.* New York: Harper and Brothers.

Taylor, F. (1947b). *The Principles of Scientific Management.* New York: Harper and Brothers.

Taylor, F. (1947c). *Testimony Before the Special House Committee.* New York: Harper and Brothers.

Thompson, C. B. (1974). *The Taylor System of Scientific Management.* Easton, PA: Hive.

Towne, H. (1888). Gain sharing. *Am. Soc. Mech. Eng. Trans.* 10:600–614.

Urwick, L. (1933). *Management of Tomorrow.* London: Nisbett.

Urwick, L. (1937). Organization as a technical problem. In: Gulick, L., Urwick, L., eds. *Papers on the Science of Administration.* New York: Institute of Public Administration, pp. 47–88.

Urwick, L. (1938). *Scientific Principles and Organizations.* New York: American Management Association.

Urwick, L. (1944). *The Elements of Administration.* New York: Harper and Brothers.

White, L. (1926). *Introduction to the Study of Public Administration.* New York: Macmillan.

White, L. (1936). The meaning of principles in public administration. In: Gaus, J., White, L., Dimock, M., eds. *The Frontiers of Public Administration.* Chicago: University of Chicago Press, pp. 13–25.

Willoughby, W. (1919). Introduction: The modern movement in efficiency in the administration of public affairs. In: Weber, G., ed. *Organized Efforts for the Improvement of Methods of Administration in the United States.* New York: Appleton, pp. 3–26.

Willoughby, W. (1927). *Principles of Public Administration with Special Reference to the National and State Governments.* Baltimore: John Hopkins Press.

Wren, D. (1979). *The Evolution of Management Thought.* 2nd ed. New York: Wiley.

# 3

# Performance Measurement and Citizen Participation

**KATHE CALLAHAN**
*Rutgers, The State University of New Jersey, Newark, New Jersey, U.S.A.*

*Not everything that can be measured is important, and not everything that is important can be measured (Albert Einstein).*

## I. INTRODUCTION

Performance measurement is an old idea that has taken on renewed importance. It was almost seventy-five years ago when the International Cities Managers Association (ICMA) issued "Measuring Municipal Activities" with suggestions on ways for local governments to assess how well services were being delivered (Fischer, 1994, p. 3). Over sixty years ago, Clarence Ridley and Herbert Simon (1938, Prix) discussed the importance of appropriate measures of performance that would enable managers, elected officials, and citizens to determine whether they were getting "efficient government or inefficient government." In 1947, the Hoover Commission was established to study and investigate the methods of operation of the Executive Branch of Government and to make recommendations on ways to streamline government operations, making them more efficient and ultimately improving service. And, almost twenty-five years before "reinventing government" came into vogue and the Gore Commission attempted to create a government that "works better and costs less", Harry Hatry and his colleagues at the Urban Institute were pioneering methods to measure the performance of government programs.

This renewed interest in performance measurement can be attributed, in part, to resolutions by various professional organizations such as the American Society for Public Administration, the Government Accounting Standards Board, and the International City Manager Association urging governments to institute systems for goal-setting and performance measurement. Certainly, the 1993 Government Results and Performance Act, which mandates that strategic plans and performance goals be established for select federal agencies, and requires that agencies show results before new appropriations are made, has had an impact.

The added emphasis can also be attributed to quality of life issues that are of growing concern in communities around the world. Movements toward greater environmental quality, sustainable development, and healthy communities are evidence of a push for an improved quality of life. Thanks to Robert Putnam (1993, 2000), more and more people are concerned with building and sustaining social capital, networks of trust and civic engagement that foster cooperation and community building. Research indicates there is a link between government performance and social capital (Putnam, 1993; Pierce et al., 2002). A high level of social capital in a community is likely to indicate a high performing government. Communities where citizens are active and involved, where a strong degree of trust and cooperation are present, tend to perform better than communities where citizens are disengaged and lack trust in each other and in public institutions.

Communities interested in developing and sustaining social capital typically develop vision statements, or goals for improving the overall quality of life in their community. In order to determine if goals have been met, or visions realized, measures of achievement (performance) must be established. As a result, as more and more communities engage citizens in community vision efforts we will see an increased role for citizens in articulating and establishing meaningful measures of municipal performance that attempt to link broad community goals and visions with measures of local government performance.

## A.  Chapter Overview

This chapter explores the relationship between performance measurement and citizen participation. The value of involving citizens in the measurement of state and local government performance is discussed, as are the challenges associated with developing and sustaining meaningful participation techniques. Several questions are addressed, such as: How do public administrators develop indicators of performance that are meaningful to citizens *and* public managers? How can public managers effectively communicate measures of performance to the public so that citizens can hold government accountable for results? How can public administrators develop appropriate participation techniques to foster and sustain citizen involvement?

## B.  Overview of Performance Measurement

Performance measurement in the public sector is frequently defined as the systematic and continuous assessment of how well services, and in some instances products, are being delivered (Holzer and Halachmi, 1996; Ammons, 1996). There is no universally accepted term for measuring an organization's performance. As a result, many terms such as productivity, work measurement, and effectiveness have been used synonymously with "performance measurement." As Paul Epstein (1988) suggests, the simplest way of thinking about it is that performance measurement is government's way of determining whether it is providing a quality product at a reasonable cost.

Performance indicators are objective measures of accomplishments: miles of road paved, number of students passing the high school proficiency test, or percentage of residents who feel safe in their neighborhood. Measures such as these can be compared over time to determine if performance improves from quarter to quarter or year to year, as well as across departments or across jurisdictions to determine how performance compares to others providing similar services. A good performance measurement system can increase knowledge about public sector service delivery and therefore enhance the decision-making process of elected officials and public managers. It can also strengthen accountability systems in that the public has an increased understanding of what they are getting, or not getting, for their tax dollar (Hatry et al., 1990).

A good performance measurement system should include a variety of measures: input (how much), output (how many), outcome (how well), and efficiency (at what cost). It should also include a few pertinent and easy to understand indicators that relate to the broader goals and objectives for a community or agency, rather than numerous scattered indicators. In this case, less is better. Identifying two to three meaningful measures for each service is more valuable than collecting reams of data that have little practical or social relevance. Too much information overwhelms the reader and does not contribute to enhanced knowledge or decision making. Likewise, a good performance measurement system should not include data for data's sake. Just because the data are collected does not mean they need to be reported or that they add value to the decision-making process. The usefulness of a performance measurement system increases to the extent that the measurement system reflects and relates to a coherent set of goals and strategies covering major agency programs and activities (Wholey, 1999, p. 220). Data not tied to a vision, goal, or objective are less valuable than those that are linked to a broader picture. Poister and Streib (1999) refer to this as the DRIP syndrome: data rich and improvement poor, where the data collected do not contribute to meaningful decision making.

A good performance management usually contributes to the following (National Center for Public Productivity).

> *Better decision-making*: it provides managers with information to make informed decisions;
> *Performance appraisal*: it links both individual and organizational performance to aspects of personnel management and when properly utilized can motivate public employees;
> *Accountability*: it fosters responsibility on the part of managers and informs the public so they hold managers accountable;
> *Service delivery*: improvements in public service performance can be realized when there are measurable standards to achieve and outcomes to meet;
> *Public participation*: clear reporting of performance measures can stimulate the public to take a greater interest in and provide more encouragement for government employees to provide quality services; and
> *Improvement of civic discourse*: it helps to make public deliberations about service delivery more factual and specific.

## II.  CITIZEN-DRIVEN PERFORMANCE MEASUREMENT

Citizen-driven performance measurement involves the use of measures or indicators that are socially relevant to citizens. Socially relevant measures are understandable to the average citizen and inform him or her about the quality of life in their community and the quality of service delivered by a government agency. Socially relevant performance measures provide citizens with comprehensible data that enable them to hold government officials accountable for performance and enable them to answer the question, "Am I getting value for my tax dollar?" So, for example, in addition to collecting data on the tonnage of refuse collected in a quarter, a public works department might also collect data on street cleanliness. The cleanliness rating of a street means more to the average citizen than the overall amount of garbage collected.

Citizens, and elected officials, can use relevant data such as cleanliness ratings to hold public administrators accountable for their performance. A citizen, with a copy of numerical street ratings in hand, can intelligently ask their elected officials, "How come streets in my neighborhood are ranked three, which means they're garbage-strewn, while in neighborhood A they're all ranked one, meaning there's not a piece of litter in sight?" In this way citizens' concerns or complaints can be objectively expressed. Typically, citizen concerns are voiced in a very subjective manner with no hard data available to back them up, such as, "The streets in my neighborhood are in terrible shape." What exactly does that mean? The vagueness of such a complaint makes it easy to ignore. Armed with objective data citizens are more likely to be taken seriously and it will become more difficult to dismiss their complaints.

Equally important is the enhanced ability for public administrators to make informed decisions about community needs and priorities. Rather than rely on strictly subjective data, generated primarily by citizen complaints, the public works department can respond to objective numerical ratings and justify their decisions on hard data. Data such as these can also be used as benchmarks to improve service over time and foster competition among service departments and providers.

Socially relevant performance measures equip citizens with the information necessary to ensure accountability; to make sure that governments and public agencies do what they are supposed to do and ultimately improve the quality of people's lives. Ideally, citizen-driven performance measurement entails citizens being involved in the establishment of appropriate performance indicators. In addition, in some instances, citizens may actually collect data. If citizens are not directly involved, public administrators, at the very least, should consider the value the performance measurement system, or specific indicators, have for citizens and should willingly share performance data with the public in a very timely and understandable way.

Citizen involvement in performance measurement may help public managers stay focused on what really matters in their communities. Citizen involvement can increase the impact of performance measurement by encouraging managers to look beyond traditional output measures (that often have little meaning to citizens) and instead focus on quality of life issues and community goals. When you think about it, why do managers care about government performance? They want to improve the quality of service delivery and ultimately the quality of life in the communities they manage.

The overall goal of involving citizens in performance measurement is to ensure that the measurement systems put into place reflect the needs and concerns of citizens. Citizens and public managers together can establish performance measures that are meaningful to both parties. So, for example, instead of just calculating the number of passengers riding a specific bus or subway line, transit officials might calculate the percentage of trips on schedule or ask passengers to rate the cleanliness of the buses and subway cars. Instead of counting the number of squad cars deployed to specific neighborhoods, public managers could ask citizens how safe they feel in their own neighborhoods or in city parks.

The relevance of performance measures increases when managers incorporate citizens' perceptions. A powerful management tool results when public managers combine or compare traditional output measures with outcome measures that reflect citizens' perceptions. For example, city managers might learn that an increased police presence in a residential area has no correlation to a citizen's feeling of safety in that neighborhood. Yet, increased police presence in public areas, such as city parks and business districts, has a direct impact on a citizen's feeling of safety. Meaningful measures that the average citizen can understand provide citizens with the opportunity to assess government performance, and influence how government services can be made more responsive to community needs and priorities.

The difference between a performance measurement system that is management-driven and one that is citizen-driven is summarized in Table 1. The steps listed in the left-hand column are steps that should typically be included in developing a performance measurement system.

## A. The Challenge of Getting Citizens Involved

Although citizen participation can ultimately improve the level and quality of municipal service provision by making services more responsive to the needs of citizens, it is often difficult to achieve. Citizen involvement typically results in effective policy and meaningful public sector programs (Stivers, 1990; King and Stivers, 1998; Box, 1998; Schacter, 1997), however, active citizenship is often perceived as burdensome, costly, and time consuming (Timney, 1996; Thomas, 1995). Performance measurement systems may be easier to design and implement when citizens are excluded and managers are the ones determining what will be measured and how it will be measured. Although easier to implement, such performance measurement systems fall short in terms of measuring what matters most in a community. Citizen involvement increases the social relevance of indicators by combining facts (hard data) with value (how citizens feel).

Tangible benefits can be derived from effective citizen involvement and participation not only in performance measurement, but in public decision making as well. Thomas (1995) indicated in *Public Participation in Public Decisions* that public involvement can increase the effectiveness of public managers and the decisions they make. For example, decision quality may improve as citizens and citizen groups add to the information available for making decisions. The added information provided by citizens, who understand issues from first-hand experience, might prevent repetitions of many ill-advised public decisions (e.g., high-rise public housing and large-scale residential displacement from urban renewal areas). With citizens involved in making decisions, acceptance of the decision may increase, enhancing the likelihood of successful implementation and reducing the amount of vocal opposition. As involvement increases, citizen understanding of governmental operations may increase and criticisms of governmental agencies may lessen, improving the plight of the often-criticized public administrator (Thomas, 1995, p.180).

The benefits of meaningful citizen involvement are known to most public administrators, but the traditional role for citizen involvement in the decision-making

**Table 1**   Comparison of Managerial-Driven and Citizen-Driven Performance Measurement

| Performance measurement system | Managerial-driven | Citizen-driven |
|---|---|---|
| Identify the program to be measured | Managers and department directors determine priorities | Citizens have a voice in determining priorities |
| State the purpose and identify the desired outcome | Department or agency establishes goals, objectives internally (managerial objectives) | Citizens are included in establishing goals and objectives; participate in strategic planning process |
| Select measures or indicators | Managers determine what measures to collect; mostly quantitative | Citizens help determine what data to collect; quantitative and qualitative; socially relevant measures |
| Set standards for performance and outcomes (targets) | Managers establish performance targets. How good is good enough? | Citizens and managers establish performance standards. What is quality service? |
| Monitor results | Administrators and staff monitor their own performances | Citizens monitor through surveys, as trained observers, through data and reports provided |
| Report on performance | Managers determine what and how to report, whether report is distributed internally or externally | Reports are shared with public, media, elected officials |
| Utilize performance information | Managers use information in planning; goal setting; continuous improvement | Citizens utilize to improve quality of life; identify strengths and opportunities for improvement; hold elected officials accountable |

process of government is still rather limited. The traditional role for citizens in the deliberative process is to attend and speak out at public hearings or meetings of governing bodies, write letters to elected officials, and, if concerned enough about a specific issue, possibly organize a petition drive. Public hearings are usually poorly attended due to the nature of the hearings, the way information is shared with citizens, and the feeling on the part of citizens that decisions have already been made and the public hearing is being held because they are required by law, not because elected officials and government administrators desire to establish policy, measure performance, or craft a budget based on citizen input.

## B. Getting Citizens Involved

Citizens can be brought into the process in a variety of ways. Community outreach through meetings, workshops, and focus group discussions is a good way to start. It is important to find out how citizens determine whether their local government is doing a good job of delivering municipal services. On what sort of measures do they rely? If it is a community new to performance measurement, citizens, as well as elected officials and municipal managers, will most likely rely on subjective measures. Are the streets clean? Do I feel safe? Are there any vacant storefronts? The idea behind a citizen-driven performance measurement program is to move from the subjective measures of what people perceive to objective measures that are data driven, and to make sure the objective measures that are introduced mean something to the general public, in addition to the public managers and elected officials.Generally, meetings with citizens should involve elements of one or more of the following.

> *Structured focus groups*, where themes surrounding service delivery, quality, and value shape the discussion;
> *Workshops*, with elements of training, role playing to view the jurisdiction from multiple perspectives, and structured idea generation techniques (e.g., to identify goals and performance indicators) are incorporated;
> *Information, feedback, and discussion sessions*, to obtain citizen reaction to the process and suggestions for improvement, to stimulate "civic conversations," and develop consensus among citizens and managers; and
> *Outreach meetings*, which are particularly important to ensure representation of a broader range of citizens than those who take the extra time to attend performance measurement meetings. Attend meetings of the Kiwanis Club, Civil Rights Commission, Landlord–Tenant Association, and League of Women Voters (to name a few) and hear what they have to say about government performance.

The Citizen-Initiated Performance Assessment (CIPA) project in Iowa, which is funded by the Alfred P. Sloan Foundation, convened a series of meetings to engage large numbers of citizens. Citizens were asked during their first meeting to identify elements of public service that matter to them. Professionalism, timeliness, quality, accessibility, and safety were frequently identified and therefore formed the basis for developing performance measures (Ho and Coates, 2002).In the process of generating performance measures that would have relevance to both citizens and public managers, the Iowa team utilized a worksheet that contained the following elements (Ho and Coates, 2001, p. 6).

> Are the measures helpful to citizens in evaluating the performance of the service? Can an ordinary citizen understand the measure?
> If a service has strategic goals and functional objectives established by the city council or another citizen committee, how are the measures tied to them?
> If the service has legal and professional standards, would citizens like to adopt them?
> Are the measures quantifiable?
> Are the measures clearly defined?
> Can the measures really show what they are intended to measure? Are there too many intervening factors that challenge the validity of the measures to reflect

government performance? If yes, can the measures be modified to control for some of the intervening factors? Should these intervening factors also be measured and reported?
Are there data available? Is it too costly and time consuming to collect the data?

Citizen surveys are used quite often to determine citizen satisfaction, or dissatisfaction, with government services and to establish priorities for a community. Citizens, as the recipients of government services, are in the best position to assess which areas of government are functioning well and which ones are in need of improvement. They can be instrumental in identifying how best to improve quality, and possibly efficiency, and for this reason surveys, when properly designed, administered, and analyzed can be a valuable tool for policymakers.

The typical citizen satisfaction survey will ask citizens to rate specific services on five-point Likert scale. Data collected the first time a survey is administered can serve as a baseline and comparisons can be made over time. Survey data can also be used to benchmark performance with neighboring communities. Benchmarking over time, with neighboring communities and even with departments within a community, encourages competition and ultimately helps improve performance. Individuals and units will strive to outperform each other and better last year's satisfaction rate.

Surveys can provide a great deal of information about citizens' perceptions of satisfaction and overall quality of life; as with any type of survey, however, there are limitations. A survey is only as good as its questions, and if not properly administered, can produce biased results. Poorly worded or leading questions will favor some outcomes over others. If the survey sample, or survey respondents, are not representative of the entire community questions of validity will arise. For example, a low-income minority family may perceive the police department differently than a white, upper middle-class family. Different perceptions fall not only along racial and economic lines, but also different age groups, same-sex households, and families with or without children will have different perspectives about the quality and need for various public services. Surveys can be valuable in determining if there is disparity in service delivery among neighborhoods, but can only do so if the response rate from the various neighborhoods is comparable.

Many communities have citizen advisory committees for a variety of issues such as budgeting, downtown beautification, and parks and recreation. Although citizen advisory committees are plentiful, very few deal explicitly with performance measurement. One of the exceptions is North Carolina's Citizen Efficiency Review Committee (CERC). The City of Winston-Salem created a citizen committee to review the efficiency and effectiveness of all City services. This volunteer committee of over 100 citizens examined each department with the goal of reducing costs and improving services. The review process also provided opportunities for City staff to learn new ideas from citizens and provided opportunities for citizens to learn more about their government.

Citizen Review Teams, led by representatives of the business and university communities, evaluated City services by using benchmarking information, best practices information, citizen and employee surveys, financial data, interviews with employees, worksite visits, and improvement ideas submitted by both citizens and employees. They met on a regular basis with each other and with management teams to formulate recommendations for improvement. In order to make these recommendations, CERC relied heavily on performance data collected by the municipality. CERC members found some performance data to be extremely helpful; other data totally useless. For example, when trying to determine whether the city should modify its bus transportation service, the cost per mile and the marginal change in that cost did not assist the committee in making informed decisions. CERC's continuous requests for information on which to base their recommendations prompted the city of Winston-Salem to improve its performance management system and to survey its citizens on a regular basis to ensure the measures reflected citizen perceptions (Dusenbury, 1999).

Citizen advisory committees might possibly be the easiest and most cost-effective way to involve citizens, but there are inherent limitations with this model of participation. In particular, advisory committees have been criticized because membership may not be representative of the community and members, as well as the elected officials who appoint them, may have their own political agenda. Appointed committee members may be perceived as insiders, and the average citizen feels excluded. In spite of these limitations public administrators should strive to improve the process, increase the representative nature of these committees, replicate them in other communities, and enhance the model to improve the effectiveness, the representation, and the role of citizens.

Many communities have geographic-based citizen groups that advocate for the needs of specific neighborhoods or geographic areas within a larger community. Priority boards in Dayton, Ohio are possibly the most widely recognized example of this type of citizen participation. Citizens are elected to serve on seven neighborhood priority boards representing seven distinct neighborhoods within the city of Dayton. Priority board members do as their name suggests, identify and articulate neighborhood priorities and see that the governing body of Dayton is informed of each neighborhood's concerns. Neighborhood needs and improvement requests are factored into the city's budget process before the departments prepare their annual budget estimates. Since 1997, Dayton has been involved in a project funded by the Alfred P. Sloan Foundation to develop quality-of-life indicators—performance measures that indicate how satisfied citizens are with the overall quality of life in Dayton. These measures will be linked to the city's strategic plan in an attempt to ensure that citizen concerns are addressed.

Another way to involve citizens in data collection is to have citizens function as trained observers. In this capacity citizens are taught to assess community conditions using a consistent rating scale. So, rather than having municipal employees rate street or park conditions, properly trained citizens would do the rating. Some trained observer initiatives are more scientific than others. For example, the Fund for the City of New York, another Sloan-funded initiative, utilizes citizen volunteers and handheld computers to document street-level environmental conditions such as potholes, abandoned vehicles, and faulty fire hydrants. In addition to the handheld computers, volunteers are equipped with digital cameras so they can take photographs of the violations. In this way the trained observers can enter the exact location of the violation into the computer, a pothole at the intersection of Park Avenue and 79th Street, as well as a digital image of the pothole.

Photographs can be powerful tools for measuring performance. In two other Sloan-funded programs, citizens in Montclair, New Jersey and Hartford, Connecticut used photographs to communicate conditions. In Montclair, one citizen, upset with the dirty condition of municipal parking lots, took a series of photographs showing varying degrees of litter in five different lots. He submitted the photographs to the local newspaper and the published images generated serious discussion among citizens, public managers, and elected officials. Needless to say, the maintenance of the parking lots increased.

In Hartford, high school students have been trained to assess conditions in local parks. In addition to completing rating forms that indicate if swings are broken and basketball courts are in disrepair, students use digital cameras to take photographs of the conditions they are reporting. The images, once again, strengthen the data that are collected. Students attend council meetings and report their findings to the elected officials. So, not only are the elected officials presented with objective data indicating park conditions, they are presented with powerful images that are hard to deny.

Although these suggestions may seem reasonable, a recent study of performance measurement in municipal government indicated that fewer than three percent of the 674 municipalities surveyed involved citizens in the development of performance measures despite the fact that citizen demands prompted the municipalities to start measuring performance in the first place (Poister and Streib, 1999). Citizens and public managers need to seriously address this abysmal figure and develop ways for citizens to become meaningfully involved.

There are a variety of approaches that can be used to include citizens in performance measurement, as previously discussed in this section. Meaningfully involving citizens is not a one size fits all approach and it is important to find the right approach for each jurisdiction. A poorly thought out or half-hearted approach will only add to the level of frustration and cynicism many citizens already feel toward government. Citizens and public managers need to reflect on their communities and determine the most appropriate ways to involve citizens in this process. In all likelihood, a multifaceted approach will be the most appropriate way to foster and sustain involvement. Approaches that include public meetings and workshops, focus group discussions, citizen surveys, and citizen advisory committees provide myriad opportunities for citizens to get involved. In this way a larger and more diverse group of citizens is likely to take part in the initiative and the initiative is likely to sustain itself.

## C.  Communicating Results

Just as photographs can be a powerful communicator of conditions, other methods of communicating results to stakeholders need to be as powerful. We have all suffered through mind-numbing reports—pages and pages of text with a few elementary bar graphs or pie charts interspersed throughout. Reports like this tend to attract little attention or generate meaningful discussion. When communicating results, reports, Web sites, and press releases need to capture the reader's attention and provide relevant information without too much time and effort invested on the part of the reader. Graphics that accurately display the quantitative and qualitative findings should be used when appropriate. Information should be detailed and yet simple: make sure the average citizen reading the report understands the content.

Possibly the best example of effective communication is the Straphangers Campaign, which was founded in 1979 by the New York Public Interest Research Group (NYPIRG) and since that time has been a voice for the nearly seven million daily subway riders in New York City. Relying on Metropolitan Transit Authority data and data collected from subway riders through surveys and observations, the Straphanger

Campaign compares the performance of 19 subway lines to each other and over time. The overall ranking of service is presented on their website to riders in the form of a dollar value on a MetroCard. For example, a subway ride in New York in 2001 cost $1.50. If you happen to ride the Q line, which was the highest performing line that year, the value on your MetroCard would show $1.25. If you happen to ride the C line, the worst performing line in 2001, your MetroCard value would be $0.65. The presentation is colorful and graphic and sends a powerful message to the rider and to the MTA. The overall performance value is calculated through a weighted formula explained on the Straphanger's Web site. So, rather than just telling riders the percentage of on-time trains, or the percentage of passengers with seats during rush hour, riders know the value they are getting for their fare. Riders are also informed of what their ride was worth the previous year so they instantly know whether service has improved.

## III. CONCLUSION

It may be costly and time consuming to include citizens in the measurement of government performance, however, ultimately the performance measurement system developed will be extremely useful and meaningful. Ideally, the data collected will have an impact on policy and program administration. The performance measurement system, rather than focusing on managerial accomplishments and administrative achievements, will address quality of life and community goals and aspirations. Government will be measuring to make government more responsive to the needs of the citizens they serve, not just to justify their budget or other internal controls. Perhaps most important, if performance measurement contributes to solving problems and improving conditions that are important to citizens, citizens will be more willing to support government and become more involved in their communities.

## REFERENCES

Ammons, D. (1996). *Municipal Benchmarks: Assessing Local Performance and Establishing Community Standards.* Thousand Oaks, CA: Sage.

Box, R. C. (1998). *Citizen Governance: Leading American Communities into the 21st Century.* Thousand Oaks, CA: Sage.

CERC. City of Winston-Salem. Citizen Efficiency Review Committee. Available at: www.cofws.org.

Dusenbury, P. (1999). *Communicating with Citizens about Government Performance, Governing-for-Results and Accountability.* Washington, DC: The Urban Institute.

Epstein, P. D. (1988). *Using Performance Measurement in Local Government: A Guide to Improving Decisions, Performance and Accountability.* Denver, CO: National Civic League.

Epstein, P. D. (1992). Measuring the performance of public service. In: Holzer, M., ed. *Public Productivity Handbook.* New York, NY: Marcel-Dekker, pp. 161–194.

Fischer, R. (1994). An overview of performance measurement. *Public Manage.* 76(9).

Fund for the City of New York. Available at: www.feny.org.

Grizzle, G. (2002). Performance measurement and dysfunction: the dark side of quantifying work. *Public Perform. Manage. Rev.* 25(4):363–369.

Hatry, H. P., Fountain, J. R. Jr., Sullivan, J. M., Kremer, L. (1990). *Service Efforts and Accomplishments Reporting: Its Time Has Come.* Washington, DC: Government Accounting Standards Board (GASB).

Hatry, P., Fisk, D. (1992). Measuring productivity in the public sector. In: Holzer, M., ed. *Public Productivity Handbook*. New York, NY: Marcel Dekker, pp. 139–160.

Ho, A., Coates, P. (2002). Citizen-Initiated Performance Assessment—The Initial Iowa Experience. Paper presented at the Van Riper Symposium of the 63 National Conference of the American Society for Public Administration (ASPA), Phoenix, AZ, March.

Holzer, M., Halachmi, A. (1996). Measurement as a means of accountability. *Int. J. of Public Admin.* 19(11 & 12):1921–1944.

King, C. S., Stivers, C. (1998). *Government Is Us: Public Administration in an Anti-Government Era*. Thousand Oaks, CA: Sage.

King, C. S., Feltey, K. M., Susel, B. O. (1998). The question of participation: toward authentic public participation in public administration. *Public Admin. Rev.* 58(4):317–326.

National Center for Public Productivity. Available at: http://newark.rutgers.edu/~ncpp/.

Pierce, J. C., Lovrich, N. P., Moon, C. D. (2002). Social capital and government performance: an analysis of 20 American cities. *Public Perform. Manage. Rev.* 25(4):381–397.

Poister, T., Streib, G. (1999). Performance assessment in municipal government: assessing the state of the practice. *Public Admin. Rev.* 59(4):325–335.

Putnam, R. (1993). *Making Democracy Work: Civic Traditions in Modern Italy*. Princeton, NJ: Princeton University Press.

Putnam, R. (2000). *Bowling Alone: The Collapse and Revival of American Community*. New York: Simon and Schuster.

Ridley, C. E., Simon, H. A. (1938). *Measuring Municipal Activities: A Survey of Suggested Criteria and Reporting Forms for Appraising Administration*. Chicago: International City Managers Association.

Schacter, H. (1997). *Reinventing Government or Reinventing Ourselves: The Role of Citizen Owners in Making a Better Government*. Albany, NY: SUNY Press.

Stivers, C. (1990). The public agency as a polis: Active citizenship in the administrative state. *Admin. Soc.* 22(May):86–105.

Straphangers Campaign. Available at: www.straphangers.org.

Thomas, J. C. (1995). *Public Participation in Public Decisions*. San Francisco: Jossey-Bass. Publishers.

Timney, M.M. (1996). Overcoming NIMBY: Using Citizen Participation Effectively. Paper presented at the 57th National Conference of the American Society for Public Administration, Atlanta.

Wholey, J. (1999). Quality control: Assessing the accuracy and usefulness of performance measurement systems. In: Hatry, H., ed. *Performance Measurement: Getting Results*. Washington DC: Urban Institute Press.

# 4

## Decision Making and Managerial Capacity in the Public Sector

**GERASIMOS A. GIANAKIS**
*Suffolk University, Boston, Massachusetts, U.S.A.*

## I. INTRODUCTION

"Managerial capacity" refers to the ability of public sector managers to make decisions that are responsive to the needs of the political jurisdictions that employ their expertise. The complex nature of many public sector issues, the generalist orientation or amateur status of most elected legislators, and the time and analysis required to respond to public problems mean that professional public sector managers must enjoy some discretion in their decision making, and this discretion must be exercised responsibly. In order to fulfill the promise of professional public administration, public sector managers must make decisions that are responsive and responsible. This raises the immediate questions of "responsive to whom" and "responsible for what."

The discipline of public administration has tended to sidestep these questions by compartmentalizing the field of public management into its constituent parts, and then focusing its energy on the techniques associated with each part. However, the sum total of these techniques does not equal the whole of public management. The questions are admittedly difficult ones, and boil down to reconciling the antidemocratic nature of expertise, which is inherently exclusionary and elitist, and the egalitarian nature of democracy, which is participative and inclusive. But public administration's failure to address these issues has left the practice of public management vulnerable to attacks from market-oriented theorists who view public management as private management that is somehow dysfunctional, and who proffer private management solutions to the problem of public sector managerial decision making. It is held herein, that these tend to diminish public sector managerial capacity.

When Woodrow Wilson (1887) invited the United States government to adopt a professional administrative apparatus, he went to great lengths to demonstrate that professional administration was not necessarily tied to any particular political system. In the United States, professional public administration had long been associated with despotic governments. The increasing cultural diversity, social differentiation, economic segmentation, and technological complexity that was transforming the nation, however, demanded a professional public sector that could respond efficiently and effectively to the social and economic issues and problems this transformation was engendering. At the same time, Wilson recognized that these administrators must enjoy "large powers" and considerable discretion in decision making in order to be able to exercise their expertise, as well as to be held justifiably responsible for the resulting actions.

Wilson also posited a conceptual difference between politics and administration, which even he recognized would be problematic to separate in practice. The autonomy needed by the cook to exercise his or her expertise must be balanced with the rights of the diners to make sure they are getting what they want. However, it was this conceptual difference that took hold in the field of public administration, rather than the idea that administrators should enjoy "large powers." The politics/administration dichotomy has crippled theory building in the field by allowing theorists to ignore its essential and definitive issue: the role of the expert in a democratic society. Theoretical approaches to decision making in the public sector have both reflected and augmented this distortion.

Public sector managers make decisions in political institutions, that is, the organizations in which public managers exercise their decisions, making discretion public policy (Cook, 1998). In order for the collective actions embodied in public policies to be considered legitimate in a democratic society, they must at least appear to pursue some version of the public interest (Downs, 1957). Because of the difficulties involved in reaching consensus regarding the substance of the public interest in a particular policy area, the United States defines the public interest in procedural and due process terms in regard to decisions made in the legislative, executive, and judicial branches. As long as certain procedural and due process rules are followed, the outcomes of political competition are deemed to be legitimate, and the "losers" are assuaged by the continuous and incremental nature of policy making. However, the manner in which the public interest is pursued in professional political institutions has never been fully articulated. The politics/administration dichotomy has served as a mechanism for avoiding this issue.

In the context of decision making, the relationship between the discretion exercised by individual managers and their organizations emerges as a crucial variable in addressing the legitimacy issue (Cook, 1998). The professional public institution is an inherently political organization, and the salient question becomes the political nature of the public manager in his or her decision-making capacity. This is not to say that private sector organizations do not exercise political power, only that they do so as individual political actors rather than as public institutions. In fact, many theoreticians have approached public institutions from the private sector perspective, particularly at the federal level. This makes them part of the political competition that legitimizes public policies in procedural terms, but this weakens the case for a *professional* public administration. Expertise and democracy must be reconciled, not merely melted into each other.

Another alternative is surrender to the "professional state" or technocracy on which citizens have come to depend (Stillman, 1991). The public interest is determined through the application of analytical techniques by substantive public policy experts. These experts employ the rational model described above to make decisions in pursuit of the optimal mix of public services. In this scenario, the political process is subverted, and policy "losers" are stripped of the safety net provided by the continuous nature of the political process. Given the multiplicity of interests manifested by the public, it is difficult to see how this approach can be responsive or responsible.

This chapter seeks to develop a normative theory of public sector decision making. It begins with an overview of existing decision-making approaches. However, this subject is inseparable from the nature of professional public administration, its relationship to democracy, and the relationship of the individual manager to his or her public organization. The professional public organization is a political institution, and the exercise of discretionary decision making within it is an exercise of political power. The exercise of political power by professional experts raises important issue for public administration and its relationship to democracy.

## II. MODELS OF DECISION MAKING

This section reviews several approaches to decision making in the public sector. Each approach holds implications for the broader issues outlined above. The review is far from comprehensive, because decision making is the definitive administrative phenomenon and virtually everything written about public administration can be approached as a theory of decision making.

## A. The Rational Model

The promise of professional public management has long been tied to the rational model of decision making, the elements of which are:

1. Identify goal
2. Identify every possible course of action to achieve goal
3. Identify all consequences of all alternative actions
4. Select alternative that optimizes goal attainment
5. Evaluate selection

The rational model seeks to determine the most efficient means to achieve a given end. Even if one assumes the reality of the politics/administration dichotomy, the limitations of this approach to decision making are obvious: costs, time, lack of information regarding consequences, and consideration of alternatives that are not politically feasible. In the public sector, organizations often pursue multiple, ambiguous, and sometimes contradictory goals. But a significant question is whether the implementers of the course of action influence the determination of the goals.

When Wilson's conceptual distinction between politics and administration met the "machine model" of organizations pursued by the early scientific management school (Morgan, 1997), the concept was concretized as the politics/administration dichotomy. The optimization of the control function through the design of hierarchically structured organizations operating under clear rules and regulations, job descriptions, and lines of authority and communication also appealed to the various groups that comprised the reform movement at the beginning of the twentieth century. The goal of such an organization was determined outside the organization—that is, through formal political processes—and deciding became rule following.

This is the model described by Max Weber (Gerth and Mills, 1946) as the administrative apparatus associated with the modern "legal-rational" society. His model of bureaucracy was designed to maximize efficiency in the delivery of goods and services. But his description of the bureaucratic model as an "ideal type" meant simply that he was describing a conceptual model of an efficient tool for achieving a given end. He feared, however, that in the real world bureaucracy would come to dominate its putative political masters, because of its control of information and the very expertise on which society comes to depend. Political questions become redefined as administrative ones, and the polity withers. What emerges from this process is the technocratic state described above.

During the 1930s and 1940s, the politics/administration dichotomy and the pursuit of efficiency became public administration orthodoxy (Svara, 1998). However, this was a period of national crises, and the values that guided the discretionary decision making of increasingly powerful professional public organizations were taken for granted; they were democratic ones and the emphasis was on getting the job done. After World War II, in part because professional bureaucrats had become involved with a greater range of public policy areas, this orthodoxy came under a series of blistering attacks from a variety of directions. Appleby (1949) pointed to the inherently political nature of public administration, and Dahl (1947) contended that problems of values and methods were inseparable in the practice of public administration. Waldo (1952) focused on the public nature of public administration and the democratically based values that should guide decision making, whereas Simon (1976) put decision making squarely in the center of his approach to administration.

Herbert Simon (1976) sought to create a science of decision making. He dismissed the previous orthodoxy as consisting of mere proverbs of administration. He showed how an organization can yield rational, goal-oriented decisions from the managers of the many components that comprised it, despite the influence of the "informal organization" introduced by Barnard (1938) and the emotional needs of "social man" unearthed in the Hawthorne experiments (Mayo, 1933). He also recognized that man had limited information-processing capacities and weak cognitive abilities. Simon brought Max Weber's "ideal type" model of bureaucracy to life by demonstrating how an actual complex organization could pursue goals in a fairly rational, efficient manner, despite the stringent requirements of Weber's conceptual model and the limitations outlined above.

For Simon, decision making was the central activity of organizations. Making a decision means making a choice among alternatives, and this implies some level of analysis. The formal and informal socialization processes in organizations and the special fields where organizational experts are educated, coupled with the structural elements of the bureaucratic form serve to "bound" and focus the limited information-processing capacities. Decision makers are only "intendedly rational," in that they seek to make rational decisions but do not have the cognitive ability to do so in the context of the organization as a whole (Simon, 1976). Organizational members are also induced to accept authority and contribute to the pursuit of the organization's goal through incentives and rewards. The decisions made by individual decision makers in limited spheres of authority and within the parameters, or "decision premises" established by the organization may not represent the best or most optimal choice, but they are usually satisfactory enough to provide for the efficient pursuit of the organization's goals. Simon combined elements of psychological/emotional man, economic man, and the informal organization to create administrative man, who "satisfices," or picks the first satisfactory choice within the established parameters, and this is good enough to ensure the overall rationality and efficiency of the organization (Simon, 1976).

Simon (1976) recognized that the acts of analyzing alternatives and choosing among them were made up of both a factual and an evaluative component. In his zeal to establish a science of decision making based on behavioralism or the study of observable behaviors, he ignored the latter; for him, values were the stuff of philosophy rather than science. The goals of the organization are treated as a given, and he focused on how a purely instrumental rationality can be achieved. This created a "generic management" school, in that it eliminated from its cosmology that which makes public administration unique. The value/fact schism also mirrors the politics/administration dichotomy, and it helped to perpetuate the latter. Once again, theorists compartmentalized public administration into its constituent parts and concentrated their efforts on the techniques associated with the parts.

Simon's model does not provide for the building of managerial capacity as defined herein. Goals are "out there" and managers are not encouraged to question these or change them; hence, responsive action is dictated to them. They cannot assume responsibility for them, because they are responsible for the pursuit of instrumental rationality in regard to a small part of the overall goal structure. From this it is possible to extrapolate the idea that the formal political processes determine goals and public administrators merely implement them. The emphasis here is on control, and this compromises the capacity of public administrators to be effective. For Perrow (1979), it also raised the question of whether hierarchies exist because people are stupid, or whether hierarchies make people stupid.

Dwight Waldo (1952) recognized that decision making in professional public organizations was influenced by values other than efficiency. He pulled public management away from "generic administration" and toward political science by highlighting the role that these organizations played in constituting public policies. He believed that basic democratic values should be consciously adopted and pursued by professional public managers to guide their discretionary decision-making power. The definition of democratic values may differ among people, but one that was clearly emphasized was citizen participation and direct engagement of the polity. Waldo's approach culminated in the "New Public Administration" (Marini, 1971), which was a product of the political activism that characterized the 1960s. In the New PA, professional public managers were to become advocates for more substantive public values, principally social equity. This more proactive stance cast public administrators in the role of independent political actors, and efficiency receded into the background.

The rational model reached its zenith in practice in the form of the Planning-Programming-Budgeting-System adopted by the administration of Lyndon Johnson in the middle of the 1960s. In PPBS, the President and his staff identified long-range goals and programmatic and resource allocation decisions would be based upon the degree to which a program successfully pursued one or more of these goals. PPBS gave birth to the program evaluation industry, and the use of cost-benefit analysis and other analytical techniques to demonstrate efficiency and effectiveness in the pursuit of identified goals became widespread. The system shortly collapsed, however, under the weight of its own analytical requirements and the loss of the political consensus necessary to dictate goals from the top down.

Despite the unrealistic informational demands of its pure form, the rational model continues to exert considerable prescriptive/normative influence in public administration. Simon's model holds out the promise of democratic control of managers' discretionary decision-making powers, and the pursuit of efficiency is the principal reason that professional administrators are employed. His model does not provide for the development of managerial capacity; indeed, it is the organization as a whole that provides for rational decision making and the efficient pursuit of its given goal through its structure and socialization processes. By consigning individual managers to purely instrumental roles, Simon's model allows the field of public administration to avoid its essential dilemmas and definitive issues. Waldo acknowledged the constitutive role of public managers, but he generally failed to provide values to guide their discretionary decision making.

## B. The Science of "Muddling Through"

Simon's model certainly does not reflect the realization of the classical rational model of decision making. He was obviously pessimistic regarding man's cognitive capacity to realize a comprehensive level of rationality required by PPBS, for example. He demonstrated that hierarchy and organizational controls are necessary for organizations to function in a rational manner. The concept of satisficing meant that policy making would be inherently incremental, in that the first satisfactory response to a choice situation would most likely be a small change from the status quo; organizational controls virtually assured this. This is a far cry from the policy strides promised by PPBS and the application of the classical rational model.

In his classic article, "The Science of 'Muddling Through,'" Charles Lindblom (1959) provides a devastating critique of and an alternative to the "rational-comprehensive" approach to policy making. He demonstrated that an incremental approach to policy making did not simply represent a limitation of the rational model, but was actually a better way to make decisions regarding public policy given the nature of the problems that public organizations attempted to address. These are often "wicked problems" (Harmon and Mayer, 1986), or problems that are subject to multiple definitions, around which it is difficult to put boundaries, and which escape direct measurement.

In what Lindblom (1959) labeled the rational-comprehensive, or "root" model, the test of a "good policy" was whether it could be demonstrated that it was the most appropriate means for achieving a given end. The time, resource, and informational demands of this approach, coupled with the cognitive limitations identified by Simon, made this model untenable. Lindblom also pointed out that political consensus regarding goals was often fleeting and usually elusive. The goals identification process was a continuous one, and the goals themselves were subject to continuous change. He described a model of "successive limited comparisons," or the "branch method" of decision making, which has the following characteristics.

1. The selection of goals and the analysis of actions are not distinct from each other, but rather are closely intertwined.

2. Hence, means-end analysis is often an inappropriate approach to decision making, or the approach is severely limited.

3. "The test of a 'good' policy is typically that various analysts find themselves directly agreeing on a policy (without their agreeing that it is the most appropriate means to an agreed objective)" (Lindblom, 1959, p. 80).

4. Analysis is limited because important possible outcomes, alternative actions, and affected values are neglected.

5. The nature of the policy-making process makes a succession of comparisons more appropriate, and greatly reduces reliance on theory.

It was the political imposition of goals from the top down and the attempt to develop theories of public problems that could be widely applied that drove the PPBS manifestation of the classical rational model. In Lindblom's approach, decision makers concentrated on what was in front of them at the time of the decision, and they took action by selecting from the range of choices immediately available. The goal was to satisfy the various actors with a stake in the particular program under consideration, and this usually entailed a process of bargaining, negotiation, and compromise, which Lindblom (1959) labeled "partisan mutual adjustment." Rational analyses of public programs by experts become a part of this process, but these analyses are never value-free; hence Lindblom (1965) referred to the process of rational analysis as "partisan analysis."

Lindblom's approach to policy making is inherently incremental, and it seeks to avoid potential costly errors associated with action based on analytical studies or theories that purport to solve "wicked" public programs by ensuring that goals are pursued in correctable "baby steps." Some would point to the negative externalities that emerged from the PPBS-based programs of the "Great Society" as validation of his approach. Although the approach appears to be nonrational and unsystematic, Lindblom refers to the process of "muddling through" as a "science," in that it ultimately brings more information to bear on seemingly intractable problems than the top-down, rational, theory-based approach. He captures the essence of his approach in the title of his book *The Intelligence of Democracy* (1965).

In this model, professional public administrators are cast as part of the political process. Their decision-making processes are responsive to the public interest to the extent that they contribute to the development of consensus regarding short-term actions. It would seem that they take responsible action to the extent that nonincremental actions are avoided, because Lindblom's model is both descriptive and prescriptive in nature. Public managers enhance their managerial capacity by honing their bargaining and negotiating skills, and their ability to sell their unavoidably partisan analyses and to garner political support for their programs.

Lindblom's approach defines professional public administrators as politicians in a pluralistic society who pursue their version of their self-, professionally, or organizationally based interests. The need to garner political support in this process may cause administrators to appeal to narrow constituencies, and compromise their capacity to respond to the general public interest. This may be particularly true at the federal level, where professional public organization can be conceptualized as individual political actors in the absence of an umbrella organization.

In Simon's model, the discretionary decision making of managers is controlled through organizational structure; in Lindblom's model, control is exercised through the nature of the policy-making process. In his Madisonian society there is little left of Wilson's (1887) version of the Hamiltonian expert who exercises "wide powers." But the discipline of public administration has not acknowledged the Madisonian world and the place of the professional public administrator in it. The field continues to assume a Hamiltonian world, and it does not arm its managers with value systems and professional orientations to be the kind of "politicians" that the public expects from experts. For Lindblom, the public interest is simply what emerges from the pluralist competition that makes up the policy-making processes. Once again, procedures and due process legitimate this in the legislative and elected executive branches, but not in the professional public organization.

The consensus-building role of the professional public administrator has been receiving increasing attention (Nalbandian, 1999; Behn, 1998). This should focus on the entire political community and not on just on an attentive public pursuing narrow self-interests. Lindblom also presaged current approaches to decision making that are more sensitive to the immediate decision context, and less optimistic regarding the utility of external theories (King and Stivers, 1998; Hummel, 1991). In his positivistic/ behavioral approach to decision making, Simon tended to decontexualize the immediate decision, and he relied on the theory embodied by the organization to steer decision making in a rational direction.

Another model that is related to Lindblom's approach in its apparent non-rational, process-oriented approach to decision making is the "Garbage Can Model" (March, 1994; March and Olsen, 1987; Cohen, et al., 1972). These theorists characterize decision making in organizations that "have ambiguity preferences and identities, ambiguous experiences and history, ambiguous technologies, and fluid participation in decision making. They are loosely coupled" (March, 1994, p. 193). These organizations are loosely coupled because they tend to deal with ambiguity, uncertainty, and, hence, risk taking in decision making through decentralization and delegation. This allows different parts of the organization to deal with the information demands of the multiple, often inconsistent environments of the organization. "The cost of such a strategy is inconsistency among the various actions of the organization over time and from one subunit to another. The process yields a set of actions that cannot be rationalized as stemming from a coherent set of organizational objectives" (March, 1994, p. 194). This process generates enormous centrifugal forces in the organization, as subunits develop their own clients, objectives, and informational frameworks.

Choices among problems, solutions, and decision makers are what characterize decision making in garbage can organizations. The preconditions of the rational model are not met, in that the context of choice making is a shifting combination of problems, solutions, and decision makers (Cohen, et al., 1972, p. 23). "Problems and solutions are attached to choices, and thus to each other, not because of any means-ends linkage but because of their temporal proximity. At the limit, for example, almost any solution can be associated with almost any problem—provided they are evoked at the same time" (March, 1994, p. 200).

These organizations come to resemble "organized anarchies" (Cohen et al., 1972). However, the absence of a strict means-end analysis does not necessarily mean that the choices that emerge from this process are irrational. Indeed, the process itself represents a rational approach to a particular environment. Delegation of responsibility can encourage managers to learn from their actions, even if it is not clear what happened or why (March and Olsen, 1987). This is not the accumulation of causal knowledge, but rather the experiential learning that comes from thoughtful reflection. March (1994, p. 206) describes the reactions of "enthusiasts" to this seemingly chaotic organization: "They seek to discover the intelligence of temporal sorting as a way of organizing attention, to see the flows of problems and solutions as a form of market, to find elegance in the ambiguity of preferences and identities and in the unfolding nature of the linkages between problems and solutions." In short, they seek to build their managerial capacity to read a choice situation, and to make the best choice possible.

## C.  The "Mixed Scanning" Approach

Yehezekel Dror (1965) criticized Lindblom's article, partly on the basis that the "rational-comprehensive" model and the "successive limited comparisons" approach constituted a false dichotomy because it precluded the development of other models. The pure "rational-comprehensive approach" constitutes an impossible goal and its opposite encourages inertia and supports the status quo. In his article "Mixed-Scanning: A Third Approach to Decision Making," Amitai Etzioni (1967) outlined the elements of an approach to decision making that constituted a middle ground between pure rationalism and incrementalism. The mixed scanning approach seeks to reduce the resources and informational detail demanded by the rational model and overcome the conservatism inherent in the incrementalist model.

Etzioni differentiated between fundamental decisions, which involved the identification and development of long-range goals, and the more limited decisions that are made within the decision-making context established by these ends. Incremental decision making proceeds within such a framework in any case, but this is limited to the status quo, periodically redefined by major decisions, such as a declaration of war. In Etzioni's view, "a more active approach to societal decision making requires two sets of mechanisms: (a) high order, fundamental policy making processes which set basic directions and (b) incremental processes which prepare for fundamental decisions and work them out after they have been reached. This is provided by mixed scanning" (1967, p. 388). However one should not read this as a restatement of the politics/administration dichotomy. Etzioni recognized that the two types of "scanning" could be divided into several levels, which would vary in the degree of detail and coverage each entailed; this implies a decision-making continuum along which a conceptual shift occurs. Neither of these two decision types is necessarily tied to a particular level of the organizational hierarchy (Etzioni, 1959).

Etzioni (1967) also pointed out the salience of the nature of the organization's environment in determining the prevalence of decision types. In a stable environment, an incremental approach would be adequate, but when environmental conditions are rapidly changing, or the initial course deemed to be wrong, a more "encompassing" approach would be appropriate. Another important environmental factor is the capacity of the actor. What is the point of engaging in encompassing scanning, if the decision maker has neither the resources nor control to respond? Another factor is the capacity to build consensus regarding strategic outcomes.

The mixed scanning model has become institutionalized as the formal model of strategic planning and the less formal "visioning" process. Rational planning is made more feasible when it is limited to the overall goals that serve as a framework for further decision making. This process also makes goals and values manifest. Etzioni held that "incrementalists reject the notion that policies can be guided in terms of central institutions of a society expressing a collective 'good'" (1967, p. 387). Although incrementalism is clothed in the trappings of free competition, its outcomes reflect power in place and basic societal innovations are likely to be ignored. Thus incrementalism is also value-based, but its goals and values are hidden. He casts the small-stepping incrementalists, whose steps are just as likely to lead in circles or nowhere in particular, as passive, or de facto defenders of the status quo.

The encompassing scanning process, or strategic planning, however, casts the professional public servant as an active politician. Strategic planning is likely to be most effective where it is least needed; that is, consensus regarding goals is more likely to be reached where consensus already exists. In the absence of political consensus, the professional public manager becomes the expert who dictates goals based on professional expertise and analytical models. In the absence of consensus, to which of the many publics do the mixed scanners attend? They would probably attend to the same publics that drive the incremental approach, or they would assume advocacy roles as championed by the "New Public Administration" (Marini, 1971). Indeed, strategic planning is often approached as an administrative process, and its political implications are overlooked. This is Weber's nightmare (Gerth and Mills, 1946). Some theoreticians have contended that public administrators have an "obligation to lead" (Behn, 1998) in policy development given the breakdown of other political institutions. Others suggest that managers of public agencies should have the discretion to choose among their political masters in the development of public policy, and this power is justified because it mirrors the checks-and-balances "spirit of the Constitution" (Spicer, 1995).

The mixed scanning model would seem to grant professional public administrators the "large powers" endorsed by Wilson (1887) without providing for the responsible and responsive exercise of their discretionary decision-making powers. At best, public administration has provided spiritual guidance in the appeal to democratic values (Waldo, 1952) or the "regime values" that constituted our nation (Rohr, 1998), but these do not provide practical guidance in specific decision situations. These general principles reduce to an appeal to public participation in the policy making that occurs in professional political institutions, but in practice participation is reduced to the attentive publics who simply pursue vested interests.

The field has sought to protect democracy through the concept of representative bureaucracy (Kelly, 1998; Rosenbloom, 1997; Krislov, 1974). This view holds that any policy making that occurs within a professional public organization is in the democratic spirit and would likely be responsive to the needs of the general public, because the personnel who comprise the organization are probably more representative of the general public than those who are elected to formal policy-making bodies. This representativeness refers to demographic factors, and this view assumes that cultural, ethnic, racial, and gender groups share basic values to which each member would subscribe. However, it is unlikely that these values would point to specific stances regarding public policies, and these highly abstracted values would serve no better as guides to action than "democratic values." This view also suggests that individual organizational actors have the power to substantively influence public policies, which is not likely to be the case in Simon's (1976) model of limited authority or Lindblom's (1965, 1959) incremental world. However, even if some "invisible hand" were to ensure that policy outcomes emanating from professional political organizations reflected the public interest because the actors represented the broad range of public value preferences, these personnel were appointed to exercise their expertise, not to represent the public.

Lindblom (1965) redefined rationality as the pluralistic Madisonian "intelligence of democracy," but Simon (1976) and Etzioni (1967) demonstrated that the rational model could be at least imperfectly realized in formal organizations. Simon neatly sidestepped the issue of values on epistemological grounds, and limited discretion through organizational structure. He did not consider responsiveness to the public interest, and responsibility was limited to accountability for following the rules and regulations in his approach (Harmon, 1995). Etzioni (1967) granted public administrators the "large powers" espoused by Wilson (1887), but his failure to provide a normative basis for the exercise of these powers limited the ability of public managers to build their capacity for responsible and responsive decision making. Nevertheless, by showing how organizations can yield rational action in pursuit of specific goals (even in "garbage can" organizations), Simon and Etzioni demonstrated that organizations can be instruments of power (Perrow, 1979). The issue of values that can serve as guides to discretionary decision making in public organizations becomes more salient.

## D.  The New Public Management

James Q. Wilson (1989) contends that what distinguishes private sector managers from public sector managers is the greater control of the factors of production exercised by the former. These factors are money, people, and things. The capacity of public managers to act is constrained by the controls placed on their use of money in the form of budgetary and financial systems. They face civil service systems that hamper their ability to motivate and deploy their personnel efficiently. They must endure legal constraints and formal bidding procedures when they need to purchase materials. This is why it is held herein that it is comparatively more difficult to be an effective public sector manager than an effective private sector manager; by the same token it is more difficult to survive as an ineffective private sector manager than as an ineffective public sector manager. The bottom line serves as a handy measure of effectiveness and a tidy executioner of the ineffective. The difficulty in defining the public interest as a bottom line makes escape to simple rule following attractive to some in the public sector.

The New Public Management (Hood, 1995) seeks to loosen the administrative shackles that bind the discretion of public managers, and to provide a bottom line in order to hold managers accountable for their exercise of this enhanced discretionary decision-making power. It is rooted in the "reinventing government" movement (Osborne and Gaebler, 1992), which advocated streamlining administrative processes such as purchasing and making budgetary and personnel controls more flexible. At the same time, however, the reinvention advocates believed that professional public managers should "row rather than steer" (Osborne and Gaebler, 1992) the ship of state. This view reconstituted the politics/administration dichotomy, and held that the newly "liberated" public managers were to focus on the efficient implementation of public policies. Managers would not simply be held accountable for the inputs consumed by their programs, but rather they would be held responsible for how successfully they had attained the goals of their programs. The problems involved in designing accurate and acceptable outcome measures were often overlooked (Bour-kaert, 1993; Grizzle, 1985), as was the constitutive role of public managers in the policy-making process (Cook, 1998).

According to Terry (1998), the New Public Management is comprised of the "liberation" management strategies described above and market-driven management, which reflects a strong belief in the benefits of competition and a suggestion that private sector management practices are somehow superior to those typically em-ployed in the public sector. This model adopts an economic view of human nature, and casts the public manager as someone who pursues his or her personal self-interest and is, thus, not to be trusted. The creation of internal markets in public bureaucracies (as well as competition from external organizations through privatization) will lower costs and increase efficiency, and also provide for the policing of public managers. Once again, however, such a system is only as effective as the measures that constitute the bottom line for public managers.

The "reinvention" seemed to limit its enthusiasm for managerial entrepreneu-rial leadership to streamlining administrative systems and providing for a "customer service" orientation (Osborne and Gaebler, 1992), although it may have overlooked the policy implications of constructing mission-driven, results-oriented enterprises. The New Public Management would seem to be more supportive of public managers assuming a leadership role in the policy process as well. There are at least three possible explanations of his view. First, those assuming an ideological perspective might conclude that the aim of this school of thought is to reduce the size of government to an absolute minimum so that public policy leadership on the part of professional public managers becomes a less significant issue. If policy choices are determined by outcome measures, the design and selection of these measures give legislative bodies or elected executives the opportunity to micromanage professional agencies. An institutional view might hold that most of the successful manifestations of this model have occurred in parliamentary states (Loffler, 1997; Boston et al., 1996; Aucoin, 1996), where policy goals, power, and leadership are established at the time of the elections and policy battles generally do not spill into the professional bureaucracy. In the United States, elections settle little because political power is so fragmented and diffuse, and the bureaucracy simply constitutes another policy battlefront (President Lyndon Johnson briefly enjoyed the powers of a prime min-ister in the middle 1960s, when he was able to implement top-down PPBS). Third, because these theories rest on the assumptions associated with economic man, legitimate public policy is simply viewed as the outcome of the pursuit of individual self-interest on the part of the members of the polity, including the professional managers. The idea of a public interest to be discovered and pursued by a collectivity is foreign here.

The New Public Management would seem to contradict "the emerging con-sensus of public administrationists . . . . that public and private management are, to cite Wallace Sayre's old saw, fundamentally alike in all unimportant respects" (Henry, 1995, p. 41). Even Herbert Simon, the father of "generic management" felt that "the attempts of the new institutional economics to explain organizational behavior solely in terms of agency, asymmetric information, transaction costs, opportunism, and other concepts drawn from neo-classical economics ignore key organizational mech-anisms like authority, identification and coordination, and hence are seriously incomplete" (Simon, 1995, p. 293). Authority systems transmit decision premises, identification with the mission of the organization provides motivation, and coordination is achieved through authority systems rather than markets. All of these are required to maximize efficiency.

Public administrationists have reacted with criticism of the feasibility of implementing across-the-board administrative systems, such as those detailed in the Government Performance and Results Act (the federal manifestation of the New Public Management), in a system as complex and differentiated as the federal bureaucracy (Radin, 1998). Others have rallied to the values that must be considered by public managers in addition to efficiency (Fredrickson, 1997), such as those advocated by Waldo (1952) and Dahl (1947). Still others have sought to soft pedal the implications of the model by assuring all that "a strong theory of public entrepreneurship requires a strong theory of citizenship" (Bellone and Goerl, 1992, p. 133) and active participation in the policy-making process by the polity as a whole. However, the market-driven aspects of the New Public Management could drive organizations to attentive publics pursuing their own self-interest. According to Lynn (2001), public administration has mounted only a weak opposition to the challenge of the New Public Management.

The "liberation" goal of the New Public Management would seem to expand managerial capacity. But in the absence of a public interest, on whose behalf is this capacity exercised? In a market-driven environment managers would be encouraged to pursue their own interests or those of their particular agencies. The blind commitment to efficiency that characterizes market mechanisms ignores the issue of efficiency toward what end. To whom and for what are these managers responsible? The answer is the measures that are designed to hold them accountable for the discretion that they would enjoy in the deployment of resources. Once again, this raises the issue of micromanagement by legislative bodies. Weak measures expose public agencies to external competition, and the agenda of shrinking the size of government is also highlighted. In addition, there seems to be an incremental bias in the market-based invisible hand, in the same way that it was manifested in Lindblom's politics-based invisible hand. Despite the call for entrepreneurialism, public sector decision makers tend to be risk aversive, and failed experiments are not well tolerated by the public (Frank and McCollough, 1992). This risk-aversive tendency is particularly strong when managers are under the close scrutiny of elected officials (Bozeman and Kingsley, 1998).

The New Public Management constitutes a direct attack on the craft of public management, as well as the prospects for effective collective action. Competition among public managers in the same professional public organization limits the amount of expertise that can be brought to bear on public problems and, hence, the range of potential responsive actions. It augments the centrifugal forces that characterize highly differentiated public organizations. However, the vulnerability of the field to these attacks is rooted in its inability to account for the policy role of the professional public manager. The New Public Management neatly sidesteps the issue of values, and therein lies its attractiveness for some theoreticians.

## E.  Other Approaches to Decision Making

Lee Roy Beach (1997) recently reviewed the psychology of decision making, and he identified three theoretical approaches to decision making: prescriptive, behavioral, and naturalistic theory. Prescriptive theories are derived from the rational school that is rooted in the discipline of economics. The emphasis here is on optimizing the pursuit of an objective. This school does not consider how decision makers actually behave, because the formal models are so self-evidently logical that any deviation is simply viewed as error. Cost-benefit analyses, decision trees, and payoff tables are the relevant tools in this approach, as well as less formal models such as the decision participation model developed by Vroom and Yago (1988). There is clearly a normative element here, as there is in any prescriptive theory. The behavioral approach focuses on how decision makers actually behave. Once again, however, as we have seen in the review of Simon's (1976) approach, effective behavior is often judged on the basis of the degree to which the result reflects that which would have been attained through a stringently rational approach. Simon described structural arrangements and cultural influences that helped decision makers approach rational decision making.

Simon's work also forms the basis of naturalistic decision theory, which borrows from behavioral theory. But "naturalistic decision theory departs from both pre-scriptive and behavioral decision theory in its almost exclusive focus on how decisions are made, rather than on how they 'should' be made" (Beach, 1997, p. 9). According to Beach (1997), organizational theorists tend to focus on the organization as the unit of analysis, whereas behavioralists center on the individual decision maker; the natural-istic approach highlights the organizational *context* of individual decision makers. Decision makers place observed events in a context that gives them meaning; this is the process of framing. "A frame is a mental construct consisting of elements, and the relationships between them, that are associated with a situation of interest to a decision maker. The elements are the salient current events and associated past events" (Beach, 1997, p. 23–24). Organizational actors come to share frames through shared values and experiences, as well as through organizational culture. The relationship to Simon's (1976) "decision premises" is obvious.

Decision makers also develop "policies" consisting of behaviors that have been employed in the past, and which the decision maker can apply to current situations through analogy or inference. Sometimes the situation is sufficiently unique that the recognition that emerges from policies can only guide the decision maker, and do not directly determine action. This approach has been formalized as recognition-primed decision making or the RPD model (Klein, 1989), and social judgment theory (Ham-mond, et al. 1975). The latter holds that people constantly process information, or cues, and their perceptual systems make unconscious inferences, which are limited by the particular frame in use. People can build more effective decision-making policies when they are provided cognitive feedback regarding the nature of the optimal policy. In Klein's (1996) research on the RPD model, he finds that decision makers in crisis situations deny that they even had time to make a decision. They rely on intuition that depends on experience to recognize key patterns that give them a picture of the dynamics of the situation. But these cues can be subtle, and decision makers often cannot indicate which cues they employed. Beach (1997) also develops the concept of image theory, which assumes that decision makers come to the decision situation with beliefs and values regarding what really matters, perceptions of what comprises worthwhile future goals, and instrumental knowledge regarding how to attain those goals. The sum total of these individual decisions constitutes organizational decision making, but the individuals are embedded in an organizational context that also influences their images.

The development of policies and contextual cultures may be a means of bringing more information to bear on the decision-making situation and overcoming the centrifugal forces that typically characterize highly differentiated public sector organizations. Structural solutions and decision premises tied to specific job descriptions tend to atomize organizational decision makers, who pursue suboptimal outcomes or substitute processes for substantive goals. Hierarchy also tends to formalize and distort communication, which is the lifeblood of decision making (Simon et al., 1950). Shared policies and cultures can tie the individual decision maker to the political institution. In this way, a community of experts takes responsibility for pursuing the public interest through a legitimate political institution, and the political power of the individual decision maker is guided and legitimized. However, cultures and decision policies are not easily developed or manipulated (Morgan, 1997). This argument is developed further in the next section.

Karl Weick (1995) views decision making as an act of interpretation rather than choice. For him, "decision making consists of locating, articulating, and ratifying that earlier choice, bringing it forward to the present, and claiming it as the decision that has just been made....The recent history is viewed in retrospect, with tentative outcomes at hand, to see what decision could account for that outcome" (Weick, 1995, p. 185). This is a process of "retrospective sensemaking," in which people create reality retrospectively. "People make sense of things by seeing a world on which they already impose what they believe" (Weick, 1995, p. 15). This is not to trivialize decision making, only to point out that the experience, memory, and values of the decision maker are crucial to the act of interpretation, as are the premise controls described by Simon (1976), which serve to facilitate interpretation and, thus, "decision making." For Weick, what is crucial in sensemaking is a good "story"; one that is plausible, coherent, reasonable, and embedded in past experience and expectations. As in Beach's review (1997) above, this points to the salience of what Perrow (1979) refers to as "unobtrusive controls" in organizations.

Hummel (1991) reinforces the idea that decision making occurs in what are often idiosyncratic contexts, which must be interpreted by managers. Managers report making decisions based on intuition and judgment, but "conversations with managers can show that they can think critically about their own thinking" (Hummel, 1991, p. 32), and they communicate this knowledge through "story telling." Managers are suspicious of blindly applying theories that were produced outside the specific decision situations they face, as well as of rational analyses of the problem that purport to present an optimal solution. Managers will consider these data, but they are more comfortable communicating with persons who are also involved in the decision context. Together they build a reality that is the basis for action. This is supported by studies that show that managers display a preference for face-to-face personal communication over a short time span (Mintzberg and Quinn, 1996, p. Hummel, 1991), rather than written communications that are analytically based. Hummel's work mirrors the concept of the "reflective practitioner" developed by Donald Schon and Chris Argyris (Schon, 1984; Schon and Argyris, 1978). A commitment to thoughtful reflection and educative action forms the basis for the professional's claim to autonomy. As Denhardt (1984) suggests, this does not entail a formal analysis of the day's events, but rather simple reflection that is the basis of learning and capacity building. This view also forms the basis for responsible action when it is contrasted with the simple application of unconscious biases, external theories, acontextual rules and regulations, and "value free" analyses, which at best provide for accountability, but often at the loss of effectiveness.

Morgan (1997) demonstrates how actions can be made more effective if the decision situation is viewed from a variety of perspectives. He outlines a series of "metaphors" that he characterizes as ways of seeing. However, each metaphor is also a way of not seeing, in that its assumptions blind the decision maker to other possibilities. It is imperative that judgment be suspended until a variety of perspectives has been employed. The results of this diagnostic reading are integrated into the "most effective story line," and this forms the basis for action. These approaches cast the professional public manager as an active participant in the policy-making process, but the negotiations, bargaining, and exchange of "stories" that comprise these approaches are not simply part of a political process as described by Lindblom (1959). They seek to create a rational definition of the decision situation so that contextually rational action can be taken.

This is, however, not a simple task, given the Madisonian world described by Lindblom (1959). Allison (1969) outlines three conceptual models of public policy outcomes that he employed to examine the Cuban missile crisis. The first reflects the assumptions of the rational actor model, and it seeks to demonstrate how a nation state chooses a policy in response to a strategic problem with which it is presented. In this "frame of reference," the state is treated as a monolithic body, and a unitary decision maker is implied. The "organizational process" model holds that "large acts are the consequence of innumerable and often conflicting smaller actions by individuals at various levels of bureaucratic organizations in the service of only partially compatible conceptions of national goals, organizational goals, and political objectives" (Allison, 1969, p. 690). In this view, what appear to be choices are actually outputs of many organizations pursuing their individual internal routines and standard operating procedures. In the "bureaucratic politics" model, what appear to be rational choices are "characterized as outcomes of various overlapping bargaining games among players arranged hierarchically in the national government" (Allison, 1969, p. 690). The salient force here is the play of political power among people, groups, and organizations that are often pursuing different goals. Allison concludes that the frame of references chosen by the analyst attempting to explain policy outcomes influences the nature of the conclusions, and he implies that all three should be employed. Once again, this requires that the analyst, or decision maker, must synthesize multiple perspectives in order to widen his or her range of possible actions.

The complexity of public sector decision making is succinctly captured in Thompson and Tuden's (1959) typology of decision-making strategies. When organizational stakeholders agree about goals and how to attain them, decision making is a matter of computation; the rational model is applicable here and issues of efficiency take center stage. If there is agreement on goals but disagreement on the causal relationships necessary to achieve them, decision making requires judgment regarding implementation. Judgment is exercised on the efficacy of alternative instrumental means. Disagreement of goals and agreement on cause and effect relationships requires bargaining, negotiations, and compromise. If there is disagreement in both areas, decision making demands some sort of inspirational intervention. Unfortunately, many of the issues faced by public sector managers seem to fall into the fourth category. Once again, Harmon and Mayer (1986) refer to these as "wicked problems": problems that are hard to define, bound, and measure.

## III.  BUILDING MANAGERIAL CAPACITY IN THE PUBLIC SECTOR

In his highly influential book *The Intellectual Crisis in American Public Administration*, Vincent Ostrom (1974) contends that efficiency in the delivery of public goods and services has no meaning if those goods and services are not responsive to the needs of the public. Ostrom was writing from a market, or public choice, perspective, and he suggested that goods and services should be provided by the smallest unit of government possible. Economies of scale may be lost but responsiveness is enhanced, because it is easier to aggregate individual preferences in smaller governments. The proliferation of governments delivering a wide range of goods and services would create a "market" of governments among which citizens could "shop" for the mix of goods and services that met their preferences. He overlooks the fact that the nature of many of these goods and services are determined by professional bureaucracies rather than elected bodies, even on the local level, where the latter tend to be comprised of part-time politicians who do not have access to supportive bureaucracies of their own (such as the Congressional Budget Office). Is it feasible to enhance responsiveness in this scenario, or are citizens left to "vote with their feet?"

A colleague and myself (Gianakis and McCue, 1999) recently examined the issue of managerial capacity, or the capacity to act responsibly and responsively, in the context of the job of the local government budget and finance professional. We concluded that responsible action was rooted in the reason that finance professionals are hired as substantive experts. The core responsibility of the finance function is to ensure the long-term financial viability of the enterprise. This responsibility is particularly important in local government, because there is no political constituency for this end. Elected officials rarely see beyond the next election, and citizens tend to perceive the collective long-term interests of the city in terms of their own short-term interests. This core responsibility legitimizes the participation of the finance professional in the policy-making process; long-term financial viability also requires effective and efficient current services, so the budgetary expert is grouped with the finance expert. The central point is that responsibility is rooted in the core functions that the expert is hired to perform.

However, this leaves the problem of responsiveness, because there is no single way to optimize long-term financial viability or to provide a responsive mix of current services. The professional must engage the public in order to determine its aggregate preferences. But the finance professional cannot act responsibly by taking the role of a unitary political actor, nor can he or she act responsively by engaging only attentive publics or narrow constituencies. The budget and finance professional must act as a part of the professional political organization created by the polity to meet its needs. As outlined above, all political institutions in a democracy are responsive to the general public and responsible for the pursuit of the public interest.

The core responsibilities of each expert tie him or her to this enterprise. But how can the variety of experts housed in the typical local government professional organization—one of the most highly differentiated organizations in the world that is subject to enormous centrifugal forces in the form of narrow constituencies and particular frames of reference—be integrated into a unitary political institution? We began our analysis with the budget and finance professional because it is only during the formal budget process that each of these individual pockets of expertise must acknowledge being part of a larger enterprise. The budget process, particularly the zero-base process as described in our book (Gianakis and McCue, 1999), holds promise as an organizational development tool in a program to raise the expert's decision-making frame of reference from an individual expert pursuing his or her own self-interest or the interests of his or her own agency and attentive publics, to one that reflects his or her status as a member of a community of experts engaging the entire political community. A "fourth generation" of information technology has also facilitated the sharing of information and, hence, communication between agencies (Landsbergen and Wocken, 2001).

We also began with the finance professional because efficiency is an element in all positions held by professional managers. Efficiency encapsulates the promise of professional public managers, and it is the concept that unites the various strands of expertise that make up the professional public organization. This efficiency cannot be achieved through structure alone without compromising effectiveness and responsibility; it precipitates suboptimization and simple accountability to rules and regulations. "Liberation management" must be pursued in order to realize the promise of professional public management, but this end is optimized more effectively through cooperation rather than competition. One of the emerging roles of the "entrepreneurial" city manager is to coordinate divergent perspectives manifested by substantively unique departments (Nalbandian, 1999). This end cannot be optimized through the development of structurally based "decision premises" tied to specific jobs. The key to optimizing resource allocation schemes and providing for the long-term financial viability of the jurisdiction is to develop an overarching organizational culture that supports cooperation rather than encouraging political competition. In this way, the professional organization takes responsibility for the pursuit of the public interest, and each manager is linked to this responsibility and to the organization as a whole.

However, the professional public organization cannot simply develop the public interest; it must be discovered. The public as a whole must become engaged in this process, and this, too, will be a difficult task given the extent to which the public has apparently lost confidence in its formal political institutions (Behn, 1998). The scenario described here also demands another kind of culture-building effort in the form of an educative relationship among the general public and elected officials and the professional public organization. The first two describe the desirable and the last outlines the possible and alternative paths to achieving it. Public managers must also be able to manage the inevitable conflict that arises when alternative futures are considered by the polity; "getting closer to clients generates considerable potential for increasing the unanticipated in public management" (Kiel, 1994).

The design summarized here allows more information to be brought to bear on the problems targeted for collective action. But despite the participation of the citizenry, questions of accountability remain. We suggest that when all of the managers of the professional public organization are focused on meeting the public interest as defined through democratic engagement, the managers themselves serve to hold one another accountable. If a manager's decision-making perspective is focused on his or her own agency, peer accountability is less likely to occur. The managers are also responsible to one another for the definition of the public interest, and technological top-down responses should not be tolerated; this reflects Waldo's (1952) and others' commitment to democratic values. This approach also calls for the reflective practitioner who takes educative action as described by Schon (1984), Denhardt (1984), and others. The professional's claim to a degree of autonomy in decision making and the "liberation" of public managers demands such an orientation.

Productivity in the public sector cannot be achieved through administrative systems or market mechanisms. Productivity is the measure of the capacity of public managers to make decisions that are responsive to the needs of the polity and for which the managers take responsibility on the basis of their autonomy. If policy making has moved to the professional public organization due to their complexity and the demand for expertise, then in order to survive democracy must also move into the public organization.

## IV. CONCLUSIONS

This chapter has reviewed various approaches to decision making in the public sector in an effort to develop a normative approach to decision making that could mitigate the tension between expertise and democracy inherent in a democratic society. It was suggested that the values necessary to guide the discretionary decision-making powers of public managers could be extrapolated from the core functions of distinct areas of expertise. These values are legitimized by the fact that they are rooted in the reasons why the expert is retained by the polity.

However, the frame of reference within which these values are pursued must be the polity as a whole, in order to provide for the pursuit of the public interest. The pursuit of the public interest legitimizes the outcomes of political institutions. Actions must be taken at the level of the public organization as a whole; actions taken below the level where the entire polity is represented across the variety of public services delivered are simply those of individual political actors representing attentive publics and narrow interests. This approach calls for a shift in the competitive organizational cultures that dominate most public organizations to cultures that emphasize collaboration and collective action on the part of the organization. Clearly, the mechanics of this approach are more feasible at the local level, but its spirit is widely applicable and forms an alternative to the challenges posed by the New Public Management.

Reinvention, devolution, and reform have "increased the scope and discretion front-line public servants exercise and [have] created an environment in which bureaucratic decision making is scrutinized against an increasingly complex set of standards" (Vinzant and Crothers, 1996, p. 457). Decision making is closely tied to the core issues of public administration as a field of study. As do Behn (1998), Frederickson (1997), and Meier (1997), the author believes that the "problem" of bureaucracy is actually a problem in governance. "This suggests a normative orientation, with public administration concerned with how governance should be structured and operated rather than just how the bureaucracy should implement public policy.... [P]ublic administration must redefine its focus because no other discipline, field, or profession is concerned with these problems" (Meier, 1997, p. 197).

## REFERENCES

Allison, T. (1969). Conceptual models and the Cuban missile crisis. *Am. Polit. Sci. Rev.* 63(3):689–718.

Appleby, P. (1949). *Policy and Administration*. Tuscaloosa, AL: University of Alabama Press.

Aucoin, P. (1996). *The New Public Management: Canada in Comparative Perspective*. Montreal: Institute for Research on Public Policy.

Barnard, C. (1938). *The Functions of the Executive*. Cambridge, MA: Harvard University Press.

Beach, L.R. (1997). *The Psychology of Decision Making*. Thousand Oaks, CA: Sage.

Behn, R. D. (1998). What right do public managers have to lead? *Public Admin. Rev.* 58(3): 209–224.

Bellone, C. J., Goerl, G. F. (1992). Reconciling public entreprenuership and democracy. *Public Admin. Rev.* 52(2):130–145.

Boston, J., Martin, J., Pallot, J. (1996). *Public Management: The New Zealand Model*. New York: Oxford University Press.

Bourkaert, G. (1993). Measurement and meaningful management. *Public Product. and Manage. Rev.* 17(1):31–44.

Bozeman, B., Kingsley, G. (1998). Risk culture in public and private organizations. *Public Admin. Rev.* 58(2):109–118.

Cohen, M. D., March, J. G., Olsen, J. P. (1972). A garbage can model of choice. *Admin. Sci. Quart.* 17:1–25 (March).

Cook, B. J. (1998). Politics, political leadership, and the public management movement. *Public Admin. Rev.* 58(3):225–230.

Dahl, R. A. (1947). The science of administration: Three problems. *Public Admin. Rev.* 7(1):1–11.

Denhardt, R. D. (1984). *Theories of Public Organizations*. Monterey, CA: Brooks/Cole.

Downs, A. (1957). *An Economic Theory of Democracy*. New York: Harper Collins.

Dror, Y. (1965). Muddling through—science or inertia? *Public Admin. Rev.* 24(3):151–158.

Etzioni, A. (1959). Authority, structure, and organizational effectiveness. *Admin. Sci. Quart.* 4 (June):43–69.

Etzioni, A. (1967). Mixed scanning. *Public Admin. Rev.* 67(4):385–392.

Frank, H. A., McCollough, J. (1992). Municipal forecasting practice: Demand and supply side perspectives. *Int. J. Public Admin.* 15(9):1669–1696.

Fredrickson, H. G. (1997). *The Spirit of Public Administration*. San Francisco: Jossey-Bass.

Gerth, H. H., Mills, C. W. (1946). *From Max Weber: Essays in Sociology*. Oxford, UK: Oxford University Press.

Gianakis, G. A., McCue, P. (1999). *Local Government Budgeting: A Managerial Approach*. Westport, CT: Quorum.

Grizzle, G. (1985). Performance measures for budget justifications: Developing a selection strategy. *Public Product. Rev.* 16(Spring):33–44.

Hammond, K.R., Rohrbaugh, J., Mumpower, J., Adelman, L. (1975). Social decision theory: Applications in policy formation. In: Kaplan, M., Schwartz, S., eds. *Human Decision and Decision Making in Applied Settings*. San Diego: Academic, 54–63.

Harmon, M. M. (1995). *Responsibility as Paradox*. Thousand Oaks, CA: Sage.

Harmon, M. M., Mayer, T. (1986). *Organization Theory for Public Administration*. Burke, VA: Chatelaine.

Henry, N. (1995). *Public Administration and Public Affair*. 6th ed. Englewood Cliffs, NJ: Prentice-Hall.

Hood, C. H. (1995). Contemporary public administration: a new global paradigm. *Public Policy Admi.* 10(2):104–117.

Hummel, R. P. (1991). Stories managers tell: why they are as valid as science. *Public Admin. Rev.* 51(1):31–41.

Kelly, R. M. (1998). An inclusive democratic polity, representative bureaucracies, and the new public management. *Public Admin. Rev.* 58(3):201–208.

Kiel, L. D. (1994). *Managing Chaos and Complexity in Government*. San Francisco: Jossey-Bass.

King, S., Stivers, C., eds. *Government Is Us: Public Administration in an Anti-Government Era.* Thousand Oaks, CA: Sage.

Klein, G. A. (1989). Recognition-primed decisions. *Advances Man-Made Syst. Res.* 5:47–92.

Klein, G. A. (1996). *Sources of Power: The Study of Naturalistic Decision Making.* Mahwah, NJ: Lawrence Erlbaum.

Krislov, S. (1974). *Representative bureaucracy.* Englewood Cliffs, NJ: Prentice-Hall.

Landsbergen, D. Jr., Wocken, G. Jr. (2001). Realizing the promise: Government information systems and the fourth generation of information technology. *Public Admin. Rev.* 61(2): 206–220.

Lindblom, C. E. (1959). The science of muddling through. *Public Admin. Rev.* 19(1):79–88.

Lindblom, C. E. (1965). *The intelligence of democracy: Decision making through partisan mutual adjustment.* New York: Free Press.

Loffler, E. (1997). *The Modernization of the Public Sector in an International Comparative Perspective: Implementation in Germany, Great Britain, and the United States.* Speyer, Germany: Forshungsinstitut Fur Offentliche Verwaltung.

Lynn, E. Jr. (2000). The myth of the bureaucratic paradigm: What traditional public administration really stood for. *Public Admin. Rev.* 61(2):144–160.

March, J. G. (1994). *A primer on Decision Making.* New York: Free Press.

March, J. G., Olsen, J. P. (1987). Organizational learning and the ambiguity of the past. In: March, J. G., Olsen, J. P., eds. *Ambiguity and Choice in Organizations.* 2nd ed. Bergen, Norway: Universitatsforlaget, pp. 54–68.

Marini, F., ed. (1971). *Toward a New Public Administration: The Minnowbrook Perspective.* Scranton, PA: Chandler.

Mayo, E. (1933). *The Human Problems of Industrial Civilization.* New York: Macmillan.

Meier, K. J. (1997). Bureaucracy and democracy: The case for more bureaucracy and less democracy. *Public Admin. Rev.* 57(3):193–199.

Mintzberg, H., Quinn, B. (1996). *The Strategy Process: Concepts, Contexts, Cases.* Upper Saddle River, NJ: Prentice-Hall.

Morgan, G. (1997). *Images of Organization.* Thousand Oaks, CA: Sage.

Nalbandian, J. (1999). Facilitating communication, enabling democracy: new roles for local government managers. *Public Admin. Rev.* 59(3):187–197.

Osborne, E., Gaebler, T. (1992). *Reinventing Government.* Reading, MA: Addison-Wesley.

Ostrom, V. (1974). *The Intellectual Crisis in American Public Administration.* Tuscaloosa, AL: University of Alabama Press.

Perrow, C. (1979). *Complex Organizations: A critical essay.* 2nd ed. Glenview, IL: Scott-Foresman.

Perrow, C. (1997). *Organizational Analysis: A Sociological View.* Belmont, CA: Wadsworth.

Radin, B. (1998). The government performance and results act (GPRA): a hydra headed monster or flexible management tool? *Public Admin. Rev.* 58(4):307–315.

Rohr, J. A. (1998). *Public Service Ethics and Constitutional Practice.* Lawrence, KS: University Press of Kansas.

Rosenbloom, D. (1997). *Federal Equal Employment Opportunity: Politics and Public Personnel Administration.* New York: Praeger.

Schon, D. (1984). *The Reflective Practitioner: How Professionals Think in Action.* New York: Basic.

Schon, D., Argyris, C. (1978). *Organizational Learning: A Theory of Action Perspective.* Reading, MA: Addison-Wesley.

Simon, H. A. (1976). *Administrative Behavior: A Study of Decision-Making Processes in Administrative Organizations.* 3rd ed. New York: Free Press.

Simon, H. A. (1995). Organizations and markets. *J. Public Admin. Res. Theor.* 5(3):273–294.

Simon, H. A., Smithberg, D., Thompson, V. (1950). *Public Administration.* New York: Knopf.

Spicer, M. W. (1995). *The Founders, the Constitution, and Public Administration: A Conflict of World Views*. Washington, DC: Georgetown University Press.

Stillman, R. J. (1991). *Preface to Public Administration*. New York: St. Martin's.

Svara, J. H. (1998). The politics/administration dichotomy as aberration. *Public Admin. Rev.* 58(1):51–58.

Terry, L. D. (1998). Administrative leadership, neo-managerialism, and the public management movement. *Public Admin. Rev.* 58(3):194–200.

Thompson, J. D., Tuden, A. (1959). Strategies, structures and processes of organizational decisions. In: Thompson, J. D., ed. *Comparative Studies in Administration*. Pittsburgh: University of Pittsburgh Press, pp. 195–216.

Vinzant, L., Crothers, L. (1996). Street-level leadership: Rethinking the role of public servants in contemporary governance. *Am. Rev. of Public Admin.* 26(4):457–475.

Vroom, H., Yago, G. (1988). On the validity of the Vroom–Yetton model. *J. Appl. Psychol.* 63(1):151–162.

Waldo, D. (1952). Development of theory of democratic administration. *Am. Polit. Sci. Rev.* 46(1):81–103.

Weick, K. (1995). *Sensemaking in Organizations*. Thousand Oaks, CA: Sage.

Wilson, J. Q. (1989). *Bureaucracy*. New York: Basic Books.

Wilson, W. (1887). The study of administration. *Polit. Sci. Quart.* 2(June):197–222.

# 5

# Public Sector Values and Productivity

**MONTGOMERY VAN WART**
*University of Central Florida, Orlando, Florida, U.S.A.*

## I. INTRODUCTION

Public sector values determine the instruments of democratic accountability and responsibility, the structures, cultures, and processes of organizations, the way employees are treated, and even the definition of the concept of "publicness." Despite the value-free notions of productivity that are often employed for reasons of simplicity, such an idea at a more abstract level is a quaint myth. For example, although while it is appropriate to talk of the most efficient way to conduct a process in terms of timeliness and the most effective way to produce in terms of cost reduction, it is naïve to assume that these values are the only, or even necessarily the most important, values in any given situation. Important though they are, due process, transparency, access, and representativeness (to mention only a few) might be more important in a given personnel action, procurement protocol, or case management technique.

The challenges of public sector values are manifold to be sure because they are numerous, often competing, and changing. This means that they are many times exceedingly complex and subtle. For example, public sector administrators use individual values (e.g., those related to their own status and role), professional values (e.g., those related to expert training and professional independence), organizational values (e.g., those related to organizational interests, structures, and leadership), legal values (e.g., those related to the significance of law), and public interest values (e.g., those related to the good of the public) (Van Wart, 1996, 1998). Although these value sets often function in concert, frequently some organizational values function at the expense of others. For example, killing is universally deplored, however, those in the military and police must sometimes use lethal force, doctors occasionally make life and death decisions about who shall live or about removing terminally ill patients from life-support, corrections officials in some states have to execute prisoners, and so on. To make matters still more difficult, values do shift over time, sometimes dramatically and radically, and sometimes subtly. In American history it is easy to see the growth of individual rights of citizens through the abolition of slavery, discrimination laws, due process laws, and so on. Within the public service it is easy to see the growth of individual rights as well in the legal establishment of merit, tenure, and due process principles. Yet even the most highly cherished values are reinterpreted over time due to society's changing perceptions of the means and degree of expressing certain values.

Therefore values have more than a passing importance to public administrators in general, and in their pursuit of productivity. First, values determine the very definition of productivity, as well as the definition of an appropriate organizational culture, structure, process, and the like. Although public administrators often take these values for granted or are only aware of them at an unconscious level, they exert a powerful influence. Second, when values shift, definitions of productivity also shift. Changing definitions of values shift notions of the "right" purpose, vision, expectations, and the use of human capital. Third, and most important, confusion about values inevitably reduces productivity. Values confusion increases working at cross-purposes and infighting, while it reduces motivation and focus. In simpler cases, values confusion is the result of ignorance, egotism, or outdated beliefs. Yet often values confusion is far more difficult to clarify and rectify, especially in situations in which values competition and value shifts are endemic. Indeed, occasionally this confusion is an inevitable healthy transitional state that should not be terminated until a vigorous values debate has occurred, a fuzzy problem is better understood with all its value implications, or a more creative solution involving a different mix of values can be found.

For these reasons, then, the importance of values is critical in enhancing productivity, and hence the importance of public administrators being able to discern the important values issues, articulate them dispassionately, and be able to facilitate values discussions (Reich, 1988). Administrators who are unclear about the underlying principles and values of given situations are far more likely to act out of impulse rather than reason. Certainly they will be poor at clarifying the contrasting or competing values at stake and at facilitating dialogue when necessary. Administrators who understand values but are poor at articulating them will generally be less able to motivate, facilitate, and even inspire. Administrators able to discern and articulate, but not facilitate, may be unable to handle the most difficult situations in which discussion and debate are necessary to uncover issues, perspectives, and problems.

This ability to discern underlying value structures, articulate them so that they are understood even when values competition exists, and facilitate them in those less common but extremely important situations when discussion and debate are necessary are characteristics of those persons considered public sector exemplars. Such an example is cited after a broad discussion of public sector values and their relationship to productivity.

The purpose of this chapter is to assist administrators in values clarification skills by discussing the nature of values, by identifying some important value clusters, and by relating some of the more difficult value shifts (and clashes) currently occurring in public administration.

This chapter begins with a review of what values are, especially with reference to the public sector. The concept of values is one of the most slippery in all of social science so this discussion is an important point of reference for the essay. Then macrolevel types and sources of values in public administration are discussed, focusing primarily on political, economic, and social sources. The argument is made that only at a very high level of abstraction can examples of values be found that are nearly timeless in public administration, and that even these abstract stable values are re-interpreted in operational terms in each age. Examples of these midlevel values that shift slowly but importantly every 50 years or so are provided. Finally, some of the contemporary administrative value clashes are discussed and related to the previous discussion about shifting beliefs.

## II. WHAT ARE VALUES?

As Harold Gortner (2001) points out, it is difficult to get a full sense of what the concept "values" means unless one looks at the different perspectives provided by the different social sciences—psychology, sociology, philosophy, and history. These distinctions are not just those of experts in different fields; these distinctions mirror the very different connotations found in lay use of the term as well.

He begins by pointing out that administrators live in a world of both facts and values (Simon, 1957; for a postmodern rejection of this assertion see Kelly and Maynard-Moody, 1993). Facts are the raw data and indisputable part of knowledge. Putting aside the significant philosophical and operational difficulties that lie immediately below the surface of this assertion (because facts are not our focus here), values come into play as soon as one has to decide what facts mean, which facts to give priority to, how to assemble facts, or how to act upon them. Although many will urge public administrators to live as much in the world of facts with their perceived neutrality as possible, in a strict sense, this is not entirely possible. For example, a caseworker may be given highly specific operational guidelines about how to dispense services provided by the government. The caseworker interviews the client to glean facts largely supported by documentation, evidence, or the possibility of fact-finding review in cases of dispute or concerns over veracity. Yet even in this highly fact-determined case, values will intrude (Dicke and Ott, 1999). First, it is impossible to build guidelines so comprehensively that all situations are defined; therefore at least some modest level of discretion (which inevitably depends on individual values) is always present. Second, specific facts may be interpreted differently because of language subtleties. Third, the values of the caseworker will not only affect how much state assistance is given, but the way in which it is given, such as the amount of time allotted in the interview, the tone, and the type of affiliated suggestions and help. Many public administrators live in a professional world where their discretion about values is far more substantial. Middle managers are constantly interpreting the difficult cases and solving problems rich in values. Senior administrators are charged with enormously important value responsibilities rife in leading organizations and making policy recommendations.

Psychology emphasizes the innate and individual aspects of values as expressed in drives/urges, preferences/attitudes, and beliefs/principles. Although macrolevel theory in psychology focuses on generalized levels or stages of needs/values (Jung, 1923; Maslow, 1954; Kohlberg, 1981), microlevel research demonstrates the extraordinary range of needs/values at the individual level (captured in the nearly universal use of Likert scales). Therefore all individuals have different value structures; even the most similar siblings will differ slightly over what motivates them, what they feel, and how they choose to act. Sociology, on the other hand, emphasizes the communal aspects of values. What are group standards of desirable beliefs, priorities, and behaviors as judged in art, finance, education, and so on that condition individuals in society (Goodenough, 1971; Wallace, 1970; Geertz, 1973)? Unless operationally defined more narrowly, then, values refer to the preferences and priorities stemming from both individual and social contexts.

A major aspect of the study of history is understanding the actual value structures of societies through the ages, as well as the contributions and variations of specific individuals in those historical contexts (Schlesinger, 1987). If the Persians had overrun Greece in 480 B.C., it is likely that Western values would be significantly different today. Or if a strong-willed Henry VIII had not broken with the Pope, it is unlikely that the English would have valued independence from the Continent so highly for the next 500 years. Philosophy, on the other hand, tends to examine the proper or ideal value structures for society and individuals. It may be expressed through religion (e.g., the proper way to worship God), politics (e.g., the proper way to organize a state), economics (e.g., the proper way to organize an economy), or "pure" philosophy (e.g., the proper way to justify action such as a reliance on intrinsic virtue versus on doing the most good for the most people).

At their broadest level then, values are inner conceptions of what is desirable at one end of the spectrum to what is right or good at the other that subsequently shape outward expressions and behavior. The sources of values are from both individuals and society, and can be discussed from either an actual or ideal mode. In the case of public sector productivity values all these elements are extant. How work is accomplished involves individual and group conceptions of the desirable, right, and good ways to do it. Actual productivity is constantly contrasted against notions of ideals as expressed through comparisons or in a vision of a better future. The key is not necessarily using a narrower definition of values, but rather, it is simply being careful to define usage for the particular context. It should be noted that the study of productivity, because of its purpose, tends to emphasize group, organizational, and social needs as the ultimate ends, and individual values merely as a means.

## III. WHAT ARE THE MACROTYPES AND SOURCES OF VALUES IN PUBLIC ADMINISTRATION?

In the simplest sense, it can be asserted that most public administration macrolevel values are derived from the political system of which they are part. The political system, in its turn, is a rough barometer of the economic and social trends of society. For the purpose of this discussion, however, political, economic, and social sources are differentiated.

Schein (1985) pointed out that values range from those that are extremely long-lasting, stable, and largely assumed (basic assumptions), to those that are moderately long-lasting, moderately stable, and frequently a point of debate (beliefs), and finally to those that can be relatively evanescent, fleeting, and/or explicit in linguistic or physical dimensions (patterns of behavior and artifacts). Ott (1989) and Van Wart (1998) have translated these notions into public sector settings.

Basic assumptions—worldviews and overarching philosophies of life—are values that may last centuries in a stable society and are the bedrock upon which other values are situated. The seeds for most basic assumptions in U.S. culture were sown in the seventeenth and eighteenth centuries, and were formalized between the American Revolution and 1800. Basic assumptions establish the types of political, economic, and socioreligious systems within which a society will operate. Beliefs—the patterns of meaning, long-term attitudes, and ideologies—are values that generally shift significantly over a period of decades. In American public administration, these shifts are commonly identified in administrative eras: the Federalist with its staid, elitist style, the Jacksonian with its emphasis on greater political representativeness and political responsiveness, the Progressive and its emphasis on merit principles and technical management, the New Deal and its emphasis on stability and growth, and the New Public Management and its interest in flexibility and entrepreneurialism (Van Wart, 1996). The patterns of behavior and artifact level of values (specific means of communicating, the manners and habits of people, rites and symbols, styles) are what we here call tastes. Some tastes shift as the tangible reflection of a shift in beliefs. As the Progressives' belief in merit principles took hold, the taste for merit examinations and independent merit boards increased. In administrative terms we classify most administrative aspects such as organizational work structures and work processes as administrative tastes (for the purpose of this discussion). However, the examples are at a fairly high level and represent a combination of mid- and microlevel values in Schein's value scheme. Some tastes shift in less ideological ways simply as a result of physical or historical evolution. In public administration examples of evolutionary changes in tastes include the preference for electronic formats (both internally in organizational communication and externally with the public being served), and increased casualness in dress. See Figure 1 for a graphic representation of the relationship among basic assumptions, beliefs, and tastes.

## A. Politically Derived Values in Public Administration

Political values focus on the use of the power of the state, most pronounced in police and military powers, and the allocation of public resources, most pronounced in budget processes. Most basic assumptions that are politically derived stem from the Constitution. Some of the important basic assumptions include:

A democratic system of representative government
A strong federal system
Separation of powers with check and balances
A relatively weak executive (at least compared to absolute monarchs or prime ministers during their tenure)

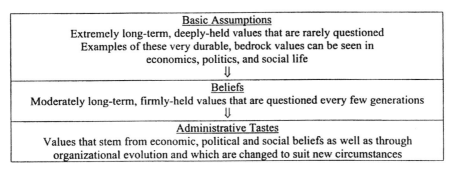

**Figure 1** The relationship of different levels of values.

An independent judicial branch with strong interpretive powers
Division of church and state, and
State as a guarantor of private property rights and contracts

Although these basic assumptions seem unequivocal within our own historical context (which is the essential nature of basic assumptions), a few comparisons highlight the profoundly different perspectives possible. For example, the Articles of Confederation predating the Constitution embodied a weak federal system and did not define a national judiciary. Today many countries blend church and state functions, from formalistic affiliations such as England to substantive fusions such as Iran. Many countries have nondemocratic systems where there are hereditary rulers (e.g., many Arabic states) or rulers who are essentially heads of government for life (e.g., China, Cuba, and much of Africa).

Contemporary political, economic, and social beliefs seemed to shift about 1990.[1] These beliefs (respectively noted by terms such as postmodern, new economy, or New Public Management) are still coalescing although their outlines are becoming relatively clear. To highlight them, New Deal/Great Society beliefs (generally the 1940 to 1990 era) are reviewed in each of these areas first.

The New Deal period was typified by the following political beliefs stressing the desirability of:

Enhancing individual rights (e.g., due process)
Enhancing minority rights (e.g., EEO and AA)
Enhancing separation of church and state (e.g., disallowal of school prayer)
Enhancing "public" sector power (e.g., expansion of number of agencies, expansion of functions)

The desirability of enhancing public sector power was particularly influential and stemmed from three major events: the success of the Progressive and Scientific Management movements to "clean up" and rationalize government, the failure of the market in the Great Depression, and the success of the government in winning World War II (Yergin and Stanislaw, 1998). These political beliefs had ramifications in terms of the tastes in administrative practices. For example, tenure rights of public employees were introduced and strengthened during this period, both through civil service systems and organized labor contracts. Minority hiring and promotion were legally required throughout the public service as the era progressed, from the integration of the military and schools, to Equal Employment Opportunity legislation, and finally to proactive Affirmative Action provisions. On the other hand, religious-based programs were excluded from public oversight and subsidy, except as charitable donations. Finally, taxes were raised proportionately to increase services and redistribution, and state regulation was encouraged in many areas where public and consumer safety needed an "even" hand.

The postmodern political era seems to be a relatively strong reaction to the perceived excesses that resulted from both the New Deal and Progressive eras. Some of the important political value trends that seem to be emerging relate to the desirability of:

Curbing the excesses of individualism
Returning to greater uniformity of treatment among groups (e.g., reverse discrimination)

Integrating religious institutions and beliefs in inoffensive ways that do not imply
state sanction (e.g., faith-based organizations receiving federal assistance to
provide social services or silent prayer in schools)
Returning as much power to the private sector as possible (e.g., contracting of
functions and agencies)

Cascading from these changing beliefs, some of the changing administrative
tastes are changing significantly too. There has been a clear trend to look for ways
of curbing the tenure rights of public employees (Condrey and Maranto, 2001), even
though movement in this area has been slow. There has been an elimination of affirmative action (but not EEO) as an explicit policy in all but egregious cases, although
many organizations pursue aggressive diversity philosophies. Inclusion of religious-
based organizations as service providers if appropriate alternatives exist is being
introduced, although judicial and legislative challenges have slowed movement in this
area. Finally, there has been an effort at tax abatement (or at least plateauing) through
several means. One is outright load shedding through service termination or privatization. Another is with more aggressive consideration of contracting out to the private
sector. Although overall tax rates have been under great pressure since the initial tax
revolt in California (Proposition 13 of 1978, after which the rate of local government
slowed considerably), fee-based services (which reduce redistribution) have become
more popular (Henry, 1999).

## B.　Economically Derived Values in Public Administration

Although the United States was founded in a mercantilist era in which European
powers wanted to amass bullion, establish colonies, and create a favorable trade balance through industry and mining, it was partially rebelling against this system in the
American revolution. However, in 1776 Adam Smith was articulating the advanced
form of mercantilism, later called capitalism, in which the economic emphasis shifted
importantly toward the formation of capital among a broader socioeconomic base and
in which free competition was enhanced as the ideal means of creating wealth. This
discouraged the use of tariffs and import bans as a means of national economic control
and later diminished the importance of absolute monetary standards. Capitalist
principles were easy to embrace because they became part of the rationale for independence. Although mercantilist states use the power of the state extensively to drive
and protect the economy, capitalist states ideally allow "the invisible hand" of the
market to settle economic competition and supply-and-demand issues. The state's role
is to make sure that competition is fair (an important regulative role) so the market can
perform adequately and to attend to those select areas in which the market cannot be
expected to perform well (e.g., public welfare, safety, defense). Broad basic assumptions of the American economy include:

A capitalist system based on:
　　Individual wealth production by a large number of people,
　　Competition as the primary organizer of market-based exchange, and
　　State regulation of the economy only to ensure that market forces are in
　　　balance and to make sure that competition is fair.
The public sector subordinate to the private sector in economic terms in all but
　　narrowly defined purposes.

It is easier to understand these basic assumptions in comparison. Oligopolies can be capitalist but still not foster broad-based wealth production and ownership (e.g., many Latin American countries). It is easier for states to ascribe to a truly free market when: economic times are good, the state is highly competitive in a sufficient number of areas to balance trade, and the country's economy does not depend too heavily on low-priced commodities (e.g., most raw materials). In times of depression, or when a country is not competitive because of education or size, or when it relies primarily upon raw materials or low-end manufactured goods, it is much more difficult to maintain capitalist principles. Finally, the subordination of the public sector to the private is not the only model. Many European countries have had successful mixed economies with strong public sector involvement and direct ownership over select consumer production areas.

New Deal beliefs were also shaped by the Great Depression and the increased reliance on the state to curb the excesses and weaknesses of the market. Although the New Deal did not overturn American capitalistic basic assumptions, it greatly relaxed those assumptions in many areas. During that era economic trends that were perceived as desirable included:

> The state monitoring a fair playing field (e.g., less competition during the Great Depression and more antitrust activity later);
> Although the state must avoid excessive intervention in the economy (especially consumer goods), the state has a special role in terms of
> Robust humanitarian needs,[2]
> Public safety and consumer protection needs,
> Public goods/services that are important and largely indivisible (water, electric, telephone, dams, roads, etc.), and
> Broadly defined economic emergencies or depressed economic areas needing direct economic stimulation.

It is easy to see how these beliefs shaped administrative tastes during that era. Although antitrust was weak during the Depression and World War II eras,[3] it resumed its importance by the 1960s. The classic case was the massive breakup of Bell Telephone. Increasingly fundamental humanitarian assistance became a state responsibility, rather than a family, nonprofit (e.g., church), or private responsibility. Thus administrative tastes in this area emphasized larger social safety nets and welfare standards including both financial assistance (e.g., Social Security and AFDC) and services (e.g., Medicare, Medicaid, and developmental assistance for handicapped individuals, etc.). Administratively, public safety was more broadly defined to encompass consumer protection including safeguards against faulty and dangerous products (e.g., the Consumer Product Safety Commission), regulation against harm in the work environment (e.g., OSHA and ERISA[4]), and nondisclosure in complicated products (e.g., insurance, car and house buying, etc.). Important "mass" services that were difficult to divide into competitive units were often allowed to be run by the public sector such as water, electric, dams, roads, airports, and so on. Those services not easily divided and prone to monopoly or quasimonopoly in which public sector ownership was not direct were heavily regulated (e.g., telephone, airlines). Public sector intervention in the economy was broadly defined in some cases because of regional stimulation (e.g., Tennessee Valley Authority, regional development banks, the Saint Lawrence Seaway Development Corporation, the Bonneville Dam, and the Columbia

Project, etc.), economic distress (examples including various types of federal insurance for farmers, flood plain residents, etc., railroad corporations—Conrail and Amtrak, or the Chrysler Loan Guarantee Act of 1979), or economic stability (e.g, the Federal Home Loan Mortgage Corporation, Federal Deposit Insurance Corporation, Federal National Mortgage Association, etc.). These interventions are complex because of the mixed rationales and the fact that they were sometimes part of the executive functions of federal, state, or local governments (e.g., the Federal Corps of Engineers or the Department of Housing and Urban Development), but were often hived off as various types of public enterprises (a city redevelopment corporation or county civic center). Nonetheless, the public sector played a large *direct* role in the economy by American standards.

The new economy is clearly reinstating a "purer" version of capitalism in terms of the beliefs that are commonly promoted and the administrative tastes that are subsequently reflected. The differences are subtle but profound in terms of what is considered desirable.

> The state should allow greater corporate flexibility except in areas of special public interest (e.g., the environment, public safety).
> The state should avoid any intervention in the economy except when:
>
> > Minimal levels of humanitarian assistance are necessary,
> > Public safety and consumer protection needs exist,
> > Service indivisibility cannot be overcome, or
> > Narrowly defined economic needs exist such as areas of economic stagnation, or targeted indirect economic stimulation.

Administrative (and judicial) tastes reflect the modest shifts in the belief level of American capitalistic assumptions. For example, although the Federal Trade Commission and the Justice Department have been successful in blocking mergers that would clearly endanger competition in many industries,[5] it appears they were unsuccessful in the very important Microsoft case[6] in which the Justice Department sought the breakup of the company in the same vein as it had with Bell Telephone. Humanitarian assistance has been curbed in welfare (e.g., the Personal Responsibility and Work Opportunity Act of 1996) and Medicaid. Pressures continue to mount in Social Security and Medicare although no reversal has yet occurred in these popular programs.

The new welfare philosophy is that people should be held more accountable for their personal actions and future, and that a greater share of personal humanitarian assistance should come from private and nonprofit sources. There has been little abatement for the taste in robust public safety as evidenced by such phenomena as the massive growth in school police personnel and huge cigarette court settlements.[7]

The sensibility of what indivisibility means has shifted dramatically, however, aided by the growth of technological alternatives. This has been most significantly seen in largely private sector industries (regulated by the public sector) such as electricity and telephone where attempts at increasing competition are being or have been implemented. (Of course, in some cases deregulation has allowed decreased competition despite the claims of proponents.) It has also been seen in traditionally public sector industries such as sanitation in which many cities have split their services among several providers,[8] and postal service in which the U.S. Postal Service was changed from a cabinet-level department with primary responsibility to Congress into an independent federal agency with primary responsibility to a postal rate commission and complete self-sufficiency in 1970.[9] Tastes in economic redistribution of tax dollars through block grants (e.g., Community Development Block Grants) or direct executive agency services (e.g., public sector housing units) have shifted slightly to vouchers at the federal level (i.e., competition rather than regulation) and tax subsidies at the state and local levels (i.e., reducing tax revenues) to enhance business enticement or expansion. State and local governments have also engaged more aggressively in economic stimulus packages than in the past, such as underwriting sports arenas (Swindell and Rosentraub, 1998). In many cases these trends are muted because of an inability to wean those specifically benefiting from support and services in the older economic regimes into newer philosophical preferences of the public at large.[10]

## C.  Socially Derived Values of Public Administration

Because individuals were often seeking religious, economic, and political freedom, a rugged individualism is one of the hallmarks of American culture. Examples of colonies founded on principles of religious freedom (at least for themselves) included most of New England, Pennsylvania, and Maryland. Economic freedom was a hallmark of most of the southern colonies and New York. This strong sense of personal independence continued to be particularly keen during American history wherever the frontier might be and it was typified in legendary figures such as Daniel Boone and the American cowboy. Thus there was a sense that virtue and personal decisions should determine the type of obligations one should have to meet. Organizations, on the other hand, were given fairly wide parameters to curb individual choice (because they were freely chosen) through contracts or covenants, and to structure themselves within certain social parameters, be those organizations churches, businesses, or social groups. For example, Alexis de Tocqueville in his famous study of America in the 1830s spent a great deal of time reflecting on the health and heterogeneity of American social institutions such as social clubs, volunteer organizations, and professional groups. Some of the more important basic assumptions of American society include:

> The primacy of individual choice in politics, religion, and livelihood and lifestyle (the pursuit of happiness);
> A strong preference for independent determination of virtue and independent decision making about what is good, rather than the imposition or regulation of the state to determine duty; and
> A strong belief in the right and ability of individuals to find sustenance in a large number of organizations (religious, social, and economic), and to give those organizations fairly wide latitude to focus the interests of members and provide discipline.

Contrasts with these strong Western social values are most obvious with the classical value structure in Asian countries in which a strong state and strong clan structures predominated over individual wants and desires. Duty to the state, family, and economic class were primary virtues, and personal choice was subordinate. Few organizational structures beyond those established or determined by the state and clan were considered necessary, no matter whether it was for religion, commerce, or social interaction.[11]

American social beliefs in organizations, by the middle of the twentieth century, leaned heavily toward large hierarchical structures in both the private and public sectors. Companies were getting larger in general by replicating services in many locations (A and P, Sears and Roebuck, Edison Electric) and/or by the use of mass production technologies (e.g., Ford, General Motors, General Electric, and IBM). The model of standardized service through a large hierarchical organization was established by the Post Office which dominated federal employment in the nineteenth century. Furthermore, there was a strong belief in the special and distinctive roles of the private and public sector, even though their organizations often functioned and looked remarkably similar. That is, a general New Deal belief was that the role of the private sector was to be the engine of growth, but that the public sector was to focus on the many areas in which the private sector could not be trusted: regulation of the market to ensure fairness, public safety, national safety, a social safety net, and commonly held public goods (roads, schools, parks, etc.). The public generally trusted the oversight provided by legislatures, the executive, and the judicial branch. Socially derived beliefs, then, included:

> A belief in strong hierarchical organizations in both the private and public sectors,
> An emphasis on the special and distinctive roles of the two predominate sectors, and
> An emphasis on competition as the primary control mechanism for the private sector where natural monopolies did not exist and external control (legislative, executive, and judicial) for the public sector.

These New Deal beliefs substantially affected administrative tastes. Public organizations tended to have steep hierarchies that were carefully layered in terms of cascading responsibility. Bureaucratic structures emphasizing expertise were favored, even though that expertise might be based on extreme specialization. Large public organizations with monopolistic characteristics could structure themselves as closed systems with relatively static inputs that were not significantly affected by output productivity. A strong reliance on cascading formal authority and stable processes was generally instituted. The size of public organizations was largely unquestioned, as long as those organizations were considered inherently governmental functions. Long-time examples of such functions—postal service, national defense, police protection, and public services such as roads and public infrastructure—were joined by enhanced social needs such as social welfare and social engineering. Although the public sector was allowed to grow, it continued to be controlled almost exclusively by nonmarket forces (especially legislative and executive oversight).

However, beliefs in the current era have been shifting former New Deal beliefs dramatically. Replacing the belief in large, hierarchical, bureaucratic organizations has been an increasing belief in organizational heterogeneity. Organizations are now emphasizing customization, small-batch work, one-stop service, self-help service through automated services (coproduction), and related types of work processes. Just as there has been a merging of information systems in society (e.g., computers, telephones, televisions, stereo systems, etc., are merging into integrated systems), there has also been an increased interest in better integration of systems and organizations in society. For example, in the private sector airline alliance systems can get you anywhere in the world; and there has been a new emphasis of strong partnerships with other companies rather than vertical integration. There is also an increased interest in integration of services in government and between the sectors as well. For example, certified development corporations are partially funded (and fully insured) by the Small Business Administration (through the 504 Loan Program), partially funded by private banks, and administered by nonprofit organizations (generally by councils of government). Finally, there is an increased belief that much of government is service-related, not really inherently governmental, and should be subjected to competitive forces. This is combined with a deep suspicion that public organizations have become too insulated, too large, and too nonresponsive to public needs. That is, there is a perception that often classical means of external control have not worked sufficiently for the large public sector that evolved in the second half of the twentieth century. In sum, some of the new socially derived beliefs include:

A belief in greater organizational heterogeneity in both major sectors,
An emphasis on integrated roles of the sectors, and
Increasing the competition in both sectors and decreasing monopolies in the
    public sector.

Although the change in rhetoric has probably been more dramatic than the actual changes that have occurred in administrative tastes as reflected in structures, processes, and ways of doing business, virtually no large organizations today are exempt from some demonstrable shifts in practices. For example, many public sector organizations have made an effort to become flatter, sometimes eliminating a full layer of middle management in large organizations.[12] A trend toward more work teams and more worker generalists is pronounced, necessitating cross-training. Public sector organizations have become more "open," meaning that they have a much greater customer/client orientation. To be more responsive, they have had to devolve and decentralize to some degree, allowing more decision making at lower levels and in the field. There has been a greatly enhanced emphasis on innovation coming from a larger number of people in the organization, which also encourages organizational hetero-geneity. Systems integration has been difficult to achieve, but one-stop shopping for clients seeking services has become common in social service agencies (e.g., welfare, unemployment insurance, job assistance, etc.), building trades (e.g., zoning information, permits, and inspections), and environmental services (e.g., seeking air, water, and land permits and inspections). Other examples of system integration include law enforcement agencies working together to share databases and therefore have com-patible and interlinked computer systems, and renewed efforts to have greater city–county collaborations. Finally, the increased use of competition has been most visible in education in which the growth of charter schools, school vouchers, and expanded student choice of schools within systems has been extensive.

## IV. CASE EXAMPLE OF THE CONNECTIONS AND COMPLICATIONS OF RELATING PUBLIC SECTOR VALUES TO PRODUCTIVITY: THE FIRST EPA DIRECTOR

William D. Ruckelshaus, the first EPA Director, had an exciting and important job (Dobel, 1992). He assumed the position as director of an agency in an era when, through the publication of books such as Rachel Carson's *The Silent Spring* and ecological scandals such as the oil spill off Santa Barbara and the burning of the Cuyahoga River, the American public was increasingly aware of, and dissatisfied with, the amount of ecological and human damage being done by both the private and public sectors. The limitations of the market in the environmental area had become clear; that is, the costs of most pollution were not being paid by polluters. And although many laws were passed in the 1960s, they had yet to really have the significant effect that had been hoped for. When Ruckelshaus took over the newly formed Environmental Protection Agency in 1970, with the more rigorous Clean Air Act of 1970 in the offing, he had much to accomplish and many new tools.

The challenges were probably greater than the opportunities, however, in terms of actually producing a cleaner and safer environment. His own organization was a patchwork of divisions and offices that had been cobbled together with a Presidential Executive Order. Its culture was highly inconsistent and organized around both different media (i.e., air and water, and pesticides, radiation, and solid waste) and functions (i.e., planning, enforcement, and monitoring). The divisions of the agency immediately tended to act as separate fiefdoms with significantly different values. With an agency of less than 6000, his resources were limited in what he could allow the agency to tackle at any given time. Politically the agency was often caught trying to navigate between an activist and more conservationist Congress and a cautious President. Much of the 1970s legislation set precise standards beyond the capacity of known technologies to get industry to innovate faster and more seriously, whereas the Administration was concerned by excessive demands on industry.

The complexity of the public sector productivity values was particularly vexing. The law is often the first among equals when public sector values compete for administrators; that is, the law is satisfied before other considerations, or special consideration is given to the law to make sure that compliance occurs. However, Congress had given the agency more mandates, work, and higher standards than were possible to achieve. The Administrator had unusual discretion in interpreting which part of the law would be implemented in those early years. The efficient and effective implementation of public policy was complicated by the heavy role of the courts and the tendency of many issues to receive attention due more to judicial action, than legislative action or executive decisions. Strong pressure was exerted by the President for relaxation of standards and by OPM for reducing the negative economic effects on private companies and the government itself. Of course environmental groups wanted fast action to make up for the accumulated damage that had occurred; however, polluters (including millions of drivers) were concerned about ease of implementation and avoidance of undue burden. Finally, although much of the expense was passed back to polluters and indirect consumers, much direct expense was passed back to taxpayers who were increasingly anxious about higher taxes.

Ruckelshaus won wide praise for his ability to build the agency, move the environmental agenda forward, and balance competing values with integrity. A hallmark of his style was information gathering and public input. Not only did he make sure that the various media of his agency, Congress, and the Executive Branch were heard, but he pioneered the effective use of the administrative public hearing on a national basis. Having made sure that he was well informed on all sides of an issue, he was able to articulate the underlying values with great clarity and balance, so that his use of the law and his discretion were clearly understood. Pragmatically, he elected not to focus on strict compliance of all polluters immediately inasmuch as this was virtually impossible, but to focus on the serious polluters first. In such cases he decided that boldness and courage were necessary, and he used his legal background as both a state and later federal assistant attorney general. Within the first sixty days of the agency, it brought five times more enforcement than any of its predecessor agencies. Ruckelshaus also used the threat of legal action against Union Carbide for pollution in West Virginia, even though his statutory authority was dubious in that case. He used public opinion to great effect in this case, in which he released a letter to the press which gathered significant public support (Landy et al., 1994).

The lessons to be learned from this exceptional administrator are relatively clear. Values were complex and shifting in the environmental policy area. Ruckelshaus was adept at identifying the changing values and leveraging the information-gathering process itself to gain credibility. Even though it was impossible to provide decisions that pleased everyone, his decisions were widely understood because of their clarity, and respected because of their fairness. Because of the values shift, new methods of productivity (in this case environmental protection) were necessary. Productivity had to be more centralized (the creation of EPA itself), methods had to be more robust (e.g., taking or threatening legal action), and initial efforts had to be more focused. Furthermore, productivity was not just reducing emissions and cleaning up waste sites, it was also education, public relations, and forging workable compromises regarding implementation strategies. Because of his ability to understand the underlying values and communicate them to a vast number of powerful constituencies, he was able to keep values confusion to a minimum, and to avoid the dysfunctionality of excessive values competition.

## V. CONCLUSION

Public sector values are numerous, competing, and changing. Although the values most associated with productivity—efficiency and effectiveness—are generally among the most important to consider, in the larger picture these largely organization-level values must be tempered with other fundamentally different values such as due process, representativeness, access, transparency, various types of responsiveness (e.g., to political masters, clients, taxpayers, etc.), and various types of accountability (e.g., to self, profession, and the public interest). To make the situation even more difficult for public administrators to master, these numerous and competing values change over time.

Yet no matter how difficult, it is critical for public administrators to understand public sector values if they are to do their jobs well. Productivity is defined by the values we hold. This occurs directly in our sensibilities about the best way to efficiently produce a service, but also indirectly in our sensibilities about how to structure and lead public organizations, how to include clients in the process, and the scope of the services to be provided. Although public administrators may emphasize technical efficiency, and the democratic process of accountability may emphasize the political role of elected officials in designing program effectiveness, it is not possible to demarcate a sharp line. Public administrators use values as implementers (e.g., their use of technical discretion and authorized midlevel policy decision making); also, they promote values as particularly important players in the policy creation process. Because values at the belief and taste levels are constantly evolving, it is important for public administrators to be in tune with the larger picture of values if they are to facilitate values consensus and coherence, rather than simply impose their own preferences where discretion exists. And because values confusion creates the opportunity for enormous inefficiencies, confusion, and frustration, it is critical that public administrators be able to discern what values are at issue, articulate them clearly, and facilitate some degree of working consensus. This skill and art may be a technical process of explication and education in some cases, or in others it may require a robust public dialogue before balanced and fair decisions can be reached.

Also complicating values elucidation is the complex nature of their sources. Values emanate from both society at large and individuals. Society creates the values climate through its numerous acculturation processes and subtly sets standards for the good of the group, especially the shaping of duty. Individuals interpret these values from their own unique perspectives and must make sense of them in fulfilling their personal destinies and sense of virtue. Values can also be construed as concrete standards derived from history, the law, and contemporary attitudes, or philosophical ideals that provide an inspirational model for which to strive. Public administrators must balance duties and their own sense of virtue, as well as blend high ideals with pragmatic realities, as they struggle with competing demands.

Public administrators must be able to determine the level of values they are considering first. At the highest level, what are the basic assumptions inherent in the American political system, economic system, or social system? Basic assumptions take centuries to change. The next level down are beliefs which change over a period of many decades and tend to be subtle reinterpretations of basic assumptions. These beliefs are ultimately evidenced as administrative tastes: the processes used, the concrete patterns of behavior, and the preferences that can shift quickly in the shortterm. For example, it is important for public administrators as part of the political system to know constitutional values (largely basic assumptions that are nearly immutable principles) and be able to discriminate them from the changeable beliefs and tastes of the age.

Only a few of the many New Deal values and administrative tastes that are shifting were discussed in this chapter; however, these shifts and the concomitant difficulties are in evidence in nearly every chapter in this volume. Some of those political and economic trends (no matter whether we like these shifts or not) include the weakening of administrative tenure rights, the curbing of more activist minority and female hiring and promotion guidelines, the pressures to curb tax increases, the emphasis on deregulation and devolution, and the move toward greater personal responsibility for economic security. The social–cultural trends discussed in this chapter are reshaping public sector organizations. New beliefs in organizational heterogeneity, role integration, and enhanced competition are leading to organizations that are flatter, use more teams and cross-training, emphasize "customer" values far more, and accentuate much more innovation and appropriate risk-taking.

The exemplar of responsible values management was William D. Ruckelshaus, the first EPA Administrator. He had to deal with old historical values of laissez-faire environmentalism of both the private and public sectors, and the new, idealistic legal realities. He had to try to comply with the ideals of legal mandates to provide improved health and ecological sustainability, while pragmatically dealing with a disorganized and incoherent agency, limited resources, and legislation that was often vague. Furthermore, the President who appointed him and to whom he reported was often a potential adversary because of his natural tendency to favor business interests and a more moderate course of action than Congress. Ruckelshaus succeeded in this complex, competing, and changing values environment because he understood the importance of values. He went to great pains to investigate the values of all the major players, and to listen to them carefully and deeply. By genuinely including them in the discussion of policy implementation, he gained their trust as being fair, even when specific interests would disagree with specific decisions that he would make. Finally, when Ruckelshaus used his discretion, which he did regularly and powerfully, he was able to explain his rationale, be understood, and know that he had the political, legal, and moral justification to carry out his decisions.

Because the value shifts occurring in the postmodern political environment, the new economy, and New Public Administration are only going to accelerate for the next ten to twenty years, understanding and managing values will only become more important for public administrators interested in fostering organizational productivity.

## NOTES

1. Of course the selection of any specific date is arbitrary and transitional periods are inevitably decades long. Substantive shifts in political, economic, and social trends were emergent in the 1970s with events such as the rise of government bashing, the challenge to American business supremacy, and increasing concerns about social decay.
2. Corporate and agriculture "welfare" needs, which are certainly very substantial, could be included in this list but are not because the overall emphasis has not shifted significantly from the New Deal and postmodern eras.
3. Indeed, to handle the vicissitudes of the Great Depression and World War II greater reliance was placed on noncompetitive strategies such as price supports and the use of monopolies.
4. The Occupational Safety and Health Administration created in 1970 as a part of the Department of Labor; Employee Retirement Income Security Act of 1974, also part of the Department of Labor.
5. During the Reagan–Bush–Clinton eras the threshold standard for endangering competition was increased significantly, so that generally only the more egregious cases were challenged.
6. At the writing of this chapter the disposition of the case has not been completed but it seems likely that Microsoft will be penalized but not suffer a breakup.
7. Of course there has been a subtle but pronounced shift to greater private security through the growth of private security guards and technological means. Such a shift reflects a fee-for-service mentality.
8. Such providers might include the city itself which may not want to relinquish some capacity to protect against private sector failure.
9. The Postal Reorganization Act of 1970 as well as the Postal Reorganization Act Amendments of 1976.
10. Social Security and Medicare are prime examples.
11. Of course Asian cultures have been enormously affected by Western values since World War II so that stereotype has extremely limited usefulness today.
12. However, at the federal level the trend toward increasing political management over the executive agencies has continued largely unabated for the last forty years. This trend toward the "thickening" of government at the top, with the hollowing of management and line functions, has caused many analysts great concern.

## REFERENCES

Condrey, S. E. Maranto, R., eds. (2001). *Radical Reform of the Civil Service*. Lanham, MD: Lexington.

Dicke, L. A., Ott, J. S. (1999). Public agency accountability in human services contracting. *Public Product. Manage. Rev.* 22(4):502–516.

Dobel, J. P. (1992). William D. Ruckelshaus: Political prudence and public integrity. In: Cooper, T. L., ed. *Exemplary Public Administrators: Character and Leadership in Government*. San Francisco: Jossey-Bass.

Geertz, C. (1973). *The Interpretation of Cultures*. New York: Basic.

Goodenough, W. (1971). *Culture, Language, and Society*. Reading, MA: Addison-Wesley.

Gortner, H. F. (2001). Values and ethics. In: Cooper, T. L., ed. *Handbook of Administrative Ethics*. New York: Marcel Dekker.

Henry, N. (1999). *Public Administration and Public Affairs*. 7th ed. Upper Saddle River, NJ: Prentice-Hall.

Jung, C. G. (1923). *Psychological Types*. New York: Harcourt Brace.

Kelly, M., Maynard-Moody, S. (1993). Policy analysis in the post-positivist era: engaging stakeholders in evaluating the economic development district program. *Public Admin. Rev.* 53(2):135–142.

Kohlberg, L. (1981). *The Philosophy of Moral Development: Moral Stages and the Idea of Justice*. Vol. 1. New York: HarperCollins.

Landy, M. R., Roberts, M. J., Thomas, S. R. (1994). *The Environmental Protection Agency*. New York: Oxford University Press.

Maslow, A. (1954). *Motivation and Personality*. New York: Harper.

Ott, J. S. (1989). *The Organizational Culture Perspective*. Chicago: Dorsey.

Reich, R. B. (1988). *Policy Making in a Democracy: The Power of Public Ideas*. Cambridge, MA: Ballinger.

Schein, E. H. (1985). *Organizational Culture and Leadership: A Dynamic View*. San Francisco: Jossey-Bass.

Schlesinger, A. Jr. (1987). *Cycles in American History*. New York: Houghton Mifflin.

Simon, H. (1957). *Administrative Behavior*. 2nd ed. New York: Free Press.

Swindell, D., Rosentraub, M. S. (1998). Who benefits from the presence of professional sports teams? The implications for public funding of stadiums and arenas. *Public Admin. Rev.* 58(1):11–21.

Van Wart, M. (1996). The sources of ethical decision making for individuals in the public sector. *Public Admin. Rev.* 56(6):525–534.

Van Wart, M. (1998). *Changing Public Sector Values*. New York: Garland.

Wallace, A. (1970). *Culture and Personality*. New York: Random House.

Yergin, D., Stanislaw, J. (1998). *The Commanding Heights: The Battle Between Government and the Marketplace that is Remaking the Modern World*. New York: Simon and Schuster.

# 6

# Privatization

**MARC HOLZER and BYRON E. PRICE**
*Rutgers, The State University of New Jersey, Newark, New Jersey, U.S.A.*

**HWANG-SUN KANG**
*KonKuk University, Seoul, South Korea*

## I. INTRODUCTION

Despite government's "businesslike" innovations in quality, human resources, and technology, the rush to privatize government has seemingly gained unstoppable momentum. Touted regularly by politicians and emphasized by the media, it is now virtually an unquestioned assumption (Holzer and Callahan, 1997).

The logic of privatization proponents is that turning over services to the private sector—through contracts or through abandonment—produces large savings with virtually no loss of quality or reduction in service levels (Savas, 1992). Proponents of privatization "have lived by the mantra that anything government can do, business can do better" (Katz, 1991). Advocates hold that outsourcing can efficiently deliver a much greater portion of services which are now public.

But the concept of privatization is not new. Privatization is an ancient approach to supposedly enhanced efficiency and effectiveness. Farazmand (2001) asserts that the history of privatization can be traced to ancient times if we consider contracting out. "For example, contracting out was tried as a tool of administration for provision of public services and for governmental performance under Darius the Great during the Persian world-state Achaemenid Empire (559 to 330 B.C.), in which two financial banking houses in the Babylonian Satrapy, Marashu & Sons and Egibi (one Persian and one Jewish), were contracted out by the state for collecting fixed property taxes" (Farazmand 1991, p. 261; Olmstead 1948, pp. 185–194). Greek mercenaries were contracted out to fight in the Persian army as well as to build major public works, such as irrigation canals, bridges, and more (Farazmand, 1991).

Donahue (1989, p. 32) states, "that the privatization movement is not solely a response to contemporary fiscal panic because business writer Peter Drucker (1978) was using the term as far back as 1968 and a Rand Corporation analyst discussed, in detail, the private delivery of public services in a 1972 study." Donahue emphasizes that large fractions of federal, state, and local budgets have always gone to purchase goods and services from suppliers outside government. Donahue (1989) ascribes this to the durable American taste for free enterprise, which, he contends, has always had a bias for the private alternative. Additionally, Donahue cites the former Bureau of the Budget's issuance of an edict in 1955 discouraging federal agencies from producing for themselves any "product or service [that] can be procured from private enterprise through ordinary business channels" (BOB, 1955, p. 6). He documents that this policy was reiterated regularly and underscored at regular intervals. This impetus encouraged the successor agency, the Office of Management and Budget, to issue Circular A-76 in the late 1960s. "Circular A-76—which would become familiar as the institutional label for federal-level privatization—was revised and amended but essentially reaffirmed by both Democrat and Republican administrations" (OMB 1983, p. 21).

The recent momentum for privatization and contracting out, according to Donahue, began in the early 1980s with the big push by the Conservative Right under President Ronald Reagan and the British Prime Minister Margaret Thatcher. The administrations of both leaders, as a matter of policy, pressed for the selling of government assets, privatizing community governmental functions, reducing the government's sphere of activities in the economy and society, deregulating the market, and intensifying the role of private corporate sector organizations in society, economy, and governance (Farazmand, 2001). Their common rationale emphasized free competition within a market system. Small government and minimal taxes were preferred. An important assumption was that the welfare state imposes substantial taxes and regulation on free market mechanisms so as to distort the free flow of capital. Thus the welfare state (big government) is necessarily confronted with economic stagflation under which economic depression and inflation simultaneously occur. They argue for "small but strong" government.

Public choice theorists have added further impetus to privatization. They argue that decision making in government does not follow principles of economic rationality; rather, most decisions are made as a function of political bargaining. In the process, many interest groups, politicians, business groups, and so on are involved. And public policies produced by that process are implemented by big government. Public choice theorists, therefore, consider government bureaucrats as maximizers of self-interest, just like business groups. Just as business groups pursue profit maximization, government bureaucrats, according to public choice theorists, pursue "budget maximization." As a result, interest groups, politicians, business groups, and government bureaucrats establish a "budget-spending coalition." Public services provided by the budget-spending coalition cannot but be inefficient, they argue.

Moe (1987) believes that once historians and scholars begin to study government in the 1980s, they are likely to argue that "privatization" was the most influential concept of the decade. Additionally, he contends that the consensus of the historians' studies will illustrate the fact that public administration as a field was profoundly altered by more than a few ideas that together have become known as privatization.

"But privatization, as today's fiscally ambitious, ideologically charged phenomenon, began as a British import" (Donahue, 1989, p. 22). As the British shed major assets and responsibilities throughout the 1980s (Pirie, 1985), conservative intellectuals in the United States set out to emulate the British example (Donahue, 1989). According to Donahue, E. S. Savas (1977), while serving as a Reagan appointee in the Department of Housing and Urban Development, published an influential book entitled *Privatizing the Public Sector.* Implicit in Donahue's comment (about Savas's authorship of the volume while in office) is that the book served as an impetus for the beginning of the privatization movement. Additionally, Donahue points out that the Privatization Task Force of the Private Sector Survey on Cost Control (or the Grace Commission as it was known) sounded a clarion call for cutting the federal payroll by half a million jobs, or roughly one-sixth, through contracting out governmental functions. With the stage set for privatization, privatization proposals and briefing papers by conservative and well-connected Heritage Foundation personnel began to flow, and culminated in 1985 in a publication entitled *Privatizing Federal Spending: A Strategy to Eliminate the Deficit,* by Heritage director Stuart M. Butler.

According to Morris (1997), more conventional government functions are increasingly being turned over to the private sector. In addition, he contends this issue has taken on added salience since the Republican sweep of the 1994 midterm Congressional elections, due to traditional conservative support for privatization as a means to reduce the size and scope of government activity.

Hanke (1987) declares that some objectives of privatization are: (1) the improvement of the economic performance of the assets or service functions concerned; (2) the depoliticization of economic decisions; (3) the generation of public budget revenues through sales receipts; (4) the reduction of public outlays, taxes, and borrowing requirements; (5) the reduction in the power of the public sector; and (6) the promotion of popular capitalism through the wider ownership of assets.

Since the 1970s, interest in the privatization of public services in occidental countries has developed and increased significantly. During the 1980s, interest again spiked when conservative social policy and the political climate proved propitious for the reduction of government functions. The financing and management of social programs became a major issue during the Reagan era, as influenced by the Thatcher administration.

Auger (1999) writes that privatization has gained prominence in state government in the 1990s. She also asserts that the new programs were a byproduct, or corollary, of unparalleled devolution of public programs and responsibilities from Washington; they were spurred by unrelenting pressures for smaller, less bureaucratic government from the grass roots, inducing states to be more amenable to the concept of privatization and the tools through which privatization could be brought to fruition. In addition, Auger (1999) avers that the earliest years of the decade found state administrators buffeted by ideologically driven debates that promulgated privatization as (1) the universal remedy for all governmental ills, and (2) as anathema to sound government. At the end of the decade Auger (1999) found state privatization discussions had shifted onto a decidedly more pragmatic plane free of the dogmatism of the 1980s.

## II. DEFINITIONS OF PRIVATIZATION

According to Barnekov and Raffel (1992): "Part of the problem of any discussion of privatization is that the meaning of the term is confusing because it has been used to refer to several types of policy initiatives."

The concept of privatization derives from the word private, which has roots in the Latin term "privatus," meaning separate from the state, deprived of office, of or belonging to oneself. "Privatization is defined as the policy or process of making private as opposed to public; the act or process of regarding as personal or separate; the concept of an institution activity, discipline, etc., seen in terms of its relation to the individual rather than to society generally or to a part of society; to alter the status of (as a business or industry) from public to private control or ownership" (Oxford Dictionary, p. 802). Higgins asserts that privatization has both a mechanical and figurative interpretation. Mechanically, he asserts, privatization should be viewed as a word used to explain an implementation process, which can be viewed as any effort to reconstruct the role of the state in producing, financing, or regulating the supply of a good service. Higgins (1986, 1987) contends that privatization is also a word invented by politicians and circulated by political journalists intended to clarify analysis but as a "symbol intended by advocates and opponents of the process it describes to dramatize a conflict and mobilize support for their own side."

Hanke (1987) contends that privatization has come to mean the transfer of assets or service functions from public to private ownership. In addition, the term privatization has taken root and, as defined in the marketplace (Bowman et al., 1992), it is loosely used to refer to reduced government involvement in the commercial sector. According to Lipman, privatization as a concept has five characteristics: sale of government-owned assets; abolition or relaxation of monopolies held by nationalized industries; the build-operate-transfer agreement under which a private company agrees to build a major project and to operate it for an agreed-upon length of time; financing by customer fees—"pay for use"—rather than by taxes; and the contracting out of public services to the private sector (Lipman, 1989).

Privatization is described by De Aless (1987) in the context of transferring government functions to the private sector. He contends that the term privatization is typically used to illustrate the transfer of activities from the public to the private sector. This also includes contracting out as well as reducing or terminating the provisions of some goods and services by government. More pointedly, privatization is a move towards private property and away from not only government and common ownership, but also from government regulations that constrain individual rights to the use of resources (Hanke, 1987).

Auger (1999) proposes that privatization is best understood from a diverse perspective consisting of an array of methods designed to encourage more involvement on the part of the private sector in the organization or financing of traditional governmental services. She finds that in the late 1980s and early 1990s use of the term privatization in state dialogues was accepted to mean service shedding or termination of governmental functions. This belief sparked vigorous rejection in some states of any discussion of privatization because it was interpreted to mean an attenuation of governmental responsibilities for dealing with public concerns. As used today in state discussions, however, "privatization has far more to do with the relocation of service implementation activities from public to private for-profit or nonprofit venues than with the elimination of governmental functions" (Auger, 1999; p. 457).

Farazmand (2001) views the term "privatization" as a value-laden concept, which is grounded in the political Right and its orientation toward smaller government. The political Right's catechisms about privatization are often popular black and white assumptions. At one end of the continuum, privatization can be viewed as the sale of state-owned assets and public enterprises. It may also be looked upon as deregulation, the application of user fees, contracting out public services to private sector providers, marketization, corporatization, and myriad reforms intended to introduce market forces into the public sector (Henig et al., 1988; Starr, 1989; Suleiman and Waterbury, 1990; Farazmand, 1996a, 1996b).

A shift from publicly to privately produced goods and services constitutes Starr's (1987) concept of privatization and he concludes that the conservative proponents of privatization perceive a zero-sum tradeoff between government and the economy. The bigger the public sector, the smaller is the private economy; the more public spending, the less private savings and investment. Based on this perspective, Starr believes privatization is certain to increase savings, investment, productivity, and growth. On the other hand, Berg and Berg (1997, p. 357) contend that "privatization in the broadest sense means giving private actors a greater role in decisions about what, where, and how to produce goods and services." In addition, Prager (1997, p. 613) holds that "Privatization in its broadest sense entails a simultaneous retrenchment of the government sector and expansion of the private sector."

Moe (1987) asserts that different advocates and adversaries of privatization define it in different ways, but the "movement" itself is held together by a shared ethos that the public sector is too large and that many functions presently performed by government might be better assigned to private sector units, directly or indirectly, or left to the play of the marketplace. Moreover, Moe contends that implicit in the discourse of the privatization movement is a view shared by other scholars that the public and private sectors are alike, both subject to the same set of economic incentives and disincentives. He also asserts that some advocates of privatization go too far by contending that nearly all public sector activities are potentially amenable to being transferred to the private sector.

## III. FORMS OF PRIVATIZATION

Gormley (1991) believes that there are four strategic forms of privatization: contracting out, vouchers, sale of assets, and load shedding. In the United States, the primary type of privatization is contracting out, and it is spread across all levels of government. Similarly, according to Savas (1977) there are four representative forms of privatization: contracting out, vouchers, franchising, and sales. We follow Gormleys' typology below. Gormley (1991) also argues that many governments have decided to transfer or relocate responsibility for a range of public services to the private sector. Additionally, he asserts, many governments have opted for privatization in an effort to reduce burdens on the public purse, maximize consumer choice, and promote other goals. In the 1990s in the United States, most local governments accepted privatization to some degree, while the federal and state governments were more reluctant to pursue privatization.

> To adherents, privatization invokes visions of a beleaguered government bureaucracy ceding responsibility for vital public services to unreliable private entrepreneurs. To other observers, privatization inspires neither rapture nor alarm, but rather cautious interest. At its best, privatization can reduce the costs of government and introduce new possibilities for better service delivery. At its worst, privatization can raise costs and has the potential to undermine other important values, such as equity, quality, and accountability (Gormley, 1991).

## A.  Contracting Out

When the government decides to contract out a public service as a form of privatization, it does not abdicate its financial support responsibility, but rather employs a private company to provide the service. In other words, the government creates a principal and agent relationship when it contracts out a public service to a private entity. The primary motivation for many governments to contract out is to reduce government costs by using more economically efficient private vendors. Contracting out also allows public agencies to take advantage of the efficiency and specialized skills believed to be offered by the private sector, capacities that may be unavailable within government. In addition, the private sector is typically believed to be more efficient than government in performing commercial activities because private firms are driven by a profit motive or by a desire to maximize shareholders' wealth. Private organizations, therefore, have a powerful incentive to seek innovative approaches to reducing costs; presumably no comparable incentive exists for the public sector (Moore and Butler, 1987).

Butler has acknowledged that privatization may not break up the "public spending coalitions, but the effect would actually be to enlarge them." Butler (1987, p. 14) contends that "contracting out expands the set of claimants on the public treasury." In a similar vein, Peterson (1996, p. 20) posits the following.

> Consider, for example, the contracting out of "public" services. When a privately owned firm, which previously served only the private sector, receives a government contract, its relationship with the government necessarily changes. This is especially true if the firm receives a franchise—a monopoly privilege. Government funding brings government control, and the government contractor may soon find himself responding to political pressures, rather than market incentives.

According to Linowes (1988) contracting out occurs when government enters into contracts with private firms to provide goods and services used by the government or demanded by the public. In addition, Linowes asserts that contracting out logically leads to cost savings because the process is opened to competition among vendors, and therefore contracting out has grown very popular at the state and local levels.

Utt (1991, p. 80) contends that:

> Contracting-out is the process whereby government hires, under contract, a private firm to perform, over a defined period of time, some specific service that might otherwise be provided by public employees using government equipment and facilities. Contracting-out is most appropriate for those governmental functions whose value can only be defined in terms of a franchise to perform a certain function such as accounting, rubbish removal, building security, vehicle maintenance, and so on.

Worsnop (1992) holds that privatization in the United States has no particular pattern that it follows, although the most common form is contracting out. In this capacity, "the government contracts with a private sector organization to provide a specific service, such as processing Medicaid claims or janitorial services, instead of providing the service itself " (Worsnop 1992, p. 980).

Overall, then, under contracting out the government can delegate to a company its authority to produce and deliver a public service. It can accomplish that transfer via a competitive bid during a limited period. Through contracting out, the assumption is that government can provide better services at lower cost because of competitive bids between private companies. Some state governments are using a contracting out strategy in order to stimulate public employees who might well see their jobs privatized if the performance of their organizations is not satisfactory.

When a government contracts out a service to a company, it should pay detailed attention to whether the company can sustain an acceptable quality of service after it is contracted out. And government should check if the company persistently maintains its responsibility to citizens. Government should treat private companies that are participating in a competitive bidding process in an equitable manner.

Possible services to be contracted out are vehicle maintenance, public hospital services, garbage collection, security services, and management of public facilities such as libraries, cafeterias, and other professional services. According to Savas (2000), the average American city contracts out 23 percent of its 64 common municipal services to the private sector. The average American state contracts out 14 percent of its activities.

## B. Vouchers

A voucher allows a citizen who needs a specific service to choose a service that meets his or her needs. Cordes et al. (2001) contend that vouchers represent a powerful tool that the government employs to finance the provision, for example, of social services. The authors describe how in the 1990s the federal government began to heavily promote the use of vouchers in publicly subsidized child care via the 1990 Child Care Development Block Grant (CCDBG). With the implementation of the Child Care Block Grant, according to the authors, the use of vouchers in certain forms of childcare became a standard financing mechanism. Also, they posit that voucher programs are predicated on the interplay of two important factors: choice for consumers and competition among producers (Steuerle 1998).

Gibelman and Lens (2002, p. 209) are of the opinion that "Vouchers are a method of subsidizing a person's needs (for example, housing, day care, health care, food tuition) on the open market." Typically, according to Gibelman and Lens (2002), people who qualify (usually based on financial eligibility) are given a voucher, which may be in the form of a redeemable coupon or stamp and worth a certain amount of money that must be spent on a specified service or product (Barker 1999). Also, the authors posit that although the voucher is financed through public monies, the consumer retains ultimate control over how much money is spent for its target purpose (Gibelman and Lens, 2002).

Utt (1991, p. 77) suggests, "vouchers represent the earmarked equivalent of a cash payment from the government to some qualified beneficiary for the acquisition of some specific product or service from private sector providers". In addition, the author suggests that vouchers are the primary means by which the Federal government provides basic social services to the poor or to other groups deemed worthy of assistance. Similarly, McDermott (2000, p. 13) contends that "a voucher plan is any program through which a set amount of public funds is made available to a family to spend at the public or private [educational] institution of its choice."

Possible services to be provided via vouchers are food, housing, education, health care, transportation, and social services.

## C.  Franchising

Through a franchise, a government can award a company a specific authority under which the company can produce a service for a limited period, and for which the company pays the government a fee. Franchising has been described by Hirsh (1989, p. 536) "as government conferring on a private entity the right to produce and sell the final product at a market-determined price, possibly at a regulated and/or subsidized price". In addition, according to Linowes (1988, p. 2), "Franchising is commonly used for services such as water, electricity, gas, telephone, and cable television." However, Pasour (1996) portrays franchising as an award of monopoly privilege to a private firm to provide a particular service, usually with price regulation by an agency of government. In addition, Pasour (1996, p. 8) asserts, "Whereas the government pays the producer for services contracted out, the consumer pays the producer for franchise services."

Benton and Menzel (1992, 437) define franchising as follows.

> Franchising refers to a situation in which local government gives a private firm the exclusive right to provide a service within a certain geographical area. It implies, therefore, that local government removes itself completely from service delivery while continuing to guarantee that (1) the service is available, (2) minimum performance standards are met, and (3) rates/prices are set at a reasonable level.

Through franchising, government can take advantage of private capital and provide better services for citizens with no great financial pressure to build expensive infrastructures. For example, a company might build a public parking lot on public land, manage the operation of the structure, and provide an income stream to the governmental entity.

**Table 1**   Institutional Arrangements for Providing Public Services

| Service arrangement | Arranger | Producer | Who pays? |
|---|---|---|---|
| Government service | Government | Government | Government |
| Government vending | Consumer | Government | Consumer |
| Intergovernmental agreements | Government (1) | Government (2) | Government (1) |
| Contracts | Government | Private sector | Government |
| Franchises (exclusive) | Government | Private sector | Consumer |
| Franchise (multiple) | Government and consumer | Private sector | Government and consumer |
| Grants | Government and consumer | Private sector | Government and consumer |
| Vouchers | Consumer | Private sector | Government and consumer |
| Free market | Consumer | Private sector | Consumer |
| Voluntary service | Voluntary association | Voluntary association | N.A. |
| Voluntary service with contract | Voluntary association | Private sector | Voluntary association |
| Self-service | Consumer | Consumer | N.A. |

## D. Sale of Assets

According to Berg and Berg (1997, p. 360), "the classic type of privatization is the sale of full or partial ownership of a state enterprise by public offering on stock exchanges, by competitive bidding for shares or assets or by noncompetitive placement of shares." If the state engages in this method, the state sells to the general public, through the stock market and other financial institutions, all or a substantial part of the stock it holds in a going concern (Berg and Berg, 1997).

Worsnop (1992, p. 980) argues that the public sector very seldom sells public assets to private interests in the United States, "at least not at the federal level." The reason for this position is supposedly obvious: "In contrast to many other nations, the United States has no tradition of government ownership of the commanding heights of the economy—railroads, airlines, telecommunications, mining, the steel industry and so on." Moreover, Worsnop (1992, p. 981) argues that "sale of public assets to private purchasers opens up additional opportunities for government economies, privatizers say."

Table 1 summarizes the four privatization arrangements described above as well as others (Savas, 2000).

## IV. EFFECTS OF PRIVATIZATION

Farazmand (2001) holds that no variable other than privatization has been more important in terms of economic forces. The author attempts to support this assertion by contending that the proponents of privatization have argued that demand and supply via capitalist economic systems have improved resource distribution to the benefit of consumers who can obtain more money to pay for public goods and services; the welfare state once considered imperative for the system no longer has a role in the system.

The case for privatization also includes other benefits besides improved efficiency, budget savings, and increased economic growth. The operative word is choice. Advocates of privatization purport that it will broaden the range of choice for individuals while serving the same crucial functions as do traditional programs. Additionally, proponents of privatization maintain that greater choice would serve the interests of equity. According to the privatizers, greater freedom of choice would generally lead to a more just distribution of benefits.

Advocates of all these forms of privatization assert that they are efficient and cost effective. They claim that the private sector, for example, can finance, construct, service, and operate most types of correctional facilities more efficiently than can government. These claims are buttressed by a number of independent studies which conclude that private companies can finance new facilities without the need for voter-approved bond issues, and can construct them more quickly and cheaply than government (Chaiken and Mennemeyer, 1987). Other studies have found that private contractors, freed from unwieldy public personnel policies and unionized work forces, are able to run correctional institutions and related programs more efficiently and cheaply than their competitors, the public operators.

The raison d'être most generally provided for the superior performance of the private sector is twofold. "Government lacks management flexibility because of union constraints on decisions, which would reduce the number of workers, better using existing capital. . . . A second reason is the absence of competition. As a monopoly, the government has no incentive to increase productivity even if labor unions would allow this type of flexibility" (Savas, 1977, p. 51). "Evidence does suggest, however, that when an agency must compete with a contractor, it can be made more productive and even match the contractor's performance" (Savas, 1977, p. 49).

Another claim centers around the view that privatization is part of the formal political agenda as a function of problems encountered by governments at every level. Bulging budget deficits and the seeming cost savings of privatization are leading to greater use of this implementation tool. Proponents of privatization or public choice supporters claim that government participation has become too widespread and that governments have certain characteristics which make successful correction of market failure extremely difficult, if not unlikely. "Whatever the cause that government fails to advance, the social good is clear. Public choice theory, although not as fully developed as those which analyze market behavior, does offer some explanations concerning failures, which are utilized in the privatization literature" (Maupin, 1990, p. 210).

Bailey (1987) states that despite the confusion of what exactly is meant by the term privatization, there is a clear unifying thread in all its conceptualizations: maximization of efficiency. The supposition among promoters of privatization is that, intrinsically, private managers can deliver at lower costs services similar or superior to those of public managers. Moreover, Bailey contends that privatization adds another policy apparatus to the tools of the public manager and policy maker. However, Bailey (1987, p. 30) asserts, "Although privatization may provide a good tool for the public manager and add an interesting dimension to the political discourse, the concept, even after eventual clarification, will not offer as much as its advocates claim."

Farazmand (2001) points out that the debate over the role of government in society has been central for over three millennia. Farazmand (2001, p. 25) also posits that "conservative political economy and public choice theorists have argued in favor of small government, little or no government intervention in the economy, and free market enterprise that would operate without government constraints and regula-tions, except for protecting the market organizations from unwanted competitors (an irony) and from possible collapse (an irony)."

But Auger (1999) points out that privatization's constituency continues to broaden, transcending both party boundaries and jurisdictional terrain and can no longer be viewed as only a conservative argument. She argues that privatization efforts are today being vigorously pursued, even led, by Democratic as well as Republican governors and legislators and are represented in the work of state agencies from Maine to Texas and from Maryland to California.

Starr (1987, p. 45) puts forth a hardheaded view:

> [A] pragmatic public policy must recognize when private alternatives might work better and by the same token where new forms of public provision may ameliorate the endemic shortcomings of the market. Most of all it must recognize that the markets are not natural creations. They are always legally and politically structured. Hence, the choice is not public or private, but which of many public-private structures works best. And "best" cannot mean only most efficient, for a reasonable appraisal of alternatives needs to weigh concerns of justice, security and citizenship.

Privatization, when defined as the custom of contracting with private sector firms and individuals for the stipulation of products or services customarily supplied by the public sector, does tender some advantages for government. For example, a review of historical and contemporary private sector involvement in corrections reveals several key factors that are pertinent to any discussion of privatization in general: (1) historically, private sector involvement has produced both significant advances in corrections, as well as flagrant abuses; (2) traditionally, government has been and currently continues to be resistant to privatization of institutional corrections while accepting private sector provision of specialized and community-based correctional facilities and services; (3) contemporary approaches to privatization have contributed to polarization and mistrust; (4) performance of the pioneer companies has been less dramatic than promised, but privatization is gradually gaining broader acceptance; and (5) research has demonstrated that the private sector can improve institutional corrections (Cox and Osterhoff, 1993, p. 47). Wolfe (1990, p. 18) also sees an additional dimension: The differential effect of privatization on capital and labor is evident. Although privatization expands profit opportunities as well as profits, it also replaces (often ineffective) political control of public sector unions with control by the market.

Berg and Berg (1997) see privatization as a fiscal tool. They view the main objectives, explicit or implicit in most privatization programs, are fiscal relief by cutting government subsidies to money-losing SOEs and/or by generating new revenues from their sale; increased enterprise efficiency; increased efficiency of the entire economy through more competitive markets and better allocation of resources across firms and sectors; increased political support and broadened institutional underpinnings for a market-based economy or further liberalization; stronger financial markets; increased investment; and the stimulation of entrepreneurship.

For Worsnop (1992, p. 982), however, the chief argument or benefit of privatization, "is that it introduces competition into the supply of basic services, benefits all parties—government, the private sector and taxpayers."

## V. WEAKNESSES OF PRIVATIZATION

Walker (1984, p. 10) reminds us that the existence of public services is a function of the inability or unwillingness of the private sector to engage in particular activities (i.e., market failures) thought necessary by the collective. "Privatization of these services cannot be assumed to result in greater efficiencies unless, of course, the federal government engages in subsidization and regulation."

Authors such as Geis (1987) and Thayer (1987) extend the examination of the market place to a quasi-empirical analysis of privatization in specific policy areas. Geis (1987, p. 45) raises the possibility that "in the interests of maximizing profit, private corporations charged with operation of prisons will maximize inmate populations through changes in public policy, such as increasing mandatory sentencing." This concern is echoed by others (Palumbo, 1986; Palumbo and Maupin, 1989; Robbins, 1986; Starr, 1987).

Shenk (1995, p.16) states that "privatizers tempt us with the promise of a mature marketplace with competition, high quality, and low costs; but the reality is that the government often must buy things no one else wants and its markets are more like used-car lots than computer superstores: few choices, questionable quality—with a hustler for a salesman."

Morris and Morris (1997) state that the review of literature points to four main issues in the privatizations (of prisons):

Privatization is often carried out as a means to provide a public service at a lower cost, thus savings public revenues;

The agent (the private company or public authority) must remain accountable to the principal (the state);

An issue of importance is a philosophical question of whether the state can (or should) abdicate its power of coercion to a nonstate entity; and

Privatization may result in a loss of capacity on the part of the state to deliver an important service.

Their final point coincides with other critics of privatization who assert that, by privatizing public services, the government risks not being able to respond to public needs, especially when only two private agencies control most of the market (AFSCME, 2000). What happens if they go bankrupt? This could spell serious consequences for the government inasmuch as there is a high likelihood that government would not be able to take over critical services in a short period of time.

As it concerns legal questions, Bozeman (1988) poses a vital question before privatization is pursued: at what point will a balance be maintained between corporate economic concerns and accountability for the critical services rendered, and for the maintenance of human rights of the clientele on the other hand? Shichor (1993) states that several scholars of privatization have raised this concern, concluding that "...the public and private sectors have distinctive characters and that these distinctions are premised on legal principles, not economic or social science theories...the public sector is being profoundly altered, and ultimately harmed by the deliberate blurring of these public and private characteristics" (Moe, 1988, p. 674).

One of the major problems perceived with the diminishing public and private distinction in the privatization literature is that the government delegates some of its powers and functions to a party whose legitimacy is not always clear (Moe, 1988). Shichor (1993) asks the following. What are the legal guarantees to the government if a corporation is bought out or sold out by its parent company? What happens if a corporation is taken over by a foreign company, a situation that occurs quite frequently? Is it acceptable that a foreign corporation will handle American prisoners or welfare clients or the mentally ill and make a profit?

Furthermore, Shichor asks what would happen if a private prison corporation, for example, declares bankruptcy. What would be the legal obligations of the government vis-à-vis the creditors of the prison corporation (American Bar Association, 1986)? How would it affect the legal and other obligations of the private corporations themselves toward the government, and how would it affect the government agency? How will a formerly private prison continue to operate? Scholars contend that legal and constitutional issues must be resolved before considering such critical areas as prison privatization. In addition, a method of cost analysis must be developed to reduce the difficulty of comparing private and public delivery of services such as prisons in order to determine, objectively, which relationship is superior. Shichor states that Robbins (1986, 1989), schooled in the legal aspects of correctional privatization, demonstrates that privatization will not ease government liability for the handling of prisoners. He points out that under 42 U.S.C.Sec.1983, the government will be liable for any civil rights violations against inmates in private prisons (Thomas and Hanson, 1989; Pelliccotti, 1987).

Critics of prison privatization argue that since the incarceration of individuals is so deeply associated with the fundamental function of government, government should not abdicate this responsibility by turning over the administration of incarceration to a private entity. Advocates of privatization argue, however, that a distinction must be made between the choice to punish and the administration of punishment. Under this line of reasoning, scholars assume it is perfectly acceptable to recognize, as the government's responsibility, the decision to punish an individual and equally acceptable to allow a private entity under governmental supervision to administer the punishment, that is, operate the prison, implying social contract theory (Hansen, 1997). In other words, Hanke (1987) asks if the profit motive has an appropriate function in the incarceration of citizens. He continues this line of questioning by asking if it will lead to disciplinary policies within the prison institution that will serve to maintain full capacity.

Moreover, public policy governs both the allocation of resources and the way in which state authority is employed. Kolderie (1986) contends that gradual increases in the proportion of public goods and services delivered by private contractors slowly privatize public policy. As private contractors play a larger role in the delivery of public goods and services, Gilbert (2001) holds that their influence within the public policy arena increases, and the influence of governmental agencies decreases. Gilbert believes that the opportunity for private sector abuse of public interests increases dramatically when both the production and the policy are controlled by the private sector.

The introduction of privatization into the criminal justice system, or what Stolz (2001) calls the subsystem, may signal the possibility of change in that subgovernment, she contends. One would anticipate contributions by private corporations, not only in the contracting process, but also at other decision points in the criminal justice policy-making process in order to have an effect on a multiplicity of legislative and administrative policy choices pertinent to privatization (Gilbert, 1996b). Changes in those involved in criminal justice and participation in the criminal justice subgovernment are of great consequence not only because of those participating in changes, but because such changes have further ramifications for subgovernment politics according to Stolz. Additionally, Stolz (2001) considers the fact that when participants change in the subsystem, this may affect the goals and stakes sought, techniques used, decision points, and overall subgovernment dynamics.

The participants within each component of a criminal justice subgovernment are believed to have vested interests, and, according to Stolz, they seek to achieve particular goals. Those goals are: "material," "solidary," or "purposive," as well as wide-ranging and narrow. She also contends that the involvement of private corporations introduces profit, through contracts, as a stake and goal with the criminal justice subgovernment. Because privatization introduces profit, it has the potential to change the reward system of the criminal justice subgovernment, the author asserts. Privatization provides more opportunities for material rewards (Stolz, 2001). For instance, the author juxtaposes the relationship between participants in a traditional criminal justice subgovernment and a private agency administering criminal justice, and concludes that corporations may be better able to meet the campaign finance goals of the elected officials, implying that this has implications for policy making. That is, private for-profit organizations have greater opportunities to meet the material goals of elected officials directly through campaign contributions (Stolz, 2001), which again suggests implications for policy making.

With the advent of privatization initiatives, access and decision points in the policy-making process change, Stolz asserts. Decisions regarding whether to privatize criminal justice have involved legislative decisions for the most part. If the decision is made to privatize, questions arise as to what should be privatized, how, and under what conditions (Gilbert, 1996a). In prison privatization, that usually includes whether administrative functions only should be privatized, certain services, or complete privatization. Again, Stolz (2001) revisits the implications for policy making by those parties in the subgovernment of privatization when she contends that

**Table 2**  Public Strategies for Private Prisons

| Reasons to privatize | Reasons not to privatize |
| --- | --- |
| 1. Private operators can provide construction-financing options that allow the government client to pay only for capacity as needed in lieu of encumbering long-term debt. | 1. There are certain responsibilities that only the government should meet, such as public safety and environmental protection. To provide incarceration, the government has legal, political, and moral obligations. Major constitutional competition between both public and private issues revolves around the deprivation of liberty, discipline, and preserving the constitutional rights of inmates. Related issues include use of force, loss of time credit, and segregation. |
| 2. Private companies offer modern state-of-the-art correctional facility designs that are efficient to operate and built based upon value engineering specifications. | |
| 3. Private operators typically design and construct a new correctional facility in half the time of a comparable government construction project. | |
| 4. Private vendors provide government clients with the convenience and accountability of one entity for all compliance issues. | 2. Few private companies are available from which to choose. |
| 5. Private corrections management companies are able to mobilize rapidly and to specialize in unique facility missions. | 3. Private operators may be inexperienced with key correctional issues. |
| 6. Private corrections management companies provide economic development opportunities by hiring locally and, to the extent possible, purchasing locally. | 4. Operator may become a monopoly through political ingratiation, favoritism, etc. |
| 7. Government can reduce or share its liability exposure by contracting with private corrections companies. | 5. Government may lose the capability to perform the function over time. |
| 8. The government can retain flexibility by limiting the contract duration and by specifying facility mission. | 6. The profit motive will inhibit the proper performance of duties. Private prisons have financial incentives to cut corners. |
| 9. Adding other service providers injects competition between both public and private organizations. | 7. Procurement process is slow, inefficient, and open to risks. |
| | 8. Creating a good clear contract is a daunting task. |
| | 9. Lack of enforcement remedies in contracts leaves only termination or lawsuits as recourse. |

*Source*: Cunningham 1999.

participants in the subgovernment can be expected to seek access to the decision points where these decisions are made in order to influence policies.

Cunningham (1999) has put forth a summary that presents the chief reasons either to accept or reject the privatization concept (Table 2). These motives to accept or reject privatization can be ascribed to the prime desire of many states and local governments to rapidly increase desperately needed prison bed capacity and to reduce prison operational costs. Others have raised the issue of whether private prisons can improve the quality of care for inmates (including enhanced protection from harm for inmates and staff) and reduce litigation (Austin and Coventry, 2001). Levinson (1985) contends that advocates for more private sector involvement in functions traditionally performed by public agencies support their position with three types of arguments: philosophical, economic, and issues regarding efficiency. Proponents for less private involvement in the public sector bolster their view with an additional set of arguments—ethical issues. Levinson provides a summary of reasons to support or not support private prisons, for example, in Table 3.

Arguments against privatization center on the assumption that the supposed benefits are short-lived or nonexistent, according to Worsnop (1992). Worsnop (1992, p. 981) also contends that private agencies are notorious for lowballing, which he defines as "submitting an artificially low bid." The purpose of this tactic according to Worsnop (1992, p. 981) is to acquire the contract or job and then "extract higher prices from the government once the opportunity to switch contractors has passed."

## VI. CRITERIA FOR PRIVATIZATION

Nelson (1980) suggests guidelines for when to contract services.
Supplier considerations:

> Existing or easily established suppliers,
> Ability to substitute suppliers (one supplier is as good and acceptable as another), and
> Ability to post performance bonds, if necessary.

Service Considerations:

> Services with routine procedures requiring limited, independent decision making,
> Services better tendered outside large institutions,
> New service populations,
> Controversial services or services confronting highly sensitive value issues,
> Service where the size of the user population is unknown or fluctuates greatly, and
> Services where funding is variable (especially if funding is outside the control of the government unit) or where continuous funding is questionable.

Government considerations:

> Difficulty acquiring capital,
> Contract administration units are available or easily established, and
> When government specifically knows what services it wants and how to measure them.

**Table 3**  Privatization—Positives and Negatives

| Philosophical issues | |
|---|---|
| Positives | Negatives |
| 1. Provides a standard against which to compare the public sector.<br>2. Helps break up public sector monopolies, which unfairly compete in areas where private enterprise can perform.<br>3. Helps reduce "too much government." | 1. Overly simplistic notion that private sector can do all tasks better and more cheaply; abdication of responsibility since public sector still ultimately accountable.<br>2. Private sector's first loyalty is to firm (profits, shareholders) and not to public good.<br>3. Creates "phantom government" doing parallel work but without public control over decisions and loss of focus on mission of public agencies in the interest of expediency; undermines citizenry's confidence in government by projecting image of public sector being unable to fulfill its basic duties and responsibilities. |
| Economic issues | |
| 1. Helps trim budgets by holding the line on taxes.<br>2. Saves jobs and creates new ones.<br>3. Aids a private sector faced with depressed markets.<br>4. Through lobbying can obtain resources denied public sector. | 1. More costly due to need to show profit, pay taxes; additional "hidden costs": to prepare, administer, monitor contract; inspect use of public sector facilities and equipment; and to train displaced public sector employees.<br>2. Jobs are eliminated to reduce costs; less regard for working conditions and paying a living wage.<br>3. Tendency to reduce/eliminate unprofitable services even though may still be needed; possibility of contractor's bankruptcy, which would require rapid, costly interim arrangements.<br>4. Funds shifted from less influential areas, but for which there may still be a need for resources. |
| Efficiency issues | |
| 1. Has stronger motivation to do well.<br>2. Provides better services.<br>3. Improves the delivery of services.<br>4. Leads to better management by introducing sophisticated costcutting practices.<br>5. Provides short-term solutions.<br>6. Serves as an information transfer source.<br>7. Permits rapid initiation of new approaches without large capital outlays.<br>8. Cheaper. | 1. May attempt to restrict services to only the "better" clients; reluctance to objectively evaluate program effectiveness or to identify problem areas.<br>2. Used to mask inadequacies of public officials who cannot manage; loss of control over qualifications of personnel hired by contractor.<br>3. Possibility of subcontracting by original awardee to less qualified firm.<br>4. Rather than promised better management, savings produced by hiring inexperienced, less well-trained individuals at lower wages and benefits, and/or ignoring contract requirements such as providing supervision. |

**Table 3** Continued

| Positives | Negatives |
|---|---|
| | Efficiency issues |
| 9. Provides expertise not available in, and too costly to recruit by, public sector. | 5. Possible short-term advantages do not outweigh long-term disadvantages. |
| 10. Frees time of public administrator for planning. | 6. Need for public sector supervisors to train contractor's employees, thereby taking them away from their own duties. |
| | 7. High staff turnover rates reduce efficiency/productivity; poor coordination with other public agencies; reduction in public sector employee morale/ productivity due to anxiety over job security. |
| | 8. Cost overruns; any modification in original contract results in additional charges; "lowballing": making very low initial bid then subsequently increasing price after agency comes to rely on, and cannot back out of, contract; lack of cost-accounting system along with contractor's reluctance to provide necessary documentation precludes making accurate cost comparisons. |
| | 9. Necessary to maintain public sector inhouse backup capability in case contractor fails to reach agreed-upon objectives. |
| | 10. Extremely difficult to write contract specifications covering every contingency; contractor has clear right to refuse to do anything not in original contract, thereby lessening government's flexibility to respond in unanticipated situations. |
| | Ethical issues |
| 1. We are not crooks! | 1. Fosters political spoils system; contract irregularities: collusion, conflict of interest, "kickbacks," bribery; contractor may lack expertise as originally claimed. |

*Source*: Levinson 1985.

The following criteria for accepting a specific privatization mode are provided by Hirsh (1989, p. 537).

Within our framework, the decision to adopt a specific privatization mode, e.g., contracting out, will depend primarily on expectations regarding its effect on (a) efficiency, (b) quality of output and accountability for it, and (c) distributional effects. The basic argument of our framework is that privatization, for instance, in the form of contracting out as opposed to government production, will have either positive or negative effects on each of the three factors, and summing over these three factors will yield an estimate of the net benefit (or cost) of contracting out. In the abstract, as long as the net benefit is expected to be positive, a government will contract out; conversely, if contracting out is expected to yield a negative net benefit, the service will be produced in the public sector.

Wallin (1997, p. 13) cites Massachusetts Governor Weld's edict about privatization as offering some simple criteria for selecting privatization projects: "(1) the service involved must be one you can define distinctly in an RFP; (2) the privatized function must have measurable performance standards; and (3) there must be more than one vendor able to perform the service, or you lose the benefits of competition." Similarly, Benton and Menzel (1992, p. 438) point out that the decision to privatize is predicated on the factors: "(1) cost reductions, (2) escalation of service demands caused by rapid growth, (3) fiscal pressures and stresses, and (4) political inducements and obstacles."

The core of a privatization strategy is to imbue the public sector with competition and an ethos of innovation. Although the transfer of property rights and government functions from the public sector to the private sector has been a prominent part of efforts to institutionalize competition and innovation in the public sector, the management strategies of public organizations are fundamentally different from those of private organizations. Those two types of organizations have very different organizational goals: pursuit of the public interest versus profit maximization. Considering the weaknesses of privatization, it might be more desirable to identify other strategies for sustaining competition and innovation in the public sector, as well as those privatization options mentioned above.

## VII.  CONCLUSION: PARTNERSHIPS, NOT PRIVATIZATION?

In sum, privatization is marketed as a solution, which will (Holzer and Callahan, 1997):

> Lower costs, while improving quality,
> Allow economics of scale,
> Allow public versus private comparisons of cost and performance,
> Avoid large startup costs,
> Provide access to specialized skills and training,
> Promote flexibility in the size and mix of services,
> Make it possible to hire and fire as necessary,
> Allow for experimentation in different modes of service provision,
> Reduce dependence on a single supplier,
> Bypass inert bureaucracies, and
> Allow quicker response to new service areas.

But skeptics hold that many services are necessarily government's responsibility, and a public to private shift will not automatically enhance productivity in a jurisdiction or department (Barnekov and Raffel, 1992). They and other critics (Stahl, 1988, p. 42; Ogilvy, 1986–1987, p. 15) suggest questions the public manager needs to answer when considering whether to privatize in order to enhance productivity. Before a public service is privatized, then, there are several points to be considered.

> What was the original goal of the service that will be privatized? All public services have targeted goals and recipients. If the services were provided

by the private sector, would those original goals and target populations be maintained?

Should governments really be responsible for the service? Some services might not be appropriate to the private sector.

Is the privatization policy of a government compatible with the societal need and national goals of the city, state, or country? For example, citizens in developing and underdeveloped countries may need more extensive public services from government than those in developed countries.

Specifically, to what extent is privatization likely to:

Interfere with accountability,
Degrade responsiveness,
Reduce services,
Lower employee morale,
Result in incomplete contracts,
Produce cost overruns,
Lower quality at the expense of quantity,
Place short-term profits over long-term planning,
Negate the service ideal inherent in public service,
Provide opportunities for graft and corruption, or
Duplicate services?

A recurring theme in the privatization literature is that what makes a difference is competition between the sectors, not privatization itself, and that private monopolies are no better than public ones (Donahue, 1984). Cost-saving competition will, for instance, encourage innovation by allowing for experimentation in different modes of service provision, bypassing inert bureaucracies, and allowing quicker response to new service areas.

Privatization, however, is only one form of competition. An equally productive alternative is an expanded form of competition in which public organizations are competitive bidders. Some cities, such as Phoenix and Indianapolis have pioneered public–private competition, and in head-to-head competition with private bidders have often won those bids.

In Phoenix, the Department of Public Works established a program that utilizes a nontraditional approach to competing with private industry in order to increase productivity and significantly cut agency costs. Faced with growing budget problems, Phoenix was increasingly awarding municipal contracts to private organizations. In response, the Department of Public Works created Competition with Privatization to enhance the competitive atmosphere in which it operates through increased technology, labor–management cooperation, innovative practices, and community involvement and support. The focus of the program is on solid waste collection, which has an impact on every household and provides citizens a means to evaluate municipal services on a firsthand basis. In 1995, savings and cost-avoidance totaled approximately $3.3 million dollars.

The program has also engendered improved employee morale and labor–management relations, which has resulted in productivity enhancements, innovations (e.g., retread tires), and participation in the competitive bidding process by department employees, as well as cooperation between unions and the City. The City of Phoenix earned back all contracts that were previously lost to private contractors.

Although competition is certainly an important assumption, it is not the only paradigm. The "flip side" of competition—cooperation—is also an essential productivity enhancement strategy, and one that is very often overlooked in the shadow of pressures for privatization. Yet joint public–private initiatives are options to which innovative public officials often turn, and cooperative arrangements for service provision are increasingly evident as the public sector seeks creative ways to stretch resources.

In contrast to privatization, these new relationships are joint problem-solving efforts, or partnerships, which may be initiated by either "side." Frequently recognized are working alliances between the workforce and management; between levels of government and between neighboring local governments; and between government and citizens, government and corporations, government and not-for-profits. These innovations have proven to be effective arrangements aimed at improving government services and cutting costs. Because they represent the ability to think and act outside the rigid but familiar "bureaucratic box," they can be essential for pooling resources and improving productivity in an increasingly resource-scarce atmosphere.

## REFERENCES

American Bar Association. (1986).

AFSCME American Federation of State, County, and Municipal Employees (2000). *The Evidence Is Clear: Crime Shouldn't Pay*. Washington, DC: American Federation of Statem, County, and Municipal Employees.

Auger, D. A. (1999). "Privatization, contracting, and states: Lessons from state government experience." *Public Product. Manage. Rev.* 22(4):435–454.

Austin, J., Coventry, G. (February 2001). *Emerging Issues on Privatized Prisons*. Washington, DC: National Council on Crime and Delinquency, Bureau of Justice Assistance, Office of Justice Programs, U.S. Department of Justice.

Bailey, R. W. (1987). Uses and misuses of Privatizationp. In: Hanke, S. H., ed. *Prospects for Privatization*. New York: Academy of Political Science.

Barker, R. L. (1999). *The Social Work Dictionary*. 4th ed. Washington: DCNASW.

Barnekov, T. K., Raffel, J. (1992). Public management of privatization. In: Holzer, M., ed. *Public Productivity Handbook*. New York: Marcel Dekker, pp. 99–115.

Benton, J. E., Menzel, D. C. (March 1992). Contracting and franchising county services in Florida. *Urban Affairs Quart.* 27(3):436–456.

Berg, A., Berg, E. (Winter 1997). Methods of privatization. *J. Int. Affairs* 50(2):357–390.

BOB. Bureau of the Budget Bulletin. (1955).

Bowman, G. W., Hakim, S. (1992). *Privatizing the United States Justice System: Police, Adjudication, and Corrections Services from the Private Sector*. Jefferson, NC: McFarland.

Bozeman, B. (March/April 1988). Exploring the limits of public and private sectors: Sector boundaries as Maginot Line. *Public Admin. Rev.* 672–674.

Brakel, S. J. (1992). The privatization of jails: A management perspective. In: Bowman, G. W., Hakim, S., eds. *Privatizing the United States Justice System: Police, Adjudication, and Correction Services from the Private Sector*. Jefferson, NC: McFarland.

Butler, S. M. (1985). *Privatizing Federal Spending: A Strategy to Eliminate the Deficit*. New York: Universe.

Butler S. M. (1987). Privatization and the management of public policy. Proceedings of Annual Meetings of the American Political Science Association. Chicago.

Chaiken, J. M., Mennemeyer, T. (1987). *Lease-Purchase Financing of Prison and Jail Construction*. Washington, DC: U.S. Department of Justice, National Institute of Justice, Office of Communication and Research Utilization.

Cordes, J., Henig, J. R., Twombly, E. C. (Winter 2001). Nonprofit human service providers in an era of privatization: Toward a theory of economic and political response. *Policy Stud. Rev.* 18(4):91–110.

Cox, N. R., Osterhoff, W. E. (1993). The public-private partnership: A challenge and an opportunity for corrections. In: Bowman, G. W., Hakim, S., Seidenstat, P., eds. *Privatizing Correctional Institutions*. New Brunswick, NJ: Transaction.

Cunningham, D. (1999). Public strategies for private prisons. Proceedings of Private Prisons Workshop, at the Institute on Criminal Justice: University of Minnesota Law School.

De Aless, L. (1987). Property rights and privatization. Proceedings of Private Prisons Workshop, at the Institute on Criminal Justice: University of Minnesota Law School.

Donahue, J. D. (1989). *The Privatization Decision: Public Ends, Private Means*. New York: Basic.

Drucker, P. (1978). *The Age of Discontinuity*. New York: Harper & Row.

Farazmand, A. (1996). *Public Enterprise Management: International Case Studies*. Westport, CT: Greenwood Press.

Farazmand, A. (1996). The comparative state of public enterprise management. In: Farazmand, A., ed. *Public Enterprise Management: International Case Studies*. Westport, CT: Greenwood.

Farazmand, A., ed. *Privatization or Public Enterprise Reform? International Case Studies with Implications for Public Management*. Westport, CT: Greenwood.

Geis, G. (1987). The privatization of prisons: Panacea or placebo. In: Carroll, R., Conant, W., Easton, T. A., eds. *Private Means Public Ends: Private Business in Social Service Delivery*. New York: Praeger.

Gibelman, M., Lens, V. (October 2002). Entering the debate about school vouchers: A social work perspective. *Children & Schools* 24(4):207–221.

Gilbert, M. (1996). Private confinement and the role of government in a civil society. In: Mays, G. L., Gray, T., eds. *Privatization and the Provision of Correctional Services: Context and Consequences*. Cincinnati: Anderson.

Gilbert, M. (1996). Making private decisions without getting burned: A guide for understanding the risks. In: Mays, G. L., Gray, T., eds. *Privatization and the Provision of Correctional Services: Context and Consequences*. Cincinnati: Anderson.

Gilbert, M. J. (2001). How much is too much privatization in criminal justice? In: Shichor, D., Gilbert, M. J., eds. *Privatization in Criminal Justice: Past, Present, and Future*. Cincinnati: Anderson.

Gormley, W. T. (1991). The privatization controversy. In: Gormley, W. T., ed. *Privatization and Its Alternatives*. Madison, WI: The University of Wisconsin Press.

Hanke, S. H. (1987). *Prospects for Privatization*. 36. 3, vols. New York: Proceedings of the Academy of Political Science.

Hansen, M. (February 1997). *Senate Fiscal Agency, Issue Paper, Private Operations of Prisons and Jails: An Analysis of Philosophical, Practical, and Economic Concerns*. Washington, DC: In a Series of Papers Examining Critical Budgetary Issues Facing the Michigan Legislature.

Henig, J. R., Hamnett, C., Feingenbaum, H. (1988). The politics of privatization. *Governance*, 442–468.

Hirsh, W. Z. (August 1989). The economics of contracting out: The labor cost fallacy. *Labor Law J.*, 536–542.

Holzer, M., Callahan, K. (1997). *Government at Work*. Thousand Oaks, CA: Sage.

Katz, J. I. (June 1991). Privatizing without tears. *Governing Mag.* 38–42.

Keane, C., et al. The perceived impact of privatization on local health departments. *Am. J. Public Health* 92(7):1178–1180.

Kolderie, T. (July/August 1986). Two different concepts of privatization. *Public Admin. Rev.* 46:285–291.

Levinson, R. B. (1985). Okeechobee: An evaluation of privatization in corrections. *Prison J.* 65(2):91.

Linowes, D. F. (1988). *Privatization Toward More Government: Report of the President's Commission on Privatization.* Urbana and Chicago: University of Illinois Press.

Lipman, I. (December 1989). The global trend toward privatization. *Lipman Report.*

Maupin, J. R. (1990). The political economy of privatizationPhD dissertation. Arizona State University.

McDermott, K. A. (2000). Questioning vouchers. *Equity Excellence Educ.*

Moe, R. C. (November/December 1987). *Exploring the Limits of Privatization.* Congressional Research Service, Library of Congress.

Moe, R. C. (March/April 1988). Law versus performance as objective standard. *Public Admin. Rev.*,, 674–675.

Moore, S., Butler, S. M. (1987). *Privatization: A Strategy for Taming the Federal Budget.* Washington, DC: Heritage Foundation.

Morris, J. C. (1997). The distributional impacts of privatization in national water-quality policy. *J. Politics* 59(1):56–72.

Morris, J. C., Morris, E. D. (1997). Privatization in Mississippi corrections, Chapter 5. In: *Impact, Economic, Financial, and Management Analysis: For the Mississippi Department of Corrections.* Mississippi State: The John C. Stennis Institute of Government.

Nelson, B. J. (1980). Purchase of services. In: Washis, G., ed. *Productivity Improvement Handbook for State and Local Government.* New York: Wiley.

Ogilvy, J. A. (1986–1987). Scenarios for the future of governance. *Bureaucrat* 13–16.

Olmstead, A. T. (1948). *History of the Persian Empire: The Achaemenid Period.* Chicago: Chicago University Press.

OMB. (August 1983). Office of Management Budget, Circular A-76, rev.

Oxford Dictionary: 802.

Palumbo, D. J. (1986). Privatization and correction policy. *Policy Stud. Rev.* 5(3):598–606.

Palumbo, D. J., Maupin, R. (1989). The political side of privatization. *J. Manage. Sci. Policy Anal.* 6:24–40.

Pasour, E. C. (1996). Privatization: Is it the answer. In: Reed, L. W., ed. *Private Cures for Public Ills: The Promise of Privatization.* Irvington-on-Hudson: Foundation for Economic Education.

Pellicciotti, J. M. (1983). 42 U. S. C. Sec. 1983 correctional officials liability: A look to the new century. *J. Contemp. Crim. Justice* 3:1–9.

Peterson, W. H. (1996). Privatization: The rediscovery of entrepreneurship. In: Reed, L. W., ed. *Private Cures for Public Ills: The Promise of Privatization.* Irvington-on-Hudson: Foundation for Economic Education.

Pirie, M. (1985). *Dismantling the State: Offers a Representative Summary of the British Approach to Privatization.* Dallas: National Center for Policy Analysis.

Prager, J. (Winter 1997). Contracting out as a vehicle for privatization: half speed ahead. *J. Int. Affairs* 50(2):613–632.

Robbins, I. P. (1986). Privatization of corrections: Defining the issues. *Judicature* 69(6):325–331.

Robbins, I. P. (1989). The legal dimensions of private incarceration. *The Am. University Law Rev.* 3:531–554.

Savas, E. S. (1977). Policy analysis for local government: Public vs. private refuse collection. *Policy Anal.* 3(1):49–74.

Savas, E. S. (1992). Privatization and productivity. In: Holzer, M., ed. *Public Productivity Handbook.* New York: Marcel Dekker, pp. 79–99.

Shenk, J. W. (1995). The perils of privatization. *Washington Monthly* 27(5):16–24.

Shichor, D. (1993). The corporate context of private prisons. *Crime, Law, Social Change* 20:113–138.

Stahl, O. G. (1988). What's missing in privatization. *Bureaucrat* 41–44.

Starr, P. (1987). The limits of privatization. In: Hanke, S. H., ed. *Prospects for Privatization.* Montpelier, VT: Capital City.

Starr, P. (1989). The meaning of privatization. In: Kamerman, S., Kahn, A., eds. *Privatization and the Welfare State.* Princeton, NJ: Princeton University Press.

Steuerle, C. E. (1998). Common issues for voucher programs. Proceedings of Vouchers and Related Delivery Mechanisms: Consumer Choice in the Provision of Public Services. Washington, DC.

Stolz, B. A. (2001). Policy-making arena and privatization: Subgovernment in flux. In: Shichor, D., Gilbert, M. J., eds. *Privatization in Criminal Justice: Past, Present, and Future.* Cincinnati: Anderson.

Suleiman, E., Waterbury, J., eds. *The Political Economy of Public Sector Reform and Privatization.* Boulder, CO: Westview.

Thayer, F. C. (1987). Privatization: Carnage, chaos, and corruption. In: Carroll, R., Conant, W., Easton, T. A., eds. *Private Means Public Ends: Private Business in Social Service Delivery.* New York: Praeger.

Thomas, C. W., Hanson, L. S. (1989). The Implications of 42 U.S.C. 1983 for the privatization of prisons. *FL State University Law Rev.* 16:933–962.

Utt, R. D. (1991). Privatization in the United States. In: Ott, A. F., Hartley, K., eds. *Privatization and Economic Efficiency.* Brookfield, VT: Edward Elgar.

Walker, A. (1984). The political economy of privatization. In: Legrand, J., Robinson, R., eds. *Privatisation and the Welfare State.* London: George Allen and Unwin.

Wallin, B. A. (January/February 1997). The need for a privatization process: Lessons from development and implementation. *Public Admin. Rev.* 57(1):11–20.

Wolfe, J. D. (1990). In: Wolfe, J. D., Foglesong, R., eds. *The Politics of Economic Adjustment.* New York: Greenwood.

Worsnop, R. I. (November 1992). Privatization. *CQ Researcher* 2(42):979–986.

# 7

# Public Management of Privatization and Contracting

**DEBORAH A. AUGER and JEFFREY A. RAFFEL**
*University of Delaware, Newark, Delaware, U.S.A.*

## I.  INTRODUCTION

Americans are culturally predisposed to adopt a distinctive set of expectations about private firms and public bureaucracies, private markets, and public policies. True or not, the private sector is assumed to be inherently dynamic, productive, and dependable, and private institutions thought to be superior to plodding overbureaucratized public institutions for the delivery of a wide range of goods and services. These expectations are so broadly held that assertions and ideas in accord with them are often defined as natural and inevitable whereas alternative views are dismissed as unrealistic and unworkable. The current movement toward privatization at the local, state, and federal governmental levels illustrates these tendencies.

Private delivery of public services has always played an important role in the United States; however, in the last two decades a number of commentators and public officials have offered proposals to expand the role of the private sector by shifting from public sector provision of goods and services to private sector alternatives. The justifications include improving the performance of public assets or service functions, cutting back public expenditures and taxes, depoliticizing policy decisions, and generating budget revenues through the sale of public assets (Hanke, 1987, p. 2). Unfortunately, all too often the evidence to support privatization initiatives has been anecdotal rather than based on careful empirical analysis. Nonetheless, these initiatives have attained a great deal of currency as the best way to improve the contemporary productivity of government.

Enough words have been written about privatization and contracting over the past decades to fill many library shelves, too many for the busy public manager to sort through to distinguish those initiatives that offer real promise for the improvement of services from those that are based largely on unexamined assumptions about the responsiveness and efficiency of private institutions. Our goal is to do the sorting. We will try to get past the rhetoric both for privatization, for example, it allows "escaping the heavy hand of the state" (Hodge, 1999), and against it, for example, as tantamount to "selling the family silver" (Hodge, 1999) to provide some guidance about where and under what circumstances there is compelling evidence that shifting the provision of goods and services from public to private or nonprofit sector hands can enhance productivity. (Readers seeking success and horror stories illustrating the best and worst of privatization and contracting are referred to an excellent "pro" Web site, the Reason Foundation's www.reason.org and an excellent "con" web site offered by the American Federation of State, County, and Municipal Employees, www.afscme.org.) In the end, we seek to offer some suggestions for the public manager who is considering whether privatization is a viable option for improving the delivery or lowering the cost of a particular type of public goods or service and suggestions about the process of managing privatization and contracting.

We recognize that privatization could be considered within the larger context of the New Public Management and macro reform models of governance. Peters (1996), for example, has suggested four models of governance as alternatives to the present public administration system: the market model (utilization of market or quasi-market mechanisms to replace or modify government, e.g., privatization), participatory model [empowerment and motivation of employees, e.g., total quality management (TQM)], flexible government model (utilization of temporary organizations, sunset legislation), and deregulated government (reduction of red tape). Denhardt and Denhardt (2000) argue that the New Public Management and quasi-market approaches to government should be compared not to the traditional bureaucratic model of government but to a New Public Service paradigm. Others importantly highlight weighty philosophical concerns in privatization and quasi-market approaches to governing such as the transformation to a "Hollow State" (Milward, 2000) and the negative aspects of the value of entrepreneurism (DeLeon, 1996). In this chapter, however, we take privatization as a current potent influence on government activities, and focus more on the pragmatic issues surrounding it, addressing more managerial than philosophical concerns (Raffel et al., 1999).

## II. DEFINITION OF PRIVATIZATION

Part of the problem of any discussion of privatization is that the meaning of the term is confusing because it has been used to refer to several disparate types of policy initiatives. These include the shift to private provision of public goods or services (through contracting out or voucher arrangements) while maintaining public financing, the use of public–private partnerships where financing and project design are shared functions, the sale of public assets, and the disengagement or withdrawal of government from specific responsibilities under the assumption that private institutions (firms, families, voluntary organizations) will take care of them. The thread that runs through the differing concepts of privatization is the belief that inefficiencies of government linked to bureaucratization and government monopoly control can be relieved by subjecting traditionally publicly provided goods or services to market forces. Competition among firms, freedom from red tape, and flexibility in hiring, firing, and compensation practices, it is believed, create pressures and opportunities for efficiency and cost savings that cannot be achieved under current public sector arrangements.

Two distinct and quite different objectives are pursued under the name of privatization: the improvement of the delivery of goods or services by taking advantage of competitive efficiencies and, alternatively, the reduction or full termination of public support of particular goods or services altogether (load shedding). In the first case privatization does not eliminate government accountability for the results of its expenditures; it simply shifts the locus of service delivery. The means of policy implementation is privatized but not the functional sphere of government action (Starr, 1987, p. 125). What is relinquished, according to Sundquist (1984, p. 307), "may be the easiest part—the doing. The conceiving, planning, goal-setting, standard-setting, performance-monitoring, evaluating, and correcting all remain with the government."

In the second case, government withdraws or reduces its role as a buyer, regulator, standard setter, or decision maker in particular service areas (Kolderie, 1986, p. 288). According to some, this constitutes "real" privatization because it breaks up public spending coalitions and genuinely reduces the scope of government commitments (Butler, 1985). But others argue that it is "false" privatization because for government to abandon a program or responsibility is not to privatize it; for privatization to occur, government must retain responsibility for assuring that something happens on the private side (Sundquist, 1984, p. 307). We adopt the second view.

Our concern here is with productivity and performance in service provision. Our assumption is that government retains responsibility for a function or activity and will continue to finance it. The question is: can the good or service at issue be more effectively provided by government directly or by private firms or nonprofit organizations through contracting out, vouchers, grants, tax credits, or other tax preferences? As we use the term, privatization refers to the transfer of the production of goods or services from public to private or nonprofit providers. Financing and oversight of the function or activity continues to be the domain of government. As Fixler and Hayes (1989, p. 75) point out, although privatization "is used by contemporary philosophers and practitioners who wish, for philosophical reasons, to see the government sector reduced . . . [it is also] simply, a method, deserving of practical examination."

By far the most utilized form of privatization in the United States is contracting out. Gormley (1994) notes there are several other types of privatization beyond contracting, including vouchers, partnerships, and asset sales, as well as "bounty-hunting" or third-party enforcement. For example, under the federal Clean Water Act, private parties, including individuals or organizations, are authorized to sue polluters and this serves as a quasi-private alternative to total government regulation. Another privatization alternative is franchising, a modified form of load shedding where government grants a special privilege to a private operator (Seidenstat, 1996). The federal government under the National Performance Review (NPR) has allowed a number of agencies to sell their services to federal organizations through the Franchise Fund Pilot Program (Halachmi, 1996). Government subsidies have been provided to various nonprofit, community, and cultural institutions such as universities, hospitals, and art museums. Vouchers have been used in the housing, vocational rehabilitation, and educational arenas to a limited extent. Publicly provided services are engaging the energies of private citizens through recruitment and use of volunteers (Brudney, 1996). But even with these various forays into a broader set of privatization alternatives, privatization in practice remains almost entirely a "contracting out" phenomenon.

## III.  CLAIMS FOR AND AGAINST PRIVATIZATION

The literature is filled with a variety of claims about the benefits of privatization and warnings about its dangers. Siegel (1999) and O'Leary (1996) have compiled excellent lists of pros and cons. Those who favor privatization argue that virtually any government activity has been or could be improved if it were privatized, even prisons, fire departments, school systems, public safety, and the Brooklyn Bridge (Brody, 1989; see also Eggers and O'Leary, 1995). For opponents, privatization leads to corruption and diminished services. Unfortunately, much of the debate is clouded by ideological biases. The arguments for privatization are based primarily on analyses of productivity that emphasize economy rather than a broader set of considerations. It is argued that competitive bidding by profit-maximizing firms for a well-specified output guarantees that services will be provided at the lowest cost because private providers are compelled to be less wasteful and more cost effective than government agencies. An entrepreneur seeking to make a profit presumably has a powerful incentive to find the optimum mixture of personnel, resources, technology, and organization to accomplish a particular objective; otherwise he or she will lose business to a competitor who has found a more efficient combination. A government official, on the other hand, is rewarded for expanding the size of the agency he or she directs, not for how efficiently the work is performed. The bureaucratic incentive is to increase expenditures, not to seek cost savings (Savas, 1987, 2000).

Opponents respond that it is naive to expect that, in the long run, privatization will decrease the costs of service delivery. As the sole or major purchaser of services, government may become hostage to the inefficiencies of single sellers of services (Bailey, 1987, p. 142). Furthermore, those who point to the cost savings and efficiency improvements of privatization overlook the profit-based inducements for private providers to service only the easy and profitable customers, whereas the difficult and unprofitable are neglected, a process called creaming. Opportunities are also created for bribery or kickbacks when government buys from the private sector. Indeed, say the critics, the American experience with the defense industry, highway construction, and medical care should alert us to the potential of private contractors for manipulation of political decisions, exploitation of contract incentives, and cost overruns. If these outcomes are to be avoided, resources must be spent to ably regulate and monitor private providers of goods and services. Kohn (1986) argues that the advantages of competition, the cornerstone of the privatization approach, "often prove illusory or short-lived or selective." Finally, it is argued that some part of the savings from privatization results from lower wage levels and the greater use of part-time workers with fewer fringe benefits. Thus privatization is really a means of securing reduced costs through losses imposed on public employees.

Those who oppose privatization focus on values other than economy such as accountability, equity, service quality, and governmental capacity. Opponents raise concerns that when service delivery is privatized, government loses control of the operations it is financing. The result may be reduction or even termination of benefits to the poorest and neediest clients. In addition, opponents argue that studies showing efficiency improvements from privatization usually lack evidence about its impact on the quality of services, thereby making it difficult to judge whether lower costs result from greater efficiency or deteriorating quality (Starr, 1987, p. 129).

Another concern is that privatization results in diminished citizen input by removing decisions from the public realm where open discussion creates opportunities for criticism and mutual persuasion. In the marketplace, "private firms have fewer obligations to conduct open proceedings or to make known the reasons for their decisions" (Starr, 1987, p. 132). Furthemore, democratic politics opens up choices that are not available in the market where people with more money in effect have more "votes." When markets fail to provide particular goods and services, democratic processes enable the public to elect to purchase them (Starr, 1987, p. 133). Finally, it has been argued that privatization weakens government by deflecting attention from making governmental institutions work as they ought to work, by undermining investments in government's organizational capacities (Sanger, 2000) and even more disturbing, by encouraging a turning away from governmental institutions altogether. In the end, says James Sundquist (1984, p. 318), "government is an instrument that must be used for an extensive and irreducible range of purposes . . . to permit [it] to fail . . . is to imperil this country's unity and progress at home and its position in the world." This statement echoes more recent concerns about the ultimate impacts of "hollowing out" the state.

Proponents dismiss these concerns as overstated and argue that, in fact, privatization leads to improved accountability and better services. When a service is contracted out, public officials are forced to take a serious look at defining objective performance measures for it. With careful writing of contracts and monitoring, they can assure that services are provided to all those who are eligible. In addition, in those forms of privatization where users pay directly for a service (such as vouchers), consumer choice provides feedback to ensure that the service is delivered in a satisfactory manner (Steuerle et al., 1999). Furthermore, by utilizing the talents and experience of private and nonprofit organizations, the range of choices for the way in which a service is provided is enlarged, the reach of services into hard-to-reach communities is extended, and the opportunities for innovation are enhanced. (Salamon, 1997). Finally, contractors can offer governments greater expertise, the ability to invest in the latest equipment and help government avoid huge capital costs, and the advantages of economies of scale (Siegel, 1999).

In short, proponents of privatization are convinced that the private sector typically does a more efficient job than the public sector in delivering services; opponents are sure that privatization is associated with corruption and a reduction or loss in service to the poor. This would seem to be an ideal subject on which research could shed light and definitively indicate whether privatization leads to positive or negative results.

## IV. RESEARCH ON PRIVATIZATION

The public manager would like to know if a given service were privatized, would the provision of the service be improved, especially with respect to the criterion of productivity. We must first note that this is a complicated research question. As we indicated above, there are many forms of privatization. The impact of a change to contracting may be quite different from a switch to vouchers. There may be differences in the delivery of services by nonprofit and profit-making organizations within the sphere of privatization. There is also more than one criterion by which to judge the change from public to private provision. At a minimum, efficiency concerns must be joined with concerns about effectiveness and equity. We cannot expect that a particular form of privatization will have the same effect along the dimensions of efficiency, effectiveness, and equity as well as across different service areas and different types of jurisdictions. It is clear then that the question goes beyond whether privatization generally results in increased productivity. Rather, we need to determine under what conditions and in what jurisdictions a particular form of privatization will have an impact on service cost, quality, and equity.

## A.  Research Design

The ideal way to answer these questions would be to build a research design based on random selection of a set of jurisdictions in which a given service function is privatized. Then the results could be compared to another set of randomly selected jurisdictions in which the same service function continues to be publicly provided. Bailis (1984) has described the characteristics of the research necessary and desirable in the human services arena but his statement can be generalized to all service areas.

> A definitive empirical analysis of the claims that privately funded human service activities are more efficient than those conducted under public auspices would require a comparison of public and private efforts to deliver the same types of service to roughly the same target population. In other words, the ideal study would resemble a controlled experiment in which all aspects of two programs are identical except that one is funded and/or administered through a private sector initiative and the other through a traditional public program.

The reader should note that the research base on privatization does not include many such studies. Indeed, too much of the work on privatization is journalistic in nature and/or reported by those who implemented the action. Fitzgerald's (1988) book, for example, presents an interesting but journalistic description of a very wide array of privatization alternatives. Likewise, Cigler (1988–1989) argues, in reviewing Savas' 1987 book, that "empirical research on many of the activities is still quite sparse." Unfortunately it is still much the case today as Hatry alleged in 1983 (p. 9).

> Unfortunately, little systematic, objective evaluation of most of these alternatives is available. Most available information is descriptive, anecdotal, and advocacy or public-relations oriented. Information on the consequences of the uses of these approaches, when mentioned at all, is usually provided by the government that undertook the action, and such information is usually limited to assessments in the first year of the activity— before longer-term consequences have been identified.

Even the more formal research literature has shortcomings. The bulk of privatization research is based on cross-sectional data analysis and natural experiments, not the most externally valid research methods. Cross-sectional research indicating that private sector services are less costly than public ones may be simply discovering the impact of creaming of clients in which the private sector discourages from participation those clients with chronic problems or who seek costly services (Starr, 1987; Gibelman, 1996). Thus a research finding that private provision is more efficient than public provision may really indicate a difference in service levels and/or quality and not greater efficiency or productivity. Bendick (1984, p. 165) notes a "prevalence of unsubstantiated claims," such as the assertion that private hospitals are more efficient than public hospitals, when there is a lack of data about the types of patients and treatments involved. Examining "natural experiments," where a jurisdiction switches from public to private service provision, may entail a similar problem. Those jurisdictions having productivity problems with provision of a service are the ones most likely to be searching for an alternative delivery system (Fisk et al., 1978). If costs are found to decrease when services are switched to private provision, it may be a result of the extreme initial values, a type of regression to the mean. In addition, if the contractors' bids are not lower than estimated inhouse delivery costs, the government is likely to avoid contracting out and never report these "negative" results.

Alternatively, the act of change itself may be the reason for an increase in efficiency. For example, on the question of whether selection of school boards by election or appointment is better, some have suggested that perhaps the important thing is to change the method every decade. The Hawthorne Effect would suggest that improvement of service delivery occurs under privatization simply because more attention has been paid to it. There may be other explanations as well. Positive initial results may reflect lowballing by an eager contractor rather than savings that can be maintained over time.

Even if the research design were adequate, a further problem in research is that the measurement of service quality is much more difficult than the measurement of changes in costs. Thus many studies provide reliable cost data but lack evidence about the impact of privatization on the quality of services (Starr 1987, p. 127) making it difficult to judge whether lower costs reflect greater efficiency or deteriorating quality. Although economy can then be indicated in research, without a clear sense of service quality one cannot determine how productivity has been affected.

Recent studies highlight the methodological difficulties of privatization research. Fernandez and Fabricant (2000) examine two cases from the State of Florida Child Support Enforcement Program to illustrate methodological problems in determining the effects of privatization. They show how weak methodology has an impact on effects measurement. Florida assigned the FSE contractor the most difficult cases, those where no support payments had been collected in six months, and then found that the contractor's collection rate was lower than that of the inhouse staff and their benefit–cost ratio inferior. When a followup study was conducted and cases assigned randomly to the contractor and inhouse staff, the results were reversed, although the difference was quite small (22.2% vs. 19.0%) and the benefit–cost ratio, favoring the contractor, not significantly different. But even these results were open to question given issues about appropriate costing methodology and evidence of the problem of "reactivity," meaning that the focused attention given to the performance of the State workers during this experiment might have enhanced their performance. The authors call for attention to research design in such studies with greater use of randomized experimental designs and sensitivity analysis given the variability of key cost and benefit factors.

Such methodological problems are certainly not unique to Florida. A comprehensive study of the results of privatization in prisons in the United States (Austin, 2001) concluded that only a few studies were helpful in estimating the effects of privatization because in general studies failed to control for inmate differences on key attributes, that is, age and other variables related to inmate conduct. Thus differences in costs between private and public prison facilities may be due to the difficulty of dealing with the different types of prisoners. The study concluded that the average saving from privatization was 1%, noting that others have projected such savings at the 20% level.

## B.   Reviews of Research on Privatization

The privatization literature is now replete with reviews of research that note general conclusions, lessons, prescriptions, and summaries about contracting and other privatization approaches. These analyses fall into several categories, from comprehensive reviews to summaries based on level of government, geography, and service area. We discuss several of each below. It is helpful and illuminating to begin by comparing two comprehensive reviews of privatization that use different methodologies and come, not surprisingly, to quite different conclusions.

E. S. Savas is a "champion" of privatization (Nordin, 2001), and his latest book, *Privatization and Public Partnerships* (2000), is a feast for privatization advocates. To Savas, privatization is the only solution to public revenue constraints. "There is but one message in his book—privatization is a good thing. No. Make that privatization is the *best* thing." Savas ignores all other tools and the important issue of "what functions are inherently governmental" (Nordin, 2001, p. 303). Essentially, all of the cited references are in support of privatization. Savas provides the theory underpinning privatization, myriad examples of how privatization has been successfully applied worldwide, and how to overcome obstacles to privatization such as fear of loss of control, labor unions, and political and legal barriers. The style of the book is anecdotal and it is extremely well stocked with references and examples. The book could have been titled "The Handbook *For* Privatization."

Graeme Hodge (1999 and 2000) has taken quite a different path to summarize and analyze the research literature on contracting. Like Savas he reviewed the rationales for privatization, although Hodge provides a critique along the way. Rather than weave the literature into an advocacy statement on privatization, Hodge conducted a rigorous meta-analysis, focusing on the size of the effect for research studies that included a hypothesis and statistical significance tests. Hodge sifted through 1400 journals and 6000 nonserial publications to identify 129 studies that had the potential to meet his criteria. Only 28, conducted between 1976 to 1994, had research design integrity and reported appropriate statistical results, which, as we suggest above, reflects the state of the world of privatization research in general: few studies meet rigorous research design criteria. A majority of the studies were U.S.-based. Sixty-eight percent of the studies were based on measurements of the effects of local government contracting.

Hodge found that the average cost reduction resulting from contracting was 8 to 14% but the savings varied greatly by service area. Contracting out maintenance, cleaning, and refuse collection services saved the most money but cost savings were not significantly different for police/security, health, fire, training, and support services. Because few of the studies included the costs of the contracting process such as contract development and monitoring, Hodge reduces his estimated cost savings to the range of 6 to 12%. Hodge also found that the more recent and more rigorous studies indicated less of a savings than the older and less rigorous studies. Hodge concludes that contracting saves money, especially in the traditional manual services area (e.g., street and building cleaning, refuse removal), but "Translating these findings into rhetoric that blindly pursues contracting out of all government services however, involves a significant leap of faith," which is not supported by the evidence and ignores other impacts of this reform (1999, p. 467).

This chapter focuses on privatization in the United States, but clearly the privatization movement and resulting research literature are now global in scope. In Eastern Europe the movement from communism toward democracy and capitalism has led to extensive load shedding and asset sales. In England "Thatcherism" generally and the Local Government Act of 1988, which called for compulsory competitive tendering, have led to an extensive literature. In developing nations the movement from socialism to capitalism has generated numerous books about privatization (see Morgan, 1995 and David et al., 2000 for more for discussions of global privatization). There are articles and books analyzing privatization by country, for example, Overman (1995) on "Privatization in China, Mexico, and Russia," Boorsma and De Vries (1995) on "The Dutch Experience," Morgan (1995) on England, collections of case studies on various nations such as France, Germany, Australia, Iran, and India (Farazmand, 2001), and articles on a variety of countries including Zimbabwe (Logie and Woodroffe, 1993). We can truly report that privatization now ranges across the world from A through Z! Indeed, globalization and privatization have become intertwined, partly because global institutions and Western capitalist nations push for privatization in developing nations; for example, the World Bank demands privatization for nations seeking its assistance (Farazmand, 2001). With few exceptions, this vast global literature focuses on asset sales and load shedding.

In the United States, general reviews of privatization have been written (see Seidenstadt, e.g., 1996), however, researchers have more frequently analyzed the privatization movement at one of the three levels of government.

In the United States, Auger (1999) recently reviewed expanding privatization activities of state governments under devolution and drew seven lessons from their privatization efforts, including cautions about the diversity of service-by-service, state-by-state experiences; the need to think about distinctions between ancillary support services and state agencies' mission-based service core; and the need for priority attention to contract management and monitoring after the "make or buy choice" has been made.

At the national level the focus has been on the National Performance Review led by then-Vice President Al Gore. But the NPR was preceded by the federal government's long history of contracting for defense, space exploration, and other technologically grounded needs. After reviewing federal experiences in four areas (including defense and energy), Kettl (1993) concludes that government needs to build its capacities to be a "smart buyer," understanding clearly the relationships between buyers and sellers in the marketplace.

At the local level, using ICMA survey data, Greene (1996) compared privatization in American cities from 1982 to 1992. He found that privatization had increased significantly over the decade in the 596 cities studied. The percentage of ICMA-surveyed functions in which a city employs private service delivery increased from 12.6 to 27.8%, an increase of 121%. The trend was up in 57 of 59 service levels including street repair, snow plowing, bus transit systems, and fire prevention, through insect/rodent control and programs for the elderly. In his recent book on cities and privatization, Greene (2002) notes that even Chicago's Mayor Daley has privatized 40 services. Dilger et al. (1997) followed up the 1992 survey in the summer of 1995 with a more indepth survey of the 100 largest cities in the nation. The 66 responses indicated that the average number of privatized services was a shade under seven and only three cities had no privatized service. "City officials in America's largest cities were relatively satisfied with their city's privatization experiences, but it was clearly not viewed as a panacea. Satisfaction levels were highest with the privatization of street lighting/ signals, solid waste collection, and printing services." They were least satisfied in the areas of drug/alcohol treatment, employment, and training, thus adding evidence that soft services are less successfully privatized than hard services. The city respondents indicated cost savings in the 15 to 20% range. They also indicated an increase in service quality. The results were best summarized by one city official who concluded that ". . . privatization is no panacea. It has tremendous political implications. There are good and bad contractors. Overall our experience has been good. Contract administration is the key to success."

Given the results of studies of contracting, it is not surprising to find that local officials have adopted a pragmatic view of privatization. Warner and Hebdon's (2001) study of chief elected township and county officials in New York State "confirm that local governments are guided in their choice of service delivery systems primarily by pragmatic concerns with information, monitoring, and service quality." Privatization and contracting out are viewed in a larger nonideological context that also includes intermunicipal service agreements, reverse privatization (contracting back in), cessation of services, and government entrepreneurship (government contracting its services to private or nonpublic sector clients). Public works, public safety, and administrative support were the service areas most likely to have been restructured since 1990, but about half of the local governments had not enacted any such restructuring from 1990 to 1997. Asking, "Where are we in local government contracting?" Siegel (1999) answers that local governments and local officials are generally satisfied with the results of contracting but there still exists a need for improvement in the precontracting period. Improving cost accounting systems, allocating interdepartmental service charges, and improving service effort and accomplishment reporting standards would improve the contracting process.

Given all these empirical studies and reviews of research and critiques of such reviews, what consensus exists? There is general agreement that privatization can lead to improved service and lower costs in areas that are measurable, monitorable, and technical in nature. Honadle (1984, p. 304) contends that "contracting lends itself more to those functional areas in which the output can be clearly described and measured." Pack (1987, p. 535) argues that "the more complex the product, the more complex and uncertain the technology, the harder it is to specify, measure, and monitor output, then the higher the transactions costs of the contract." Similarly, Bendick (1984, p. 154) concludes that privatization is more efficient "where the good or service demanded is relatively straightforward, simple, and technological. However, the evidence justifies only a very cautious and skeptical stance when the public need being addressed is complex, long-run, and sociological." Finally, Donahue (1989, p. 83) argues that "if a task allows for clear evaluation by results, then the bias should be toward turning the task over to profit-seekers." But if the task is so complex that myriad constraints and specifics are necessary in the contract, "it may be better to . . . set up a bureaucracy."

There is also an extensive literature that includes research reviews and collections of privatization studies in many discrete service areas including housing (Linneman and Megbolugbe, 1994), transportation (Hakim et al, 1996), prisons (Austin, 2001), water resources, and health care (Shaw, 1999). Given that a general conclusion from the privatization literature is that one should be careful about general conclusions, we examine the literature in a limited number of service areas below to gain additional insights for implementing and managing privatization.

## 1. Solid-Waste Collection

Over a decade ago Savas (1987, p. 124) concluded that:

> The service studied most extensively and most thoroughly to determine the relative performance of different arrangements is residential solid waste (or refuse) collection. The evidence is overwhelming and clear: contract collection is substantially more efficient than municipal collection, and no less effective.

Savas referred to nine studies, including his own work, conducted over a decade which indicated that municipal collection costs about 35% more than contract collection. Apparently the lower cost was not a function of lower service quality. Savas cited a national survey of households which indicated that about 90% of respondents thought their refuse collection was good or excellent independent of the type of collection. He argued that the increase from 21% in 1975 to 35% in 1982 in the percentage of U.S. cities using contracting was attributable to the increasing evidence that contracting for refuse saves money without decreasing service quality.

In his most recent book, Savas (2000, p. 160) repeats his earlier findings because "Privatization of this issue is a settled issue; it no longer attracts much attention from researchers." Indeed, Siegel (1999) cites over 30 studies conducted on solid waste collection in local government but only one was published after the publication of Savas' 1987 book. In that study Ammons and Hill (1995) returned to survey the six competitive service cities studied by Savas in 1981. Savas had found that in five of the six cities the cost per household of contracted as opposed to municipal service was lower. The study a decade later indicated that the competitive, public–private systems remained viable. Cost increases in the five cities that had maintained the competitive system were lower than increases in the consumer price index and national average costs for solid waste management expenditures per capita. (New Orleans had opted to move to contracting out all such services in 1987.) And best practices were shared across public/private lines; private firms learned from city employees and vice versa.

Shetterly (2000) combined the 1992 ICMA survey of alternative delivery, data from the County and City Data Book of 1994, and his survey of 109 jurisdictions in 1997 (41 were completed) to address the question not of whether contracting out saved money but rather whether contract design influences contractor performance in refuse collection. He found that penalty provisions, that is, contract deductions for nonperformance, are greatly related to contractor cost but performance specification, sealed bid, and contract length had only a weak association to the annual refuse collection cost per resident. Shetterly's work is illustrative of a shift in research in contracting out more generally from whether privatization saves money to what aspects of the contracting process are related to privatization savings and success.

Solid waste or refuse collection contracting remains the showcase of privatization advocates but it is not clear that we can generalize findings from this service area to others. Cost savings appear relatively consistent, however, several authors have found this area to show different results than others (e.g., Hodge, 2000; Hirsch, 1995). As Walsh (1995, p. 224) states: "A cynical view would be that what we know, given the narrow range of studies, is that the contracting out of refuse collection leads to a short term reduction in costs . . . .broad conclusions about the value of market mechanisms may have been built on a limited base."

Although privatization has been shown to increase productivity in solid-waste collection, it is problematic in areas where the outcomes are long range, holistic, and unmeasurable. Two areas where this can be illustrated are human services and education. In the former, there is a great expansion in the use of contracting and some evidence about its impact; in the latter, there is much debate and some recent privatization innovations but limited empirical evidence.

## 2.  Human Services

The longstanding tradition of linkage between public sector and private sector providers of social services has been well noted in the literature (Salamon, 1995; Salamon and Abramson, 1982; DeHoog, 1984). In state government, use of privatized contracted services has been a practice of significance in select social service sectors for more than thirty years (Smith and Lipsky, 1993). Yet devolution of additional human service responsibilities to states throughout the 1990s has expanded this privatization trend. Review of state experience suggests privatization is both broadening and deepening in social service arenas (Auger, 1999). Contracted services are being employed in a far wider scope of human service areas. Longstanding contracting out of services for child welfare, substance abuse, and mental health have been supplemented by new areas added since 1990, including vocational rehabilitation, child and family support services, foster care and adoption, child care, and child support enforcement (Chi and Jasper, 1998; GAO, 1997a). And in the aftermath of passage of welfare reform legislation in 1996, a whole new set of welfare-to-work services such as job readiness, job training/placement, teen pregnancy prevention/support, and parenting education have been heavily contracted out (DeVita and Twombly, 1999; Sanger 2000; Twombly, 2000). Far greater shares of the social service budgets of government are being placed in the hands of private contractors at the start of the twenty-first century.

Within individual contracted social service areas, the literature also reflects contracting's deepening reach, with governments acting to privatize an even more inclusive set of service functions. In the past 10 years, government has begun to contract out far beyond conventional front-line service delivery activities, and to cede to the hands of contractors an even more fundamental array of social program management responsibilities, such as client eligibility/benefit determination, case oversight and management, social program design and specification, program evaluation, and even the ongoing management of entire "networked" social service systems. The for-profit service provider Lockheed Martin, for example, is under contract with the state of Texas to perform a comprehensive set of program design, program management, and program evaluation functions for the state's welfare-to-work services. At the subnational level in the United States, social services have arguably become the most extensively contracted out of all government services.

One central question confronting governmental managers considering privatizing any new human service area is whether cost savings can be attained. The answer,

unfortunately, is not clear. Substantial cost savings claims have been made by a number of state governments in conjunction with their social service privatization efforts (GAO, 1996a, 1997a; Chi and Jasper, 1998). But these claims are rarely backed by adequate empirical investigation (Gibelman, 1996). Both substantial cost savings and substantially higher expenditures have been linked to different social service privatization efforts in the empirical literature. (See Johnston and Romzek, 1999 on Medicaid services to the elderly; Milward and Provan, 1998 on mental health; GAO, 1996b on child support enforcement; see also Gibelman, 1996).

In truth, variation is so great among the *types* of social services contracted, and adequate controls for service quality so elusive and neglected in the difficult-to-measure human service area that it is unlikely that a clear generalizable picture of privatization cost savings in human services will ever be available to guide public manager's choices, leaving the decision to be based on other service criteria (e.g., projected capacity for greater innovation, advantages in reaching hard-to-reach clients, deeper nonprofit experience in newly emerging areas of social policy, and ties to the community that advance more tailored service responses). Yet there is a certain logic embedded in the special relationship that exists between government and the nonprofit sector agencies which dominate contracted human services, a logic that suggests that at least some level of cost savings is likely to result when human services are contracted to nonprofit providers.

In contrast to other public services like transit and solid waste, privatized human service systems have a distinctive cross-sector character. Privatization in human services has largely meant the "nonprofitization" of government services (Nathan, 1997; Gronbjerg and Smith, 1999). Nonprofit organizations have been alleged to provide more than half of all governmentally supported human services (Salamon, 1995; Smith, 2003). Conversely, it has been estimated that more than half of the organizational revenues of social and legal service nonprofits in the United States are now derived from governmental sources (Weitzman et al., 2002). The result is a heavy mutual dependence between government and nonprofit social service agencies that has major relevance for the issue of not only potential cost savings but also for longer-term governmental contract management functions.

The likelihood of cost savings under human services contracting stems from the fact that nonprofits, in general, appear to offer lower wage and benefit packages to their employees than those offered by government, yielding reduced front-line service expenditures (Johnston and Romzek, 1999; Mann and Gibelman, 1996; Becker et al, 1995). Furthermore, experienced nonprofits often function to reduce government service costs even more greatly as a result of their capacity to leverage other resources that help support the service provision effort. These include the donated labor of the nonprofit's volunteers and additional monetary resources derived from the combination of tax exemption, private donations, and foundation grants that financially underwrite nonprofit operations (Auger, 1997). Some governmental service contracts even explicitly seek to capitalize on nonprofits' aptitudes for "resource leveraging" by requiring bidders to supply a specific "in-kind match" in support of the service enterprise as part of their contract bid (Gibelman, 1996). This practice, while producing cost savings for government in the short run, imposes substantial burdens upon largely "undercapitalized" nonprofit providers, who are often inadequately compensated by government for their full overhead costs. Over the longer term, overburdening nonprofits resource leveraging capacities may serve to ultimately weaken

these providers, to the extent that government overexploits these advantages in order to "bottom out" its contract costs. In the face of these wage and leveraging elements, however, the allegations of cost savings gains from social service contracting with nonprofits appear to have some foundation in truth.

Ongoing governmental resource limitations and continued political support for privatization mean human service contracting is likely to continue its expansionary trend. Yet government managers need to be keenly aware that *the conventions of privatization practice in other service areas do not fit well in the human services arena.* Both the unique characteristics of the human services as a public service area and the mutually dependent nature of government's relationship with nonprofit sector entities pose special productivity challenges for government managers seeking to effectively privatize in this area.

First, human services are intensely personal services, whose impact on individual clients can have deep quality-of-life implications (Gibelman, 1996). As a result, "continuity of service" considerations matter in ways that are less true for other public service areas (De Hoog, 1996; Smith and Lipsky, 1993). It is readily apparent that it is a far weightier matter for public managers' contract decisions to compel a mentally ill juvenile to change his longstanding therapist than for a public manager to compel a household to shift to a new trash collector. It is a far cry different to switch child protective services providers who may be tracking children at risk of abuse and neglect than to change to new toll collection agencies on a public bridge. In human services, there are high costs imposed on the individual as a result of government's contract choices that are not built into our conventional competitive contracting models. This is not to argue that government contract agents should be unwilling to change providers where contracted services are deemed ineffective or far too costly compared to other available options, only that genuine productivity would dictate that alongside standard contract decision criteria of cost and performance, that the value of service continuity be included in some explicit way in contract processes employed by public agencies.

Secondly, in contrast to other types of contracted public services, the human services tend to be populated by a fragmented and complex network of relatively small, autonomous, and highly specialized front-line service provider organizations (DeHoog, 1996). The fragmented and highly specialized character of social service provision poses some special challenges for government managers seeking to contract out. Productivity of the service enterprise is highly dependent upon the effective assemblage of these disparate private organizations into a functioning, interconnected, service system—a network capable of offering the public access to a relatively seamless, full-spectrum "continuum of care" (Wernet, 1999) .

Important work by Milward and Provan and others highlights the new centrality of government managers' responsibilities for such "network management" functions (Milward and Provan, 1998; O'Toole, 1997). Yet the dictates of effective network management are often at odds with conventional contracting practices premised on "competitive contracting" models which tend to emphasize contracting of discrete, separate service activities, and to encourage individual contract providers to view one another as competitors rather than collaborators.

This fragmented yet interdependent character of the human services can be illustrated using the mental health examples offered by Milward and Provan. In mental health it is often the case that one provider may provide a suicide hotline, another

inpatient crisis intervention; a third may specialize in longer-term talk therapies, and a fourth might operate group homes in the community. Yet despite the fragmented nature of the provider system, the effectiveness of overall treatment of a client can be seen to depend heavily upon cooperative behaviors among these service providers, a willingness of agencies to refer clients to other service agencies even though they may be competitors in other arenas, a willingness to devote uncompensated time to information sharing and to joint problem-solving related to client progress even after the client is in another contract provider's care, and willingness to collaborate with the public contracting agency and other providers to collectively identify and address emerging service gaps as they become apparent. These reflect critical cooperative investments in an integrated service system infrastructure, and have parallels in the experience of other human service networks as well, including disabilities services, child welfare services, AIDS-related services, and welfare-to-work initiatives (De Hoog, 1996; Mordock, 1999; Bielefeld et al., 1995; Sanger, 2000).

Unlike productivity in individual services, productivity in service networks is contingent on cooperation. Provider agencies' willingness to engage in cooperative behaviors and to sacrifice their own short-term interests for the good of the network is premised on a series of presumptions: that other contract providers will reciprocate at a future point, that cooperative efforts will be rewarded, and that the network will remain stable long enough for both to occur (Milward and Provan, 1998). These are ill-served by our prevailing competitive contracting models.

Competition has long been a central anchor of the privatization literature (Savas, 1987; Donahue, 1989; Kettl, 1993), and competitive contracting has been discussed as a generally valuable model by many, including this chapter's authors in previous articles (see Auger, 1999; Raffel et al., 1999). But new work suggests that for the social services, competitive contracting models, if insufficiently tempered by considerations about system well-being, can prove counter to productivity aims. Overemphasizing adversarial competition and focusing solely on agency individualism rather than on collaborative investment, can undermine rather than reinforce provider inclinations to devote time to system-building and maintenance functions for the service network. Moreover, although competitive contracting models advocate very frequent (often annual) rebidding of contracts, too frequent rebidding can have the effect of routinely destabilizing service networks, thereby introducing disincentives for cooperative behaviors because time is insufficient for agencies to expect their investments to be recouped. Crafting new contracting models that temper competition with inducements for peer provider cooperation and network support remains a major new challenge for government contracting agencies.

A third set of new privatization challenges in human services relates to the rapid expansion of for-profit providers in the human service contracting arena. For-profit firms have had longstanding involvements in niche areas such as nursing homes and child care, however, government regulations in many human service areas historically either mandated that only nonprofit entities be eligible to receive government contracts, or stipulated a preference for them (Smith and Lipsky, 1993; Gronbjerg and Smith, 1999). Recent evidence indicates these strictures have given way and that for-profit expansion in the contracted human services is booming (Salamon, 1997; Ryan, 1999; Frumkin and Andre-Clark, 2000). For-profit enterprises are not only expanding in home health care and day care services, but also in child support enforcement, services for at-risk youth, disabilities support services, and other areas

(Ryan, 1999). Recent growth has been markedly dramatic in welfare-to-work related services (such as job readiness and employment training), where large well-capitalized for-profit corporations such as Maximus, Lockheed Martin, and Curtis and Associates have captured a significant share of state and local contracts under welfare reform (Frumkin and Andre-Clarke, 2000; O'Regan and Oster, 2000).

This dramatic rise in contracting with new for-profit human service enterprises is a profound change that raises many difficult questions for government contract managers. What are the consequences for clients of contracting with for-profit enterprise? How can government managers make a considered choice between for-profit and nonprofit human service providers? Some empirical studies find nonprofit human services superior to those provided by for-profits, as measured by client and client families' satisfaction (Weisbrod, 1988 study of nursing homes) or by staffing ratios and professional credentials of front-line staff (Willer, 1988 in day care, as cited in Gormley, 1994; also Mauser, 1998). Other studies directly contradict this view (Herzlinger and Krasker, 1987 in health care) or report mixed results (Heinrich, 2000 in job training).

Although full empirical evidence is sorely lacking, many seasoned scholars assert that nonprofits bring particular strengths to human service arenas: that they are more likely to be effective in assisting severely disadvantaged clients or reaching hard-to-reach populations (such as immigrants or racial minorities) given their traditions of serving those groups (Salamon, 1997); that they are able to bring to the treatment of clients an intimate knowledge of the community in a way that recently arrived for-profits cannot (Sanger, 2000); that they are less prone than for-profits to engage in creaming (i.e., treating only the easiest to treat and/or discouraging use of expensive services out of cost considerations) as a result of a strong peer-reinforced occupational subculture that views such practices with strong disfavor (Frumkin and Andre-Clarke, 2000); that they contribute more extensively to critical civic engagement and social capital development functions (Alexander et al., 1999 ). Others make the case for favoring nonprofits on different grounds. Ryan (1999, p.136), for example, notes reports of for-profit scandals, alleging "Some of the most sensational abuses in recent years [have occurred] in for-profit juvenile detention centers...and at for-profit psychiatric facilities . . ." (For other for-profit scandals see AFL-CIO, 1997.)

In addition, studies by other authors raise some grounded concerns about limited longevity and commitments among newly emerged for-profits seeking contracts. Writing from field observations on contracting under welfare reform, Sanger cautions, "When caseloads decline and clients are scarce, [for-profits] are likely to move on to other human service areas where they can increase their market share, economies [of scale], and profits." In her view, this risks the community's loss of both important "institutional memory" and of built service capacities. Government agencies, then, should also ask in making contract decisions, what the likelihood is that the community will retain these governmental investments and what the consequences are should for-profit providers decide to pack up and move on. (Sanger, 2000; Ryan, 1999).

A final set of challenges noted in recent human service privatization is familiar. Public managers need to devote far more time and attention to contract management efforts. Findings of inadequate staff expertise and insufficient financing of contract management in privatized human services are widespread (GAO, 1997a, 1997b; Auger, 1999; Milward, 1996; Dicke and Ott, 1999; Smith and Smyth, 1996). Moreover, in their recent review of contracted Medicaid services, Johnston and Romzek (1999) conclude that the process of contract management becomes even more complex and difficult as certain conditions apply: as the proportion of private benefits decreases, as outcomes become less tangible, as the time frame needed to effectively gauge outcomes lengthens, as provider supply decreases—all of which apply in most human service areas. With new paradigms of contracting out now encompassing not just direct service provision but program design, eligibility processes, and even management of entire human service networks, it is clear that our contract management practices have failed to keep pace with the growing scale and complexity of contracted human service delivery systems. Contract monitoring in contemporary human services needs both further conceptual attention and greater practical investment.

## 3. Education

There are few analysts who do not now see a crisis in American education, and there is certainly strong evidence that the productivity of this nation's public schools has declined (Poole, 1980). Fitzgerald (1988) notes, for example, that the position of America's students in international comparisons has deteriorated and SAT scores have declined while at the same time expenditures on public education have increased. American students now sit in classrooms with fewer classmates and have access to many more professional specialists in their schools but the quality of student achievement has not improved. Despite the agreement over the existence of a problem, there is no agreement about how to enhance educational productivity. A number of privatization alternatives have been suggested to solve America's educational crisis. These include performance contracts, tuition vouchers, tuition tax credits, and a public sector version of the private market, charter schools.

Performance contracting, an agreement between a contractor and a local school district for instruction of a specified group of students with payment according to achievement as measured on standardized tests, was tried and abandoned in the early 1970s (Bendick, 1984; Hali et al., 1972) but recently implemented in Baltimore, Maryland, and Hartford, Connecticut. Both Baltimore and Hartford contracted with Education Alternatives Incorporated (EAI) to operate schools. From 1992 to 1996 EAI ran nine schools in Baltimore but the contract was terminated when municipal officials determined that EAI was spending more per pupil but student performance was not any better than in comparable schools (Mintrom and Vergari, 1997). In 1994 Hartford and EAI agreed to a five-year contract for the firm to operate all 32 schools in the city district. In January 1996 the newly elected school board terminated the contract after a dispute over finances and union opposition to resource changes. Reportedly the company subsequently decided to avoid "volatile and political" school districts, that is, urban, after this experience (Mintrom and Vergari, 1997).

In 1993 an urban school district (almost certainly Baltimore) contracted with a private company (presumably EAI) to provide remedial instruction in reading and mathematics in six elementary schools; the following year the program was expanded to seven elementary and two middle schools. In a careful and well-designed study Johns Hopkins' researchers MacIver and Stringfield (2000) found positive results on student achievement in math but no impact on reading comprehension. The authors could not determine why students improved in math and whether the result could or could not be replicated in public schools. Thus experience with performance contracting suggests that implementation in the urban context is a difficult task and, to the extent results are measured, little improvement in student achievement can be observed.

More recently, there has been debate over the relative efficiency and effectiveness of public as compared to private schools and arguments have been put forth about the likely effects of tuition vouchers and tuition tax credits to spur competition and increase attendance in nonpublic schools (Lieberman, 1989; Savas, 1987). Unfortunately, empirical data on the issue are overwhelmed by a plethora of conjecture and argument.

Tuition vouchers, advocated in the modern era by Milton Friedman (1962), would provide each student with a specified amount of funds to attend any school of choice, public or private. There is little empirical research on vouchers because the proposal has been implemented only on a very limited basis. An experiment in Alum Rock, California, in the early 1970s, limited to public schools, was terminated in midcourse, too soon to allow the possible positive effects of competition and choice to occur (Hatry, 1983). Vermont has allowed towns to finance students at nonsectarian private schools for decades, but 92% of the state's students attend public schools (Fitzgerald, 1988). And President Ronald Reagan's initiative to establish a voucher program for students eligible for federal compensatory funds in 1983 was not accepted by Congress (Savas, 1987) and a similar plan from George W. Bush was recently killed in Congress. However, two local voucher programs have been implemented in the 1990s.

Milwaukee, Wisconsin, which had perhaps the nation's best-developed school choice plan based on magnet schools in the city and an interdistrict desegregation plan that sent city students to suburban schools, adopted an experimental school choice plan in 1990 allowing a limited number (about 1000) of Milwaukee's children from poor homes with incomes less than 175% of the federal poverty level to attend private as well as public schools. State Representative and former welfare recipient Annette "Polly" Williams introduced the legislation and Republican Governor Tommy Thompson worked to see the bill passed (Percy and Meier, 1996). Vouchers equivalent to the state per student aid to the city schools are provided to these students. Sectarian schools were not allowed to accept these students. Professor John Witte of the LaFollette Institute of Public Affairs at the University of Wisconsin and his colleagues concluded in 1994 that "There is no systematic evidence that choice students do either better or worse than MPS [Milwaukee Public School] students once gender, race, income, grade and prior achievement are controlled" although parental opinion of choice students was quite positive. This report caused a firestorm of academic and political countercharges (Percy and Meier, 1996). Levin (1998, p. 377) has concluded that "Although much has been made of the Milwaukee experiment by both advocates and detractors of vouchers, its potential for providing evidence is far more limited than its use by policy analysts" because of high attrition rates of participants, the small number of participating schools, and missing data problems. The very small mathematics gain made by participants beyond their peers who were not in the program, not matched by any positive results in reading comprehension, may be the result of the higher motivation and educational support of those families who participated in the voucher experiment. After studying data from both Milwaukee and Cleveland, a GAO report in October 2001 (Toppo, 2001) concluded that there was not definitive proof that voucher programs raised test scores.

In Cleveland 1500 students from low-income families were allowed to use their vouchers at participating private, religious, or suburban public schools. Like Milwaukee, Cleveland's program expanded so that 3700 students were involved by 2001. However, in March 2001 the program was declared unconstitutional by the Sixth Circuit U.S. Court of Appeals, and the constitutionality of voucher programs which include sectarian schools remained in question. In June 2002 the U.S. Supreme Court upheld the constitutionality of this program. Although Governor Jeb Bush has pushed for an expanded program, in Florida vouchers are available only to those students in chronically inadequate schools and with disabilities. In 2001 only 50 students were in the "failing school" program. Although there are few examples of publicly supported vouchers, in the last decade many private voucher programs have been established. By the end of 1997, 30 programs modeled after the program begun by J. Patrick Rooney, an Indianapolis insurance executive, were in operation around the nation in cities from New York to San Antonio (Savas, 2000). Rooney's program offered to pay half of 500 students' tuition at any private (including religious) school. These programs are extremely popular with parents but their impact remains unknown. Savas (2000) reports a waiting list of over 40,000 families.

Tuition tax credits to reduce the tax liability of those who send their children to nonpublic schools have also been intensely debated. The likely effects of such credits on educational achievement, racial and class segregation, and common democratic values, however, are problematic, as suggested by James and Levin's (1983) useful collection of papers on this privatization alternative.

The attractiveness of both vouchers and tax credits depends in large part on the assumption that nonpublic schools are more effective than public schools. This assumption is quite questionable. Coleman et al. (1981) found, in a study that has been the focus of much of the past debate about the comparative research on public and private schools, that students who attend public high schools do not achieve as much as those who attend nonpublic, particularly, Catholic, high schools. This analysis of the differences between public and parochial schools in fostering academic achievement, however, has undergone a good deal of scrutiny (Levin, 1987, 1998). Critics point out that controlling for socioeconomic status but not for pre-high school achievement led to the appearance of positive Catholic school effects on cognitive achievement but these were actually a function of the student selection criteria used by Catholic schools (Alexander and Pallas, 1983). Levin argues that even if the differences were real, they are so small that they are of trivial importance (1987).

A related area of controversy is the relative economy of public versus private schools. Levin concludes that the finding that private schools do a better job at a lower cost is the result of faulty accounting. It cannot be assumed that private school tuition equals costs and volunteer labor cannot be ignored in assessing costs (Levin, 1987; James and Levin, 1983). Lieberman (1989), in a volume advocating the privatization of education, argues the opposite, claiming that the true costs of public schools are masked by an accounting system that leaves out capital expenses.

Although some argue that the governance must change in the direction of privatization for public schools to improve, others insist that privatization is not necessary and that restructuring within the public schools is desirable and possible (Sizer, 1984), that instructional technology should be improved to increase educational productivity (Walberg, 1984), and that choice within public school systems may be sufficient (Boyd and Kerchner, 1988). Accounting for only a small percentage (less than one percent) of America's public school students, about 500,000 now attend about 1700 charter schools in 38 states and the District of Columbia (Olatoye, 2000; Hoff, 2001; Center for Education Reform, 2001). Charter schools are intended to increase choice and innovation by remaining free of many state and local district policies and regulations. Charters are a quasi-market alternative that are now receiving much positive publicity but there is certainly no systematic evidence that students achieve more in charter schools than they would have in their assigned public school. Charters may be linked to private sector service provision. The Edison Schools, a private management company founded in 1992 as The Edison Project, has been contracting with charter schools in several states, including Michigan and California and by 2001 had implemented its program in 113 public schools serving over 57,000 students (Mintrom and Vergari, 1997; Edison Schools, 2001). In 2001 Pennsylvania's Governor Tom Ridge asked Edison to analyze the troubled Philadelphia school system, an anticipated first step toward Edison running part or all of one of the nation's largest districts.

Simon (1996), testing the basic assumptions of the market model by assessing whether those communities with more of a marketlike system in education generated a higher student achievement level, found that more children in nonpublic schools did not lead to higher achievement in public schools. Despite the arguments, despite the rhetoric, despite the hype, when all is said and done and analyzed, MacIver and Stringfield's (2000, p. 375) conclusions seem accurate: "there exists little objective research about the effects of different privatization models on student achievement."

## V. CRITERIA FOR EVALUATING PRIVATIZATION ALTERNATIVES

Examination of the studies, claims, and counterclaims across these service areas suggests that broadbrush generalizations about the effect of privatization on productivity will not assist the public manager in determining whether privatization is a feasible alternative when considering how to improve the delivery or lower the cost of a particular type of good or service. Fortunately, a number of analysts have proposed criteria on which to make such a decision about privatization alternatives. Hatry (1983) suggests evaluating alternative approaches to service delivery along the following dimensions: the cost of the government service, the financial cost to citizens, the degree of choices available to service clients, the quality/effectiveness of the service, the potential distributional effects, the staying power and potential for service disruption, the ease of implementation, and overall impact (see also O'Leary, 1996; Allen et al., 1989; Ross, 1988; Marston, 1987; Savas, 1987; Ferris and Graddy, 1986; Meyer and Morgan, 1979; Fisk et al., 1978). Hodge (1999) suggests that a broader view of privatization would include not only economic but also social, democratic, legal, and political "performance" considerations. There are also a number of publications that offer detailed information about how to privatize. Meyer and Morgan (1979), for example, have developed a guide to help municipal administrators make more informed decisions about contracting for municipal services (see also Marston, 1987; Hayes, 1985; Hatry, 1983; Fisk et al., 1978), whereas others advise how to anticipate and respond to public employee concerns (Denhardt et al., 1995).

Our review suggests that there are several principal questions the public manager needs to answer when considering whether to privatize to enhance productivity.

(1) What programmatic activities are the best candidates for privatization? (2) Is there a reasonable amount of evidence that privatization is feasible for the goods or services under consideration? (3) How do the costs of public and private provision of these goods or services compare? (4) How can accountability be ensured?

## A.   Potential for Privatization

A preliminary judgment must be made as to which areas of governmental activity provide the best prospects for achieving productivity gains by shifting to private providers. Here the public manager must turn to the experience of other jurisdictions or agencies and to an assessment of local circumstances. Unfortunately, as we have indicated above, productivity data are insufficient bases from which to draw firm conclusions about the relative merits of public versus private delivery of most government functions. Available evidence certainly does not justify extreme advocacy of privatization, particularly with regard to social programs (Kamerman and Kahn, 1989, p. 261; Johnston and Romzek, 1999, p. 384). As noted above, productivity gains are most likely to be achieved in areas that are "predominantly straightforward, immediate, measurable, amenable to monitoring, and technical in nature–such as refuse collection, data processing, and streetlight maintenance" (Bendick, 1984, p. 107). Yet both ICMA surveys of cities and counties and the Council of State Government's survey of the states (Chi and Jasper, 1998) indicate that although tangibleness and simplicity of output are clearly important variables in predicting contracting out usage, there is a rising volume of contracting out of health and human services.

When considering which programs or activities are the best candidates for privatization, the public manager should identify those that are most amenable to the clear specification of performance standards and goals. For the most part, those that can be subjected to explicit arms-length monitoring and control should be selected. As Bendick (1984, p. 113) points out, entire programs may fall within this category. It is frequently the case, however, that for many areas of governmental activity, only selected aspects of programmatic activities can be readily delegated to private agencies or firms. Furthermore, when distributional goals are important, such as targeting benefits to minority or low-income groups, the prospects for productive privatization diminish because the ability to achieve these goals through contract specification is difficult (Ferris and Graddy, 1986, p. 333). Private firms tend to provide benefits as cheaply as possible, not necessarily in ways that have been politically determined to be socially desirable.

## B.   Feasibility of Privatization

There are legal, marketplace, and political barriers to privatization. Legal barriers can range from minor restrictions to blanket prohibitions. Some states require municipalities to obtain approval before they can contract out services, or certain powers may be vested only in local jurisdictions, such as the right of the police to take a person into custody (Fisk et al., 1978, p. 5). There may also be limits on the application of user fees and vouchers, requirements that any private contractors establish wage rates equivalent to the public sector, or other stipulations that are onerous to private firms or nonprofits.

The absence of an existing alternative to public sector provision is, of course, a second principal limitation. In the case of contracting, if there is an insufficient supply of for-profit or nonprofit agencies with the resources, personnel, facilities, or equipment to supply a type of good or service, then the feasibility of effective privatization is called into question. Louisville, Kentucky, for example, has had to provide special needs adoption services inhouse because of a lack of bidders, despite its preference for contracting (Allen et al., 1989, p. 163). There are ways to change the bidding process, or to break up a service area into its component parts to increase the supply of prospective providers, but in some cases the number of suppliers may still be insufficient to guarantee effective competitive bidding for contracts. Consequently, any savings from contracting out are likely to be reduced (although there may still be other compelling reasons, such as diversity, community knowledge and ties, and deeper expertise, to pursue privately contracted provision anyway).

Privatization must also be politically feasible. Powerful employee organizations may be able to block efforts to privatize by negotiating restrictions into labor contracts or by organizing opposition through media campaigns, public demonstrations, strikes or slowdowns, or pressure on elected officials (Magid, 1990; McNichol, 1990; Savas, 1987, 2000). Constituent organizations may block privatization if some segments of the community fear that services will be diminished or disrupted. For some public goods, the very appearance of buying and selling undermines the claims of the state to be acting impartially on behalf of the entire community (Starr, 1987, p. 133). These include the administration of justice, the exercise of coercive power, and the collection of taxes. But the boundaries of this concern may be changing. For example, many communities are now encouraging and supporting private mediation services. For the most part, however, where life and property are concerned, the public generally prefers "to maintain unambiguous lines of responsibility, and avoid any possible public–private conflict of interest, even at the loss of whatever increased inefficiency and innovations might be attained through privatization" (Sundquist, 1984, p. 310).

## C.  The Cost of Public Versus Private Provision

For the goods or services under consideration, the public manager should make a comparative analysis of the respective costs of public and private provision. On the public side, "real" costs include not simply the costs that appear in published budgets of operating agencies. Real costs also include such things as capital and maintenance expenditures for facilities, vehicles, and equipment, as well as interest on capital expenditures; supplies and labor that may be currently incorporated as part of the budgets of supporting agencies; future capital needs; fringe benefits (including pensions); training costs; and overhead costs of executive and staff agencies (Savas, 1987, p. 259; Fisk et al., 1978, p. 101).

With respect to the private provision alternative, there are a number of costs that must be considered in addition to anticipated direct payments for services (including overhead, fees, or profit). Noteworthy here are legal costs to government in preparation of contracts, and administrative costs in conducting the bidding process, evaluating bids, and awarding contracts. There are also costs associated with developing inhouse capability to monitor contracts that need to be included and which, according to Savas (1987, p. 260), typically range from two to seven percent of contract cost. The costs of resuming the service if privatization does not work or the private agency withdraws, of termination pay and finding alternative jobs for displaced employees, and other associated expenses must also be considered. Many of these factors can be easily overlooked when conducting cost comparisons and lead public managers to inappropriately favor private delivery, much as overlooking public costs "hidden" in various agency budgets can stack judgments in favor of government provision. Despite assertions by privatization advocates, there are many reasons to be cautious about automatically concluding that privatizing will save dollars and enhance productivity and performance. Not only are there many financial costs in making the transition to and regulating private delivery which may be unanticipated, but there is also the larger and more important question of whether the quality of the service or function will be sustained. Furthermore, as indicated above, there may be difficult legal, political, and distributional considerations to be factored in.

On the other hand, a rigorous comparison of the advantages and disadvantages of public versus contracted provision can reveal situations in which resources are being allocated inefficiently or management is inadequate. Periodic reviews of the efficiency and quality of government services can have a beneficial effect on service delivery, particularly when a wide range of alternatives to existing arrangements is considered. Hatry (1983, p. 96) reminds us that when the current delivery system is found to be inefficient or ineffective, public agencies should first be given an opportunity to improve before the risks and uncertainties of a new delivery system are too quickly assumed to be the resolution.

## D.  Managing Privatization

The literature on how to manage contracts and public–private arrangements is a growing one. A number of summaries of this literature point the governmental manager toward successful contract administration. O'Leary (1996, p. 271), for example, summarizes the literature in ten macro and six micro lessons in managing contracts and grants. Her lessons include, "move incrementally in hiring contractors and selecting grantees" but "move quickly (but within the boundaries of due process) when waste, fraud, and abuse are suspected." For a systematic overview of contract management issues it is helpful to view the contracting process as a series of questions to be addressed.

The government policy maker or manager faces many choices and decisions in the contracting process. Under what circumstances should the contract be made with a for-profit or nonprofit agency (Gormley, 1994)? In social or educational services, where the "difficult to treat" client might be threatened by the potential for for-profit agency creaming, or where minority or low-income constituencies suggest an important "value-added" element to a provider's community knowledge and roots, non-profits may prove better contract targets (Sanger, 2000; Salamon, 1997). Should the contract be performance-based or process-oriented? As a general rule, it is not easy to specify service outcomes that a contractor should achieve and to assess the quality of delivered services, even for simple services such as cleaning (Walsh, 1995). The more difficult the specification of desired service outcomes and the more problematic accurate measurement of those outcomes in the short term, the further away from any performance-based contract system one should lean (Johnston and Romzek, 1999). Behn and Kant (1999, p. 479) offer up some helpful hints on the use of performance-based contracts, urging contracting officials to clearly "Understand the difference and relationship between the mission and the measures." Should the contract be punishment-grounded or use a cooperative contractual approach? Cooperative contracts must be based on trust and are more reliable "when there is continuity in client and contractor interaction" (Walsh, 1995, p. 114), when there is ongoing mutual government–provider investment in cross-sector partnership arrangements (DeHoog, 1996; Smith and Smyth, 1996), or where such contracts are compelled by difficulties in checking contractor performance.

What type of contract should be negotiated: block, cost and volume, or case contracts? As Walsh explains, England's government has defined these three distinct models. Block contracts are "agreements to provide a given range of services for a stated cost with very little clarity on service quality." Volume contracts state the costs for units of service and specify the frequency of provision allowed. Finally, contracts can be written on an open-ended cost-per-case basis where no particular number of cases is specified. Should the contract be cost-plus or fixed price? Fixed price contracts have an advantage of predictability, but the concern is that fixed price contracts may lead to quality reductions, as in the case of patients being discharged from hospitals too soon in the 24-hour baby delivery controversies.

How complex should contracts be? Walsh warns that contracts which are multistage and multiparty can lead to multiheadaches for contract managers (Walsh, 1995). How short or long term a contract should be used? The answer is, "It depends." The types of discrete, physical, or ancillary services that are the focal point of the work of Savas and others are appropriate for the kind of frequent annual rebidding they recommend to keep contractors "on their toes" (Savas, 1987, 2000). Yet in cases where the "network of services" government seeks to make available has importance beyond the import of any single service offering (as in the human services), substantially lengthened contract periods (biannual or multiyear contracts) are needed to induce contract providers to "invest" in collaborative behaviors that support the network as a common enterprise (Milward and Provan, 1998; De Hoog, 1996).

Finally, how can governments ensure adequate contract monitoring and accountability? Johnston and Romzek (1999) caution to expect greatly expanded contract monitoring complexity where the contracted service has less individualized private benefits and more collective social benefits; where service outcomes are less tangible, more difficult to measure, and have a longer time horizon to show service impacts; and where provider supply is limited. Auger (1999) urges critical financial investment in contract management capacities commensurate with the new burdens contracting strategies impose. And Walsh highlights the value of three distinct approaches to contract management and oversight functions: using mechanisms such as performance bonds or quality assurance systems, selecting contractors with the "appropriate" (i.e., consonant) service values (a major reason for the use of nonprofits in social services), and subjecting contract failure to sanctions such as default notices and payment delays or even termination. The key problem here may be that the more severe the penalty, the less attractive this action is to government (Will it find another contractor? What will the press report? What will the political fallout be?). Thus "relatively few contracts have been terminated because of failure of the contractor" (Walsh, 1995, p. 129).

A major current thrust of the recent research on contract administration is a questioning of the utility of the classical model of market competition. Beinecke and DeFillippi (1999, 491) argue that "contracting may be conceptualized as a continuum from the classical contract to a relationship agreement." In classical contracting the service is simple, the contract short-term, contractor options plentiful, and the contract easily moved to an alternative supplier in competitive bidding based on price. But the reality is often quite different: the services are complex, few or no alternative suppliers are available, the contract cannot be kept simple, and both government and the contractor must deal with changing circumstances and uncertainty. Despite an impetus for detailed attention to contract planning and specification, Walsh concludes, "Contracts are never complete" (1995, 130). Sooner or later, government and contractors have to work out new arrangements and details and ultimately trust will play a role in this process. Thus Dicke and Ott (1999) discuss the idea of a "treaty" approach to contracting, certainly a different approach than one based on classic market conceptions. And Behn and Kant (1999) conclude, "Be prepared to learn, change, improve, and learn some more as you work collaboratively—not adversarially—with contractors."

## VI. CONCLUSIONS

The shift from public to private provision of a service is no panacea for public managers seeking greater productivity and performance. Our review of current privatization research and thought indicates that private provision of services may well result in economy (i.e., saving money), but the achievement of genuine productivity (i.e., enhanced efficiency and effectiveness) is more problematic. The best opportunity for improving productivity with privatization occurs where the service is easily measured and monitored (as in refuse collection or ancillary support services), but the jury is either hung or still out where the situation is more complex, as in human services and education.

Yet the contemporary realities are such that privatized strategies that blend service implementation arrangements across sectors are likely to continue regardless of the jury's current verdict. So ubiquitous is the impetus for privatization that it has led to calls for public managers to think in terms of specialities in intersectoral administration, raising the question of whether privatization isn't more properly subsumed within a broader conceptualization of governance arrangements (Henry, 2002). Still, there is much the public manager can learn from the existing literature and debate over privatization. Approaches used by private and nonprofit organizations being considered as alternatives to government agencies may be useful in informing and reforming the work of the public sector. The use of choice and competition (e.g., within public education), and attention to measuring services quantitatively (e.g., in solid-waste collection), may be adopted within an environment of public service provision. In addition, private sector alternatives may be attractive in instances where government is considering expanding a service or adding a new function, particularly in those areas where inhouse capacity has not been developed or cannot currently be afforded. When contracting is the preferred service delivery alternative, adequate attention must be paid to the need for informed and skillful contract administration.

Sophisticated public managers hoping to increase productivity need to consider privatization alternatives in the context of their jurisdiction's current circumstances, the potential for, the feasibility of, and the costs and risks inherent in privatization. But they should also be aware that when it comes to privatization and contracting, the devil is in the details. Given the complexity of accumulated research, broad generalizations about privatization and contracting should be viewed skeptically—except for this one, of course.

## ACKNOWLEDGMENT

The authors thank Tim Barnekov for his contributions to the original chapter on privatization authored with Jeff Raffel, which served as the foundation for this work. His research, insights, and writing provided a superb basis for this updated chapter.

## REFERENCES

AFL-CIO (1997). *Contracting Human Services: Recurring Scandals and Malperformance.* Washington, DC: AFL-CIO.

Alexander, J., Nank, R., Stivers, C. (1999). Implications of welfare reform: Do nonprofit survival strategies threaten civil society. *Nonprofit Voluntary Sector Quart.* 28(4):452–475.

Alexander, K. L., Pallas, A. M. (1983). Private schools and public policy: New evidence on cognitive achievement in public and private schools. *Sociol. Educ.* 56:170–182.

Allen, J. W., Chi, K. S., Devlin, K. A., Fall, M., Hatry, H. P., Masterman, W. (1989). *The Private Sector in State Service Delivery: Examples of Innovative Practices.* Washington, DC: Urban Institute.

Ammons, D. N., Hill, D. J. (1995). The viability of public-private competition as a long-term service delivery strategy. *Public Product. Manage. Rev.* 19(1):12–24.

Auger, D. A. (1997). The nonprofit-government relationship in an era of devolution: Emerging perspectives on the states. In: Proceedings of the Annual Meeting of the American Political Science Association, Boston, September 2–6.

Auger, D. A. (1999). Privatization, contracting, and the states: Lessons from state government experience. *Public Product. Manage. Rev.* 22(4):435–454.

Austin, J. (2001). *Emerging Issues on Privatized Prisons.* Washington, DC: U.S. Department of Justice, Office of Justice Programs.

Bailey, R. W. (1987). Uses and misuses of privatization. In: Hanke, S. H., ed. *Prospects for Privatization.* New York: Academy of Political Science. pp.435–454.

Bailis, L. N. (1984). *Comparative analysis of the delivery of human services in the public and private sectors.* (Manuscript). Waltham, MA: Heller Graduate School, Brandeis University.

Becker, F. W., Silverstein, G., Chaykin, L. (1995). Public employee job security and benefits: A barrier to privatization of mental health services. *Public Product. Manage. Rev.* 19(1):25–33.

Behn, R. D., Kant, P. A. (1999). Strategies for avoiding the pitfalls of performance contracting. In: Raffel, J. A., Auger, D. A., Denhardt, K. G., eds. Privatization and contracting: Managing for state and local productivity. *Public Product. Manage. Rev.* 22(4): 470–489.

Beinecke, R. H., DeFillippi, R. (1999). The value of the relationship model of contracting in social service reprocurements and transitions: lessons from Massachusetts. In: Raffel, J. A., Auger, D. A., Denhardt, K. G., eds. Privatization and Contracting: Managing for State and Local Productivity. *Public Product. Manage. Rev.* 22(4):430–501.

Bendick, M. Jr. (1984). Privatization of public services: Recent experience. In: Brooks, H., Liebman, L., Schelling, C. S., eds. *Public private partnership: New opportunities for meeting social needs.* Cambridge, MA: Ballinger, pp. 153–171.

Bielefeld, W., Scotch, R. K., Thieleman, G. S. (1995). National mandate and local nonprofits: Shaping a local delivery system of HIV/AIDS services. *Policy Stud. Rev.* 14(1/2):127–137.

Boorsma, P. B., De Vries, P. (1995). The drive for public productivity: The Dutch experience, 1980–1993. *Public Product. Manage. Rev.* 19(1):34–45.

Boyd, W. L., Kerchner, C. T. (1988). *The Politics of Excellence and Choice in Education.* New York: Falmer.

Brody, M. (1989, November 27). Buy the Brooklyn Bridge: Privatized toll roads will profit from financial gridlock. *Barrons*, pp. 11.

Brudney, J. (1996). Designing and implementing volunteer programs. In: Kettl, D. F., Milward, H. B., eds. *The State of Public Management*. Baltimore: Johns Hopkins University Press, pp. 193–212.

Butler, S. M. (1985). *Privatizing Federal Spending: A Strategy to Eliminate the Deficit*. New York: Universe.

Center for Education Reform. (2001). Available at http://edreform.com/charter-schools/law/ranking-2001.htm.

Chi, K., Jasper, C. (1998). *Privatization Practices: A review of Privatization in State Government*. Lexington, KY: Council of State Governments.

Cigler, B. A. (1988–1989). Review of E. S. Savas. *Privatization in Policy Stud. J.* 17(2):458–460.

Coleman, J., Hoffer, T., Kilgore, S. (1981). *Public and Private Schools*. Chicago: National Opinion Research Center.

David, J., Ossowski, R., Richardson, T., Barnett, S. (2000). *Fiscal and Macroeconomic Impact of Privatization*. Washington, DC: International Monetary Fund.

DeHoog, R. H. (1984). *Contracting Out for Human Services: Economic, Political and Organizational Perspectives*. Albany: State University of New York Press.

DeHoog, R. H. (1996). Contracting for social services: What we have learned and an Rx for the future. *J. Health Hum. Serv. Admin.* 19(1):13–25.

DeLeon, L. (1996). Ethics and entrepreneurship. *Policy Stud. J.* 24(3):495–510.

Denhardt, K., Raffel, J., Auger, D., Jacobson, E., Lewis, J. (1995). Employee issues in privatization. *Manage. Inf. Serv. Rep.* 27(10). Washington, DC: International City/County Management Association.

Denhardt, R. B., Denhardt, J. V. (2000). The new public service: Serving rather than steering. *Public Admin. Rev.* 60(6):549–559.

DeVita, C. J., Twombly, E. (1999). Nonprofit organizations in an era of welfare reform. In: Boris, E. T., Steuerle, C. E., eds. *Devolution and Government Retrenchment*. Washington, DC: Urban Institute, pp. 213–234.

Dicke, L. A., Ott, J. S. (1999). Public agency accountability in human services contracting. *Public Product. and Manage. Rev.* 22(4):502–516.

Dilger, R. J., Moffett, R. R., Struyk, L. (1997). Privatization of municipal services in America's largest cities. *Public Admin. Rev.* 57(1):21–26.

Donahue, J. D. (1989). *The Privatization Decision: Public Ends. Private Means*. New York: Basic.

Edison Schools. (2001). Available at http://www.edisonschools.com/home/home.cfm.

Eggers, W. D., O'Leary, J. (1995). *Revolution at the Roots: Making our Government Smaller, Better, and Closer to Home*. New York: Free Press.

Farazmand, A. (2001). *Privatization or Public Enterprise Reform? International Case Studies with Implications for Public Management*. Westport, CT: Greenwood.

Fernandez, S., Fabricant, R. (2000). Methodological pitfalls in privatization research: Two cases from Florida's child support enforcement program. *Public Perform. Manage. Rev.* 24(2):133–144.

Ferris, J., Graddy, E. (1986). Contracting out: For what? With whom? *Public Admin. Rev.* 46(4):332–344.

Fisk, D., Kiesling, H., Muller, T. (1978). *Private Provision of Public Services: An Overview*. Washington, DC: Urban Institute.

Fitzgerald, R. (1988). *When Government Goes Private: Successful Alternatives to Public Service*. New York: Universe.

Fixler, P. E. Jr, Hayes, E. C. (1989). Contracting out for local services. In: Hayes, E. C., ed. *The Hidden Wealth of Cities: Policy and Productivity Methods for American Local Government*. Greenwich, CT: JAI, pp. 71–109.

Friedman, M. (1962). *Capitalism and Freedom*. Chicago: University of Chicago Press.

Frumkin, P., Andre-Clark, A. (2000). When missions, markets, and politics collide: Values and strategy in the nonprofit human services. *Nonprofit Voluntary Sector Quart.* 29:141–163. Supplement.

GAO. U.S. General Accounting Office. (1996a). *Child Support Enforcement: States' Experience with Private Agencies' Collection of Support Payment.* Washington, DC: (GAO/HEHS-97-11).

GAO. U.S. General Accounting Office. (1996b). *Child Support Enforcement: Early Results on Comparability of Privatized and Public Offices.* Washington, DC: (GAO/HEHS-97-4).

GAO. U.S. General Accounting Office. (1997a). *Social Service Privatization: Expansion Poses Challenges in Ensuring Accountability for Program Results.* Washington, DC: (GAO/HEHS-98-6).

GAO. U.S. General Accounting Office. (1997b). *Child Support Enforcement Privatization: Challenges in Ensuring Accountability for Program Results.* Washington, DC: (GAO/T-HEHS-98-22).

Gibelman, M. (1996). Contracting for social services: Boon or bust for the voluntary sector? *J. Health Hum. Serv. Admin.* 19(1):26–41.

Goodsell, C. T. (1985). *The Case for Bureaucracy: A Public Administration Polemic.* Chatham, NJ: Chatham House.

Gormley, W. T. Jr. (1994). Privatization revisited. *Policy Stud. Rev.* 13(3/4):215–234.

Greene, J. D. (1996). How much privatization? A research note examining the use of privatization by cities in 1982 and 1992. *Policy Stud. J.* 24(4):632–640.

Greene, J. D. (2002). *Cities and Privatization: Prospects for the New Century.* Upper Saddle River, NJ: Prentice-Hall.

Gronbjerg, K. A., Smith, S. R. (1999). Nonprofit organizations and public policies in the delivery of human services. In: Clotfelter, C. T., Ehrlich, T., eds. *Philanthropy and the Nonprofit Sector in a Changing America.* Bloomington: Indiana University Press, pp. 139–171.

Gurin, A. (1989). Governmental responsibility and privatization: Examples from four social services. In: Kamerman, S. B., Kahn, A. J., eds. *Privatization and the Welfare State.* Princeton, NJ: Princeton University Press, pp. 179–205.

Hakim, S., Seidenstadt, P., Bowman, G. W. (1996). *Privatizing Transportation Systems.* Westport, CT: Praeger.

Halachmi, A. (1996). Franchising in government: Can a principal-agent perspective be the first step toward the development of a theory? *Policy Stud. J.* 24(3):478–494.

Hali, G. R., Carpenter, P., Haggart, S. A., Rapp, M. C., Sumner, G. C. (1972). *A Guide to Educational Performance Contracting.* Santa Monica, CA: Rand Corporation.

Hanke, S. H. (1987). *Prospects for Privatization.* New York: Academy of Political Science.

Hatry, H. P. (1983). *A Review of Private Approaches for Delivery of Public Services.* Washington, DC: Urban Institute.

Hayes, E. C. (1985). Contracting for beginners. *Urban Resources* 2(4):44–46.

Heinrich, C. J. (2000). Organizational form and performance: An empirical investigation of nonprofit and for-profit job-training service providers. *J. Policy Anal. Manage.* 19(2):233–262.

Henry, N. (2002). Is privatization passé? The case for competition and the emergence of intersectoral administration. *Public Admin. Rev.* 62(3):374–378.

Herzlinger, R. E., Krasker, W. S. (1987). Who profits from nonprofits? *Harvard Bus. Rev.* 65:93–106.

Hirsch, W. Z. (1995). Contracting out by urban governments: A review. *Urban Affairs Rev.* 30(3):458–472.

Hodge, G. A. (1999). Competitive tendering and contracting out: Rhetoric or reality? In: Raffel, J. A., Auger, D. A., Denhardt, K. G., eds. Privatization and contracting: Managing for state and local productivity. *Public Product. Manage. Rev.* 22(4):455–469.

Hodge, G. A. (2000). *Privatization: An international review of performance.* Boulder, CO: Westview.

Hoff, D. J. (2001). School choice programs growing more rapidly outside the U.S. *Educ. Week* 20(41):5.

Honadle, B. W. (1984). Alternative service delivery strategies and improvement of local government productivity. *Public Product. Rev.* 8(4):301–313.

International City Management Association. (1982). Alternative approaches for delivering public services. *Urban Data Serv. Rep.* 14(5).

James, T., Levin, H. M. (1983). *Public Dollars for Private Schools: The Case of Tuition Tax Credits.* Philadelphia: Temple University Press.

Johnston, J. M., Romzek, B. S. (1999). Contracting and accountability in state Medicaid reform: Rhetoric, theories, and reality. *Public Admin. Rev.* 59(5):383–412.

Kamerman, S. B., Kahn, A. J. (1989). Childcare and privatization under Reagan. In: Kamerman, S. B., Kahn, A. J., eds. *Privatization and the Welfare State.* Princeton, NJ: Princeton University Press.

Kettl, D. (1993). *Sharing power: Public governance and private markets.* Washington, DC: Brookings Institution.

Kohn, A. (1986). *No Contest: The Case Against Competition.* Boston: Houghton Mifflin.

Kolderie, T. (1986). The two different concepts of privatization. *Public Admin. Rev.* 46(4):285–291.

Levin, H. (1987). Education as a public and private good. *J. Policy Anal. Manage.* 6(4):628–641.

Levin, H. M. (1998). Educational vouchers: Effectiveness, choice, and costs. *J. Policy Anal. Manage.* 17(3):373–392.

Lieberman, M. (1989). *Privatization and Educational Choice.* New York: St. Martin's.

Linneman, P. D., Megbolugbe, I. F. (1994). Privatisation and housing policy. *Urban Stud.* 31(4–5):635–652.

Logie, D. E., Woodroffe, J. (1993). Structural adjustment: The wrong prescription for Africa? *British Med. J.* 307(6895):41–44.

MacIver, M. A., Stringfield, S. (2000). Privatized delivery of instructional services for urban public school students placed at risk. *Educ. Eval. Policy Anal.* 22(4):375–382.

Magid, M. (1990). Cottage cheese or chicken? An AFSCME fight for public food service. *Labor Res. Rev.* 9(l):53–59.

Mann, E., Gibelman, M. (1996). Symposium: Contracting out for human services introduction. *J. Health and Hum. Serv. Admin.* 19(1):3–12.

Marston, L. (1987). Preparing for privatization: A decision-maker's checklist. In: Hanke SH, ed. *Privatization and Development.* San Francisco: Institute for Contemporary Studies, pp. 67–76.

Mauser, E. (1998). The importance of organized form: Parent perception vs. reality in the day care industry. In: Clemens, W. W., Powell, E., eds. *Private Action and the Public Good.* New Haven, CT: Yale University Press, pp. 124–136.

McNichol, L. (1990). Fighting on many fronts: SEIU in Los Angeles. *Labor Res. Rev.* 9(l):53–59.

Meyer, M. E., Morgan, D. R. (1979). *Contracting for Municipal Services: A Handbook for Local Officials.* Norman, OK: Bureau of Government Research.

Milward, H. B. (1996). Conclusion: What is public management. In: Kettl, D. F., Milward, B., eds. *The State of Public Management.* Baltimore: Johns Hopkins University Press, pp. 307–312.

Milward, H. B. (2000). Governing the hollow state. *J. Public Admin. Res. Theor.* 10(2):359–380.

Milward, H. B., Provan K. G. (1998). Governing service provider networks. In: Proceedings of Association of Public Policy Analysis and Management, New York, October 28–31.

Mintrom, M., Vergari, S. (1997). Education reform and accountability issues in an intergovernmental context. *Publius* 27(2):143–166.

Mordock, J. (1999). Current practices in public child welfare. In: Wernet, S. P., ed. *Managed Care in Human Services*. Chicago: Lyceum, pp. 53–70.

Morgan, P. (1995). *Privatization and the Welfare State: Implications for Consumers and the Workforce*. Aldershot, UK: Dartmouth Publishing.

Nathan, R. P. (1997). *The Newest New Federalism for Welfare: Where Are We Now and Where Are We Headed*. Albany, NY: Rockefeller Institute of Government.

Nordin, J. (2001). Chronicle, description, and remedy. *Public Perform. Manage. Rev.* 24(3): 301–304.

Olatoye, O. (2000). School choice and equality: An interview with Joseph Viteritti, research professor. *Wagner Rev.* 136–140.

O'Leary, R. Managing contracts and grants. In: Perry, J. L., ed. *Handbook of Public Administration*. 2nd ed. San Francisco: Jossey Bass, pp. 236–275.

O'Regan, K. M., Oster, S. M. (2000). Nonprofit and for-profit partnerships: Rationale and challenges of cross-sector contracting. *Nonprofit Voluntary Sector Quart.* 29:120–140. Supplement.

O'Toole, L. (1997). Treating networks seriously: Practical and research based agendas in public administration. *Public Admin. Rev.* 57(1):45–52.

Overman, E. S. (1995). Privatization in China, Mexico, and Russia: a comparative study. *Public Product. Manage. Rev.* 19(1):46–59.

Pack, J. R. (1987). Privatization of public sector services in theory and practice. *J. Policy Anal. Manage.* 6(4):523–540.

Percy, S. L., Maier, P. (1996). School choice in Milwaukee: Privatization of a different breed. *Policy Stud. J.* 24(4):649–665.

Peters, B. G. (1996). *The Future of Governing: Four Emerging Models*. Lawrence, KS: University Press of Kansas.

Poole, R. W. Jr. (1980). *Cutting Back City Hall*. New York: Universe.

Raffel, J. A., Auger, D. A., Denhardt, K. G. (1999). Privatization and contracting: Managing for state and local productivity. *Public Product. Manage. Rev.* 22(4):430–434.

Rein, M. (1989). Social structure of institutions. In: Kamerman, S. B., Kahn, A. J., eds. *Privatization and the Welfare State*. Princeton, NJ: Princeton University Press, pp. 63–65.

Ross, R. L. (1988). *Government and the Private Sector: Who Should Do What?* New York: Crane Russak.

Ryan, W. P. (January–February 1999). The new landscape for nonprofits. *Harvard Bus. Rev.* 77(1):128–136.

Salamon, L. M. (1995). *Partners in Public Service: Government-Nonprofit Relations in the Modern Welfare State*. Baltimore, MD: Johns Hopkins University Press.

Salamon, L. M. (1997). *Holding the Center: America's Nonprofit Sector at a Crossroads*. New York: Nathan Cummings Foundation.

Salamon, L. M., Abramson, A. J. (1982). *The Federal Budget and the Nonprofit Sector*. Washington, DC: Urban Institute.

Sanger, M. B. (2000). When the private sector competes: Lessons from welfare reform. Proceedings of the Annual Conference of the Association for Public Policy Analysis and Management, Seattle, WA, November 1–4.

Savas, E. S. (1987). *Privatization: The Key to Better Government*. Chatham, NJ: Chatham House.

Savas, E. S. (2000). *Privatization and Public–Private Partnerships*. New York: Chatham House.

Seidenstadt, P. (1996). Privatization: Trends, interplay of forces, and lessons learned. *Policy Stud. J.* 24(3):464–477.

Shaw, E. P. (1999). *New Trends in Public Sector Management in Health: Applications in Developed and Developing Countries*. Washington, DC: World Bank Institute.

Shetterly, D. R. (2000). The influence of contract design on contractor performance: The case of residential refuse collection. *Public Product. Manage. Rev.* 24(1):53–68.

Siegel, G. B. (1999). Where are we on local government service contracting? *Public Product. Manage. Rev.* 22(3):365–388.

Simon, C. A. (1996). Private school enrollment and public school performance: Assessing the effects of competition upon public school student achievement in Washington State. *Policy Stud. J.* 24(4):666–675.

Sizer, T. (1984). *Horace's Compromise: The Dilemma of the American High School.* Boston: Houghton Mifflin.

Smith, S. R. (2003). Social Services. In: Salamon, L. M., ed. *The Resilient Sector: The State of Nonprofit America.* Washington, D.C.: The Brookings Institution.

Smith, S. R., Lipsky, M. (1993). *Nonprofits for Hire: The Welfare State in the Age of Contracting.* Cambridge, MA: Harvard University Press.

Smith, S. R., Smyth, J. (1996). Contracting for services in a decentralized system. *J. Public Admin. Res. Theor.* 6(2):277–296.

Starr, P. (1987). The limits of privatization. In: Hanke, S. H., ed. *Prospects for Privatization.* New York: Academy of Political Science, pp. 277–296.

Steurele, C. E., Ooms, B. D., Peterson, G., Reischauer, R., eds. *Vouchers and the Provision of Public Services.* Washington, DC: Urban Institute.

Sundquist, J. L. (1984). Privatization: No panacea for what ails government. In: Brooks, H., Liebman, C., Schelling, S., eds. *Public Private Partnership: New Opportunities for Meeting Social Needs.* Cambridge, MA: Ballinger, pp. 303–318.

Toppo, G. (2001, October 2, A5). GAO seeks more study of vouchers. *Wilmington News Journal.*

Twombly, E. C. (2000). Assessing the adaptive responses of human service nonprofits in devolving social service systems. Proceedings of the Annual Conference of the Association for Public Policy Analysis and Management, Seattle, WA, November 1–4.

Walberg, H. (1984). Improving the productivity of American schools. *Educ. Leadership* 41(8):19–30.

Walsh, K. (1995). *Public Services and Market Mechanisms: Competition, Contracting and the New Public Management.* Houndmills, UK: Macmillan Press.

Warner, M., Hebdon, R. (2001). Local government restructuring: Privatization and its alternatives. *J. Policy Anal. Manage.* 20(2):315–336.

Weisbrod, B. (1988). *The Nonprofit Economy.* Cambridge, MA: Harvard University Press.

Weitzman, M. S., Jalandoni, N. T., Lampkin, L. M., Pollak, T. H. (2002). *The New Nonprofit Almanac and Desk Reference.* Washington, DC: Urban Institute and Independent Sector.

Wernet, S. P. (1999). An introduction to managed care in human services. In: Wernet, S. P., ed. *Managed Care in Human Services.* Chicago: Lyceum, pp. 1–22.

# 8

## Productivity Barriers in the Public Sector

**DAVID N. AMMONS**
*University of North Carolina, Chapel Hill, North Carolina, U.S.A.*

## I. INTRODUCTION

Capable managers of productive organizations are adept at finding ways to overcome barriers to productivity. No successful manager has been spared this challenge, because no organization is immune to such obstacles. Appearing in various forms and combinations, they threaten the efficiency and effectiveness of operations. Managers who lead productive units have found ways to outmaneuver, neutralize, or eliminate the obstacles that would otherwise thwart the organization's accomplishments.

All barriers to productivity improvement are not equal. By the same token, neither are all administrators. Some officials are simply more adept than others at identifying and sizing up potential obstacles, developing effective strategies to overcome, avoid, or otherwise cope with those obstacles, and building a record of successes in organizational innovation and productivity improvement.

Public and private sector executives face many similar impediments to organizational change, but some obstacles that are common in one sector are rare, nonexistent, or at least different in the other. In this chapter, attention is directed to a variety of hurdles that restrict the ability of public sector managers to improve the productivity of their organizations (see Ammons, 1992 for an earlier version of this discussion). Presented here is an extensive, but not exhaustive, list of productivity barriers. No effort is made to recite general impediments that recognize sector boundaries only faintly, if at all (e.g., broad accusations of poor management, insufficient basic skills, apathy, and shoddy workmanship are criticisms over which neither the public sector nor the private sector holds a monopoly).

**Table 1**   Common Barriers to Productivity Improvement in the Public Sector

*Environmental barriers*[a]
    Absence of market pressures
    Political factors that influence decision making
    Public's lack of patience with operational changes
    Lack of enthusiasm for gradual gains
    Dominant preference for the status quo
    Productivity's lack of political appeal
    Short time horizon of politicians and top administrators
    Subordination of efficiency to secondary status
    Limited options for achieving economies of scale
    Procurement and personnel procedures
    Legal restrictions and court rulings
    Anti-innovation and anti-productivity effects of some grants and other intergovernmental
        programs
    Intergovernmental mandating of expenditures
*Organizational barriers*[b]
    Bureaucratic socialization process
    Lack of accountability
    Focus on output rather than outcomes
    Perverse reward system
    "Spend it or lose it" budget rules
    Inadequate management commitment to productivity
    Barriers to monetary incentive plans
    Union resistance
    Perceived threat to job security
    Excessive layers of middle management
    Supervisory resistance
    Ambiguous objectives
    Reluctance to abandon
    Insufficient analytic skills or analytic staffing
    Inadequate cost-accounting systems
    Inadequate performance data within/across jurisdictions
    Inadequate performance evaluation/appraisal
    Inadequate dissemination of program information and reluctance to use what is known
    Fragmentation of government
    Bureaucratic rigidities, including an extreme focus on rules and procedures
    Fragmented authority or uncertainty about where decisions can be made
    Turf-protecting tactics
    Inadequate research, development, and experimentation
    Requirement of large initial investment for productivity improvement efforts
    Performance myths
    Overselling productivity
*Personal Barriers*[c]
    Inadequate control of time/workday
    Conceptual confusion
    Risk avoidance
    Proclivity to "paralysis by analysis"
    Managerial alibis

[a] Barriers common to virtually all public sector operations (i.e., obstacles that are part of the public sector environment).
[b] Barriers found at varying degrees in many public sector organizations (i.e., obstacles whose presence and magnitude are likely to vary from one organization to another).
[c] Barriers that stem from the traits, attitudes, and behavior of individuals.

Common barriers to productivity improvement in the public sector are grouped into three clusters (Table 1), more for the sake of convenience of presentation than as an ideal typology:

Environmental barriers, including factors that most clearly distinguish the public sector environment from that of the private sector and confound productivity initiatives;

Organizational barriers, including common characteristics found at varying degrees in public sector organizations; and

Personal barriers, including individual traits, attitudes, and behavior that may influence an administrator's inclination and ability to tackle productivity improvement opportunities.

None of the three clusters is inviolate. It would be easy to argue that several of the barriers belong in a different cluster than the one in which they are placed. More than a few barriers, in fact, could qualify for two or for all three clusters.

## II. ENVIRONMENTAL BARRIERS

The public sector environment is in many ways less conducive to productivity improvement than is the private sector environment. Many candidates for public office pledge to run government like a business, but when elected most discover inhibiting factors that are far from inconsequential.

### A. Absence of Market Pressures

Public sector agencies are rarely pushed by the competition to be more innovative or productive. Instead, they operate as "unregulated monopolies" and, not surprisingly, tend to behave accordingly (Osborne and Plastrik, 2000, p. 157; Savas, 2000, p. 31, 1987, p. 97; Harlow, 1977, p. 334; Niskanen, 1971; Downs, 1967; Tullock, 1965). In a competitive market environment, innovative, cost-conscious businesses that produce goods or services desired by their clientele are rewarded, whereas noninnovative, wasteful, unresponsive businesses are punished with declining market shares and perhaps even bankruptcy. In the absence of such pressures, organizations operating with the luxury of monopoly status—a status enjoyed by some private sector and the vast majority of public sector organizations—can become complacent and unresponsive.

### B. Political Factors That Influence Decision Making

Government is not a business. Public sector decisions are rarely guided by concern for financial profit. The "bottom line" on issues in government may refer less often to a financial balance sheet than to a quick box score on winners and losers in the competition for public programs, or to the likely impact of a decision at the polls, either public opinion or electoral. Recommendations that make good business sense, such as suspending operations that drain agency resources while providing benefits to a very limited clientele, may be rejected for political reasons. As noted by Osborne and Plastrik (2000, p. 39), political biases, personal whims, and the legislative process can turn "even well-thought-out strategies into sausage."

The success of the governing body is not measured by return on investment or shareholder dividends. Instead, a successful governing body is known collectively for its leadership and the favorable public opinion it enjoys and, individually, for the reelection prospects of its members and their potential for higher office. For that reason, public decisions often are governed less by productivity considerations than by political factors.

## C. The Public's Lack of Patience with Operational Changes; Lack of Enthusiasm for Gradual Gains

Effective productivity improvement initiatives often require new strategies or patterns of operation producing net benefits over a multiyear period. Rarely are substantial gains immediate or individualized. Benefits, perhaps in the form of cost savings for a given service, typically are modest at the outset, as conversion or startup expenses for a new system or procedure are absorbed and broadly diffused among the taxpayers. In contrast, program changes often seem disruptive and threatening to citizens who partake of services of the program undergoing alteration. Even program changes that eventually are accepted and appreciated by clientele often are resented and resisted at the outset. Unless substantial improvements are made in the quality or quantity of a given service, affected clientele are apt to rail against productivity-inspired program change, whereas the public at large, unimpressed by benefits of perhaps only pennies a day for individual taxpayers, are unlikely to rally in defense of productivity improvement.

When the public mood intermittently turns toward improving the efficiency of government, quick action and immediate results are desired rather than the more gradual pace of steady, analytically based productivity improvement. The periodic appointment of blue-ribbon committees and establishment of high-profile programs to improve government performance heighten public expectations that a quick fix is possible and increase public frustration when it is not immediately forthcoming.

## D. Dominant Preference for the Status Quo

If groups having the power to influence change are generally satisfied with the services provided to their members and see little reason to push changes for the benefit of powerless groups, little encouragement is likely to be generated for experimentation and innovation in service delivery (Marris and Rein, 1973, p. 45).

## E. Lack of Political Appeal

As a political cause, improving the quality and efficiency of government services lacks the appeal of promises to resolve social issues, the allure of program expansion or capital improvements, the grand implications of long-range planning and economic development strategies, or the widespread personal implications of tax policy. Policy issues capture the morning headlines and evening news coverage much more often than do stories of operational successes and failures in routine governmental functions.

Government officials can get good mileage from a strategy that, while not neglecting to maintain government operations within the broad band of acceptable performance, nevertheless puts primary emphasis on high-profile policy successes. Policy issues simply have greater political appeal than do matters of operational efficiency and effectiveness. Accordingly, that select group of administrators with reputations earned on the strength of productivity improvement has followed a route less frequently traveled than the broader path that leads to acclaim via policy recommendations.

## F. Short Time Horizon

Campaigning for office is a constant endeavor for many, and perhaps most, elected officials. Only the intensity level changes with the official kickoff of a new campaign. Awareness of their own political mortality affects the patience of most politicians and top government executives for long-term productivity improvement initiatives carrying large front-end price tags and the promise of only gradual returns on investment. These officials frequently have a short time horizon for such matters, one that extends only as far as the next election. After all, why incur major expenses and perhaps short-term tax increases that are almost sure to earn the wrath of voters, while producing long-term benefits that may only be enjoyed by one's successor?

## G. Subordination of Efficiency to Secondary Status

Public sector agencies are tugged in a variety of directions. Multiple objectives, often conflicting with one another, are facts of life in the public sector environment. Efforts to characterize principal objectives have spawned various lists. Morgan and England (1999, p. 178), for example, observe that governments at the local level pursue the goals of efficiency, effectiveness, responsiveness, and equity.

In public sector conflicts between the value of efficiency and one or more of the other values, efficiency frequently loses. Professional associations, employee organizations, client groups, neighborhood associations, and service regulators all constitute formidable interest groups that tend to value efficiency on a level secondary to other goals, if at all. Not surprisingly, the values that compete with efficiency are often given political and administrative priority.

## H. Limited Options for Achieving Economies of Scale

Although private firms may encounter relatively few barriers to expanding their markets and thereby spreading various capital and fixed costs over a larger customer base to achieve economies of scale, government managers typically find their market expansion options to be more limited. For instance, a municipality cannot simply offer its services to the residents of adjacent communities just because it would like to expand its market. Although economy-of-scale options are available through intergovernmental service agreements, merger, annexation, or intergovernmental cooperation in securing contract services, these options cannot be exercised quickly or unilaterally simply because market expansion makes good business sense to an efficiency-minded government.

## I. Procurement and Personnel Procedures

Among the advantages touted by proponents of privatization is the freedom private contractors enjoy from the cumbersome procurement and personnel procedures common in government (Osborne and Plastrik, 2000). Private firms can purchase equipment and hire employees quickly. They are less encumbered by rules restricting their choices. Often they enjoy greater flexibility to pay market rates, to deploy workers as needed, and to reward superior performance.

Public sector managers typically operate in a more restricted environment. Customary procurement regulations provide little managerial discretion, thwart speedy acquisition, and make the "low bid," rather than the "best bid," the favored option and path of least resistance. Similarly, rules and procedures designed to remedy the problems of favoritism and prejudice in public employment often have restricted supervisors' ability to adjust assignments, and sometimes even their ability to extend differential treatment and rewards for varying levels of employee performance. Having hundreds or even thousands of job classifications unnecessarily restricts managerial options and adds needless complexity to personnel systems (Osborne and Plastrik, 2000, p. 412; National Commission on the State and Local Public Service, 1993). Furthermore, the well-intended but time-consuming requirements stipulated in civil service hiring processes for the purpose of securing the best candidate for the job may instead cost public sector organizations their top candidates, as the most desirable applicants tire of waiting and accept job offers elsewhere (Savas and Ginsburg, 1973).

Somewhere along the way, the concept of merit has become overgrown with practices and procedures that have relegated employee performance to secondary status in matters of human resource administration. A review of the federal personnel system led Kettl et al. (1996, p. 1) to observe, "the civil service process too often hinders, not helps, the federal government as it struggles to get its work done. Problems of recruiting and retaining good workers, many government managers believe, have worsened service delivery and hurt productivity."

## J.  Legal Restrictions and Court Rulings

Legislative actions and judicial interpretations of the law can dramatically affect the nature of public services, how those services are delivered, and how they are funded. With little regard for operational efficiency or local priorities, the courts have usurped or have been deeded the decision-making prerogatives normally reserved for legislative bodies and administrative personnel on controversial issues ranging from jail facilities, special education, and air quality to matters of service equity and accessibility.

## K.  Anti-Innovation and Anti-Productivity Effects of Some Grants and Other Intergovernmental Programs

The elimination of the General Revenue Sharing program in the mid-1980s represented a major loss to state and local governments both in federal dollars and in local discretion over the expenditure of intergovernmental revenues. Remaining behind is an assortment of grant programs that often inhibit innovation and productivity improvement through rigidity and restrictive stipulations.

In the mid-1990s, for instance, federal funds used for the training of narcotics-sniffing dogs were initially denied to the city of Portland, Oregon, for the training of a creature that already had demonstrated a gift for this type of duty. The animal, named Harley, did not qualify for these funds, because Harley was a potbellied pig. Although the city's request was consistent with the antidrug objectives of the federal program and might, in fact, have led to the discovery of better means of achieving the desired ends, the funds were initially denied because the animal was not a canine, as prescribed by program rules. White House action designating Harley an "honorary dog" cleared the impasse (Gore, 1995, p. 34).

Similarly, when state officials working on Oregon's welfare reform efforts proposed the use of welfare savings to fund a poverty prevention program, their idea met federal resistance. It was not that anyone thought Oregon's plan was a bad idea; it simply had not been prescribed in the program's rules. Only after several rounds of review consuming eight months' time did Oregon get its approval (Macy, n.d., p. 12).

Regulations governing grant-supported programs tend to be written with an eye toward controlling the behavior of the least responsible governments (Anderson et al., 1983, p. 182), often resulting in tightly prescribed and cumbersome operating procedures that lead to red tape and delays, while eliminating flexibility in the development of improved methods. Few grant programs over the years have rewarded the productive, or penalized the unproductive, use of federal funds; many have included maintenance-of-effort provisions, prohibiting any reductions in local expenditures; and some formula-based grants have rewarded local governments for increased expenditures in a given program (Multi-Agency Study Team, 1979; GAO, 1978; Hayward and Kuper, 1978). These factors, coupled with the tendency of many officials to spend grant dollars less carefully than own-source revenues, have had the unintended effect of undermining productivity.

## L.  Intergovernmental Mandating of State and Local Expenditures

When higher levels of government order lower levels to provide specified services or facilities, those mandates are rarely, if ever, issued with operational efficiency as a high priority. The U.S. Advisory Commission on Intergovernmental Relations (ACIR) counted 36 significant mandates having major effects on state and local governments and their resources as of 1980 (ACIR, 1984), but this number soared during the next decade with 27 new mandates enacted by Congress between 1981 and 1990 (Conlan and Beam, 1992, p. 7).

A larger category of incursions into state and local prerogatives is comprised of statutes in which state and local authority is preempted by federal action mandating activities or services meeting minimum federal standards. Congress has enacted more than 400 preemption statutes since its inception in 1789, with more than half of them enacted in the relatively short span since 1969 (ACIR, 1992). State legislatures have proven no more reluctant to impose mandates on their local government counterparts.

Mandates address state and national policy issues ranging from safe drinking water to education to civil rights, but they also have intervened in more routine local matters—such as operating hours of libraries and wage levels for local government employees—in a manner characterized by the ACIR as questionable or clearly inappropriate (ACIR, 1978, p. 3). On more than a few occasions, individual governments have been ensnared by rules written for others but applied to all. When compliance is expensive and seems unnecessary, frustration is a common result.

> Is it surprising that taxpayers in Phoenix, Arizona, which averages seven inches of rainfall a year, question federal mandates that force the city to devote large sums every year to monitoring runoff from practically nonexistent rainstorms? Is it any wonder that citizens in Midland, Michigan, resent EPA regulations that make the community spend far more than necessary to dispose of solid waste? (Sitting on seventy-five feet of clay, Midland's landfill would be perfectly safe without the federally required liner.) (Nivola, 2000, p. 9)

John Kincaid (1989, p. 22), former ACIR Director, succinctly addressed the problem of excessive regulation.

> For too long, we have tried to reform the intergovernmental system according to a UPS model of federalism. UPS, which says that it runs "the tightest ship in the shipping business," has exhaustive rules governing every facet of its operations, down to the hand that delivery-truck drivers should use to fasten their seatbelts (the left hand)... Such rules cannot work in the intergovernmental arena if we are to have an efficient federal democracy in which state and local elected officials make many decisions about who gets what, when, and how.

The costs imposed on localities by unfunded federal mandates in fiscal year 1993 alone were estimated at $11.3 billion by the accounting firm, Price Waterhouse (Gullo and Kelly, 1998). State mandates drive costs higher still. Some state governments have stipulated vacation time for local government employees, established standards for working hours, or even required equal numbers of officers on each police shift (Moore, 1988; Savas, 2000, p. 34).

As concern for the problem of mandating increased, some states passed laws requiring that cities and counties be reimbursed for the costs of implementing new mandates. Several of these states, however, have generally ignored their own legislation. A General Accounting Office (GAO) report, for example, noted that 57 mandates had been enacted by the Illinois General Assembly, costing local governments an unreimbursed $148 million in less than a decade following the enactment of that state's mandate reimbursement law in 1979 (Moore, 1988). At the federal level, enactment of the Unfunded Mandates Reform Act of 1995 (UMRA) produced a greater flow of information to Congress on the impact of various mandates, which figured prominently in congressional debate (Gullo and Kelly, 1998). Nevertheless, in 1996 "significant new mandates and preemptions were passed, while state and local victories were largely achieved in modifying how new mandates were to be implemented, not in determining whether new mandates would be enacted" (Posner, 1997, p. 53).

## III. ORGANIZATIONAL BARRIERS

A second category of productivity barriers includes impediments that are found at varying degrees in many public sector organizations. Some organizational barriers may be major impediments in a particular agency or jurisdiction and relatively insignificant in others.

### A. Bureaucratic Socialization Process

The informal process by which veteran employees introduce new employees to the ways of an organization or work unit (i. e., providing cues on what is expected, subtly molding new employees to fit the organizational culture, "showing them the ropes") can have a powerful influence on subsequent performance. Organizations that have lost their zeal for excellence may find great difficulty in attempting to break from that pattern. "The socialization of new recruits by socializing agents with little interest in change" (Fainstein and Fainstein, 1972, p. 517) can create a cadre of bureaucrats resistant to innovation.

## B. Lack of Accountability

Among the harshest criticisms of government is the claim that few government managers or employees are held accountable for their actions or for their failures to act. Observers have even noted that some officials prefer vague goals and objectives "so that progress cannot be measured" (Schick, 1996, p. 61). To the extent that these allegations are true, government operations are deprived of a fundamental mechanism of direction and control. More important, an organizational culture that eschews accountability is unlikely to foster the level of pride and devotion to one's work that comes with being responsible for or being in charge of some program, operation, or facility, however great or small.

## C. Focus on Outputs Rather than Outcomes

Many government managers are inclined to focus on their department's activities or workload—its outputs—rather than on the bigger picture of whether their efforts are achieving positive changes in the lives of citizens or producing other results they were designed to bring. By fixating on simply maintaining or expanding the activities of the department, they may overlook opportunities, perhaps procedural innovations or fundamental service delivery alternatives, to improve the results or outcomes of these activities (Osborne and Gaebler, 1992, pp. 138–165; Osborne and Plastrik, 2000, p. 31).

## D. Perverse Reward System

Even as early as 1888, James Bryce noted a special irony in the American bureaucracy. It was odd, he thought, that the system offered few rewards or even assurances of continuing employment to government workers demonstrating the prized American qualities of personal industry and efficiency.

> It [seems] strange that a people so eminently practical as the Americans acquiesced in a system which ... gives nobody the least security that he will gain a higher post or even retain the one he holds, by displaying the highest efficiency. [Bryce, 1888; cited in Schiesl, 1977, p. 25]

In a perverse twist, governments at all levels not only fail in most cases to provide adequate rewards and recognition for superior performance, but they often reward managers who have expanded their budgets and increased the number of persons they supervise. Unfortunately, the department head who finds ways to minimize the resources necessary to continue operating effectively can expect, instead of accolades and a substantial pay increase, the reassignment of current funds to cover the overruns of a less efficient department and a reduction in his or her own department's appropriation for the upcoming year. The absence of substantial material incentives for managerial innovation and productivity improvement is seen by many as a fundamental impediment to productivity improvement, one that contributes to many other barriers.

## E. "Spend It or Lose It" Budget Rules

Few governments allow their departments or agencies to carry forward to subsequent years all or even a portion of any savings remaining in the current year's budget. Any "under-expenditure" is simply returned to the government's treasury for reappropriation. From the agency's perspective, the funds have been "lost." Worse still, their under-expenditure might be perceived as evidence that the agency needs fewer resources in the future.

Rather than losing funds or jeopardizing future appropriations, many agencies believe it is more rational to lower their guard against spending on low-priority items in the last month or two of the fiscal year, if a budget balance remains (Gore, 1993a, 1993b). They make expenditures that would not have passed muster early in the year, simply because they see no advantage and plenty of disadvantages in saving the money.

## F. Inadequate Management Commitment to Productivity

Most government managers recognize operational productivity as an objective. The same can be said, however, for many other pressing issues that compete with productivity improvement initiatives for managerial time and attention. Often, the latest crisis or the most explosive issue facing a government unit holds an attention-grabbing advantage over more deferrable efforts to analyze and improve day-to-day operations. Philosophical commitment to productivity improvement, perhaps with rhetorical accompaniment, and actual commitment are two very different things.

## G. Barriers to Monetary Incentive Plans

Monetary incentive plans in the public sector often are stalled not only by restrictive civil service regulations and assorted legal barriers but also by inadequate human resource administration systems (Davis and West, 1985) and the resistance of the general public, legislators, supervisors, and even employees themselves. Without adequate job classification and performance appraisal systems, monetary incentive plans lack a suitable foundation and are more likely to lead to dissatisfaction and frustration than to success.

Although government reinvention enthusiasts urge greater personnel management flexibilities, including financial and nonfinancial awards (Osborne and Plastrik, 2000, pp. 127–130), vocal segments of the general public are often quick to criticize plans that would increase the pay of a bureaucracy they consider to be already overpaid and underworked. Opposition from legislators often stems from a desire to avoid adverse citizen reaction, to maintain tight control over wages, and to protect scarce resources not only by avoiding additional expenses, but also by returning to the legislature for reappropriation all savings from improved performance rather than committing to a plan for distributing a portion of such savings to employees. Some supervisors and managers raise objections to monetary incentives in the belief that such programs induce a factory mentality inappropriate to public service. High-achieving employees and their supervisors worry that poor performers will ride the coattails of top performers if group incentives are prescribed. Employees themselves often fear that the reward system will be administered inequitably if the plan calls for individual awards.

## H. Union Resistance

Unlike the national trend that saw union membership slide to 9% of private sector workers in 2000, unionization of the public sector workforce is on the upswing. Union membership grew from 12% of all federal, state, and local government employees in 1955 to 37.5% in 2000 (Bureau of Labor Statistics, 2001; Persinos, 1989). The influence of public sector unions stems from their size, the degree of control their members hold on the production of government services, the essential nature of many of those services, and the status of union members not only as employees, but also as a formidable block of voters.

Organized labor's opposition to privatization and other management efforts to reduce public employment or cut labor costs is well documented in the popular media, as are union efforts on behalf of the seniority principle and the establishment of work rules limiting management discretion in dealing with employees. Unions have tended to oppose differential treatment based on productivity (Balk, 1980), employee reductions, civilianization, contracting out government functions (Stanley, 1972), and innovations in personnel deployment or technology when the result is considered disruptive or threatening to employees (e.g., Greiner et al., 1981; Chaiken and Bruns, 1978; Walker, 1978).

Unions have consistently supported measures that would expand employment or increase staffing requirements. The International Association of Fire Fighters, for example, has strongly supported efforts to enact National Fire Protection Association standard 1710 that would establish minimum staffing levels for fire service responses (i.e., four-person staffing) and emergency medical responses (i.e., two paramedics on advanced life support calls) (Fitch and Associates, 2001; IAFF, 2001). Spokespersons for the National League of Cities, National Association of Counties, International City/County Management Association, and other associations of city and county officials have argued that staffing and deployment decisions should be left to local governments themselves (Borut, 2001; Fletcher, 2001).

Despite a record of support for expanded employment and opposition to a variety of productivity improvement initiatives, the power of unions and their significance as a productivity barrier might be commonly overstated. At the federal level, President Reagan's 1981 firing of 11,000 striking air traffic controllers signaled limits to the ability of labor to impose its will and delivered a sharp blow to the power of public sector unionism. At the local government level, the city of Indianapolis' celebrated program of managed competition at first felt the wrath of city employees' unions, but eventually won their cooperation in the effort to outbid private competitors (Goldsmith, 1997; Eggers and O'Leary, 1995). Even in the mid-1970s, Hayes (1977) noted that major conflicts between management and organized labor had occurred in relatively few instances, and suggested that most municipal employees view productivity improvement with "equanimity, if not indifference." Where management and political leaders have been truly committed to achieving a particular objective, union opposition rarely has been sufficient to rebuff their efforts. Moreover, in some instances, as in Indianapolis, adversaries have become allies with major productivity gains achieved through the cooperative efforts of management and organized labor (e.g., Goldsmith, 1997; Steisel, 1984).

Clearly, where the opposition of organized labor occurs, it cannot be ignored. Organized labor's principal threat to productivity, however, may be less in its push for higher wages than in its insistence on restrictive work rules and, as noted by Morgan (1984), in the cumulative effects of greater bureaucratic autonomy as reflected in an increasingly unresponsive workforce.

## I.  Perceived Threat to Job Security

Many employees are skeptical of productivity improvement initiatives, fearing that the term productivity is simply a pseudonym for "speedup" or "automation." The likely result in either case is a reduction in the number of employees required to complete the same amount of work. Seen in those terms, cooperation with productivity improvement efforts is an irrational act, for in doing so, an employee could be helping to eliminate his or her own job. To neutralize this source of potential resistance, many employers have established "no layoff" policies, promising that any employment reductions resulting from productivity improvement initiatives will be achieved through reassignment of employees or normal attrition.

## J.  Excessive Layers of Middle Management

Top-heavy administrative structures are in part the product of excessive controls put in place to prevent errors and improprieties. A bloated layer of management can also be the result when incompetent managers are "kept on even after others have been hired to improve the level of performance" (Kaufman, 2001, p. 34). Where government departments have been forced to compete with the private sector, some have discovered that streamlining operations and trimming the ranks of middle managers are keys to competitive success (Goldsmith, 1997).

Without doubt, effective supervision contributes to an organization's productivity. When layers of supervision exceed what is truly needed, however, the effect on costs undermines the unit's efficiency.

## K.  Supervisory Resistance

Supervisors are ideally situated in the organizational ranks to thwart any productivity improvement initiatives they oppose. For that reason, the prospect of supervisory resistance is potentially one of the most formidable of all productivity barriers. Supervisors who feign support for, or cooperation with, productivity improvement initiatives in the presence of superiors but downplay the importance and applicability of those initiatives in their absence can severely damage the prospects for success.

Supervisors may oppose productivity improvement efforts for any of a variety of reasons. They may be personally uncomfortable with change in an operation they have grown to know very well over a period of many years. They may fear that their own skills or those of valued subordinates will be inadequate for adapting to revised procedures or the application of new technologies. They may be aware of inefficiencies in their operation, but prefer the pace and performance level that has heretofore been acceptable. They may resent the intrusion of an outside analyst telling them how their operation should be run. Or they may fear that good ideas coming from outside their unit will reflect poorly on their own innovativeness and managerial ability.

Strategies to gain the cooperation—or minimally, the acquiescence—of supervisors are likely to be important for the success of a productivity improvement initiative. Keeping supervisors well informed and enlisting their input throughout the process are recommended elements of such a strategy. Often, however, upper management begins its efforts to secure supervisory support much too late. Unless management values have been nurtured among supervisors over a period of months and years, last-minute appeals for cooperation and loyalty are likely to be received coolly. Where management fails to secure the allegiance of front-line supervisors as part of its ranks and to instill management values at that level, those failures may prove costly.

## L. Ambiguous Objectives

Too many public sector organizations allow their managers to become complacent in their work, drifting from day to day without a real commitment to or a plan for long-term improvement of operations. They handle routine matters and various problems that arise from time to time and convince themselves that they have thereby fulfilled their supervisory or managerial responsibility. The public expects its services to continue and the manager's job, they reason, is to keep them coming. Period. They give little thought to service enhancement, performance targets, or departmental objectives. If pressed, they often will express objectives only in lofty and ambiguous terms: "to ensure public safety," or "to enhance the standard of living." But having only ambiguous objectives is very much like having no objectives at all.

Lofty objectives may be good for speeches, but they are of little value in serious efforts to improve performance and productivity. What is needed are clear, concise, measurable objectives on which a manager and work unit can focus. As noted by Drucker (1980, p. 103), "To have a chance at performance, a program needs clear targets, the attainment of which can be measured, appraised, or at least judged."

## M. Reluctance to Abandon

Government programs may sometimes achieve their objectives completely, seizing the opportunity or defeating the problem that prompted their establishment. In other cases, well-intentioned programs may utterly fail, demonstrating no progress toward the achievement of their objectives. In either of these two events, it probably is time to abandon the program and redirect resources. The moment has been seized or lost for such programs, and funding is more appropriately directed to the continuation of programs that show progress toward achievement of objectives, or to new programs that deserve to be tested. But the inability to abandon is a common malady of government, a characteristic Drucker (1980) places at the top of his list of public administration's "deadly sins." Government programs often take on lives of their own and tenaciously cling to life long after they have achieved their objectives or have repeatedly failed.

## N. Insufficient Analytic Skills or Analytic Staffing

Systematic productivity improvement customarily has an analytical base. Procedural improvements are carefully contemplated and designed. The costs and benefits of various operational options are studied. Equipment alternatives and configurations are scrutinized. Resource and expenditure ramifications—short- and long-term—are analyzed.

Some public sector organizations are prepared to conduct systematic analyses; many, however, are not. It is an unfortunate paradox that those organizations with slack resources, the least pressing need for a team of analysts to find ways to save money, and the least tendency to adopt cost-cutting strategies are most likely to have such analysts (Levine, 1979). On the other hand, those organizations most in need of analytic talent are most likely to be without it, choosing to cut analysts rather than police officers or other front-line service deliverers when the budget crunch arrives.

## O.  Inadequate Cost-Accounting Systems

The National Performance Review detected among federal agencies uncoordinated budgeting and accounting systems that rarely provided program managers with fundamental operating information (Gore, 1993b). When reform-minded officials have examined the systems in state and local governments, they often have arrived at similar conclusions upon discovering the absence of basic unit cost information for various services (Goldsmith, 1997).

The budgets of many governmental units understate the expenditures for individual programs and activities (Savas, 2000, 1979). Rarely is the understatement a matter of deliberate deceit. More often, it is simply the result of budgeting and accounting practices that fail to assign full overhead and capital expenses to the various programs that actually require or benefit from those expenditures. Consequently, administrators often have inaccurate perceptions of the costs of various services, a condition that could lead to managerial complacency if reported costs seem to lie within acceptable bounds or to the inappropriate rejection of privatization options that incorrectly appear to offer no financial advantages (Savas, 2000, 1987).

## P.  Inadequate Performance Data Within/Across Jurisdictions

Without a good system of performance measurement, assessments of a unit's work tend to be subjective and anecdotal. As noted by Lord Kelvin (as quoted in Lehrer, 1983, p. 25) in 1883:

> I often say that when you can measure what you are speaking about and express it in numbers, you know something about it; but when you cannot express it in numbers, your knowledge is of a meagre and unsatisfactory kind; it may be the beginning of knowledge, but you have scarcely, in your thoughts, advanced to the stage of science, whatever the matter may be.

Comprehensive performance measurement systems are not yet commonplace in the public sector. Where they exist at all, most measurement systems tend merely to tabulate workload indicators—the number of calls answered, the number of cases processed, the number of applications received—and to offer few gauges of efficiency or effectiveness. As a result, few managers are adequately prepared to declare how their operations fare compared to other jurisdictions, other units in the same jurisdiction, or even compared to themselves at an earlier point in time.

## Q.  Inadequate Performance Evaluation/Appraisal

Systematic assessment of performance at either the program or individual level is the exception in the public sector rather than the rule. Few public sector programs are evaluated systematically to determine whether they are achieving their objectives and doing so in a reasonably efficient fashion. Informal judgments of program effectiveness and efficiency tend to be subjective, based on anecdotes of program success or failure, the glowing testimonials of program proponents, or the harsh criticisms of program opponents.

By the same token, the appraisal of individual employee performance tends to be handled in a perfunctory manner, if at all. Many supervisors view performance appraisal duties as an interruption of their primary responsibilities rather than as an integral part of them. Failing to recognize the importance of honest feedback for performance improvement, many appraisers hope to avoid the sometimes emotionally wrenching aspects of the process by awarding all subordinates virtually the same rating, all acceptable, for example, or all exceptional. Under such circumstances, the organization derives no developmental benefits through employee counseling, no motivational benefits through meaningful pay-for-performance adjustment of wages, no special insights into the training needs of the organization, and no advantages in forecasting long-term staffing needs in relation to the aptitudes and skills of current employees. Inadequate evaluation at both the individual and program levels unfortunately leaves public officials with a dubious information base as they make staffing and resource allocation decisions.

### R. Inadequate Dissemination of Program Information and Reluctance to Use What Is Known

Many observers believe that public sector performance would be improved if information on successful programs and services in other agencies or jurisdictions were more readily available. Although research suggests that the eagerness of public sector managers to get their hands on productivity improvement information might be somewhat overstated (Ammons and King, 1983), greater awareness could inspire some improvements.

A hurdle greater than the information gap is the reluctance of public officials to adapt information about successful programs of which they are aware for use in their own jurisdictions. Too often, successes elsewhere are dismissed summarily on the basis of selected conditions that differ somewhat from those found in a public official's own jurisdiction. Rarely will conditions in one government unit be replicated precisely in another. The innovative official finds ways to adapt programs or overcome inhospitable conditions where possible.

### S. Fragmentation of Government

For years, scholars and government reformers have insisted that the fragmentation of government impairs the coordination of planning and decision making, and reduces the effectiveness and efficiency of service delivery. Conventional wisdom has long suggested that the proliferation of separate municipalities in a small geographical area, overlapped by county government and a variety of special-purpose districts, obscures lines of accountability, promotes unnecessary duplication, and forfeits opportunities for economies of scale. Competing views, however, have begun to challenge conventional thinking. Researchers have found that some fragmented local governments have secured through intergovernmental cooperation many of the benefits of a more unified system, including economies of scale, without giving up the advantages of smallness (e.g., Parks and Oakerson, 1989; Oakerson and Parks, 1988; ACIR, 1987).

Fragmentation of government, it appears, may be a less formidable and consistent barrier than once thought. Nevertheless, where traditions of interjurisdictional jealousy and distrust preclude opportunities for coordination and economy, fragmentation remains an impediment to productivity gains.

## T.  Bureaucratic Rigidities, Including an Extreme Focus on Rules and Procedures

"Red tape" is a label commonly attached to one of the least popular manifestations of bureaucratic rigidity. The authors of bureaucratic rules in the public sector have rarely placed innovation and efficiency among their greatest concerns. More often, burdensome procedures that often are maddening to the clerks, administrators, and clients who must adhere to them have been written to maintain control over the bureaucracy, limit opportunities for corruption, and ensure a system of checks and balances. Tight rules and regulations have been prescribed to ensure the application of merit principles in employment practices, equity in service delivery, and uniformity of performance (see, e.g., Kaufman, 2001).

Recent observers have discovered that greater rigidities often exist in organizations that are unclear about their goals and objectives, and uncertain about the means of achieving them. Organizations having clear goals and objectives, strategies aligned with their objectives, and employees committed to achieving them have less need to control actions (Osborne and Plastrik, 2000, pp. 129–130).

## U.  Fragmented Authority and Uncertainty About Where Decisions Can Be Made

"Bureaucratic runaround" is an unfortunate symptom of fragmented authority. Like the authors of bureaucratic rules, the architects of organizational structures in the public sector have placed the importance of control, checks and balances, and other values ahead of innovation and efficiency.

Unfortunately, bureaucratic hierarchies often restrict opportunities for innovation and productivity improvement while only partially upholding the values their architects sought. Bureaucratic organizations typically require a would-be innovator to pass through several rounds of approval to effect organizational change. Forcing innovators to run the organizational gauntlet can have a devastating effect on the will to even try. "All in all," writes a former budget director for the City of New York, "our state and local governments are superbly equipped to do tomorrow what they did yesterday. But these governments are not designed to be highly efficient, responsive, flexible, or innovative" (Hayes, 1972, pp. 7–8).

The cost of fragmented authority is often measured in operational inefficiency and lost opportunities. It also can be measured in terms of organizational ineptness and occasional corruption. A story of apparent ineptness stemming from fragmented authority, for example, appeared in the *Tampa Tribune*, to the dismay of county officials (Gurwitt, 1989). It seems that heavy rainfall and the threatened flooding of two area lakes brought two county pumping crews to the rescue at the behest of separate commissioners. The efforts of those crews, however, proved futile, as each unknowingly pumped water from its assigned lake into the lake of the other. Fragmented authority, built into the system intentionally, perhaps prevented undue concentration of power, but did so at the expense of efficiency and effectiveness.

A pattern of similar fragmentation of authority among county commissioners in Mississippi led to more than wasted efforts and embarrassment (Zolkos, 1989). Following an FBI "sting" operation that netted more than four dozen county supervisors allegedly "on the take," more than half of Mississippi's 82 counties rejected the longstanding "beat system" of road management in which each of five county supervisors had his own geographical fiefdom for road maintenance. In its place, the voters adopted a unit system through which road maintenance is directed by an appointed road manager under the control of the entire board of supervisors.

## V. Turf-Protecting Tactics

Turf-protecting tactics arise when a government, department, agency, or individual work unit takes steps to rebuff cooperative efforts, operational inquiries or studies, or other steps deemed to be intrusive out of fear that authority, control, or resources will be lost. Such tactics may appear in the form of opposition to city–county consolidations and other jurisdictional mergers. They may also appear as opposition to interdepartmental sharing of personnel or equipment. Or they may appear as opposition to cooperative service delivery arrangements that would replace unilateral decision making with decisions based on negotiation and compromise.

Kaufman recalls turf battles among the Forest Service, Park Service, and Bureau of Land Management over control of federally owned land, as well as battles over ambulance calls in New York City among the emergency medical services operated by the police department, fire department, and the Health and Hospitals Corporation (Kaufman, 2001, p. 31).

Thomas (1999, pp. 114–115) argues for rejection of the old public sector paradigm with its prescriptions that frustrate cooperation and block productivity, such as the following six classic turf-protection tactics:

Refuse to share information within or outside an agency;
Charge fellow agencies for every tiny service rendered;
Create enemies of fellow units or agencies;
Refuse to accept assistance from outside the agency;
Create an illusion or the reality that others need to ask our permission; and
Always just say "no."

## W. Inadequate Research, Development, and Experimentation

New approaches to the solution of government problems, especially approaches featuring the application of technology, are reported regularly. For example, loop detectors installed in the streets of Los Angeles now communicate with transponders in local buses and traffic signals on selected routes, timing the signals and reducing passenger travel time by 25% (Kittower, 2001, p. 54); wireless systems and laptop computers allow building inspectors, code enforcement officials, and other field employees in Greensboro, North Carolina, and other municipalities to maximize productive time in the field and minimize downtime and time in transit to and from the central office (Gold, 2001); and handheld devices with digital camera attachments enable animal control officers in Lincoln, Nebraska not only to retrieve forms and information about a particular animal while still in the field, but also to photographically document animal and health violations (Solomon, 2001). Many governments have enhanced their electronic capabilities to allow citizens to apply for permits, register for programs or courses, access public documents, and pay taxes, fees, and fines online (PTI/ICMA, 2001).

Despite impressive advances, gains through research, development, and experimentation have been less than the size of the government market would seem to justify. Given the number of government jurisdictions in existence and the array and magnitude of functions they perform and problems they confront, instances of operational experimentation are less numerous and the creative application of technology less rapid than might be expected. The public sector represents a substantial component of the national economy and, therefore, would seem to be an enticing target for private research and development. However, below the federal level the multiplicity of state and local governments and special districts offers a disjointed market with a history of only gradual adoption of the latest technology.

## X. Requirement of Large Initial Investment for Productivity Improvement Efforts

Modest productivity improvement sometimes can be achieved with little or no additional expense. In some cases, for example, a good idea from a current employee may be implemented with ease, producing immediate benefits in service quality or cost reduction. Often, however, productivity gains require substantial front-end investments that must be recouped before net benefits can be realized. Similar investments often are required for initial analysis of improvement opportunities and for various expenses related to startup or conversion to a revised operational system, typically including equipment and other capital items.

The requirement of large initial outlays with the prospect of only gradual recovery of that investment works against productivity initiatives in the competition for scarce resources. Despite the long-term advantages of such investments, substantial pressure often exists for the allocation of all discretionary resources to the immediate enhancement of basic services (e.g., hiring police officers rather than analysts), or to addressing a current crisis.

## Y. Performance Myths

A variety of myths erroneously accepted as management gospel or as immutable truths of public sector service delivery hinders the prospects of productivity improvement. Research has demonstrated, for example, the inadequacy of the homily, a happy employee is a productive employee. Although both employee happiness and organizational productivity are desirable objectives that should be pursued by conscientious officials, one does not necessarily lead to the other (Katzell and Yankelovich, 1975). Similarly, the choice of service delivery options is handicapped by the conflicting myths revered in two extreme camps: according to one, the public sector will always perform public service functions better than the private sector because the public sector is less plagued by greed and corruption, it is not compelled to make a profit, and its employees are more caring; but in the view of the other camp, all answers lie in the private sector. An open-minded review of the evidence reveals the frailties of both myths (e.g., Downs and Larkey, 1986). Strict adherence to one or the other denies an agency or jurisdiction important options.

Prevailing thought on service delivery routines in basic government functions is often laden with myths. Conventional wisdom at various times, for example, has disdained the thought of competition in the public sector, while nevertheless arguing that competition improves private sector services; has contended that emergency dispatch duties should be handled by sworn officers, not entrusted to civilians; has suggested that individual employee incentives were fairer and therefore superior to group incentives; has held that one-person refuse vehicles were too dangerous to justify their use; and has argued that the deployment of two-officer patrol cars was a superior strategy to the use of one-officer cars. Conventional wisdom has been reconsidered in each case.

## Z.  Overselling Productivity

Advocates of productivity improvement initiatives, especially those requiring the expenditure of substantial resources at the outset, sometimes find aggressive promotion of these initiatives to be necessary to gain authorization to proceed. However, when promises are made that cannot be kept, even moderately successful programs engender disappointment and become vulnerable (Osborne and Plastrik, 2000; Weaver, 1996; Downs and Larkey, 1986; Barbour, 1980). Productivity improvement involves organizational change; change is disruptive and perhaps even threatening to those employees and program clients who prefer the status quo; and disgruntled parties are more than willing to point out any instances in which reality falls short of promise.

## IV.  PERSONAL BARRIERS

Not all productivity barriers are features of the system, that is, impediments stemming either from the public sector environment or from the characteristics of a particular organization. Some barriers are more personal in nature. Aspects of the various traits individuals bring with them to the workplace, including the manner in which they respond to environmental and organizational conditions, may affect the ability and willingness of a manager to cope with a given hurdle. Obstacles that might appear to be minor to one administrator may be magnified by the adverse personal reaction of another.

## A.  Inadequate Control of Time/Workday

Most government managers, like their counterparts in the private sector, work long hours. Studies routinely place the average workweek of government executives at more than 50 hours per week (e.g., Ammons and Newell, 1989; Stillman, 1982; Lau et al., 1980). Downs and Larkey (1986, p. 42) suggest that if critics would "look in on the offices at the White House, the Office of Management and Budget, the National Security Council, the Pentagon's E and A rings, the State Department, the Central Intelligence Agency, or any city hall or police department on a Sunday afternoon— any Sunday afternoon," they would be surprised by the number of executives and staff members they would find hard at work.

The demands that force long working hours for public executives fracture the typical workday, splitting it into myriad pieces that send most administrators flitting from one issue, task, or crisis to another. Upon concluding a study of private sector executives, Carlson (1951, p. 52) wrote, "I always thought of a chief executive as the conductor of an orchestra, standing aloof on his platform. Now I am in some respects inclined to see him as the puppet in the puppet show with hundreds of people pulling the strings and forcing him to act in one way or another."

Time constraints and the pressures of competing demands for managerial attention constitute a barrier to productivity improvement. Many executives have a figurative or even a literal file of good ideas to tackle when they get a little extra time. Unfortunately, very little time is all that most administrators get for such matters. For some, the enormous demands on managerial time constitute a major barrier; for others, more adept at time management, including prudent priority setting and the art of effective delegation of duties, that obstacle is somewhat less formidable.

## B.   Conceptual Confusion

Confusion over the meaning and ramifications of productivity in the public sector complicates communication, undermines analytic and planning efforts, and limits achievement (Balk, 1984). Those who view productivity improvement narrowly, simplistically, or apprehensively, restrict opportunities and reduce the likelihood of success. The notions of "more bang for the buck" and "working smarter, not harder" only begin to capture the essence of productivity improvement; equating it to forced speedups or cutback management captures even less.

## C.   Proclivity to "Paralysis by Analysis"

A conscientious administrator or researcher would prefer to base important decisions on logic and thorough analysis of complete data. Unfortunately, the information can never be complete; the analysis can never be perfect. At some point, the productive manager has to move forward with a decision based on careful analysis of good, but rarely perfect or complete, data (Osborne and Plastrik, 2000, p. 42).

Managers who are unable to move forward following a conscientious and reasonably complete analysis may inadvertently lock in place a status quo operation, despite opportunities for improvement. They are paralyzed by the thought that a little more analysis would clarify the decision and reveal an obvious course of action. "Paralysis by analysis" is a self-inflicted malady. In some cases, it is produced by perfectionism and in others it is merely an avoidance mechanism for an administrator who would prefer not to have to make a difficult recommendation or decision.

## D.   Risk Avoidance

The possibility of a substantial return on investment is a tantalizing inducement to the taking of moderate or even substantial risks. The success of junk bonds, race tracks, lotteries, and Las Vegas gambling casinos is testimony to that allure. Risk taking of a somewhat different kind is necessary to start a new business or buy one that is struggling, to take calculated gambles to keep an existing company ahead of its competitors or help it catch up, to step out on a limb to seize an opportunity, or to divert scarce resources to prepare for conditions no one else has yet predicted. Those who take these and other risks in the private sector expect to be rewarded when their actions prove beneficial to their companies. They also understand the penalty when executive decisions are short-sighted or ill-advised or when an entrepreneur fails.

Entrepreneurial managers are found less frequently in the public sector and often are less daring because their regard for public resources demands greater certainty before taking calculated risks, but public sector entrepreneurs do exist. The risks these entrepreneurs take are inspired by their commitment, their professionalism, or their perspective on public service, rather than by the incentive of personal reward that inspires many of their private sector counterparts. Successful risk taking in the public sector simply does not offer tangible rewards on a similar scale. The hazards for failure, however, can be substantial, especially for upper-level public executives.

"It is a familiar truth in ... government," notes Szanton (1981, p. 63), "that if you do the job the old way and something goes wrong, that's an act of God; but if you do it a new way and something goes wrong, it's your neck." Some observers suggest that the high probability of public criticism for unsuccessful risk taking and the low probability of tangible rewards for success produce the "relatively low risk threshold of most public officials" (Steiss and Daneke, 1980, p. 170). Others perceive an even more serious barrier than the failure to encourage risk taking, suggesting that "innovation is seemingly discouraged by the recruitment into civil service jobs of people with high risk avoidance" (Fainstein and Fainstein, 1972, p. 517). In other words, "a consequence of these asymmetric incentives is adverse selection, namely that innovative people do not choose careers in the public sector" (Borins, 2000, p. 500).

## E.  Managerial Alibis

Public sector managers confront substantial barriers to productivity improvement. For some, the barriers seem so ominous and impenetrable that any attempt to defeat, surmount, or circumvent them appears futile. The complaints of such managers are familiar.

> "Our hands are tied by legal restrictions."
> "He's a problem employee, but we can't fire him. We're civil service, you know."
> "We've always done it this way. The legislature would never approve a change."
> "The folks in the central offices force us to do it this way with all their silly rules."

Innovative determined managers find ways to work within legal restrictions, civil service regulations, and other administrative rules, or they find ways to work around or to change them. For these officials, bucking tradition may be difficult but not impossible.

In contrast, many public sector managers attempt to excuse their failure to deal effectively with difficult circumstances by complaining about political factors, rules and regulations, and various organizational rigidities that make their jobs difficult. Government managers, it seems, have a long history of offering alibis. Even in the 1970s a survey conducted for the National Center for Productivity and Quality of Working Life concluded that many of the complaints against so-called productivity inhibitors were simply excuses for inaction. The authors of the survey report noted, "Government managers do not shoulder responsibilities and authority that are allowed by the system; presumably because these are unpleasant to exercise" (Hayward and Kuper, 1978, p. 4). A more recent analysis conducted by the National Performance Review discovered that many of the rules criticized as onerous and routinely blamed on lawmakers, headquarters, or some other rule-making agency have, in fact, been developed and self-imposed by the operating agencies themselves, often in a manner that restricts operations more tightly than the original regulation or legislation required (Gore, 1993c, p. 7). Agencies that were granted greater purchasing authority, for example, sometimes chose through their internal regulations not to accept or take advantage of it.

## V.  COPING WITH PRODUCTIVITY BARRIERS

Coping is the operative word when it comes to productivity barriers. Some barriers can be removed; some cannot. Some can be overcome directly and perhaps even quickly; others must be circumvented. To the frustration of idealists, the practical reality of limited time, resources, and control occasionally requires that some impediments must be tolerated—at least to a degree and for a period of time—and productivity gains of less than optimum magnitude accepted. Whether removed, circumvented, or temporarily tolerated, potential obstacles must be identified and considered carefully. Few, if any, productivity barriers can safely be ignored.

To cope effectively, a manager must be able to recognize potential productivity barriers, assess their magnitude, and devise an appropriate strategy for achieving desired results despite those obstacles. A good plan, however, is not enough. An effective manager must also marshal necessary resources, including the enthusiasm, or at least, acquiescence, of organizational leaders and the support of program personnel.

Few meaningful improvements in operations can be achieved without confronting obstacles of one kind or another. Administrators who are easily discouraged will have careers of modest impact. More aggressive and unrelenting administrators can take encouragement from the knowledge that others before them have encountered and coped with a variety of environmental, organizational, and personal barriers to productivity improvement, and have won. The improvements that have occurred in public sector operations, even in the face of long odds, are their legacy.

## REFERENCES

ACIR. Advisory Commission on Intergovernmental Relations, United States (1978). *State Mandating of Local Expenditures (A-67)*. Washington, D.C.: U.S. Government Printing Office.
ACIR. Advisory Commission on Intergovernmental Relations, United States (1984). *Regulatory Federalism*. Washington, D.C.: ACIR.
ACIR. Advisory Commission on Intergovernmental Relations, United States (1987). *The Organization of Local Public Economies*. Washington, D.C.: U.S. Government Printing Office.
ACIR. Advisory Commission on Intergovernmental Relations, United States (1992). *Federal Statutory Preemption of State and Local Authority: History, Inventory, and Issues*. Washington, D.C.: ACIR.
Ammons, D. N. (1992). Productivity barriers in the public sector. In: Holzer, M., ed. *Public Productivity Handbook*. New York: Marcel Dekker, pp. 117–136.
Ammons, D. N., King, J. C. (1983). Productivity improvement in local government: its place among competing priorities. *Public Admin. Rev.* 43(2):113–120.
Ammons, D. N., Newell, C. (1989). *City Executives: Leadership Roles, Work Characteristics, and Time Management*. Albany: State University of New York Press.
Anderson, W. F., Newland, C. A., Stillman, R. J. II. (1983). *The Effective Local Government Manager*. Washington, D.C: International City Management Association.
Balk, W. L. (1980). Organizational and human behavior. In: Washnis, J., ed. *Productivity Improvement Handbook for State and Local Government*. New York: Wiley, pp. 477–502.
Balk, W. L. (1984). Productivity in government: a legislative focus. *Public Product. Rev.* 8(2):148–161.
Barbour, G. P. Jr. (1980). Law enforcement. In: Washnis, G. J., ed. *Productivity Improvement Handbook for State and Local Government*. New York: Wiley, pp. 927–970.

Borins, S. (November/December 2000). Loose cannons and rule breakers, or enterprising leaders? Some evidence about innovative public managers. *Public Admin. Rev.* 60(6):498–507.

Borut, D. J. (May 28, 2001). Not another mandate! *Nation's Cities Weekly* 24(21):2, 12.

Bryce, J. (1888). The *American Commonwealth*. Cited in Schiesl, M. J. (1977). *The Politics of Efficiency*. Berkeley: University of California Press.

Bureau of Labor Statistics, United States (January 18, 2001). Labor Force Statistics from the Current Population Survey: *Union Members Summary*. Available at *http://stats.bls.gov/newsrels.htm*.

Carlson, S. (1951). *Executive Behavior: A Study of the Work Load and the Working Methods of Managing Directors*. Stockholm: Strombergs.

Chaiken, J. M., Bruns, W. (1978). *Improving Station Locations and Dispatching Practices in Fire Departments: A Guide for Fire Chiefs and Local Government Executives*. Washington, DC: U.S. Department of Housing and Urban Development.

Conlan, T. J., Beam, D. R. (Fall 1992). Federal mandates: the record of reform and future prospects. *Intergovern. Perspect.* 18(4):7–15.

Davis, C. E., West, J. P. (1985). Adopting personnel productivity innovations in American local governments. *Policy Stud. Rev.* 4(3):541–549.

Downs, A. (1967). *Inside Bureaucracy*. Boston: Little Brown.

Downs, G. W., Larkey, P. D. (1986). *The Search for Government Efficiency: From Hubris to Helplessness*. New York: Random House.

Drucker, P. F. (1980). The deadly sins in public administration. *Public Admin. Rev.* 40(2):103–106.

Eggers, W. D., O'Leary, J. (1995). *Revolution at the Roots: Making our Government Smaller, Better, and Closer to Home*. New York: Free Press.

Fainstein, N. I., Fainstein, S. S. (1972). Innovation in urban bureaucracies. *Amer. Behav. Sci.* 15(4):511–531.

Fitch and Associates (2001). NFPA membership approves standard—Cities to appeal. *Manage. Focus Providers Emerg. Med. Serv.* 16(2):1–3.

Fletcher, J. (July 16, 2001). National coalition protests fire, EMS staffing mandate. *Nation's Cities Weekly* 24(28):1, 6.

GAO. General Accounting Office (1978). *State and Local Government Productivity Improvement: What Is the Federal Role?* Washington, DC: U.S. Government Printing Office.

Gold, B. M. (Spring 2001). A productivity panacea. *Electron. Govern.* 2(1):26–27.

Goldsmith, S. (1997). *The Twenty-First Century City: Resurrecting Urban America*. Washington, D.C.: Regnery Publishing.

Gore, A. (September 7, 1993a). *Creating a Government that Works Better and Costs Less: Report of the National Performance Review*. Washington, DC: National Performance Review.

Gore, A. (September 1993b). *Creating a Government that Works Better and Costs Less: Improving Financial Management*. Washington, DC: U.S. Government Printing Office.

Gore, A. (September 1993c). *Creating a Government that Works Better and Costs Less: Transforming Organizational Structures*. Washington, DC: U.S. Government Printing Office.

Gore, A. (1995). *Common Sense Government: Works Better and Costs Less: Third Report of the National Performance Review*. Washington, DC: U.S. Government Printing Office.

Greiner, J. M., Hatry, H. P., Koss, M. P., Millar, A. P., Woodward, J. P. (1981). *Productivity and Motivation: A Review of State and Local Government Initiatives*. Washington, DC: Urban Institute.

Gullo, T. A., Kelly, J. M. (September/October 1998). Federal unfunded mandate reform: a first-year retrospective. *Public Admin. Rev.* 58(5):379–387.

Gurwitt, R. (1989). Cultures clash as old-time politics confronts button-down management. *Governing* 2(7):42–48.

Harlow, L. F. (1977). *Without Fear or Favor*. Provo, UT: Brigham Young University Press.

Hayes, F. O'R. (1972). Innovation in state and local government. In: Hayes, F. O'R., Rasmussen, J. E., eds. *Centers for Innovation in the Cities and States*. San Francisco: San Francisco Press.

Hayes, F. O'R. (1977). *Productivity in Local Government*. Lexington, MA: D. C. Heath, Lexington Books.

Hayward, N., Kuper, G. (1978). The national economy and productivity in government. *Public Admin. Rev.* 38(1):2–5.

IAFF. International Association of Fire Fighters (2001). *Historic victory: NFPA standard approved, Across the IAFF*. Available at *www.iaff.org/across/news/archives/072001nfpa. htm.*

Katzell, R. A., Yankelovich, D. (1975). *Work Productivity, and Job Satisfaction: An Evaluation of Policy-Related Research*. New York: Psychological Corporation.

Kaufman, H. (January/February 2001). Major players: Bureaucracies in American government. *Public Admin. Rev.* 61(1):18–42.

Kelvin, Lord, as quoted in Lehrer, R. N., ed. (1983). *Whitecollar Productivity*. New York: McGraw-Hill

Kettl, D. F., Ingraham, P. W., Sanders, R. P., Horner, C. (1996). *Civil Service Reform: Building a Government that Works*. Washington, DC: Brookings Institution.

Kincaid, J. (1989). Currents of change in the federal system. *Intergovern. Perspect.* 15(4):19–22.

Kittower, D. (October 2001). Putting technology to work. *Governing,* 15(1):48–54.

Lau, A. W., Newman, A. R., Broedling, L. A. (1980). The nature of managerial work in the public sector. *Public Admin. Rev.* 40(5):513–520.

Levine, C. H. (1979). More on cutback management: hard questions for hard times. *Public Admin. Rev.* 39(2):179–183.

Macy, C. H. (n.d.). *The Oregon Option: A Federal-State-Local Partnership for Better Results*. Baltimore: Annie E. Casey Foundation.

Marris, P., Rein, M. (1973). *Dilemmas of Social Reform*. Chicago: Aldine.

Moore, W. J. (November 1988). Crazy-quilt federalism. *Nat. J.* 26:3001–3005.

Morgan, D. R. (1984). *Managing urban America*. 2nd ed. Monterey, CA: Brooks/Cole.

Morgan, D. R., England, R. E. (1999). *Managing Urban America*. 5th ed. New York: Chatham House.

Multi-Agency Study Team (1979). Report to the National Productivity Council, November. *Reprinted in Public Product. Rev.* 4(2):167–189.

National Commission on the State and Local Public Service (1993). *Hard Truths/Tough Choices: An Agenda for State and Local Reform*. Albany, NY: Nelson A. Rockefeller Institute of Government.

Niskanen, W. A. (1971). *Bureaucracy and Representative Government*. Atherton, Chicago: Aldine.

Nivola, P. S. (June 2000). Last rites for states rights? *Reform Watch*. No. 1. Washington, DC: Brookings Institution.

Oakerson, R. J., Parks, R. B. (1988). Citizen voice and public entrepreneurship: The organizational dynamic of a complex metropolitan county. *Publius* 18(4):91–112.

Osborne, D., Gaebler, T. (1992). *Reinventing Government: How the Entrepreneurial Spirit is Transforming the Public Sector*. Reading, MA: Addison-Wesley.

Osborne, D., Plastrik, P. (2000). *The Reinventor's Fieldbook: Tools for Transforming Your Government*. San Francisco: Jossey-Bass.

Parks, R. B., Oakerson, R. J. (1989). St. Louis: The ACIR study. *Intergovern. Perspect.* 15(1):9–11.

Persinos, J. F. (1989). Can AFSCME parlay its social-issues savvy into another decade of growth? *Governing* 2(10):44–49.

Posner, P. L. (Spring 1997). Unfunded mandates reform act: 1996 and beyond. *Publius* 27(2):53–71.

PTI/ICMA (February 27, 2001). *Is Your Local Government Plugged In?* Washington, DC: Public Technology, Inc., and International City/County Management Association.

Savas, E. S. (1979). How much do government services really cost? *Urban Affairs Quart.* 15(1):23–42.

Savas, E. S. (1987). *Privatization: The Key to Better Government.* Chatham, NJ: Chatham House.

Savas, E. S. (2000). *Privatization and Public-Private Partnerships.* New York: Chatham House.

Savas, E. S., Ginsburg, S. G. (Summer 1973). The civil service: a meritless system? *Public Interest* 32:70–85.

Schick, A. (1996). *The Spirit of Reform, State Services Commission.* New Zealand: Wellington. Available at *www.ssc.govt.nz/spirit/Strategic.asp?MenuID = 52.*

Schiesl, M. J. (1977). *The Politics of Efficiency.* Berkeley: University of California Press.

Solomon, P. (July 2001). More than an address book. *Techtrends 2001: Supplement Govern. Tech.* 20–22.

Stanley, D. T. (1972). *Managing Local Government Under Union Pressure: Studies of Unionism in Government.* Washington, DC: Brookings Institution.

Steisel, N. (1984). Productivity in the New York City department of sanitation: the role of the public sector manager. *Public Product. Rev.* 8(2):103–126.

Steiss, A. W., Daneke, G. A. (1980). *Performance Administration: Improved Responsiveness and Effectiveness in Public Service.* Lexington, MA: D. C. Heath, Lexington.

Stillman, R. J. II. (1982). Local public management in transition: A report on the current state of the profession. In International City Management Association. *The Municipal Year Book 1982.* Washington, DC: ICMA, pp. 161–173.

Szanton, P. (1981). *Not Well Advised.* New York: Russell Sage Foundation and Ford Foundation.

Thomas, C. J. (1999). *Managers, Part of the Problem? Changing How the Public Sector Works.* Westport, Connecticut: Quorum.

Tullock, G. (1965). *The Politics of Bureaucracy.* Washington, DC: Public Affairs.

Walker, W. E. (1978). *Changing Fire Company Locations: Five Implementation Case Studies.* Washington, DC: U.S. Department of Housing and Urban Development.

Weaver, R. K. (1996). Reinventing government or rearranging the deck chairs? The politics of institutional reform in the 1990s. In: Patrick, Weller, Glyn, Davis, eds. *New Ideas, Better Government.* Brisbane, Australia: Allen & Unwin, pp. 263–282.

Zolkos, R. (December 1989). Mississippi counties streamline operations. *City State* 5:3, 45.

# 9

# The Implementation Game

**EVAN M. BERMAN**
*University of Central Florida, Orlando, Florida, U.S.A.*

## I. INTRODUCTION

Processes of productivity and performance improvement require clear answers to the question, "*What* are we going to improve?" as well as "*How* are we going to implement the proposed improvements?" This chapter focuses on the "how" question. An important task of the manager in productivity improvement is to get others to follow him or her in new efforts. This is no small feat, as even the best of intentions usually is inadequate to ensure success. Managers need detailed knowledge and experience in implementing change, as organizations and the people within them are notoriously resistant to change. The failure to successfully implement customer service, employee empowerment, performance measurement, information technology, and other productivity improvement efforts is seldom because these strategies are difficult to intellectually comprehend. More often, the failure to successfully implement productivity improvement rests with inadequate analysis and skills in dealing with the dynamics of organizational processes, which must come to embrace and support new productivity improvement efforts. In short, implementation is a key to success (Berman, 1998; Gaebler et al., 1999; Osborne and Plastrick, 2000; OECD, 1997; Cohen and Eimicke, 1996).

A productive mindset or outlook on the matter at hand is informed by the following considerations. First, despite numerous challenges to success that exist, many managers are successful in implementing productivity improvement. Many challenges to productivity improvement can be overcome, numerous case studies of successful change exist in the literature, and many organizations have managers who are known for their effectiveness (Donahue, 1999; Holzer and Callahan, 1998; Kettl and DiIulio, 1995; Gore, 1995). Second, no organization presents a manager with perfect conditions for change. All organizations have their challenges, and the task of the astute manager is to recognize them and overcome with them in productive ways. The fact that one's organization is not perfect is no excuse for not improving it. Third, the task of the manager is to improve one's organization or workteam, not to make it perfect. As the saying goes, "Perfect is the enemy of the good." Present managers take satisfaction in making their workplace a better place, while leaving it to future managers to make it even better.

The latter is of quite some career relevance for managers, too. Careers are furthered by reputations for effectiveness, and productivity improvement is often taken as a measure of managerial professionalism. Successful implementation of productivity improvement enables managers to promote their reputation for effectiveness by creating a record of change and accomplishment (Berman and West, 1999, 1998a; Altshuler and Zegans, 1997). It is not necessary to create the perfect organization or the perfect work process. Careers and reputations do not depend on that. Rather, productivity improvement is a multiyear effort with numerous semiannual targets along the way that are all causes for celebration and rewards. Managers plan for these successes. In short, the art of productivity improvement is the art of the practical improvement, not the unfeasible dream.

## II. CONDITIONS FOR SUCCESS

Productivity improvement efforts are often thought of as things that managers must "do." Although productivity improvement requires considerable activity, reflection is an appropriate place to start. Two organizations may achieve vastly different outcomes in productivity improvement efforts due to the different starting conditions that they face. The success of productivity improvement requires that managers analyze the conditions at hand and ensure that conditions for success are in place. Without these conditions, managers face an uphill and maybe even a losing battle. Success will be hard to come by. There are at least five necessary conditions for success: higher officials' support, a need for change, a critical mass of people, a specific initial project, and organizational trust.

### A. Higher Officials' Support

The first condition for success is higher officials' support. The definition of "higher" is the manager's boss and, as necessary, the boss' boss. In local government, the latter could be an elected official or, possibly, a political appointee in federal or state government. Higher management support is necessary for a variety of reasons: to provide resources (such as for training or information technology), to provide authorization for changes (such as personnel changes) and overall legitimation, or to gives a "green light" to continue. However, higher management is also practically important to prevent end-runs from lower managers or employees around the manager working toward productivity improvement. End-runs are a powerful way of blocking or redirecting productivity improvement efforts by discrediting others and their efforts. The tactics of end-runs are often leaks and gossip ("Did you know that . . .?"). It is difficult to be successful at productivity improvement when others are doing an end-run around the manager in charge. When higher managers sanction the productivity improvement efforts of lower managers, the end-run path is blocked (Kanter et al., 1992; Kotter, 1995; Strebel, 1996).

Sometimes support for productivity improvement involves elected officials and political appointees. This is not the typical case, however, it does deserve discussion. Unlike senior appointed managers, who often readily grasp its importance, productivity improvement is seldom a main concern to elected officials and political appointees, who usually focus on policy and program development. Although the latter conflict with the needs of productivity improvement (Cope, 1997; Thompson, 2000), support from elected officials may be forthcoming because such improvement is consistent with the development of the organization, because the potential fallout for higher officials is minimal, and because very little is asked of them—only legitimacy, resources, and support against end-runs. Thus, support from these elected officials may require little more than presentation of coherent and compelling arguments and feasibility planning. Of course, support is not guaranteed, and astute managers therefore usually have a few different productivity improvement strategies in mind; a little flexibility goes a long way when seeking support from political officials. There are many different ways to improve organizations and units, indeed.

Some managers claim the lack of legal authority as a reason for not undertaking productivity improvement. This argument is dubious because the scope of management responsibility is usually sufficiently broad to find something that a manager can do to improve the organization. It seems incredulous to maintain that there is nothing that a manager can legally do to improve the organization short of political support or passing new laws. Others have noted that turnover of elected and political appointed officials creates new policy agendas which may impede productivity improvement (Ammons, 1992). Yet this need not always be the case: the two are seldom linked, change creates opportunity for new support, and many productivity improvement efforts occur at relatively low levels of the organization that are not affected by political turnover. One implication for productivity improvement efforts that are connected in this way is to structure them so that they produce phased, short-term results.

Clearly, productivity improvement efforts are more likely to succeed when adequate resources, authority, and protection are available. Such support need not involve political officials, but it might. In any event, productivity improvement is furthered when managers find improvement opportunities for which the support of higher officials is available, and then work within (or around) the constraints that exist in order to make productivity improvement happen.

## B.  An Urgent Need for Change

It is frequently observed that in the U.S. political system crisis leads to consensus and change. For example, environmental disasters are often catalysts for major new environmental legislation. Airline accidents are known to spur increased regulatory activity. The second condition for success is the existence of a crisis or urgent need for change. At any point, organizations have numerous areas in which they could be improved. All of these potential targets for improvements are vying for attention and consideration. Yet there is nothing like a crisis to draw immediate attention to action. Urgent crises often also draw attention from higher management, hence, furthering their support, and, possibly, resources, authority, and protection against end-runs.

It is not always clear why an issue becomes viewed as an urgent crisis, but it seems that those labeled as such usually threaten the existence or credibility of an agency in some important way. The link with productivity improvement, then, can be direct or indirect. For example, a public transportation agency that has one of its passengers murdered is apt to call into question the ability of the agency to provide safe transportation. The need to restore public confidence is clear; the productivity improvement implication, if any, is not. In other instances, the linkage is direct. A regulatory agency facing a backorder of three months for service requests is facing a crisis that demands productivity improvement. The situation becomes a crisis when its clients make the situation a focus of media or legislative attention.

Regrettably, the reality of productivity improvement is that not every productivity opportunity has a major "crisis" associated with it. Neither can managers create or promote crises without the risk of severe personal backfiring. In the absence of a crisis or urgent need, productivity improvement may be relegated to the set of issues that are both important and of nonimmediate significance. Managers, like politicians, then have to make their case to other organizational members for support. In the absence of media attention, the above problem of backorders might still be perceived as an "urgent need" (rather than crisis) by others inside the organization. It follows that managers need to learn how to be effective advocates for their proposals by getting others to see them as desirable responses to urgent needs. In the absence of a crisis, managers may spend months persuading others that something is an urgent need.

Persuasion is a fine art, indeed. Faced with competing opportunities, a cogent case must be made. First, managers need to show that the proposed productivity improvement saves or even increases agency revenues. Reductions in staff time needed to process something are easily translated into cost savings. Reducing the number of errors that need rework is also a cost savings. Electronic interactions that promise both are also savings, though not without outlays, too. Second, others will need to be persuaded that the improvement helps the organization as a whole, not merely the department of the manager. When something helps the organization as a whole, it may also help other managers, thus gaining their support. Third, managers need to show that they are confident, and not afraid of being held accountable. A feasibility assessment should be undertaken, and an implementation plan that gives accounting for timelines and which includes performance measures.

In short, when urgent needs or crises are present, productivity improvement becomes easier because it is easier to obtain higher officials' support which, in turn, induces others to support it as well. Often, managers will need to successfully persuade others that productivity improvement responds to an important organizational problem.

## C.  A Critical Mass of Support

Managers cannot do productivity improvement alone. Employees do much of the work, and the job of the manager is to get employees to do the work. Productivity improvement requires a "critical mass" of people at different levels of the organization, including workers. A critical mass is the third necessary condition for success, providing the initial support that gets the project going and keeps it moving along. The critical mass consists of supporters who enthusiastically set out to make the productivity improvement idea work in practice, and who generate some initial successes that validate the idea around which others can later rally (Beer et al., 1990).

Managers must often cultivate their initial critical mass of support. In organizational development, the 25–50–25 rule states that no matter what is being proposed,

25% of one's audience will enthusiastically embrace it, 25% will oppose it, and 50% will sit on the fence, ambivalent about the proposed effort. This is an ideal-type rule; although not tested in practice, many practitioners feel that it is approximately correct. Fence sitters may yet come to embrace the idea if it proves to have "staying power" in the organization. The implication of this rule of thumb is that managers must identify and work with the 25% of employees and managers who support the proposed effort. These persons must be given reasons and motivation to rally around the proposed idea. In the absence of a committed group of followers, the critical mass, the proposed productivity improvement is destined to die for lack of support. The effort simply fails to "take off."

This perspective challenges some prevalent gut instincts of less experienced managers; they often try to persuade those who initially resist the proposed effort. The implied reasoning is that if resisters can be persuaded, then managers need fear no further resistance during the effort. This reasoning is flawed, in part because resisters may include cynics and others who are not receptive to persuasive argument. Also, it is irrational to believe that fence sitters will embrace the proposed change in the absence of some proof that it works and that it is embraced by the organization. In short, resisters will always exist. Thus the implementation strategy is to begin work with supporters, not resisters. Initially, resisters should be ignored. In due time, when the productivity improvement works, the legion of supporters will grow, and some of the initial resisters may be converted. Some resisters may even leave the organization. Others will just have to be tolerated to some extent, as they probably already are.

## D.  Successful Initial Project

Successful productivity improvement efforts are often characterized by having one or more initial (trial or pilot) projects that are characterized as successes. These are also sometimes called productivity improvement test sites. Having such sites is the fourth condition for success. An early success "feeds" one's supporters, and provides something to be persuaded about to those still sitting on the fence. An early success provides momentum to early productivity improvement efforts. The initial effort is often a simple easy application chosen because it will be successful; it is also called a "ripe apple." Productivity improvement is easier when managers have identified such a project.

However, some managers seem to choose a difficult project instead. The implied reasoning is that difficult projects provide greater learning opportunities. Challenging projects also provide evidence of the merit of productivity improvement efforts. This thinking is faulty, because it ignores the significant challenge of gaining organizational acceptance. Difficult projects are more likely to fail and thereby provide ammunition to one's challengers or resisters. Moreover, productivity improvement is not akin to a demonstration or feasibility project. The task of the manager is to make the organization better, not perfect. It truly suffices to choose easy targets of improvement, leaving more difficult targets for later after organizational support has been gained.

At times, the nature of some productivity improvement efforts makes them unsuitable for an initial project because the change must be organization- or unitwide. For example, reorganizations often must be implemented in an encompassing manner. Then the possibility of failure and learning by trial and error must be acknowledged.

Managers expect complications, and so does everyone else. It is hoped that support rather than punitive action is forthcoming when things do not work out as planned. Such a helpful and conciliatory tone can do much to win over the skeptics who, like everyone else, have no choice but to participate in the new way of doing business.

## E.  Trust

The fifth condition for success is the existence of trust among employees and managers. This is the most abstract of conditions and yet, according to many, one of the most critical determinants of success. Trust is necessary because productivity improvement implies that employees must give up their known ways of getting the job done for new untested ways. They must also give up known rewards associated with these ways for unknown future rewards, and accept heightened risk of failure with potentially lower rewards or even increased punishment. Trust is the "glue" that allows employees to accept these diminished working conditions. Specifically, trust allows workers to accept managers' promises that things will work out and that no harm will come to them; good things might even happen! By contrast, when trust is absent, the rationale for accepting managers' promises appears hollow and worthy of deep suspicion. Those who would be sitting on the fence might now resist the effort, and those who would have supported the effort with reservation, might turn against it, too (Goodstein and Burke, 1990; Berman and Van Wart, 1999; Berman and West, 1998b).

It is interesting to note that trust is not a feature that characterizes persons, but rather the cognitive consequence of interactions. Trust is associated with emotions that are born from reflection about experiences with others. Specifically, trust is created when others "do as they say" and act in consistent ways over time that are benevolent to us rather than do harm. In productivity improvement, managers need to have established trust with workers by projecting their effectiveness and showing their support for workers who "do the right thing." When workers trust managers to be successful and not invoke harm to them, productivity improvement goes much smoother than when workers perceive managers as being ineffective and harmful or uncaring. Trust is seldom an accidental event in organizations. Managers who inspire trust are apt to have worked hard at it. They also work consistently at it because, as many people know, one act of unkindness erases ten good deeds that aimed to inspire trust.

Trust is also associated with organizational environments that are favorable for productivity improvement and modern management philosophies. Bardwick (1995), for example, distinguishes between organizational cultures of revitalization, fear, and entitlement. In cultures of fear, and entitlement, little trust exists between employees and managers. Cultures of revitalization are characterized by optimism and accountability, and require trust in order for workers to be innovative and exercise initiative in meeting organizational goals.

In short, when these five conditions are present (higher officials' support, a need for change, a critical mass of people, a specific initial project, and trust), productivity improvement is much easier than when any one of them is missing. Being aware of these conditions is important, and may cause managers to pause before rushing into productivity improvement. Indeed, an astute manager might well take up to a year to ensure that these conditions are in place before proceeding with any specific productivity implementation strategy discussed below.

## III.  STRATEGIES FOR IMPLEMENTATION

The success of implementation is increased when following a strategy. From the early 1970s, various studies have sought to identify pathways or strategies that improve the probability of success. This literature is sometimes referred to as "planned change" (e.g., Robertson and Seneviratne, 1995). Managers enhance their success by following the steps below, even though implementation efforts do not always mirror these proposed steps exactly. We first discuss strategies for making change in a small unit (a supervisor with six to ten employees), and then organizationwide change that could involve several thousand employees.

### A.  Small Scale Change

The implementation process for productivity improvement in a small unit is straightforward, although not without pitfalls that need to be avoided. Many of these steps are analogous to project management, yet the intention of productivity improvement is that change should be ongoing rather than timebound (e.g., Davidson Frame, 1995). Small unit change can follow these steps:

1.  Getting a mandate to start the project;
2.  Stating a clear reason for the project;
3.  Explaining the goals and target dates;
4.  Stating faith that the goals and target dates can be achieved, and giving some examples that this can be done;
5.  Completing initial first steps and, if appropriate, a pilot project;
6.  Empowering people to operationalize the plan;
7.  Monitoring implementation: keeping the project on track, moving it forward, and being available for crisis intervention.

The first step reminds managers to get support from higher officials. Even when no additional resources are involved, support from higher officials provides legitimacy and reassurance that others consider the proposed improvement meritorious. Support from higher officials also deals with the problem of end-runs by foreclosing them. The second step provides employees with a rationale for the proposed productivity improvement; that is, explaining the nature of the problem that the productivity improvement addresses, why the problem is important (or even critical), and why the productivity improvement initiative is a sensible approach to dealing with the problem.

The third and fourth steps bring the productivity improvement effort closer to reality by showing specifics and manager commitment. By stating specific goals, the manager is implying that he or she is not afraid of making claims to which he or she can be held accountable. By being specific, the manager also tells employees exactly what is being asked of them. By offering the goals and target dates with enthusiasm, the manger conveys a sense of unwavering support and confidence in the proposed plan. Enthusiasm and accountability are important, because the manager surely expects that of employees, too. By showing enthusiasm, accountability, and specifics, the manager is creating a framework for success.

An important consideration regarding Steps three and four is whether the managers should expect cooperation from all employees, or only some. The 25–50–25 rule is certainly in effect, but much depends on the specific context. In some settings, employees cannot withhold their support; they can be directed what to do (e.g., army personnel). In other settings, employees can withhold their support or through foot dragging threaten the success of the plan (e.g., research scientists). In all settings, it is wise to start the productivity improvement efforts as a pilot project that involves only volunteers from those who are among the 25% who are enthusiasts. If the productivity improvement must involve all of the workers, it might be a good idea to give the 25% who are supporters a leadership role in the effort, and to ensure that resisters are not assigned critical aspects of the plan.

Another consideration is the "tone of voice" of the manager. Managers need enthusiasm and commitment, and so a supportive and coaching style of leadership is preferred over leadership that is directing or autocratic in nature which may breed resistance. An analogy can be made with teachers, because employees along with the manager are learners as they try to apply the proposed productivity improvement to their unique situation (Berman, 1998; Lynch, 1992). As good teachers, managers should tell employees why the effort is important, and how it benefits them (or the mission to which they ought to be committed). The manager-as-teacher should be enthusiastic and persistent about pursuing the success of the effort, have an endless range of examples to prove his or her point, and help employees-as-students learn from mistakes that are inevitable with any new endeavor. The manager should welcome contributions from all employees, regardless of their motives or past reluctance. The manager-as-teacher knows when enough support exists to continue with the effort, and should treat everyone fairly and with dignity, not building any hills that employees can't climb. The manager should also be in control of the productivity improvement effort, while holding the line with resisters. These considerations also are the hallmark of many excellent teachers.

The rule of three states that some people are reluctant to take something seriously unless it has been said a few times. A lot of managers say a lot of things that later turn out to be inconsequential or not followed up on; it is thus reasonable to assume that something that has been said three times has some commitment of the person saying it. Thus managers should expect to have to repeat much of what they say, perhaps as often as three times. A related rule is the rule of seven, which states that people need to practice something seven times before they master it. Although seven times may be an exaggeration in some instances, the notion of a learning curve is clearly established in the literature.

The above steps and considerations set the tone, expectations, and modus operandus for subsequent steps. The fifth step is the actual pilot project or other first steps of the productivity improvement effort. Here managers-as-leaders will lead by example, working with employees to make the productivity improvement successful. It is important to choose an initial effort that is easy and simple, and which can serve as a template or model from which subsequent applications can be drawn. The initial efforts serve as learning exercises. After the initial effort(s), the manager then, in Step six, empowers employees to proceed on their own, applying the productivity improvement effort to new situations. Some applications may be progressively more difficult, thus requiring employees to continue to work together and share information. Managers lead in this effort by ensuring that workers follow up and learn implementation lessons. Such sharing of information and accountability can be a temporary feature of regular staff meetings in which this is discussed.

The seventh step involves managers as monitors of productivity improvement implementation. After several applications, the effort should be routine, but managers will still need to keep an eye on the effort to ensure that it continues moving forward. Managers, after all, are accountable to higher officials for its success. To this end, managers might require periodic updates. They should also be available as trouble-shooters as new challenges inevitably arise. These might involve conditions that are beyond the scope of control of employees, such as other departments that drag their feet, rules that need interpretation, clients with unusual requests, and the like.

The empowerment and broader diffusion of productivity improvement implies that at some point managers will have to deal with the matter of resisters. A hope is that initial skeptics will eventually come around as positive results are shown and more employees support the project. The latter implies a smaller audience for the critics, which may affect their decision to go along. Also, during implementation managers have ample opportunity to reach out and try to understand the reasons for employees' misgivings, and address them. But one cannot ignore the real possibility of those who, no matter what, refuse to give support. At that point, managers may want to consider the opportunity costs of dealing with such resisters. First, managers should ask whether these employees really damage the effort. If not, then doing nothing is certainly an option. Maladaptives are a fact of life. Benefits of ignoring cynics are the avoidance of headaches, and increased benefits such as merit pay and rewards for other employees; clearly, resisters should not expect excellent performance appraisals. A second option is to encourage such employees to transfer to other positions that may be better suited to their talents. A third option is to threaten to seek dismissal through the usual human resource management process of reprimanding and the like. Such threats may cause the resister to comply. A fourth option is actual dismissal which often is still quite trying. In short, in the imperfect world of organizations, the question to ask is whether the costs of removing resisters is worth the incremental gain in productivity improvement. Often, it is not.

## B. Large Scale Change

Productivity improvement also occurs throughout entire agencies, and may involve thousands of employees. Some federal agencies are quite large, as are state agencies that have branches or divisions in each of their counties and major population centers. How can productivity improvement be implemented in very large agencies?

Some productivity improvement implementation efforts may take up to five years. Of course, this does not mean that managers wait five years for results. Rather, productivity improvement is implemented in small steps, in different parts of the organization, with each effort producing a definable positive result for the organization and those involved. Slowly, as more and more divisions of the agency implement the productivity improvement effort, more positive results occur, until the effort is implemented throughout the entire organization. Widespread diffusion may take up to five years, even though each effort is about three to six months long and is designed to produce positive results. Also, the fact that some efforts take that long does not imply that one manager oversees the entire effort. Such a commitment is wildly unrealistic in many instances. Rather, the impetus for productivity improvement comes from different people at different points in time; each time, the need for productivity improvement must be successfully argued by those who want it. Thus some efforts might not make it throughout the entire agency, such as when circumstances change and the initial effort is no longer appropriate or is superseded by more promising productivity improvement efforts. (Beckhard, 1990; Laszlo and Lauge, 2000; Berman, 1998; O'Toole, 1996).

In practice, large scale projects proceed in many different ways, reflecting the unique exigencies of organizations. The following is an idealized way in which such change might occur, taking into account the above issues and conditions for success. Large scale change can involve the steps:

1. Creating awareness about the need and feasibility of change among senior managers;
2. Reaching consensus among senior managers regarding trying one or several pilot projects;
3. Creating a group of middle managers/senior employees responsible for the implementation of the pilot project;
4. Providing training, resources to middle managers/senior employees for implementation, and implementing the pilot project;
5. Diffusing the effort by identifying new targets in new departments, and using previously involved employees/managers as leaders or internal consultants on those projects;
6. Further diffusion through more replication in other settings, replicating the effort until each unit has one or more of the productivity improvement efforts; and
7. Formalizing any changes to operating procedures and appraisal systems as needed.

The first step creates awareness about the need for and the feasibility of change. Although the initial idea for change can arise from anywhere inside or outside the organization, the need for resources, legitimacy, and protection against end-runs implies that productivity improvement is likely to fare better when higher officials are brought on board. Lower managers will need to find at least one such senior manager to support the effort. Typically, that senior manager will need to persuade other senior managers as well, which is Step two. Such persuasion requires having some preliminary ideas about how the improvement might be implemented, which lower managers might be doing what, and the costs and benefits of the proposed effort. Often, a specific pilot project is also discussed. Depending on the scope and complexity of the proposed change, getting support from other senior managers may involve as little as their notification in a meeting, or as much as the creation of a separate task force to study the matter in greater detail.

Figure 1 shows these first two steps. The arrows denote the source of the original idea for change. The solid line denotes a formal reporting relationship between the chief senior manager supporter and the middle manager who "champions" the productivity improvement effort. The middle manager could be the person who brought the proposed need to the senior, although not necessarily. The three dotted lines in the figure represent the involvement of three senior managers whose advice is being sought. Figure 1 further shows some other middle managers and (groups of) employees who might be involved in any proposed effort. Note that although Figure 1 depicts top management, in practice a "senior manager" is likely to be one's boss or at most the boss' boss. Thus the senior manager is not necessarily a top manager.

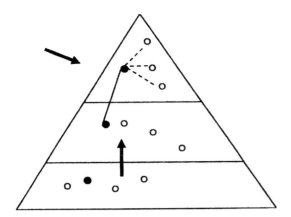

**Figure 1**   Initial exploration.

Step three involves the initial implementation. As discussed earlier, it is important to choose a good "ripe apple" test site for implementation that creates experiences and successes in making the proposed effort work. Those involved in the pilot project should gain the experience and confidence to subsequently apply the effort in other areas (Berry, 1991). However, the design of the initial pilot project should take into consideration that after the pilot project other organizational members must be asked to undertake pilot projects in their own units. Thus initial pilot projects are often accompanied by the involvement of middle managers and employees who follow the initial project (perhaps even as an "advisory group") so that they can learn from it for their subsequent execution. These participants might also be asked to support the middle manager in the initial pilot project effort, thus giving them an active role. This involvement is shown in Figure 2, as the dotted lines that involve other middle managers and, perhaps, some employees.

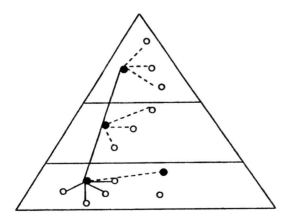

**Figure 2**   A pilot effort.

As in any new effort, the 25–50–25 rule applies. As discussed earlier, senior managers do well to identify a middle manager who supports the effort of the initial pilot project. The middle manger, in turn, will need to draw on employees who support the effort. In large agencies, senior managers should have little difficulty identifying a good site location. The actual request to implement a pilot project can take the form of a structured "psychological contract" discussion, whereby both the senior and middle managers clarify their expectations of each other regarding support, accomplishment, and rewards. The same might also be true for the discussion that follows between the middle managers and the employees (Rousseau, 1995).

Typically, there is little need for an agencywide announcement of the pilot project. The trying out of a new idea is a routine occurrence. Organizational commitment has certainly not yet been given to any widescale deployment. Thus most employees and managers may not even be aware of the new effort, and many will not know until subsequent efforts have been tried.

Step four involves ensuring adequate resources and expertise for the success of the pilot effort. The nature of resources depends on the specific productivity improvement effort. Consultants are sometimes used in these early efforts as "experts" or people who have experience implementing the effort elsewhere. These persons can lend an ear as others grapple with applications. Later, consultants might be used as facilitators assisting other units in their applications. The role of consultants is to help managers and employees learn how to make the productivity improvement work; they should not be doing the productivity improvement for them.

A successful pilot project lays the ground for subsequent diffusion. Step five is the first-time diffusion effort that, in large part, is led by those who have been involved as advisory group members in previous efforts. Such previous participants are shown in Figure 3 as the middle managers and employees shaded or light gray. Although some managers and many employees will be new to the effort, it is hoped that each team has at least one person who can then speak from the experience of having participated on the pilot team. Doing so is a highly effective way of facilitating the learning curve and taking advantage of institutional memory. In this way, one pilot project advisory group of seven members can spawn at least seven new efforts. The

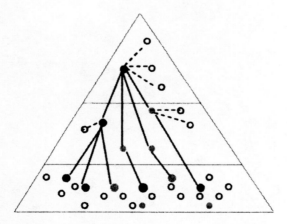

**Figure 3**  Diffusion.

idea is captured in Figure 3, which also shows new advisory groups associated with the new efforts.

Step six is mere repetition of the above application and diffusion processes. The seven diffusion efforts in Step five now give rise to fifty or more projects in Step six, and so on. A third diffusion effort would virtually be agencywide, as it could involve a couple of hundred different implementation efforts. We should note, however, that there is nothing automatic about the diffusion effort. Management and employee turnover, as well as changes in the environment of the agency, require that each subsequent diffusion is argued on merit. With regard to resisters, one hopes that the success and momentum of initial efforts is sufficient to cause initial fence sitters to become supporters. Some resisters may become fence sitters and, eventually, reluctant but cooperating participants. Die-hard resisters will find shrinking audiences and they might, eventually, be cast somewhat as loners who are going against the tide of events.

We should also note the viewpoint of large-scale productivity improvement when seen through the eyes of employees, rather than managers. Many employees may be unaware of the productivity improvement effort until well into Steps four or five. The decision to implement the effort in their work unit will be seen as being put upon them from above; these employees have not been part of the managerial learning curve. Managers need to carefully explain to employees the prior background of the proposed effort, and to present it as a tentative experience to be evaluated further (Scharitzer and Korunka, 2000).

Step seven is the formalization of the productivity improvement effort that occurs at the end of all diffusion. By then, for most organizational members the productivity improvement has become the normal way of doing business. Such formalization is likely to be seen as routine news. Note, too, that Step seven is likely to occur three to five years after the initial idea (Step one). In an agency with normal turnover of five to nine percent annually, this means that many workers, up to half of the agency, could be new to the organization. They will have entered the organization in some advanced stage of the productivity improvement implementation effort. For them, the new approach is all that they have ever experienced at the agency. The productivity improvement is the normal, already existing way of getting the job done. It has been fully absorbed in the organization, and employees and managers are now ready to get on with the next productivity improvement effort.

## IV.  CONCLUSION

Productivity improvement requires consideration for both "what" and "how" it will be done. This chapter discusses the "how" of productivity improvement. Specifically, it suggests that managers should be aware of conditions that increase the likelihood of success. No organization offers perfect conditions for success, but managers can succeed nevertheless by acknowledging them. The task of the manager is to make the organization better, not perfect. Important conditions for productivity improvement are: higher officials' support, a need for change, a critical mass of people, a specific initial project, and trust. This chapter also discusses "planned change" strategies that can enhance a manager's success. The steps for managing change in small groups are: (1) getting a mandate to start the project; (2) stating a clear reason for the project; (3) explaining the goals and target dates; (4) stating belief that the goals and target dates can be achieved and giving some examples of how this can be done; (5) completing the initial first steps and, if appropriate, a pilot project; (6) empowering people to operationalize the plan; and (7) monitoring implementation by keeping the project on track and being available for crisis intervention.

By being aware of change strategies, managers exercise foresight and strategy in overcoming barriers to change. This chapter also discusses the steps for implementing productivity improvement in a (very) large agency. Managers need to get senior management support, implement a few pilot efforts, train other managers and employees to implement the productivity improvement in their units, and implement the effort in a growing number of units. This is more complex, and takes more time. When managers follow these steps, they can increase their success. In doing so, managers make organizations better, and thereby increase both the organization's and their own reputation for effectiveness.

## REFERENCES

Altshuler, A., Zegans, M. (1997). Innovation and public management. In: Altshuler, A., Behn, R., eds. *Innovation in American Government*. Washington, DC: Brookings Institution, pp. 68–82.

Ammons D. (1992). Productivity barriers in the public sector. In: Holzer M., ed. *Public Productivity Handbook*. New York: Marcel Dekker, pp. 117– 136

Bardwick, J. (1995). *Danger in the Comfort Zone*. New York: AMACON.

Beckhard, R. (1990). Strategies for large system change. In: Kolb, D., Rubin, M., Osland, J., eds. *The Organizational Reader*. Englewood Cliffs, NJ: Prentice-Hall.

Beer, M., Eisenstat, R., Spector, B. (1990). Why change programs don't produce change. *Harvard Bus. Rev.* 68:158–166.

Berman, E. (1998). *Productivity in Public and Nonprofit Organizations*. Thousand Oaks, CA: Sage.

Berman, E., Van Wart, M. (1999). The ethics of productivity. *Int. J. Org. Theor. Behav.* 2:413–430.

Berman, E., West, J. (1998a). Productivity enhancement efforts in public and nonprofit organizations. *Public Product. Manage. Rev.* 22:207–219.

Berman, E., West, J. (1998b). Responsible risk-taking. *Public Admin. Rev.* 58:346–352.

Berman, E., West, J. (1999). Career risk and reward from productivity. *Public Person. Manage.* 18:453–471.

Berry, T. (1991). *Managing the Total Quality Transformation*. New York: McGraw-Hill.

Cohen, S., Eimicke, W. (1996). *The New Effective Public Manager*. San Francisco: Jossey-Bass.

Cope, G. (1997). Bureaucratic reform and issues of political responsiveness. *J. Public Admin. Res. Theor.* 7:461–471.

Davidson Frame, J. (1995). *Managing Projects in Organizations: How to Make the Best Use of Time, Techniques, and People*. San Francisco: Jossey-Bass.

Donahue, J. (1999). *Making Washington Work: Tales of Innovation in the Federal Government*. Washington, DC: Brookings Institution.

Gaebler, T., Blackman, J., Bruce,, Blessing, L. (1999). *Positive Outcomes: Raising the Bar on Government Reinvention*. Burke, VA: Chatelaine.

Goodstein, L., Burke, W. (1990). Creating successful organization change. *Org. Dynam.* 19(4): 5–17.

Gore, A. (1995). *Common Sense Government: Works Better and Costs Less*. Washington, DC: U.S. Government Printing Office.

Holzer, M., Callahan, K. (1998). *Government at Work: Best Practices and Model Programs*. Thousand Oaks, CA: Sage.

Kanter, R., Stein, B., Jick, T. (1992). *The Challenge of Organizational Change*. New York: Free Press.

Kettl, D., DiIulio, J., eds. *Inside the Reinvention Machine: Appraising Governmental Reform*. Washington, DC: Brookings Institution.

Kotter, J. (1995). Leading change. *Harvard Bus. Rev.* 74(2):59–67.

Laszlo, C., Lauge, F. (2000). *Large Scale Organizational Change: An Executive's Guide*. Woburn, MA: Butterworth-Heinemann.

Lynch, R. (1992). *LEAD! How Public and Nonprofit Managers Can Bring Out the Best in Themselves and Their Organizations*. San Francisco: Jossey-Bass.

OECD. *Organization for Economic Co-Operation and Development. In Search of Results: Performance Management Practices*. Washington, DC: OECD.

Osborne, D., Plastrick, P. (2000). *The Reinventor's Fieldbook: Tools for Transforming Your Government*. San Francisco: Jossey-Bass.

O'Toole, L. (1996). Critical incidents and emergent issues in managing large-scale change. In: Kettl, D., Milward, B., eds. *The State of Public Management*. Baltimore: Johns Hopkins University Press.

Robertson, P., Seneviratne, S. (1995). Outcomes of planned organizational change in the public sector: a meta-analytic comparison to the private sector. *Public Admin. Rev.* 55:547–558.

Rousseau, D. (1995). *Psychological Contracts in Organizations: Understanding Written and Unwritten Agreements*. Thousand Oaks, CA: Sage Publications.

Scharitzer, D., Korunka, C. (2000). New public management: evaluating the success of total quality management and change management interventions in public services from the employees' and customers' perspectives. *Total Quality Manage.* 11:S941–S953.

Strebel, P. (1996). Why do employees resist change? *Harvard Bus. Rev.* 75(3):86–95.

Thompson, J. (2000). Reinvention as reform: assessing the national performance review. *Public Admin. Rev.* 60:508–522.

# 10

## Government Reinvention

**BEVERLY A. CIGLER**
*Pennsylvania State University, Harrisburg, Pennsylvania, U.S.A.*

## I. INTRODUCTION

Over the past two decades, governments worldwide have accomplished extraordinary changes in how their bureaucracies operate, internally and in delivering services to their "customers." In some cases, these sweeping changes have been accompanied by a dramatic transformation of the role of government in society, especially government's relation to citizens and the nonprofit and private sectors. We are beginning to speak less about "government" and more about "governance," the interplay among and between the public, private, and nonprofit sectors in service production and delivery and in policymaking. Especially useful commentary on the sweeping changes found in the governance system is found in Peters and Pierre (1998), Milward and Provan (2000), and Kettl (2000). Similarly, we have expanded concern with "intergovernmental relations" to include intersector relations. Agranoff and McGuire (2001), for example, examined the search for management models within the context of a changing American federalism and O'Toole (1997) wrote about the implications for democracy in a networked bureaucratic world.

As the internal workings of government were being reshaped to serve its customers, other reforms were being made to change what is meant by citizenship and to engage citizens more broadly in the governance system that includes government's policy-making and service delivery roles. Roberts (1997), for example, refers to public deliberation as an alternative approach to crafting policy and setting direction.

As the standards and norms that shape the behavior of public employees and bureaucracies have changed, so too has the language of government. With a strong focus on private sector tools and techniques, the language of business is now mirrored in public sector management. The term most used to depict the administrative changes worldwide is the "New Public Management" (NPM), however, there are vast differences in the nature, size, and approach to reforms across countries (e.g., Pollitt, 1993).

## II. REINVENTION IN THE AMERICAN CONTEXT

In the United States, the favored terminology is "reinventing government," the depiction popularized by David Osborne and Ted Gaebler (1992) in their book, *Reinventing Government* (see also Barzelay and Armajani, 1992). Their prescriptions were widely read and used by elected and appointed officials at all levels of government and adapted by the Clinton Administration for its national-level government reform program called the National Performance Review (NPR), under the direction of then-Vice President Al Gore (Gore, 1993; Clinton and Gore, 1994). States and larger cities and counties adopted many of the same reforms, as did nonprofit organizations (Moon and deLeon, 2001; Kearney et al., 2000; Berry and Wechsler, 1995).

The National Performance Review aimed to make the national government work better and cost less by becoming performance-based, results-oriented and customer-driven, with empowered employees who could be held accountable. The NPR, which had its name changed to the National Partnership for Reinventing Government, was officially dismantled on January 16, 2001. It was one of the longest sustained and most well-known executive branch reform initiatives in U.S. history (Frederickson, 1996; Williams, 2000). As would be expected, it left a mixed legacy. Criticisms were quick and sustained (e.g., Moe, 1994; Carroll, 1995; Ingraham, 1997; Thompson, 2000; Haque, 2001; Gilman, 1999). The strongest criticism was lodged at the market-based foundation of many reforms (e.g., DeLeon and Denhardt, 2000; Frederickson, 1999).

The NPR began roughly simultaneously with the information technology (IT) revolution that transformed the U.S. economy and, by the late 1990s, government agencies were asked to take actions to advance electronic government. IT-based procurement reforms, such as buying through online reverse auctions, often yielded substantial savings. Federal agencies developed and used information technology to give individuals with disabilities access to government information and data. Launched in September 2000, FirstGov.gov links access to Web sites at all government levels, offering the public a single access point for information for thousands of government Web sites. The NPR reforms spanned a very wide range of government functions, including procurement, budgeting, and many other aspects of management. The area of public personnel management was a special target of reform (Peters and Savoie, 1994). Attempts were made to decentralize authority and make changes in selection procedures, position classification, and the use of incentives.

It's difficult to judge long-term success and/or to credit the NPR with the claimed $137 billion saved because of the impossibility of separating NPR-driven reform from other productivity efforts. Many agencies are visibly more customer friendly and hundreds are online. The federal workforce was cut by 377,000 (17%), but that sometimes reduced or eliminated institutional memory and created work backlogs. Personnel cuts sometimes came before IT systems were in place to handle eliminated jobs. Agency computers are plagued with security problems.

As with most reform efforts, the promise was greater than the reality. However, government reinvention didn't stop with a change of administrations. When President George W. Bush assumed the presidency in 2001, the NPR ended—but largely in name only. For example, in early 2002, the Bush Administration issued new guidelines for developing a "smarter" regulatory system that incorporated cost-effective rules. The President's Management Agenda for fiscal year 2002 (*http://www.whitehouse.gov/omb/ budget*) included government-wide initiatives that built on what was begun with the NPR. This included strategic management of human capital, competitive sourcing, improved financial performance, expanded electronic government, and budget and performance integration. It also included nine program initiatives that targeted some principles from the NPR. The Bush Administration's vision for government reform was guided overall by three broad principles: citizen-centered, not bureaucracy-centered government; results-oriented government; and market-based government. The first two principles clearly build on the NPR.

The reforms associated with the NPR are unlikely to die, even though the NPR Web site was relegated to the "cyber cemetery." There has been a lasting shift of attention from the classic notions of good public administration characterized by hierarchical control, specialization, reduced duplication, and clearly defined rules and procedures (Ostrom, 1974). The accumulation of changes in public bureaucracies at all levels in the United States in terms of how government business is conducted are so great in quantity, so lasting in effect, and of such continuing interest that a new presidential administration or turnovers in elected officials at any level are unlikely to halt the changes. Put simply, the goal of making government work better and cost less remains strong. This does not mean that everything has been a success but it does mean that the pragmatic toolkit of reform strategies and techniques is such that organizations can pick and choose those that work for them, and discard others.

## A. New Governance Reforms

During approximately the same time period that NPM and government reinvention ideas and practices took hold, other changes, sometimes labeled as the New Governance, began to forge new patterns of interaction among and between governments and society. New governance ideas and practices essentially change the meaning of government itself (McKnight and Kretzmann, 1993; Barber, 1998). Governance is achieved through a complex of networked relationships, placing the quality of inter-organizational, intergovernmental, intersector, and citizen–government relations at center stage. A focus on government's role within the governance system leads to a significantly different focus than what has typically been described as government reinvention (Peters and Savoie, 1996; Agranoff and McGuire, 1999; Alter and Hage, 1993; Alexander, 1995; Cigler, 2001).

The NPR, in its narrowest sense, was a driver of a set of management reforms. Other factors, such as a global concern for increased social equity, democratization, and empowerment fueled a spate of other government reform efforts. Still other concerns, such as a realization of the lack of policy coherence, fueled other reform efforts (Cigler, 1990). Changes in technology and communications, especially in information technology, were additional drivers of change.

Governance encompasses the gamut of mechanisms, processes, relationships, and institutions by which citizens articulate their interests and mediate their differences through collective action. Who exercises power is important to governance so political context must be understood. Governance institutions include the legal system; democratic institutions (e.g., legislatures); civil society, including community-based organizations or nongovernment organizations (NGOs), churches, and so on; economic markets such as business and labor groups; and the public sector. All of the institutions and processes of governance are changing, largely in response to fiscal pressures and globalization.

Instead of debating whether government should be more of a steerer or rower (but see Denhardt and Denhardt, 2000), as done with the NPM and the NPR, the focus is more on government as a relationship builder—a facilitator, broker, and manager of the complex networks that operate within the seemingly self-steering capacity of society (Kickert, 1997; Cigler, 1998). The complex set of collaborative relationships within the governance system does not focus attention on what is done alone by government or another sector. Instead, coproduction of services, coregulation, coguidance, and costeering of societal systems largely replace top-down and central steering by government. Interorganizational networks are characterized by interdependence and resource exchange, suggesting several key questions. What is or should be the role of government within a networked society? What changes or reforms would improve that role? How can accountability to citizens be accomplished in a networked world?

New governance thinking and practice, for example, does not treat citizens as customers in a reactive role to what government does, as is the case with the more limited government reinvention theory and practice. Citizens are considered "owners" who should have more active roles in deciding government's agenda and policies, including service delivery. Timney (1998) and Schachter (1995, 1997) offer especially good insights on the role of citizen owners and ways to overcome administrative barriers to increased participation. The NPM and the NPR stress continuous quality improvement, performance management, and other techniques to enable organizations to compete more effectively in a globalized society. New governance principles promote collaborative relationships. The two emphases are not necessarily incompatible. Successful businesses have learned to compete and cooperate at the same time, coining a new term, "coopetition." This is the challenge for reconciling "government reinvention" with the nature of governance.

The remaining sections of this chapter examine the bundle of ideas that can be identified as "government reinvention" and "the new governance" in the United States at all levels of government. The sections are as follows.

> Identify the underlying principles and assumptions that are reshaping public sector bureaucracies and government's role within the broader governance system;
> Describe and categorize the general patterns of administrative change that define government reinvention (sometimes referred to as REGO) within public bureaucracies and the role of government within the larger context of civil society and its governance system;
> Suggest explanations for these unprecedented efforts toward change; and,
> Assess progress and the likely next steps in government reform.

The amount and types of changes that have occurred are of such magnitude that no one catch-all term, such as the New Public Management or Reinventing Government captures what has been attempted and implemented by national, state, and local bureaucracies. The New Governance terminology is broader ranging but embraces some traditional reinventing government tenets. Most contemporary public administration writing on government reform has focused on changes within internal bureaucracies, to the relative neglect of the massive changes that have occurred in the broader governance system. Research and practice regarding multicommunity collaboration, a reshaping of intergovernmental and intersector relations, improved interorganizational relations, and a reshaping of democratic discourse and citizen engagement are topics that must be included when examining "government reinvention." The scholars who have been critical of the practices and theories related to the NPM and the NPR have sometimes offered new governance thinking in their critiques without apparent awareness of the literature on governance.

There is also no single or simple explanation for the emergence of the gamut of reforms over the last two decades, or the interest in their continuation. The mix of new management tools and ideas is truly a worldwide phenomenon, although differing structures and organizations characterize implementation. There is also varied success, which highlights the difficulty of transplanting basic management tools to different political and historical contexts. Government reinvention within the United States must be understood within the context of its particular social and political environment, that is, within the context of the overall governance system. Reform efforts stem from assumptions and principles about changing society and its governance system, including which values should be endorsed in making changes.

## III.  PRINCIPLES AND ASSUMPTIONS RESHAPING GOVERNMENT

Elsewhere (Cigler, 1998), I set forth twelve assumptions and principles—sometimes compatible and sometimes in conflict, all intertwined—that underline the transformation of public bureaucracies and government's role in society. These include the bundle of views underlying the NPM and government reinvention as well as the new governance ideas. The assumptions and principles are as follows.

*One.*  The view that monopoly government is not necessarily the most appropriate way to meet the needs of society or public responsibilities for a given service or function. That is, the rationale for government action is being reassessed. Consumers are increasingly being offered more options, for example, managed care and health maintenance organizations. K-12 education includes public schools and private schools, but also an array of such options as charter schools, school choice, and vouchers. Privatization, for both the production and the delivery of services, and outsourcing of government operations (e.g., payroll, bill collection, prison administration) is becoming commonplace. This extends to delivering, measuring, and monitoring human services such as juvenile and family services, home care and nursing homes, and some welfare activities.

Flexibility, choice, and discretion in the use of policy instruments are also more prevalent than in the past. Market-oriented approaches, such as vouchers, user charges, contracting out, and demand rationing, are now part of the policy tool kit. Centralized, rule-bound, inflexible, and process-oriented approaches have given way to decentralization, flexibility, and cost-effective approaches to allocation and management of finances. The financing and delivery of services is driven more by consumers, not programs.

*Two.*  The perception that government should be less of a direct funder, service provider, and regulator than in the past and more of a facilitator, catalyst, enabler, convenor, information generator and disseminator, standard setter, broker, and capacity builder. In effect, a major new role for government is evolving, that is, that of relationship-builder among people and groups across all sectors and government levels. State governments, for example, are more likely to award grant funds to local jurisdictions if they are willing to collaborate. Building the managerial, financial, and technical capacity of local government has become an important role of both states and the national government. Information on best practices or model policies, the development of measurement guides and monitoring and evaluation systems, and other ways to facilitate continuous learning are frequently provided by one level of government for a lower level, as well as throughout government for its bureaucracies.

*Three.* Holistic approaches to complex and intertwined problems must be forged, it is assumed, because of the complexity of problems, fiscal constraints, and accelerated changes in technology and communication. Global competitiveness has pushed the public sector toward boundary-spanning roles in building relationships for the development of self-sufficient regional economies. This includes holistic approaches to workforce skill development, high-quality physical infrastructure development, leveraged financial and technical resources, and adequate provision of the basics for quality living (e.g., affordable, quality health care and housing). These holistic approaches require new forms of intergovernmental and intersector collaboration. More and more the emphasis is on watersheds, laborsheds, commutersheds, and ecosystem management.

The last decade has seen the emergence of hundreds of "values-based organizations" that are committed to promoting and supporting the social justice, health, economic equity, and well-being of all people. Such organizations promote values that dovetail with many of the guiding principles outlined here: valuing diversity, equality, and equity; promoting civic participation; inclusionary approaches to individuals in decision making and social change processes that affect their lives within the workplace and externally; learning as individuals and collectively as an organization and community; and enhancing scientific, professional, and public capacity to use information and share knowledge.

*Four.* Regional approaches to the delivery of goods and services, whether through the regionalization of services, mergers, consolidations, or more informal collaborative processes, are assumed necessary in the global economy. The key questions no longer revolve on whether there is regionalization, but on who will be in charge. Will regional approaches be mandated or will incentive-based systems be developed to induce regional cooperation?

*Five.* Another operating assumption is that entities that supply services to the public should operate at the community level, individually or collectively. Improved institutional capacity and revitalized governing boards are high on reform agendas as are a wide variety of training programs to build managerial and governance skills. The assumption that programs are best operated at the community level also fuels interest in regionalism inasmuch as no one government or organization alone has the capability to deal with complex problems. By combining resources and people across communities, appropriate responses may be developed.

*Six.* Increasingly, the principle that resources should be concentrated on the people, organizations, and places in greatest need, with more self-reliance expected of recipients of government aid, is promoted. To ensure accountability, the trend is toward providing aid directly to individuals, rather than to bureaucracies. School programs with vouchers for low-income families are an example. Health care programs that include benefit packages that reflect ability to pay are another. Although state aid to municipalities has decreased, property tax relief for the needy has been increased by state legislatures. Welfare benefits are now dependent on completing high school and job training. High school dropouts can lose the privilege of having a driver's license in some states. Parents who do not maintain child support obligations may have funds automatically deducted from their paychecks or lottery winnings, or they may be arrested. Welfare recipients are asked to become more self-reliant through lifetime limits on eligibility and work requirements. Major place-specific programs assist areas or individuals in greatest need, such as state enterprise zones or community development corporations.

*Seven.* It is assumed that an appropriate balance should be restored between citizen rights and responsibilities. Changes in welfare policies are one example. Others include the loss of gun ownership if convicted of domestic violence, including child and spousal abuse, and prison fee programs that require prisoners to pay for room and board and other services. A "three strikes and you're out" law that automatically sends offenders with a third felony conviction to prison for life is another example. More delegation of authority in the changing management structures aims to encourage individuals to take personal responsibility.

*Eight.* Give governments increased mandate, regulatory, and fiscal flexibility when working with each other and with the private sector, and internally. The trend is away from overly prescriptive mandates that dictate how activities must be carried out toward those that specify goals to be accomplished. This is assumed necessary for achieving economic and social advantage. Streamlined facility permitting by states and local governments or integrated permitting and incentive programs are examples at the subnational level. Brownfield legislation lends flexibility in assessing liability for toxic wastes on old industrial sites turned into greenfields.

Another trend is the combination of mandates with capacity-building tools and inducements such as technical assistance or financial aid. A state might require local governments to prepare comprehensive land use plans and tie noncompliance to the withholding of state aid. Or, a state might reward a local government with a grant-in-aid and/or technical assistance for plan development, rather than issue highly prescriptive rules regarding the content of local plans. Certain procedures for plan development, but not content, might be required by a state. Less coercive approaches by higher-level governments may enhance local innovation and the ability to shape solutions for uniquely local circumstances. Increased flexibility in the regulatory arena includes regulatory negotiations, which bring together all stakeholders early in the process to design approaches for avoiding later problems. Alternative dispute resolution techniques encourage intergovernmental cooperation and save money.

*Nine.* An important guiding assumption or principle is that accountability for performance be stressed over processes, input, and bean counting. Strategic planning and strategic thinking processes, performance measurement and benchmarking, performance monitoring, and consultative processes are widely used among midsized and larger governments and agencies. As relief from stringent regulations is given, there are requirements to abide by stringent performance standards. Contract for performance procedures offer stronger roles for employees and/or lower levels of government, but demand more accountability. Partnership approaches within, among, and between governments, employees, citizens, and all sectors are prevalent. Greater attention is paid to analyzing impacts, risk assessment, user design, and information disclosure to citizens than has been the case in the past. The devolution of programs and responsibilities from one level to another is an ongoing trend.

Flexibility in work arrangements and the use of resources, a focus on performance, and enhancement of skills and competencies of management staff is promoted. Open participative approaches are used to promote performance management processes in the workplace. This includes setting and achieving performance objectives; building trust and cooperation within and across organizations; balancing the goals of the organization and the development needs of those who work in it; designing organizational structures to achieve effectiveness, consistency of response, and speed of decision making; devolving responsibility and establishing new accountability mechanisms; adopting value for money approaches; and a motivating and rewarding work environment, including development by negotiation of appropriate reward systems.

As responsibility, authority, and discretion have devolved to lower levels in an organization and/or to lower levels of government, accountability requirements have increased through the use of benchmarks, standards, and performance reviews. The rapid emergence of charter schools across the states is a policy example. Charter schools operate free of most state regulations; they are under performance contracts and different funding formulas than traditional schools, however. The notion of a performance review is also embodied in the concept of school report cards issued annually to the community, and parent surveys of school performance.

New arrangements for authority and accountability require more proactive approaches to managing and developing human capital within the workplace. This includes attention to sound recruitment and retention policies, workload distribution, career planning, organizational skills planning, job satisfaction, and performance management. More attention to teamwork, flexible reporting arrangements, and adequate recognition and reward systems for good performance are valued.

The effort to reconcile the demands of a clean environment, successful economic development, and equity for all (i.e., sustainable development) has led to a variety of flexible approaches in state–local relations. Broad goals are established for guiding state and local plans to achieve sustainability in the use of natural and financial resources, but local jurisdictions are permitted to choose how and where development occurs.

"Let managers manage, but require managers to manage" is a phrase that expresses the wide-ranging reinvention management strategies that are tied to accountability. Attention is increasingly devoted to measurement, monitoring, quality performance, goals and objectives, and strategic processes. Regional indices to gauge the success or failure of regional strategies are another example of this. So, too, are community scorecards, which provide indicators of service quality and quality of life, generally based on some type of benchmarking.

*Ten.* Deliberative democracy as the basis for policy decisions is another underlying assumption of government reinvention. New ways to engage citizens in designing future governance are promoted. Study circles, citizen forums, civic journalism, focus groups, citizen juries, and other strategic tools aim at creating dialogue that is issue- and knowledge-based and nonconfrontational. Such community conversations promote collegial learning and dialogue to develop approaches to social and political problems. These strategies collectively aim to build the civic infrastructure by developing greater trust relationships as a basis for increased collaboration.

Internal to the workplace, open participative approaches that aim to achieve joint ownership by management, staff, and unions are highlighted. Effective consultation and participation by all concerned and affected parties are replacing adversarial approaches to changes. Similarly, a customer service orientation means that customers or consumers are consulted more than in the past about their needs and what is important to them, including the type of service expected. Customer satisfaction is more systematically tracked than in the past. Openness and transparency are key goals. For citizens, the aim is for services to be more responsive than before, with more information available to them about actions and decisions taken on their behalf.

*Eleven.* Another guiding principle is that experimentation, cautious risk taking, and innovation should be encouraged and rewarded, not avoided and penalized. In a retreat from past practice, the public sector is learning to tolerate failure and copy success. Selective policies and programs are being favored over radical change. Voluntary programs are promoted over those imposed on people and communities. Single comprehensive approaches are giving way to multistaged experimental approaches based on pacing and sequencing strategies. It is argued that public service values such as accountability and responsiveness can be reinforced, not replaced, by such entrepreneurial behavior.

A movement toward child-first systems (placing less emphasis on keeping abused children with their parents and more willingness to place children in foster homes is an example of experimental innovation. Others include alternatives to the institutionalization of the elderly and nonviolent criminals. Corrections policy examples range from the development of private sector options for incarceration to expanded pretrial intervention and alternative sentencing. Instead of building new prisons, community-based penalties can be expanded, sentences of nonviolent offenders adjusted, and community policing instituted to have policy focus not solely on regulation and enforcement, but also on collaborative community building and facilitation. Results and outcomes—to community, neighborhoods, families, and individuals—are emphasized over programs and services.

*Twelve.* A focus on prevention, to avoid more complex and costly problems later, is another guiding assumption or principle that is reshaping government. Early childhood development, immunizations, Head Start, and other programs improve children's health and prepare them for school success. Checkups, screening, and immunization lower Medicaid costs. Integrated human service networks that focus on "families at risk" deal with child abuse and neglect, teen pregnancy, school dropouts, and other problems of children in poverty. Homes for unwed mothers, now called "second chance homes," offer adult supervision to teen mothers and help in early child development.

Prevention strategies dovetail with holistic approaches to social, health, and other societal problems such as violence prevention. Comprehensive community initiatives (CCI) is a term that covers the full range of initiatives that take a comprehensive approach to change communities in order to improve the well-being of their residents. Such initiatives pursue change at many levels, including individual, family, institutional, and communitywide, through processes that involve collaboration and coordination within the community and between the community and the broader society.

## IV.  GOVERNMENT REINVENTION CHARACTERISTICS

Among the twelve assumptions and guiding principles, several underlie one or more of the tools, techniques, and management styles of what is labeled "government reinvention" or the "new public management." These characteristics are as follows.

> Apply private sector management models, tools, or techniques (e.g., such as strategic planning and accrual accounting). This also includes the introduction of competition and rivalry into public sector provision via term contracts, contracting out, and other alternatives. It includes the use of monetary incentives linked to measured performance.
>
> Use alternative models for the production and/or provision of public services by the public, private, and nonprofit sectors, emphasizing the importance of cost, choice, and quality above other values.
>
> Utilize a revised role for government in the overall provision of public services.
>
> Utilize what are called market and quasimarket mechanisms to coordinate the supply and demand for public services and contractual mechanisms (e.g., contracting with the private sector or intergovernmental agreements) for service provision.
>
> Attempt to decouple political decision making from the management of public services.
>
> Promote a new role for public managers and government itself, to provide entrepreneurial leadership in a competitive results-based environment that is in constant pursuit of the bottom line. Risk taking and other entrepreneurial behaviors are seen as catalysts for more effective government.

In these reinvention reforms government entrusts its agencies with increased flexibility in using resources in exchange for holding them responsible for results. The tools used to ensure accountability include strategic and operational plans, performance measures and targets, contracts for personal and organizational performance, separating service delivery from policy making, new rules for accountability, annual reports, active use of evaluation and auditing, and financial inducements. The intent is to create more openness and transparency through a free flow of information between government and the consumers of services. This holds potential both for improving governmental performance and increasing citizen trust. It can be argued that the management tools of government reinvention are actually policy tools used to advance specific values, primarily efficiency.

As with any type of reform, moderation is a good thing. It is misguided, for example, to assume that public sector management need only import private sector management. This overlooks the fundamental differences in the political, legal, and societal environment in which public administration operates. The private sector has a different relationship with society than does government and has nothing comparable to the relationship between administrative agencies and elected officials or politics.

Legislative oversight, presidential or gubernatorial management, control over appointments—these and other political control structures are absent in private management. In terms of market exposure, formal legal constraints, political influence, coerciveness, scope of impact, public expectation, and goal complexity, the two sectors differ in fundamental ways.

An appropriate amount of entrepreneurial behavior can help bureaucracies to be more innovative and adaptive to change. On the other hand, there is potential conflict between entrepreneurial autonomy or discretion and democratic accountability (Bellone and Goerl, 1992). Public sector performance is more difficult (and sometimes impossible) to measure than private sector performance. Administrative rules and regulations may hamper performance but also help ensure public accountability. Hood and Jackson (1991) explained several value patterns: (1) effectiveness and parsimony, (2) honesty and fairness, and (3) robustness and resilience. Each may contradict the other, however, primarily focusing on the first pattern might sacrifice the others and harm bureaucratic performance. Another concern is that thinking of citizens solely as consumers and worrying about their satisfaction may compromise the role of a citizen in a democracy (Schachter, 1997). As I wrote elsewhere (Cigler, 1995–1996), "Citizens and leaders. . . must reinterpret, redefine, and reeducate themselves about. . . civic obligations or responsibilities. Without that, there will be no. . . reinvented government."

In reality, government reinvention is largely a set of best practices and not a fully coherent, tested prescription for management. It is best viewed as a large toolkit with many good ideas that have to be mixed and matched and carefully considered in light of other concerns. The most significant questions about government performance involve tough political choices with conflicting values. Frederickson (1996) refers to the "wrong-problems problem" in arguing that tough political choices that deal with real public problems are intentionally ignored by a fixation on better management as the universal solution. Carroll (1995) pointed out that government reinvention and the NPM introduce a contemporary form of the policy–administration dichotomy in that consideration of politics is ignored in the reforms promoted. Ingraham (1997) echoed the point by treating management reform as a subset of all government reform.

Although the interest in and application of the reforms of government reinvention have been amply discussed and critiqued, the same commentators have not addressed the new governance ideas or reforms that have occurred simultaneously with government reinvention. One reason may be that it is at the local level that new governance is most prominent and mainstream public administration has traditionally not included large numbers of faculty or programs that specialize in local affairs. Similarly, those who study intergovernmental relations have been at the forefront of examining networks, networked relationships, and partnership building but this is a small group among public administration scholars. New governance focuses explicitly on government's role in the political system and not so much with the internal workings of bureaucracy, which tends to dominate mainstream public administration attention.

Local government is the level of face-to-face interaction with citizens and the changes in the last decade especially have been widespread in terms of government–citizen relations and the creation of new accountability frameworks. Importantly, the Clinton Administration, including its National Performance Review, clearly embraced new governance ideas and put them into practice. In fact, the NPR changed its name to the National Partnership Review at one stage.

The academic literature on new governance comes primarily from disciplines that have not been well integrated into public administration, which has relied on such fields as political science and business management. Research on networked organizations and collaborative processes is found in those fields but is most heavily found in sociology, planning, applied psychology, democratic political theory, and regional economics, among other fields not well integrated into public administration.

## V. PRINCIPLES RELATED TO NEW GOVERNANCE

Among the twelve assumptions and guiding principles discussed earlier are some that differ significantly in the values advanced from those underlying government reinvention. These define what has been labeled "new governance," which is guided by the following types of thinking.

*Governance* is broader than government, covering all sectors and both policy making and service delivery. Interdependence among and between organizations and individuals shapes key relationships, not solely competition.

*A new role for government* is that of network manager and relationship builder, as well as facilitator, enabler, broker, and capacity builder. Contrary to government reinvention, government's role may actually expand as it takes an active, not passive, role in the governance system. Basic good management skills are not unimportant, however, new skills of collaborative decision making, social entrepreneurship, the ability to work with diverse groups, mutual adjustment, and so on are of key importance (Cigler, 1988; Rhodes, 1997).

*Networks and network organizations* are the key institutions within the new governance, compared to the focus on markets and against hierarchy, associated with government reinvention. Public administration is improved not merely by reform of internal structures, but by improving the quality of interorganizational relations, vertically and horizontally and across all levels and sectors in the complex governance system (Mandell and Gage, 1990). Relationship building is the "continuous quality improvement" focus of the new governance. Results-oriented governance depends on multiple actors with differing amounts of authority, resources, and responsibility for outcomes.

*Policy making* cannot and should not be separated from service delivery. In fact, NPM and government reinvention are treated as a policy subfield by academics interested in new governance.

*Citizenship* must be reinvented, not just the tools and techniques of management and service delivery (King et al., 1998). Contrary to mainstream government reinvention ideas, in which citizens are customers who largely react to the actions of administrators, new governance requires responsible informed citizens. Administrators and governments can and should play a key role in building "social capital," the glue that holds society together by working more closely with citizens and all sectors within civil society.

*More user-friendly policy information* should be available to citizens about government in a democracy. This feature of new governance dovetails with the analytical, performance measurement, and reporting tools associated with reinvention. However, it is more comprehensive in including public policy information as well as service delivery concerns.

*New governance promotes more of a balance* between efficiency values and others (e.g., equity, liberty, fairness) to protect the general social welfare. Similarly, new governance is cautious about the indiscriminate substitution of market mechanisms for government regulation, which poses problems for accountability, transparency, and public participation. For example, although contracting may sometimes be cost effective, there is still a need for regulation of the service through careful monitoring of the contractor's performance.

*Entrepreneurial behavior* of public employees and government is not opposed, however, entrepreneurship is expanded to include social entrepreneurship that seeks a balance among building citizens, civil society, and the public interest concerns and economic-based entrepreneurial behavior (Cigler, 1988). The concept of the "public interest" remains vague, but new governance ideas focus less on promoting methodological homogeneity in the governance system (e.g., through analytical performance-based techniques) and more on ensuring representativeness and inclusiveness in the policy-making system. Underlying this is the belief that government still has an important role in redistributive initiatives in the design of public policy in the public interest, compared to the private sector emphasis on amassing wealth for private gain. Although other types of entrepreneurial behavior are not opposed, social entrepreneurship is concerned that the impact of an entrepreneur's tendency to break rules and manipulate the policy process may undermine the governance process. Similarly, the concern is that the public entrepreneur will place a premium on innovative change, to the neglect or undermining of the core values of the public service.

## VI. EMERGENCE OF THE UNDERLYING ASSUMPTIONS AND PRINCIPLES OF GOVERNMENT REINVENTION AND NEW GOVERNANCE

Government reinvention and new governance ideas evolved over decades. Why did the underlying assumptions, principles, and characteristics that drive reform emerge in the first place? There is no consensus regarding the triggering events or mechanisms for reforms, especially changes in government roles, service delivery responsibilities, and the core values of public service. Some of the structural reinvention or NPM reforms that began in the 1980s were ideologically driven by conservatives who sought to diminish the size of government by replacing much of bureaucracy with market mechanisms. Concerned more with management than policy and advocating such strategies as decentralization, customer-driven behavior, and organizational flexibility, reforms were largely responses to social and political conditions of the times. Despite the importance of the technical merits or drawbacks of specific tools and techniques within the government reinvention toolkit, reinvention's roots are best understood within the context of the political system in which the reforms occurred.

Some view NPM, NPR, and other government reinvention efforts as doctrinal, in part, because of the perceptions that some reforms have been antibureaucracy and antigovernment. Efficient and responsive government is the primary object of the reinvention initiatives, with the notion that good business practices can improve the public sector. Such thinking is not new, however. It is the bundle and mix of strategies used that represents the major shift from traditional public administration. The use of market-based techniques and "liberation management" is different. It's not assumed that government bureaucracies and managers do not perform well because they are poor managers; instead, the contention is that managers and employees are trapped in bad systems with unnecessary rules and regulations. If internal regulations are lifted, performance will be improved. This drives the deregulation of internal management and the decentralization and streamlining of management processes such as budgeting, personnel, and procurement. The underlying idea is that the internal systems of government bureaucracies should imitate the market, with competitive market pressure replacing internal hierarchical controls. If good people are trapped in bad systems, the creation of new incentive structures might improve performance. For reinvention advocates, this means competition through building rivalry into the internal market of the public sector. Entrepreneurial behavior becomes necessary for survival.

The aim of improving governmental performance by making it more results-oriented is supported by all parts of the political spectrum. The notion of importing business management ideas and techniques is driven more by theory, experience, and practices, than by ideology. For example, the performance-based administrative techniques of reinvention are widely embraced. These include financial and management reforms that stress greater management autonomy, explicit standards and performance measurement, emphasis on output and outcomes, the dismantling of low performance entities, greater competition via privatization and among agencies, assimilation of private sector management styles, and efficient resource use.

Reinvention and new governance ideas both flowed from perceptions about economic and regulatory issues related to globalization. Technological innovations enabled private markets to transform their production, finance, and investment practices largely free of government intervention. With boundaries becoming increasingly irrelevant and regulatory roles inconsistent with changes in the international economy, efficiency was touted as a key role for the public sector rather than its traditional economic and regulatory responsibilities. National governments in the United States and elsewhere began to serve as intermediaries in the transnationalization of private sector production, marketing, distribution, and financial deregulation activities.

It is in these activities that NPM and government reinvention are somewhat aligned with new governance ideas inasmuch as government emerges as a facilitator of relationships in the globalized international economy. Government has more of an explicit role today in protecting the interests of actors in the market than it did in the past. Government efforts to cope with and respond to the pressures of globalization helped spawn the marketization of the public sector internally and the adoption of NPM-type reinvention ideas. A government that is competitive, flexible, market-oriented, and better equipped to contend with rapid external change in a global economy is widely appealing. The notion of entrepreneurial government and entrepreneurial managers also dovetails with attempts to make government less monopolistic in service delivery, including delegating responsibilities through privatization and retrenchment policies such as downsizing.

Still another reason for the emergence of reform ideas is found in efforts to decrease government's traditional role in advancing social agendas, specifically, the welfare state. In part, this began in the 1980s due to budget shortfalls; however, an increasingly affluent society is a contributing factor. Welfare policy in the United States is no longer an entitlement and recipients of transitional assistance are required to assume more responsibilities. There has been a shift from the former trends of redefining wants to be needs and needs to be rights (Cigler, 1995–1996). Today, all sides of the political spectrum ask for more balance between rights and responsibilities.

Government reinvention and the new governance are not fully coherent or inclusive philosophies of either public administration or governance. Neither has a universal agenda nor do they necessarily represent a paradigmatic change in the operation of bureaucracy or in defining government's role. Some scholars, in fact, question whether the NPM or government reinvention represents much new at all or whether they simply offer insight into old issues. One could argue that U.S. reinvention is a continuation of past reform efforts to professionalize the public service.

Another reason for the emergence of the NPM and government reinvention is found in the economic theories that are central to many of the basic assumptions of these reforms. These theories have explicit views about the role of government in the economy, with less to say about the best way to deliver services. Williamson (1975), a key proponent of the theories that shape the assumptions advocating various structural reforms, clearly prefers markets to hierarchies. The conservative ideologies in the 1980s that launched some of the public sector reforms later called the NPM and reinventing government sought to decrease the size of the public sector and its perceived inefficiencies by satisfying "customers." Structural reforms were, thus, dominated by modeling such business practices as attempts to flatten bureaucracies in order to shift power to lower-level workers, giving them more voice within the organization. Clients, customers, and stakeholders were also empowered. Government reinvention sought to make both the workplace and the decision-making process more democratic, as well as to increase the potential for acquiring new ideas by creating more inclusionary participatory processes. Structural reforms also included the decentralization of authority within organizations and from the national government to state and local governments and from states to local governments. New governance accommodates these trends by focusing on ways to create interactive citizen–government relations within the decentralized structures.

Traditionally, governing structures concentrated control of human and financial resources at the center with operational responsibility for delivering services at the bottom of organizations. Government consisted of controllers and the public was controlled. Government issued rules, monitored compliance with the rules, and intervened, as it thought appropriate. The public was expected to comply.

Process reengineering reforms adapted business reengineering processes to public sector service delivery bureaucracies, especially at the local level. These reforms also changed public resource allocation decisions, including how the decisions were made. Early efforts to incorporate flexibility in public bureaucrats included revisions of civil service systems and even abolishment, most notably at the state level. Public managers were given more latitude in hiring, firing, promoting, and offering awards to employees.

A complex and multiple set of economic theories and ideas influenced the early reinventing government reforms, especially the family of rational choice theories, which include public choice theory, agency theory, new institutional economics, and transaction cost economics (TCE). These theories assume that individual or group behavior is opportunistic and rational, that is, that behavior is essentially based on self-interest (Buchanan, 1978; Chan and Rosenbloom, 1994; Williamson, 1975). This implies skepticism about public servants being concerned with the common good and assumes that they attempt to maximize their own utility through larger budgets and greater influence (Niskanen, 1971). These theories advocate the separation of advisory, regulatory, and delivery functions of the public sector and argue that public services should be contestable and contracted out or privatized when possible. It's also argued that clear lines of accountability, incentives, and sanctions should be put in place to align the interests of "agents" with those of their "principals."

Government reinvention reforms are also influenced by the postbureaucratic paradigm in that the way to achieve economic ends and to overcome the problems of self-interest is to remove differences between the public and private sectors, thus shifting the emphasis from process accountability toward accountability for results. Managerial skill and autonomy, output measures and performance targets, corporate plans and mission statements, a host of accountability mechanisms, performance-linked pay, efficiency, and cost cutting are key tools of government reinvention.

"Decentralized centralization," involving the fragmentation of larger public service bureaucracies into independent components with devolved management control is another reinvention approach, as are centralized reporting and monitoring focused on efficiency and performance. Fragmentation supports a gradual movement toward privatization because the operations of some fragments may be transferred to private sector agencies whereas others can remain in the public sector. Users of public services, conceptualized as consumers or customers, have the ability to choose and purchase wanted services. Consumer rights are related to the idea that, for many public services (e.g., public education), consumers cannot "exit" unsatisfactory services because the exit option is too expensive.

Transaction cost economics argues that the ideal organizational structure minimizes contract costs, which are affected by the nature of the goods and services and the economic environment. Williamson (1975) initially argued that structures could be aligned along a continuum, with hierarchy and market at opposite ends. Later, he acknowledged that hybrid structures called "networks" occupy an intermediate position on the continuum, with many transactions occurring in networks. According to transaction cost economics, each of the structure types has distinctive features and is appropriate for particular transactions.

The assumptions made about network structures are important in light of the underlying assumptions of opportunism and bounded rationality that suggest distrusting relationships among network members. TCE often uses game theory ideas to suggest ways to have "credible commitments" in light of contract terms, for example, that give particular benefits or impose punishment so that stated commitments are honored. A distrusting TCE model offers insight about some network relationships undertaken by the public sector. The contracting out of production or distribution of a service can be improved by writing strong contract specifications at the outset and using strong contract monitoring throughout the relationship. Lack of trust poses danger to information sharing and exerts pressure on contractual terms and requirements for their prespecification. Above all, public sector managers must be aware that the major burden for accountability is on them.

New governance ideas also rely on economic theories, especially resource dependency, exchange relationships, and transaction cost economics. Research has shown that some networks are a new and distinct type of structure or organization for which assumptions of opportunism are not applicable. Network members' behavior is not necessarily to achieve their own selfish ends. Trust and the building of trust relationships is essential to the functioning and success of truly collaborative networks. Network effectiveness is dependent on the ability to obtain and use information so that information sharing is essential. For information sharing to occur, a level of trust among members must be developed. However, few of the reformed structures are the types of markets as theorized by transaction cost economics. And, only some of the reforms lead to quasi-markets that consist of a single purchaser, multiple competing sellers, and transactions consistent with market notions. Instead, the trans-actions involved are generally ones in which there is an inability to prespecify requirements. The need for judgment and for longer-term, ongoing, coordinated arrangements is present, compared to the short-term clear requirements of a market.

What is emerging is governance by a complex arrangement of networks, rather than markets or quasi-markets. A network might be more flexible than a hierarchy, but is also more complex to manage (Mandell, 2001) due to the requirements for coordination, cooperation, and collaboration. Because a network may be composed of independent member organizations, each will have its own objectives that may conflict with the network's objectives. The tension between the network's objectives and each member organization's objectives requires new types of management skills.

The economics literature from which new governance draws is that of resource dependence (Thompson, 1967; Pfeffer and Salancik, 1978), transaction cost (Arrow, 1983; Williamson, 1975; Powell, 1990), and organization–environment relations (e.g., Aldrich and Pfeffer, 1976). These literatures make the case that organizations need to manage both their organizations and their environments, often by entering into exchange relationships with external parties to acquire resources. Exchange relationships form the basis for interorganizational collaboration. New governance ideas extend dependence-reducing strategies beyond simple contractual service delivery arrangements to include joint ventures, partnerships, mergers, and the gamut of collaborative options. Just as TCE is used to help make decisions about whether to produce and/or deliver a service internally or to contract out, the same theories can be applied to making decisions on what types of networking, cooperation, coordination, and/or collaboration ventures to participate in to moderate transaction costs. These can be informal or formal, short- or long-term and inter- or intraorganizational. Organizational environment relations theory is yet another rationale for explaining the formation of networks. It is important that relationships among and between organizations and their environments are negotiated and increased legitimacy is a goal.

Regulatory reform is another area of public sector reform, stemming in large part from the perception that governments must respond rapidly and effectively to globalization, cultural diversity, new technologies, and the like if societal needs are to be met appropriately and swiftly. Countries compete internationally not only in the marketplace but also on the quality of their public sectors so that governments must improve competitiveness across the board. Regulations are essential tools for securing justice and protecting welfare, but traditional public administrative control and oversight processes, it is argued by reformers, do not ensure cost effectiveness or policy coherence and regulators are increasingly technocratic and vulnerable to capture by certain interest groups.

Based on these assumptions, recent regulatory reforms include ways to build regulatory management capacity for initiating change and coordinating cross-cutting issues, reform the processes for developing new regulations so that regulation is used only when necessary and when high quality standards are met, and upgrade the quality of existing rules, including some deregulation. The objective of the regulatory reforms is to have less intrusive government. Government would be a steerer, not rower, with other systems, most notably the private sector, providing the dynamic that drives society. Government's role would be that of an umpire adjudicating transgressions of the rules. As such, government is considered just one of several forms of societal governance. Government also facilitates the development of other, nonstate forms of governance and more complex collaborative alliances, including public–private partnerships.

Public–private partnerships are not new. When government merely steers, however, they become more numerous and politically significant. The complex networks that result present greater management challenges for those in the smaller public sector, at the least requiring greater skills in coordination and persuasion over core values as distinct from only functional values. This is vastly different from exercising unquestioned authority.

Partnerships are both a challenge and opportunity for those in the nongovernmental sectors. Greater involvement in partnerships requires the development of greater management capacity, for example, for welfare organizations. Over time, however, the networks can be an alternative form of governance that can get new items on public agendas. The boundaries of government become more porous with the development of more partnerships. In partnerships, the actors negotiate their roles and responsibilities. Government must tend to matters central to the democratic process, such as equity, justice, and equal access to services, but their partners in such negotiations may not value these principles to the same extent.

How can these new public–private partnerships be held accountable? Can government ensure principles of fairness, equity, and justice as just one segment of a partnership? Will government itself become less accountable because of the complexity of networks and partnerships? Will these emerging new governance structures become a phenomenon too large for a shrunken state to effectively control? How can government obtain the information necessary to determine whether responsibilities are being met and those responsible held fully accountable? Accountability is traditionally derived from the Hobbesian doctrine of covenant, with a consequent social contract checks-and-balances between elected officials and public bureaucracies. The emerging networks break the separation of powers doctrine, thus tampering with the foundation of the accountability chain built into democratic governance systems.

In the move from government to governance and intergovernmental to intersector approaches, the evolution of NPM highlights the growing complexity in steering patterns and power distribution in modern democracy. New types and layers of steering mechanisms have been built on top of old ones. Hierarchies and traditional public administration are all around, but are now operating along with a wide variety of other steering tools: decentralization, performance contracting, privatization and outsourcing, public competition, enterprise accounts, benchmarking, report cards, transformative leadership development, and so on (Cigler, 1998). The numerous types of steering mechanisms create cross-cutting problems leading to issues of accountability. "Who or what should give accounts to whom, for what, and when, how" are now central questions related to management within a democracy.

## VII.  ACCOUNTABILITY ISSUES

Accountability is an integral part of basic democratic principles, producing the trust needed for effective governance. Without trust there is no democracy and no effective citizenship because trust is the key vehicle for achieving societal coherence. As such, government reinvention must be cognizant of and responsive to issues of accountability. Democracies don't survive because citizens are forced to comply with rules and regulations, such as paying of taxes. They survive because citizens believe in the system and therefore comply. In effect, trust translates to legitimacy for governmental actors and institutions. Legitimacy to whom? Accountability of whom to whom? These questions are at the foundation of democracy and are not simple technical issues for resolution. Instead, they involve societal decisions about the source of the distribution of power.

## A. Types of Accountability

*Legal Accountability.* A foundation of democracy is the idea that actions taken by civil servants are grounded in law and that law is not made retrospectively. Instead, it is generalizable with citizens able to calculate the effect of their actions and their rights. Legal accountability is based on the notion that flexibility does not override the rule of law. In a governance system rapidly moving toward so much power by those other than the elected leaders, it is not possible to legally pin down accountability. Legal accountability means conforming to statutes, laws, and regulations.

*Fiscal Accountability.* Who should be held accountable for public budgets and spending patterns, as well as economic policies that contribute to positive economic growth? Much of government reinvention appears to give primacy to questions surrounding fiscal accountability. What should our tax levels be? Who should pay the national economic debt? What are the obligations of one generation to the next for social security?

*Policy Accountability.* In a democracy, the notion that elected officials are held accountable for policy output and the performance of the civil service lies at the heart of the system. Managers "doing the right thing" are operating programs in conformance to the policy goals set by the governing body.

*Process Accountability.* This includes meeting internal requirements for planning, budgeting, accounting, and reporting activities to facilitate auditing of performance, whether program or financial.

*Democratic Accountability.* There is no democracy unless basic democratic values are adhered to and respected, including the rule of law and respect of and protection for basic human rights.

*Efficiency Accountability.* This ensures that programs are operated efficiently. "Doing it right and doing the right thing."

*Ethics Accountability.* This implies that actors comply to codes of general moral standards or with specific professional ethics.

*Effectiveness Accountability.* This measures actual outcomes against objectives to determine if the job is getting done.

Accountability in a multicentered governance system is contingent upon differing relationships and conflicting rationales for public action. There is no necessary conflict among the types of accountability, but there can be. Different actors evoke different types under different circumstances.

From a *technical perspective*, accountability involves questions of how to write good specifications for contracts, what incentives to build into a particular steering system, what information should be gathered, processes, and so on.

From a *political vantagepoint*, legitimacy holds center stage.

From a *normative viewpoint*, accountability concerns require dealing with what values should inform the actions of public administrators. The common values of working for the collective good are largely what hold together traditional public administration, that is, the hierarchical and machinelike model of bureaucracy. In a multicentered system of policy dominance (Cigler, 1990) and a decentralized, devolved management system, there is little opportunity for expressing the normative ideals of public service, either at the policy level or through internal activities.

As is the case with other reforms, reinvention and the NPM have different and somewhat hidden assumptions or basic contradictions (Hood and Jackson, 1991). If micromanagement is eliminated or reduced and more autonomy is given to public organizations, then control and congruency over governmental actions, policies, and projects become an issue. Accountability is a problem but the potential for loosely coupled organizations to resolve social problems is also problematic (Ostrom, 1974).

Many proponents of reinvention techniques suggest that the reforms are simply a set of technically neutral techniques designed to cope with increasing governance complexity and to reconcile demands for better steering and less rowing. However, market-based mechanisms, customer-focused culture, and evaluations of outcomes are matters of negotiation among different actors within the governance system. In democratic countries, bureaucracies are already tightly controlled and supervised but they can defend different agendas (Niskanen, 1971). The institutional framework of democracies allows inefficient controls that block governmental efficiency and innovation. If the political system still has control of the bureaucracy, it is very difficult to increase the freedom of bureaucracies to assure good management. Performance-oriented budgets are one important approach, but they require a huge effort of negotiation among actors within a political system.

Many problems faced by traditional public administration, however, have not disappeared. Uncertainty is still a constant of organizational behavior and power structures persist. Government reinvention may be understood as an alternative approach to facing the complex and contradictory nature of organizational and institutional behavior (or collective action). To understand whether the reforms will work is to ask whether individual and organizational behavior can change—age-old questions (Selznick, 1949; Crozier, 1964). Can behavior change if institutions, defined as rules and norms whether formal or informal, and organizational structures are built in ways that provide incentives for rational behavior and customer-oriented attitudes that are structured through market mechanisms? The argument is that flexibility must be provided so that bureaucracies have more freedom for action and more mobile structures to respond to particular problems with specific answers rather than using cookie-cutter approaches. Added flexibility, however, leads to heterogeneous values among actors that could possibly deny the original values of the reform effort. The tensions between flexibility and control may increase when heterogeneous values increase. It is highly unlikely that there will be a consensus of homogeneous values, thus there is no consensus regarding outcomes and output to be obtained by governmental actions.

## B. Decline of Policy Coherence

Governments' ability to steer policy through increasingly complex political and economic environments is now a constant concern regarding contemporary governance. Privatization, contracting, and devolution may have the unintended effect of hampering the ability of government to ensure policy coherence because these reforms exacerbate government's coordinating capacity (Fredericksen and London, 2000; Agranoff and McGuire, 1998; Cigler 2001; Peters and Savoie, 1996). Organizational restructuring, especially in the late 1980s and early 1990s, was characterized by a tension between public choice-based prescriptions for increased political control and reforms aimed at improving management capacity. Advice from political appointees was favored over advice from bureaucrats, along with decreasing the policy orientations of central agencies responsible for ensuring coordination in government action. The "hollowing out" thesis raises fundamental questions regarding the viability of government bureaucracy as a managing agent of public policy. Government contracting, for example, increases fragmentation and diminishes government's direct role in the policy process.

Public administration in the twenty-first century consists of a variety of alternative models. Traditional or "old" public administration, with its hierarchical and rule-laden bureaucracies is still needed and very much in operation. A vast variety of mechanisms that draw from government reinvention ideas, especially regarding market-based options and competition, is also in operation. New governance ideas that focus on networks and partnership building, with government as a facilitator, are powerful. All have strengths and weaknesses. None alone leads to "the best" government performance. Together, government reinvention and the new governance have truly led to a transformation of governance in the United States.

## REFERENCES

Agranoff, R., McGuire, M. (1998). Multinetwork management: collaboration and the hollow state in local economic policy. *J. Public Admin. Res. Theor.* 1:67–91.

Agranoff, R., McGuire, M. (1999). Managing in network settings. *Policy Stud. Rev.* 16:18–41.

Agranoff, R., McGuire, M. (2001). American federalism and the search for models of management. *Public Admin. Rev.* 61(6):671–681.

Aldrich, H., Pfeffer, J. (1976). Environments of organizations. *Ann. Rev. Sociol.* 2:79–105.

Alexander, E. R. (1995). *How Organizations Act Together: Interorganizational Coordination in Theory and Practice.* Amsterdam: Gordon & Breach.

Alter, C., Hage, J. (1993). *Organizations Working Together.* Newbury Park, CA: Sage.

Arrow, K. (1983). The organization of economic activity: Issues pertinent to the choice of market versus nonmarket allocation. In: Arrow, K., ed. *General Equilibrium: Collected Papers of Kenneth Arrow.* Cambridge, MA: Belknap Press of Harvard University.

Barber, B. R. (1998). *A Place for Us: How to Make Society, Civil Society and Democracy Strong.* New York: Hill & Wang.

Barzelay, M., Armajani, B. J. (1992). *Breaking Through Bureaucracy: A New Vision for Managing in Government.* Berkeley, CA: University of California Press.

Bellone, C.J., Goerl, G.F. (1992). Reconciling public entrepreneurship and democracy. *Public Admin. Rev.* 52(3):130–134.

Berry, F., Wechsler, B. (1995). State agencies' experience with strategic planning: findings from a national survey. *Public Admin. Rev.* 55(2):159–168.

Buchanan, J. (1978). *From Private Preferences to Public Philosophy: The Development of Public Choice, The Economics of Politics.* London: Institute of Economic Affairs.

Carroll, J. (1995). The rhetoric of reform and political reality in the National Performance Review. *Public Admin. Rev.* 55(3):302–312.

Chan, S., Rosenbloom, D. (1994). Legal control of public administration: a principal-agent perspective. *Int. Rev. Admin. Sci.* 64(12):559–574.

Cigler, B. A. (1988). Trends affecting local administrators. In: Perry, J. L., ed. *Handbook of Public Administration*. San Francisco: Jossey-Bass, pp. 40–53.

Cigler, B. A. (1990). Public administration and the paradox of professionalization. *Public Admin. Rev.* 50(6):637–653.

Cigler, B. A. (1995–1996). Governance in the re____ing decade of the 90s. *Public Manager.* 24(2):3.

Cigler, B. A. (1998). Emerging trends in state-local relations. In: Hanson, R.L., ed. *Governing Partners: State-local Relations in the U.S.* Boulder, CO: Westview, pp. 53–74.

Cigler, B. A. (1999). Pre-conditions for the emergence of multicommunity collaborative organizations. *Policy Stud. Rev.* 16:86–102.

Cigler, B. A. (2001). Multiorganization, multisector, and multicommunity organizations: Setting the research agenda. In: Mandell, M. P., ed. *Getting Results Through Collaboration: Networks and Network Structures for Public Policy and Management*. Westport, CI: Quorum, pp. 71–85.

Clinton, W., Gore, A. (1994). *Putting Customers First: Standards for Serving the American People*. Washington, DC: U.S. Government Printing Office.

Crozier, M. (1964). *The Bureaucratic Phenomenon*. Chicago: Chicago University Press.

DeLeon, L., Denhardt, R. (2000). The political theory of reinvention. *Public Admin. Rev.* 60(2):89–97.

Denhardt, R., Denhardt, J. (2000). The new public service: serving rather than steering. *Public Admin. Rev.* 60(6):549–559.

Frederickson, G. (Summer, 1996). Comparing the reinventing government movement with the new public administration. *Public Admin. Rev.* 56(3):263–270.

Frederickson, G. (1999). Public ethics and the new managerialism. *Public Integrity* 265–278.

Fredericksen, P., London, R. (2000). Disconnect in the hollow state: the pivotal role of organizational capacity in community-based development organizations. *Public Admin. Rev.* 60(3):230–239.

Gilman, S. (1999, Spring). Public-sector ethics and government reinvention: Realigning systems to meet organizational change. *Public Integrity* 175–192.

Gore, A. (1993). *From Red Tape to Results: Creating a Government That Works Better and Costs Less, Report of the National Performance Review*. New York: Times Books/Random House.

Haque, S. (2001). The diminishing publicness of public service under the current mode of governance. *Public Admin. Rev.* 61(1):65–82.

Hood, C., Jackson, M. (1991). *Administrative Argument*. Croft Road, Vt: Darmouth Press.

Ingraham, P. (1997). Play it again, Sam; It's still not right: searching for the right notes in administrative reform. *Public Admin. Rev.* 57(4):325–331.

Kearney, R., Feldman, B., Scavo, C. (2000). Reinventing government: city manager attitudes and actions. *Public Admin. Rev.* 60(6):535–548.

Kettl, D. (2000). Public administration at the millennium: the state of the field. *J. Public Admin. Res. Theor.* 10(1):7–34.

King, C. S., Stivers, C., et al. (1998). *Government Is Us*. Thousand Oaks, CA: Sage.

Mandell, M.P., ed. (2001). Getting Results Through Collaboration: Networks and Network Structures for Public Policy and Management. Westport, CT: Quorum Books.

Mandell, M. P., Gage, R. W. (1990). *Strategies for Managing Intergovernmental Policies and Networks*. New York: Praeger.

McKnight, J. L., Kretzmann, J. P. (1993). *Building Communities from the Inside Out: A Path Toward Finding and Mobilizing Community Assets*. Evanston, IL: Center for Urban Affairs and Policy Research, Northwestern University.

Milward, B., Provan, K. (2000). Governing the hollow state. *J. Public Admin. Res. Theor.* 2:359–379.

Moe, R. (1994). The 'reinventing government' exercise: misinterpreting the problem, misjudging the consequences. *Public Admin. Rev.* 54(2):111–122.

Moon, J., deLeon, P. (2001). Municipal reinvention: managerial values and diffusion among municipalities. *J. Public Admin. Res. Theor.* 3:327–351.

Nalbandian, J. (1999). Facilitating community, enabling democracy; new roles for local government managers. *Public Admin. Rev.* 59(3):187–197.

Niskanen, W. A. (1971). *Bureaucracy and Representative Government.* Chicago: Aldine-Atherton.

Osborne, D., Gaebler, T. (1992). *Reinventing Government: How the Entrepreneurial Spirit is Transforming the Public Sector from Schoolhouse to Statehouse, City Hall to the Pentagon.* Reading MA: Addison-Wesley.

Ostrom, V. (1974). *The Intellectual Crisis in American Public Administration.* Tuscaloosa, AL: University Press.

O'Toole, L. (1997). The implications for democracy in a networked bureaucratic world. *J. Public Admin. Res. Theor.* 3:443–459.

Peters, G., Pierre, J. (1998). Governance without government? Rethinking public administration. *J. Public Admin. Res. Theor.* 2:223–243.

Peters, G., Savoie, D. (1994). Civil service reform: misdiagnosing the patient. *Public Admin. Rev.* 54(5):418–425.

Peters, G., Savoie, D. (1996). Managing incoherence: the coordination and empowerment conundrum. *Public Admin. Rev.* 56(3):281–290.

Pfeffer, J., Salancik, G. (1978). *The External Control of Organizations: A Resource Dependence Perspective.* New York: Harper and Row.

Pollitt, C. (1993). *Managerialism and the Public Services: Cuts or Cultural Change in the 1990s?* 2nd ed. Cambridge, MA: Basil Blackwell.

Powell, W. (1990). Neither market nor hierarchy: Network forms of organization. In: *Research in Organizational Behavior.* Vol. 12. Greenwich, CT: JAI, 295–336.

Rhodes, R.A. (1997). It's the mix that matters: from marketisation to diplomacy. *Australian J. Public Admin.* 56(1):40–53.

Roberts, N. (1997). Public deliberation: an alternative approach to crafting policy and setting direction. *Public Admin. Rev.* 57(2):124–132.

Schachter, H. L. (1995). Reinventing government or reinventing ourselves: two models for improving government performance. *Public Admin. Rev.* 55(6):530–537.

Schachter, H. L. (1997). *Reinventing Government or Reinventing Ourselves: The Role of Citizen Owners in Making a Better Government.* Albany: State University of New York Press.

Selznick, P. (1949). *TVA and the Grassroots.* CA: University of California Press.

Thompson, J. (1967). *Organizations in Action.* New York: McGraw-Hill.

Thompson, J. (2000). Reinvention as reform: assessing the national performance review. *Public Admin. Rev.* 60(6):508–521.

Timney, M. M. (1998). Overcoming administrative barriers to citizen participation: Citizens as partners, not adversaries. In: King, C. S., Stivers, C., et al. , eds. *Government is Us.* Thousand Oaks, CA: Sage, pp. 88–101.

Williams, D. (2000). Reinventing the proverbs of government. *Public Admin. Rev.* 60(6):522–534.

Williamson, O. (1975). *Market and Hierarchies: Analysis and Antitrust Implications.* New York: Free Press.

# 11

## Productivity and Ethics

### The Leadership Challenge

**JAMES S. BOWMAN**
*Florida State University, Tallahassee, Florida, U.S.A.*

**RUSSELL L. WILLIAMS**
*University of North Florida, Jacksonville, Florida, U.S.A.*

## I.  INTRODUCTION

Productivity, doing things right, and ethics, doing right things, are reciprocally integral to success: together they mean doing right things right. Technical expertise, knowing how to do one's job, is critical. Indeed, the temptation is to define a "professional" as simply one who is technically proficient. It also makes it easy to equate public administration with corporate management; "[t]he field of administration is a field of business," according to Woodrow Wilson (1887, p. 209).

Being ethically sound, knowing why one does one's job, is at least as important as being technically capable. Ethical competence, revealed by a less frequently quoted part of Wilson's seminal work, calls for a civil service cultured and self-sufficient enough to act with sense and vision ... to straighten the paths of government ... purify its organization, *and to crown its duties with dutifulness* (1887, p. 201; emphasis added). While calling for the same technical competence found in the private sector, public administrators are charged with a concern for, and devotion to, the greater good. Governmental managers, in short, have an obligation not only to work productively, but also to wisely husband public assets.

To address this challenge, this chapter first briefly defines productivity and ethics, and presents a decision-making framework to integrate them. Agency internal and external relations are then examined and illustrated by a recent case study showing how productivity and ethics intersect. The discussion concludes by arguing that authentic public service requires attention to productivity and ethics, but not necessarily in that order.

## II.  DEFINING AND INTEGRATING PRODUCTIVITY AND ETHICS

### A.  Defining Terms

Productivity and ethics have always been intimately related core values: the former deals with what and how much should be produced, the latter with why and how things should be accomplished. Berman (1998, pp. 5–6) sees productivity as "the effective and efficient use of resources to achieve outcomes" (effectiveness is "the level of outcomes" or accomplishments, and efficiency is "the ratio of outcomes [and outputs] to inputs"). Achieving productivity is generally straightforward when the organization has a clear purpose (e.g., making money), a simple policy-making structure (a dominant chief executive), and ample resources applied to limited objectives (assembly-line production of widgets). Being "productive" is usually thought of in terms of tangible measurements such as the number of tires a company manufactures in a year.

Productivity in government is seldom so easily comprehended. Market forces and the bottom-line numbers they produce do not readily define it. Setting goals (or benchmarks against which productivity might be evaluated) is an arduous task.[1] What results to gauge and how to make those measurements is frequently problematic and subject to discretion, interpretation, and controversy. In trying to determine the public interest, productivity may become victim to "fuzzy math." It is not simple for public agencies to be productive in the private sector sense because productivity is about what is "good" for the populace; the business concept of profitability is of little help in this determination.

Yet the definition of productivity is clear compared to ethics, which further compounds the difficulty of combining them in government service. Top management may define public service productivity, however, the personal ethics of each civil servant is hardly irrelevant. Given that personal ethics differ, it is incumbent upon an organization to create an environment that clarifies what is considered ethical action. Defining the value of "right," as in "to do the right thing," is a complex undertaking. A business can say it is ethical if it legally earns a profit without knowingly harming someone. If compensation, benefits, and the workplace are adequate (with low turnover rates, few labor disputes or discrimination suits, and high productivity), then it can claim it treats its employees fairly. The range of values to be satisfied in this environment is narrow.

In contrast, the multiple stakeholders, intractable problems, and limited resources make determining the "right thing" difficult in the public sector. Van Wart (1998, p. 317) notes,

> the emphasis on nonprofitable goals—social equity, due process, the appearance of propriety, openness, financial conservatism, rigorous standards of legally defined fairness to employees, notions of contribution to the common good and so on—is far greater than in the private sector ... [C]hoices are made even more difficult because values in [public sector] value systems often change.

He correctly indicates the considerable scope of ethical issues. National defense, for instance, is a clear responsibility of government and benefits all citizens. Yet it is difficult to make the case that the military engages in fair treatment when some of its personnel receive wages so meager that they must rely on food stamps.

Ethics, according to Van Wart (1998), is both (1) a matter of laws, rules, and procedures as well as (2) an overarching value system. The first perspective, the "low road," assumes individuals act ethically if they stay out of trouble. Administrators who merely follow the rules, however, run the risk of being "soulless bureaucrats," unresponsive to changing popular needs. They may be efficient, but likely not effective when public service is the ultimate goal. The second definition, the "high road," assumes people will aspire to "do the right thing." Perversely though, doing so may lead to illegal or questionable acts if an organization's or an individual's value system does not conform to stated rules. Ethical action is possible, but productivity may suffer because of conflicting priorities. There may be no one best way to be ethical or productive in the public sphere.

## B. Integrating Terms

In differentiating ethics and productivity—and ultimately transcending the tension between them—it should be evident that both are central to management. Indeed, they are complementary dimensions of leadership: doing right things is the purpose of an organization and doing things right is the means to achieve that purpose. Competency in ethics is the top line for everything managers do and competency in productivity is the bottom line. A genuine commitment by leaders to the agency, its employees, and the citizenry will enhance productivity in a manner that fosters the achievement of the ethical goals for which they also are responsible.[2]

Unfortunately, there is limited empirical evidence[3] and few practical tools to demonstrate the mutual dependency of productivity and ethics. However, if ethics are seen in terms of right and wrong, and productivity in terms of good and bad, then both concepts can be maximized by use of an integrative decision-making model. A *right–good* decision is not only ethically correct (right), but also economically productive (good). Decisions can also be characterized as *right–bad* (ethical, but unproductive), *wrong–good* (unethical, but seemingly productive), as well as *wrong–bad* (unethical and unproductive).

Case 1 presents an ethics versus productivity case involving a staff assistant and discusses how city managers responded to it. As shown, four quite different decisions emerge: right–bad (employee termination), wrong–good (condoning the problem), wrong–bad (personnel transfer), and right–good (suspension). From an ethical and productivity perspective, the last response creates a "win-win" solution. Regarding ethics, it acknowledges the organization's responsibility to reduce opportunities for unethical behavior, but also sanctions the employee in a just manner proportionate to the offense. Concerning productivity, and recognizing that no money or operational capability was lost, the decision permits the city, department, and the individual to continue to be effective after discipline has been levied. Other members of the organization will see that management values both ethics and productivity, thereby nurturing a desirable work environment.

**Case 1**   Petty Cash

---

International City/County Management Association conferees were given a set of ethical dilemmas and asked to respond with a "yes" or "no" to the question presented by each scenario. One involved a highly valued staff assistant who did exceptional work. However, one day she admitted "borrowing" (and repaying) small amounts from petty cash and writing false receipts to cover the withdrawals, a clear cause for dismissal under personnel rules.

A substantial proportion (44%) of the over 700 managers recommended termination in this early 1980s study. *Public Management* magazine subsequently agreed by arguing that a felony had been committed, and by asking, "What would other employees think if her behavior was excused?" "How has she repaid the 'trust and value' in which she was held?" and, "If the same situation occurred with another employee would leniency be used?"

Yet was this really the best—"right–good"—course of action (see Figure 1)? Might not it actually be a right–bad decision, right because of the felony, but bad since the employee is an otherwise exemplary person, perhaps as indicated by her repayments and ultimately by her confession? Alternatively, a "wrong–good" choice can be envisioned where the behavior is condoned and the work unit continues to benefit from her services. Yet doing nothing, no matter how economically "good" it may be, sends the wrong ethical message to the employee and others. Another decision would be "wrong–bad," for instance, to transfer (or even promote) the person to another area. Here not only is the ethical problem ignored, but it is passed along and, in addition, the original department loses her services. A "right–good" approach then may be to suspend the employee without pay, place her on notice that future offenses will result in termination, remove petty cash from her duties, and establish a two-signature requirement for future withdrawals by authorized personnel.

*Source*: Bowman 1995, pp. 66–68.

Of course, this solution will not satisfy everyone, but that is hardly the point. Rather, the process of seeking right–good decisions highlights a key management function: generating alternative courses of actions, evaluating them based on consistent criteria, and making a considered judgment (Figure 1). The result is not a muddled compromise, but a conscious attempt to reconcile productivity and ethical value claims.

Being ethical may well be more important than being productive. Yet, recognizing that productivity is not automatically antithetical to principled decision making increases the likelihood that ethics will be taken seriously. Both ethics and productivity are essential. Indeed, decisions are made frequently without recognition that ethical judgment is involved because ethics are often masked by other, often productivity-

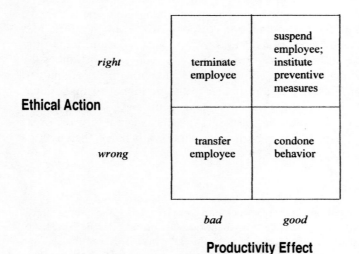

**Figure 1** Integrative decision-making model. (From Bowman 1995, p. 67.)

related, factors. Although policy-making uncertainties will always exist, the willingness to give ethics as well as productivity weight is a crucial step toward resolving such uncertainties.

This is not merely an aspirational, Pollyannaish suggestion; it is a professional requirement in as much as modern American public administration has never been solely a technical endeavor. The question can be asked, "Would the public rather have a productive, morally corrupt or an unproductive, morally pure government?" Perhaps many would sacrifice moral purity. Then-President Clinton's rise in popularity, while the economy was booming and his personal ethics wanting, confirms this gloomy assessment (Rozell and Wilcox, 2000). Yet Woodrow Wilson's earlier description of public service couples business efficiency and moral dutifulness. Neither extreme—productivity at the expense of ethics or ethics at the expense of productivity—is desirable.

To summarize this section, although ethics and productivity are difficult to define, that does not stop policies from being made. The above decision-making scheme encourages an explicit weighing of these key values. In fact, the mutual trust required between public organizations and their stakeholders demands such an effort.

## III. PRODUCTIVITY AND ETHICS IN ORGANIZATIONS

The matrix in the previous section may assist officials in their work. However, the leadership challenge, by definition, includes emphasis on not only the individual policy maker, but also the organization as a whole. Although the final responsibility for actions taken rests with each public servant, promoting ethical conduct is not solely the duty of any one person. Nurturing one's own decision-making strategy is necessary, but not sufficient to foster productivity and ethics in government. "Nothing of value happens without individuals," a wise observer once said, "but nothing is lasting without institutions." This section examines internal and external agency strategies for balancing productivity and ethics. This is then followed by a case study illustrating why such balancing is crucial.

### A. Internal Relations

As guardians of democratic and professional principles, public organizations have a collective moral duty. This can be discharged not only by developing an ethics code, but also by creating an infrastructure to ensure the department does not then hypocritically publish it, but do nothing to implement it.[4] To make the statement a living document:

> An agency-specific credo should be developed (or reexamined) with maximum employee participation;
> The credo should:
>> Be prefaced with a letter by the organization's leadership that puts it in the context of the department's traditions and mission statement, summarizes its rationale, and personally commits the signer(s) to its precepts;
>> Include guidance on its use in decision making by having implementation procedures, case materials and study resources, and commonly asked questions and answers;

Be integrated into the personnel system, from recruitment through training
to evaluation, and

Provide the basis for periodic ethical audits to identify issues confronting
the agency.

Cultivating an ethos does not simply mean one is trying to do the right thing; it also
means trying to be the kind of person in the kind of organization that does the right
thing.

A comprehensive set of built-in affirmative procedures—displaying the code in
the workplace and in major agency publications, utilizing it in decision making,
applying to it in job descriptions, making it a criterion in performance in personnel
reviews, using it to evaluate organizational programs—would be difficult to flaunt. An
ethics statement assumes people are disposed to do the right thing, and the agency is
structured to support them. It is less important that rules fit a given situation than to
raise the question, "What sort of person/organization are we becoming by pursuing
this policy?" Even with their well-known limitations, codes of ethics can serve as a
bridge between the individual and the organization, between productivity and ethics.

There is, of course, nothing automatic about internal systems (or external controls such as media, hotlines, unions, inspectors general; see below) as they can only
supplement an act of will on the part of agency leadership sustained by a program of
action. As moral custodians of collective goals, a task force of employees and managers could validate and operationalize recruitment and training activities by ensuring agency standards are followed. It could act as an "angel's advocate" in decision
making, as an appeal board, and as an ombudsman in the policy process. It could also
publish advisory opinions, formulate ethical impact statements, design an employee
bill of rights, provide space on standard forms for dissenting opinions, and specify
when the whistle must be blown (e.g., knowledge of a felony). Organizational development techniques (e.g., team building, participatory decision making, feedback
mechanisms, employee development programs) and an empowerment strategy (e.g.,
granting discretion with authority and responsibility) can reinforce task force activities. In other words, the mere profession of ethical principles in a code, without full
commitment at the senior level, continual practical training throughout the organization, and monitoring their effectiveness, can become a public relations exercise
rather than real accountability.

By thinking about internal ethics first, the context for improved internal productivity is established. Workers belonging to an agency whose leadership is genuinely
committed to exemplary conduct are relieved of several burdens. Issues related to job
security, promotional opportunities, salary increases, and management–employee relations can be less contentious in an environment where ethical conduct engenders
mutual trust. In like manner, performance appraisal sessions, for example, although
never fated to be popular, become more of the developmental opportunities they
purport to be rather than the adversarial proceedings they often are.

Internal ethics are not a panacea for internal productivity problems. Work may
still be hard or tedious, the hours long, the agency understaffed, and the salaries low;
things will go wrong, problems and inefficiencies will occur, and there will still be some
less than inspiring managers, and less than admirable employees. However, a visible,
viable, and vibrant commitment to ethics in the workplace diminishes management's
likelihood to make punitive or arbitrary personnel decisions, as well as workers'

tendencies to engage in management bashing during difficult times. Such an environment, over the long term, will be more productive than one marked by the rancor inherent in situations where people do not trust one another.

In short, the operative core concept is, "Ethics may only be instrumental, it may be only a means to an end, but it is a necessary means to an end" (Thompson, 1992, p. 255). In this vein, to achieve an ethical workplace means not only having a good place to work, but also having an organization better able to serve the public.

## B. External Relations

There is an easy sensibility to the need for ethical action related to productivity inside an organization. It should be a better and more efficient department if employees understand how people are to be treated and what is expected. However, what is the bond between productivity and ethics in organizational external relations?

Because it is not possible to satisfy all interests at all times, the critical role of ethical action in the pursuit of productivity is now evident: no organization that is not trusted can be successful. Trustworthiness is a result of scrupulous ethical action and is the hallmark of professional administration. In external relations, it means that agencies carrying out even the most onerous tasks, such as those by the Internal Revenue Service, will be less apt to face charges of inefficiency and ineptitude. The same quality shields against partisan tinkering during changes in political power. Although it may appear idealistic to tie productivity to ethics, one need only look at the flagging fortunes of the National Aeronautics and Space Administration in the wake of the *Challenger* and *Columbia* disasters or the Federal Bureau of Investigation since the Ruby Ridge shooting, the Timothy McVeigh–Oklahoma City investigation, and the 9–11 terrorist attacks. It is apparent the citizenry lost, without replacement, a portion of the public goods those agencies furnish: be they the wise use of tax dollars in the space program or the sense of security and reliability that a law enforcement agency must provide.

The four basic elements of an ethics code discussed in the preceding section are also germane for external relations. However, it would be useful to include a fifth component; the credo should: commit employees to treating other agencies, groups, or individuals in a manner that builds or reinforces their agency's reputation for integrity. This provision recognizes that agency trustworthiness, which may ultimately determine its external productivity, is often based on how a few of its members interact with other stakeholders. An actual failure to incorporate this concept, along with the rest of the internal and external relations dimensions of productivity and ethics, including component five, is discussed below.

---

**Case 2**  Inspecting the Inspectors

---

Inspectors general (IG) hold a special place in government; any federal, state, or local department that receives an affirmative report from its jurisdiction's IG can cite it as evidence that the agency is internally and externally productive and ethical. To carry out its own mission, the IG's office itself must, of course, be above reproach; to be any less is to invite doubt regarding its own productivity and ethics. A recent incident in the Pentagon's Office of the Inspector General illustrates clearly how productivity and ethics interact with organizational internal and external relations.

In the Department of Defense (an agency with 670,000 civilian and approximately 2.7 million uniformed employees and an annual budget approaching 300 billion), the Office of Inspector General (OIG), "directs the Pentagon's battle against waste, fraud, and abuse in the military industrial complex. The office is also in charge of combating hackers trying to raid the military's computers. Overseeing 1,200 employees, spending 230 million a year, the IG is comparable to the director of the FBI" (Wilson, 2000). On May 22, 2001 Defense Secretary Donald Rumsfeld received a letter from Senator Charles Grassley (D-Iowa) stating: "I am ... conducting an oversight investigation of allegations that 12 to 15 officials in ... [your OIG] ... tampered with audit materials to alter the outcome of a Peer Review required by law. This is a major integrity violation" (Grassley, 2001).

The "Peer Review" process (itself an institutional response to Juvenal's famous question, "Who watches the watchmen?") is a triennial intragovernment audit of IG offices, conducted by other federal inspectors general, to ensure the integrity of completed reports. A passing grade must be earned to receive accreditation; failure to do so severely affects an OIG's ability to carry out its mission of finding and eliminating fraud, waste, and abuse as the quality of any audit by an unaccredited office could easily be called into question. The OIG, although accredited during the 1997 Peer Review, had fared poorly. In 2000, the designated peer auditor, the Treasury Department's Inspector General for Tax Administration, randomly identified eight audits, from the hundreds generated over the preceding three years, for examination.

Senior Defense IG officials believed one of the audits would not meet established standards, resulting in the loss of certification. Subsequently deciding to rework the report, original papers were destroyed, and a new set of documents created. This required backdated papers signed by staff members not involved in the "re-creation" process. When the Treasury audit later awarded accreditation, an anonymous source alerted Grassley.

The effect on agency external relations was easy to see. Senator Grassley (2001) said, "If the IG can't be trusted, then we are in trouble. Who can we trust? This unfortunate episode puts a dark cloud over the entire IG community." By its actions, the Defense Department's OIG compromised its ability to be productive inside the Pentagon, in government as a whole, and outside the public service. The falsified report apparently took over 950 work hours (the equivalent of nearly six months), at a cost of at least $63,000, to produce (Margasak, 2001). The time expended to rework the documents meant that other projects were left undone. Subsequent investigations cost additional hours and dollars. By fabricating data, the Pentagon office fooled the IG for Tax Administration into giving a favorable report and embarrassed it by having to retract the evaluation. This negatively affected its ability to work with that agency and, by extension, other agencies, including, perhaps especially, Congress. Because the Defense Department works with contractors outside government, they are now in a position to question the accuracy of audits of their expenditures. This too can only lead to a loss of productivity. The sad irony of an OIG doing the very things it is charged with preventing, as presaged in point five of the above credo, is apparent.

The impact on internal relations was equally damaging. When senior officials order patently unethical and illegal activity, the basis of healthy employer–employee relations is severely eroded. These relations were further affected when high administrators were "cleared," by their own internal investigation, of any wrongdoing and junior personnel were made subject to discipline. Employing the matrix terms discussed earlier, the decision to prepare a fraudulent audit was "wrong" ethically and "bad" productively, one that had serious internal and external consequences. These policymakers may have been technically smart in what they did, but they were—profoundly—ethically unwise.

Such cases, to say nothing of the accounting debacles of the Enron era, clearly establish the crucial bond between productivity and ethics. They demonstrate that the productivity–ethics link is certainly more than an abstraction for the professional administrator. This official, charged with rendering public service, must deal with that nexus, the subject of the conclusion.

## IV. CONCLUSION

Many professionals today work in transparent and inclusive organizations; in such institutions, forming deep relationships with internal and external stakeholders is key to high performance. For this to occur, reputation matters and that reputation depends not only on what it can do, but also on what it should do. To make a real difference in public service means genuine progress in both productivity and ethics.

As this chapter has shown, managers must have technical and ethical competencies; yet the terms themselves are difficult to define and there is little literature that explains their interactions. Nonetheless, they can be, and are, integrated into decision making. Indeed, high-performing organizations with ethical cultures emphasize productivity improvement (Berman, 1998); such is the result when the fundamentals of good work, productivity and ethics are in harmony. When not given the attention that they deserve, the internal and external relations of the entire organization can be endangered if not destroyed. A profession, in the end, is only as good as its ethics.

Aligning productivity and ethics means recognizing that ethics often trump productivity: efforts to improve ethics by empowering employees usually heighten ethics and productivity. However, the converse is not true: programs designed to promote productivity can undermine both productivity and ethics (Osborne and Gaebler, 1992).[5] High performance, stated differently, requires committed people and that, in turn, requires an organization to earn that commitment (Zadek, 1998, p. 423).

There is no reason to believe that such circumstances will be less important in the new century, and herein lies the leadership challenge. No shortcut to improving productivity and ethics exists. Sound initiatives require a needs assessment gauging: the likelihood of political support, the receptivity of the organization's culture, the necessary leadership commitment, the availability of resources, and the willingness of employees to participate. Without such planning, agencies may fall victim to pseudo-solutions such as exhortations to improve (with no provision for identifying how or what) and/or old-fashioned management pressure and "bash-the-bureaucrat" politics. The public deserves better.

## NOTES

1.  Assume, for instance, that a late season storm in excess of the number originally projected by the National Weather Service severely damaged property along the Eastern seaboard. The public would not be sympathetic if the Federal Emergency Management Agency could not provide the same level of service to those affected by the "extra" storm as those in earlier, predicted storms. The Weather Service would be criticized for failing to predict the storm in its annual projections. Both organizations would be viewed by many as neither efficient nor effective, and therefore not productive.
2.  Some of the discussion that follows is adapted from Bowman (1995).

3. Although the relationship between productivity and ethics has not been conclusively established, Menzel and Carson's (1999) review of the literature suggests that intriguing consistent evidence exists to suspect that ethics have a positive influence on performance. Gueras and Garofalo point out that the attempt to demonstrate statistical relationships on this matter is flawed because, "trust, accountability, and responsibility do not lead themselves to measurement ..." (2002, p. 265).
4. The next several paragraphs are derived from Bowman (2000, 1986).
5. Thus profits are not the goal of a business, but the means that permit it to continue providing goods and services. Likewise, cutting (or raising) taxes is not the goal of governments, but the means that allows them to meet public needs.

## REFERENCES

Berman, E. M. (1998a). Public cynicism: Manifestations and responses. In: Berman, E. M., West, J. P., Bonczek, S. J., eds. *The Ethics Edge*. Washington, DC: International City/County Management Association, pp. 207–215.

Berman, E. M. (1998b). *Productivity in Public and Nonprofit Organizations*. Thousand Oaks, CA: Sage.

Bowman, J. S. (1986). Restoring citizen confidence in bureaucracy: Beyond civil service reform. In: Calista, D., ed. *Reforming American Bureaucracy*. Greenwich, CT: JAI, pp. 245–260.

Bowman, J. S. (1992). Quality circles for the 1990s. In: Holzer, M., ed. *Public Productivity Handbook*. New York: Marcel Dekker, pp. 499–515.

Bowman, J. S. (1995). Ethics and quality: A "right-good" combination. In: West, J. P., ed. *Quality Management Today*. Washington, DC: International City/Country Management Association, pp. 64–69.

Bowman, J. S. (2000). Towards a professional ethos: From regulatory to reflective codes. *Int. Rev. Admin. Sci.* 66:6773–6787.

Geuras, D., Garofalo, C. (2002). *Practical Ethics in Public Administration*. Vienna, VA: Management Concepts.

Grassley, C. (2001). Letter to the Secretary of Defense from the Chairman of the Senate Finance Committee dated May 22, 2001. Available at http://www.d-n-i.net/FCS_Folder/grassley_ig_audit.htm.

Margasak, L. (2001, June 6). Anti-fraud agency fakes documents. *AP online*. Available at http://web.lexis-nexis.com

Menzel, D. C. (1966). Ethics stress in public organizations. *Public Product. Manage. Rev.* 20:70–83. September.

Menzel, D. C., Carson, J. (1999). A review and assessment of empirical research on public administration ethics. *Public Integrity* 1:239–264.

Mosher, F. (1982). *Democracy and the Public Service*. 2nd ed. New York: Oxford.

Osborne, D., Gaebler, T. (1992). *Reinventing Government*. Reading: Addison-Wesley.

Rozell, M., Wilcox, C. (2000). *The Clinton Scandal and the Future of American Government*. Washington, DC: Georgetown University Press.

Thompson, D. F. (1992). Paradoxes of government ethics. *Public Admin. Rev.* 52(3):254–259.

Van Wart, M. (1998). *Changing Public Sector Values*. New York: Garland.

Wilson, G. (2000, November 20) Commentary: Get a new top cop for the Pentagon *GovExec.com* (Online Journal). Available at http://govexec.com/dailyfed/1100/112000nj2.html.

Wilson, W. (1887). The study of administration. *Polit. Sci. Quart.* 2(2):197–222.

Zadek, S. (1998). Balancing performance, ethics, and accountability. *J. Bus. Ethics* 17:1421–1441.

# 12

# Trust, Performance, and the Pressures for Productivity in the Public Sector

**MARC HOLZER and MENGZHONG ZHANG**
*Rutgers, The State University of New Jersey, Newark, New Jersey, U.S.A.*

## I. INTRODUCTION

This chapter first examines the theme of trust and performance in the context of the intellectual history of public administration. The main focus of the chapter is the link between government performance and public trust, analyzing the relationship and revealing the complications using empirical evidence, among trust, performance, and ongoing pressures for productivity in the public sector.

Three pillars of public administration values have gradually been recognized: efficiency, effectiveness, and equity. Earlier scholars of public administration emphasized efficiency, that is, the machinelike task of getting the job done at the lowest cost in resources. The "one best way" approach of performing each task was identified with the works of Taylor (1903, 1911, 1923). The efficiency orientation is reflected again in the late twentieth century with the privatization initiative under the new public management practices. The scientific management approach, grounded in business organization, gave rise to a number of supposedly universal "principles." For example, Gulick (1987) created the acronym POSDCORB (planning, organizing, staffing, directing, coordinating, reporting, and budgeting) for the tasks of chief executives, and Urwick (1952) identified "Ten Principles" as guidelines for organizational design. The descriptions of administrative organizations by the above-mentioned authors, as well as Fayol (1949) and others fits within the framework of the bureaucratic model as defined by Max Weber. The Weberian model of bureaucracy was conceptualized as a vehicle for facilitating the efficiency and effectiveness of organizational development. In practice, however, the public views bureaucracy with negative connotations of hierarchy, unresponsiveness, red tape, and inefficiency (Holzer and Gabrielian, 1998).

Both efficiency and program effectiveness gained momentum from the 1970s onwards, initially under the rubric of the "productivity movement," and then under various other labels such as "reinventing government." The values of equity were emphasized by the Minnowbrook participants in 1968 and began to gather more momentum as one of significant pillars of public administration (Marini, 1971). With the coming of the new millennium, an all-encompassing term is public performance, which conceivably embraces all the previous values (efficiency, effectiveness, and equity) in public administration.

What does the history of public administration tells us about performance and trust? First, performance, either public or private sector, is positively associated with efficiency and effectiveness. Second, trust plays a more prominent role in public administration than the majority of public administration scholars have assumed. In *The Study of Administration*, Wilson (1987) emphasized trust:

> It is clearing the moral atmosphere of official life by establishing the sanctity of public office as a *public trust* (p. 18).
>
> Suspicion in itself is never healthful either in the private or in the public mind. *Trust is strength in all relations of life;*... so it is the office of the administrative organizer to fit administration with conditions of clear-cut responsibility which shall insure *trustworthiness* (p. 20).
>
> Self-government does not consist in having a hand in everything... The cook must *be trusted* with a large discretion as to the management of the fires and the ovens (p. 21).

In the context of this history, Section II examines the relationship between trust and economic performance. Section III reveals the extent to which public trust and American society relate to each other. Section IV presents data on government performance, confidence, or declining public trust, with empirical evidence from historic and comparative data. Section V discusses the causal linkage between trust and performance. In conclusion, Section VI discusses some of the ways that trust might be reconstructed and performance improved.

## II.   TRUST AND ECONOMIC PERFORMANCE

This section focuses on the relationship between trust and economic performance within an organization and between trust and economic performance at the country level. In effect, this is a review and extension of Fukuyama's model in his provocative book *Trust: The Social Virtues and the Creation of Prosperity* (1995).

### A.   Trust Within an Organization and the Organization's Economic Performance

The traditional approach toward an organization's economic performance is closely associated with physical, financial, and human capital, but not much light is shed on the cultural aspects such as social capital. Fukuyama's proposition is not wholly original, because some twenty years ago Kenneth Arrow said that "virtually every commercial transition has within itself an element of trust" and "much of the economic backwardness in the world can be explained by the lack of mutual confidence" (Galston, 1996, p.129). Fukuyama's thesis changed the attitudes toward factors influencing an organization's economic performance. To Fukuyama, an organization's economic performance is surely dependent on the trust of the people working in that organization. Fukuyama tries to quantify these reasons and concludes that eighty percent of an organization's economic performance could be attributed to rational self-interest and twenty percent to culture and tradition. People do not behave simply to maximize utility, as economists believe within the rational actor model. Rather, they act for a whole host of reasons—many based on culture, belief, and tradition—that do not fit with economists' models (Gewen, 1995).

Two situations are addressed by Fukuyama: organizational performance in low-trust cultures and societies such as China, South Korea, Italy, and France, and in high-trust societies such as Japan, Germany, and the United States. Fukuyama proposes that the higher the trust among people, the larger the industrial and commercial organizations that might be developed. In this direction, his argumentation is a successful endeavor. In the case of Chinese culture, Hong Kong, Taiwan, and Singapore share some common traits. Trust is highest within family, and then could be extended to kinship and to some extent to close friends. From the societal perspective, people generally do not trust each other, voluntary association is rare and corporations could seldom expand to the large scale as compared to the largest companies in the United States and Japan. Although Fukuyama's accounts might explain the conditions of Hong Kong, Taiwan, and Singapore, the same logic is not necessarily applicable to the situation in mainland China. Voluntary associations in China have been prohibited, and a market orientation is a recent (about twenty years old) phenomenon. Not long ago, a command economy with state-owned enterprises was dominant in mainland China. The net effect has been to suppress the private economy, and therefore many production organizations operate under the Chinese government, rather than under the paradigm of voluntary cooperation between individuals. The relationship between trust and corporate performance (in the standard of corporation scale) will have to be tested a number of years from now; however, Fukuyama's illustration of the situation in France, South Korea, South Italy, Hong Kong, Taiwan, and Singapore is persuasive. Namely, the low-trust relationship among people has resulted in small-scale corporations. Low-trust societies are unable to develop either the large-scale corporate organizations or the widespread networks among small businesses that are essential for successful modern economies (Galston, 1996).

By contrast, high-trust societies, such as Japan, Germany, and the United States, are superpowers marked by a highly developed sense of societal trust and communal solidarity. These countries readily developed large-scale enterprises and professional management. American Protestant churches, German mediaeval guilds, and Japanese samurai all have provided some forms of social glue. Indeed, they could be regarded as a communitarian orientation, with a collective sense of voluntary association. In the case of Japan, the lifetime employment system is a good example of trust between employees and management. In some cases, there are written contracts that employees agree not to seek a better job or a higher wage elsewhere, and the company agrees not to fire its own employees or raid employees of another firm. Typically, the agreement rests on moral pressure rather than on law.

But with the recession of the Japanese economy in the 1990s, it has been hard to follow a written or unwritten agreement of lifetime employment. Japanese firms responded to the harsh reality in a number of ways, such as forced early retirement. Nevertheless, the lifetime employment system restricted Japanese companies from downsizing and wholesale layoffs to gain productivity advantages as many American corporations did in the 1980s and 1990s. Lifetime employment in Japan is a testimony to the fact that each side has a high degree of confidence that the other will live up to its promise (Fukuyama, 1995). As for German industry, the idea of a community of interest between workers and management was given an institutional form in 1920. Although Germany is marked by significant class differences and obstacles to social mobility, there is a high degree of pride in labor that "allows German workers to identify not simply with their social class but with their industry and its managers. This sense of professionalism and calling has moderated the inclination toward class warfare in Germany and has led to a very different set of workplace relationships than might otherwise have been the case" (Fukuyama, 1995, p. 233). In contrast to the classic management model of specialization of work, each German worker is trained to do a number of different tasks and has a great amount of flexibility to do whatever is needed based on daily requirements. This practice demands trust between employees and management, and German workers are frequently considered as team players.

In the United States, there is a deep-rooted culture of liberalism and individualism on the surface. Fukuyama (1995, 276) captured the ingrained cooperative characters of American workers in the following paragraph.

> Consider the transcontinental agricultural commodity trade that developed in the mid-nineteenth century... In those days, it would be very difficult for a dealer in Chicago to negotiate detailed contracts with another in Abilene or Topeka, much less sue for breach of contract. A great deal of this trade therefore depended on *trust*.

In short, Fukuyama's test as to the relationship between trust and corporate performance (by the standard of capacity to expand the company size) is convincing. Although Fukuyama is unable to run a statistical regression analysis for the hypothesis of the relationship, the comparative study between societies with low and high trust as to corporate performance does make sense.

## B. Trust and Economic Performance at the Country Level

It seems that Fukuyama also suggests that there is a linear relationship between trust and economic performance at the country level. However, the results of his endeavors are, at best, mixed. First, comparing the economic performance at the societal level between the high-trust countries of Japan, Germany, and the United States, the result is not quite clear. With a continual decline in public trust in the United States, the economic performance of the country is still strong. Why can't Japan and Germany surpass the United States in per capita income if social capital such as trust is that important? At the societal level, many factors influence aggregate economic performance. After all, if Fukuyama is correct, trust only accounts for twenty percent of the final outcome.

As for low-trust societies, South Korea has been performing well in the past decades, with some large corporations supported by the state. France is similar in this approach in that the state has a hand in industry. In the case of Hong Kong, Taiwan, Singapore, and Italy, small businesses are flourishing. In mainland China, the majority of state-owned enterprises are not earning profits or, even worse, are losing money at the expense of the state. However, private businesses and collective companies, as well as joint ventures with international corporations, are prosperous. As a whole, these low-trust societies generally performed well by economic standards. Why does not low social capital lead to poor economic performance? Again, many factors play roles in the process of economic performance at the societal level, such as political system, economic structure and foundation, cultural tradition, economic policies, environment, international investment, and so forth. In the end, trust may or may not account for twenty percent of the outcome.

Although Fukuyama convincingly demonstrated that trust has a great impact on firm size, it is not clear to him, however, whether the prosperity of a country can only be brought about by large corporations.

> It is possible to imagine futures in which large, complex, and sophisticated corporations take the lead in creating wealth, as well as futures dominated by small, nimble, and innovative ones. Since we cannot predict future directions in technology, we cannot know which of these futures will materialize. What we can say is that the impact of cultural differences in the propensity for sociability will have a large, but at the moment indeterminate, impact on economic life (Fukuyama, 1995, p. 342).

## III. DECLINING TRUST OF THE PUBLIC IN GOVERNMENT

Public confidence and trust in government have been declining over the past decades. This section serves as an empirical test of that proposition as a basis for understanding whether the public's attitudes toward government, society, and even their own value orientations have changed over the past decades.

### A. Americans' Attitudes Toward Governments (Executive, Legislature, and Judicial Areas)

*Americans' Confidence in the Executive Branch of Government.* From survey results, we know that only 11% of Americans had a great deal of confidence in the executive branch of government, and 35% had hardly any confidence in it, in 1994. This was an improvement from 42% who had hardly any confidence in 1974 when the Watergate investigation heavily influenced American attitudes toward government. However, the percentage of people who had a great deal of confidence also declined from 14% in 1974 to 11% in 1994. In 1998 the situation improved a little bit, with 14% of respondents indicating a great deal of confidence, and 35% who had hardly any confidence (National Opinion Research Center, 1972–2000).

*Americans' Confidence in the Congress.* From survey results, we know that Americans had little confidence in Congress. Worse yet, public confidence in Congress had been declining from 17% who had a great deal of confidence in 1974 to 8% in 1994. People who had hardly any confidence in Congress increased from 21% in 1974 to 39% in 1994. However, the situation improved a little bit in 1998, with 10% of respondents expressing a great deal of confidence, and 30% hardly any confidence, in Congress (National Opinion Research Center, 1972–2000).

*Americans' Confidence in the Supreme Court.* The percentage of Americans who had hardly any confidence in the Supreme Court increased from 14% in 1974 to 16% in 1994, and the percentage of people who had a great deal of confidence decreased from 33% in 1974 to 30% in 1994. In 1998, the percentage of Americans who had hardly any confidence in the Supreme Court fell to 14%, and the percentage of people who had a great deal of confidence increased to 31%. Overall, if we combine the percentage of people who had a great deal of confidence and the people who had only some confidence as one category, the percentage was 81% in 1998 as well as in 1974. This number indicates that Americans maintained confidence in the Supreme Court (National Opinion Research Center, 1972–2000).

*Americans' Confidence in Public Officials.*   The majority of Americans do not think that public officials are interested in the problems of the average man or woman. In 1974, 64% of survey respondents agree that most officials were not really interested in the problems of the average person. In 1994, 74% shared this view (Mitchell, 1996, p. 77). In short, they do not have much confidence in public officials.

     In summary, as for the attitudes of Americans toward American government— the executive, the Congress, the Supreme Court, and public officials—the degree of trust has been declining from 1974 to 1994. Comparatively speaking, the degree of confidence in the Supreme Court is higher than in the Executive and Congress. Furthermore, about three-quarters of Americans did not think public officials were interested in their problems in 1994.

## B.   Americans' Attitudes Toward the Military

The majority of people had some or a great deal of confidence (85%) in the military in 1994 and 1998, and the percentage of people who had hardly any confidence in the military was 12% in 1994 and 1998. In 1974, the figure was similar, with 84% of people having some or a great deal of confidence in the military, and 13% of people indicating hardly any confidence in the military (National Opinion Research Center, 1972–2000). This suggests that the majority of Americans maintain a confidence in the military.

## C.   Americans' Attitudes Toward Education

Americans' favorable attitudes toward education have declined. As for those who have a great deal of confidence in the people who are running education, the percentage declined from 49% in 1974 to 25% in 1994. Combining people who have some degree of confidence and a great deal of confidence, the percentage declined from 90% to 81% over 20 years, and people who had hardly any confidence in education increased from 8% in 1974 to 17% in 1994. In 1998, this situation improved somewhat, with 27% of people having a great deal of confidence in the people who are running education, and 16% of people had hardly any confidence in education (National Opinion Research Center, 1972–2000).

## D.   Americans' Attitudes Toward Life

*Are Things Getting Worse?*   More than two thirds of Americans in 1994 perceived that the lot of the average person was getting worse, not better. The percentage of the respondents who shared this view increased from 59% in 1974 to 67% in 1994 (Mitchell, 1996, p. 74).

*Who Should Help the Poor?*   The percentage who strongly agree that the government should be responsible for improving the standard of living of the poor declined from 39% in 1974 to 26% in 1994. The percentage who are of the opinion that poor people should take care of themselves increased from 23% in 1974 to 28% in 1994 (Mitchell,

1996, p. 51). That is, the government was less likely to be perceived as the means to solving problems of the poor.

*Whose Responsibility is Health Care?* More than half of respondents agree that government should be responsible for health care. From 1974 to 1994 there was no noticeable change. Only about 20% believe that people should take care of themselves (Mitchell, 1996, p. 83).

## E. Personal Outlook

The degree of trustworthiness of others declined from 1974 to 1994. In 1974, 39% of respondents believed that most people can be trusted, whereas the percentage was 34% in 1994. In 1974, 56% of respondents believed that you cannot be too careful, and this number increased to 61% in 1994. The situation improved in 1998, with 37% of respondents agreeing that most people can be trusted and 56% believing that one cannot be too careful (National Opinion Research Center, 1972–2000). In 1974, 62% of respondents believed that other people try to be fair; this figure decreased to 53% in 1994. In the meantime 31% of people thought others would take advantage of them in 1974, and 39% in 1994. In 1974, 56% of respondents believed that others try to be helpful, although the figure declined to 46% in 1994. The percentage of people who believed that others were just looking out for themselves increased from 37% in 1974 to 47% in 1994. As for the membership in organizations, it declined slightly in church-affiliated groups (42% to 33%), school service groups (18% to 16%), and fraternal groups (14% to 10%) from 1974 to 1994. Membership in professional or academic societies, however, increased from 13% in 1974 to 19% in 1994 (Mitchell, 1996, pp. 349, 352, 355, 371).

**Table 1** Summary

| Americans' attitudes toward | | | Comments |
|---|---|---|---|
| A | Government | Executive | Confidence declined from 1974 to 1994 ▼ |
| | | Congress | Confidence declined from 1974 to 1994 ▼ |
| | | Supreme Court | Confidence declined from 1974 to 1994 ▼ |
| | | Public officials | Confidence declined from 1974 to 1994 ▼ |
| B | Military | | Confidence declined from 1974 to 1994 ▼ |
| C | Education | | Confidence declined from 1974 to 1994 ▼ |
| D | Life | Things getting better | Agree from 1974 to 1994 ▼ |
| | | Who should help the poor? | Taken care of by govt. ▼ (from 1974 to 1994) |
| | | Health care | No noticeable change ◄──► (from 1974 to 1994) |
| E | Personal Outlook | Trustworthiness of others | Most people can be trusted ▼ (from 1974 to 1994) |
| | | Fairness to others | Most people try to be fair ↓ (from 1974 to 1994) |
| | | Helpfulness to others | Most people try to be helpful ▼ (from 1974 to 1994) |
| | | Membership in organization | Slightly declined in three out of four groups (from 1974 to 1994) ↓ |

In short, in most cases, the trust of Americans toward government, society, and others has been on the decline from 1974 to 1994 (Table 1). The hypothesis that public confidence and trust in the government had been declining over the past decades is, therefore, tentatively confirmed.

## IV.  GOVERNMENT PERFORMANCE AND PRODUCTIVITY

In Section III, we surveyed opinions of Americans toward government and society in 1974, 1984, and 1994. Our conclusion is that Americans do not feel as confident in government and other organizational leaders as they did two or three decades ago. Generally speaking, the degree of Americans' trust in government and society has declined over the past decades.

Is there something wrong with the performance, or perceived performance, of government in the United States? We might, then, hypothesize that American government's performance has been declining over the last decades.

Below, we focus on two dimensions: historical comparisons of current performance with previous performance, and international comparisons with major industrialized democracies.

### A.  Economy

The average real GDP in billions of dollars in the period of 1990 to 1995 was: United States (6024), Japan (2356), France (1052), West Germany (1365), United Kingdom (930), Canada (544), and Sweden (143) (OECD, 1994). From the above number, we see that the United States is still a dominant force with regard to average GDP in advanced democracies. The annual rate of growth in real GDP in the United States, however, has been continually declining over the last three and a half decades. From 1960 to 1969 in the United States, the annual rate of growth in real GDP was 3.84%; then 2.82 (1970 to 1979); then 2.51 (1980 to 1989); then 2.00 (1990 to 1995). The annual rate of growth in real GDP has similarly shown a declining trend among the other six democratic countries (Bok, 1996, p. 25).

Over the long term, the unemployment rate in the United States has steadily increased: 3.92% (1964 to 1969), 6.03% (1970 to 1979), 7.16% (1980 to 1989), and 6.40% (1990 to 1994) (OECD, 1995), although there was some improvement in the latter 1990s. From this number, it appears that unemployment rates in the United States continually increased from the 1960s to the 1980s. Although in the 1990s the unemployment rate declined to a somewhat lower level compared with that of the 1980s, it was still higher than the 1960s and 1970s.

In short, in the United States, the annual rate of growth in real GDP was not as high in the 1990s as in the previous three decades. The unemployment rate in the 1990s was generally higher than those of the 1960s and 1970s. This economic outlook may have led to unsatisfactory sentiments and doubts as to government performance, and eventually a loss of confidence in government.

### B.  Education

How does the competence of American students compare with students from other countries? The high school graduation rate in the United States (75.7% in 1992) was only a little bit higher than that of Canada (68.4%), although lower than those of the other four countries (Japan: 92.2%, France: 78.2%, United Kingdom: 80.1%, and West Germany: 109.6%) (Bok, 1996, p. 61). The real worry, however, is the poor performance of American students in math and science as compared with students in other countries. Tests of math and science administered by the International Assessment of Educational Progress (IAEP) in 1988 showed that, out of twelve participating countries, American students ranked twelfth in mathematics and ninth in science, with none of the participating countries doing significantly worse than United States. (Medrich and Griffith, 1992).

By and large, American students do not perform well compared with students in advanced countries in math and science. But who is responsible for this disappointing result? Parents are unlikely to blame themselves. A natural scapegoat is the schools. To be fair, however, other reasons might be found in factors such as family, reference groups, media (TV), and social environment, all of which influence the behavior of students.

## C. Quality of Life

*The Economist* (December 25, 1993 to January 7, 1994) ranked America eighth out of twenty-two countries (Bok, 1996, p. 151) in terms of quality of life. According to the satisfaction levels expressed by citizens, the combined results of numerous surveys ranked the United States eleventh among thirty-eight countries (Bok, 1996, p. 152). This suggests that Americans may not be satisfied with the quality of their lives as compared to people in the top ten countries on the list.

## D. Health Care

Comparing Canada, France, West Germany, Japan, Sweden, the United Kingdom, and the United States, an American's life expectancy is the lowest among those countries, and the infant mortality rate is the highest. This picture may be dismaying. Given unfavorable health care system comparisons, it is hard for the public to accept that the cost of health care is the highest in the United States (Bok, 1996, pp. 223–225).

## E. Life of the Aged

Among five countries, the poverty rate of the elderly in the United States (23.9%) was the second highest in 1978 to 1980. The percentage of the elderly with incomes below the official U.S. poverty line was the second highest (16.1%) in those years. After income transfer programs, the percentage of the elderly living in poverty (29.3%) was the highest in the United States (Palmer et al., 1988).

In summary, for purposes of historical comparison, out of 73 policy areas, 18, or about 25%, worsened in the 1990s as compared with the 1960s in the United States (see Table 2, Summary 1). As an international comparison, out of 70 areas, America ranked at or near the bottom in 33 areas, or 47.1% among seven countries (see Table 2 Summary 2).

These figures are revealing. Subjectively, then, Americans may increasingly and collectively believe in the poor performance of American government, even if each of these conditions was a function of multiple conditions as we suggest below.

**Table 2**   Summary 1. U.S. Policy Areas that Became Worse in the 1990s Compared with the Early 1960s

| | |
|---|---|
| 1 | Economy: minimizing unemployment |
| 2 | Research and technology: share of worldwide high technology exports |
| 3 | Housing: affordability for renters[a] |
| 4 | Neighborhoods: concentration of poverty in urban neighborhoods |
| 5 | Perception of personal safety in neighborhoods |
| 6 | Health care: cost (percentage of GDP) |
| 7 | Job security: percentage of workforce with some form of legally sanctioned representation |
| 8 | Job security: Percentage of workforce laid off per year |
| 9 | Job security: unemployment insurance (percentage of unemployed receiving) |
| 10 | Violent crime: incident (per 100,000 people) |
| 11 | Violent crime: success in solving crime (clearance rate) |
| 12 | Violent crime: fear for personal safety |
| 13 | Personal responsibility: obeying the law (extent of crime) |
| 14 | Personal responsibility: percentage of children born out of wedlock |
| 15 | Personal responsibility: cheating on exams |
| 16 | Personal responsibility: percentage of income given to charity |
| 17 | Personal responsibility: community service |
| 18 | Personal responsibility: percentage of eligible voting |

[a] "Affordable" indicates the percentage of people paying more than 30% of their income for housing.
*Source*: Bok, 1996, pp. 360–363.

**Table 2**   Summary 2. United States compared with six other industrial democracies (Canada, France, West Germany, Japan, Sweden, and the United Kingdom); the U.S. record in the following areas is at or near the bottom

| | |
|---|---|
| 1 | Economy: growth rate of per capita income (1960–1990) |
| 2 | Economy: growth rate of productivity (1960–1990) |
| 3 | Economy: net investment in plant and equipment as percentage of GDP (1960–1990) |
| 4 | Education: student achievement (math) |
| 5 | Education: student achievement (science) |
| 6 | Labor market policy: percentage of GDP spent on training (public and private) |
| 7 | Labor market policy: percentage of workforce receiving training |
| 8 | Housing: affordability for entire population |
| 9 | Neighborhoods: degree of segregation by income in cities |
| 10 | Neighborhoods: degree of segreation by race in cities |
| 11 | Neighborhoods: length of commute to work |
| 12 | Environment: percentage of waste recycled |
| 13 | Children's well-being: infant mortality |
| 14 | Children's well-being: percentage enrolled in preschool |
| 15 | Children's well-being: percentage in poverty |
| 16 | Health care: life expectancy |
| 17 | Health care: cost as percentage of GDP |
| 18 | Health care: coverage by health insurance |
| 19 | Health care: public evaluation of system |
| 20 | Job security: percentage of workforce with some form of representation |
| 21 | Job security: protection from arbitrary discharge |

**Table 2** Continued

| | |
|---|---|
| 22 | Job security: assistance in case of layoffs |
| 23 | Violent crime: incidence (per 100,000 people) |
| 24 | Violent crime: success in solving crimes |
| 25 | Violent crime: fear for personal safety |
| 26 | Old age: percentage in poverty |
| 27 | Old age: access to affordable long-term care |
| 28 | Personal responsibility: violations of criminal laws |
| 29 | Personal responsibility: incidence of teenage pregnancy |
| 30 | Personal responsibility: voting rates |
| 31 | Providing for the poor and disadvantaged: percentage of population with incomes below poverty line |
| 32 | Providing for the poor and disadvantaged: severity of poverty (aggregate poverty gap as percent of GDP) |
| 33 | Providing for the poor and disadvantaged: effectiveness of government income transfer programs |

*Source*: Bok, 1996, pp. 368–371.

## V.  CAUSAL LINKAGE BETWEEN TRUST AND PERFORMANCE

We have discussed the relationship between trust and economic performance in the private sector. We have also examined the decline of trust in terms of Americans' attitudes toward government and society, as well as the decline of American government performance in historical and international perspectives. In this section, we further conceptualize the framework of the relationship between trust and performance, building the causal linkage between trust and performance at the organizational and societal levels, respectively.

We now focus on the relationship between trust and government performance.

## VI.  THEORETICAL HYPOTHESIS: THE HIGHER THE GOVERNMENT'S PERFORMANCE, THE HIGHER THE PUBLIC TRUST TOWARD GOVERNMENT

### A.  Operational Hypothesis: The Higher the Government's Performance, the Higher the Public Confidence in Government

In Section III, we indicated that the majority of Americans had lost some degree of confidence in government, society, and others in most of the fourteen categories in the 1994 survey as compared with the 1974 survey. In Section IV, we concluded that, for historical comparison, out of 73 policy areas, 18 policy areas, or about 25%, worsened in the 1990s compared with the 1960s in the United States (see Table 2, Summary 1). As for international comparisons, out of 70 areas, America ranked at or near the bottom in 33 areas, or 47.1% among seven countries (see Table 2, Summary 2). This is to say that the American government did not do as well in one out of four areas in 1990 as compared with the 1960s. Compared with six other leading democracies, America ranked at or near the bottom in 33 out of 70 areas, or 47% area, among seven countries (see Table 2, Summary 2). We might cautiously say that government performance in the United States was poor to some degree in comparison with its history and with other advanced industrialized countries.

We must acknowledge that a group of factors were influencing the public's confidence in government; thus government's performance is only one of the factors, although an extremely important one. For this purpose, Joseph Nye (1997) at the Kennedy School of Government at Harvard University tested seventeen hypotheses where the government's performance was not a significant fact influencing public confidence in government. Although Nye's category of government performance is questionable (for he separated aspects such as government scope, economic slowdown, and economic inequality from performance), there is reason to argue that economic policy is one important function of government. Nye's table can at least illustrate the range of elements that will influence the decline of confidence in government.

For theory building, it is possible to construct these two formulas:

$$Y_1 = F (X_1, X_2, X_3, X_4, \ldots)$$
$$X_1 = F (Y_1, Y_2, Y_3, Y_4, \ldots),$$

where:          $Y_1$ = public trust in government, operationalized as public confidence in government,
                $X_1$ = government performance (a group of indices),

$X_2, X_3, X_4, \ldots$ and $Y_2, Y_3, Y_4, \ldots$ are a number of other factors such as crime, environment, health, life expectancy, and so on.

The first formula indicates that a number of factors (including government performance) influence public trust in government. The second formula indicates that a number of factors (including trust) influence government performance. From these two functions, we see that trust and government performance are two endogenous variables. We might then understand that trust, as one sort of social capital, has a great impact on government performance, although this impact might only be perceived over the long-term period. According to Nye (1997, p. 100):

> While there are differences of degree between loss of confidence, dissatisfaction, cynicism, and hatred, the steady devaluation of government and politics over long periods could affect the strength of democratic institutions. If people believe that government is incompetent and cannot be trusted, they are less likely to provide such crucial contributions as tax dollars and voluntary compliance with laws, and bright young people will not be willing to go into government. Without these resources, government cannot perform well, and if government cannot perform, people will become even more dissatisfied and distrustful. Such a cumulative downward spiral could erode support for democracy as a form of governance.

Thus, the relationship between public trust in government and government performance is a two-way track. These two factors interact with each other, especially in the long term.

## VII.  CONCLUSION: RECONSTRUCTION OF TRUST AND IMPROVEMENT OF PUBLIC PRODUCTIVITY

In Section IV of this chapter, we presented a number of areas wherein government performance declined compared with historical records, and especially with six other advanced countries. Although 18 out of 73 policy areas were worse in the 1990s as compared with the early 1960s, 49 out of 73 policy areas (67%) actually improved (Bok, 1996). Nevertheless, responses to poll questions usually suggest the public distrusts the federal government, stressing poor performance as characteristic of government service. For example, 81% of respondents agree that government is wasteful and inefficient, and 79% said the government spends too much on the wrong things (Nye, 1997).

As a nation where individualism takes hold, America's notable achievements rely primarily on individual talent and creativity. Under such conditions, America's major universities, research scientists, teaching hospitals, artists, and popular culture have come to lead the world. The country has also supplied a favorable environment for creative entrepreneurs. In these cases, able and enterprising individuals have received the opportunities, support, and incentives they needed for success. The country has also attracted talented people from other places to meet the demands of its development. However, in areas such as alleviating poverty, improving the public schools, and protecting the environment, where the skills of coordinating many organizations, cooperating with community groups, and creating efficient bureaucracies and programs are necessary, America may not have performed as well as other industrial nations (Bok, 1996).

Two candidates for blame are the policy-making process within Congress and program administration within the executive branch of government. Members of Congress spend the least amount of time doing what the public would most expect them to do—making laws. Rather, they spend more time on "pork-barrelling" and casework in order to gain advantages toward reelection (Cann, 1998). "The best-known examples are the dams, roads, research facilities, and other tax-funded projects that are sometimes allocated so as to satisfy influential legislators and local interest groups, rather than to maximize public benefits" (Bok, 1996, p. 415). The practice of such kind of activities within Congress creates substantial waste and inefficiency. In terms of administration, tales of $60 hammers and $300 toilet seats, examples of waste which are not indicative of the high performance levels of most agencies and programs, are fodder for the media and politicians. These and other problems prompted conservative critics of government such as Ronald Reagan to say, "Government is not the solution to our problems; government is the problem."

There are problems in government, as in the private sector. But government is also the solution to the problems that the public encounters. Americans treasure a clean environment, equality of opportunity, old-age benefits, and many other goals. If the public sector is drastically cut back, how might government realize the objectives most Americans desire? To solve this contradiction, Bok proposes two approaches. Either Americans could be persuaded to give up some of their basic goals, or someone could demonstrate that a big government is not essential to fulfill the tasks American want. To require Americans to give up their basic goals seems unrealistic. Small government cannot reach the goals most Americans desire. In the end, Americans have to trust that the public sector and public employees are doing a very good job. Americans can only rely on government to solve many of the pressing problem they now face.

Optimistically, although 18 out of 73 policy areas were worse in the 1990s compared with the early 1960s, 49 out of 73 policy areas (67%) actually improved (Bok, 1996). Thus, viewing the glass as "half full," American government had been improving its performance substantially.

**Table 3**   Total Taxes Collected from All Sources, as Percentage of GDP

| Country | Canada | France | West Germany | Japan | Sweden | U.K. | U.S. |
|---------|--------|--------|--------------|-------|--------|------|------|
| Taxes   | 43.1   | 46.1   | 45.3         | 34.4  | 60.0   | 38.8 | 32.2 |

*Source*: OECD 1994, and Bok 1996 p. 309.

A major problem, however, is the international comparison. Out of 70 areas, America ranked at or near the bottom in 33, or 47%, among seven countries (see Table 2, Summary 2). However, America's effective tax rate is the lowest (32%) among the seven leading nations (see Table 3).

A Chinese proverb states, "If you want a horse to run with energy, you need to give her grass to eat." American government is not armed with adequate revenue for the investments the public demands. And a high percentage of the national budget goes to the military. American government simply needs more resources (physical capital, human capital, financial capital, and social capital) to accomplish its missions. But to attract those resources it needs to improve its performance. Americans do not want to hear stories of $60 hammers and $300 toilet seats again. Instead, they want to know a much more productive public sector is providing the high-quality public goods and services they need, and is doing so efficiently and productively. We need to break the vicious chain of "low trust—low resources—poor perceived government performance—public distrust" at some point. Rather, this trend should be a cumulative upward spiral of "high trust—more resources—excellent perceived government performance—high trust."

## REFERENCES

Bok, D. (1996). *The State of the Nation: Government and the Quest for a Better Society*. Cambridge, MA: Harvard University Press.

Cann, S. J. (1998). *Administrative Law*. 2nd ed. Thousand Oaks, CA: Sage.

Fayol, H. (1949). *General and Industrial Management*. London: Pitman Publishing.

Fukuyama, F. (1995). *Trust: The Social Virtues and the Creation of Prosperity*. New York: Free Press.

Fukuyama, F. (1999). *The Great Disruption: Human Nature and the Reconstitution of Social Order*. New York: Free Press.

Galston, W. A. (Winter 1996). Trust—But Quantify. *Public Interest*. Winter p. 129.

Gewen, B. (June 5–19, 1995). Contradicted by the facts. *The New Leader*. Vol. 78. p. 5–7.

Gulick, L. (1987). Notes on the Theory of Organization. In: Shafritz, J.M., Hyde, A.C., eds. *Classics of Public Administration*. 2nd ed. revised and expanded. Chicago: Dorsey.

Holzer, M., Gabrielian, V. (1998). Five great ideas in American public administration. In: Rabin, J., Hildreth, W. B., Miller, G. J., eds. *Handbook of Public Administration*. 2nd ed. New York: Marcel Dekker.

Marini, F., ed. (1971). *Toward a New Public Administration: The Minnowbrook Perspective*. Scranton, PA: Chandler.

Medrich, E. A., Griffith, J. E. (1992). International Math and Science Assessments: What Have We Learned? 26, National Center for Education Statistics.

Mitchell, S. (1996). *The Official Guide to American Attitudes: Who Thinks What About the Issues That Shape Our Lives*. Ithaca, NY: New Strategist.

National Opinion Research Center. (1972–2000). Roper Center for Public Opinion Research. National Opinion Research Center—General social survey cumulative data file.

Nye, Joseph S. (Fall 1997). *In Government We Don't Trust. Foreign Policy.* pp. 99–108.

OECD. (December 1994). Economic Outlook, Statistics on Microcomputer Diskette 56.

OECD. (December 1995). Economic Outlook, A25.

Palmer, J., Smeeding, T., Torrey, B. (1988). The Vulnerable. Urban Institute Press.

Taylor, F. (1903). *Shop Management.* New York: Harper and Row.

Taylor, F. (1911). *The Principles of Scientific Management.* New York: W. W. Norton.

Taylor, F. (1923). *Scientific Management.* New York: Harper and Row.

Urwick, L. F. (1952). *Notes on the Theory of Organization.* New York: American Management Association.

Wilson, W. (1987). The study of administration. In: Shafritz, J. M., Hyde, A. C., eds. *Classics of Public Administration.* 2nd ed. revised and expanded. Chicago: Dorsey.

# 13

# Monitoring Quality and Productivity in the Public Sector

**THEODORE H. POISTER**
*Georgia State University, Atlanta, Georgia, U.S.A.*

## I. INTRODUCTION

As has been established elsewhere in this volume, performance measurement systems are indispensable for managing government agencies productively. Public administrators who are committed to results-oriented management need to (1) set goals and objectives, standards, or targets; (2) allocate resources accordingly and provide direction and control over people and programs so as to focus energy on attaining those goals; (3) monitor performance so as to identify strengths and weaknesses as well as measure overall success; and (4) stay on course or make midcourse corrections as indicated in order to improve performance. This is the sine qua non of effective management practice and applies to every level in an organization from top executives down to first-level supervisors.

To some extent performance measurement systems—tracking key indicators of agency or program performance at regular intervals over time—have been a staple in the public manager's toolkit for some time (Poister and Streib, 1989). However, with the passage of the Government Performance and Results Act (GPRA) of 1993 at the federal level and similar legislation or executive mandates in most states, there has been a tremendous renewal of interest in performance measurement at all levels of government over the past several years. And there are a number of resources that make performance measurement tools and approaches accessible to public managers for practical application in public agencies (Center for Accountability and Performance, 1997; Ammons, 2001; Hatry, 1999; Poister, forthcoming).

Particularly with the passage of GPRA and similar state and local government mandates, attention focuses now more than ever on measuring *outcomes*, the end

**231**

results or real impacts produced by public programs. This is obviously a very positive development, because it is impossible to know whether programs are effective or whether they are really making a difference if outcomes are not being measured. Such measures of outcomes or effectiveness are, or at least should be, the bottom line in assessing a public agency's performance. However, there are a number of other criteria of program or agency performance that are also important to monitor although they are subordinate to effectiveness, precisely because they are linked to producing desired outcomes. This chapter, therefore, examines the use of performance measures focusing more specifically on quality and productivity in public sector operations.

## II. MONITORING PRODUCTIVITY

As used in this volume, and throughout the public management literature, the term *productivity* is used at two different levels. At a macro level productivity is almost synonymous with overall performance, a kind of composite of efficiency, effectiveness, and cost effectiveness. At this level a productive organization is one that is functioning efficiently to deliver effective public services. At a micro level, however, productivity refers more specifically to the relationship between input or the factors of production and the immediate products, or output, produced. Thus productivity monitoring is actually more output-oriented, focusing on the amount of work completed, units of service provided, or number of clients served rather than looking at actual outcomes, which are the real impacts that are generated out in the field or in a target population as a result of services being delivered or clients being served. However, the two are directly related inasmuch as improving productivity will lead to increased output which will lead in turn to greater impact, assuming an effective intervention strategy.

At this level productivity is very closely related to internal operating efficiency in that they both relate output to input. However, whereas efficiency indicators relate output to the overall direct cost of providing it, usually expressed as unit costs, productivity measures relate the output produced to the amount of specific kinds of resources needed to produce it. By far the most common type of productivity measure refers to labor productivity, but other types of productivity measures, such as those focusing on the use of equipment, are sometimes also incorporated in productivity monitoring systems. Productivity measures must also have a time dimension in order to be meaningful. In a government printing office, for example, labor productivity might be measured by the number of images produced per full-time equivalent employee (FTE) per week, whereas equipment productivity might be measured by the number of images produced per large press per hour.

Thus the most common kinds of performance measures tracked by systems designed to monitor productivity and the factors that influence it include:

Volume of output,
Labor productivity,
Equipment productivity,
Availability of resources, inventories,
Equipment downtime,
Cycle time, turnaround time,
Pending workload, backlog of cases, and
Utilization rates, flow of cases.

For the purposes of real productivity analysis, these kinds of factors are often monitored with respect to an operating system or service delivery system as a whole, but they may well also be applied to component processes that make up that system.

## A. Output-Oriented Systems

Some monitoring systems are designed primarily as output-oriented systems because the management imperative they are developed to support is principally concerned with increasing output, often through improving productivity. For example, for several years the top priority of the Pennsylvania Department of Transportation was to improve the condition of the state highway system and reduce the backlog of deferred maintenance needs by making the county-level maintenance units more productive. Over time the Department restructured the maintenance organizations, strengthened management capacity in the county-level units and made them more accountable to the formal chain of command, invested heavily in employee training, and used quality improvement tools to improve work processes, all aimed at making these units more productive.

Table 1 shows a small excerpt from a monthly activity report which PennDOT uses to track success along these lines. This part of the report covers four particular highway maintenance activities in the six counties that constitute the Department's District 1. The most important measures contained in this report for the month of June, 1995, concern the actual amount of output produced by each activity: tons of manual patching material applied to fix potholes, tons of patching material applied with mechanized patching, gallons of liquid bituminous surface treatment applied, and tons of "plant mix" surface treatment completed. This report also compares the actual data on work completed against "plan," or targets that were set at the beginning of the fiscal year. Thus it shows, for example, that for the fiscal year as a whole, Mercer and Crawford Counties applied more tons of material than targeted by their plans, and Venango County was only able to achieve 56% of its targeted output.

In addition, this activity report tracks the efficiency of these operations; for instance, the cost per ton of manual patching material applied ranges all the way from $150 per ton in Warren County to $300 in Erie County. These actual costs are contrasted with each other and assessed in the face of the statewide average cost of $198 per ton. Furthermore, the report presents data on labor productivity, measured by the number of man-hours per ton of material applied. This ranges from 4.86 hours per ton in Warren County to 9.85 in Erie County, as compared with the statewide average of 6.7 hours per ton and the standard of 7.5 hours per ton applied.

## B. Using Standard Hours

Sometimes it is possible to measure both the numerator and denominator of productivity indicators with the same scale. For example, although the varied output of a government printing office can be summarized in terms of images produced, it can also be measured in another common metric, the number of "billable hours" produced during a given time period. Each job coming into the plant is assessed in terms of volume of work and degree of difficulty, and from that is derived the number of billable hours, the number of hours the job should require given the work standards in place. Productivity can then be measured as the ratio of billable hours produced by the plant in a week to the number of production hours worked that week (after subtracting

**Table 1** Morris Highway County Management Summary Activity/Production Cost Report Redbook For the Month of June 1995 District 01-0

| Act/units | Description | County name | Annual Plan | Annual %Comp | Dept. Plan | Dept. Actual | Dept. %Comp | Contract Plan | Contract Actual | Contract %Comp | YTD unit cost ($) | Hist unit cost ($) | Average man-hours per unit |
|---|---|---|---|---|---|---|---|---|---|---|---|---|---|
| 711 7121 Tons | Roads-paved patching manual | Crawford | 851 | 111 | 851 | 949 | 111 | 0 | 0 | 0 | 205.19 | 228.35 | 7.84 |
| | | Erie | 3030 | 92 | 3030 | 2814 | 92 | 0 | 0 | 0 | 300.42 | 325.58 | 9.85 |
| | | Forest | 535 | 101 | 535 | 543 | 101 | 0 | 0 | 0 | 159.44 | 192.68 | 6.48 |
| | | Mercer | 218 | 135 | 218 | 294 | 135 | 0 | 0 | 0 | 172.60 | 237.88 | 6.11 |
| | | Venango | 636 | 56 | 636 | 358 | 56 | 0 | 0 | 0 | 256.22 | 236.95 | 9.81 |
| | | Warren | 1420 | 98 | 1420 | 1404 | 90 | 0 | 0 | 0 | 150.52 | 192.90 | 4.86 |
| | | -Total- | 6690 | 95 | 6690 | 6564 | 95 | 0 | 0 | 0 | 235.24 | 265.41 | 7.97 |
| | | St-hist unit cost: $211.46; St-avg unit cost: $198.05; St-avg mhrs/units: 6.66; Std.mhrs/unit | | | | | | | | | | — | 7.50 |
| 711 7124 Tons | Roads-paved patching-mec | Crawford | 5133 | 106 | 2633 | 2505 | 95 | 2500 | 2945 | 117 | 69.65 | 64.37 | 1.06 |
| | | Erie | 2600 | 98 | 2600 | 2565 | 98 | 0 | 0 | 0 | 75.67 | 78.87 | 1.21 |
| | | Forest | 2320 | 95 | 2320 | 2207 | 95 | 0 | 0 | 0 | 50.69 | 64.38 | .56 |
| | | Mercer | 2780 | 107 | 2780 | 2993 | 107 | 0 | 0 | 0 | 82.24 | 90.12 | 1.71 |
| | | Venango | 170 | 100 | 170 | 0 | 0 | 170 | 170 | 100 | .00 | .00 | .00 |
| | | -Total- | 13003 | 102 | 10533 | 10269 | 99 | 2670 | 3115 | 116 | 70.77 | 74.65 | 1.18 |
| | | St-hist unit cost: $51.86; St-avg unit cost: $54.16; St-avg mhrs/units: .01; Std.mhrs/unit | | | | | | | | | | — | 1.10 |
| 711 7124 Gals | Roads-paved surf treat liq bit | Crawford | 449695 | 98 | 449695 | 443828 | 98 | 0 | 0 | 0 | 1.42 | 1.26 | .01 |
| | | Erie | 300500 | 99 | 300500 | 300447 | 99 | 0 | 0 | 0 | 1.51 | 1.55 | .01 |
| | | Forest | 12672 | 104 | 12672 | 13286 | 104 | 0 | 0 | 0 | 1.29 | 1.59 | .01 |
| | | Mercer | 351000 | 100 | 351000 | 352377 | 100 | 0 | 0 | 0 | 1.34 | 1.26 | .01 |
| | | Venango | 300285 | 100 | 300285 | 300410 | 100 | 0 | 0 | 0 | 1.12 | 1.09 | .01 |
| | | Warren | 174748 | 92 | 174748 | 161351 | 92 | 0 | 0 | 0 | 1.26 | 1.60 | .01 |
| | | -Total- | 1500900 | 98 | 1588900 | 1571699 | 98 | 0 | 0 | 0 | 1.34 | 1.20 | .01 |
| | | St-hist unit cost: $34.70; St-avg unit cost: $130.04; St-avg mhrs/units: .01; Std.mhrs/unit | | | | | | | | | | — | .01 |
| 711 7125 Tons | Surface treatment 1" plant mix | Forest | 600 | 99 | 600 | 595 | 99 | 0 | 0 | 0 | 41.33 | 54.09 | .67 |
| | | Mercer | 4200 | 107 | 4200 | 4516 | 107 | 0 | 0 | 0 | 45.23 | 96.35 | .55 |
| | | Venango | 8675 | 100 | 0 | 0 | 0 | 8675 | 8675 | 100 | .00 | .00 | .00 |
| | | Warren | 715 | 99 | 715 | 714 | 99 | 0 | 0 | 0 | 121.31 | 47.75 | .32 |
| | | -Total- | 14190 | 102 | 5515 | 5825 | 105 | 8675 | 8675 | 100 | 54.37 | 65.15 | .53 |
| | | St-hist unit cost: $34.70; St-avg unit cost: $36.04; St-avg mhrs/units: .30; Std.mhrs/unit | | | | | | | | | | — | .01 |

*Source:* Pennsylvania Department of Transportation 1995.

setup time, time spent in training, time spent in cleanup, etc.). If this ratio is less than one for any particular week, that signifies that the plant did not produce as many billable hours as it should have been expected to produce given the productivity standards in place.

As seen above, PennDOT has established standards regarding the number of production hours allowed per unit of output produced by each one of its programmed highway maintenance activities. For instance, the standard is 7.5 hours per ton of manual patching material applied to the roads, as compared with only 1.1 hours per ton of mechanized patching completed. Beyond looking at any one activity, these standards can be used to aggregate maintenance crew productivity over a number of maintenance functions. First, the amount of each kind of output produced (e.g., tons of patching material applied, gallons of seal coating, miles of guardrails replaced) can be converted to a common metric, task hours completed, representing the number of hours that would be allowed for each of these activities based on the standards. Secondly, because PennDOT keeps track of the production hours actually worked (the total hours worked by maintenance crews minus check-in time, travel time to work sites, etc.) the total task hours completed can be divided by production hours to obtain a generic measure of labor productivity.

For example, Figure 1 shows data on task hours per production hour in each of PennDOT's eleven districts, for both 1987 and 1994. The maintenance functions included in this measure include 10 "big ticket" activities such as manual and mechanized patching, surface treatment, crack sealing, shoulder grading and shoulder cutting, and drainage pipe replacement. When maintenance crews are working right at the standards, the value of this labor productivity measure will be one task hour completed per production hour worked. As seen in Figure 1, however, in 1987 districts 2 and 8 fell substantially below this standard whereas districts 6 and 9 were just slightly below it. Eight of the eleven districts improved their labor productivity between 1987

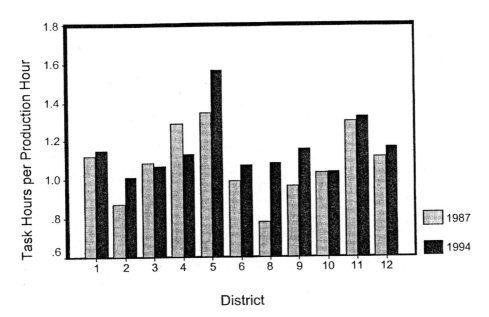

**Figure 1**   PennDOT labor productivity by District: 1987 to 1994.

and 1994, however, and in 1994 all the districts performed at or above the standard of one task hour of work completed per production hour worked. Some, such as district 5 and district 11, exceeded the standard by substantial margins.

## III.  MONITORING SERVICE QUALITY

As the quality revolution has swept through government over the past fifteen years, it has made an indelible mark on the public management landscape (Carr and Littman, 1990; Berman and West, 1995; Hyde, 1997). Now more than ever, managers of public programs are challenged to improve the quality of the services they deliver as well as customer satisfaction with those services. From a performance measurement perspective this means tracking indicators of the quality of input, and especially the output produced and, as shown below, customer satisfaction. Typically, the dimensions of quality that are considered as being the most important in the quest for improving customer service include:

> Timeliness, total time required, waiting time;
> Accuracy, thoroughness, reliability, fairness;
> Accessibility, hours of service, convenience;
> Decor, cleanliness, and condition of facilities;
> Personal safety and security; and
> Courtesy, politeness, and professionalism.

Interestingly, these and other dimensions of service quality can usually be measured with quantitative indicators. This is usually a matter of defining what constitutes acceptable quality standards and then tracking the number or percentage of cases in which those standards are achieved or in which performance falls short of the standards. Looking at decentralized operations for renewing driver's licenses, for example, managers might want to monitor the (1) percentage of customers who have to wait in line for more than twenty minutes before being served, (2) the average time required for a customer to complete the license renewal process, and (3) the percentage of renewals that are processed correctly the first time.

### A.  Quality and Productivity

In the past, managers often thought that quality improvement was antithetical to maintaining or increasing productivity. They felt that if they were forced to focus too much on achieving high-quality service, operations would slow down and productivity would necessarily suffer. More recently, though, advocates of the quality movement have pressed the argument that improving quality actually leads to greater productivity in the long run, largely by eliminating *rework*, or cases that have to be processed over again because they were done incorrectly the first time.

For example, an office supply operation in a state government would monitor productivity in terms of "lines" of product shipped to customers per employee per day or the number of orders filled per employee per week. Quality, on the other hand, would be measured by the percentage of orders shipped within two days of receipt of the order, the percentage of orders filled completely the first time (without having to backorder some items), and the percentage of orders shipped that contained all the correct items. Clearly, shipping more lines per employee per day will speed up the time in which customers receive the materials they order, but what about the effect of the accuracy measure on productivity? In the short run, taking greater pains to assure that the right items are included in the shipment could conceivably slow down the operation somewhat and reduce the number of lines shipped per employee, but in the long run it will reduce the number of items that have to be returned and replaced with the correct ones, which constitutes rework, and thereby improve overall productivity in the long run.

Thus quality and productivity are more often seen today as mutually supportive or complementary performance criteria. The Williamsport, Pennsylvania, Bureau of Transportation, for example, annually tracks the overall performance of its City Bus system through measures of quality and productivity, as well as overall utilization and cost effectiveness, as shown in Table 2. Actual performance is compared against predetermined standards as well as statewide averages for other similar public transit systems in Pennsylvania. Labor productivity is measured by the number of vehicle miles per employee, per bus operator, and per maintenance employee, and vehicle productivity is measured by the number of miles and hours of service operated per vehicle.

Service quality is measured first of all in terms of schedule reliability, the percentage of bus trips that depart from identified bus stops within plus or minus five minutes of the times shown in printed schedules. This is tracked separately for both peak and nonpeak periods. WBT tracks the percentage of passenger trips that require transfers from one bus to another because this is an important indicator of convenience from the customer perspective. Safety is monitored by the number of collision accidents per 100,000 vehicle miles operated, and the overall reliability of the service is measured by the number of vehicle miles operated per road call required (instances in which a service truck must drive out to attend to an operating problem on a bus) and the number of vehicle miles between service interruptions, in which buses actually break down en route due to mechanical problems. These latter two measures are indicators of the quality of service provided by the maintenance department.

Overall utilization of the system is measured first by the number of passenger trips per capita per year, which is really a measure of the service area's usage of the transit system. The other measures of utilization shown in Figure 2, which relate the number of passenger trips served by the system to the number of vehicle miles or hours of service provided, along with the ratio of passenger miles traveled to vehicle miles operated, really represent the overall productivity of the system in a somewhat larger sense. Finally, the operating cost per passenger trip, revenue per passenger trip, net cost per passenger trip, and percentage of total expenses recovered through the farebox are all indicators of the system's overall cost effectiveness.

## B. Disaggregated Measures

As indicated earlier, quality and productivity measures are often monitored in the aggregate but also broken down into the constituent elements of an operating system. Tracking such measures for individual work units or individual field offices delivering services, for example, provides much more detailed information regarding the strengths and weaknesses, or the locus of problems, within an overall operating system.

Continuing along the lines of the public transit illustration above, Table 3 shows some of the same productivity measures for individual routes in the City Bus system.

**Table 2**  Williamsport Bureau of Transportation City Bus Performance

| | WBT standard | WBT actual 1999 | Statewide average for class 3 systems |
|---|---|---|---|
| Productivity standards | | | |
| Vehicle miles per employee | ≥15,000 | 16,799 | 14,635 |
| Vehicle miles per operator | ≥22,000 | 24,190 | NA |
| Vehicle miles per maintenance employee | ≥80,000 | 100,793 | NA |
| Vehicle hours per vehicle | ≥2,000 | 2,232 | 1,903 |
| Vehicle miles per vehicle | ≥28,000 | 31,829 | 25,486 |
| Service quality standards | | | |
| Percent trips ± 5 minutes | | | |
|   Nonpeak periods | ≥95% | 97.4% | NA |
|   Peak periods | ≥90% | 96.0% | NA |
| Percent transfers | ≤10% | 17.6% | NA |
| Collision accidents per 100,000 vehicle miles | ≤3.0 | 0.7 | NA |
| Vehicle miles between road calls | ≥3,500 | 6,171 | NA |
| Vehicle miles between service interruptions | ≥25,000 | 60,756 | NA |
| Utilization standards | | | |
| Annual rides per capita | ≥15 | 16.2 | 11.4 |
| Passenger trips per vehicle mile | ≥2 | 2.1 | 1.7 |
| Passenger trips per vehicle hour | ≥28.0 | 30.5 | 22.3 |
| Passenger miles per vehicle mile | ≥6.0 | 5.7 | 6.2 |
| Cost effectiveness | | | |
| Cost per passenger trip | ≤$1.85 | $1.57 | $2.14 |
| Revenue per passenger trip | ≥$0.70 | $0.58 | $1.04 |
| Net cost per passenger trip | ≤$1.15 | $0.99 | $1.10 |
| Percent cost recovery | ≥35% | 37% | 49% |

*Source*: Williamsport Bureau of Transportation 1999–2000.

Although the aggregate data for the system as a whole accumulate almost automatically over the course of a year from WBT's routine recordkeeping systems, however, obtaining some of the same measures for individual routes requires a special effort involving additional work on the part of the bus drivers. Thus these disaggregated data pertain to one particular week only.

Because many of the quality and efficiency indicators monitored in the aggregate above are a function of overall policies and procedures or the centralized maintenance function and are therefore truly measures of systemwide performance, the disaggregated data shown in Table 3 focus primarily on system productivity as influenced by

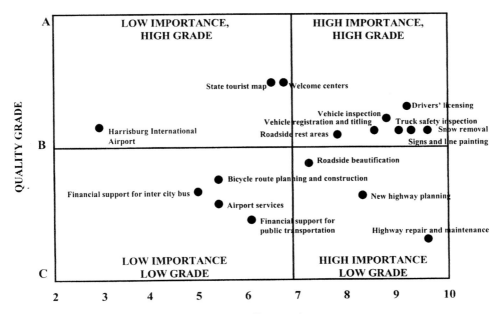

**Figure 2** PennDOT services importance/quality matrix.

**Table 3** City Bus Passenger Statistics by Route (December 8–13, 1997)

| Route | Passenger trips per bus trip | Passenger trips per vehicle hour | Variable cost per passenger trip ($) | Revenue per passenger trip ($) | Net cost per passenger trip ($) | Variable cost per recovery (%) |
|---|---|---|---|---|---|---|
| Newberry | 32.2 | 54.9 | 0.87 | 0.53 | 0.34 | 61 |
| Montoursville | 16.1 | 32.1 | 1.93 | 0.57 | 1.36 | 29 |
| Garden view | 18.3 | 33.9 | 1.55 | 0.55 | 1.00 | 35 |
| Loyalsock | 18.1 | 30.6 | 1.57 | 0.54 | 1.03 | 34 |
| Market street | 5.4 | 24.9 | 2.36 | 0.48 | 1.88 | 20 |
| West third street | 19.5 | 38.2 | 1.31 | 0.53 | 0.78 | 40 |
| South side | 6.6 | 15.2 | 2.93 | 0.56 | 2.37 | 19 |
| East end | 9.1 | 21.0 | 2.11 | 0.51 | 1.60 | 24 |
| Nightline east | 15.2 | 36.7 | 1.32 | 0.57 | 0.74 | 44 |
| Nightline west | 14.1 | 50.2 | 1.33 | 0.63 | 0.70 | 47 |
| Hill's express | 6.1 | 36.5 | 1.66 | 0.59 | 1.07 | 35 |
| PM shuttle | 19.8 | 49.5 | .83 | 0.43 | 0.40 | 52 |
| Muncy/mall local | 20.5 | 18.1 | 2.99 | 1.01 | 1.98 | 34 |
| Lycoming mall | 31.1 | 45.3 | 5.75 | 1.92 | 3.84 | 70 |
| Total | 15.9 | 33.0 | 1.56 | $0.50 | $1.00 | 32 |

ridership levels. And these measures vary substantially from route to route. The number of passenger trips per bus trip, for instance, ranges from 32.2 on the Newberry Route to only 5.4 on the Market Street Route. In general, these comparisons show that in addition to the Newberry Route, the strongest performers are the Lycoming Mall Route, the Nightline West Route, and the PM Shuttle, and the Montoursville, Garden View, Loyalsock, West Third Street, Nightline East, and the Hill's Express Routes are fairly productive routes across this set of measures. The Market Street, South Side, East End, and Muncy/Mall Local Routes, on the other hand, are clearly the weak links in the system. These more detailed performance data provide greater insight as to where WBT might focus service enhancements and/or service trimming strategies in order to improve overall system productivity.

## C.  Quality and Productivity Improvement

As suggested by the example above, quality and productivity measures are often monitored at fairly detailed levels. Whereas performance measures designed to track success in achieving an agency's strategic goals or monitor the overall performance of a major program may tend to be more "global" and observed at a macro level, perhaps on an annual basis, quality and productivity measures often tend to be analyzed at a more micro level. What has become the conventional quality improvement process (which in practice usually focuses on improving productivity as well as service quality) typically involves analyzing work processes to identify problems and develop solutions to improve the operation. This work is necessarily carried out in some detail. Thus public agencies often define quality and productivity indicators in detail, focusing on the operating level, and observe them quite frequently.

As an example, the U.S. Social Security Administration (SSA) contracts with a state agency in each state to adjudicate claims for disability benefits; if the claim is found to be eligible, the claimant then begins to receive the benefits. The work of determining eligibility itself is a serious and onerous responsibility, and the workload is heavy. The Georgia Disability Adjudication Section of the Georgia Department of Human Resources, for instance, receives nearly 100,000 new claims each year. It has on the order of 300 full-time equivalent employees and an annual budget of approximately $30 million to determine for each case whether the claim should be approved or denied. In managing the adjudication program, the SSA has established at least three standards:

Cases should be closed within 70 working days of receipt of the claim;
The initial accuracy rate should be maintained at 95% or higher; and
The pending workload should be kept within 10 weeks.

Looking at the Southeast Region, Table 4 shows the kind of performance indicators tracked on a weekly basis to monitor this operation in each state. First, the number of new claims received during the week by each state is compared against the number of claims received in the same week of the prior year, to take seasonal variation into account. Then, claims received year to date (YTD) are compared against the previous year. Secondly, the number of cases cleared by each state are tracked in the same way. On a regional basis these agencies cleared more cases than they received during the week, thus reducing the backlog somewhat. On a year-to-date basis, the cases cleared have increased by 27% and receipts have only increased by 14%.

**Table 4** Disability Determination Performance Tracking Report, Report Week: February 18, 1999 (Week 21)

| | Claims | | | | Dispositions | | | |
|---|---|---|---|---|---|---|---|---|
| | Claims received 2/18 | FY 98 receipts (week 21) | FY 99 YTD receipts | Receipts % change YTD 98–99 | Cases cleared 2/18 | FY 98 dispositions (week 21) | FY 99 YTD dispositions | Dispositions % change YTD 98–99 |
| Alabama | 1,118 | 1,235 | 32,243 | 21 | 934 | 1,263 | 34,102 | 49 |
| Florida | 3,319 | 2,352 | 71,527 | 16 | 3,578 | 2,676 | 68,999 | 23 |
| Georgia | 1,673 | 1,488 | 39,350 | 3 | 2,162 | 1,790 | 38,284 | 15 |
| Kentucky | 1,526 | 1,522 | 33,614 | 16 | 1,124 | 1,584 | 35,408 | 30 |
| Mississippi | 1,157 | 1,114 | 28,202 | 17 | 1,373 | 1,423 | 29,073 | 41 |
| North Carolina | 1,564 | 1,417 | 36,149 | 9 | 1,816 | 1,812 | 37,745 | 21 |
| South Carolina | 812 | 792 | 20,498 | 6 | 1,098 | 849 | 22,009 | 35 |
| Tennessee | 1,566 | 1,545 | 35,275 | 19 | 1,556 | 1,220 | 37,011 | 21 |
| Region | 12,746 | 11,482 | 297,104 | 14 | 13,657 | 12,635 | 302,901 | 27 |

Workload and productivity

| | | | Work dispositions | | Quality and efficiency | |
|---|---|---|---|---|---|---|
| | Cases pending | % over 70 days | Weeks pending | Per FTE work year | Initial accuracy 3-month rolling qtr. (%) | Cumulative cost per case ($) |
| Alabama | 14,603 | 24.8 | 8.8 | 267.1 | 98.7 | 272 |
| Florida | 28,716 | 20.9 | 8.4 | 272.0 | 92.4 | 23 |
| Georgia | 22,549 | 29.4 | 10.2 | 249.9 | 95.8 | 310 |
| Kentucky | 15,028 | 19.5 | 8.2 | 269.9 | 91.2 | 251 |
| Mississippi | 11,492 | 22.9 | 7.7 | 287.4 | 94.2 | 247 |
| North Carolina | 9,987 | 11.7 | 4.9 | 292.9 | 96.0 | 236 |
| South Carolina | 8,405 | 17.0 | 7.3 | 271.8 | 93.2 | 247 |
| Tennessee | 12.284 | 12.4 | 6.9 | 254.5 | 96.2 | 262 |
| Region | 123,102 | 21.1 | 7.9 | 269.8 | 94.6 | 252 |
| Nation | | | | | 94.0 | 304 |

Regionwide there were 123,102 cases pending at the end of this particular week, and over 20% of them had been in process for more than 70 days; in Georgia almost 30% of the pending cases had not been cleared within 70 days, thus falling short of the standard set by SSA. The Georgia agency also had slightly more than 10 work weeks of caseload pending, while all the other states had less of a backlog on that score. For the region as a whole, these agencies were on track to close almost 270 cases per FTE, but that varied from a high of 292 in North Carolina to a low of 249 in Georgia. With respect to accuracy, several states were achieving the standard of exceeding the 95% initial accuracy rate, but Florida, Kentucky, Mississippi, and South Carolina all fell below this standard. Finally, the cumulative cost per case closed was $252 in the Southeast Region, ranging from $213 in Florida to $310 in Georgia, but for the most part the region still compared favorably with the national average of $304. Overall, then, the Georgia agency compared favorably in terms of quality but rather poorly in terms of productivity and operating efficiency. Although these kinds of short-term, very specific measures may not be particularly helpful for purposes of strategic planning or policy making, they are indispensable to the SSA for monitoring both the quality and productivity of this ongoing case adjudication process.

## IV.  MONITORING CUSTOMER SATISFACTION

Most public agencies that emphasize quality improvement are also concerned at the same time with customer service and customer satisfaction with the services they provide. Thus they are often interested in soliciting customer feedback on a regular basis. Although that customer feedback might well focus for the most part on the same performance criteria addressed by the quality indicators, obtaining satisfaction measures directly from customers themselves provides feedback from a different source which might or might not be consistent with the results generated with the programmatic data. In general, agencies solicit or receive direct input and feedback from customers through the mechanisms of:

Advisory groups, customer councils,
Focus group sessions,
Complaint systems,
Customer surveys, and
Response cards.

The latter three of these channels often provide a basis for accumulating data on a regular ongoing basis so as to facilitate monitoring performance indicators over time. Complaint systems principally record negative feedback from customers and therefore cannot be expected to provide a balanced picture of customer attitudes, however, they can be useful in tracking the extent to which customer dissatisfaction and perceived problems change over time. Surveys can be conducted on a systematic basis to solicit unbiased customer feedback, and if they are replicated on a regular basis they will also allow managers to track trends in customer satisfaction over time. Response cards, which actually constitute very brief surveys focusing attention on specific instances of service delivery, can be conducted continuously on an ongoing basis and provide an indication of trends over time.

Broad-based customer surveys seem to be the favored method of soliciting feedback on the range of services offered by a government organization. Figure 2, for example, shows ratings of services provided by the Pennsylvania Department of Transportation by a sample of nearly 7000 residents across the state, cross-plotted against the average importance level assigned to each service by these respondents. This survey asked respondents to rate the quality of these services with the kind of grades typically used in schools, in which A = Excellent, B = Good, C = Fair, D = Poor, and F = Failing. This kind of plot can be particularly compelling in that it shows that although some services may be seen as not particularly important although they are of high quality, customers may see other services as being much more important but of lower quality. PennDOT customers see the Department doing a good job with respect to such services as driver licensing, truck safety inspections, and snow removal, all rated as being very important, but they also rated other very important services such highway construction and highway repair and maintenance as still needing improvement.

## A. Comparative Measures

As reflected in several illustrations above, there is growing interest in the use of comparative performance measures (Coe, 1999; Kopczynski and Lombardo, 1999; Morley et al., 2001), and this extends to customer satisfaction measures as well as other kinds of indicators. Comparing actual performance data against the same measures for other agencies or programs provides a context for interpreting the results of performance measures and sometimes serves to identify leading edge performers that might be helpful as benchmarking partners.

Table 5 shows comparative data from passenger surveys conducted by the Williamsport City Bus System and several other local public transit agencies with smaller and medium-size service areas in Pennsylvania. Respondents were asked to rate their system on the basis of five particular criteria as well as provide an overall rating of the service. These comparative data exist because the state funding agency, PennDOT, requires each system receiving state assistance to conduct such a survey once every three years, to contain at a minimum items on these five specific elements. These common elements include vehicle cleanliness, driver courtesy, fares, on-time performance, and personal safety. Table 5 compares the percentage of passengers on the City Bus system who indicated that they were satisfied with each of these criteria

**Table 5**  Percentage of Customers Satisfied with Pennsylvania Public Transit Systems

|  | Williamsport city bus (%) | Other systems (%)[a] |
|---|---|---|
| Vehicle cleanliness | 89 | 64–93 |
| Driver courtesy | 92 | 75–94 |
| Fares | 88 | 45–95 |
| On-time performance | 84 | 63–94 |
| Personal safety | 91 | 74–97 |
| Overall service | 98 | 69–98 |

[a] Includes Harrisburg, Lancaster, Reading, Erie, Allentown/Bethlehem, State College, York, Wilkes-Barre, Scranton, Altoona, and Johnstown, Pennsylvania. *Source*: On-board passenger surveys conducted by the participating transit systems.

against the range of the percentage satisfied in the other eleven systems. Clearly WBT is at the top of the range in terms of overall passenger satisfaction with the service provided, and it compares favorably with the other systems in terms of vehicle cleanliness, driver courtesy, and personal safety. However, it is only in the middle of the range—still a respectable rating—in terms of on-time performance, or schedule reliability. Even though the passenger feedback on the City Bus System is obviously quite positive, comparing these ratings against those on other systems helps to put these results into perspective.

## V. CONCLUSIONS

This chapter has attempted to present the kinds of performance measures used most frequently to monitor productivity and service quality in public agencies, and to illustrate how they are used with a variety of examples. Rather than linking to overall program goals, policy objectives, or substantive strategic initiatives, tracking quality and productivity measures tends to focus more on the nuts and bolts of service delivery systems and ongoing operations. As compared with performance measurement systems that are intended to support strategic management processes, or budgeting systems with annual data, for example, systems designed to monitor quality and productivity tend to focus on more detailed indicators of performance at the operating level, and often very frequently, perhaps on a monthly, weekly, or even daily basis.

The examples presented in this chapter also illustrate the importance of converting performance data into useful information through setting up comparisons of actual performance against standards or targets, trends over time, comparisons across operating units or programs, or benchmarking external comparisons against other agencies or programs. Assuming that the measures are designed deliberately for this purpose, and that the performance data are interpreted appropriately, such monitoring systems can indeed help managers improve both quality and productivity in public agencies and programs.

## REFERENCES

Ammons, D. N. (2001). *Municipal Benchmarks: Assessing Local Performance and Establishing Community Standards*. Thousand Oaks, CA: Sage.

Berman, E. M., West, J. P. (1995). Municipal commitment to total quality management: a survey of recent progress. *Public Admin. Rev.* 55(1):57–66.

Carr, D. K., Littman, I. D (1990). *Excellence in Government: Total Quality Management in the 1990s*. Arlington, VA: Coopers & Lybrand.

Center for Accountability and Performance (1997). *Performance Measurement: Concepts and Techniques*. Washington, DC: American Society for Public Administration.

Coe, C. (1999). Local government benchmarking: lessons from two major multigovernment efforts. *Public Admin. Rev.* 59(2):111–115.

Hatry, H. P. (1999). *Performance Measurement: Getting Results*. Washington, DC: Urban Institute.

Hyde, A. (July 1997). A decade's worth of lessons in continuous improvement. *Govern. Exec.* 58–68.

Kopczynski, M., Lombardo, M. (1999). Comparative performance measurement: insights and lessons learned from a consortium effort. *Public Admin. Rev.* 59(2):124–134.

Morley, E., Bryant, S. P., Hatry, H. P. (2001). *Comparative Performance Measurement.* Washington, DC: Urban Institute.

Pennsylvania Department of Transportation (June 1995). *County Management Summary.*

Poister, T. H. (forthcoming). *Measuring Performance in Government and Nonprofit Organizations.* San Francisco: Jossey-Bass.

Poister, T. H., Streib, G. (1989). Management tools in municipal government: trends over the past decade. *Public Admin. Rev.* 49(3):240–248.

Williamsport Bureau of Transportation (1999–2000). *Performance Report and Plan Update.*

# 14

# Evaluation Research and Performance Measurement

*Dealing with Issues of Purpose and Perspective*

**ARIE HALACHMI**
*Tennessee State University, Nashville, Tennessee, U.S.A.,
and Zhongshan University, Guangdong, Guangzhou, China*

## I. INTRODUCTION

Evaluation research can provide managers with a basis for an informed decision for starting, modifying, or terminating a program. Managers may emphasize results or the process for getting them as a prime consideration. Therefore the evaluation should be designed with the decision-makers's needs in mind. This chapter offers a conceptual framework to help managers and evaluators relate the purpose of an evaluation to the perspective the decision maker prefers. The political context of public agencies may not be conducive to productivity improvement through evaluation research, but the chapter suggests that the proposed framework can help increase the productivity of the evaluation itself.

Suchman (1967) differentiated between evaluation and evaluation research. The former, he said, is used in a general way to refer to the social process of making judgments of worth. It is basic to all forms of social behavior, whether that of an individual or a complex organization, but it does not require any systematic procedure for collecting and presenting evidence to support the judgment. Evaluation research, however, is restricted to the utilization of scientific research methods and techniques. Hence evaluation research refers to the use of common procedures for collecting and analysis of data for the purpose of proving, rather than asserting, the value of a program (Suchman, 1967). According to Weiss (1972), the purpose of evaluation research is to provide information for decision making about programs.

Public agencies are expected to achieve goals that were formulated as a result of a political process. The relative value and importance of the goals can be subject to political scrutiny by politicians, philosophers, and social critics. For administrators, the question is how to get the most out of the definite amount of resources that are available to them in the pursuit of these goals. Evaluation research can help managers improve the utilization of resources or the effectiveness of the effort to achieve various goals. At the same time, it can provide participants in the political process with the necessary arguments for redefinition of goals and priorities.

Because it is impossible to separate program evaluation from politics, all evaluation efforts can be dysfunctional to the practicing administrator. Evaluation results may invite pressure for change, and they may expose the shortcomings of agencies, including poor judgment or lack of accountability. In anticipation of such consequences, the Governor of Kansas was advised in 1977 to stop an effort by the Highway Safety Administration to evaluate the licensing of drivers in his state. The adviser reckoned that if it is working, why bother to evaluate it, and if it is not working, we do not have the resources to correct it (Halachmi, 1982). As noted by Wholey et al. (1986) "evaluators have functioned well as critics, pointing out where and when organizations have failed to meet their objectives or produced negative side effects that outweigh positive accomplishments". It seems that the Kansan advisor to the Governor made the same observation on his own.

Growing demands at the turn of the century for more government accountability, better and more services, and opposition to new taxes resulted in legislative initiatives that encouraged (if not mandated) evaluation and performance measurement (Halachmi, 2002). Typical of such initiatives were the Government Performance and Results Act of 1993 (GPRA) in the United States and the introduction of new public management practices that were derived from the concepts of Citizen Charters and Best Value/Value for Money in the United Kingdom (Halachmi and Montgomery, 2000; Bovaird, 2000). Such initiatives induce administrators to use evaluation research to support their claim to use public resources in general and to pursue various options of performance measurement (e.g., Benchmarking or Balanced Score Cards) in particular (Bovaird and Halachmi, 1999).

The thesis of this chapter consists of the following elements.

1.  Although it is impossible to separate evaluation, and thus performance measurement, from politics, it is possible to reduce the cost of their dysfunctional attributes by enhancing their usefulness for creating value. As noted by Pawson and Tilley (1997, pxii), the great promise of evaluation is that it purports to offer the universal means with which to measure "worth" and "value." "Evaluation, in short, confers the power to justify decisions." From a pragmatic point of view, that means, first of all, that ultimately evaluation and performance measurement must serve managers and agency employees as a tool for increasing productivity. This notion was articulated and written into GPRA. Second, evaluation and performance measurement should help outside stakeholders hold program managers accountable.

2.  The goals of enhancing productivity and enhancing the prospect of a more rigorous external scrutiny may not always be consistent with each other, however,

proper selection of the approach or focus of performance measurement and evaluation may reduce any resulting dysfunctions (Halachmi, 2002).

## II. CLASSIFYING APPROACHES TO EVALUATION RESEARCH

Various authors suggested taxonomies for classifying different approaches to evaluation research. For example, House (1980) reviewed various approaches to evaluation research and developed an eight-by-four matrix for representing a taxonomy that differentiates among eight different models: system analysis, behavioral objectives, decision making, goal-free, art criticism, professional review, quasi-legal, and case study. The differences among the models are derived by reference to four characteristics: major audiences/reference groups, assumptions, methodology, and the nature of the findings. Morris and Fitz-Gibbon (1978) offered a less elaborate approach. Using a normative approach (i.e., what the evaluation should emphasize), they offered a classification that involves only six models: goal-oriented evaluation, decision-oriented evaluation, transactional evaluation, evaluation research, goal-free evaluation, and adversary evaluation.

The purpose of this chapter is to address evaluation research as it pertains to productivity enhancement in the public sector, therefore it is not possible to address the phenomenological and epistemological dimensions of evaluation research beyond the above reference to taxonomies. The chapter approaches the issue of evaluation research and performance measurement by suggesting a conceptual framework for selecting an evaluation design or a performance measurement scheme. Since the first edition of this handbook, some of the questions that influenced the development of the proposed framework have been articulated by Wholey et al. (1994) when they asserted that some basic questions should be asked about any program being considered for evaluation or monitoring.

1. Can the result of the evaluation influence decisions about the program?
2. Can the evaluation be done in time to be useful?
3. Is the program significant enough to merit evaluation?

In addition to these questions, the proposed framework evolves from a modest attempt to answer some additional questions such as, how can the opportunity cost of carrying out an evaluation or performance measurement be minimized in order to reduce the diversion of resources from operations to overhead.

The proposed framework allows administrators to think about evaluation and performance measurement by reference to two dimensions, the purpose of the evaluation or the measurement and the perspective from which the activity is conducted. The assumptions here are: (1) that ultimate, or primary, institutional user(s) of the results of the evaluation of the performance measurement (e.g., managers, legislators, central staff units, organizations representing various stakeholders) are known before the activity (or activities) take place; (2) that said user(s) are keenly aware of how and when they are going to use it; and (3) that they are capable and may influence the design of the evaluation of the measurement to induce reports that are highly useful to them.

These assumptions are based on the various claims that derive the value of evaluation and performance measurement from the extent that they are "real"

(Pawson and Tilley, 1997) or the "utilization focus" (Patton, 1986; Wholey et al, 1994) of the effort.

## III. A PROPOSED CONCEPTUAL FRAMEWORK FOR EVALUATION RESEARCH

Wholey (1983) claims that there are two contrasting pictures of government: results (outcome) -oriented management, and process-oriented management.

Results-oriented managers establish realistic, measurable, outcome-oriented program objectives in terms of which they assess and manage their programs. Process-oriented managers, according to Wholey (1983), look at resource structure, program activities, information followup, and use of information. Our *purpose* and *perspective* dimensions correspond to Wholey's *result* and *process* postures of management in government entities. However, this chapter sees the two as different dimensions rather than as contrasting, that is, mutually exclusive, options.

The proposed conceptual framework for evaluation research is presented as a two-by-two matrix in Figure 1. This framework can help a public manager focus the evaluation and tailor it to his or her preferences and the situation at hand. The proposed framework can thus increase the utility of the evaluation. The framework is useful even though the manager may change either the purpose or the perspective, or both, of the evaluation. Such change may occur after the manager gets feedback from important constituencies while the research is carried out or after preliminary drafts of the findings become available. The proposed framework suggests that in order to make the necessary adjustments and to be responsive to political changes, the manager can move in any one of three directions. By considering this framework, the manager can have not only a better grasp of the changes in the focus of the decision-making process, but also a basis for selecting an evaluation design strategy (Fink and Kosecoff, 1978; Patton, 1980).

By using this framework, the decision maker can organize effective presentations to evaluators and outsiders about the issues and the kinds of decisions that need to be made. As noted by Suchman (1972), "Perhaps the most crucial question to be asked before an evaluation is undertaken is, what decisions about the program or its objectives will be affected by the results of the evaluation?"

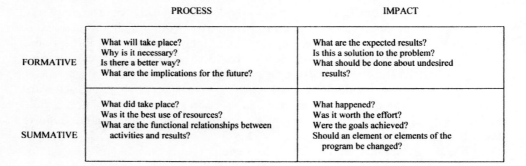

**Figure 1**  Evaluation research: Purpose and perspective.

## A. Two Purposes of Evaluation

It is possible to identify two purposes for the conduct of evaluation. One purpose is to provide the necessary information for making a decision to authorize the implementation of a proposed program. In this case, the evaluation takes place before the beginning of the program and is exploratory in nature. The other purpose for doing an evaluation is to provide the necessary input for making a decision about the future of an existing one.

### 1. Summative Evaluation

According to Patton (1978), summative evaluation is aimed at determining the essential effectiveness of a program. It is particularly important in making decisions about continuing or terminating a project. The purpose of summative evaluation is to judge the worth of a program after it has been in operation (Weiss, 1972a). In the words of Palumbo (1988), the main question in summative evaluation is, "What difference does the program make?" For example, a summative evaluation can be a promising way to determine the impact of a health program. According to Borus et al. (1982), in order to assess the impact of health programs, there is a need for several essential sets of information. First, data that are necessary for determining the continuation of the program; second, which of the alternative programs achieved the greatest gains for a given cost; third, what mixes of components within a program are most effective for a given expenditure so that a maximum operating efficiency can be achieved; fourth, the first three kinds of information should be provided for persons with different characteristics so that the decision maker may determine which individuals are best served by each program; finally, data should be gathered to suggest new methods for providing healthcare delivery. Borus et al. (1982) note that "few impact evaluations of health programs have provided all of this information."

A summative evaluation may also be used to assess the process, to establish what took place and how it contributed to the alleged results. In a summative evaluation of impact, the results are the dependent variable. The questions are: What are the outcomes, and what can be said about them? When the process is evaluated, the impact is assumed to be given. The questions are: What is the causal relationship between the outcomes and the various activities, and is there a better way of doing things?

In order to get the highest return on investment in the summative evaluation, it is necessary to plan it in advance. Such planning calls for definition of the data that could be used to assess effectiveness and efficiency. When direct measurement of the actual results is impossible, for example, because the different components of the result materialize over time or take a very long time to manifest themselves, there is a need to identify primary and secondary indicators of the potential results. In line with the logic of scientific research, it may be necessary to stipulate before the implementation of a program what levels of performance or what results will amount to what levels of success. This is because as a program comes closer to achieving its ultimate results, it may be harder (and more expensive) to effect a marginal improvement over the past. For example, a program that is designed regarding the vaccination of children may be quite successful initially when concerned parents bring the children to the clinic to get the shots. The program may experience difficulties and require more effort and resources for reaching children in remote areas or where parents are not cooperative.

The summative evaluation facilitates decisions about the continuation of a program by analysis of data that pertain to one or all of the following issues.

THE EXTENT THAT PRESCRIBED GOALS WERE ACHIEVED AND THE NATURE OF THE CAUSAL RELATIONSHIPS BETWEEN THE PROGRAM AND THE RESULTING EFFECTS.  This part of the evaluation generates data that are important for assessing effectiveness. It requires the evaluator to establish in advance the measures or analytical tools that are going to be used; the data that are going to be collected; the person responsible for collection of the data; the instruments that are going to be used for data collection; and when the analysis of the data should take place. (Wholey, 1983, pp. 109–123).

THE PROSPECT THAT THE RESULTS WERE OBTAINED DUE TO THE PARTICULAR DESIGN AND DELIVERY OF THE PROGRAM AND NOT DUE TO THE MERE EXISTENCE OF THE PROGRAM.  For example, a summative evaluation may help the decision maker find out whether the virtue of a "Meals on Wheels" program has to do with the provision of food or with the opportunity to interact with the people who deliver it. In the latter case, the same benefits may be achieved by the use of an effort that consumes less resources. This part of the evaluation helps to assess the efficiency of the program.

THE ECONOMY OF RESOURCE UTILIZATION FOR IMPLEMENTING THE PRO-GRAM.  This implies the verification that the program did not consume more resources than were needed, and that scarce (or expensive) resources were not used when adequate but cheaper ones were available. This part of the evaluation may involve calculation of the opportunity cost, the cost of forgoing the benefits that would have resulted from using the same resources for the next- most-desirable project. This, too, helps to assess program efficiency.

THE OPTIMIZATION OF THE EFFORT TO CARRY OUT THE PROGRAM.  Here the summative evaluation needs to establish whether the scope of the program was optimal. Because a change in scope may change the economics of the effort, the product is treated as the independent variable and the elements of the effort to generate them are the dependent variables. A program may be labeled as less than optimal when a marginal (qualitative or quantitative) change to input or process can lead to a major (qualitative or quantitative) improvement of the output over past performance. By the same token, a program may be less than optimal if a marginal reduction of the output (in terms of quality or quantity) can generate a major saving of resources. This element of the summative evaluation can help the decision maker deal with the cost effectiveness of the program.

THE VALUE OF UNINTENDED AND UNANTICIPATED RESULTS.  Even when the byproducts of a program are desired, the decision maker needs to consider comparative data. The efficiency and cost effectiveness of the program in question must be compared to the corresponding (actual or estimated) cost of a separate program for achieving said byproducts. When the unintended results are undesired, the policymaker needs to assess whether they can be minimized, if not prevented, and whether the net benefits of the program can justify its continuation. It is important to remember that sometimes it is impossible to separate the undesired side effects from the desired ones. The decision about the continuation, modification, or termination of a program must be reached only after comparing the ratio (or net value) of desired to undesired results for the case under consideration with corresponding data for other alternatives.

CAPACITY ASSESSMENT WITH SPECIFIC REFERENCE TO ORGANIZATIONAL CHARAC-TERISTICS THAT SEEM TO INFLUENCE THE NATURE, MAGNITUDE, OR DISTRIBUTION OF SPECIFIC RESULTS.  In capacity assessment, the results are treated as the dependent variable. Capacity assessment may include references to the adequacy of organizational structure (i.e., division of labor), technology (process or hardware) that is used to generate the results, facilities, and quality and size of the labor force. In addition, the administrator should be provided with information about the reserve capacity, the ability of the organization to increase its level of operation (e.g., to house more inmates, school more children) without changing the structure or fixed cost. To use an analogy, assessment of the reserved capacity should tell the administrator the number of additional passengers that can board a train without changing the configuration of the train or the crew. The information about the optimization of the program provides the administrator with data about the economics of the program. Capacity assessment provides the necessary data input for decisions that involve modifications of existing programs. For example, in an office situation, the fit between the specifications of the copying machine and the copying needs of the office has to do with optimization. What else the copying machine can do, independently of a given need, has to do with capacity. Because there may be a difference between optimal use of resources and optimal use of capacity, an assessment of the latter may put the assessment of the former in perspective.

## 2.  Formative Evaluation

Some writers use the initial definitions of Scriven (1967) to define formative evaluation as a step in the implementation process. According to Posavac and Carey (1980, p. 15), formative evaluation is done "to improve the plan for services or their delivery, to raise the outcomes of programs, or to increase the efficiency of service." King et al. (1990) assume that the formative evaluation provides the program planner and staff with information to help adjust the plan to the setting and improve it. This approach to formative evaluation has to do with the fine-tuning of operations. It is different from the summative evaluation only in the implied assumption that the decision about the continuation of the program was made, that it is a positive decision, and that it calls for some minor changes in the program. With this approach, evaluation becomes a management tool for monitoring performance, for creating a database for decision making, and for justifying a corrective action. When formative evaluation is expected to take place after implementation of the program has begun, it is hard to tell it apart from the summative evaluation. The first one supposedly looks at the process, and the latter looks at the total impact of the program (Morris and Fitz-Gibbon, 1990).

The confusion about the difference between summative and formative evaluations was augmented after the introduction of the concept of program evaluability in the mid-1970s. Evaluability has to do with the value of the information that becomes available as a result of an evaluation research. Wholey (1977) suggested the following sequential steps for bounding and refining the evaluation.

1.  *Bounding the problem/program.* Determining what federal, state, or local activities and what objectives constitute the program: what is the unit and what is to be analyzed.
2.  *Collection of program information.* Gathering information that defines the program's objectives, activities, and underlying assumptions.
3.  *Modeling.* Developing a model that describes the program and the interrelationships of activities and objectives from the point of view of the intended user of the evaluation information.

4.  *Analysis.* Determining to what extent the program definition, as represented by the model, is sufficiently unambiguous that evaluation is likely to be useful. This step also includes the identification of evaluation studies.
5.  *Presentation to management/intended user.* Feedback of the results of assessment and determination of the next steps that should be taken.

Rutman (1977, p. 61) suggested that formative evaluation can assist in determining the program evaluability by monitoring the actual operation of the program. In his words, "It is by identifying the factors which appear to influence the program's operation and its outcomes that formative research contributes to increasing program evaluability." Rutman's (1977, p. 62) formative evaluation involves "monitoring" and "data collection on the actual operation of the program" to "determine whether there are uniform activities that are implemented in a systematic manner." It makes the difference between formative and summative evaluations one of timing: formative evaluation starts with the implementation; summative evaluation starts later on.

The approach we take in this chapter is that formative evaluation precedes the implementation or even the approval of a program. It is done in order to ascertain the existence of the capacity to reach a desired goal in terms of organizational preparedness, adequacy of technology, personnel, and so on. The formative evaluation is also useful for creating the justification for the program and the fiscal commitments to carry it out. Thus the purpose of formative evaluation is to provide the decision maker with vital information about the prospects of reaching the goal. It is an effort for generating the necessary proof that what looks good on paper can be materialized if the necessary conditions and resources are provided. Formative evaluation allows evaluability assessment because it mandates that the program be clearly articulate, that goals or expected effects be clearly specified, and that causal assumptions linking the program to the goals and/or effects are plausible. These are also the necessary preconditions for evaluating program effectiveness (Rutman, 1977a).

Formative evaluation requires an experimental or a quasi-experimental (Campbell and Stanley, 1963) design to establish the existence of the capability to carry out the program under consideration or to achieve the desired results. In either case, there is an effort to control for intervening variables. The purpose of such designs is to establish that the plan for implementing the program is capable of creating the desired results. This requirement is one of the differences between formative and summative evaluations. In the case of summative evaluation, experimental or quasi-experimental designs may not be possible. The reason is that it is very difficult to introduce the necessary measures for controlling the effects of various variables after the fact. It follows that a prudent administrator should anticipate the possible need for such an evaluation and introduce the necessary controls before beginning to implement the program. Indeed, the collection of data for doing a summative evaluation on a regular basis may induce an evaluation even when there is no operational need for it. Under such circumstances, the manager may be free to learn about the effectiveness and efficiency of the organization without the commitment to take an immediate action.

In addition to exploring the capabilities of the organization or the proposed program of action to lead to the desired results, formative evaluation may involve other analyses of the program or the organization. Thus the evaluation may be used to explore the nature of the objectives. This exploration, in turn, may provide important insights that can be used for designing the summative evaluation to determine the impact of the program. For example, is the objective unitary or multiple; that is, are we seeking a single change or several changes? What is the desired magnitude of the effect? When is the desired change to take place? What is the hierarchy of objectives, and what is the relative importance of various objectives (i.e., can achieving more of a lower objective compensate for lesser achievement of a higher one)? Who is the target of the program (Suchman, 1967)?

Formative evaluation may provide a decision maker with important background information about the some or all of the following.

What are the problems with which the program intends to deal?

What are the causes of these problems?

What specific groups are affected?

How widespread are the problems now and in the future?

How significant are the problems?

What are the program objectives (e.g., eliminate the cause of a problem, stop its spread, treat those affected)?

What measures can be used to assess progress toward achievement of these objectives?

How does the program intend to deal with a problem? What is the nature of the effort to achieve the objectives?

What other public or private organizations or groups are already involved in activities that relate to a problem or the target population, or have a stake in what will be done about it?

What are the major alternatives for dealing with the problem?

What are the different criteria for assessing the advantages of each alternative? What should be the relative weight/importance of each criterion in selecting the alternative for action?

What legal, political, social, or economic issues should be considered in selecting an alternative?

What can be said about the relationship between the expected benefits and costs for dealing with the problem, for achieving the state objectives, and for selecting each alternative of action?

What is the feasibility of each course of action? What are the constraints on action, or the use/availability of resources? What is the opportunity cost? What are the funding sources?

What issues may be involved in collecting the necessary data for a summative evaluation?

What is the program's statutory authority?

Who is going to be in charge of the program? Who are the other key people? What do they think about it? Do they have previous experience or involvement with a similar problem?

What facilities are going to be used for implementing the program? How adequate are they? What are the involved costs?

## B. Two Purposes of Performance Measurement

Performance measurement can be designed to ensure accountability, or it can be used to enhance productivity (Halachmi, 2002) as illustrated in Figure 2. The two efforts may have synergetic relations: pressures for greater accountability may lead to better

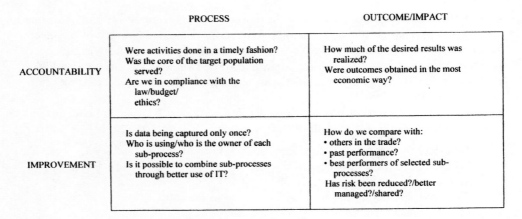

**Figure 2** Performance management: Purpose and perspective.

performance, and enhanced productivity may result in greater accountability. However, as pointed out elsewhere (Halachmi, 2002), there are cases where the need for greater accountability may get in the way of greater performance and vice versa. For example, the need to keep meticulous records and to make them available to public scrutiny may inhibit innovation and experimentation. By the same token, pressures to get better performance numbers may push administrators to use tactics that are not condoned by the public. A case in point is the public complaining about the heavy hand of the Internal Revenue Service (IRS) in the 1990s because performance of IRS regions, and thus the careers of those who managed them and those working under them, was assessed by the use of benchmarks. The pressures on the IRS resulted in higher collection of money but not in better accountability, as in some cases the IRS was wrong to collect or wrong in the selection of the methods of collecting. In response to congressional pressures on the IRS to use fluctuation in the number of public complaints as a performance measure, the IRS reduced the scope of tax audits and ended up collecting less than it should have been collecting.

It follows that if the two purposes of performance measurement can be inconsistent, the evaluator must start the design of a performance measurement scheme by deciding on the primary purpose of the activity. Is it meant to enhance accountability, or is it meant to help improve productivity? Following the decision, the analysts must match up the kind of quastions that should be answered by measuring performance with the selected purpose of the evaluation.

## IV.  EVALUATION: TWO PERSPECTIVES

The purpose of the formative and summative evaluation is to provide the administrator with the necessary data for making an informed decision about starting, continuing, modifying, or abolishing a program. Impact and process evaluations, however, represent the two perspectives for designing evaluations to generate such data. Using one perspective, evaluation may concentrate on the results or the impact of the program and attempt to answer the question, "Are we doing the right things?"

Using the other perspective, the evaluation may concentrate on the process or the activities for implementing the program. In this case, the evaluation is meant to answer the question, "Are we doing things right?" As pointed out by Wholey (1983), by using a process or a results-oriented perspective, the public manager decides on priorities and selects the relevant criterion for decision making.

## A. Process Evaluation

According to Nachmias (1979), process evaluation is concerned with the extent to which a particular policy or program is implemented according to its stated guidelines. Such an approach limits the usefulness of the examination of the process to summative evaluation. Indeed, it has been suggested that in operations analysis the emphasis is on means or operations of the program without specific attention to ends (Rieken, 1972). According to the conceptual framework of this chapter, such an examination is useful even in the case of a formative evaluation. As a matter of fact, when it comes to issues of productivity, studying the attributes of the process may contribute more in the case of formative evaluation, when changes can be made, than in summative evaluation. The proposed framework treats process evaluation as an effort to provide the administrator with information about the following.

### 1. Activities

What activities take place (or should take place) in connection with a planned effort? What is the necessary sequence among them and why? What (or who) governs (or regulates) that sequence? In the case of formative evaluation, this information will allow the decision maker to understand what it takes to produce the desired results. In the case of a summative evaluation, it should provide possible explanations for differences between what took place and what could or should have taken place according to the program documents. In the absence of other qualitative or quantitative indicators about the actual results, the appropriateness of the activities that make up the process becomes an indicator of quality. The assumption here is that using the right process increases the odds of achieving the desired result, whereas a faulty process rules it out. By evaluating individual activities and the functional interdependencies among them, process evaluation provides the opportunity for establishing the advantage of using a specific process over another even when both alternatives are adequate. Thus process evaluation can help a decision maker address issues of coordination and consistency across the board. It should be noted that for public administrators, issues of due process may prevail over considerations of effectiveness and efficiency. By studying data about the characteristics of the process for implementing a given (or a proposed) program, the administrator may identify possible discrepancies among the legal, political, and economic considerations that should guide him or her. Having this information is the first step for taking a corrective action to remedy the situation.

### 2. Side Effects and Byproducts

What other activities take place (or could take place) in the same area or using the same facilities, means, or personnel without noticeable adverse effect on the results of the effort, and who (what) regulates them? The purpose of this information is to provide the manager with information on important side effects or byproducts. Information about these can be used in mobilizing support for the program or for fine-tuning operations in order to get more out of resources that are being used for the program. The comparison of actual and potential returns on the use of resources as part of process evaluation can help a manager assess efficiency. In assessing efficiency, the manager must follow one of the common methodologies of benefit cost analysis and remember that the agency in charge of the program under evaluation is a party with a vested interest (Stillman, 1991). This implies that the public administrator cannot spare any effort in defining what constitutes a benefit and what constitutes a cost. By changing the definitions of what is a cost and what constitutes a benefit, an unscrupulous administrator may turn a marginal failure into a major success. An independent process evaluation that verifies whether there is a general consensus and wide support for the definitions of the benefits and the cost of the program may discourage attempts to influence the appearance of things.

### 3.  Staffing and Personnel

Who will be (or must be) involved in the implementation of the program? What are the implications of such involvement for the institutional ability to sustain current or desired levels of activity in other areas? What activities can be contracted out in order to avoid hiring employees on a temporary basis? Who (individual or organization) will be asked to cooperate or provide assistance in carrying out the program?

### 4.  Resource Utilization and Costs

What resources are necessary in order to meet salary demands, contractual obligations, capital expenditures, and debt service, and the need for materials, supplies, and the use of facilities and equipment? What is the fixed cost and what is the variable cost of delivering the service (product) under the most favorable conditions, under expected conditions, and under the most adverse circumstances? What is the overhead for managing the program, and how does it compare with the overhead figures for other programs of the same agency and/or sister agencies? What are the changes in the expected demands for resources when the discount rate is changed, using realistic projections, from the "most favorable" one to the "most unfavorable" one? Are there alternative sources of funding, for example, budget transfers from other agencies, grants, user fees, bonds, or pay-as-you-go arrangements? What commitments is the agency making about the use of resources in the future? What are the most and least favorable estimates for the startup cost, the cost of keeping the program going without major changes, and the cost of terminating the program, that is, the sunk cost?

## B.  Impact Evaluation

All public service and action programs have multiple effects. Such differential effects will reflect the varying impacts of different segments of the total program, the variations among different populations which lead some groups to be affected more than others, the different times at which the effects may be measured, and the different situations or conditions under which the evaluation is made (Suchman, 1967). Impact evaluation requires the evaluator to establish the reliability and the validity of the different measures that will be used before designing the evaluation itself. After the data have been collected, any question about the validity or reliability of the measures may undermine the usefulness of the evaluation.

Nachmias (1979) contends that impact evaluation is concerned with examining the extent to which a policy causes a change in the intended direction. Scriven (1972) points out that evaluation of the impact should be independent of the original intentions. Comparing the impact to the intended results may not reveal the whole value. The value of some important byproduct of the program often exceeds the value of the intended results. For example, HeadStart was a program that was meant to affect children. Changes in the attitudes of parents (of HeadStart children) toward school, the community, and government were a bonus, albeit one that would have been harder to achieve as a primary objective of an independent program (Halachmi, 1977).

According to Scriven (1972), using a goal-free evaluation will allow managers to make decisions on the basis of the true value of the results. It will allow the manager to decide in favor of a program even when its proven results are different from or disappointing in comparison with the original intent as long as they are of value in themselves. Indeed, Scriven suggests that the evaluator remain deliberately uninformed about the formal goals to reduce possible bias. The attractiveness of goal-free evaluation from a political point of view is obvious; yet its usefulness is limited to summative evaluation. In the case of formative evaluation, the manager cannot speculate that the residual or unintended effects of a program will be valuable enough to justify it.

The Urban Institute and the International City Management Association under the direction of Harry Hatry came close to endorsement of a goal-free evaluation. In their *Measuring the Effectiveness of Basic Municipal Services* (Hatry, 1974), they recommend that evaluation of effectiveness attempt to measure such aspects as:

> The degree to which the intended purposes of the service are being met;
> The degree to which unintended adverse impacts of the service on the community occur;
> The adequacy of the quantity of the services provided relative to the community's need, desires, and willingness to pay;
> The speed and courtesy displayed in responding to citizen requests; and
> Citizen perceptions of satisfaction with the service (even though these may not be in agreement with "factual" observations).

## V. TWO PERSPECTIVES ON PERFORMANCE MEASUREMENT

Performance measurement, as illustrated in Figure 2, can use a *system perspective* and, in particular, focus on the administrative process used to carry out a program, or it can examine it from the *outcome/impact perspective*. Using the system perspective and concentrating on the process involves performance measurements that could facilitate Business Process Reengineering (BPR) Hammer and Champy, 1993; Halachmi, 1995; Halachmi and Bovaird, 1997). Such a perspective may result in greater improvement of productivity due to better application and use of resources and information technology. However, subsequent improvements may be limited to suboptimization, allowing subelements of the system to perform better but not contributing directly to overall improvement of system performance. Studying performance from the outcome and impact has the potential to contribute directly to systemic improvement by allowing better allocation of resources across the board, that is, by providing decision makers with better ideas about the functional relations between a given pattern of resource allocation and ultimate performance of the system as a whole.

The various performance measurement schemes correspond to various evaluation perspectives. This allows the evaluator to select the mix of performance measurement that is likely to facilitate the selected evaluation perspective, either by concentrating on elements of the operation as a system (i.e., input, process, and output), or by concentrating on the outcome and the impact.

## VI.  EFFICIENCY, EFFECTIVENESS, AND EVALUATION OF PRODUCTIVITY

Most people understand that efficiency has to do with the use of resources: getting the most out of them. They also know that effectiveness has to do with impact: making progress toward the achievement of a desired goal. Indeed, most people can assess an existing or proposed program as one that is high or low in efficiency or effectiveness. However, because they may not agree on what is the right measure for judging effectiveness or efficiency, they may assess a given program in different ways. Heffron (1989) suggests that in the midst of this diversity, the consensus seems to be to agree to disagree. However, such an agreement is of little help to the practicing public administrator.

The common notion and the prevailing expectation is that a government program should get a high score in both respects. Yet the problem in the public sector is not limited to the issue of selecting the "right" approach or measure of effectiveness or efficiency. The real issue of productivity in the public sector has to do with solving the problem that results when the optimal solution to an existing problem calls for a program that is high in one respect but not necessarily in the other.

Figure 3 illustrates a situation in which the administrator may have to make a choice between considerations of effectiveness and efficiency in making a decision when a fancy high- technology machine with a hefty price tag is purchased by a rural hospital. Although the possibility of a high rating on both efficiency and effectiveness (upper left cell) is the most desired, it is not necessarily the most feasible. Hence the administrator may have to compromise deliberately in one respect to avoid a situation in which the hospital is worse off in both respects (lower right cell). The difficulty of

EFFECTIVENESS

|  | HIGH | LOW |
|---|---|---|
| **EFFICIENCY HIGH** | Hi-tech machine used around the clock. Some users are from out of town. | Patients referred to clinics in neighboring cities. Results mailed to physician. |
| **EFFICIENCY LOW** | Machine is used only part-time but is ready for service. | Machine is not used because physician does not know how to read its results. |

**Figure 3**  Effectiveness and efficiency.

making the choice has to do with the reaction and expectations of service recipients and the political context of programmatic decisions in the public sector.

Those who benefit most from a given program will support it by reference to the effectiveness side even if it means less-than-economic use of the resources that are available to society. Those who are not the main beneficiaries of the program will stress the need for efficiency. The inherent problem of using considerations of effectiveness and efficiency to judge public agencies was not lost on recent writers on organization theory. Harmon and Mayer (1986) claim that efficiency and effectiveness assume, at best, second-order criteria for judging the adequacy of organizational action. They point out that Weick (1979) has already advised managers to be wary of institutional pressures toward valuing the criteria of efficiency and/or effectiveness when the important issue may be what to do, not how best to do it.

Program evaluation and the conceptual framework that is offered in this chapter cannot provide the administrator with definite answers to questions about launching a program, modifying it, or doing away with it. However, the conceptual framework that is offered here can facilitate the design of evaluation effort for meeting the decision-making needs of the administrator. Thus, even though the proposed approach is not a panacea for productivity problems in the public sector, it can increase the productivity of evaluation efforts.

## REFERENCES

Borus, M. E., Buntz, C. G., Tash, W. R. (1982). *Evaluating the Impact of Health Programs.* Cambridge, MA: MIT Press.

Bovaird, T. (2000). Best value in the united kingdom: using benchmarking and competition to achieve value for money. *International Review of Administrative Sciences* 66(3):415–431.

Campbell, D. T., Stanley, S. C. (1963). *Experimental and Quasi-Experimental Designs for Research.* Chicago: Rand McNally.

Fink, A., Kosecoff, J. (1978). *An Evaluation Primer Workbook.* Beverly Hills, CA: Sage.

Halachmi, A. (1977). The use of policy evaluation in policymaking. *Indian J. Public Admin.* 284:1035–1052.

Halachmi, A. (1982). Action research and evaluation. *H.K. J. Public Admin.* 4(2):44–69.

Halachmi, A. (1995). Reengineering and public management. *Int. Rev. Admin. Sci.* 61(3):329–342.

Halachmi, A. (2002). Performance measurement: a look at some possible dysfunctions. *Work Study* 51(5):230–239.

Halachmi, A., Bovaird, T. (1997). Process reengineering in the public sector: Learning some private sector lessons. *Technovation* 17(5):227–235.

Halachmi, A., Montgomery, V. L. (2000). Best value and accountability. *International Review of Administrative Sciences* 66(3): 393–414.

Hammer, M., Champy, J. (1993). *Reengineering the Corporation.* New York: Harper Business.

Harmon, M. M., Mayer, R. T. (1986). *Organization Theory for Public Administration.* Boston: Little, Brown.

Hatry, H. P. (1974). *Measuring the Effectiveness of Basic Municipal Services (Initial Report).* Washington, DC: Urban Institute and International City Management Association.

Heffron, F. (1989). *Organization Theory and Public Organizations.* Englewoods Cliffs, NJ: Prentice-Hall.

House, E. R. (1980). *Evaluating with Validity.* Beverly Hills, CA: Sage.

King, J. A., Morris, L. L., Fitz-Gibbon, C.T. (1990). *How to Assess Program Implementation.* Newbury Park, CA: Sage.

Morris, L. L., Fitz-Gibbon, C. T. (1978). *Evaluator's Handbook*. Beverly Hills, CA: Sage.

Nachmias, D. (1979). *Public Policy Evaluation*. New York: St. Martin's.

Palumbo, D. J. (1988). *Public Policy in America: Government in Action*. San Diego: Harcourt Brace Jovanovich.

Patton, M. Q. (1978). *Utilization-Focused Evaluation*. Beverly Hills, CA: Sage.

Patton, M. Q. (1980). *Qualitative Evaluation Methods*. Beverly Hills, CA: Sage.

Pawson, R., Tilly, N. (1997). *Realistic Evaluation*. London: Sage.

Posavac, E. J., Carey, R. G. (1980). *Program Evaluation: Methods and Case Studies*. Englewoods Cliffs, NJ: Prentice-Hall.

Rieken, H.W. (1972). Memorandum on program evaluation. In: Weiss, C. H., ed. *Evaluating Action Programs: Readings in Social Action and Evaluation*. Boston: Allyn and Bacon, pp. 85–104.

Rutman, L., ed. (1977). Formative research and evaluability assessment. In: Rutman, L., ed. *Evaluation Research Methods*. San Francisco: Sage, pp. 59–71.

Scriven, M. (1967). The methodology of evaluation. In: Tyler, R.W., Gagne, R.M., Scriven, M., eds. *Perspective on Curriculum Evaluation*. Chicago: Rand Mcnally, pp. 69–83.

Scriven, M. (1972, December). Pros and cons of goal-free evaluation. *Eval. Comment J. Educ. Eval.* 34:1–7.

Stillman, R. J. (1991). *Preface to Public Administration: A Search for Themes and Direction*. New York: St. Martin's.

Suchman, A. E. (1967). *Evaluative Research: Principles and Practice*. NY: Russell Sage.

Suchman, E. A. (1972). Action for what? A critique of evaluative research. In: Weiss, C. H., ed. *Evaluating Action Programs: Readings in Social Action and Evaluation*. Boston: Allyn and Bacon, pp. 52–84.

Weick, K. (1979). *The social psychology of organizations*. 2nd ed. Reading, MA: Addison-Wesley.

Weiss, C. H. (1972). Evaluating educational and social action programs: A treeful of owls. In: Weiss, C. H., ed. *Evaluating Action Programs: Readings in Social Action and Evaluation*. Boston: Allyn and Bacon, pp. 3–27.

Wholey, J. S. (1977). Evaluability assessment. In: Rutman, L., ed. *Evaluation Research Methods*. San Francisco: Sage, pp. 41–56.

Wholey, J. S. (1983). *Evaluation and Effective Public Management*. Boston: Little, Brown.

Wholey, J. S., Ambramson, M.A., Bellavita, C., eds. (1986). Performance and Credibility: Developing Excellence in Public and Non Profit Organizations. Lexington, MA: Lexington Books.

Wholey, J. S., Hatry, H.P., Newcomer, K.E., eds. (1994). *Handbook of Practical Program Evaluation*. San Francisco: Josey-Bass Publishers.

# 15

# Program Evaluation
*Pragmatic Support for Better Government*

**GEORGE JULNES**
*Utah State University, Logan, Utah, U.S.A.*

## I. INTRODUCTION

For those interested in promoting public productivity, a key concern is knowing whether and in what way given initiatives contribute to valued increases in productivity. For example, does the implementation of a performance measurement system in a federal agency really lead to productivity gains? Does the statewide adoption of educational standards really lead to more effective teaching? Program evaluation, and the related activity of policy evaluation, is intended to address these concerns. But program evaluation has proved controversial. In particular, the early view of evaluation as an extension of good social science (e.g., Campbell, 1969) has been criticized with regard to the values that it embodies, its assumptions about social policymaking, and the methods employed.

These controversies have had a polarizing effect on the evaluation community in the United States, resulting in what has been called the paradigm wars in evaluation (see Reichardt and Rallis, 1994). Such conflicts between the opposing ideological approaches may have been stimulating intellectually, but they also reinforced barriers between alternative approaches and, in addition, distracted attention from the more important task of helping people make more informed decisions. With many now recognizing the excesses of these paradigm wars, there is an emerging reconciliation of approaches that emphasizes evaluation as a pragmatic activity to address different needs in different contexts.

This chapter develops this emerging view by first reviewing the debates over key issues in evaluation and then developing a more pragmatic approach that grounds evaluation in terms of the practical questions that are typically asked of evaluators.

This pragmatic approach holds several advantages for public administrators in that theory is viewed not as an end in itself but as a tool to help administrators answer their questions. Specifically, the task for evaluation theory is to begin with these practical questions and articulate a conceptual framework that guides the design and analysis choices required in evaluation according to how the practical questions can best be addressed in particular contexts.

## II. LESSONS LEARNED FOR THE PRACTICE AND THEORY OF EVALUATION

Evaluation of public sector programs and policies is premised on the belief that appropriate information can support public sector decision making. To improve the capacity of the evaluation field to deliver on this promise, we need to consider the lessons learned over the past thirty years. We address these lessons by reviewing some of the recent controversies in evaluation, referred to as "paradigm wars." These paradigm wars were not a contest between only two views, but, rather, involved a series of critiques against and defenses of a view of evaluation that came from the social sciences. For simplicity we can focus on three paradigms: social science-based evaluation, utilization-focused evaluation, and constructivist evaluation.

### A. Social Science-Based Evaluation and the Modernist Project

In the early work in evaluation in the 1960s, beginning with the approach associated with Campbell (1969; Campbell and Stanley, 1963) and other early evaluators (e.g., Suchman, 1967), the emphasis was on the concerns that still dominate quantitative social science methodology: using research designs and analyses that enhance the internal validity of conclusions, including use of random assignment to experimental groups, the hypothetico-deductive approach to testing theory, and sophisticated statistical analyses. Because of the dominance of this approach in areas such as psychology and sociology, we refer to it as the social science approach, although we recognize that all of the social sciences have strong qualitative traditions as well. The presumption of these evaluators was that if they did their jobs right, valid information would lead to better policies and programs (Shadish et al., 1991).

This view can be called a modernist approach because it represented a continuation of the modernist project that began in the age of enlightenment, a belief that the rational application of knowledge will result in an inevitable movement toward social progress (Schwandt, 1997). Thus the modernist approach to evaluation presumes that we can use methods developed in social sciences to arrive at an accurate understanding of social problems and the best available solutions. These identified solutions would be incorporated into public policy and so would resolve the social problems. Further efforts would be applied to resolving other social problems, and the result would be the modernist view of progress. In short, the goal is "better living through evaluation," with better evaluation involving the use of more rigorous methods.

### B. Emphasizing Decision Makers: Utilization-Focused Evaluation

One of the early critiques of the social science approach to evaluation was that theorists such as Campbell were naive about the political context in which evaluation operated (Shadish et al., 1991). Instead of seeing the active use of information to reform the "experimenting society" that Campbell (1969) envisioned, some evaluators with political experience (e.g., Weiss, 1977) pointed out that policymakers rarely use evaluation findings to make decisions. If the results of the rigorous, social science approach are not used in decision making, this would seem to call into question the value of the whole enterprise.

One reason for such lack of use is that the goal of evaluation in the social science approach may not fit the information needs of policy makers. In particular, the social science approach emphasizes the importance of supplying valid information about program impacts, devoting substantial time and resources to developing valid measures, coordinating comparisons with experimental or quasi-experimental designs, and conducting analyses with sophisticated statistical controls. Accordingly, a second approach to evaluation is concerned less with the validity of the information and more with conducting an evaluation that produces information that can and will be used by decision makers (Shulha and Cousins, 1997). The underlying assumption is that it is better to recognize the artificiality of the social science goals and focus instead on the actual information needs of the identified users of evaluation (Wholey, 1994).

This focus on use, or utilization of findings, is characteristic of what has been called the utilization-focused approach to evaluation (Patton, 1997). The goal of utilization-focused evaluation is to help the major decision makers make better decisions. The methods of this approach are geared to finding out what decisions need to be made and then providing the information that would help with those decisions. Rather than rely on the rigor of experimental methods, utilization-focused evaluation tends to use simple designs and analyses, providing real-time feedback to primary decision makers.

Typically the decision makers emphasized in this approach are public sector administrators and policy makers (or their counterparts in business organizations when applied to the private sector) although one could also emphasize citizens as decision makers. Working in a political context, these individuals will be focused more on wanting information that will help them achieve political goals. For example, government administrators might be concerned that a social services program provides the most effective services to those most in need; however, they are likely also concerned that nothing about the operation of the program will result in negative publicity that will embarrass their agency and have an impact on their careers. Accordingly, such administrators might prefer evaluators to provide real-time information that will help them anticipate program problems and allow damage control before their problems are reported by the media. Even when long-term evaluations are commissioned, the most salient goal of the policymakers may be less one of trying to establish the "truth" about causal relationships and more one of developing "evidence" that justifies policy positions already preferred by those involved (Weiss, 1998).

## C. Acknowledging Power and Politics: Constructivist Evaluation

A third approach, referred to here as constructivism, provides even greater opposition to the social science paradigm than that offered by the utilization-focused approach. The basic idea of the constructivist approach is that the world that we inhabit and interact with is not an objective thing, but rather a subjective reality that we construct from our interpretations. A variety of implications are drawn from this basic idea. One implication is that the rational view of public programs is merely a convenient construction, with many other versions equally real (Lincoln, 1990). As such, rather than attempting to generate true information, evaluators should focus on giving voice to divergent perspectives and engaging stakeholders in dialogues to attempt to reach meaningful convergence.

Another implication concerns the goals of the programs being evaluated. Some of the early approaches to evaluation assumed that the stated program goals were of primary interest to all stakeholders, that programs existed as rational responses to identified problems. In contrast, those with a more political orientation contended that public programs were rarely established and funded for rational reasons (Schwandt, 1997). For example, public programs can be established to provide jobs that translate into political support, to placate potential opposition with minimal resources, and to make symbolic gestures in line with political promises. These types of goals offer little for a traditional approach to evaluate.

This emphasis on power and politics applies to analysis itself, with some (e.g., Fischer, 1995) contending that public programs and efforts to analyze them are inherently political. Specifically, there is a power issue with regard to who gets to choose what is to be measured, how it is to be analyzed, and in terms of what values the findings should be interpreted. The social science approach of allowing the evaluator to make these choices is an unwarranted presumption of the objectivity and appropriateness of one set of values. On the other hand, favoring the values of administrators and basing the evaluation on them, as is characteristic of utilization-focused evaluation, is equally unwarranted. In either case, a rational gloss is applied to a political act (Guba and Lincoln, 1989).

This recognition that values pervade what are often presented as neutral decisions about evaluation design raises the question of the proper role of evaluators. In the social science view, evaluators should be neutral observers who simply comment on ongoing activities. Constructivists reject this view, and some argue that, given that we are all affected by the values around us, we need to acknowledge and accept our biases and become advocates for these value-based biases.

## III. MAKING SENSE OF THE PARADIGM WARS

What are we to make of the above critiques? Although the debates among these three approaches have been heated, there is a retrospective sense that the debates were less important than they seemed at the time. One reason for this change in perspective is that it now seems clear that the opposing sides each had meaningful insights to offer. More generally, these conflicts illustrate the confusion that can result when we give too much meaning to artificial dichotomies: "Too often social scientists create needless controversies by seizing upon one side of a dualism and proclaiming it the more important" (Thompson et al., 1990, p. 21). To move beyond an endless focus on the controversies and toward actions based on the insights from the controversies, many evaluators have begun advocating more pragmatic foundations for practice. We introduce some of these pragmatic themes and then consider the implications for two of the primary tasks in evaluation: understanding program impacts and supporting value judgments about these impacts.

### A. Pragmatic Evaluation

Pragmatism (Dewey, 1966; Putnam, 1995) is a well-established paradigm in American thought that takes a different approach to the dualisms that fueled the paradigm wars and yet also avoids the limitations of some utilization-focused approaches. Part of its strength comes from the pragmatic view of the role of theory in guiding practice. In short, theory—whether in the humanities, the sciences, or evaluation—is an evolved tool, one that has evolved because of the benefits that it provides. This is not to say that theory need not in some way correspond to our world; there are reasons why some theory tools yield more benefits than others. Pragmatic evaluation is an evolved tool as well, one that is of value because of the way it supports our natural decision-making abilities. This is in contrast to a rational/technical view that presumes that the proper application of validated methods yields judgments that are superior to, and should be substituted for, informed decision making. That is, the pragmatic view begins with the assumption that administrators and other involved stakeholders are often quite good at recognizing that some programs are effective and others not, at recognizing that some program changes lead to desired improvements whereas others do not. But public programs are generally complex, both with regard to program elements and to the contexts in which they operate. Evaluation contributes by working through this complexity and clarifying it so that the natural decision-making capacities of administrators and other stakeholders are supported.

The pragmatic view develops this notion of evaluation as a tool and offers an approach that, rather than forcing a choice between extreme positions, is informed by an understanding of the limitations and insights associated with the different perspectives. In terms of limitations, as the constructivists point out, the utilization-focused approach makes the questionable assumption that the values of established decision makers, or some other set of powerful stakeholders, are to be given precedence over others (Schwandt, 1997). The constructivists, however, are vulnerable to the charge that, in exposing the false rationality of programs and in dismissing the notion of progress, they have painted themselves into a corner of irrelevance, that an evaluator who accepts all interpretations as equally meaningful and all values as equally warranted may make people feel good but contribute little else (Henry and Julnes, 1998). All of us can imagine a public program that clients and agency personnel both support as valuable, for example, a drug rehabilitation program that attempts to increase the self-esteem of users, but which fails to achieve any public goal, such as reducing actual drug use. Programs have real effects on real people, and some effects are legitimately more desired by society than others.

As for the insights offered by the different evaluation paradigms, from the utilization-focused approach, we recognize the need to be explicit in matching the questions of greatest concern with the methods to be used in addressing them. From the constructivist approach we recognize that what we represent through evaluation is not objective in the way that the social science paradigm had presumed and that, particularly in political contexts, the value issues are not as straightforward as we might have hoped. Finally, the social science paradigm, for its part, offers a critique of methodology that needs to be considered, even if the needs of particular evaluation contexts override the recommendations from the social science perspective. Taking these points seriously, we can develop an alternative that seems more in line with our experiences as decision makers, evaluators, and citizens.

As for the lack of direct, or instrumental, use of evaluation, this point may have been overstated in that other evaluators have found, and Weiss (1998) has more recently acknowledged, that instrumental use is common in some contexts. Increasing use may be a function of making greater efforts to improve the fit between the primary practical questions of policy makers and the analytic questions that evaluators are trained to answer. In that these practical questions diverge in differing evaluation contexts, this argues for a purpose-driven approach to evaluation wherein the most relevant purposes for a particular context are used to drive decisions about methodology (Mark et al., 2000). This emphasis on fitting evaluation to its context applies also to the roles of evaluators, implying that it may be particularly useful for evaluators to maintain a neutral role in some contexts while being more engaged as advocates in other contexts. Other aspects requiring a context-sensitive approach to evaluation include what are often the two major tasks: understanding program outcomes and supporting social valuation.

## B. Understanding Program Impacts

To promote more effective government, it is not enough to document that programs are accountable with regard to activities; one wants to hold programs accountable to achieving objectives. This highlights a major controversy in evaluation over how to identify program outcomes or impacts, with some even questioning whether it is important to understand program impacts. There are certain aspects to this conflict that are of particular relevance to those wanting to use evaluation to improve policies and programs. The first involves a potential conflict between those promoting performance measurement and those defending the impact evaluation tradition, and the second is the conflict between what are characterized as quantitative and qualitative paradigms.

### 1. Impact Evaluation and Monitoring

An important controversy in the public productivity field hinges on the meaning of the word "outcome." In one sense, measuring program outcomes is strictly a descriptive activity of collecting data on such things as test scores in schools, number of complaints about public agencies, and satisfaction levels of program participants. Performance measurement is based on this type of descriptive monitoring (de Lancer Julnes and Holzer, 2001; Wholey, 1994). Another sense of "outcomes," however, is that the outcomes of a program are those that were caused by the program. This entails making causal inferences, something that goes beyond simple description. Rather than view these two approaches to understanding outcomes as contradictory, we can instead view both as falling under the broad tent of evaluation and argue for developing guidelines for when each approach is likely to be particularly useful. To understand when these two approaches are most useful, it helps to review the criticisms of each approach.

First, as argued by those who focus on utilization issues, impact evaluation is often derided as providing too little, too late, to be useful for policy change (Weiss and Bucuvalas, 1980). Many evaluations take years to complete, involve an array of complicated analyses, and are not focused on the information needs of the decision makers. On the other hand, monitoring has long been criticized as offering unreliable information to decision makers. For example, Pressman and Wildavsky (1973) define monitoring (e.g., of clients, program activities, and client outcomes) as "quasi-evaluation" and note that "quasi-evaluations either ignore or obscure causality: 'What,' not 'why,' is their question. Each of these forms of evaluation serves a purpose, but each is inherently limited in its capacities to produce knowledge" (Pressman and Wildavsky, 1973, p. 189; see also Perrin, 1998).

## 2. Quantitative and Qualitative Approaches to Evaluation

The most visible (or at least most heated) aspect of the recent paradigm wars in evaluation has involved the quantitative social science and the qualitative constructivist paradigms. In trying to reconcile these approaches, it is important to recognize that the differences involve more than just whether numbers are used. Indeed, one important distinction derives from differing views of causality.

Although they resist the association with positivism, evaluators who rely on quantitative methods are similar to positivists of the past in viewing causality in terms of the covariation of program activities and outcomes (Cook and Campbell, 1979). We are most confident, in this view, that a program causes a positive outcome when we find that this positive outcome is always, or almost always, associated with the program. Recognizing, however, the potential for spurious conclusions based on such covariation, the quantitative paradigm has evolved some other features to support making causal inferences. First, it is viewed as more compelling if the covariation was predicted or deduced rather than being discovered by post hoc analyses. Second, planned control over the treatment variable, such as through random assignment to experimental and control groups, is viewed as central to the most compelling designs for making causal inferences.

Qualitative evaluators, in contrast, contend that aggregate covariation is of limited use in understanding causality and prefer to rely on the insights from the study of individual cases. By seeking aggregate findings, and not conducting case analyses instead, one is losing the complexity of what is really happening to individuals (Yin, 1994). Instead, one needs to observe the interactions of individuals to understand what caused desirable or undesirable outcomes. Use of the deductive method alone is deemed inappropriate because the particular context being studied is so complex that only the most basic relationships can be anticipated; to understand the complex dynamics involved, an inductive approach is better suited to research.

## 3. Pragmatic Alternative

The pragmatic alternative to the conflict between impact evaluation and monitoring is to recognize the value of each in different circumstances (Julnes and Mark, 1998; Mark et al., 2000). Impact evaluation is more important in contexts where (1) the quality of the causal inference is important (where the costs of the wrong inferences or the benefits of the right inferences are high), (2) it is reasonable to delay some decisions until after the evaluation results become understood, and (3) current understanding is not adequate to make informed decisions (e.g., the dynamics are complex or there are multiple stakeholder groups with different, though undetermined, information needs).

Monitoring, on the other hand, is more appropriate when (1) the quality of the causal inferences is less important (e.g., decisions can be reversed easily as more information becomes available), (2) decisions need to be made frequently and in real-time, and (3) the results of monitoring are patterns that can be interpreted with minimal ambiguity (although the degree of ambiguity is typically not known until the data are examined).

Guidance such as this can be valuable, however, it is also important to remember that each approach can be enhanced to be more useful in other contexts. Impact evaluations can be more timely and responsive to stakeholder needs, and monitoring efforts can provide less ambiguous results when the measurement is more frequent and regular and a greater variety of relevant indicators is measured.

As for the qualitative–quantitative debate, the pragmatic alternative to this conflict begins with the recognition that the paradigm wars presented an artificial dichotomy. As Bhaskar (1989, p. 12) points out, choosing either the quantitative-experimental or radical qualitative paradigms results in a choice between "either a conceptually impoverished and deconceptualizing empiricism, or a hermeneutics drained of causal import and impervious to empirical controls." Instead, there has been recent interest in the use of mixed, or multiple, methods (Caracelli and Greene, 1997; Datta, 1997; Frechtling and Sharp, 1997). This mixture of methods can occur in individual studies, as when one begins with a deductive approach with quantitative data, engages in extensive interviews of key individuals, and then tests new hypotheses with additional quantitative data. However, any single evaluation is unlikely to embody all methodological possibilities and research priorities (Julnes and Foster, 2001). As a result, policy is best informed by an array of evaluations that use different methods. Taken separately, the different methods can be tailored to different needs; taken together, the resulting findings can be complementary and provide a fuller picture of the underlying policy and its impact. Without some coordination, however, diverse approaches can create as much confusion as insight, producing results that are difficult to reconcile or that even appear contradictory (Datta, 1997).

## C.  Supporting Social Valuation

For evaluation to be a valuable tool in service of better government, there must be some confidence that evaluation can help us understand not only the impacts but also the value of the various alternatives that lay before us. And yet, confidence in this capacity is called into question when we recognize that there are competing values, each with associated criteria and standards and each presenting a different account of the evaluand (the "thing," being evaluated, be it a program, person, or product) that can legitimately be used to evaluate the social program or policies. Each of the three paradigms discussed above—social science, utilization-focused, and constructivist—maps out different stances on the important value-related questions. The resulting lack of consensus on the appropriate values for evaluation has challenged the warrant for the claim that evaluation in the social domain can contribute to improving our social condition. Without arguing for a formal resolution of the problem that is posed by competing values and criteria, we can take solace and avoid skeptical paralysis by building on the recent insights of philosophers and evaluators in emphasizing human needs and the role of evaluation in supporting our natural capacities for making value judgments (Henry and Julnes, 1998).

## 1.  Challenge of Identifying Foundational Values

The problem confronting evaluators can be seen in the now familiar account of the controversy: whereas early evaluators like Campbell tended to presume objective values (e.g., "impact x is unambiguously good; programs that yield more x are better than those that yield less"), some came to recognize that programs and policies often have unanticipated consequences that are not tracked as well as the anticipated variety

(Scriven, 1993), while others pointed out the genuine conflict among values in a democratic society (Berlin, 1990; Hurley, 1989; Okun, 1975). This recognition of offsetting consequences and conflicting values, and the way that supposedly objective values had political impacts in promoting the interests of some groups over others, was particularly damning in that it appeared to take away any justification for using evaluation to improve the social condition (Schwandt, 1997).

An important result of this postmodern critique is that most current approaches to evaluation can be understood in terms of the ways that they attempt to counter this critique and claim an ethical high ground for evaluation (Schwandt, 1997; Shadish et al., 1991). On the one hand, some evaluators, particularly those in the qualitative evaluation tradition, have attempted to refine the value foundation of evaluation by identifying the most fundamental, and defensible, values. Pursuing this goal, there is a cluster of evaluation approaches, such as emancipation and empowerment evaluation, that emphasizes equality over the elitist values that serve social control (Fetterman et al., 1996; Mertens et al., 1994). Criteria for such approaches include measures of opportunity and achievement for those least well-off in society and measures of the gap between those who are marginalized and those who flourish in society.

Another cluster of evaluation approaches, however, identifies the good society as one that is efficient in responding to the preferences of all citizens. One criterion for this value of efficiency involves using benefit-cost analysis to generate measures of the comparative levels of aggregate utility provided by alternative program options (Gramlich, 1990). It is supported by the Kaldor–Hicks criterion (i.e., choose the option that yields the largest net present value; if this value is positive, then the winners could, in theory, adequately compensate the losers and still be ahead).

The thrust of the postmodern view of values is that efforts to establish foundational values are not as straightforward as common sense might suggest. In particular, the foundational value emphasized by one group of scholars tends to conflict with the "self-evident" foundational value promoted by other scholars. For example, the two values just described, equality and efficiency, are both desirable, but increasing aggregate value (or utility) often conflicts with the equality criterion, as Berlin (1990) and Okun (1975) pointed out.

## 2. Limits of Value Relativism

Taking a different approach in responding to the postmodern critique are those who recognize the subjectivity of choosing one value foundation over another and so feel that it is presumptuous for evaluators to impose their own values. The so-called fourth-generation camp identified by Guba and Lincoln (1989) rejects the notion of objective values and so focuses on representing the value perspectives of stakeholders. Interestingly, the social science evaluation approach that was targeted by much of the postmodern critique by the qualitative evaluators also derives justification from that critique. If objective values are indeed a myth, better for the evaluator to embrace value relativism and focus instead on making a contribution by identifying the impacts of programs and policies, leaving it to others in a democratic society to judge the value of these impacts.

The problems associated with the value relativists are of equal concern. Leaving aside for now Scriven's (1993) claim that these people are not evaluators, both the fourth-generation constructivists and the social science practitioners are inclined to use criteria and standards that may distort the attribution of value to social programs. The constructivists are inclined to what House (1995) describes as the fallacy of relativism, the view that all value positions are equally deserving of representation in evaluations. In contrast, our commonsense view would suggest that the values of hate groups or particularly deviant individuals may not warrant equal standing with other values. Most constructivists would, of course, not value giving voice to hate groups, but they have something of a dilemma in making this choice without appearing to support one value stance over others. As noted, the social science approach shares this limitation of relativism wherein use of benefit-cost analysis requires that, by implicit appeal to higher-order values, the costs and benefits to some groups are often deliberately excluded, as when the business losses of drug dealers are not allowed the same standing in evaluating a social intervention as the benefits experienced by children playing on safer streets.

## 3. Relying on Client Values

Although also a value-relativist, the utilization-focused evaluator is less likely to provide an explicit representation of all value positions but more likely to commit other of House's fallacies. In particular, the lack of a value-based anchor for choosing criteria that represent value makes it easier for these evaluators to be influenced by the values of the paying sponsors and/or clients of the evaluation [this influence leading to the fallacies of valuation that House (1995) refers to as clientism, contractualism, and elitism/pluralism]. For example, not being able to measure or describe everything, evaluators, whether qualitative or quantitative, make decisions that often reflect value perspectives and which can influence the characterization of the program or policy being evaluated. When these choices are the result of client interests alone, the result is what House (1995, p. 29) refers to as "clientism," making evaluation decisions on the basis of "the claim that doing whatever the client wants or whatever is to the benefit of the client is ethically correct." Allowing assessment of value to be based on the interests of the powerful is a problem that the postmodern critique had identified and sought to change, but it is the fallacy that the utilization-driven evaluators are most vulnerable to committing. If one is interested in supporting the public good, one may need to address value issues that the client would rather neglect (Chelimsky, 1997).

## 4. Pragmatic Alternative

Thus we see three opposing value stances—appeal to foundational values, value relativism, and clientism—that seek to provide a grounding that legitimizes the evaluation enterprise, each with its shortcomings (Schwandt, 1997). In that most recognize the problems associated with trying to ground evaluation on either abstract principles or attempted value neutrality (and pretty much everyone recognizes the problem of clientism/elitism), we would like a framework that offers an alternative, one more in line with our commonsense understanding of the issues to consider in making value judgments.

The pragmatic approach begins with the presumption that public programs have real effects and evaluators need to help others understand these effects. Furthermore, in line with our commonsense experience, we do not value all outcomes equally. Putnam (1987, p. 79) describes this commonsense value stance in terms of human needs: "It is because there are real human needs, and not merely desires, that it makes sense to distinguish between better and worse values, and for that matter, between better and worse knives."

As such, while respecting the constructivist critique of rationality and the claim that personal and organizational goals are often central in developing a particular program, a pragmatic view also recognizes that programs are always justified to the public in terms of the extent to which they address real social or individual needs. Even when our understanding of those needs changes, as when HeadStart shifted from a program to address cognitive deficits to one aimed at social deficits, real social needs are always discussed when talking about the social worth of the program. This indicates that even in the most political contexts it is relevant for evaluation to consider social needs and to assess the degree to which public programs contribute to meeting those needs.

Having placed human needs, imperfectly understood as they are, at the center of evaluation, we still need to consider the task of the evaluator in representing the values associated with these human needs. One of the controversies in this regard is whether evaluators should simply describe the values held by others or instead become involved in arriving at value judgments based on an understanding of stakeholder values. The pragmatic alternative to this controversy is an intermediate position which recognizes that the goal is not simply description of values but neither do we presume to prescribe value choices. Rather, the goal for the pragmatic evaluator is to *support* the value judgments of major stakeholders. Values inquiry is used to understand the most relevant values of stakeholders, with subsequent analyses and presentation of results keyed to being organized around those values. Consistent with the positions of many pragmatists of the past century, this suggests that the goal of evaluation is not to begin with abstract values and derive judgments, but rather to support judgments in particular contexts and then try to understand the values involved.

A second controversy raised by the debates between approaches is over the value of rational accounts of the benefits and costs of programs. Although the utilization-focused evaluators would emphasize the benefits and costs as seen from the policy-maker perspective, the constructivists are more concerned with involving different perspectives on the value of program impacts. For example, Schwandt (1997) offers his values-critical approach as one that is guided by and supports practical wisdom of diverse stakeholders. One practical task for a "values-critical evaluator," having recognized that values are inevitably embedded in evaluation, is how to manage the value bases of our evaluations.

## IV. CRAFTING EVALUATIONS TO SUPPORT EFFECTIVE GOVERNMENT

We have considered several of the conflicts that have characterized evaluation in the previous decades and introduced the theory of a pragmatic alternative. In this section we want to highlight the decisions that are involved in designing a pragmatic evaluation that seeks to support more effective government. We begin by reviewing the pragmatic vision of evaluation, particularly its emphasis on designing evaluations that are appropriate for specific contexts. We then address the major choices required in designing context-sensitive evaluations: (1) selecting evaluation purposes to address stakeholder needs, (2) selecting and combining methods to address the selected evaluation purposes, and (3) conducting these tasks with regard to addressing value issues as well as program impacts.

## A.  Decisions Required in Pragmatic Evaluation Practice and Theory

As developed above, for pragmatic evaluation, theory is valued not as a formal foundation from which to dictate practice but rather as a tool that organizes practical wisdom. This highlights the antiformalism of the pragmatic approach, a stance that views formal models as conceptual supports, not as ideals that necessarily yield conclusions more valid than our informal judgments: "[The] revolt against formalism is not a denial of the utility of formal models in certain contexts; but it manifests itself in a sustained critique of the idea that formal models . . . describe a condition to which rational thought either can or should aspire" (Putnam, 1995, p. 63).

For evaluation theory, therefore, we are not looking for a formal theory that prescribes one correct way to conduct evaluations but rather for a framework that guides us in making decisions required for developing appropriate evaluations for particular contexts (Julnes et al., 1998). One consequence of this emphasis on pragmatic evaluation is that it focuses the debate not on abstract concepts but on the practical questions confronting administrators. Table 1 presents some of the decisions that confront evaluators if they attempt to design evaluations that can contribute to policy and program debates. Although the philosophy of science that underlies the decisions covered in Table 1 is only alluded to here, it is detailed elsewhere (Bhaskar, 1975; Cook and Campbell, 1979; House, 1991; Julnes and Mark, 1998; Mark et al., 2000; Putnam, 1987) and is of value in providing a coherent foundation for critique and recommendations.

## B.  Selecting Evaluation Purposes to Address Stakeholder Needs

If we want an evaluation approach that is useful for promoting more informed public policies and programs, we need to begin with an appreciation of the different questions that stakeholders want evaluation to address. A critical task for evaluators, therefore, is to understand the particular questions that are most relevant to a given context.

**Table 1**   Decisions Required for Design of Context-Sensitive Evaluations

| Decisions | Major concepts/scholars |
| --- | --- |
| Selecting evaluation purposes | Practical questions (Weiss, 1998)<br>Primary and secondary purposes (Mark et al., 1999) |
| Selecting and combining evaluation methods | Degree of causal confidence (Scriven, 1967; Julnes and Mark, 1998)<br>Importance and limits of moderated relationships (Cronbach, 1975) |
| Selecting methods to support judgments of program value | Descriptive vs. prescriptive valuation (Schwandt, 1997)<br>Contextual valuation (Henry and Julnes, 1998)<br>Stratified valuation (Henry and Julnes, 1998) |

Weiss (1998, p. 6) offers a practical view of the major questions that administrators need help in addressing:

> Many people want (and need) to know: How is the program being conducted? What is it actually doing? How well is it following the guidelines that were originally set? What kinds of outcomes is it producing? How well is it meeting the purposes for which it was established? Is it worth the money it costs? Should it be continued, expanded, cut back, or abandoned? Should people flock to it, sign up selectively, or stay away in droves? Does it work for everybody or only some kinds of people?

Two points stand out in this quote from Weiss (1998). First, these questions are ones that every evaluator has heard from stakeholders, but note the diversity of these questions. There is no reason to expect the same types of evaluation designs to be appropriate for all or even for many of these questions. Instead, if we want evaluation to contribute to making better public sector decisions, we would benefit from having a framework that acknowledges the diversity of tasks confronting evaluators and provides guidance in planning evaluations that are appropriate to their contexts. The other point to emphasize is that Weiss is not restricting these questions to administrators; many people are stakeholders in the sense of having a stake in the running of public programs, and all have some need for information.

Recognizing that different people have different information needs to be addressed by evaluation, we nonetheless would like a framework that organizes these different types of information questions. Combining Weiss's set of questions with some of her other points (such as on how to improve programs), we can identify five practical decision-contexts that are particularly important for evaluators (Weiss, 1998, pp. 25–26).

1. Midcourse Corrections: The program is running, but there is a desire to make changes either to strengthen it before a summative evaluation or in response to some interim feedback.
2. Testing Program Ideas: This is similar to midcourse corrections in that one is varying an existing program to test whether new ideas result in improved programs.
3. Changing Program Scope: The program is established, and now faces a decision about whether to expand, institutionalize, or reduce (or kill) the program.
4. Continuation of Funding: If a funding agency is deciding whether to kill an ongoing program, this is similar to the previous point; if deciding funding among projects, then this is similar to the next point.
5. Choosing Among Alternatives: This is the classic decision when buying a new car or hiring from an applicant pool; it is less common in public sector program evaluation to confront direct comparisons of two or more available programs that are operating in similar contexts.

The point of lists like this is not that every meaningful decision-making task is included in the list nor that every evaluation should address only one of these decision-types (Mark et al., 2000). Rather, this list can help evaluators be clearer about the practical questions that need to be addressed. Recognizing the practical questions being asked of an evaluator, we are in a better position to select methods (often combining available methods) that actually address those questions. Before moving to method decisions, however, it is useful to recognize that the practical questions tend to be translated by evaluators into what can be called evaluation purposes. That is, training in evaluation tends to emphasize a small number of analytic questions that evaluators are inclined to address. For example, some evaluators emphasize addressing the question of how to improve a program (Preskill and Torres, 1999), others emphasize using evaluation to yield overall judgments of value (Scriven, 1993), and still other emphasize the question of whether the agency being evaluated is complying with mandated regulations (Wholey, 1994). This suggests a list of three evaluation purposes: program improvement, assessments of value, and accountability (a fourth purpose, knowledge development, is often included as a secondary purpose).

Figure 1 illustrates the relationship among the three practical purposes in terms of an outcome line (Mohr, 1995). To aid interpretation, consider an example in which resources (e.g., personnel and money) are allocated to developing a Web site to help citizens renew their automobile registrations online. The proximal, or somewhat immediate, outcomes are many people renewing their registrations online and shorter lines in the Bureau of Motor Vehicles offices. The shorter lines are believed to increase citizen satisfaction (and reduce their frustration), and this increased satisfaction is presumed to be a good thing, that in some meaningful way, society is better off (e.g., the more satisfied citizens become more involved in supporting a democratic society).

In this example, accountability is served by monitoring, either in terms of resource use and activities being in compliance with expectations (e.g., Web site is being developed appropriately) or in terms of outcomes matching expectations (e.g., people are using the Web site to renew registrations online). Assessment of value involves a judgment of the overall value that results from a particular allocation of resources (e.g., citizens are pleased with the better service and view the investment as a good one). This purpose is distinguished from accountability in that it is not enough to document outcomes, one needs to establish a causal linkage between activities and outcomes. Program improvement requires judgments about individual linkages such that changes can strengthen these linkages. For example, one might evaluate alternative ways to enter automobile renewal information on the Web site in terms of how long the online registration takes to complete (with the presumption that shorter is better). Evidence of one alternative requiring less time for registration than another is

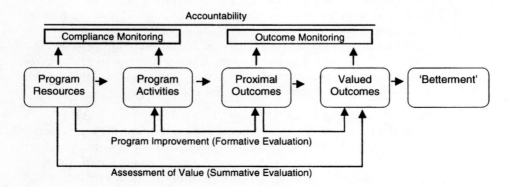

**Figure 1**  Multiple evaluation purposes.

accepted as evidence that the Web site change represents a genuine improvement, without considering the larger issue of citizen satisfaction.

## C.  Selecting and Combining Methods According to Evaluation Purpose

Once one identifies the most relevant purposes for an evaluation, the task becomes one of selecting and combining the methods that support those purposes. This task is complicated by the paradigm wars of the recent past in evaluation, when one was encouraged to choose between the quantitative and qualitative methodologies. The quantitative approaches presumed a Humean notion of causality and a hypothetico-deductive logic to strengthen causal conclusions; the qualitative approaches were inductive, concerned less with the problem of spurious conclusions and more with the problem of trivial conclusions that can result from studying only the hypotheses that were deduced before beginning the evaluation.

### 1.  Decisions About Methods

Although there are situations in which a purely qualitative or quantitative approach might be appropriate, most people today acknowledge the value of both qualitative and quantitative methods. The problem that results from this open-mindedness is the need to make decisions about which methods to use in particular contexts. One consideration suggested by the quantitative–qualitative debate is the degree of confidence required in the causal conclusions of an evaluation. In situations in which the conclusions of an evaluation will lead to largely irreversible decisions to devote massive funding to one program rather than another, the strong causal conclusions that result from randomized social policy experiments can be essential (Orr, 1998). In other situations, it may be more important to receive ongoing information about program effectiveness and to modify program activities frequently in response to outcome monitoring that does not emphasize the validity of causal conclusions (Wholey, 1994).

These decisions about methods also require considering the audiences for evaluation findings; policy makers may make little use of complex evaluations whereas researchers may believe a simple monitoring design provides little insight into complex problems (Greenberg et al., 2000). Similarly, in selecting an analysis and reporting strategy, aggregate findings (e.g., overall gains in achievement scores) have an attractive simplicity that must be balanced against the added insights of more complex analyses. For example, although policy makers are accustomed to some subgroup analyses (e.g., distinguishing outcomes by urban vs. rural regions), there are diminishing returns to adding ever-finer disaggregations (e.g., combining the cross-tabulations of urban vs. rural with: parents with high school diploma vs. without; family receiving food stamps receipt vs. not; and ethnicity). Different stakeholders are likely to prefer different resolutions, but some balance is required (Julnes et al., 1998).

### 2.  Combining Methods

The importance of addressing multiple purposes argues against exclusive reliance on any one evaluation method. For example, accountability is often best served by reporting systems that provide administrative data on expenditures and client outcomes, whereas program improvement generally benefits from survey or interview methods that capture the interpretations and insights of program personnel. Furthermore, a concern with value issues, that children are treated fairly and given equal opportunities to succeed, argues for qualitative methods that give voice to the perspective of the children and their families. This is particularly important for groups, the poor, ethnic minorities, girls and women, and persons with disabilities, who have been neglected in the past by policy makers (Mertens et al., 1994).

The idea that evaluators are more effective when using multiple perspectives is not new. For example, Cook and his colleagues (Cook, 1985; Shadish et al., 1986) proposed *critical multiplism* as a nonfoundational approach that uses multiple perspectives to compensate for the limitations of any single perspective or method. According to Cook, this multiplism could involve:

> value stances,
> program theories,
> operationalization of constructs,
> methodology paradigms,
> professional affiliations of investigators, and
> contexts for inquiry.

The basic insights of critical multiplism continue to be developed in evaluation. For example, Caracelli and Greene (1997) argue for a *mixed-method* approach involving the coordination of different paradigms (such as the quantitative and qualitative paradigms). Nonetheless, despite such calls for multiplism, most evaluations and policy analyses are motivated and shaped by a single tradition. In part, this narrow focus often reflects the inertia that comes from training in a particular approach to evaluation. Another obstacle, however, is that the complexity implied by critical multiplism can be immobilizing. Without some sense of priorities, arguments for multiple methods often devolve into recommendations to "do everything." Few if any evaluations can or should aspire to such comprehensiveness. Recognizing this need for guidance, evaluators have begun to develop frameworks to assist us in sorting through the desired multiplisms by relating method choices to the evaluation purposes that are most appropriate in particular evaluation contexts (Mark et al., 2000).

## 3.  Addressing Contextual Factors

Many areas of public policy have revealed inconsistent and ambiguous results from evaluations: performance measurement systems seem successful in some situations, less so in others (de Lancer Julnes and Holzer, 2001); educational innovations are shown to raise scores in some studies but not others (Drickey, 2000). An obvious reaction to this failure to demonstrate consistent effects is to investigate the conditions under which the program might be most effective. Quantitative analysis allows for this through the study of moderated relationships using interaction terms; embedded case study design can accomplish the same effect for qualitative analyses (Yin, 1994). The challenge in pursuing this, however, is that, as Cronbach (1975) pointed out long ago, whatever moderated relationship is discovered is itself moderated by some other factor. For example, the impact of the agency Web site may be greater for automobile registration in urban than in rural areas. However, additional analyses might reveal that this urban advantage represents use of online registration only for those adults who also have a computer at home, and so on.

Cronbach's critique is valid but should not be used as an excuse to ignore moderated relationships. There is value in choosing a middle road between the neglect of moderated relationships and the commitment to analyze every possible interaction term. The key to selecting the most relevant moderated relationship is to use the insights of experts and other stakeholders. Through this dialogue, as noted by Julnes and Mark (1998, pp. 40–41), evaluators can "turn from the question, Is the program effective? to the more textured question, For whom is the program effective, with what program elements, and under what conditions?"

In the example of the Web site for automobile registrations, past research should lead to an evaluation of the relevance of prior computer use as a factor that might lead citizens to benefit or not from the online registration resource. Evaluations of such programs should therefore investigate the specific characteristics of the registration Web sites that make them most effective. In investigating these moderated relationships, however, it is useful to recognize that, despite the demand of traditional approaches, it is not necessary that all moderated relationships of interest be specified in a priori hypotheses. It is possible to engage in a "principled discovery" process that explores these relationships in an orderly way that retains rigor in avoiding being misled by chance relationships (Julnes and Mark, 1998; Mark et al., 2000).

## D. Pragmatic Approach to Values Inquiry

Above we argued that the pragmatic approach to making value judgments has several distinctive features. First, formal theories of values are seen as useful, but only as guides. House (1995, p. 45) supports this practical view in claiming that "use of formal philosophic theories, such as Rawls's (1971) theory of justice, can serve to inform and critique our positions but need not be used to determine judgments in every evaluation, or how certain interests should be weighted in advance of the study."

Second, evaluators need to consider both the descriptive and the prescriptive aspects of values, at times describing stakeholder values and at other times using their understanding to develop value-laden conclusions. With regard to these value-laden conclusions, the goal for evaluation is not to substitute its methods and findings for the value judgments of others. Rather, the goal for the pragmatic evaluator is to support the value judgments of major stakeholders (Henry and Julnes, 1998). Values inquiry is used to understand the most relevant values of stakeholders, with subsequent analyses and presentations of results keyed to being organized around those values. Consistent with the positions of many pragmatists of the past century, this suggests that the goal of evaluation is not to begin with abstract values and derive judgments but rather to support judgments in particular contexts and then try to understand the values involved. This includes avoiding both the value-neutral relativism and exclusive commitment to a single value. There is an intermediate path that allows some objectivity to value judgments without returning to the unreflective objectivity of positivism: the "fact-value distinction, although analytically defensible, obscures the extensive interpenetration of facts and values in the real world" (Thompson et al., 1990, p. 22).

These distinctive features of the pragmatic approach help us avoid needless conflicts but also complicate our efforts to make the necessary decisions for context-sensitivists. First, consider that, in spite of the difficulties in articulating a consistent and coherent account of values, we are generally capable of making appropriate value-

**Table 2**   Tasks of Values Inquiry

|  | Representation of values | Relating values and outcomes |
| --- | --- | --- |
| Operational value claims | A. Representation of stakeholder values | B. Analytic support for valuation by stakeholders |
| Betterment (community) | C. Representation of public values | D. Critical Review in the context of public values |

based choices in everyday life. The goal for methods of values inquiry, therefore, is not to "determine value" but to support our natural abilities in understanding values. We can, then, describe two general ways that evaluators can contribute to the natural valuation of those involved in the deliberative democratic processes: representing the values of relevant stakeholders and relating those values to the outcomes of social programs and policies. Furthermore, given the distinction made above between operational definitions of value (e.g., higher test scores, more satisfied citizens, more efficient production) and the longer-term approach of attempting to contribute to a better society, there needs to be some balance in attending to the short- and long-term outcomes. As shown in Figure 1, this involves both the linkage between proximal outcomes and valued outcomes and, somehow, also the linkage between the valued outcomes and the final attainment. The tasks related to these two sets of factors are shown in Table 2 (see Fischer, 1995).

One task presented in Table 2 is the representation of stakeholder values, to be accomplished through both qualitative and quantitative methods. In the case of the decision to privatize a school, we might use focus groups as a qualitative method and the use of surveys in support of quantitative methods of representation. Another task involves relating the represented values to the identified outcomes in ways that support the valuation by stakeholders of the policy or program. In addition to distinguishing the ways that different stakeholders are affected, performing this task properly requires analyses that are sensitive to the contextual factors that affect the value judgments made in everyday life. A third task requires moving from an individual level to a community or societal level, and for this we elaborate our discussion of survey methods to include the use of surveys to assess "public values." Finally, a fourth task is to relate public values to societal outcomes, an interpretative task that we illustrate with a discussion of the methods that support a critical review of the societal value of programs and policies.

## V.   SUMMARY

In sum, from the pragmatic view, evaluation can be an important tool in promoting more effective government, but conflicts within the field can end up interfering with using this tool to best effect. We have detailed the paradigm wars that led to this pragmatic approach and described the key tasks associated with pragmatic evaluation.

The value of the pragmatic approach lies in its commonsense response to the extreme choices promoted by more traditional approaches to evaluation. For assessing impacts, a mixed methods methodology was described that should strengthen evaluation and make it more useful. Supporting value judgments of stakeholders also benefits from the pragmatic view in that we can distinguish key tasks (e.g., support conclusions about the operational value of programs); in contrast, evaluators also want to consider whether the operational value that has been defined is related in a meaningful way to the ultimate goal of a better society.

## REFERENCES

Berlin, I. (1990). In: Hardy, H., ed. *The Crooked Timber of Humanity: Chapters in the History of Ideas*. Princeton, NJ: Princeton University Press.

Bhaskar, R. A. (1975). *A Realist Theory of Science*. Leeds, UK: Leeds Books.

Bhaskar, R. A. (1989). *Reclaiming Reality*. New York: Verso.

Campbell, D. T. (1969). Reforms as experiments. *American Psychol.* 24:409–429.

Campbell, D. T., Stanley, J. C. (1963). *Experimental and Quasi-Experimental Designs for Research*. Chicago: Rand McNally.

Caracelli, V. J., Greene, J. C. (1997). Crafting mixed-method evaluation designs. In: Greene, J. C., Caracelli, V. J., eds. *Advances in Mixed-Method Evaluation: The Challenges and Benefits of Integrating Diverse Paradigms*. New Directions for Evaluation No. 74. San Francisco: Jossey-Bass, pp. 19–32.

Chelimsky, E. (1997). The coming transformations in evaluation. In: Chelimsky, E., Shadish, W. R., eds. *Evaluation for the 21st Century: A Handbook*. Thousand Oaks, CA: Sage, pp. 1–26.

Cook, T. D. (1985). Postpositivist critical multiplism. In: Shotland, L., Mark, M. M., eds. *Social Science and Social Policy*. Thousand Oaks, CA: Sage, pp. 21–62.

Cook, T. D., Campbell, D. T. (1979). *Quasi-Experimentation: Design and Analysis Issues for Field Settings*. Skokie, IL: Rand McNally.

Cronbach, L. J. (1975). Beyond the two disciplines of scientific psychology. *Am. Psychol.* 30:116–127.

Datta, L-e. (1997). Multimethod evaluations: using case studies together with other methods. In: Chelimsky, E., Shadish, W. R., eds. *Evaluation for the 21st Century: A Handbook*. Thousand Oaks, CA: Sage, 344–359.

de Lancer Julnes, P., Holzer, M. (2001). Promoting the utilization of performance measures in public organizations: an empirical study of factors affecting adoption and implementation. *Public Admin. Rev.* 61(6):693–708.

Dewey, J. (1966). *Democracy and Education: An Introduction of the Philosophy of Education*. New York: Free Press.

Drickey, N. (2000). A comparison of virtual and physical manipulatives in teaching visualization and spatial reasoning to middle school mathematics students. Unpublished doctoral dissertation, Utah State University, Logan, UT.

Fetterman, D., Kaftarian, S. J., Wandersman, A. (1996). *Empowerment Evaluation: Knowledge and Tools for Self-Assessment and Accountability*. Thousand Oaks, CA: Sage.

Fischer, F. C. (1995). *Evaluating Public Policy*. Chicago, IL: Nelson Hall.

Frechtling, J., Sharp, L. (1997). *User-Friendly Handbook for Mixed Method Evaluations*. Arlington, VA: National Science Foundation.

Gramlich, E. M. (1990). *Benefit-Cost Analysis for Government Programs*. 2nd ed. New York: McGraw-Hill.

Greenberg, D., Mandell, M., Onstott, M. (2000). The dissemination and utilization of Welfare-to-Work experiments in state policymaking. *J. Policy Anal. Manage.* 19:367–382.

Guba, E. G., Lincoln, Y. S. (1989). *Fourth Generation Evaluation*. Thousand Oaks, CA: Sage.

House, E. R. (1991). Realism in research. *Educ. Res.* 20:2–9.

House, E. R. (1995). Putting things together coherently: Logic and justice. In: Fournier, D., ed. *Reasoning in Evaluation: Inferential Links and Leaps*. New Directions for Evaluation, No. 68. San Francisco: Jossey-Bass, pp. 33–48.

Henry, G., Julnes, G. (1998). Values and realist valuation. In: Henry, G., Julnes, G., Mark, M., eds. *Realist Evaluation: An Emerging Theory in Support of Practice*. New Directions for Evaluation, No. 78. San Francisco: Jossey-Bass, pp. 53–72.

Hurley, S. (1989). *Natural Reasons: Personality and Polity*. New York: Oxford University Press.

Julnes, G., Foster, E. M. (2001). Crafting evaluation in support of welfare reform. In: Julnes, G. Foster, E. M., eds. *Outcomes of Welfare Reform for Families Who Leave TANF*. New Directions for Evaluation, No. 91. San Francisco: Jossey-Bass, pp. 3–8.

Julnes, G., Mark, M. (1998). Evaluation as sensemaking: Knowledge construction in a realist world. In: Henry, G., Julnes, G., Mark, M., eds. *Realist Evaluation: An Emerging Theory in Support of Practice*. New Directions for Evaluation, No. 78. San Francisco: Jossey-Bass, pp. 33–52.

Julnes, G., Mark, M., Henry, G. (1998). Promoting realism in evaluation: Realistic evaluation and the broader context (conceptual review of *Realistic Evaluation* by R. Pawson and N. Tilley). *Evaluation* 4:483–503.

Lincoln, Y. S. (1990). The making of a constructivist: A remembrance of transformation past. In: Guba, E. G., ed. *The Paradigm Dialog*. Thousand Oaks, CA: Sage, pp. 67–87.

Mark, M. M., Henry, G. T., Julnes, G. (2000). *Evaluation: An Integrated Framework for Understanding, Guiding, and Improving Policies and Programs*. San Francisco: Jossey-Bass.

Mertens, D. M., Farley, J., Madison, A., Singleton, P. (1994). Diverse voices in evaluation practice: feminists, minorities, and persons with disabilities. *Eval. Prac.* 15(2):123–129.

Mohr, L. B. (1995). *Impact Analysis for Program Evaluation*. 2nd ed. Thousand Oaks, CA: Sage.

Okun, A. M. (1975). *Equality and Efficiency: The Big Tradeoff*. Washington, DC: Brookings Institution.

Orr, L. L. (1998). *Social Experiments: Evaluating Public Programs with Experimental Methods*. Thousand Oaks, CA: Sage.

Patton, M. Q. (1997). *Utilization-Focused Evaluation: The New Century Text*. Thousand Oaks, CA: Sage.

Perrin, B. (1998). Effective use and misuse of performance measurement. *Am. J. of Eval.* 19:367–379.

Preskill, H., Torres, R. T. (1999). *Evaluative Inquiry for Learning in Organizations*. Thousand Oaks, CA: Sage.

Pressman, J. L., Wildavsky, A. (1973). *Implementation*. Berkeley, CA: University of California Press.

Putnam, H. (1987). *The Many Faces of Realism*. LaSalle, IL: Open Court.

Putnam, H. (1995). *Pragmatism*. Oxford, UK: Blackwell.

Rawls, J. (1971). *A Theory of Justice*. Cambridge, MA: *Harvard University Press*, Belknap Press.

Reichardt, C. S., Rallis, S. F., eds. *The Qualitative-Quantitative Debate: New Perspectives*. New Directions for Program Evaluation No. 61. San Francisco: Jossey-Bass.

Schwandt, T. A. (1997). The landscape of values in evaluation: Charted terrain and unexplored territory. In: Fournier, D., Rog, D. J., eds. *Progress and Future Directions in Evaluation: Perspectives on Theory Practice, and Methods*. New Directions for Evaluation No. 76. San Francisco: Jossey-Bass, pp. 25–40.

Scriven, M. S. (1967). The methodology of evaluation. In: Tyler, R. W., Gagne, R. M., Scriven, M. S., eds. *Perspectives of Curriculum Evaluation*, AERA Monograph Series on Curriculum Evaluation, No. 1. Skokie, IL: Rand McNally, pp. 39–83.

Scriven, M. S., ed. *Hard-Won Lessons in Program Evaluation New Directions for Evaluation* No. 58. San Francisco: Jossey-Bass.

Shadish, W. R. Jr., Cook, T. D., Houts, A. C. (1986). Quasi-experimentation in a critical multiplist mode. In: Trochim, W. M. K., ed. *Advances in Quasi-Experimental Design and*

*Analysis*. New Directions for Program Evaluation, No. 31. San Francisco: Jossey-Bass, pp. 29–46.

Shadish, W. R., Cook, T. D., Leviton, L. C. (1991). *Foundations of Programs Evaluation: Theories of Practice*. Thousand Oaks, CA: Sage.

Shulha, L. M., Cousins, J. B. (1997). Evaluation use: theory, research, and practice since 1986. *Eval. Pract.* 18(3):195–208.

Suchman, E. A. (1967). *Evaluative Research: Principles and Practice in Public Service and Social Action Programs*. New York: Russell Sage Foundation. *Eval Pract.* 18(23): 195–208.

Thompson, M., Ellis, R., Wildavsky, A. (1990). *Cultural Theory*. Boulder, CO: Westview.

Weiss, C. H. (1977). Research for policy's sake: The enlightenment function of social research. *Policy Anal.* 3:531–545.

Weiss, C. H. (1998). *Evaluation: Methods for Studying Programs and Policies*. Upper Saddle River, NJ: Prentice-Hall.

Weiss, C. H., Bucuvalas, M. J. (1980). *Social Science Research and Decision-Making*. New York: Columbia University Press.

Wholey, J. S. (1994). Assessing the feasibility and likely usefulness of evaluation. In: Wholey, J. S., Hatry, H. P., Newcomer, K. E., eds. *Handbook of Practical Program Evaluation*. San Francisco: Jossey-Bass, pp. 15–39.

Yin, R. K. (1994). *Case Study Research: Design and Methods*. 2nd ed. Thousand Oaks, CA: Sage.

# 16

## Balanced Measurement in the Public Sector

### Stakeholder-Driven Measurement

**MARC HOLZER**
*Rutgers, The State University of New Jersey, Newark, New Jersey, U.S.A.*

**HWANG-SUN KANG**
*KonKuk University, Seoul, Korea*

## I. INTRODUCTION

This chapter discusses balanced measurement of the public sector from two perspectives. From an intraorganizational perspective, it deals with the balanced scorecard as an example of balanced measurement. From an interorganizational perspective, the stakeholder approach to performance measurement is discussed. Integrating the two perspectives, stakeholder-driven measurement is introduced.

## II. THE STUDY OF PERFORMANCE MEASUREMENT

After the Government Performance Results Act of 1993 was enacted, substantial research on government performance measurement accelerated. What are the main themes of that research?

### A. Conceptual Theme—What Is Performance Measurement?

How is performance measurement adopted and implemented (Berman, et al., 1999; Few and Vogt, 1997; Halachmi and Bouckaert 1996; Hatry et al., 1994; Wye et al., 1997)? Generally, performance measurement is a managerial tool for performance improvement in the public sector. Conceptual studies accept performance measurement as a kind of value-free tool that could be generalized across organizational cultures, structures, and social environments in the public sector. Thus performance measurement is described as initiated by the political leadership and managed by a few professional work divisions or employees. Recent studies have addressed how to effectively integrate performance measurement indicators with strategic and long-term organizational goals so as to build a strategic planning mechanism. For example, the balanced scorecard illustrates how long- term goals can be incorporated into multiple indicators: financial, customer, internal process, and learning/growth (Kaplan and Norton, 1996).

## B.  Practical Theme—How to Design the Measurement Indicators?

What kinds of indicators do we have for each kind of public service (Hatry, 1999; Hatry and Fisk, 1992)? In large part, performance measurement is a technical tool. In particular, Harry Hatry has provided substantial and helpful knowledge concerning the whole process of designing measurement indicators, from identifying the program's mission, objectives, and outcomes, to finding the best indicators for each outcome. Joseph Wholey is also a significant figure in this arena of study.

## C.  Theoretical Theme—What Should Be Measured?

What is a clear definition of effectiveness, efficiency, and productivity in the public sector (Hatry, 1999)? Is citizen satisfaction a valid indicator (Gilbert et al., 1999)? Beyond the technical issues of performance measurement, theoretical studies deliberate the philosophical issues. For example, can the concept of productivity in public management be defined in the same terms as that in business management? Can government performance be measured by the formula of efficiency only? Assuming that is not the case, what are possible additional indicators?

## III.  BALANCED SCORECARD: A MULTIDIMENSIONAL MEASUREMENT APPROACH

## A.  Background

Financial indicators have been primary indicators of performance measurement in both the public and private sectors. Of late, however, the financial accounting model is being challenged by a total resources management strategy (TRM). TRM in this chapter refers to a transition from the period of exploitation to the period of exploration. In the exploitation period, the financial accounting model was the primary measurement method of corporate performance, and economic efficiency was the first principle of government and corporate performance. But financial accounting methods necessarily neglect an organization's intangible and intellectual assets, such as motivated employees, flexible and predictable internal processes, organizational learning capacity, and even time resources (Kaplan and Norton, 1996). In particular, a capacity for creating knowledge emerges as an important organizational resource. Modern organizations are required not only to exploit their tangible resources, but also to apply their intangible resources.

The Balanced Scorecard (BSC) was introduced to cope with environmental changes surrounding modern organizations (Kaplan and Norton, 1992). BSC uses performance measurement not just as an accounting system tool, but also as a technique for strategic management. BSC interlinks performance measurement systems with organizational goals and internal business processes. For instance, when an organization sets "customer-focused management" as its goal, it must be able to pinpoint the definition of customer-focused management and then design a measurement system for the new organizational goals. In addition, it should check to see if its internal business process is appropriate for those organizational goals. BSC enables an organization to establish a strategic management system, aligning organizational goals and internal business processes with the performance measurement system. Kaplan and Norton (1992) explained the essence of the concept as follows.

> Think of the balanced scorecard as the dials and indicators in an airplane cockpit. For the complex task of navigating and flying an airplane, pilots need detailed information about many aspects of the flight. They need information on fuel, air speed, altitude, bearing, destination, and other indicators that summarize the current and predicted environment. Reliance on one instrument can be fatal. Similarly, the complexity of managing an organization today requires the managers be able to view performance in several areas simultaneously.

BSC consists of four interlinked perspectives: financial, customer, internal business process, and learning/growth perspective. Through this family of measurement indicators, a BSC can illustrate how an organizational vision and goals are cascaded into many daily practices, leading to measurement of how the organization achieves its ultimate goal.

The Procurement Executives' Association (OECD, 1999) has operationalized the four BSC perspectives for deploying an organization's strategic direction, communicating its expectations, and measuring its progress toward agreed-upon objectives:

> Some indicators are maintained to measure an organization's progress toward achieving its vision; other indicators are maintained to measure the long term drivers of success. Through the balanced scorecard, an organization monitors both its current performance (finance, customer satisfaction, and business process results) and its efforts to improve processes, motivate and educate employees, and enhance information systems—its ability to learn and improve.

## 1. The Four Perspectives of the Balanced Scorecard

*Financial.* In the government arena, the "financial" perspective differs from that of the traditional private sector. Private sector financial objectives generally represent clear long-range targets for profit-seeking organizations, operating in a purely commercial environment. Financial considerations for public organizations have an enabling or a constraining role, but will rarely be the primary objective for business systems. Success for public organizations should be measured by how effectively and efficiently they meet the needs of their constituencies. Therefore, in the government, the financial perspective emphasizes cost efficiency, that is, the ability to deliver maximum value to the customer.

*Customer.* This perspective captures the ability of the organization to provide quality goods and services, the effectiveness of their delivery, and overall customer service and satisfaction. In the governmental model, the principal driver of performance is different than in the strictly commercial environment; namely, customers and stakeholders take preeminence over financial results. In general, public organizations have a different, perhaps greater, stewardship/fiduciary responsibility and focus than do private sector entities.

*Internal Business Processes.* This perspective focuses on the internal business results that lead to financial success and satisfied customers. To meet organizational objectives and customers' expectations, organizations must identify the key business processes at which they must excel. Key processes are monitored to ensure that outcomes will be satisfactory. Internal business processes are the mechanisms through which performance expectations are achieved.

*Learning and Growth.* This perspective looks at the ability of employees, the quality of information systems, and the effects of organizational alignment in supporting the accomplishment of organizational goals. Processes will only succeed if adequately skilled and motivated employees, supplied with accurate and timely information, are driving them. This perspective takes on increased importance in organizations, such as those of the PEA members, that are undergoing radical change. In order to meet changing requirements and customer expectations, employees may be asked to take on dramatically new responsibilities, and may require skills, capabilities, technologies, and organizational designs that were not available before.

## B.  Values of the BSC Rationale in the Public Sector

The success of BSC in the public sector takes shape differently from that in the private sector. The BSC approach to government performance measurement is worthwhile not just because of the comprehensiveness of its measurement indicators, but also because of the broad scope of stakeholders.

Since World War II, the policy sciences have been dominated by positivism and its techniques. Positivism-dominated approaches could be said to contribute to rational decision making and technical development of policy science. Positivism-dominated policy science, however, has been criticized as endangering the development of democratic policy science to the extent that it blocks citizen's intervention and participation in the decision-making/implementation process. According to Robinson and Morrison (1995), there are several reasons why individuals are frustrated in a group and/or society. First, when they have no opportunity for communication, individuals do not know what they are expected to do. Second, when they sense a great asymmetry between themselves and others, they think they may not make any difference in the group and/or society; individuals usually do not trust other people or their organizations when they feel two kinds of asymmetry: power asymmetry and information asymmetry (Hindmoor, 1998). Third, when they feel the relationship between others and themselves is unfair, they come to have low commitment to the group and/or society. This analysis provides a good basis for recognizing why positivism-dominated policy science blocks citizens' intervention and participation in the decision-making/implementation process. According to Schneider and Ingram (1997), that positivism brings about the professionalism of policy science. And professionalism and its jargon are barriers to communication between bureaucracy and citizens (Throgmorton, 1994). Some empirical studies show that professionalism and its associated jargon cause citizens to become frustrated with their intervention and participation in the public bureaucracy. In addition, many street-level bureaucrats have been systematically isolated from important decision-making processes under a strict hierarchy of government bureaucracy, although they possess useful experience and knowledge for the improvement of government performance. Thus modern policy science as dominated by positivism and methodological empiricism must be criticized for having endangered societal and organizational democracy.

As a reaction to that problem, scholars began to pay much greater attention to "stakeholder approach evaluation." (Atkinson et al., 1997; Mercier, 1997) Professional policy analysts have usually taken responsibility for evaluating public policies. Weiss (1983) points out five problems in this traditional approach to policy evaluation: narrow, unrealistic, irrelevant, unfair, and unused. Professional analysts exercise an exclusive authority when they implement and evaluate a public policy. Other stakeholders in government activities, such as citizens, interest groups, media, and street-level bureaucrats, have few opportunities for influence during the process. Yet policy experts have only limited knowledge and perception as to the various preferences of those stakeholders. Moreover, those stakeholders do not have incentives to participate in the traditional policy process. Stakeholder-approach evaluation attempts to include those various stakeholders in the process.

As an example of the stakeholder-approach evaluation method, the BSC measurement approach in the public sector has a great advantage in that it can include many stakeholders in a government performance measurement system.

## C. How Does Balanced Measurement Work? Charlotte's BSC and Its Weaknesses

The City of Charlotte was the first municipality to have adopted a balanced scorecard in the public sector. Charlotte presented a favorable environment in which the balanced scorecard approach could be well established as part of the performance measurement system. Citizen involvement and collaboration with government activities were extensive, and the city won first prize in the City Livability Awards. Citizen involvement in government management does not produce results immediately. There are several conditions for effective citizen participation, such as citizen education, public employees' acceptance of citizen involvement, and valid communication channels between citizens and government.

The city had a long history of performance measurement of city services, especially Management by Objectives (MBO). Those who study performance measurement in the public sector hold that there are many factors that affect successful establishment of performance measurement. Most of all, public employees should accept that their performances are measured by some indicators, and it is not a foregone conclusion that public employees will cooperate with performance measurement.

Under the leadership of the city manager, Ms. Pamela Syfert, Charlotte applied Kaplan and Norton's balanced scorecard to five focus areas: Community Safety, Transportation, Economic Development, City Within a City, and Restructuring Government. The four perspectives in the original model for Kaplan and Norton's balanced scorecard were modified in Charlotte's (see Figure 1). A customer perspective takes first place.

Figure 2 is an example of Charlotte's balanced scorecard. According to the City Manager, their traditional performance measurement systems, such as MBO, told them what the city was doing, not why they were doing the work. MBO is a good

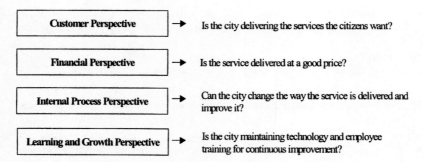

**Figure 1** Four perspectives of balanced scorecard.

tool for control and audit, but not for strategic management. Before a public program is launched, MBO indicates to public employees how they should go about implementing a program. The balanced scorecard indicates why they have to implement the program.

Charlotte's balanced scorecard remains as a strategic tool managed by a group of professional planners and managers. The balanced scorecard project was implemented by three teams: leadership, core, and liaison. The leadership team consisted of city managers, several business executives, the budget director, finance director, and planning director. The group acted as the steering team for the project. Budget analysts Schumacher and Elliott served as the core team, or the staff group. The liaison team consisted of a contact person in each city department. The contact people applied the main balanced scorecard to each departmental balanced scorecard. Thus Charlotte's balanced scorecard was a strategic performance measurement system of the professional, by the professional, but for the public. Citizens could input their opinions into the balanced scorecard project through a citizen survey "customer comment response card." But a citizen survey does not necessarily mean that Charlotte's

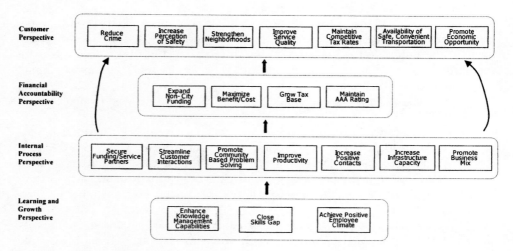

**Figure 2** An example of Charlotte's balanced scorecard.

performance measurement effort is a citizen-driven model (Epstein et al., 2001). Thus Charlotte's BSC is a typical example of adopting the BSC methods in the public sector, but is not an example of balancing measurement as a reaction against positivism-dominated policy science.

According to Monahan (2001) and Whittaker (2001), who are extensively and intensively reviewing many best practices utilizing the BSC approach in federal and local government organizations, most of those BSC practices have been driven by performance measurement experts. It seems that BSC in the public sector at this moment is a managerial tool that integrates organizational long-term goals (qualitative vision) and short-term strategies (quantitative objectives).

In this chapter, we emphasize that balanced performance measurement has multiple usages not only for performance improvement, but also as a strategic channel of democratic communication between government and stakeholders such as citizens and business groups.

## IV. STAKEHOLDER-DRIVEN BALANCED MEASUREMENT IN THE PUBLIC SECTOR

"Stakeholders" in this chapter refers to individuals or groups in society who are affected both negatively and positively by a public policy. Oregon Benchmarks is now widely known as a cooperative goal-setting approach for local development by a public–private partnership. The City of Jacksonville is a good example of stakeholder-driven balanced measurement in the public sector.

Under the philosophy of expert-driven performance measurement, it is assumed that governments or policy experts clearly recognize the needs of their constituents and better respond to them than do other groups. But we question whether public problems should be solved by governments and a few policy experts alone, or with the public as well.

Citizens know and can voice what they need. In addition, they may well know how to solve problems in their communities. Recently, scholars and government managers have increasingly recognized that citizens, especially, can play multiple roles in government, from coproducers to issue framers (Epstein et al., 2001). Thus citizens and all social groups are great potential resources in the whole policy process of government. This shift applies to performance measurement.

When governments design and implement stakeholder-driven balanced measurement, three core issues must be considered.

FIRST, GOVERNMENT SHOULD DEFINE WHO THEIR STAKEHOLDERS ARE. Public policy is a product of political negotiation. When a performance measurement system is designed for a public service, governments should impartially identify who is affected both negatively and positively by the public service. Donnelly (1999) holds that these types of stakeholders should be involved in the public sector:

1. Users and consumers,
2. Future or potential users,
3. Excluded and nonusers,
4. Citizens,
5. Local communities,
6. Elected members,

    7.   Decision makers,
    8.   Public employees,
    9.   Other public agencies,
  10.   Commercial and voluntary sector partners,
  11.   Professional associations, and
  12.   Society as a whole.

No stakeholders mentioned above should be excluded throughout the decision-making process. All stakeholders are potentially helpful in designing a reliable and valid performance measurement system. However, it is not necessary for government to get all stakeholders involved concurrently. Some might be somewhat less active or important in certain aspects of performance measurement than in others. It would be much better if governments would embrace as many stakeholders in their performance measurement systems as possible. Performance measurement is, in part, an art of social integration so that government might listen to more balanced voices from all stakeholders.

SECOND, GOVERNMENT NEEDS TO DEVELOP A FAMILY OF MEASUREMENT INDICATORS. Many experts in performance measurement in the public sector agree that some measurement indicators in a performance measurement system are not valid or reliable. Thus the number of indicators may need to be reduced. However, the nature of measurement indicators should be multidimensional. For instance, narrowly based quantitative indicators may have serious limitations in measuring complicated aspects of government performance. There should be a balance point at which quantitative and qualitative indicators are reasonably mixed.

In addition, the timeliness of a measurement indicator should be balanced. Organizational objectives often refer to short-term targets, and organizational goals to long-term vision. Organizational performance in the public sector is hardly measured by those short-term objectives and indicators. Governments may need to invest much more in terms of resources for inefficient work. For example, state governments sometimes take over financially stressed schools for low-income students in order to continue to provide them with educational services. Such investments cannot produce immediate results. It might be more desirable for those long-term goals to be hierarchically cascaded so as to reflect specific performances of front-line units of each department. Through this network of organizational goals and strategies, each unit would have more opportunities to cooperate with others in order to achieve the organization's goals.

THIRD, GOVERNMENT SHOULD COMMUNICATE WITH ITS VARIOUS LEVELS OF PUBLIC EMPLOYEES SO THAT IT CAN REFLECT MORE BALANCED VOICES IN ITS PERFORMANCE MEASUREMENT SYSTEMS. Public officials can create a cooperative network via performance measurement within a public organization. Performance measurement clearly pinpoints what each department should do and what each individual is expected to do in order to contribute to achieving organizational goals. Also, performance measurement can provide an interdepartmental link for cooperation in a public bureaucracy. Departments realize that they have to cooperate with each other in order to achieve performance goals explicitly identified via performance indicators. In addition to this horizontal cooperative network, performance measurement provides a chance for a public organization to establish a vertical cooperative network between managerial employees and street-level bureaucrats. In designing their performance measurement system, managerial employees typically realize that it is very important to lead street-level officials to commit themselves to performance measuring activities. Although public officials may not want to take any responsibility for performance measurement, some governments have begun to get public officials involved in designing performance indicators. They communicate past results of organizational performance measurement to all employees and ask for their constructive thoughts for enhancing their next round of performance. This strategy is closely related to knowledge management.

## V. IMPLICATIONS IN THE PUBLIC SECTOR

Performance measurement in the public sector has multiple uses. If we see performance measurement as merely a managerial tool, we might not see those multiple possibilities. The BSC approach guides us to more extended phases of performance measurement in the public sector. The approach includes "customer perspectives" as a core element, although several public organizations using the BSC approach define their customers' perspectives via "expert judgment." In short, performance measurement "of experts," "by experts," but "for citizens" is the general picture of current performance measurement in the public sector.

Figure 3 illustrates the utilization spectrum of performance measurement in public organizations. Many public organizations are implementing a control-driven performance measurement system. Performance measurement indicators have typically been linked to the budget process and personal performance appraisal. But many governments have become interested in establishing a strategic planning system via performance measurement in their organizations, and the state governments of Texas, Oregon, and Florida have shown that citizen and business groups can be very useful partners in performance measurement systems.

The State of Washington's Department of Personnel (2001 plans for 2002) has applied the BSC as shown in Table 1.

In spite of so many enthusiastic initiatives for administrative reforms throughout the history of public management and administration, most have been short-lived. Why is a "sustainable administrative reform" so difficult to establish? Reform

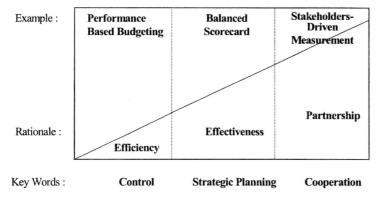

**Figure 3** Utilization spectrum of performance measurement.

**Table 1** Balanced Scorecard—Overall Priorities FY 2002

DOP mission

To support and facilitate state government's efforts to attract, develop, and retain a
productive and diverse workforce that is capable of delivering quality services to the
citizens of Washington State.

Value perspective

Cost-effective statewide human resource infrastructure support and leadership exemplified
by operational excellence, customer focus, and innovation

Customer Perspective

Right people, right jobs, right time
Responsive accessible service
Useful information readily available and timely
Human resource systems, rules, policies that are efficient, effective, adaptable,
understandable

Financial Perspective

Rates commensurate with services
Increase entrepreneurial revenue
Improve cost efficiency

Business Processes

Right people, right jobs, right time:
Workforce planning information and guidance
Qualified, available, diverse candidates as soon as possible
Classification system that flexes with changing business needs
Training and development options for workforce capability and progression
Special services to support workforce productivity and retention
Rule and human resource policy streamlining and reform
Knowledgeable consistent advice, consultation, and interpretation
Research and development: human resource innovations
Prompt effective communications, marketing, and information access
Improve internal processes to optimize service delivery

Internal Capacity

Performance expectations, development, and reviews timely and linked to organizational
strategic objectives
Recruitment/retention/diversity strategies within DOP
Internal awareness/understanding of DOP direction and progress
Data-based decision making
Overall employee satisfaction

refers to change, and any kind of change involves pain and burden. Before public managers and politicians try to ask their stakeholders to take on the pain and burden necessary for change and reform, they should first ask whether they are ready to do so. Indeed, consensus does matter in administrative reform efforts (OECD, 1999).

We recommend stakeholder-driven performance measurement in the public sector. We are, of course, aware of many problems of expert-driven public policy. Government innovation initiated and implemented by a few experts and political leaders could be efficient in the short-term. However, government activities should not be calculated to a short-term formula. Some radical scholars of public policy evaluation have asserted that expert-driven public policies are neither efficient nor effective in the long run.

Those who have proposed stakeholder approaches to performance measurement point out that expert-driven measurement activities (Atkinson et al., 1997; Mercier, 1997) often fail to:

Adequately highlight the contributions that employees and suppliers make to help the organization achieve its objectives;

Identify the role of the community in defining the environment within which the organization works; and

Identify performance measurement as a two-way process, which enables management to assess stakeholders' contributions to the organization's primary and secondary goals, and enables stakeholders to assess whether the organization is capable of fulfilling its obligations to them now and in the future.

Stakeholder-driven performance measurement is very important in the public sector, where so many conflicting stakeholders are competing. It values mutual collaboration between those stakeholders in developing measurement indicators and implementing the entire process of measurement activities.

## REFERENCES

Atkinson, A., Waterhouse, J., Wells, R. (Spring, 1997). A stakeholder approach to strategic performance measurement. *Sloan Manage. Rev.* 25–37.

Berman, E., West, J., Wang, X. (1999). Performance measurement in US counties: new research findings. In: Proceedings of the American Society for Public Administration, Orlando, FL.

deLeon, P. (1997). *Democracy and the Policy Sciences.* New York: SUNY Press, 1997.

Donnelly, M. (1999). Making the difference: quality strategy in the public sector. *Manag. Serv. Quart.* 9(1).

Epstein, P, Wray, L., Marshall, M., Grifel, S. (2001). Engaging citizens in achieving results that matter: a model for effective 21st century governance. Available at *http://www. citizenleague.net/cl/SLOAN/whole.htm* [2001-10-25].

Few, P., Vogt, J. (Winter, 1997). Measuring the performance of local governments. *Popular Govern.* 41–54.

Fischer, F. (1993). Citizen participation and the democratization of policy expertise: from theoretical inquiry to practical cases. *Policy Sci.* 26:165–187.

GASB (2000). State and local government case studies on use and the effects of using performance measures for budgeting, management, and reporting. Available at *www.gasb.org* [2000-15-25].

Gilbert, R., Nicholls, J., Roslow, S. (1999). Measuring public sector customer service satisfaction. *Public Manage.* 21–25.

Halachmi, A., Bouckaert, G. (1996). *Organizational Performance and Measurement in the Public Sector: Toward Service, Effort, and Accomplishment Reporting*. Westport, CT: Quorum.

Hatry, H. (1999). *Performance Measurement*. Washington, DC: Urban Institute.

Hatry, H., Fisk, D. (1992). Measuring productivity in the public sector. In: Holzer, M. ed. *Handbook of Public Productivity*. New York: Marcel Dekker, pp. 139–160.

Hatry, H., Gerhart, C., Marshall, M. (September, 1994). Eleven ways to make performance measurement more useful to public managers. *Public Manage*. 15–21.

Kaplan, R. (1999). *City of Charlotte*. Harvard Business School case study 9-199-036.

Kaplan, R., Norton, D. (1996). *Balanced Scorecard*. Boston: Harvard Business School Press.

Mercier, C. (1997). Participation in stakeholder-based evaluation: a case study. *Eval. Prog. Plan*. 20(4):467–475.

Monahan, K. (2001). *Balanced Measures for Strategic Planning: A Public Sector Handbook*. Vienna: Management Concepts.

Morrison, E. W., Robinson, S. L. (1997). When employees feel betrayed: a model of how psychological contract violation develops. *Acad. Manage. Rev*. 22(1):226–256.

National Partnership for Reinventing Government (2001). Balancing measures: Best practices in performance management. Available at *http://www.npr.gov/library/papers/bkgrd/balmeasure:html* [2000-10-25].

OECD (1999) Governance in Transition: Public Management Reforms in OECD Countries. Procurement Executives' Association. Guide to a Balanced Scorecard Performance Management Methodology. Available at *http://oamweb.osec.doc.gov/bsc/guide.htm#d%20Chapter%20Two*.

Robinson, S. L., Rousseau, D. M. (1994). Violating the psychological contract: not the exception but the norm. *J. Organi. Behav*. 15:245–259.

Schneider, A. L., Ingram, H. (1997). *Policy Design for Democracy*. Pitt, KS: University of Kansas Press.

Syfert, P. (1998). Decision making in the age of accountability. In: Proceedings of the Managing for Results Conference, Austin, Texas.

Throgmorton, J. A. (1994). The rhetorics of policy analysis. *Policy Sci*. 24(3):153–179.

Washington State, Department of Personnel (2001). Available at *http://hr.dop.wa.gov/geninfo/dop_bsc.htm*.

Weiss, C. (1983). The stakeholder approach to evaluation: Origins and promise. *In Stakeholder-Based Evaluation: New Directions for Program Evaluation*, no.17. San Francisco: Jossey-Bass.

Whittaker, J. (2001). *Balanced Scorecard in the Federal Government*. Vienna: Management Concepts.

Wye, C., et al. (Fall, 1997). Forum: Implementing the result act. *Public Manage*, 3–46.

# 17

## Measurement as Accountability

**MOHAMAD G. ALKADRY**
*West Virginia University, Morgantown, West Virginia, U.S.A.*

**ALI FARAZMAND**
*Florida Atlantic University, Fort Lauderdale, Florida, U.S.A.*

## I. INTRODUCTION

The beginning of the twentieth century witnessed a great deal of debate on government accountability. Wilson (1887) had just written his landmark article calling for a separation of politics from administration. Taylor (1911) conducted his time and motion studies and called for the adoption of his productivity measures in government organizations as well as the private sector. Weber (1946) wrote his landmark essay on accountability and the role of the administration and parliament in a democratic political system. Writings in Great Britain criticized the so-called bureaucratic despotism whereby administrators were acting without prior political orders (Kingsley, 1944).

The century ended unlike it had started. As we headed into the twenty-first century, concerns about political accountability were replaced by calls for performance accountability. Political leaders in both major political parties in the United States and those who held power in society came to a consensus that government ought to be accountable for its effectiveness and efficiency. Key administrators, or managers, would be accountable for achieving efficiency and effectiveness goals. The notion of a democratic government that dominated the writings of the late nineteenth and early twentieth centuries was replaced by the notion of performance government by the end of the twentieth century (Halachmi and Bouckaert, 1996; Popovich, 1998).

In this chapter, we argue that new theories of governance, including New Public Management, Good Government (UN), managerialism, reinvention, and Performance Government advocate a form of measurement or performance accountability that shuts out political accountability. This form of accountability is detrimental to the notion of popular sovereignty that underlies most western political systems.

In order to understand the notion of performance accountability, it is important to examine the pervasive mood, or hysteria, of performance government as well as its implications for traditional forms of accountability. A number of conditions contributed to the pervasiveness of performance government. These conditions include the rise in New Right movements in most of the influential western world, the resurgence of managerialism as a guiding ideological force in the reform movement, calls for reinventing government, and the rise of the new ideological and intellectual ethos of Public Management (or New Public Management) based on globalization of capital and the reemerging of the New Right. The result of these conditions is a form of Public Management that places more value on small and efficient government than it places on political accountability.

At the turn of the twentieth century, values of equality and sovereignty of the people were valued more than values of performance accountability, or efficiency and effectiveness, in other words. This shift from political accountability to performance accountability transforms debates on government from political debate about issues to technical debate about numbers and results.

## II.  PERFORMANCE GOVERNMENT

Performance measurement is not a new concept to the field of public administration. It is rather, "an old idea that has taken on renewed importance" (Poister and Streib, 1999, p. 325). As early as 1938, The International City/County Managers Association published a book entitled *Measuring Municipal Activities: A Survey of Suggested Criteria for Appraising Administration*. One could also argue that Taylor's (1911) time and motion studies and attempts to implement Taylorism in the public sector in the 1920s have all acted to introduce the notion, and essentially the practice, of performance measurement into the public sector. Prior to the 1980s, performance measurement appeared in the shape of performance-based budgeting (Grizzle, 1985; Poister and Streib, 1999). In a survey of states, Melker and Willoughby (1998) suggested that 47 of 50 states used results-oriented budgeting and a performance reporting system. In the 1990s, performance measurement became the norm that most government agencies aspired to achieve (Garsombke and Schrad, 1999; Melkers and Willoughby, 1998; Behn, 1998; Martin and Kettner, 1996).

Performance measurement reduces all outcomes and output of an administration to numbers and measurable results. Under the notion of performance measurement, managers of service institutions obtain and use the feedback from performance measures "to build self control from results into their system" (Drucker, 1973, p. 158). Performance government therefore implies the measurement of results and accountability based on achievement of these results (Broom, 1995; Wechsler and Clary, 2000). Performance government is summed into the goals of the National Performance Review Act, which "calls upon managers to formulate both strategic and performance plans, monitor program delivery by tracking performance indicators and assess policy and program outcomes" (Newcomer, 1998, p. 129). The dominant administrative values under performance government are efficiency and effectiveness. Performance measures therefore result in tipping the scale toward efficiency and effectiveness against equity and quality of service (Pollit, 1990; Thompson, 2000).

The economic invasion of public administration was prefaced with a set of conditions related to governing in an information age and the involvement of citizens in government performance measurement. Performance government was marketed as a tool to deal with two important government issues: the scarcity of resources and public hostility issues. Performance measurement could act as a tool to ensure that the available and scarce resources were being spent with due regard to economy and efficiency.

Measurement of performance by itself does not ensure an increase in productivity. Indeed, Sutermeister (1969) argues that increasing the productivity of individuals in organizations involves the nature of work relations, the knowledge and ability of individuals, and the level of technological advancement of the workplace among many other things. What measurement does, however, is provide a step toward improving productivity through providing the tool to monitor performance changes. The second use of productivity measurement is benchmarking. Many of the new government initiatives, such as the National Performance Review and the Government Performance and Results Act of 1993 (GASB), emphasize the importance of measuring an organization's own performance against providers of similar services in the public and private sectors (Martin and Kettner, 1996). This benchmarking, by itself, offers a great deal of information on identifying the best practices of an organization among its peers. Perhaps the most significant function of measuring the performance of public organizations is putting an end to rumors, myths, and sentiments about the inefficiency of those organizations.

As the available resources to spend on government programs become more scarce, inefficiency is less and less tolerated. The resource problem is driving governments to make decisions based on resources, thus the terms "across the board cuts" and "program gutting." At the same time, governments are faced with the challenge of having to "do more for less." Political decisions therefore have been transformed into economic decisions.

On the other hand, government inefficiency is increasingly becoming an issue with the citizenry. Citizens are becoming less and less tolerant of low government productivity. As a result of this perceived low productivity, citizens receive fewer services and/or pay more taxes. With the information revolution, citizens have better access to government. There is also an increase in the number of academics and practitioners who call upon citizens to partake in the performance-based decision-making process. There is one clear thing: governments need to become more productive. Efficiency seems to have reemerged as the new bottom line for public organizations around the world and especially in Canada and the United States.

There are a number of measures that were implemented to emphasize this culture of performance measurement, thus officially declaring a state of performance emergency. The first is the establishment of the General Accounting Standards Board in 1989. Following that was the National Performance Review at the federal level headed by then- Vice President Al Gore. The National Performance Review aimed to free organizations from past regulations and policies that constrained members and to provide new incentives to reward performance managers (Roberts, 1997). The Democratic administration's zest for performance measurement implementation was not particularly new to government. These were the general attitudes presented by Thatcher in the United Kingdom, Mulroney in Canada, and Reagan in the United States (Savoie, 1994).

The federal government also introduced the Government Performance Results Act in 1993 to require all federal agencies to report to Congress with their five-year strategic plans by 1997. The Act also required federal agencies to report annual performance plans to the Office of Management and Budgeting by 1999. Legislating performance measurement acts as an indication of the seriousness of the federal government in implementing performance government. It is also a response to claims that bureaucracy and politicians are behind the failure of performance measurement volunteer implementation (Garsombke and Schrad, 1999). Such legislation vindicates politicians as the engineers of reform and not its opponents. At the same time, it affirms claims that volunteer implementation of performance measurement would result in no implementation of performance measures. The Government Performance Results Act is performance measurement's affirmative action legislation.

The prevalence of performance measurement is not nearly as important as its pervasiveness in the American political culture. Government at the state and local levels followed the footsteps of the federal government. The speed with which performance measurement has dominated administrative organization in the 1990s is indeed remarkable. In the early 1990s, the term "performance measurement" was as ubiquitous among government officials as the Internet. At the end of the decade, most government organizations had either implemented some form of performance measurement or were aspiring to do so. In a survey conducted in 1997, after establishing the General Accounting Standards Board, 26% of the 553 respondents indicated that they had some form of output or outcome measure (Kopczynski and Lombardo, 1999). In a study by Garsombke and Schrad (1999), 71% (or 82 cities) of responding cities and 67% (or 63 state agencies) of responding state agencies indicated that they used performance measurement systems. National associations of administrators at all levels rushed to endorse performance as their response to the prevailing antigovernment sentiment (Poister and Streib, 1999). The National Academy of Public Administration and the American Society of Public Administration passed resolutions and took solid steps to jump on the performance measurement bandwagon. The International City/County Manager's Association formed the Local Government Comparative Performance Measurement Consortium that would capture and report data in several service delivery areas and from several participating local governments (Kopczynski and Lombardo, 1999).

Performance measurement is not the only results-oriented management tool of the twentieth century. There are many similar management reforms that emphasize results such as strategic planning (Bryson, 1995), strategic management processes (Koteen, 1991; Vinzant and Vinzant, 1996), and quality management programs (Cohen and Brand, 1993). However, performance measurement is the results-oriented management tool that has the widest prevalence.

In an article entitled "Performance driven government: Using measures to manage," Walter (2000) argues that most governments have moved now from measurement of performance to establishing ways to use that information in management decisions. This means that performance measures would be used to review programs and as a decision-making tool. The measures, and not those doing the measurement, would assume the role of decision making and politics would retreat to the role of passive observation of the measures at work.

Although some regard performance measurement to be a way of the future and a tool, some still caution that it has many shortcomings. Thompson (2000) warns that performance measures can induce gaming behavior. Carter et al. (1992) argue that performance measures disregard those measures that can not be quantified. In an age when research methods scholars are increasingly realizing the significance of qualitative methods in social research, performance measures focus solely on quantitative methods (also see Wholey and Hatry, 1992). Radin (1998) argues that performance measures act to further fragment an already fragmented government by devising performance measures for each division within agencies. He argues that performance measurement promotes the notion of fragmented agencies. This poses a challenge to the ability of performance accountability to deliver accountability of the whole if government is fragmented. Based on his case study of the implementation of performance measurement in the Social Security Administration, Thompson (2000) argues that performance accountability constrains the discretion of administrators. Roberts (2000) argues that performance measurement is a "synoptic" approach to strategic management where top executives plan and implement while having a tendency to ignore political environment or context.

Performance government is based on the ability of public managers to quantify and measure their results. As a measurement-based system of accountability, performance government fails to adhere to "methodological pluralism." In this sense performance government is methodologically narrow-minded. Given its adoption of the economic principles of public choice and the New Right, one would suspect that performance government is ideologically innocent. Implying the notion of performance government ideologically would become more obvious as other theories of governance converge with performance government on the same economic principles.

## III. MANAGERIALISM AND THE NEW RIGHT

Managerial reform in the 1980s in the United States, Great Britain, and Canada was introduced by three conservative leaders with a strong interest in reducing the size of government in their own countries. The three political leaders championed what is often termed as the New Right Movement. This New Right Movement made government administration its primary target. The main strategy of this movement was to portray government administration as inefficient, ineffective, and unaccountable. The goal was to superimpose private sector management tools on public organizations that would get leaner and meaner. Thatcher even went as far as privatizing policy making by delegating this function to right-wing think tanks (Gray, 1995).

Thatcher, Reagan, and Mulroney commissioned private-sector leaders to recommend public sector reforms. These private sector gurus were not sensitive to the notion of popular sovereignty nor to that of constitutional bureaucracy. The respective Rayner, Grace, and Nielsen Commissions were more concerned with reducing the cost of government than improving its performance. For instance, Rayner starts his Commission report by stating that the "two greatest enemies of government operations are paper and tyranny of the past" (Savoie, 1994). This statement only reflects the indifference of this reform engineer to the main purpose of procedures, rules, and controls as key elements of the administration. One of the main consequences of New Right policies has been the ideological resurgence of managerialism as the guiding management trend in the west.

Managerialism is defined as a "set of beliefs and practices, at the core of which burns the seldom tested assumption that better management will prove to be an effective solvent for a wide range of economic and social ills" (Pollit, 1990, p. 4). Managerialism has already affected the public administration of many western countries especially with the rise of the New Right movement in Canada, Great Britain, and the United States. Reform practitioners often looked to the private sector for answers to public sector problems. The Grace Commission and the financial management initiatives sold the idea that efficient techniques used in the private sector would be applicable to the production of services in the public sector.

According to Terry (1998), neomanagerialism is rooted in liberation and market-driven management (also Aucoin, 1990, 1996). Liberation management is "guided by the idea that public managers are highly skilled and committed individuals who already know how to manage" (Terry, 1998, p. 195). Therefore, administrative performance would be improved by tackling the problems of bad systems and red tape.

Pollit (1990) argues that the notion of managerialism is similar to neo-Taylorism and the scientific management movement in the western world. Managerialist approaches started taking shape more than a decade before Pollit wrote his book. Under managerialism, society responds to whatever managements of various organizations can gain in their transactions with each other. This is a complete reversal of the founding principles of the bureaucracy. The bureaucratic organization was designed to serve society and not be served by it. Enteman (1993) argues that under managerialism, managers are engaged in some sort of a complex and hidden conspiracy that enables them to run the country. Enteman is concerned that managerialism is lethal to democracy. It ignores the role of citizens in this process. Voting and political participation are irrelevant in a managerialist state.

The effects of globalization are evident in the spread of managerial principles across the developing and developed world, with different countries implementing different versions Maor (1999) compares the implementation of managerialism in Australia, Canada, the United Kingdom, and New Zealand. He suggests a great difference between the practice in the United Kingdom on one hand and Canada, New Zealand, and Australia. In the United Kingdom, government created "an elite class of executives known as the Administrative Class." In other countries, the New Managers came from the civil service ranks. Although representing an ideological shift to the right, managerialism consistently drove executive decisions into backroom discussions of technical performance.

Some of the major criticisms to managerialism came from academic sources. Academics who valued political accountability feared that this accountability would be replaced by a form of accountability based on numbers and measured results. Managerialism's indifference to traditional values of political accountability was evident in Osborne and Gaebler's (1993) *Reinventing Government*, a book referred to by the then-Governor Clinton as "the blueprint of reforms." Osborne and Gaebler hailed the elimination of public administration policies and procedures as best practices, with such policies and procedures replaced by measures of performance and achieving results.

Government initiatives, practices, and the newest management paradigms suggest empowering bureaucrats. Public service new managerialist practices all flow in the same stream of viewing public servants as managers and not as administrators. Managerialism places no value on the issue of political control of the bureaucracy. Chapman 1990) agrees that most literature on managerialism has generally lightly considered the accountability issue.

There are some criticisms particularly of the role of managerialism and its effect on democratic theory. Terry (1998) and Reed (1999) argue that managerialism conflicts with democratic theory. Managerialism prescribes different relationships between citizens and states and represents a move into market-based government. The emphasis of managerialism is on productive values—essentially economic—and not political values. In this model of government, the public administrator is the policy entreprener and an agent of change (Terry, 1997). Reed (1999) argues that Neo-Managerialism is a combination of Taylorism, Public Choice, and Agency Theory. As such, managerialism is tainted with the same problems of public choice theories in terms of its inability to protect the poor and marginalized who would be repressed by virtue of their powerlessness. This is especially true because under managerialism, these individuals would have no power to affect policy (Farazmand, 2001; Timney and Kelly, 2000).

Managerialism, therefore, is fundamentally an ideological shift from the center to the right. It is a movement of the New Right, which does not vary much from the old right except for its incremental approach to change. It is often accompanied by contracting out, privatization, and reduction in the size of government, measures suggested by the old right among Public Choice theorists. Arguments for such government rightist moves are prevalent in political and economic theories (on this issue, see Downs and Larkey, 1967; Niskanen, 1971; and Savas, 1974).

## IV. PUBLIC MANAGEMENT

Like other subtheories of government such as managerialism and performance government, the New Public Management serves to distinguish the old public administration from the new public management. The documentation of the rise in the field of "Public Management" by Lynn (1996) is another piece of evidence that public administration theory as we knew it has been replaced by current practices of managerialism, reinvention, and empowerment. Lynn quotes Garson and Overman (1983, p. 278) on the list of differences between public administration and public management:

1. The inclusion of general management functions such as planning, organizing, control, and evaluation in lieu of discussion of social values and conflicts of bureaucracy and democracy;
2. An instrumental orientation favoring criteria of economy and efficiency in lieu of equity, responsiveness, or political salience;
3. A pragmatic focus on midlevel managers in lieu of the perspective of political or policy elites;
4. A tendency to consider management as generic, or at least minimize the differences between public and private sectors in lieu of accentuating them;
5. A singular focus on the organization with external relations treated in the same rational manner as internal operations in lieu
6. A strong philosophical link with the scientific management tradition in lieu of close ties to political science or sociology.

What is emerging is a new field closer to the field of business administration than to the field of public administration. The two fields have different "questions" and concerns as Behn (1995) and Kirlin (1996) demonstrate on two different occasions. Public management regards procedural rules as impediments to productivity (Behn,

1995). Public administration of responsibility and accountability to democratically elected officials (Kirlin, 1996).

In the book that guided the Gore Commission findings, Osborne and Gaebler (1993) cite the case where one of the rule books of the Department of Defense was cut down from 400 to 4 pages. The rule book was even totally waived in one pilot project. Regarding such cases as successful is fairly simplistic. What if one of the base commanders makes a wrong decision based on his own values and perceptions as compared to rules? What would this commander be held accountable against? It is only logical to assume that a person could be held accountable in accordance with the rules of his or her office. One can't, at least in the civil service, hold people accountable in accordance with their own values or the values of their superiors.

Not to be mistaken with antidiscretion moves, rules protect the public from the whims of administrators. Immigration officers, for instance, might be more efficient if they were to make decisions based on their personal judgments of immigration applicants and irrespective of any guiding legislation, rules, and procedures. But one can only imagine the damage that could be caused by such discretionary power if it were to be misused by officers to discriminate against people. Indeed, even in the presence of rules and procedures, some officers manage to use their little discretionary power in order to make value judgments that may be interpreted as acts of discrimination.

The distinction between public administration and public management is more than an issue of semantics. In an essay on reforming the United States Civil Service, Heclo objects to referring to civil servants as public managers:

> A public manager is a task-oriented achiever of goals; a civil servant is an official in service to the state and public. A public manager thinks about an organization as a kind of historical vehicle meeting certain goals; a civil servant lives in a world of institutions with historically derived identities and distinctive capacities. A public manager does a job; duties are defined by the managerial task at hand. A civil servant occupies an office; his duties extend beyond any given task and are derived from a shared concept of office.

Some authors argue that the New Public Management brings market economics closer to public sector management. They would also argue that public management has much to learn from private management (Wilson, 1994).

PS2000, the major public administration reform initiative in the Canadian public sector, shares the same blueprint with many administrative reforms in the United States, Australia, and Great Britain. Johnson identifies the problem with the most recent suggested or applied public sector reforms. He argues that

> the heart of the failure . . . was that the advocates of comprehensive reforms did not adequately cope with the question of how the reforms would "fit" in parliamentary government . . . How can reform be made workable in the political environment that government operates in, when every exercise of responsibility, and every answer in the name of accountability, is judged in political terms?

Commenting on administrative reforms in Canada between 1962 and 1991, Johnson argues that reformers tend to overlook the interaction of their proposed reforms with the principles of parliamentary democracy.

Managerial reforms and the shift to the New Public Management have not been consistent with conservative (Republican in the United States and Tories in Canada and Britain, for instance) political leaders. Such reforms have also been endorsed and adopted by the nonconservative leaders in Britain and the United States. Micklethwait and Wooldridge (1996) argue that Blair and Clinton have been equally eager to adopt the managerial ideologies of the New Right in their respective countries. Political leaders adopted this ideology of managerialism and referred to it with different labels. The goals of this newly prevalent ideology extend beyond the confines of administration. Indeed, theories of governance represent little less than an all-out war against government and the public administration that serves the broad-based public.

## V. SAME WINE, DIFFERENT BOTTLES

Managerialism, Performance Government, and the so-called New Public Management are different manifestations of the invasion of public administration by public choice theorists and economists (Farazmand, 1994, 2001). With the exception of a few academic, but ineffective, albeit astute, criticisms, the admission of economics into public administration practice has occurred with no resistance. Public administration schools offered public policy degrees with emphasis on public policy analysis (Stone, 1997; Lynn, 1996). Public sector reforms focused on program evaluations and productivity measurement and comparison. Economic reasoning substituted for cognitive reasoning. In other words, political accountability has been replaced by performance and economic accountability. Globalization helped enforce and spread this "system of governance without government, management, or control" (Kettl, 2000, p. 492). The challenge is to be able to examine implications of performance or measurement accountability on shaping the new political system. Here, we examine one particular implication, which is the danger of substituting politics with economics.

"Inspired by a vague sense that reason is clean and politics is dirty, Americans yearn to replace politics with rational decision making" (Stone, 1997, p. 373). With these words, Stone refers to the public tendency to accept reason and denounce politics. This is an explicit goal of many reinvention engineers. In her criticism of the dominance of policy analysis in the field of public administration, Stone takes issue with the rationality of policy analysis and refers to it as "reasoning by calculation." This reasoning by calculation "rests on estimating the consequences of actions, attaching values to the consequences, and calculating to figure out which actions would yield the best results" (Stone, 1997, p. 375). Martin and Kettner (1996) hail performance measurement as the "New Accountability" with the ability to incorporate three accountability perspectives, efficiency, quality, and effectiveness, into one. Martin and Kettner's measurement accountability is precisely what Stone defines as reasoning by calculation.

The effect of performance accountability on the principle of popular sovereignty is one of the more often-cited warnings about replacing politics with measurement. Kettle (2001, p. 492) writes, "shared values, which shaped governmental policies in the past, have yet to emerge. National sovereignty has shrunk along with government's capacity to understand and shape the emerging issues and the conflicts that underlie them." In what Timney and Kelly (2000) call the "demise of popular sovereignty," the notion of performance accountability shuts citizens out of administration (Farazmand, 1999, 2001). Administrative accountability becomes a factor of how well administrative results are quantified and measured. This reduces the role of citizens to that of monitoring measured performance. This is not a far cry from reality. For instance, some states and local governments issue reports on productivity measures to "empower" citizens. The Office of the Auditor General in Canada, the General

Accounting Office, and various inspector generals in the United States conduct performance audits where they measure and make judgments. The major public sector reforms resulting from the actions of the National Performance Review are evidence of this empirical focus. This form of economic rationality precludes the option of deliberation of processes and limits the role of politics and especially the role of citizens.

Zanetti and Adams (2000, p. 534) assert, "theories of governance collectively known as the New Public Management shift the focus from the social contract to the economic contract." They argue that the net result of this subverting of democracy by these new theories is that "democracy receded in importance" and has taken a distant second place "to issues of efficient allocation of services" (p. 550). This certainly is a colonizing factor that eases the globalization of capital (Farazmand, 2001).

In a sense, this notion of performance accountability brings us back to the old and arguably utopian separation between politics and administration (Rosenbloom, 2001; Lynn, 2001). The main difference between Wilson's politics–administration dichotomy and the new theories of governance is that the theories of governance blur the scope of issues that are subject to politics. Under this existing system of governance, politics seems to mean little beyond theatrics, for example, the Condit–Levy affair, the Clinton–Lewinsky affair, and similar scandals. Political debates about health insurance policy, welfare policy, or energy policy in the 1990s are absent from the public eye. Debate of such policy issues occurs in neither the political nor the administrative stages of governing. Public participation has been successfully eliminated from both politics and administration, and that is the true threat to popular sovereignty.

In conclusion, one cannot but remember the words of prominent governance advocates in suggesting that their landmark book on reinventing government is "about governance, not politics" (Gaebler and Osborne, 1993, p. 267). If this is the case, then governance will be unable to ever lead us beyond the "political and social status quo" (Ventriss, 2000). Under this political and social status quo, performance is the focus of accountability and citizens are customers who would merely monitor measured performance (Khademian, 1998; Ventriss, 2000). What more could capitalism want from public administration? Finally, the words of Felts and Jos (2000, p. 520) remind us that this victory of market ideals should not come as a surprise:

> The rise of the new public management has sparked considerable criticism because of its affinity with the private sector and market models generally and has ignited a new round of efforts to sharply distinguish public and private organizations. But this serves to obscure the historical reality that public bureaucracy owes at least part of its ascendancy to the demands of capitalist enterprise.

Indeed, public bureaucracy and the institutions of government have become instruments of globalization of capital, of promoting corporate organizations, of social control, and of establishing and maintaining a hegemonic corporate state (Farazmand, 1999, 2001).

## REFERENCES

Aucoin, P. (1990). Administrative reform in public management paradigms, principles, paradoxes, and pendulums. *Governance* 3(2):115–137.

Aucoin, P. (1996). *The New Public Management: Canada in Comparative Perspective*. Montreal: Institute for Research on Public Policy.

Behn, R. D. (1998). What right do public managers have to lead. *Public Admin. Rev.* 58(3):209–224.

Broom, C. (1995). Performance-based government models: Building a track record. *Public Budget. Finan.* 15:13–17.

Bryson, J. M. (1995). *Strategic Planning for Public and Nonprofit Organizations.* San Francisco: Jossey-Bass.

Carter, N., Klein, R., Day, P. (1992). *How Organizations Measure Success: The Use of Performance Indicators in Government.* London: Routledge.

Chapman, R. (1990). Simple answers, complex problems: Administrative reforms in Australia, 1970–85. In: Kouszmin, A., Scott, N., eds. *Dynamics in Australia in Public Management: Selected Essays..* Melbourne: Macmillan, pp. 200–221.

Cohen, R., Brand, S. (1993). *Total Quality Management in Government: A Practical Guide for the Real World.* San Francisco: Jossey-Bass.

Downs, G. W., Larkey, P. D. (1986). *The Search for Government Efficiency: From Hubris to Helplessness.* New York: Random House.

Drucker, P. (1973). *Management: Tasks, Responsibilities, Practices.* New York: Harper and Row.

Enteman, W. F. (1993). *Managerialism: The Emergence of a New Ideology.* Madison, WI: University of Wisconsin Press.

Farazmand, A. (1999). Globalization and public administration. *Public Admin. Rev.* 59:509–522.

Farazmand, A. (2001). Public organizations in the ages of accelerated globalization. *Public Organ. Rev. Global J.* 1:5–11.

Felts, A. A., Jos, P. H. (2000). Time and space: The origins and implications of the new public management. *Admin. Theor. Praxis* 22(3):519–533.

Gaebler, T., Osborne, D. (1993). *Reinventing Government: How the Entrepreneurial Spirit is Transforming the Public Sector.* New York: Plume Books.

Garsombke, H. P., Schrad, J. (1999). Performance measurement systems: Results from a city and state survey. *Govern. Finan. Rev.* 15(1):9–12.

Garson, G. D., Overman, E. S. (1983). *Public Management Research in the United States.* New York: Praeger.

Gray, J. (1995). The strange death of Tory England. *Dissent, 42* Fall:447–452.

Grizzle, G. A. (1985). Linking performance to funding decisions: What is the budgetor's role? *Public Product. Rev.* 41:33–44.

Halachmi, A., Bouckaert, O. (1996). *Organizational Performance and Measurement in the Public Sector: Toward Service, Effort, and Accomplishment Reporting.* Westport, CT: Quorum Books.

Kettl, D. (2000). The transformation of governance: Globalization, devolution, and the role of government. *Public Admin. Rev.* 60(6):488–497.

Khademian, A. M. (1998). What do we want public managers to be? Comparing reforms. *Public Admin. Rev.* 58:269–273.

Kingsley, J. D. (1944). *Representative Bureaucracy: An Interpretation of the Bristish Civil Service.* Yellow Springs, OH: Antioch Press.

Kirlin, J. J. (1996). The big questions of public administration in a democracy. *Public Admin. Rev.* 56:416–423.

Kopczynski, M., Lombardo, M. (1999). Comparative performance measurement: Insights and lessons learned from a consortium effort. *Public Admin. Rev.* 59(2):124–134.

Koteen, J. (1991). *Strategic Management in Public and Nonprofit Organizations.* New York: Praeger.

Lynn, L. E. Jr. (1996). *Public Management as Art, Science and Profession.* Chatham, NJ: Chatham House.

Lynn, L. E. Jr. (2001). The myth of the bureaucratic paradigm: What traditional public administration stood for. *Public Admin. Rev.* 61(2):144–160.

Maor, M. (1999). The paradox of managerialism. *Public Admin. Rev.* 59(1):5–18.

Martin, L. L., Kettner, P. M. (1996). *Measuring the Performance of Human Service Programs.* Thousand Oaks, CA: Sage.

Melkers, J., Willoughby, K. (1998). The state of the states: Performance-based budgeting requirements in 47 out of 50 states. *Public Admin. Rev.* 58(1):66–73.

Micklethwait, J., Wooldridge, A. (1996). Managing to look attractive. *New Statesman* 125, 125(8):24–25.

Newcomer, K. E. (1998). The changing nature of accountability: The role of the inspector general in federal agencies. *Public Admin. Rev.* 58(3):129–136.

Niskanen, W. (1971). *Bureaucracy and Representative Government.* New York: Aldine-Atherton.

Osborne, D., Gaebler, T. (1993). *Reinventing Government: How the Entrepreneurial Spirit is Transforming the Public Sector.* New York: Plume Books.

Pollit, C. (1990). *Managerialism and the Public Sector: The Anglo-American Experience.* Oxford: Basil Blackwell.

Popovich, M., ed. (1998). *Creating High-Performance Government Organizations.* San Francisco: Jossey-Bass.

Poister, T. H., Streib, G. (1999). Performance measurement in municipal government: Assessing the state of the practice. *Public Admin. Rev.* 59(4):325–335.

Radin, B. A. (1998). The Government Performance and Results Act (GPRA): Hydra-headed monster or flexible management tool? *Public Admin. Rev.* 58(4):307–316.

Reed, C. M. (1999). Managerialism and social welfare: A challenge to public administration. *Public Admin. Rev.* 59(3):263–266.

Riccucci, M. M. (2001). The "old" public management versus the "new" public management: Where does public administration fit in. *Public Admin. Rev.* 61(2):172–175.

Roberts, A. (1997). Performance-based organizations: Assessing the Gore plan. *Public Admin. Rev.* 57(6):465–478.

Roberts, N. (2000). The synoptic model of strategic planning and the GPRA: Lacking a good fit with the political context. *Public Product. Manage. Rev.* 23(3):297–311.

Rosenbloom, D. H. (2001). History lessons for reinventors. *Public Admin. Rev.* 61(2):161–165.

Savas, E. (1974). Municipal monopolies versus competition in delivering urban services. In: Haley, W., Rogers, D., eds. *Improving the Quality of Urban Management.* Beverly Hills, CA: Sage.

Savoie, D. J. (1994). *Thatcher, Reagan, Mulroney In Search of a New Bureaucracy.* Toronto: VTP.

Stone, D. (1997). *Paradox: The Art of Political Decision Making.* New York: W. W. Norton and Company.

Sutermeister, R. A. (1969). *People and Productivity.* New York: McGraw-Hill.

Taylor, F. W. (1911). *The Principles of Scientific Management.* New York: Harper and Row.

Terry, L. D. (1998). Administrative leadership, new-managerialism, the public management movement. *Public Admin. Rev.* 58(3):194–200.

Thompson, J. R. (2000). The dual potentialities of performance measurement: The case of the Social Security Administration. *Public Product. Manage. Rev.* 23(3):267–281.

Timney, M. M., Kelly, T. P. (2000). New public management and the demise of popular sovereignty. *Admin. Theor. Praxis* 22(3):555–569.

Ventriss, C. (2000). New public management: An examination of its influence on contemporary public affairs and its impacts on shaping the intellectual agenda of the field. *Admin. Theor. Praxis* 22(3):500–518.

Vinzant, S. H., Vinzant, J. (1996). Strategy and organizational capacity: Finding a fit. *Public Product. Manage. Rev.* 41(2):139–157.

Walter, J. (2000). Performance-driven government: Using measures to manage. *Governing* 13(4):69–73.

Weber, M. (1946). *From Max Weber: Essays in Sociology.* In: Gerth, H. H., Mills, C. W., eds. New York: Oxford University Press (trans.).

Wechsler, B. (1994). Reinventing Florida's civil service system: The failure of reform? *Rev. Public Person. Admin.* 14(2):64–76.

Wechsler, B., Clary, B. (2000). Implementing performance government: A Symposium Introduction. *Public Product. Manage. Rev.* 23(3):264–266.

Wholey, J. S., Hatry, H. P. (1992). The case for performance monitoring. *Public Admin. Rev.* 52(6):604–610.

Wilson, D. (April, 1994). Is there a new public management. *Parliament. Affairs* 47:315–317.

Wilson, W. (1887). The study of administration. *Polit. Sci. Quart.* 2(2).

Zanetti, L. A., Adams, G. B. (2000). In service of the leviathan: Democracy, ethics and the potential for administrative evil in the new public management. *Admin. Theor. Praxis* 22(3):534–554.

# 18

# The Measurement of Human Services

**RAY GONZALES**

*Rutgers, The State University of New Jersey, Newark, New Jersey, U.S.A.*

## I. INTRODUCTION

Human service, social intervention, or impact programs exist with the explicit intent of ameliorating the effect of a social ill. Examples include: substance abuse and HIV prevention and treatment programs, mental health and crisis counseling, basic services provided to at-risk or needy populations, and job training and placement programs. The nature of these services makes measurement efforts more difficult in comparison to other public services. Consequently, this chapter aims to provide the reader with an understanding of performance measurement as it operates in these organizations, paying special attention to the role of nonprofits, from academic and applied points of view. The chapter maintains that performance measurement in human services is grounded in evaluation because of the importance of causal reasoning in effectiveness arguments. Because this is the case, attention needs to be paid to the evaluation literature when addressing the mechanics of any outcome assessment system. Several recommendations are made to address this in resource-scarce environments. Before starting, it is important to understand some of the history as well as basic concepts that make performance measurement useful as part of a managerial tool.

## II. PERFORMANCE MEASUREMENT

Performance measurement is designed to enhance the performance and accountability of government agencies and programs. Hatry (1999, p. 3) defines it as the "...measurement on a regular basis of the results (outcomes) and efficiency of services of programs." Ammons (1996) situated performance measurement in the context of municipal services, but his account of Peter Drucker's view of effective organizations is appropriate here. Drucker defines a successful service organization by its ability to clearly define the nature and scope of its function, mission, and activities; set clear objectives; set priorities, concentrate on the most important objectives and set standards of performance; measure performance, analyze the results, and work to correct deviations from established standards; and regularly conduct audits of performance to ensure that the management system continues to function properly (p. 10). This description of successful organizations is an illustration of how the concept of performance measurement is woven into a managing-for-results philosophy. Managing-for-results is ". . . a customer-oriented process that focuses on maximizing benefits and minimizing negative consequences" (Hatry, 1999b, p. 3). What constitutes a managing-for-results organization can vary but, most often, public organizations claiming to be results-oriented will do at least some of the following: define goals/outcomes, create measures, benchmark progress, survey clients (customers), include stakeholders in the development of programs, make use of performance-based budgeting, award funds to programs and people based on results, evaluate programs, report results, and use the information to make improvements in programs (See also http://govinfo.library.unt.edu/npr/library/papers/bkgrd/cover.html.)

The idea that performance information be used as a point of comparison to assess progress is the basis of *benchmarking*. It distinguishes itself from performance measurement in that it is the act of establishing standards for a given service or good based on information provided by a performance measurement system (Fine and Snyder, 1999). Adopted from the private for-profit sector, one organization compares itself with another, operationally better (a.k.a., best-in-practice), organization. Organizations mimic the most effective behaviors to enhance performance, and create a more competitive and innovative environment than that which existed in the past. The use of the terms "most effective behaviors" invokes the notion of *best practices*. Best practices are those actions believed to be the most successful regarding providing any given service or good. In the case of public goods provision, *best practices reviews* involve making the best practices public, so that other entities can benefit (Wray and Hauer, 1996).

## A.  Foundations

Depending on the area of the field, the origins of performance measurement can vary. In public administration, performance measurement principles have been around since the managerial modernism of the early 1900s, developing through the 1940s with Herbert Simon and work published by the ICMA. It reappeared again in the 1960s with the concern for evaluating federal social intervention programs. Some place the origins in general management theory inclusive of private and public organizations (Aristigueta, 1999; Easterling, 2000; Ehrenhalt, 1994; Ellis, 1975; Sawhill and Williamson, 2001). Ehrenhalt (1994) and Aristigueta (1999) tie Planning Programming Budgeting System, Zero-Based Budgeting and Management By Objectives, Reinventing Government, and Total Quality Management to performance measurement. In fact, a number of local governments, until recently, grounded their performance measurement systems in something other than managing-for-results.[1] More recently, Congress, via the Government Performance and Results Act (GPRA) of 1993, the Governmental Accounting Standards Board (GASB), the International City/County Management Association (ICMA), the United Way of America, and the Urban

Institute have led in the development of performance measurement systems in federal, state, and local levels of government and nonprofit organizations.

The GPRA, a framework for the management of federal programs, intended to hold federal agencies accountable for the expenditure of public monies by requiring the use of performance measurement, a response to the belief that government is wasteful and inefficient. Managing by making use of performance information should enhance program efficiency, effectiveness, accountability, service quality, customer satisfaction, service delivery, congressional decision making, internal management, and most important, restore confidence in government (Government Performance Results Act, 1993). Federal managers are required to formulate and regularly update strategic and performance plans, and publish program performance reports. There is still an issue as to whether the GPRA has worked but its principles have spread to state and local governments (Ammons, 1996; Aristigueta, 1999; Brooks, 1997; Kearns, 2001), and have become a regular part of federal funding requirements. Discussions with the Office of Personnel Management suggest that federal government measurement efforts are at a crossroads (Kearns, 2001). In the years since implementation of the GPRA, success has been mixed. The cost-reduction implications taken from the National Performance Review forced many federal programs to make reductions in the area of professional evaluation and outcomes assessment. Unfortunately, the GPRA still required performance information. Thus some programs perform monitoring functions under resource constraints. Further still, the data being collected are aggregated at a level so large that the intended aims of measurement systems are missed and inapplicable to smaller offices. Currently the federal government is working to correct the problem by atomizing data sets, making them more applicable to government functioning.

The GASB and ICMA have done much to advance performance measurement at the state and local level. Since the mid-1980s, the GASB, responsible for setting financial reporting guidelines for state and local governments, has stressed efficiency and effectiveness by encouraging governments to engage in Service Efforts and Accomplishment (SEA) reporting. A series of SEA publications were intended to get governments to develop measurement systems in a number of areas from public health to road maintenance. The ICMA's Performance Measurement Consortium reflected quality management principles by beginning under the premise of continuously improving the quality of public services via interjurisdictional comparison. In 1994, 44 municipalities agreed to standardize the application of performance measurement systems in four areas including fire, police, neighborhood, and support services, creating databases from which governments could compare progress. Today, there are over 130 participating municipalities with a number of cities vying to be one of five jurisdictions admitted into the program each year. Unfortunately, research into the role of performance measurement in municipal government is largely descriptive and inconsistent. The most current shows that slightly less than half of all municipalities use performance measures (Poister and Streib, 1999).[2]

In the name of developing nonprofit capacity, the United Way of America has produced training materials for national and community-based organizations, assessed the status of performance measurement efforts in nonprofits (United Way of America, 1998), and stressed the importance of measuring program results in social service provision (United Way of America, 1996). An unfortunate characteristic of nonprofit programs is that their assessment systems are notoriously bad (Edwards and Hulme, 1996; Lipsky and Smith, 1989). Limited resources in conjunction with the high cost of outcome assessment, lack of formal training in evaluation, the difficulty in defining purpose, unclear goals, the inflexibility of program staff, a history of reporting output exclusively, and difficulty in operationalizing abstract outcomes has made measuring performance an undertaking of mamooth proportions. In understanding performance measurement, there is more utility in knowing about its conceptual underpinnings than in looking at history—specifically as those underpinnings reflect private-sector thinking and the field of evaluation.

A survey of *Public Productivity and Management Review* articles shows that performance measurement has received much attention since the late 1980s.[3] Hatry (1999b) believes the recent emphasis on performance measurement has been the result of private-sector thinking seeping into public-sector programs. Almost all contemporary approaches to public management reflect the assumption that what works for the for-profit private entities will work for public organizations, tacitly or explicitly embracing market ideas and viewing public goods in private terms. Managing-for-results, for example (encompassing the concern for accountability, performance, and trust in service provision articulated by the GPRA), conceptualizes taxpayers as "customers." In classic economic theory, the usefulness of the metaphor is dependent upon a direct exchange mechanism. Crudely put, a person pays money for some immediate; and in most instances, quantifiable, benefit or good. The problem, articulated by Samuelson (1954), is that public benefits can be, and often are, diffuse. Thus just because one person pays for a service, that person may not be the only recipient of the benefit. And in some instances he or she may not receive any direct benefit at all. It is this characteristic of public goods that has caused a problem for theorists attempting to marry market analogies to the public sector. The concern is that government attempts to treat citizens as customers, or to conceptualize public goods as private goods, when in many instances, they are anything but these things (see Schachter, 1997 for a theoretical critique of citizen–government conceptualizations). Furthermore, one would think that using performance measures based on erroneous assumptions about the nature of citizen–government relations would render measures impotent or misinterpreted. The success of and approaches to the overall effort are patchy and varied. Privatization has been shown to be successful for some services (Edwards and Hulme, 1996) and either not successful or inappropriate for others. Economist conceptualizations in the area of spatial finance illustrating private-sector concepts in the provision of public goods have met with only indirect evidence speaking to the accuracy of their models (Dowding et al., 1994). And research on the effectiveness of performance measurement systems looks promising in some instances (Bernstein, 2000a) and disconcerting in others (Streib and Poister, 1999).

The other area of interst revolves around the relationship between performance measurement and evaluation. Without evaluation (at least in principle) performance measurement cannot exist, and depending upon the type of service provided, emphasis on evaluation can vary. Typically, in human services the locus of evaluation is the progress or status of an individual or group of individuals. Hence issues relating to causation and methodological rigor become prominent. Many in the field of evaluation (e.g., Dawson and Tilley, 1997; Fetterman, 1997; Sanders, 1997; and Scriven, 1981) take issue with this view of evaluation from a definitional point of view but the fact is inescapable: evaluation and performance measurement in the context of human services must rely on the tenets of social science explanation in order to establish the effectiveness of program activity. The credibility associated with the method (via the natural sciences) makes their use a step short of necessity, even if the evaluation field does not always see it the same way (Stufflebeam, 2001). Thus, to understand the foundations of performance measurement as a practice, one needs to understand evaluation.

Evaluation exists differently in different disciplines and definitions vary to speak to this. The one commonality is that evaluation is the determination of worth. Variations can be slight and are often lengthened to address disciplinary needs (e.g., Aristigueta, 1999; Rossi and Freeman, 1993). Rossi and Freeman's (1993) definition works well for human service organizations in that evaluation is "the systematic application of social research procedures in assessing the conceptualization and design, implementation, and utility of social intervention programs." To assist in defining evaluation, Scriven (1981) discussed it in terms of what it is not. First, evaluation is not exploratory research because it does not lead to the generation of testable hypotheses. Second, it is not research because there is no hypothesis testing. Third, although it is somewhat like measurement (more so than it is like hypothesis testing), the construction of tools is often arbitrary so it remains divorced from the field of measurement. These observations are important because not only have they served to help practitioners and academics think about the evaluation field and how it fits into the social sciences, but they apply to performance measurement, adding clarity to its characteristics and limitations.

Other perspectives distinguish between performance measurement and evaluation by looking at the purposes of each. Wholey and Hatry (1992) and The General Accounting Office (US General Accounting Office, 1998) are in accord in viewing performance measurement as the constant monitoring of program progress and seeing evaluation as more of a resource-intensive summative function relating to end-judgment or, as previously described, determinations of worth. But the point is moot for a couple of reasons. First, similar skill sets are needed regardless of whether outcomes are monitored regularly (stressed in Hatry's (1999b) definition of performance measurement) or summatively. Second, managers generally use monitoring information to evaluate programs anyway (Scheirer and Newcomer, 2001). As a field, evaluation has gone from being a professional practice to a "transdiscipline" (Scriven, 1999). This means that evaluation acquires labels and methodological approaches based on the demands of the field of use. In government activity, evaluation exists under the rubric of *performance measurement* (Holzer, 1992), *outcome monitoring* (Aristigueta, 1999), or *productivity measurement* (Hatry and Fisk, 1992).

## B. Important Concepts in Performance Measurement

To this point, we have tried to minimize the use of performance measurement jargon. However, some concepts relevant to the field of evaluation and performance measurement need to be explained to understand points made later. The terms described below are grounded in *theory-driven evaluation*—a distinct approach to evaluating programs—developed to conceptualize social intervention programs and performance measurement concepts such that there is congruence across initiatives, permitting the sorting of programs and program characteristics at a very broad level. It is highly likely that someone else in this book has already explained this so it will be kept brief.

Input is the resources that go into a program, and can be expressed in terms of the number and/or qualifications of people, amount of money, or time. *Process* or *activities* are the things a program does to achieve its stated goal or goals. *Output* is the direct result of program activity, comprising products and/or services, and countable such as the number of counseling hours provided or the miles of road paved. Output does not necessarily show that a program has achieved its goal (Hatry, 1999b). *Outcomes* are much more complex in their meaning and are discussed in greater detail below, but they can be simply thought of as the consequences of program action. *Performance* indicators are the numerical representations of the various components of a performance measurement program; they can represent input, output, or outcomes. *Outcome Indicators*, closely associated with performance indicators, are characteristics of a person, service, or program that has acquired some benefit, improved condition, or status signifying the achievement of an outcome. Outcomes are divided into multiple forms. The most common are defined either temporally or by locus of attention. When outcomes are defined temporally, they are labeled as *long* or *end, intermediate*, or *short-term outcomes* (United Way of America, 1996). The significance of this grouping allows programs to utilize logic models and map out progress from a big-picture point of view, meaning that programs can identify progress along a temporal continuum. Theoretically, the long-term outcomes represent the achievement of the program goal whereas shorter ones reflect the achievement of milestones. An additional, more useful, conceptualization is possible, however. In this view, outcomes are defined by locus of attention; they can be labeled as either *performance* or *impact outcomes*. Performance outcomes generally reflect organizational goals emphasizing the provision of a service (e.g., increasing the capacity of a program to provide service). This means that a good has been achieved, but usually it is an improvement in organizational or program functioning, rather than a benefit to a client or service recipient. Examples of these include: increased customer satisfaction with refuse removal, increasing the number of enrollees in drug abuse prevention programs, and shortened response time in providing relief services subsequent to or during a critical incident. Impact outcomes are the meaningful benefit received by clients, normally expressed in terms of new knowledge, increased or acquired skill, changed attitude, or improved condition (e.g., the number (or percentage of persons remaining drug free after two years of rehabilitation program exposure). This is the classical definition of an outcome as articulated by the Urban Institute and the United Way of America. In presenting this conceptualization, it may alreadybe in existence somewhere; to date, there have only been suggestive distinctions drawn in the social work literature (Mullen and Magnabosco, 1997). The importance of the aforementioned concepts to the present discussion warrants a detailed example.

There are a number of programs aimed at enhancing the academic performance of at-risk or underprivileged youth to ensure the successful completion of compulsory education. At the federal level, there is the HeadStart program. Through grants or service contracting, personal and academic counseling and tutoring are provided; progress is tracked via teacher reports, standardized tests, and/or report cards. The input of such programs would be people (teachers, counselors, and tutors), the time they spent with the children or engaging in activities, the dollars invested in materials and people, and the facilities used to house the activities. The activities would be the counseling and tutoring services. The output would be the counseling or tutor hours provided or the number of clients participating in the program. The outcomes would be the stated goals of the program: improved attendance (shorter-term outcome), passing into the next grade or increases in grade-point average (intermediate outcomes), or graduation from high school and enrolling in college (long-term). Performance indicators would include the number of federal dollars invested (input), range of activities provided (activities), number of tutoring hours provided (output), and the number of children who increased their grade-point average (outcome/outcome indicator/impact outcome). The performance indicator just described fulfills three conceptual roles. It is an outcome in that it is a consequence (at least theoretically) of program activity; it is an outcome indicator because a child with a high GPA can be considered someone with a better chance of completing school than a child with a low GPA, ceteris paribus; finally it is an impact outcome in that the benefit is experienced by the participant. Meanwhile, a process outcome would be the ability of the program to reduce the number of persons on its waiting list.

In sum, these are the most important facets of theory-driven evaluation/ performance measurment. Most authors adhere to this view, sometimes fine-tuning, but the concepts remain the same. For example, Ammons (1996) believes performance measures take four forms, workload, efficiency, effectiveness, and productivity measures. Workload measures indicate the amount of work performed (e.g., in municipal services, the amount of garbage collected, i.e., output). Efficiency measures express the work performed and the resources required to perform it (usually in numeric terms representing an amount of output for a given input). These are expressed as unit costs, but can be couched in other terms such as cost per-person. Effectiveness measures depict the degree to which performance objectives are achieved or reflect the quality of local government performance (i.e., outcomes). Often they take the form of quantitative assessments of goal achievement (e.g., recidivism rates among rehabilitated inmates or satisfaction levels with fire services). Productivity measures are somewhat more complex and combine efficiency and effectiveness in a single indicator (e.g., the number of accidents per mile of newly paved highway).

## III. THE ROLE OF NONPROFITS

Nonprofit organizations are diverse in type; however, this chapter is concerned only with those providing human services. Consistent with this definition, Lipsky and Smith (1989) describe differences between government and nonprofit organizations. First, nonprofits can attend to client needs before adhering to organizational policies and procedures. Second, nonprofits define their client base in terms of their ability to be successful with them, whereas government defines them with the notion of equity as an organizing principle. Although these differences do not conjure laudable implications for performance measurement, nonprofits do possess some characteristics making them attractive as service providers. They are known for community volunteerism, civic dependability, and a neighbor-helping-neighbor image. In the 1980s and 1990s, they expanded their role by increasing the number of services provided for government. The theoretical advantages were numerous. The proximity of nonprofits to community needs, specialized skill, and expertise allowed government to respond more quickly to social problems than if they were to establish social service mechanisms from scratch. Public officials could also change program direction, at whim, by cutbacks or earmaking funds more easily than in government programs. Government could further take advantage of the credibility associated with nonprofit initiatives, and by purchasing a service, accountability shifted to the nonprofit sector. Finally, government could save money by having nonprofits bid on service contracts. These ideas, grounded in public choice theory, are the driving force behind the privatization of social services (e.g., reduction in the size of government, quality of service and efficiency issues, accountability, etc.). Despite these theoretical arguments for the effectiveness of nonprofits, nongovernmental organizations, and community-based organizations, there is no reliable evidence assessing impact, and what information is available suggests that these organizations do not perform as effectively as once thought (Edwards and Hulme, 1996).

Given the unique role nonprofits play in providing human services, there is value in understanding how performance measurements operates in these organizations and how it has come to be a major concern for nonprofit managers. National human service organizations are applying performance measures, emphasizing outcomes, to social intervention programs (Hendricks, 2000; United Way of America, 1996, 1998). One of the most common responses from the human services nonprofit camp was that their efforts were effective because their caseloads were increasing (Edwards and Hulme, 1996). Their reservations went unnoticed because outcome reporting and evaluation have become a regular requirement for organizations receiving philanthropic dollars, placing a disproportionate amount of weight on the accountability function and reducing the organizational improvement aspects of performance measurement. Also, trends in philantropic giving and government spending priorities invoke economic exchange metaphors such that requests for charitable contributions or tax dollars echo a "grants-as-investment paradigm." (Easterling, 2000; Hatry, 1999a; United Way of America, 1996, 1998). The good provided is in the form of information on the service recipient (or social indicators) status/progress (outcomes), showing a meaningful contribution to society, or the responsible allocation of charitable/public resources. Fine et al. (2000) looked at measurement efforts in nonprofits that regularly monitor performance. They surveyed 178 organizations and found that over half of all evaluation efforts were conducted to assess impact, and fifteen percent did it to improve program planning. Note that these data do not speak to the practices of all nonprofits, only those regularly using performance measurement. Technically speaking, measuring performance in nonprofits is nothing new if one uses the federal government's definition of performance indicators. Nonprofits have been tracking output information for years. The novelty exists in the act of tracking outcome information.

## IV. RESEARCH REVIEW

Examining the writings on performance measurement and evaluation closely, it becomes clear that the purpose are twofold: it serves to strengthen decision-making capabilities among stakeholders (Bernstein, 2000a, 2000b, 2000c, 2000d, 2000e, Epstein and Campbell, 2000; Hoffman et al., 1999; Poister and Streib, 1999; Streib and Poister, 1999), and establish accountability (Ammons, 1995; Bernstein, 2000a, 2000b, 2000c, 2000d, 2000e; Easterling, 2000; Epstein and Campbell, 2000; Fine et al., 2000; Poister and Streib, 1999; Scriven, 1999; United Way of America, 1996, 1998). In some instances it can serve a third function, resource procurement. Authors such as (Chelimsky (1997), Epstein (1992), Halachmi (1992), Halachmi and Bouckaert (1996), and Hatry and Fisk (1992) attempt to artificially increase the number but their divisions are just subcategories of the aforementioned two. For example, Epstein (1992) says evaluation exists to improve decision making, accountability, and performance. Implicit in improved performance is the idea that enhanced decision making occurs during program activity. The point is, very often the functons of evaluation and performance measurement can be explored at length but their purpose ultimately boil down to a few simple principles. This notwithstanding, research explores the status of measurement use (Aristigueta, 1996; Bernstein, 2000a, 2000b, 2000c, 2000d, 2000e; Edwards and Hulme, 1996; Epstein and Campbell, 2000; Fine et al., 2000; Hendricks, 2000; Poister and McGowan, 1984; Poister and Streib, 1999; United Way of America, 1998), and a number of dimensions of system quality (Bernstein, 2000c, 2000e; Bouckaert, 1993; Divorski and Scheirer, 2000; Easterling, 2000; Epstein and Campbell, 2000; Fine et al., 2000; Hatry, 1999b; Hatry et al., 1994; Jennings and Staggers, 1999; Johnson, 1998; de Lance Julnes and Holzer, 2001; Kaplan, 2001; Kirchoff, 1997; Poister and Streib, 1999; Sawhill and Williamson, 2001; Sheehan, 1996; Streib and Poister, 1999; Wholey, 1998; Wray and Hauer, 1997). Unfortunately, almost all this work is descriptive in nature, and there is almost no programmatic research looking at the relationship between measurement and performance.

Accountability in governmental performance measurement efforts operates solely to restore citizens' trust in government. If this is true then the communication of measurement results is essential to this. Poister and Streib (1999) note that less than twenty percent of respondents reported that citizen groups received performance information. Case studies published by the GASB are consistent with this (Epstein and Campbell, 2000; Bernstein, 2000b, 2000c). In nonprofits, it works somewhat differently because of the greater number of funding parties involved. Stakeholders can include governmental bodies, individual donors, foundations, and service recipients. Of interest is that although accountability may be a major concern in philanthropic giving (Easterling, 2000; Fine et al., 2000; United Way of America, 1996), research shows that of those nonprofits that do engage in performance measurement, a little less than half do it for accountability purposes (Fine et al., 2000). Scriven (1999) took a funder's perspective in discussing some of the more subtle accountability issues. In his view, funders want to see whether (1) the intervention is worth what it cost, (2) there are unintended consequences, (3) the methods used in the intervention are appropriate by professional and ethical standards; and (4) there are better ways to do the same thing.

Enhanced decision-making capacity is the other primary consequence of performance measurement. Research shows how the integration of this function can enhance service provision in behavioral health services in the context of a quality management scheme (Hoffman et al., 1999). And in some instances, municipalities use efficiency and effectiveness as organizing principles in structuring assessment systems (Bernstein 2000a, 2000b), devising creative ways (e.g., incentive systems for program managers) to encourage the efficient provision of service (Bernstein, 2000a). This information is illuminating, however, it is also anecdotal. The work that hints at systematic program improvement has other weaknesses. Poister and Streib (1999) surveyed over 1200 administrators from municipalities with populations larger than 25,000 with the intent of learning how cities with centralized performance measurement systems develop and apply their measures. Almost every city surveyed indicated that performance measurement was adopted to make better managerial decisions. Perceptions of "improved quality of decisions" were favorable (approaching eighty percent), and approximately seventy-one percent of jurisdictions believe that performance measurement has resulted in either "substantial" or "moderate" improvement in service quality. In these studies respondents were asked to self-report the impact of performance measures on various aspects of municipal service provision, relying on subjective assessments of program improvement. This is not bad but it lacks a full account because it does not consider the opinions of service recipients in some areas (e.g., improved service quality); what is more, there may be more objective indicators for some of these constructs than self-report items. Research in the area of public economics regularly uses macrolevel datasets to reflect different characteristics of municipal service provision (e.g., per-capita expenditure as a measure of efficiency). Operationalizations such as these will never be able to show that the use of performance measurement results in increased savings, but if used in conjunction with survey research giving evidence at this conclusion, a reasonably strong argument can be made.

The concept of system quality in performance measurement embodies a number of conceptual areas including data and measure quality, procedure, participation, usefulness, and measurement system focus. There is little disagreement but a lot of ideas about what constitutes a quality system. They usually have good measures (Bouckaert, 1993; Sawhill and Williamson, 2001; Sheehan, 1996; Poister and Streib, 1999; Streib and Poister, 1999) and data (Divorski and Scheirer, 2000; Jennings and Staggers, 1999), focused designs (Easterling, 2000; Kaplan, 2001), reasonable expectations of system performance (Easterling, 2000; Sawhill and Williamson, 2001), stakeholder participation (Bernstein, 2000c, 2000e; Bouckaert, 1993; Epstein and Campbell, 2000; de Lance Julnes and Holzer, 2001; Kirchoff, 1997; Wray and Hauer, 1996), adequate resources to collect and analyze data (Hatry, 1999b; Easterling, 2000), enjoy support from management (Hatry, 1999b), and are useful (Fine et al., 2000; Hatry, 1999b; Hatry et al., 1994; Johnson, 1998; Wholey, 1998).

Easterling (2000) says that to have a good evaluation system, set clear and reasonable expectations; use logic models; build evaluation capacity while it is being conducted and have grantors play by the same rules. Sawhill and Williamson (2001) believe organizations need to identify missions that are measurable, maintain simplicity in the measurement process, make measures marketable and appealing to donors, and make use of the organizational improvement, as well as accountability capacities of performance measurement. Fine et al. (2000) argue that the strongest systems document programmatic successes, employ a focused design, provide a tool for program planning, and make use of stakeholders and outside evaluators. Kaplan (2001) believes that good systems place the organizational mission at the heart of an evaluation program. Hatry (1999b) sees quality grounded in four prerequisites relating to data processing, analysis, support from upper management, patience, and time. The commonality in these perspectives resides in four areas. They stress the importance of maintaining focus (at the theoretical level and in terms of measurement), not having unrealistic expectations, incorporating expertise into the system, and understanding the uses of information.

Not to be overlooked is the concept of data quality because it has a substantial impact on decision making and system integrity. Frequently data are judged on their accuracy/validity and reliability. Reliability is more of a measurement issue but it has a direct impact on data quality. The core ideas when thinking about data quality are the control of impurities, understanding the nature of the data, having a plan to guide the data collection process, having clarity about the problem for which data are being collected, constructing ways to report the data, and identifying the types of statistics that may be used prior to data collection (Jennings and Staggers, 1999). Divorski and

Scheirer (2000) identify four approaches to asses and improve data quality at the federal level. The first deals with building organizational commitment to achieving high-quality data. Next, assessing the quality of existing data; and third, responding to those limitations identified during the second phase. Finally data quality needs to be "built into" performance information (p. 83). The demand for evaluation has led to the mass quantification of results in the nonprofit world (Edwards and Hulme, 1996). Due to many limitations on nonprofit capacity most nonprofit data look like propaganda rather than performance information (Edwards and Hulme, 1996; Lipsky and Smith, 1989).

Gregory Streib and Theodore Poister (Streib and Poister, 1999; Poister and Streib, 1999) indirectly took data quality to task by looking at the quality of performance measures. Twenty-six percent of municipalities report "usually" having problems measuring the quality of their services (Poister and Streib, 1999). The remaining areas, focusing on clarity, capability, relevance, and support, are "usually" a problem no more than fifteen percent of the time at most. The other study (Streib and Poister, 1999) departed from the descriptive nature of research by examining the validity of performance measures from a framework developed by Geert Bouckaert, assessing capability, practices, and qualifications of staff in an effort to tap the extent to which measures were a manifestation of organizational goals (validity), a collaborative effort reflecting the input of multiple stakeholders (legitimacy), and the information collected was used in the development of municipal program (functionality). Both studies found many weaknesses in municipal performance measures.

## V.   PROBLEMS IN THE ASSESSMENT EFFORT

It is clear that procedural and content problems pervade performance measurement efforts. At this point, we wish to expand upon some of these problems and present solutions as they reflect activity in human service organizations, beginning with the problems inherent in causal reasoning. From one point of view, program administrators are interested in showing that the activities conducted are working toward the goals (outcomes) established by a steering committee, board of directors, city council, and/or focus group. Managers have to show that their program is causing intended, and at the very least unintended, benefits to be experienced by program participants. In the social sciences, there is a variety of ways to explain events, including functional, structural, materialistic, and rational choice explanations. Often, when using one or more of these approaches, a causal elements is involved such that a given outcome can be attributed to (or is the result of) some other process or event that came before it. Asserting a causal relationship involves meeting several criteria: first, a claimant must be able to say that two things are related; second, there must be an element of time-order involved; and finally, there must be nothing else affecting the explanandum (what is being explained) other than the explanans (what is believed to do the explaining). This final requirement is known as the criterion of *nonspuriousness* (Singleton et al., 1993). To say that a causal relationship is spurious is to say that something else, other than the explanans is affecting the explanandum. Although the aforementioned perspective seems obvious, it is the foundation upon which all quantitative (and some qualitative) social science research and outcome assessment exists.

The strength of experiments in the social sciences is measured in terms of how well they adhere to the tenets of causal reasoning described above. A true experiment consists of random assignment, manipulation of some independent variable, a pretest, posttest, and at least one control group. Random assignment means that any given participant has an equal chance of being assigned to either the treatment or control group. This is done to evenly distribute the effects of potentially extraneous (spurious) variables (Toothaker and Miller, 1996). The treatment group is the group upon which the manipulation of the independent variable (the cause) occurs, whereas the control group receives no manipulation. Theoretically, if the two groups are randomly assigned (hence extraneous influences are evenly distributed across both groups) and they receive a pretest prior to manipulation (to determine their level on the dependent variable (where the effect is sought) prior to treatment, and posttest (measurement of the dependent variable) after treatment, then they have met the requirement of a true experiment. Granted, the design could be stronger to eliminate maturation effects, but these are the quintessential elements.

Quasi-experimental designs, on the other hand, are more diverse in type and considerably more relaxed in their requirements. For example, they do not require randomization, or a pretest, and under some circumstances, no manipulation of the independent variable. They do lend themselves well to field research because the bulk of the reasoning process (comparison of one group to another) is intact. Randomized field experiments are usually the preferred way to show cause in evaluation and carry the greatest amount of methodological weight because they adhere to the greatest number of causal explanation requirements. Nevertheless, the biggest problem with quasi-experimental designs is an overreliance on external comparison groups (Dean et al., 1999).

Interrupted Time Series (ITS) utilizes the concepts of counterfactuals and Autoregressive Integrative Moving Averages (ARIMA). There are two approaches to conducting ITS in which the error terms are determined by past research and theory, or by the data set under examination. What is significant about ARIMA is that it was developed in 1975 to enhance the validity of quasi-experimental designs. Often evaluators had to work with datasets not robust to unseen spurious influences or poor control groups (Dean et al., 1999). The idea was that if an indicator of interest could be tracked across time, the manipulation of the independent variable would be visible in the variability of the indicator of interest. This sounds overly simplistic but presently, entire careers are made out of working with this technique (a.k.a., regression analysis, econometric modeling, path analysis). Orwin (1997) provides some good examples of how the method has developed and how it functions in the evaluation field.

Multimethod evaluations operate along the same principle as triangulated research. Multiple approaches (e.g., in-person interviews and secondary data sources) can be used to verify preliminary findings (Datta, 1997). Methodologically independent sources of information serve to validate information on the assumption that any weaknesses in the studies do not influence the results in the same way. Similar to the multimethod approach is cross-design synthesis (Droitcour, 1997), an offshoot of work done in the area of metaanalysis and originally used in medical evaluation. It has three main ideas: for some questions, no single evaluation design will do; work can be stronger if two designs complement each other (in the area of strengths and weaknesses); and a strategy is needed to capture the value of different methods. Apart from first main idea, it smacks of the calculated use of multimethod evaluation.

The larger point is that showing cause in any assessment is difficult because of the compromises in method: stemming from a need to balance naturalism and rigor. There is a large body of work looking at this issue, resulting in imaginative ways to enhance the robustness of findings (See Aiken et al., 1998; Dean et al., 1999; Pituch, 1999; Staines et al., 1999). In the absence of true experiments all method violates, at some level, one or more of the above assumptions and/or processes in causal analysis and, if extreme enough, can nullify outcome claims, undermining the credibility of outcome assessment programs. Hatry (1999b) and others address this weakness, although in lesser detail, and explore others such as the use of social indicators and proxies.

Social indicators are macrolevel statistical representations of some population characteristic. They are of use to many social intervention programs because they can represent the bottom line of program effectiveness. Take HIV prevention programs, for example. In theory, if a prevention program works then the rate at which HIV spreads in the population should slow or stop. Social indicators will not indicate whether it was any given program that caused the reduction, but they can provide intuitive evidence that the program(s) is (are) working. The problem for service providers is that programs are seldom large enough to have an impact on the values of any given indicator because they simply do not serve enough people or are not geographically pervasive enough to mathematically influence the statistical estimates. A problem of another type, although somewhat related, deals with the use of proxies. Proxies are substitutes for a preferred outcome or outcome indicator. To use the same example, we know that it would be difficult for a small program to use social indicators to assess effectiveness, and we further assume that periodic sampling and blood testing of service recipients would not be feasible. A program could track the frequency of unprotected sex and intravenous drug use among participants, instead. The strong statistical relationship between infection and these behaviors means that a reduction of at-risk behavior should correspond to an assuagement of the disease. The problem with proxies is that they are not exactly what is sought so it can make effectiveness claims appear tenuous. Sometimes, it is the best that can be done (for a more thorough discussion, see Hatry, 1999b).

Data collection is as important as measure and data quality, and generally more difficult for human services than for other types of programs (Mowbray et al., 1998). Several authors (Cozzens, 1997; Figueredo and Sechrest, 2001; Hatry, 1999b; Hendricks, 2000; Kopcynski and Lombardo, 1999; Mowbray et al., 1998) identify a number of problems relating to effective data collection:

> Attrition resulting from low participation rates among the target population (e.g., the homeless or minority populations), lack of trust, and previous negative experiences for program participants (Mowbray et al., 1998);
> Problems when trying to collect information on variables for which data quality is notoriously low (sensitive or embarrassing information);
> Length of time it takes human service outcomes to be realized (Cozzens, 1997; Mowbray et al., 1998);
> Maintaining client records (Mowbray et al., 1998);
> Technology (Hatry, 1999b);
> General expense compared to other forms of evaluation and monitoring (Figueredo and Sechrest, 2001; Hatry, 1999b);
> Lack of congruence among funding cycles, length of program funding, and realized outcomes (Cozzens, 1997; Mowbray et al., 1998);
> Maintaining focus on outcomes and not simply collecting information on output (Hendricks, 2000); and
> Using experimental designs in assessing impact (Figueredo and Sechrest, 2001).

Of significance is that these issues are key to defining the evaluative/performance measuring context of human service organizations. If one or more of these challenges is egregious in nature, the impact on data quality is obvious. Fortunately, procedures exist to ameliorate the effects of these problems. The literature provides guidance in terms of identifying elements that are most likely to serve this purpose:

> Presence of a workgroup to oversee the measurement effort (Hatry, 1999b);
> Keeping measures current (Streib and Poister, 1999);
> Enhancing stakeholder involvement in creating measures (Bouckaert, 1993);
> Having a data collection plan (Jennings and Staggers, 1999);
> Taking steps to reduce attrition (Mowbray et al., 1998); and
> Making use of benchmarks and focus groups (Hatry, 1999b).

These reflect both traditional and contemporary views on the procedural elements of human service assessment systems. In theory, they affect data quality and subsequent overall system quality, buttressing causal and effectiveness arguments.

## A.  Issues of Concern to Nonprofits

The special nature of nonprofit organizations in providing human services makes some challenges, particularly relevant. We are hesitant to mention all of the obstacles because some might think it a "lost cause" and decide to study something else. Nevertheless, using the literature and professional experience, problems have been sorted into four areas relating to organizational/program focus, standards of performance, available help, and measure/data quality.

*Organizational/Program Focus.*  Nonprofits have a difficult time distinguishing among impact, performance outcomes, and output. According to Hatry (1999b) the conceptual similarity between output and outcomes confuses some and often output is reported as outcomes. Hendricks (2000) argues that many nonprofits need to work on maintaining focus on outcomes and organizational goals. Sawhill and Williamson (2001) illustrate how a lack of focus can lead to the selection of an excessive number of indicators, collapsing a performance measurement system entirely, and rendering efforts incomplete. Many agencies do not work through the conceptual elements of an initiative from a theory-driven evaluation/performance measurement perspective. That is, models lack a smooth logical connection among the organizational goals, the activities of the program, measures, output and outcomes. Further still, initiatives tend to set multiple goals for themselves and attempt to assess that many outcomes. The dilemma is that if each activity requires assessment, then the cost of assessment increases with the number of activities. In small nonprofits, this has the effect of pulling resources away from where they are needed, helping service recipients. Hendricks (2000) identifies other problems with target setting including the routine changing of targets to avoid comparison information, creaming, premature target setting (a lack of baseline information), and goal displacement.

*Standards of Performance.*  One time a program, providing counseling services, reported a one hundred percent success rate. This appeared nice until we read further. By their reasoning, a person was counted as a "successful outcome" if he or she received any counseling. Unfortunately, this did not speak to the quality of the counseling, or more importantly, to the result of that counseling. Hence, reported outcomes were not actually outcomes. Events like this are common in nonprofit assessment systems (Hendricks, 2000) and carry with them serious implications for data quality, turning performance information into false advertisement (Edwards and Hulme, 1996).

*Available Help.*   Bozzo (2000) reviewed 26 publications and resources for nonprofits and found materials to be excessively technical and prescribed measurement systems that could not be sustained from within an organization. Consistent with this observation, we had to "strip down" the United Way of American (1996) model to make it digestible to nonprofit employees responsible for monitoring program progress. We simplified definitions and disregarded certain elements of what constitutes an ideal system just to lay the schematic foundation for future learning about outcome assessment. The United Way manual presupposes the existence of large amounts of resources and makes use of an esoteric vernacular that is not readily applicable to some community-based organizations. Furthermore, there was little mention of organizational capacity and a lack of specificity in terms of methodology and decision making. Hendricks (2000) notes how there is no centralized source of information to help nonprofits, and when help is available, it is usually available in service-specific formats. We regularly refer nonprofits to the online resources of the American Evaluation Association (n.d.). Memberships are reasonably priced and come with interesting, high-quality journals. Of particular use is their free discussion group called EVALTALK. Postings can be mind-numbingly off-topic at times but it is a way to gain access to resources and (normally expensive) information relating to outcomes and many of the common problems in performance measurement, from professionals experienced in assessment. There is a searchable archive where organizations can find references to tools and techniques related to outcomes and outcome indicators, which can keep initiatives from "reinventing the wheel" for some constructs.

*Measure and Data Quality.*   It is not uncommon for agencies providing educational services or employment training to assess progress via a standard pre- or posttest format. A number do this incorrectly by assessing perceived skill and/or knowledge acquisition instead of the more appropriate actual skill and/or knowledge acquisition. This amounts to asking a participant, "How much do you think you have learned?" and is a sorry excuse for an evaluation process. Evaluation work looking at the effectiveness of these forms of measures (a.k.a. retrospective pretest methodology) shows that a relationship exists between objective assessors and retrospective pretests (Pratt et al., 2000). For our purposes, this means that if people say they, "Learned a lot," statistically speaking, they probably did. However, looking at the correlation coefficients reveals $r$ values between .2 and .27, accounting for, at most, 8% of the variability in scores. This means that although there may be a relationship, it is a weak one, suggesting that evaluators should find better predictors of objective knowledge.

Problems relating to measure quality are perhaps the most serious for performance measurement purposes because they generate bad data. Using content analysis, Sheehan (1996) assessed the capacity of nonprofit measurement systems in terms of their ability to assess mission statement effectiveness. He found that 90% of nonprofits project making a meaningful change outside the organization (e.g., impact outcomes) on their mission statements, however, only 14% of organizations, with reliable measures, actually possess the ability to assess this type of effectiveness. This means that although nonprofits are saying that they are measuring outcomes, the truth of the matter is something quite different. Further still, this result makes no mention of those organizations with unreliable measures, which, by definition do not assess anything. Initiatives that do not have good measures are not measuring the things they say they are and their reported impact outcomes are rendered baseless. Similarly, a number of initiatives report the achievement of abstract outcomes but have no proof of these accomplishments. The typical scenario is of an agency reporting that their clients are more "self-sufficient" than in the past. However, a statement to this effect is the extent of the proof offered, making no claim about concrete behavior that may be indicative of a person who is "self-sufficient." Other times, outcome information is too perfect. Some initiatives report that their success rate is 100%. Low standards notwithstanding, the one consistent thing in conducting the evaluation of social intervention programs is that nothing is ever 100% effective. Responses to this effect suggest that programs may be developing a creative relationship with the truth.

## VI. CONCLUSION

Conclusions and recommendations in this chapter are presented on two fronts, those for practitioners, and those for academics. For academics, programmatic theory-driven research is needed, especially when looking at the relationship between measurement and enhanced performance. The work in this area shows promise but lacks the elements needed to fortify assertions about the extent to which measurement efforts have improved program performance. Finding objective indicators of efficiency and effectiveness should help with this: explore how performance outcomes relate to impact outcomes in managerial contexts, looking particularly closely at budget-measure interaction. The first twelve GASB case studies danced around the issue, generating a number of worthwhile hypotheses. Communication in the context of local government–citizen relations is an area in need of exploration because it is the vehicle through which one of the primary objectives of performance measurement is accomplished. Research would do well to look at relationships among methods and frequency of performance information exposure, and perceptions of government. Finally, the performance measurement and evaluation literature pertaining to system quality is full of prescriptive information aimed at facilitating the development of viable performance measurement systems. The popular opinion is that good performance measurement systems take time, patience, and commitment to develop (Hatry, 1999b; United Way of America, 1996) or turns on the idea that systems meet predetermined criteria for success (Bouckaert, 1993; Hatry, 1999b; Hatry et al., 1994; Wholey, 1998). Future research should pair up expert opinion with what program managers see as quality measurement systems.

On the applied side, hire a professional or someone with training in evaluation. Chances are pretty good he or she will be able to provide you with higher-quality data than someone without formal training. However, should resources not permit, programs need to select those outcomes and outcome indicators that do the best job of speaking to "effectiveness" as it is conceptualized in the mission accomplishment literature, keeping the assessment effort simple (government programs, and government-sponsored programs will almost always have more resources with which to conduct assessment activities so this may not apply to them). The up-side is that the system can speak to the main point of the program, showing focus and clarity of purpose while saving resources. The down-side is that the assessment effort will not provide a comprehensive view of organization performance, selling the program short to potential funders. If an organization decides to go this route, be aware of both the organizational and program mission-statements when designing the system. Keeping these in mind throughout the process (especially during measure selection) will result in much less wasted effort. Practitioners should be aware of the notion of cause because it is the key to demonstrating program worth. Causality is a simple concept, at times requiring the application of sophisticated techniques to arrive at nothing more than common sense. Some services require greater rigor than others so adjust the effort to the service (often easier said than done). Finally, as public human services are increasingly contracted out to private organizations, more resources need to go to developing nonprofit capacity.

Ultimately the worth of the performance measurement movement will be determined via a multidimensional test relating to the motivating factors behind using it. If it is done for accountability purposes, the primary test is citizen trust, in either government or nonprofit spending practices. If it is done with the intent of enhancing performance, numerical benefit-maximizing and cost-reducing information are needed to argue success, not perceptions of that information. A further indicator can be added for nonprofits: the extent to which measurement efforts have served to fortify pecuniary resources. Other tests relating to the functionality of performance measurement systems are steps along the way to ascertaining success, but are ancillary to our concerns relating to the performance and accountability of public organizations.

## NOTES

1. For example, Winston-Salem, North Carolina situated their program in management by objectives. Tucson, Arizona began using performance measures in the 1970s as a part of its Planning Programming Budgeting System.
2. The results of most studies vary, most likely due to a number of methodological reasons relating to year of the study, definitions and types of performance measurement instruments, and the manner in which performance measurement was operationalized.
3. Two years ago I sorted ten years of *Public Productivity and Management Review* articles to determine the most popular themes in public management research. I never attempted to publish or presentthe information but I identified four themes inclusive of methodological considerations and content areas. I found the case-study method to be the most popular form of research method and decision making, productivity measurement, and Total Quality Management to be the three most popular content areas.

## REFERENCES

Aiken, L. S., West, S. G., Schwalm, D. E., Carroll, J. L., Hsiung, S. (1998). A comparison of a randomized and two quasi-experimental designs in a single outcome evaluation: Efficacy of a university level writing program. *Eval. Rev.* 22(2):207–244.

American Evaluation Association. (n.d.) Available at: http://www.eval.org.

Ammons, D. A. (1995). Overcoming the inadequacies of performance measurement in local government: The case of libraries and leisure services. *Public Admin. Rev.* 55(1):37–47.

Ammons, D. A. (1996). *Municipal Benchmarks: Assessing Local Performance and Establishing Community Standards*. Thousand Oaks, CA: Sage.

Aristigueta, M. P. (1999). *Managing for Results in State Government*. Westport, CT: Quorum.

Bernstein, D. J. (2000). GASB SEA case study: Prince William County, Virginia: Developing a comprehensive managing for results approach. In: *Governmental Accounting Standards Board, Performance Measurement for Government:* In: *State and Local Government Case Studies on Using Performance Measures for Budgeting, Management, and Reporting. Norwalk, CT: Governmental Accounting Standards Board.*

Bernstein, D. J. (2000). GASB SEA case study: Tucson, Arizona: An evolving performance measurement culture. In: *Governmental Accounting Standards Board, Performance Measurement for Government: State and Local Government Case Studies on Using Performance Measures for Budgeting, Management, and Reporting. Norwalk, CT: Governmental Accounting Standards Board.*

Bernstein, D. J. (2000c). GASB SEA case study: City of Winston-Salem, North Carolina: Focusing on government efficiency and public confidence. In: *Governmental Accounting Standards Board, Performance Measurement for Government: State and Local Government Case Studies on Using Performance Measures for Budgeting, Management, and Reporting. Norwalk, CT: Governmental Accounting Standards Board.*

Bernstein, D. J. (2000). GASB SEA case study: Portland Oregon: Pioneering external accountability. In: *Governmental Accounting Standards Board. Performance Measurement for Government: State and Local Government Case Studies on Using Performance Measures for Budgeting, Management, and Reporting.* Norwalk, CT: Governmental Accounting Standards Board.

Bernstein, D. J. (2000). GASB SEA case study: Multnomah County, Oregon: A Strategic Focus on Outcomes. In: *Governmental Accounting Standards Board. Performance Measurement for Government: State and Local Government Case Studies on Using Performance Measures for Budgeting, Management, and Reporting.* Norwalk, CT: Governmental Accounting Standards Board.

Bouckaert, G. (1993). Measurement and meaningful management. *Public Product. Manage. Rev.* 17(1):31–43.

Bozzo, S. L. (2000). Evaluation resources for nonprofit organizations: Usefulness and applicability. *Nonprofit Manage. Leader.* 10(4):463–472.

Brooks, R. A. (1997). Evaluation and auditing in state legislatures: Meeting the client's needs. In: Chelimsky, E., Shadish, W., eds. *Evaluation for the 21st Century*. Thousand Oaks, CA: Sage, pp. 109–120.

Chelimsky, E. (1997). The coming transformations in evaluation. In: Chelimsky, E., Shadish, W., eds. *Evaluation for the 21st Century*. Thousand Oaks, CA: Sage, pp. 1–26.

Cozzens, S. E. (1997). The knowledge pool: Measurement challenges in evaluating fundamental research programs. *Eval. Program Plan.* 20(1):77–89.

Datta, L. (1997). Multimethod evaluations: Using case studies together with other methods. In: Chelimsky, E., Shadish, W., eds. *Evaluation for the 21st Century*. Thousand Oaks, CA: Sage, pp. 344–359.

Dawson, R., Tilley, N. (1997). An introduction to scientific realist evaluation. In: Chelimsky, E., Shadish, W., eds. *Evaluation for the 21st Century*. Thousand Oaks, CA: Sage, pp. 405–418.

Dean, D. H., Dolan, R. C., Schmidt, R. M. (1999). Evaluating the vocational rehabilitation program using longitudinal data. *Eval. Rev.* 23(2):162–189.

de Lance Julnes, P., Holzer, M. (2001). Promoting the utilization of performance measures in public organizations: An empirical study of factors affecting adoption and implementation. *Public Admin. Rev.* 61(6):693–708.

Divorski, S., Scheirer, M. A. (2000). Improving data quality for performance measures: Results from a GAO study of verification and validation. *Eval. Program Plan.* 24(1):83–94.

Dowding, K., John, P., Biggs, S. (1994). Tiebout: A survey of the empirical literature. *Urban Stud.* 31(4/5):767–797.

Droitcour, J. A. (1997). Cross design synthesis: Concept and application. In: Chelimsky, E., Shadish, W., eds. *Evaluation for the 21st Century*. Thousand Oaks, CA: Sage, pp. 360–372.

Easterling, D. (2000). Using outcome evaluation to guide grantmaking: Theory, reality, and possibilities. *Nonprofit Volun. Sect. Quart.* 29(3):482–486.

Edwards, M., Hulme, D. (1996). *Beyond the Magic Bullet*. West Hartford, CT: Kumarian in association with Save The Children.

Ehrenhalt, A. (1994). Performance budgeting, thy name is . . . . *Governing*, 8, 9.

Ellis, L. O. (1975, April). The evaluation of resource usage in the not-for-profit environment. *Woman CPA*, pp. 6–8.

Epstein, P. (1992). Measuring the performance of public services. In: Holzer, M., ed. *Public Productivity Handbook*. New York: Marcel Dekker, pp. 161–194.

Epstein, P. D., Campbell, W. (2000). GASB SEA case study: City of Austin. In: *Governmental Accounting Standards Board, Performance Measurement for Government: State and Local Government Case Studies on Using Performance Measures for Budgeting, Management, and Reporting*. Norwalk, CT: Governmental Accounting Standards Board.

Fetterman, D. M. (1997). Empowerment evaluation and accreditation in higher education. In: Chelimsky, E., Shadish, W., eds. *Evaluation for the 21st Century*. Thousand Oaks, CA: Sage, pp. 381–395.

Figueredo, J. F., Sechrest, L. (2001). Approaches used in conducting health outcomes and effectiveness research. *Eval. Program Plan.* 24(1):41–59.

Fine, T., Snyder, L. (1999). What is the difference between performance measurement and benchmarking? *Public Manage.* 81(1):24–25.

Fine, A. H., Thayer, C. E., Coghlan, A. T. (2000). Program evaluation in the nonprofit sector. *Nonprofit Manage. Leader.* 10(3):331–339.

Government Performance Results Act (GPRA) of 1993. (1993). (Online), Available at: *http://www.whitehouse.gov/omb/mgmt-gpra/gplaw2.html*.

Halachmi, A. (1992). Evaluation research: Purpose and perspective. In: Holzer, M., ed. *Public Productivity Handbook*. New York: Marcel Dekker, pp. 213–226.

Halachmi, A., Bouckaert, G. (1996). *Organizational Performance and Measurement in the Public Sector: Toward Service Effort and Accomplishment Reporting*. Westport, CT: Quorum.

Hatry, H. (1999). Mini-symposium on intergovernmental comparative performance data. *Public Admin. Rev.* 59(2):101–104.

Hatry, H. (1999b). *Performance Measurement: Getting Results*. Washington, DC: Urban Institute.

Hatry, H., Fisk, D. (1992). Measuring productivity in the public sector. In: Holzer, M., ed. *Public Productivity Handbook*. New York: Marcel Dekker, pp. 139–160.

Hatry, H., Gerhart, C., Marshall, M. (1994). Eleven ways to make performance measurement more useful to managers. *Public Manage.* 76(9):15.

Hendricks, M. (2000, February). Outcomes measurement in the nonprofit sector: Recent developments, incentives and challenges. *American Society for Public Administration, Center for Accountability and Performance Symposium on Leadership of Results Oriented Management in Government, Washington DC*.

Hoffman, F. L., Leckman, E., Russo, N., Knauf, L. (1999). In it for the long haul: The integration of outcomes assessment, clinical services, and management decision-making. *Eval. Program Plan.* 22(2):211–219.

Holzer, M., ed. (1992). *Public Productivity Handbook*. New York: Marcel Dekker.

Jennings, B. M., Staggers, N. (1999). A provocative look at performance measurement. *Nursing Admin. Quart.* 24(1):17–30.

Johnson, R. B. (1998). Toward a theoretical model of evaluation utilization. *Eval. Program Plan.* 21:93–110.

Kaplan, R. S. (2001). Strategic performance measurement and management in nonprofit organizations. *Nonprofit Manage. Leader.* 11(3):353.

Kearns, J. (2001). Associate Director, Eastern Management Development Center, Office of Personnel Management, Shepherdstown, WV. Interview, August 16, 2001.

Kirchoff, J. (1997). Public services production in context: Toward a multilevel, multi-stakeholder model. *Public Product. Manage. Rev.* 21(1):70–85.

Kopcynski, M., Lombardo, M. (1999). Comparative performance measurement: Insight and lessons learned from a consortium effort. *Public Admin. Rev.* 59(2):124–134.

Lipsky, M., Smith, S. R. (1989). Nonprofit organizations, government and the welfare state. *Polit. Sci. Quart.* 104(4):625–648.

Mowbray, C. T., Bybee, D., Collins, M. E., Levine, P. E. (1998). Optimizing evaluation quality and utility under resource constraints. *Eval Program Plan.* 21:59–71.

Mullen, E. J., Magnabosco, J. L., eds. *Outcomes Measurement in the Human Services.* Washington DC: National Association of Social Workers.

Orwin, R. G. (1997). Twenty-one years old and counting: The interrupted time series comes of age. In: Chelimsky, E., Shadish, W., eds. *Evaluation for the 21st Century.* Thousand Oaks, CA: Sage, pp. 443–466.

Poister, T. H., McGowan, R. P. (1984). The use of management tools in municipal government: A national survey. *Public Admin. Rev.* 44(3):215–223.

Poister, T. H., Streib, G. (1999). Performance measurement in municipal government: Assessing the state of the practice. *Public Admin. Rev.* 59(4):325–335.

Pituch, K. A. (1999). Describing school effects with residual terms. *Eval. Rev.* 23(2):190–211.

Pratt, C. C., McGuigan, W. M., Katzev, A. R. (2000). Measuring program outcomes: Using retrospective pretest methodology. *Am. J. Eval.* 21(3):341–359.

Rossi, P. H., Freeman, H. F. (1993). *Evaluation: A Systematic Approach.* 5th ed. Beverly Hills, CA: Sage.

Samuelson, P. (1954). The pure theory of public expenditure. *Rev. Econ. Statist.* 36:387–389.

Sanders, J. R. (1997). Cluster evaluation. In: Chelimsky, E., Shadish, W., eds. *Evaluation for the 21st Century.* Thousand Oaks, CA: Sage, pp. 396–404.

Sawhill, J. C., Williamson, D. (2001). Mission impossible?: Measuring success in nonprofit organizations. *Nonprofit Manage. Leader.* 11(3):371.

Schachter, H. L. (1997). *Reinventing Government or Reinventing Ourselves.* New York: SUNY.

Scheirer, M. A., Newcomer, K. (2001). Opportunities for program evaluators to facilitate performance-based management. *Eval. Program Plan.* 21(1):63–71.

Scriven, M. (1981). *The Logic of Evaluation.* Inverness, CA: Edgepress.

Scriven, M. (1999). *The Nature of Evaluation. Part I: Relation to Psychology.* Washington, DC: ERIC Clearinghouse on Assessment and Evaluation (ERIC identifier, ED435710).

Sheehan, R. M. (1996). Mission accomplishment as philanthropic organization effectiveness: Key findings from the excellence in philanthropy project Nonprofit Volun. *Sect. Quart.* 25(1):110–123.

Singleton, R. A., Straits, B. C., Straits, M. M. (1993). *Approaches to Social Research.* 2nd ed. New York: Oxford.

Staines, G. L., McKendrick, K., Perlis, T., Sacks, S., De Leon, G. (1999). Sequential assignment and treatment-as-usual. *Eval. Rev.* 23(1):47–76.

Stufflebeam, D. L. (2001). *Evaluation Models.* San Francisco: American Evaluation Association/Jossey-Bass.

Streib, G. D., Poister, T. H. (1999). Assessing the validity, legitimacy, and functionality of performance measurement systems in municipal governments. *Am. Rev. Public Admin.* 29(2):107–123.

Toothaker, L. E., Miller, L. (1996). *Introductory Statistics for the Behavioral Sciences*. Pacific Grove, CA: Brooks/Cole.

United Way of America (1996). Measuring Program Outcomes: A Practical Approach. Alexandria, VA: United Way of America.

United Way of America. (1998, April). *Update: Outcome Measurement Activities of National Health and Human Service Organizations*. Alexandria, VA: United Way o America.

US General Accounting Office (1998). *Performance Measurement and Evaluation: Definitions and Relationships*. Washington, DC: USGAO.

Wholey, J. (1998). Assessing the quality and usefulness of performance measurement systems. *Public Manage*. 27(3):23.

Wholey, J., Hatry, H. (1992). The case for performance monitoring. *Public Admin. Rev.* 52(6):604.

Wray, L. D., Hauer, J. A. (1996). Best practices reviews for local government. *Public Manage.* 78(1):7.

# 19

# Performance Measurements, Accountability, and Improving Performance

**ARIE HALACHMI**
*Tennessee State University, Nashville, Tennessee, U.S.A.*

## I. INTRODUCTION

Gormley and Weimer (1999, p. 197) suggest that "the organizational report card is only one of several techniques that policy entrepreneurs may employ in the quest for accountability or quality." Allen (1996, p. 11) notes that "continuing pressures for improved accountability and greater value-for-money performance have prompted governments at all levels to recognize the need for program performance measurement. Many jurisdictions, particularly in the United States, even have legislated performance measurement of programs." But, one might ask, are the same schemes for measuring performance for accountability as suitable for facilitating better performance or a greater value for money?

In 1936 Harold Lasswell observed that politics has to do with *who gets what, when, and how* (Lasswell, 1936). In recent years, the *how* in Lasswell's equation was sometimes equated with performance measurement; in other words, performance results determined funding. Although disagreements about what constitutes the proper approaches to performance measurement and the use of it to establish accountability are common, which performance measures can lead to better performance is anybody's guess. The reason is that the availability of information about performance and rate of progress is a necessary condition for improving performance, however, obtaining this performance information is not a sufficient condition to bring about such improvement. At the end of the day, political considerations and pressures from various interests influence funding decisions rather than objective value-free analytical assessments, assuming that such assessments are possible at all. On their face, performance measurements are supposed to protect and isolate decisions about allocation of resources from political pressures by providing objective and undisputed data. In reality, data about poor or superior performance seem to become just another instrument in the battle to influence favorable budget allocations. Thus the political context of performance measurement influences, if not determines, the instrumental value of performance reports to managers, policy makers, and the public at large, let alone professional employees in public agencies and their clients. For that reason, being in a position to influence what is being measured, when, and how, is by itself of political significance.

If performance measurement is just another ball in the political football game, one must wonder whether the cost of performance measurement can always be justified. As noted by Halachmi (2002) there is a question about the extent to which the instruments that foster accountability (e.g., by establishing whether a planned action was carried out as promised) can be as useful for enhancing performance or productivity (e.g., by generating new ideas, innovations, and experimentation for the purpose of assuming a proactive posture or improving performance). With these questions in mind, this chapter asserts that performance measurement may have some serious dysfunctions that should be considered when organizations review existing performance measurement schemes or decide to introduce them in the first place.

The chapter starts by discussing the problematic nature of the need to assess the benefit and cost of performance measurement, paper pointings out, among other things, that although we may seem to agree on the desirability of performance measurements, in principle, we know little about their economic (vs. political or symbolic) benefits and opportunity costs from societal and systemic points of view. The chapter concludes that certain performance measurements can facilitate better accountability but when it comes to improving performance, such measurements can hinder progress, innovation, and experimentation, slowing down adjustment to changing circumstances and adaptations to new situations.

## II.  BETTER ACCOUNTABILITY: SYMBOLIC POLITICS AND REAL VALUES

Sacrificing the margins of an organization's capacity for action or an agency's scope or level of service is often justified in the name of two important values: the need to assure accountability and the need to improve performance. Each of the two values by itself is not controversial, so little attention has been paid to the prospect that for many organizations it may not be possible or affordable to maximize both values at the same time. A case in point is the American Government Performance and Results Act (GPRA) of 1993. As illustrated in Section 2 of GPRA shown below, Congress assumed that more data equal better accountability (see (b)1 and (b)5) while at the same time it can improve performance (see (b)3, (b)4). To understand why this perception, which may or may not be true, is being held as a self-evident truth, one must study the current perspectives on accountability, transparency, governance, and civil society. An in-depth discussion of these things is outside the scope of this chapter, however, a brief examination of some opinions about the notion of accountability may provide some clues.

**Section 2** Findings and Purposes

(a) Findings: The Congress finds that—

 1. Waste and inefficiency in Federal programs undermine the confidence of the American people in the Government and reduces the Federal Government's ability to address adequately vital public needs;
 2. Federal managers are seriously disadvantaged in their efforts to improve program efficiency and effectiveness, because of insufficient articulation of program goals and inadequate information on program performance; and
 3. Congressional policymaking, spending decisions and program oversight are seriously handicapped by insufficient attention to program performance and results.

(b) Purposes: The purposes of this Act are to—

 1. Improve the confidence of the American people in the capability of the Federal Government, by systematically holding Federal agencies accountable for achieving program results;
 2. Initiate program performance reform with a series of pilot projects in setting program goals, measuring program performance against those goals, and reporting publicly on their progress;
 3. Improve Federal program effectiveness and public accountability by promoting a new focus on results, service quality, and customer satisfaction;
 4. Help Federal managers improve service delivery, by requiring that they plan for meeting program objectives and by providing them with information about program results and service quality;
 5. Improve congressional decisionmaking by providing more objective information on achieving statutory objectives, and on the relative effectiveness and efficiency of Federal programs and spending; and
 6. Improve internal management of the Federal Government.

*Source*: Section 2, "Findings and Purposes," Government Performance & Results Act of 1993.

For our purposes here, the prospect that a scheme of performance measurements for better accountability can be equally as useful for improving performance cannot be accepted at face value. Put differently, my claim is that we are not in a position to conclude that a good measurement for better accountability can be as useful for improving performance due to the lack of well-developed polemics about the desired scope, timing, or responsibility for developing and implementing meaningful schemes of performance measurement and report cards for either better accountability or improved performance. At this time we know we do not know enough about the ultimate benefits and costs of performance measurement from a systemic or societal point of view although we tend to agree that performance measurement is desirable.

Little has been said so far in any of the leading publications on public management concerning the opportunity cost of an improved ability to hold officials and agencies accountable. The vast amount of writing on performance measurement and report cards offers few models or algorithms for calculating the tangible or intangible value of the tradeoffs hat result from augmenting the capacity to measure performance or evaluate programs, policies, or whole agencies versus the corresponding reduction in capacity to deliver services. Diminishing an agency's capacity to affect reality in important ways (due to the siphoning of resources from operations to overhead) in return for an improved capacity to enhance accountability, which can be questionable when accountability is only a symbolic value, might be seen as a luxury few communities can afford. The many writings about organizational report cards and performance measurement in recent years extol the virtues of performance measurement and improved accountability (Gormley and Weimer, 1999), but such writings do so without addressing the real and full systemic or social cost in comparison to the proven meager benefits. The reason, I claim, is the unproven assumption that the act of introducing performance measurement always results in enhancement of accountability as a symbolic societal value.

Consider, for example, the tangible and intangible costs and benefits involved in the administration of the matriculation exams at schools and universities so that educators and educational institutions can be held accountable. Some of the resources that might have been applied toward "real" education of students are used instead for underwriting the effort to score well on specific tests that are mandated by an outside agency. The selection of a test and what it should measure is based on a review of what is assumed to be important at that time rather than what might be important in the future, inasmuch as determining the latter is impossible. In each case the test results, as a measure of instruction quality, are expected to help establish accountability of a school, district, or university (and their respective teachers). Yet such test results, even if they are genuine, can tell little about the students' improved education as a result of attending the respective institutions of learning because some students do well in spite of bad teachers. The test scores may tell us how well the students have been prepared for taking specific tests, but even that information is questionable inasmuch as some get extra help outside the classroom (e.g., by attending a Kaplan test preparation program). Most important, tests tell us little, if anything, about students' general education or skills not covered in the tests.

It is important to note that improved accountability does have a social benefit but that this benefit may be marginal and symbolic in comparison to the real values society wants to maximize.

For example, the scores on certain tests, where cheating by students has been helped (if not encouraged) by teachers, were the subject of news reports about Michigan (Walsh-Sarnecki, 2000; Franklin, 2001) and Hong Kong (Hong Kong Mail, 2000). As a result of this mass cheating, test scores turned out to be misleading and thus of no value whatever.

Yet even if they had been valid, they would represent, at best, a questionable benefit in terms of accountability or a help to decision makers and perhaps an even lesser benefit to the students. The reason is that test scores may tell more about students' test-taking skills than about their scholastic gains from taking certain classes. For the students, and thus from the societal point of view, the consumed instruction time (to prepare for the specific test instead of studying important topic(s) not covered in the test) is a "cost" that is not going to be reflected by the test scores. This possible "hidden (or opportunity) cost" along with the bad behavioral example set by the educators involved in Michigan and Hong Kong, was the "cost" of those efforts to enhance accountability through testing. The cost to society, as expressed by educational benefits that are not realized when students have been drilled only for taking a specific test, may exceed the value that was meant to be realized in terms of a marginally better accountability. The purpose of the tests in the cases cited above was to use accountability measures to ensure performance quality, but in reality, both in Michigan and in Hong Kong, the means (i.e., accountability) became a more important objective to attain than the ultimate goal (i.e., better education).

Yet my argument about the ratio of possible (or questionable) benefits to the certain costs of performance measurement must be qualified. It should be noted that in theory, any introduction of performance measurement involves a cost and that the cost results from the siphoning of resources to underwrite more overhead. In practice, however, this may or may not be the case. In practice, the introduction of performance measurement might be an improvement on the previous use of resources, for example, where there is a lot of organizational slack. In such cases, introduction of performance measurement (which becomes a new component of overhead) may not come totally at the expense of operations. It follows in theory that when performance measurement is underwritten by the use of slack resources, it may help reduce waste without affecting performance. If anything, the possible reduction in waste may even improve the utilization of the remaining resources as managers, cognizant of the effort to relate the consumption of resources to outcomes, become more careful about how they use resources across the board. This, in turn, may help the attainment of prescribed goals of economy, efficiency, and effectiveness.

When considering the theoretical prospect that the introduction of performance measurement may improve resource utilization, the reader should consider some possible counterarguments. First, the likelihood that managers will identify, mobilize, or volunteer slack resources for underwriting performance measurement is very low (there are several possible reasons for this, but a complete discussion of them is beyond the scope of this chapter). Second, given the constant reduction in the amount of resources available to public organizations in recent years in comparison to the relative increase in their service load, most government agencies have already been left with very little slack. Thus, even if managers are willing to use slack resources to underwrite new work assignments due to the introduction of performance measurement, they are not likely to be able to tap such idle resources easily.

If accountability, as an important value of governance, is the main reason for the introduction of performance measurement, proponents of such new initiatives face a difficult question. Can organizations address the hazard of trading in some of their important capacity for action in order to enhance the abstract, although desirable and symbolic, values of transparency and accountability? For example, how can a responsible and ethical manager in a human service agency deal with a service recipient who is complaining about a long waiting period to see a care provider? Can that manager minimize the wrath of that service recipient by explaining that in order to make the agency's operation more open to public scrutiny (i.e., more transparent) there was a need to eliminate some caregiver positions in order to underwrite new positions the agency must fill in order to comply with new reporting requirements? From a service recipient's (or professional employee's) point of view, the answer to the question "accountable to whom?" might be very different from what legislators, policy makers, or budgeting or auditing agencies have in mind.

As this writer sees it, at the end of the day, societal interests and benefits are more likely to be a function of the benefits to the service recipient from the use of resources to produce a service than a function of holding officials and the agency accountable or making operations more transparent. The prospect that an agency has done now wrong is not as important, from a systemic point of view, as the prospect that a deserving citizen was deprived of quality service. To use an analogy, the notion that the operation was successful but the patient is dead is not a message of good news.

The current emphasis on accountability is based on a questionable assumption that without outside review and scrutiny public employees may become derelict in their efforts to attain prescribed objectives. Accountability in that sense has to do with the ability to review and verify hard data about performance. According to performance measurement schemes such as the 1993 American GPRA or the 1997 Public Sector Accountability Act (PSAA) of Ontario, Canada, such accountability may result from the comparison of actual performance to the strategic plans that were used to obtain resources in the first place.

Yet, as any long-time student of public administration may recall, there were simply too many cases in which government officials reported what was accomplished as if it were the objective they set out to achieve in the first place. Such practices have been very common during the late 1960s and early 1970s with American programs such as HeadStart or the Teachers Corps (Halachmi, 1973). Acknowledging this practice, Scriven (1972, 1978, 1991) advocated years ago the use of what he called "Goal Free Evaluation" (GFE) over the so-called "Goal Bond Evaluation" (GBE). Goal free evaluation concentrates on establishing the merit and desirability of the obtained result to facilitate decisions about continuation of funding, program modification, or its termination. Goal bond evaluation compares actual performance to the planned one for arriving at the same conclusions.

To ensure that legislatures are carrying out their oversight function as expected by the public, parliamentarians, as articulated in Section 2 of the American 1993 Government Performance and Results Act, wish to get agencies' reports on performance that correspond to the budget requests they submitted in the first place. By facilitating the prospect of accurate comparison of plans to performance, deputies can get involved in micromanagement that may seem to their voters as constituency service and which they are likely to bill (though it might be misleading!) as a pursuit of the public interest. By comparing planned action to delivery, they can avoid the need to take a position on whether a given achievement is very positive or not so good. As pointed out elsewhere (Halachmi, 1998), politicians find it easier to address administrative issues than to take a position on matters that involve conflicting interest and ambiguous values.

## III. WHAT IS PERFORMANCE ACCOUNTABILITY?

According to Bob Sendt (2000), NSW Auditor General, in the public sector, shopping around for services is not generally possible. Limited functions—particularly in the budget-funded sector—are subject to competition. Most services are provided free or with limited user contribution, so private-sector providers can exist only where it is possible for them to substantially differentiate their services through quality, access, or status (e.g., private schools), in effect, operate in a separate market. In the private sector, inefficiencies translate into higher prices, leading to market share loss, or reduced profits, leading to shareholder action. Either way, management gets a clear message. Similarly, a reduction in quality of a service or product, unless accompanied by lower prices, will lead to loss of market. For goods and services provided by the public sector, however, market signals are generally weak. Equally, simple bottom-line measures (such as profit/loss) are not that meaningful for much of what government does. Despite these possible difficulties, Sendt (2000) claims, taxpayers have a right to be able to find out if their financial contributions to the State are being used effectively and in a value-for-money manner. Thus discussing the topic of this chapter in a meaningful way requires us to pause and to ascertain what we mean by the term accountability. I suggest that one way of doing it is to examine how it is used in different places in an effort to identify some common themes.

It may be that the most basic notion of accountability as honesty and keeping of the public trust is expressed by the mission statement of the Philippine Foundation for Transparency and Public Accountability Today and Tomorrow, Inc., also known as the TAPATT Foundation Inc., or simply TAPATT. According to TAPATT (2001):

> While other organizations in civil society choose to advocate human rights, anti-crime measures, a gunless society, press freedom, gender equality, environmental protection, freedom from debt, third sex acceptability, animal rights, etc., we choose to concentrate on transparency and accountability in government.
>
> We believe that any credible program to perform government must begin and end with transparency and accountability, in the continued absence of which predatory politicians and public officials, their relatives and cronies, will continue to proliferate and prosper like maggots on a decaying carcass. As citizens and taxpayers of this country, we have the right to demand transparency and accountability in and from government, the present as well as future ones. And we have a responsibility to future generations to make this country work; it is the only country we have.
>
> To this end, we will use the Internet and other means to demand transparency and accountability in government, to force politicians and public officials to be transparent and accountable in the performance of their public duties.

This document embodies some important elements of accountability that can be found in many other documents around the world. It suggests that accountability has to do with communication about the proper management of public assets in the public interest and living up to the public trust. The means for ensuring "good government" according to this mission statement involves openness and easy public access to accounts of government activities. This notion is consistent with the views of James Madison (*The Federalist*, No. 37) when he said that "The genius of republican liberty seems to demand... not only that al power should be derived from the people, but that those entrusted with it should be kept in dependence on the people..."

Barker (2000) suggests that "governmental accountability—that is, the duty of public officials to report their actions to the citizens, and the right of the citizens to take action against those officials whose conduct the citizens consider unsatisfactory—is an essential element, perhaps the essential element of democracy." This general definition of "government accountability" does not offer obvious answers to questions such as: what is subject to reporting to the citizens, how and when (how frequently) should reports be made, and what is unsatisfactory conduct.

Isn't reelection to office a vote that one is found to pass the accountability-to-the-public test? As illustrated by the impeachment of President Clinton, "government accountability," "public accountability," "reporting to the public," or "public satisfaction" are not always clear and precise terms.

According to the Auditor General of NSW (Sendt, 2000), the 1974 Royal Commission on Australian Government Administration (RCAGA) was established at the Commonwealth level to inquire into concerns about the size of government, its administrative inefficiencies, and the lack of accountability of public entities. "The Commission supported expanding the scope of external audit in the public sector to incorporate assessment of economy and efficiency, planting the early seeds for what we know today as performance audit."

It should be noted that said Commission regarded the assessment of program effectivenens as political in nature and thus something that should specifically be excluded from audit (Sendt, 2000). With that in mind, the reader should consider the possible implications for governance, politics, and managerialism of the recent interest in Australia and in other countries to expand the scope of audits and accountability reports to include issues of effectiveness that were left out in the past.

According to Sendt (2000), up until that period when the Commission was compiling its report, the notion of accountability was mainly concerned with a breakdown of input, with a distinct emphasis being placed on any underexpenditure of appropriations and reasons for any variations in the proposed budget from current expenditure results.

According to Sendt (2000), many of the recent changes were brought through reforms in response to greater public demand for improved efficiency, economy, and effectiveness of government programs. Thus he concludes (Sendt, 2000),

> There are indications that in particular it is effectiveness accountability with which the public appears to be most concerned. And this makes sense. It is natural that the public would want to know what results are being achieved with the money they provide. The concept of accountability now firmly and overtly encompasses the notion of account-ability for results or performance.

In Canada (Ontario, 1998), the 1997 Ontario Budget proposed the Public Sector Accountability Act to ensure that each publicly funded organization prepare a specific business plan and that these plans be made available to the Legislature and the public. The Act requires these organizations to report on their financial activities in accord-ance with the recommendations of the Canadian Institute of Chartered Accountants. The Act also requires these organizations to prepare a corporate plan and annual report that details objectives, resources required, and performance against the plan. Benchmarks, against both private and public sector practices, are also required. The PSAA of Ontario resembles GPRA in many ways, such as the stipulations about the developing of business plans and tying annual reporting to them. However, PSAA is similar to both GPRA and the Australian approach as illustrated by the case of NSW (Sendt, 2000) in its emphasis on auditlike examination of records against established standards of bookkeeping.

This notion of accountability as having to do with "accounts" is made clear in the case of British Columbia. According to the Auditor General of British Columbia (British Columbia, 1995),

> Accountability—the obligation to account for responsibilities conferred—is a concept fundamental to our democratic system. It clearly establishes the right of the citizen to know what government intends to achieve on behalf of its citizens and how well it has met its intentions. In British Columbia, it means that government is accountable to the Legislative Assembly for the way in which it manages the power and resources entrusted to it. In turn, the Legislative Assembly, on behalf of the people, is responsible for ensuring that this accountability takes place.

This approach to accountability asserts that accountability is a relationship within a chain or a chain process, that accountability is not between government employees and the public but between government employees and the legislature that is entrusted with an oversight function on behalf of the public. In other words, performance reporting is not a proxy for direct democracy. This notion (and the similarity to GPRA) is clear when one reads the Executive Summary, which goes on to state:

> Over the past year, the Auditor General of British Columbia and the Deputy Ministers' Council have been working together to bring about a focus on results for the range of government activities. This report represents the first step in that process, outlining the basis for an accountability framework—that is, a way of clearly addressing:
>
>> who is accountable to whom and for what;
>> what information should be reported;
>> how much information should be reported;
>> what the quality of the information should be;
>> how the information should be verified;
>> how accountability information should be provided;
>> when accountability information should be provided; and
>> what the Legislative Assembly should do with the information it receives.
>
> In this report, we recommend that accountability information be conveyed between various levels of governing: from the individual to the program level; from the program level to the corporate level; from the corporate level to the government level; and from the government level to the Legislative Assembly, on behalf of the people. We also recommend that accountability be comprehensive in its scope, applying to ministries, Crown corporations, and funded agencies (such as regional health boards and school boards), as well as government as a whole.
>
> We believe an effective accountability framework requires that government be clear about both its intended and actual results. Therefore, the framework should be closely integrated with performance management system that includes:
>
>> clear objectives;
>> effective strategies;
>> aligned management systems;
>> performance measurement and reporting; and
>> real consequences for the success or failure of programs.
>
> This information should cover the range of government activities to allow an assessment of its financial performance, its legal compliance and fairness, equity and probity, and its organizational and program performance. Of course, the type of information and level of detail to be provided would vary according to the level of accountability, but it would be based on the same information a government requires for effective management.

Two years later (Moses, 1997) in British Columbia, the notion of accountability get a much more direct and simple treatment. According to Moses (1997), a ranking Civil Service Commission employee:

> Accountability can be thought of as enforcing or explaining responsibility. Accountability involves rendering an account to someone who has authority over you, such as Parliament or a superior, on how and how well one's responsibilities are being met (including the actions of subordinates), on actions taken to correct problems and ensure they do not reoccur. It also involves accepting personal consequences for problems that could have been avoided had the individual acted appropriately. These could include

formal consequences, such as discipline, or informal consequences such as embarrassment, or effect on your professional reputation.

Moses (1997) elaborates on the issue of personal consequences in connection with accountability and points out the possible confusion that results from the use of related, but imprecisely defined, terms:

> The Task Force uses the term "answerability" to describe a key aspect of accountability, the duty to inform and explain—without getting instructions. Thus, answerability does not include the personal consequences that are a part of accountability. The concept of answerability is sometimes also used in circumstances where full and direct accountability is not an issue. For example, public servants are answerable before parliamentary committees, not accountable to them. And the Task Force would say that public officials are answerable to the public—providing the public with information about their activities.
> But, the Task Force found that too many public servants and members of the public appear to believe that these are old-fashioned values, and that they are changing. There appeared to us to be confusion on issues of responsibility, accountability, answerability and blameability for both Ministers and public servants. As new organizational forms are designed, it is worth thinking about what could go wrong if mistakes are made. This could provide useful discipline in defining how accountability would work in protecting the authority of elected persons in the conduct of government.

In 2001 the Auditor General of British Columbia released a publication, *Auditing for Better Public Sector Accountability and Performance*, that sheds some light on the actual nature of the issue of "accountability" and where it belongs institutionally. The document (Auditor General of British Columbia, 2001) starts by defining the vision for and the mission of the Office of the Auditor General in the following way.

> Our Vision: Making a difference for the people of British Columbia by contributing to accountable and well-performing government
> Our Mission: To serve the Legislative Assembly and the people of British Columbia by providing independent assessment and advice that enhance government accountability and performance

What follows makes clear the purpose and nature of the audit and where it fits institutionally. The document (Auditor General of British Columbia, 2001) goes on to say the following.

> *Accountability and Performance*
> People have the right to be kept informed about government performance. Government today affects the lives of its citizens through a wide range of social and economic activity. For this reason, people have the right to be kept informed about what their government intends to achieve and what it has actually accomplished. Put another way, government must be accountable to its citizens.
> The challenge, however, is that government is large and complex, and the intended results of programs are not always easily explained. Even though the public routinely receives extensive information on government programs and activities, most British Columbians still don't have a clear idea of how well their government is performing at any given time.
> *What is Accountability?*
> Accountability is a relationship between two parties. In the case of government, the contract is between the public and their government: the public gives government the responsibility to govern and manage public resources, and the government in turn is accountable to the public through the Legislative Assembly for its performance. This

concept is fundamental to our democratic system. It establishes the right of a citizen to know what government intends to do and how well it has met its goals.

*The Role of the Auditor General*

The Office of the Auditor General provides a critical link in the chain of public accountability, a role that is both unique and vital to the democratic process of responsible government. The Office's role is to assist the legislature in overseeing the management of public money, by providing independent assessments of, and advice about, government accountability and performance.

Unlike the Auditor General of NSW (Sendt, 2000), the Auditor General of British Columbian in 2001 makes no distinction between issues of efficiency and the political nature of issues that have to do with effectiveness. Thus one cannot avoid pondering whether the issue addressed by the document is the issue of accountability or rather another issue: who is in charge of establishing accountability in British Columbia? In other words, the 2001 document deals with internal politics. The Auditor General of British Columbia in 2001 is consistent with the position of that office in 1995, but the emphasis in the 2001 document on the role of the Auditor General as the instrument of Parliament in establishing and verifying accountability makes it clear that performance measurement is an issue of audit, not of management, that is, performance.

This issue of audit versus performance becomes complicated when one examines the deliberations about accountability at the British Parliament. According to the Report of the Select Committee on the Public Service (1998), accountability to Parliament is, of course, only one aspect of accountability and some witnesses drew specific attention to accountability to the public as a different issue than accountability to Parliament. According to the said report, one witness, for example, spoke about the impact of agencies in this regard.

> Agencies now have very clear targets which are published, they are not just published in business plans, in many cases they are published in local offices around the country, so for the first time, I think, people, customers, clients, whatever you want to call them, can hold the agency to account. You can hold the agency to account and, as a Permanent Secretary, I can too. They have business plans which set out clearly their objectives in the coming year and beyond. They produce annual reports. The chief executives and their senior managers are very much more visible than I think Civil Servants traditionally have been, and I think visibility is an important part of accountability. It is very difficult to hold someone accountable if you cannot recognize them or find them. Management responsibility has been sharpened . . . the chief executives are on fixed term contracts, and whether or not those contracts are renewed will depend upon their performance (Select Committee on Public Service, 1998).

Thus the introduction of agencies (as elements of the accountability chain) appears to have had an impact both on accountability to Parliament and on accountability to the public. This impact, the Report (Select Committee on Public Service, 1998) claims, caused the Committee

> to consider various more specific questions in relation to accountability. Among them were:
>
>> Is there now a consistent approach to accountability throughout the different institutions of the public service?
>> What does accountability cost?

> Is it possible—or, indeed, desirable—to distinguish between policy and operations so as to hold Ministers accountable for policy and Chief Executives accountable for operations within agencies?

While raising additional important questions, the Select Committee Report (1998) does not introduce a new perspective or a new definition of accountability beyond the basic concept of equating responsibility for or before with the results of examining the records, the accounts. The deliberation at the House of Lords does not help us deal with the question of whether performance measurement has to do as much with management as it has to do with audit, that is, whether it has to do with the functional relationships among units of government or between government and the polity or whether it has to do also, to a larger or smaller extent, with progress, innovation, and reforms.

The proposal to enhance the functions of the Philippine Audit Commission (UNDP, 2001) suggests the following.

> One of the characteristics of good governance is accountability. Accountability refers to the imperatives for citizens or key broad-based elites to make public officials responsible for government behavior and responsive to the needs of the citizens. Accountability at the micro level implies that government structures are flexible enough to offer beneficiaries the opportunity to improve the design and implementation of projects. Similarly, outcomes of macro-policies affecting the economy as a whole, ultimately, depend on the support and cooperation of those groups affected. This may necessitate some degree of consultation, ranging from narrowly conceived consultative committees to a broadly-based elected legislature...

> Accountability also means establishing criteria to measure the performance of public organizations as well as oversight mechanisms to ensure that standards are met...Accountability must also include the existence of mechanisms to evaluate the economic and financial performance of public institutions.

This document introduces the element of consultation as a possible element of accountability. This element might help as we attempt to understand accountability in terms of meeting expectations. Although I may be reading into that text something that was not intended to be there, I believe it is important to bring up this point, as it has the potential of broadening the discussion and understanding of performance measurement beyond the limited notion of audit.

As noted by Parasuraman et al. (1988), the measurement of service quality has to do with meeting and exceeding service expectations (Boulding et al., 1993). Meeting service expectations is "audit," but exceeding it has to do with management of performance, productivity enhancement, and so on, which common audits do not, cannot, or should not address.

According to Ayeni (1998), Robert Pyper has rightly observed, "the concept of accountability is often used as a basic benchmark against which systems of governments can be judged. Accountable government is deemed to be good government, and carries with it connotations of advanced democracy." Ayeni (1998) asserts that public accountability is about how those who exercise powers in the name of the public fulfill their duties and obligations, and the process by which they are made to answer and account for their actions. It is about the responsibility of officials and agencies, ways to minimize abuse of power and authority, and strategies to ensure that those in authority comply with acceptable standards, and can be sanctioned whenever necessary. Thus,

Ayeni (1998) concludes, accountability refers to more than a mere duty to provide answers because of its added connotation of the possibility of sanction. It establishes a relationship between the people as "stewards" who entrust their powers and on the other hand for a variety of ends and in different institutional contexts, accountability can be viewed from a range of interrelated perspectives. Ayeni (1998) quotes Pyper again, saying, "The basic information about the matters for which the relevant political and official actors are accountable—their role and personal responsibilities—is a vital key to understanding accountability [that is] to consider the numerous agents and agencies to which [they] might be considered accountable." Accordingly, Ayeni (1998) suggests, some authors have conceptualized accountability from the perspective of its sources, others spoke of a directional model, and yet others have viewed it in terms of process. The direction and the process perspective can be related to what was addressed previously in this chapter as the concern about the chain of responsibility and the information collection (what information? how collected?), respectively.

## IV. CAN MEASUREMENT COMPROMISE PERFORMANCE?

Is it possible that the performance measurement for accountability and for enhanced productivity are inconsistent with each other? In "The Fall and Rise of Strategic Planning," Henry Mintzberg (1994) suggests that strategic thinking and planning are two terms that are not consistent with each other, although many use the term "strategic planning" for both concepts. Strategic thinking involves tacit knowledge of the use of "soft data" and synthesis, and it involves intuition and creativity (Mintzberg, 1994; p. 108). Planning, however, other involves rational and systematic analysis using "hard data." As Mintzberg (1994, p. 108) says, planning is "about breaking down a goal or a set of intentions into steps, formalizing those steps so that they can be implemented almost automatically, and articulating the anticipated consequences or result of each step." Mintzberg's concept of planning is conducive to the way mechanistic (bureaucratic) organizations operate, and his notion of strategic thinking is more consistent with the notion of organic organizations.

My claim here is that performance measurement activities that are meant to facilitate accountability (or transparency) are a natural extension of the logic of planning as articulated by Mintzberg. The generation of performance report cards to enhance performance, on the other hand, is more akin to Mintzberg's notion of strategic thinking. Therefore, studying performance to improve productivity may require a different kind of report card from the kind needed to establish accountability. The possible dichotomy between the attributes of performance measurement (as one of the means for fostering greater accountability) and the attributes of scorecards that are meant to enhance performance may resemble Mintzberg's (1994) dichotomy between strategic thinking and planning. If this analogy is correct, managers and decision makers must decide what they want performance measurement to do; enhance accountability or boost performance. Current management theory and public laws that mandate performance measurement make no allowance for this prospect.

To improve performance, scorecards may have to be different from one agency to another or even for the same agency at different times. Such reports must include the option of saying that even though the organization is very efficient and effective, its mission has become obsolete. These report cards should encourage creativity, innovation, and experimentation, with special rewards for lessons derived from failures.

To improve accountability, however, scorecards must have a consistent content over time and across the board. This notion of performance measurement is consistent with Hatry's (1999, p. 3) definition of performance measurement as "measurement on a regular basis of the results (outcomes) and efficiency of services or programs." To be meaningful scorecards should be based on data that relate expenditures to results (e.g., as is done in SEA reporting), data on customer satisfaction, and data on actual progress to projected performance targets (e.g., as is done under Citizen Charters). Accountability report cards grade organizations on their ability to score well in respect to those dimensions that were considered important in the past, that is, when resources were allocated. Because these dimensions or performance targets may or may not be as important for the future of the agency or society after a while, they may assist with accountability but necessarily with improved performance. The reason is that such reports may not facilitate the efforts to derive lessons that can lead to proactive actions and thus to better future performance.

From managers' points of view, performance reports should be able to grade organizations on their ability to meet the challenges they face as they are toiling to carry out their mission. Unfortunately, most accountability oriented performance measurements, that is GPRA-like schemes that emphasize comparison of planned versus actual achievements, still fall short of meeting this challenge. This, in turn, is raising a question about the justification of the cost for underwriting performance measurement.

## V. IMPROVED PERFORMANCE

One of the symbolic values that is used to justify the current interest in performance measurement is improved performance. This objective is expressed by terms such as economy, efficiency, effectiveness, quality, and responsiveness. The roots of the current interest can be traced to two intellectual efforts to reduce uncertainty about production functions: Scientific Management (Taylor 1911) and the Principal–Agent approach (Halachmi, 1998; Jensen and Meckling, 1976) of neoclassical institutional economics.

Following the teaching of Frederick Taylor (1911), it was accepted that the best way to improve performace was to record and collect data about ongoing activities, subject them to careful analysis, and follow a controlled process of trial and error to isolate or synthesize the "one best way." Although the logic of Taylor's Scientific Management is not disputed, its unpopularity among managers, employees, and unions suggests a possible inherent conflict between the effort to keep records and the effort to improve performance. This can be translated into a possible incongruity between accountability (which involves the generation and keeping of records) and improved performance. Those opposed to Taylor showed concern about the consequences of the prospect of being held accountable. Managers were concerned that data would show that in the past they were inefficient. Employees were concerned that their trade secrets and experience would lose their value and that they would lose control over their work situation as data analysis would help the organization establish a better way of doing things. Unions were concerned that the data analysis would show that each employee could produce more and the number of needed employees was lower than was assumed in the past. In other words, the opposition to Taylorism was not an opposition to progress per se, but a resistance to the process that was going to be used to bring it about—the greater transparency and scrutiny by people who are not involved in getting the job done.

The assumption that improved performance may result from careful analysis of performance data is related to another questionable assumption that alleges that hired hands treat organizational resources differently from how they treat their own. This assumption is a key element of the Principal–Agent approach. According to this perspective (Halachmi, 1998, p. 46; Jensen and Meckling, 1976), the Agent has interests that are inherently inconsistent with those of the Principal and is likely to exploit the asymmetry between the information available to her or him and the performance information available to the Principal. In other words, the Agent is likely to take advantage of the situation to use the Principal's resources to his or her own benefit at the expense of the Principal.

The recent fashion of contracting out is, among other things, an attempt to reduce the informational asymmetry of the involved Principals and Agents. By using a performance contract, the Agent is compensated only when the agreed-upon result is accomplished. In addition to reducing the prospect that the Agent consumes too many resources for delivering the desired results, a performance contract involves sharing the risks or even shifting the risk altogether to the service provider, that is, the Agent. Thus both sides, the Principal and the Agent, are aware up front of the final cost and the expected benefits of entering into the contract. The logic of American Government Performance and Results Act of 1993 (GPRA) is exactly that except that the Principal is the Legislature and the Agents are the various departments that make the Executive Branch remain a public entity.

There is an interesting similarity between the logic of the current quest for better performance through better record keeping, analysis, and performance measurement and the ideas advanced by the Scientific Management and Principal–Agent approaches. This similarity may explain, in part, why so little attention has been paid to the prospect that enhancing accountability may be inconsistent with the effort to enhance performance.

To understand the possible conflict between the effort to promote accountability and the effort to enhance performance, one must recognize that accountability can be established only under conditions of certainty and linearity, that is, when there is some consensus on where things are and where they are expected to be at the end of a given period of time when the report card is compiled. The grades on the report card and the performance measures document the extent of the expected progress, but they leave no room for grading organizations on unplanned achievements. Unless substitutions (that can open the door to all kinds of manipulations) are allowed; for example, when goal free evaluations (Scriven, 1972) are possible, efforts to seize the opportunity to generate such unscheduled improvement does not help with accountability. The GPRA stipulation that strategic plans must be developed before performance measurement is conducted is a good example of this notion of the necessary conditions for establishing accountability. The tests used in Michigan and Hong Kong, where students were caught cheating with the help of their teachers, were developed knowing in advance what the students were expected to know at graduation. Institutions and officials were to be held accountable for achieving prescribed results regardless of how valuable these achievements were going to be to either the individual students or society. In other words, the tests were generated to establish accountability which is past-oriented rather than performance which is future-oriented.

It is true that it is much more complicated to hold a manager accountable at the end of a period when the desired outcomes are not established in advance, but grading managers on actual achievements rather than the planned ones may greatly help to improve performance. Unfortunately, current theory and practice of performance measurement offer no help on how this can be done.

## VI.  CONCLUSION

As I have pointed out elsewhere (Halachmi, 1996), establishng accountability by reference that is limited to the deviation from the "approved" blueprint may be counterproductive. Discouraging anything that is outside the four corners of the contract that is established when the Legislature provides the budget to fund a proposed government program or agency has merit when it comes to accountability. However, when it comes to better productivity, such an approach may be dysfunctional because it may discourage a shift from "doing things right" to the more important "doing the right things." For example, such an approach may work against moving from the production curve that was acceptable to the Legislature (when the budget was approved) to a higher curve that could not have been predicted when the budget proposal was compiled. From the accountability point of view only a move to a higher point of the production curve is allowed. Thinking outside the box or straying outside the envelope may be inconsistent with common notions of accountability within government. Thus measurement for better accountability may discourage a quick translation of organizational learning into new organizational structures, administrative procedures, or redefinition of missions, visions, or performance targets. An overemphasis on scoring high on accountability measures encourages disregard of changing environmental conditions before the evolution of political or social consensus about the "new reality" and the desired way(s) of coping with it. It also discourages analysis of any possible faults in the assumptions that guided the development of the plan because such analysis may not put those involved with the planning in the past in a good light. In other words, performance may suffer when for accountability reasons managers are reluctant to make necessary adjustments to operations in midcourse. Managers who seek an unqualified audit report might be willing to compromise their duty to be proactive and forgo necessary adaptations as circumstances change. They might be doing things right to satisfy the auditors but not the right things from the societal or systemic point of view.

A recent review of the War on Cancer in the United States (Sobel, 2001) illustrates this point. At the beginning of the War on Cancer, a select group of bureaucrats dictated the research agenda, funneling hundreds of millions of dollars into the hypothesis in vogue at the time, cancer-causing viruses. The assumption was that cancer was one disease rather than a multiplicity of diseases, that a single cure was likely, and that success could be measured only by a complete and final victory. Only research grants that incorporated what we know in hindsight were misguided assumptions were funded. Only research results that had to do with the "approved" hypothesis were considered worthy, even though we now know they were worthless.

Under the current approach to performance measurement, generating such research results may have earned the involved parties high marks on their organizational report cards. The performance scorecard for the resulting outcomes of the research from a societal point of view, however, is very low (Sobel, 2001).

The case of the War on Cancer is also a good illustration of the tendency of government employees to cover their tracks. In this case, funding was made available only to those research proposals that were consistent with mainstream science at the time. Improved performance requires innovation and experimentation, whereas the tendency to play it safe (the bureaucratic modus operandi that discourages, in principle, new initiatives and innovation because they might involve additional work for the involved employees), along with the new emphasis on accountability, is sure to stifle creativity and experimentation. Between the forces that foster bureaucratic inertia and the current emphasis on accountability, the "Skunkworks" of Tom Peters (Peters and Waterman, 1982), which made it possible to invent the Post-it™ note at 3M, is unlikely to happen in the public sector. Improved performance is likely to be preempted by the red tape and reporting required for accountability requirements.

To answer the question of whether the same performance measurement schemes can lead to better accountability and to better public productivity one must consider the inherent differences between the two purposes. Some of the main differences between performance measurement for accountability and performance measurement for enhancing productivity (or enhanced performance) are summarized in Table 1.

As can be seen from the table, performance measurement for accountability may not be conductive to breaking away from current practices with the aim of reaching better productivity. By the same token, changing the data that are being collected, experimenting, and innovation can render any effort to establish accountability an impossibility. Thus although performance measurement can help accountability and better productivity, a given scheme might be more conductive to one than the other.

**Table 1**  Accountability Measures vs. Performance Measures

|  | Accountability measurements | Performance measurements |
|---|---|---|
| Orientation: | Historical (past) perspective | Future (proactive) perspective |
| Purposes: | Doing things right | Doing the right things |
|  | Moving to a higher point on the curve | Moving to a higher/different curve |
| Activities involved: | Comparing planned to actual | Experimentation and innovations |
| Data used: | Hard data (predefined) | Hard and soft data as needed or as available |
| Performance graded by: | Accountants, auditors, lawyers, judges, elected officials, professionals, public | Service recipients and providers, programs administrators, elected officials public |
| Ideal | Think inside the box | Think outside the box |
|  | Stay within the "contract" | Break away |

## REFERENCES

Allen, J. R. (1996). The uses of performance measurement in government. *Gov. Finan. Rev.* 12(4):11–16.

Auditor General of British Columbia (2001). Auditing for Better Public Sector Accountability and Performance. Victoria, B.C.

Ayeni, V. O. (1998). *New dimensions in promoting accountability in public administration: International and theoretical overview.* Proceedings of the Workshop on Accountability & Corruption in the Pacific: Evaluating the Roles of Ombudsmen & Leadership Codes, Australian National University, Canberra, 6–7, 9–10.

Barker, R. S., (2000). Government accountability and its limits. *Issues of Democracy: An Electronic Journal of the U. S. Department of State, 5* (2). Available at: http://usinfo.state.gov/journals/itdhr/0800/ijde/barker.htm.

Boulding, W., Kalra, A., Staelin, R., Ziethaml, V. (1993). A dynamic process model of service quality: From expectations to behavioral intentions. *J. Market. Res.* 30(1):7–27.

British Columbia (1995). *Enhancing accountability for Performance in the British Columbia Public Sector.* Auditor General of British Columbia Deputy Ministers' Council. Available at: *http://learnet.gc.ca/eng/lrncentr/online/speech.htm.*

Hong Kong Mail. (2000, October 4). College duo convicted of exam leak.

Gormley, W. T., Weimer, D. L. (1999). *Organizational Report Cards.* Cambridge, MA: Harvard University Press.

Halachmi, A. (1973). Survival and evaluation: Commentators' use of labels. *J. Appl. Behav. Sci.* 9(3):173–194.

Halachmi, A. (1996). Promises and possible pitfalls on the way to SEA reporting. In: Halachmi, A., Bouckaert, G., eds. *Organizational Performance and Measurement in the Public Sector.* Westport, CT: Quorum, pp. 77–100.

Halachmi, A. (1998). Franchising in government: An idea in search of a theory. In: Halachmi, A., Boorsma, P., eds. *Inter and Intra Government Arrangements for Productivity.* Boston: Kluwer Academic, pp. 44–58.

Halachmi, A. (2002). Performance measurement, accountability, and improved performance. *Public Perform. Manage. Rev.* 25(4):370–374.

Hatry, H. P. (1999). *Performance Measurement: Getting Results.* Washington, DC: Urban Institute.

Jensen, M. C., Meckling, W. H. (1976). Theory of the firm: Managerial behavior, agency cost and ownership structure. *J. Finan. Econ.* 3:305–360.

Lasswell, H. D. (1936). *Politics: Who Gets What, When, How.* New York: McGraw-Hill.

Mintzberg, H. (1994). The fall and rise of strategic planning. *Harvard Bus. Rev.* Reprint no. 94107:107–114.

Moses, J. (1997, May 27). *Ethics, accountability and new organizational forms.* Proceedings of the Tenth Annual Public Sector Financial Management Workshop, Civil Service Commission, Victoria, British Columbia. Available at: *http://learnet.gc.ca/eng/lrncentr/online/speech.htm.*

Ontario (1998). *Legislative Proposals to Improve Public Accountability: Status of Recommendations for Amendments to the Audit Act.* Annual report of the Auditor, Office of the Provincial Auditor, Ontario, Canada.

Parasuraman, A., Zeithaml, V., Berry, L. (1988). Servqual: A multiple-item scale for measuring consumer perceptions of service quality. *J. Retail.* 64(1):12–40.

Peters, T:, Waterman, R. (1982). *In Search of Excellence: Lessons from America's Best-Run Companies.* New York: Warner.

Scriven, M. (1972). Pros and cons of goal-free evaluation. *Eval. Comment* 3(4):1–7.

Scriven, M. (1978). *Goal-free evaluation in practice.* Proceedings of the annual meeting of the American Educational Research Association, Toronto, Ontario, Canada.

Scriven, M. (1991). Pros and cons of goal free evaluation. *Eval. Pract.* 12(1):55–76.

Select Committee on Public Service Report. (1998, January). *Summary of General Evidence on the Public Service and the Committee's Conclusions and recommendations: Accountability, House of Lords.* Available at: *http://www.parliament.the-stationery-office.co.uk/pa/ld199798/ldselect/ldpubsrv/055/p srep01.htm.*

Sendt, B. (2000). *Accountability issues in the public sector.* Proceedings of the ICAA Members in Commerce Group. The Audit Office of New South Wales, Sydney.

Sobel, R. (2001, June 18). Volleys in the cancer war. *U.S. News & World Report*, pp.42.

TAPATT. (2001). *Our mission statement.* Available at: http://www.tapatt.org/.

Taylor, F. (1911). *The Principles of Scientific Management.* New York: Harper.

UNDP, United Nations Development Programme (2001). *Proposed preparatory assistance document enhancing the public accountability programme of the Philippine commission on audit.* Available at: http://www.surfsouthasia.org/NEW/SURF/GOV/UNDPPROJ/PHI/97/022.shtm.

Walsh-Sarnecki, P. (2000). *Detroit school accused of cheating on MEAP test.* Detroit: Free Press.

# 20

# The Utilization of Performance Measurement Information

## Adopting, Implementing, and Sustaining

**PATRIA DE LANCER JULNES**
*Utah State University, Logan, Utah, U.S.A.*

## I. INTRODUCTION

Public productivity improvement has been the goal of the many government reform strategies of the last century. Under the guise of a variety of names such as scientific management, PPBS (Planning, Programming, and Budgeting Systems), ZBB (Zero-Based Budgeting), TQM (Total Quality Management), reinventing government, and now management for results, efforts have sought to improve productivity by focusing on accountability, efficiency, effectiveness, and responsiveness (Elden and Sanders, 1996; Berman, 1998). A consistent force in these efforts has been performance measurement. Measurement in the public sector, assessing what government is accomplishing with a given amount of resources, has been touted as the core management strategy for improving productivity since at least 1943 (Ehrenhalt, 1994).

Given this centrality of performance measurement to the improvement of public productivity, it is surprising that the use of performance measures is not as prevalent as one might expect (Berman and Wang, 2000; Greiner, 1996). Instead, using measurement information to improve productivity is often limited to reporting a list of workload measures to embellish budget documents (Hatry, 1996). One is led to conclude, therefore, that, at least when it comes to performance measurement, efforts to improve or reform government, and particularly government productivity, have not fulfilled their potential.

In this chapter we argue that the utilization of performance measurement information is a special case of knowledge utilization and thus its purported lack of use should be examined from a knowledge utilization framework. Building on previous theories, we used a two-stage model of performance measures utilization derived from survey data, and then proceeded to elaborate and verify the model based on data from telephone interviews. This last procedure added one more stage to the original model and shed light on the questions: does performance measurement work and what does it mean to work?

## A.  Government Reforms: In Support of Better Performance?

In analyzing the failures of the many government reform efforts in the United States (141 at the federal level alone between 1945 and 1995 according to Light, 1997), Ott and Goodman (1998) concluded that government reform efforts have problems in common which contribute to their failure. First, reform efforts often contradict and nullify each other. Just as implementation of one reform begins, a new reform is proposed that erodes the support base for the prior one. Second, government reforms are often implemented without conducting any form of systematic pilot testing.

These problems suggest that there has been a lack of fit between organizational needs and prescribed management solutions (de Lancer Julnes, 1999). This is particularly a problem with management reforms that require organizations to develop performance measurement systems. As with the Procrustean bed of Greek mythology, the problem is often one of trying to fit the organization to the proposed solutions rather than the other way around. Lessons from experience repeatedly make clear that this imposition should be avoided (Bobrow and Dryzek, 1987; Fischer, 1986; Pfeffer, 1981; Harvey and Mills, 1970).

Even though these lessons have been recognized and brought into theory, they have failed to have a cumulative force. As a result, we see repeated efforts towards reinventing the wheel of informed practice. Noting this problem, Cibulka and Derlin (1998) have examined the sustainability of performance accountability in state education reform. They contend that sustaining such efforts has proven to be a major problem in the past and question whether the current emphasis of performance accountability at the center of education reform will be more successful than past policies.

Notwithstanding past failures, our repeated attempts to improve government productivity through accountability and efficiency, and the new concerns for transparency and responsiveness, indicate that we believe these are worthwhile goals. Thus if we believe that new efforts such as managing for results, and the Government Performance and Results Act (GPRA) in particular with its emphasis on performance measurement, can contribute to these goals, it is incumbent upon us to come up with appropriate strategies so that these efforts too do not end in familiar disappointment. It is especially important to recognize that achieving these goals will necessitate the utilization of performance measurement information.

## II.  PERFORMANCE MEASUREMENT INFORMATION AS KNOWLEDGE—TOWARD A THEORETICAL FRAMEWORK

The field of knowledge utilization was launched by the recognition, over three decades ago, that social science research often had little impact on policy making. Concerned that public decision makers were not making the best use of available information, scholars sought explanations for this lack of use.

One avenue of explanation, the "two-communities" metaphor, built on the sociological analysis of differences between researchers and policy makers (Dunn, 1980). Another approach involved the recognition that direct or instrumental use of findings was only one form of utilization, with other forms often at least as important (Weiss, 1979, 1997). Other approaches have focused on explaining research utilization in terms of organizations' culture, their political or economic environment (Oh and Rich, 1996; Cohen, 1977; Weiss, 1972), or have used bureaucratic theory and psychosocial approaches to advance the understanding of what constitutes usable knowledge (Rich and Oh, 1994).

These explanations represent steps forward, but they have not produced empirically validated theories or models of knowledge utilization (Rich and Oh, 1994; Wingens, 1990; Bozeman and Bretschneider, 1986). One might respond to the apparent limitation of available theories by claiming that it is inappropriate to expect predictive models in such a complex domain. Alternatively, it is possible that, for a variety of reasons, we have restricted ourselves unnecessarily in our efforts to develop more adequate frameworks (Wingens, 1990; Huberman, 1987, 1989, 1994).

The contention that knowledge utilization theory remains weak can be understood in terms of suggestions for further development that have been offered as the field matured. One suggestion has been to expand the scope of inquiry. According to knowledge utilization scholars, the "two-communities" metaphor, which provided some valuable ways to gain insights when knowledge utilization was created as a field, continues to be the dominant model of inquiry (Wingens, 1990; Nelson et al., 1987; Dunn, 1980). The problem with this simple metaphor, however, is that it often leaves out important contextual factors, namely, social, political, and economic conditions, and individual and information characteristics, because it does not go beyond the cultural differences of the two communities (Stehr, 1992; Wingens, 1990; Holzner and Fisher, 1979; Nelson, 1981). This suggestion that we need to expand the scope of inquiry leads to the important observation that to understand knowledge utilization we need a more comprehensive and systematic approach based on existing substantive theories (Oh and Rich, 1996; Rich and Oh, 1994; Wingens, 1990; Huberman, 1987, 1989, 1994). Although Rich and Oh (1994, p. 86) noted that "there have been a few attempts to understand comprehensively how information is used in the decision making process," they also contended that we still lack a framework that can help assess the role of sets of variables and the causal relationships among them.

Another recommendation for advancing the field is to refine our definitions by moving away from defining utilization as an attitude toward social science research or a perceived need for research (Rich and Oh, 1994). Instead, we need to also pay attention to potential uses of information. This latter point is akin to Weiss's (1997) typology of knowledge use being direct or instrumental versus other types of uses, including enlightenment use. Further refinement of what constitutes knowledge use was suggested by Stehr (1992), who differentiated two types of social science knowledge: practical (or knowledge designed to serve as capacity for action) and action knowledge (or knowledge translated into action). The notion of knowledge as capacity for action means that "it may remain unused or dormant" (Stehr, 1992, p.4). As we take stock of the advances in the field, we find that if the field is to move to the next level, we need to take these insights seriously.

As in other contexts for knowledge utilization theory, the concern here is that public decision makers are not making use of performance measurement information, even when their organization has developed such information (Hatry et al., 1990;

Kamensky, 1995; GASB, 1997; Fountain, 1997; Berman and Wang, 2000). Thus the lack of use of performance measurement information is a particularly helpful case example for the purpose of advancing knowledge utilization theory. In particular, it, (1) allows the systematic assessment in one study of many factors often addressed in isolation, and (2) allows us to expand the meaning of knowledge utilization in a way that suggests reconciliation of past controversies by distinguishing at least three phases of utilization: the initial adoption of a performance measurement system, the subsequent implementation of the system in making decisions, and finally the accommodation and sustained use of the system.

## A.  Performance Measurement in Support of Rational Decision Making

Performance measurement is geared to the production of knowledge that can be used by an organization's stakeholders to make better decisions. Like a program or policy evaluation, performance measurement at its best can provide information (through performance indicators) that would allow users to assess the economy, efficiency, and effectiveness of government, that is, productivity (Hatry et al., 1990; Holzer, 1992). This can provide a rationale for the development of goals and objectives, resource allocation, monitoring results, and modifying plans to enhance performance, making the information useful to management, citizens, and elected officials (Hatry et al., 1990; Colwell and Koletar, 1984). It allows public organizations to be accountable, responsive, and improve planning and budgeting (Berman, 1998).

In the broad sense of the word, performance measurement has long sought to bring more rationality into the decision-making process. The impetus for performance measurement and rational decision making in public organizations started with an effort to improve efficiency—equated with productivity—and the subsequent application of scientific management (Bouckaert, 1992; Martin, 1992). These efforts have continued in many forms, ranging from mandating that public organizations implement such tools as PPBS and cost benefit analysis, to adding new features to performance measurement systems, such as an emphasis on results (de Leon, 1988; Newcomer, 1997). Regardless of the form taken, these efforts have been based on the general assumption that performance improvement can be attained through the adoption of technical and scientific methods. These points are evident in the new performance measurement emphasis on management for results, which is an outgrowth of the private sector's total quality management movement (OEI, 1994; Milankovich, 1990).

In the traditional rational view, organizations are believed to be instruments for efficient goal attainment and the purpose of their managers is to replace "irrationality" with technically rational actions (Perrow, 1972; Fischer, 1986). The orientation of this model is mechanistic in that organizations are viewed as made of different parts which can be modified by applying rational planning based on scientific analysis to achieve the efficiency of the whole (Gouldner, 1959). As such, based on traditional beliefs, in terms of performance measures, public organizations' adoption and use of performance information will depend on whether certain conditions are present, such as experts in charge, managerial control, systematic standardization, and work fragmentation and mechanization—the principles of scientific management (Howard and Schneider, 1994). As long as the organization has the capacity to produce and process the knowledge, knowledge utilization will occur.

However rational performance measurement is touted to be, a rational view of performance measures utilization may not be helpful on its own at explaining why such information is not more widely used. The experiences of some government organizations that have experimented with performance measurement suggest that the explanation for lack of use is rather complex. They indicate that there are deep issues involved that go beyond the rational or technical factors to include political and cultural issues (Cannon, 1996; Marshall, 1996; Berry and Ikerd, 1996). Thus performance measurement holds promise for developing theories of knowledge utilization for two reasons: the goal is using available information for better decision making; and a variety of factors work against the utilization of performance measurement information. How those factors work is explained in the following section.

## III. FIRST STUDY: PERFORMANCE MEASUREMENT UTILIZATION AS A COMPLEX PROCESS

The first step toward promoting better government through performance measurement utilization is to recognize that utilization is a process much like the processes of innovation and policy change. In a study conducted in 1997 we proposed the notion that initial utilization of performance measurement information is composed of at least two stages—adoption and implementation—each distinctively affected by factors that can be understood in the tradition of the rational/technocratic model and the political/cultural model (de Lancer Julnes and Holzer, 2001). This section provides only an abridged version of the theory used in that study; the reader is referred to the above citation for a more detailed discussion. The findings of this study and of the discussion in the previous section suggested the following general model of performance measurement information utilization presented in Figure 1.

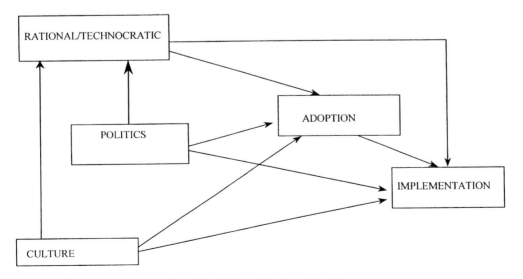

**Figure 1** Suggested general model of the utilization of performance measures.

The distinction between the adoption, or development, of performance measures and implementation, or actual use, can be appreciated if we liken it to Stehr's (1992) distinction of social science knowledge discussed earlier. Adopting or developing performance measures represents developing a capacity to act. The implementation or actual use represents knowledge converted into action. Thus having developed performance measures gives decision makers the ability to use those measures in making decisions that could affect the programs. As with any policy for change, however, when performance measurement moves from adoption to implementation, the effort faces challenges that were either not present or not as predominant at the adoption stage (Cibulka and Derlin, 1998; Palumbo and Calisto, 1990; Cronbach and Associates, 1980).

Let us consider budget decisions as an example. In rational terms performance measurement information, as explained earlier, can help improve this decision process. However, budgets are political struggles in terms of the amounts allocated, which implies an inevitable "win" for some and "lose" for others, and what the budget process itself will be (Miller, 1991; Meld, 1974). Any action that makes a claim against the resources of the organization is political (Pettigrew, 1973). Thus, for example, even if performance measures indicate that a program is not efficient, if it serves a strong group, the agency may not only fail in decreasing the program's budget "but may actually see the appropriations increased as this threat mobilizes the affected interests" (Wildavsky, 1988, p.74).

We developed the points made above by proposing and finding that rational/ technocratic factors—resources (data, people, time, benchmarks), information about performance measurement (workshops, conferences, and publications), and goal orientation—are particularly important in influencing the adoption stage of performance measures (de Lancer Julnes and Holzer, 2001). On the other hand, political and cultural factors such as support from elected officials and citizens, having incentives and openness to change, have a preponderance of influence on implementation, the stage with the greater risk to political agendas.

In theory, performance measurement is supposed to provide organizations with the knowledge to change the way they do business. However, as implied by Korman and Glennerster (1985) policy makers do not necessarily expect policies for change to be implemented. They are in many ways enacted to satisfy some political pressure. Thus public servants "know that they need not strain themselves too hard to achieve results" (Korman and Glennerster, 1985, p.7). Therefore, by looking at performance measurement as a process we are better able to focus our attention on developing strategies for success that are appropriate for each stage of the process. In what follows, we briefly describe the methodology used to collect and analyze the data and discuss the structural linkages suggested by the findings.

## A.  Methodology

The study presented in this section is based on self-reported data from a questionnaire mailed to 704 state and local government employees who responded to a national survey conducted by the GASB in 1996. The questionnaire was also sent to a random sample of those employees who did not respond to the GASB's survey. In total, 934 questionnaires were mailed. Of those, we received 513 completed responses for a 55% response rate.

With a few exceptions, all the variables are factors identified through factor analyses. These factors were then used in regression analyses to estimate the relationships presented earlier in Figure 1. The components of the model are summarized in Appendix I.

## B. Structural Linkages and Discussion

Figure 2 shows the structural linkages of the model suggested by de Lancer Julnes and Holzer's (2001) research. It is an estimated path model explaining the utilization of performance measures. This figure shows the mechanisms by which different factors affect adoption and implementation of performance measurement information.

In general, a path model decomposes the total causal effect into direct and indirect effects. The direct effects are calculated by regressing all the variables (those that precede the dependent variable and those that intervene or mediate the relationship between the dependent and independent variable). For example, a direct effect is graphically represented by an arrow going directly from the dependent to the independent variable (of the form: $x \rightarrow y$). Five multiple regression models make up the causal path model presented here. That is, there is a model that explains adoption ($R^2 = .58$), one that explains implementation ($R^2 = .68$), one explaining resources ($R^2 = .62$), one explaining goal orientation ($R^2 = .45$), and another explaining access to information ($R^2 = .29$). Each of these models is significant at less than the .01 level and all factors or variables included in the estimated path model are significant at less than the .05 level.

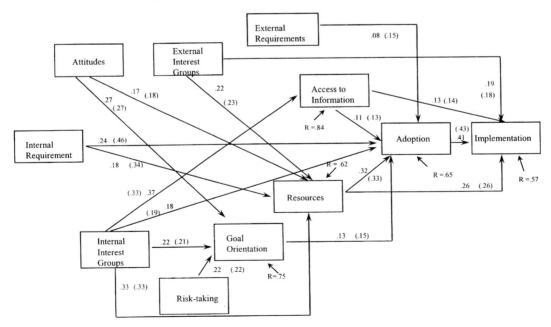

**Figure 2** Estimated path model of the utilization of performance measures. All Factors significant at <.05; the numbers are estimated regression coefficients; number in parentheses are standardized coefficients; R is the residual path coefficient or $(1-R^2)^{1/2}$.

The numbers along the path lines shown in Figure 2 represent the estimated standardized direct causal effect of each factor on each of the outcomes. To help the reader assess the theoretical importance of each factor, unstandardized coefficients are included in parentheses (Achen, 1982).

Indirect or mediated effects, on the other hand, are a result of the sum of the products of the coefficients from the independent variable to the dependent variable through intervening variables (of the form $x \rightarrow m \rightarrow y$). In this example, the value of the indirect path from $x$ to $y$ is obtained by multiplying the coefficient from $x \rightarrow m$ by the coefficient from $m \rightarrow y$. In Tables 1 and 2 below we show both the direct and indirect effects of each predictor factor on the two outcomes and the total estimated causal effect of each predictor for the entire model. For simplicity, only those factors with a direct effect on one of the two main outcomes have been included in the tables.

Even though GASB had found a larger percentage of state departments and counties and a smaller percentage of municipalities reporting developing performance measures, in this study such differences did not appear to be significant at the adoption stage. However, our findings indicate that once adoption has occurred, implementation is more likely at the municipal or city level. This may mean that at the local level, once adoption has occurred barriers to implementation are more easily overcome than at other levels of government. Another reason suggested by Walters (1997) is that states have a harder time tying resource allocation and street-level results because legislators are not used to seeing dollars tied to outcomes.

## 1.  Direct Effects on Adoption and Implementation

As one would expect, adoption has an important and direct effect on implementation. The estimated standardized coefficient shows that this factor has the largest direct effect on implementation with an estimated standardized coefficient of .43. Also, as measured by its unstandardized coefficient (.41), this factor is the most important predictor of implementation. The effects of all other factors are described below.

*Rational/Technocratic Factors.*  Figure 2 shows that all of the rational technocratic factors—resources, goal orientation, and access to information—have a direct effect

**Table 1**  Direct, Indirect, and Total Effects to Adoption

| Factor | Estimated causal effects to adoption | | | |
| | Direct | Indirect via | Total to adoption | Model total |
|---|---|---|---|---|
| External requirements | .08 | | .08 | .11 |
| Internal requirement | .24 | Resources = .06 | .30 | .50 |
| Internal interest groups | .18 | Resources = .11 | .36 | .66 |
| | | Goal orientation = .03 | | |
| | | Access to information = .04 | | |
| External interest groups | | Resources = .07 | .07 | .35 |
| Resources | .32 | | .32 | .72 |
| Goal orientation | .13 | | .13 | .19 |
| Access to information | .11 | | .11 | .30 |

**Table 2** Direct, Indirect, and Total Effects to Implementation

| | Estimated causal effects to implementation | | | |
| --- | --- | --- | --- | --- |
| Factor | Direct | Indirect via | Total to implementation | Model total |
| Adoption | .43 | | .43 | .43 |
| External requirements | | Adoption = .03 | .03 | .11 |
| Internal requirement | | Adoption = .10 | .20 | .50 |
| | | Resources = .05 | | |
| | | Resources and adoption = .05 | | |
| Internal interest groups | | Adoption = .08 | .30 | .66 |
| | | Resources = .09 | | |
| | | Resources and adoption = .05 | | |
| | | Goal orientation and adoption = .01 | | |
| | | Access to information = .05 | | |
| | | Access to information and adoption = .02 | | |
| External interest groups | .19 | Expertise = .06 | .28 | .35 |
| | | Expertise and adoption = .03 | | |
| Resources | .26 | Adoption = .14 | .40 | .72 |
| Goal orientation | | Adoption = .06 | .06 | .19 |
| Access to information | .13 | Adoption = .06 | .19 | .30 |

on adopton. Of the three, the largest direct effect as shown in Figure 2 and Table 1 is from resources, with an estimated standardized coefficient of .32. The second largest standardized effect on adoption is goal orientation (about .13).

In contrast, the figure shows that only two of those factors have a direct effect on implementation, resources, and access to information. The estimated path coefficients are .26 and .13, respectively.

*Politics.* As depicted in Figure 2 both internal and external requirements have direct effects on adoption, but not on implementation, and the effect of internal re- quirements is larger than that of external requirements. The estimated standardized coefficients are about .24 and .08, respectively. The unstandardized coefficient is about .46 ($p < .01$ level) for internal requirements, compared to .14 ($p < .05$) for external requirement.

The factor of internal interest groups is a direct precursor of adoption of performance measures, with a standardized effect of about .18 ($p < .01$). Controlling for adoption, internal interest groups have a negative effect on implementation. However, the effect was not included in the final representation of the model because it did not meet the .05 significance level. Had this structural relation been included in the model, the total effect of internal interest groups would have been reduced to .56 from .66.

The effect of external interest groups, as expected, was found to have a direct impact at the implementation stage of utilization. This political factor has a direct standardized effect of about .18 ($p < .01$).

## 2.  Indirect (Mediated) Effects on Adoption, Implementation, and Total Effect

*Politics.*   Although the external requirements factor has an indirect effect on through adoption, this effect is minimal. Table 2 shows that the indirect effect of external requirements on implementation is just .03, found by multiplying the coefficients in the paths from external requirement to adoption and adoption to implementation (.08 * .43). Overall, of all the factors with a direct effect on adoption or implementation, the factor external requirements appears to have the least explanatory power on the utilization of performance measures.

The effect of internal requirements on implementation, as shown in Figure 2 and in Table 2, is through several paths including the path to adoption and the path to the factor resources, and through the effect that the factor resources has on adoption. The total indirect effect on implementation is .20 (.10 + .05 + .05).

The internal interest groups factor also has an indirect effect on adoption. This indirect effect is due to its explanatory effect on all three rational/technocratic factors. In Table 1 we show that the indirect standardized causal effect is .18. Figure 2 and Table 2 also show that the estimated causal effect of internal interest groups on implementation is through six indirect paths. These paths go through and include access to information, access to information and adoption, adoption, goal orientation and adoption, resources, and resources and adoption; the total indirect effect is .30. Overall, this factor appears to have one of the highest explanatory powers (.66 standardized coefficient) on the utilization (adoption and implementation) of performance measures.

Our findings indicate that the factor external interest groups has a small effect on adoption through its explanatory effect on resources (.07). The indirect effect on implementation is through two paths: resources (.06) and resources and adoption (.03). The total causal estimated effect of external interest group is .35.

*Culture.*   As depicted in Figure 2, the effect of attitudes and risk taking on our two outcomes is primarily through their explanatory power on the rational/technocratic factors (not shown in Tables 1 or 2). The effect of attitudes on adoption is through its explanatory power on resources and goal orientation (.10 unstandardized). The effect of attitudes on implementation, as shown in Figure 2 is through three paths. These paths include resources, resources and adoption, and goal orientation and adoption (.11 unstandardized). Our estimated path model shows that the factor risk taking affects both adoption and implementation indirectly through its effect on goal orientation (.03 and .01 unstandardized, respectively)

## C.  Conclusions from First Study

As indicated by our findings, the factors that influence adoption, or development of knowledge, do not operate in the same manner when it comes to implementing or actually using the knowledge. In this study, the structural analysis indicated that internal factors such as internal interest groups and internal requirement to use performance measures appear to have a direct effect on adoption but only an indirect effect on implementation. In contrast, external interest groups seem to have a direct influence on the actual use of knowledge but a small and indirect effect on adoption.

Attitudes toward change, risk taking, and internal requirements have an indirect effect on the actual use of knowledge mostly through the effect of the rational/technocratic factors and other mechanisms created to facilitate performance measurement. These are contextual issues that must be taken into consideration when analyzing knowledge use.

Although the findings of our model are a good step toward understanding utilization of performance measurement and provide some insights that suggest strategies for supporting the process, the model requires further inquiry for two reasons: the model is tentative, and several questions remain unanswered. Thus verification and further elaboration are necessary. Verification will allow us to assess the extent to which the patterns of responses we found are consistent. It will also help determine whether our interpretations of the responses are appropriate. Elaboration, on the other hand, can give further insight as to what dynamics might be responsible for the mechanisms described here. In addition, further inquiry can help shed light on the challenges that lie ahead of the performance measurement utilization effort and the strategies for overcoming these challenges.

## IV. SECOND STUDY: VERIFICATION AND ELABORATION

In this section we discuss how the previously presented structural model was elaborated and its accuracy in interpreting responses verified. Of particular interest is the fact that this verification and elaboration led to the addition of at least one more stage to the model—sustaining.

## A. Methodology

Although data for the structural model were collected by means of a mailed survey, verification and elaboration were achieved by conducting telephone interviews with 18 state and local government employees. These individuals who agreed to participate were part of a randomly selected group of 75 who were in the sample surveyed in 1997. Respondents held positions such as finance directors, city administrators, budget directors, and legislative auditors.

The interviews lasted anywhere from 20 to 40 minutes depending, in most cases, on whether the organization had developed systematic performance measurement systems. In order to verify and elaborate our model, respondents were asked a series of closed- and open-ended questions that were similar to those asked in the mailed survey of 1997.

## B. Discussion of Findings

### 1. Adoption: Developing a Capacity for Action

As part of the verification process, respondents were asked about the types of performance measures that had been developed in their organization. Table 3 shows the frequency distribution of these measures. Consistent with the 1997 study, input and output measures are the most common form of performance measures developed in public organizations. The second most common are outcome measures, followed closely by efficiency measures.

**Table 3**  Performance Measures Developed

| Measures | Number and percent responding |
| --- | --- |
| Inputs | 15 (83%) |
| Output | 15 (83%) |
| Outcomes | 12 (67%) |
| Efficiency | 11 (61%) |
| Effectiveness | 5 (28%) |
| Other (workload, quality, explanation) | 4 (22%) |

Based on the current and previous findings, we could speculate that adoption itself may consist of several stages. The easiest stages may be developing output and input measures, and the most difficult stages being developing more refined measures such as outcome and efficiency measures. With regard to outcomes, for example, one respondent indicated that it is difficult to develop those measures because "in so many of the programs the clients get away and you can't catch up with them to see what happened."

Notwithstanding the four types of measures identified above, categories that have been recommended by GASB, it is worth noting the possibility that perhaps more organizations have developed these measures but because they give them a different name, such measurement efforts may not be reflected in current performance measurement studies. For instance, at least two respondents indicated that they are moving away from labeling their efforts to quantify or explain activity as performance measurement because the term has a negative connotation. Another comment was that they do not use labels such as outcome, output, or efficiency measures because many people can't tell the difference among them. For that reason, they have resolve to use names like workload, goals, and success indicators.

## 2.  Implementation: Knowledge Converted into Action

Understanding what it really means for performance measures to be implemented is an important part of our verification process. Verificaton of this aspect of our model was attempted in two ways: we asked an open-ended question about use and then went over a list of specific uses that were included in the 1997 survey. That performance measures don't drive decisions but are important and somehow influence action was a common theme among respondents when queried about actual use of the measures. This assertion brings to mind Weiss's arguments about how knowledge can be used in an instrumental way and for enlightenment.

The responses to the open-ended questions fell into two loose categories, political use and rational use. Political use refers to using performance measures for budget-related purposes. Budgets, as explained earlier, are political struggles. In this study, political use or purposes included such responses as justifying funding requests (e.g., for explaining why they need more money, or to show what they've done with the money). Political use also included using performance measures for transparency purposes. In some ways, this type of use seems more closely related to enlightenment because the measures provide awareness and allow for reflection about programs. About 50% of the comments fell in this category.

Rational use, on the other hand, refers to focusing on monitoring the progress toward specific goals, and evaluating performance. This type of knowledge use is called instrumental in the evaluation literature. Respondents spoke of performance measures as giving them the ability to monitor their goal attainment, thus helping organizations move in the right direction. Of all the comments, 38% were in this category.

When respondents were given discrete choices of use, overall, the percentages of reported implementation were lower than those of adoption. Table 4 shows the distribution.

The responses depicted in Table 4 are consistent with those we obtained in the mailed survey. Resource allocation and monitoring were the most often-cited uses. Reporting to citizens or the media was the least often-cited use. The numbers, nonetheless, require certain qualifications because they may appear to contradict our assertion at the beginning of the chapter that substantive use or implementation of performance measurement information is scant.

First, and as an example of elaboration, an analysis matching the discrete responses to the open-ended question indicates that implementing performance measures for resource allocations means that the agency is using the information as part of the budgeting process. Sometimes it is used by executive or legislators to ask questions regarding why a certain target was achieved or not. A respondent stated that "they are used to analyze what's going on in the program and to bring it to the attention of the city council." Another said, "They are also used to explain, not necessarily for decision making." Again, this brings up the issue that implementation need not require instrumental use and, therefore, the fear of performance measurement reported in the literature and by some of the respondents may be greater than the reality. All of the respondents who used the term resource allocation as an example of use of performance measures indicated that if at all used, they are rarely used to cut budgets in cases of poor performance. In many cases, issues such as increased demand for the service drive allocation decisions.

Second, according to the responses from the telephone interviews, implementing performance measures by actually using them in strategic planning really means that the measures are included in their five-year plan as targets. The third qualification is that in terms of reporting to elected officials, respondents stated that this is done through the budget document. That is, the performance measures are part of the

**Table 4** Implementation of Performance Measures: Discrete Choices

| Uses | Number and percent responding |
|---|---|
| Strategic planning | 9 (50%) |
| Resource allocation | 11 (61%) |
| Monitoring of programs | 11 (61%) |
| Reporting to internal management | 8 (44%) |
| Reporting to elected officials | 9 (50%) |
| Reporting to citizens or media | 6 (33%) |

budget process. No other form of systematic reporting was indicated. Likewise, reporting to citizens and the media meant that the budget document was made available, often at the library and, in some instances, through the Web. This seems to be a very passive way of disseminating performance information.

Given this information, a response to the question of whether performance measures work will be relative in that it will depend on how the organization has decided to implement the information. As shown here, the implementation of performance measures can range from being subtle, as in the case of reporting measures in the budget document, to concrete, as in the case of a restructuring of services or the creation of new goals after systematic monitoring of performance.

Notwithstanding the above reported uses, there were a few respondents that showed certain skepticism about the contributions of performance measurement information. For example, one respondent said, "I don't know what the [performance measures] do for anybody." This particular individual said that he had seen other efforts (specifically PPBS and ZBB) come and go and he expected the same thing will happen to managing for results. Another respondent thought that performance measurement made things worse, "because there are many things you can't quantify and [decisions] should not be driven by measure systems that simply count things."

## C.  Verification and Elaboration of Path Model

### 1.  Factors that Promote or Hinder Adoption

As in the mailed survey of 1997, in the phone interviews what was categorized as internal interest groups dominated the responses to the question of whether there were individuals, groups, or circumstances that were particularly influential in promoting development of performance measures. Management (including department/agency heads, city or county manager) and nonmanagement employees, sometimes working in informal teams, were cited the most as having an important effect on adoption.

Elected officials such as the governors, legislators, county boards, and city councils were mentioned several times. According to the responses, however, their influence seemed to be more through their power to require the development of performance measures. That is, when asked about circumstances that had been influential, respondents attributed adoption to legislation, laws, or simple expectation and requests that performance measures be included in the budget process. Other responses included: attending seminars or training, because it came from the top, revenue shortfall, and requirements from GASB.

Respondents were also asked what groups or individuals and circumstances had complicated development. Most of the comments were related to attitudes toward performance measures. Respondent explained that the existing culture within their organization hindered development efforts because it resulted in staff and management not buying in. According to one of the respondents, one of the consequences of no buy-in is that it may lead to half-hearted efforts with measures that then are not useful. One respondent stated that "Because agency heads did not buy in, they did a poor job on their performance plan." One respondent indicated that long-term employees in particular tend to have a negative attitude toward performance measurement, often arguing that it is not part of their job. Another commented that when department heads are not "overly excited" about developing performance measures, the process is rarely successful. Furthermore, misperceptions about performance measures, fears on the part of managers of getting their budgets cut, being told what to do, or being punished if their program is found not working also seem to have a negative impact on development. Legislators were also cited as fearing loss of control because they are used to line item instead of program appropriations and as not having the time to review all the performance information. Thus in those cases they opt for mandating that the adoption effort be discontinued.

Other important factors that hindered adoption fall under the rational/technocratic domain of our study. Respondents thought that their lack of time, data, and other resources made development of performance measures difficult. According to one respondent, "Department heads feel strapped for resources; thus, they do the minimum required. Other related problems included the need for training on how to develop performance measures as well as the belief that developing a good performance measurement system takes a lot of effort.

## 2. Factors that Promote or Hinder Implementation

The responses to the question on factors that influenced implementation followed to a great extent the patterns found in the mailed surveys. Consistent with the findings depicted earlier in Figure 2, when respondents in organizations where performance measures had been implemented were asked about the individuals or groups that were most influential on the implementation of performance measures, most cited elected officials (governor, legislators, county boards, city councils, and mayors). In particular, some indicated that using performance measurement information has to begin at the top. Some influence was also attributed to city managers, department heads, and county administrators.

As far as circumstances positively influencing implementation, most responses highlighted the importance of a changing culture. Respondents talked about the culture having changed mostly because "performance measurement is not going away." Two other comments indicated that providing incentives to use it helped. Only two comments were related to resources and two others mentioned the need for formally requiring use.

When asked which individuals or groups have complicated implementation, most respondents mentioned management. Specifically, resistance or just mild support from department and agency heads was reported as complicating actual use of performance measures. Another problem seemed to be that elected officials did not use performance measures. Respondents cited the lack of use and active participation of legislators and county board members as factors that complicate implementing performance measurement information. A respondent from a state indicated that because they have a part-time legislature, members "don't have time to digest it [performance information] and therefore the measurement effort is wasted."

Circumstances cited as complicating implementation included fear of being held accountable, particularly of outcomes, and of "setting nice goals that can't be achieved." Another issue cited was the learning curve of performance measurement. Respondents identified the difficulty in understanding performance measurement systems as contributing to the lack of use. Related to that, lack of training on how to use performance measures was viewed as a problem as well. However, a respondent suggested that simply learning how to use the information is not the issue, the real issue is that deciding "what to do with the information is a political decision."

Finally, cultural issues were also cited as having a negative impact on implementation. For example, one respondent said that turf issues had complicated the process. Another indicated that in order for implementation to occur in her organization, there was a need to create an atmosphere to accept change. Related to that was a third comment on the need to change the perception that performance measurement is a waste of time.

### D.   Sustaining Performance Measurement Information: A Third Stage in the Utilization Process

In talking with the respondents, another stage in the utilization process—sustaining implementation—emerged. Indicating that it was not enough to adopt and initially implement performance measures, respondents identified several challenges for sustaining implementation. Three of the most often-cited challenges related to obtaining buy-in as a form of culture change, following through the implementation stage, and the characteristics of the measures.

With regard to the first, getting buy-in across the organization, including elected officials and those who see performance measurement as extra work, was seen as a major challenge. Respondents recognized that without this support and change in the culture of the organization, performance measures will remain underused at best, poorly developed at worst. The second major concern stressed by respondents was related to the initial implementation. Specifically, respondents mentioned issues such as how to interpret successes and failures and how to adjust accordingly, how to best report on results, and, generally, how to translate the measures into action. The third major challenge identified by respondents relates to developing a meaningful performance measurement system. According to respondents, such a system requires agreement as to the measures to develop and the purpose; it also needs to be easily understood and must link systematically to what is being done.

Another challenge also identified was the need for continuity. Respondents spoke of the need to make performance measurement part of the culture so that it will continue being important even after the administration that supported the process changes. A respondent said that "we must develop the system and stick to it." This particular comment goes back to Ott and Goodman's (1998) criticism of government reform efforts constantly being replaced by new efforts. At the same time, respondents said that there is a need to keep performance measurement as a living and viable thing. If the measures are not allowed to change according to demands, then the process will stagnate. Thus there is a need for accommodation on the part of the performance measurement system itself and the organization.

Three other challenges are worth noting. The first is a concern with accounting for outcomes. That is, there is a perception that measuring outcomes is difficult for certain types of services. The second challenge is related to resources. One respondent indicated that although they are given the responsibility to develop performance measures, they are not given extra time or people to do it, thus performance measurement becomes an added activity to their daily job responsibilities. Finally, the third challenge deals with fear. One respondent made the comment that "People are afraid when they can't explain in quantifiable terms the services and actions they are performing."

### 1.  Strategies for Addressing Challenges

Not only were respondents very insightful in identifying the challenges to sustaining the implementation of performance measures, they were equally insightful in providing suggestions for addressing such challenges. Three of the strategies most often mentioned by them were having top management use performance measures, providing training on performance measurement, and particularly implementation and taking small steps.

Most of the respondents seemed to believe that if their governing body uses the information "so that people see it," then it will become part of what people do. A respondent from a state noted that "The legislature must start using it for its funding decisions. That will make agency heads use it." A related comment was made by another respondent who indicated that use has to be a directive from the board (county board) and not from the (county) administrator. That will give performance measurement more power. Unfortunately, the simple strategy of mandating performance measurement does not necessarily work. As reflected in the literature and the findings discussed here, there are other factors that contribute to the success or failure of performance measurement.

Some respondents concluded that an appropriate strategy is for the governing body to emphasize performance measurement and use the information because that will create an expectation for use on the part of management. You need to "Push from the top; if not there will always be resistance," said another respondent. Conversely, one respondent thought that one strategy should be involving customers, "So that department heads see that it is them who want it and not the administration telling them what to do." Perhaps multiple strategies need to be implemented if performance measurement efforts are to succeed.

Respondents also suggested that another strategy that can help overcome the challenges to the whole utilization process may be training on adoption and implementation. Some suggested bringing in consultants. Other respondents suggested that having an inhouse consultant would be ideal. In this regard, Wholey (1999) has concluded that as public agencies move toward heavier involvement in performance-based management, not only there will be an even greater need for training but also a need for managers and staff skilled in the measurement process.

Furthermore, getting agreement on goals, objectives, and type of measures developed, according to one respondent will help show that performance measurement is a management tool to do the job better, "and not an accountability hammer to significantly change budget allocation." That will make performance measurement successful. Unfortunately, as suggested by Newcomer (1997) within public agencies, stakeholders with authority to decide what to measure have different world views from one another, which could make reaching agreement difficult.

With regard to the third strategy, respondents felt that performance measurement efforts would be more successful if they started with small baby steps. Likewise, performance measurement efforts need to be built into the day-to-day operations. One respondent suggested that the utilization of performance measurement means that you have to change the way you do business and such a change takes time. Therefore, for performance measurement to be successful you have to "grow it, and don't expect results right away." This assessment concurs with the criticism that government officials have a tendency to not undertake experiments or pilot projects to test reform (Ott and Goodman, 1998; Light, 1997). And, even when government undertakes a pilot project to test reform, "the temptation is to go government-wide" (Light, 1997, p. 4).

Other strategies were suggested as well. One strategy suggested was to show examples to those involved in performance measurement that performance measurement works, "that it can be done," and that it can be used to improve operations. This will help in overcoming resistance, particularly from those who think that performance measurement is a wasted effort. Documenting successful and even unsuccessful applications of performance measurement has been suggested by scholars such as Greiner (1996) as a strategy for supporting performance-based management.

Finally, some respondents indicated that people should be rewarded for using performance measures. In particular, one respondent intimated that agencies should reward when goals are attained. However, as suggested by another respondent, in order for goals to be achieved, they need to be attainable. Thus, it is important for performance goals to be realistic by taking into consideration the context in which the organization operates.

### E.  Conclusions from Second Study

In this section we showed how using telephone interviews allowed us to verify and elaborate a model developed from data gathered through a mailed survey. By and large, this procedure allowed for the verification of the accuracy with which we interpreted the responses of those who participated in the mailed survey.

As with the mailed survey, we were able to distinguish stages in the utilization process of performance measures. In particular, the telephone interviews allowed us to assess the importance of the main factors believed to affect adoption and implementation. For example, respondents showed a proclivity to believe that internal interest groups have a very important effect on adoption. Implementation, as found in the earlier study, seemed to be more influenced by external interest groups.

An important contribution of the telephone interviewing process was a more refined understanding of how the different mechanisms affect the utilization process. Of particular importance was the understanding that actual use or implementation can vary from enlightenment to instrumental use, each important in its own context. Finally, another contribution of this procedure was that we identified at least one more stage of the utilization process, sustaining. As with the different levels of use, implementation is not a one-time accomplishment in the utilization process. Therefore, strategies need to be devised to sustain it.

### V.  CONCLUSION

In this chapter we have discussed a model of utilization of performance measures. It was shown how the model was developed and later verified and elaborated. We began with the observation that lack of use of performance measurement information was the fundamental problem. Although we may think that performance measurement is a rational activity, the utilization of the information is not, at least not in the traditional rational view. And, therefore, studies keep reporting scant use of performance measures.

This suggests that performance measures utilization is a complex process that needs to be supported by developing strategies that go beyond a simple focus on traditionally rational values. The adoption, implementation, and maintenance of performance measures is affected by political, cultural, and rational factors all at the same time.

Likewise, in order to support the process, it is important to understand how performance measures are actually implemented given the purpose of the implementation. If the purpose is instrumental as in the case of monitoring to assess achievements, then that is successful implementation. If the purpose is enlightenment because it allows for reflection, then that too can be classified as implementation. To expect the use of information always to be instrumental is to miss the other important contributions that performance measures can make.

Strategies appropriate for supporting each stage of the utilization process were suggested. To summarize, strategies for supporting adoption include training and gaining the support of management and nonmanagement employees. Strategies for supporting implementation include a "teach by example approach" on the part of elected officials. If they use performance measures, then they will create the expectation of use and in the long run also contribute to sustaining implementation. Strategies for sustaining implementation include working toward changing negative attitudes toward performance measures and misperceptions as to their real purpose.

## APPENDIX I. COMPONENTS OF THE MODEL

Unless otherwise stated, the following are underlying factors validated through factor analysis.

### A. Dependent Variables

The dependent factor Adoption measured how extensively output, outcome, and efficiency measures have been developed for programs in the organization and range from 1, not developed for any, to 4, developed for all.

The factor Implementation measured the frequency of use of output, outcome, and efficiency measures in each of the following activities: strategic planning, resource allocation, program management, monitoring, evaluation, and reporting to internal management, elected officials, and citizens or the media. Answers ranged from 1, for never, to 4, for always.

### B. Independent Variables

The variable External Requirements is an additive index representing the number of external requirements (Law or Administrative Regulation) to use performance measures.

Internal Requirement is a dichotomous variable that measured whether there was an internal policy requiring the use of performance measures.

The factor Internal Interest Groups measured the extent of support for performance measures by management and nonmanagement employees. This factor was based on answers to four questions (two for each employee category). The questions asked to what extent had management and nonmanagement employees taken the initiative to promote the development and implementation of performance measures and to what extent had nonmanagement employees formed working groups (formal or informal) to promote the development and implementation of performance measures. The response choices ranged from 1, for not at all, to 4, for to a great extent.

External Interest Groups, also a factor, measured the extent of support for performance measures by elected officials and/or citizens based on answers to three questions. The questions related to involvement of external constituents in promoting accountability and efficiency, elected officials taking the initiative to promote the development and implementation of performance measures, and whether elected officials had formed working groups (formal or informal) to promote the development and implementation of performance measures. Like the previous factor, these were also scale items with the same response choices.

The factors Attitudes and Risk taking represent measures of organizational culture and how open these organizations were to change. Attitudes is based on perceptions about innovation and change in general and performance measures in particular as reflected in the extent of agreement with these statements: (1) Management is willing to implement appropriate organizational innovation and change; (2) Management views performance measures as an important aspect of decision making (resource allocation, strategic planning, etc.); (3) Nonmanagement employees willingly accept organizational innovation and change; and (4) Nonmanagement understands and views performance measurement as a vehicle for performance improvement. Responses ranged from 1, strongly disagree, to 4, strongly agree. Risk taking represents the extent to which individuals agreed with the statements: (1) there is a reward/incentive system in place in the organization that encourages improving performance; and (2) there is a reward/incentive system in place in the organization that encourages risk taking (using innovative ideas with the goal of improving performance).

The factor Access to Information is one of the three rational/technocratic factors and reflects the extent to which management and nonmanagement employees had access to performance measurement-related information. It is based on three questions asking how often employees received or had access to publications or online services relating to performance measurement, and how often management and nonmanagement employees attended conferences or workshops related to performance measurement. The answer choices included never, sometimes, frequently, and always (1 to 4).

Resources, another rational/technocratic factor, measured the extent to which the organization had available relevant technical expertise and resources for performance measurement. The questions included in the factor analysis were: (1) to what extent the organization has committed resources (time, people, money) to be used in measurement of program performance; (2) to what extent the organization has assigned staff for evaluation of program performance; (3) to what extent the organization has an assigned department for evaluation of program performance; (4) to what extent the organization collects relevant and reliable data that can be used to assess performance; and (5) to what extent the organization uses benchmarks for evaluating performance (1, not at all, to 4, great extent).

Goal Orientation, the third of the three rational/technocratic factors, measured the extent to which the organization was oriented toward efficient goal achievement. This factor was created from answers to questions including: (1) to what extent is management trained in applications such as TQM, MBO, or computer-based decision making; (2) to what extent are programs and departments guided by goals and objectives; (3) to what extent do programs and departments clearly communicate strategies for achieving objectives; and (4) whether there is agreement that the organization's mission, as practiced, promotes efficiency. All these questions were in a 4-point scale.

## REFERENCES

Achen, C. (1982). *Interpreting and Using Regression*. Beverly Hills, CA: Sage.

Berman, E. (1998). Productivity in Public and Nonprofit Organizations. *Strategies and Techniques*. Thousand Oaks, CA: Sage.

Berman, E., Wang, X. (2000). Performance measurement in U.S. counties: Capacity for reform. *Public Admin. Rev.* 60(5):409–420.

Berry, M., Ikerd, J. (1996). *Outcome Budgeting: Catawba County, NC*. Washington, DC: ASPA's Center for Accountability and Performance.

Bobrow, D., Dryzek, J. (1987). *Policy Analysis by Design*. Pittsburgh: University of Pittsburgh Press.

Bouckaert, G. (1992). Public productivity in retrospective. In: Holzer, M., ed. *Public Productivity Handbook*. New York: Marcel Dekker, pp. 5–46.

Bozeman, B., Bretschneider, S. (1986). Public management information and system: Theory and practice. *Public Admin. Rev.* pp. 475–487, special issue.

Cannon, J. (1996). *Utah Tomorrow*. Washington, DC: ASPA's Center for Accountability and Performance.

Cibulka, J., Derlin, R. (1998). Accountability policy adoption to policy sustainability. *Educ. Urban Soc.* 30(4):502–515.

Cohen, L. H. (1977). Factors affecting the utilization of mental health evaluation research findings. *Prof. Psychol. Nov.* pp. 526–534.

Colwell, W. L., Koletar, J. W. (1984). Performance measurement for criminal justice: The Federal Bureau of Investigation (FBI) experience. *Public Product Rev.* VIII(3):207–224.

Cronbach, L. J., Associates (1980). *Toward Reform of Program Evaluation*. San Francisco: Jossey-Bass.

de Lancer Julnes, P. (1999). Lessons learned about performance measurement. *Int. Rev. Public Admin.* 4(2):45–55.

de Lancer Julnes, P., Holzer, M. (2001). Promoting utilization of performance measures in public organizations: An empirical study of factors affecting adoption and implementation. *Public Admin. Rev.* 61(6):693–708.

de Leon, P. (1988). *Advice and Consent. The Development of the Policy Sciences*. New York: Russell Sage.

Dunn, W. (1980). The two-communities metaphor and models of knowledge. *Knowledge* 1:515–536.

Ehrenhalt, A. (1994 November). Performance budgeting, thy name is .... *Governing* 8:9.

Elden, M., Sanders, S. L. (1996). Vision-based diagnosis: Mobilizing for transformational change in a public organization. *Public Product. Manage. Rev.* 20:11–23.

Fischer, F. (1986). Reforming bureaucratic theory: Toward a political model. In: Calista, D., ed. *Bureaucratic and Governmental Reform*. Greenwich, CT: JAI, pp. 35–53.

Fountain, J. (1997). Are state and local governments using performance measures? *PA Times* 20(1):PM 2–PM 8.

Gouldner, A. W. (1959). Organizational analysis. In: Merton, R. K., et al., eds. *Sociol. Today*. New York: Basic, pp. 404–405.

GASB Governmental Accounting Standard Board (1997). *Report on Survey of State and Local Government Use and Reporting of Performance Measure*. Norwalk, CT: First Questionnaire Results.

Greiner, J. (1996). Positioning performance measurement for the twenty-first century. In: Halachmi, A., Bouckaert, G., eds. *Organizational Performance and Measurement in the Public Sector*. Westport, CT: Quorum.

Harvey, E., Mills, R. (1970). Patterns of organization adaptation. In: Zald, M., ed. *Power in Organizations*. Nashville, TN: Vanderbilt University Press, pp. 181–213.

Hatry, H. (1996). Foreword. In: Halachmi, A., Bouckaert, G., eds. *Organizational Performance and Measurement In The Public Sector*. Westport, CT: Quorum.

Hatry, H. P., Fountain, J. R. Jr., Sullivan, J. M., Kremer, L. (1990). *Service Efforts and Accomplishments Reporting: Its Time Has Come*. CT: Governmental Accounting Standards Board (GASB).

Holzer, M. (1992). Mastering public productivity improvement. In: Holzer, M., ed. *Public Productivity Handbook*. New York: Marcel Dekker.

Holzner, B., Fisher, E. (1979). Knowledge use. Considerations in the sociology of knowledge application. *Knowl. Creation, Diffusion, Utilization* 1(2):219–244.

Howard, R., Schneider, L. (1994). Worker participation in technological change: Interests, influence, and scope. In: Fischer, F., Sirianni, C., eds. *Critical Studies in Organization and Bureaucracy*. Rev. ed. Philadelphia: Temple University Press, pp. 519–544.

Huberman, M. (1987). Steps toward an integrated model of research utilization. *Knowl. Creation, Diffusion, Utilization* 8(4):586–611.

Huberman, M. (1989). Predicting conceptual effects in research utilization: Looking with both eyes. *Knowl. Soc.* 2(3):6–24.

Huberman, M. (1994). Research utilization: The state of the art. *Knowl. Policy: Int. J. Knowl. Transfer Utilization* 7(4):13–33.

Kamensky, J. M. (1995). Program performance measures: Designing a system to manage for results. In: Halachmi, A., Holzer, M., eds. *Competent Government: Theory and Practice. The Best of Public Productivity and Management Review, 1985–1993*. Burke, VA: Chatelaine, pp. 239–246.

Korman, N., Glennerster, H. (1985). Closing a hospital: The Derenth Park project. *Occasional Papers on Social Administration*. No. 78. London: Bedford Square Press.

Light, P. (1997). *The Tides of Reform: Making Government Work 1945–1995*. New London, CT: Yale University Press.

Marshall, M. (1996). *Development and Use of Outcome Information in Government, Prince William County, Virginia*. Washington, DC: ASPA's Center for Accountability and Performance.

Martin, D. W. (1992). The management classics and public productivity. In: Holzer, M., ed., *Public Productivity Handbook*. New York: Marcel Dekker, pp. 47–62.

Meld, M. (1974). The politics of evaluation of social programs. *Soc. Work*, 445–448.

Milankovich, M. (1990). Total quality management for public sector productivity improvement. *Public Product Manage. Rev.* (XIV,19–32.

Miller, G. J. (1991). *Government Financial Management Theory*. New York: Marcel Dekker.

Nelson, C. E., Roberts, E., Maederer, J., Wertheimer, C., Johnson, B. (1987). The utilization of social science information by policy makers. *Am. Behav. Sci.* 30(6):569–577.

Nelson, S. (1981). The three coins on diffusion research. In: Rich, R., ed. *The Knowledge Cycle*. Beverly Hills, CA: Sage.

Newcomer, K. (1997). Using performance measurement to improve programs. *New Direct. Eval.* 75:5–14.

OEI. Office of Evaluation and Inspections. *Practical Evaluation for Public Managers*. Washington, DC: Office of Inspector General, Department of Health and Human Services.

Oh, C. H., Rich, R. F. (1996 Spring). Explaining use of information in public Policymaking. *Knowl. Policy Int. J. Knowl. Transfer Utilization* 9(1):3–35.

Ott, J. S., Goodman, D. (1998). Government reform or alternatives to bureaucracy? Thickening, tides and the future of government. *Public Admin. Rev.* 58(6):540–545.

Palumbo, D. J., Calisto, D. J. (1990). *Implementation and the Policy Process: Opening Up the Black Box*. New York: Greenwood.

Perrow, C. (1972). *Complex Organizations*. Glenview, IL: Scott, Foresman.

Pettigrew, A. (1973). *The Politics of Organizational Decision-Making*. London: Tavistock.

Pfeffer, J. (1981). *Power in Organizations*. Cambridge, MA: Ballinger.

Rich, R., Oh, C. H. (1994). The utilization of policy research. In: Nagel, S., ed. *Encyclopedia of Policy Studies*. 2nd ed. New York: Marcel Dekker, pp. 69–92.

Stehr, N. (1992). *Practical Knowledge. Applying the Social Sciences*. London: Sage.

Walters, J. (1997 June). Performance and Pain. *Governing* 26-31.

Weiss, C. H. (1972). The politicization of evaluation research. *J. Soc. Issues* 26(4):57–68.

Weiss, C. H. (1979 September/October). The many meanings of research utilization. *Public Admin. Rev.* 426–431.

Weiss, C. H. (1997). *Evaluation: Methods for Studying Programs and Policies*. Upper Saddle River, NJ: Prentice-Hall.

Wholey, J. (1999). Performance-based management: Responding to the challenges. *Public Product. Manage. Rev.* 22(3):288–307.

Wildavsky, A. (1988). Political implications of budgetary reform (1961). In: Schick, A., ed. *Perspectives on Budgeting*. Washington, DC: ASPA, pp. 68–78.

Wingens, M. (1990). Toward a general utilization theory. *Knowl. Creation Diffusion, Utilization* 12(1):27–42.

# 21

# Performance, Productivity, and Budgeting

**GERALD J. MILLER**
*Rutgers, The State University of New Jersey, Newark, New Jersey, U.S.A.*

**DONIJO ROBBINS**
*Grand Valley State University, Grand Rapids, Michigan, U.S.A.*

## I. INTRODUCTION

Is productivity achieved through public budgets? As part of management systems, budgets are designed to achieve an amalgam of values, including productivity. To understand the relationship between productivity and budgets, this chapter outlines purposes attached to budget systems, and draws their implications for achieving greater productivity in government organizations.

First, we describe large-scale budget reform structures in terms of their relationship to productivity; we find that productivity is not the central aim. Therefore we look at productivity-friendly changes in budgeting in more detail and then look at budget-friendly productivity-oriented reforms. Finally, we look at the latest efforts to join productivity and budgeting by examining what are known as expenditure control budgets, target-base budgets, and performance-base budgets.

## II. PRODUCTIVITY AND HOW BUDGETS ENCOURAGE IT

A definition of productivity reveals links to normative ideas about what budget reforms could do. Many conveniently think of productivity as economic efficiency, a surplus of the goods or services produced over those resources used in their production. Closely akin to this idea are two others: achieving the highest levels of effectiveness for a given investment and choosing the least costly investment that will yield a given level of performance. These often translate into micromanagerial incentives for greater, error-free performance.

   In macroeconomic terms, productivity often means reduced government expenditure and increased private sector investment. Ideologically, this definition suggests major differences in each sector's ability to perform; therefore a more nearly neutral view might argue for greater investment in projects with large durable returns on investment. Budgets can favor productivity by encouraging choice and favoring alternative investments that have larger returns for the public resources committed to projects, agencies, and activities.

   In the ordinary view of budgets, designers have created a process that forces managers to consider different programs often in competition within and between government departments. Managers commonly employ a simple economic idea: that any alternative must be judged in terms of other alternatives. Budgeting for productivity involves analysis, and proponents of analysis argue that explicit or systematic examination of alternative policies allows the public to hold its public officials accountable for performance.[1]

   Which public officials should be held accountable for what draws public productivity into questions of organization structure and into politics. A budget design can either increase or decrease the amount of discretion afforded to the manager, agency head, or the one preparing the initial budget. Devolving discretion to the agency level from top management and especially from political leaders, while also holding agency managers accountable for results, may improve productivity and performance. Therefore budget styles and formats vary not only in the amount of analysis they permit but also in the degree to which agency discretion is either limited or boundless.

## III.  TYPES OF BUDGETS AND THEIR CONTRIBUTIONS TO PRODUCTIVITY

In summarizing the financial and productivity problems facing public officials, one noted government productivity expert has outlined two problems: increasing the amounts of revenue and using present amounts to their best advantage. The second, he says, is the more difficult to solve: "without open market or profit test, there are no clear widespread indications of what . . . government services are wanted, in what quantity, at what quality, and what prices" (Hatry, 1972, p. 263). Lacking the marketplace on which to base decisions, government officials must choose courses of action "which contribute most to government objectives . . . [and, rationally] . . . insure maximum use of scarce resources" (Grossbard, n.d., p. 4). Those who design budget methods and procedures, then, must bear the responsibility of making the choice process contribute to productivity.

### A.  Budget Principles and Practices

At its narrowest, a budget is a plan. That plan estimates proposed expenditures for a given period, usually a calendar or fiscal year, and relates planned spending to an estimate of means needed to finance the plan. The planned spending, moreover, contributes to the achievement of a series of objectives. Thus the budget relates objectives, spending plans, and the means of financing the attainment of these objectives.

The budget is also a control device, used to conserve resources, directing that only the amount specified in the budget be spent; in this sense, budgets control the amount of resources fed into the governmental system. As a control device, the budget also directs managers toward certain objectives and away from other objectives, limiting discretion. In this additional sense, budgets combine input control with output controls to give managers a bottom-line; efficiency, output, and performance measures tell whether government programs give the people who pay for them their money's worth. During an operating period, the budget as a control device may be a means of comparing actual results with planned results so that the variances may be analyzed and improvements made.

The budget process is one in which decision makers allocate scarce resources to their highest and best uses. Should citizens decide to devote all resources needed to satisfy every claim for government action, a government budgeting process would be irrelevant. Thus budgeting represents choices. Moreover, the most important claims change over time, making budget processes necessary to reallocate among prior and new claims.

In addition, a budget is a promotion device. The budget's transparency, as well as its purpose in being an accountability device, requires that the budget call attention to some matters, perhaps telling those who must abide by the budget what to heed and what to ignore. In calling attention, the budget provides incentives to act or not to act, to act efficiently, effectively, or equitably.

Finally, budgets grant discretion. Should more or less discretion be allowed at the agency or department level? Or should the bulk of discretion be left to the executive or the legislature? Some argue that discretion, when passed on to managers, increases the level of productivity for that agency, and hence government as a whole. However, opponents view greater agency discretion as the prime cause of fraud and abuse. Some budgets afford more discretion than others.

If we consider, like Sundelson (1935, p. 243) and others (Stourm, 1917, pp. 144–168; Shirras, 1936; Wildavsky, 1986, 2001), what the technical features of an ideal budget might be, we would find a set of generally agreed-upon ideas relating the requirements of informed voters and responsible decision makers. These ideas include comprehensiveness, exclusiveness, unity, annularity, accuracy, clarity, and publicity. Comprehensiveness requires that the budget hold all authority for government expenditure and revenue. Exclusiveness reflects the importance attached to separating fiscal matters from substantive ones; the budget should include financial matters, not other matters of substance. Unity suggests the need to relate all of the parts of the budget to each other, what revenues support what expenditures if earmarked. Annularity forces regular review of expenditures and revenues by commanding the length of the period between reviews. Accuracy means that estimates of needs and resources are near the mark rather than the product of wishful thinking, political strategy, or simply, poor forecasting. Clarity demands that who pays what and how much as well as what is spent be unmistakable rather than confusing or simplistic. Finally, budget making must seek publicity, especially the airing of needs, grievances, and the policy positions of representative and represented.

Sundelson's (1935) eight principles might be compressed to one. According to Burkhead (1956, p. 106):

> There is probably only one principle which is likely to be useful—that of operational adequacy. The budget cycle and the budgetary process must be capable of coping with

the governmental problems at hand. The budget must emphasize flexibility and adaptability not an ideal that never changes.

Burkhead comes closest to our understanding of productivity and performance.

Within all of these images and principles are the basic tenets for defining a resource management device, and specifically a budget. The actual practices of governments today are more often at the one extreme of meeting the very basic definition we started with—a plan relating revenues to spending with little thought to discretion one way or the other—than at the other extreme which combines planning, control, allocation, incentives, and discretion.

What budget methods have governments used traditionally and where do they fall along this scale? We apply this scale in succeeding portions of this chapter: first, the line-item budget as a rudimentary way of assessing expenditures and means; early performance budgeting as a method of going one step beyond the line-item budget by classifying items by function and determining the efficiency of the budgeted expenditures; program budgeting, as a means of combining planning, budgeting, and economic analysis of allocation choices; and budgeting to decentralize decision making and reorient budgets among old and new programs through zero-base budgeting. Later we go beyond budget reforms as they have appeared up to and through zero-base budgeting to investigate productivity-friendly budgeting practices including measurement and incentives and then describe other budget systems that have come into being in the late twentieth century for the specific purpose of pursuing government productivity and performance.

## B. Line Item Budgeting: The Control Orientation

An early approach to budgeting, a line-item or object of expenditure budget, is still a popular approach in government due to its simplicity and the strict accountability or control it allows. This budget, however, has limited utility as a management tool.

The line-item budget allocates funds to specific items or objects. For example, salaries, office supplies, and printing costs are forecast for the next year, limiting the administrator to a certain increment per object over the amount budgeted for that object the last fiscal year.

The Jeffersonian line-item approach was implemented again around the turn of the twentieth century as a means to reform uncontrollable spending (Smithies, 1955; Cleveland, 1915). Line-item budgets were devised to hold governmental units accountable for expenditure by setting an item-by-item spending schedule.

The greatest advantage of line-item budgeting is the control it exerts on financial administration. The intentions of governmental decision makers are defined as to what will be spent on what. This, in turn, provides some control over work by casting expenditures along departmental lines and characters of expense.

Grossbard (n.d., p.6) argues the insufficiency of the line-item budget. He views line-item budgeting as a result of "short run thinking and a tendency to put off both expenditure increases and revenue measures until a later period." The problem with the traditional line-item budget format, he further argues, is that "it does not do enough." Specifically, the budget is difficult to relate to objectives. There is no relation of expenditures to accomplishment, no concept of alternatives to policy, and no integration of planning, budgeting, and control. Line-item budgeting promotes inertia in that changes are produced only as marginal changes from the previous year. Levels of service, organization structure, and methods of operation become permanent, although they may be unsatisfactory.

Anton (1964), in his study of politics and budget practice in three Illinois cities, depicted the marginal or incremental practices of line-item budgeting. Because the only information available to a city was the past year's budget and the marginal increases asked by each department, the budget hearing was found to provide the only clues as to what to cut and what to leave as it was. He observed (1964, p.16):

> Precisely because the "stakes" are inherently so political in meaning, the criteria used to decide [budget] question are seldom relevant to departmental goals. Instead, the deciding criteria become such political factors as power and influence of the department head, the ability of the department to mobilize support for its demand, or the ability of the council to gain prestige by granting or refusing the demand.

The increases in the budget were, and in other cases usually are, not based on any demonstration that services from any particular department would improve or suffer because of increases or cuts. The line-item budget is a first step toward holding government accountable to voters for spending decisions, but it is many steps short of encouraging productivity and performance.

## C. Early Performance Budgeting and an Orientation Toward Management

Due to limitations in line-item budgeting and increasing spending, local and then the federal government began turning to a new approach, a classic productivity enhancement approach, with the invention of a "performance" budget (Burkhead, 1956, Chapter 6). This management approach related expenditures to a government's performance of functions expressed in law and the budget. Legislators appropriated money to activities—jobs to be performed—rather than line items or objects of expenditure. The new concept introduced operational analysis, a method of measuring input—personnel services, contractual services—against output or the cost per unit of activity. Generally, the budget called for more information on what the activity was, what the procedures used were, and what level of service could be provided for what amount.

This new performance budgeting approach provided distinct advantages over the line-item concept. By its orientation to management, performance budgeting helped administrators calculate the work efficiency of operating units by developing budget categories in functional terms and providing work-cost measurements to yield insight into the efficient performance of prescribed activities. At the height of performance budgeting's acceptance, Ridley and Simon (1943) identified four types of measurement needs: results, costs, efforts, and performance, the last three of which were their measures of "administrative efficiency" and, commonly today, productivity. For the first time, standards were set based on the measurements made, worker hours, cost accounting, and a ratio of personnel to activity.

Many found disadvantages in performance budgeting's application in the federal government. There were inherent difficulties in measuring government work with precision. It was easy to measure government purchases, generally easy to measure government products, but "perennially difficult to measure government output except for repetitive discrete products such as postal service" (Burkhead, 1972, p. 73).

Performance budgeting also lacked the tools to deal with long-range problems. With planned expenditures set within a one-year perspective, "almost all options [for future action] have been foreclosed by previous commitments" (Schick, 1966, p. 258). The performance budget encouraged efficiency, in other words, sacrificing effectiveness and ignoring equity.

## D.  Program Budgeting: An Emphasis on Goals

Program budgeting suffers a severe identification crisis in the budgetary literature. It is used synonymously with performance budgeting as well as with the planning, programming, and budgeting system (PPBS). Even when the Hoover Commission introduced the term performance budget, its task force report utilized the term program budget interchangeably with performance budget. Schick (1966, p. 250) observed, "no uniformity in usage, some preferring the program budgeting label, others performance budgeting to describe the same things. The level of confusion has been increased by the association of the term with the PPB movement."

Program budgeting, a product of World War II efforts to assign priorities and control production of war materials (Novick, 1968), emerged in an attempt to distinguish between work performance and work goal achievement. Burkhead (1956, p. 139) attempted to distinguish between performance budgeting and program budgeting. A program may be defined in relation to a higher level of organization than performance. Because a program may encompass several performing organizational units, the program budget is broader and more integrative than a performance budget. Program costs are broad summary costs which may be developed through aggregation of part or whole performing units' costs. Performance details need not be incorporated into a program budget, inasmuch as it is not necessarily based on performing units.

Also, a department or agency may be involved in several programs simultaneously, but operating units or functions within a department are directly responsible for performance. In terms of organizational structure, the program budget may respond to higher-level organizational imperatives, whereas the performance budget may serve lower-level operating needs.

The program budget has a longer range and is forward looking. Performance budgets are based on records of past performance and accomplishments, whereas program budgets are built around estimates of what performance is reasonable to expect in the future. Program budgets are thus better prepared to project the social and economic policies of government.

According to these distinctions, these two types of budgets serve different purposes. A program budget is more suited to the requirements of overall budgetary planning, including review by the central budget office, the chief executive, and the legislature. It is most useful for decision making at or above the departmental level. Performance budgets must likewise provide information for review purposes, but must also be detailed enough to serve management purposes at or below the departmental level.

Program budgeting involves an attempt to arrange budget expenditures around program or functional needs in order to meet broad objectives. Relating input to output facilitates benefit-cost analysis which serves the analyst's need to allocate resources to the most efficient and effective means for achieving ends. The key elements of the process include long-range planning, goals setting, program identification, quantitative analysis, including benefit-cost measurement, and performance analysis.

There are several essential steps in the construction of a program budget:

1. Definition of the ends to be achieved;
2. Definitions of the method and timetables by which they are to be achieved;
3. Determination of the costs for each action required; and
4. Determination of measurements of success, whether goals are actually being achieved through the budgeted programs.

Program budgeting focuses on goals and outcomes, and helps provide perspective for budget expenditures. The budget requires consideration of future implications of programs and effects of current actions. It also emphasizes the role of planning in budget decision making.

Program budgeting falls short of the productivity ideal. Economic, social, and political events, for one thing, may not follow a pattern anticipated in the plan and may undermine the intentions of program budgeting's long-range planning efforts. Analysis of relationships between input and output does not necessarily consider unintended consequences or side effects of actions taken or proposed. Both problems may suggest a model of equity in the real world different from that in planners' heads. Moreover, quantitative measurement of output may not be possible; even where quantitative analysis is feasible, the criteria of efficiency may preclude the consideration of effectiveness.

## E. PPBS: The Planning Orientation

PPBS, or Planning, Programming, Budgeting System, has been characterized as a rational means of fusing planning processes, programming efforts, and the budget system. Many have found little new among the components but a revolutionary concept in the combination. Planning is the determination of the basic goals of the organization and the selection of the programs best calculated to achieve these goals. Programming entails the scheduling and execution, as efficiently as possible, of the specific projects required to implement these programs. Budgeting is the process of converting the goals, programs, and projects into money estimates for review within the administrative branch and final action by the legislative branch, PPBS emphatically embraces rational decision making.

There are disadvantages, however, in the PPB system, both internal and external. First, internal difficulties concern the dynamics of the structure itself, the goal-setting procedure, and benefit–cost analysis. Within the procedural structure of PPBS budgeting, there is a tendency to centralize decision making. The responsibility for goal setting and policy choice is centrally determined, resulting in better coordination of activities, but at the cost of innovation and development of new alternatives at lower levels of policy making.

Its stress on the cross-structural nature of goals and objectives diminishes the importance of existing organizational boundaries. This approach disrupts present channels of communication between administrative agencies. Because there will be different cross-structural arrangements for each objective, the PPBS approach has not been found to establish a single channel to replace it.

Goal setting itself is difficult because of both the complexity of problems and the different outlooks of each goal setter. Wildavsky (1969, 1966, pp. 292–310) notes the ultimate problem with PPBS: budgeting, in PPBS, is intimately linked to policy; however, the basic problems in policy formulation and development stem from the fact that we do not know what it is that we are trying to accomplish.

Benefit–cost analysis itself is not sufficiently sophisticated yet to meet all demands placed upon it. Most important, such variables as social systems and highly intangible services elude measurement. Given the fact that analysis serves political as well as administrative decision making, some argue that analysis should include all considerations, especially political costs and benefits. The opposing view points out that political matters will drive out economic considerations or even rational administrative ones.

There are other major political problems as well. In the very process of changing systems, existing programs have built up definite constituents convinced of the validity of the present approach; "members of an organization and their clients have a vested interest in the policies of the past" and fight change (Wildavsky, 1966, p. 294).

The PPB system, on paper at least, is a well-developed way of achieving some level of effectiveness (through planning) and efficiency (through programming and budgeting). The political problems, usually arising at even low departmental levels (constituent-departmental belief in programs) much less at the legislative level, reveal a marked ignorance of equity in those budget methods, an ignorance PPBS has in common with line-item, performance, and program budgets.

## F.  Zero-Base Budgeting as Decentralized Program Evaluation

Theoretically, zero-base budgeting (ZBB) could remedy some equity problems, those emerging when departments rebel at the top-down insistence of plans, programs, and budgets. That is, ZBB nominally requires that each previously funded program or new program proposal be justified, without regard to previous funding levels. This procedure is designed to promote objective comparisons among diverse programs requesting resources, based on their merits alone and negating the effects of historical bias.

In practice, the definition of ZBB is much less comprehensive. Peter Pyhrr (1970), an early proponent of ZBB and to many its inventor, recognizes the impracticality of a true zero-base budget and leans toward a more practical definition, one in which evaluation has a profound effect but not an exhaustive use. He urges reliance on the evaluations of those who actually implement policy and carry out programs, the departments.

ZBB has at least ten productivity advantages, as a result. First, ZBB yields increased information from managers throughout the organization, particularly operating managers who are responsible for the actual performance of the activity for which they budget. Second, it results in improved plans and budgets which themselves result from combining planning and goals setting, budgeting, and operational decision making into one process requiring detailed scrutiny of every activity. Third, ZBB encourages the use of continued evaluation of program efficiency and effectiveness throughout the budget or operating year. Fourth, programs and managers who have committed themselves to certain levels of performance can be reviewed during the operating year to gauge progress. Fifth, ZBB's priority ranking system facilitates assigning cutbacks or reductions when necessary. Sixth, ZBB helps set priorities and sharpen overall objectives. Seventh, the ZBB approach shifts budget attention away from incremental approaches to last year's budget and focuses on minimum levels of operation. Eighth, ZBB promotes the search for alternatives to programs, performance, and funding levels and may be most useful in reallocating funds among programs within an agency. Ninth, the ZBB approach can readily identify low-yield or low-priority programs that may be eliminated. Finally, ZBB reduces the opportunity for manipulation of budget presentation information, or "gamesmanship." If the information is present in ZBB formats, attempts at gaming become transparent.

The disadvantages of ZBB include problems of implementation: users are threatened by the need to reevaluate pet projects. Also, the number of decision packages generated can overwhelm managers reviewing them; the paperwork produced can have more volume than meaning. ZBB is limited to use with only those controllable elements in budgets. In the federal budget, controllables may amount to no more than 25% of the total. The ranking system remains susceptible to subjective decision, and ZBB does not aid in judging priorities among dissimilar activities such as defense, education, and energy. ZBB is difficult to apply to state and local programs whose genesis is not local but federal and whose support does not lend itself to their control. In addition, there is difficulty identifying appropriate decision units, in gathering accurate supporting data to produce effective analysis, and in determining minimum levels of effort. ZBB requires vast improvements in agency evaluation systems necessary to make program comparisons and rankings and it is expensive and time consuming to implement.

Practically, ZBB's disadvantages include its failure to fundamentally change the practice of budget making. Second, managers often decide priorities in a vacuum, without knowledge of how interrelated programs might be affected by rankings done partially by others. Thus Program A may have been related to Program B, but A was included in a set of priorities distant from B; one's operation may have depended on the other but one's fate could not be revealed to the other. In the end, the increased effort to gain efficiency and equity may have sacrificed effectiveness. ZBB also ignores the equity in an outmoded tax system.

## G. Budgeting and Productivity

Budget reforms have tried to force budget decision makers to comprehend more information as well as consider goals other than who gets what, when, where, and how—political logrolling's emphasis. Some argue that performance, and the administrative discretion necessary to achieve it, takes a backseat to politics. And given all the efforts to make the process more effective and efficient—from different budgeting formats such as ZBB and PPBS, to different restrictive remedies such as the line-item veto by the executive or term limits for elected decision makers—politics still overshadows economic efficiency. "The failures of past efforts, such as PPBS, are largely a result of an inability to account for politics. No set of budget techniques can substitute for political decisions about who wins and who loses" (Joyce, 1993, p. 15). Thurmaier's (1995, p. 456) research also supports this. He suggests that "conflicts between political and economic imperatives are handled subtly in practice, but it appears that economic and technical calculations are subordinated to prior political determinations." Aucoin (1991, p. 121) sums it up best: "If restraint, despite the rhetoric, has not led to a revolution in the political will of politicians to secure efficiency, then perhaps the reason lies in the capacities of politicians to do so." He proposes that productivity and performance are achieved through agency discretion and financial management flexibility.

The reforms vary, but they all try to handle both efficiency and effectiveness concerns; none really combines all aspects of productivity. That is, fiscal stress constantly reminds managers of the important choices between spending less and spending the same amount more efficiently. Parsimony and efficiency may be the longest standing goals of budgeting (Miller, 1991) and among the most traditional links to productivity improvement. However, among the early thoughts about budgets is that of linking budgeting to a third goal, management improvement. Burkhead (1956, p. 284) argues that budgets should also include, "Ways and means to 'save money by spending money.'" By spending money for innovative projects, budgeteers might actually become more effective.

Legislators and other political leaders often do not seem quite so oriented toward parsimony, efficiency, or effectiveness. Their scrutiny tends toward finding out who will bear the burden and who will reap the benefit of government programs. Equity, then, and however defined, has as much or greater say in the outcome of budget decisions than anything else (DeParle, 1991a). Some representatives argue for a fair, more nearly equal distribution; some argue for a progressive distribution, and some argue for a distribution weighted toward investment. In all cases, good predictions for productivity underlie the argument. Because government budget decisions made by elected decision makers have a significant influence on government agency productivity, the principle by which they are made often dictates the principle to be used by agency managers in determining their own allocation as they implement or execute legislative imperatives.

Budgeting technologies, therefore, are not value-free. Ideological positions, on which these technologies are based, compete. In fact, budgets are quite often framed, if not in productivity terms, in ways aimed to achieve parsimony, efficiency, effectiveness, or equity nevertheless. Yet, in terms of productivity, budgets should help attain at least three of the four ends. Productivity concerns exist in all efforts to increase efficiency, effectiveness, or equity, because each comprises both sides of the budget equation: how much input contributes what output or outcomes. A productivity-oriented budget would be that method which yields greater efficiency, greater effectiveness, and greater equity than all other budget methods.

Unqualified measurements of budget efforts toward these goals, however, come only grudgingly. In fact, the most often-cited problem with budgets is the reliance on geographical distribution, logrolling, and other simpleminded conflict resolution rules in place of measurement. Compromise-driven politics tend to dampen any resolve to increase equity, effectiveness, or efficiency. Much more emphasis gets placed on maintaining the existing distribution of budget resources; making innovative choices seems irrelevant to the process (Wildavsky, 1992). Is there room for change from this state? Can budgets encourage productivity? Can productivity improvement efforts include budgets?

## IV.  HOW CAN WE INDUCE PRODUCTIVITY-ORIENTED SPENDING DECISIONS

What else can be done? Realizing differences among levels of government, as well as budget formulation and implementation, we present two basic approaches to the productivity budgeting problem. The first seeks those budget elements that might make the budget process "productivity-friendly," reducing the budget process' outright exclusion of one or another of productivity's goals. The second approach, however, is to force productivity programs to work inside budget routines, as they exist. We call these reforms "budget-friendly" productivity elements.

In referring to budgeting, we have to admit that there might be huge differences in budgeting at the federal and state/local levels. Heretofore, the major difference seemed to be the amount of discretion allowed. The budget at the federal level has had far more to do with making strategic choices; discretion existed and that made for logrolling, as we discussed earlier.

Does there exist this sort of discretion any longer? Straitjackets now bind most governments in the United States, making strategic choices much less possible and executing the plan to which they are straitjacketed more likely (Wildavsky, 1992). Therefore, budgeting processes across U.S. governments may be becoming less discretionary; size may be the only distinguishing aspect.

Truly, there are differences between management analysis and politics. By distinguishing management analysis from politics, Grizzle (1998) observed the difference in the ordering of organization goals and the competition among competing goals in the budget process. Productivity analysis seems to relate most successfully to the ordered goals side of analysis than otherwise.

Finally, most discussion of productivity budgeting should admit the differences between policy and management. Policy decisions in budgets, normally, come from the executive and legislature. Managers have the job of providing choices and eliminating those that are politically or managerially impossible to sustain. Managers also have some impact on the implementation plan implicit within the policy choices. This plan is part of the process to which we refer most often in the proposals that follow.

### A.  Productivity-Friendly Budget Elements

Lauth (2001) warns of the pitfalls of using budgeting as the handmaiden for productivity improvement. The budget is simply too cumbersome to help, he says. Rather, the budget can be made to be less hostile and friendlier to the ideas underlying productivity improvement. Three major groups of efforts to make the budget friendly or at least neutral are described: technical modifications, measures, and incentives.

### 1.  Technical Modifications

Lauth (2001) and Grizzle (2001) observe that typical budget procedures forestall productivity efforts. However, small technical modifications could overcome some of the barriers between budgeting and productivity, they maintain. First and foremost, the budget process exerts unnecessary control and reduces cost savings in forbidding budget transfers among object classes or line-items without legislative approval. Purchases or repairs may be deferred due to this restriction, to illustrate, forcing more costly ones later. Agencies must often also forgo discounts for advance payments.

Second, the insurmountable budget barrier between personnel costs and other costs may unwittingly reduce cost savings. That is, budgeted personnel lines can seldom be converted to any other object class or vice versa. Thus consultants may be allowed for manyfold times the expense of a fully trained, permanent employee.

Finally, central finance offices often pull back the salary savings of productive line units that they achieve from attrition, unpaid leaves, or other temporary absences. The department is left stranded oftentimes, but the department is shackled to lower-level performance—fewer people to do the same amount of work—without the opportunity to use the same salary savings to reward employees for what might be a temporary bulge in workload.

## 2. Support for Measurement

Productivity and budgets have often stood at arms length when the performance-to-budget dollar measurements became complicated or numerous. In truth, much public sector work performance can only be measured from the input side (dollars given to school districts, for instance). Many blame time limits, training gaps, and primitive computing capability for the lack of development in the other areas, however.

In one of the clearest insights into the operation of budget offices, Grizzle (2001) dispels much doubt about the ability to solve these problems. She finds that many efforts to create time and develop information would involve negligible amounts of the central budget office's work year and little cost.

Her view is that measurement problems could be less considerable and more mythical than is thought, if measurement were merely a technical problem. When measurement is a political problem, it becomes one of several behaviors for which budget officers blame incentives.

## 3. Incentives

The motivation to perform productively gets caught in the crosscurrents produced by budgets. There are, first of all, incentives to misrepresent information in budgeting thereby confusing the measurement problem still further (Jones and Euske, 1991). For example, a rapid program reduction tends to accelerate efforts to justify it, mobilizing constituencies and data on its behalf.

Just as there are incentives to misrepresent, there are incentives to perform productively. Incentive pay is the best-known variation. Lauth (2001, p. 199) describes the Counselor Performance Appraisal System used by Georgia's Division of Vocational Rehabilitation as typical.

> Performance goals were set for each counselor through negotiation between the counselor and his or her supervisor. Counselors were eligible to earn incentive pay based on their levels of goal achievement (for example, successful rehabilitation-case closures, according to agreed-upon criteria). Incentive pay did not become a part of base salary and had to be earned each year. Funds for incentive pay came from internal management and salary savings (realized from increased employee productivity).

Obviously, the availability of funds for incentives was important, as were the agreed-upon criteria.

Group incentive plans are another variation. As reported by the U.S. General Accounting Office (1983) almost two decades ago, for example, North Carolina state employees could propose programs for which they would be rewarded as a group with a quarter of the savings if greater productivity were realized. The state budget office chose those for whom documentation might provide clear assessments of savings.

Lauth (2001, p. 199) stated that the legislature terminated the program in less than ten years because of the

> belief on the part of some legislators that some projects were chosen more for their pay-incentive opportunities for employees than for their cost-saving utility for the state; a sentiment in some legislative quarters that it was the responsibility of state employees to perform their work efficiently without special incentives to do so; and a concern that although all work-unit employees shared equally in the pay-incentive plan, not everyone contributed equally to the work effort. During the years in which the plan operated, work crews in the Department of Transportation tended to be among the major beneficiaries of the program. Because ability to document savings is an important criterion in receiving incentive pay, agencies with well-developed cost-accounting systems and responsibility for tasks that lend themselves well to measurement are likely always to benefit more than other agencies in incentive pay programs.

Considerable antipathy to group incentive programs emerges as the program's design more clearly designates the type of work it rewards and those it cannot.

Increasing agency discretion acts as an incentive booster for agency and department heads to improve operations and achieve efficiencies. This could also lead to reductions in funding requests by agencies. Allowing for more agency discretion "may serve to reduce bureaucratic resistance to restraint; more management flexibility can be an explicit *quid pro quo* for giving agencies less money" (Aucoin, 1991, p. 135).

## B. Budget-Friendly Productivity Elements

At another level, the productivity program can profit by major changes in the budget system, making it part of a productivity improvement project. The budget system itself has been changed, in this case to one of two major systems, an expenditure control budget or a target-base budget. Short of wholesale system change, retained savings plans remove the biggest disincentive to productivity improvement, the transfer of budget surpluses to the central treasury at the end of the fiscal year. Still short of a savings plan, calculating mechanisms may be added to budget systems. Finally, research on policy and program outcomes suggests that more effort in this direction holds considerable promise.

### 1. Budget Systems

Two types of budgets appear to work expressly to accommodate concerns in productivity programs, expenditure control budgeting and target-base budgeting. The productivity concerns with which they contend were best expressed by Usilaner (1978) who urged that specific budget policy ground rules be issued in advance in budget proceedings as a way of specifying the basis for staffing levels, eliminating arbitrary productivity assumptions, providing for some degree of agency sharing in productivity gains, and defining the consideration to be given to productivity analyses in manpower requirements decisions. The two budget systems live up to Usilaner's demands, each in its own way.

*Expenditure Control Budgeting (ECB).* First developed in California cities in the 1970s, ECB has several elements, according to Herzik (1991). First, the system relies on a base budget figure adjusted for population and price-level changes. Second, ECB-base budgets assume existing service levels and require explicit approval of changes. Third, departments create retained savings plans, developed through productivity plan-induced savings, to finance changes in service levels or increases in programming. Fourth, central budget offices permit departments to carry forward savings gained from underspending their budgets. Fifth, ECB relies on line-item control of spending.

The most important aspects of ECB are selection of a base year and maintenance of department head interest in service delivery innovation. Base years may be different for agencies due to the fact that at any time some have unique expenditures, such as capital projects, and others do not. Careful scrutiny prevents one department's base budget from being inflated, creating unfairness.

Second, a department normally having considerable political clout and able to gain bigger budgets to meet service demands may feel unfairly treated under ECB. Inasmuch as all expansion must be paid out of savings, the department resists. Top management action to force attention to innovation consists of making the sole route to expansion underexpenditure.

*Target-Base Budgeting.* Target-base budgeting relies on excellent revenue forecasting to establish a target (Rubin, 1991; Lynch, 1990; Wenz and Nolan, 1982). Given that accuracy, central budget offices allocate a target figure to departments within which existing service delivery costs must fit. New programs must pass muster separately in budget requests.

The existing services or target budget, even though revenue-driven, forces priority setting and often forces innovations. Rubin (1991, p. 5) points out that the targets are assigned as a percentage of the base budget for a department. The targets "may be less than the department's base, by a percent that varies from year to year, and may vary from department to department." The target is protected, however, in that it is often appropriated lump sum, with review of productivity or performance goals and not spending proposals, allowing a variety of tradeoffs and transfers within departments, between lines, between programs, and even between operating and capital budgets.

The unprotected or new budget requests to expand services compete with those of other departments. The list of a department's projects is submitted in priority order. All lists get substantial scrutiny from budget examiners, Rubin states. These lists force detailed scrutiny to the margin, making target-base budgeting rational but not comprehensive.

## 2.  Retained Savings Plans

Although ECB explicitly mandates retained savings and target-base budgeting creates savings that may be reallocated, such savings plans may exist independently of a budget system fashioned with it in mind. Klay (2001) reviews these savings plans and describes two types, conditional appropriations and discretionary savings plans.

*Conditional Appropriations.* Klay (1978) proposed that legislatures give state agencies direct incentives to innovate by appropriating the agency's funds in two parts, one unconditionally and the other conditionally. The legislature would authorize a part of an agency's program on the condition that the agency generate savings in its unconditionally appropriated program. If the agency is given appropriations for normal service delivery and the highest priority program expansions in its unconditional appropriation, the legislature might also allow the agency to use savings on lower priority expansions. For example (Klay, 1978, p. 28),

> An agency desiring to test the impact of service offices in neighborhood shopping areas could be given conditional authority, if sufficient savings were generated, to rent space and to move people and equipment from the central office. Agencies which administer transfer payments could be authorized to disburse "dividends" on a one time basis to their most needy recipients if savings could be generated by reducing overhead, detecting ineligible recipients sufficiently so that they no longer require help. Agencies which administer grants-in-aid could be authorized to encourage recipients to be cost conscious and to turn back unspent funds so that more of the original applicants could be funded. Those who are able to turn back funds from grants might be rewarded by being given some type of preference in subsequent competitions for awards.

Beyond these examples, the legislature might actually premise supplemental appropriations (especially when revenues are underestimated) on the generation of savings.

*Discretionary Savings Plans.*  To retain some leverage over agencies, especially when the agencies that generate savings are not agencies which central budget offices or legislatures consider to be well managed, finance officers might distribute savings, at their discretion, when productivity goals are met. Boynton et al. (1977) argue the need for greater administrative discretion as a reward for good management. Klay (2001) argues that giving these same well-managed agencies their savings as well would provide substantial incentives.

Discretionary savings plans might also be used in cases where several agencies competed in supplying essentially the same or very similar services. Many have pointed out the productivity potential of interagency competition, especially among agencies such as city governments, school boards, county governments, and independent districts that perform some similar services. State oversight agencies that have some control over the subnational governments might retain discretion to reward those which produce the service most efficiently or develop the greatest level of innovation. The ability to use retained savings might provide an incentive, and merger of service providers might aid in gaining effort toward either efficiency or innovation.

## 3.  Calculating Mechanisms

Beyond the behavioral incentives to act in different and more innovative ways, budget systems could benefit by calculating mechanisms that shed light on other aspects of the allocation problem.

One calculating mechanism, percentaging analysis (Nagel and Malis, 1987), is a form of citizen/member/customer-oriented allocation of resources. The strength of favor citizens/organization members/customers (members) feel toward a budget item and then report, the greater the proportion of total budget the item should receive. The analysis follows these steps:

1. Design a questionnaire for members in which they register the favor for items their dues finance;[2]
2. Average members' reaction scores;
3. Divide each item's reaction score by the sum of all action scores to get a proportion of total "favor";

4.  Multiply the budget by the favor proportion to get an "optimum" budget;
5.  Compare optimum to actual budgets to calculate the degree of under- or overfunding;
6.  Determine membership subgroup differences; and
7.  Ascertain reasons for over- or underfunding.

In the seventh step, Nagel and Malis point out that income-producing activities are likely to be overfunded and less popular than other activities. Likewise, expensive items may be underfunded.

To strengthen the analysis, Nagel and Malis add income and expense, handling them in much the same way as attitudes. In the end, they recommend that expenses be subtracted from income, item by item, and then divided by total expense (assuming a balanced budget). These items are weighted in proportion to attitudes as desired.

Separately, they recommend marginal analysis, relating items. Taking budgets and attitudes at two different times, they could relate them statistically, determining, essentially, the "return" on a budget dollar by attitude change. Two time points risk validity threats, however, especially because other events could have created attitude or budget change; therefore long data series are needed to perform this sort of marginal analysis.

A more important view of percentaging analysis lies in the larger issue of how much to trust attitudinal measures in making budget decisions. Stipak (1984) argues that what citizens respond to in surveys of their attitudes may not be the level of agency performance in delivering the particular service. Others (Brown and Coulter, 1983; Fitzgerald and Durant, 1980; Parks, 1984) view attitudes in much the same way.

## 4.  Outcomes Research

Ultimately, budget-friendly productivity elements must include outcome measures. Providing equitable incentives across agencies may instill a will to innovate, to be efficient, or to attain goals. Attitudes may portray the needs of association members, organization customers, or agency clients. Allocation, however, demands more: an unbiased measure of achievement to which incentive programs may urge effort and against which attitudes may be viewed and balanced. To force budget-friendly performance decisions, therefore, we need outcome measures and a system to monitor work with these measures and evaluate performance itself.

*Measurement.*    In a classic and pioneering study of public sector productivity, Fisk (1983, p. 2) warns of trouble. "Specification and measurement of output are the most difficult problems in measuring the productivity of state and local government," he points out. If output measures are difficult to come by, we maintain, outcome measures are even scarcer.

SEVERAL TYPES OF MEASURES.    There are, according to Fisk, three basic types of measures, operational, immediate, and consequential. Operational measures are those that suggest the internal efficiency of an agency. Fisk mentions number of reports produced, audits completed, and equipment downtime as examples. Such measures help in day-to-day management of an agency, but, strictly speaking, they are not productivity measures, as are immediate and consequential measures.

Immediate measurements are those that depict the final organizational output divided by the resources used to produce it or its input. For example, tons of garbage collected per employee hour provides a ratio, a technical efficiency measure. The shortcoming of these measures relates to their lack of power in explaining why we are collecting garbage, for example (public health or aesthetics), or how well we are doing it. Knowing that we are collecting garbage for public health reasons tells managers what priority to assign kinds of garbage and, therefore, where to go to collect it.

Such a measure is a consequential measure, according to Fisk (1983, p. 2); it "addresses the issue of a program's impact on society and whether the program makes optimum use of resources to achieve its goals." An example of a consequential measure is jobs created per employee hour for an economic development project or the deaths prevented per employee hour for a fire department (the reasonably foreseeable deaths minus the actual deaths). These measures directly relate organization members to the organization's work.

"CHAIN OF OUTPUT" MEASURES. Although immediate and consequential measures have dominated recent performance measurement research in government agencies, relating them to the budget is an effort that demands more attention. How would such research proceed? Swiss (1991) uses the concept of "output chains" to show that budget-friendly productivity elements can be both valid and highly relevant to managers. That is, chains relate the question, "Did we perform the job without wasting resources?" to the other question, "Did the job achieve the desired result?" In our fire department example, we would establish first the number of fires fought (internal efficiency), then the cost per fire fought or fire fought per employee hour, and finally deaths prevented per fire or per employee hour.

Of what validity or relevance is the chain idea? Swiss (1991, p. 146) maintains:

> It forces managers to think through what they really want to measure and how measurable it is; this moves them away from the temptation of choosing indicators on the basis of availability. Developing a chain before designing a management system also alerts managers to likely displacement problems (the further [toward technical efficiency] an indicator is, the more prone to displacement) and to measurability problems (the closer [to the consequential end], the more difficulty in measurement). It alerts them to difficulties with environmental impacts on the indicator (the further [toward consequential], the more outsiders can affect it) and helps them balance the system (the measurements should include at least some indicators [weighted toward the consequential]).

Because budgets, although some more than others, are based on an implicit chain of output, developing budget-friendly productivity elements demands considerable work relating technical efficiency measures to immediate measures, and to consequential measures.

RELATIONSHIP TO INPUT. The measure of input used in immediate and consequential measures has traditionally been that suggested by labor productivity. The reasons seem straightforward. Labor costs, which dominate budgets, are relatively easy to calculate, are available readily in existing data sets, and have private sector data available for comparison. Difficulty in determining a more accurate measure of labor costs has led to widespread use of hours paid as the primary input measure.

*Monitoring and Evaluating.* Feedback systems that use the outcome measures have budget consequences. What the measures emphasize may or may not jibe with the organization's goals, with fairness, or with the budget's emphasis. Consider lessons for social welfare entitlement programs learned from one past program initiative (Danziger, 2000; Randall, 1979) and the budgeting process connected with it. Measures were developed for overpayments and ineligible recipients. The system was monitored and state agencies administering the program sanctioned when their rates substantially exceeded federal standards. Yet the system did not ferret out those underpaid or those who were eligible but not receiving benefits. Truly, the organization's goals were minimized, unfairness increased, and the initiative forced displacement of the long-term economic goals of budget policy.

The initiative also splintered efforts to evaluate the program and guide its development in a budget-friendly way. First, the effort to evaluate the program went in two directions, one political to buttress the claim that the program had eliminated welfare cheats, the other economic to justify the use of transfer payments to provide income floors—a safety net—for the young, the disabled, and the poor.

Second, the initiative failed to guide budget-friendly productivity efforts. The initiative, as many who oppose it now look back and see, failed to discourage dependency. It did nothing to offer alternatives to transfer payments, more or less emphasizing greater spending in the future as transfer payment dependency reached future generations (DeParle, 1991b). Moreover, the initiative's implicit budget policy became cost-centered. Cost-centered budgeting, generally, rewards projects that cost little whatever their productivity value. Cost-centered budgeting leads eventually to zero-sum gaming where increased spending in one area means decreased spending in others and where deferred maintenance (keeping destitute or needy individuals whole) supports new projects.

## V. THE NEW PERFORMANCE-BASE BUDGETING

How, then, can outcome measures support budget-friendly productivity efforts? In the late 1980s, 1990s, and into the new century new, productivity-oriented, performance-based budgeting systems have appeared. The new systems have incorporated and borrowed elements from private sector budget practices and preserved valued features of old budgetary reforms. The new performance-base budgeting also collides with political decision making and poses new questions about how choices should be made and what role budgets should play in management improvement.

### A. Performance-Based Budgets

Fiscal stress and budget deficits, as well as constant dissatisfaction with government performance led to concerted efforts, beginning in the 1980s, to find consensus about the characteristics of good budgeting. In one influential study, several groups in the United States formed the National Advisory Council on State and Local Budgeting (1997) and proposed criteria for a good modern budget. The groups proposed that a budget clearly define policy direction, translate taxes and revenues received into concrete levels of service, show consequences of increases or decreases in service and communicate this to stakeholders, facilitate control over expenditures, motivate and give feedback to employees, and evaluate employee and organization performance and make adjustments.

The criteria came to life in the Government Performance and Results Act (GPRA) of 1993 (Radin, 1998), and likewise in state and local Results Acts and executive orders (Melkers and Willoughby, 1998). GPRA emphasizes program results and agency accountability for them. The Act focuses managers' attention on setting goals, measuring program performance against those goals, and reporting publicly on progress made. Obviously, one of the foremost purposes of the Act is to instill confidence in the public about federal government managers' ability to solve problems and meet citizen/taxpayers' needs.

To implement the federal Results Act, each agency must, first, develop strategic plans covering a period of at least five years. The strategic plan must include a mission statement, outcome-related, measurable goals and objectives, and plans agency managers and professionals intend to follow to achieve these goals through their activities and through their human, capital, information, and other resources. Those in the agency must consult Congress and others interested in or affected by plans; in other words, they must consult stakeholders. As with the private sector budget model, agency managers and professionals must develop annual performance plans that include performance indicators that will cover relevant output, service levels, and outcomes. With these performance plans, "Congress intended. . . to establish a direct annual link between plans and budgets" (U.S. GAO, 1999, p. 3) and to capture the long-range implication of choices and decisions with new methods of recognizing and measuring transactions in the budget (U.S. GAO, 2000; see also GASB, 1999). The U.S. Office of Management and Budget in the President's Executive Office consolidates these measures in the federal budget each year. Agency managers and professionals provide, in annual performance reports to Congress, information on how well they have achieved their goals and performance measures in the previous fiscal year.

Performance-based reforms deal widely with organization change. Budget reform, often undertaken alone, becomes part of the larger government performance enhancement effort. Yet there are even stronger reasons why a management reform will have a greater likelihood of success when the reform includes budgeting. First, no other decision-making system has the leverage to pressure departments to improve program management as does the budget. Second, the budget process always has and always will be the place where everyone raises questions of efficiency, economy, effectiveness, productivity, impact, and results of government activities. Third, the power of the purse is a formidable weapon in getting results. Finally, only budget offices can stimulate, goad, and even inspire agencies to strengthen their programs, operating systems, and organizational structures (Schick, 1966; Caiden, 1998).

Overall, the aim of the Results Act is high, intuitive, and in keeping with traditional reform ideas of accountability and governance. The aim is high given the consolidation of information that a performance budget would provide, everything everyone accomplished, how he or she accomplished it, and how much it cost. The aim is intuitive, as Niskanen (1971, p.42) simply states ". . . a bureau that performs better than expected is likely to be rewarded by higher future budgets." The aim is in keeping with traditional reforms which have held that "systematic presentation of performance information alongside budget amounts" will enrich budget decision making (U.S. GAO, 1999, p. 2).

## B.  The Private Sector Model for the New Performance-Based Budgeting

The current reform efforts reflect private sector concerns. A private sector model of budgeting takes a definite input, output, outcome form (Lazere, 1998; Churchill, 1984;

Hax and Majluf, 1984; Knight, 1981; Trapani, 1982). First, forecasts of the economy, regulations governing business, and markets—customers and competitors—establish some horizon of opportunities and threats. Strategic goal setting follows with analysis of organization strengths and weaknesses. Specific goals result, including what market share the business and its business units can achieve over five or so years and what new business units might be created with what new products or services. The goals translate into annual or tactical performance plans, essentially what should be done and who should do it this year. Plans include targets so that one knows whether one is making progress in achieving strategic business unit goals. The business unit also establishes measurable output and outcomes called substantive and financial scorecards, weighting them in such a way that they balance emphasis according to the strategy the firm has adopted. Budgets, in lump sum and having few process controls, follow plans and give considerable discretion to lower-level managers. Budgets also count in accrual terms in that future spending gets discounted to the present. Finally, individual employee performance plans follow from annual plans. Just as important, these individual plans and their measurable objectives tie into each individual's compensation. Finance underlies and integrally relates all of these components: what does it cost and how much will that cost leverage in earnings? Present decisions must accord with long-term goals. By focusing stronger attention on outcomes and results rather than simply inputs, private sector budgets complement, even motivate, decentralized organization structures and lump sum grants.

## C.  The New Performance-Based Budgeting and Other Budget Reforms

The new systems have borrowed from the successes of budget reforms in the past. In fact, new performance-based budgeting may be understood as drawing on all previous reform efforts. Reform efforts have differed, however, as Larkey and Devereux (1999, p. 167) point out, yet the new performance-based budgeting draws from them all.

First, rationalizing reforms have emphasized enhanced analysis and reason. Those reforms included economic analyses of costs and benefits or marginal utility, especially Planning, Programming Budgeting Systems and zero-based budgeting. New performance-based budgeting's reasoning improvements cover the inclusion of planning, relative value comparisons, and productivity analysis.

Second, there have been ad hoc norm-related reforms, as Sundelson (1935) outlined, that have evolved over the last 150 years or so in Western democracies. The concepts of budget balance, comprehensiveness, and annularity belong to the second, ad hoc norm tradition. Ad hoc norms among performance-based reforms include what Larkey and Devereux call "decisional efficiency," primarily the savings in time and effort that come with decentralization, and "feasible comparisons," the stimulation of competition or cooperation, as appropriate, among agencies in solving particular problems.

Third, there are democratizing reforms that seek to open the decision processes to inform and involve citizens better. Freedom of information and sunshine laws belong to the democratizing movement. Performance-based budgeting's democratizing reforms come from the wider scope of accountability problems the reforms try to tackle with explicit attention given to greater stakeholder and citizen participation and involvement.

Fourth, there are power-shifting reforms such as line-item vetoes that adjust authority and responsibility for budgeting, particularly between executives and legislatures. In performance-based budgeting, power-shifting reforms relate to the broad decentralization of power over budgets, the implicit incentives to reallocate funds from lower to higher priority programs, and the retention of savings when efficiency improvements provide them.

Fifth, there are control reforms such as auditing, tax limitations, and balanced budget amendments that attempt to impose external constraints on decisional behaviors. Greater fiscal control is usually developed to address "the problems of fraud, waste, and abuse in the handling of public money... [with] audits auditing the auditors who audit the auditors, all overseen by legislators looking for political advantage and a sporadically attentive public" (Larkey and Devereux, 1999, p. 178). Performance-based reforms yield a reversal of the traditional fiscal control emphasis on increasing input controls to provide greater output controls as dictated by the accomplishment of specific outcomes or results.

The present concern for results or performance nevertheless builds on the past while contributing much that is new. According to Cothran (1993, p. 450), performance-based budgeting reforms differ in that they

> are generally simpler, more streamlined, and require less paperwork and analysis. They involve more discretion by line managers than did the earlier reforms, and there is a much greater emphasis on accountability than under the older formats. Finally, the recent reforms are motivated by a desire to change fundamentally the culture of public management by turning bureaucrats into entrepreneurs. Previous budgetary reforms pursued legality, efficiency, and effectiveness. The present wave of budgetary reform aims to stimulate motivation. The new approaches incorporate most of the goals of the previous reforms, but they seek to achieve them through decentralized incentives that give program managers greater authority to combine resources as they think best but that hold the managers accountable for the results.

To Cothran there is much of the old, but a newer decentralized emphasis provides managers much discretion.

## D. The Politics of the New Performance-Based Budgeting

The performance-based reforms have also come at a time of clashing national priorities and movements at all levels of government. The setting for reform has come in a period of change that has seen budget cutting and surplus dividing, sometimes at the same time, making this a different era for reform. As Radin (1998, p. 311) observes, "[The Results Act accentuates] planning. The tradition of planning is embedded in an era of growth; plans are most often used as a way to choose new directions or to expand programs." Strategic plans in performance-based reforms, therefore, must deal with issues not as new initiatives added on to existing programs but as reallocations that eliminate an existing program if a new one is proposed.

The nature of government service delivery now runs counter to the direction of traditional reforms. Devolution and privatization, compounding the existing fragmentation in decision making, play against strategic planning's usual emphasis on centralization. The fundamental nature of entitlements and block grants reduces much of the budget's ability to force compliance with state and national spending and performance priorities.

The mixed ideological motives of those who support performance-based reforms also loom large. Again, Radin observes (1998, pp. 311–312; Shin, 1997), "It is clear that some proponents of the legislation are those who advocate good government for its own sake, but ... [while] performance measures could give an agency that's targeted for extinction proof of its effectiveness, such standards could also provide Members [of Congress] determined to sink an agency just the ammo they need."

## E.  The Budgetary Theory Underlying the New Performance-Based Budgeting

The budget theory underlying the Results Act, however, is not beyond dispute, and therein lies the eventual path these performance-based reforms will take toward budgeting success or failure. Since empirical research began building, much has appeared to tell budgeteers to "avoid too good results" (Wildavsky, 1964, p. 93). Why?

The danger of claiming superb accomplishments is that Congress and the Budget Bureau may reward the agency by ending the program. "Why would you need five more people in the supervisory unit?" John Rooney inquired of the Justice Department. "Since you are doing so well, as we have heard for fifteen minutes, you surely do not need any more supervision." However good it may be said that results are, it is advisable to put equal stress on what remains to be done. "Progress has been realized in the past," the Civil Defense agency asserted, "but we cannot permit these past accomplishments to lull us into a false sense of security" (Wildavsky, 1964, p. 93).

At least one empirical test confirms Wildavsky's view and rejects Niskanen's assertion (Warren, 1975). Other budget behavior observers, such as Schick (1978, p. 179), have agreed, pointing out that the "budget process conventionally confronts managers with the uncomfortable risk of a loss of funds if they try to purge inefficiencies from their agencies." The fact that an agency performs well does not inform the decision about the need for additional resources: "... should it be provided with more resources to do an even better job, or should it be cut back on the grounds that its purpose has been achieved and it is no longer needed? ... If a program is doing badly, and showing few results, does this mean it should be terminated, or provided with more resources to do a better job?" (Caiden, 1998, p. 44). In broader issues of resource allocation, Caiden finds performance somewhat irrelevant in deciding "whether a given sum of money is too little, too much, or just right to preserve a species, operate a system of trauma centers, or monitor or control contagious diseases." Political popularity and the necessity of balancing budgets often become the sole reasons for budget decisions. In addition, the technology of performance measurement has not, overall, developed to the point where program results may be understood unequivocally.

Very cautious optimism exists. Joyce (1993, p. 14) predicts deliberate but eventual acceptance of performance-based reforms and budgets. He notes that experience suggests a large impact on budgets' main reason for being, tradeoffs, illustrating that

> If the choice were between a job training and an air pollution program, we might know that adding $100 million more to the EPA budget would make the air cleaner by X amount, while costing Y amount of lost wages from workers who had not been trained. If we had all of these data (and we believed them), that would make decisions more informed.

He adds that knowing what is traded off against what does not make the choice between cleaner air and higher incomes through job training easier.

The caution comes with ingrained tendencies in budgeting. In the sense of how budgeting works now, performance-based reforms discourage micromanagement. The current budget system tends to encourage excessive attention on budget input by political leaders, excessive control over individual budget line-items, rather than the macromanagement of values that Key (1940) suggests as the sole prerogative and most important function of politics. The question of whether political leaders will assume a textbook role remains an open one.

How will performance-based reforms influence budgets, then? Observers argue that eventual acceptance will come as the result of a culture change brought about by valid information and acceptance of new budget roles, but we add agreed-upon measures of results, clearly articulated authorizations and appropriations, and the delegation of management to public administrators whose discretion the budget rewards.

From a different point of view, by not forcing performance information into a decisive role in budgeting but forcing budgeteers to oversee management improvements, reforms will change budgeting. The reforms have forced management improvement into the budget office through what is seen when the M appears in OMB, the office of management and budget in federal, state, and local governments. At the same time, budget offices have become more independent of finance offices, traditionally the tax collection, accounting, purchasing, debt management, and budgeting office, and more allied with the Chief Administrative or Operating Officer or the Chief Executive Officer. Questions about the capacity of a budget office, possibly knowledgeable about costs and concerned most with overall spending and tax levels, to review managerial issues and performance quickly emerge. Questions remain about whether a budget office can cope with management improvement on top of budget examination and control and whether they should.

Others are not as optimistic and even see a period in which budget offices may drift and lose their comfortable anchors. At the federal level, the Results Act came after reductions on the management side of the U.S. Office of Management and Budget (Moe, 1994). What will budget officers do? According to Schick (1990, p. 33),

> The old controller role is slipping away and, along with it, the leverage that budget officials exercised over departments as well as a part of their database for monitoring expenditures. Central staff understand that it does not suffice for them to make the big decisions while ceding all the details to spenders. They hope that performance measures will substitute for the lost information and controls while giving them an important niche in the management process. Yet they are not sure things will work out this way. While the budget offices . . . generally support decentralization, they worry that the new performance-based system will leave them without effective roles or controls. They are not confident that performance measurement will go beyond technique to the behavior of managers. Departments will "take the money and run," one budget official protested. But he also conceded that the old controls are no longer viable.

Thus decentralization and devolution as well as a results orientation in performance-based reforms are replacing traditional structures and institutions. The budget theory is not clear although eventual use of performance information in budgeting seems imminent.

Performance-based reforms have become a major movement and are now often compared to the reform era of the late 1800s and early 1900s. This reform movement, for budgeting however, resembles much that has happened in previous budget reform episodes. Budget offices in the past have changed from staffs of accountants to staffs of economists. Whether budget offices will now be staffed with organization and management theorists and what the basic forces of budgetary decision making will be remain to be seen.

## VI. CONCLUSION

Budget matters and managerial or productivity concerns have existed independently of each other in the history of reform in government. Productivity-friendly budget changes that have appeared transfer discretion across budget accounts or line-items, decentralized control, and discretion over salary savings, greater attention to performance measurement, and individual or group reward and incentive plans. Budget-friendly productivity changes that have appeared include new budget systems such as expenditure control budgeting and target-base budgeting, retained savings plans, new methods of soliciting feedback from those affected by programs, and greater attention to outcomes in budgeting. Both productivity-friendly budget changes and budget-friendly productivity improvements promise a closer connection between budgeting and management in government.

Moreover, the newest reform, performance-based budgeting, has introduced an even tighter connection. Performance-based budgeting has promise as a truly revolutionary movement, borrowing from valued parts of reform movements in the past and also adopting components of successful private sector budgeting processes. This budgeting reform has the potential not only to strengthen management improvement efforts with the action forcing potential of budgets, but the reform also may change budgeting by forcing management improvement or productivity to become a major concern of budgeters.

## NOTES

1. Through analytical methods, budgets also consider different personnel and performance combinations. For example, *utility theory* examines the relative worth of various alternatives measured subjectively and generally incorporating probability and the decision makers' attitudes toward risk. *Cost-effectiveness analysis* measures the relative efficiency of various technologies in achieving an already decided maximum result. *Cost–benefit analysis* measures the relative efficiency of projects economically, asking whether the intended effects are worth the cost.
2. Nagel and Malis used a -2, -1, 0, + 1, + 2/strongly disagree ⇔ strongly agree scale that United Artisan League members used in answering the question, "The following activities are important to me."

## REFERENCES

Anton, T. J. (1964). *Budgeting in Three Illinois Cities*. Urbana, IL: Institute of Government and Public Affairs.

Aucoin, P. (1991). The politics and management of restraint budgeting. In: Blais, A., Dion, S., eds. *The Budget Maximizing Bureaucrat: Appraisals and Evidence.* Pittsburgh: University of Pittsburgh Press, pp. 119–141.

Boynton, R. P., Medina, W. A., Covello, L. S. (1977). How you always wanted to manage but were not allowed to try. *Bureaucrat* 6:131–151.

Brown, K., Coulter, P. (1983). Subjective and objective measures of public service delivery. *Public Admin. Rev.* 43:50–58.

Burkhead, J. (1956). *Government Budgeting.* New York: Wiley.

Burkhead, J. (1972). The budget and democratic government. In: Fremont, J. L., Miller, E. G., eds. *Planning, Programming, Budgeting.* Chicago: Markham, pp. 63–77.

Caiden, N. (1998). Public service professionalism for performance measurement and evaluation. *Public Budget. Finan.* 18(2):35–52.

Churchill, N. C. (1984). Budget choice: Planning vs. control. *Harvard Bus. Rev.* 62(4):150–164.

Cleveland, F. A. (1915). Evolution of the budget idea in the United States. *Ann. Am. Acad. Polit. Soc. Sci.* 62:15–35.

Cothran, D. A. (1993). Entrepreneurial budgeting: an emerging reform? *Public Admin. Rev.* 53(5):445–454.

Danziger, S. (2000). Approaching the limit: Early lessons from welfare reform. Proceedings of the Conference Rural Dimensions of Welfare Reformed, sponsored by the Joint Center for Poverty Research, Northwestern University/University of Chicago.

DeParle, J. (1991a, September 26). Painted by numbers, 1980's are rosy to G.O.P., while Democrats see red. *New York Times* B10.

DeParle, J. (1991b, December 9). In new social era, Moynihan sees "new" social ills. *New York Times* A13.

Fisk, D. (1983). *Measuring Productivity in State and Local Government. Bulletin 2166, U.S. Department of Labor, Bureau of Labor Statistics.* Washington, DC: U.S. Government Printing Office.

Fitzgerald, M., Durant, R. (1980). Citizen evaluations and urban management: service delivery in an era of protest. *Public Admin. Rev.* 40:585–594.

GASB (Government Accounting Standards Board). (1999). Statement No. 34: Basic financial statements—and management's discussion and analysis—for state and local governments. Norwalk, CT: GASB.

Grizzle, G. (1998). Budgeting and financial management: propositions for theory and practice. In: Rabin, J., Hildreth, W. B., Miller, G. J., eds. *Handbook of Public Administration.* 2d ed. New York: Marcel Dekker, pp. 223–263.

Grizzle, G. (2001). Linking performance to funding decisions: What is the budgeter's role? In: Miller, G. J., Hildreth, W. B., Rabin, J., eds. *Performance-Based Budgeting.* Boulder, CO: Westview, pp. 203–214.

Grossbard, S. I. (n.d.). *PPBS for State and Local Officials.* Kingston, RI: Bureau of Government Research, University of Rhode Island.

Hatry, H. P. (1972). Reflecting the consumer viewpoint in state and local government fiscal and expenditure decision. *Nat. Tax J.* 25:260–273.

Hax, A. C., Majluf, N. S. (1984). The corporate strategic planning process. *Interfaces* 14(1):47–60.

Herzik, E. B. (1991). Improving budgetary management and fostering innovation: expenditure control budgeting. *Public Product. Manage. Rev.* 14:237–248.

Jones, L. R., Euske, K. J. (1991). Strategic misrepresentation in budgeting. *J. Public Admin. Res. Theor.* 1:437–460.

Joyce, P. G. (1993). Using performance measures for federal budgeting: proposals and prospects. *Public Budget. Finan.* 13(4):3–17.

Key, V. O. (1940). The lack of a budgetary theory. *Am. Polit. Sci. Rev.* 34:1137–1144.

Klay, W. E. (1978). A legislative tool to encourage agency efficiency. *Public Product. Rev.* 3(1):23–31.

Klay, W. E. (2001). Management through budgetary incentives. In: Miller, G. J., Hildreth, W. B., Rabin, J., eds. *Performance-Based Budgeting*. Boulder, CO: Westview, pp. 215–227.

Knight, H. C. (1981). Budgeting: a contrast of preaching and practice. *Cost Manage*. 55(6):42–46.

Larkey, P. D., Devereux, E. A. (1999). Good budgetary decision processes. In: Frederickson, H. G., Johnston, J. M., eds. *Public Management Reform and Innovation: Research, Theory and Application*. Tuscaloosa: University of Alabama Press, pp. 166–188.

Lauth, T. P. (2001). Budgeting and productivity in state government: Not integrated but friendly. In: Miller, G. J., Hildreth, W. B., Rabin, J., eds. *Performance-Based Budgeting*. Boulder, CO: Westview, pp. 191–202.

Lazere, C. (1998). All together now: Why you must link budgeting and forecasting to planning and performance. *CFO* 14(2):28–36.

Lynch, T. E. (1990). *Public Budgeting in America*. 3rd ed. Englewood Cliffs, NJ: Prentice-Hall.

Melkers, J., Willoughby, K. (1998). The state of the states: Performance-based budgeting requirements in 47 out of 50. *Public Admin. Rev.* 58:66–73.

Miller, G. J. (1991). *Government Financial Management Theory*. New York: Marcel Dekker.

Moe, R. (1994). The reinventing government exercise: misinterpreting the problem, misjudging the consequences. *Public Admin. Rev.* 54(2):111–122.

Nagel, S., Malis, B. (1987). Using percentaging analysis for more productive budgeting. *Public Product. Rev.* 44:65–92.

National Advisory Council on State and Local Budgeting. (1997). *A Framework for Improved State and Local Government Budgeting and Recommended Budget Practices*. Chicago: Government Finance Officers Association.

Niskanen, W. A. (1971). *Bureaucracy and Representative Government*. Chicago: Aldine-Atherton.

Novick, D. (1968). The origin and history of program budgeting. In: Hyde, A. C., ed. *Government Budgeting*. 2nd ed. New York: Harcourt Brace, pp. 342–348.

Parks, R. (1984). No apologies. *Public Admin. Rev.* 44:552.

Pyhrr, P. A. (November–December 1970). Zero-base budgeting. *Harvard Bus. Rev.*, 111–121.

Radin, B. A. (1998). The Government Performance and Results Act (GPRA): hydra-headed monster or flexible management tool. *Public Admin. Rev.* 58(4):307–315.

Randall, R. (1979). Presidential power versus bureaucratic intransigence: the influence of the Nixon administration on welfare policy. *Am. Polit. Sci. Rev.* 73:798–800.

Ridley, C. E., Simon, H. A. (1943). *Measuring Municipal Activities*. Washington, DC: International City Managers Association.

Rubin, I. S. (1991). Budgeting for our times: target base budgeting. *Public Budget. Finan.* 11:5–14.

Schick, A. (1966). The road to PPB. *Public Admin. Rev.* 26:243–258.

Schick, A. (1978). The road from ZBB. *Public Admin. Rev.* 38(2):177–180.

Schick, A. (1990). Budgeting for results: Recent developments in five industrialized countries. *Public Admin. Rev.* 50(1):26–34.

Shin, A. (1997). On the front burner. *Nat. J.* 21:1289.

Shirras, G. F. (1936). *The Science of Public Finance*. 2 Vols. London: Macmillan.

Smithies, A. (1955). *The Budgetary Process in the United States*. New York: McGraw-Hill.

Stipak, B. (1984). Comment on performance. *Public Admin. Rev.* 44:551–552.

Stourm, R. (1917). Thaddeus, Plazinski, ed. *The Budget*. New York: Appleton.

Sundelson, J. W. (1935). Budgetary principles. *Polit. Sci. Quart.* 50(2):236–263.

Swiss, J. E. (1991). *Public Management Systems: Monitoring and Managing Government Performance*. Englewood Cliffs, NJ: Prentice-Hall.

Thurmaier, K. (1995). Decisive decision making in the executive budget process: Analyzing the political and economic propensities of central budget bureau analysts. *Public Admin. Rev.* 55:448–460.

Trapani, C. S. (1982). Six critical areas in the budgeting process. *Manage. Account.* 64(5):52–56.

U.S. GAO. U.S. General Accounting Office. (1983). *Increased Use of Productivity Measurement Can Help Control Government Costs.* Washington, DC: U.S. Government Printing Office.

U.S. GAO. U.S. General Accounting Office. (1999). *Performance Budgeting: Initial Agency Experiences Provide a Foundation to Assess Future Directions (GAO/T-AIMD-GGD-99-216, July 1).* Washington, DC: General Accounting Office.

U.S. GAO. U.S. General Accounting Office. (2000). *Accrual Budgeting: Experiences of Other Nations and Implications for the United States (GAO/AIMD-00-57, February).* Washington, DC: General Accounting Office.

Usilaner, B. (1978). Productivity: A management tool for controlling government spending. *Public Product. Rev.* 3(2):25–34.

Warren, R. S. (1975). Bureaucratic performance and budgetary reward. *Public Choice* 24:51–57.

Wenz, T., Nolan, A. (1982). Budgeting for the future: Target base budgeting. *Public Budget. Finan.* 2:88–91.

Wildavsky, A. (1964). *The Politics of the Budgetary Process.* Boston: Little Brown.

Wildavsky, A. (December 1966). The political economy of efficiency. *Public Admin. Rev.* 26:292–310.

Wildavsky, A. (March–April 1969). Rescuing policy analysis from PPBS. *Public Admin. Rev.* 29:189–202.

Wildavsky, A. (1986). *Budgeting.* Rev. ed. Piscataway, NJ: Transaction.

Wildavsky, A. (1992). *The New Politics of the Budgetary Process.* 2nd ed. New York: Harper/Collins.

Wildavsky, A. (2001). Transformation of budgetary norms. In: Swedlow, B., ed. *Budgeting and Governing.* Piscataway, NJ: Transaction, pp. 235–248.

# 22

## Benefit–Cost Analysis

**GERALD J. MILLER**
*Rutgers University, Newark, New Jersey, U.S.A.*

**DONIJO ROBBINS**
*Grand Valley State University, Grand Rapids, Michigan, U.S.A.*

## I. INTRODUCTION

Government allocation decisions have a significant influence on the nation's productivity—its economic efficiency—and, particularly, on government productivity. Specific allocation decisions, those in budget and regulatory policies, have a profound effect on societal and economic affairs as well. Therefore, understanding allocation decision making can provide insight about just how and with what consequences allocation decisions are made to enhance productivity as well as to mollify contending social forces.

One allocation tool, benefit–cost analysis (BCA), has grown in popularity at least among policy analysts, in the four most recent presidential administrations, as the tool of choice in determining allocations. Therefore, this tool takes on greater significance, and we should wonder how well we understand its foreseen and unforeseen consequences.

Allocation refers to government action to define the country's needs and set priorities for fulfilling them. It is through allocation policy, substantially, that public expenditure policy and regulatory policy are made. Both spending and regulation decisions determine in concrete terms what government agencies and staff members do and how they do it.

Allocation technology is not value-free. In allocation, ideological positions compete for the critical premise or assumption. Allocation policy is quite often framed in terms of equity versus efficiency. Equity dictates that policies and programs give to each according to his needs from each according to her abilities whereas efficiency suggests that projects should result in at least one person being better off and no one worse off.

As a result, determining what technology to employ in making allocation choices has great allure and controversy. One controversial method of organizing information is benefit–cost analysis, and in this chapter, we look at its rationale and methods. Then we critique the use of BCA in achieving productivity. We define productivity as economic efficiency—benefits exceed costs—and seek to determine whether productivity can be achieved with the methods provided by BCA.

## II.  RATIONALE AND METHOD OF BENEFIT–COST ANALYSIS

One of the reasons a government exists is to act as the agency of last resort. Government usually gets asked to do those things everyone else is either unwilling or unable to do. Formally, therefore, one of the major concerns of government policy makers has to do with compensating for what markets fail to provide or leave as a consequence of what they do provide. For the purpose of description here, we call government action to remedy market failures the provision of public goods. This section describes the way governments make choices in coping with market failure. First, we reintroduce the fiscal allocation role of government and briefly explain how governments fulfill it. Second, we explain how market failure occurs. Third, we discuss the decision-making process that is used to determine the proper amounts of public goods that should be produced by governments. Finally, we discuss the relatively new concept of "non-market failures" and the contributions of economic reasoning to the financial management of government agencies.

### A.  Fiscal Functions of Government

There are certain goods that few will produce, often leaving it to government to provide some things every one needs. For instance, national defense, the classic case, is a commodity that is too expensive, too complicated, and in general, too hazardous to society to leave for each citizen to provide for himself or herself.

In any case, we find government as the provider of last resort when "market failure" occurs. Market failure strikes when the normal processes of the giant auction we call the economy does not work efficiently, specifically when rationing is neither feasible nor desirable (Stiglitz, 1988; Musgrave and Musgrave, 1980).

Rationing is not feasible when no one can be excluded from use of a product or service. Fire services to a complex of abutting apartments may not be feasible, inasmuch as containing a fire in one gives benefits to all. Because no one is excluded, all except the one who pays become free riders. No price system for rationing makes sense.

Rationing may also be undesirable even though feasible. For instance, an uncrowded bridge could be paid for with a toll device forcing drivers to pay as they enter. Because the bridge is uncrowded, the toll may actually decrease traffic and provide an incentive to seek alternative routes to avoid the tariff.

In both cases, rationing through normal market mechanisms does not work as it would otherwise. Other methods must be used to decide allocation: how much each apartment dweller should pay for fire protection and how big a bridge to build.

Government's allocation functions relate to the provision of public services. Generally, the problem is to decide how much and what type of public goods to provide. Decision makers need some sort of mechanism for deciding these questions, and luckily, they have not just one but four mechanisms: basic economic feasibility, Pareto optimality, the Kaldor criterion, and democratic voting.

## 1. Economic Feasibility

Economic feasibility or economic efficiency is simply when the benefits from a public program exceed the costs of that program. Consider the following two programs, each costing society $10,000 but yielding different benefits. The first program, program A, is not economically feasible; benefits are less than costs. Program B is economically feasible because benefits to society as a whole, the summation of all individual benefits, exceed societal costs. Policy makers, if using only this method, would choose program B. In the end, however, program B does not meet productivity standards; that is, efficiency and equity are not realized because one person is made worse off in the end. See Tables 1 and 2.

## 2. Pareto Criterion

Named after the nineteenth century economist, the Pareto criterion guides selection of a policy by favoring those in which at least one person is better off and no person is worse off as a result of the policy. It goes one step further than economic feasibility, allowing for more equity.

What policies have such an unambiguous goodness attached to them? Education might, but some suffer lost earnings from going to school that they will never recoup. What about water and air quality? There are sunk costs in pollution that we could say one would suffer loss in remedying.

Consider program B where efficiency is achieved but equity is lacking. Using the Pareto criterion, although the majority of individuals is made better off, there is one person, C, whose position is made worse; the individual costs are more than the individual benefits. Under this criterion, then, policy makers would not fund program B.

Program C, on the other hand, would be funded because it is both economically feasible and meets Pareto optimality (see Table 3); at least one person, here A, B, D, and E, is made better off without making any one worse off.

## 3. Kaldor Criterion

Another method of dealing with welfare, the Kaldor criterion, is slightly less demanding. This method begs the question, should we or should we not accept a

**Table 1**  Program A

| Individual | Benefits ($) | Costs ($) | Surplus (loss) ($) |
| --- | --- | --- | --- |
| A | 3,000 | 2,000 | 1,000 |
| B | 2,500 | 2,000 | 500 |
| C | 500 | 2,000 | (1,500) |
| D | 500 | 2,000 | (1,500) |
| E | 2,000 | 2,000 | 0 |
| Total | 8,500 | 10,000 | (1,500) |

**Table 2**  Program B

| Individual | Benefits ($) | Costs ($) | Surplus (loss) ($) |
|------------|--------------|-----------|--------------------|
| A | 3,000 | 2,000 | 1,000 |
| B | 3,500 | 2,000 | 1,500 |
| C | 1,000 | 2,000 | (1,000) |
| D | 3,000 | 2,000 | 1,000 |
| E | 2,500 | 2,000 | 500 |
| Total | 13,000 | 10,000 | 3,000 |

policy if those in the community benefiting from the policy compensate those who lose by the policy, especially if the winners or beneficiaries still have some gain left over?

Consider this example. If the strict private goods only requirement were not relaxed (libertarianism), we would never get such goods as pristine ocean beaches. One finds it extremely difficult to slice up pieces of the ocean in order to allocate maintenance responsibilities to protect the beach. Moreover, nature's ways in forcing erosion and so on would make such coercion folly. Will one person maintain the beaches? Not by the table of benefits, especially when those benefits are held down by the inability to divide the resource or exclude others from its use.

But should the beaches be maintained? If costs equal the expense of maintaining the beaches and benefits equal the sum of everyone's perception of betterment, if economic feasibility occurs then common sense would tell us yes. For example, the $10,000 program, program C, provides greater benefits to some than to others. The gains range from $500 for E to $1,500 for B.

We might say that the $10,000 version of beach cleanup is less equitable than it is efficient. Defining productivity as a balance between equity and efficiency, we want to find the program that would achieve both. The Kaldor criterion is meant to suggest a way to find that program.

Recall that the Kaldor criterion provides for winners compensating losers in a given situation. Without assuming any losers, however, we can still create a Kaldor-like result, as Table 4 illustrates. To ensure that the winners bear their fair share of the costs and still stand to reap some gain, the maximum project would have to be $13,999. We can compute this amount by distributing the costs in the same way as the original surpluses so that one person gains $1 of surplus, whereas all others have benefits that equal their costs.

**Table 3**  Program C

| Individual | Benefits ($) | Costs ($) | Surplus (loss) ($) |
|------------|--------------|-----------|--------------------|
| A | 3,000 | 2,000 | 1,000 |
| B | 3,500 | 2,000 | 1,500 |
| C | 2,000 | 2,000 | 0 |
| D | 3,000 | 2,000 | 1,000 |
| E | 2,500 | 2,000 | 500 |
| Total | 14,000 | 10,000 | 4,000 |

**Table 4** Program C

| Individual | Benefits ($) | Costs ($) | Surplus ($) |
|---|---|---|---|
| A | 3,000 | 2,999 | 1 |
| B | 3,500 | 3,500 | 0 |
| C | 2,000 | 2,000 | 0 |
| D | 3,000 | 3,000 | 0 |
| E | 2,500 | 2,500 | 0 |
| Total | 14,000 | 13,999 | 1 |

The dispersion of benefits and costs underlies the progressive tax structure and distribution of income programs that have guided the construction and maintenance of the American version of the welfare state for more than fifty years. More to the point of this chapter, however, the Kaldor criterion underlies the measurement of productivity and, like benefit–cost analysis, the Kaldor criterion argues that as long as the benefits exceed the costs of a project, the project should go forward.

## 4. Voting

The problem with mathematical approaches to determine public program funding is the determination of benefits, especially those that are intangible and immeasurable. In a country where individualism and decentralized decision making reign, we assume that each person can value a policy alone. The sum of those values becomes the public welfare. However, this makes it difficult to calculate individual benefits. Instead the political system, specifically the voting system, takes care of that.

But what vote should be required—unanimity? Three-fourths? Two-thirds? Fifty percent plus one? Plurality? The answer lies in the analysis of voting by legislative bodies. Following Buchanan and Tullock (1962), the analysis falls on the interaction of two variables: the loss of value that occurs when we do not include in any decision each individual's own calculation of benefit from a given project, and the cost of making an effort to ascertain each individual's preferences.

The price system determines what and how much of a public good to produce. Voting, on the other hand, applies in finding the expected cost to the individual and to the group or public of implementing a public project. How much effort to exert in finding these individual preferences, or specifically, in determining when we can feel sure we have solicited the opinions of enough people and when enough people desire a project to warrant its implementation constitutes the basis of voting analysis.

Voting analysis demands that we know individuals' preferences toward a project. Obviously, 100% voting participation resulting in a consensus decision on the project would guide decision makers in making a valid decision. The first variable in voting analysis, therefore, is the probability of violating the Pareto criterion as we depart from unanimous consent. Such a problem occurs in sampling as well as in choosing majority rule over consensus.

Nevertheless, gaining unanimity has drawbacks, not the least of which is the cost entailed in cajoling participation and informing voting. The counterbalance to total participation and consensus is the cost that both would entail. The closer we get to total participation and consensus in voting, the higher the cost of the voting process.

The lower the cost of the voting process, the less likely it is that we will have valid facsimiles of the voters' preferences. That is, the majority of votes of the number of voters may not be valid expressions of the preferences of the total population even though such an election may cost less than any methods we could use to secure unanimity.

Obviously, the appropriate system of voting involves trading off the cost of exclusion against the cost of the election, a calculation easier than it looks. We seldom have a single issue where an individual has two choices and perfect information about them both. Rather, we have a continuous stream of issues about which individuals have varying levels of intensity of preferences.

It can be shown through studies of public opinion that our knowledge of and attention paid to issues facing members of Congress is relatively low. Given that there are over 10,000 or so measures members see in every session, we, as voters, probably know something (if anything at all) about less than one percent and have intense preferences about even fewer, say one tenth of one percent. Moreover, we probably have full and complete knowledge of even less, perhaps one-hundredth of one percent.

Also the intensity of preferences among voters tends to form a regular pattern. Very few voters feel intensely either way about an issue. The vast majority, the middle, has no feeling at all about an issue and probably does not find the issue itself salient.

Such arrays of preferences yield themselves to vote trading—logrolling—as well as coalition building. In cases where we have public provision of private goods, we have the conditions for bargaining: costly participation, isolated issue salience, and unclear estimates of who benefits through policies and by how much. These conditions create one of two things, overspending (Buchanan and Tullock, 1962) and underspending (Downs, 1960).

Consider an example Buchanan and Tullock (1962) offer as support for the idea that logrolling tends to create more expenditure than would ordinarily be the case if economic efficiency controlled. Consider the case of one hundred farmers in a locality, each of whom is served by a separate access road requiring maintenance. Maintenance of a specific road must have the consent of a majority of voters and, if so, is financed out of general tax revenues levied on all hundred farmers equally. If each road's maintenance is voted on separately and no logrolling takes place, no road improvements would pass under general tax financing. Each road improvement benefits only one person but the cost is borne by several.

Suppose vote-trading agreements can take place. In order to have his road repaired, each farmer must agree to support the road repairs of fifty other farmers in order to get the fifty-one votes required for his own road repairs. The benefit to one farmer is having his own road repaired. The cost to the farmer willing to trade votes is his share of the repairs to be done on the other fifty roads he agrees to support. In the general case, each of the farmers will attempt to secure an agreement with fifty other farmers and the agreements will probably be overlapping, inasmuch as all one hundred farmers want to get their own roads repaired. In the end each farmer will have secured agreement to have his road repaired. In determining the level of road repairs on each road, the benefit to the farmer whose road is being repaired is weighted against the costs of fifty farmers of repairing it. The costs incurred by the other forty-nine farmers not included in that particular agreement are neglected. Overall, the cost to all farmers will exceed the benefits from the chosen level of repairs in each road. The logrolling process will have resulted in overexpenditure.

Anthony Downs (1960) demonstrates the opposite case, the case for spending less than would be necessary. If we consider the same example above but substitute higher education for road repair, we might find that the calculation of benefits each farmer made would result in undervaluing the public expenditure. Arguments, except for the agricultural experiment station, the cooperative extension service, and the college of agriculture at the state land grant university, would probably tend toward belittling most benefits and accentuating higher education's costs because the farmers believe the funding should support farming and like activities. In the end, higher education might be underfunded, given some notion of adequate or efficient funding, and the entire government budget made smaller than economic efficiency might otherwise dictate.

In the end, allocation may be approached through logrolling or through benefit–cost analysis. Benefit–cost analysis is that allocation principle in which a project is selected if the benefits and costs are weighted and the result makes society better off. The problem with benefit–cost analysis lies in implementing shared benefits in such a way that those who bear most of the costs get enough of the benefits to offset their losses.

Logrolling, using the political process to allocate, examines a project in the context of all projects on the agenda for study at one time. The supporters of a project ultimately get their way only because they trade favors with supporters of other projects. The result is a sharing of benefits and costs so that both sets of supporters, as a whole, are better off. The problems with logrolling tend to be those related to overspending, a condition supporters of logrolling think is a function of viewing of the needs of the individual as greater than the needs of society. That is, those who favor benefit–cost analysis, and who believe logrolling results in overspending, tend to be those who favor the right of the individual to reach her goals in competition with others without help from the government. Those who favor logrolling rather than benefit–cost analysis see the needs of society as paramount, at least those needs which, in the end, are believed to make societal benefits greater than the costs to society.

## III. ALLOCATION, ORGANIZATION, ANALYSIS—MICRO AND MACRO

Benefit–cost structures drive project-by-project or budget-by-budget decisions. For simplicity purposes, we follow Schmid's (1990) organization. At the micro or project level, an analyst delves into the preferences for that project versus its cost. At the macro or budget level, decision makers must cope with combining, into some meaningful whole, projects that have overcome microlevel constraints. The systematic aggregation of microdecisions is not truly a macrodecision. In reality, budgets are conducted from both microviews and from some systematic macroview (often called an ideology or a political platform) that details how the entire basket of public goods should be chosen. This section describes both levels of analysis and some practical ways the two levels may complement each other.

### A. Micro—Benefit–Cost Analysis

To begin a benefit–cost analysis, at least one project needs to be studied. In this case, the concept is straightforward: determine benefits and costs; then find the ratio of dollar-quantified benefits, at their current value, to dollar-quantified costs, at their current value (B/C). If that ratio is greater than one, the analysis suggests, because benefits are greater than costs, that the project should be considered for inclusion in the jurisdiction's budget.

This concept includes the major ideas influencing the analysis. First is the notion of measuring benefits and costs. This involves estimating, forecasting, and costing them, all difficult to do in the public goods sector. The second idea is measuring benefits and costs at their current value. This requires the knowledge of preferences about the time value of money and the impacts of inflation.

## 1.   Uncertainty and the Measurement of Benefits and Costs

Measuring benefits and costs involves carefully considering both the obvious and not so obvious elements that a project will entail, forecasting changes that will occur and affect these elements over time, and including (costing) the elements properly, that is, in both accounting and economic terms. Here, we describe the hazards of estimating, forecasting, and costing.

*Estimating*.   The first element of measurement is estimation. Estimation deals with the type of cost or benefit to be counted and benefits and costs that are real or pecuniary types, tangible or intangible, as well as direct or indirect benefits. First, real benefits and costs are those that have a real or absolute consequence for society as a whole. That is, on balance the benefit or cost to society is not one in which the cost to one group of individuals is offset by the benefit to another group of individuals. The benefit or cost is not merely redistributed, as a pecuniary benefit or cost would describe, but an absolute change in the wellbeing of society as a whole.

Second, tangible and intangible benefits and costs describe the difference between those that can be priced or where society can agree relatively easily on a price and those that cannot. A tangible benefit–cost to many is a project such as a dam, with its measurable construction costs and irrigation, flood control, and recreation benefits. An intangible cost might be the endangered species that are destroyed as a result of the dam's displacement and destruction of the species' habitat.

The last type of benefit and cost that must be confronted in estimating the numbers that feed the benefit–cost analysis is the direct–indirect contrast. Direct costs are those immediately apparent from the project. The dam example, both tangible costs and tangible benefits, illustrates this idea. The indirect or secondary costs of the dam's construction might include things such as poorer or better drainage of streams and marshes that feed the undammed stream; greater air and noise pollution as a result of recreational equipment used on reservoirs created by the dam; and even climate changes resulting from large bodies of water replacing water flows.

In each case, the analysis would not be complete without considering the pecuniary, intangible, and indirect benefits and costs of a project. Most analyses suggest this to be difficult and controversial.

*Forecasting*.   The policy problems and consequences of forecasting are often not based on political differences. No forecaster can know the future and, instead, must monitor various data sets, therefore judgments must be made about what to consider important enough to follow closely, what is novel, and what is a trend. One's assumptions, built not only through political views, but also through organizational and professional effort, guide one to search for answers to all three questions (Pierce,

1971, p. 53). Thus forecasting has a great interpretive potential. Likewise one can influence the course of events. If one's view is substantially influential, the guidance this forecast provides can influence the course of events (Pierce, 1971, p. 41). As Klay (1985) has pointed out, what one wants to see can happen; views do become self-fulfilling prophecies.

Many different classification schemes help to understand forecasting as a rational exercise. Quantitative methods are those depending on empirical data and in which theories play a central role. Qualitative methods also may come into play; forecasters may have only a fuzzy understanding of their theories' production under various conditions. Finally, forecasters may combine both forms, implicitly reflecting organizational biases; forecasters may even reason backward from a desirable conjectured state of affairs to data and assumptions necessary to support the conjecture (Dunn, 1981, p. 195).

Quantitative methods are those forecasting methods involving data and mathematical analysis. The purpose of these methods is to determine a relationship, specifically causal, among a variety of variables. Causal relationships are those having the characteristics of: a statistical association, time order, nonspuriousness, and randomness when samples are used. Governments rely on econometric and mathematical models to forecast the future and determine the impacts of public programs. These methods encompass a variety of different designs, from cross-sectional to time series analysis, but the general notion is to create a model of explicitly stated relationships among variables that portray an abstraction of some phenomenon such as taxes and economic growth. Most models build on history but, in addition, on elaborate theoretical relationships such as involving the curvilinear relationship among productivity, tax rates, and revenue yields (Wanniski, 1978).

More specifically, an econometric model is a system of analysis in which the economic system of a country is represented by a complex system of statistically estimated mathematical equations. The number of equations that are needed to adequately represent the economy depends on the number of actors that are to be considered. The larger the number of equations, the greater the number of subtle economic variations that can be accounted for by the model.

The same model can also be used for policy analysis. To investigate any specific set of possible government actions, the policymakers simply insert the change into the model and solve to find out what the impact of the action is *likely* to be. In periods of inflation, the figure for taxes might be raised and expenditures lowered. In periods of depression, the opposite actions might be taken.

An econometric model allows the government to predict the effects of a policy action before enacting it. The quality of the model depends on the accuracy with which it can attempt to depict the economy by a set of statistically estimated mathematical equations. Particular emphasis is placed on having as many variables as possible explained within the system of equations, on the use of hard economic data, and on the simultaneous solutions of the model without the introduction of other considerations.

Qualitative forecasting models, on the other hand, are those in which subjective estimation predominates. Such methods have greatest utility in murky or confusing areas of activity, those areas where our knowledge of the relevant variables and the patterns of interaction among these variables may not be well developed. Often quantitative methods' loudest partisans are those who reject a priori reasoning or positive theory.

The most basic qualitative forecasting technique is the judgmental forecast. Using judgment, individuals create a relatively unstructured and informal process. Those people with information relevant to the phenomenon being considered essentially pool that knowledge and make educated guesses about the future. Hunches and intuition play a large role in the outcome of a judgmental forecasting process.

The delphi technique is a well-known form of judgmental forecasting (Brown and Helmer, 1962). To employ this method, one empanels a group of experts. These experts respond to a sequence of interrogations in which their responses are communicated to one another. Specifically, their responses to one questionnaire are used to produce a subsequent questionnaire. Any set of information available to some experts and not others is passed on to the others through this sharing process. This information, the method envisions, sharpens judgment among experts and focuses attention and forecasts.

Brainstorming is another information-gathering technique, one useful in aiding judgment and forecasting future events (Osborn, 1953). This method follows a very disciplined format. Criticism of any source of information or of the information provided is banned. In fact, farfetched ideas are encouraged as an aid to eliciting a large number of practical ideas. The quantity of data is emphasized. The first step in the process—the generating phase—rests primarily on creativity. The second phase is a winnowing-out phase in which individuals evaluate ideas generated earlier. The third phase builds on the best ideas surviving the second phase by focusing attention on synthesizing these best ideas. Finally, the evaluation phase forces the elimination of all but the best idea or forecast.

Finally, many organizations employ the nominal group technique (Delbecq et al., 1975) to forecast future events. A nominal group is a group composed of the pooled output randomly chosen individuals who have worked alone.

Forecasting has its problems. In government, forecasting is hardly ever the prerogative of only one group. Intergroup effort, in fact, describes what takes place when both legislative and executive bodies cooperate, of course (Kamlet et al., 1987), but such effort is also required among different offices within the executive branch (Pierce, 1971).

Common to all whose task is forecasting is ambiguity. Seldom is there a clear definition of cause–effect relationships. Less seldom is there agreement about what one wants to happen. Thus forecasting is often a judgmental process, one especially influenced by forecasters' social construction of reality.

To understand the judgmental process, and thus revenue forecasting, it is necessary to understand the elements that interact to construct cause–effect relationships and desired outcomes. The interaction among actors in forecasting, as in all organizational and judgmental exercises, assumes that all want stability; all participants interact and confine behavior in ways to trade stable expectations about behavior.

Explaining reality construction solely as an economy of social interactions is incomplete. March and Olsen (1989) suggest that the market centers on bias; that solutions, rather than problems, are the driving force behind change. Specifically they offer that "when causality and technology are ambiguous, the motivation to have particular solutions adopted is likely to be as powerful as the motivation to have particular problems solved, and changes can be more easily induced by a focus on solutions than by a focus on problems" (March and Olsen, 1989, p. 62). All parties to making judgments have a solution in mind. Judgment in a collective choice situation is a matter of convincing other parties of the connection between a preferred solution and the problem at hand.

The argument about one's preferred solution may be easier to make when the party realizes the importance of sequential attention. Parties to the making of a judgment have limited time and limited willingness to devote more than a fair share of that time to a given judgment call. Any party realizing the limited time problem can choose whether to focus attention on a given solution.

One's ploy may well be to focus on the aspect of the problem where a given solution seems most capable of resolution. Or one's time may best be spent in characterizing a problem where a favorite solution has always been chosen by the group to use. In fact, Brunsson (1989) argues that it is possible to sustain a coalition among members who have what appear to be strictly inconsistent objectives because of sequential attention. Moreover, by using "technology and expertise [executives] can manage the assumptions and judgments which must be made to combine . . . forecasts in some reasonable way and predict . . . change" (Pierce, 1971, p. 50).

The recognition of biases, and the understanding that differences may be useful, underscores much research in judgment making (Wright and Ayton, 1987). That is, differences create a healthy skepticism about others' views and assumptions, bringing them out in the open (Golembiewski and Miller, 1981). Research (Klay, 1983, 1985; Ascher, 1978) suggests that airing such differences may reduce overreliance on outdated core assumptions, or "assumption drag," in forecasts, improving their accuracy.

*Measuring Benefits and Costs.* Finally, benefit–cost analysts must cope with the assignment of some quantitative value to the stream of benefits and costs. This has special difficulty in the public goods sector, since markets have not "priced" these goods, owing to market failures in either rivalry or divisibility. Specific costing problems that bedevil analysts are estimating shadow prices, final prices, opportunity costs, transfers, and inflation.

First, the cost of a project or the benefit of it may often be estimated by analogy, that is, shadow prices. Some equivalent market may exist for a project, somewhere; that equivalent is employed as the basis for costing out the elements of the projected-for analysis. The problems associated with finding such a shadow price, or of using the most nearly correct one, still creates problems. Would a roller coaster ticket price mirror a subway fare?

Second, the lack of a shadow price leads to additional problems. That is, most public goods tend to be oriented toward outcomes rather than mere output. Therefore determining final prices becomes a difficult task. Outcomes are extremely hard to envision much less estimate in dollar-denominated consequences. For example, street sweeping and cleaning are often touted as popular programs, even though they have no meaningful output (pounds of garbage collected, raves from residents) but they have definite outcomes. "Clean streets" has a meaning all its own and is an end in itself. Such an end in itself is hard to measure for benefit–cost analysis.

Next, a project without a shadow price always carries an opportunity cost that might be measurable and meaningful for analysis. The opportunity cost of any project is the benefit and cost of another project forgone to proceed with the present one. The true worth of any project, therefore, is the cost (and benefit) of the most obvious substitute. Clean streets may carry the cost of an opportunity, such as a rat amelioration program forgone. The illustration also suggests the problem of lack of adequate quantifiables in opportunities forgone, the biggest problem in calculating costs.

Fourth, a transfer of payment from one individual to another should not be included in the calculation of benefits and costs. Transfers are not included because "there are no economic gains from a pure *transfer payment* because the benefits to those who receive such a transfer are matched by the costs borne by those who pay for it" (U.S. Office of Management and Budget, 1992, p. 5).

Finally, inflation has an impact on the future values of benefits and costs. The U.S. Office of Management and Budget (1992, p. 7) suggests that "analysts should avoid having to make an assumption about the general rate of inflation whenever possible." But if a rate is necessary, they recommend, "the rate of increase in the Gross Domestic Product deflator from the Administration's economic assumptions for the period of the analysis."

*Summary.* Problems abound in estimating, forecasting, or costing project elements for analysis. Estimating benefits and costs accurately requires knowledge far exceeding that available to an analyst. Forecasting demands objectivity and knowledge of theoretical relationships far beyond what is normally expected of economics and social observers. Costing public programs has special difficulties in that few analogous, meaningful, or quantifiable projects exist on which to base estimates.

## 2. Valuation over Time and by Different Selection Criteria

The selection of projects through benefit–cost analysis is commonly derived from an investment theory utilizing comparisons between a stream of benefits and a stream of costs measured at their current value. Generally, these comparisons are made on the basis of one or the other of two calculations, net present value (NPV) or internal rate of return (IRR).

The NPV measures future streams of benefits and costs by "netting" or subtracting current value costs from current value benefits (benefits minus costs). A variation of this measure is the more popularly known ratio of current value benefits over current costs, benefit–cost ratio (B/C). The criterion for selection in the former is a positive number; the criterion for the ratio is a number greater than unity (1).

A second method of selecting a project is to determine its rate of return. This calculation suggests projects with current value benefits exceeding their current value costs by a given rate, or percentage, are better than those that do not.

The difference between the NPV/BC ratio and IRR is in the former's discrimination in favor of larger numbers. That is, IRR corrects for extremely large differences in scope among projects. It is more appropriately applied at the macrolevel where projects compete against other projects than at the microlevel where a project's benefits compete against its odds.

*Discounting.* Nevertheless, the calculation of NPV and the BC ratio depend on establishment of current value benefits and costs. Current value benefits and costs are also known as discounted elements.

Discounting is based on a preference for the time value of money. For example, if given the choice between $100 now and $100 a year from now, most people would prefer to have the $100 now. That is, according to Henny Youngman, *nem di gelt*: "Don't believe all the baloney people tell you about what they'll do for you tomorrow.

Take the money" (Youngman, 1990). If forced to wait, we would want the year-from-now choice to be equal in value to the $100 today alternative. The amount that would make the $100 a year from now equivalent in value to the $100 today alternative is our preference for the time value of money. Under some circumstances, some of us prefer more than others. To illustrate: the delay in getting the $100, such as when we lend money to a college student, daughter, or son to buy an automobile in return for the promise to repay it, we would want to have compensation for the delay. What would the time preference be?

The calculation of time value may shed light on finding preferences. Consider that if you put $100 in a bank at 5% interest, you would have $105 in one year, if the interest were compounded annually. The future value of that $100 (the amount it would be worth in one year) is $105, or:

$$\text{Future Value of } \$100 = \$100 \times (1 + 0.05) = \$105.$$

A sum of $100 now is equivalent to $105 one year from now at a 5% annually compounded interest rate. A person's choosing not to put money in the bank tells us that the $100 sum we have today is equivalent to an amount next year of at least $105 and maybe much more. If the person feels that having $100 today or $105 one year from now are equivalent, then the 5% interest rate represents the time value of money, of waiting one year for the money (future value).

If we know the interest rate that reflects the tradeoff for the citizens of a community between $100 in benefits today versus some greater level of benefits in later years, we can convert the value of the future benefits into their present-day worth. Some examples illustrate the need to know the present value of future benefits. In the first case, many governments often buy fleets of automobiles for their police forces and for many other departments. The government's decision makers face the quandary, "Should we buy or should we lease the automobiles?" Present valuing the terms of the lease is the only true way to compare, in financial terms, the buy-versus-lease alternatives.

In a second case, governments often sell bonds in the marketplace to finance capital improvements such as roads and bridges. These bonds will be redeemed with principal payments the government will make annually over a period of years. The bond financing is, more often than not, competitive. Ordinarily, investment banks bid on bonds by offering an interest rate for each annual principal payment. If a bond financing covered a redemption period of ten years, an investment bank would often bid on each of ten annual payments or maturities. The government decision maker who evaluates the competing bids must calculate the present value of each principal payment on which the bank submitted a bid because, presumably, the interest rates the banks bid were different, leading to different total amounts of interest the government would pay.

Essentially, we calculate the present value in the opposite way we calculate interest earnings of future value. That is, assume the formula for the future value of a sum of money is

$$FV = PV(1 + i),$$

where $FV$ is the future value, $PV$ represents the present value, $i$ denotes the interest rate, and $(1 + i)$ symbolizes the discount factor. Using algebra, we can determine the present value using the formula:

$$PV = FV \div (1 + i).$$

In other words, if we know any two items—future value, interest rate, or present value—we can find the third. And if we know the future benefits of a project with any certainty at all, as well as the interest rate, we can find the present value of the project.

We should note one fact about terminology related to the time value of money. The rate used to calculate future value is best thought of as an interest rate; most of us are familiar enough with that process through savings accounts and like investments. However, the rate used in present value calculations is known as the discount rate because the value of a benefit we receive at some future time is smaller today by comparison because we deduct an amount to compensate us for the delay. In other terms, we deduct from the future value by a factor that relates time and the discount rate. In addition, we need to understand the impact of inflation on the interest rate. The interest rate banks offer are nominal rates. Say the bank offers a 5% interest rate. We have to take into account the potential for inflation ($\pi$) over the next year. At the end of the year, if inflation was 2%, the real interest rate ($r$) is 3%. This is known as the Fisher Effect ($r = i - \pi$). Higher inflation rates are more (less) conducive for borrowers (lenders) because they reduce the "real" amount of interest to be paid back.

Projects often begin to have benefits much later than one year after they have been built. The construction of a project, for example, may take three years. The benefits, although forecast to be a certain amount, may have to be adjusted because of the delay. The adjustment would be done in the same way as three separate one-year present value calculations. That is, if the present value of a forecasted benefit of $1000 (at 5%) for one year were

$$PV = \$1000 \div (1 + 0.05) = \$952.38,$$

the present value for the second year would be equal to

$$\$952.38 \div (1 + 0.05) = \$907.03$$

and the present value of the third year would be

$$\$907.03 \div (1 + 0.05) = \$863.84.$$

This can be simplified using the formula:

$$PV = FV \div (1 + i)^t.$$

Thus, by adding the essence of time ($t$), or power, to the discount factor (for this example we are cubing the discount factor), we calculate precisely what the present value would be had we used the longer method, calculating the present value for each year.

Many projects have costs and benefits continually over a period of years. In other words, these projects have a benefit (or cost) stream. To find the total value of the stream from this succession of periods, we add terms to the basic formula for present value that we looked at earlier. If a project had annual benefits for $t$ years, we would use the formula:

$$\text{Present value} = \text{Annual value} \times \frac{(1 + \text{discount rate})^t - 1}{\text{discount rate}(1 + \text{discount rate})^t}.$$

Consider the following example. A city is offered $1800 for a piece of property today. The city has been leasing that property to another business; the lease is to run for five more years at $300 a year, paid at the beginning of the year, with the option given to the business to purchase the property at the end of the lease period for $500. Which option would you advise the city leaders to choose, sell or continue leasing? Using a discount rate based on the opportunity cost of capital of 5%, and assuming both the sale and the lease took place today, let's consider the two alternatives shown in Table 5.

We would probably advise the city to sell the property. Of course, the difference is small because, above all, we are dealing with rather small sums. Yet, if the differences were small even with bigger numbers, other considerations would be called into play to decide the question, such as the disposition of the property, given other city policies, if sold; the reliability of payments by the present lessor; other plans the city might have for adjoining property; and so on.

The city's main advantage in knowing the present value of the lease is the ability to compare directly the value of a sale and the value of the lease. These types of calculations make comparisons meaningful, because the cash flow from the lease, [(5 × $300) + $500] = $2000, might have led decision makers to believe that the lease's value was more than it actually was.

## B. Macro—Benefit–Cost Analysis or Portfolio Construction

On a project-level evaluation of benefits and costs, the net present value idea has some merit. Certainly, a government decision maker hesitates to spend taxpayers' money on

**Table 5**   Lease Versus Buy Decision

| | | |
|---|---|---|
| 1. | The lease | |
| | Annual benefit, paid today and each year for four more years | = $300 |
| | PV annual benefit | |
| | This year | = $300 |
| | Next four years | = $300 × $[(1.05)^4 - 1] / 0.05 (1.05)^4$ |
| | | = $1063 |
| | Total PV annual benefit | = $300 + $1,063 |
| | | = $1363 |
| | One time benefit, at the end of the lease, five years from now | = $500 |
| | PV one time benefit | = $500 $/(1.05)^5$ |
| | | = $392 |
| | Total benefit of the lease | = $1363 + $392 |
| | | = $1755 |
| 2. | The sale | |
| | The sale would take place today; therefore its present value is $1800 | |
| 3. | Comparing the two alternatives | |
| | Lease/purchase | = $1755 |
| | Sale | = $1800 |

projects where worth cannot be shown readily. However, selection problems occur when the comparison is between projects of unequal size or projects of unequal economic or useful lives, as well as when an entire budget of projects is being selected. We find two strategies normally used to overcome these selection problems: a scheduling strategy and a strategy to construct portfolios.

## 1. Benefit–Cost Analysis Without Constraint

First, capital projects are often submitted with no expenditure ceiling specified. Consequently, more projects are submitted than can be funded. Setting priorities is necessary to achieve the required cutbacks.

Decision makers frequently achieve prioritization by scheduling. Scheduling helps alleviate waste by ensuring construction of facilities required initially, that is, before primary construction. For example, sewers will be scheduled for construction prior to building a street so that it will not be necessary to cut new pavement during sewer construction.

A danger of prioritization by scheduling is that rarely are projects eliminated. More often they are postponed and placed further down the schedule. As projects stay on the schedule for several years there can be a maturation effect: they may become bona fide projects with funding even though they logically do not have a high priority.

Prioritization requires review to ensure the project relates to the overall goals and policies of the jurisdiction. Projects must be scrutinized to find the value they add to programs, even if the programs are of different value. Using program or zero-base budgeting, rather than the department or functional approach, managers can force these comparisons.

## 2. Marginal Rate of Return Analysis

A second approach to cost–benefit analysis is one that overcomes the scheduling problems and employs marginal analysis in selecting productive projects. This method has greatest utility when projects are quite different in scale or useful life.

Marginal analysis requires several steps. First, a range of discount rates is evaluated to determine the likely field of opportunity costs for projects such as those being evaluated. Second, the analyst determines the internal rate of return for the entire set of projects and discards those that fall below the opportunity costs of capital. Third, the preferred choice is selected by finding that project which has the highest internal rate of return for the employment of capital.

*Finding the Range of Discount Rates and Opportunity Costs.*  An opportunity's cost is the cost of another project or set of projects forgone. That is, if one chooses one project over another, the true value of the choice is the value forgone to gain it. Consider the example of desserts. If we forgo one that contains 1000 calories for one that has 100 calories, we value the one we chose at its 10:1 savings rate. The one we chose is 10 times the value of the one we did not choose.

In this same sense, public projects compete with private sector projects. If we decide to spend money on public capital projects, we forgo the economic benefits of leaving the money in the private sector, where, presumably, it generates economic growth.

Because we cannot grasp the long-term benefits and costs of collective goods very well, the opportunity cost gets fixed as a discount rate by which we judge what costs and benefits we do know. We measure costs and benefits and discount this stream by the opportunity cost of capital.

Many consider the market to have done this costing for us, at least in constructing a range of opportunity costs for portfolio purposes. The difference between the tax-free yield on municipal bonds and the taxable yield on these bonds or on corporate bonds of equal risk of default might serve as the floor in our range. The yield on federal long-term bonds might be our range's ceiling.

Why these? If the opportunity cost of capital is value forgone, the small difference in the former represents such a comparison. The tax exemption represents the subsidy or cost of pushing investment dollars from the private to the public sector. These bonds would not be sold, or the projects they finance built, we assume, if they had to be offered at market rates.

The top of the range is that market rate which attracts capital. The federal government's long-term taxable bond rate is such a rate.

*Determining the Internal Rate of Return of the Projects.* Instead of determining a benefit–cost rate, many analysts follow the private sector practice of solving for the rate of return on investment, or the internal rate of return. Having discovered this internal rate, analysts discard those projects whose rates are less than the opportunity cost of capital, the floor of rates.

Consider the example of a project with an initial outlay of $20,000, annual costs of $10,000 and annual benefits of $13,000, all of which are paid or received at the end of the fiscal year. The projected life of the project is 10 years, and there is no residual benefit at the end of the project. This project's costs and benefits are represented with the cash flows shown in Table 6.

To find the IRR, we determine that discount rate at which the net present value (or net discounted costs and benefits) is zero. In Table 7, we show four possible discount rates and the net current value for the cash flows in Table 6. Given the numbers that appear in the table, the discount rate of 10.41% brings the discounted benefits and costs into equality. That is, the net costs and benefits are almost zero.

The internal rate of return of a given set of cash flows (outflow in payments for construction and such, inflow in benefits received) is that discount rate at which the current value of the inflow equals the current value of the outflow. Finding the IRR

**Table 6** Project Costs and Benefits

| Year | Costs ($) | Benefits ($) |
|---|---|---|
| 1 | −30,000 | +13,000 |
| 2 | −10,000 | +13,000 |
| 3 | −10,000 | +13,000 |
| 4 | −10,000 | +13,000 |
| 5 | −10,000 | +13,000 |
| 6 | −10,000 | +13,000 |
| 7 | −10,000 | +13,000 |
| 8 | −10,000 | +13,000 |
| 9 | −10,000 | +13,000 |
| 10 | −10,000 | +13,000 |

**Table 7**   Project A

| Project | Discount rate (%) | | | |
|---------|------|------|-------|-------|
|         | 5    | 10   | 15    | 20    |
| A       | 4118 | 253  | −2334 | −4088 |

is a matter of eliminating all those discount rates at which the two flows are not equal.

Take for illustration, three projects with unique cash flows, each over 10 years, as shown in Table 8. With a computer spreadsheet, it is possible to find the rate (see Table 9), since hunting for it is time consuming and tedious.

Just as large numbers may make projects less practical, even though benefit–cost ratios make them look better, projects that have large internal rates of return also may not be practical. This may be particularly so in situations where there are limited budgets. For example, a budget with a limit of $15,000 simply cannot afford any of the projects, no matter what their IRR. Not only does the internal rate of return calculation limit the population of possible projects to those that exceed the minimum rate or the opportunity cost of capital but, obviously, it also limits projects to those the government can afford.

*Selecting Projects by Their Marginal Rates of Return.* The actual method of choosing a portfolio of projects that has internal rates higher than the minimum is by determining marginal rates of return among those that have not been weeded out already. This method operates on the principle that each additional dollar invested in a project should have at least the same, if not a higher, rate of return than the last. We would first employ the minimum acceptable rate criterion to projects to weed out those projects that alone could not produce a rate of return great enough to justify taxation to finance it. Then we would ask which combination of projects yields the highest marginal rate of return.

Taking the projects just described, and establishing a 7% minimum acceptable rate, arriving at net current values and benefit–cost ratios comes first. The net current values and ratios are displayed in Table 10. Then the process requires finding the differences between any and all projects. The marginal analysis method requires comparison between successively larger projects—between one project and another with larger capital requirements—and not the other way around (Gohagan, 1980, pp. 209–211).

In our example, our process requires moving from Project A to Project B (and on to Project C) or from Project A to Project C. We ask whether it is justifiable to spend

**Table 8**   Projects A, B, and C Costs and Benefits

| Project | Capital costs ($) | Annual costs ($) | Annual benefits ($) |
|---------|------|------|------|
| A       | 20,000 | 10,000 | 14,000 |
| B       | 30,000 | 10,000 | 15,000 |
| C       | 50,000 | 17,000 | 25,000 |

**Table 9**  Finding Internal Rate of Return

| | Discount rate (%) | | | |
| --- | --- | --- | --- | --- |
| Project | 5 | 10 | 15 | 20 |
| A | 11,839 | 6,396 | 2,684 | 103 |
| B | 10,037 | 3,450 | −993 | −4,038 |
| C | 14,155 | 3,702 | −3,328 | −8,127 |

additional capital to mount a larger project. The marginal additions are portrayed in Table 11.

The analysis suggests two facts. There is no additional benefit to be gained by investing in Project B rather than Project A. However, because we set the rate of return at 7%, the move from A to C would be justifiable, because the $30,000 extra dollars, invested in what we presume to be a popular project, would return at least that minimum. Because of our analysis, the marginal internal rate of return calculation would suggest Project C to be the most productive use of the public's money.

## 3.  Portfolio Construction

A third approach to benefit–cost analysis deals with the most productive combination of projects by using investment portfolio approaches of choice. Finding this combination is the subject of capital budget deliberations. How does one build a portfolio?

Constructing a portfolio requires several steps. First, we set the minimum rate of return for capital. Second, we determine the marginal internal rate of return for each project or combination of projects over each other project or combination. Finally, we choose that combination which exceeds our minimum rate by the greatest margin.

*Setting the Minimum Rate.*   In our last example, we set the minimum rate at 7%. We now use the same data, however, let's make the hurdle a higher one, 10%, inasmuch as we are dealing with large net current values as Table 12 reveals.

*Determining Marginal Rates for All Combinations.*  As with the last group of projects, we now determine marginal rates, but with the portfolio approach, we also combine projects and calculate IRR and MIRR for these combinations as well. For an illustration of this with our project data, see Table 13. In it we report only the largest capital projects. The marginal rate of return is the rate of return on the extra capital invested in projects with higher capital requirements. In the A + C versus A + B example, the A + C required $20,000 more capital than A + B; therefore the marginal rate is the return on that extra $20,000.

**Table 10**  Projects' Net Values

| | | Net present value | | |
| --- | --- | --- | --- | --- |
| Project | Capital required | @ 7% | BC ratio | IRR (%) |
| A | 20,000 | 9,403 | 1.11 | 20.2 |
| B | 30,000 | 7,081 | 1.07 | 13.7 |
| C | 50,000 | 9,460 | 1.06 | 12.4 |

**Table 11** Projects' Additions in Returns

| Marginal increase | In capital | Annual costs | Annual benefits | MIRR (%) |
|---|---|---|---|---|
| From A to B | 10,000 | 0 | 1,000 | 0 |
| From A to C | 30,000 | 7,000 | 11,000 | 7.06 |

*Choosing the Best Combination.*   The criterion of choice is based first on total present value, then marginal benefit–cost ratios, and finally the marginal internal rate of return. In setting up the last comparison, we took only the portfolio wit the highest total present value, A + C with $10,098. Then we compared it to those projects just smaller in capital requirements to determine whether the expenditure of the extra money was justified. The extra $20,000 resulted in at least equal costs and benefits when compared to the combination of A + B and a positive benefit–cost ratio when compared to Project C. Each of the MIRR measures, that compared to A + B and that compared to C, were greater than the 10% hurdle we set up. We conclude that the extra $20,000 was a justifiable expenditure on these measures.

If A + C is a justifiable set of projects, what about the next one, B + C, which requires larger amounts of capital? Is the extra $10,000 expenditure justifiable when we select B + C over A + C? According to the chart, it is not. The extra $10,000 represents substantially greater costs than benefits (a marginal benefit cost ratio of 0.68). Also, the extra capital brings no return at all.

We conclude with the choice of a simple portfolio of Projects A and C. The total current value of benefits and costs was a positive $10,098. The marginal gain over the next lower capital cost alternatives was above the minimum rate of return we established as well.

## IV.  THE RESEARCH

To test the assumption that the marginal internal rate of return method will provide the best guide to projects to select, we conducted a research project involving seasoned state government executives. We asked them to compute the rates of return, but then asked them to select the best portfolio, not only using their calculations but also their experience as a guide. The research can suggest some of the important steps actually used in considering which projects are apparently in the best interest of a public authority to fund.

**Table 12** Project Comparison on Calculated Outcomes

| | Capital($) | Annual benefits($) | Annual costs($) | Net present value @ 10% | BC @ 10% |
|---|---|---|---|---|---|
| A | 20,000 | 14,000 | 10,000 | 6,396 | 1.08 |
| B | 30,000 | 15,000 | 10,000 | 3,450 | 1.04 |
| C | 50,000 | 25,000 | 17,000 | 3,702 | 1.02 |
| A + B | 50,000 | 29,000 | 20,000 | 9,847 | 1.06 |
| A + C | 70,000 | 39,000 | 27,000 | 10,098 | 1.04 |
| B + C | 80,000 | 50,000 | 27,000 | 7,152 | 1.03 |

**Table 13**  Marginal Gain Among Projects

|  | Marginal BC | Marginal IRR (%) |
| --- | --- | --- |
| A + C over A + B | 1.00 | 10.41 |
| A + C over C | 1.08 | 20.24 |
| B + C over A + C | 0.68 | 0.00 |

## A. Methods

Thirty state government analysts, acting as research subjects, were given a benefit–cost analysis to conduct as they saw fit. They were divided into five groups for analysis and discussion, in order to ensure that whatever special expertise existed in urban problems was spread evenly across the groups. The choice concerned the best use of $250,000 in state funds for an economically and socially destitute but politically sensitive (hometown of the governor) area of the state. The groups were given one month to decide their portfolios. The five project choices are briefly described below.

*A Transportation Project.*  A wooden trestle bridge, having an estimated economic life of 25 years, would cost $80,000 for initial construction and would need annual maintenance costing $4000. The wooden bridge would have to be rebuilt after 25 years, which would require a one-month closure to traffic. The wooden bridge would be built in an area subject to flooding, one in which the "100-year flood" probabilities indicate some likelihood of a flood that would destroy the bridge up to three times during a 50-year period. There would be intangible, tourism-related benefits to such a structure.

*A Transportation Project.*  A steel replacement bridge, constructed on the same site as, but instead of, the wooden bridge, would have a 50-year economic life. The initial cost would be $160,000 with annual maintenance of $2000. The bridge would be invulnerable to the 100-year flood.

*A Job Training Program.*  The journeyman-training program would recruit 100 trainees per year for six years, 50% from the hard-core unemployed and 50% from nonunion construction workers (who now make $8000 per year). The trainees would enter a four-year training program. Once in, students would be paid $7000 and upon successful completion, would be hired at $14,000. A trainee dropout rate of 10% per year could reasonably be anticipated; graduated journeymen would face an average 10% unemployment rate. Administrative costs for the program would be $100,000 per year.

*A Job Training Program.*  The clerical training program would also recruit 100 trainees per year over a six-year period. The trainees would enter a one-year program and be placed in jobs that paid $7000 upon successful completion but receive nothing while training. Ninety percent of the trainees would come from the hard-core unemployed. Administrative costs for the program would be $100,000 per year.

*An Urban Renewal Project.*  The redevelopment project covers a 100-block area of an urban area and involves land purchases, resident relocation, redevelopment and improvements, public facilities, and administrative costs. The total of tangible costs equals $4.6 million. The total tangible benefits equal $3.7 million. However, planners and proponents suggest large intangible benefits.

The respondents were asked to use the internal rate of return method to establish relative worthiness and the marginal rate of return methods to help identify components of the best mix. They were also asked specifically to include the managerial implications of the portfolio and change recommendations, in that light especially considering fraud and abuse and difficulty in evaluating project success substantively.

## B. Findings

Five major sets of findings emerged from the research. First, the benefit–cost analysis could be swayed by both the assumptions built into the projects as well as assumptions projected by the analyst onto the study. For example, many questioned the low dropout rate in the training programs, and this assumption was crucial to the benefit stream. Also, the subjects divided equally over the forecast unemployment rate, with those otherwise favoring the project forecasting a lower unemployment rate than graduate trainees would face in future job markets.

Second, intangibles tended to play a large part in the analysis of social infrastructure programs such as the urban renewal project. Arguments made to include intangibles pointed toward all manner of benefits from redevelopment, from better health of residents to pride in community. Hardheaded numbers analysts deprecated these measures and discarded this project from their portfolios.

Third, all subjects pointed out the fraud potential of the projects and added this factor into their analysis. Urban renewal was the consensus choice of the project most prone to abuse. Training programs were thought to be abused but able to be quarantined from such a problem by good management, an intangible cost.

Fourth, subjects suggested that a short-term bias pervaded analysis. This short-term bias affected judgments about training programs particularly, because their benefits and social consequences may not be apparent for a generation. The short-term bias was also manifested in the consumption orientation of the analytical approach. Conservation or patrimony benefits often are difficult to envision much less measure owing to their intergenerational quality.

Finally, undergirding all of the findings was the constant presence of political considerations. In other words, what would "sell" politically, subjects always wondered. Despite its advantage in IRR terms, "Would a wooden bridge be politically as well as physically vulnerable?" one subject asked. "Could the bridge be explained in the face of conventional opposition, much less justified in the battle for funding by interest groups representing other proposals?"

Some pointed out that the benefit–cost analysis imputed values and demands to individuals without actually verifying them. The value of a bridge, for instance, was the individual's opportunity of traveling the next best route. However, no one ever asked an individual whether that was the route he would take or whether he would take that trip at all if there were no bridge. Some mentioned that the analysis would skirt politics when the political process was the only true gauge of what real individuals wanted or were willing to tax themselves to finance.

Politics, in the form of equity, also became an issue. One subject argued, "Cost–benefit analysis is not particularly sensitive to the way in which income is distributed in society." The subject noticed that benefit–cost analysis tended to infer the same amount of value to rich and poor individuals. Also apparent to this subject was the method's conservatism; when used with the five alternatives here, the method tended to minimize the need for government intervention on behalf of the poor.

## C. Summary

Despite. the large number of caveats made to an otherwise quantitative analysis, subjects generally agreed that there are "serious public policy implications in undertaking a project that is not rational with respect to tangible costs that exceed benefits, particularly in times of fiscal austerity." The number of biases that emerge in analyzing the benefits and costs of a range of projects—fraud potential, short-term returns, consumption overwhelming conservation, tangible items to measure—suggested the extreme conservatism of the method to the subjects. Yet the last comment on fiscal austerity is revealing. It suggests that the political environment for tax policy, the willingness of individuals to pay taxes, and the civic mindedness of taxpayers serve to condition analysts to the need to be conservative or otherwise in the assumptions and use of bias in analysis. Presumably, times other than fiscal austerity might prompt different analytical procedures.

This research has tested the idea that the internal rate of return method of benefit–cost analysis would guide seasoned state executives in their choice of an optimal, even if hypothetical, portfolio. The findings suggest that a large number of other considerations, both managerial and political, guide judgment in addition to quantitative techniques. However, the surprising finding was the large role that the IRR calculation actually played: that it is not sound, "not rational," to select a project in which tangible costs exceed benefits. Moreover, surprisingly, subjects were loathe to project their own political leanings or their social philosophies on the analysis, content instead to act conservatively, in hopes, we would infer, that the political process would take over where they left off in creating an equitable as well as efficient portfolio.

## V. ECONOMIC REASONING IN GOVERNMENT FINANCIAL MANAGEMENT

We now place benefit–cost analysis within the even larger body of literature characterizing economic reasoning in government. This review forms a critique and is meant both to support the research findings of the previous section, and to suggest the larger sources and consequences of the benefit–cost analysis approach for choice.

Economic decision making tends to be deductive. Because of that, economics has an elegant and mathematics-based precision in detailing "proof." Economics also provides a sense of practical worldliness. Having based microeconomics, or the theory of the firm, on the idea that firm owners maximized economic theory asserts something called optimal public decisions.

The fundamental principle of economic reasoning applied to the public sector states that "ureaucratic officials, like all other agents in society, are motivated by their own self interests at least part of the time (Downs, 1957, p. 2). That is, political actors seek advantage for both themselves and their constituents and tend to maximize gain and minimize loss. Both bureaucratic and political actors reach their targets through a maze of rules, communication and coordination rules for bureaucratic officials and voting rules for political actors. The world within which behavior bends around rules is an unpredictable one. The actors, therefore, constantly calculate what is literally a risk–return relationship, given their fundamental preferences for different kinds of advantages.

The BCA approach has its limits in government decision making, as the research reported here has suggested. That is, BCA is often used to justify ex post facto a position already taken; the most significant factor in BCA is often its sponsor. Benefit–cost analysis tends to neglect the distributional consequences of a choice. The method systematically undervalues projects that improve the distribution of wealth and systematically overvalues projects that exacerbate economic inequality. In the Kaldor terminology, benefit–cost analysis would recommend a course of action that could potentially allow the winners to compensate the losers so that no one is worse off, but the method does not guarantee that the winners *will* compensate the losers.

Over and above the operational problems with BCA, and by extension economic reasoning in government, there are intangibles of fundamental importance that BCA cannot conceive. For example, a moral significance in the duties and rights of individuals to each other and of government to all individuals is not comprehended in the measurement of consequences alone. With benefit–cost analysis, certain rights such as due process of the law or broad public participation and discourse, cannot be conceived simply because they are processes valued for themselves rather than outcomes.

Benefit–cost analysis has been blamed for damaging the political system. Some argue that politics is superior to analysis because of the wider scope of ideas and concepts the people practicing politics can fathom. Others argue that analysis enfranchises unelected policy analysts and disenfranchises those who do not understand, do not believe, or cannot use analysis to make their arguments to government. Such a situation creates a loss of confidence in government institutions, at the very least, and, more fundamentally, subverts democratic government.

To return to BCA's basis in economics, others argue that the basis insofar as it describes or prescribes government action has flaws. That is, BCA assumes that there can be no market failure. There are always opportunity costs and shadow prices with which public sector goods and services can be valued. Research on markets suggests that markets are not perfectly competitive, that the lack of competition leads inevitably to failure, and that the public goods are produced to remedy that failure. Without a way to value public goods and services, therefore, benefit–cost analysis fails to inform the decision-making process.

Another economic idea, that any alternative must be judged in terms of other alternatives, lends support to analysis. These proponents of BCA argue that there is no alternative to BCA, none as explicit or systematic. In fact, BCA analysts' formalized explicit nature allows the public to hold its public officials accountable to a larger extent than under normal politics and management. Systematic analysis is less likely to overlook an important fact or consideration which when placed in an adversarial process such as politics, may lead to the determination of the public interest far sooner than mere impressionistic surmise.

However, opponents of benefit–cost analysis argue about what it systematically reveals. They say that it reveals only values related to conserving resources to the exclusion of all others; the overriding value, in fact, is economic efficiency rather than others that are possible: those associated with justice, domestic tranquility, the general welfare, and the blessings of liberty. As Dryzek (1993, p. 222) points out, "[A]ll that matters is how much of the target value [efficiency] is achieved." Moreover, benefit–cost analysis never questions the given resource constraints, a matter that is questioned in political debate.

The controversy over the use, misuse, or lack of use of analysis often pits those who believe in government against those who see the market as the predominantly positive force in society. Typically, what BCA overlooks is what most progovernment action proponents find government most useful in providing, equity and to an even larger extent broad participation in self-government. Promarket proponents argue that government intervenes for spurious reasons and, in doing so, creates more problems than it solves, certainly leading to less rather than more economic efficiency.

## VI. CONCLUSIONS

We have identified productivity in terms of both equity and efficiency in this chapter. We have also shown that the Kaldor criterion for allocating government services fulfills that criterion in theory. In demonstrating the Kaldor criterion, we have shown BCA and have elaborated most of its important technical facets. In doing so, we demonstrated that benefit–cost analysis, and productivity, rely on comparisons made among programs at the suborganization, then organization, then interorganization levels, and that the real outcome of these comparisons is the construction of portfolios of investments. The technology that might be used to improve these comparisons, and thus improve productivity, we argued, could be borrowed from portfolio construction models in business investment practice, inasmuch as they too are based on benefit–cost analytic principles.

We further argued the heuristic, if not the absolute determinative value of this technology. Moreover, we demonstrated through a small piece of research that BCA is a crucial learning tool in understanding policy problems. Nevertheless, the research revealed the limited nature of this technology: real decision makers in a simulated situation used other, different criteria in making final choices. These other, different criteria, often more heavily weighted than benefit–cost analysis, included managerial feasibility and a project's tendency toward encouraging fraud and abuse.

In the end, we classed BCA as a method that ignores intuition, feeling, and other means of informing decisions. Although practical in a limited way, the analytical methods underlying benefit–cost analysis are often self-defeating. Especially inappropriate to government productivity, the methods defy reality, an administrative reality that must reconcile plural views, each of which describes more than monetized utility, in allocation policy choices.

## REFERENCES

Ascher, W. (1978). *Forecasting: An Appraisal for Policymakers and Planners.* Baltimore, MD: Johns Hopkins University Press.
Brown, B., Helmer, O. (1962). *Improving the Reliability of Estimates Obtained from a Consensus of Experts.* Santa Monica, CA: Rand Corporation.
Brunsson, N. (1989). *The Organization of Hypocrisy.* Chichester, England: Wiley.
Buchanan, J. M., Tullock, G. (1962). *The Calculus of Consent.* Ann Arbor, MI: University of Michigan Press.

Delbecq, A. L., Van de Ven, A. H., Gustafson, D. H. (1975). *Group Techniques for Program Planning: A Guide for Nominal Group and Delphi Processes.* Glenview, IL: Scott, Foresman.

Downs, A. (1957). *An Economic Theory of Democracy.* New York: Harper & Row.

Downs, A. (1960). Why the government budget is too small in a democracy. *World Polit.* 12:541–563.

Dryzek, J. S. (1993). Policy analysis and planning: From science to argument. In: Fischer, F., Forester, J., eds. *The Argumentative Turn in Policy Analysis and Planning.* Durham, NC: Duke University Press, pp. 214–232.

Dunn, W. N. (1981). *Public Policy Analysis.* Englewood Cliffs, NJ: Prentice-Hall.

Gohagan, J. K. (1980). *Quantitative Analysis for Public Policy.* New York: McGraw-Hill.

Golembiewski, R. T., Miller, G. J. (1981). Small groups in political science. In: Long, S., ed. *Handbook of Political Behavior.* Vol. 2. New York: Plenum, pp. 1–71.

Kamlet, M. S., Mowery, D. C., Su, T. T. (1987). Whom do you trust? An analysis of executive and congressional economic forecasts. *J. Policy Anal. Manage.* 6:365–384.

Klay, W. E. (1983). Revenue forecasting: An administrative perspective. In: Rabin, J., Lynch, T. D., eds. *Handbook of Public Budgeting and Financial Management.* New York: Marcel Dekker.

Klay, W. E. (1985). The organizational dimension of budgetary forecasting: Suggestions from revenue forecasting in the states. *Int. J. Public Admin.* 7:241–265.

March, J. G., Olsen, J. P. (1989). *Rediscovering Institutions: The Organizational Basis of Politics.* New York: Basic.

Musgrave, R. A., Musgrave, P. B. (1980). *Public Finance in Theory and Practice.* 3rd ed. New York: McGraw-Hill.

Osborn, A. (1953). *Applied Imagination: Principle and Procedures of Creative Thinking.* New York: Scribners.

Pierce, L. D. (1971). *The Politics of Fiscal Policy Formation.* Pacific Palisades, CA: Goodyear.

Schmid, A. A. (1990). *Benefit–Cost Analysis: A Political Economy Approach.* Boulder, CO: Westview.

Stiglitz, J. E. (1988). *Economics of the Public Sector.* 2nd ed. New York: Norton.

U.S. Office of Management and Budget (1992). Memorandum for heads of executive departments and establishments. Circular No. A-94 Revised. Washington, DC. Available at http://www.whitehouse.gov/omb/circulars/a094/a094.html.

Wanniski, J. (1978). Taxes, revenue and the 'Laffer Curve.' *Public Interest*, Winter, 3–16.

Wright, G., Ayton, P. (1987). *Judgmental Forecasting.* Chichester, England: Wiley.

Youngman, H. (1990, July 31). Nem di Gelt (Take the money). *New York Times* A19.

# 23

# Indicators of Living Conditions

## Challenges and Opportunities
## for Accountability and Governance

**MARIA P. ARISTIGUETA**
*University of Delaware, Newark, Delaware, U.S.A.*

## I. INTRODUCTION

Government reform and devolution are serving as the impetus for accountability to the funding source and to the public. The current reforms have at least two measurement models associated with them: social indicators, sometimes called benchmarks or milestones, and performance measures. Ideally, these improvements to include social indicators will enhance productivity, alter policy making, and policy management by facilitating the emergence of "outcome based accountability systems, systems-wide coordination and integration efforts, performance-based competitive service models, and public sector privatization and democratization schemes" (Corbett, 1997, p. xix). "The necessity for productivity improvement is a recurring theme in economic, technological, and social arguments" (Holzer, 1995, p. 413), an argument that is continually emphasized by heads of state, the media, international agencies, corporations engaged in international trade, economists, public administrators, and the public. Adding to the complexity are the effects of globalization, increased market competition, downsizing in the private and public sectors, tax reductions, budget cutbacks and reduced social benefits on personal and community well being.

Simply stated, social indicators are nothing more than "quantitative data that serve as indexes to *socially important conditions* [italics added] of the society" (Biderman, 1966, p. 69). What could possibly be more vital to the well being of society than information on socially important conditions, so that policy may be instituted to address those conditions in need of attention? Vogel (1997, p. 104) asserts, "Providing the social indicators to chart the process of change is still the most urgent challenge confronting us today, as it was 30 years ago." Yet, because social indicators are based on the social and economic state of society over which government programs may have no control and little influence, developing indicators of living conditions provides challenges for accountability and performance.

"Accountability to citizens is the ultimate accountability" (Liner et al., 2001, p. 38). Providing regular information to the public about the progress in addressing social problems is likely to increase people's interests, confidence, and support in government and nonprofit agencies, especially if such reports are presented in a balanced way, presenting both accomplishments and areas in need of improvements. Examples are available of use of indicators in Florida to inform the public of the limitations of government and solicit assistance from the community in addressing social problems (see Aristigueta, 1999).

This chapter provides an overview of the history of social indicators, discusses the differences between social indicators and performance measures, and offers criteria to develop the indicators. The reader will also find a discussion on the uses and misuses of the social indicators, and lessons learned from practice and the literature.

## A.  Past and Present of Social Indicators

The practice of quantifying societal phenomena for public decision making dates back to the seventeenth century. The term "statistics" refers to "matters of the state," and the earliest were simply governmental record-keeping systems output (Innes, 1990). "Sometime in the 1920s, the idea began to take place that a society would produce a quantitative picture of itself and its changes" (Innis, 1990, p. 92). The idea of a social report was conceived to communicate trends in factors affecting the well being of individuals in society to a wide audience. A presidential committee appointed in 1929 was charged with producing a quantitative picture of society and its changes. In 1933, this committee produced the report, *Recent Social Trends* (Innes, 1990). This document compiled information on the health, environment, quality of life in rural and urban areas, families, crime, and the arts in American society.

In the late 1950s and 1960s, interest in social indicators was triggered by a rethinking of priorities in American society; for example, earlier Russian success led to an expansion of the space program and concentration on scientific research and education. The report, *Social Indicators*, described the need to monitor how a major technological change, such as the space program, might affect society (Bauer, 1966).

In 1967, Senator Mondale proposed a bill to create an annual social report. This mandate evolved into the book, *Toward a Social Report*, prepared by the United States Department of Health, Education, and Welfare and published in 1969 (Mc Call, 2001). This was followed by a series of reports in 1973, 1976, and 1980 titled *Social Indicators* and published by the Bureau of the Census (Bauer, 1966).

By the late 1980s, the social indicator movement had lost a great deal of steam. Indicators were still in use by governmental agencies and nongovernmental organizations (NGOs) but referred to as variables for analysis instead of social indicators (Mc Call, 2001). During the same period, the concepts of sustainable development and social development were expanded and refined. The United Nations, the World Bank, and other international agencies further expanded their analyses of developing nations. They also used the term "social development" to describe the level of living to be used as a measure by developing nations interested in the state of human welfare.

Governments were urged to use caution in addressing social welfare activities. Carley (1981, p. 88) warned that politicians might not want research that "stirs up waters better left calm." Clearly the advocacy was toward implementation of social welfare policies after serious evaluation of the specific needs of the individual society.

The 1990s witnessed a reemergence of the social indicators in a variety of applications in the United States, although they often were not referred to as such. For example, social indicators are found among the strategies to manage for results in state government, where these are most often referred to as benchmarks or milestones. A frequently recognized effort in state government is the Oregon Benchmarks that began in 1989 from the twenty-year vision for strategic development and was accompanied by indicators that reflect quality of life issues.

> Oregon Shines suggests that we have an opportunity to achieve sustained economic prosperity and to enhance our enviable quality of life. [To do that, it concluded]...we must invest our resources in our people to produce a quality work force, and we must preserve our quality of life...Capable people and good living conditions are worthwhile ends in themselves, yet they also attract and nurture the industries of the 21st Century (Oregon Progress Board, 1999).

Social indicator data do not measure the results of a single program; instead they are the overall signs of social and economic health. "The data on the indicators are intended to inform decisions about policy priorities at both the State and departmental levels" (Aristigueta et al., 2001, p. 255).

## B. Social Indicators Versus Performance Measurement

The public administration literature often does not distinguish between social indicators and performance measures (see, for example, Hatry, 1999; Kopcynski and Lombardo, 1999; U.S. GAO, 1995). Other writing on performance-oriented management focuses on agency performance measurement while omitting the issue of social indicators (see, for example, U.S. GAO, 1992; Wholey, 1983; and Wholey and Hatry, 1992). Authors use the term outcome measurement to refer to both social indicators and performance measures that are outcome oriented. Social indicators may be overlooked in the outcome-oriented literature because they provide an overall view of trends, whereas performance measures focus on specific government activities whose outcomes are believed to be more easily influenced by program intervention. The distinction is crucial for appropriate use.

Innes and Booher (1999a) write of several types of indicators with distinct uses: (1) systems performance indicators, used to provide feedback to the health of a community; (2) policy and program indicators, used to provide policy makers with feedback about the operation of a specific program or policies; and, (3) rapid feedback indicators, used to assist individuals and businesses in making decisions on a day-to-day basis. Although these distinctions are helpful, there is need for further clarification between the social indicators and the performance measure.

Bauer (1966) defines social indicators as measures to assess where we stand and are going with respect to values and goals. The social indicators are influenced by a variety of sources, in many cases, beyond the control of programs and program managers. The focus of social indicators should be to promote communication and general enlightenment rather than to function as a performance-monitoring tool. On the other hand, performance measures may be used as a limited performance-monitoring tool as defined by Hatry (1999, p. 3); performance measurement is "measurement on a regular basis of the results (outcomes) and efficiency of services or programs."

Advocates of performance management tools for program accountability voice opposition to the use of the social indicator; the problem remains regarding who will be held accountable for the achievement of the indicators (see Aristigueta, 1999). The social indicators, like performance measurement, are not explanatory and therefore should not be used for individual accountability or to replace more thorough program evaluation. The movement toward focusing on the outcomes through performance indicators and performance measures, as well as the costs of public services has become strong at all levels of government and in the nonprofit sector. However, "progress is slowed by such factors as unfamiliarity with outcome measurement, concern over the possible cost of new data collection requirements, and fears that public managers, who often have limited influence over many of their program outcomes [and much less over social indicators], will be unfairly blamed for outcomes that are less than expected" (Liner et al., 2001, p.1).

In practice, the use of social indicators is widely accepted and recognized as an important tool in shaping social policies. "The question is no longer about whether there is a need for social indicators, but rather, about the quality of those used" (Ben-Arieh, 2000, p. 3). Equally important is how social indicators are used. Vogel (1997, p. 104) calls for a return to the "original purpose of social indicators: to send signals to governments, business, other organizations and the general public by placing quality-of-life issues on the political agenda," however, support is provided through this discussion for the use of social indicators beyond general enlightenment to a governance tool in the iterative outcome-based accountability model found in state government models with the components shown in Figure 1.

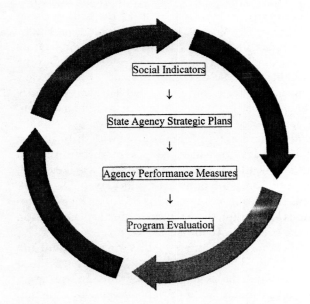

**Figure 1**   Components of an outcome-based accountability system.

## II. SOCIAL INDICATORS DEFINED

The term "social indicator" was coined by Bauer and his colleagues as an analogy to the term "economic indicator" and they defined social indicators as statistics, statistical series, and all other forms of evidence that enable us to assess or benchmark progress toward our values and goals (Bauer, 1966). "Social indicators are the repeated measurements made of the same phenomena over time" (Rossi and Gilmartin, 1980, p. xiii). Whether they are labeled social indicators, milestones, benchmarks, or population outcomes, the distinguishing characteristic is that they are time series measurements allowing for the identification of long-term trends, periodic changes, and fluctuations in the rate of change in conditions affecting the well being of individuals and communities. The purpose of the indicator is "to yield a concrete, comprehensive picture of individual living conditions that can be understood by the general public" (Vogel, 1997, p. 105).

The intent today, as in the past, is to provide quantification of societal phenomena for policy decision making, internal management, and informing the general public. In practice, the use of social indicators has been expanded to include their use as basic tools of governance for state and local planning initiatives, advocacy, program design and administration, resource allocation, intergovernmental relations, and alignment with program performance measures in order to create an outcome-based accountability system (Aristigueta et al., 2001). In addition, federal and state contracts are imposing performance requirements on local governments and nonprofit organizations. In ideal practice, the performance contract will call for performance measures, and these will be aligned with the broader social indicator.

## A. Examples of Social Indicators

Perhaps the most readily recognized social indicators are Kids Count, a project of the Annie E. Casey Foundation (1999), an effort to track the status of children in the United States that is described on their Web page as follows.

> This signature initiative of the Foundation examines the economic, educational, physical, and social well-being of children in the United States and informs public debate about innovative and promising strategies to improve outcomes for the most vulnerable children. The initiative's principal activity is the annual publication of the *KIDS COUNT Data Book*, which uses the best available comparative data to track conditions affecting children in the 50 states and the District of Columbia. By providing policymakers and citizens with benchmarks of child well-being, KIDS COUNT seeks to enrich local, state, and national discussions concerning ways to secure better futures for all children.

At the national level, the principal activity of the initiative is the publication of the data book with these indicators as the measures of children's well being:

Percentage of low birth-weight babies,
Infant mortality rate,
Child death rate,
Rate of teen deaths by accident, homicide, and suicide,
Teen birth rate,
Percentage of teens who are high school dropouts,

> Percentage of teens not attending school and not working,
> Percentage of children living with parents who do no have full-time, year-round
>     employment,
> Percentage of children in poverty, and
> Percentage of families with children headed by a single parent.

The Foundation also funds a nationwide network of state-level projects that provide a more detailed community picture of the conditions of children. These reports include data for the conditions of children in the respective state; some break out the information further. For example, in Delaware, the three counties in the state separate the eleven indicators and the state data are compared to those of the United States. The underlying goal of this project is to provide information for advocacy and action to improve the well being of children.

States' efforts, which include the monitoring of cross-sector well being in communities such as the *Oregon Benchmarks* and *Minnesota Milestone* and the monitoring of children and families such as the *Families Count in Delaware*, published in conjunction with *Kids Count in Delaware*, often trickle down to local governments and nonprofits. In state government, the developers of the Oregon Benchmarks, the Oregon Progress Board, were the pioneers in this effort, developing the indicators with stakeholder input. In 1992, the Oregon Progress Board received the Vanguard Award in recognition of their impact and excellence in state development policy. The award described Oregon benchmarks as "the first workable system in the country that makes economic development and human investment strategic planning real in the public sector" (Oregon Progress Board, 1993). In addition, Oregon's use of benchmarks is viewed as bringing public accountability out of mere politics and into day-to-day governance, by calculating progress toward defined developmental results, rather than simply counting the program input number. Municipal and county governments in Oregon (as in other states) are following the lead of the state by adopting their own benchmarks (Walter, 1995). Similar efforts are found in United Way of Portland that is also actively involved in establishing benchmarks.

The Bureau of the Census, the National Center for Education Statistics, and the National Center for Health Statistics produce other social indicator reports in the United States. Among international groups, the Organization for Economic Cooperation and Development (OECD, 2001) published *Society at a Glance: OECD Social Indicators 2001 Edition*, with the following description.

> Social policy covers a great number of issues that do not stand on their own but, as is increasingly recognized, are both diverse and interlinked. For example, tackling social exclusion involves simultaneously addressing barriers to labor market reintegration, health care issues and educational aspects. Social indicators have been developed to provide the broad perspective needed for any international comparison and assessment of social trends and policies. By linking social status and social response indicators across a broad range of policy areas, social indicators help readers to identify whether and how the broad thrust of public social policies and societal actions are addressing key social policy issues. . . . This publication captures in a nutshell information covering a wide range of topics, amongst others: fertility rates, asylum seekers and refugees, employment, retirement ages, early childhood education and care, replacement rates, relative poverty, the gender wage gap, social expenditure, potential years of life lost, health infrastructure, suicide, group membership and prisoners.

## B.  Criteria to Develop Social Indicators

The criteria to develop social indicators should include an assessment of well being across a broad array of outcomes, behaviors, and processes. This requires the disaggregation of data. Disaggregation may be done by ascribed characteristics (such as age, sex, race, ethnicity), well-being characteristics (such as education, employment, income), or by contextual variables (size of community, type of occupation). The OECD provides several purposes for the disaggregation of data: (1) normative considerations to assess equity and justice in the distribution of goods and services; (2) to detect nonuniformity and covariations in the data to uncover possible influences; and (3) to determine if a targeted population is being reached (OECD, 1976).

Aggregation of measures can encounter problems with meaning. For example, the Rand McNally Index loses meaning when air quality, housing prices, and school quality are combined into a single index without a clear basis for their weighting system (Landis and Sawicki, 1988). In addition, "aggregated measures reflect a particular theory or set of value judgements about the society and what is important," and these values may not be shared by members of society (Innes and Booher, 1999b, p. 8). Aggregation may also hide useful findings. For example, an overall lower infant mortality rate may not reveal higher rates among ethnic/racial groups.

The public and the policy makers should easily and readily understand social indicators. To interpret the indicators, some explanations should be provided with care not to influence the data. See, for example, Figure 2. In addition, the *Delaware Families Count/Kids Count* book contains a program statement to inform the public of programs the state has in place to address and try to influence the indicator:

> By providing medical and social services during pregnancy and after a baby is born, Delaware strives to prevent infant deaths. Through the Home Visiting Program, all first time parents are offered in-home support and referrals for needed services. In addition, the Perinatal Board has assumed statewide leadership to save babies lives by examining the causes of infant mortality and providing information that promotes healthy family behavior through community outreach projects. In concert with those efforts, the Division of Public Health works to prevent Sudden Infant Death Syndrome (SIDS) through the "Back to Sleep" campaign, which promotes healthy sleeping positions for infants.

Moreover, indicators need to be valid and reliable, should assess positive and negative aspects of well being, and be reflective of social goals (Moore, 1997). Social goals require the involvement of stakeholders in the process and design of the indicators of well being. The development of the indicators should be done with these two questions in mind: How important is the information to decision makers? How useful is the information?

Development of multiple indicators is required in order to provide a comprehensive picture of the societal condition. For an example, refer to the Casey Foundation's reporting of risk factors for children's well being in the fifty states as shown in Table 1. This information is further measured by high school dropouts and risk factors, teen parenthood and risk factors, risk factors by race/ethnicity, and location (Annie Casey Foundation, 1999, p. 6). Other factors may benefit from examining additional correlations, for example, low-birth weight and infant mortality.

Finally, as a society, we must examine equity issues that may be hidden by a statistic. For example, overall the state may be experiencing less teenage pregnancy.

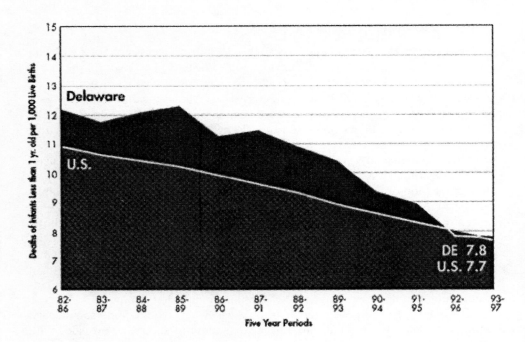

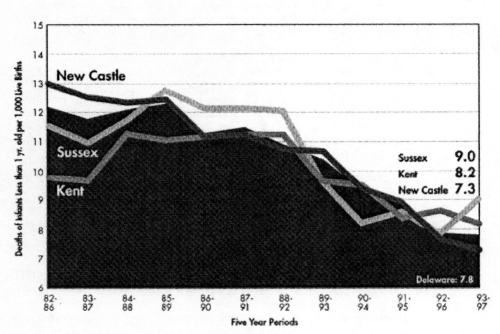

**Table 1** Percentage of Children with Certain Risks

| Factors | Risk (%) |
| --- | --- |
| Children not living with two parents | 32 |
| Household head is high school dropout | 19 |
| Family income is below the poverty line | 21 |
| Child is living with parent(s) who do not have steady full-time employment | 28 |
| Family is receiving welfare benefits | 12 |
| Child does not have health insurance | 15 |

*Source*: March 1998 Current Population Survey conducted by the U.S. Census Bureau found in the Annie Casey Foundation, 1999.

The lower rate is the result of lower rates in the higher populated urban area, yet the more rural parts of the state may in fact have seen an increase of births among its teen population. The information should be processed by answering the question, what can and should the information of social conditions mean to program management and policy makers.

## C. Use of Social Indicators: Creating Opportunities for the Challenges

Social indicators have multiple uses. For example, we see the advocacy role that they play in the policy agenda through the Kids Count efforts. They are also used as organizing frameworks for the Governor's Priority in Arizona. In Delaware, social indicators are used for alignment with agency performance measures. Alignment occurs when an organization's activities, core processes, and resources are aligned to support the mission and assist the organization in achieving its goals.

A limited study by Sturgis (1999) of nonprofits in Delaware found the state's social indicators in use for policy decision making, internal management, accountability to the public, professional knowledge, and awareness. As a result of the data, interested groups will sometimes develop community projects to address the issues.

Social indicators affect the whole range of public decision making, from problem formulation to policy and program design. Johansson (1982) regards social reporting as a joint activity linking the various actors in the political arena: citizens, elected officials, political parties, and other interest groups. For example, in Delaware an elected official learned of problems with infant mortality through statistics brought to

---

**Figure 2** Infant mortality: The infant mortality rate represents the number of deaths of children under one year old per 1000 live births. This rate is important because it is associated with a variety of factors, such as maternal health, quality of and access to medical care, socioeconomic conditions, and public health practices. Certain conditions increase the risk of infant mortality. These risks include maternal age (less than 19 or over 40), timing of pregnancy (leaving less than 18 months between births), poor maternal health or nutrition, and inadequate prenatal care. According to a national study, poverty is a key factor that affects the life expectancy of a child. The mortality rate for children born into families in poverty is 50% higher than that of children born into families with incomes above the poverty line. (From Delaware Kids Count.)

his attention by the news media; programs were designed and implemented to provide pre- and postnatal care as a result of this information.

Innes and Booher (1999b, p. 6) found in their work on communities that "indicators can help with public dialogue and community self-management." They further believe that it is the process that matters most, as this is how the indicators are internalized as part of the system. People then act on the indicators because the ideas the indicators represent have become second nature and part of what they take for granted (Innes, 1998).

Indicators have been influential in the public policy arena. For example, the national unemployment rate, the gross national product, and the consumer price index are used for public policy making (de Neufville, 1975). Data on race in schools has had an effect on policy related to desegregation (Weiss and Gruber, 1984). Nonetheless, Innes and Booher (1999b) point out that indicators do not drive policy and the conversion and learning require more than reading a report or seeing the results of data from an indicator. Indicators must measure something that is publicly valued and must be associated with a policy or set of actions. The indicators' greatest influence is attained through the collaborative learning process that indicator development and maintenance requires.

Indicators are also useful for comparisons or benchmarking. These comparisons are referred to as comparative performance measurement (CPM) and classified by Morley et al. (2001a) as falling into these categories.

1. Consumer-oriented comparisons—examples of these are *Places Rated Almanac, Money Magazine's* "Best Places to Live" and *U.S. News and World Report's* "America's Best Colleges".
2. Advocacy group comparisons—examples include the Annie E. Casey Foundation's *Kids Count Data Book* and *Governing Magazine's* "Grading the States: A Management Report Card".
3. Mandated reporting and comparisons—the FBI's Uniform Crime Reporting System requires the annual reporting of *Crime in America, United Kingdom Local Authority Performance Indicators,* and *Vermont Community Profiles.*
4. Self-initiated cooperative comparisons—includes *International City/County Management Association's Local Government CPM Consortium, North Carolina Institute of Government's CPM Project,* and the *Long Beach Police Department Peer Comparison.*

Note: Morley et al. (2001a) do not distinguish social indicators from performance measurement.

Finally, performance measures of a single agency do not typically address the cross-cutting goals of most large organizations. Social and economic indicators are broader and therefore may be appropriately used as an organizing framework. In Delaware, the Family Services Cabinet Council's initiative to develop coordinated and collaborative services across state agencies provided the impetus for social indicators by making the need for data on more global indicators apparent. "As a result, the indicators project was initiated to provide data to identify and plan appropriate initiatives and monitor changes in the status of children and their families" (Aristigueta et. al., 2001, p. 265). For example, the organizing framework may be illustrated by the statewide goal: healthy children. Social indicators such as the rate of teen death by injury, homicide, and suicide support this goal. At the child mental health agency level, one of the performance measures is the proportion of children who are readmitted to a hospital within thirty days of their release. Although mental health alone is not expected to have an observable influence on the social indicator, the alignment is able to illustrate steps that are taken to address the issue.

## D. Misuse of Social Indicators: Adding to the Challenges

Social indicators are sometimes misused. Unevenness of coverage of quantifiable societal conditions sometimes occurs due to personal or political areas of interest. It is impractical to think that value-free indicators may be developed. Instead, Innis (1990) recommends that we insulate (not isolate) the statistics from immediate day-to-day politics in order to strike a balance between political and programmatic considerations.

Problems are encountered when using social indicators as program performance measures. Agencies may be held accountable for social indicators when the influencing factors are beyond the agency's influence such as societal trends or changing demographics. At a recent American Society for Public Administration conference, Martin (2001) left the audience with the following questions: Do we really want stakeholders to start equating:

> The performance of job training programs with decreases in the unemployment rate?
> The performance of adoption programs with decreases in the numbers of children in foster care?
> The performance of STD clinics with the community STD rates?

However, this does not mean that programs working toward alleviating those conditions should not track progress with their own clients and align performance measures and identified social problems. For example, Morley et al. (2001b, p. 15) provide the following example from Gaston Skills, Inc. in Dallas, North Carolina, which provides vocational rehabilitation programs.

> For its supported employment program, it used such outcome indicators as number and percent of clients placed in jobs in the community: average hourly wages; average number of hours worked per week; number and percent of clients stabilized in the workplace (able to function with minimal support from the organization's job coach): and number and percent of successful case closures (defined as having an appropriate job match and the ability to function independently after the training period).

These measures provide a picture of what is being done in the community to alleviate unemployment and of the accomplishment toward this end. These program outcomes may be aligned with social indicators. However, this is quite different from a specific program being held responsible (or claiming success) for the unemployment rate in a community.

Data sometimes are presented without analysis and interpretation, leaving the reader to interpret the patterns and meanings without appropriate guidance. "Without narrative interpretations, the interconnectedness of the different aspects of well-being could not be described; the reasons for the selection and organization of particular data series could not be explored; and above all, the reader could not be

**Table 2**  Uses and Misuses of Social Indicators

| Uses | Misuses |
|---|---|
| Comprehensive picture of individual's living conditions | Performance monitoring tool |
| | Presenting data without analysis |
| Tool to shape social policy | Basing need for program on social indicator alone |
| General enlightment | |
| Advocacy | Individual accountability |
| Public dialogue | |
| Community self-management | |
| Accountability to the public | |
| Internal management | |
| Professional knowledge | |
| Awareness | |
| Comparisons or benchmarking | |
| Organizing framework | |
| Decision making | |

alerted to the dangers of unwarranted conclusions or the possibilities of alternate explanations" (Johnston, 1978, p. 7). More recently, the State of Florida released its social indicators without explanation, intentionally leaving interpretation to the public and policy makers. One cannot help but wonder how much this led to the demise in 1998 of social indicators as a state effort. For more on this subject refer to Aristigueta (2000).

Societal indicators may also present a problem when used alone to determine need for a program. Innes and Booher (1999b, p. 9) claim, "all too often the public or analysts declares that some policy has failed when in reality we would be worse off without it, or when we would have different results if we just changed it a bit." The uses and misuses of social indicators are summarized in Table 2.

Technology has facilitated the collection of data; and the abundance and ease of access to data have increased the incidence of inappropriate use of data (Mc Call, 2001). Policy makers may alter the original purpose of the data or not use the information or social indicators available because they are not in agreement with the cause of or solution to the social problems being measured (Biderman, 1966; Carley, 1981; Kingdon 1995).

## III.  LESSONS FROM THE LITERATURE AND PRACTICE

The efforts made in the area of social reporting are toward a more informed policy process and public. The optimism endures for the overall well being of society and the democratic process. Lessons learned are discussed below.

1.  Having the data does not necessarily mean you have a good indicator. Policy makers in haste to publish reports have been known to develop indicators because the data were available. The focus should be on utility, not on availability. Recommendations for action as seen in Table 1 are a good way to alert others on how these issues may be addressed.

2. There is no such thing as a value-free indicator. Indicators should reflect the social values of the community. This is best accomplished by including in the process and development the stakeholders who will use and learn from them. By the same token, indicators need to reflect the voices of those who are experiencing the effects.

3. The indicator should be conceptually clear and meet the requirements for appropriateness, reliability, and validity, and be widely understood and accepted by the experts and stakeholders alike (Innes, 1990).

4. Recognize that identifying indicators implies at least a potential challenge to established political institutions by posing a variety of questions. Are the indicators reflective of the values of the institution and the community that it represents? What are the expectations that the community will place on the government to alleviate these problems?

5. Some of the movement's founders were overly optimistic about the uses of social indicators for performance monitoring. Experience has shown that social indicators are primarily useful for general enlightenment, for advocacy and influencing of the political agenda, and for social planning (Vogel, 1997).

6. Be aware of the quality of data used for social indicators and how useful these data are for comparison. Hatry (1999) warns of the potential for data manipulation and suggests a data quality control process. When conducting comparisons, one needs to make sure the data reported were obtained or calculated in comparable ways.

7. New indicators are needed to supplement those of the past and reflect current societal trends including: indicators of job security, the number and regularity of working hours (due to the rise of the contract employee), perception of government (examples of this appeared in Florida's social indicators), political participation (examples may be found in Virginia's social indicators).

8. The development of good indicators often requires controversial discussion. One of the most controversial and dynamic discussions for developing measures for children's well being includes asking the child. Ben-Arieh (2000, p. 239) believes that it is necessary to raise the child's stature in the policy process by "emphasizing the child as a unit of observation, reflecting the child's voice and perceptions, and enhancing children's rights." Asking the adults is simply not enough and neither is measuring the success into adulthood. De Lone (1979) argues that children are instrumentalized by the forward look perspectives in the sense that their good life is postponed until adulthood; childhood should be considered a stage in and of itself.

9. Indicators do not provide answers; rather they are a starting point for discussion and potential action. It is not the indicators themselves or the reports that matter, but the learning and change that take place during the course of their development and the way the learning leads to new shared meaning and changed discourses (Innes, 1990, 1988).

## IV. CONCLUSION

Today's government reform movement includes an enhanced interest in effectiveness as demonstrated by the emphasis on results. At the same time, reform efforts represent an important reemphasis on values, including the elevation of efficiency in comparison to other dimensions of performance (Cigler, 1995). Others are predicting that in the coming years equity will join efficiency and effectiveness as a key component of government performance (Greiner, 1996). In line with these concerns is strong support for the amplification of the public's voice in government (Chapin and Denhardt, 1995).

Social indicators are a basic tool of governance in the outcome-based accountability infrastructure; in addition, they provide an opportunity to address equity issues and to amplify the public's voice in government. An indicator developed in a thoughtful informed way, with input from the agencies and stakeholders, can help disclosure about conditions and communicate to the public with leadership about problems, needs, and opportunities. An indicator meeting these requirements is one that will continue to be effective over time because the people who produce and use it regard it as valuable (Innes and Booher, 1999b).

Nonetheless, social indicators provide accountability challenges for management structures that are based upon individual performance and may be threatening to political environments where there are expectations to act on the data. In the use of social indicators, the requirement to serve the public may best be fulfilled by shifting the focus of accountability and performance from the individual or program to societal learning through information sharing. The broader definition of accountability involves not only formal oversight but also public scrutiny in terms of public confidence and trust (Kearns, 1996). Social indicators provide the opportunity for governments, community, nonprofits, and the private sectors to work toward common goals, often requiring the involvement of multiple agencies. Other indicator results are heavily influenced by societal trends and conditions. In order for effective collaborations to occur, the pressure for individual performance must be alleviated and the emphasis must be shifted to the communication process for improving policy making, accountability, and governance.

Social indicators are important for governance and critical in times of increased accountability and performance requirements coupled with reduced social benefits on personal and community well being. Along with indicators, explanations must be provided to include conditions that are beyond the control of government. This may help to ease the tensions that are created by unrealistic expectations for the role of government in addressing social problems. In addition, providing information on programs that are in place to help address the problem will let the public know that the problem is not being ignored, as was shown in Figure 2. "If we accept the basic notion that the most important task of politics is to improve living conditions for everyone...then social indicators must be regarded as an essential tool for assessing progress toward that goal." (Vogel, 1997, pp. 107–108).

To extend institutions by developing democratic methods for governing bureaucracies is, perhaps, the crucial problem of our time (Blau 1963). Social indicators serve as an investment in democracy by aiding multiple purposes. To the extent that social indicators become accepted in public discourse, they give a voice to the voter. They provide an objective measure of progress toward the defined goals, for example, healthy children or public perception of government. Social reporting demystifies politics. It provides a common ground on which everyone involved can learn something about the status of the community's well being. Thus social reporting performs an important function in a representative democracy by illuminating trends and comparing dissimilarities and patterns of inequality. As Vogel (1997, p.108) reminds us, social indicators are a "cheap investment in democracy."

Finally, from a management perspective, social indicators provide an umbrella for political and organizational priorities, and for alignment to agency performance measures. A managing for results system that includes social indicators is better able to communicate to the public on issues of societal and community well being, and contribute to a better informed policy-making process.

## REFERENCES

Annie Casey Foundation. (1999). KIDS COUNT DATA BOOK. Baltimore, MD. Available at www.aecf.org

Aristigueta, M. P. (1999). *Managing for Results in State Government*. Westport, CI: Quorum.

Aristigueta, M. P. (2000). The rise and fall of the Florida benchmarks. In: Neely, A., ed. *Performance Measurement—Past, Present, and Future*. Cambridge, UK: Fieldfare, pp. 16–23.

Aristigueta, M. P., Cooksy, L. J., Nelson, C. W. (2001). The role of social indicators in developing a managing for results system. *Public Perform. Manage. Rev.* 24(3):254–269.

Bauer, R. A. (1966). *Social Indicators*. Cambridge, MA: MIT Press.

Ben-Arieh, A. (2000). Beyond welfare: measuring and monitoring the state of children—New trends and domains. *Soc. Indicat. Res.* 52(3):235–257.

Biderman, A.D. (1966). Social indicators and goals. In: Bauer, R.A., ed. *Social Indicators*. Cambridge, MA: MIT Press, pp. 68–153.

Blau, P. M. (1963). *The Dynamics of Bureaucracy*. Chicago: University of Chicago Press.

Carley, M. (1981). *Social Measurement and Social Indicators: Issues of Policy and Theory*. London: Allen & Unwin.

Chapin, L. W., Denhardt, R. B. (1995). Putting citizens first in Orange County, Florida. *Nat. Civic Rev.* 84:210–217.

Cigler, B. A. (1995). County governance in the 1990s. *State Local Gov. Rev.* 27:55–70.

Corbett, T. J. (1997). Foreword. In: Hauser, R. M., Brown, B. V., Prosser, W., eds. *Indicators of Children's Well-Being*. New York: Russell Sage Foundation, pp. xix–xxi.

Delaware Kids Count. Available at http://www.deKidscount.org/ (accessed on September 17, 2003).

De Lone, R. H. (1979). *Small Futures: Children, Inequality, and the Limits of Liberal Reform*. New York: Harcourt Brace Jovanovich.

de Neufville, J. I. (1975). *Social Indicators and Public Policy: Interactive Processes of Design and Application*. Amsterdam: Elsevier.

Greiner, J. M. (1996). Positioning performance measurement for the twenty-first century. In: Halachmi, A., Bouckaert, G., eds. *Organizational Performance and Measurement in the Public Sector*. Westport, CT: Quorum, pp. 11–50.

Hatry, H. P. (1999). *Performance Measurement: Getting Results*. Washington, DC: Urban Institute.

Holzer, M. (1995). The public productivity challenge. In: Halachmi, A., Bouckaert, G., eds. *The Enduring Challenges in Public Management*. San Francisco: Jossey-Bass, Inc., pp. 413–448.

Innes, J. E. (1988). The power of data requirements. *J. Am. Plan. Assoc.* 54:275–278.

Innes, J. E. (1990). *Knowledge and Public Policy: The Search for Meaningful Indicators*. New Brunswick, NJ: Transaction.

Innes, J. E. (1998). Information in communicative planning. *J. Am. Plan. Assoc.* 64:52–63.

Innes, J. E., Booher, D. E. (1999a). Metropolitan development as a complex system: a new approach to sustainability. *Econ. Devel. Quart.* 13:141–156.

Innes, J. E., Booher, D. E. (1999b). Indicators for sustainable communities: a strategy building on complexity theory and distributed intelligence. *Working Paper, Institute of Urban and Regional Development*. Berkeley, CA: University of California, Berkeley Press.

Johansson, S. (1982). *Towards a Theory of Social Reporting*. Sweden: Swedish Institute for Social Research.

Johnston, D. F. (1978). Federal social indicators reports: a critique and plans for the future. Proceedings of the Annual Meeting of the American Sociological Association.

Kearns, K. P. (1996). *Managing for Accountability: Preserving the Public Trust in Public and Non-Profit Organizations*. San Francisco: Jossey-Bass.

Kingdon, J. W. (1995). *Agendas, Alternatives, and Public Choices*. New York: HarperCollins.

Kopcynski, M., Lombardo, M. (1999). Comparative performance measurement: insight and lessons learned from a consortium effort. *Public Admin. Rev.* 59(2):124–134.

Landis, J., Sawick, D. (1988). A planner's guide to the Places Rated Almanac. *J. Am. Plan. Assoc.* 54(3):336–358.

Liner, B., Hatry, H. P., Vinson, E., Allen, R., Dusenbury, P., Bryant, S., Snell, R. (2001). *Making Results-Based State Government Work*. Washington, DC: Urban Institute.

Martin, L. L. (2001, March 10–14). Social indicators as program performance measures: a really bad idea! Proceedings of the National Conference, American Society for Public Administration, Newark: NJ.

Mc Call, L. (2001). Measuring the social health of Native American communities in New Mexico: applying the social health index to reservations and counties. Doctoral dissertation. Los Angeles: University of Southern California

Moore, K. A. (1997). Criteria for indicators of child well being. In: Hauser, R. M., Brown, B. V., Prosser, W., eds. *Indicators of Children's Well-Being*. New York: Russell Sage Foundation, pp. 36–44.

Morley, E., Bryant, S. P., Hatry, H. P. (2001a). *Comparative Performance Measurement*. Washington, DC: Urban Institute.

Morley, E., Vinson, E., Hatry, H. P. (2001b). *Outcome Measurement in Nonprofit Organizations: Current Practices and Recommendations*. Washington, DC: Independent Sector and Urban Institute.

OECD. Organization for Economic Cooperation and Development. (1976). *Measuring Social Well Being: A Progress Report on the Development of Social Indicators*. Washington, DC: OECD Publication Center.

OECD. Organization for Economic Cooperation and Development. (2001). *Society at a Glance: OECD Social Indicators 2001 Edition*. Available at http://electrade.gfi.fr/cgibin/ OECD BookShop.

Oregon Progress Board. (1993). *Oregon Benchmarks*. Portland, OR: Oregon Progress Board.

Oregon Progress Board. (1999). Achieving the Oregon Shines vision: The 1999 benchmark report highlights. Report to the Legislative Assembly. Portland, OR: Oregon Progress Board.

Rossi, R. J., Gilmartin, K. J. (1980). *The Handbook of Social Indicators: Sources Characteristics, and Analysis*. New York: Graland STPM Press.

Sturgis, J. (1999). Families count in Delaware: One state's efforts with an indicator initiative. Master's analytical paper. Newark, DE: University of Delaware.

U.S. GAO. U.S. General Accounting Office. (1992). *Performance Measurement: An Important Tool in Managing-for-Results*. Washington, DC: U.S. General Accounting Office.

U.S. GAO. U.S. General Accounting Office. (1995). *Managing for Results: State Experiences Provide Insights for Federal Management Reforms*. Washington, DC: U.S. General Accounting Office.

Vogel, J. (1997). The future direction of social indicators research. *Soc. Indicat. Res.* 42:103–116.

Walter, J. (1995). *Building the American Community: What Works, What Doesn't*. Washington, DC: National Academy of Public Administration.

Weiss, J. A., Gruber, J. E. (1984). Deterring discrimination with data. *Policy Sci.* 17:49–66.

Wholey, J. S. (1983). *Evaluation and Effective Public Management*. Boston: Little, Brown.

Wholey, J. S., Hatry, H. P. (1992). The case for performance monitoring. *Public Admin. Rev.* 52(6):604–610.

# 24

# The Human Side of Productive Work Environments

**MARY E. GUY**
*Florida State University, Tallahassee, Florida, U.S.A.*

## I.  INTRODUCTION

The test of a productive work environment is whether it challenges staff to perform at their best and whether doing their best results in quality service to the public. Meeting these criteria brings bonuses above and beyond quality output: At the societal level, it fulfills an obligation to use tax dollars efficiently; at the personal level it enhances employees' quality of worklife.

Money cannot buy the intangible commitment that causes employees to perform at their best—nor can direct orders command such commitment. The desire to achieve is generated by the relationship between management and workers, pride in workmanship, and belief in the mission. Intangible but essential are rapport, commitment, and conscientiousness among staff amid an atmosphere conducive to productivity, all within a context that maximizes quality and quantity. What is required to achieve such an environment? This is the question addressed here. A good place to start the discussion is with the elements of a productive work environment, demonstrating how they apply to the work setting. First comes an understanding of the environment in which work takes place.

## II.  EXTERNAL AND INTERNAL ENVIRONMENTS

For lack of a better expression, the work environment has both near and far elements. The *far environment* includes those contextual factors external to the organization. These invisible factors comprise the complex web of political, economic, legal, and social influences that surround the agency and shape its actions. It affects workers less as they go about their daily tasks and more in terms of the pride they feel in being associated with the agency. Manifestations of the far environment include both positive and negative media stories, political campaign rhetoric, and public opinion. These features directly affect organizational design and indirectly affect productivity. For example, U.S. taxpayers are hostile toward the Internal Revenue Service because of its mission to collect income tax. To maintain its credibility and minimize criticism, the IRS is attentive to its image and the communications that shape it. To a greater extent than most public agencies, it employs centralized decision making and constricted information flows to the outside.

Across all agencies, lower-level staff are sealed off from the effects of the far environment as they go about their usual tasks, but they are affected nevertheless. A positive public image promotes a sense of pride and identification with the agency. It also makes recruitment and retention easier because a popular agency is a train on which many people want to ride. When public opinion is hostile, employees tire of defending their work to their friends and families. After being reminded of negative headlines too many times, they psychologically distance themselves from the agency. As their commitment diminishes, so does their productivity. This scenario discourages workers from enjoying a sense of ownership in the organization's overall performance as they struggle to dissociate themselves and their work from that which is criticized.

The *near environment* is the general milieu, or atmosphere, within the workplace. It is manifested in a number of ways: the nature and quality of communication between people; the amount of candor that exists when people discuss activities, assignments, and plans; the tenseness versus lightheartedness in the air; the atmosphere that pervades agency/client interactions; the pride that workers have in doing their jobs well; and the norms that guide employees' personal assessments of how much work they should be expected to produce and for what level of quality they should be held accountable.

Although there are obstacles to controlling either, managers have more control over the near than the far environment. Manipulable variables include incentive systems, project assignments, performance standards, rewards and sanctions, staffing patterns, communication channels, and workflow. In optimal circumstances, thoughtful supervision and effective leadership combine to maneuver these variables into a synergy that results in productive work environments. Although the far environment affects the near, the discussion in this chapter now focuses on the near because that is where managerial control can have the greatest impact on worker behavior.

## III.  PRODUCTIVITY IS A PEOPLE ISSUE

It is people who control the productivity of any organization. From fire chiefs to public health officers to public works directors to job training supervisors, management matters. It matters not so much for its own sake as for its ability to motivate the workforce to function as the hands and feet of important public purposes. To a large degree, it is managerial skill, not financial largesse, that determines productivity; after a certain point, more dollars and more automation will not improve performance. People improve performance. Managers, the traffic cops who direct the flow of work, have the responsibility to make this happen.

**Table 1** Managerial Techniques for Improving Productivity

| Techniques |
| --- |
| Coaching |
|    Build on strengths |
|    Harness enthusiasm of influential personnel |
|    Delegate but do not dump |
|    Reward desired behavior |
|    Keep in touch with employees |
| Goal setting |
|    Set meaningful goals |
|    Clarify priorities |
|    Allocate sufficient resources |
| Contingency strategies |
|    Deal with troublemakers |
|    Be prepared for change |
|    Use creative problem solving |
|    Keep an open mind |

*Source*: Guy 1992, p. 310.

Managerial tasks range from technical oversight to interpersonal relations. These tasks have the capacity to change an organization's climate, communication patterns, interdepartmental relations, and staffing patterns, as well as to generate technological initiatives. The easiest way to make quick productivity gains is to mechanize a process. The more difficult, but most enduring, way to make gains is to develop each worker's desire and ability to be maximally productive. For example, after researching libraries, Damanpour and Evan (1984) concluded that the adoption of administrative initiatives triggers the adoption of technical initiatives more readily than the reverse. Those libraries that adopted administrative initiatives had a greater payoff in the end because the changes caused by the initiatives paved the way for technological changes.

Multiple dimensions of organizational life are brought to bear in the effort to create and nurture work environments that reinforce productivity. Interpersonal relations, culture, climate, communications, and needs of the workforce come readily to mind. It is management's responsibility to diagnose the needs of a workplace and then select and implement those initiatives that will have the greatest likelihood of nurturing productivity. The starting point is to diagnose the near environment. After identifying its strengths and weaknesses, it is possible to determine which activities are necessary to maximize strengths and minimize counterproductive features. Table 1 lists techniques that combine to improve productivity. These items presume capacity building through capitalizing on human behavior.

## IV. MANAGING KNOWLEDGE WORKERS

In pursuit of a productive work environment, managers' responsibilities include articulating where the agency is going, for what purpose, and how it is going to get there. To this end, characteristics of a productive work environment include team building, open communication, flexibility in the midst of predictability, and balancing the needs of the organization with the needs of the workforce. This is especially true in public service, where most of the work is done by knowledge workers.

As Peter Drucker instructed years ago, knowledge workers differ from industrial workers. They expect more autonomy and their productivity is often dependent on rapid communication with peers, subordinates, and superiors. They have expertise that managers do not, thus those higher in the chain of command are dependent on those lower to figure out how to accomplish goals. Rather than the pyramid-shaped hierarchies of old, today's organizations are concentric, overlapping, coordinated rings, with knowledge workers at their core. In comparison to the assembly-line workers accounted for by traditional scientific management theory, knowledge workers are their own capitalists because they own the means of production, that is, knowledge (Drucker, 1980).

Reliance on individual workers presumes decentralization and flexibility. Half a century ago, Drucker (1954) urged a departure from the standardization that scientific management preached. He argued that practices should have no more uniformity than the concrete task requires. How true that is today. No one person knows all aspects of a job, so staff work in teams in order to bring all areas of expertise to the table. This is why team building is essential.

"Team building" is a term that means to bring people together to develop the linkages necessary for them to work interdependently toward the accomplishment of a goal. In one sense, it relates to the entire workforce cooperating to achieve the overall goals of the agency. Effective team building involves cross-faulting strengths and weaknesses of personnel so that workers who are weak in one area are complemented by others who are strong in that area but perhaps weak in the area of their teammates' strengths. Staffing patterns that are developed with a conscious awareness of individual strengths and weaknesses allow workers to use their strengths, doing what they do best, while their weaknesses are compensated by the strengths of others.

Team building is necessary to overcome structural divisions that otherwise establish barriers between workers. Different departments, different professions, and different functions predispose staff to parochialism when representatives of various work units discuss organizational goals and strive for consensus on how to achieve them. The advantage to organizing by department is that it brings together staff with similar job tasks. The drawback is that it isolates staff from one another. Team building is the remedy to establish durable links between departments.

In effective teams, staff assignments are sufficiently stable that members develop a personal identification with the team, assuming an "us versus them" pride in their group's performance. Work groups cannot establish smooth operating procedures unless team membership is stable. Members must be part of the team long enough to be comfortable making mutual adjustments for each other and to have a personal identity with their collective performance (Guy, 1985). Once team identification occurs, then interteam bridging structures are important. The formation of bridges, such as task forces and member exchanges, is necessary so that the "us versus them" attitude is bridled by an understanding that each team's success depends on the relations it maintains with other work units.

Having said this, attention now turns to the techniques listed in Table 1. What is involved in coaching, goal setting, and contingency strategies in a setting of knowledge workers and teams? The following paragraphs describe these tools. Then a case is provided that demonstrates how a productive work environment turned upside down. After the case, discussion follows that explains how the absence of techniques listed in Table 1 resulted in high turnover, lowered morale, and a downturn in productivity.

## A.  Coaching

The manager is a catalyst, the coach who spurs workers to do their best, to figure out how to work smarter. The manager works through others to accomplish the goals of the organization. Five techniques capture this process: building on strengths, harnessing the enthusiasm of influential personnel, delegating without dumping, rewarding desired behavior, and keeping in touch. This is not an exhaustive list but, rather, is indicative of the frame through which effective managers view their work.

### 1.  Build on Strengths

Employees expect the opportunity to do their jobs; to be kept informed of matters affecting their work; to receive appropriate rewards for their contributions; to receive feedback about how well they are doing; and to receive whatever support, guidance, and training are necessary. For this to occur, the manager must be able to communicate personal expectations to employees clearly and to give feedback on what they are doing right and what needs improvement. Effective management involves coaching employees to be as good as they can be and rewarding desired behaviors. Good coaches create a culture with identifiable heroes, villains, and rebels. The heroes personify the characteristics prized by the organization. Villains personify that which is unwanted, and rebels define the margins of acceptable behavior. The attributions reveal norms the agency rewards and those that it penalizes.

### 2.  Harness Enthusiasm of Influential Staff

Harnessing the interest and enthusiasm of opinion shapers eases the amount of hands-on persuasion required of managers. Opinion shapers are those who are respected by their peers, are wired into the grapevine and know what is going on, and those to whom others turn when they want rumors verified and events interpreted. They sway opinion and convince peers to go along with, or resist, changes.

### 3.  Delegate but Do Not Dump

Delegating is an essential skill; dumping is an abrogation of responsibility. Delegating implies that duties and responsibilities are assigned to subordinates for them to implement according to their best judgment and to report back on the activities. Dumping implies that duties and responsibilities are assigned to subordinates with or without their consent, never to be asked about the status of the work again. Delegation implies that a choice is present to accept or refuse the responsibilities on the part of the subordinate and that the superior retains interest in the assignment. Dumping implies that no choice is present to the subordinate, and once the tasks are assigned, the superior will not be assisting with the tasks in any way, even insofar as showing meaningful interest. Delegating means that the resources to do the job are provided; dumping often means that the task is assigned without requisite resources to be successful.

## 4.  Reward Desired Behaviors

Only when an employee perceives a reward to be meaningful does it become an inducement. For some workers, a convenient parking space is a reward; for others it is time off work. For some, being highlighted in the agency newsletter is rewarding, whereas others value a luncheon in their honor.

One technique for highlighting good performance is through a Positive Incident Report. This is a variation on the euphemistic "Unusual Incident Report," in which an accident or otherwise potentially damaging event is reported and used as the basis for disciplinary action. A positive spin can be put on this reporting procedure by documenting innovative actions that otherwise would be overlooked. A daily or weekly review of positive incidents accompanied with positive feedback enhances the confidence of staff and fosters positive attitudes about the work environment in general. It also helps staff identify new ways to solve problems.

## 5.  Keep in Touch with Employees

Communicate, communicate, communicate. Employees need easy access to accurate information. Communication is the unseen infrastructure of the organization. The lifeblood of a vibrant organization is its ability to move information and ideas from the bottom to the top and back down again in a continuous dialogue. Hardening of the arteries is a threat not only to human health but to the health of communication flows. When lines of communication become rigid and inflexible, they lose their usefulness and reliability as information channels.

The concept of climate is intertwined with communication. The climate may be one of warmth and support or one of cold uncaring. The amount of communication and degree of coordination on a unit affects how smoothly the unit operates and how much support there is for individual needs and concerns. In turn, climate affects turnover. In more supportive climates, staff are more likely to enjoy their work and remain. In colder climates, there is less social fulfillment and employee turnover is higher.

Communication is a management tool. Keeping abreast of what is going on and the forces that are helping or hindering employees' work pays dividends. Employees want to know that superiors appreciate what they do, care about their welfare, and are paying attention to their work. Managers must be able to communicate expectations in a way that motivates workers. Clear instructions and meaningful compliments encourage employees to be productive and take pride in their work.

Some messages are communicated more clearly when a combination of channels is used. Channels include email, electronic bulletin boards and chat rooms, hang-on-the-wall bulletin boards beside the water fountain, memoranda, as well as the ever-present "grapevine" of informal communication.

One of the most persuasive reasons for flattening hierarchies as much as possible is to reduce the number of people that messages must pass through before arriving at their destination. Each time a message is interpreted and paraphrased by intermediaries, it is modified. By the time it arrives at its destination, it has undergone numerous alterations.

Despite their labor-saving advantages, computers and the Internet have added to labor instead of shrinking it. To a great degree, knowledge workers are drowning in information while starving for certainty. There is an optimal level of information that any one person can integrate and comprehend. With too little information, employees feel they are not being kept abreast of everything they need to know. At the other extreme, too much information is an overload, producing confusion over which direction to take. Job satisfaction increases with increasing amounts of information, but past some optimal point, too much information leads to decreased decision quality. Although this presents a quandary for management as well, it is a challenge facing every worksite.

## B. Goal Setting

Goals guide performance. They provide a direction to travel and a common destination. For projects to generate shared values, the workforce must have common understandings about what is important and what is being achieved. One of the purposes of goal setting is to provide a forum where everyone can share their ideas about what is achievable and reach a consensus on specific goals.

### 1. Set Meaningful Goals

It is management's responsibility not to set the goals, per se, but to create an atmosphere where workers set their own goals, goals they are committed to achieving. Goals too high serve neither as motivators nor benchmarks. Goals too low also fail to motivate because they fail to challenge. Workers who have actively participated in goal setting have a clearer understanding of the goals and their importance than workers who were not involved in setting them.

### 2. Clarify Priorities

The variety of demands on a worker's time and attention keeps growing. Take the job of fire chief, for example. In many communities the fire chief is responsible for a broad array of functions: emergency medical services, identification and disposal of hazardous materials, fire prevention programs, enforcing building codes, compliance with regulatory mandates, inspection and maintenance of water mains and hydrants, communications systems for disaster preparedness, and staying current with the latest equipment. As the population ages, the need for expanded emergency medical services will continue to escalate, whereas the demand for fire protection and other services currently provided will continue as well (Walters, 1990). How should a fire chief go about setting goals and priorities? The variety of functions makes it impossible to set uniform performance standards for the entire force. On the other hand, relying only on the overall mission to protect and promote the safety and health of the community's citizens is too broad to lend guidance to supervisors as they struggle to set reasonable performance expectations. Clearly, each division must assess its own capacities and set performance standards based on the responsibilities it bears. Yet the standards of each division must contribute to the overall goals of protecting and promoting safety and health.

By setting priorities on the functions performed, the fire chief accomplishes several things. First, priorities let employees know what absolutely must be done versus what should be done. Second, it helps personnel set goals and know how to rank them in order of importance. And third, it lets employees know what the fire chief thinks is important, which in turn gives them insight into the activities that the chief watches most closely.

### 3.  Allocate Sufficient Resources

Resources must be shifted along with production goals so they are consistent with one another. For example, take the case of a county health department that is responsible for monitoring the immunization records of all children enrolled in the public school system. When only one person is given the responsibility to visit all the schools in five different districts and make home visits to educate parents about their children's immunizations, the whole job cannot be done. Sufficient workers must be assigned to the task or the goal must be diminished.

Staff know that when they are not supplied with resources necessary to achieve their goals, the goals are meaningless. Disparities among expectations, words, and deeds dampen motivation. When this happens, goals lose their ability to motivate and they become meaningless—and managers lose an easy productivity tool. Ideally, goals are their own performance criteria. Workers know when they meet them and know when they come up short. If resources are lacking to achieve goals, then the goals themselves are worthless.

### C.  Contingency Strategies

Circumstances dictate methods. Varied management styles and organizational characteristics produce different approaches to leadership, motivation, communications, decision making, teamwork, and management control. Strategies must be compatible with the work environment, which means that they must make sense within the managerial and technical system; suit the skills, training, and understandings of personnel; fit with organizational and work patterns; and comply with the traditions and culture of the workforce. The internal milieu created by the near environment affects the speed with which changes are introduced and accepted, the way organizations solve problems, and the overall rate of productivity. Four types of strategies are described: dealing with troublemakers, being prepared for change, using creative problem solving, and keeping an open mind. To some degree these overlap, and to a greater degree, many more strategies will be encountered by managers, but these provide a few examples.

### 1.  Deal with Troublemakers

Sooner or later, every work unit will have an outlaw or two, workers whose behavior is noticeably deviant from that of the others. Their behavior, in fact, defines the normal by what their behavior is not. They fall into one of several categories. There will be those who take a stance contrary to whatever the majority propose. There will be those who are not bad enough to fire but not good enough to be productive members of the organization. And there will be those who form cabals to promote their own self-interest at the expense of everyone else's.

How to deal with troublemakers depends on which variation is represented. One way to deal with outlaws is by co-optation, that is, bringing them into the decision-making process rather than isolating them outside it. This is a desirable route for dealing with deviants who are influential opinion shapers. A good rule of thumb is to identify what motivates the person, match that interest with a project where the person can excel, and put the person at the front of the parade. In other words, harness the person's energy and influence and make it work for the organization rather than against it.

To deal with marginal employees, those who are not bad enough to discharge but not productive enough to be a constructive member of the team, there are several choices depending on how much control one can wield. Although not desirable, this author has witnessed a perverse, though effective strategy. A large state-operated facility identified a single work unit and assigned marginal producers and troublesome employees, the outlaws, to it. The facility allocated sufficient resources to the unit so that goals could be achieved. Even though employees elsewhere ostracized those assigned there, the unit created its own MASH-like identity and the work got done (Guy, 1985). A more constructive route is to mainstream outlaws, assigning each to a group that is motivated, productive, and cohesive. The insertion of the miscreant risks disturbing a smooth functioning work group, but takes the chance that the positive characteristics of others will have a salutary effect on the performance of the problem employee.

## 2. Be Prepared for Change

Flexibility in the midst of predictability is essential. It is valuable to promote innovative ideas, "thinking out of the box," and questioning usual and customary procedures. On the other hand, it is also important to maintain consistency where it matters. A workforce that has been kept abreast of events is more willing to adapt when changes are necessary than a workforce that has been kept uninformed. In environments where there is too much change, the unpredictability of the situation causes employees to distance themselves psychologically. Instead of promoting an identity with the group, it foments displeasure and fosters anxiety. Change presents both threat and opportunity. An old shoe that pinches but is predictable is often more comforting than a new shoe that has yet to be broken in.

It is less top management's role to identify and solve problems than to create an environment in which workers identify and solve their own problems. To do this requires a clear vision of where the organization is headed and the strength to steer it there. As an analogy, if one is lost on a highway, a road map is useful. However, when lost in a swamp, the road map is useless and a compass is necessary to indicate the general direction to be taken. The mission and goals of the agency become that compass.

## 3. Use Creative Problem Solving

"Thinking out of the box" is another effective strategy. The way a problem is framed determines the alternatives that are considered. Thus, thinking differently about the same old problem can produce new insights and new approaches, approaches that may be more effective than those used earlier. Brainstorming and nominal group OD techniques are vehicles for generating new ways of thinking about old problems.

## 4. Keep an Open Mind

Although not necessarily a separate category from creative problem solving and being prepared for change, an open-minded approach to issues establishes an atmosphere conducive to creativity and flexibility. With the reliance on knowledge workers and teams comes an increasing variety of perspectives. Welcoming ideas for new ways to solve problems generates beneficial alternatives.

## V. APPLICATION OF CONCEPTS

They have always experienced change, but today's public organizations are experiencing change at warp speed. The following case depicts a community-based agency that experienced a change in management style,[2] setting in place a series of events that resulted in lower productivity and high turnover. Following the description of the circumstances, the elements discussed above are applied to demonstrate how the problems that arose were both predictable and avoidable.

Case   Changes at the Wood Center

The Wood Center, a community-based nonprofit facility under contract with the statewide Department of Children and Youth Services, offered three programs for juvenile offenders: the community school, case management, and the transitional aftercare unit.

Initially the center was directed by Paul Adam, a fellow well known and widely regarded by juvenile justice workers around the state. He had directed the Center since it opened four years ago and was respected by the workers at the Center. Adam had a participatory management style and an open door policy for all employees.

When Adam retired, Anthony Kennedy was hired to take his place. Although Kennedy had worked for the Department of Children and Youth Services for 15 years, he had no experience working in community facilities such as the Wood Center, which served an urban area marked by racial and ethnic diversity. The only similar experience he had was gained from a short assignment in a small rural county that was demographically homogeneous. Following Adam's retirement, the staff expected Kennedy to run the Center as Adam had. Most of the staff had worked at the Center since it had opened and were comfortable with the management style that had evolved.

It soon became clear that Kennedy's style was distinctly different from Adam's. Whereas Adam was a hands-on manager and "one of the guys," Kennedy preferred a laissez-faire style best described as management-by-exception. Only when something outside the norm arose did he attend to it. When issues demanded his attention, his approach was to resort to the policy manual and follow the rules. When a major human resource problem arose, he contracted with outside consultants to solve the problem rather than tackle it himself.

It did not take long for staff to become frustrated and disgruntled, but they reasoned that Kennedy's tenure would be short. His lack of leadership and psychological distance from the work of the center led staff to think of him as missing-in-action. They carried on with their work much as they had during Adam's tenure and things rocked along. The staff worked well with one another, adapted their schedules to accommodate each other's needs, and the Center's services were performed to everyone's satisfaction. They surmised that Kennedy had his eye on a post with the Department of Children and Youth Services and that this was just a stepping stone. Most of Kennedy's time seemed to be consumed in developing political connections around the state in order to promote his candidacy for the appointment. Once Kennedy gained his next position, they assumed that one of the long-term program managers would be promoted to the position and that things would be back to normal, running much as they had when Adam had been Center Director.

True to speculation, Kennedy landed the job with the state agency within the year. Although staff had assumed that one of their peers would take Kennedy's place, that was not to be. Two changes occurred in rapid succession, one at the agency level and one at the Center. First, the state agency that contracted with Wood Center had a name change, from the Department of Children and Youth Services to the Department of Juvenile Justice. Second, the Wood Center was reorganized to comply with the state agency's revised mission.

The department's name change signaled a narrowing of mission from a focus on comprehensive social services for youthful offenders to one of criminal justice programs for youth. The department's responsibilities were now solely the supervision of delinquent youths and they were completely separated from the social service side.

The Center's case management units were separated into residential and nonresidential programs and the community school and transitional aftercare unit were combined. The

Board of the Wood Center selected its new director from candidates suggested by the agency rather than by staff at the Center.

Karen Oldman was hired by the state agency to be the liaison between the agency and the Center. The state had come under fire through several high-profile cases of juvenile repeat offenders whom the public believed were released too soon from detention centers. Although none of these cases had been at the Wood Center, the agency clamped down on procedures at all the Centers that performed contractual services for it. One of the results of the heightened attention was the hiring of Oldman to monitor contract compliance. An employee of the new Department of Juvenile Justice, Oldman had worked her way up the ranks within the agency and did not have first-hand experience with youthful offenders.

Sandy Day became the new Center director. Prior to assuming her position, Day had been the program manager of a small eight-bed group home in a nearby city. Although an employee of the former Department of Children and Youth Services for fifteen years, she was not familiar with case management work or the type of offenders being serviced at Wood Center. Neither Day nor Oldman had any experience with the supervision of large staffs or with the large caseloads that the Wood Center experienced.

Day, upon assuming her position, issued a number of edicts designed to rein in the autonomy that staff had enjoyed since the Center had opened its doors. Her policies centralized control in her office. No staff were to communicate with Oldman or any other staff in the state agency without first consulting her; case managers could no longer authorize the apprehension of a juvenile without the authorization of a manager; and all extensions of detention for youth awaiting residential placement had to be requested in writing and submitted to her. These were striking changes and altered the work for the professional staff. Instead of teams making treatment decisions and implementing them as had been the usual procedure, all decisions became recommendations to be sent to Day's office for her approval.

Until Day had been named Center Director, three case managers were attending graduate school part-time, working on masters' degrees. Three secretaries were working on their undergraduate degrees. It had been an unwritten policy at the center to work around these staff members' schedules so they could pursue their education. Day sent a memo to all staff advising them that she considered their jobs to be their first priority and that school schedules were not to conflict with work schedules. If there was a conflict, staff were instructed to quit school or to seek other employment. All those who were in school left shortly after receiving the directive.

As the liaison between the agency and the center, Karen Oldman also instituted changes that required increased paperwork and documentation. First, she required that all screening decisions for punishment of juveniles would have to be approved by her before being implemented; nonresidential placement of youths would have to occur within ten days, or an extension would have to be requested along with a written justification for the delay; and case managers' file entries would have to include specific references to treatment plan objectives. Oldman increased the number of contacts that case managers had to have with the juveniles and their families. She also required a written report for any juvenile whose release had to be revoked, a report that detailed where the treatment plan had failed.

Staff were insulted that they had not been consulted prior to these changes and resented the imposition of additional requirements without their consent. They also lacked respect for the new "rulemakers," believing that neither Day nor Oldman had the work experience or knowledge necessary to understand the pressures they felt. Day had worked with smaller caseloads of youth who had been charged with less serious offenses and were on probation, living at home with their families. The life experience of the juveniles with whom she was familiar was far gentler than the experience of the youth who found their way to the Wood Center. In the Center, caseloads of 100 juveniles were common, all of whom had been committed to the state and charged with serious crimes. Oldman, though an experienced administrator, did not appreciate the workload of the Center staff and failed to understand how the increased reporting standards would draw time away from essential treatment services.

Resentment was high and morale plummeted. A staff that had worked together for years and been committed to the work of the Center looked for escape routes. Within a year after the reorganization, four case managers, three secretaries, and another four staff members left the Center, including a program manager who took early retirement. Turnover was so high that the Center's Board of Directors began doing exit interviews to learn why so many staff were leaving.

## A. What Went Wrong?

What factors transformed Wood Center from a productive worksite with little turnover to a site where staff left in droves and productivity plummeted? A review of the case shows that from the time Adam retired, the elements essential to a productive work environment dwindled away. While Anthony Kennedy directed the work of the Center, he ignored the human element of service work, failed to comprehend the culture that had made the Center run smoothly prior to his tenure, and did not take the time to connect with staff. He spent most of the time away from the office, leaving it without leadership. When a major personnel problem occurred he hired the services of an outside consultant without any attempt at personally resolving the problem, further demonstrating that he was an "outsider." Nevertheless, there remained a camaraderie among staff and their well-oiled method of getting the work done moved things forward. However, the strength of the team could not survive the additional changes. When Day and Oldman came on board, the systems that had been in place were completely disrupted. Control of work processes moved from the professional staff to the Director's and the Liaison's offices and staff fled.

What can we learn from this case? Both the near and the far environments changed at the Wood Center. For the first four years of its existence, an orderly evolution of processes and procedures evolved. Staff adapted themselves to the far environment—the relationship with the Department of Children and Youth Services—just as they bent the near environment to adapt to them. As with any discussion of work culture, personalities matter. The system that evolved and worked smoothly while Adam was Director required his sort of hands-on management style. Once he retired, the system continued under Kennedy's leadership as if in a holding pattern, waiting for an Adam-like director to reappear. Instead, both the far and near environments changed.

When the state agency refocused its mission and contractual expectations, the casework that had been valued by staff was marginalized. When Day replaced Kennedy, the near environment changed. The mutual adjustment among workers that accommodated those who were taking college classes was no longer allowed. The reliance on team decision making disappeared. The autonomy to make rapid decisions was denied. The discussion that follows uses the productivity techniques listed in table 1 to frame the wrong turns at the Wood Center.

### 1. Coaching and Goal Setting

Although Kennedy did not build on strengths of the workforce, at least he was able to rely on their strengths such that he was free to focus on other issues and let the center run itself. Although he dumped rather than delegated tasks, staff were willing to tolerate this because they sensed his tenure would be short. Although he failed to keep in touch with employees, even relying on an outsider to settle personal conflicts among workers, this was tolerated because the work team was stable enough to persevere as long as they felt leadership would improve shortly. The goals being pursued continued to be those agreed upon during Wood's tenure. When Kennedy was replaced by Day and the agency hired Oldman to monitor contract compliance, however, too many changes happened too fast. Strengths disappeared, goals became mixed, and priority shifted from a focus on output to one on process, all without buy-in from staff. Instead of harnessing the enthusiasm of the opinion shapers and letting a new culture evolve,

Day and Oldman elected to move speedily, wresting control from staff to clarify who was in charge and how operations would be conducted. They disrupted the usual routines and by doing so, altered the near environment and staff morale.

Although this case does not provide information sufficient to assess which behaviors Day and Oldman rewarded, it is reasonable to assume that the productive workers exited as they felt their work was not valued. Sandy Day, as center director, relied on the authority of her position in dealing with staff. She made little attempt to see the work from their perspective and to learn their perceptions of the challenges they faced. She initiated changes based on her own perceptions and attempted to run the center as she had run the group home where she had worked before joining Wood Center. Day neglected the center's culture of mutual adjustment in her dealings with staff who were taking college classes. Mandated changes reduced the autonomy of case managers, the loss of which created further distrust, disloyalty, and lack of motivation. Even the exodus of significant numbers of staff did not alter her position. Karen Oldman also approached her new position from one of hierarchical control. The changes she initiated reduced staff autonomy and consolidated decision making in her office. These changes contributed to staff feeling overworked, disrespected, and frustrated.

The culture that had taken root during Adam's tenure was durable and shaped staff understandings, meanings and perceptions, which made it difficult for new leadership to institute rapid change. When the department's name changed, focus groups to explore what the change signified in terms of the mission, goals, and philosophy would have helped to clarify the new environment for everyone. Day could have conducted a series of meetings with staff to determine what the change meant to them and how the viewpoints between the old and the new could be reconciled. She should have recognized the center's culture that promoted staff educational advancement and acknowledged its importance to the symbolic functioning of the organization as well as to staff retention.

By their actions, Oldman and Day seemed to ignore symbols that were important to staff. The change of the department's name signified a redefinition of scope from a social work orientation to a criminal justice orientation. Although many of the staff had criminal justice backgrounds, an equal number were social workers. Many had been with the Center since it opened and were comfortable functioning under a mixed orientation. Neither leader acknowledged the change, however, or the effect the new policies had on staff or the goals to be achieved.

## 2. Contingency Strategies

Culture change can be achieved two ways. One way is for the opinion shapers who were committed to the old way of doing things to leave and be replaced by new opinion shapers. The downside is that this creates a void while new staff learn the ropes and informal leaders emerge. Moreover, the development of new informal leaders is no guarantee that the new culture which emerges will emphasize the norms that Center leadership want. The other way is to work intensively with the opinion shapers, soliciting their ideas, and using artful persuasion to change elements of the culture more gradually. Neither is easy. The former is disruptive as staff leave, organizational memory is lost, and positions remain vacant while new staff are recruited and trained. The latter is less disruptive to productivity but requires patience, perseverance, and many hours of discussions, meetings, and compromises.

Day's and Oldman's autocratic style was too divergent from the acceptable norm that had evolved at the Center since its start years earlier. Failing to understand knowledge workers put another nail in the coffin. In the world of knowledge work, organizations exist to serve both the organization's purposes as well as those of the people who work there. Helping staff who were pursuing college degrees would have built a bond between Day and the staff that would have benefited the organization in the long run. Oldman lost sight of the fact that the fit between the organization and the people has to be good in order for both to be successful. Instead of imposing standards, she could have met with the center's case managers to discuss strategy and goals. She missed an opportunity to understand the ethos of the Center and to build a bond with them.

While Kennedy's approach to dealing with troublemakers was to hire an outside consultant, it served to distance workers from him and probably cemented them closer together. When there are troublemakers who disrupt the work of others, management has an obligation to step in and resolve the problem in such a way that those whose behavior is constructive are rewarded and those whose behavior causes problems are sanctioned. This is an opportunity to manage symbols, to highlight heroes, and to demonstrate which behaviors are not tolerated.

When Day took the reins of the Center, she would have done well to focus on the change that her arrival foretold and to deal with this openly rather than by top-down edicts. Creative problem solving with opinion shapers at the Center may have prevented the exodus that occurred. Finally, Day and Oldman's attempt to build structure and control violated the norms of the Center. Had they assumed their posts with an open mind, it is likely that they would have gathered more information before closing the door and insisting on centralization, increased paperwork, and top-down management strategies.

There were several ways that Kennedy, Day, and Oldman could have reframed their approaches. They should have kept in mind that productivity is a people issue and should have communicated more effectively with staff, soliciting their opinions and coming to an understanding of the nuances of the work norms at the Center. To do so would have increased trust and loyalty and allowed staff to develop respect for the skills which they, as new leaders, brought with them. It would also have capitalized on the organizational memory of staff. Kennedy lost the trust of center personnel when he used the services of an outside consultant to resolve an internal problem. Day and Oldham had to convince staff that they knew about the work of the Center and understood the pressures involved.

All in all, Kennedy, Day, and Oldman each walked into a strong culture that was not welcoming to outsiders. Rather than coaching staff to adapt to new pressures and constraints, they each tried to deal with the situation: Kennedy by letting things run as they always had; Day and Oldman by trying to implement change through direct orders. All three missed the opportunity to ally with Center personnel. If they had formed an alliance with the Center's staff they could have applied the use of their position power more effectively. Failing to recognize the expertise and network power of Center staff, Day and Oldman found themselves on the margins, issuing orders that had little effect. Instead of facilitating the use of alliances and networks, Day tried to cut off communication between staff and other professionals external to the Center. She used old-fashioned assembly-line management only to watch it fail as staff simply quit and went to work elsewhere.

## VI.  SUMMARY

Productive work environments rarely just happen. They require effort, planning, and most important, a genuine commitment to employee input and patience. There must be commitment from all levels in the chain of command and a sense of individual responsibility for the common good of the group. When only one person is responsible, then everyone else is free from responsibility. But when each one is responsible, then everyone is responsible, both individually and collectively.

The bottom-line to productive work environments is that they require harnessing those elements that are healthy and productive and reinforcing them. This means placing people where they can build on their strengths and do what they do best. It means placing people in supervisory and managerial positions who are most capable of supervising and managing well. It means keeping the lines of communication open, being flexible, and achieving a reasonable balance between the needs of the organization and the needs of workers.

## NOTES

1. The author is grateful to Karen Fowles for her contributions to this chapter.
2. The facts of the case have been preserved, although the names of the people and of the center have been disguised to protect those involved.

## REFERENCES

Damanpour, F., Evan, W. M. (1984). Organizational innovation and performance: the problem of "organizational lag". *Admin. Sci. Quart.* 29:392–409.

Drucker, P. F. (1980). *Managing in Turbulent Times.* New York: Harper & Row.

Drucker, P. F. (1954). *The Practice of Management.* New York: Harper & Brothers.

Guy, M. E. (1985). *Professionals in Organizations: Debunking a Myth.* New York: Praeger.

Guy, M. E. (1992). Managing People. In: Holzer, M., ed. *Public Productivity Handbook.* New York: Marcel Dekker, pp. 307–319.

Walters, J. (1990, January). Paul F. Reincke: the politics of fire. *Governing*, pp. 44–49.

# 25

# The New American Workplace

**WILLA BRUCE**
*University of Illinois, Springfield, Illinois, U.S.A.*

**DOROTHY OLSHFSKI**
*Rutgers, The State University of New Jersey, Newark, New Jersey, U.S.A.*

## I. INTRODUCTION

Competition makes organizational efficiency a priority in both the public and the private sectors. For many organizations, organizational efficiency translates into initiating cost-cutting measures inside the organization. Because personnel costs represent a substantial portion of the cost of most goods and services, the personnel function is a likely place to target for cost savings. Efforts to increase productivity by tightening internal operating efficiencies of the personnel process, however, should proceed with the recognition that the issues and assumptions that guided thinking about personnel have changed. What workers do, how they do it, and who they are is different than it was even fifteen years ago.

Technology has changed the content of work and it has also changed the connection between the workers and the work itself. Automated manufacturing processes computerization, and robotics have replaced physical labor with office work. Production work, that previously used manual laborers, now requires a more educated employee who understands automated processes and can competently manage those processes. Manual laborers, who previously could find employment without special talents are finding themselves without work opportunities in a service economy.

Productivity issues are not the only reasons for concern. Quality of life issues have surfaced as the old assumptions about motivational incentives, the nature of family life, and the availability of a support network break down. When supporting a family required only one full-time paycheck, and there was a full-time person maintaining the household, employers could impose geographical requirements, rigid work rules and schedules, and the employees were able and willing to comply. Now supporting a family usually requires two paychecks and there is no full-time person providing support for the adults and children. Flexibility, not rigidity, is needed to support the important work and family values. Quality of life issues also emerge as the workforce ages. Those incentives that were attractive when the employee was 25 years old no longer apply when the employee is 60.

The goal of this chapter is to examine some topics that are emerging as major issues in public personnel administration, especially the two large trends of changes in the nature of work and organization, and changes in the nature of the workforce. Both of these are discussed with respect to the public sector.

## II. THE CHANGING NATURE OF THE WORK

### A. Characteristics of the Workforce in a Global Economy

The global economy has eliminated geography as a major consideration in business decision making. Because of advances in communication and transportation technology, private sector organizations can control the locations of their businesses. Every facet of production can be duplicated anywhere in the world, with the important exception of the skills of the workforce. Workers are location bound. Consequently, nonretail businesses can choose to locate anywhere an adequately skilled workforce can be found. Private sector organizations can choose to train the workforce or they can move to find a workforce with the skills for which they are looking.

Obviously, the public sector has no such freedom. It is bound by geography and responsibility for public welfare. Governments try to attract private investment and they compete with each other and with foreign countries for the opportunity to host business ventures. An important part of the government's promotional package is its ability to offer an efficient and effective public service. So at the same time the governments are courting businesses to locate in their region, they are in competition with them for the skilled educated workers needed to support an effective public service. For governments, the crux of the competition is their ability to present their public services as efficient and economical, their locale as a comfortable and attractive site, and their citizens as a willing and able labor force.

The definition of an employable labor force has changed as the United States moves away from manufacturing to a service economy; the types of jobs and the skills required of the workforce are different. Unskilled labor is no longer the marketable commodity that it was even fifteen years ago. In both an agrarian and a manufacturing economy, physical capabilities determined the worth of an uneducated unskilled laborer; but in a service economy, intellectual capabilities supersede physical ones in determining the worker's worth. To compete globally, Reich (1990) maintains that the most important competitive asset of the nation is the skills of the workforce.

In the past, uneducated and untrained workers have been able to find work as laborers and in the past that type of work paid a livable wage. Now they cannot. Manual labor jobs, which used to employ people regardless of educational level, have become scarce, and the pay for that labor is very low, reflecting the changes in the economy in general. The economy can no longer absorb these workers, whereas at the same time there are not enough educated workers to fill the need. For example, in 1989,

New York Telephone tested 57,000 people before it found 2100 qualified to become operators and repair technicians. This situation is not an isolated case. The National Institute for Literacy, created by the National Literacy Act of 1991, conducted a survey in 1992 and found that between 21 and 23% of the adult population (approximately 44 million people) could not read well enough to fill out an application, read a food label, or read a simple story to a child. The same group conducted an international survey in 1997 in which only Poland outdid the United States for the worst adult literacy skills of industrialized Western countries (National Institute for Literacy, 2000).

The balance between the economy's need for skilled and unskilled workers has shifted, but this problem of inadequate skills does not solely rest with adults whose skills have become obsolete because of technological innovations. The nation's educational system is not producing enough skilled young people who are competent to join the workforce. The U.S. Department of Labor's Occupational Outlook projects that occupations that are in decline are those that required no advanced education and, other than farming, these occupations are largely clerical or low-skill jobs associated with manufacturing. Those occupations in which that the Department of Labor projects increases are knowledge workers in jobs such as computers and nursing that require at least a college degree (Bureau of Labor Statistics, 2001).

Government jobs do not offer a haven for those without skills, inasmuch as most public sector jobs are requiring advanced education. So the public sector finds itself grappling with twin problems: where to find the skilled workers, for both public and private jobs, who are needed for an increasingly technical service economy, and what is to be done about those citizens who are unqualified for employment. Although not specifically a public personnel problem, this is a public problem with implications for public personnel administration and policy. First, competent public employees are critical for an efficient and effective public service and, looking at the other side of the coin, public employment will surely be some part of the solution for dealing with an unskilled unemployed segment of the population.

The magnitude of the change involved in moving from an unskilled to skilled labor force has not been thoroughly addressed. The changed nature of work that initiated this need for an educated skilled workforce has created problems of its own. New technologies have changed the way workers relate to their work (Zuboff, 1988). New computing capabilities have almost eliminated the tactile quality of some types of work. For many processes that once intimately involved the person, with the advent of automation and computerization have been transferred into explicit data displayed on computer terminals. Many assembly workers no longer touch the products being assembled; they monitor the process via remote terminals. Secretaries may no longer touch the letters they type. In most instances, they are on computer, and although the screen is visible, the typists cannot feel the work, and many times do not understand where the work has gone (Zuboff, 1988). At the end of the workday, the product produced or the work completed may not be obvious, and many times it is not even visible. The outbox is not a real fixture on the desk; it is now an icon. The technology is so sophisticated and the presentation of the data that monitor the processes is so sterile that it can obscure the fact that the data on the computer screen represent a tangible product or process.

The intangible nature of work has always been present at the higher levels of organizations. The higher one rose in the organization, the further removed one became from the actual work of the organization. This has not been the case at the lower levels of the hierarchy where the technology may obscure the actual task being conducted. The problem then is: if the technology does not make sense, the employees do not understand the connection between what they are doing and the accomplishment of the task.

Sophisticated technology requires that the personnel working with the technology have a minimal competency in the basic skills. As an entry-level requirement this is a higher standard than that required of entry-level employees in the past. Furthermore, the extent of the intellectual competencies needed of the personnel who work with technologies has been profoundly underestimated. The ability to decipher the information provides employees with the connection between what they are doing and the work itself. In high technology areas such as the nuclear power or the chemical industry, the possibility of extreme negative consequences due to employee failure to accurately understand the data or to see relationships between important sets of data illustrates how critical a thorough understanding of technology is to the competent performance of high-technology jobs. The ability of the worker to understand how his or her actions are connected to the work being performed has an impact not only for the consumer of the product or service, but it also has important implications for the employee's level of motivation, job satisfaction, and commitment, and the quality of the product. Quality work can be produced only if the relationship between the worker and the work is clear and understood.

## B.  Characteristics of Managerial Jobs

The nature of managerial work in this more complicated environment is undergoing change. People used to work in offices. Now, thanks to technology, people work from home, the plane, or the shared desk in an office hotelling arrangement. They attend meetings without leaving their work space using teleconferencing and they interact with team members they have never met face-to-face via virtual work spaces. Email, faxes, and cell phones means work is never very far away. The environment is fast paced and organizational structures and processes have been adapted to accommodate the volatile times. The management of this fast-paced approach builds upon diverse, multifunctional project teams where power and authority are not clearly assigned. In the face of competitive pressures, organizations are forced to become leaner, less bureaucratic, and more entrepreneurial (Kanter, 1989). As hierarchy is deemphasized, the manager's job changes. Project teams proliferate, causing rank and formal structure to be less important as a source of power. Exerting influence becomes a function of networks and team membership, not hierarchy.

These horizontal work relationships require new skills of the manager: negotiation skills overshadow traditional command relationships. Persuasive abilities become just as important as logical presentation skills. Motivational strategies are short-circuited as career paths are no longer straightforward and predictable (Kanter, 1989; Pynes, 1997).

Kanter's data (1989) were drawn from private sector organizations, and it is unlikely that the public sector organizations will follow the same path. An increasingly competitive environment is driving the private sector's move to deemphasize hierarchy. However, a highly political environment drives government bureaucracy. Paul Light (1999) sees a continued layering of the federal government with a proliferation of titles created especially for those positions near the top of the pyramid. He argues that downsizing has hit the lower levels of the hierarchy the hardest, where the turnover is greatest and the pay is low. And although there may be fewer workers in the federal government, there are more titles and a greater distance from the front lines of the bureaucracy to the top. Concurrently, the public sector faces increasingly scarce resources, and this is coupled with the trend to privatize and outsource many government operations. As the bureaucracy sheds functions it begins to resemble what Milward and Provan (2000) call the "hollow state," here the task of government management is not so much about doing as it is about overseeing what is being done by nongovernment employees. The unrelenting pressure on government to stay small has created a growth industry in the private and not-for-profit sectors that now produce the goods and services that government once delivered inhouse (Light, 1999). In many parts of the federal government and increasingly at the state level, contract negotiation and administration are the important skills.

## C.  Changing Nature of Work

The changing nature of work raises some important issues for the personnel administrator. Workforce skill requirements have changed to reflect the movement of the United States away from manufacturing toward a service economy, therefore securing an educated workforce, both for employment in the public sector and to work in the private sector, has become of paramount importance to governments at all levels. A related problem involves the public policy problem of unemployable persons.

Second, the intellectual content of lower-level jobs that involve technology has been underestimated. At a minimum, the employee must be able to read and do arithmetic. Motivation to do a job and a commitment to producing a quality product or service, however, depend upon the employer's ability to interpret the data presented and make a reasonable connection between his or her actions and the actual work. Literacy is a minimum competence needed here.

Third, hierarchy is just one of many organizational forms prevalent in the private sector. In government, hierarchy is still alive but it is not as permanent a structure as we would have thought fifteen years ago. Reengineering efforts have severely curtailed the role of middle management in some parts of the government; the U.S. Customs Service is one example (Hammer and Chappy, 1993; Hammer, 2001). In addition, the unrelenting demand by the public and politicians to limit the scope of government has dramatically reduced the size of government.

Adjusting job entry requirements, training, and aligning employee expectations to the new dynamics created by an increasingly technical work environment are issues that personnel administrators now face. At the same time that the nature of work is being examined, the composition of the workforce is undergoing substantial change. The changing workforce is another important issue for the personnel manager to address.

## III.  CHANGING WORKFORCE

The characteristics of the workforce itself will be different than in the twentieth century: older, more culturally diverse, and more female. The continuing presence of women in the workforce raises issues of the employer's response to pay issues and to the problems of managing family responsibilities and parenting. As the workforce ages, family responsibilities increase as employees are challenged to care for aging parents. The changing nature of the workforce calls into question traditional notions of employee motivation and reward, and thus raises additional issues for the public personnel manager.

## A. Maturing Workforce

The maturing of the workforce presents a series of challenges to the public sector in the twenty-first century. The greatest challenge may be overcoming the stereotypes about aging. For instance, a 1988 survey of human resource managers that defined older workers as "50 and older" found that the majority of respondents see the older worker as different, less competent, and less innovative than their younger workers. Two-thirds of the respondents reported that older workers are "complacent and lacking in motivation," and "clogging the promotion pipelines" (*Omaha World Herald*, 1988).

The findings of that survey, however, may say more regarding stereotypes about older workers than they say about their actual characteristics. To say that age 50 is the mark of an "older employee" and to conjure up the stereotypes of "complacent" and "lacking in motivation" are absurd when one considers that by 2005 about 37% of the workforce is expected to be 45 or older and that most of this group will be between the ages of 50 and 60. By then, 14.5% of the workforce will be age 55 or older (*Christian Science Monitor*, 2001). The ratio of workers age 25 to 64 to workers age 65 and older will increase dramatically. In 1995, 51.6% of the workforce was between the ages of 25 and 64, and only 12.6% were over 64. By 2030 the Census Bureau projects that 20.2% of the workforce will be aged 65 or older, and the younger group decreases to 47.4% (Judy and D'Amico, 1999, p. 95). In addition, recent legislation has raised the Social Security retirement age in increments, and retirement age is scheduled to increase to age 67 by the year 2027.

Those in positions to employ others appear to believe that replacing older workers with younger ones improves the bottom-line and that a young workforce gives the impression that an organization is vibrant and innovative (Goldberg, 2000). Assumptions that older workers are less capable and less interested in their work continue into the twenty-first century, and discrimination against older workers is still evident. "In 1998, it took those aged fifty to sixty more than 65 percent longer to find a new job than it took someone thirty-five to forty" (Goldberg, 2000). Goldberg believes this is because of the negative stereotypes about older workers.

Research indicates that the government workforce is older than its private sector counterpart. "The proportion of older government workers aged 45 to 64 has raised from 36.8 percent in 1994 to 41.7 percent in 1998. In the same time period private sector proportions are up only from 25.3 percent in 1994 to 27.8 percent in 1998" (Ehrenhalt, 1999). One can predict a continuing increase in the number of older workers because increasingly there are incentives to stay in the workforce. For example, the tax on earnings of those aged 65 to 69 has been reduced and, starting in 2003, the Social Security retirement age will begin to increase (Barone, 2001, p. 1). In addition, persons 65 and older can now receive full social security benefits without penalty, even if they are employed.

In fact, retirement, as we know it today, may become obsolete. In its place will be "self-driven investment opportunities that allow workers to take their savings with them from employer to employer. The promise of retirement will no longer lure workers to the government sector" (Green, 2000, p. 435). Ready or not, older workers will be major contributors to the productivity of the twenty-first century.

> All this comes at a time when "American organizations are in a crisis as they face the tightest labor market in 30 years" (Kolman, 2001, p. 9). The debunking of stereotypes about capacities of older workers will be crucial to the management of the twenty-first century work force. In the 1980s, commonly accepted belief that older employees reach a point in their careers when motivation declines significantly … is due in part to organizationally created self-fulfilling prophecies…. Lowered motivation may result, not from aging itself, but *from managerial expectations and treatment of older employees* (Rosen and Jerdee, 1985).

At this point in history, there is a growing demand for older workers because there are not enough skilled workers available for jobs in either the public or private sectors while there is a growing supply of these older workers. How to recruit, motivate, and encourage older workers will dramatically affect the activities of human resource managers in the twenty-first century (Doverspike et al., 2000, p. 445). Research is needed to learn if age and maturity demand different motivational strategies than now in good currency. Will the work of Maslow, Hertzberg, and McGregor be as powerful for mature workers? Will Expectancy Theory still explain how to challenge workers to greater levels of productivity? The time is now ripe to explore different motivational strategies in relation to years of experience on the job and in the world of work.

In their report *Workforce 2020*, (Judy and D'Amico (1999, pp. 104–106), observe that people who stay employed after the traditional retirement age will "pose serious challenges" to organizations as well as benefits. To meet the challenges employers will need:

1. Creative workforce planning,
2. Creative ways for younger workers to advance,
3. Creative benefit packages that provide parental care as well as child care, and
4. Creative ways to provide medical insurance and health care.

In addition to changing the terms and conditions of work, employers will need to acknowledge and debunk the prevailing assumptions that serve to denigrate older workers. Goldberg (2000, pp. 113–118) identifies "the most damaging assumptions" that compare older and younger workers as follows: older workers are not as creative; older workers are ill more often; older workers are less flexible; older workers don't learn as quickly; older workers find it hard to take orders; older workers cost more. She then offers evidence to suggest that these assumptions are merely false stereotypes.

Her counterarguments are: older workers temper creativity with practicality, thus offering more usable suggestions; although older workers have more chronic illnesses, they have fewer accidents and fewer workmen's compensation claims; older workers bring wisdom in place of curiosity; older workers learn as well as younger workers; older workers have lower turnover; supervision of older workers is not different from supervision of younger workers; and they are not more expensive than younger employees, although the expenses are different.

A maturing workforce is a reality of the twenty-first century. It is time to quit making assumptions about older workers. It is time to celebrate their abilities, their contributions, and their willingness to work.

## B.  Multicultural Workforce

The first immigrants to the United States were a cultural hodgepodge. America was known as "the great melting pot" or "tossed salad" where one's status was limited only by one's ability and willingness to work. While "masses yearning to be free" came from Europe and Asia, Africans were captured and brought in chains. But, come they all did, with their different cultures and different languages.

By the beginning of the twentieth century, however, immigrants were expected by both themselves and others to submerge their own culture and become part of an American amalgam of English-speaking, upwardly mobile, competitive individualists. Those who did, achieved financial rewards. Those who did not were relegated to unskilled labor pools where they became contributors to the industrial and agricultural development of this country. Those who could not adapt to the economic system were reluctantly supported by the welfare system.

Adaptation to the market economy and its inherent socioeconomic system became the norm, so that by the 1980s being different in the workplace was seen as somehow unacceptable. Workers were expected to submerge their uniqueness into corporate America's image of the employee: to speak the same language, wear the same type clothing, accept the same cultural norms.

Yet the workforce of the twenty-first century is different. Not all workers speak fluent English—or want to. Not all workers share the traditional Protestant work ethic, or the current Japanese work ethic, both of which require high levels of energy and interest directed toward the workplace. Not all workers have the same cultural understanding of nonverbal behaviors.

As one young worker confided to one of the authors, "I'm never sure if I'm supposed to look away when my supervisor talks with me, or if I'm supposed to look him straight in the eye. My mother," she went on to say, "is Polish. When she's giving me directions, she says, 'Look at me so I'll know you're paying attention to what I say.' But my dad's Hispanic. To look him in the eye is a sign of disrespect. He slaps me."

Herein lays the dilemma of an employee raised in a culture other than mainstream American. Yet mainstream America is fast losing its influence on those who work in its organizations, for more and more workers come from countries and cultures other than our own. New immigrants now account for one-half of the workforce growth, whereas in the 1980s they accounted for only one-fourth of workforce growth (Judy and D'Amico, 1999, p. 98) That's a tremendous increase and it is gradually changing the composition of the American workforce.

In 1995, 76% of the workforce was white non-Hispanic. Projections indicate that by 2005, the percentage of white non-Hispanic workers will decrease to 73%, and by 2020 to 68%. The percentage of black non-Hispanic workers is expected to remain constant at about 11%, and Hispanics will increase from 9% in 1995 to 14% in 2020. The rate of change is much more rapid in parts of the West and South, whereas changes in the Northeast and Midwest are minuscule (Judy and D'Amico, 1999, pp. 109–110). In response to 2000 Census questions, multiracial people are being identified. "Officially, one in 40 Americans calls himself or herself the product of two or more racial groups according to the 2000 census. In addition, 14 of the nation's 100 largest cities boast a multiracial group that represents 5 percent or more of their populations" (Belsie, 2001, p. 3). Most of the multiracial group are part Hispanic.

The increasing variety of cultural heritages will influence the workplace and challenge the human resource manager in the twenty-first century. It will have a significant impact on the government workplace, which the U.S. Office of Personnel Management calls "a pace setter in employing minorities" (Kampeas, 2001, p. 5).

At this point in history, immigrant, black, and Hispanic workers are not as educated as their white-European counterparts. Even when they have college degrees, the degrees are more often in lower paying fields (Judy and D'Amico, 1999, p. 116.) Many immigrant workers are poorly educated as well. "Current law may permit the immigration of too many uneducated workers who will lack the skills to prosper in tomorrow's economy" and "most minority workers will be significantly less well-educated than most of their white counterparts" (Judy and D'Amico, 1999, p. 114). At the same time, large companies are asking for a loosening of immigration restrictions for highly educated, technologically sophisticated immigrants.

The education and earning potential of immigrants seems polarized as we begin the twenty-first century. These workers are either undereducated or highly educated. The American educational system has a new challenges as it prepares the next generations of workers. At the same time, employing organizations will be challenged to find adequately qualified employees for highly sophisticated work.

## C.   The Employee as Spouse, Parent, and Child

The traditional family, with male breadwinner, female helpmate, and 2.5 children is rapidly becoming obsolete. Two-earner families in which both husband and wife are employed increased from 39% in 1980 to 62% in 1998. This trend is expected to continue, as is the trend that more and more mothers of young children hold jobs: 64% in 1998 (U.S. Census Bureau, 1999, p. 417). Employees in the twenty-first century will also increasingly have responsibility for care of their own parents. A recent survey by the Families and Work Institute reports that "one in five working parents has been part of the so-called 'sandwich generation' during the past year—both raising children and caring for elderly relatives" and that 25% of employees provided elder care during 1996 (Galinsky, 1999, p. 15).

Even though the character of the workforce is changing, the myth of separate worlds, first identified by Kanter (1977), still exists. The twentieth-century myth about job commitment, described by Orthner and Pittman (1986), continues to pit the organization and the family against each other as they demand the time and energy of the worker. Before women were in the workforce in such numbers, the organization benefited from female spouses of managerial men. Companies and top-level government agencies literally got a "two-for-one" deal in which the wife worked unofficially and behind the scenes to promote the man's accomplishments and advance his career. Such assistance and support will be less and less possible as successful women move into top-level positions. The most recent data indicate that 85% of U.S. workers live with family members and have day-to-day family responsibilities. A family member is defined as "anyone related by blood, marriage, or adoption, as well as partners to whom employees are not legally married" (Galinsky, 1999, p. 5). Men and women will each have to succeed or fail on their own merits, for spouses will be in parallel careers also struggling to succeed. Workplace expectations must change to address this new reality.

Another myth carried over from the Judeo-Christian heritage, is that all workers in families are heterosexual and legally married. This myth has prompted what few family support policies that do exist to ignore domestic partnerships in which unmarried partners live together in "an intimate and committed relationship of mutual caring" (Swan, 1990). Such partnerships include both heterosexual and homosexual relationships, and their numbers are increasing. A 1986 study by the U.S. Bureau of the Census revealed 2.2 million heterosexual domestic partners and 1.5 million homosexual domestic partners for a total of 3.7 unmarried partners. The 1999 census data report a total of 5.29 million unmarried partners (U.S. Census Bureau, 2001). That is a tremendous increase which leads to the conjecture that persons living in partnered relations will comprise a growing chunk of the workforce. Yet very few organizations offer insurance and other benefits to unmarried partners.

Clearly workplace policies of the twenty-first century need reevaluating and refurbishing. Policies rooted in long-held traditions do not always address current realities. Where familied workers are concerned, this is increasingly the case, whether or not those workers are married.

## 1.  Single-Parent Workforce

Many single parents are in the workforce and managing a single-parent workforce presents a special set of challenges. In 1988, 73% of the 3 million single women in the workforce were single parents, as were 80% of the 4.5 million women who are widowed, divorced, or separated. (U.S. Census Bureau, 1999, p. 417). In 1999, 27% of the employed single parents were men (Galinsky, 1999, p. 5). In 1988, data indicated that one out of five children and more than half of all black children will grow up in single-parent homes (Winfield, 1988). The numbers are increasing. The most recent data available (1998) show that, of those children living in single-parent homes, 24% are white, 62% are black, and 36% are Hispanic (U.S. Census Bureau, 1999, p. 64). Single parents comprise a significant segment of the workforce.

Expectations of single parents have not caught up with the reality of their lives. American society continues to be in transition. Single parents in the workforce face the challenges of child-rearing alone, while also managing jobs and careers and those who juggle career and home are on the frontier of a world of conflicting expectations. If they are women, they are expected to be the homemakers and caretakers society remembers from the television sitcoms of the mid-twentieth century. On the other hand, they are expected to be so self-sufficient that neither welfare nor child care assistance will be needed. They are expected to earn their bread and make it too.

In the 1980s, corporate America created the "mommy track" where women who are mothers and employees could be placed. This term referred to the "dead-end, but often high-pressure, jobs where working mothers could be parked" (Lundstrom, 1999, p. 1). Women on the "mommy track" were not expected to devote their lives to their career. They were not expected to advance either. The notion that women, whether or not they are single mothers, are not interested in advancement is another stereotype that must be overcome. Neither marital status nor home responsibilities are factors that should be considered in encouraging and rewarding productivity.

Rather, organizations, both public and private, should develop family-friendly policies that enable employees to successfully balance home and work. Congressman George Miller (California), Chair of the Select Committee on Children and Families stated in 1988: "Evidence derived by my committee suggests that there is a very substantial benefit to be derived by the corporation by being 'employee friendly.' These people are part of your future, part of your profits—they are, in fact, a real resource"... (Winfield, 1988, p. 7). The public sector can be a trend-setter for family-friendly benefits. Several public sector examples are identified (Naff, 2001): Ventura

County, California has developed a model on-site childcare program and advises business on creating their own. The Bay Area has developed a "One Small Step" program that shares information on childcare availability among over 300 employers and 300,000 employees. San Diego created a Work and Family Coalition that utilizes representatives from organizations with successful childcare programs to provide information and assistance to others. Another example of public sector encouragement of employers is the city of Austin, Texas which has developed a list of "Fifty Things Employers Can Do to Support Families in the Workplace" and posted them on their Web site (Linehan, 2001).

Business and government entities that offer family-friendly policies have increased over the past decade. Indeed, "family friendliness has grown from a piecemeal collection of human resource benefits into a social movement by leading companies using a strategic comprehensive approach" (Galinsky, 1999, p. 1). The social movement has not had much impact on the workplace, however, when one considers that only 20% of U.S. employers provide childcare information and referral, just 11% provide on-site childcare, and only 25% provide eldercare information and referral. Such assistance is even more important for single parents than for other workforce members, because they must juggle home responsibilities alone.

## 2. Dual-Earner Workforce

Managing a dual-earner workforce (DEF) will be a challenge for public organizations in the twenty-first century for at least the following reasons. The first is the sheer numbers of DEFs in the workforce, numbers that are on the increase. More than three out of four married employees have spouses or partners who are also employed. This is an increase from 66 to 78% over the past twenty years (Galinsky, 1999, p. 5).

The second reason DEFs will be a challenge to the public sector is that many public organizations restrict employment of two members of the same family by means of antinepotism rules (Reed and Cohen, 1989). Yet such rules are being challenged in both federal and state courts. The challenges emerge from the "arguments that antinepotism rules discriminate against women and interfere with the right to marry" (Reed and Cohen, 1989). Although the trend in court decisions has been in favor of managerial rights (Cooper, 1985), the prospect of such challenges requires that the informed public administrator be knowledgeable about DEFs and what they bring to (and expect from) the workplace.

The third challenge presented by DEFs is to traditional work ethic values which assume that each employee is a discrete, autonomous individual unencumbered by a career-oriented spouse or significant other. Dual wage-earner family members, while committed to achieving success in their chosen profession, are also highly committed to achieving a balance between work and family. The presence of a second paycheck frees them to consider recreation and balance leisure with work (Sekaran, 1986).

Professionals may refuse an opportunity for promotion or transfer when that opportunity conflicts with a spouse's career. They also may make employment decisions based on opportunities for advancement and development that maximize the potential of both members, rather than just on an opportunity for one member alone (Rapaport and Rapaport, 1976). This means that employers will have less flexibility in transferring employees to different geographic areas.

This does not mean that DEFs are less loyal, less dedicated, or less ambitious than their single-career family counterparts. The contrary appears true. Once a DEF identifies niches in which both members can grow and develop, they are likely to demonstrate great organizational loyalty and commitment to career longevity in those employing organizations (Gilmore and Fannin, 1980).

When dual-earner family members become parents another set of issues emerges. In a 1989 article in the *Harvard Business Review*, Rodgers and Rodgers indicate that employed men and women who are also parents spend long hours in the two job worlds of home and work. This has not changed in the twenty-first century. In fact, employees are working longer today than they did previously. Between 1977 and 1997, men's total hours at their job (or jobs) increased from 47.1 hours to 49.9 hours per week. During this same period, women's working hours increased from 43.6 to 47.1; and both men and women want to work less (Galinsky, 1999, p. 8). There is nothing to indicate that the time DEFs spend on home-related work has decreased in the last decade.

## 3. Women's Pay Issues

A group which has had and will continue to have a great impact on the government workforce of the twenty-first century is women. The most recently available statistics (1998) indicate that women constitute 46% of the civilian workforce (U.S. Census Bureau, 1999, p. 413), although they only hold 30.7% of the middle-management jobs and 24.2% of the senior-level positions (Kampeas, 2001).

The percentage of women employed by government has increased at a greater rate than women's participation in all sectors. In 1988, only 31% of the entire federal workforce was female (Naff, 2001). By 2000, women held 43.8% of the federal jobs and 46.6% of the jobs in the private sector (Kampeas, 2001). Women have consistently been employed in greater numbers at the state and local government level. In 1987, 41.8% of the state and local government employees were women. In 1999, 44% of the employees were women (U.S. Census Bureau, 1999, p. 339).

Most of the low-income workers are women. Women earn 76 cents to every dollar that a man earns. They spend an average of 11.5 years out of the workforce caring for children, and only 30% are in jobs with a pension, although they live, on average, six years longer than men (Goodman, 2001, p. 5). Low pay and low financial security may mean that women will stay in the workforce longer than their male counterparts. This means that society will have longer access to their talents and skills. Research indicates that women are more productive than white men at the same federal grade level, yet they are being held to levels below their abilities. They are being kept beneath the mythical "glass ceiling" that inhibits their career advancement (Naff, 2001, p. 76).

Despite women's presence in the workforce, their salaries are still substantially lower than those of men. In 1982, the median annual earnings of women who completed four years of college were only 58.7% of those earnings made by men with four years of college (Center for Women in Government, 1987, p. 5). In 1997, women with Bachelor's degrees earned 63% of what men earned with that same degree (U.S. Census Bureau, 1999, p. 481). Even though gender disparities do not appear in either college enrollment or grades, pay equity has not been achieved (Infante, 2001).

A public sector responsive to the issues of equality and fairness will be required to reassess pay grades and job classification systems, as well as hiring and promotion policies to provide a working environment where women do indeed have equal opportunity with men.

## IV.  CONCLUSIONS AND RECOMMENDATIONS

### A.  The Nature of Work

#### 1.  The Global Economy

The most important factor needed to compete in a global economy is a skilled workforce. Investment in the education and training of citizens and improving local infrastructure and services in order to be able to host business enterprises is presently the responsibility of local government. This is an issue of economic development that has been carried by the local communities but it is too important to be left at that level. Education and training, because of their importance to the country's prosperity, should be a priority at the national level.

Furthermore, the linkage between workforce skills and economic prosperity should be made clear and explicit by local, state, and national decision makers. The clearer the link is drawn, the more likely financial support for skill training will gather advocates and supporters. Education and training should be promoted and supported by all levels of government and private sector organizations, not only because it is in the interest of the individual, but because it is in the interest of maintaining a healthy economy.

#### 2.  Development of a Skilled Labor Force

At the individual level and closely related to the need for education and training to maintain global competitiveness, is the need for education and training so that the individual can find employment. Creating a more employable labor force should emphasize skill development, but the skills must lead to jobs. Moreover, the jobs that will be the focus of the training will be more sophisticated, so the training effort will need to be substantial. At the same time that the newly created jobs require more knowledge and skill to competently perform, they may pay less than the former jobs that have disappeared. A Detroit auto worker with fifteen years experience is not likely to find a job outside that occupation at a comparable salary. This is a troubling point that will make the transition more difficult.

#### 3.  Complicated Technologies in the Workplace

Technology has changed work. At the turn of the century, the wisdom accompanying the introduction of automation implied that as machines do more, people do less. This wisdom held with mechanical automation because the technology was, at its base, understandable. The sophisticated technology of the twenty-first century is a different story. Advanced computer technology relieves people of repetitive or structured tasks, but the processes performed by computers are not readily understandable to the layperson, nor is the work that computers perform tangible and visible. Although an automated, mechanical work process may require a less actively involved workforce, an increasingly technological, computerized work process requires a more sophisticated employee.

Sophisticated technology allows more work to be completed with fewer people. At the same time, it puts increased demands on the employees to be able to interpret the data generated by the technology. Employees need to understand the technology and be able to evaluate and troubleshoot the processes being performed. Failure to understand the computerized process results in a decrease in

motivation and commitment of the employees and threatens the effective performance of the work.

The labor force in a high technology environment needs more information and
training in advanced technologies, how they work, and how they fit into the overall
work that is being performed. The technicians also need to be more responsible for
interpreting and evaluating the data they generate and manipulate. Decision-making
authority can then devolve to lower levels in the organization as the technicians take
more responsibility for their work.

## 4. Managerial Work

The job of the manager is less secure, less predictable, and more volatile than in the
past. Although hierarchy is on surer footings in the public sector than it is in the
business community, the public sector trends toward reengineering and privatization
have disturbed what used to be a stable secure work life. Those entering the workforce
today can predict that their career paths will be unpredictable. A career in a single
organization, common in the 1960s and 1970s, will not be the norm. And because the
technology is advancing so quickly, professional development will not end with the
college or graduate degree.

Managers working in this setting need flexibility and innovativeness when the
incentives and rewards of a government job still tend to be centered on the quality of
the work itself. Extrinsic rewards are still not readily available in the public sector.

The turbulent water analogies of Peter Vaill (1989) and Gareth Morgan (1988)
and the chaos illustrations of Tom Peters (1987) surely apply to the chaotic pace of
technological change in the private sector where competitive pressures require close
attention to new technologies. But the public sector is more insulated here. Public
sector turbulence is created by public demands for justice or equity, and by major
policy disputes and environmental events. Government is rarely on the cutting edge of
technology. Public accountability makes it extremely difficult for a public decision
maker to risk public money on untried technologies. Leaner organizations may emerge
in response to budget reductions, but the government itself was not designed to be
efficient; it is designed to be responsive, deliberative, and predictable.

## B.  The Changing Workforce

### 1.  Maturing Workforce

In the public sector, managers cannot afford to hold on to inaccurate stereotypes
about the mature worker. With the constraints of cost cutting, reduced numbers of
competent young people, and the restrictions of both antidiscrimination legislation
and pension plans, these "older employees" are likely to be the bulk of the workforce for the foreseeable future. Government organizations need to learn how to
maximize their continued competence, not wring their collective hands about the
graying of the workforce.

Recognizing that the average age of the workforce is increasing requires that
recruitment and incentive strategies be directed toward older workers. While
research suggests that age is not an indicator of competence, many managers and
supervisors fear that it is. Consciousness raising and sensitivity training akin to that
provided in earlier decades to teach organizations to deal with minorities and women
is necessary.

Data indicate that women will retire later than men. Many of them got a later start in the workplace due to family responsibilities and many of them have earned about two-thirds of what their male counterparts earned. They often cannot afford to retire. It is, thus, possible to predict that more older women than older men will continue to work, thus requiring that organizations continue to concentrate on equal opportunities for women. It would be a shame, but a real possibility, if the salary gap between men and women continues into their old age.

As the workforce ages, organizations will need to reassess health care benefits; perhaps providing cafeteria programs that provide insurance for children of younger workers, dependent insurance for those responsible for elderly parents, and long-term care insurance for those who work after traditional retirement age.

## 2.  Multicultural Workforce

Just as the workforce of the twenty-first century will be older than in past centuries, it will be more culturally diverse. Organizations will need to teach those born in the United States to understand and accept cultures that may be foreign to them. They also have an obligation to teach long-held North American organizational and cultural norms to those who come from other heritages. The 1988 version of this chapter suggested that businesses who hire ethnic minorities will have a competitive edge and identified two reasons the public sector will benefit from a multicultural work force. In 2001, there is no need to encourage organizations to hire workers from various ethnic groups. They are the fastest growing component of the workforce. They hold our future.

For persons of different cultural heritages to work together, it will be necessary to take steps to ensure that managers and workers communicate in such a way that foreign-born workers understand what is expected. It will also be necessary to reassess the culture of the organization. The traditional American values of competition and individualism may be confusing for those from cultures where community and mutual support are the norms. Yet the United States is one of the few countries in the world that views diversity as normal and desirable. Diversity exists in a climate of tolerance and compromise. Creating an environment where such a climate will flourish will be the challenge to twenty-first century organizations.

## 3.  Family-Centered Issues

As the numbers of familied workers increase, organizations will have to acknowledge the legitimacy of family responsibilities. The Family and Medical Leave Act of 1993 (29 CFR Ch. V, 7/1/97 Edition) provides a safety net for working family members, while also balancing the rights and concerns of employers. Under this act, a worker who has been with the organization twelve months or longer is entitled to unpaid leave, job protection, and continued participation in group health insurance for up to twelve work-weeks for one of the following situations: birth, adoption, or becoming a foster parent, to care for a spouse, child, or parent who is seriously ill, or for personal serious illness. In this Act domestic partners are not considered spouses, and no family care benefits are available for them.

Family responsibilities do not exist only after work hours and they are not confined to personal care for sick relatives. Government, by example, and in policy, should enable people to act responsibly toward their families. Presently public policy does not bolster families. In some cases, particularly the welfare policy, it discourages positive behavior toward family responsibilities. By attempting to be neutral, government policy disregards most family issues altogether. The losers in the arrangement are the children.

A recent list of "Fifty Things Employers Can Do to Support Families in the Workplace," prepared by the Bureau of National Affairs in Washington, DC contains suggestions for initial planning steps, work time and workplace policies, leave policies, information policies/programs, telephone access policies, counseling policies/programs, financial support, childcare services, and other policies and programs (Linehan, 2001). This list can be accessed on the City of Austin, Texas Web site. It demonstrates the complexity of issues that employers need to consider to enable workers to balance job and family responsibilities.

A concerted effort to retain employees through greater consideration of their family responsibilities should naturally lead to a more successful organization and more productive employees. With the growing shortage of qualified workers, such assistance makes good business sense as well as demonstrates humane management.

## REFERENCES

Barone, M. (2001, May 14). Delay the golden years. *U.S. News World Rep.* 130(19):25.

Belsie, L. (2001, July 17). Profile rises for multiracial people. *Christian Science Monitor*, p. 3.

Bureau of Labor Statistics. (2001). *Occupational Outlook Handbook 2000–2001*. Washington DC: U.S. Government Printing Office.

Center for Women in Government. (1987). *Statistics on Women and Minorities in Public Employment*. Albany, New York: NYS Division for Women.

Christian Science Monitor. (2001, July 12). *Baby boomers*, p. 7A.

Cooper, P. (1985). Conflict or constructive tension: the changing relationship of judges and administrators. *Public Admin. Rev.* 54(6):643–652.

Doverspike, D., Taylor, M. A., Shultz, K. (2000). Responding to the challenge of a changing workforce. *Recruit. Nontrad. Demograph. Groups* 29(4):445–459.

Ehrenhalt, S. (1999). *Government Employment Report* 6:19–22.

Family and Medical Leave Act of 1993 (29 CFR Ch. V, 7/1/97 Edition).

Galinsky, E. (1999). Families and Work. Available at http://www.familiesandwork.org/announce/workforce.html.

Gilmore, C. B., Fannin, W. R. (1980, May–June). The dual career couple: a challenge to personnel in the eighties. *Bus. Horizons*, pp. 36–41.

Goldberg, B. (2000). *Age Works*. New York: Free Press.

Goodman, E. (2001, July 30). An uninsured 401(k) isn't a very good safety net. Springfield (IL). *State Journal Register*, p. 5.

Green, M. (2000). Beware and prepare: The government workforce of the future. *Public Person. Manage.* 29(4):435–444.

Hammer, M. (2001). The superefficient company. *Harvard Bus. Rev.* 79(8):82–91.

Hammer, M., Chappy, J. (1993). *Reengineering the Corporation*. New York: Harper.

Infante, V. (2001). Why women still earn less than men. *Workforce* 80(4):31.

Judy, R., D'Amico, C. (1999). *Workforce 2020*. Indianapolis, IN: Hudson Institute.

Kampeas, R. (2001, July 17). Government lacks diversity at middle decision-making levels. Springfield (IL). *State Journal Register*, p. 5.

Kanter, R. (1977). *Men and Women of the Corporation*. New York: Basic Books.

Kanter, R. (1989). The new managerial work. *Harvard Bus. Rev.* 67(6):85–92.

Kolman, S. (2001). Taking the pulse of personalized and online employee communication strategies: the second annual survey of major employer trends. *Employee Benefits J.* 26(1):9–12.

Light, P. (1999). *The New Public Service.* Washington, DC: Brookings.

Linehan, J. (2001). Fifty things employers can do to promote families in the workplace. City of Austin, Texas Web page. Available at http://www.ci.austin.tx.us/childcare/50ways.htm.

Lundstrom, M. (1999, December 2). The new mommy track: chief executive, cook, and bottle washer. *Bus. Week on Line*, pp. 1–4.

Milward, H., Provan, K. (2000). Governing the hollow state. *J. Public Admin. Res. Theor.* 2:359–379.

Morgan, G. (1988). *Riding the Waves of Change.* San Francisco, CA: Jossey-Bass.

Naff, K. (2001). *To Look Like America: Dismantling Barriers for Women and Minorities in Government.* Boulder, CO: Westview.

National Institute for Literacy. (2000). Available at http://www.nifl.gov.

Omaha World Herald. (1988, September 11). Innovation urged to fully use skills of older people, pp. 1G, 3G.

Orthner, D., Pittman, J. (1986, August ). Family contributions to work commitment. *J. Marriage Family*, 48:5793–5781.

Peters, T. (1987). *Thriving on Chaos.* New York: Knopf.

Pynes, J. (1997). *Human Resources Management for Public and Nonprofit Organizations.* San Francisco: Jossey-Bass.

Rapaport, R., Rapaport, R. N. (1976). *Dual Career Families Reexamined—New Integrations of Work and Family.* New York: Harper and Row.

Reed, C., Cohen, L. (1989). Anti-nepotism rules: the legal rights of married co-workers. *Public Person. Manage.* 18(1):27–44.

Reich, R. (1990). *The Power of Public Ideas.* Cambridge: Harvard University Press.

Rodgers, F., Rodgers, C. (1989). Business and the facts of family life. *Harvard Bus. Rev.* 67(6):121–130.

Rosen, B., Jerdee, T. (1985). *Older Employees: New Roles for Valued Resources.* Homewood, IL: Dow-Jones-Irwin.

Sekaran, U. (1986). *Dual Career Families: Contemporary Family and Organizational Issues.* San Francisco: Jossey-Bass.

Swan, W. (1990). The development of the concept of domestic partnerships. Proceedings of the 1990 National Conference of the American Society for Public Administration.

U.S. Census Bureau. (1999). *Statistical Abstract of the United States.* 119th ed. Washington, DC: U.S. Government Printing Office.

U.S. Census Bureau. (2001). *Special Report, Profile 2000.* Washington, DC: U.S. Government Printing Office.

Vaill, P. (1989). *Managing as a Performing Art.* San Francisco: Jossey-Bass.

Winfield, F. (1988). *Work and Family Sourcebook.* Greenvale, NY: Panel.

Zuboff, S. (1988). *In the Age of the Smart Machine.* New York: Basic.

# 26

# Broadening Workplace Participation

**MEREDITH A. NEWMAN**
*University of Illinois at Springfield, Springfield, Illinois, U.S.A.*

## I. INTRODUCTION[1]

> The fact is that society today is not a race-neutral society. It's not a color-blind society. Opportunity is not distributed without regard to race, and therefore, in order to have a racially integrated student body, it is necessary to pay attention to race in the admissions process (Lehman, 2001).

The recent Public Broadcasting System's *News Hour* reporting on "Admitting for Diversity" reflects an ongoing public interest in the issue of *equal access*—to institutions of higher learning and, more generally, to positions of administrative and political authority. It also illuminates the controversial nature of issues of diversity and inclusivity, and highlights a perception of "winners" and "losers" caught in a zero-sum equation.

This chapter is informed by the public debate, but it addresses the issue of diversity and broadening workplace participation by going beyond the numbers. That is, diversity in the public workplace is examined both in terms of a demographically diverse workforce, and also in terms of diversifying the work itself. The chapter proceeds with an examination of the demographic composition of the current and projected workforce. The representativeness of the workforce is discussed by reference to employee categories of sex, race, ethnicity, age, and disability. The challenges to broadening workplace participation are identified, and managerial strategies available to promote broadening are presented in turn. The chapter concludes with a discussion of the importance of diversity broadly construed for our increasingly entrepreneurial public workplaces.

## II.  HOW BROAD IS WORKPLACE PARTICIPATION?

There are currently 140.9 million persons in the civilian labor force (16 years old and over), up from 125.8 million in 1990. Of this total, women number 65.6 million (46.6%), blacks number 16.6 million (12%), and Hispanics (of any race) number 15.4 million (11%) (U.S. Bureau of Labor Statistics, 2001).[2]

Population projections suggest that the labor force will become increasingly heterogeneous over the next several decades. According to the 2000 Census, of a total population of 281.4 million, whites comprise 75% of the total (down from 80.3% in the 1990 Census). Whites are projected to decline to 73.8% in 2040. If whites of Hispanic origin are excluded, the percentage of the American population that will be white in 2040 will drop to 56.4%. Blacks comprise 12.3% of the total population (only a slight increase from 12.1% in 1990). An influx of immigration from Latin America, together with high birth rates among Hispanics, will downgrade the status of blacks as the nation's largest racial minority (Payne, 1998, p. 134). Hispanics, who currently comprise 12.5% of America's population, will constitute almost 20% by the year 2040. Asian and Pacific Islanders comprise 3.8% (up from 2.9% in 1990) (U.S. Census Bureau, Statistical Abstract of the United States, 2000, No. 17, p. 18). The Asian population is expected to double its current size by 2009, triple by 2024, and quadruple by 2038 (Payne, 1998, p. 134). Native Americans (including Eskimo natives) currently comprise 9% of the total population (U.S. Census Bureau, 2000, No. 17, p. 18), up from 7% in 1990.[3]

More women will enter the workforce and stay, and people of color will increase their share of new entrants into the labor force. The average age of the population and the workforce is projected to rise substantially, and the pool of young workers entering the labor market will correspondingly shrink (Patton et al., 2002, p. 24). The implications of each of these changes for human resource management are examined in turn.

## A.  Gender

The workplace has been permanently altered by the dramatic change in women's labor force participation in the last half of the twentieth century, especially with regard to married women, including mothers with young children (Newman and Mathews, 1999, p. 34). As social and economic conditions evolved, women entered the workforce and tended to be employed even after they married and had children (Guy, 2002). Initially, it was older married women (over age 35) who were drawn into the labor force. Given the fertility patterns of the time, they tended to have school-age or grown children by that age. One of the most significant shifts over the past thirty years has been the substantial growth in labor force participation among younger married women, many of whom are mothers of young children (Blau and Ehrenberg, 1997, p. 1). In 1970, there were 3.9 million married women with children under 6 in the labor force. In 1999, that number had almost doubled, to 7.2 million (U.S. Census Bureau, 2000, Table 653, p. 409).

Table 1 shows the increasing proportion of women workers from 1970 through the year 2008, as projected by the U.S. Bureau of Labor Statistics. The percentage of women in the labor force has increased steadily over the last three decades, from 43.3% in 1970 to 60% in 1999 (and a projection of 61.9% in 2008). The number of women in

**Table 1**  Gender of the Civilian Labor Force and Participation Rates with Projections: 1970 to 2008

| Year | Civilian labor force (in millions) | | Participation rate (%) | |
|------|-------|------|-------|------|
|      | Women | Men  | Women | Men  |
| 1970 | 31.5  | 51.2 | 43.3  | 79.9 |
| 1980 | 45.5  | 61.5 | 51.5  | 77.4 |
| 1990 | 56.8  | 69.0 | 57.5  | 76.4 |
| 1995 | 60.9  | 71.4 | 58.9  | 75.0 |
| 1999 | 64.9  | 74.5 | 60.0  | 74.7 |
| 2008 | 73.4  | 81.1 | 61.9  | 73.7 |

*Source*: U.S. Census Bureau, 2000, p. 403.

the labor force has shown a dramatic increase over the same period, from 31.5 million in 1970 to 64.9 million in 1999. This number is projected to reach 73.4 million in 2008.

The increase in the number of women in the labor force, and the number of mothers of young children, are driving reconsideration of how work is organized, performed, and evaluated. Family-friendly workplace policies represent a first step toward accommodating employees (especially women) as they struggle to balance work and family demands.

Nevertheless, despite the increasing number of women in the workplace and some accommodation to their needs, only about 20% of women have advanced to the middle and upper levels of management in state and federal agencies (Kelly et al., 1991; Guy, 1992; Newman, 1993; Naff, 1995, 2001). The overwhelming majority of women are still found at the lower levels of organizations, in positions that do not allow them to advance beyond a certain point and where they have little opportunity to reach line positions. They are typically on truncated and shorter career tracks than their male counterparts, more likely to be in staff than line positions, and more likely to be in part-time jobs. Many women remain segregated into quintessential female-type occupations that contribute to the enduring pay gap between women and men. These glass ceilings and glass walls continue to limit the successful integration of women into middle- and upper-level management positions, and still represent powerful barriers to broadening workplace participation across organizational hierarchies.

## B.  Race/Ethnicity

The "face" of the workforce is also changing in terms of the increasing entry of people of color.[4] Table 2 sets forth figures on the current racial diversity of the labor force, and displays the U.S. Census Bureau's projection for labor force characteristics in the year 2008.

As illustrated in the table, white non-Hispanics are the largest group in the labor force. However, blacks and Hispanics have steadily increased their representation in the U.S. labor force over the last two decades. The number of Hispanics in the labor force has more than doubled between 1980 and 1995, and their numbers are projected to more than triple between 1980 and 2008. The Hispanic labor force is projected to be larger than the black labor force by 2008.

**Table 2**  Race/Ethnicity of the Civilian Labor Force and Participation Rates with Projections: 1970 to 2008

| | Civilian labor force (millions) | | | Participation rate (%) | | |
|---|---|---|---|---|---|---|
| Year | White (non-Hispanic) | Black | Hispanic (all races) | White (non-Hispanic) | Black | Hispanic (all races) |
| 1970 | 73.6 | 9.2 | (NA) | 60.2 | 61.8 | (NA) |
| 1980 | 93.6 | 10.9 | 6.1 | 64.1 | 61.0 | 64.0 |
| 1990 | 107.4 | 13.7 | 10.7 | 66.9 | 64.0 | 67.4 |
| 1995 | 112.0 | 14.8 | 12.3 | 67.1 | 63.7 | 65.8 |
| 1999 | 116.5 | 16.4 | 14.7 | 67.3 | 65.8 | 67.7 |
| 2008 | 126.7 | 19.1 | 19.6 | 67.9 | 66.3 | 67.7 |

*Source*: U.S. Census Bureau, 2000, p. 403.

With the face of the workforce changing from white to a collage of colors come adjustments in workplace habits. Tolerance for those of different races and cultural backgrounds is essential, in words as well as deeds. Cultural differences and traditions must be incorporated into the workplace milieu (Guy and Newman, 1998, p. 78) and should extend to the type of work done itself.

For the most part, however, this does not appear to be occurring. The representation of people of color across middle- and upper-organizational levels is even more severely limited than that of women, generally speaking. For example, people of color hold 29% of the jobs in the federal government, but only 10% of the senior-level positions are held by persons of color (U.S. Merit Systems Protection Board, 1996, p. 11). The MSPB's report concludes, in part, that "not all of the differences can be explained by differences in education, experience, and other measurable merit-based factors" (p. xi). Rather, "subtle race- and sex-based biases continue to influence subjective judgments on employment-related matters" (p. xii). This finding is supported by reference to the scholarly literature (e.g., Grandjean, 1981; Borjas, 1982; Lewis, 1997). Recent high-profile lawsuits in the private sector—such as allegations of systematic discrimination against black employees by Texaco leading to a settlement of some $176.1 million—underscore the reality that America is not a color-blind society, and highlight the fact that deliberate steps must continue to be taken toward the goal of a more representative and inclusive workplace (Payne, 1998, p. 107).

## C.  Age

Women and people of color are not the only nonmainstream groups in the public workforce. The median age of the workforce, which was 34.6 years in 1980 and 36.6 years in 1990, now stands at 38.7 years. The median age of the workforce is projected to be 40.7 years in the year 2008 (Fullerton, 1999, p. 30). In 1998, 46.5% of the labor force was age 40 or older; by 2008, more than half the labor force will be in this age category (Fullerton, 1999, p. 31). The graying of the workforce has occurred despite the entry of Generation Xers (born between 1965 and 1981). Table 3 displays the age distribution

**Table 3**  Age of the Civilian Labor Force and Participation Rates with Projections: 1970 to 2008

| | Civilian labor force (in millions) | | | | | Participation rate (%) | | | | |
|---|---|---|---|---|---|---|---|---|---|---|
| | 1970 | 1980 | 1990 | 1999 | 2008 | 1970 | 1980 | 1990 | 1999 | 2008 |
| Male (years) | | | | | | | | | | |
| 16–19 | 4.0 | 5.0 | 4.1 | 4.3 | 4.8 | 56.1 | 60.5 | 55.7 | 52.9 | 52.9 |
| 20–24 | 5.7 | 8.6 | 7.9 | 7.3 | 8.3 | 83.3 | 85.9 | 84.4 | 81.9 | 81.4 |
| 25–34 | 11.3 | 17.0 | 19.9 | 17.3 | 17.1 | 96.4 | 95.2 | 94.1 | 93.3 | 93.2 |
| 35–44 | 10.5 | 11.8 | 17.5 | 20.4 | 18.3 | 96.9 | 95.5 | 94.3 | 92.8 | 92.3 |
| 45–54 | 10.4 | 9.9 | 11.1 | 15.4 | 19.0 | 94.3 | 91.2 | 90.7 | 88.8 | 88.8 |
| 55–64 | 7.1 | 7.2 | 6.6 | 7.5 | 10.8 | 83.0 | 72.1 | 67.8 | 67.9 | 69.4 |
| 65 + | 2.2 | 1.9 | 2.0 | 2.3 | 2.8 | 26.8 | 19.0 | 16.3 | 16.9 | 17.8 |
| Female (years) | | | | | | | | | | |
| 16–19 | 3.2 | 4.4 | 3.7 | 4.0 | 4.6 | 44.0 | 52.9 | 51.6 | 51.0 | 52.4 |
| 20–24 | 4.9 | 7.3 | 6.8 | 6.6 | 7.5 | 57.7 | 68.9 | 71.3 | 73.2 | 74.6 |
| 25–34 | 5.7 | 12.3 | 16.1 | 14.8 | 15.3 | 45.0 | 65.5 | 73.5 | 76.4 | 79.0 |
| 35–44 | 6.0 | 8.6 | 14.7 | 17.5 | 16.6 | 51.1 | 65.5 | 76.4 | 77.2 | 80.0 |
| 45–54 | 6.5 | 7.0 | 9.1 | 14.0 | 17.8 | 54.4 | 59.9 | 71.2 | 76.7 | 80.0 |
| 55–64 | 4.2 | 4.7 | 4.9 | 6.2 | 9.8 | 43.0 | 41.3 | 45.2 | 51.5 | 57.7 |
| 65 + | 1.1 | 1.2 | 1.5 | 1.7 | 1.9 | 9.7 | 8.1 | 8.6 | 8.9 | 9.1 |

*Source*: U.S. Census Bureau, 2000, p. 403.

of the labor force and the U.S. Census Bureau's projection for labor force characteristics in the year 2008.

The sustained trend over the last three decades is the aging of the American workforce (both in terms of numbers of older workers and their increased rate of participation within the workforce). As shown in Table 3, the number of female workers aged 45 to 54 years has doubled in the years 1980 to 1999 (from 7 million to 14 million), and is projected to be as many as 17.8 million in the year 2008. Female workers aged 55 to 64 years are projected to number 9.8 million in the year 2008, more than double their 1980 figure. Participation rates of these female age cohorts are also high, and they are increasing steadily over time.

Different age cohorts have different expectations of what it means to "work." Generation Xers are broadly viewed as a nonidealistic generation, expecting immediate rewards from their work rather than trusting institutions to reward them in the future (Guy and Newman, 1998, p. 85). For their part, many older workers remain underutilized and undervalued in the workplace. Henderson (1994, p. 86) refers to the subtle discrimination experienced by older workers as the "Detroit syndrome" devalue them, demote them, discount them, and dump them. "Ageism is manifest at work when older middle- and lower-level employees are relegated to positions with little responsibility. The perception that older workers are less productive than their younger colleagues then becomes a self-fulfilling prophecy as the less productive assignments result in their being less productive, reinforcing the stereotype" (Guy and Newman, 1998, p. 85).

## D.  Workers with Disabilities

The Americans with Disabilities Act of 1990 (ADA) defines disability as a substantial limitation in a major life activity. In 1997, 52.6 million people (19.7% of the population) were coping with some level of disability and 33.0 million (12.3% of the population) were managing their lives hindered by a severe disability.[5] It is noteworthy that the likelihood of having a disability increases systematically with age. Among those 45 to 54 years old, 23% of the population suffered some form of disability, and 14% had a severe disability. For those 65 to 69 years old, the comparable estimates are 45% and 31%, respectively. Women make up the majority of the individuals with disabilities: 28.3 million women compared with 24.3 million men. Disability status is also associated with sharp differences in levels of educational attainment. For individuals 25 to 64 years old with a severe disability, 33% had not finished high school compared with 11% of those with no disability. In 1997, 9% of those with a severe disability had graduated from college compared with 29% of those with no disability (McNeil, 2001). How do these figures translate to the workplace?

The largest underemployed minority group in the United States is composed of persons with disabilities. In 1990 there were 21.4 million persons with a work disability; of this total, 23% were employed, 14% were full-time employees, 75% were not in the labor force, and 11% were unemployed (U.S. Census Bureau, 2000, No. 667, p. 415). Individuals with a severe disability had an employment rate of 31% and median earnings of $13,272, compared with 82% and $20,457 for those with a nonsevere disability, and 84% and $23,654 for those with no disability (McNeil, 2001).

Not surprisingly, persons with disabilities are underrepresented at all levels within public agencies (National Performance Review, 1993, p. 62). The passage of the ADA was the impetus for an increasing number of people with disabilities to enter the workforce and to seek opportunities equal to those of their nondisabled peers (Guy and Newman, 1998, p. 79). However, in 1990 only 6% of federal employees had disabilities, and only 1% had severe disabilities (National Performance Review, 1993, p. 62). These data, however, should be viewed with some caution due to the difficulty in obtaining reliable information and the fact that the definition of a disability continues to evolve. With respect to the latter point, many sources of information define the term disability in medical terms: as a conditional or a functional impairment. The newest view is that disability refers to an interaction of a person possessing a restrictive condition or impairment with their environment (Hale, 2001).

Regardless of the distribution of employees with disabilities, employers are required under the ADA to make reasonable accommodation for disabled workers. With the dawning tolerance for those with disabilities come additional responsibilities on the part of employers to ensure that the workplace is as worker-friendly as possible (Guy and Newman, 1998, p. 79).

Taken together, there appear to be both the opportunity and the necessity to broaden workplace participation generally, and, more specifically, across all organizational levels. Women and people of color continue to be underrepresented in middle- and upper-management positions, and across certain occupational categories. The increase in the number of age discrimination cases filed with the Equal Employment Opportunity Commission over the years represents strong evidence that many older workers remain marginalized in the workplace (U.S. Equal Employment Opportunity Commission, 2001). Among those groups who are at a disadvantage in the workplace, those persons with a work disability may be the most underutilized group in the workforce. As the newest census population and labor force data suggest, managers will increasingly have opportunities to expand their already diverse workforces. What might preclude their taking full advantage of these opportunities?

## III. THE CHALLENGES TO BROADENING WORKPLACE PARTICIPATION

Antidiscrimination legislation[6] and judicial rulings of the past four decades have, for the most part, eliminated the more overt sex, race, age, and disability discrimination in the contemporary workplace. However, as noted above, subtle forms of discrimination continue to define the work experiences of many women and people of color, as well as many older workers and those with work disabilities. There is a rich literature on the barriers to the successful integration of "others" into the middle- and upper-management ranks of public organizations (for example, Lewis, 1988 ; Kelly 1991; Guy, 1992; Newman, 1993; Naff, 1995, 2001; Kelly and Newman, 2001). A recurring theme in this body of research is the power of stereotypes to limit opportunities of "others" at work.

### A. Myths and Stereotypes

Despite the extensive legal framework that prohibits discriminatory practices, human resource decisions relating to selection, hiring, promotion, training, and the assignment of challenging job assignments all involve a considerable degree of subjective judgment. As such, the actual criteria underlying these decisions may not be captured by formal adherence to employment laws. Indeed, any resultant disparate impact may remain invisible to those responsible for making these decisions. Anecdotally, a former departmental chair (who is a white male) once said to me, "I don't know what all the fuss is about the glass ceiling. I've never seen it." The irony of this remark is telling. The implication is that a failure to "see" the problem precludes taking any action to address it.

Negative stereotypes continue to shape the work experiences of nontraditional employees. Stereotypes about the appropriateness of "place" oftentimes relegate women into "women's" jobs and men into "men's" jobs. Sex segregation across jobs reflects stereotypical notions about the kinds of work that are appropriate for women and men (Maume, 1999, p. 484). Women and people of color have easiest access to "bad" jobs characterized by low pay, low advancement opportunities, poor working conditions, and instability. The same dynamic operates in reverse: white males tend to enjoy the many opportunities typical of "good" jobs (Ospina, 1996, p. 82). Women tend to be overrepresented in the nonprofessional job categories that are peripheral to the mission of organizations and that involve a substantial amount of "caring" work, and correspondingly underrepresented in the more "rational" scientific and more valued technical jobs (see, e.g., Thomas and Mohai, 1995). The emotional labor research (much of which is conducted by sociologists and feminist economists) suggests that more women than men hold jobs that require them to engage in organizationally prescribed displays of emotion. Because women are perceived to be naturally able to perform these functions, their work is considered unskilled and, as such, remains undervalued and unrewarded. This reinforces an already prevailing stereo-type regarding women's limited potential for the "tough" demands of leadership positions (Norton and Fox, 1997, p. 42).

Job segregation occurs both horizontally and vertically. Horizontal segregation refers to the distribution of women and men across occupations, such as women as secretaries and men as truck drivers or women in staff posts and men in line posts. Vertical segregation refers to the distribution of women and men in the job hierarchy in terms of status within an occupation, such as women as hygienists and men as dentists, women as paralegals and men as lawyers, women as staff assistants and men as directors (Guy and Newman, forthcoming 2004). According to Jacobs (1989), over half of all employed women would have to change their occupational category to equalize occupational distribution by gender. The stubborn persistence of sex-segregated occupations represents a barrier to breaking through glass ceilings and glass walls and limits the opportunity for broadening workplace participation.

Similar processes are at work with respect to racially segregated occupations "Racialized" jobs are those in which black managers tend to be placed in liaison jobs linking the organization to the black community or to advocates for black equality. This results in the concentration of black women and black men in agencies with black clients, such as social welfare or corrections. Maume (1999) refers to these jobs as "The Relations": the community relations, the public relations, and the personnel relations types of administrative positions. For the most part, these are jobs that are not at the core of an agency's functions. In addition, they are not the types of jobs that prepare the incumbents for executive line positions (p. 389). Moreover, negative stereotypes about people of color persist (Naff, 2001, p. 124) and are manifest, for example, in the use of the term "qualified minority" the presumption is that minority applicants are not automatically presumed to be sufficiently qualified.

Stereotypes of Asian Americans tend to shape their work experiences in several ways. Asian Americans are variously referred to in the literature as the silent, the invisible, or the model minority (Xin, 1997, p. 335). By all accounts, they have achieved spectacular economic and social mobility in recent decades. Although they constitute less than 4% of the population, Asian Americans are currently 19% of the student body at Harvard and 11% of all the physicians in the United States (Thernstrom and Thernstrom, 1997, p. 534). Asian American professionals tend to be held in high regard as employees, however, they are seldom selected to become members of management teams (Naff, 2001, p. 89). As Xin (1997, p. 337) reports, "If they are so impressive, why is nobody impressed?" One explanation relates to the stereotypic perception of Asian Americans as being nonassertive and lacking in the "forceful" leadership qualities valued by the dominant culture (Xin, 1997, p. 335). Moreover, an "impression gap" may further explain the discrepancy between Asian American educational attainment and upward organizational mobility. Asian Americans tend to use different impression management tactics compared to European Americans. Asian Americans "report using significantly less self-disclosure and less self-focused and supervisor-focused impression management tactics" than European Americans. Not seeing anything "more impressive" than they expected, supervisors tend to carry forward their initial views on Asian Americans and thus do not see them as potential supervisors or leaders (Xin, 1997, p. 349). In this way, Asian Americans may be trapped by their cultural values of maintaining modesty and being passive in communicating with superiors (Xin, 1997, p. 352).

Stereotypes also extend to those with a work disability. Considerable research is available indicating that disabled people tend to be perceived negatively (Mamman, 1996, p. 455). Negative attitudes of coworkers, in turn, can affect the performance of a disabled employee adversely and reinforce the negative attitudes in question. These dynamics limit the level of integration and adjustment into the workplace on the part of the disabled.

## B. Sexual Harassment

Sexual harassment continues to be a pervasive problem in the U.S. workplace. A multistate study of upper-level public administrators in state agencies reported that from 6 to 16% of administrative-level female public administrators have experienced unwanted sexual advances in connection with their work. The same study reported that up to 24% of the women surveyed experienced requests for sexual favors, up to 36% experienced offensive physical contact, and up to 57% suffered as victims of offensive verbal behavior (Kelly, 1995, p. 196). At the federal level, the incidence of sexual harassment is similarly widespread. According to the latest study on sexual harassment conducted by the U.S. Merit Systems Protection Board (1995), 44% of female respondents and 19% of male respondents reported some form of unwanted sexual attention during the preceding two years.

Sexual harassment appears to affect work style, self-perception, and a woman's ability to perform particular job functions, especially those workplace functions linked most directly to line leadership and management (Kelly, 1995, p. 206). Sexual harassment serves to remind women of their place, and broadcasts a "no entry" message to those who aspire to upward mobility in their carrer. As such, sexual harassment represents a barrier to broadening workplace participation when victims are no longer willing to stay the course at work and instead decide to leave. This pattern of revolving doors for women has resulted in only a slight decline in occupational segregation since 1970 (Maume, 1999, p. 505). For those who choose to stay, sexual harassment too often serves to limit women's effectiveness and demeans women's status and authority at work.

## C. The Cloning Effect

The cloning effect refers to the concept of homomorphy or homosocial reproduction and involves the twin elements of risk and trust (Rizzo and Mendez, 1990). Social similarity greatly "facilitates the formation of alliances and social networks, access to channels of information, the acquisition of a similar definition of reality and of the vocabulary and style to impress others with allegedly superior knowledge, and consensus concerning the course of action to be followed" (Murphy, 1988, p. 163). As such, social similarity acts as a mechanism of exclusion or inclusion in organizations. The most convenient answer to questions such as, "Whom can I trust" and, "Whom can I communicate with accurately and efficiently" might very well be: someone who looks like me, talks like me, and acts like me (Ospina, 1996, p. 142). One consequence of this dynamic is conformity and uniformity among those who aspire to become managers. That is, as employees in the lower levels are socialized into the organizational culture, they recognize the power of the cloning effect and try to adapt their own attitudes and behaviors to reflect the traits that managers value and reward. It is not coincidental that women who make it to the top of the organizational hierarchy tend to be more like their male counterparts than the women whom they have left behind. It should be noted that the cloning effect is not confined to white males. Research suggests that women and people of color also engage in homosocial reproduction for similar reasons (e.g., Eisinger, 1982; Hindera, 1993a, 1993b; Lewis, 1989; Mladenka, 1989a, 1989b; Riccucci, 1986; Selden, 1997). However, given that white males are disproportionately represented in the middle and upper levels of management, this effect will have a disproportionate (negative) impact on women and people of color.

## D. Perceptions of Inequitable Treatment

Elsewhere I identified self-limiting concepts as representing a barrier to women's career advancement (Newman, 1993). This may stem from a perception of limited opportunity for advancement, which may lead to less commitment to their organizations, diminished motivation, and lessened desire to succeed. Kanter (1977) refers to this self-fulfilling prophecy dynamic as a "downward spiral of opportunity." With respect to public sector settings, it has been noted that "A substantial number of women and people of color in the government do perceive their opportunities to be limited" (Naff, 2001, p. 158). With reference to the responses of approximately 13,000 federal employees to the Workforce Diversity Survey administered in 1993, Naff (2001, p. 158) reports that "[m]ore than half of women believe they must outperform their male colleagues to be promoted, and nearly half of African Americans and more than one-quarter of Asian Pacific Americans and Latinos believe that their organizations are reluctant to promote people of color into supervisory positions." For the most part, white males do not share those same views. "To the extent that perceptions of disparate treatment contribute to the desire of women or people of color to leave government employment, or deter them from applying for promotions" (Naff, 2001, p. 133), such perceptions make it difficult to achieve broad workplace participation.

In sum, challenges to broadening workplace participation include negative stereotyping, segregated occupations, sexual harassment, the cloning effect, and perceptions of inequitable treatment. Taken together, these barriers limit the successful integration of "others" into positions of authority within public workplaces. Women and people of color continue to be compressed into the lower levels of organizations, and concentrated into what are conventionally considered to be sex- and race-appropriate occupations. Salary inequities are reflected in this segregation. Frederickson (1990) reminds us that for workplace participation to be broadly conceived, we must go beyond the numbers themselves (block equality) to a consideration of where the numbers reside (segmented equality). That is, it is not enough to increase the numbers of nontraditional workers in our public organizations unless we also take into account their integration at all levels therein. This chapter extends this concern for a more demographically diverse and more representative bureaucracy to a consideration of diversifying the work itself.

## IV. MANAGERIAL STRATEGIES

Diversity is a fact of life. How public sector managers respond to the changing workforce demographics will shape, if not predict, the current and future performance of their public agencies. The literature suggests that there are typically two different approaches to "managing diversity." One approach can be characterized as ignoring "difference," the other approach recognizes (even emphasizes) those same differences. According to Thomas and Ely (1996, p. 80), organizations either encourage and expect women and people of color to blend in, or they set them apart in jobs that relate specifically to their backgrounds and, as noted above, assign them to areas that require them to interface with clients of the same identity group.

The first (and most common) approach to managing diversity is that of assimilation. This discrimination-and-fairness paradigm idealizes assimilation and color- and gender-blind conformism (Thomas and Ely, 1996, p. 83). Under this paradigm, the focus is on equal opportunity, fair treatment, recruitment, and compliance with federal EEO requirements. Accordingly, progress in diversity is measured by how well the organization achieves its recruitment and retention goals rather than by the degree to which conditions in the organization allow employees to draw on their personal assets and perspectives to do their work more effectively (Thomas and Ely, 1996, p. 81). The workers get diversified, but the work does not.

By contrast, the access-and-legitimacy paradigm is predicated on the acceptance and celebration of differences, of differentiation. Under this approach, "the objective is to place different people where their demographic characteristics match those of important constituents and markets" (Thomas and Ely, 1996, p. 86). However, managers may be "too quick to push staff with niche capabilities into differentiated pigeonholes without trying to understand what those capabilities really are and how they could be integrated into the company's mainstream work" (p. 83). Difference is valued in the organization, but not valued enough that the organization attempts to integrate it into the very core of its culture and practices (p. 83).

Thomas and Ely (1996, p. 81) propose an alternative integrative approach that incorporates aspects of the first two paradigms, but goes beyond them by specifically connecting diversity to approaches to work. This learning-and-effectiveness model "lets the organization internalize differences among employees so that it learns and grows because of them" p. 86). In order to make the most of their own pluralism, organizations have developed an outlook on diversity that enables them to incorporate employees' perspectives into the main work of the organization and to enhance work by rethinking primary tasks and redefining strategies, missions, organizational practices, and even culture (p. 85). Managers "realize that increasing demographic variation does not in itself increase organizational effectiveness. They realize that it is *how* a company defines diversity—and *what it does* with the experiences of being a diverse organization—that delivers on the promise" (p. 81, emphasis in the original). With this model of integration in mind, the fundamental requirement for broadening workplace participation is a genuine commitment of management.

## A. Management Support

As the anecdotal quote above suggests, managers and supervisors must first "see" that employment policies and procedures oftentimes lead to differential outcomes for nonmainstream groups, and must acknowledge their pivotal role in facilitating a more level organizational playing field. Tacit support is not sufficient; rather, managers must be willing to visibly support the effort with organizational resources and communicate that support throughout the organization (Naff, 2001, p. 197). Senior managers must provide the leadership so that line managers, in turn, are motivated to pursue this goal. What can managers do?

First, pay close attention to the numbers. Communicate a zero-tolerance stance towards sexism, racism, homophobia, ageism, and sexual harassment. Procedures related to recruitment, selection, retention, promotion, performance appraisal criteria, and career development programs should be examined for potential bias and be revamped as necessary. Targeted recruitment can ensure that nontraditional employees are encouraged to apply for openings at all organizational levels. Employers can also work closely with high school and college officials who can locate minority candidates. Part-time, work study, and summer jobs programs can serve to introduce potential long-term minority employees into the organization (Braddock and McPartland, 1987, p. 24). At the job selection stage, screening methods must be scrutinized to ensure that the selection standards are objective, job related, and valid. The same vigilance against subjectivity and potential bias similarly applies at the promotion stage.

Second, closely monitor where the numbers reside. The representation of groups at all levels and occupations in the organization should be closely monitored. Periodic audits should take place. Managers and supervisors should be held accountable for their success in broadening workplace participation across organizational levels and across occupations. The provision of ongoing employee training can promote an understanding of the importance of diversity goals and allow for the development of skills necessary to work more effectively in a diverse workforce. The implementation of formal or informal mentoring programs can further facilitate the career advancement of nontraditional workers.

Third, look beyond the numbers to the work itself. A more diverse workforce presents managers with a real opportunity to rethink the way work is organized, performed, and evaluated, as well as what it does with the experiences of being a diverse organization. That is, it enables managers to rethink the work of the organization. Managers should strategize over how best to make diversity work for the organization by explicitly connecting diversity to approaches to work. A strategic reexamination of the organization's culture, structure, processes, and systems is a necessary first step. Rethinking primary tasks, redefining strategies, missions, and organizational practices are at the core of an integrative approach and represent the best means to realize the promise of an increasingly diverse workforce. Rather than attempting to fit nontraditional workers into traditional structures, employees' perspectives are incorporated into the main work of the organization. In this way, the diverse workforce and approaches to work are brought into closer alignment.

The way work is organized and performed is already undergoing a shift. Organizations are increasingly utilizing team-based approaches to the performance of work. For teams to function well, members must be able to see beyond skin color and stereotypes. Team building is essential to creating a work environment that is conducive to developing strong bonds and cooperative relations among coworkers (Rubaii-Barrett and Beck, 1993, p. 517). Although work group cohesiveness tends to be stronger in homogeneous work groups, diverse teams enable the consideration of various cultural perspectives in thinking through workplace problems.

In addition, family-friendly workplace policies are in place in most public organizations. These benefits are intended to accommodate diversity in employee needs relative to work location, schedules, benefit choices, dependent care (child and elder care), and employee wellness (Roberts, 2000, p. 6). These nontraditional programs include flexible work schedules, permanent part-time employment, childcare arrangements, job sharing, and telecommuting. The main focus of many of these programs is on accommodation, as workers (especially women) struggle to balance their work and family obligations. Although these programs have been criticized on these grounds (McCurdy et al., 2002), they can also be viewed favorably to the extent that they encourage managers to rethink traditional approaches to work.

To continue the transition to an integrative approach to managing diversity, managers are rethinking what their organizations do. Managers can encourage their employees to make explicit use of their background cultural experiences and knowledge gained outside the organization to inform and enhance their work (Thomas and Ely, 1996, p. 89).

> Individuals often do use their cultural competencies at work, but in a closeted, almost embarrassed, way. When people believe that they must suggest and apply their ideas covertly, the organization ... misses opportunities to discuss, debate, refine, and build on those ideas fully.

It follows that managers must ensure that employees feel safe to be themselves. Managers are best placed to ensure that organizational trust remains intact in an increasingly heterogeneous workplace by setting a tone of honest discourse, by acknowledging inevitable workplace tensions, and by resolving them sensitively and swiftly (Thomas and Ely, 1996, p. 90).

More important, nonmainstream workers bring more than their "insider information" to the workplace. "They bring different, important, and competitively relevant knowledge and perspectives about how to actually *do work*—how to design processes, reach goals, frame tasks, create effective teams, communicate ideas, and lead" (Thomas and Ely, 1996, p. 80). In the process, basic assumptions about an organization's functions, strategies, operations, practices, and procedures are reevaluated, enabling fresh and meaningful approaches to work to develop in turn. Broadening workplace participation is the principal means to this end.

## V. CONCLUSION

The contemporary American workplace is undergoing irreversible changes. The widespread public service reforms that are associated with New Public Management and Reinventing Government are moving us farther away from traditional civil service systems toward an increased reliance upon the private and nonprofit sectors to deliver public services. Market-oriented action and a bottom-line mentality have increasingly become the norm for contemporary government. In the process, many public sector administrators are being recast in the mold of public entrepreneurs and contract managers. As a function of these reforms, the size of the public workforce is decreasing at the same time as organizations are being called upon to maintain or enhance productivity. The face of the workforce has also changed as more women and people of color enter and stay engaged in careers and as the workforce ages. Moreover, the pace and impact of new technologies on human resource management is changing the very definition of what it means to work.

Upon this ever-shifting ground, there is one important constant—that workplace diversity is here to stay. The question is no longer, "How can the problem of diversity be resolved?" Instead, the proper question to be addressed is, "How can managers best embrace the opportunities that ensue from a more diverse workforce and integrate the varied perspectives and approaches to work that members of different identity groups bring to the workplace?" The reasons why we should be committed to doing so are at least threefold.

The argument for representative bureaucracies is central to the notion of democratic governance. The powerful symbolic legitimacy accorded a governmental bureaucracy representative of all members of the society it serves has long been recognized in the scholarly literature (e.g., Krislov, 1974; Kranz, 1976; Krislov and Rosenbloom, 1981). The theory of representative bureaucracy postulates that in reflecting the demographic makeup of the nation, the agencies of government will manifest the values of the citizenry in their work (Naff, 2001, p. 7). Hence, the argument for diversifying the workplace calls for having the workforce proactively reflect the gender, cultural, and ethnic complexity of each local community, and American society as a whole (Patton et al., 2002, p. 93). According to Guy and Thatcher (in press), a diverse workforce represents "democracy in action."

From a more utilitarian perspective, there is a strong economic imperative to broaden workplace participation. The government is paying an enormous cost for the glass ceiling that keeps women, people of color, older workers, and disabled persons underrepresented at the middle- and upper-management levels in governmental bureaucracies. It is making poor use of a major segment of its human resources. The benefits that accrue from leveraging diversity include increased profitability, however, they go beyond financial measures to encompass learning, creativity, flexibility, organizational and individual growth, and the ability of an organization to adjust rapidly and successfully to market and other changes (Thomas and Ely, 1996, p. 80). In short, enhanced performance is more likely to accrue to organizations that embrace diversity. More fundamentally, there is the moral imperative to broaden workplace participation in the service of distributive justice in the workplace (Ospina, 1996, p. 46).

In sum, this chapter has sketched out the changing nature of the workforce, the persistence of lingering discrimination, and managerial strategies available to expand employment opportunities, especially for nontraditional employees. The central premise is that it is necessary but insufficient to examine workplace participation by strict attention to the numbers, either in the aggregate or at various levels within organizations. Rather, the more appropriate approach to diversity is to stress the importance of integration by explicitly linking diverse workers to diverse approaches to the work itself, including the way work is organized, performed, and evaluated, as well as what the organization does in service to its mission. The essence of high-performing organizations may very well reside in management's unequivocal commitment to this emerging paradigm of the cultivation and exploitation of the benefits of workplace diversity.

## NOTES

1. The author is grateful to Nicholas Lovrich for his editorial comments.
2. The U.S. Bureau of Labor Statistics has no information on the labor force status of Native Americans, and only limited information regarding Asians and Pacific Islanders (Howard Hayghe, Supervisory Economist, Office of Employment and

Unemployment Statistics, Bureau of Labor Statistics, personal communication, October 5, 2001).

3. The increase in the number of Native Americans stems from the willingness of more whites to classify themselves as Native Americans, based on their mixed racial heritage (Payne, 1998, p. 134).

4. The term "people of color" refers to the three race/ethnic groups identified by the U.S. Bureau of Labor. They are blacks, Hispanics, and Asians, Pacific Islanders, American Indians, and Alaska Natives.

5. "Severe" disability is defined as any of the following criteria: use of a wheelchair, a cane, crutches, or a walker; a mental or emotional condition that seriously interferes with everyday activities; receipt of federal benefits based on an inability to work, Alzheimer's disease, or mental retardation or another developmental disability (McNeil, 2001).

6. For a detailed examination of this extensive legal framework see, for example, Guy and Newman (1998).

## REFERENCES

Blau, F. D., Ehrenberg, R. G., eds. *Gender and Family Issues in the Workplace.* New York: Russell Sage Foundation.

Borjas, G. J. (October 1982). The politics of employment discrimination in the federal bureaucracy. *J. Law Econ.* 25:271–299.

Braddock, J. H. II, McPartland, J. M. (1987). How minorities continue to be excluded from equal employment opportunities: Research on labor market and institutional barriers. *J. Soc. Iss.* 43(1):5–39.

Eisinger, P. K. (1982). Black employment in municipal jobs: The impact of black political power. *Am. Polit. Sci. Rev.* 76:380–392.

Frederickson, H. G. (1990). Public administration and social equity. *Public Admin. Rev.* 50(2):228–237.

Fullerton, H. N. Jr. (November 1999). Employment outlook: 1998–2008 Labor force projections to 2008: Steady growth and changing composition. *Month. Labor Rev.* 19–32.

Grandjean, B. (March 1981). History and career in a bureaucratic labor market. *Am. J. Sociol.* 86:1057–1092.

Guy, M. E. (1992). *Women and Men of the States.* Armonk, NY: Sharpe.

Guy, M. E. (2002). The difference that gender makes. In: Hays, S., Kearney, R., eds. *Public Personnel Administration: Problems and Prospects.* 4th ed. Englewood Cliffs, NJ: Prentice-Hall, pp. 256–270.

Guy, M. E., Newman, M. A. (1998). Toward diversity in the workplace. In: Condrey, S. E., ed., *Handbook of Human Resource Management in Government.* San Francisco: Jossey-Bass, pp. 75–92.

Guy, M. E. Newman, M. A. Women's jobs, men's jobs: Sex segregation and emotional labor. *Public Admin. Rev.* 64(3):forthcoming.

Guy, M. E. Thatcher, J. B. Diversity, administration and governance. In: A. Farazmand R., Carter, eds. Sound Governance: Policy Innovation and Administration. Westport, CT: Greenwood. In press.

Hale, T. W. (Septemper 17, 2001). Personal communication (Economist, Bureau of Labor Statistics), September 17.

Henderson, G. (1994). *Cultural Diversity in the Workplace: Issues and Strategies.* Westport, CT: Qourum/Greenwood.

Hindera, J. J. (1993a). Representative bureaucracy: Imprimis evidence of active representation in the EEOC district offices. *Soc. Sci. Quart.* 74(1):95–108.

Hindera, J. J. (1993b). Representative bureaucracy: Further evidence of active representation in the EEOC district offices. *J. Public Admin. Res. Theor*, 3:415–429.

Jacobs, J. (1989). *Revolving Doors: Sex Segregation and Women's Careers*. Stanford, CA: Stanford University Press.

Kanter, R. M. (1977). *Men and Women of the Corporation*. New York: Basic.

Kelly, R. M. (1995). Offensive men, defensive women: Sexual harassment, leadership, and management. In: Duerst-Lahti, G. J., Kelly, R. M., eds. *Gender Power, Leadership, and Governance*. Ann Arbor, MI: University of Michigan Press, pp. 195–209.

Kelly, R. M., Newman, M. A. (2001). The gendered bureaucracy: Agency mission, equality of opportunity, and representative bureaucracies. *Women and Polit.* 22(3):1–33.

Kelly, R. M., et al. (1991). Public managers in the states: A comparison of career advancement by sex. *Public Admin. Rev.* 51(5):402–412.

Kranz, H. (1976). *The Participatory Bureaucracy: Women and Minorities in a More Representative Public Service*. Lexington, MA: Lexington Books.

Krislov, S. (1974). *Representative Bureaucracy*. Englewood Cliffs, NJ: Prentice-Hall.

Krislov, S., Rosenbloom, D. H. (1981). *Representative Bureaucracy and the American Political System*. New York: Praeger.

Lehman, J. (August 21, 2001). Admitting for Diversity. Online News Hour. Available at: www.pbs.org/newshour/bb/education/july–dec01/. Accessed September 28, 2001.

Lewis, G. (1988). Progress toward racial and sexual equality in the federal civil service? *Public Admin. Rev.* 48(3):700–707.

Lewis, G. (1997). Race, sex, and performance ratings in the federal service. *Public Admin. Rev.* 57(6):479–489.

Lewis, W. G. (1989). Toward representative bureaucracy: Blacks in city policy organization, 1975–1985. *Public Admin. Rev.* 49(3):257–268.

Mamman, A. (1996). A diverse employee in a changing workplace. *Org. Stud.* 17(3):449–477.

Maume, D. J. Jr. (1999). Glass ceilings and glass escalators. Occupational segregation and race and sex differences in managerial promotions. *Work Occupations* 26(4):483–509.

McCurdy, A. H., Newman, M. A., Lovrich, N. P. (2002). Family-friendly workplace policy adoption in general and special purpose local governments: Learning from the Washington State experience. *Rev. Public Person. Admin.* 22(1):27–51.

McNeil, J. (2001). *Americans with Disabilities: 1997. Household Economic Studies. Current Population Reports P70–73 U.S. Census Bureau*. Available at: www.census.gov/hhes/www.disability.html. Accessed September 28, 2001.

Mladenka, K. R. (1989a). Barriers to Hispanic employment success in 1,200 cities. *Soc. Sci. Quart.* 70(2):391–407.

Mladenka, K. R. (1989b). Blacks and Hispanics in urban politics. *Am. Polit. Sci. Rev.* 83(1):165–191.

Murphy, R. (1988). *Social Closure: The Theory of Monopolization and Exclusion*. Oxford: Clarendon.

Naff, K. C. (1995). Perceptions of discrimination: Moving beyond the numbers of representative bureaucracy. *Policy Stud. J.* 23(3):483–498.

Naff, K. C. (2001). *To Look Like America: Dismantling Barriers for Women and Minorities in Government*. Boulder, CO: Westview.

National Performance Review. (September 1993). Reinventing Human Resource Management. Accompanying Report of the National Performance Review, Office of the Vice President, Washington DC.

Newman, M.A. (1993). Career advancement: Does gender make a difference? *Am. Rev. Public Admin.* 23(4):361–384.

Newman, M. A., Mathews, K. (1999). Federal family-friendly workplace policies: Barriers to effective implementation. *Rev. Public Preson. Admin.* 11(3):34–48.

Norton, J. R., Fox, R. E. (1997). *The Change Equation. Capitalizing on Diversity for Effective Organizational Change.* Washington, DC: American Psychological Association.

Ospina, S. (1996). *Illusions of Opportunity. Employee Expectations and Workplace Inequality.* Ithaca, NY: Cornell University Press.

Patton, W. D., Witt, S. L., Lovrich, N. P., Fredericksen, P. J. (2002). *Human Resource Management. The Public Service Perspective.* Boston: Houghton Mifflin.

Payne, R. J. (1998). *Getting Beyond Race. The Changing American Culture.* Boulder, CO: Westview.

Riccucci, N. M. (1986). Female and minority employment in city government: The role of unions. *Policy Stud. J.* 15(1):3–15.

Rizzo, A., Mendez, C. (1990). *The Integration of Women in Management. A Guide for Human Resources and Management Development Specialists.* Westport, CT: Greenwood.

Roberts, G. E. (Spring 2000). An inventory of family-friendly benefit practices in small New Jersey local governments. *Rev. Public Person. Admin.* 12:35–47.

Rubaii-Barrett, N., Beck, A. C. (1993). Minorities in the majority: Implications for managing cultural diversity. *Public Person. Manage.* 22(4):503–521.

Selden, S. C. (1997). *The Promise of Representative Bureaucracy: Diversity and Responsiveness in a Government Agency.* Armonk, NY: Sharpe.

Thernstrom, S., Thernstrom, A. (1997). *America in Black and White. One Nation, Indivisible.* New York: Simon & Schuster.

Thomas, D. A., Ely, R. J. (September-October 1996). Making differences matter: A new paradigm for managing diversity. *Harvard Bus. Rev.*, 79–90.

Thomas, J. C., Mohai, P. (1995). Racial, gender, and professional diversification in the Forest Service from 1983 to 1992. *Policy Stud. J.* 23(2):296–309.

U.S. Bureau of Labor Statistics. (2001) Available at http://stats.bls.gov/cpsaatab.htm#empstat. Accessed September 17, 2001.

U.S. Census Bureau (2000). Statistical Abstract of the United States: 2000, No. 644, p. 403.

U.S. Equal Employment Opportunity Commission. (2001). EEOC Enforcement Statistics and Litigation. Age Discrimination in Employment Act (ADEA) Charges. Available at http://www.eeoc.gov/stats/enforcement.html. Accessed October 2, 2001.

U.S. Merit Systems Protection Board. (October 1995). *Sexual Harassment in the Federal Workplace: Trends, Progress, Continuing Challenges.* Washington, DC: U.S. Merit Systems Protection Board.

U.S. Merit Systems Protection Board. (April 1996). *Fair & Equitable Treatment: A Progress Report on Minority Employment in the Federal Government.* Washington, DC: U.S. Merit Systems Protection Board.

Xin, K.R. (1997). Asian American managers: An impression gap? An investigation of impression management and supervisor-subordinate relationships. *J. Appl. Behav. Sci.* 33(3):335–355.

# 27

## Merit Pay and Employee Performance

**GERALD T. GABRIS**
*Northern Illinois University, DeKalb, Illinois, U.S.A.*

**DOUGLAS M. IHRKE**
*University of Wisconsin, Milwaukee, Wisconsin, U.S.A.*

## I. INTRODUCTION

Tracing the history of public management's fixation on merit pay is not easy because using incentive pay to reward rated past performance of individual employees has been around in various incarnations for quite some time. At a very minimum, rewarding performance with pay can be traced to the differential piece-rate system first deployed by Frederick Winslow Taylor at the turn of the century (Schachter, 1989). More recently, and perhaps the clearest manifestation of the merit pay logic, was the program begun at the federal level in connection with the Civil Service Reform Act of 1978 (Ingraham and Ban, 1984). With the passage of this legislation at the federal level, compensation systems at all levels of government on how to reward and motivate public employees with incentive pay have not been the same since.

The purpose of this chapter is severalfold. Merit or incentive pay is a powerful idea that is unlikely to wither away soon just because of its complexity or because public organizations find it difficult to implement. On the contrary, in this era of performance management and reinventing government (Osborne and Gaebler, 1992), merit pay may take on an even larger role in how public employees are compensated in government organizations. Given the probability that merit pay appears to possess a staying power that transcends its occasional failures, this chapter focuses on the following themes.

Why is the theory and logic of merit pay so compelling?
What are the continuing problems connected with merit pay in the public sector?

How might compensation systems design better, more effective, incentive pay components?

## II. MERIT PAY THEORY

If for no other reason, merit pay may remain so popular today because of its rather seductive logic. Typical merit pay reasoning runs something like this. Employees who perform well are engaging in behavior that if rewarded, will continue. In short, behavior follows rewards. Although simple, this logic conveys a persuasive elegance. Moreover, this logic seems to be borne out in reality and to possess face validity. Yet life never is simple.

Edward Lawler (1983), one of the codevelopers of expectancy theory (Vroom, 1964), suggests that although a connection exists between rewards and behavior, this linkage is subject to subtle nuances that can dramatically influence the strength and intensity of the relationship. One key ingredient is the "valence" or value that an employee places on a specific reward. This can be explained as follows.

Consider a clerical employee who performs very well during the year. His supervisor informs him that he will receive a $600 merit pay increase for his high performance. The $600 will be divided into 12 monthly installments of $50 and after taxes the employee might receive approximately $38. Now, this employee may not be jumping up and down in his chair in exultation over this reward. On the contrary, he may even feel slighted, and the impact of the merit pay on his behavior will likely be marginal.

Lawler points to another force that influences how pay and performance connect. Employees need to feel that they have a good "chance" of being rewarded if they achieve a specific level of performing behavior. Take graduate students in a course on human resources management. If they study 10 hours for an exam they may expect to earn a grade of A. But this is not guaranteed. Thus, how motivated employees become in a merit pay system depends on whether they genuinely feel they can win the reward if they perform at a certain level.

By combining the value of a reward along with the probability of attaining it, one arrives at the essence of expectancy theory. It may be possible to have an extremely valued reward connected with a low probability of attainment (which explains why people purchase lottery tickets even though their chance of winning is one in several million) or, conversely, a low reward with a high probability of winning. The key is to understand that these forces "interact" in determining the level at which a merit pay plan might motivate any particular employee.

Of course, there are other assumptions associated with merit pay logic. One of the more common suggests that in any given organization there exists a certain percentage of "deadwood employees." For elected officials, the perception that a certain percentage of public employees are unproductive has become a quintessential norm in our political culture. Therefore, it becomes the responsibility of fiscally conservative elected officials to protect the public against these freeloaders. Translated, merit pay and performance appraisal make public employees accountable for their work. If they do not perform up to snuff or perform below expectations then they should not be financially rewarded. What better way to send a message home than by paychecks? This notion was openly advocated by former-President Jimmy

Carter as part of his rationale for the Civil Service Reform Act of 1978 (Ingraham and Ban, 1984).

Another assumption, perhaps less obvious, can be derived from "implicit" contract theory (Rosen, 1985). In this perspective, by providing employees with incentive pay, they may "feel" obliged to work harder. This idea stems from the classic assumption that an honest day's work is due for an honest day's pay. If we pay public employees for their higher performance they will feel obligated to perform well. There exists, in essence, an unwritten contract between the employee and the employer.

How this might work can be demonstrated via a management by objective (MBO) performance system. It is not uncommon for these systems to state rather explicitly what level of accomplishment is required for the employee to earn a specific performance score. For example, if an employee is expected to secure 10 contracts during the year as part of her performance for an exceptional rating, and she does so, then she feels she has completed her end of the bargain. Given this performance the organization can justify the incentive pay on the grounds that this pay reflects the level of work produced.

One final assumption regarding the logic of merit pay involves what has come to be known as equity theory (Adams, 1965). This concept makes a lot of intuitive sense. Suppose two workers doing basically the same job vary substantially in their individual performance. Worker A compares herself to Worker B. Worker A is the high performer, producing an output twice as effectively as Worker B. If at compensation time Worker A receives essentially the same level of compensation as Worker B inasmuch as they are technically both in the same position), Worker A may become quite upset. Worker A probably feels that distributive justice warrants a greater differential in reward or pay. If this does not ensue this theory predicts dire consequences will follow.

So, how might we summarize the persuasive elements of merit pay logic? Why is it so appealing?

1. Merit pay rewards behavior associated with high performance. This will presumably lead to repetition of this behavior and cause poorer performers to improve.
2. Merit pay will punish the deadwood and freeloaders. They may even decide to quit.
3. Merit pay makes public employees accountable to the electorate and their representatives.
4. Merit pay serves as a contract between government and employees: an honest day's work for an honest day's pay.
5. Merit pay serves as a tool for distributive justice and fairness in compensation. High performers will lose motivation if they are not rewarded.

The above reasons provide a rather convincing argument for merit pay, right? The fact of the matter is that while merit pay sounds like an excellent idea on paper, it often runs into trouble in practice. In a vein analogous to what Woodrow Wilson said about the U.S. Constitution, it is easier to "frame" a merit pay plan than to "manage" one. Let us now turn briefly to several recurring problems.

## III.  PRACTICAL PROBLEMS THAT NAG AT MERIT PAY SUCCESS

There is probably no single thing that makes a merit pay plan fail. More often, it is the accumulation of multiple wounds that usually brings down the beast. A good summary of potential pitfalls can be found in Robert Heneman's (1992) assessment of merit pay, and at best this chapter can only provide a quick summary of the key issues. Unlike some students of merit pay, however, we do not think that most merit pay plans are the products of evil management minds (Thayer, 1978; Adams, 1996). On the contrary, most merit pay plans are the result of a complex decision-making processes that are usually very sensitive to employee reactions. In fact, from the earliest reports about supervisory perceptions of merit pay and employee evaluations, writers have found supervisors to be quite chary toward these processes (McGregor, 1957; Gabris, 1986).

Nonetheless, the best laid plans of mice and men can and do go awry. Summarized below are some of the most common problems encountered by these authors.

1.  The merit plans are not managed. The plans are left to run on automatic.
2.  There is often very little difference in the reward compensation given to high and low performers.
3.  There is insufficient funding for the level of rewards necessary to make a difference to employees.
4.  Merit pay plans lead to increasing distance between high performers and low to average performers. The plans do not motivate low to average performers to perform better.
5.  The rules and implied contract for receiving rewards are fuzzy and inconsistent. There is no clear target. Rules change from year to year. Rules make it very difficult to reward employees.
6.  Measurement systems to assess past individual performance are ineffective and inadequate.

The authors admit that more could be added to this list, but feel that these highlight most of the problems. How do these problems manifest themselves in typical public organizations?

Strangely, after investing time, money, and energy into developing a merit pay plan, many public organizations simply let the plans run on automatic, and seem surprised when they inevitably skid off the road. What gives? There are multiple subissues associated with this larger one. In the first place, implementing merit pay plans requires an organization to address problematic issues glossed over during initial formulation. Concerns involving merit pay policy, interpretations of policy, measurement standards, supervisory training, and even communication of merit policy to employees often arise.

In the experience of one of the authors with a municipal merit pay plan, a city continually shifted its merit policy to address unexpected issues that surfaced. This resulted in a kind of seat-of-the-pants approach that satisfied no one. Whenever something came up that was not addressed in the original policy, policies were constructed on the spot only to be changed shortly by newer policies dealing with even newer contingencies. The merit pay plan became so convoluted no supervisor nor employee clearly understood it. Employees were not communicated with, and many complained they learned more about their merit pay plan from a local newspaper than from management. Supervisors were untrained. Some supervisors were applying very stringent standards in their units and in some others, supervisors were extremely lenient and used the merit pay to reward all employees working with them. Eventually, the plan came to be viewed as an unfair messy system that when given an early burial, no one mourned its passing.

Organizations need a strategy on how to implement merit pay. Implementation must be managed and carefully assessed. So many things can go wrong that it becomes imperative for management to closely watch how these plans work and, when necessary, to correct course. Too often, public organizations simply design the plans and then think they will manage themselves. No one takes responsibility for getting them to succeed. Without detailed attention, they fail.

Connected with the problem of letting the plans run on automatic, is the corollary issue of insufficient funding. Too often, public organizations create win–lose payoff scenarios, do not link performance to sufficient pay to make a difference in behavior, or strive to game the system to reward everyone even though they may not deserve it. Each of these possibilities creates a distinct set of unanticipated consequences that are usually not good for the public organization.

The win-lose concept can be stated in simple terms. Pay increase are normally tethered to the base salary levels of employees within an organization. From year to year, one can determine approximate salary increases for a unit by multiplying the salary base of the unit by a projected raise percentage. Thus if the raise increase is supposed to be five percent, most employees expect a five percent increase to their base. In the win-lose scenario, Worker A may receive an eight percent raise, but only if Worker B receives the paltry increase of two percent. In short, one worker's gain in another's loss.

As harsh as this logic may seem today, it was at the heart of the earliest federal merit pay payouts. Needless to say, this type of reward system did not last long. Associated with this notion was the idea that only a certain percentage of workers would be eligible for a raise at any given time, even though employees may have met stated performance standards in an absolute sense. Sometimes this has been described as giving only the top 25% of performers a merit raise. If employee performance follows a normal curve, then by definition, only a small percentage can really be at the highest level. What this concept fails to consider is that perhaps the standards are so high, that even modest performers are already performing well enough. To punish them by not rewarding them could create a disaffection that gradually reduces their motivation to perform.

Underlying this problem is the organization's unstated objective of intending to fund the merit plan in a niggardly fashion. It is cheaper to give a smaller percentage of workers merit raises even though a larger number have met the absolute standards. Such systems are normally not well received by employees or supervisors who find them extremely difficult and painful to implement. The only advantage of this system and the win-lose model is that the organization, by giving out so few merit raises, may have sufficient resources to give a few large ones that are viewed as substantive by employees. But on balance, the negatives of this approach seem to outweigh any benefits.

This leads to the last funding dilemma, namely, gaming the system to reward as many employees as possible. In this case, just about every employee is given a high performance appraisal score, known variously as positive leniency or halo (Latham and Wexley, 1981). If everyone receives a high performance score, then by definition all should receive a relatively equal merit payout. This is in fact what actually happens. Supervisors achieve the effect of an across-the-board salary increase under the guise of a merit pay plan. So, will this make everyone happy? Well, only sort of.

Truly high performers may feel victimized by such a strategy and see themselves as subsidizing the raises of lower performers. Initially, they may not complain so as to not rock the boat. But as equity theory predicts, they will not tolerate this type of redistributive injustice indefinitely. Literal pay equality will irritate high producers if in fact they are performing at higher levels. Moreover, lower performers are then over rewarded and have even less incentive to improve their performance. Why should they?

What the across-the-board strategy does is to take a marginal merit pay increase and spread it out so all benefit to some extent. It is a kind of extreme win-win logic. This may make sense when the amount of dollars in a raise pool is small to begin with. It may not be worth the hassle and difficulty of objectively appraising individual performance if the end result is a very small merit increment. Because public organizations put so little money into merit raise pools, this option may make sense under austere conditions. Alternatively, this kind of mock reward system undermines any real sense of linking performance to pay and probably delegitimizes the merit pay concept as a tool for making substantive merit pay rewards in the future.

There is another problem connected with the logic of merit pay. This involves the assumption that merit pay will remotivate employees who are average to below average in their job performance. Ostensibly, when these employees see others reaping rewards of their hard work, this should stimulate similar behavior in the hearts and minds of the less motivated. This logic implies a cause and effect that may not exist in nature, but it sounds commonsensical on the surface.

Gabris and Mitchell (1988) suggest that what does happen is merit pay actually motivates the high performers, who do expect to receive merit increments. This reward serves to reinforce their conception of self-worth. They feel they deserve the merit increment because they have earned it as suggested by implied contract theory. At the same time, this assumption may not apply to low to average performing employees.

Employees experiencing difficulty with performance may simply give up. They may feel they can never satisfy their supervisor, that they can never really compete with the high performers, and so they refrain from becoming more productive. These employees eventually come to see merit pay as a kind of punishment, as an unmotivator. Instead of trying to beat the system by performing better, they often blame the system for their situation. They will often claim their supervisors are biased against them, that the measurement process is subjective and unfair, and that even when they do try no one seems to notice. So, they give up. Over time, this can lead to a real disparity between the high and low performers, which Gabris and Mitchell (1988) term the Matthew Effect. Here, the rich become richer and the poor, poorer. Although this may not be the intent of a merit pay plan it can be a consequence. As such, merit pay plans have a very hard time building acceptance and legitimacy within an organization's culture, because so many perceive such systems as exclusive and punitive.

This leads to a final set of problems. Many public organizations change their merit policies annually, in part to reflect budget realities, but also because they lack effective tools for measuring employee performance. The result is a hodgepodge of expectations and rules that are often fuzzy, inconsistent, sometimes contradictory, and not very motivating. Moreover, when merit raises are given, they are based on instrumentation that is often very subjective and potentially arbitrary. How might these concerns be observed in a typical public organization?

On the matter of performance appraisal instrumentation, many public organizations still rely on "trait" systems. These are appraisals that require a supervisor to rate a subordinate's "innovativeness," "teamwork," or "work attitude" among other traits. The problem stems from the flaws in this model. First, employee traits are at best vaguely job related. What kind of work attitude, for instance, should employees demonstrate that is related to what they do on the job? The second drawback involves a lack of interrater agreement as to the meaning of these terms which results in very low interrater reliability. One rater may perceive an employee's challenging remarks as a positive indicator of assertiveness, whereas to another rater, the same employee may be perceived as a complainer.

Many public organizations rely on trait appraisals because they are easy to develop and implement. They may also convey a sense of face validity. However, when one begins asking tough questions about the validity and fairness of these instruments their shallow nature normally rises to the surface in short order. They are not sound systems for making merit pay decisions.

Some public organizations also change their merit pay policies frequently, often as a strategy for balancing their budgets rather than for solid analytical reasons. Merit pay plans can become pawns within the annual budgeting process, where budget issues rather than the motivational potential of the merit concept drive how much money is set aside for incentive pay. Perhaps this cannot be entirely avoided. But the impact often translates into rapidly and frequently changing sets of rules on how much merit pay an employee can earn based on a specific level of scored performance. Because the rules change often they are akin to a moving target. Such plans are simply too convoluted and complex for most employees to comprehend and, as such, appear to have little real value regarding performance and motivation.

Given these common problems with merit pay plans, how might public organizations design better system components? How might merit pay systems be constructed to work better, smarter, and more effectively?

## IV. DESIGNING BETTER MERIT PAY SYSTEMS

We should begin with the assumption that no single system or approach works best for all public organizations. Merit pay systems are very organization-centric, and should take their bearings from the local organization culture, the environment, and what works practically for any particular organization. That said, there are some common patterns of merit pay that we have found that seem to work for many public organizations in some combination. These are highlighted below.

1. Merit pay should be just one component of a pay system, not the sole component.
2. Merit pay should be based on valid performance appraisal instrumentation that measures what employees actually do at work.

3. Merit pay should be significant enough to make a real difference in an employee's take-home pay. This difference should be noticeable and substantive.
4. Merit pay policy should be consistent and be given time to work. Rules should not change dramatically or quickly.
5. Public organizations should expand their conceptualization of "merit reward" to include nonmonetary incentives.
6. Related to Number 5, merit rewards need to be designed for motivating employees that merit pay plans do not ordinarily reach or motivate.
7. Merit pay plans should be extended to group as well as individual performance.

What follows is a brief discussion of each of these seven items with the hope of showing how they can be configured to make a merit pay program more effective. At the same time, the authors caution the reader again that there is no one best way to implement merit pay, and that merit pay should never be construed as a panacea for general organizational problems. How we choose to define merit pay comes from the introductory sentence of this chapter which borrows heavily from Heneman (1992, p. 6). Namely, merit pay is compensation based on the rated performance of an individual for a past period of time. The question becomes how this can be done effectively, fairly, and practically in public organizations.

Based on several consulting experiences, some public agency officials make the bold claim that all pay for their employees is awarded meritoriously. Yet when we delve into what this means, the accuracy of the claim almost always diminishes substantially. In the first place, most public organizations utilize multiple compensation components for determining the pay of their workers. These normally include such elements as

Market rates and pay grades,
Cost-of-living adjustments,
Internal equity adjustments to pay,
Skill-based pay,
Automatic step increases (seniority), and
Individual merit pay increments.

Market rates are normally assigned to benchmark jobs. These rates are used to develop pay grades for different jobs, and the level of pay considered externally fair (Wallace and Fay, 1988). Public organizations could not even attract or retain good employees if they did not pay market rates. It is important to note that market rates have nothing to do with the performance of individual employees. They pertain primarily to benchmark jobs.

Most employees feel that they should receive some type of cost-of-living increase in typical years, just to stay even with the changing economy. Many public organizations use various kinds of consumer price indices for measuring cost of living, and typically give employees some annual pay boost based on this statistic. Again, this makes sense and is very popular among employees. Yet this has little to do with employee performance. It is simply given to all employees according to a fixed percentage rate that is added to their existing salary base.

Internal equity adjustments are another feature of compensation that is becoming more common. Internal equity involves how valuable a job is for a particular organization based on its factors of importance rather than the market. Some jobs may be very strategic to an agency's mission: they may require complex skills and they may involve supervision. All these internal values may escalte the worth of a job for a particular agency.

By measuring internal worth through such techniques as job evaluation, organizations can develop statistical models for determining predicted pay for a certain level of internal value. This enables the organization to develop policies for paying some jobs more than the market would bear based on internal value. This kind of compensation can address inequities that have been historically linked to gender or some other factor, where although the work is highly valued, it receives less attention in the external market (nurses, secretaries, and teachers, for example). Like the external market, internal equity adjustments are based on the value of a "job" not the person in the position. Individual merit plays little if any role here.

Skill-based pay is yet another way of adding components to a pay system that reward employees for achieving new skill levels. Examples would be public works employees learning how to operate new equipment or cross-training for other jobs. Another would be teachers who earn a master's degree in a specialized area. These employees by expanding their knowledge become more valuable to the work organization via the acquisition of new skills.

Automatic step increases represent the kind of annual pay increase management has trouble with but most employees like the best. These systems reward an employee essentially for being on the job and for seniority rather than performance. Usually employees are bumped up a step or two once or twice a year as long as their job performance is satisfactory. Employees like this increase because they perceive it as predictable, consistent, fair, and stable. They can plan on it. It is a pay increase not connected with any risk other than performing satisfactorily. Managers do not like it for many of the same reasons employees prefer it. Managers feel it over rewards low performers, it is taken for granted, it is not linked to performance, and that it is a give-away.

Typically, but not always, cost-of-living and step increases account for the largest share of an employee's annual pay increase. This leaves some wriggle room for merit pay increases, which are the only increases based solely on rated or scored performance. In the work organizations the authors have researched and consulted with, the merit component is typically small, amounting to maybe 10 or 20% of the annual increase. But is this all that bad?

Given the problems associated with merit pay highlighted earlier, it may be wise to not place too much emphasis on merit pay as a major component of a compensation program. Employees perceive it as risky, it is highly changeable, the rating instruments are perhaps subjectively and perceptionally biased, and not enough resources may be available anyway for it to make a big difference. We recommend that merit pay be a component of a compensation system, but remain a small part, where the higher up the hierarchy an employee resides, the more emphasis is given to merit pay. That said, we feel a mixed compensation system, utilizing the elements commonly found in most pay systems is the more practical way to go most of the time.

It is obvious that performance appraisal instruments used for evaluating employees should be reliable and valid. They should be job related and possess a high dose of face validity. Normally, the kinds of instruments that reflect these technical specifications involve either behavioral measures or management by objectives (Latham and Wexley, 1981; Daley, 1998; Bernardin and Beatty, 1984). More typically, the kinds of performance instruments found in many public organizations are of the trait system type. Here raters are asked to judge employees according to their degree of perceived dependability, innovativeness, citizen contact, and work attitude among other traits.

In an annual classroom exercise we request students to bring samples of the performance appraisal instruments from their work or intern organizations. Invariably, the majority of these are trait instruments with a scattering of MBOs and or behavioral measures. Most are very simplistic where the same instrument is utilized across many different job lines and in some cases, serves as a one-size-fits-all instrument for a public agency's positions.

As stated above, trait instruments possess very low interrater reliability and, therefore, are technically invalid instruments for measuring employee performance. The same employee could be rated differently by several supervisors on the same criteria. Moreover, these instruments possess weak to nil job relatedness. For example, some assess an employee's "leadership" for jobs that do not require any specific kind of leadership. This is unfair, because such employees are probably scored low on this measure when in fact they do not perform any leadership tasks. Nonetheless, trait instruments remain popular and common, why might this be the case?

It is our hunch that trait instruments are common because they are so easy to construct. A person could design a trait-based performance instrument in little less than a day. Also, they are convenient because one trait instrument can be applied to a wide variety of jobs. Hence there is no fuss with job relatedness issues. One instrument does everything. Finally, a manager can stretch the argument that at least some traits do measure important "good citizenship" behaviors that may be job related, such as "comes to work on time," or is a "team player." Thus it is the very simplicity and ease of implementing trait instruments that may account for much of their continued popularity and frequency, in what would otherwise be considered generally sophisticated, progressive public organizations.

We feel this is a big mistake. These instruments can be easily abused either intentionally or otherwise and can generate employee distrust toward management's performance measurement systems. They lend themselves to error, bias, and unreliability. No wonder many public employees dislike being evaluated. It may be they just do not want important personal compensation decisions that greatly affect the quality of their lives based on flawed instruments.

We encourage organizations to design specific instruments for each job along behavioral and or MBO lines. This chapter is not constructed to go into these possibilities in any detail, but we feel enough research and utilization of these options exists so that public organizations should have no trouble developing them.

The next element in an effective merit pay system involves the size of merit rewards. They need to make a noticeable difference (Heneman, 1992). Again, this may sound simple but frequently, incentive pay rewards are so small they have virtually no motivating effect and may even be counterproductive. One way to increase the perceived size of a merit reward is to give it in a lump sum. The authors have worked for organizations where lump sum bonuses range from about $1000 to over $5000. By giving the bonus as a lump sum, the employee receives the benefit of his or her performance all at once. This can have an impact on any employee's financial condition. We feel this makes better sense than stretching out a merit increment over time to a point where the increments are so small, they are hardly noticeable to the employee.

Where the merit raise becomes an addition to an employee's base salary, we have found through our survey research that employees need between six and eight percent increases in base pay for them to take notice. Obviously, this can be quite expensive, and may be a reason why bonuses have become popular. Bonuses must be earned every year. They are generally a lump sum based on one's performance appraisal score. This has the added benefit of allowing topped-out employees in a pay range to receive extra compensation for outstanding work, without blowing the pay ranges within their work organization. In short, the pay must make a noticeable difference for it to motivate employees.

Perhaps one of the more difficult needs for making merit pay successful in the public sector involves the stability and consistency of merit pay "policy" over time. Too often, merit pay becomes a pawn within the budgeting process, and is redesigned frequently to meet financial rather than motivational requirements. So, how can public organizations improve on this score?

First, public organizations should spend considerable initial effort in designing the general merit policy and link this to absolute rather than relative standards. By this, the authors mean linking merit pay payouts to specific score or performance levels that are uniform, stable, and consistent over time. Once this linkage is made, the merit increment connected with different levels of performance should be reasonable enough to make a difference to employees, but not so large that they become annual budget gaming targets. If the merit component of a compensation system is kept reasonably small, say twenty of the total, this should not be a problem. Then, when employees score at a specific performance level, they have knowledge of their approximate merit payoff.

A second suggestion is to train all supervisors responsible for rating on the details of the merit pay policy. In this way, there is a common core knowledge and interpretation of the rules. Many managers claim ignorance regarding the content of their organization's merit pay policies and, consequently, often give employees erroneous or contradictory information. This should be a resolvable problem via training and clearer communications. One further step would be to train employees about the policy and how it works. This would demystify the merit policy process.

A third suggestion is rather simple. The public agency should realize that in the first year or two of implementation, most merit pay systems will face unanticipated problems, and will engender some employee resistance. No matter how elegant a merit plan is, no matter how much preplanning was involved, unexpected problems and issues will arise, guaranteed. To deal with these nascent troubles we recommend that the public organization make fine-tuning adjustments as necessary, but fundamentally to stick with the plan for at least two to three years before assessing its success or lack thereof. Merit plans need time to gain employee acceptance. They are often the target of skeptical comments by employees unsure of the outcome. Thus the organization needs to practice patience and allow the plan to be fine-tuned so that over time it can become accepted. Alternatively, many public organizations make snap decisions to terminate merit pay plans at the first whiff of employee resistance or lack of acceptance. Then they try something new and different only to arrive at the same result. Merit pay requires patience, patience.

One possibility is that a public organization is truly faced with a budget emergency, and therefore needs to zero out any funds budgeted for merit pay during a specific fiscal year. If this happens, one suggested solution is to utilize a rolling average performance appraisal score so that employees who score high on performance during merit-payless years, are not completely unrewarded once the budget allows for merit payouts in subsequent years. This concept is not difficult to implement and evens out an employee's performance appraisal score over two to three years. This reduces the stress associated with having a good year go completely unrewarded.

There is one related concept that can help stabilize merit pay plans for the public sector that does not directly involve dollars. Namely, the organization can develop noneconomic incentives that nonetheless motivate employees and reward them for high performance (Gabris and Giles, 1983).

The idea here is to identify various noneconomic incentives that would motivate employees in the absence of monetarily based merit pay. For example, many public employees are motivated by extra time off. If extra vacation time could be made available to high performing employees, or possibly accummulated for a payoff at retirement, this might be sufficient to motivate employees enough to maintain high levels of productivity or to even increase current levels of output. Nonmonetary incentives should never become the sole basis for reward, but could supplement and augment relatively skimpy merit pay pools. It provides public organizations with an alternative that few have endeavored to develop, yet could help make the difference between a marginal and successful plan.

The ideas connected with noneconomic incentives also raise possibilities for motivating perpetually low performers who do not appear motivated by traditional merit pay plans. Research and applied programs dealing with this specific motivational problem are sparse. Often managers find themselves dealing with severe work attitude problems with some employees where the easiest strategy is to just ignore them. This only reinforces their behavior and can allow it to spread to other employees. What might one do with poorly motivated workers?

Leader member exchange (LMX) theory offers one plausible solution (Graen and Uhl-Bien, 1995). Managers need to include employees typically associated with informal "outside" groups at work, as "insiders." Insiders are given special perks, extra assignments, and autonomy. Their job satisfaction is usually high. Outsiders are given only assigned work, they are not trusted, and, in turn, they can become chronic complainers. By including more employees in the inside group managers may reduce the number of discontents to a less dysfunctional level. Furthermore, good behavior and performance for these borderline employees needs continual reinforcement. Many probably suffer from low esteem and the attitude that "they cannot achieve hard goals even if they try." They need to learn that this is not the case, and that they can achieve complex goals if they learn to focus.

To reinforce constructive behavior and attitudes, managers need a bundle of incentives at their behest to reward this kind of employee more frequently. Again, various noneconomic or low-cost incentives might work, such as time off for good work, special perks connected with advanced training, positive management attention, and more autonomy on the job. This may also mean these kinds of employees need more frequent performance appraisal and quicker feedback on how well they are doing. If they are doing well and improving, they should be rewarded.

Although this concept deals only indirectly with traditional merit pay, it addresses a flaw in merit pay patterns where only the best performers are rewarded. Management should anticipate that by rewarding only high performers, many average to low performers may become disaffected and develop bad work attitudes. This strategy provides one practical way for dealing with this possibility.

Finally, most traditional merit plans reward individual not group performance. Yet in many public organizations, not only is group performance easier to measure, it also reflects more of the actual type of work in which most public employees routinely engage. In the private sector, rewarding group productivity has been more commonly done, and is referred to under a variety of labels such as the Scanlon plan (Moore and Ross, 1978) and gainsharing (Graham-Moore and Ross, 1990). Very little is written on this type of group reward concept in the public sector even though it offers some interesting possibilities (Gabris and Mitchell, 1985; Jarrett, 1990).

The basic gainsharing concept runs something like this. Suppose governmental unit B in Agency X has budgeted $100,000 for project ABC, and that 10 employees work for unit B. Assume unit B has been exceptionally prudent and creative in how it pursues and accomplishes project ABC to the extent that the total costs for achieving this goal amount to $80,000. Using a simple 50/50 split formula, $10,000 would go back into Agency X's budget coffers and $10,000 would be set aside as a group bonus for the employees in unit ABC. If divided equally, each employee would receive an additional $1,000 bonus. By encouraging creative thinking, efficiency, and smart project implementation, all members of unit ABC are rewarded. Presumably, this would be a sufficient and noticeable incentive to maintain high levels of group performance that would save Agency X money. Unfortunately, few public organizations use this kind of gainsharing for many of the reasons cited below.

Perhaps the biggest red flag that gainsharing "appears" to raise involves budget overestimates that make it seem the unit is saving money when, in fact, the unit has more money than it actually needs from the start. In short, units have fat in their budgets. By accomplishing a project for less money than was budgeted risks giving the appearance to policy makers that the unit has been systematically inefficient, and should not receive as much money from year to year as it has been. Thus being efficient carries the paradoxical risk of making it appear that a unit is inefficient.

Others contend that any savings, meaning all savings, need to be returned to the agency and perhaps to the taxpayer as a rebate. If projects can be accomplished for less money, why should the public spend more than it needs to for getting the work done? By providing a group bonus, the public would be subsidizing performance that should be occurring anyway. Therefore, group bonuses should not be necessary for nurturing high levels of group performance.

Even though these problems may exist, it is hard to dispute the fact that much of the work done in public organizations is produced by intact work groups and project teams. Indeed, extracting out of team-based output the contributions of isolated individuals for merit pay rewards may be much more difficult than identifying the level of group performance. What we may need are tools and measurement systems for identifying group output more clearly and how these high performance efforts save the taxpayer money. Should these be rewarded? Our answer is in the affirmative. Rewarding group productivity is essentially no different from rewarding individual performance with merit pay. Why should the individual receive more recognition than the group? Many individuals could not achieve their high output without group support-yet the individual, rather than the group, normally gets all the credit. If we reward individuals for high performance it seems that rewarding effective teams may be equally valid, and would go a long way toward invigorating potentially lethargic bureaucratic organizations. The fact that we have not done this does not mean it is impossible, but that we have not yet created innovative mechanisms for accomplishing this. Rewarding group performance may be the future of merit pay in the public sector, we just need to learn how to do it and do it well.

## V.  CONCLUSION AND SUMMARY

We have argued in this chapter that merit pay is likely to continue to be a tool in the arsenal of management techniques used to motivate public employees and improve productivity, even though it possesses numerous warts and problems. Merit pay is perceived by many as a mechanism for ensuring employee accountability to important policy goals and performance expectations. Merit pay is viewed by many as a "fair" way of rewarding public employees, and alternatively, as an effective tool for punishing the deadwood.

Whether merit pay does in fact accomplish these objectives is open to debate. But as Heneman (1992) contends, perceptions about merit pay may be more important than the realities. If elected officials and policy makers think it works and does improve performance, this may be a sufficient reason for continuing it even if the association between merit pay and increases in employee performance are fuzzy at best. Merit pay simply sounds too good not to be true. Thus we in the public sector will likely see many new and improved merit pay plans that replace earlier models that faltered. Public managers need to brace themselves for this eventuality.

Our recommendation is for public administrators to take the offensive in this matter. By designing innovative new merit pay plans that potentially use noneconomic incentives, combine monetary with nonmonetary incentives, or reward outstanding group performance, public managers may stay ahead of the curve. The key for success also involves designing carefully balanced compensation systems that provide sufficient incentive for high performance, but that also reinforce job security, skill development, and even to some degree, seniority in service. Merit pay should only be one facet of a more comprehensive compensation package available to employees. Finally, public managers should realize that traditional merit pay systems are unlikely to reinvigorate low to moderate performers and somehow magically transform their behavior. It may be necessary to target innovative programs that appeal to these employees for this purpose. Will all of this happen?

Our surmise on this point is pure conjecture, but speculating on the future generally fits at least some portion of an academic's job description. Our general response is that merit pay reform will continue to occur almost endlessly, but unless more fundamental reforms occur in basic bureaucratic structure, then the great majority of merit pay innovations will slip through the cracks. This is not a new argument nor necessarily ours. Robert T. Golembiewski has been making this same argument for over 40 years and counting.

As Golembiewski (1995) sees it, those who hallow the current bureaucratic state (Goodsell, 1994; Wamsley et al., 1990), and those who wish to hollow it (Osborne and Gaebler, 1992) share a common flaw. Namely, they retain classic bureaucratic structure as the organizational vehicle for accomplishing their mission. As long as bureaucratic structure persists it will repeat over and over the same problems it has always experienced. These will impede merit pay reform.

Bureaucratic structure by definition creates rather narrow and specialized job descriptions. Over time, employees learn all they can and experience little room for either vertical or horizontal growth. They adapt to this by possibly abandoning their need to grow (Hackman and Oldham, 1981) exhibiting relatively low energy levels. Specialized units compete over scarce resources, communications become inefficient and laborious, and a shutdown in any one specialized unit can essentially shut down the whole system. Bureaucratic structures work reasonably well in stable environments where tasks are routine and the technology is relatively simple. In more turbulent environments a flatter, less bureaucratic type of structure seems to work better (Golembiewski, 1995; Lawrence and Lorsch, 1967).

Wherein does the future of merit pay reside? Perhaps a rephrasing of a Winston Churchill aphorism best describes this future and present. Never has so much fuss been made about a type of pay for so many public employees that has produced so few meaningful results. Moreover, we may get merit pay right in the end, but not without first exhausting all other possible alternatives.

## REFERENCES

Adams, J. S. (1965). Injustice in social exchange. In: Berkowitz, L., ed. *Advances in Experimental Social Psychology*. New York. Academic, pp. 267–299.

Adams, S. (1996). *The Dilbert Principle*. New York: Harper Collins.

Bernardin, H. J., Beatty, R. (1984). *Performance Appraisal: Assessing Human Behavior at Work*. Boston: Kent.

Daley, D. (1998). Designing effective performance appraisal systems. In: Condrey, S., ed. *Handbook of Human Resource Management in Government*. San Francisco. Jossey-Bass, pp. 368–386.

Gabris, G. T. (1986). Can merit pay systems avoid creating discord between supervisors and subordinates: Another uneasy look at performance appraisal. *Rev. Public Person. Admin.* 7:70–90.

Gabris, G. T., Giles, W. (1983). Improving productivity and performance appraisal through the use of non-economic incentives. *Public Product. Rev.* 7:173–191.

Gabris, G. T., Mitchell, K. (1988). The impact of merit raise scores on employee attitudes: The Matthew effect of performance appraisal. *Public Person. Manage.* 17:369–387.

Golembiewski, R. T. (1995). *Practical Public Management*. New York: Marcel Dekker.

Goodsell, C. (1994). *The Case for Bureaucracy*. Chatham, NJ: Chatham House.

Graen, G. B., Uhl-Bien, M. (1995). Relationship based approach to leadership: Development of leader-member exchange (LMX) theory of leadership over 25 years: Applying a multi-level multi-domain perspective. *Leadership Quart.* 6:219–247.

Graham-Moore, B., Ross, T. (1990). *Gainsharing: Plans for Improving Performance*. Washington, DC: BNA Books.

Hackman, R., Oldham, G. (1981). *Work Redesign*. Reading, MA: Addison-Wesley.

Heneman, R. (1992). *Merit Pay*. Reading, MA: Addison-Wesley.

Ingraham, P., Ban, C. (1984). *Legislating Bureaucratic Change*. Albany, NY: SUNY Press.

Jarrett, E. J. (1990). Gainsharing and the Government Sector. In: Moore, B. G., Ross, T. L., eds. *Gainsharing: Plans for Improving Performance*. Washington, DC: Bureau of National Affairs, pp. 174–193.

Latham, G., Wexley, K. (1981). *Increasing Productivity Through Performance Appraisal*. Reading, MA: Addison-Wesley.

Lawler, E. (1983). *Pay and Organizational Development*. Reading, MA: Addison-Wesley.

Lawrence, P., Lorsch, J. (1967). *Organization and Environment*. Boston: Harvard Business School.

McGregor, D. (1957). An uneasy look at performance appraisal. *Harvard Bus. Rev., May-June*, 89–94.

Moore, R., Ross, T. (1978). *The Scanlon Way to Improved Productivity*. New York: Wiley.

Osborne, D., Gaebler, T. (1992). *Reinventing Government*. Reading, MA: Addison-Wesley.

Rosen, S. (1985). Implicit contracts, a survey. *J. Econ. Lit.* 23:1144–1175.

Schachter, H. (1989). *Frederick Taylor and the Public Administration Community*. Albany, NY: SUNY Press.

Thayer, F. (1978). The President's management "reforms", theory X triumphant. *Public Admin. Rev.* 38:309–314.

Vroom, V. (1964). *Work and Motivation*. New York: Wiley.

Wallace, M., Fay, C. (1988). *Compensation Theory and Practice*. Boston: PWS-Kent.

Wamsley, G., Backer, R. N., Goodsell, C., Kronenberg, P., Rohr, J., Stivers, C., White, O., Wolf, J. (1990). *Refounding Public Administration*. Newbury Park, CA: Sage.

# 28

# Nonmonetary Incentives for Productivity Enhancement

**ROE ANN ROBERTS**
*Midwestern State University, Wichita Falls, Texas, U.S.A.*

## I. INTRODUCTION

This chapter reviews a number of nonmonetary approaches to productivity enhancement in the workplace. A survey of over 700 human resource professionals conducted by the Society for Human Resource Management (SHRM) found that businesses are shifting from designated benefits, such as sick leave and vacation leave, to more flexible offerings such as telecommuting and flexible scheduling (Paul, 2001). Identifying those offerings that meet employees' needs is essential.

To be successful, nonmonetary approaches to productivity enhancement require managers to display a increased concern and understanding of what motivates their employees. This concern is especially important in an ever-changing job market. In 2001 job cuts were estimated at 1.6 million. These cuts have an impact on both the remaining and the laid-off workers' motivation and commitment to the organization. Managers must quickly remotivate these workers or suffer a large economic and psychic drain on the organization until these employees' energies can be productively rechanneled. Yet theory X-style managers continue to hire motivated workers who are excited about working for the company, then treat them like wayward children, and then simply replace them when they become less motivated and lose their high commitment levels (Harter, 1997). This "personnel practice" only makes sense if the following conditions are true.

1. There is no cost in training new workers.
2. A limitless supply of trained and highly motivated workers exists.
3. Constant turnover does not have a negative impact on morale.

Unfortunately for theory x-style managers, none of these conditions exists, nor have they ever truly existed, in the job market. So it makes more sense for the manager to strive to revitalize those employees who have lost their motivation. According to Jefrey Saltzman, that accounts for about ninety percent of all employees (Gladstone, 2001). Some ways to increase motivation and improve worker productivity are to (Blanchard, 1989; Anonymous, 2001) survey workers and establish what motivates them; provide employees with information about the organization and their place in it, especially financial data; give employees meaningful responsibilities such as allowing them to make decisions that affect their own work; rely on employees' judgments and trust them to do their jobs; look for and praise things workers do well; reward desirable behaviors; and provide education and training that build careers and job knowledge. Applying these seven approaches to improving employee motivation may save the agency both time and money, two pressures that both public and private agencies often face. A number of other internal and external pressure exist that have fueled the drive to identify nonmonetary approaches to productivity enhancement.

## A.  Forces Affecting Increasing Productivity Pressures

The recent emphasis on enhancing productivity arises in part from internal and external pressures that have a negative impact on productivity. Historically, managers have used financial incentives as tools to increase productivity. Yet, as Maslow and others have demonstrated, motivation often is derived from nonmonetary incentives once the basic needs of survival have been met (Hertzberg, 1959; Maslow, 1943).

Systems theory identifies a number of external forces that influence an organization (Sylvia et al., 1985). A review of these forces reveals a number of items affecting the organization's drive to increase productivity, including:

1.  Economic pressures to cut costs and increasing competition from imported goods;
2.  Legal issues relating to equity and environmental impacts such as the 1990 Clean Air Bill and the Americans with Disabilities Act;
3.  The changing culture in America;
4.  Technological changes such as fax machines, computers, and the Internet;
5.  Increasing demands for more and better education;
6.  Specialization needs due to increasing technological dependence;
7.  Politics;
8.  Social changes stemming from the influx of Asians and Hispanics and their cultural mores;
9.  Demographic changes such as the aging and feminization of the American workplace; and
10. The expansion of the European Commonwealth and the breakup of the Warsaw Pact.

Several of these external forces are the direct result of societal changes. These societal changes in turn have increased the pressures within the organization to alter the organization's structure and behavior to better respond to these changes. When faced with these complex problems a systems approach offers the manager a way to rationalize the current situation and practices and suggests directions for improvement (Stewart, 2001). Some of these pressures have resulted from employee turnover created by cost-cutting efforts and increasing demands for enhanced quality and productivity; client complaints as the formerly unheard and often pliant masses increasingly exercise their civil rights; and increasing employee litigation due to cost-cutting efforts and complaints of discrimination based on race, sex, sexual orientation, disabilities, and age. Naisbitt and Aburdene (1985) and Ackoff (1974) pointed out that there are many significant changes occurring in society, which will continue to have an impact on the structure of organizations for decades to come.

The forces for change that have been explored in this chapter are only a few that are, or will be, influencing the American workplace in the next decade or more. Having established that the need for change exists, if productivity is to be enhanced, managers must appreciate the amount of support that currently exists for these changes.

In 1988, attitudinal questionnaires were sent to a random sample of 1000 union workers in the United States. Data collected from the respondents indicate a desire for work environments that include some degree of worker participation, productivity bonuses, teamwork, and employee training and retraining programs. The questionnaires seemed to show strong philosophical support for such work environments, especially from managers and recently hired workers. The majority of those surveyed support the types of changes which will be necessary to develop the proposed work environment (Premeaux et al., 1989). A more recent study found that the more opportunities workers had to participate in workplace decision making the higher their job performance. (Sako, 1998).

The four approaches discussed in this chapter, systemwide, or departmental, analysis, organizational ombudsmen, quality circles, and job description analysis and redesign, are intended to provide managers with methods that can be used to change the present work environment by reevaluating the job tasks as well as the work environment. The process of reevaluation and assessment will allow the manager to eliminate existing and potential problems, thus improving productivity and decreasing worker dissatisfaction.

## II. SYSTEM, OR DEPARTMENTAL, ANALYSIS

System analysis is a commonly used device designed to implement computerization in the work environment (Waters and Murphy, 1983). Waters and Murphy's approach has been modified in this chapter to better suit the goal of increasing productivity by enhancing work performance. Analyzing the organization or one of its departments serves a number of purposes, as it allows the manager to identify employee dissatisfaction, backlogs, and gaps between departmental and organizational goals.

It will also set the groundwork for productive change and enhanced employee involvement within the organization if the committee's results are acted upon in good faith. This approach can be used in establishing quality circles or organizational ombudsmen.

### A. Steps in System, or Departmental, Analysis

System, or departmental-level, analysis is composed of a number of steps.

1. First a committee should be developed composed of workers from the department(s) to be analyzed as well as one or two administrators. The committee goals should include increasing productivity and job satisfaction.

Roberts

2. In order to achieve these goals, data must be collected by the committee. Collecting data may mean conducting

    a. Employee interviews/surveys,
    b. Tracking job tasks to identify backlogs,
    c. Reviewing current paperwork trails, and
    d. Obtaining the mission statement with each department's goals and objectives.

3. Problem spotting, identification, and formulation should be carried out by the committee as it gathers these data. This step can be accomplished by identifying recurring employee complaints and dissatisfaction; identifying why job backlogs are occurring; identifying incomplete, unnecessary, or repetitious paperwork; identifying any discrepancy between the mission of the organization and the departmental goals and objectives.

4. Developing alternative solutions to the problems identified by the committee is another important step in this process. These solutions should be arrived at by consensus and employees should be actively encouraged to make recommendations. The conclusions of the committee should be summarized and presented to top management; after being reviewed by top management, the committee should be notified as to what recommendations will be enacted and which will not be and why not. Management should allow feedback from the committee as to the final decisions.

This fairly simple set of steps (if followed) should set the stage for improving productivity in the work environment by increasing worker morale and involvement along with identifying ways in which to improve the functioning of the organization or department.

## III. ORGANIZATIONAL OMBUDSMEN

The idea behind organization ombudsmen stems from the use of ombudsmen in the health arena as a tool for identifying employee and consumer complaints. Dave Stum, senior vice president at Aon Consulting in Ann Arbor, Michigan, said, "Management expects HR to be the advocate, ombudsman or listener for superior–subordinate issues, one of many roles it plays" (Bredemeier, 2001). However, organization ombudsmen, like health care ombudsmen, should not be wearing several hats; they should be primarily concerned with identifying and solving employee and consumer complaints. To be successful, complaint handling must involve a series of steps or techniques:

1. Identify the nature of the complaint;
2. Investigate it by gathering data;
3. Report the results of the investigation to the interested parties;
4. Develop solutions to the complaint;
5. Implement the solution(s); and
6. Evaluate the solution(s).

These steps are similar to those utilized in successful decision-making processes.

The concern with responding to complaints and attempting to solve them can increase organizational participation by both the workers and the public. It can decrease litigation and promote positive consumer and employee relations. The use of positive reinforcement techniques can also be utilized by management to support behaviors that have been identified by the ombudsman as effective in reducing complaints. This type of reinforcement has previously been proven to result in increased morale and productivity (London et al., 1999). Therefore, organizational ombudsmen can have an impact on three areas in an organization: quality of working life, productivity, and organizational development.

If the organization decides to use ombudsmen, the job should assume a staff or advisory position in the organizational structure, as its objectives are similar to those of the personnel department. If an ombudsman is to be effective, he or she should have close contact with both the clients and the staff.

Many organizations already have informal ombudsmen. They are charismatic leaders who represent their coworkers and voice their complaints to management. The successful manager should become aware of who they are, and generate a productive relationship with them to utilize their input in attempts to increase productivity. Ombudsmen should focus on their communication skills and use a wide variety of behavioral techniques for handling complaints, ranging from passive listening to confrontational approaches. They must rely more on personal charisma than on their position in the organization. Ombudsmen can become part of a sound employee relations program that can have a positive impact on productivity (Rolnick, 1989).

## A. Creating an Ombudsman Program

Creating a new program requires at least four major steps: conducting an environmental assessment, developing program guidelines that match the assessment, outlining the program's position in the organization, and starting up the program and performing periodic evaluations.

The first step in creating an ombudsman program entails conducting an environmental assessment of the organization's power structure and isolating where the program can fit into it without creating power struggles. The next step is to identify the organizational participants, and uncover their attitudes toward this program. Will the organizational climate support an ombudsman program? What are the occupations of the different organizational work groups? What are the organization's expectations, attitude, and commitment to the program? What are worker/consumer expectations, attitudes, and commitment to the program? What communication modes predominate in the organization? How will the program fit into the formal and informal communication channels? Can resistance be expected and from whom? And what potential or current inter- and intragroup conflicts exist in the organization that might influence the program's effectiveness?

After completing the first step in which the organization's environment has been assessed and determined, the next step is to design a program that matches the organizational climate. To do this, a number of items must be clearly identified.

1. What are the organization's goals and objectives?
2. What are its target groups: workers, management, and/or consumers?
3. What is the ombudsman's job description?
4. What are specific complaint areas with which he or she deals?
5. What are the authority limits of the position?
6. What guidelines for confidentiality and information use should apply to the program?

The third step in creating the program should include an outline of the actual structure of the program in terms of organizational authority: line or staff, the total numbers of workers in the program, and the internal communication and authority structure of the program. How does the program support the organization's long-term goals in planning, organizational development, directing, leading, and controlling?

Implementation follows this step, starting up and operating the program. Periodic progress evaluations of the program's effectiveness in terms of morale and productivity should be carried out. Another way of approaching the problem of complaint identification and resolution is through the use of quality circles.

## IV. QUALITY CIRCLES

Quality circles (QCs) are normally groups of 4 to 10 employees doing similar kinds of work. In 1997 26% of managers in a survey reported utilizing QC concepts (Flores and Utley, 2000). A QC seeks to use the expertise of each member in identifying and solving problems related to the work the group performs. As QCs continue to grow in the United States, management needs to better understand how such groups function internally (Sule and Strack, 1983). The Japanese have used small group participation, the main principle behind QCs, with great success.

A survey carried out at Alfred Teves Engineering (South Africa) reveals that the majority of workers desire to do a good job and to make suggestions to management regarding organizational improvements. However, workers feel that although management listens to suggestions, little change is implemented. If QCs are to be utilized they must be part of an organizationwide approach combining top-down and bottom-up management to encourage better communication. The greatest emphasis must be placed on training and communication efforts designed to improve attitudes, knowledge, and skills (Heath, 1989). Almost twenty years after this study, QCs continue to exist in most of the Fortune 500 companies and studies suggest that the financial investment in them has been returned sixfold (Anonymous, 1999).

Before implementing any new program, a number of questions must be answered.

1. What are the organization's goals, values, and culture? How do they "fit" with the concept of quality circles?
2. What work groups and/or individuals are to be included in the quality circle?
3. What are the primary duties of the circle?

   a. What are the allowable topics of the group?
   b. Are confidentiality guidelines needed?
   c. What organizational data might be needed by the circle and how will they be used?

4. How will the circles be structured (e.g., consensus)?
5. What psychosocial aspects are to be considered:

   a. Employee/management expectations, attitudes, and commitment;
   b. Resistance by both workers and managers; and
   c. Handling intra- and intergroup conflicts?

6. Where do the circles fit into the organizational management scheme in terms of planning, organizing, development, directing/leading, and controlling?

Implementation of QCs should only be carried out after these questions have been successfully answered or failure may result. Management should periodically evaluate the effects of QCs on employee motivation and productivity in concert with the involved employee groups.

## V. JOB DESCRIPTIONS UPDATE AND REDESIGN

Evidence from a British study was used to evaluate a conceptual framework entitled quality of working life (QWL). This focuses, in part, on job redesign and employee participation. Although the purpose of QWL is to serve as a humanizing agent in the workforce, the study revealed that job redesign practices are often implemented solely for productivity reasons. Employee participation measures enacted by the companies studied were often designed to increase managerial control (Hales, 1987). Yet, as has been previously discussed, numerous studies have shown that increasing worker participation results in both increased productivity and increased worker satisfaction.

Job descriptions must be periodically updated and jobs must be redesigned in response to both technological changes and workers' needs. Employees should be actively solicited for their input during this activity. This can be accomplished by conducting interviews, surveys, and so forth. Managers must also review and compare current job descriptions against the actual job tasks performed. This can be done through the use of flow charts, flow diagrams, or other types of workload analysis. The results of this review and the employee interviews must then be specified in terms of the types of tasks that must be performed for the position. The job position must be delegated the necessary power and/or influence needed to complete tasks, and the educational requirements of the position must be delineated. The job's position in the organizational hierarchy must be clearly stated and the possibilities for upward mobility afforded by the job must be included in the description.

The second group of approaches focuses on the restructuring of the work environment in order to increase worker satisfaction and to encourage strong social ties in the workplace. These approaches include job teams, flexible job time and telecommuting, employee merit/recognition systems, employee education programs, as well as child daycare and elder care.

## VI. JOB TEAMS = JOB ROTATION AND TEAM BUILDING

The use of team building as a successful productivity improvement program depends on several elements. The first element, communication, means that honest and complete communication must exist between the managers and workers, between the low- and mid-level managers, and between the managers and the customers.

The second element in building a successful job team is based on the organizational and worker commitment to the team. This commitment must be promoted by:

1. Involving workers in goal setting, planning, and other tasks;
2. Making the team's goals measurable and observable;
3. Developing a reward program, and basing it on workers' suggestions for improving both individual and team efforts; and
4. Matching workers and tasks carefully.

The third element is based on allocating time for monitoring progress, recognizing accomplishments, redirecting efforts when glitches occur, and revitalizing the team when energies run low (Deeprose, 1989).

Tektronix Graphics Workstation Division (GWD) is one of several companies that have employed job rotation successfully as a productivity-enhancement tool. Because GWD desired to involve and develop employees in the company's goals, jobs were rotated so that everyone became a coordinator for a week. The company found that communications with vendors improved with the changes, and "breakthrough thinking" led to several significant changes in the company. Julie Vincent of GWD says that flexibility is the key to cost-effectiveness (Mangiapane, 1988).

Enacting job rotation and team-building programs require that the manager survey and identify jobs that can be shared or performed in groups. Once these jobs have been identified, the manager must meet with employees in such jobs and solicit their input and ideas as to how their positions could fit into a team. Techniques for soliciting input include active listening approaches and brainstorming sessions.

Starting with a pilot group of employees, identification of their current levels of productivity and morale is the first step. If the workers have a negative expectancy valence, it is possible that they will make a poor pilot study group. The valence-expectancy model states expectancy is the subjective probability of success (SPS) at a given task. Choosing to work at a task is different from working hard to perform well. Expectancy can be viewed as the individual group member's belief as to his or her ability to achieve in a given situation (Eden, 1988).

If the workers have positive expectations and high morale, a cross-training program can be set up so that each individual can learn the other employee's job. A variety of educational approaches can be used to achieve this end; however, involving workers in the process of training each other should provide a positive boost to their self-esteem.

Once the workers have been cross-trained, they should be encouraged to develop their own team's work schedule. This allows them to share, split, or exchange jobs as suits the team's needs. After a few months the team's productivity and morale levels should be reviewed using surveys, interviews, and productivity studies. Increases in either morale or productivity levels will support further use of this approach in the organization, but only after careful analysis of the jobs being teamed together and the employee temperaments.

## VII. FLEXIBLE JOB TIME AND TELECOMMUTING

The use of flex-time on the job means the manager must establish shift patterns that better suit the needs of the employees. For example, a mother with small children may need to drop them off at a daycare center which may open at 7:00 A.M. and close at 3:00 P.M. Why not have a 7:30–2:30 schedule for this parent instead of the traditional 9 A.M. to 5 P.M. schedule. Or even better, why not a daycare center on site that has hours that match the company's workday? Another approach offered by 25% of companies surveyed was job sharing in which two part-time workers split the job hours in ways that meet both of their needs as well as the company's. These workers could be college students, husband and wife teams, or two workers who can only work part-time owing to childcare responsibilities. Other companies (31%) offered compressed workweeks and/or telecommuting options (37%). In addition, 26% of companies now provide paid family leave beyond the Family and Medical Leave Act (FMLA) minimum requirement (Paul, 2001).

Census figures show that most women no longer leave the workforce after having children. Thus many working women experience conflicts as they try to meet both work and family expectations. In the past, when a child was sick it was assumed that the mother would leave work to care for it as she usually was the lowest salary earner as compared to the father. However, as women's salaries increase, men may also find themselves responsible for fulfilling traditional childcare responsibilities. Or, companies may have to revise existing corporate practices concerning work schedules to meet the needs and expectations of dual-career couples and single parents.

A small but growing number of U.S. companies are beginning to develop responses to the family pressures on their workers by sponsoring various programs designed to help ease work versus family conflicts. To help workers combine parent and employee roles, these companies are providing flexible time schedules and benefits and extended leave programs. Research that has been done in this area suggests that corporate response to family issues can mean reduced absenteeism, turnover, and tardiness, and increased morale, loyalty, and productivity (Spruell, 1986). Merck and Company is an example of one company that sponsors a childcare center near its home office and also offers flex-time. In addition, parents are allowed to work part-time or at home after maternity leave (McKay-Rispoli, 1988).

## VIII. EMPLOYEE MERIT/RECOGNITION SYSTEMS

Rewarding workers who suggest methods that improve the quality and quantity in production is not new. In Britain during World War II, suggestion schemes were widespread and encouraged by the government. Reward programs have other benefits besides increasing production and lowering expenses. For example, workers see themselves as important valued contributors to the organization, not just as merely replaceable cogs in a vast machine. Such programs help to develop mutual respect throughout the organization (Stewart, 1989).

How do we reward workers who contribute to the organization? Studies have shown that employees rank recognition for a job well done higher than raises and pay for performance as a motivator. Productivity improvements occur when companies link the reward programs to clearly defined goals that are achievable for the majority of employees. A reward program must convey the feeling to employees that the company cares about them (Rawlinson, 1988). Employees can be nominated for recognition by managers or by coworkers. Rewards can take the form of public recognition, such as yearly dinners that recognize the top ten workers who have contributed to the organization that year, or special parking places with their names on them.

Rewarding workers who increase their individual productivity can also be useful to management. In 1974, Union National Bank of Little Rock (UNB), Arkansas, utilized B.F. Skinner's principles of behavior change to solve productivity problems. Using Skinner's approach, the bank identified several problem areas: punitive management, long-delayed rewards, salary separated from performance, group pay-offs, workers rewarded for "busyness," lack of feedback, and, finally, arbitrary work standards. Using three workers as subjects, the bank identified the highest producer each week. The productive worker was congratulated each week, and in six weeks' time, performance had increased 200%. This system was then applied to another department with the same results (McNally, 1988).

## IX. EMPLOYEE EDUCATION AND WELLNESS PROGRAMS

Managers are responsible for creating a work environment in which the worker's full potential can be developed. This environment must offer clear challenging goals to the workers that are supported by sound education programs. Successful development of this environment can only happen if the manager recognizes that employee motivation, productivity, and commitment can be achieved only if open communication, interpersonal trust, and acceptance exist. To gain the worker's support in creating this environment, individual needs in the form of a sense of belonging, identity, accomplishment, and self-esteem must be met. Meeting individual needs requires honest communication. This communication will enable workers and managers to gain a better understanding of each other's needs and will reduce organizational alienation. Part of the process of creating this new open work environment is the need to eliminate significant demotivating factors, including minimal job training, lack of clearly defined goals, lack of performance feedback, inefficient work areas, environmental distractions, and monotony (Anonymous, 2001).

The creation of clear challenging goals can be accomplished if communication and training occur. Tellabs has committed itself to an ongoing training program of 80 to 120 hours each year, along with $7000 in tuition assistance. Education programs offered by some companies may include health promotion classes that focus on stress reduction and diet (Shen et al., 2000). Two ways to encourage better training are using the flex-time concept to allow workers to attend college or technical courses, which will qualify them for promotions, and developing inhouse programs, which will allow workers to perform their jobs more efficiently and/or qualify them for promotions. Workers who complete programs or courses should be recognized for their accomplishments. Managers also must keep in mind that the workers' opinions and attitudes toward either of these two types of programs will be strongly influenced by the groups to which they belong, and that credibility is essential if morale is to be maintained (Honeycutt, 1989; Anonymous, 2001).

## X. CHILD DAYCARE AND ELDER CARE

Women traditionally are the primary caregivers in the United States. As such they are often solely responsible for caring for young children and frail elderly relatives. However, about 17% of men also perform childcare duties according to the 1995 census. In addition, as of 1997, 5.5 million children resided with their grandparents, double the number in 1970 (Alford, 2001). However, even though women are still the primary caregivers, they also account for over half of the labor force.

In 1990, 60% of mothers with young children were working (Houppert, 2001). As working mothers continue to enter the workforce in increasing numbers and little federal support exists for childcare, organizations are either supplying or looking for childcare alternatives for employees.

Studies have shown that the shortage of good child daycare is probably the most pressing problem for working parents. Moreover, there is the problem of juggling time schedules and the accompanying stress. Guilt and anxiety also can affect many working parents, guilt resulting from the need to leave the child in daycare and anxiety as to whether the child is receiving proper care (McKay-Rispoli, 1988). One of the oldest corporate daycare programs in New England was created in 1971 and is located at the Stride Rite Corporation (Lawrence, Massachusetts). Stride Rite executives responded quickly when they realized the negative effects this guilt and anxiety could have on worker morale and productivity. A few years later Stride Rite again set the standard when it began offering elder care as well.

It's unclear how many companies have followed Stride Rite's lead and now offer on-site daycare. An early survey conducted in 1987 by the U.S. Department of Labor found only 2% of all companies provided on-site daycare, but most of the top 25 companies identified in a recent employee satisfaction survey in Chicago now provide this benefit or one like it (Shen et al., 2000). Another survey found 24% of companies allow parents to bring children to work in emergency situations, and 13% provide emergency/sick childcare (Paul, 2001). Private sector companies seem to be far ahead of their public counterparts in this area. The number of public agencies providing daycare facilities was almost nonexistent until as recently as 1989. In the early 1990s daycare centers had just been opened at several federal offices across the country, including Hawaii, Washington, D.C., and Seattle, Washington. However, other firms and public sector employers that do not have facilities available for providing on-site childcare centers provide other services, such as assistance with childcare expenses, referral services (20%), and counseling. It is not uncommon for smaller companies to pool resources and share childcare facilities. In some locations, businesses have formed childcare "consortiums" that, at times, include government agencies (Barnes, 1989; Paul, 2001). Therefore a range of options is available to employers wishing to assist workers with childcare. These options usually include providing on-site child care, supplying information and referrals to community childcare centers, parents permitted to bring children to work in emergency situations, emergency/sick childcare available, partially subsidizing the cost of child care, and/or offering collective child-care programs with other agencies or even private companies.

Linda C. Tout, director of the First Atlanta Corporation's (Georgia) child daycare center, states that close proximity of the company daycare center enhances parents' peace of mind and so enhances productivity (Lydenberg and Beffart, 1984). So, not only the need for daycare, but also its practical application to productivity enhancement is receiving increasing organizational attention. A study conducted at two southeastern textile companies revealed that company daycare centers were positively associated with higher job satisfaction, increased commitment, positive perceptions of organizational climate, and lower absenteeism (Youngblood and Chambers-Cook, 1984). These findings were supported by a study of the Zale Corporation's (Dallas, Texas) on-site childcare center. On-site daycare is coming of age in larger companies. CDW Computer Centers not only offers on-site childcare facilities but also a $3000 bonus for adoption assistance. Tellabs new headquarters will include a daycare center for 200 children, and Motorola combines on-site daycare with flexible schedules to meet the needs of its workers (Shen et al., 2000).

Even though many companies that sponsor childcare and elder care centers must subsidize them, the company receives benefits in the form of lower employee turnover, an improved corporate image in the community, and increased employee loyalty. Zale's center was carefully planned to provide a sense of teamwork between parents and staff. However, all of the studies on child daycare are careful to point out that not all agencies or businesses would benefit from providing on-site childcare facilities. A cost–benefit study must be done to determine whether such a program is viable in each individual case (Romaine, 1982).

Funding for daycare centers may often be supplemented by outside sources. Red Rope Industries (Bristol, Pennsylvania) opened a childcare center in 1972. At that time the company did not qualify for federal funding for the center, but did qualify for a 50% corporate tax credit through the Neighborhood Assistance Act. Another study by Abt Associates (Cambridge, Massachusetts) found over 10% of employee needed child daycare, so the company decided to participate in founding a child daycare center. The Abt Associates' center opened using employee-donated care time each week, and with partial company subsidies in 1972. Abt still partially subsidizes the center, but it is now open to the nearby business community members as wel (Fooner, 1981). Recent changes in the tax laws may provide new financial impetus for companies to open new, or improve existing, company-sponsored daycare facilities. In 2002 employers who provided on-site childcare received a 25% tax credit, up to $150,000, to pay for the expenses of renovating and staffing childcare facilities (St. Pierre, 2001). In addition to the cost factor, there are also issues of liability, regulations, and equity involved in establishing daycare operations.

The average charge for elder care services is about $140 a week. Many workers who are now entering their most productive years will find themselves facing this financial burden, along with the emotional stress of finding quality daycare for their frail elderly parents. More than 22 million households now care for an older person (Franklin, 2001). Corporate executives are recognizing that as the workforce ages (the mean age in America in 1999 was 35.5 years) so do their parents. As a result, 19% of companies now offer elder care referral services and some offer additional services for elderly dependents, 5% provide emergency elder care and 2% provide company-supported elder care centers (Paul, 2001).

## XI. CONCLUSIONS

A decline in productivity is not only a labor problem, but also a failure of management. The key to improving productivity is a radically improved attitude toward human resource management. Human resource management must be an integral part of every organization's planning. A systematic management approach that uses feedback and positive reinforcement must be developed which arises from a sincere desire by management to create a partnership with the workers. Organizations must focus on the long-term prosperity of the company rather than quick dividends. That is, management must become future oriented.

## REFERENCES

Anonymous. (1999). Quality circles are alive and well. *Office Syst.* 16(2):12.
Anonymous. (2001). What drives employee satisfaction? *Community Bank* 10(7):42–43.
Ackoff, R. L. (1974). *Redesigning the Future*. New York: Wiley.
Alford, R. (2001). More grandparents bring up babies. The Associated Press, July 25th.
Barnes, R. (1989). Childcare grabs benefits spotlight. *Nat. Underwriter (Property/Casualty/ Employee Benefits)* 93(15).

Blanchard, M. (1989). Motivating people to top performance. *Exec. Excell.* 6(6):11–12.

Bredemeier, K. (2001). Job loss creates doubts, worries about rights. On the job. The Washington Post, E01, June 25th.

Brown, C., Reich, M. (1989). When does union-management cooperation work? A look at NUMMI and GM-Van Nuys. *Cal. Manage. Rev.* 31(4):26–44.

Deeprose, D. (1989). Three key elements of a productivity improvement program. *Supervis. Manage.* 34(11):7–11.

Dilks, C., Croft, N. L. (1986). Child care: Your baby? *Nation Bus.* 74(12):16–24.

Eden, D. (1988). Pygmalion, goal setting, and expectancy: Compatible ways to boost productivity. *Acad. Manage. Rev.* 13(4):639–652.

Flores, G.N., Utley, D.R. (2000). Management concepts in use—a 12-year perspective. *Eng. Manage. J.* 12(3):11–17.

Fooner, A. (1981). The bottom line on day care. *Inc.* 3(5):94–102.

Franklin, M.B. (2001). On-the-job aid for caregivers. Kiplinger's Person. *Finan. Wash.* 55(8): 82–84.

Gladstone, R. (June 3, 2001). Motivating workers in uncertain times. *New York Times.* Late ed. June 3.

Halcomb, R. (1986). Women at work. *Incent. Market.* 160(4):72–80.

Hales, C. (1987). Quality of working life, job redesign and participation in a service industry: A rose by any other name? *SO Serv. Indust. J.* 7(3):253–273.

Harter, N. W. (1997). The shop floor Schopenhauer: Hope for a theory-X supervisor. *J. Manage. Educ.* 21(1):87–96.

Heath, P. M. (1989). The path to quality achievement through teamwork plus commitment. *Int. J. Qual. Rel. Manage.* 6(2):51–59.

Hertzberg, F., Mausner, B., Synderman, B. (1959). *The Motivation to Work.* New York: Wiley.

Hitchings, B. (1985). Today's choices in child care. *Bus. Week* 2888:104–108.

Honeycutt, A. (1989). Creating a productive work environment. *Supervis. Manage.* 34(11): 12–16.

Houppert, K. (2001). Working moms, then and now. *Parenting* 14(10):74–75.

LeRoux, M. (1985). Youth marketing-for-profit centers open doors to daycare. *Ad. Age* 56(12):30, 32–33.

London, M., Holt Larsen, H., Nellemann Thisted, L. (1999). Relationships between feedback and self-development. *Group Organ. Studies* 24(1):5–27.

Lydenberg, S. D., Beffart, M. (1984). Who's taking care of the children? First Atlanta "comes in first" with daycare. *Nat. Assoc. Bank Women J.* 60(3):11–16.

Mangiapane, A.R. (1988). Empowering people to improve a process. *Manufact. Syst.* 6(1): 18–24.

Maslow, A. H. (1943). A theory of human motivation. *Psychol. Rev.* 50:370–396.

McKay-Rispoli, K. (1988). Small children: No small problem. *Manage. World* 17(2):15–16.

McNally, K. A. (1988). Compensation management in practice: Managing the workplace for maximum productivity. *Compen. Benefits Rev.* 20(5):13–17.

Naisbitt, J., Aburdene, P. (1985). *Reinventing the Corporation.* New York: Warner.

Nordstrom, R., Rucker, G., Hall, R. (1988). Performance management in city government: A case study. *Public Person. Manage.* 17(2):159–165.

Paul, P. (2001). Flexing our options. *Am. Demograph.* 23(7):10–12.

Paull, J. (1986). How to boost productivity—Put a nanny on your payroll. *Canad. Bus.* 59(3): 122–123.

Premeaux, S., Mondy, R. W., Bethke, A., Comish, R. (1989). Managing tomorrow's unionized workers. *Personnel* 66(7):61–64.

Rappaport, M. (1984). Childcare comes of age. *Manage. World* 13(10):30–32.

Rawlinson, H. (1988). Make awards count. *Person. J.* 67(10):139–157.

Rolnick, A. L. (1989). Shape up or ship out. *Bobbin* 30(8):122–128.

Romaine, M. F. (1982). Zale's corporate child care program. *Tex. Bus. Exec.* 8(1):20–25.

Sako, M. (1998). The nature and impact of employee "voice" in the European car components industry. *Hum. Res. Manage. J.* 8(2):5–13.

Schwandt, D. R., Hillman, L. W., Bartz, D. E. (1989). Clarifying performance expectations. *Supervis. Manage.* 34(11):17–21.

Shen, T., Zivan, D., Mongomery, C. (2000). The best places to work. *Chicago* 49(10):100–111.

Shields, M. I. (1985). Childcare. *Inc. Madison Ave.* 27(3):76–82.

Spruell, G. (1986). Business planning for parenthood. *Train. Devel. J.* 40(8):30–35.

St. Pierre, N. (2001). Daily briefing—Tax reform with a feminine accent. *Bus. Week Online.* July 25th.

Stewart, I. (1989). Worker reward schemes. *Manage. Decis. (UK)* 27(4):80–81.

Stewart, J., Ayres, R. (2001). Systems theory and policy practice: An exploration. *Policy Sci.* 34(1):70–94.

Sule, D. R., Strack, D. E. (1983). Analyzing the quality circle process using GERTS III. *Indust. Manage.* 25(4):7–13.

Sylvia, R., Meier, K., Gunn, E. (1985). *Program Planning and Education for the Public Manager.* Monterey, CA: Brooks/Cole, pp. 2–17.

Thomas. (1989). Productivity improvement through people: Some new approaches. *Manage. Decis. (UK)* 27(4):55–65.

Tiner, T. (1985). Kids at work. *Executive (Canada)* 27(7):24–29.

Waters, K., Murphy, G. (1983). *Systems Analysis and Computer Applications in Health Information Management.* Gaithersburg, MD: Aspen.

Youngblood, S. A., Chambers-Cook, K. (1984). Child care assistance can improve employee attitudes and behavior. *Person. Admin.* 29(2):45–46, 93–95.

# 29

# Training and Development for Productivity

**MONTGOMERY VAN WART**
*University of Central Florida, Orlando, Florida, U.S.A.*

## I. INTRODUCTION

The wave of government reinvention in the 1990s brought many opportunities to the public sector to rethink how it does business. At its best, the wave of reform in its many guises—quality management systems, team-based government, reengineering, the New Public Management, the learning organization, and the like—brought needed freshness, innovation, and opportunities for radical reforms in select areas. Yet as often as not, reinvention efforts in the 1990s led to failed attempts at administrative reform, partially dismantled systems with nothing to replace them, and more confused cultures with less coincidence of espoused and practiced values. Although it is dangerous to generalize across the tens of thousands of public sector jurisdictions in the United States, it seems that more often than not training and development in the public sector fall in this latter category of unmet expectations and unfulfilled opportunities. It remains to be seen whether the reinvention of training is simply taking longer than anticipated, or whether it is hopelessly stalled. To use Kurt Lewin's (1951) classic metaphor of change, it is as though training had accomplished an "unfreezing" but has been unable to accomplish the "change" phase, much less the "refreezing" of the successfully implemented new practices and values.

Some examples might help. The quality management reform preached a systems approach to problems, and what could be more a part of the system than training, and yet training more often than not was disenfranchised or privatized in the 1990s. Establishing team cultures takes a great deal of acculturation over time that must have substantial training support but examples of such support are exceedingly rare. Reengineering was never even taught in the public sector, requiring those interested (primarily executives) to go to private sector training programs to learn how to do it. The New Public Management preaches a new entrepreneurial and/or competitive spirit in the public sector, yet this spirit has rarely occurred (with some notable exceptions) in training circles. The single most important reform for our purposes is the learning organization because it is a knowledge- and learning-based conceptualization of excellence. It changes the emphasis (for high-performing organizations that already have technical competence under their belts) from basic forms of learning to advanced forms. Yet to date, there may only be a few handfuls of organizations in the public sector that could seriously lay claim to that title.

There are four challenges, then, for organizations that want to use training and development for greater productivity.[1] Training and development must be used more strategically, which in turn, will mean a tactical overhaul of most training systems themselves. Training systems must be assessed, both for what they can do currently and what they should do in a robust organization bent on producing both routine operational quality and flexibility and innovation in operations and programs. Also, because almost all of the reform initiatives being undertaken require more decentralization, empowerment, job expansion, and power sharing, more broadly trained employees are necessary. Technical skills are no less important but advanced general skills (e.g., skills formerly largely restricted to supervisors and systems analysts in the past but now devolved to line workers) will need a greater emphasis. This occurred initially with the wave of TQM programs in the early and mid-1990s but has fallen off dramatically. In addition, the more strategic use and design of training systems, and a broader training agenda, cannot detract from a renewed emphasis on training basics. Organizational and training systems may change over time but human nature and how people learn do not. Core learning and teaching principles need to be reinforced. Untutored trainers, most often, are poor trainers. Finally, there also needs to be a reemphasis on curriculum and instructional design as training programs and systems are rebuilt. This is particularly true with new emphases on self-training, certification systems, and higher levels of accountability as well as immense changes in technology that are often poorly understood and thus badly used.

With these four challenges in mind, we now turn to a review of organizational learning needs, organizational competency clusters, individual learning needs, and individual training methods.

## II. ORGANIZATIONAL LEARNING NEEDS

In keeping with a productivity orientation, we start with organizational needs—that is, strategic needs—and move to individual needs, rather than vice versa. This section starts with the strategic questions that can be asked from an organizational perspective. Next it looks at the types of learning that occur and divides learning into two tiers, basic and advanced learning, each of which is further divided into less and more sophisticated levels.

### A. The Strategic Assessment

As always with strategic planning, the assessment phase is the most important. Without the right questions and good data, how can good decisions be made? Five questions are proposed here. Each should be asked with skepticism because ongoing systems frequently "make do" for such a long time that more robust questioning is unaccustomed.

*What is the Quality of Training?* This is a technical question and needs a technical analysis. Generally the assessment is made primarily based on user perceptions or training evaluations. This is a good place to start but it is hardly sufficient. In fact, sole reliance on user perceptions will warp the training system over time. Equally important are the evaluations of supervisors and those interacting with the trainees after the training. This information is not difficult to get, either through interview or survey methods. Still another dimension of quality that can really only be accurately assessed by experts is curriculum and instructional design from a technical point of view. The basics of such an analysis are reviewed in the last two sections of this chapter on individual learning needs and training methods.

*How Appropriate Is the Training That Is Being Offered?* No one sets out to offer inappropriate training, but it is remarkable how training quickly becomes dated and loses vibrancy because of trainer substitution. Is the training as work-related as it might be; for example, is it embedded with the cutting-edge issues affecting the organization? Is accountability appropriately distributed to both trainees and trainers? Do trainees have learning thresholds to meet? What performance measures of individual learning and the training's effect on organizational productivity are in place? Although knowledge, skill, and performance assessments are generally unpopular with both trainees and trainers, they are nonetheless powerful motivators for participants and useful data for those seeking to improve training programs.

*Are the Resources and Support Adequate for the Training System?* Needless to say, all systems can use more resources in their quest for improvement or excellence, but the chronic underfunding of development activities in the public sector with its heavy personnel-driven workload makes this question pressing. Executives who believe that the training is truly strategic to their goals, whether that is operations improvement, morale boosting, or cultural realignment, are more likely to fight for increased budget allocation. Senior managers, too, are more likely to reallocate their scarce resources. This may even mean decisions to sacrifice personnel lines for the increased productivity of fewer employees; that is, putting more dollars into fewer well-trained people. This question becomes especially important for those organizations ready to ascend an entire level. At one end of the spectrum, a remarkable number of small or decentralized agencies (e.g., towns, counties, special districts, etc.) have little formal training at all and need to establish a baseline of basic training, sometimes in concert with other entities because of critical mass and expertise. At the other end, a relatively small number of organizations have well-established and articulated training systems and are able to consider "evolving into" a learning organization with the relatively lush development resources that it takes to be one.

*Is the Suitability and Substitutability of Training Properly Balanced?* For any given problem, training may be the correct, partial, or incorrect response. More training on a bad procedure may help in the short term but largely misdiagnoses the problem. More training to correct inefficiencies that are driven by perverse incentives (e.g., caseloads judged entirely by volume without having counterbalancing accuracy measures) is largely a wasted effort. Furthermore, sometimes training may be a suitable response but a substitute might be more effective. The classic example here is in recruitment.

Why spend the time and expense of long basic training and education programs if the marketplace already has sufficient applicants with such experience? Because of constant market shifts in this regard, the agency may need to review recruitment as regularly as the training program itself.

*Does the Training System have the Requisite Comprehensiveness or Complexity for Its Current Stage of Development?* To answer this question takes a big picture perspective. Are different types of training available both for organizational and individual learning needs (addressed immediately below)? Are there different learning structures for both informal and formal needs, as well as based on worker locations, time constraints, learning styles, and the like? Are the elements of the system easily understood by its consumers and is it well publicized?

## B. The Tiers of Learning

One way of assessing the training system in a strategic analysis, especially the issue of comprehensiveness, is to look at tiers of learning that may be met in an ascending order of learning needs. The two tiers, shown in Table 1, are basic and advanced learning.

*Basic learning* occurs primarily by acquiring basic knowledge and skills and dominates much of the literature and our thinking about training and development. It can be further divided into the routine level and the professional level. New initiates to

**Table 1**   A Synopsis of Basic and Advanced Tiers of Learning

| TIER 1: Learning by acquiring basic knowledge |
|---|

1.   Learning by using study and practice (such as technical knowledge, skill acquisition, basic interpersonal skills, basic problem solving)
    Routine learning
    Professional learning (more sophisticated basic learning)

| TIER 2: Learning by expanding, creating, or transmitting knowledge |
|---|

2.   Learning by sharing
    Teaching
    Discussing
    Teaming
3.   Learning by comparing
    Systematic examination of past personal experience
    Systematic examination of others' experience
    Experimentation
4.   Learning by systems thinking
    Quality management
    Reengineering
5.   Learning by competing
    Goal setting
    Striving and risk-taking
    Learning through failure
6.   Learning by suspending disbelief
    Challenging standard ideas
    Playing with new ideas

first-tier learning may be thought of as the young child, the first-year student, the pre-service MPA student, the new trainee, or inexperienced user of technology. Still in the basic learning tier but at the high-performing end of the continuum are those at the professional level who are seen, after long periods of hands-on learning and experience, as craftspeople, masters, and operational experts.

We learn by acquiring knowledge and practicing skills throughout our lives. In the world of work, this is especially true of the vast areas of technical material that we must routinely master. Technical material includes the content area in which we specialize (e.g., law enforcement, social welfare, health, land management, etc.) as well as the processes by which we apply that knowledge: laws, regulations, organizational policies, and job requirements. Technical information doubles every seven years according to many experts and is clearly increasing at a faster and faster pace. Today, unlike the past in which most basic learning was completed by the end of formal schooling, we must continue to learn throughout our lives if we are not to become obsolete.

Underlying the acquisition of knowledge and skills today are the basic competencies of reading, writing, computation, listening, and oral communication skills. We often think of these skills as learned in primary school and mastered in secondary school. However, research indicates that many in society are functionally illiterate and never successfully gain these basic competencies. Those in adult education know that many adults have let their basic learning skills atrophy and have lost much of their learning confidence. Those returning to school take some time to reacclimate and regain assurance.

Because the proficiencies of knowledge and skill acquisition are so extensive, only a few are mentioned here. Rehearsal strategies are those techniques in which individuals repeat and review information (or skills) to move them from short-term memory to long-term memory. Some rehearsal strategies include subvocalization, simple note-taking, drill, discussion, and memorization. Most knowledge and skills do not "stick" without some rehearsal strategies, although highly adept learners may be unaware of their own extensive use of them. Elaboration strategies make connections with new information and prior knowledge. Such strategies focus on testing connections by paraphrasing and summarizing, relating examples to personal experience, taking "full" notes, and by expanding information and connections through questioning. Organizational strategies are those that work at connecting the information in ways that are personally meaningful. They involve clustering techniques at a simple level to mental maps at a more sophisticated level. Monitoring strategies involve the discipline of making sure that learning occurs as expected, so that learning modification can occur if it does not. Such strategies include "self-questioning about the nature of the task, consciously focusing attention on a task, giving positive self-reinforcement during the process, and realistically coping with error and correction" (Carnevale et al., 1990, p. 52). Good learners and trainers are consciously aware of the need for rehearsal, elaboration, and organizational and monitoring strategies, and they build opportunities for them into the learning experience. The ability to "absorb" information and skills is almost totally dependent on their use.[2]

The differences between routine training and professional training (also commonly referred to as continuing education) are a matter of sophistication rather than a matter of kind. Experts still acquire knowledge and refine skills, but at a higher level of complexity and intricacy. Public agencies are full of programs that are for mature professionals who are reviewing bodies of knowledge and practice areas for up-to-date information, detailed explication of rules and policies, and cutting-edge solutions to operational issues. Indeed, continual learning needs to take place at this level for a lifetime, without even considering advanced learning. Yet despite its fundamental importance and the new emphasis on lifelong learning, this is widely bemoaned as an area that is weaker than it should be (Holzer, 1995, pp. 441–444; Cohen and Eimicke, 1995, p.xvi).

The basic tier of learning, including both the routine and professional levels, is roughly what Argyris and Schön (1974, 1978) call single-loop learning or what Senge refers to as personal mastery. Without knowledge and skills we cannot be experts, and to give them their due, public bureaucracies generally excel at acquiring expertise (Weber, 1946).

The next tier, *advanced learning*, goes beyond simple knowledge and skill acquisition to involve learning that expands, creates, and transmits knowledge (Garvin, 1993). There are many images used in second-tier learning such as perfecters, improvers, adapters, and innovators, and at a still more high-performing level, artists, inventors, applied researchers, and scientists. The two levels within this tier can be thought of roughly as problem solvers at the simpler level and as systems designers at the more sophisticated level. This tier of learning involves four of Senge's five disciplines for learning organizations and is what Argyris and Schön referred to as "double-loop" learning. The five types of learning that are included in this advanced tier are learning by sharing, comparing, systems thinking, competing, and suspending disbelief (Van Wart, 1997).

Learning by sharing is particularly powerful in the affective domain, which is often the gateway to the other two domains of learning, cognitive and psychomotor. Affective learning is where we learn to believe in and value some things as opposed to others and therefore is generally a key to motivation. Learning by sharing takes a number of forms including teaching, discussing, and teaming. Learning by teaching is contrary to what we intuitively assume, that is, that we learn by being taught. However, teaching generally forces people into more advanced modes because it requires teachers to be clear, logical, and organized; to practice themselves and anticipate problems; to respond to questions; to see things through others' eyes; and even, as the old saying goes, to know things backward as well as forward. Learning by discussing is one of the most important forms of advanced learning because it leads to the discovery of nonroutine problems, anomalies, contradictory perspectives, hidden assumptions, and complementary ideas. Learning by teaming was introduced as an antidote to excessive hierarchical tendencies in organizations in the 1980s, and became popular in the 1990s (Katzenbach and Smith, 1993). Learning by teaming encourages high levels of trust, shared purpose, mutual responsibility for learning, and performance discipline.

Learning by sharing is particularly important for organizations experiencing rapid process and product changes, because many changes must be shared and collaboratively overcome, without being slowed down by excessive organizational structures. Thus both team-based and project-based organizations are especially sensitive to this mode of advanced learning.

Learning by comparing is the basis of the scientific method that compares the past with the present (various types of time series), the "normal" with deviations and anomalies, and, in some restricted setting, control groups with experimental groups.

From these comparisons come hypotheses about the relationships of phenomena, which subsequently can be proven, disproved, or modified by further systematic observation. Given the tremendous success of the scientific method in modern history, there can be little doubt of its power. Three types of learning by comparing are worth stressing here. Learning by systematic examination of past experience refers to one's own experience, whether that is defined as the person, group, or organization. People who take the time to reflect and compare events in their lives (e.g., the performance data related to their work), with a discipline to act on what they discover, generally perform with higher quality and accomplish more. Learning from systematic observation of others' experience is commonly called benchmarking in the management literature (Bogan and English, 1994). Although benchmarking can have a number of meanings, the most common refers to comparison with industry leaders whose performance is among the best. The idea is not to discover the single best procedure or method and implement it intact; the idea is rather to compare differing successful strategies, find those that are most compatible, and modify the best practices to suit the unique situation of the recipient (Light, 1994). Learning by experimenting is indeed a robust form of comparison, but it is not always possible. Individuals and/or organizations perform experiments by changing a practice and measuring the change, such as a change in an intake procedure or technology, with both experimental and control groups.

In all these types of learning by comparing, several guidelines are important to remember. First, comparing does little good if at the end of contrasting, the objects of comparison have been allowed to become too contaminated with numerous extraneous influences because such contaminated information can actually lead to the wrong conclusion. Second, a strong initial commitment to use the results provides a great impetus to conduct the comparison well in the first place, and to use the learning derived from the comparison afterward. Too often comparisons are for the sake of information rather than action.

Systems thinking is the hallmark of advanced learning for Peter Senge who makes this "discipline" the one that fuses all the other advanced forms of learning "into a coherent body of theory and practice" (Senge, 1990, p. 12). Systems thinking is the antidote to tunnel vision, turfism, stove-piping, and other bureaupathologies that accrue from overspecialization of function and responsibility. Despite the contributions of specialization in the past, contemporary organizational learning finds it more often than not a major inhibitor (Kettl, 1994). Senge and Kettl are not alone in urgently calling for a greater emphasis on systems thinking. The quality management movement is a form of systems theory that is easily seen in the work of Deming, Crosby, Juran, and others. Even the reengineering craze in the United States in the mid-1990s had as its base the radical realignment of organizational processes to conform to a systems rationality, in contrast to incremental improvements which can actually do more harm than good (in the worst cases) by concealing poor systems design (Hammer and Champy, 1993; Hammer, 1995; Champy, 1995; Mechling, 1994). Ironically, front-line workers and middle management were encouraged, until recently, not to take a systems approach. Executives and senior managers were the strategists, planners, and systems thinkers; others could not hope to see the "big picture" and need not try. Instead, workers and most lower managers were expected to specialize and focus on the task at hand, which was normally a small piece of a much larger process. The bulk of problem solving was generally done at a senior level or by systems analysts. Negative side effects for other departments or areas were often of little consideration. The problem with this mindset for the contemporary organization is that the changes are typically too many, too fast, and too technical to keep up with for a few senior managers and design experts. Furthermore, customization of response is an increasing priority and can only be done by a widely practiced systems-oriented mentality, not by strict regulations and work/decision protocols designed to protect the system from its own employees.

The ability to learn through competition is captured by the expression "necessity is the mother of invention" and through the underlying capitalistic belief that competition causes innovation and creativity to flourish in the long-run. What Rosabeth Moss Kanter noted for the last decade still holds true, "The question most appropriate for the 1990s is not *what* the competitive world organization should look like but *how* to become one" (Kanter et al., 1992, pp. 1–2). Competition can lead individuals to learn by requiring them to determine what they want to achieve, by driving them toward that achievement or level of excellence, and by creating both incentives for succeeding and disincentives for floundering. Competition itself can be broken down into a number of component parts including goal setting, striving and risk-taking, and failing. Setting goals can be likened to competing with oneself. Numerous studies have indicated the power of goal setting to produce results, especially the motivational effect of hard realistic goals (Carnevale et al., 1990, p. 235). Learning by striving and risk-taking are newfound (or at least newly re-discovered) qualities for most of the public sector. However, given the widescale policy and management reforms that are being promoted, modest risk-taking is considered a normal part of the learning and adapting process (Levin and Sanger, 1994, p. 147). Examples include pilot projects, demonstration projects, higher performance goals, and competitive bidding (among the services that public agencies themselves offer). Risk-taking suggests that not all ventures will succeed, whether because of planning, implementation, or simply bad luck. People must not only be willing to learn from success but failure as well. As Somerset Maughan once said, "Only mediocre people always succeed."

Of all the modes of advanced learning, none is more commonly discussed, but more difficult to do, than suspension of disbelief. This mode of learning requires the ability to suspend current beliefs about the proper way to do something, the proper way to value, or the nature of truth. We unquestioningly use habits, routines, and belief systems most of the time or we would need to go back constantly to first principles. Yet some of the greatest learning is by seeing the world afresh, discarding (at least temporarily) our mental models, and trying out new ideas, perceptions, and beliefs. Most great scientists and inventors are masters at this type of learning, which leads to changes in old dysfunctional routines and discovery of new patterns or ways of doing things. However, this mode requires an ability to tolerate ambiguity and messiness that is contrary to the orderly notions and discipline that are normally prized (Balk, 1995; Wheatley, 1992; Mintzberg, 1994). One way that suspension of disbelief is demonstrated is through the challenging of one's own mental models when there is evidence that there are new ways of operating, a new environment requiring a new mindset, or problems that seemingly cannot be resolved through current pro-cesses. Although such a tack is motivated by the need to change, another tack is to play with ideas simply for the fun and creativity of the act. Both of these mindsets can be augmented by strategies such as brainstorming (in which critical observations are temporarily suspended) and visioning (in which nonexistent ideal futures are imagined).

Although an examination of organizational learning needs is useful at the most strategic level, organizational needs can and should be examined from a more operational perspective as well. Like individuals, organizations must have competencies to carry out their business. It is to a competency perspective that we now turn.

## III. ORGANIZATIONAL COMPETENCY CLUSTERS AND TRAINING TYPES

Organizations have various types of functions that they must perform and in the training and development literature these are generally known as types of training (Van Wart et al., 1993). There are three metacompetency clusters: technical training, general skills training, and management training.[3] No strategic analysis of an organization would be complete without an assessment of the strengths and weaknesses of the various types of training or, in some cases, an assessment of the types of training that are altogether absent.

### A. Technical Training

Three types of technical training are identified here: procedural, mechanical, and professional. Procedural training focuses on laws, codes, rules, or procedures that are required for compliance with agency mandates and for coordination and flow of work. It is sometimes called operations or administrative training. The most common type of procedural training is new-employee orientation that focuses on employee benefits and agency policies. Some of the other common types of procedural training cover topics such as agency overviews, personnel procedures, selection/hiring procedures, promotional guidelines, discipline rules, procurement processes and warehouse requisitions, security systems and safety procedures, travel policies, audit procedures, grievance protocols, diversity training, sexual harassment training, employee appraisal systems, and so on. Procedural training tends to focus on information and practice more than on skill building per se. It also tends to have broad audiences and tends to be scheduled for relatively short time periods. In the very smallest organizations procedures training is generally done on the job by the supervisor; however, as organizations become larger, the need for formalized procedural training increases because of the complexity of the organization's operating systems. The challenge of procedural training is to be sure that it does not rely solely on lecture.

Mechanical training (also known as mechanical-technical training) focuses on how things operate, how they are built, how they can be fixed if broken, and how they can be maintained. Manual or physical skills are a large part of the training. One of the most common types of mechanical training is training on computers, such as learning word processing programs, graphics packages, spreadsheets, and customized data systems for the organization. Clerical filing and data-entry jobs usually have extensive mechanical components. Jobs involving equipment and facilities, such as communications, transportation, building, power, and infrastructure jobs, also have extensive mechanical aspects. Many facilities management jobs have mechanical components, including building, repairing, monitoring, and cleaning. In mechanical-technical training the physical ability to do something is as important as intellectual rehearsal of the procedures. A few common examples are: computer classes of all types, the engine repair and maintenance training programs for mechanics at most large agency motorpools, and driving classes for law enforcement officers, fire service personnel, and bus and ambulance drivers. Mechanical training is a frequent part of other types of training and can be quite sophisticated in and of itself (e.g., pilot training).

Professional-technical training focuses on the select knowledge, skills, and abilities needed by practicing professionals in performing their jobs in the public sector. Because professional workers apply principles from mathematics, physical and natural sciences, law, social sciences, administrative science, education, political science, and so on, their training is inherently more theory- and principle-driven than are most types of training. Examples of professional-technical training are less frequent in general training catalogues and tend to be concentrated in technical training bulletins. Examples include most training in the traditional professions: accounting and auditing, law, medicine, architecture, education, engineering, biology and other sciences, law enforcement, fire service, forest and land management, and social assistance disciplines. Professional training has grown with the increasing complexity of society and now includes areas such as risk management, contract management, public relations, financial management, strategic planning, and so on, for both specialists and generalists in these areas.

## B. General Skills Training

Technical skills focus on the specific knowledge to do a specific job, whereas general skills focus on the skills that are needed to do any or many jobs in organizational life. Although most employees come to the organization with adequate basic skills, this assumption must be verified, especially for lower-paying front-line positions, some physical jobs, or when a significant number of employees do not have English as a first language. Basic skills include not only the classic "reading, 'riting, and 'rithmetic" but also basic listening and speaking skills and even some basic advanced skills such as speaking in public and meeting skills. Training in this area is largely remedial in nature; however, some organizations enhance employees' basic skills through courses on speed reading, technical writing, advanced math, and advanced listening (for interviewing and customer service).

Advanced general skills training focuses on making employees more effective outside their roles as subject-matter specialists. General skills training aims to improve employees' ability to learn, to work with others, to adapt, and to be productive. Such training includes courses on learning to learn, interpersonal skills, negotiation, teamwork, problem solving, creativity, goal setting, self-esteem, customer relations, and basic management tools (such as flowcharts, PERT charts, statistical process control, check sheets, etc.). For a long time most of these topics were discussed only in management training classes, if at all. However, with the excellence movement and the quality-improvement revolution, there was an explosion of interest in training all employees in these skills in the public sector in the early 1990s.[4]

## C. Management Training

The last metacluster is management training. Managers at different levels of the organization tend to have different responsibilities and functions and need different competencies (Katz, 1955), therefore, this cluster is divided into supervisory, (middle) management, and executive training. Supervisory skills training focuses on supervisors' direct interaction with subordinates and on getting work done by, with, or through other people. Specific interpersonal skills are one target and so are clearly identifiable personnel processes. Although direct contact skills are of primary importance to first- and second-line supervisors, these skills continue to be important for managers and executives as well. When a new manager comes to a position without benefit of supervisory experience, because of advancement based on professional expertise rather than on management experience, supervisory courses are appropriate. Many of the topics discussed in procedural courses in technical terms become the focus of skills training in supervisory classes. Common topics for supervisory programs are how to evaluate employees, how to conduct selection/hiring interviews, motivating people, delegation, team building, how to coach employees, train-the-trainer, conducting meetings, how to prevent grievances, problem counseling, employee goal-setting and reward systems, communication skills, active listening skills, and confidence building.

Whereas supervisory skills training focuses on specific interpersonal skills (such as progressive discipline) and specific group processes (such as discipline policy) within an organizationally determined framework, management training focuses on complex interpersonal skills (such as labor relations) and interrelated group processes (such as organizational climate) in an attempt to find organizational solutions within a changing and complicated environment. The focus shifts from individuals to groups and from problems of a unit to the management of programs. There is often a focus on the improvement of general analytic skills (as opposed to the specific analytic skills of technical professionals) and the ability to make balanced judgments based on a variety of data sources. Management training has a number of standard topics including administrative leadership, workforce planning, labor relations, program management and evaluation, project management, budgetary and financial planning, risk management, decision making and problem analysis, information management, and so on. Discussions of supervisory topics take on an organizational dimension, so that team building becomes the integration of many teams, delegation becomes the empowerment of employees for increased productivity and creativity, and listening skills become a source of data for diagnosing systemic problems.

Executive development training is the most conceptual, broadest, and most externally oriented type of training. Programs for executives tend to focus on the role of the organization in the public sector environment and facilitate the executives' skills in coping with external opportunities and threats and public relations. Typical courses for executive programs focus on media relations, public speaking and contact skills, leadership and organization assessment (generally with databases collected specifically for the training), transformational and visionary leadership, strategic planning, legislative and lobbying processes, interagency and intergovernmental teamwork, advanced management philosophy, policy analysis, organizational development, and political and social trend analysis.

So far the discussion has analyzed the differences among types of training in order to discriminate among the types of audiences and competencies that are common. But what can be said of the similarities or underlying principles common to all types of training? To find these types of commonalities we turn to the individual's perspective on learning.

## IV. INDIVIDUAL LEARNING NEEDS

Those responsible for designing and implementing learning in the more formal aspects must pay attention to at least three major learning inputs: trainee characteristics, work environment, and learning principles. Trainee characteristics include the knowledge, skills, abilities, and motivation that trainees bring to the training situation. These characteristics are important because they affect the need or lack of need for training, the design of the training, and the output of training. Without an assessment of the training needs of the targeted group, it is easy to make false assumptions in designing training. In the worst-case scenarios, most of the trainees know the specific information in advance of the program. Such assessments are generally best done prior to the program but may also be conducted at the program's beginning to refine the focus. Not only are trainee knowledge and skill levels important, but so too are motivational levels. Highly motivated groups may accept more technical information and more rigorous demands than those less motivated for whatever reasons. Good trainers adjust the sequence and motivational aspects significantly with this prior knowledge.

Nearly as important is the work environment from which trainees come and to which they will return. The work environment affects training in two important ways: through the support that comes from the work environment for training and development activities, and through the opportunity given the trainees to apply new skills and knowledge gained from the training. Certain types of support in the work environment are obvious, including monetary support for training and education, and the potential for promotions and salary increases; other types of support are less obvious such as the status of training, the encouragement to use new skills, and the opportunity to discuss training with supervisors. In the ideal training culture, training inside the organization or opportunities for training outside the organization are well funded (e.g., tuition reimbursement programs), the level of training and education is directly reflected in salary increases (e.g., skill-based pay), training itself is well regarded which leads to significantly higher motivation levels, trainees are required to use the skills learned in the classroom, and supervisors discuss the desired outcomes of training prior to a program and debrief employees upon their return.

## A. Learning Principles

In the actual design and implementation of a training program, some general principles are important to keep in mind in order to maximize the effect and efficiency of training. In substantial training programs, the omission of even one of these principles can lead to dismal results in many cases.

The first principle is the need for *goal setting* which is an important way to focus and enhance motivation (Kim and Hammer, 1976; Wexley and Latham, 1981). The first level of goals includes those that bring the employees into training. These goals may stem from employee characteristics such as belief in training and the motivation to succeed or from work-environment factors such as promotion and salary potential and encouragement by supervisors. Or the goals may be more specific, for example, a need to master minimum required competencies, raise performance to higher standards, gain cross-training for organizational flexibility, or learn about a new technology. The goals also may be developmental, such as the desire to cross-train for career breadth, explore new career opportunities, or explore current state-of-the-art theories and practices. A second level of goals is employed in the training itself. The training program usually will be composed of many learning priorities that should each have a specific learning goal. Instructors call those goals the desired learning objectives.

A second need that is important and significantly more central in training settings than in educational settings is *increasing the similarity of training to the work environment*. Early researchers stressed that if the same stimulus and response elements are in both the training and the job, transfer to the job is more likely, and retention of motor and verbal behaviors increases. This notion is called "identical elements" (Crafts, 1934; Wexley and Latham, 1981). Identical elements can include the conditions of the training program, such as the surroundings, tasks, equipment, and other physical aspects. The term also reflects the degree to which trainees attach similar meanings to the training and organizational context, that is, the psychological identity (Baldwin and Ford, 1988). Increasing similarity between the training and work settings has particular relevance when specific tasks, skills, or behavior are being taught, including relatively simple skills such as machine operation, intermediate skills such as the performance of employee evaluations or the application of procedural discipline, and complex skills, such as negotiation. Three progressive steps increase the similarity of training to the work environment: the use of examples, modeling, and simulation. The use of examples is a cognitive technique that includes simple allusions to applications to full-blown discussions of relevant cases. Modeling is a visual or graphic technique that actually shows the correct behavior to the trainees. Examples of modeling include short demonstrations, skits, and training videos. Simulations are opportunities for trainees themselves to perform the behaviors. Simulations can be nonautomated such as role plays and management games, or automated such as machine and computer simulations.

The third training principle is *using underlying principles*. Underlying principles emphasize universal or generalizeable aspects, and enhance transfer of learning from one training situation to another (Bourne, 1970). Therefore the use of underlying principles is extremely pronounced in educational venues because of the longer durability of the training. However, underlying principles do not, by themselves, teach the specifics that people need to anchor their learning and their more concrete needs. Therefore it is easy to overemphasize underlying principles to the detriment of the learning endeavor. Who has not sat in a training or university class in which the instructor was hopelessly entwined in teaching a set of principles devoid of practical examples or the goals of the audience? Some training is so skill- and task-specific that general principles are omitted altogether such as brief regulation updates or computer training. However, the omission of training principles from most substantial training settings is a fundamental error.

A fourth, surprisingly complex principle, is *increasing the organization of the material* (Gagné, 1962). A brilliant lecture may dazzle listeners, but little may be retained the next day when questions are asked of them unless the structure of the lecture is readily apparent and reinforced. Nor is organization of the material solely determined by logical structure or cognitive attributes. In fact, one of the most common mistakes is excessive cognitive emphasis at the expense of opportunities to rehearse or question. The lecturer who discourages questions "until the end" may not get any, not because the lecture answered all the questions that arose, but because the audience lost interest and the learning moment passed. Thus organization of the material means ensuring that the material makes sense from the learners' perspective, not necessarily from a simple logical flow of material. Indeed, some of the most effective learning designs violate logical flow for the sake of variety, interest, or experience, and still are organized from the learners' perspective as long as the reasons and overall structure are made clear. For example, a training video demonstrating a disastrous appraisal interview might be an excellent attention-getter, followed by a discussion of the correct elements and an eventual analysis of the wrong behaviors seen at the outset. Because there is really no correct order per se, it is the clarity of the learning structure that is critical. Devices that help in this regard are outlines, advanced readings, auxiliary questions, the use of labels and definitions, and occasional assessments of the learners' status through questions or tests.

Although *active involvement of learners* in the learning process has been reemphasized in modern research (Craik and Tulving, 1975), it is actually an ancient learning principle. The Socratic method teaches by using questions to discover truths. It requires the learner to constantly question and probe his or her experiences and understanding. Whether active involvement is stressed as a part of the initial instruction or is stressed separately after instruction, it is basically practice. There are three aspects to involvement that should be considered: manipulation of material, frequency of practice, and timing of practice. Any manipulation of the material will lead to vastly superior recall over no manipulation at all. Examples of involvement include questions and answers, discussions, exercises, small-group activities, and note-taking. Of course the frequency of practice (the amount) is directly related to the depth of learning. Although multiple cognitive exposures quickly diminish in effectiveness, multiple practice opportunities do not and can be used to anchor learning more deeply or enhance skill proficiency under supervision. Finally, the timing of practice can be either massed or distributed, but, in general, massed practice is more efficient, however, it is not as effective. Of course, involvement often takes a good deal more time than straight cognitive presentations and so the balance of principles must be assessed on a case-by-case basis.

Related to, but separate from, learner involvement is *feedback*. The term feedback refers to the knowledge of results of practice (Locke, 1980). If there is no instructor-monitored practice, there can be no external feedback. Practice includes exercises (with answers or oversight), tests, discussions, papers, and in-training observation of behavior in simulation or apprenticeships. Feedback can take many forms. It can be verbal praise and/or suggestions for improvement. It can be test scores, productivity reports, and performance measurements. Feedback can be a subtle physical behavior by the instructor: a nod or shake of the head, a smile or frown, or a pat on the arm. Good trainers tend to look for ways to increase te amount and immediacy of feedback (Yukl and Latham, 1975). Although performance of tasks has an implicit feedback function apart from the instructor, the trainee who receives instructor feedback is likely to outstrip those who are not assisted by this feedback. For example, mentoring is a particularly powerful technique because of the customized feedback on performance that participants constantly receive. Feedback reduces errors, makes training more interesting, enhances motivation, and generally leads to higher standards and better goal setting. As a behavior-shaping tool, feedback in most situations should ideally be emphasized early in training and taper off considerably as the trainee becomes proficient and confident (Komaki et al., 1980).

The final training principle is *using a variety of techniques and stimuli*. By varying techniques, a trainer can engage several of the learners' senses. If a trainee only hears something in a lecture, the chances of his or her remembering (effective encoding) after only a few days are really quite small. If a trainee hears and sees something, perhaps in a lecture and on an overhead, the chances increase that he or she will remember the material. If something is heard, seen, and written down (the tactile sense), the chances of retention increase still more. And if the learner has the opportunity to verbalize the material, the chances of remembering are at their greatest. When different sensory and cognitive channels are used in the learning process, there is a greater opportunity for encoding for all learners and it also seems to enhance interest and motivation. Research has shown that increasing learning task variety (over a constant amount of time) increases learning effectiveness until very small time increments are reached (Duncan, 1958). Excessive variety only becomes a problem because of the increased likelihood of confusion or loss of organization.

## B. Additional Teaching Considerations

Using these teaching principles and common sense, a few additional teaching considerations emerge. First, it is important to remember that not all material needs the same depth, and that depth requires more repetition and instructional variety. By using good instructional design, for example, an instructor will highlight in advance the competencies that require depth and practice in order to build the time into the lesson plan. Too often all material is treated with the same level of depth or superficiality.

Another consideration is that lack of or insufficient practice in skills may mean that when learners do practice on their own, they practice incorrectly. As these incorrect practices become more efficient over time, the behaviors become fossilized and more difficult to identify because of additional coping mechanisms that may be acquired.

A related consideration is that unlearning actually takes longer than new learning. Unlearning may be the result of correcting poor practices or practices that have become outdated but the ramifications are the same. Although learners may cognitively understand the change faster than the new learner, the fossilized behavior is difficult to extinguish physically, and reversion to old practices is psychologically tempting.

Another challenge is that to teach too much may be to teach nothing. Data overload may mean that the learner is unable to organize the material, the underlying principles are lost, involvement and feedback are shunted aside, and that variety is sacrificed. The classic example is a long abstract lecture that covers a great deal of material without much learner input. After a day learners may be hard-pressed to remember the topic, much less pertinent details of the lecture.

Finally, adult learning theory reminds us that in most situations in which adults find themselves, they come with a great deal of information and with specific questions. That means that the principles of shared goal setting, learner involvement, and extensive feedback become that much more important for the mature learner (Knowles, 1980). Indeed, in mature learning situations the learners structure their own learning experiences to answer their own learning interests, only using the instructor as a facilitator or resource.

With these principles and considerations in mind, it is time to turn to more concrete training methods.

## V. INDIVIDUAL TRAINING METHODS

Several major issues regarding training methods are reviewed. First, the structures of training have a great deal to do with how methods are utilized. Second, some of the basics of good curriculum design are discussed. Third, some of the strengths and weaknesses of instructional families are examined.

### A. Training Structures

Organizations that have strong learning cultures pay attention to both the formal and informal training systems. Both are important and can provide a positive synergy for the other. The formal structure includes the classes that are offered (both face-to-face and distance), certifications that require learners to review material and master it even though an instructor may not be present, and licenses that require strict standards of mastery. Informal structures include on the job training (OJT), mentoring, development plans, and learning resources. Because the situations of organizations vary so immensely, from large organizations with corporate universities to small organizations that are barely able to offer a new employee orientation on a regular basis, only questions to ask, rather than precepts to follow, are provided here.

In terms of the formal classes offered, is the organization at a stage where it should offer classes that enhance advanced learning and does it offer them? Has the organization assessed how well it does at offering classes in all the major competency clusters? Do full- and part-time instructors receive assistance in teaching so that they understand the basic principles of learning? Are the classes in the curriculum linked into learning sequences that are readily apparent to learners and which provide motivational inducements (such as a certificate for completing a series)? Are learners and trainers held accountable for the organizational resources that they expend? In general, does the organization have strategies to reward those who learn and monitor those who do not? Does the organization use a variety of formal learning formats and technologies, such as distance learning, for diversity and flexibility? Are expectations of the different types of formal learning situations truly realistic?

In terms of the informal learning system, is OJT a euphemism for by-the-seat-of-your-pants training? Are OJT and formal classes structurally interwoven and supported? Are supervisors and other teaching workers in the field given the tools, training, and support that they need to do a proper job with OJT and mentoring? Are learning goals an active part of individual development plans each year? Are learning resources (learning centers, technical libraries, help desks) set up with contemporary materials and staff support?

### B. Curriculum Design

Although full-blown lesson plans may not always be called for, anyone designing any training or evaluating it needs to know the basics of curriculum design. In a training context, curriculum design is how material is organized to maximize learning. There are four simple elements, all of which are critical for effective curriculum design where robust learning is important.

What are the learning objectives? This seemingly innocuous question is more honored in the breach than in custom. Too often programs and classes teach about and around something rather than teaching to a few tight objectives. Especially in training situations, what will the learners be able to do at the end of the session? Only the briefest sessions should be allowed to inform participants without really engaging in deeper forms of learning.

How will the learning occur (what will the didactic inputs be)? How will the learners receive the information and how many times? For example, will they read a manual and then discuss it with their supervisor, or will they listen to a lecture and then talk about it in small groups as it relates to their own experiences? Will they be exposed to demonstrations or models of ideal or improper behavior? The most common problem here is the lack of enough exposure with sufficient variety in the critical learning competency being targeted.

How will the learners practice the information? Will they have exercises, role plays, simulations, and practice tests? Will these be done under instructor supervision, with peer review, or strictly on their own (perhaps with answer sheets)? Will they have multiple opportunities to practice or only one? The most common problem here is to skimp, or entirely skip, the practice phase because of a lack of time. Yet from the learner's perspective, this may be the most helpful stage. Where time is a critical concern, many strategies can be employed to increase efficiency such as concurrent practice with peers, and self-monitored practice with carefully designed exercises and answers.

What are the performance measures that will be used and to what standard? Will there be a test or demonstration that the learner must perform in order to prove a sufficient level of mastery? The most common problem here is not providing learners with adequate and realistic practice opportunities to understand the test situation before they are in it. However, although strategies such as practice tests are time consuming for instructors, they are powerful learning devices for serious learners.

## C. Instructional Design

Instructional design looks at the specific methods that are used in the didactic input, practice, and performance measurement phases of curriculum design. Different instructional families tend to emphasize different learning principles, so although there is an endless variety of good configurations for good instructional design, there is also an endless variety of bad configurations as well. Six instructional families are reviewed here.

Lecture methods include the standard lecture, team teaching, guest speakers, panels, and student presentations. As a family they are strong at teaching underlying principles and increasing the organization of the material. Used strictly by themselves, they tend to be weak at setting goals, involving the learners, and giving feedback. Lecture methods are a very robust and flexible family but tend to be overused and often lead to excessively instructor-dominated curriculum designs where adult learning strategies would be more effective.

Discussion methods include question-and-answer techniques, large-group methods, small-group methods, case studies, debates, and individual conferences. Strictly by themselves, they tend to be strongest at setting goals, actively involving learners, and giving feedback. They are weakest at increasing similarity and teaching underlying principles. Discussion methods are also very time consuming. Discussion methods are often, and properly, counterbalanced against lecture and reading methods.

Printed materials include auxiliary reading materials, training manuals, and programmed instruction. Their strengths and weaknesses tend to mimic those of lecture methods; they are strong in teaching underlying principles and increasing the organization of the material and weak at setting goals, work similarity, involvement, and feedback.[5] Printed materials have as some of their advantages that they can be used outside of class and that they can be good at providing "anytime, anywhere" flexibility. Solely by themselves learners may find printed materials passive and tiring.

Practice and feedback techniques include note-taking, adjunct questions, individual exercises, demonstrations, role plays, simulations, survey and self-assessment techniques, tests, and site visits. Their strengths are generally in their similarity to the work environment, involvement, and feedback. Their weaknesses are in goal setting, teaching underlying principles, and increasing the organization of the material. These methods are particularly good for the practice and performance phases in curriculum design.

Behavior-shaping methods include coaching, apprenticeships, job rotation, self-training, embedded training, and counseling. These methods have as their strengths setting goals, increasing similarity to the work environment, active involvement, and feedback. They are particularly weak at teaching underlying principles and organizing the material. Today only more robust training systems generally make extensive use of behavior shaping methods, despite the value they contribute to the instructional design repertoire, because of the time and resource constraints.

Technology-based techniques are a category composed of audiotapes, slides, videotapes and films, computer-based instruction, teleconferencing, and various high-end technology uses such as optical discs. They tend to be strong at teaching underlying principles and increasing the organization of the material, and sometimes in increasing the similarity to the work environment. They tend to be weak at setting goals, active involvement, and giving feedback. They are rarely used in standalone situations and are increasingly being incorporated as standard elements in training programs.

## VI. CONCLUSION

Training and development for productivity requires a relatively tough-minded approach that begins with an organizational perspective of learning needs and competency clusters and only then moves to individual needs. It requires asking the tough questions about not only what is desirable to achieve from an organization but also the standards that are necessary and who will be accountable, including the trainees and trainers.

Larger well-run agencies, in particular, have a responsibility to provide more than basic learning opportunities today. They have the responsibility to make sure that there are adequate levels of professional training at the basic level, and that different types of advanced training are offered as well. Another way of looking at the balance of learning types is to make sure that all the major competency clusters are accorded adequate treatment given the maturity, resources, and vision of the organization.

At the individual level, organizations cannot afford to have trainers who are not well versed in basic training principles and precepts. In particular, subject matter experts cannot be expected not to overlook one or more important teaching dicta if not provided with the oversight and support of training experts. Nor can organizations afford not to review their formal and informal training structures to ensure balance and realism. Finally, basic elements of curriculum design cannot be omitted without significant diminution of learning outcomes; nor can curriculum design be properly implemented without a basic grasp of instructional methodology.

As demands for organizations to do more with less increase (Van Wart and Berman, 1999), training and development must be used more strategically and must be required to be well implemented both tactically and structurally. The concept of the learning organization today is popular because it allows for self-learning, self-organizing, and greater flexibility. However, not as apparent is the fact that it is spurred by the pressures coming from competition and speed. In many industries today, organizations that do not learn quickly die. That is indeed a tough performance expectation and one on which the public sector needs to keep its eyes focused.

## NOTES

1. Throughout this chapter the focus is on training and development within one organization at a time, rather than on inter-organizational training (e.g., training consortia).
2. These and other learning strategies are incorporated into the seven learning principles discussed in the section on individual learning needs.
3. In addition to the subtypes identified below, there are some other fundamental types of training omitted because of lack of relevance to this discussion. In employee enrichment training, for example, the focus is not to enhance job performance by augmenting knowledge, skills, or abilities, but is instead on the needs, interests, and well being of the learner. It may or may not have an effect on job performance. Examples include: smoking cessation, first aid, CPR, ergonomics, career development, retirement benefits training, and other lifestyle and health-related topics. It can also loosely include topics that do not specifically relate to the employee's job but are relevant for the organization at large such as public speaking for front-line employees. The more pratical examples of this type of training are included here in general skills training. Yet another example of a type of training that is not generally found in the public sector "industry" is sales training.
4. This trend seems to have since plateaued.
5. Programmed instruction is designed to have more substantial involvement and feedback components but is labor intensive to design and sometimes not well received by adults.

## REFERENCES

Argyris, C., Schön, D. A. (1974). *Theory in Practice*. San Francisco, CA: Jossey-Bass.
Argyris, C., Schön, D. A. (1978). *Organizational Learning*. Reading, MA: Addison-Wesley.
Baldwin, T. T., Ford, J. K. (1988). Transfer of training: A review and directions for future research. *Person. Psychol.* 41(1):63–105.

Balk, W. L. (1995). Managing innovation and reform. In: Halachmi, A., Bouchaert, G., eds. *The Enduring Challenges of Public Management*. San Francisco: Jossey-Bass, pp. 326–347.

Bogan, C. E., English, M. J. (1994). *Benchmarking for Best Practices*. New York: McGraw-Hill.

Bourne, L. E. (1970). Knowing and using concepts. *Psychol. Rev.* 77(6):546–556.

Carnevale, A. P., Gainer, L. J., Meltzer, A. S. (1990). *Workplace Basics*. San Francisco: Jossey-Bass.

Champy, J. (1995). *Reengineering Management*. New York: HarperCollins.

Cohen, J., Eimicke, W. (1995). *The New Effective Public Manager*. San Francisco: Jossey-Bass.

Crafts, L. W. (1934). Transfer as related to number of common elements. *J. Gen. Psych.* 13:147–158.

Craik, F. I. M., Tulving, E. (1975). Depth of processing and the retention of words in episodic memory. *J. Exper. Psych.* 104(3):268–294.

Duncan, C. P. (1958). Transfer after training with single versus multiple tasks. *J. Exper. Psych.* 55(1):63–72.

Gagné, R. M. (1962). Military training and principles of learning. *Am. Psych.* 17:83–91.

Garvin, D. A. (July–August, 1993). Building a learning organization. *Harvard Bus. Rev.* 78–91.

Hammer, M. (1995). *The Reengineering Revolution: A Handbook*. New York: HarperBusiness.

Hammer, M., Champy, J. (1993). *Reengineering the Corporation*. New York: HarperBusiness.

Holzer, M. (1995). The public productivity challenge. In: Halachmi, A., Bouchaert, G., eds. *The Enduring Challenges of Public Management*. San Francisco: Jossey-Bass, pp. 413–448.

Kanter, R. M., Stein, B. A., Jick, T. D. (1992). *The Challenge of Organizational Change*. New York: Free Press.

Katz, R. L. (1955). Skills of an effective administrator. *Harvard Bus. Rev.* 33:33–42.

Katzenback, J. R., Smith, D. K. (1993). *The Wisdom of Teams*. Boston: Harvard Business School Press.

Kettl, D. F. (1994). Managing on the frontiers of knowledge: The learning organization. In: Ingraham, P. W., Romzek, B. S., eds. *New Paradigms for Government*. San Francisco: Jossey-Bass, pp. 19–40.

Kim, J. S., Hammer, W. C. (1976). Effects of performance feedback and goal setting on productivity and satisfaction in an organizational setting. *J. Appl. Psych.* 6(1):48–57.

Knowles, M. S. (1980). *The Modern Practice of Adult Education: From Pedagogy to Andragogy*. 2nd ed. New York: Cambridge.

Komaki, J., Heinzmann, A. T., Lawson, L. (1980). Effect of training and feedback component analysis of a bahavioral safety program. *J. Appl. Psych.* 65(3):261–270.

Levin, M. A., Sanger, M. B. (1994). *Making Government Work*. San Francisco: Jossey-Bass.

Lewin, K. (1951). *Field Theory in Social Science: Selected Theoretical Papers*. New York: Harper.

Light, P. C. (1994). Creating government that encourages innovation. In: Ingraham, P. W., Romzek, B. S., eds. *New Paradigms for Government*. San Francisco: Jossey-Bass, pp. 63–89.

Locke, E. A. (1980). Latham versus Komaki: A tale of two paradigms. *J. Appl. Psych.* 65(1):16–23.

Mechling, J. (1994). Reengineering TQM and work design: An integrative approach to continuous organizational excellence. *Public Admin. Quart.* 18(1):54–63.

Mintzberg, H. (1994). *The Rise and Fall of Strategic Planning*. New York: Free Press.

Senge, P. (1990). *The Fifth Discipline*. New York: Doubleday.

Van Wart, M. (1997). Learning in non-hierarchical bureaucracies: The new learning profile. *Korean Rev. Public Admin.* 2(2):117–147.

Van Wart, M., Berman, E. (1999). Contemporary public sector productivity values: Narrower scope, tougher standards, and new rules of the game. *Public Product. Manage. Rev.* 22(3):326–347.

Van Wart, M., Cayer, N. J., Cook, S. (1993). *Handbook of Training and Development in the Public Sector.* San Francisco: Jossey-Bass.

Weber, M. (1946). Max Weber: Essays in Sociology. In: Gerth, H. H., Mills, C. W., eds. New York: Oxford University Press.

Wexley, K. N., Latham, G. P. (1981). *Developing and Training Human Resources in Organizations.* Glenview, IL: Scott, Foresman.

Wheatley, M. J. (1992). *Leadership and the New Science.* San Francisco: Berrett-Koehler.

Yukl, G. A., Latham, G. P. (1975). Consequences of reinforcement schedules and incentive magnitudes for employee performance: Problems encountered in industrial settings. *J. Appl. Psych.* 60(3):294–298.

# 30

# Rewarding and Punishing for Productive Performance

**RICHARD A. LOVERD**
*Acton, Massachusetts, U.S.A.*

Men are rewarded and punished not for what they do, but rather for how their acts are defined. This is why men are more interested in better justifying themselves than in better behaving themselves. (Thomas Szasz)

What counts is not necessarily the size of the dog in the fight—it's the size of the fight in the dog. (Dwight D. Eisenhower)

The desire of reward is one of the strongest incentives of human conduct...the best security for the fidelity of mankind is to make their interest coincide with their duty. (Alexander Hamilton)

## I. INTRODUCTION

Soon after opening his first plant, Thomas Edison noticed that his employees had a habit of watching the sole factory clock. To Edison, the inventor-workaholic, this sort of behavior made very little sense. Still, something needed to be done to keep employee minds on the job and off the clock. So Edison had dozens of clocks installed, no two showing the same time, in order to cause so much confusion that no one would care what time it was.

Ideally, employees should be so interested in their work that they do not feel tied to a clock; the work itself, the workplace, and the quality of the leaders who supervise them should be so stimulating that time flies by. Unfortunately, as so many of us can attest, reality intrudes and this too often does not prove to be the case. Instead, "lives of quiet desperation," endless self-justification, and low productivity seem to be the behavioral watchwords in the workaday world.

How can managers encourage less mediocrity and more "fight" in their employees with ways that stir them to thrive in their jobs and yield productive results? In this chapter, a number of possible answers to this question are suggested through a review of the reward and punishment strategies that can motivate people. In particular, the needs of employees, and the factors available in the workplace to meet those needs, are presented. Then, attention to the methods of reinforcing performance through rewards is considered, followed by a discussion of the degree to which employees value those rewards and believe they can achieve them. And finally, consideration of the feasibility of such reward and punishment strategies in the public workplace is explored.

As the preceding paragraph implies, more emphasis is placed upon rewards than punishment in the pages that follow. This is so because, as Fox (1979, p. 90) notes, "Punishment is a problematical procedure to use in motivating employees and should be employed only as a last resort." He goes on to suggest that punishable behavior may tend to be repeated when the punisher is absent. Then again, the punisher may be perceived as the "bad guy," with the whole relationship between superior and subordinate jeopardized. Furthermore, the subordinate may seek to retaliate against the superior in any number of ways, from slowing down work to slandering the manager (Kessler, 1974). And in the last analysis, punishment, even when well deserved, tends to be perceived as inherently unfair because "for the few who are caught and disciplined, the many who are equally guilty but undetected go scot-free" (Dowling and Sayles, 1971, p. 133).

By contrast, reward "focuses on what the employee is doing right and contributes to a positive relationship with the manager....[and] Since most people like rewards, they may modify their behavior so that they can continue to be rewarded" (Fox, 1979, p. 91). Therefore, where possible, it makes sense to emphasize rewards over punishments in managerial writings and actions.

## II. WHERE THE WORKPLACE HAS ITS OWN REWARDS

### A. Maslow's Hierarchy of Needs

Employees bring certain needs to the workplace which, in the process of being met, can spur them to do productive work. Perhaps the most popular and useful of theories describing those needs is the one articulated by Maslow some years ago (1943, 1954). As Raymond Miles (1975, p. 135) notes in his study of reward systems, Maslow's work is suitable because it is

> ...widely known ... and because it is highly relevant for the sort of explanation we are attempting here. We are not using it because it is a proven theory—in fact, recent studies have not lent precise support to the concept. Neither, however, has anyone else provided a more plausible explanation of human needs, and Maslow's explanation does exhibit a certain amount of face validity.

In his work, Maslow suggests that people seek higher and higher levels of need satisfaction through a five-level conceptual "hierarchy of needs." Starting from the lowest level, he assumes that human seek to satisfy the most primitive and urgent of human needs first and then, having met them, look for satisfaction from higher and higher levels of need. Those levels, in ascending order, begin with (1) physiological needs, followed by (2) safefy needs, (3) the need for belongingness and love, (4) the need for esteem, and (5) the need for self-actualization.

Physiological needs refer to such basic bodily needs as food, shelter, warmth, water, and sleep. Although most jobs satisfy these most basic of biological requirements, all of us have probably gone to work hungry or in need of sleep at one time or another and been reminded of their debilitating effects.

Once having met the physiological needs to a significant degree, safety needs provide the next rung to reach on the hierarchy. These kinds of needs would include actual physical safety as well as the feeling of being safe from both physical and emotional injury. Thus, in addition to the fact that some jobs are physically safer than others, the feelings of job security, economic well-being, and freedom from illness could be counted in this category.

The next level on Maslow's hierarchy, the need for belongingness and love, reflects the individual's desire for social needs. Physiological and safety needs focus on the individual's own person; the need for belongingness and love involves the need for other people. Put another way, most of us exhibit a strong urge to have contact with others, to be part of a group, and to be accepted by that group in the workplace.

Then again, beyond being part of a group and having a sense of belonging, we seek to stand out, to have self-respect, and the respect of others through esteem needs. In the process, our feelings of personal worth, adequacy, and competence should be met along with the need for respect, admiration, recognition, and status in the eyes of others.

And finally, the top level of Maslow's hierarchy suggests the need for self-actualization, which involves the attainment of full self-expression and the desire to become what each of us is fully capable of becoming. In a phrase, self-actualization reflects the need to "be all we can be" by reaching our potential and making actual what each of us wishes our perceptions of "self" to be.

For those considering rewards, Maslow's hierarchy holds several insights. It categorizes and points up the importance of different types of needs in the workplace, and in so doing provides the first clear statement that management should recognize higher- as well as lower-level needs in its motivational thinking (Rowland and Ferris, 1982). Furthermore, it suggests that managers should be aware that satisfied needs are not as strongly motivating as needs unmet; or, put another way, employees are more enthusiastically motivated by what they are seeking than by what they already have (Davis and Newstrom, p. 189). And given this observation along with the fact that different people will be at different levels of the need hierarchy at different times, it suggests that rewards should be adjusted on an individual basis; for what may satisfy (i.e., meet the need of) one employee may have little relevance to another.

## B.  Herzberg's Two-Factor Refinement of Maslow's Needs

Further discussion of the use of rewards and their relevance in motivating and satisfying human needs is provided by Herzberg et al. (1959; Herzberg, 1966, 1968) in the development of his two-factor theory of motivation. From his research with engineers and accountants, Herzberg discovered that not all job factors and reward systems are capable of motivating; some, at best, can only keep employees from being dissatisfied, and thus are categorized as maintenance, or hygiene factors. These factors, relating largely to Maslow's lower-level needs, include rewards that might be provided through an improved personal life; better pay; better working conditions; greater job security; improved company policy and administration; better relations with superiors, subordinates, and peers; and higher status. As such, they address the context surrounding a job and are extrinsic to the job itself, providing no direct satisfaction at the time work is performed, and lacking in the direct capacity to motivate employees.

By contrast, Herzerg's motivational factors do relate to the job itself and provide intrinsic rewards which yield satisfaction that the person can experience while performing the job. These factors, involving Maslow's higher-level needs, are reflected in the content of the job and provide such rewards as greater recognition, advancement, more responsibility, the possibility of further growth, a sense of achievement, and a general sense of challenge from the work itself.

As one might imagine, Herzberg's theory generated a considerable amount of controversy in reward and punishment circles. By suggesting that only rewards which meet higher-level needs can motivate, he broke with Maslow, who believed that, depending upon the level of individual development, any level of need can be a motivator (DuBrin, 1978). In so doing, Herzberg's work also tended to suggest a professional, white-collar bias because blue-collar jobs are less likely to include the needs he characterizes as motivators (Davis and Newstrom, 1989). Furthermore, some of the rewards Herzberg viewed as hygienic factors others believed could be equally motivational. Pay in particular was singled out. As Miles (1975, p. 156) observes,

> Where pay benefits are used merely to compensate for time served, they probably function much as Herzberg suggests. However, where sizable dollar rewards are linked to outstanding performance in creative reward systems, there is little question that they reinforce other forms of recognition and thus serve as motivating forces.

Nonetheless, despite the criticisms, Herzberg did help to move motivational thought forward by suggesting refinements in Maslow's ideas as applied to the work setting. Those refinements, in turn, encouraged managers to shift their attention from rewards related to lower-level, extrinsic, hygienic needs, which often yielded poor results, to the potentially powerful upper-level intrinsic needs that are satisfied through the work itself (Davis and Newstrom, 1989).

## III. FINE TUNING REWARDS AND PUNISHMENTS TO GAIN PERFORMANCE

The need theory approaches covered in the previous section provide a useful start to the discussion of reward and punishment, however, they are only a start. This is so because such approaches focus on the satisfaction of individual needs which are frequently difficult to measure, challenging to relate to performance, and ultimately only a part of the larger motivational picture. For example, how does one measure esteem needs and assess how they change over time? And even if a manager is able to obtain the knowledge necessary to calibrate employee needs, it is not altogether obvious how that information should be used, or what kind of behavior and/or performance will result. In this latter regard, although it may be clear that a particular employee's job security is threatened, the way in which he or she will be motivated to constructively deal with that need may be uncertain. To obtain greater security, he or she may (1) work harder to gain the attention of a superior, (2) join a union to protect his or her security institutionally, (3) work less hard to spread the work, (4) seek to undermine the legitimacy of the offending boss, or (5) pursue any number of other behaviors (Cummings and Schwab, 1973). Thus the point remains that, even with a knowledge of needs, it is unclear how a manager might go about measuring and channeling such needs to enhance employee performance. And in any event, as Henderson (1979, p. 45) observes, it should be stressed that the satisfaction of individual needs "is not the only force or variable that affects the things people do when working. The relative measures people make concerning the relationship between their workplace efforts and the rewards they receive possibly have far greater impact on human behavior."

## A. Of "Carrrots" and "Sticks": Skinner's Use of Behavior Modification

To avoid these sorts of needs theory deficiencies, there has been considerable interest in shifting to a motivational model that places more emphasis on performance and allows for more measurement and predictable managerial application of incentives. One such model, dubbed behavior modification, operant conditioning, or reinforcement theory, and based upon the work of B. F. Skinner (1953, 1969, 1971), has gained considerable appeal. Rather than attempt to decipher and measure internal needs, this approach takes its cue from learning theory and assumes that work behavior is a learned activity, that such behavior depends upon the consequences accompanying it, and that it is therefore possible for managers to influence and modify employee behavior by manipulating those consequences. This thinking, in turn, is based upon the law of effect, which states that behavior which is followed directly, or reinforced, by a rewarding consequence tends to be repeated, whereas behavior that is reinforced by a negative, or punishing, consequence tends not to be repeated. Therefore, the incidence of various kinds of behavior in the workplace can be seen as dependent upon the ways in which those behaviors are being reinforced by their "carrot" and "stick" consequences.

Of course, there may be instances where the consequences themselves miss the mark because they are not deemed persuasive or relevant enough to produce the desired behavior, or because the relationship between the consequences and behavior is unclear. Hence the consequences used by managers should be powerful enough to get the employee in question to respond and clear enough to evoke the proper response.

There are four different types of reinforcement that can be used to modify the behavior of employees: positive reinforcement, negative reinforcement, punishment, and extinction. *Positive reinforcement* provides a favorable consequence, a reward, that encourages repetition of a particular desired behavior. If, for example, an employee hands in a report on time and responds well to praise, then praise from the superior will encourage a repeat of such behavior in the future.

*Negative reinforcement* also encourages the reinforcing of desired behavior, but in this case the reward is not a positive one; it is instead the avoidance of unpleasant consequences. Much of our legal system is based on this form of avoidance learning; that is, we follow the law in order to avoid possible unpleasantness. And continuing with our earlier example, an employee may hand in a report on time to avoid the harassment and criticism he may have experienced with a late report in the past.

Although both positive and negative reinforcement seek to reward desired behavior, punishment and extinction are aimed at reducing undesired behavior. *Punishment* occurs when an unpleasant consequence accompanies and discourages an undesirable behavior, and there is probably little need to point out examples of its use in the workplace. Suffice it to say that if our hypothetical employee submitted his report late, he would receive penalties of one sort or another. Yet, as noted earlier in this chapter, punishment has a rather mixed record when it comes to yielding results. Indeed, Skinner himself favors extinction over punishment as a means for decreasing the frequency of undesired behaviors (Hamner, 1974).

Nonetheless, if punishment is to be used, it may be helpful to remember Douglas McGregor's "red-hot stove rule" as a means for reducing its more harmful effects. As with touching a red-hot stove, the manager should make certain that the punishment administered is immediate, with warning, consistent, and impersonal (Strauss and Sayles, 1980).

1. The burn is immediate. There is no question of cause and effect. So too should the disciplinary process occur as soon as possible after an infraction occurs.
2. You had warning. Because the stove was red-hot, you knew what would happen if you touched it. So too should the employee be aware ahead of time that if she performs in an unacceptable way, a punishment will be meted out to fit the "crime."
3. The punishment is consistent. Everyone who touches the stove is burned. Thus all those caught committing similar infractions should be punished in a similar way; one is not more severely disciplined than another.
4. The punishment is impersonal. A person is burned for touching the stove, not because of who he is. Punishment has the least negative effect if the individual feels that his or her behavior at the particular moment is the only thing being criticized, not his or her total personality.

By following these guidelines, punishment, like being burned by the stove, can help employees learn their lessons quickly and discourage a repetition of undesirable behavior in the future.

The final type of reinforcement, *extinction*, involves the withholding of rewards for undesirable behavior so that the behavior will eventually disappear. With this approach, along with no reward there is no punishment either, only a lack of reinforcement which, when repeated, causes the undesired response to become extinct. Thus, to once again use our hypothetical employee, his report, if late, would not receive rewards; most likely an indifferent silence would be the response.

Having reviewed behavior modification and its various types of reinforcement techniques, it would seem that this approach holds out the most promise for managers seeking to develop productive reward and punishment systems, and in many ways it does (Luthans and Lyman, 1973). It emphasizes performance and provides a measurable systematic way of using incentives and disincentives to reinforce productive performance (Luthans and Kreitner, 1974, 1985). In so doing, it provides a useful means for managers to control employee behavior, analyze it, and, where necessary, change it to meet managerial objectives.

The problem is that employee needs and objectives may tend to get lost in the process. As Henderson (1979, p. 52) observes, reinforcement theory assumes the following.

1. Individuals take no active role in shaping their own behavior; they are merely agents responding to outside forces.

2. The concept of needs, drives or goal-directed behavior is unacceptable because of the inability to observe, identify and measure these [internal] forces.
3. Permanent change in individual behavior results from reinforcement of a particular behavior.

Consequently the behavior modification that uses these assumptions is a noncognitive approach, one which does not take individual judgment and choice into account (Rowland and Ferris, 1982). This approach, in turn, runs counter to much modern-day thought and action which stress the need for more individual autonomy, self-determination, and self-actualization in the workplace. "At the extreme, people could be treated like rats in a training box when in fact they are intelligent, thinking, self-controlled individuals who are capable of making their own choices and perhaps motivating themselves" (Davis and Newstrom, 1989, p. 119). Thus, when viewed from this perspective, behavior modification seems strangely out of step with current humanistic thinking.

## B. Expectancy Theory as an Integrative Approach

The Machiavellian and strangely anachronistic nature of behavior modification suggests the need to continue the search for motivational models that are more cognitive (i.e., cognizant of individual needs and perceptions) while remaining performance oriented. One such integrative approach, called expectancy theory (Vroom, 1964; Porter and Lawler, 1968), looks quite promising in satisfying this search. In this regard, Cascio (1986, p. 397) notes that "While reinforcement theories focus on the *objective relationship* between performance and rewards, expectancy theories emphasize the *perceived relationships*—what does the person expect?" And Sayles (1989, p. 66) further observes that "The theory persuasively argues that employees must perceive productivity and performance as necessary steps along *their* path to satisfying *their* own goals." Consequently, individual perceptions and needs play a major role in helping to meet organizational performance with this approach.

Three key factors developed by Vroom (1964) form the foundation for the expectancy model and demonstrate the pivotal role of individual perception in this motivational scheme. For Vroom, motivation is the product of valence, expectancy, and instrumentality.

The first factor, *valence*, refers to the value or importance a particular outcome, or reward, has for a person. Obviously, the more attractive a particular reward is, as measured from the employee's point of view, the more inclined she will be to want to pursue it. If, for example, promotion is deemed important, then performance that can lead to promotion could prove quite attractive. But the two other factors related to performance itself also need to be considered. First, what is the likelihood, or *expectancy*, that the person in question can generate the effort necessary to yield the proper level of performance? And furthermore, if that performance is attained, what is the likelihood that it will be *instrumental* in gaining the outcome/reward sought?

Thus, with Vroom's view, one sees all three motivational factors at work in the employee's perceptual equation. Not only is there concern for the importance of the reward itself (valence); attention to the likelihood that a certain level of effort will produce the proper level of performance (expectancy), and interest in knowing whether that level of performance will indeed obtain the desired reward (instrumentality) are also integral considerations. And, as Nadler and Lawler (1977) observe, these expectancy views in turn suggest certain basic assumptions about the causes of behavior (i.e., performance) in organizations: behavior is determined by a combination of forces in the individual and in the environment; individuals make conscious decisions about their own behavior in organizations; different individuals have different needs, desires, and goals; and individuals make decisions among alternative plans of behavior based on their expectation of the extent to which a given behavior will lead to a desired outcome.

Nadler and Lawler (1977) then go on to suggest that, based on these expectancy assumptions, managers can help to productively motivate employees in a number of ways.

1. They should seek to determine the rewards valued by each subordinate. If rewards are to be motivators, they must be suitable for the individual. Managers can determine what rewards their subordinates seek by observing their reactions in different situations or by asking them what rewards they desire.
2. Managers should also determine the performance they desire. They must know what performance level or behavior they want so that they can tell subordinates what they must do to be rewarded.
3. Make the performance level attainable. If the subordinates feel the goal they are being asked to pursue is too difficult or impossible to reach, their motivation will be low.
4. Link rewards to performance. To maintain motivation, the appropriate reward must be clearly associated within a short period of time with successful performance.
5. Analyze what factors in the work environment might counteract the effectiveness of the reward.
6. Make sure the reward is adequate. Minor rewards will be minor motivators (Stoner, 1978, pp. 430–431).

In a similar vein, Sayles (1989, pp. 66–68) suggests a series of expectancy steps that employees might follow, and managers facilitate, to yield productive motivational success. In the case of employees, they must believe that

1. They have the capacity (based on past experience and self-confidence) to improve performance;
2. This improved performance will not be excessively costly in terms of energy, friendship, or other personal sacrifices (i.e., effort);
3. This improved performance will result in demonstrably good results, that is, something that others can measure, assess, or perceive—some significant difference from the situation before;
4. These results will be appraised as commendatory, as a positive contribution;
5. These results will be rewarded; and
6. The reward will be equitable (i.e., fair in comparison to others producing similar results).

And managers can serve as facilitators by helping employees to successfully negotiate each of the aforementioned steps in several ways:

1. Aid in providing training and experience;
2. Help redesign the job and the division of labor so that extra efforts are not excessively costly to produce improved individual performance;

3. Make certain that these efforts are complemented and not dissipated by the efforts of others;
4. Be positively responsive to improved performance;
5. Facilitate obtaining of fair compensation for this improvement; and
6. Adjust the reward to make it equitable compared to what others receive.

Having reviewed the expectancy theory and seen some of the ways it might be applied in practice, it obviously shows great promise. Yet the expectancy theory too is not without its problems. Employees may not believe that high performance is instrumental in securing rewards, and so too may they have difficulty believing that increased effort on their part will lead to effective performance (Dessler, 1978). As well, this approach also seems to assume that people use a rational decision-making process in relating effort to performance and rewards when, in practice, people often follow routine, act on impulse, copy their friends, and make decisions on the basis of limited information. And finally, the key variables are not always easy to conceptualize and measure, making research difficult (Strauss and Sayles, 1980).

Nonetheless, with its integrative approach, the expectancy theory can make the best use of other theories along with its own. It can emphasize performance while taking account of human needs. And it can even "blend easily with behavior modification [by using] the acquired information about employee perceptions of valence to select those rewards which, when applied systematically, will have a predictable effect on employee behavior" (Davis and Newstrom, 1989, p. 135).

## IV. MAKING USE OF REWARDS AND PUNISHMENTS

Having covered a number of the key approaches to reward and punishment, the question remains as to just how helpful these theories and techniques are in bringing about productive performance in the public sector workplace. In a very real sense, the answer to this question relates to the nature of the public workplace itself, to its constraints and culture (Loverd, 1997; Perry, 1995; Peters, 1995; Ott, 1989; Peters and Nelson, 1979) as much as to any predilections that employees or managers might have.

And that public workplace is not terribly receptive to productivity and motivational innovations. In fact, from the outset one could say that the government was not formed for the primary purpose of efficient management and productivity; rather, it was intentionally, indeed constitutionally, designed to be diffuse in power and difficult to run. Allison (1996, p. 459) makes this point when he stresses "the fundamental constitutional difference" between the managerial climate of government and that of business.

In business, the functions of general management are centralized in a single individual: the Chief Executive Officer. The goal is authority commensurate with responsibility. In contrast, in the U.S. government, the functions of general management are constitutionally spread among competing institutions: the executive, two houses of Congress, and the courts. The constitutional goal was "not to promote efficiency but to preclude the exercise of arbitrary power," as Justice Brandeis observed. Indeed, as *The Federalist Papers* make starkly clear, the aim was to create incentives to compete: 'the great security against a gradual concentration of the several powers in the same branch consists in giving those who administer each branch the constitutional means and personal motives to resist encroachment of the others. Ambition must be made to counteract ambition.' Thus, the general management functions concentrated in the CEO of a private business are, by constitutional design, spread in the public sector among a number of competing institutions and thus shared by a number of individuals whose ambitions are set against one another.

This diffusion of power is further reflected in a diffusion of goals. As DeMarco (1983, p. 204) notes, governments and their public personnel systems

> are designed to achieve multiple goals, and they have many unintended as well as intended consequences for public management. In addition to organizational effectiveness and efficiency, civil service regulations and procedures also seek to foster equity, merit, due process, the well-being of individual employees, and a responsive human resources policy. Thus public personnel systems can be impediments to organizational productivity and detract from productivity improvement.

Levine and Nigro (1975, pp. 99–100) make much the same goal-conflicted point regarding the "inherent and perhaps necessary contradictions and strains that exist in the real world of public personnel management" when they observe that public agencies are expected to satisfy both "juridical demands and manpower needs" which could require that they provide effective and efficient services while pursuing policies which insist that the government meet affirmative action requirements and be an employer of last resort. Writ large, Wildavsky (1988, p. 5) notes in similar fashion that perhaps much of what confounds public service performance springs from an "ideological dissensus within the political stratum, profound disagreements over equality, democracy, and hence the role of government, disagreements that create conflicting expectations that no conceivable cadre of civil servants can meet." Little wonder that one study (Mushkin and Sandifer, 1978, p. 144) goes so far as to suggest that, on the basis of an eight-city survey, "[productive] performance [of civil servants] does not appear to be the central theme of many established systems of personnel management."

Still, despite the difficult diffusion of power and goals, few would argue that productive performance should be ignored if we are to have a government that is responsive and worthy of our trust. Therefore, in order to yield productive behavior, where possible, workplace conditions should be improved to enhance the likelihood that reward and punishment systems can be put to good use (Loverd and Pavlak, 1995).

A good place to start improving working conditions lies with the merit system itself which, according to a report by the Committee for Economic Development (1978), has a number of commonly cited deficiencies, including (1) slow, unimaginative, and unaggressive recruitment by personnel offices; (2) filling/bureaucratic delays that prevent the prompt filling of job vacancies, often leading to the loss of top applicants to other job opportunities; (3) rigid classification systems that impede efficient assignment of work; and (4) managers who lack the authority to reward superior performers and discipline or fire nonperformers. As a consequence, "The supervisor does not control the selection and removal process very directly and, as protections for employee job security develop, the employee has a degree of independence" (Cayer, 1980, p. 37). And, of course, that greater independence serves to weaken the authority of the supervisor.

Related deficiencies in public service systems are also noted in reports by the Hudson Institute (1988), the Volcker Commission (Volcker, 1990) and the Winter Commission (Winter, 1993). For example, the Hudson Institute, in its report commissioned by the U.S. Office of Personnel Management, cites a "crisis of competence" facing the federal public service with low pay, low prestige, and outdated management practices contributing to a situation where few of the most talented individuals choose public service. At the state–local levels, the Winter Commission points out that highly fragmented structural arrangements hinder executive leadership and constrain performance (Elling,1994; Cox,1994; Dunn, 1994). Perhaps best known among these studies are the comments of the Volcker Commission which note the general distrust, poor public image, and low esteem Americans have for federal government service. These conditions, in turn, cause an erosion of performance and civil servant morale across America and make it all the more difficult to attract and retain, much less reward and punish, public employees effectively.

Further encompassing the bulk of the merit system deficiencies just noted are three useful categories that Hays and Reeves (1984) believe deserve our attention: the emphasis on job security, the lack of incentives, and administrative centralization. A lower-level need to be sure, the *emphasis on security*, so much a part of most merit systems, tends to jeopardize worker motivation by stifling initiative and risk-taking. It makes people less competitive and less critical of their surroundings and nurtures complacency, even among those employees who might have sought higher-level needs originally.

So too is the *lack of incentives* a problem for merit systems. As was noted in our discussion of reinforcement theory, good behavior not systematically reinforced through incentives can disappear; and the incidence of effective incentive programs in the public service is not very great. Unfortunately, most merit systems operate in a way similar to seniority systems, granting periodic salary increases to workers with little regard for the quality of their output.

And finally, Hays and Reeves (1984) note that there should be more of a shift away from *administrative centralization*, which encourages more control and more organizational rigidity and does not allow workers sufficient latitude to apply their talents and mature professionally. Instead public employees follow personnel policies, operational procedures, job descriptions, and position classifications directed centrally with little delegation and little opportunity to satisfy their needs for accomplishment, growth, esteem, or self-actualization.

In addition, beyond the categories noted by Hays and Reeves lies that much larger challenge of enhancing the overall prestige of public service. If prestige is high, many will be drawn to public service and expect to be motivated and productive in it. For example, during the 1950s, three of every four Americans "expected the federal government to do the right thing most or pretty much all of the time" (Stille, 2001, p. A13). However, as Perry and Wise (1994) observe, this has not been the case in more recent times. Instead, from the mid-1960s to the 1990s an ongoing decline in public confidence in American institutions occurred to the point where only one in four Americans believes that the government will "do what is right." This decline in public trust has made it all the more difficult to recruit and retain a high-quality public workforce, leading many to choose, and trust, private over public sector employment (Loverd, 2002).

It should be noted that for some individuals the motivation to seek and keep public employment has little to do with prestige. Instead, such key inducements as the desire to serve one's country, to help form public policy, to promote a social cause, or to redress an injustice serve as primary motivational factors (Perry and Wise, 1994).

But for many others, the overall prestige of public service can provide a major incentive.

To begin to remedy low prestige, expectations need to change outside as well as within the confines of public employment, a condition that will likely require environmental shifts regarding the way in which the public views its public servants as much as any improvements within the public service itself. To wit: the more the public perceives a need for, and appreciation of, its public servants, the more likely its prestige will rise. Therefore, when events requiring a need for governmental intervention present themselves, if public servants should demonstrate their ability to fill that public need in the most productive and effective way possible, prestige will grow.

Perhaps no better recent example of public service at its best can be cited than its response to the attacks by Muslim terrorists on the Pentagon and the World Trade Center on September 11, 2001. The response by police, fire, and emergency medical teams at the local level, and a host of state and federal agencies at higher levels, was impressive, leading Americans to rethink their relationship with their government and perhaps turn back to, and trust it, once again. Indeed, by October, 2001, one *Washington Post*/ABC News poll noted that public confidence in Washington to "do what was right" rose to 64% "within the range of public confidence in 1964, before the Vietnam protest era" (Shribman, 2001, p. A13). This was a good start for not only renewing confidence but drawing people back into public service. Still, it is only a start and may not last. As Donahue (2001, p. A39) suggests, "The public's reconciliation with government could prove as ephemeral as September's surge in church attendance." Nonetheless, he goes on to say that governmental work may once again be embraced: "A generation or two of talented young people came to shun public work as unrewarding, unglamorous, bereft of status—and most damning of all, dull. There are hints that this may be changing."

To keep such momentum for public support of government service high and provide opportunities to employ the most productive use of reward and punishment systems, public managers need to look in two directions. They need to look within their organizations and direct their attention to streamlining rules and structures, developing incentives, and modifying job security so that complacency and resignation are not the orders of the day. On the other hand, they need to look outside their agencies and reach for opportunities to prove themselves to the public so that support and trust will be more widespread and the likelihood of attracting ever greater numbers of qualified and motivated individuals is enhanced.

## V.  CONCLUSIONS

In this chapter, as a means to securing more productive behavior, we have examined the different needs of employees and the intrinsic and extrinsic factors available in the workplace to meet those needs. We have also examined a number of different methods for encouraging desirable behavior and discouraging undesirable behavior through reinforcement techniques. Then we explored the promise and challenge of expectancy theory, particularly with regard to its ability to stress perceived relationships between performance and rewards while making good use of needs and reinforcement theories.

And finally, having investigated these different types of reward and punishment approaches, we looked at the public sector context in which they might be used. In many ways, it should be clear that that context provides as much challenge as the technologies of reward and punishment methods themselves. If productivity is to be improved, constructive changes in the nature of that context, starting with the merit system and reaching out to the larger public, will need to be considered.

## REFERENCES

Allison, G. (1996). Public and private management: Are they fundamentally alike in all unimportant respects? In: Stillman, R., ed. *Public Administration: Concepts and Cases*, 6th ed. Boston: Houghton Mifflin, pp. 291–307.

Cascio, W. (1986). *Managing Human Resources: Productivity, Quality of Work Life, Profits*. New York: McGraw-Hill.

Cayer, N. J. (1980). *Managing Human Resources*. New York: St. Martin's.

Committee for Economic Development (1978). *Improving Management of the Public Workforce*. New York: Committee for Economic Development.

Cox, R. (1994). The Winter Commission report: The practitioner's perspective. *Public Admin. Rev.* 54:108–109.

Cummings, L., Schwab, D. (1973). *Performance in Organizations: Determinants and Appraisal*. Glenview, IL: Scott, Foresman.

Davis, K., Newstrom, J. (1989). *Human Behavior at Work*. 8th ed. New York: McGraw-Hill.

DeMarco, J. (1983). Productivity and personnel management in government organizations. In: Hays, S., Kearney, R., eds. *Public Personnel Administration: Problems and Prospects*. Englewood Cliffs, NJ: Prentice-Hall, pp. 203–215.

Dessler, G. (1978). *Human Behavior: Improving Performance at Work*. Reston, VA: Reston.

Donahue, J. (2001, December 13). Is government the good guy? *The New York Times*, p. A39.

Dowling, W., Sayles, L. (1971). *How Managers Motivate: The Imperatives of Supervision*. New York: McGraw-Hill.

DuBrin, A. (1978). *Human Relations: A Results-Oriented Approach*. Reston, VA: Reston.

Dunn, D. (1994). Public affairs, administrative faculty and the Winter Commission report. *Public Admin. Rev.* 54:109–110.

Elling, R. (1994). The line in Winter: An academic assessment of the first report of the National Commission on the State and Local Public Service. *Public Admin. Rev.* 54:107–108.

Fox, D. (1979). *Managing the Public's Interest: A Results-Oriented Approach*. Rinehart & Winston, New York: Holt.

Hamner, W. (1974). Reinforcement theory and management in organizational settings. In: Tasi, H. Hamner, W., eds. *Organizational Behavior and Management: A Contingency Approach*. Chicago: St. Claire, pp. 21–35.

Hays, S., Reeves, T. (1984). *Personnel Management in the Public Sector*. Boston: Allyn & Bacon.

Henderson, R. (1979). *Compensation Management: Rewarding Performance*. 2nd ed. Reston, VA: Reston.

Herzberg, F. (1966). *Work and the Nature of Man*. New York: World.

Herzberg, F. (1968). One more time: How do you motivate employees? *Harvard Bus. Rev.* 46:53–62.

Herzberg, F., Mausner, B., Snyderman, B. (1959). *The Motivation to Work*. New York: Wiley.

Hudson Institute (1988). *Civil Service 2000*. Washington, DC: U.S. Office of Personnel Management.

Kessler, C. (1974). Influencing employee behavior. *Developing the Municipal Organization*. Washington, DC: International City Management Association, pp. 84–101.

Levine, C., Nigro, L. (1975). The public personnel system: Can juridical administration and manpower management coexist? *Public Admin. Rev.* 35:98–107.

Loverd, R. (1997). *Leadership for the Public Service: Power and Policy in Action*. Upper Saddle River, NJ: Prentice-Hall.

Loverd, R. (2002). Privatization and public control: Why make public management more businesslike? In: Woolley, P., Papa, A., eds. *American Politics: Core Argument/Current Controversy*. 2nd ed. Upper Saddle River, NJ: Prentice-Hall, pp. 271–275.

Loverd, R., Pavlak, T. (1995). Analyzing the historical development of the American civil service. In: Rabin, J., Vocino, T., Hildreth, B., Miller, G., eds. *Handbook of Public Personnel Administration*. New York: Marcel Dekker, pp. 1–19.

Luthans, F., Kreitner, R. (1974). The management of behavioral contingencies. *Personnel* 51:370–396.

Luthans, F., Kreitner, R. (1985). *Organizational Behavior Modification and Beyond*. Foresman, Glenview, IL: Scott.

Luthans, F., Lyman, D. (1973). Training supervisors to use organizational modification. *Personnel* 50:38–44.

Maslow, A. (1943). A theory of motivation. *Psych. Rev.* 50:370–396.

Maslow, A. (1954). *Motivation and Personality*. New York: Harper & Row.

Miles, R. (1975). *Theories of Management: Implications for Organizational Behavior and Development*. New York: McGraw-Hill.

Mushkin, S., Sandifer, F. (1978). *Personnel Management and Productivity in City Government*. Washington, DC: Georgetown University Public Services Laboratory.

Nadler, D., Lawler, E. (1977). Motivation: A diagnostic approach. In: Hackman, J., Lawler, E., Porter, L., eds. *Perspectives on Behavior in Organizations*. New York: McGraw-Hill, pp. 101–116.

Ott, J. (1989). *The Organizational Culture Perspective*. Chicago: Dorsey.

Perry, J. (1995). Compensation, merit pay, and motivation. In: Hays, S., Kearney, R., eds. *Public Personnel Administration: Problems and Prospects*. 3rd ed. Upper Saddle River, NJ: Prentice-Hall, pp. 121–132.

Perry, J., Wise, L. (1994). The motivational bases of public service. In: Rosenbloom, D., Goldman, D., Ingraham, P., eds. *Contemporary Public Administration*. New York: McGraw-Hill, pp. 251–262.

Peters, B. G. (1995). *The Politics of Bureaucracy*. 4th ed. White Plains, NY: Longman.

Peters, C., Nelson, M. (1979). *The Culture of Bureaucracy*. New York: Holt, Rinehart & Winston.

Porter, L., Lawler, E. (1968). *Managerial Attitudes and Performance*. Homewood, IL: Dorsey.

Rowland, K., Ferris, G. (1982). *Personnel Management*. Boston: Allyn & Bacon.

Sayles, L. (1989). *Leadership: Managing in Real Organizations*. 2nd ed. New York: McGraw-Hill.

Shribman, D. (2001, October 16). A renewed interest, trust in government. *Boston Globe*, p. A13.

Skinner, B. F. (1953). *Science and Human Behavior*. New York: Macmillan.

Skinner, B. F. (1969). *Contingencies of Reinforcement*. New York: Appleton-Century-Crofts.

Skinner, B. F. (1971). *Beyond Freedom and Dignity*. New York: Knopf.

Stille, A. (2001, November 3). Suddenly, Americans trust Uncle Sam. *New York Times*, p. A11, A13.

Stoner, J. (1978). *Management*. Englewood Cliffs, NJ: Prentice-Hall.

Strauss, G., Sayles, L. (1980). *Personnel: The Human Problems of Management*. 4th ed. New York: Prentice-Hall.

Volcker, P. (1990). *Leadership for America: Rebuilding the Public Service*. Lexington, MA: Lexington.

Vroom, V. (1964). *Work and Motivation*. New York: Wiley.

Wildavsky, A. (1988). 'Ubiquitous anomie' or public service in an era of ideological dissensus. *The Campus and the Public Service*. Washington, DC: National Academy of Public Administration, pp. 1–15.

Winter, W. (1993). *Hard Truths, Tough Choices: Agenda for State and Local Reform*. San Francisco: Jossey-Bass.

# 31

# Labor–Management Partnerships
*Direct Paths to Productivity Improvement*

**SEOK-HWAN LEE**
*The Catholic University of Korea, Songsim Campus, South Korea*

**MARC HOLZER**
*Rutgers, The State University of New Jersey, Newark, New Jersey, U.S.A.*

## I. SUCCESS STORIES IN LABOR–MANAGEMENT PARTNERSHIPS

In an era of limited resources, public sector scholars, practitioners, and elected officials often discuss strategies of cutback management, downsizing, privatization, and contracting out. The underlying goal of these strategies is to reduce the role and/or costs of government by shifting service delivery to private sector organizations, assuming that utilizing the private sector is a more efficient alternative to expending funds through the public sector.

At the same time, there has been continuing attention to continuous improvement, total quality management (TQM), quality of work life (QWL), teamwork-based organization, and labor–management cooperation for productivity improvement within the public sector. A major characteristic of these strategies is to seek answers in the public sector rather than relying on resources available in the private sector. Without a harmonious relationship between labor and management, it is impossible to achieve a high level of productivity in any organization. The reason is simple. No matter what productivity improvement strategies are considered, they have to be acceptable to and supported by employees at all levels. Top management decisions that are lacking in consensus from the labor side are likely to create tensions between the two sides, thereby decreasing employees' willingness to enhance productivity.

As such, labor–management partnership is a backdrop for everything that is going on in government at all levels. Even though there are many success stories in labor–management cooperation in the public sector, those stories have not been sufficiently disseminated to inform the vast majority of public sector scholars and practitioners.

Although adversarial perceptions between the two have prevailed in the workplace, in turn hindering both sides from cooperating, many scholars and practitioners in the public sector agree that a harmonious relationship between management and workforce is the key to enhancing productivity in any government organization (Canfield and Holzer, 1977; Goldoff, 1978; Coleman, 1990; Hodes, 1991; Holzer, 1988; Grace and Holzer, 1992; Klay, 1988, Mann, 1989; Herrick, 1990; Holzer and Callahan, 1998).

Some scholars have also paid attention to the collective bargaining process and structure that are believed to foster a good relationship between the two sides (Levine and Hagburg, 1979; Lewin et al., 1981; Aaron et al., 1988; Kershen, 1983; Saran and Sheldrake, 1988). However, comprehensive research is required to identify factors affecting productive partnerships between labor and management.

It is necessary, therefore, from a comprehensive perspective to identify successful factors affecting harmonious labor–management relationships in the public sector. Based on success stories, this chapter provides a broad view of what should be emphasized in order to build labor–management cooperation for productivity improvement.

## II. CRITICAL FACTORS FOR LABOR–MANAGEMENT PARTNERSHIPS

### A. Obtaining Both Top Management Commitment and Widespread Support From All Levels

Successful management–workforce cooperation depends heavily upon a strong comprehensive commitment of top management. Grace and Holzer (1992, p. 489) note essential elements for cooperation in a labor–management relationship:

> Minimizing tension between all parties;
> Genuine understanding between union and management officials;
> Continuous sharing of information;
> An effective system for resolving conflicts, including employee grievances;
> Creating a positive environment for collective bargaining;
> Mutual interest in creating a work environment responsive to the needs and interests of employees; and
> Employees, union representatives, and supervisors working together to solve work-related problems and to improve work procedures.

Paying attention to the elements mentioned above may not, however, be sufficient to create a cooperative relationship between the two sides. This is not simple as each side may view cooperation in a different way. Grace and Holzer (1992) also point out that the elements above may fail to reflect significant institutional interests of employers and unions.

Simply having top management support is not sufficient. Many success stories in labor–management cooperation indicate that unless top management clearly signals its commitment to the partnership and gets widespread support from all employees, the initiative for partnership will dissipate. One success story, Quality Services through Partnership in Ohio, which began in 1991 and is still operating, strongly supports the importance of top management commitment and widespread acceptance among employees. At the outset, with leadership from the governor, cabinet, and the five state employee unions, labor and management perspectives merged and the partners began to create new ways of serving Ohio's citizens. The governor teamed up with cabinet directors and union leaders to identify mutual interests aimed at improving productivity and quality.

One success story in the federal government indicates the importance of top management commitment and widespread support from all related agencies. As the U.S. OPM (2000), in its report to the President, points out:

> Immediately after Executive Order 12871 was issued, the Norfolk Naval Shipyard and the Metal Trades Council, AFL-CIO, created a Partnership Council and an Executive Steering Committee to improve organizational performance through labor–management partnership. Membership was limited at first to senior management and labor officials. Management and the union soon realized, however, that meaningful change would require support from every level of the organization. To gain that kind of support, every employee at the Shipyard was offered intensive training in leadership and quality principles. Membership on the Partnership Council was enlarged significantly. The results have been impressive. Productivity gains reached $61 million dollars in FY 1999, employee satisfaction is up, the production of hazardous waste and the cost of waste disposal are both down, and the Shipyard is a recognized model.

## B.  Multiple and Ad Hoc Joint Labor–Management Committees

The importance of a joint labor–management committee is found in solving work-related problems and building trust and mutual respect between the two sides. Such committees deal mostly with critical issues such as workplace safety, work hours, training, and personnel concerns. Although committees' roles, in many cases, deal with day-to-day workplace issues, it may be possible for each side to build a level of trust through these activities over time. It may then be much easier to deal with more complicated problems that cannot be avoided in the workplace.

Furthermore, the trust established in committee meetings can have a positive impact on the relationship between labor and management, a relationship that has traditionally been considered adversarial at the bargaining table. In the case of Quality Services through Partnership (QStP), the governor established the Ohio Quality Steering Committee composed of equal numbers of union leaders and managers. The group's mission was to guide the launch of the state government's quality initiative. The steering committee completed development of a quality implementation plan for state government, and the plan served as an early road map for the first group of quality champions. In 1993, the Quality Users Advisory Committee (eventually renamed the Ohio Quality Network) was launched. Members included quality coordinators and union liaisons from all agencies. Its critical mission was to ensure that agencies learn together so they can move forward together. Therefore, from the outset, employees have been involved in every step of making important decisions through a variety of labor–management committees. The use of these joint committees was a major driver for a successful management–workforce partnership.

Tompkins County, New York has also been known for successfully restructuring cooperative labor–management tools. The county's labor–management cooperation initiative was structured around total quality management and termed "Partners for Quality." Multiple labor–management committees have been implemented in an ad hoc manner to deal with workplace conflicts or to address specific projects. The most important is that in addition to these committees a communication venue, or "Employee Council," was comprised mainly of employees (Gans and Guild, 1998).

As particular situations create different problems, it is often necessary to have more than one labor–management committee. The case of Genesee County, New York illustrates why different labor–management committees are needed to fix problems that are unique to certain agencies. Burt and Goldberg (1998 pp. 1–2), in a case study, describe two different labor–management committees.

> There are two main labor–management committees in Genesee County. The general unit labor–management committee includes most county departments, with about 320 CSEA members represented, and the Genesee County Nursing Home labor–management committee has about 150 CSEA member employees. The general unit committee was started in 1991, and the nursing home committee was started during the late 1980s. The nursing home has its own committee because of the special nature of the services it provides. It also operates as an "enterprise fund," which means that its finances are separate from the rest of the county's departments. As an enterprise fund, the nursing home is able to keep the money it earns, but when it is losing money, it cannot draw on other county revenue. Currently, the home is earning money, which has enabled the county to invest in improvements in the facility. The two committees operate within somewhat different contexts. In the late 1980s and early 1990s, the nursing home was losing money due to a change in the state's reimbursement policy for Medicare and Medicaid patients. It faced the prospect of being sold by the county legislature if it did not become self-sustaining on its own revenues. It was realized that the home had to change its mode of operating in order to survive, and that the cooperation and involvement of both management and labor would be necessary. The labor–management committee provided a good vehicle for the two groups to work together to try to improve the operations of the home. With the general unit committee, management saw great potential in improving workplace practices through the more cooperative structure provided by a labor–management committee. The county personnel officer approached the CSEA labor relations specialist, who agreed that establishing a committee was a good idea.

Ontario County, New York has also used multiple labor–management committees for successful partnerships: a countywide committee dealing with broader issues such as developing a new human services building program, and agencywide committees operating in various departments. Each committee's role is different, but each operates in a cooperative manner (Blumner and Vaughn, 1998).

## C.  Communication Channels

Grace and Holzer (1992, p. 490) argue that "the vision, once created, must be communicated clearly and frequently in a variety of ways." This assortment of transparent communication channels within the organization is the key to achieving a harmonious relationship between the two sides. Through these channels, both sides will come to understand mutual problems and discuss what should be done on a daily basis. Especially in an era of cutback management, open communication leads to diminishing of labor–management tensions.

As Simon (1997, p. 208) indicates, "Communication in organizations is a two way process: it comprehends both the transmittal to a decisional center of orders, information and advice; and the transmittal of decisions reached from this center to other parts of the organization."

In fact, following the formation of joint labor–management committees, every employee was asked to actively participate in decision making, management and the union began meeting regularly, and gradually both sides were open to the concerns of the other. Evidence suggests that regular and informal partnership meetings have contributed to decreasing the numbers of grievance filings and perceptions of unfair labor practices.

## D. Documenting and Disseminating Success Stories and Languages

Holzer and Lee (1999) point out that under the so-called "ingroup–outgroup categorization" between workforce and management, each side is inclined to attribute causes of difficult work situations to the other. Labor–management tension is getting worse because each side is unwilling to take any responsibility on critical issues in the workplace. Rather than seeking solutions together, both sides have stuck to their own interests. Because the current tension between the two is attributable, in part, to stereotypic beliefs, negative perceptions need to be eliminated to restore a cooperative relationship. In this regard, providing success stories can help to reduce this type of perception. In an organization, story generates belief, recall, and commitment (Wilkins, 1983; Berg, 1985). Examples of positive labor–management relationships typically present evidence that where success stories and positive languages are remembered and documented, both sides view each other as partners, not as obstacles.

Providing success stories can also help other agencies learn how to successfully launch cooperative relationships. The National Governors' Association releases various Governors' Guides to Improving Service Quality on a regular basis (National Governor's Association, 2002). Sharing best practices provides agencies with important advice on "what works and what does not."

OPM also reports that experiences communicated through success stories have helped changed the metaphor from conflict to partnership. The following two examples are documented on the Web (U.S. OPM, 2000).

> In the early 1990s, the Department of Labor and AFGE's National Council of Field Labor Locals embarked on a 10 year effort to transform their labor–management relationship from hostility to cooperation. Their work resulted in a new Collective Bargaining Agreement and a new relationship, both founded in the belief that labor–management relations need not be a zero-sum game where one party gains at the expense of the other. Over time, the parties learned that even the best labor–management partnerships have their ups and downs. Consistent with the President's reaffirmation memorandum, labor and management developed a revitalization plan to give their relationship a boost and make their partnership part of the agency's day-to-day business. The plan included an all-employee survey and focus groups in select field offices around the country. A labor–management team analyzed the results and developed an action plan calling for extensive training for field staff; revising the parties' existing Partnership Handbook; reemphasizing the importance of pre-decisional involvement; and reinforcing the existing commitment to partnership.
>
> In the past, an adversarial relationship between Marine Corps Base Camp Lejeune and AFGE Local 2065 led to over 200 grievances and over 100 unfair labor practice charges annually. Over time the parties agreed this was no way to do business. They formed a labor–management partnership and began to focus on dispute resolution. In

a two-year period from 1997 to 1999, unfair labor practice charges at Camp Lejeune dropped from a high of 120 down to zero. Grievances were almost always resolved at the lowest level, with only three grievances proceeding as far as the third step. The agency estimates the reduction in disputes has saved some $350,000 annually.

The Defense Megacenter (DMC) Rock Island mainframe computer processing center, through the formation of a total quality management process, has tried to replace adversarial language from previously negotiated contracts with language reflecting the idea of "partnership." An example is the "Flexi-Place" or "Work at Home" program, which was intended to give participation opportunity to employees who were unable to come to the worksite because of a disability. The partnership council proposed inserting "flexi-place" language into the contract. As a result, commitment and trust has increased, thereby improving labor relations (Brekke et al., 1998).

## E.  Continuous Training and Education

Successful labor–management cooperation must be based on a spirit of teamwork, therefore it is essential to provide both sides with training programs on how to work together as a team. Training programs for teamwork must be aimed at providing a clear understanding of both job and personal expectations. Through the teamwork experience, both sides develop a mutual understanding of work to be accomplished and a recognition of individuality and trust.

Kathy Button, President of CSEA Local 436 of the Finger Lakes Developmental Disabilities Service Office in Rochester, New York maintains (AFSCME, 1999) that "In a transition, everyone has to be open and work aboveboard. The union understands there's a give-and-take. But everybody has to be educated."

Ontario County, New York was successful in creating cooperative labor–management structures. Training middle management under a cooperative philosophy was the key to achieving a harmonious relationship with top management. It is meaningless for top management to buy into an idea without the support of middle managers (Blumner and Vaughn, 1998).

OPM's report (U.S. OPM, 2000) also places an emphasis on training in the techniques and tools of partnership.

The Defense Civilian Personnel Management Service, Field Advisory Services (FAS) Division, has provided extensive training on labor–management cooperation to union and management partners throughout the Department of Defense. Forty-five Defense installations have received training on the basic principles of partnership, twenty have received training on partnership facilitation, seventeen have received training on interest-based bargaining or interest-based problem solving, and ten have received training on mediation. During the past two years, the FAS Division at Defense has devoted over 350 classroom days to partnership training for more than 3,000 management and union officials. In addition, FAS has worked with unions to jointly deliver partnership training for the National Partnership Council and at symposia sponsored by the Office of Personnel Management and the Society of Federal Labor Relations Professionals.

In addition, one of the factors that made Ohio's QStP successful was the governor's commitment to training for teamwork. In Ohio, the Office of Quality Services introduced the Team Launch Workshop. This workshop enables a variety of teams to accomplish their common goals effectively. The first half of the workshop involves hands-on learning in which participants get indepth information on developing ground rules, experiencing the stages of team development, deciding what to measure and how to track the measurements, building the team, and ensuring team effectiveness. In the second half, each team begins its specific project, working together with its team facilitator. Each participating team

Decides on a team name;
Develops its set of ground rule;
Goes through the first steps of the continuous improvement process;
Begins analyzing its process; and
Identifies ways to measure process capability.

Following the Team Launch Workshop, the team continued its project at its own worksite, with the ongoing involvement of the facilitator (Ohio Office of Quality Service, 2000).

Another success story in labor–management partnership, at the Naval Air Station (NAS) in Brunswick, Maine, emphasizes the importance of training. At NAS, many union and management people have been jointly trained in "interest-based problem solving and alternative dispute resolution." As a result, employees' job satisfaction has increased and a harmonious relationship between the two sides now prevails (Tetrev and Wagner, 1998).

Tompkins County is also well known for providing continuous training to every employee, manager, and legislator under total quality management principles. As Gans and Guild (1998, p. 3) report,

> Tompkins County has invested heavily in training for this program. Between 1994 and 1997, the county spent just over $300,000 for outside consultants to conduct training. In 1998, the county will spend an estimated $170,000 for consultants to complete the bulk of the training (for all departments except the sheriff's department which is independent of other county government). Since 1997, in-house costs have been around $100,000. These costs will drop dramatically after 1998, when all employees, managers, and elected officials have been trained in total quality management techniques and only training for new employees and refresher courses will be necessary.

## F. Employee Empowerment

Providing employees decision-making authority improves morale and streamlines government processes. Successful management–workforce cooperation depends upon a significant level of empowerment. It is critical to get more employees involved in every stage of decision making, if at all possible. In a joint management–labor team, both managers and employees should be able to share important information necessary to make a final decision. Because the level of empowerment is also directly related to job satisfaction and organizational commitment, thereby increasing a harmonious relationship between labor and management, it is essential to create a favorable environment where employees feel empowered.

This does not necessarily mean that managers do not have to do anything. Managers' roles are recast as coaches, mentors, capacity builders, and securers of resources (Hickman and Lee, 2001).

Success stories identified in the public sector also often indicate that decisions are made by consensus rather than majority vote. In other words, no votes are taken. This means that, if any person is unhappy with a proposed solution, the solution must be reworked to the point where every member of the committee can support the final outcome. As such, this consensus rule affords each member an equal voice in decision making (Balliet et al., 1998; Personnel Department of Ulster County, 1998).

In the case of QStP, union members participated in strategic planning and/or setting departmental goals and created a Strategic Plan. Furthermore, labor and management members of the QStP Steering Committee drafted a Partnership Statement for the department at the outset. Through these activities, directors of the union planning group were supportive in developing plans for how the union could better support quality efforts. More involvement at all levels of the organization has led to a feeling of mutual respect for both sides and, just as important, a shared feeling of cooperation in working toward departmental goals (Ohio Office of Quality Service, 2000).

## III.  FROM TENSION TO PARTNERSHIP

Holzer and Lee (1999) argue that although the tension between labor and management sides rises from a variety of factors, including a difficult work environment and job characteristics, in many cases it comes from some stereotypic beliefs that each side holds. In other words, through intergroup attribution, labor management tension is getting worse. On the critical issues, such as a partnership climate, RIFs (Reduction-In-Forces), and poor performance, each group typically tries to avoid responsibility and finds fault with the other. Through this process, hostility is likely to be increased. Figure 1 illustrates how labor–management tension is likely to occur through intergroup attribution.

The management side often does not take responsibility for the difficulties of partnership, however, Robert Tobias, while President of the National Treasury Employees Union (NTEU), asserted (*Government Executive Magazine*, 1997, quoted

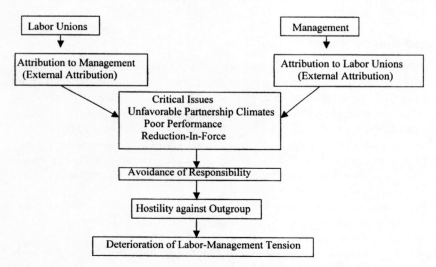

**Figure 1**   The process of labor–management tension. (From Holzer and Lee 1999.)

in Holzer and Lee, 1999) that "there is significant resistance from mid-level managers who up until now did not have to be involved in partnerships, and there has been much talk about partnerships and creating partnerships, but basically it has been at the top."

In addition, although the management would view current performance evaluation systems as fair, unions have different opinions, particularly with regard to poor performers. The fairness of performance evaluation has becomes a matter of debate between labor and management. As Bobby Harnege, President of the American Federation of Government Employees (AFGE), argues (*Government Executive Magazine*, 1999, quoted in Holzer and Lee, 1999),

> There is no such thing as one poor performer. That individual has a supervisor. If he or she is staying on the rolls, then we have two poor performers. Performance management rules, which were established by the Civil Service Reform Act, do not need to be changed. Instead, managers need to have the courage to deal with poor performance.

As such, through this intergroup attribution, tensions between the two sides may be worsening.

Assuming that the tension between the two sides is based mainly on stereotypical beliefs, lessons learned from success stories do help change the metaphor from

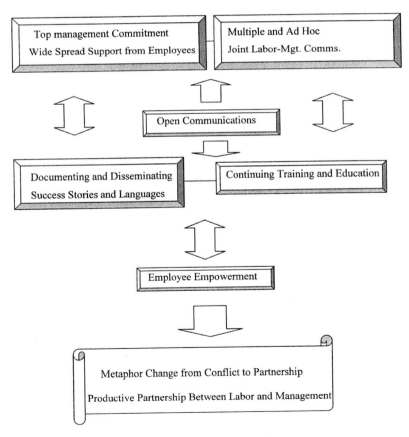

**Figure 2**   Path to labor–management partnership.

"conflict" to "cooperation." As discussed in this chapter, a cooperative productive labor–management relation is a function of top management commitment and widespread support, multiple and ad hoc joint labor–management committees, communication, documentation and dissemination of success stories and languages, continuing training and education, and employee empowerment. Figure 2 illustrates how these six factors may result in a harmonious relationship between labor and management. However, these six factors are not mutually exclusive and simultaneously affect one another. Given that adversarial perceptions prevail between the two sides, strategies for management–workforce cooperation must be focused on changing the metaphor from conflict to partnership.

## IV. CONCLUSION

Labor–management partnership is not easy. Grace and Holzer (1992, p. 495) conclude that "although the investment is substantial, the alternatives to labor–management cooperation should be unacceptable to public leaders."

It always requires sufficient time. Continuing top management support is a necessary first step in achieving a productive partnership. A successful partnership should be based on a high level of mutual trust.

Rudy de Leon, deputy Defense secretary at the Department of Defense (DoD), points out the importance of continuing top management support (*Government Executive Magazine*, 2000a).

> The Defense Department has done a good job of creating labor–management partnerships at its most senior levels, but must expand them to more individual military bases. We have made great progress in partnering, but we still have work to do together because there are places where partnerships are in the early stages of development. We also need to consider additional means to strengthen our partnerships, including thinking together about how labor–management relations can and should play a role in improving our organizational performance and meeting our program goals.

Robert Wilkerson (*Government Executive Magazine*, 2000b), Assistant Commissioner for Customer Service at the Internal Revenue Service, emphasizes that "mutual respect between the IRS and the National Treasury Employees Union (NTEU) has been crucial in negotiating successfully. The key is building trust and building a relationship. We have tried very hard to listen to each other."

Productive organization depends on productive people. When labor and management work together in a harmonious work environment, they can jointly follow a direct path to productivity improvement.

## REFERENCES

Aaron, B., Najita, J. M., Stern, J. L., eds. (1988). *Public Sector Bargaining*. Washington, DC: Bureau of National Affairs.

AFSCME (1999). AFSCME news release. Opening the door: Model programs developed through labor–management cooperation. October 14 (online). Available at http://www.afscme.org/pol%2Dleg/opend04.htm.

Balliet, L., Bruemmer, E., Fantauzzo, S., James, R., Richards, V., Roberson, D. S., Rosebraugh, W. (1998). Making government work: The Indiana statewide program (online). Available at http://www.nlma.org/8thlmc/8nlmc-21.htm.

Berg, P. (1985). Organization change as a symbolic transformation process. In: Frost, Peter, et al., eds. *Organizational Culture*. Beverly Hills, CA: Sage, pp. 281–300.

Blumner, N., Vaughn, D. (1998). Creating win-win situations: The case of Ontario county (online). Available at http://www.crp.cornell.edu/restructuring/doc/reports/aspiring_to_excellence/cases/ontario.pdf.

Brekke, V., Hess, J., Idlewine, W., Kelgord, D. (1998). Positive change despite downsizing (online). Available at http://www.nlma.org/8thlmc/8nlmc-31.htm.

Burt, L., Goldberg, L. (1998). Cooperative labor management structures in Genesee county (online). Available at http://www.crp.cornell.edu/restructuring/doc/reports/aspiring_to_excellence/cases/genesee.pdf.

Canfield, R., Holzer, M. (1977). Management-labor productivity simulation: City of deficit prone. *Public Product. Rev.* 2(4):38–47.

Coleman, C. J. (1990). *Managing Labor Relations in the Public Sector*. San Francisco: Jossey-Bass.

Gans, J., Guild, K. (1998). Cooperative labor–management restructuring tools in Tompkins county (online). Available at http://www.crp.cornell.edu/restructuring/doc/reports/aspiring_to_excellence/cases/tompkins.pdf.

Goldoff, A. C. (1978). Union-management cooperation in New York. *Public Product. Rev.* 3(2):35–47.

*Government Executive Magazine* (1997). Tobias touts partnership. April, 9 (online). Available at http://www.govexec.com/features/0699/0699s1.htm.

*Government Executive Magazine* (1999). Officials debate the future of the civil service. January, 12 (online). Available at http://www.govexec.com/dailyfed/0199/011299b2.htm.

*Government Executive Magazine* (2000a). DoD pledges to expand union partnerships. August 28, 2000 (online). Available at http://www.govexec.com/news/index.cfm?mode = report& articleid = 17072.

*Government Executive Magazine* (2000b). Labor–management partnerships said to thrive on trust. July 12, 2000 (online). Available at http://www.govexec.com/dailyfed/0700/071200m1.htm.

Grace, S. L., Holzer, M. (1992). Labor–management cooperation: An opportunity for change. In: Holzer, M., ed. *Public Productivity Handbook*. New York: Marcel Dekker, pp. 487–498.

Herrick, N. (1990). *Joint Management and Employee Participation: Labor and Management at Crossroads*. San Francisco: Jossey-Bass.

Hickman, G. R., Lee, D. (2001). *Managing Human Resources in the Public Sector: A Shared Responsibility*. Orlando, FL: Harcourt College.

Hodes, N. (1991). Achieving quality through labor–management participation in New York State. *Public Product. Manage. Rev.* 15(2):163–168.

Holzer, M. (1988). Productivity in, garbage out: Sanitation gains in New York. *Public Product. Manage. Rev.* 11(3):37–50.

Holzer, M., Callahan, K. (1998). *Government at Work: Best Practices and Model Programs*. Thousand Oaks, CA: Sage.

Holzer, M., Lee, S. -H. (1999). Labor–management tension and partnership: Where are we? What should we do? *Int. Rev. Public Admin.* 4(2):33–44.

Kershen, H., ed. (1983). *Collective Bargaining by Government Workers: The Public Employee*. Farmingdale, NY: Baywood.

Klay, W. E. (1988). Microelectronics-based automation and the future of public labor relations. *Public Product. Manage. Rev.* 11(4):57–68.

Levine, M., Hagburg, E. C., eds. (1979). *Labor Relations in the Public Sector: Readings, Cases, and Experimental Exercises*. Salt Lake City, UT: Brighton.

Lewin, D., Feuille, D., Kochan, T. A., eds. (1981). *Public Sector Labor Relations: Analysis and Readings*. 2nd ed. Sun Lakes, AZ: Horton.

Mann, S. Z. (1989). Labor–management cooperation and worker participation: A public sector perspective. *Public Product. Rev.* 12:229–236.

National Governor's Association Center for Best Practices (2002). News room (online). Available at http://www.nga.org.

Ohio Office of Quality Service (2000). Quality services through partnership (online). Available at http://www.state.oh.us/quality/mallabout.html.

Personnel Department of Ulster County (1998). Department overview (online). Available at http://www.co.ulster.ny.us/personnel/overview.html#labor.

Saran, R., Sheldrake, J., eds. (1988). *Public Sector Bargaining in the 1980s*. Brookfield, VT: Avebury.

Simon, H. A. (1997). *Administrative Behavior: A Study of Decision-Making Processes in Administrative Organizations*. 4th ed. New York: Free Press.

Tetrev, R., Wagner, C. (1998). Working toward a true partnership (online). Available at http://www.nlma.org/8thlmc/8nlmc-29.htm.

U.S. OPM. U.S. Office of Personnel Management (2000). Labor–management partnership: A report to the president (online). Available at http://www.opm.gov/lmr/report/index.htm.

Wilkins, A. L. (1983). Organizational stories as symbols which control the organization. In: Pondy, L. R., et al., eds. *Organizational Symbolism*. Greenwich, CT: JAI, pp. 81–92.

# 32

## Reducing Workplace Stress

*Prevention and Mitigation Strategies for Increased Productivity*

**ROSS PRIZZIA and GARY HELFAND**
*University of Hawaii—West Oahu, Pearl City, Hawaii, U.S.A.*

## I. INTRODUCTION: THE IMPACT OF WORK-RELATED STRESS ON JOB PERFORMANCE AND PRODUCTIVITY

In recent years, workplace stress has increasingly become associated with job performance and productivity. According to the (U.S.) National Institute for Occupational Safety and Health (NIOSH), work-related stress is defined as "harmful emotional and physical reactions that occur as a result of jobs that do not match the capabilities, resources, or needs of workers" (Scorza, 1998). NIOSH has recently estimated that seventy-five percent of workers perceive their jobs as stressful and twenty-five percent perceive their jobs as the most stressful factor in their lives (Scorza, 1998).

Recent studies have linked work-related stress to sharp increases in coronary heart disease and a multitude of other psychological and physical disorders (Bosma et al., 1997; Gushue, 1996). In a longitudinal study of stress in the British Civil Service, evidence was obtained that linked perceived lack of job control with the greater likelihood of developing coronary heart disease. After studying over 7000 male and female civil servants, the researchers concluded that the rank and file in the mid and lower levels of the hierarchy were more likely to feel a sense of helplessness combined with coronary heart disease. They concluded that "greater attention to the design of work environments may be one important way to reduce inequalities in health" (Marmot et al., 1997). This is a significant study that supports the trend over the last several decades toward increased and widespread decentralization of decision making throughout the public sector. Other studies have linked workplace stress with weakened immune systems, high blood pressure, hormonal imbalances, mood swings, acute depression, insomnia, eating and digestive disorders, excessive anxiety, frustration and anger, workplace violence, workplace accidents, substance abuse, and burnout (Cryer, 1996; Probst and Brubaker, 2001; Gushue, 1996; Grieger et al., 2000; Anderson, 1999). It does not take a great deal of reflection to realize that any one or combination of these potentially debilitating disorders can lead to poor job performance and a resulting decrease in productivity.

## II. FACTORS CONTRIBUTING TO WORK-RELATED STRESS

Figure One, which originally appeared in the first edition of the *Public Productivity Handbook* (Helfand, 1992), has been revised and expanded to include additional stress factors that have been identified and studied over the last ten years.

However, in perusing numerous recent studies that have attempted to identify the major causes of work-related stress, several factors have repeatedly emerged: (1) lack of participation in decision making and resulting sense of loss of job control, (2) poor communication, with little or no feedback about job performance, (3) widespread role confusion, (4) perceived inequitable reward system, (5) job insecurity, (6) difficulty adapting to new technology, (7) chronic underwork or overwork, (8) shift work, (9) unpleasant or dangerous work environment, (10) negative social environment, and (11) responsibility for making life and death decisions. Although each of these factors has received considerable attention in the literature of stress management, it should be emphasized that individuals react differently to the same stimuli or stressors. It is the responsibility of management to be aware of these factors as they exist within their own organization and the impact they are having on employees.

## III. REDUCING WORKPLACE STRESS: PREVENTION AND MITIGATION STRATEGIES

It is essential that action be taken to prevent or mitigate the major real and potential stressors that can adversely affect job performance and productivity. Accordingly, a stress-related organizational diagnosis should be conducted to identify all workplace stressors and the resulting impact on employees. This should be a highly participatory process undertaken with the assistance of one or more individuals with the appropriate professional training and experience. According to two recent studies, organizations can significantly prevent or reduce workplace stress by developing: (1) a life stress scale—as an adaptation of the Holmes Rahe Scale, (2) a distress symptoms input form, (3) a burnout inventory, (4) an organizational stress audit, (5) stress balancing or mitigation strategies for different positions and units, and (6) other stress-related indexes, profiles, or feedback measures as deemed appropriate for the unique characteristics of the particular type of organization in question (Cryer, 1996; Covey, 1999).

With respect to performing a stress audit, an extensively used tool is the Occupational Stress Indicator (OSI), which uses six different but interrelated questionnaires that focus on: identifying sources of pressure, general patterns of employee behavior, perceptions of degree of job control, existing coping strategies, employee health, and job satisfaction (IRS, 2000).

After the necessary instruments have been created and a stress-related organizational diagnosis is made, action must be taken to reduce the stress levels and increase

| Stress Factors (Causes) | Individual Processing | Effects |
|---|---|---|
| physical environment:<br>  – light, noise<br>  – temperature, humidity<br>  – air pollution<br>  – unsanitary working conditions<br>  – vibration, movement<br>  – aesthetically un-pleasing<br>    surroundings<br><br>organizational:<br>  – formal structure flawed<br>  – inappropriate mgt. style<br>  – inappropriate control systems<br>  – inadequate/ inequitable reward<br>    system<br>  – interdepartmental politics &<br>    conflict<br>  – missing or confusing policies on<br>    work-related issues<br>  – poor communication<br><br>work group:<br>  – interpersonal conflict<br>  – poor group cohesiveness<br>  – poor group image/low status<br>  – extreme competition among<br>    group members<br><br>job-related:<br>  – role conflict/ambiguity<br>  – work overload or underload<br>  – non-productive meetings & tasks<br>  – constant deadlines/ unrealistic<br>    deadlines<br>  – decision making responsibility<br>    (lack or too much)<br>  – technological change and<br>    uncertainty<br>  – job insecurity<br>  – shift work<br>  – required to make life and death<br>    decisions | INDIVIDUAL REACTION/<br>ADAPTATION | subjective:<br>  – frustration, anger, boredom,<br>    apathy, anxiety, depression,<br>    fatigue, guilt, &/or loneliness<br><br>behavioral:<br>  – emotional outbursts<br>  – accident proneness<br>  – excessive eating, smoking,<br>    and/or drinking<br>  – loss of appetite<br>  – drug abuse<br>  – excitability<br>  – nervous laughter<br>  – tremors/trembling<br>  – restlessness<br>  – impulsive behavior<br>  – other nervous habits (tapping,<br>    nail biting, teeth grinding, etc.)<br><br>cognitive:<br>  – memory lapses<br>  – mental blocks<br>  – poor concentration<br>  – difficulty making decisions<br>  – hypersensitivity to criticism<br><br>physiological:<br>  – increased heart rate, blood<br>    pressure, blood sugar<br>  – dryness of mouth<br>  – pupil dilation<br>  – hot (sweating)<br>    cold (chills) body sensations<br>  – tingling and numbing in limbs<br><br>organizational:<br>  – job disputes<br>  – absenteeism<br>  – turnover<br>  – increased accidents<br>  – increased job/work related errors<br>  – upsetting or disruptive<br>    organizational climate<br>  – organizational disloyalty<br>  – overall decrease in productivity |

**Figure 1** Causes and effects of work-related stress. (From Cox 1978, Gibson et al., 1988, and Hampton et al., 1987.)

the coping skills of employees. The specific actions to be taken depend, of course, on the results of the stress audit. However, based on studies undertaken over the last two decades, a number of stress prevention and reduction strategies or techniques have been identified. The most effective of these appear to be: providing first-line supervisors and mid-level managers with specialized training focusing on the prevention, recognition, and treatment of workplace stress; whenever possible, utilizing team-based group work designed to give employees a feeling of increased job empowerment; creating an Employee Assistance Program (EAP) which includes a comprehensive counseling option for the prevention and treatment of stress-related disorders; demonstrating a commitment to adequate ongoing in-service training to deal with the problem of changing technology; increasing the flexibility of work schedules whenever possible and needed by employees; providing conflict management and other interpersonal skills-based workshops for employees; and maintaining open lines of communication between upper-level management and the rest of the organization. This last strategy is vitally important to alleviate such problems as job insecurity, role confusion, fear of and resistance to change, perceived reward system inequities, and any other unusual work-related problems.

Finally, in addition to the generic studies of stress in organizations, new research has appeared that focuses on job-related stress for such specific public sector occupations as policing (Anderson et al., 1995), disaster work (Grieger et al., 2000), mass transit operators (Ragland, 2000), firefighters (Salazar and Beaton, 2000), teachers (Anderson, 1999), public defenders (Lynch, 1998), and others. A present and future challenge for the public sector is to develop stress prevention and reduction models that are customized for different types of government agencies and the specific kinds of workers they employ. Another challenge that has led to important gains in stress reduction for some categories of public workers is the collective bargaining process.

## IV. COLLECTIVE BARGAINING AND REDUCTION OF WORKPLACE STRESS IN THE PUBLIC SECTOR

Both top management and union representatives need to be involved in the process of stress reduction and creating healthy organizational change. Among the healthy organizational changes needed to reduce occupational stress are changes that will

Increase employees' autonomy or control,
Increase the skill levels of employees,
Increase levels of social support (both supervisory and coworker),
Improve physical working conditions,
Make healthy use of technology,
Provide a reasonable level of job demands,
Provide for job security and career development,
Provide for healthy work schedules,
Improve the personal coping mechanisms of employees, and
Do no harm (i.e., do not have the unintended side effect of degrading the quality of work) (Cahill et al., 1995).

To facilitate the implementation of these changes in the form of specific programs, management can begin with occupational stress workshops followed by the formation of joint labor–management occupational stress committees. These committees should include union member employees from various departments, divisions, shifts, and work groups, and management representatives with real authority in the organization. For example, a public service agency on the East Coast formed a joint labor–management stress committee after a survey of staff found serious morale problems. The ongoing committee consisted of both top administrators and union leaders, which gave it credibility with the rest of the staff. After determining what issues could be addressed by the committee, it generated a number of effective individual and structural strategies to improve the working climate of the agency. (Cahill et al., 1995)

## A.  Occupational Stress as an International Collective Bargaining Issue

The collective bargaining process in the public sector has traditionally served to improve wages, working hours, and working conditions. Contemporary collective bargaining in the public sector has expanded the scope of negotiations and the traditional contract items, including working hours and working conditions, to include the reduction of occupational stress as one of the overall qualities of work life issues. The impact of information technologies (IT) on the quality of work life (QWL) and the growing concern with occupational stress has been the subject of a recent international symposium sponsored by the International Labor Organization (ILO, 2000a).

The forces of privatization and the subsequent restructuring of public sector agencies has increased occupational stress related to workers' health and safety. A 1999 survey of 9000 public sector workers in Ontarion concluded that in almost all cases, the consequences of reorganization, restructuring, downsizing, and contracting out are increasing workloads with a corresponding rise in injuries and stress (CUPE, 1999). The 1999 Survey was a follow-up to a previous 1993 Canadian Union of Public Employees Social Services Survey on stress-related workplace violence which concluded that 65% of the workers were subjected to some form of violence through aggressive acts and that the conditions creating the violence included staff shortages, growing caseloads, and reduced health and safety in the workplace (CUPE, 1999).

Increased occupational stress identified by the 1999 survey among public sector workers in Ontario was similar to other regions of Canada and has resulted in a nationwide increase in stress-related worker compensation claims. Growing concern over the rise in stress-related worker compensation claims has given rise to a nationwide lobbying effort by employers to exclude occupational stress from compensation eligibility in civil service and contract negotiations.

Other studies have found overwork in Canada and Europe to be a primary cause of occupational stress which led to high levels of burnout, poorer health, increased risk of workplace accidents, and lower productivity (32 Hours, 1998).

Since 1998, the federal and regional governments of France, the Netherlands, Italy, Belgium, Denmark, Canada, and more recently Spain, have developed, with the cooperation of public sector unions, various incentives for a reduction and redistribution of work time. In Belgium, public sector workers have the right to choose a four-day week, while receiving 90% of their former pay (32 Hours, 1998). In Italy, collective bargaining agreements have facilitated reductions in working time as a means of reducing occupational stress and other related working conditions (EU, 2000a).

A 2001 study on mental health in the workplace conducted by the International Labor Organization (ILO) suggests that economic globalization is a contributor to the high prevalence of occupational stress, burnout, and depression (ILO, 2001). The report takes into account the origins and complexities of mental difficulties and differing workplace practices, incomes, and employment patterns of the countries studied, which included Finland, Germany, Poland, and the United States (ILO, 2001). The report concludes that the incidence of mental health problems among public sector workers is increasing with as many as one in ten workers suffering from depression, anxiety, stress, or burnout, which in some cases, led to unemployment and hospitalization (ILO, 2001).

The European Union (EU) published the preliminary results of a survey of working conditions focusing on work-related health problems including occupational stress in the public and private sector of the 15 EU member nations. The survey, conducted by the European Foundation for the Improvement of Living and Working Conditions, involved 2500 individual face-to-face interviews and concluded that the results "should ring alarm bells in the European workplace" (EU, 2000b). Results of the 1997 Australian National Survey of public employees found high levels of insecurity and an increase in employee perceptions of greater stress. The Final Report on the survey's findings included recommendations for new industrial relations legislation to address occupational stress through collective bargaining (Burgess and Campbell, 1998). A 2000 Survey conducted by the ILO among public sector workers in the Czech Republic, Hungary, and Slovakia found occupational stress as the highest priority among organizational issues that needed to be addressed through collective bargaining (ILO, 2000b).

## B. Joint Labor–Management Strategies to Reduce Occupational Stress

A comprehensive approach to the reduction of occupational stress in the context of collective bargaining was developed in 1995 for managers, supervisors, and union members (Cahill et al., 1995). The authors' contended that the most important step in reducing occupational stress in collective bargaining is to have both top management and union representatives make a serious and sustained commitment to stress reduction as an important organizational goal. The authors' suggested that joint labor–management stress committees can develop a personal stress management activity along with an organizational activity. A personal coping strategy could be targeted toward the individual staff member while an organizational, or structural, change strategy is targeted toward the larger work environment. Of the two, structural strategies are more effective in reducing long-term stress and risk of illness. Choosing projects small enough to succeed but large enough to matter may be the most effective approach to obtain momentum and gain support for the joint labor-management committee. Following are some specific strategies that parallel the broad organizational goals detailed previously to manage and reduce occupational stress. (Cahill et al., 1995).

As Table 1 shows, effective strategies for the reduction of occupational stress can be developed with the participation of representatives of both labor and management. The successful outcome of these strategies is usually dependent upon the level of commitment of top management and labor representatives to the specific goals that each strategy is designed to address. Continuous commitment and participation by key members of both labor and management in the process of reducing stress are essential to making a real difference in the long term.

## C. The Impact of Privatization on Occupational Stress in the Context of Public Sector Collective Bargaining

The environment in which governments, public sector employees, and unions are operating is changing rapidly. In many countries, a variety of external pressures is causing governments to become more efficient through restructuring and downsizing through privatization. Privatization is leading to significant shifts in the skills required

**Table 1**  Goals and Strategies for Stress Management

| Goals | Strategies |
|---|---|
| Increasing employees' sense of control and participation in the workplace | Using staff meetings more effectively to encourage participation and input |
| | Develop autonomous work groups |
| Increasing the skill levels of employees | Increased skill-based training |
| | Use of career ladders to reward skill development |
| | Use of job rotation to expand skills |
| | Use of job redesign to increase range of skills needed |
| | Healthy use of computers for skill development |
| Increasing levels of social support | Training in proactive supervision |
| | Training in conflict resolution and team building |
| | Appropriate use of staff retreats |
| Changes that improve physical working conditions | Improving indoor air quality |
| | Reducing levels of physical hazards such as noise, toxins, chemicals, etc. |
| | Job redesign to reduce incidence of repetitive strain injuries (i.e., reducing repetitive work, awkward work postures, and/or heavy lifting) |
| Healthy use of technology | Healthy use of computers |
| | Staff involvement in choosing new equipment |
| Maintaining job demands at healthy levels | Reduced use of overtime |
| | Caseload restrictions |
| | Brake mechanism (an administrative group designed to reduce the amount of change the organization initiates) |
| | Formation of "What don't we need to do?" committee (an internal group charged with finding low priority or unnecessary tasks) |
| Changes that provide for job security and career development | Extension of career ladders |
| | Expansion of responsibilities and tasks |
| Changes that provide healthy work schedules | Reduced use of forced overtime |
| | Rotating shifts in a forward (day to night) schedule. |
| | Use of flexi-time and other alternative workweek schedules |
| Strategies to improve personal coping mechanisms | Improving the diet of employees |
| | Encouraging employees to exercise |
| | Training in deep muscle relaxation techniques |
| | Training in effective cognitive strategies |
| | Training in substance abuse awareness |
| | Organizing discussion groups on healthy stress reducers |
| | Transition time |
| | Leaving stress at the front door—training on family dynamics and parenting skills |

of workers, in behaviors, and in workplace practices. However, it is important to recognize the diversity among countries and recognize that not all countries are responding to these pressures and the subsequent occupational stress in the same way.

An important factor to consider is the role of public sector unions in this process of change because in most countries, the rates of unionization in public administration are high. Effective change, therefore, cannot happen without a constructive relationship between labor and management. The views of labor and management on the current unprecedented wave of privatization are very different, however, and there is a large gap between the two in their positions on privatization and restructuring in general. There has, in fact, not been an ongoing dialogue between labor and management on many of the issues involved and many labor unions perceive themselves to be structurally and politically excluded from the privatization process. This inevitably places labor in a reactive position, only able to criticize from the outside. Moreover, collective agreements are often seen by management as an impediment to change.

## D. Factors Linking Privatization, Productivity, Public Sector Unions, and Occupational Stress

### 1. Reduced Government Spending

In virtually all countries, debt control has emerged as a major issue in the 1990s and a key goal of government has been to control public spending and balance budgets. To achieve those goals, governments have worked to restrict the scope and nature of their activities and to reduce operating expenditures, often by significant employment reductions and through privatization of the delivery of services and adoption of other modes of alternative service delivery.

### 2. A Shift in Political Philosophies

In most countries, there has been a shift in political ideologies away from a view that governments should be direct providers of a wide variety of services to citizens to a view that the private sector is best able to meet many public needs. This new view of government focuses on its role in policy development, in information brokering, and in fostering collaboration between various groups outside government. This shift in the role of government in the economy and society implies a reduction in the size of government and changes in the nature of government work often through privatization. Together, these outcomes have significant implications for the nature of skills demanded of government workers and occupational stress.

### 3. Globalization

Globalization and deregulation have raised competitive standards for efficiency, productivity, and quality in both the private and public sectors. The public sector has a significant impact on national economic performance through its direct impact as a buyer and seller of goods and services, through its indirect impact on product and labor markets, and because the regulatory environment has significant impact on the economy (Purchase and Hirshhorn, 1994).

### 4. Emphasis on Results

Increasingly, just as in the private sector, governments are being expected to define and apply performance standards in order to measure both their efficiency and their effectiveness. Typically this involves the adoption of market-type mechanisms such as privatization for the delivery of programs and services. Consequently, there is a growing emphasis on performance measurement with respect to efficiency/productivity, quality, and on-time delivery both in terms of output (efficiency) and in terms of outcomes (effectiveness). In terms of human resource impact, that means that growing attention is being given to innovative practices such as pay-for-results and performance pay, the pressures of which add to occupational stress.

## 5. Information and Communication Technologies (ICT)

The on-going spread of ICT presents governments with the opportunity to change service delivery practices. At the same time, research on the private sector shows that there is a close link between technological and organizational change. Increasingly, that research is pointing to the emergence of new forms of work organization as the use of ICT deepens within organizations. There is a tendency toward knowledge work and people-centeredness and, as problem-solving responsibilities move down the hierarchy, middle- and lower-management positions are threatened (Frenkel, 1995). Attewell (1992) notes that ICT heightens "connectivity" or "lateral dependence" in an organization. Together, the features of ICT lead to increases in complexity, responsibility, and accountability for individual workers and require new managerial approaches and new workplace arrangements some of which inevitably increase occupational stress.

## 6. Changing Demographics

Partly in reflection of the aging of the population as a whole, and partly as a result of steps that have already been taken to reduce the size of the public sector, significant aging has taken place in government workforces in most countries. Managing an aging workforce poses different challenges from the case when the workforce is composed of a mix of young, prime-aged, and older workers. As populations continue to age, governments will need to compete with the private sector for a smaller pool of young workers. Evidence from the private sector indicates that there is a general trend toward a technically skilled and more innovative labor force. As the same trend continues in government, competition for this type of worker will be particularly intense resulting in increased occupational stress for the less-skilled workers usually represented by public sector unions.

## 7. Some Examples of Negative Outcomes of Privatization Relevant to Productivity and Occupational Stress

As noted above, privatization is one of the most critical and politically sensitive government activities. It has led to fundamental shifts in the relationship between the private and public sectors in many jurisdictions. The role and scope of privatization have increased dramatically in the last ten years both in the form of contracting out of public services and in the outright purchase of government enterprises by the private sector on the national and international levels. The overwhelming concern for the increasing globalization of privatization activities tends to narrowly focus on economic factors for success at the expense of social factors for those most affected. These privatization activities often are characterized by short-term economic gains by private sector interest groups of the affected public sector agencies and community. Moreover, commonly accepted tradeoffs that occur throughout the privatization process typically create an imbalance of accrued benefits to various segments of the workforce and members of the community, in general.

Generally, privatization has negative as well as positive consequences and the negative consequences are often masked or go undetected because the effectiveness of privatization is based primarily on economic performance. As shown in Table 2, public services that are typically restructured and downsized through privatization can result in a variety of negative outcomes.

## E.  Management of the Future Unionized Workplace and Occupational Stress

What type of workplace and management strategies will best match the evolving nature of government work? The traditional civil-service model is characterized by clearly delineated job definitions, procedures for merit-based promotions, the linking of greater authority with greater knowledge and expertise and, more recently, the pursuit of equity principles. Governments argue that changes which have taken place over the 1990s call into question the extent to which the traditional model allows governments to meet its new objectives.

Trends in the size and nature of government over the past decade have had, and will continue to have, major implications for government workers and for the shape of government workplaces. Some of these impacts are the result of the process of change itself and of the significant amount of downsizing that has already taken place. Other impacts, however, are still emerging as governments struggle to define themselves and work to identify what their human resource requirements will be in the future. And questions remain as to whether the changes that are currently being experienced will continue in the long term or whether new directions will emerge if the nature of external pressures changes.

It is important to have a sense of the scale of employment change that has taken place in public administration in the 1990s. Since the early 1990s, major reductions have taken place at both the federal and local levels, with employment in public administration decreasing 18 to 20% in most countries. In fact, in most jurisdictions, the main strategy used to shrink government budget deficits has been to reduce labor costs through a combination of employment cuts and salary freezes rather than through increased taxes. This strategy has had implications for work and workers and raises a number of workplace issues.

Not surprisingly, this environment has had major implications for public sector unions and collective bargaining. In the 1990s, cuts that have taken place have seriously affected notions of job security and collective agreements have been overridden. The result is a difficult atmosphere in which to constructively negotiate new workplace "bargains." It is important to recognize as well that the nature or tone of labor–management relations at the macro level can have major implications for attitudes and the quality of relations at the workplace level.

The federal level also saw relatively strong growth among professional occupations and some growth in computer-related occupations. Very large decreases took place in the size of the clerical and secretarial groups in both levels of government. These trends parallel similar trends in the private sector, trends that partly reflect shifts that are taking place in response to the deepening use of computer-based technologies in organizations (McMullen, 1996).

**Table 2**  Some Examples of Negative Outcomes of Privatized Public Services

| Privatized public service | Year(s) | Results/outcomes |
|---|---|---|
| Lockheed Martin Inc. contracted to automate Child Support Services in California for $99m by 1997 (AFSCME, 2001) | 1992–1997 | Cost overruns of $297m With only 23 of 58 counties automated by 1997 Productivity dropped 60–70% Staff and employees experienced increased pressure and frustration and spent more time identifying problems than actually handling cases The Director of San Francisco County pulled out of the project and reactivated its old system |
| Laidaw Educational Services (LES) to provide school bus services to Charleston County School District, South Carolina (*Post and Courier*, 1999) | 1999 | Students late for school and missed out on free breakfast program Pressure on school staff and employees by students and angry parents School District withheld payments to LES pending compliance |
| TANF to provide case management and job placement services to Mississippi Department of Human Services (DHS) (Duncan, 1999) | 1996–1999 | Private and public interests did not mesh well or communicate clearly DHS was responsible for success, but it had no actual authority or means of ensuring quality and compliance with policy objectives of its privatized components DHS eliminated the privatized case management component because of high turnover rates caused by job stress |
| Wackenhut to provide security and food service operations at Austin (Texas) State Corrections Facility (Quin, 1999) | 1996–1998 | Allegations of neglect, falsification of records, and sexual misconduct Chronic staff shortage and turnover due to stress State of Texas cancelled contract and resumed responsibility of the privatized components |
| Corrections Corporation of America (CCA) to provide security services for correction facility in Youngstown, Ohio (*The Cleveland Plain Dealer*, 1999) | 1996–1998 | $1.65m paid by CCA to settle class action lawsuit that claimed facility was "unsafe" for prisoners and staff Unsafe conditions led to stress and subsequent high turnover rates |

### i.   Changes in Workplace Issues, Workforce and Work

These occupational shifts are themselves indicative of a shift in the "business" of government, however, they also raise a number of workplace issues. It is likely, for example, that workplaces composed primarily of highly skilled workers will require different sets of human resource management practices than workplaces where lower-skilled workers predominate.

Governments face a challenge on this front too. There is evidence that the message given to many, by downsizing and privatization and a lack of recruitment, is that public administration is a hostile environment for workers, especially young ones. This view can only be reinforced by current concerns around issues of morale among "survivors" of downsizing and privatization who must cope with and adapt to ongoing change. Many young people do not see employment in government as a viable career option. For those who survive privatization, occupational stress increases.

The challenge for governments is how to shape public sector internal labor markets that can compete with the private sector in terms of earnings, promotion, and career development. Governments need to examine all aspects of remuneration including nonwage earnings and the role that can and should be played by innovative practices such as performance-based pay and the use of bonuses. Because for most occupational groups compensation is bargained collectively, any new approaches that are developed must meet with union approval.

### ii.   Flexible Workforce, Pace of Work, and Occupational Stress

If a trend to employing more workers on a contract or temporary basis continues in government, a number of issues will arise. Many of these concern how managers can integrate different types of workers while recognizing that different conditions of work might apply to them. For example, do workplace rules that apply to regular workers also apply to nonstandard workers? How do managers create an atmosphere of inclusion, a sense of belonging, and commitment in workers with a less than permanent attachment to a workplace? How do nonstandard workers fit a unionized environment? What adjustments are expected of unions and how willing and able are unions to make these adjustments?

The way in which public managers answer these questions will determine the nature of the impact of privatization on occupational stress of the workforce. Given the scale of workforce reductions that have taken place in government in the 1990s, it is not surprising that issues relating to pace of work, workload, and stress are gaining profile as employees who remain after privatization and downsizing are asked to do more with less, and often in new ways. The pressure to do more with less, in shorter timeframes, and with little flexibility to manage financial and human resources are major sources of stress. Results of a recent survey of managers note that many managers feel that levels of stress among workers in their units are having a negative effect on employee productivity (Public Management Research Centre, 1997). Among both managerial and nonmanagerial workers, the amount of both paid and unpaid overtime is becoming an important concern.

## V.   CONCLUSION

The process of restructuring government through privatization is one that has involved downsizing, changing the focus or "business" of government, and shifts in the occupational and skill mix of workers. Ultimately, this process of restructuring is having major implications for the shape of government workplaces as the arena in which change takes place.

In the shorter term, issues around morale loom large as survivors of cuts adapt to increased workloads, new demands, low or nonexistent pay increases, and public attitudes that reflect a view that government employees are expendable lead to increased occupational stress and a decrease in productivity. Low employee morale can in turn have an impact not only on employee performance today but also on government's ability to recruit high-quality workers for tomorrow. In the longer term, governments need to be clear on their role in the economy and in society and act to transform traditional approaches to production and occupational stress into practices that motivate and reward workers, while creating workplaces that are both efficient and equitable.

Finally, it is also very important to note that these issues need to be examined from a management as well as a union perspective. Clearly, the reform of government is placing public sector unions in a difficult position and strategies need to be worked out that allow unions to be recognized as key players in workplace change.

All other things being equal, the presence of a collaborative and cooperative approach between labor and management to occupational stress reduction in the public sector appears to be the most important criterion for success from an international perspective regardless of country, region (i.e., North or South America, Eastern or Western Europe), or level of development.

In conclusion, it appears that throughout the world, international data from comparative analysis and case studies reveal that the reduction of occupational stress improves the potential for real productivity gains and the overall quality of work life.

# REFERENCES

AFSCME. American Federal, State, and County Municipal Employees. (2001). *Government for Sale: An Examination of the Contracting Out of State and Local Government Services.* 6th ed. Washington, DC: AFSCME.

Anderson, V. (1999). The effects of mediation on teacher perceived occupational stress, state, and trait anxiety, and burnout. *School Psych. Quart.* 14(1).

Anderson, W., et al. (1995). *Stress Management for Law Enforcement Officers.* Englewood Cliffs, NJ: Prentice-Hall.

Attewell, Paul. (1992). Skill and occupational change in U.S. manufacturing. In: Adler, Paul S., ed. *Technology and the Future of Work.* New York: Oxford University Press.

Bosma, H., et al. (1997). Low job control and risk of coronary heart disease in Whitehall II Study. *British Med. J.* 314, 558–655.

Burgess, J., Campbell, I. (1998). The nature and dimensions of precarious employment in Australia. *Labour Industry* 8(3):5–21.

Cahill, J., Landsbergis, P. A., Schnall, P. L. (1995, September). *Reducing Occupational Stress.* Proceedings of the Work Stress and Health Conference, Washington, DC.

The Cleveland Plain Dealer. (1999, March 3).*Policing the prison: settlement with private lock up in youngstown should cut violence and mismanagement* p. 8B.

Covey, F. (1999, October). Rethinking stress. Available at http://www.franklincovey.com/organizational/servprod/rts.htm/.

Cox, T. (1978). *Stress.* Baltimore: University Park Press.

Cryer, B. (1996, June). *Neutralizing workplace stress: The physiology of human performance and organizational effectiveness.* Proceedings of Psychological Disabilities in the Workplace: The Centre for Professional Learning, Toronto. Available at http://www.heartmath.com/Library/articles/neutralize.html.

CUPE. Canadian Union of Public Employees Bargaining Issues Report. (1999, December). *Overloaded and Under Fire: Report of the Ontario Social Services Work Environment Survey*, Ottawa, Ontario.

Duncan, C. (1999). *Privatization of Mississippi DHS.* Welfare to Work, 4.

EU. European Union. (2000a, May). *Reorganization and Reduction of Working Time in France.* Peer Review Summary Report, Geneva.

EU. European Union. (2000b, December). *Survey of Working Conditions* (Preliminary Report), Geneva.

Frenkel, S. (1995). Re-constituting work: Trends towards knowledge, work, and info-normative control. In: Frenkel, S., Korczynski, M., Donohue, L., Shire, K., eds. *Work, Employment, and Society* 9(4):773–796.

Gibson, J. L., Invancevich, J. M., Donnelly, J. H. (1988). *Organizations: Behavior, Structure, Processes.* 6th ed. Piano, TX: Business Publications.

Grieger, T. A., et al. (2000). Acute stress disorder and subsequent post-traumatic stress disorder in a group of disaster workers. *Depression Anxiety* 11(4):183–184.

Gushue, John (1996). Increasing workplace stress means occupational medicine will be a growth area. *Canadian Med. Assoc. J.* 155(9):1310–1313.

Hampton, D. R., Summer, C. E., Webber, R. A. (1987). *Organization Behavior and the Practice of Management.* 5th ed. Glenview, IL: Scott, Foresman.

Helfand, G. (1992). Work-related stress and productivity. In: Holzer, Marc, ed. *Public Productivity Handbook.* New York: Marcel Dekker.

ILO. International Labor Organization. (2000a, February 28). *Symposium on Information Technologies in the Media and Entertainment Industries: Their Impact on Employment, Working Conditions, and Labour-Management Relations Final Report*, Geneva.

ILO. International Labor Organization. (2000b, May). *Central and Eastern European Team Survey Report*, Geneva.

ILO. International Labor Organization. (2001). *Mental Health in the Workplace: An Introduction*, Geneva.

IRS. *IRS Employment Review.* (2000). 709(13).

IT revolution adds to workplace stress: Study. (2000, October 11). *The Times of India.* Available at http://www.timesofindia.com/111000/11hlth13.htm.

Lynch, D. (1998). In their own words: Occupational stress among public defenders. *Crim. Law Bull.* 30(6):473–497.

Marmot, M., et al. (1997). Contribution of job control and other risk factors to social variations in coronary heart disease incidence. Lancet 350:235–239.

McMullen, Kathryn. (1996). *Skill and Employment Effects of Computer-based Technology: The Results of the Working with Technology Survey III.* CPRN Study No. W/01, Ottawa: Canadian Policy Research Networks.

*The Post and Courier.* (1999, November 6). Charleston, South Carolina.

Probst, T., Brubaker, T. (2001). The effects of job insecurity or employee safety outcomes: Cross-sectional and longitudinal explorations. *J. Occup. Health Psych.* 6(2).

Public Management Research Centre. (1997). *Results of Focus Group Discussions with Senior Public Servants*, Ottawa: Public Management Research Centre.

Purchase, B., Hirshhorn, R. (1994). *Searching for Good Governance.* Kingston: Queen's University School of Policy Studies.

Quin, L. (1999, September 23). *Travis to jail: Stay out of probe: County wants inquiry into whether Wackenhut Corrections Corp. wrongly paid witness.* p. BI. Austin *American—Statesman.*

Ragland, D. (2000). Neurobiological, psychosocial and developmental correlates of drinking—

occupational stress factors and alcohol—related behavior in urban transit operators. *Alcoholism: Clinical Exper. Res.* 21(7):1011–1020.

Salazar, M., Beaton, R. (2000). Ecological model of occupational stress: Application to urban firefighters. *J. Am. Assoc. Occup. Health Nurses* 48(10).

Scorza, J. (1998). Workshops: Reduce workplace stress, increase profits. *Score* Available at http://www.score.org/workshops/reducestress.html.

32 Hours. (1998, September). *32 Hours: Action for Full Employment, Budgetary Options to Promote a Reduction and Redistribution of Work Time.* Report of Standing Committee on Finance, Government of Canada, Toronto.

# 33

# Organizational Change and Innovation

**DOROTHY OLSHFSKI and HELISSE LEVINE**
*Rutgers, The State University of New Jersey, Newark, New Jersey, U.S.A.*

## I. INTRODUCTION

Change is a given. To think otherwise is delusional. Change may be intended or unexpected; it may be positive or disruptive, radical or incremental. People may react with acceptance, resistance, or sabotage. It is probably a byproduct of globalization and our advanced technology, but both government bureaucracies and private companies are continually being challenged by change. In the private sector, pioneering new technologies, processes, and applications are increasingly recognized as central to the firm's long-term viability. In the public sector the emphasis on change has not been as strident as it is in the private sector. After all, the government is not as threatened by change. It won't go out of business. Or will it? The reinventing and reengineering movements and the emphasis on privatization and contracting out have refocused government activity and changed the size and scope of government. In a fast-changing world, the goal is to maintain relevancy. Government must maintain its relevance by adapting to the changes in society so that the role of government in society fits the times. Dealing successfully with change is how the government maintains its fit, and ensures its legitimacy.

The challenges presented by a fast-moving world are defined by public administration and management literature from diverse yet overlapping perspectives. Lane (1997), for example, refers to extant public sector change engines internally driven by deregulation, privatization, and marketization. Kettl (2001) looks at external forces of globalization and devolution as the central concerns the federal government will be faced with in the upcoming decade. Vaill (1989) depicts the changing context of organizations as a world of permanent whitewater, where the role of leader-manager must be reassessed amidst an uncertain and chaotic world. Most recently, the impending challenges to management in the public organization as it nears a "hollow state" of governance have also been recognized in public administration as a change of major proportion that must be recognized in order for the polity to begin to cope with it (Goodsell, 2001; Milward and Provan, 2000).

Despite opinion to the contrary, government bureaucracies change and innovate. Every new president pursues his own agenda and the bureaucracy follows, maybe not enthusiastically, but they have to cope with the new priorities. Agency heads set the agenda for their departments. However, they only stay in office an average of 2 1/2 years; consequently government departments are constantly adjusting to a new set of priorities. Meyer (1979) found that public bureaucracies changed constantly in his study of 270 state and local finance departments. Similarly, case studies of the Veterans Health Administration (Young, 2000), Village Creek Wastewater Plant (Nunn, 1992), Florida Department of Highway Safety (Stokes-Berry et al., 1998), and studies of innovation among public managers (Borins, 2000; Rainey, 1999), government information systems (Landsbergen and Wolken, 2001), and quality management efforts in the Pennsylvania Department of Transportation (Poister and Harris, 2000) confirm that transformation in public organizations not only takes place, but contibutes to performance improvement and productivity as well.

Regardless of the nature or cause, all organizations undergo change constantly. In this chapter we examine theoretical models of organizational change and types of change as they present themselves to public and private organizations and make some recommendations for both research and practice in dealing with change.

## II. THEORETICAL MODELS OF ORGANIZATIONAL CHANGE

Because change is a complex phenomenon and single theories can only offer a partial explanation of what is happening, we can expect no single theory of change to explain everything. Rather, the literature on organizational change offers different metaphors to aid in interpreting change. The guiding metaphor will describe the change, explain why it happened, predict where the change activity is likely to go, and generally offer the analyst a useful way to interpret events. Furthermore, the metaphors complement each other by providing alternative interpretations of the same series of events. The insight gained by the reinterpretation of events using different metaphors offers the analyst a more sensitive and sophisticated interpretation of change.

Three theoretical frameworks characteristic of change literature particular to government and business organizations are modeled after well-known paradigms in the physical and social world. Interpreting change using a mental map grounded in physics was first introduced by Kurt Lewin (1947). Lewin's three-stage change model, later echoed by a profusion of change research in both public and private sectors, adopted an open-system view of organizations that assumed that change was rational and episodic, and planned adaptations of existing organizations to the environment (Meyer, 1979; Beckhard and Harris, 1977; Beer, 1980; Moss-Kanter, 1983). Within this category there is also a subset of researchers who sees change as goal oriented and therefore the change is purposive (Marx and Engels, 1848; Fukuyama, 1992).

Next, evolutionary theorists, using biology as their frame of reference presume change as a naturally occurring phenomenon. Organizations grow, they mutate to adjust to their environments, and they survive if they are the strongest. There are two strains of thinking within the biology metaphors: lifecycle theorists who identify a developmental sequence with respect to change (Kimberly and Miles, 1980), and evolutionary theorists who see organizational mutations in response to environmental stimuli but reject the notion of a predictable sequence (Aldrich, 1979; Rothschild, 1990).

Theorists in this last category also see change as continuous and inevitable, but they focus on the irrationality, unpredictability, and uncontrollable nature of change (Waldrop, 1992). Change as navigating whitewater (Vaill, 1989) depicts the organization as trying to maintain control as it is buffeted by internal and external forces. Structures may be more unstable than we realize and organizational roles are becoming less defined. Similar to the garbage-can model of decision making (Cohen et al., 1972), change in the whitewater mode matches adaptations with situations as they emerge. Each of these metaphors is examined in the next section.

## A. Change Interpreted as a Physics Metaphor

Physics interprets nature as a series of actions and reactions. In this model the world is seen as a mixture of colliding forces and events that compete for dominance. Based on the Newtonian law of physics, this model of change has been the dominant conceptualization. Using this conception of change, the process is rational. A system becomes unstable as oppositional forces emerge and then collide to produce change. A new equilibrium is produced and it lasts a while until new oppositional forces emerge. And the process continues.

Lewin (1947) described this change process in three stages that assumes a state of disequilibrium as the precursor to change, followed by a transition stage that ultimately emerges into a new and stable, yet temporary, equilibrium. This final stage becomes institutionalized until altered by a deliberate change agent, once again causing a shift in the status quo.

Cummings and Worley (1997) list four basic activities that take place in organizations during planned change: entering and contracting, planning, implementing, and institutionalizing. During the initial stage, data are gathered, resources are committed, contracts are agreed upon, and problems and planned change efforts determined. The next step shifts the behaviors of the organization, department, or individual to a new level. Visions are created, and behaviors, values, and attitudes are developed through changes in organizational structures and processes. Finally, a new state of equilibrium emerges reinforced through the culture and policies of the organization.

Table 1 summarizes some of the "organizations as iced cube" models (Moss-Kantor et al., 1992, p. 376). Whether the stages are called unfreezing, moving, refreezing (Lewin, 1947), or a Three-Act Drama (Tichy and DeVanna, 1986), a physics-based theory of change does not assume a continuous change process. Five assumptions emerge from this analytic framework: linearity (movement is from one state to another in a forward direction through time), progressive movement, movement is toward a specific goal, disequilibrium is requisite, and the movement is planned and managed by people outside the system (Marshak, 1993, quoted in Weick and Quinn, 1999).

## B. Change Interpreted as a Biology Metaphor

Biology sees nature as constantly evolving so that change proceeds through a cycle of mutation or variation, selection, and then retention. Building on the Darwinian model, survival depends upon adapting to environmental conditions in an incremental

**Table 1** Linear Models of Change

| Model | Process | | |
|-------|---------|---|---|
| Lewin (1947) | Unfreezing | Changing | Refreezing |
| Beckhard and Harris (1977) | Present state | Transition state | Future state |
| Beer (1980) | Dissatisfaction × | Process × | Model |
| Kanter (1983) | Departures from tradition and crises | Strategic decisions and prime movers | Action vehicles and institutionalism |
| Tichy and DeVanna (1986) | Act I—awakening | Act II—mobilizing | Act III—(epilogue) reinforcing |
| Nadler and Tushman (1989) | Energizing | Envisioning | Enabling |

*Source*: Moss-Kantor et al., 1992.

fashion. The evolutionary, or natural-selection, approach to organizational change claims that those organizations best adapted to their environment survive; the rest are eliminated (Meyer, 1979; Aldrich, 1979). It is a way to look at change that assumes competitive selection and resource scarcity (Van de Ven and Poole, 1995).

Using the biology metaphor, Downs (1967) proposed a three-stage lifecycle positing that government bureaus transform, invariably, through predetermined phases. Once an agency comes into existence it struggles to establish its autonomy, then it goes into an expansion stage, and finally, a deceleration phase where the rules are recorded, gains are consolidated, and the agency becomes more rigid. Quinn (1985) expanded upon the Downs model by including a final stage where the organization manipulates its structures and processes in order to adapt to its environment. A natural expansion of this thinking is the study of organizational decline and death.

Rothschild (1990) argues that the entire economy can be viewed as an ecosystem. Organizations are built upon complex hierarchies, where some organizations are simple like a single-celled creature, and others are immensely complex. Economies evolve and adapt to environments; spontaneous order emerges from the interaction of the system's components. Following the change as biology argument, Fukuyama (1992) also describes the predictable evolution of societies toward a final goal, liberal democracy.

Viewing change using the biology metaphor encourages the analyst to focus on the organization as it adjusts itself to its environment. This model best accommodates change that is evolutionary rather than revolutionary.

## C. Change Interpreted as a Whitewater Metaphor

Instead of a quest for predictable change, the whitewater metaphor views the world as being about flux and change, and the forming and dissolving of patterns. Emery and Trist (1965) noted very early on that the environment of organizations is increasingly subjected to flux and uncertainty. The whitewater analogy finds comfort in chaos theory and tends to view managing as a performing art inasmuch as the best the manager can do is keep the organization afloat, by orchestrating the deployment of talent given the environment at any given time (Vaill, 1989).

Chia (1999) views change as the "sine qua non" of all living and social systems. From this conceptual lens, transformation and renewal emanate from an indeterminate and complex process intrinsic to all organizations, not as the outcome of an external remedy or deliberate intevention. As a result, there is no initial or stable state of equilibrium that is jarred by an external environment that needs to be fixed. Rather, change is perceived as outside the boundaries of Newtonian physics where reality is explained through spatial and temporal sequences. It is also outside the evolutionary movements of the biology metaphor that explains variation as adaptations and mutations.

The turbulent and continual movement of the change process implied by the whitewater metaphor imposes constant demands on social organizations and the people who manage them. As complexity theory explains, when applying nonlinear and "whitewater" change forces to human organizations, the organization must adapt to the world of continuous flux. This implies a constant re-creation of the organization itself in a manner analogous to the nonlinearlike nature of the change processes (Neumann, 1997).

Viewing change using the whitewater metaphor encourages the investigator to look for abrupt departure from the existing operations of the organization. This model can accommodate both radical and disruptive change. Radical change efforts navigate unexplored territory in an attempt to continually generate path-breaking and revolutionary ideas and innovations. Nadler (1998, p. 63) defines radical change efforts as a "dramatic change in strategy and abrupt departures from traditional work, structures, job requirements, and cultures, which in turn necessitate a complete overhaul of the organization." Disruptive change involves the advent of a technology that does not improve the performance of a traditional product but offers instead an opportunity to produce a new variaton on the original product that will signal a change in the criteria by which customers choose (Christensen, 2000; Christensen and Overdorf, 2000; Hamel, 1999, 2000). Christensen (2000) illustrated this point by arguing that the electric car could not compete with the traditional product (gasoline-powered cars) on the dimensions of speed, distance, or acceleration time in the year 2002. However, as electric car technology advances, these three dimensions may be replaced with cost of operating as the key decision criterion. In this case, the disruptive technology could displace the traditional product if the electric cars improved enough for speed, acceleration, and distance so that these criteria would no longer determine the customer's choice. Radical and disruptive changes are more easily identified by using the whitewater analogy because this view of organizational change anticipates big shifts in focus.

The model-in-use determines how actual organizational change will be interpreted. Theory offers description, explanation, and prediction so the particular metaphor used to characterize the change will strongly influence the interpretation in all three of those categories. The skilled analyst is aware of the model-in-use and can move among the models to expand the interpretation of the situation in the organization.

## III. CATEGORIES OF CHANGE

Change comes in two packages: planned and unplanned. Adaptation to intentional organizational change is commonly called Organizational Development or OD and it refers to proactive efforts of facilitating change via planned or intentional change agents. Golembiewski (1989) has identified three components of an organizational development effort that require attention from those directing the change: the patterns of relationships among those in the organization should be clarified and examined to guard against disruptive interaction patterns; a suitable structure to facilitate the desired change should be put in place; and appropriate policies that reinforce the OD effort should be implemented.

On the other hand, unplanned change forces the organization to adopt a reactive posture and to focus on adaptation. Externally imposed change, such as volatile political and regulatory environments (Nunn, 1992) which pose threats to an organization's viability due to reduction in market share, financial losses, and a declining industry (Mone et al., 1998) or a change in government policy (Tobias, 2000; Taylor and Pierce, 1999; Light, 2000), compels both public and private organizations to initiate change efforts.

Organizations can employ strategic planning to attempt to accommodate change in an organized and thoughtful manner, but not all change is predictable. Planned and unplanned change is a routine problem for organizational planners. In this section we discuss types of change that we can say with some certainty now have an impact on or will have an impact on public and private organizations in the near future. Technological change, administrative changes, and change in work and the workforce are issues that will continue to challenge organizations.

## A. Technological Change

The adoption of innovative information technology for improving performance has been widely discussed in contemporary public and private organizational literature (West and Berman, 2001; Landsbergen and Wolken, 2001; Borins, 2001; Stokes-Berry, 1997; Goodman and Darr, 1996; Young, 2000). The ongoing development of the World Wide Web, electronic government and business, and virtual conferencing has changed the way we collect, share, and produce usable knowledge and deliver services to customers and clients, but it also has provided an alternative to hierarchy as the primary means of information processing (Walton and Nadler, 1994; LaPorte et al., 2001).

In the public sector, the extent of the information technology network is a function of the funding and commitment of the government providing the funding. The federal level government is committed to applying technology to support their functions and to communicate with citizens (see http://www/firstgov.gov). But there is variability among states and this variability is dramatically visible when considering the information technology capabilities of local governments. Public funding of an extensive network of information technology in the United States is largely the responsibility of the separate governments and their support is largely determined by the level of sophistication of the government managers, the size of the budget, and the far-sightedness of their strategic vision. In spite of the demonstrated success of adapting information technology and computer applications to problem solving, coping with technological change is still problematic, especially at the local levels.

Research, however, has demonstrated the effectiveness of successful application of technology to public sector problems. Using case studies to examine the application of technology by two federal agencies, Landsbergen and Wolken (2001, p. 211) illustrated the importance of data-transfer technologies in cross-agency regulatory enforcement and reporting methods. Their findings "argue for the development of infrastructure for government to support more agencies in sharing information." A similar argument is considered by West and Berman (2001) in their examination of the reciprocal relationships among revitalized management practices (risk-taking, openness in decision making, and managerial and peer support to employees) and the effect of innovative technology on organizational effectiveness (service delivery improvement, wider use of knowledge sources, and stakeholder satisfaction). They found that a positive impact of information technology on organizations (efficiency, effectiveness, responsiveness, and timeliness) requires managerial support in coordinating and facilitating the change process. Borins (2001) found that the creation and use of databases for obtaining employment records to enforce child support obligations of noncustodial parents is a good example of effective technological change in public agencies. Similarly, LaPorte et al. (2001) found that the character and the quality of civic life were enhanced in their examination of the role of the Internet and the Web in transforming government administration worldwide.

Technological change has quickened the pace of our work life; it has really allowed us to do more with less faster. But it has also provided access to much more data and information than ever before. Information overload is clearly a problem for most agencies and managers. Managing information is now a pressing problem. Knowledge management is the process that attempts to organize, codify, and structure what is known by those involved in the work of the organization. Knowledge management strategies attempt to harness knowledge held by those individuals in geographically dispersed locations both inside and outside the organizations and to maintain historical records of organizational decisions and the supporting rationale. There is a wide variety of activities subsumed under the rubric of knowledge management, ranging from organizing data in a uniformly accessible manner so that it can be shared, to elaborate techniques that attempt to make tacit knowledge available throughout the organization. It is becoming a mandatory ingredient in private sector organizational structure, and increasingly it is being recognized as important to public sector effectiveness as well (Denning, 2001; Hansen et al., 1999; Ruggles, 1998). Starbucks, the gourmet coffee chain, for example, attributes continued growth and ultimate success to the "connectedness" of its 425 stores due to their use of Lotus Notes which allows shared databases of geographically disparate units (Goodman and Darr, 1996).

## B.  Administrative Change

The efficacy of the traditional bureaucratic model of public administration has been questioned in recent years as governments have adopted privatization, outsourcing, and private–public partnerships to provide public services (Osborne, 1993; Auger, 1999; Meyer, 1979; Golembiewski and Kiepper, 1988; Greer et al., 1999; White, 1999; Doherty and Nord, 1993). Administration of contracts instead of administration of an operating program is increasingly the case in government, especially at the federal level.

Furthermore, administrative change initiatives that affect the employees, such as reward systems, employee compensation, performance-based management, and performance appraisal systems, have had a strong influence on employee motivation and control (Tobias, 2000; Wholey, 1999). Contrary to traditional hierarchical models of management, performance-based management includes "delegating authority and flexibility in return for accountability for results, creating incentives for improved program performance, redesigning central management systems to focus on performance, reallocating resources or redirecting performance activities to improve performance, and developing partnerships designed to improve performance" (Wholey, 1999, p. 5). High-performing public organizations provide a reward system that has strong egalitarian features, as in having all salaried employees as opposed to white-collar versus blue-collar, is based on skills possessed, rather than specific tasks actually performed; encourages skill development, even far beyond tasks currently performed; and includes gain-sharing, ownership, or other features to enhance motivation by tying rewards to performance (Golembiewski and Kiepper, 1998). Whereas administration of traditional job-based compensation systems entails centralized and top-down decision making, decentralized decision making, employee involvement, and performance-based compensation systems, indicative of nontraditional structures, are reflective of and better suited for changing environments (Doherty and Nord, 1993). But at the same time these new administrative structures require managerial skills different from those required only twenty years ago.

Government agencies lag behind the private sector in their personnel practices. Pay-for-performance systems are used widely in the private sector, but they are not as prevalent in public service agencies (Taylor and Pierce, 1999; Light, 2000). Furthermore, Roberts (2001) posits that municipal governments trail behind the private sector in family-friendly provisions such as flex-time, flexi-place, elder care, and childcare. As Roberts (2001, p. 390) suggests in his study of benefits administration in municipal governments, "Relying on traditional benefits to attract and retain employees, given changes in employee needs and characteristics, may attenuate the abilities of municipal governments to maintain high quality work forces."

The Veterans Health Administration, one of the largest agencies in the federal government, illustrates a successful transformation effort amidst private sector competition, fiscal constraints, stakeholder pressure, increased medical technology, shift in resource priorities from inpatient-oriented tertiary care to outpatient-oriented primary care, and government regulations, obstacles the VHA was forced to overcome or perish (Young, 2000). Based on the experiences of the VHA in response to both external and internal environmental pressures, transformational leadership, perseverance, training, communication, education, and decentralization of decision making contribute to a successful change effort to improve performance in organizations generally, and public sector agencies specifically (Young, 2000).

Administrative change on the scale that is presently being applied is a relatively new phenomenon. Max Weber's (1946) hierarchy has withstood one hundred years of application but it appears that the end may be near, at least for some organizations. The trends toward changing the way work is administered are occurring both externally (privatization, outsourcing, and contracting out) and internally (pay-for-performance, decentralized decision making, devolution of authority, etc.). Public organizations can try to avoid these changes but their success in doing this is unlikely.

## C.  Changes in Work and the Workforce

Internal environmental pressures such as workforce diversity and changing demographics represent salient trends in the human resource dimension of our changing societies (Moss-Kantor, 1989; Moye, 1993; Pynes, 1997). In the decade ahead, nearly half of the workforce will be female, more than half of the new entrants into the workforce will be minorities or immigrants, half of all Americans will be over forty-five and one in three Americans will be sixty-five or older; more single parents, openly gay men and women, and people with disabilities will be part of the workforce and the majority of jobs will require a college education (Moye, 1993). The effectiveness of the organization is dependent upon the performance of the thousands of people who work in the organizations which depends, in turn, upon how well the organization has adapted to the new workplace.

It is politically correct to bemoan the early management writers who advocated the scientific approach to management practices and its mechanistic treatment of workers, by issuing a call for more trusting, committed, mature, and responsible approaches to managing people (Duck, 1993; Balfour and Wechsler, 1991; Leana and Van Buren III, 1999; Moon, 2000; Shockley-Zakabaj et al., 2000; Wright and Snell, 1998). Organization managers are advised to emphasize and manage the dynamic patterns and relationships within an organization in order to encourage the type of strategic and innovative thinking that produces anticipation of problems and opportunities before they occur. This is easier said than done. Cultural differences can create communication and cooperation problems only touched upon by diversity training. And furthermore, downsizing, competitive pressures, or other significant environmental stressors will erode trust, sharing, and commitment even in the most progressive of agencies.

From the employees' perspective, things do not look so positive. The impact of downsizing, contracting out, outsourcing, and privatization, new staples for both public and private sectors, indicate a decrease in organizational tenure. Employees can no longer expect to work for one or two organizations during their lifetimes. Rather, work instability and short-term employment will characterize the work life of an increasing number of the workforce. Couple this with the rapid increase in technology and the skills required just to keep up. The situation described here will affect the middle-class professional, who under the old rules, would have been assured work for life. This situation would be ameliorated by portable pensions and universal healthcare.

The paternalistic tradition of pension-for-service mentality and retirement as a departure-from-work-entirely concept is being replaced by a new generation of part-time employment and second career choices. To meet these changing retirement objectives and those accompanied by a more mobile and diverse workforce, the provision of portable pensions liberates the employee from the restraints of retirement savings based solely on years of service and rewards for long-term employees. The newly defined needs of the employee in today's labor market, rather, would be better addressed by being entitled to "take their account balances with them" and roll over contributions without being tied to age, length of service, or private/public transfer limitations (Schroeder-Chaplain, 1996).

The creation of the Federal Employment Retirement Service in 1987 and the Economic Growth and Tax Relief Reconciliation Act of 2001, most recently signed into law by President George W. Bush, offer some encouraging indications that pension laws are being modernized to provide adequate replacement income to fit the new changes in work and retirement patterns. However, even though the new tax law substantially contributes to changes in the portability of retirement savings (i.e., it allows tax-free rollovers among governmental 457 plans, 403(b) plans, and qualified plans under 401(a), and permits trustee-to-trustee transfers from 403(b) or 457 plans for the purchase of service credit under governmental defined benefit plans) agencies are not *required* to accept these rollover contributions. For example, under the new law, Section 457 retirement savings plans which are used by many state and local governments and other tax-exempt organizations, will now provide for vested funds to roll over among various types of qualified plans and similar arrangements without restrictions. However, implementing such retirement plan revisions would still depend on each agency's adoption specifications. Without mandated pension requirements for sponsors of all public sector retirement plans, employee uncertainty and "fit" remains problematic. For example, without further assessment of national retirement policy goals, contracting out of public services still has adverse effects on the employees who formerly provided them. These employees are either transferred to other departments or hired by the contractor at a lower salary or with fewer and perhaps, "nonportable" benefits. It would be in the best interest of public sector employees if government retirement plan regulations required agencies that do decide to privatize to include provisions of portable severance packages and retraining programs to employees as a prerequisite to contracting out their services (Pynes, 1977).

In addition, the lag of public agencies behind their business sector counterparts in implementing and sustaining variable compensation programs that accommodate the changing nature of the workplace poses serious concerns not only for those employed by government agencies, but for the long-term viability of the agency itself. For example, due to the retirement of the baby boom employees, Light (2000) warns of an impending "human capital crisis" or "massive brain drain" among civil service employees that could weaken government performance unless radical change efforts are implemented to accommodate a new generation of talent defined by the changing nature of today's workplace. Aligning recruitment, retention, and career development programs with diverse family structures, multitrack careers, and intersector job paths is a must.

With the forty-year veteran an ideal type of a bygone era, to stay competitive in private, public, and nonprofit industries, companies will be required to offer flexible reward packages, innovative retirement plans, and workplace policies that "fit" diverse employee priorities. Particularly in the public sector, offering individuals retirement packages that include greater portability of retirement funds, flexibility with respect to plan withdrawals, and lessening of regulatory burdens for the employers who sponsor or who are considering sponsoring qualified plans, will be crucial determinants in attracting younger and more diversified employees and adapting to their retirement objectives. Remaining sensitive to employees' changing needs and life choices in the decades ahead will be an integral part of maximizing human capital over the long term.

## IV.  CONCLUSION

Change is a given. Being prepared for the changes, both mentally and materially, is the challenge for the practitioner. To enhance performance and effectiveness, practitioners need to make decisions and identify their agendas using a flexible strategy that allows them to adjust to their environment and in so doing successfully innovate and change. Compensation and other work policies need to align with constantly evolving cultural values; managerial skills and knowledge need to keep up with technological demands to stay competitive in an information-rich environment; risk-taking and nontraditional ideas need to be encouraged at all levels of the organization. And we recommend that worker concerns be incorporated into organizational policy, most notably, the issue of portable pensions. Characterizing an individual's progression on the job as moving on a career ladder is no longer appropriate. Workers now face many more interruptions in their movement through their work life than the present generation has and certainly more than our parents' generation. The uncertainty and anxiety of coping with these changes will be lessened if retirement contributions are assigned to workers directly, not to the contributing organization.

Identifying the causes, effects, and effectiveness of the different types of change is the mission for the academic who is interested in organizational change. Change researchers should look to an integrative approach in a change process research design. First, performance outcomes need to be built into a change process design to study reciprocal relationships between change processes and performance outcomes. In other words, how do we measure effective reactions to change and how can we better evaluate how and why organizations change. Secondly, understanding the external and internal factors that impede or facilitate the organization's effectiveness in response to planned, unplanned, and at times, disruptive change is an essential part of the academic mission.

Although the organizational literature suggests that government bureaucracies and the public servants who staff them are faced with a particular set of barriers that inhibit change (Downs, 1967; Golembiewski, 1989), we have also provided examples of successful innovative approaches taken by public agencies within the context of a changing society. Given the pervasive nature of change, how the government will continue to surpass these barriers and implement and manage change forces in the twenty-first century and beyond will be crucial determinants of how the government maintains its fit, ensures its legitimacy, and shapes the future role of public sector organizations. After all, the government is not as threatened by change as the business sector. It won't go out of business. Or will it?

## REFERENCES

Abrahamson, E. (July–August 2000). Change without pain. *Harvard Bus. Rev.* pp. 75–79.

Aldrich, H. (1979). *Organizations and Environments.* Englewood Cliffs, NJ: Prentice-Hall.

Auger, D. (1999). Privatization, contracting, and the states: Lessons from state government experience. *Public Product. Manage. Rev.* 22:435–454.

Balfour, D., Wechsler, B. (1991). Commitment, performance, and productivity in public organizations. *Public Product. Manage. Rev.* 14:355–367.

Beckhard, R., Harris, R. (1977). *Organizational Transitions.* 3rd ed. Reading, MA: Addison-Wesley.

Beer, M. (1980). *Organization Change and Development: A Systems View.* Dallas: Scott, Foresman.

Berman, E., Van Wart, M. (1999). Contemporary public sector productivity values. *Public Product. Manage. Rev.* 22:325–347.

Borins, S. (2000). Loose cannons and rule breakers, or enterprising leaders? Some evidence about innovative public managers. *Public Admin. Rev.* 60:498–507.

Borins, S. (2001). Public management innovation: Toward a global perspective. *Am. Rev. Public Admin.* 31:5–21.

Bower, J., Christensen, D. (January–February 1995). Disruptive technologies: Catching the wave. *Harvard Bus. Rev.* pp. 27–37.

Burke, W. (1994). Diagnostic models for organization development. In: Howard, A., & Associates, eds. *Diagnosis for Organizational Change: Methods and Models.* New York: Guilford, pp. 53–84.

Chia, R. (1999). 'A rhizomic' model of organizational change and transformation: Perspective from a metaphysics of change. *British J. Manage.* 10:209–227.

Christensen, C. M. (2000). *The Innovator's Dilemma.* New York: Harper Collins.

Christensen, C. M., Overdorf, M. (2000). Meeting the challenge of disruptive change. *Harvard Bus. Rev.* 78:66–76.

Christensen, C. M., Bohmer, Kenagy, J. (September–October 2000). Will disruptive innovations cure health care? *Harvard Bus. Rev.* pp. 102–111.

Cohen, M. D., March, J. G., Olsen, J. P. (1972). A garbage can model of organizational choice. *Admin. Sci. Quart.* 17:1–25.

Cummings, G., Worley, C. (1997). *Organizational Development & Change.* Cincinnati: Southwestern.

Davenport, T. (1994). Managing in the new world of process. *Public Product. Manage. Rev.* 18:133 ff.

Denning, S. (2001). *The Springboard.* Boston: Butterworth-Heinemann.

Doherty, E., Nord, W. (1993). Compensation: Trends and expanding horizons. In: Golembiewski, R., ed. *Handbook of Organizational Behavior.* New York: Marcel Dekker, pp. 429–455.

Downs, A. (1967). *Inside Bureaucracy.* Prospect Heights, IL: Waveland.

Duck, J. (November–December 1993). Managing change: The art of balancing. *Harvard Bus. Rev.*, pp. 109–118.

Emery, F. E., Trist, E. L. (1965). The causal texture of organizational environments. *Hum. Relations* 18:21–32.

Frederickson, G. (March 2001). *Twenty-First Century Public Administration: The Folly of Experience and the Wisdom of History.* Proceedings of the 62nd National Conference American Society for Public Administration, Newark, NJ.

Fukuyama, F. (1992). *The End of History and the Last Man.* New York: Avon.

Gage, A. (2000). Profile: Group works to change attitudes toward public sector employees. *Public Manage.* 82:20–21.

Galpin, T. (1996). *The Human Side of Change: A Practical Guide to Organization Redesign.* San Francisco: Jossey-Bass.

Golembiewski, R. (1989). *Organization Development: Ideas and Issues.* New Brunswick, NJ: Transaction.

Golembiewski, R., Kiepper, A. (1988). *High Performance and Human Costs: A Public Sector Model of Organizational Development.* New York: Praeger.

Goodman, P., Kurke, L. (1982). Studies of change in organizations: A status report. In: Goodman, Paul S., and Associates, eds. *Change in Organizations.* San Francisco: Jossey-Bass, pp.1–46.

Goodman, P. S., Darr, E. (1996). Exchanging best practices through computer aided systems. *Acad. Manage. Exec.* 10:7 ff.

Goodsell, C. (March 2001). *Public Administration's Soul Reincarnated.* Proceedings of the 62nd National Conference American Society for Public Administration, Newark, NJ.

Hamel, G. (September–October 1999). Bringing Silicon Valley inside. *Harvard Bus. Rev.* pp. 7–21.

Hamel, G. (2000). Reinvent your company. *Fortune* 141:98–118.

Hansen, M., Mohria, N., Tierney, T. (1999). What's your strategy for managing knowledge? *Harvard Bus. Rev.* 24(3):538–555.

Holzer, M., Callahan, K. (1998). *Government at Work: Best Practices and Model Programs*. Thousand Oaks: Sage.

Huy, Q. N. (1999). Emotional capability, emotional intelligence, and radical change. *Acad. Manage. Rev.* 24:325–345.

Kearney, R., Feldman, B., Scavo, C. (2000). Reinventing government: City manager attitudes and actions. *Public Admin. Rev.* 60:535–548.

Kettl, D. (2000). The transformation of governance: Globalization, devolution, and the role of government. *Public Admin. Rev.* 50:488–497.

Kettl, D. (2001). What's next? *Gov. Exec.* 33:20–26.

Kilduff, M., Dougherty, D. (2000). Change and development in a pluralistic world: The view from the classics. *Acad. Manage. Rev.* 25:777–782.

Kim, P. S. (2000). Administrative reform in the Korean central government: A case study of the Dai Jung Kim Administration. *Public Perform. Manage. Rev.* 24:145–160.

Kimberly, J., Miles, R. (1980). *Organizational Life Cycles*. San Francisco: Jossey Bass.

Kirkpatrick, D. (1985). *How to Manage Change Effectively*. San Francisco: Jossey-Bass.

Kotter, J. (1995). Leading change: Why transformation efforts fail. *Harvard Bus. Rev.* 73:59–67.

Landsbergen, D., Wolken, G. (2001). Realizing the promise: Government information systems and the fourth generation of information technology. *Public Admin. Rev.* 61:206–220.

Lane, J. (1997). *Public Sector Reform: Rationale, Trends, and Problems*. London: Sage.

Lane, L., Wolf, J. (1990). *The Human Resource Crisis in the Public Sector: Rebuilding the Capacity to Govern*. Westport, CT: Quorum.

LaPorte, T., Demchak, C., Friis, C. (2001). Webbing governance: Global trends across national-level public agencies. *Commun. ACM* 44:63–67.

Larkin, T. J., Larkin, S. (May–June 1996). Reaching and changing frontline employees. *Harvard Bus. Rev.* pp. 39–48.

Leana, C., Van Buren, H. III. (1999). Organizational social capital and employment practices. *Acad. Manage. Rev.* 24:533–555.

Lewin, K. (1947). Frontiers in group dynamics. *Hum. Relations* 1:5–41.

Light, P. (2000). The new public service. *Gov. Exec.* 32:17–19.

Marx, K., Engels, R. (1848). *Selected Works*. London: Lawrence and Wishart.

Meyer, M. (1979). *Change in Public Bureaucracies*. New York: Cambridge University Press.

Milward, H., Provan, K. (2000). Governing the hollow state. *J. Public Admin. Res. Theor.* 2:359–379.

Mone, M., McKinley, W., Barker, V. (1998). Organizational decline and innovation: A contingency framework. *Acad. Manage. Rev.* 23:115–132.

Moon, M. J. (2000). Organizational commitment revisited in new public management: Motivation, organizational culture, sector, and managerial level. *Public Perform. Manage. Rev.* 24:177–194.

Moss-Kanter, R. (1983). *The Change Masters*. New York: Simon & Schuster.

Moss-Kantor, R. (1989). *When Giants Learn To Dance*. New York: Touchstone.

Moss-Kanter, R., Stein, B., Jick, T. (1992). *The Challenge of Organizational Change: How Companies Experience It and Leaders Guide It*. New York: Free Press.

Moye, H. (1993). Reassessing human resources in large-scale bureaucracies. In: Kuhn, R., ed. *Generating Creativity and Innovation in Large Scale Bureaucracies*. Westport, CT: Quorum, pp.151–156.

Nadler, D. (1998). *Champions of Change: How CEOs and Their Companies Are Mastering the Skills of Radical Change*. San Francisco: Jossey-Bass.

Nadler, D., Tushman, M. (1989). Organizational framebending: Principles for managing reorientation. *Acad. Manage. Exec.* 3:194–202.

Neal, C. (1999). A conscious change in the workplace. *J. Quality Participation* 22:27–30.

Neumann, F. (1997). Organizational structures to match the new information-rich environments: Lessons from the study of chaos. *Public Product. Manage. Rev.* 21:86–100.

Nunn, S. (1992). Organizational improvement: The case of Village Creek. *Public Product. Manage. Rev.* 16:117 ff.

Osborne, D. (1993). Reinventing government. *Public Product. Manage. Rev.* 16:349–356.

O'Toole, L. (1997). Implementing public innovations in network settings. *Admin. Soc.* 29:115–138.

Pascale, R., Millemann, M., Gioja, L. (November–December 1997). Changing the way we change. *Harvard Bus. Rev.* pp. 7–19.

Piderit, S. (2000). Rethinking resistance and recognizing ambivalence: A multidimensional view of attitudes toward an organizational change. *Acad. Manage. Rev.* 25:783–794.

Poister, T., Harris, R. (2000). Building quality improvement over the long run: Approaches, results, and lessons learned from the PennDOT experience. *Public Perform. Manage. Rev.* 24:161–176.

Pynes, J. (1997). *Human Resources Management for Public and Nonprofit Organizations*. San Francisco: Jossey-Bass.

Rainey, H. (1997). *Understanding & Managing Public Organizations*. San Francisco: Jossey-Bass.

Rainey, H. (1999). Using comparisons of public and private organizations to assess innovative attitudes among members of organizations. *Public Product. Manage. Rev.* 23:130–149.

Roberts, G. (2001). Employee benefits costs control strategies in municipal government. *Public Perform. Manage. Rev.* 24:389–402.

Rothschild, M. (1990). *Bionomics: Economy as Ecosystem*. New York: Holt.

Ruggles, R. (1998). The state of the notion: Knowledge management in practice. *Cal. Manage. Rev.* 40(3):80–89.

Shockley-Zakabaj, P., Ellis, K., Winograd, G. (2000). Organizational trust: What it means, why it matters. *Organ. Devel. J.* 18:35–48.

Stokes-Berry, F. (1997). Explaining managerial acceptance of expert systems. *Public Product. Manage. Rev.* 20:323–335.

Stokes-Berry, F., Berry, W., Foster, S. (1998). The determinants of success in implementing an expert system in state government. *Public Admin. Rev.* 58:293–305.

Strebel, P. (May–June 1996). Why do employees resist change? *Harvard Bus. Rev.* pp. 26–32.

Taylor, P., Pierce, J. (1999). Effects of introducing a performance management system on employees' subsequent attitudes and effort. *Public Person. Manage.* 28:423–452.

Thompson, J. (2000). The reinvention laboratories: Strategic change by indirection. *Am. Rev. Public Admin.* 30:46–68.

Tichy, N., DeVanna, J. (1986). *The Transformational Leader*. New York: Wiley.

Tobias, R. (2000). Realizing reform. *Gov. Exec.* 32:39–42.

Tolchin, S. (March 2001). Public Administration in 2026: Will the Field Still Exist? Proceedings of the 62nd National Conference American Society for Public Administration, Newark, NJ.

Tushman, M., O'Reilly, C. (1997). *Winning Through Innovation*. Boston: Harvard Business School.

Vaill, P. (1989). *Managing as a Performing Art: New Ideas for a World of Chaotic Change*. San Francisco: Jossey-Bass.

Vaill, P. (1996). *Learning as a Way of Being*. San Francisco: Jossey-Bass.

Van de Ven, A. H., Poole, M. S. (1995). Explaining development and change in organizations. *Acad. Manage. Rev.* 20(3):510–540.

Waldrop, M. (1992). *Complexity*. New York: Simon & Schuster.

Walker, J., Bechet, T. (1994). Addressing future staffing needs. In: Ann Howard and Associates, eds. *Diagnosis for Organizational Change: Methods and Models*. New York: Guilford, pp. 113–138.

Weick, K. (1995). *Sensemaking in Organizations*. Thousand Oaks, CA: Sage.

Weick, K. (2000). Emergent change as a universal in organizations. In: Beer, M., Nohria, N., eds. *Breaking the Code of Change*. Boston: Harvard Business School, pp. 223–241.

Weick, K., Quinn, R. (1999). Organizational change and development. *Ann. Rev. Psych.* 50:361–386.

White, R. (1999). More than an analytical tool: Examining the ideological role of efficiency. *Public Product. Manage. Rev.* 23:8–23.

Wholey, J. (1999). Performance-based management. *Public Product. Manage. Rev.* 22:288–307.

Wise, L. (1999). The use of innovative practices in the public and private sectors: The role of organizational and individual factors. *Public Product. Manage. Rev.* 23:150–168.

Wright, P., Snell, S. (1998). Toward a unifying framework for exploring fit and flexibility in strategic management. *Acad. Manage. Rev.* (23), 756–772.

Young, G. (2000). Managing organizational transformations: Lessons from the Veterans Health Administration. *Cal. Manage. Rev.* 43:66–82.

# 34

## Strategic Management and Productivity

**ARIE HALACHMI**
*Tennessee State University, Nashville, Tennessee, U.S.A.,
and Zhongshan University, China*

## I. INTRODUCTION

The lack of consensus on the exact definitions of and differences between two important terms, "strategic management" and "strategic planning", can confuse managerial thinking (Mintzberg, 1994; Halachmi, 1986). The problem is that many government entities are required by laws, such as the Government Performance and Results Act of 1993 (GPRA) in the case of Federal agencies, to use strategic planning to improve productivity—another term that is open to different interpretations and definitions (Halachmi and Holzer, 1986). The purpose of this chapter is to eliminate some of the fog that reduces the ability of practitioners and students of public management to address the issue of strategic management and productivity. We hope the discussion offered here will help practitioners and academicians in their struggle with the notion that strategizing in the public sector may be desirable but is not always possible or cost-effective.

The chapter begins by addressing the issue of public sector productivity. It points out that a statement about productivity conveys judgment rather than an objective value. Thus what may seem to be right and prudent in the short run may be prove to be much less than that in the long run. For example, the effort to reduce undesired air pollution resulted in government regulations that favored different chemical formulas to suit local climate conditions in different parts of the country. This solution seemed to work well until the energy shortages of late 2000 and early 2001 with the rolling blackout in California. Because the fuel market had been segmented due to special formulas, it was impossible to move gasoline from markets that had a glut to markets that experienced shortages. This kind of conflict between short-run results and long-term considerations can be a source of trouble for managers. The chapter goes on to suggest that productivity is a mediating variable between the organization and the environment and that it can be studied as a dependent or an independent variable. The discussion of strategizing in the public sector includes observations on who defines missions and key operational parameters in the public sector, on the difference between the public and private sectors when it comes to perceived threats and opportunities, and on how each sector deals with an apparent threat. The chapter goes on to define some of the reasons why strategizing in the public sector may not be cost-effective. The chapter concludes by suggesting that when strategic management is not cost-effective or feasible, management initiatives to enhance productivity at the subsystem level might be the way to get strategic gains, that is, to develop desired strengths and eliminate or reduce certain weaknesses.

## II.  WHAT DO WE MEAN BY STRATEGIC PLANNING OR MANAGEMENT?

Mintzberg (1998, p. 10) notes that "human nature insists on a definition for every concept." But the word "strategy" has long been used in different ways even if it has traditionally been defined in only one way. Thus Mintzberg concludes, "Explicit recognition of multiple definitions can help people to maneuver through this difficult field." He goes on to offer five alternative definitions of strategy: as plan, ploy, pattern, position, and perspective. According to Mintzberg (1998, pp. 1–15):

> Strategy is a plan—some sort of consciously intended course of action, a guideline (or a set of guidelines) to deal with a situation;
>
> Strategy is a ploy—a specific maneuver intended to outwit an opponent or competitor;
>
> Strategy is a pattern—specifically, the resulting behavior that forms a pattern in a stream of action;
>
> Strategy is a position—a means of locating an organization in what organization theorists like to call an "environment";
>
> Strategy is a perspective—its content consists not just of a chosen position, but of an ingrained way of perceiving the world.

Quinn (1988) asserts that it is strategic decisions that determine the effectiveness of an enterprise (whether its major thrusts are in the right directions given its resource potential), rather than whether individual tasks are performed efficiently.

According to Halachmi and Holzer (1986, p. 10), *strategic factors* "are elements that give the organization a particular strength or weakness. They put the organization in a position where it may exploit a given situation to its benefit." Halachmi (1992, p. 551) suggests also that "strategic management is an effort to capitalize on the strengths of the organization by taking advantage of favorable conditions inside or outside the organization. It involves minimization of cost by making operations consistent and predictable and by avoiding challenges to structure and the organizational culture." Thus he concludes that strategic management "is the process for implementing a strategic plan which integrates the organization's goals, policies, and action sequences into a cohesive whole." He notes that strategic management is required, but it is not a guarantee of success or productivity.

## A. Productivity as a Statement of Approval

What do we mean when we say that a given unit or an individual is productive, needs to be more productive, or is improving productivity? As explained below, statements about productivity imply comparison and judgment. Being labeled productive means that as a result of comparison, an individual or an organization is judged to be better than some other relevant entity in some respect. In other words, labeling something productive is a relative, rather than an absolute, evaluation. Because the attribute of being productive is the result of a specific comparison, its validity is time-sensitive. What is deemed productive at one time may not be perceived as such later on, following subsequent comparison(s) and corresponding assessment of the respective findings. In other words, the determination of productivity is an assessment whose validity needs to be proven again and again. A change in the parameters of the comparison, for example, who judges the comparison, may lead to different conclusions, which may challenge the original assessment of productivity. The judgment expressed by a statement about productivity implies the use of benchmarking. Labeling something or someone as productive, or nonproductive, is thus also an assertion of the validity or relevancy of the benchmark or the comparison.

Statements about productivity are often reflective of value judgment and, as such, cannot be understood as externally or internally valid. Thus it is not hard to find statements where data about a given operation are compared to different benchmarks, leading observers to reach different conclusions about productivity. Some of the problems concerning the selection of the "proper" measure of productivity can be illustrated by a brief examination of the following examples.

The first example involves the disagreement about the main cause(s) of productivity growth after World War II. According to Jorgenson and Griliches (1967), the growth resulted from the introduction of more capital resources. A different conclusion was offered by Denison (1969), who claimed that the productivity growth for that period was caused by increased efficiency.

The second example is based on productivity reports from the Bureau of Labor Statistics (BLS). The BLS (1998, p. 11) notes that the data on transit productivity are used for two different measures: vehicle revenue miles (VRM), which increased at an average annual rate of 2.2%, and unlinked passenger trips (UPT), which increased at an average rate of 0.5%. VRM are often categorized as the service or capacity provided, and UPT is treated as the output. The transit industry, however, views VRM as an output and UPT as an outcome. The BLS (1998, p. 11) goes onto illustrate that not only do the service measurements vary by type of measure, but also the rate of change of each measure may vary by the period examined. For example, three Employment Service measures for one peak-to-peak output cycle (1979 to 1986) show exactly the same rate of change ($-3.3\%$) for three possible measures: placement, referrals, and a service-based measure. For the preceding cycle (1974 to 1979), however, the rate of change was 4.6% for placements, 3.8% for referrals, and 2.1% for the service-based measure.

It is easy to grasp intuitively that comparisons with benchmarks may involve one's own past record(s) or the past or present record(s) of another entity. As pointed out by Dror (1968), comparisons with such benchmarks, which he calls *standards*, may be misleading, a problem that may not be evident to the untrained observer. For example, comparing what is costs to weave a rug in two countries, one using child labor and one using facilities high in capital investment, may lead to the wrong conclusions about which country is more productive when it comes to manufacturing rugs. The problems involved in generating a meaningful comparison (i.e., ensuring acceptable levels of internal and external validity) become more complex as we move from the production of tangible goods to the assessment of less-tangible products. One of the current challenges facing many countries is to make comparisons and to judge the performance of those parts of national economies involved with production and delivery of services in general and, in particular, with those services having no alternative providers in the private sector.

Although productivity assessment is not easy and can go wrong, its value to strategic analysis and management is real. Because of this value, we must understand that the nature of a productivity measurement is more important than a simple comparison. As explained below, to assess productivity is also to assess the functional relationships connecting the components of the whole production system under consideration, for example, (1) which ones have synergetic relations and which ones can undermine (or interfere with) each other, (2) which elements or steps of the process provide added value, and (3) which ones are cost centers. We must ask: What is being compared in order to assert productivity? Many analysts focus on the ratios of output to input (Hatry and Fisk, 1992). As Halachmi and Holzer (1986) have pointed out, this approach may have some serious weaknesses. The following example may illustrate one of the possible problems of using ratios as measures of productivity.

Let's assume that a tax-collection agency has two offices. One office of the agency collects $100 a day at a cost of $10, and the other office collects $1000 at a cost of $100 during the same day. Determining which office is more productive cannot be helped by reference to the ratios of output to input inasmuch as they are 1 to 10 in both cases. Productivity in this case must be determined by other means, for example, by reference to the net output (Dror, 1968). By comparing the net collection (i.e., the net output) of the first office, which is $90, to the net collection of the second office, which is $900 for the same day, a manager may conclude that the second office is more productive.

Using the conceptual framework of general systems theory (van Bertalanffy, 1968; Van Gigch, 1974), *productivity* implies an improvement in the functional relationships among components of a system. Such improvement can be absolute or relative. Thus an improvement indicates a move on the production curve in the desired direction. Simply put, productivity aims at improvement of the functional relationships among the three elements of the system: input, process, and output. Improvement results when input, process, or output promotes a greater contribution by either one or both of the other two elements of the system (Halachmi and Holzer, 1986). Productivity also implies the system's improvement, in some aspect, over the past. This notion seems to be straightforward and simple on its face, until one ponders how it pertains to the functional relationships among output, outcome, and impact. After all, if what counts at the end of the day is the impact (i.e., outcome) rather than the improved performance (i.e., process) of the system, then what was the value of any alleged productivity gain if it failed to translate into a meaningful impact? To borrow from medicine, what is the value of a successful operation that was performed more efficiently than previous ones if it did not save the patient's life? This brings up the question of the desirability and promise of suboptimization as a tool for enhancing productivity.

Suboptimization occurs when a system as a production function may be more productive but the "improved" output may not generate the expected outcome (e.g., studying longer may not make you more knowledgeable). The problem escalates when the expected outcome materializes but may not have any impact (e.g., when what counts for getting the job is who you know rather than what you know). Such suboptimization may imply productivity improvement, but it is not real progress. That is because suboptimization may indicate the necessary conditions for improvement but is insufficient to bring it about.

Public administrators know they are better off whenever they can proactively address productivity issues before questions about resources and allocations are turned by politicians into a political football. Administrators know from experience that after an election such political footballs may complicate the generation of good solutions to problems, due to the conflicting promises politicians may have made to different interest groups. A typical scenario involves a congested street: one promise, to truckers, is to consider a plan to widen the street to eliminate a traffic bottleneck; another, to residents, is to urge a plan making the street a one-way passage with some restrictions on commercial traffic. The task of finding and recommending possible ways for resolving such discrepancies and finding the resources to underwrite the cost of any proposed solution is often left to the career employees of government agencies. Public administrators who fail to be proactive often invite dissatisfaction. Such a development may get out of hand when concerns about economic efficiency or programmatic effectiveness manifest themselves as items that compete for attention on the systemic, institutional, or policy agenda (Cobb and Elder, 1972; Kingdon, 1984).

Public managers learn quickly that whenever they miss an opportunity to make decisions about operations themselves, "symbolic values" rather than "market (economic) values" are likely to dominate the considerations used by elected and appointed officials. Politicians prefer to consider symbolic values for at least two reasons: because symbolic values of proposed actions can be politically more valuable than the corresponding market values of the anticipated outcome of a proposed action; and because decisions involving the use of symbolic values may not be as difficult as proposed solutions that force reallocation of economic resources, which is likely to be resisted by those who are content with the status quo.

So how can public managers determine what will constitute a meaningful improvement in productivity? The public administrator may consider several questions.

What constitutes a genuine increase in efficiency, that is, superior utilization of available resources?

What may be considered enhanced effectiveness, that is, a different application of the same resources for attaining additional goals or other results?

What changes may lead to a qualitative amelioration, such as refined products or services?

Is it possible to attain better effectiveness or quality without augmenting the consumption of resources? Is it possible to do more with less?

Can a marginal change in the input, process, or output characteristics of a public agency make a big difference?

What are the net benefits of such a change in the short and long run?

These and similar questions confront managers all the time. Such questions demonstrate that productivity, as a concept or as a management problem, is multi-dimensional. Therefore, any effort to enhance productivity must address its various aspects.

The difficulty of comprehending productivity does not imply that it can be overlooked as a strategic consideration. Rather, the complexity of the concept of productivity, as it applies to the public sector in general, and to the provision of services and public goods in particular, suggests that public managers should pay more attention to it.

## III. PRODUCTIVITY AS A MEDIATING VARIABLE BETWEEN THE ORGANIZATION AND THE ENVIRONMENT

One of the reasons public officials experience difficulty in addressing the issue of productivity is that the relationships among the different dimensions of organizational performance are not linear. A change in one aspect that results in greater productivity in one respect may or may not indicate a corresponding improvement or deterioration in other aspects of an agency's performance. As a matter of fact, with the introduction of performance measurement schemes, those aspects of performance that are subject to performance measurement are likely to improve, but at the expense of other aspects that are not covered by a given set of measurements or indicators. In line with the logic of the general systems approach (van Bertalanffy, 1968; Van Gigch, 1974; Halachmi and Holzer, 1986), the productivity of a given system may improve under several conditions, for example, when output declines in marginal terms although the input is reduced significantly, or when a marginal increase of the input results in a major change of the output. Productivity may improve, however, not only by moving to a more desired position on the organizational production curve, but as a result of a move to a new production curve that is different and unrelated to the "old" curve. Thus improved productivity is a notion that is not limited to the improvement of an existing practice, past practices, or past output. It may involve rethinking and questioning all existing practices and organizational structures to take advantage of new information technology and of changing preferences and specific demands of service recipients. In the 1990s this notion of productivity enhancement characterized the various approaches to business process reengineering (BPR) (Hammer and Champy, 1993; Halachmi, 1995, Halachmi and Bovaird, 1997), and especially the calls to reinvent government and the public sector (Osborne and Gaebler, 1992; Gore, 1993).

Under the general systems approach the term *equifinality* represents the notion that it is possible to achieve a given outcome through different means. Equifinality is an idea at the root of the current challenge of reengineering the business process. Addressing this challenge involves the use of the powers of new information technology (IT) to explore alternative ways of getting to the same or better results.

The acronym PEG stands for certain contingencies that illustrate the main avenues for improving a given system's performance:

1. Productivity may increase (a) when a marginal increase in input leads to major improvement in the quality or quantity of output, (b) when any decline in input corresponds to a smaller output or no change in output;
2. Economy may improve when a marginal decline in output results in significant savings of resources that used to be consumed as part of input; and

3. Gains may result from a better fit between the profile of the input mix of resources and the characteristics of the process.

The three contingencies suggest various options a manager can use for influencing performance. The involved cost and benefit of each is different. Choosing the approach for enhancing productivity of a given system, for example, any public agency, will be guided by another set of considerations, namely, those concerned with distribution of the expected new costs and benefits. Because such distribution may be different under each of the three plans, selection of one over the others may not be simple or politically feasible. For example, career and elected (or appointed) officials may use different considerations for selecting the preferred approach, such as an approach that is consistent with party ideology or an approach that rewards those who support them at the expense of those who support their political opponents. Career employees, however, may use professional considerations; they may prefer the course of action most likely to be approved by other professionals on the basis of technical (i.e., economic) grounds. They are more likely than elected or appointed officials to consider long-term implications, whereas the former are likely to be more concerned about immediate results. Professional employees may opt for a Rawlsian approach (Rawls, 1971), a plan that contributes the most to the weakest elements of society, and the elected and appointed officials may prefer a plan that benefits the largest number of people or eligible voters.

Something else that complicates efforts to address productivity issues in the public sector is the need of senior decision makers to use inconsistent short- and long-term considerations simultaneously. Such actors, elected or appointed officials, must be able to show their supporters that they have accomplished something between elections. The problem public officials face is that the functional relationship between short-term productivity improvements and long-term productivity gains is very complex due to the following reasons.

1. The two may be mutually exclusive (i.e., attaining one may be at the cost of attaining the other). For example, using explosives for fishing may increase fish yield in the short run, but because of destruction of the fish themselves and of their ecological surroundings, fish yield will eventually decrease. The building of a new thruway may reduce commuting time, pollution, and energy consumption in the long run, but in the short run it can divide neighborhoods, have an impact on local business, and increase the cost of providing services such as police and fire protection, schools, and sanitation to the neighborhood while the construction is going on.

2. The functional relationship between the two is not a constant or stable one (i.e., it may exist at one point of time but not at another). For example, a temporary addition of another gate for reducing the length of the queue of cars for entering a national park is a short-term productivity improvement that may calm tempers and generate additional revenues for the park. But once news gets out that the lines are now shorter, those who avoided the park's congestion may decide to visit, exhausting the processing capacity that was enhanced by adding another gate and ensuring that those who come once will not come again.

3. The relation between short- and long-term productivity improvement is not linear (i.e., a change in one may not lead to a corresponding change in the other). For example, a neighborhood public green that offers a lot of privacy to young lovers may require them as families to expand extra efforts for supervising their young children at play.

   4.  The functional relationship between short- and long-term gains is not a direct one. For example, efforts that may lead to improved productivity by the end of a given electoral cycle may amount to a temporary suboptimization and may not contribute to long-term gains. By the same token, activities that may result in long-term gains may not be enough to prevent a change of course, such as when incumbents lose their bids for another term in office to finish what they started. In short, a productivity change in one time frame may or may not have a simple or direct correlation with a desired change in another time frame.

   Due to the complex functional relationship between short- and long-term productivity improvements, the significance of any observed productivity gain cannot be easily assessed. An effort to enhance productivity in the short run may or may not lead to an improvement in the long run, or it may hide the development of conditions that would prevent long-term productivity. The following example may help illustrate this point. The rush to promote and tenure university professors in the late 1960s was meant to improve instruction by stabilizing the faculty. At a time when the demand for qualified professors exceeded supply, early tenure was a way to ensure the availability of the necessary manpower for dealing with exploding enrollments. Twenty years later, some universities were struggling to get rid of overstaffed and nonproductive faculty. The answer to a pressing problem did work in the short run, but it proved to be quite problematic in the long run.

   A short-term shift in efficiency, in effectiveness, or in quality may be just that. It may or may not be an indicator of the shape of things to come in the long run. An improvement in any one dimension, such as effectiveness, may not last or produce a corresponding change in one (or several) of the other dimensions. Therefore, a short-term gain may be offset by a greater loss of productivity in the long run. For example, pressuring social workers to be more efficient (e.g., to see more cases per day) or to increase effectiveness (e.g., to reduce the level of recidivism) in order to improve the ratio of input to output may be temporarily effective. The resulting byproducts, however, such as burnout or high turnover, may diminish the agency's capacity to handle future cases. The human and monetary cost of restoring the lost capacity of the agency may exceed the value of the temporary gain.

   In the private sector, compromising long-term productivity for the sake of short-term gains may influence the value of a company and thus the appraisal of its managers (Ouchi, 1982). In the public sector, the situation used to be different. Traditionally, elected officials and their appointees emphasized short-term gains and career civil servants took care of the long-term effects through systematic planning. Such planning was meant to take care of the public interest and was the bureaucrats' tool of choice for securing some stability. After all, any long-term plan that sailed successfully through the approval process reduced the options open to politicians and their appointees for short-term meddling. Long-term plans that involve a substantial commitment of resources discourage initiatives to introduce new programs or to do away with old ones. Citizen charters, executive orders, and legislation such as the GPRA force current officeholders to nominally frame short-term interests in relation to their agencies' long-term results. Yet as all practitioners know, when it comes to daily operations, little ever changes.

   In the private sector, managers are accountable to boards who represent the stockholders. The goals pursued by such boards are expected to be consistent with and to be derived from the objectives sought by the stockholders. The rank and file of such organizations are expected to be committed to meeting the objectives of management, as those are the true objectives of the organization (Katz and Kahn, 1978; Hodges and Anthony, 1984). In the public sector, the situation is different, and that is one of the reasons it is even harder to reconcile short- and long-term organizational objectives. It is important to be cognizant of this difference because it may explain, in part, why it is so difficult to find many good examples of strategic planning and management in the public sector, why strategic planning may not be useful for just any public agency (Halachmi, 1986, and why productivity is a strategic factor (Halachmi and Holzer, 1986).

In the public sector, the selfish interests of both (short-term) political appointees and (long-term) career employees are presented as the articulation of the true public interest, that is, the interest of the stockholders. Unlike their counterparts in the private sector, public employees are not working for their managers, nor do they assume or accept the notion that the managers' goals are necessarily the legitimate organizational objectives. Public employees attempt to identify and to express their own selfish interests in terms of what they think or project to be the public interest. Consequently, it can be difficult to reconcile the different interests and goals of appointed and career employees when the gap between them is wide. Such a gap may result from substantive differences, such as about the right direction for action, or it may evolve when the two groups have different priorities. Such differences often appear when short- and long-term considerations cannot clearly and quickly be reconciled or, more particularly, when a balance cannot be struck between long- and short-term productivity gains. For example, during the first Reagan administration, career employees and political appointees at the U.S. Environmental Protection Agency (EPA) could not bridge the gap between their different sets of goals and priorities. The attempt of management to force its wishes backfired. Employees went directly to the "board," that is, Congress, to complain that the interests of the majority of the stockholders were not being served. They even took the matter directly to the stockholders by leaking to the media negative stories about their management. Managers who failed to understand the difference between the public and the private sector were not able to contain the damage, and the feud immobilized the agency until these managers had been replaced. The case of the EPA in the 1980s underscores the difficulty of balancing different priorities and that balancing short- and long-term considerations tends to represent choices among competing policy or subpolicy interests.

The political context in which public agencies function and the fact that on the horizon there is always the next budget hearing or election day make most managers favor short- over long-term productivity gains. In the absence of an educated media, that is, reporters sufficiently knowledgeable to expose the compromise of the public's interests for the sake of serving special interests, there are no forces to counteract the pressures of short-term considerations. As a matter of fact, an incumbent who does not expect to hold the same position after the next election may feel an incentive to take, under false pretenses, actions that will reduce the efficiency, effectiveness, or capacity of the agency to carry out its mission in the future, even without short-term gains. Such a sinister move might ensure that the incumbent's record would shine in contrast to the problems that will confront his or her successor. For example, the city charter of a certain southeastern city allows the mayor to serve only two consecutive terms. Faced with the need for a drastic and a very unpopular property tax increase, the current mayor asserted that the whole problem was due to deliberate actions and lack of actions by the previous administration. According to sources close to the current mayor, the allegation is that while in office, the previous mayor (who is a possible candidate for the mayor's job in the future) postponed essential repairs to the infrastructure of the city in order to remain popular with the voters and to tarnish the image of his successor. Political commentators in that city agree that such a scenario is not impossible.

## IV.  POLITICAL EFFECTIVENESS VERSUS ECONOMIC EFFICIENCY

Another difficulty in addressing the issue of productivity in the public sector, from a strategic point of view, is that what is effective or efficient for political ends may not be desirable from an economic or a programmatic (technical) point of view. In other words, political effectiveness (e.g., generation/maintenance of support) does not imply economic efficiency (e.g., cost-effectiveness) or technical quality. Hence the valuation of a change in productivity is a function of perspective. An improvement from one point of view may not be perceived as such by those with another perspective. For example, service recipients, social workers, administrators, public interest groups, and elected officials with different political ideologies or constituencies may use different measurements for assessing improvement in the productivity of a welfare agency. Such diverse groups may not agree on what constitutes an adequate measurement of productivity or on the right interpretation of quantitative measurements. For example, changing procedures so that caseworkers are seeing more cases per day may indicate, from one viewpoint, better administrative procedures for processing requests for service. Other viewpoints may see such change as an indication of any one of the following: better-qualified caseworkers or less attention to individual cases; exploitation of employees or smart scheduling; greater responsiveness or the deliberate creation of the conditions for private providers to replace public ones. Because the future of a public manager is most often dependent on political rather than economic circumstances, there is a built-in tendency in the public sector to be more sensitive to politics than to considerations of economy. This means that operations with the prospect of gains in political effectiveness or efficiency may prevail over acts that promise only economic or technical gains. The dominance of political rationality over economics is likely to prevail as long as the economics of the program, or the involved agency itself, is not made a political issue by other political contenders. Even under such circumstances, actions will be governed by political rather than by economic or technical consideration.

The developments in the aftermath of the Three Mile Island nuclear accident is a case in point. As a reaction to the finding that the accident was a result of human error (Todorovic, 1999; Norman, 1999; NUREG/CR_1250, 1980) due to insufficient training, a new administrative structure was put in place. The regulatory powers and scope of operations for the Nuclear Regulatory Commission and other agencies (e.g., the U.S. Department of Energy, OSHA, Civil Defense) evolved further as a political gesture. The new roles of the involved agencies may have created a regulatory overkill that can be justified in terms of its politics (i.e., showing important constituencies that their elected and appointed officials are taking care of their interests), but not from an economic or technical point of view (i.e., asking for the same information or for more information may or may not improve safety or reduce the cost of operations).

What are the implications of this common tendency to give priority to political considerations over economic or technical ones? One possible result is that expert opinion may be a necessary but not a sufficient condition for accepting or approving a strategic plan. This issue is not academic. It has immediate implications for the practicing public manager in the United States. Under the GPRA of 1993, agencies are expected to develop strategic plans and to report about their progress to achieve the goals they set for themselves. The strategic plans themselves, however, may be subject to review by the executive branch's Office of Management and Budget (OMB) or by Congress's Government Accounting Office (GAO). The reviews within the OMB and within the GAO are likely to result in different findings, because the two are likely to use different political perspectives (Halachmi, 1996b, 1999). For example, the GAO (1997) raised some questions about the procedures used within the U.S. Department of Justice in developing the necessary documents to comply with the GPRA, but the OMB had no problem with it. In comparison, Wall Street analysts can develop an objective assessment of the economic or technical merit of a corporate strategic plan that many other analysts can accept. When it comes to the strategic plans of government agencies, however, *where* the assessment is made may influence its content and thus the merit of the strategic plan. This, in turn, is likely to influence the subsequent amount of support public managers can expect from employees and outsiders when it comes to the implementation of a plan. Under these circumstances, one must ask: What is the real value of any strategic plan in the public sector? What are the odds that compliance with the GPRA is likely to enhance an agency's performance from a technical or economic point of view?

The difficulty in comprehending the complex and dynamic interrelationships among the various dimensions of productivity in any given agency is augmented by constant changes in the power matrix outside the agency. This difficulty may lead public administrators to underestimate the instrumental value of productivity from a strategic point of view. In particular, public administrators may overlook the fact that productivity, regardless of definition, is an important mediating variable between the agency and its environment.

## V. PRODUCTIVITY AS A DEPENDENT AND AN INDEPENDENT VARIABLE

From a strategic point of view, productivity can be treated as an independent variable that influences how an agency interfaces with its environment. For example, when the same program is implemented by counterpart agencies (i.e., agencies with a very similar mission in different states or local authorities), the variations in the ensuing results may correspond to the differences in levels of productivity of each agency. The productivity of the agency, rather than the objective quality of the program or the characteristics of its environment, may be used in such cases to explain success or failure. The use of such an approach (i.e., one that uses productivity as an independent variable) must be assumed whenever comparisons of performance are based on benchmarks.

As a dependent variable, changes in productivity indicate a change in the functional relationships of the various components of the production function as explained earlier in this chapter: a change in the relationships between input and process (throughput), input and output, or process and output. Looking at productivity this way implies that its measurement has to do with changes in output. Yet one must wonder whether more meaningful measures of productivity are not likely to be gained by measuring changes in outcomes or impact. After all, what counts (in order of real importance) is the impact of an activity only when impact cannot be assessed directly should the outcomes of the activity be measured. Likewise only after that, if outcomes cannot be measured, should the relevant output that made it all possible be measured. As explained below, managers often fail to see the strategic value of having and using multiple productivity measurements as a means for developing better understanding of the production process and its context. Those who are intimidated by the not-so-simple concept of multiple productivity measurements may overlook the fact that as a dependent variable, such measurements can, over time, expose subtle changes in the production function that cannot be ascertained directly, easily, or early enough by studying other kinds of data.

Experienced managers can see intuitively why productivity should be perceived as a strategic factor. One of the reasons is its functional role in influencing the ultimate results of an administrative action. An organization that requires more resources than another to carry out a given action is relatively weak. The reality, however, is that most managers consider productivity analysis as part of micro, rather than macro, management, and they leave matters of productivity to lower-level managers. They treat it as an element of the implementation stage rather than the analysis or planning stages.

Current models and schools of thinking about strategic management deal mainly with organizations in the private sector. Consequently, they incorporate and make reference only to those aspects of productivity that are of interest or importance to private-sector managers, such as return on investment or ratio of input to output. But even in the private sector we find that a comprehensive analysis of the implications of a proposed plan of action on short- and long-term organizational productivity (i.e., the treatment of productivity as a dependent variable) is often missing. One reason that productivity is sometimes treated as an administrative rather than a managerial issue may be the result of the conceptual inconsistency in thinking (1) of strategic planning as derived from stated goals and (2) of goals as set following a strategic analysis of the environment (Halachmi, 1986). In the first case, the assessment of strengths or weaknesses of the organization influences the selection of the strategy. The purpose is to maximize the ability of the organization to attain prescribed goals by taking advantage of a given situation. Followers of the second, alternative, approach assess the situation without reference to past goals. Given the strength and the weaknesses of the organization, relative to the forces in and the conditions of the environment, they define missions and goals that are likely to be met successfully.

Regardless of whether strategy follows or precedes the selection of organizational objectives, issues that influence productivity—such as employees' skills, morale, or experience; or division of labor or technology—are considered as part of the strengths or weaknesses of the organization. In either case, the tendency of senior managers is to consider the existing characteristics of the organization as independent variables. As such, these variables influence the selection of the strategy, rendering it a dependent variable. The common notion is that the strategy should take advantage of organizational strengths and shield it from threats due to weakness. In both cases, the inherent value of existing organizational characteristics is derived either from the mission (which the strategy is expected to serve) or from the assumed state of the relevant environment (which influences the definition of the mission).

The selection of a strategy may be influenced by the existence (or nonexistence) of particular skills, and the definition of a mission may be selected by the existence or nonexistence of such skills. There is little evidence, however, to support the view that strategy selection can be influenced in the opposite way, that is, that a strategy or a mission can be selected with due consideration to the probable effect on productivity, for example, on development or maintenance of important skills.

Even though productivity is a function of strategic choices, it is seldom treated as a dependent variable or as an explicit consideration during the analytical phase. It seems that the only time productivity is treated as an important variable is during the budgeting process. Under analytical frameworks such as zero-base budgeting (ZBB), agencies are asked to show and to explain the productivity implications of alternative courses of action. Because practitioners and students of public administration do not explore the productivity implications of alternative courses of action, they cannot go on record to point out that certain strategic choices would produce inefficiency. Public managers consider strategic decisions only for any immediate and direct bearing on implementation of the strategy or the attainment of goals. The long-term implications for productivity, as a dependent variable of such decisions, are usually ignored.

When organizational characteristics that determine productivity are treated as independent variables (that influence the design and implementation of the strategic plan, the dependent variable), their strategic value is obvious but limited. This is because each element can affect performance only within a certain tolerance. An organizational characteristic, like past experience, must exceed the upper limit of the critical mass that is needed to influence performance. For example, a record of forty years of service to the indigent is not likely to determine future performance any more (or less) than a record of twenty years of service to them. The maximum influence of any characteristic eventually reaches a peak. Past that point, the influence of any organizational characteristic—such as past experience, skills, motivation, or work practices—flattens out or becomes irrelevant altogether.

Public administrators understand the instrumental value of existing productivity in influencing the ultimate results of a proposed action. But sometimes they fail to see that productivity does not exist independently of the plans they want to implement.

## VI. SOME STRATEGIC FACTORS THAT MAY AFFECT PRODUCTIVITY AND STRATEGIC PLANNING FOR IT

In hindsight, it is easy to define what factors should have been considered as part of strategic analysis, strategic planning, or strategic management processes, but managers are expected to have foresight and to be proactive. This entails separation of primary from secondary strategic factors or issues and may constitute a challenge to any manager, and given the environment of public agencies, meeting the challenge is particularly difficult for several reasons. First, accurate judgment when it comes to identification of primary and secondary factors may prove elusive because in the public sector issues evolve or fade away, not only on their own merit, but due to the appearance or disappearance of other issues over which managers have no control. Because of developments in information technology, around-the-clock news coverage, and the connectivity of global financial markets, domestic issues in one country may influence the importance of various issues in many other countries. This new reality may undermine the usefulness of strategic planning in any sector of the economy. This threat should be taken seriously by public managers because a strategic plan that fails due to unanticipated changes in the environment increases the opportunity cost that results when scarce resources are diverted from one desired goal to the efforts for achieving another, from operations to planning.

A second reason for the difficulty of separating primary from secondary strategic factors is that the more salient factors can distract managers' attention and cause them to overlook less obvious, but more potent, factors. One factor that may contribute to the wrong assessment of what constitutes a primary strategic factor and what is secondary in importance is the role of the media in shaping the daily agenda of senior executives. A common routine in many government offices involves the last-minute cancellation of meetings and a change of the planned agenda for managers at all levels following a sensational headline. Agencies and elected officials are expected to respond to issues that are selected by the media according to considerations that have little to do with the public's welfare. Thus the media's interest, rather than the professional opinions and insights of public employees, often determines the priorities for government agencies. Under such conditions, it is no wonder that issues of secondary importance get prominence if they lend themselves to better picture opportunities or the so-called "human interest stories."

Members of the media who may have no expertise in a relevant field will compile news reports that reduce complicated issues to short sound bites. Unable to comprehend the complexity of many issues or the possible consequences of alternative courses of action, they tend to gravitate to the least complicated aspects of the problem, which may not be the most important ones, that is, those of primary strategic importance. In the course of their efforts to educate the public about what they, the members of the media, think is important, reporters and commentators create public expectations. Although such expectations may be wrong or misplaced, they may influence the range of choices (and even effect additional/new choices) public managers consider for dealing with any given issue, including priorities and the nature of the preferred courses of action. For example, during the investigation and impeachment trial of President Clinton, the media in general and cable TV were busy with the details of and speculations on the events of the day and the expected courses of actions by Ken Starr and Congress. The economic and governance problems in Russia or in the Far East were barely reported, even though they may have been of greater strategic importance to the welfare of America than any discrepancy between the story of Monica Lewinsky and Vernon Jordan about the breakfast they had or did not have when Monica was looking for a job.

## VII. DIFFERENCES IN HOW PUBLIC AND PRIVATE SECTORS PERCEIVE THREATS AND OPPORTUNITIES

In the private sector, strategic analysis is a search for opportunities to exploit and threats to avoid, but does that also hold true for the public sector? Before addressing this question, some other issues concerning the nature of a strategic plan as a management tool should be clarified.

The strategic plan evolves from an analytical process that includes examination: (1) reaffirmation or redefinition of the organization's mission and (2) mapping the content of relevant environments. Thus the strategic plan may establish whether the organization continues to pursue objectives that are closely related to the goals it had in the past, or whether it is starting to move in a different direction. By the same token, the strategic plan establishes the nature of the immediate or business environment in which the organization operates, the industry it claims to belong to, and whether (and how) it would consider developments and evolving trends within the national and international economies.

The strategic plan contributes to productivity by suggesting a course of action that takes advantage of the organization's assumed strengths, and by minimizing the cost due to assumed weaknesses (i.e., realized ineffectiveness or inefficiencies). The analytical process for developing the strategic plan generates important organizational learning that is of value even if the strategic plan is not adopted or implemented. This value is generated because the systematic character of the analytical process (assuming it is done correctly) allows managers as well as rank and file employees to understand what the agency or their subunit must do, and what it can and cannot do. This learning, in turn, contributes to performance in several ways. For example, it enhances the strength of the organization and its productivity by creating a common frame of reference that facilitates communication and coordination of activities across the board. By the same token, this shared understanding of the organization, its mission(s), and the challenges it faces from elements in its different environments can mold employees of different ranks and varied interests into a cohesive community with shared values. This can influence productivity by fostering loyalty and a sense of commitment that are called for when operational problems require employees to perform beyond the call of duty.

The strategic planning process facilitates a rational division of labor by striving to match relative abilities (or capacity) with needs (or demands) as recommended by classical economic theory. Indeed, from a systems point of view, underwriting the cost of the strategic planning process is justified when it ensures a division of labor (among organizations) that corresponds to their respective levels of expertise and areas of specialization.

Yet the rationale and the theory behind the concept of strategic planning in the private and public sectors are not identical. For example, at least in theory, public agencies are not supposed to look for opportunities to provide new services or products, let alone exploit opportunities for growth and expansion. As reflected by the passing of the GPRA, critics of the public sector suggest that applying business tools such as strategic planning to public agencies may boost its performance. But at the same time, agencies are forbidden to use one of the great attractions of strategic planning to private entrepreneurs, identification of growth opportunities. The reader should consider this restriction in the context of the arguments articulated by Niskanen (1971) about the "budget-maximizing bureaucrats." Niskanan uses the term to illustrate the gap between the rational businesslike procedures of the private sector and the lack of economic rationality in public management.

For public agencies, the mission and key characteristics of their operations (e.g., use of advisory boards, public hearings, appeals procedures) are established by the enabling legislation that creates them. Thus legislatures, rather than public managers, should have the burden of examining the obsolescence of agency missions. Indeed, occasional efforts such as "Sunset Reviews" (Adams and Sherman, 1978) and other kinds of evaluation and audits suggest that this important element of strategic planning is usually part of the legislative oversight function. For students of public administration, the various functions of legislatures and those performed by public managers in the strategic planning process correspond to the difference between policy making and implementation.

The notion of separation between politics and administration (Wilson, 1887) is used to explain the division of labor between legislators and public administrators. To the extent that such division does exist, legislatures may have the responsibility for adjusting the law to changing circumstances and for determining the need or justification for government to provide new products or services. The question is whether part-time legislators with their small staffs, as is the case in many state and local governments, are capable of discharging this responsibility in a timely manner. Even at the federal level, with full-time legislators and larger staffs, such a task is impossible. In addition, one must ask what the odds are that legislators can stop using delay tactics geared to enhance partisan interests and become proactive.

With the acquiescence of the legislators (and if the public managers choose to), public managers can end up playing a greater role in strategic planning than can be expected through strict interpretation of the division of labor between the executive and legislative branches of government. The GPRA stipulates that a strategic plan must be developed at the agency level. It reduces the choices public managers have about planning, but the GPRA does not eliminate their discretion. It is still up to managers at the agency level and at the executive branch of government to decide on the interpretation of missions and on whether to suggest to Congress that a given mission is obsolete and that the enabling legislation should be changed. As long as the expertise on any given topic is at the agency level, and as long as legislative bodies like Congress cannot match it, the onus of suggesting there is a need for change is on public managers, interest groups, the media, academia, and the courts. Any expectation that Congress, or any legislative body, can be proactive seems to be unrealistic.

Before going on to address some implications of the above observations, it should be noted that unlike the case of private companies in the public sector, court decisions can have great strategic significance in determining an agency's mission, permissible modes of operations, or other important variables of its operations. Yet it should also be noted that the involvement of the courts in strategic planning and management in the public sector, and thus in influencing government productivity, is unpredictable. For example, in the 1980s, federal courts took an active role in managing the correction system in Tennessee and the school district in Kansas City, although there is no case of the courts getting involved in the management of companies on behalf of plaintiffs that won a case before them. The personality of sitting judges at levels of the judicial system and the philosophy or doctrine that is communicated to lower courts by the Supreme Court can encourage or discourage judicial activism. The message from the liberal proaction Supreme Court under Chief Justice Warren is very different from the conservative minimum action message of Renquist's Supreme Court.

The involvement of the three branches of government in activities that influence the definition and interpretation of an agency's mission and how it is pursued is not without consequences. For one, this multiple involvement creates fog and confusion about who is responsible for what decision. This, in turn, does not help accountability or the pursuit of real (economic) values over symbolic ones.

Undeniably, there is a role for public managers in strategic planning. Yet given the roles and the involvement of the legislators and the courts and their influence on the implementation phase, one must wonder about the nature of this role. Is it the same role for all agencies? Does the role of public managers in strategic planning and management change over time? Is the role played an ad hoc function of the personal political ties or power base of the administrator in question? These questions become even more difficult to answer when one considers that public agencies, as organized entities rather than as individual administrators, suppress or create the opportunities that justify new interpretation (let alone definition) of a mission and modus operandi. Agencies cultivate demands for new and different services and goods when it suits their needs. They do it as an organized deliberate effort, or as the commutative result of partisan and unauthorized efforts of individual employees. Through dissemination of information they indoctrinate and facilitate the definition of new programmatic interests that can serve institutional or personal agendas. Appointed and career employees of a public agency can influence the emergence of interest groups to support those goals that serve their own agendas, while pretending to be indifferent or uninvolved. Mobilizing teacher unions, or pretending to be responsive to them, helped President Carter establish the U.S. Department of Education outside the U.S. Department of Health, Education, and Welfare. Teachers supported the proposed new department with the same vigor they demonstrated when President Reagan sought to abolish it because it was "their" agency. Interest groups articulate the demand for goods or services with which the agency should get involved and support a change in the enabling legislation. In the case of teachers, the change in the enabling legislation for establishing the U.S. Department of Education resulted not only in a redefinition of mission for HEW, but in the creation of a new environment for all other federal agencies and for intergovernmental relations, that is, for the interface of the federal government with state and local authorities. To the extent that HEW employees helped mobilize the interest to separate education from HEW, those transferred to the new department could take advantage of the opportunities they helped to create, in terms of career mobility.

Whether the reorganization of the division of labor at the federal level resulted in the generation of real new value for the general public, or whether its benefit was limited to one group (i.e., teachers), or is only of a symbolic nature is yet to be determined by researchers.

## A. Differences in How Public and Private Sectors Deal with Apparent Threats

The differences in strategic planning in the private and public sectors involve not only the different meaning of opportunities and the exploitation of strength. Those differences extend also to the way each sector deals with an apparent threat. In the private sector the appearance of a new firm offering competing services or goods is always a threat. The lifecycle of products and services in the private sector is driven by the market entry of new providers and products and the response of old providers, as they adapt business practices and products to the point that all competing goods and services become more or less indistinguishable, like commodities. The changing of prospective market shares is a threat that results from the addition of new providers or new business practices. On the other hand, growth in the number of alternative providers is not a threat in the public sector. An agency may gain strength when other agencies share similar administrative practices or standards for the goods and services they provide. The decision of one agency to imitate another agency and to introduce a new service (e.g., a credit-cardlike magnetic strip with important records) has an effect that is different from the effect of the decision of one private vendor to imitate another vendor. The reason is that imitation in the public sector may not lead to corresponding changes in the market share of the agencies involved. After all, what characterizes most agencies is that they have their own markets with little or no competition. As a matter of fact, imitation of goods, services, or administrative practices of one agency by another agency can help to legitimize the decisions by still other agencies to continue or to start such services. In contrast to the private sector, where the addition of another provider to the marketplace is a potential threat to survival, the entry of each additional agency to the relevant market may even extend the life expectancy of existing public providers.

In the public sector, a threat to an agency's structure, definition of goals, and available resources is imminent when other agencies start changing. Media reports and word of mouth about administrative reforms in one agency can create expectations for corresponding changes in other agencies. For example, in one Southeastern city the use of information technology to facilitate public access by one agency generated expectations that the same would become available to the public for dealing with other city agencies. When the expectation did not materialize, the agencies that were slow to develop Web pages and the option of using email to ask for information were accused of being unresponsive to citizens' demands. This, in spite of the fact that the records did not show any letter or any other formal request from the public for such access.

A political danger looms whenever an agency decides to abandon past practices, goals, or organizational structures. Thus, for example, under the Johnson administration, services to the poor by agencies such as the Office of Economic Opportunity (OEO) or the Department of Housing and Urban Development (HUD) were imitated by other agencies such as the Department of Agriculture (Food Stamps Program) and the Department of Labor (Job Corps Program) or Commerce (Small Business Administration). Many of these services had been provided by private charities and local agencies. Under the Reagan administration, the scaling back of services in one agency created a pressure on other agencies to follow suit. As agencies pulled out of the welfare market, their character started changing from a public to a private one. This change became evident as local and private agencies started moving in to fill the void that was created when federal agencies reduced their roles as providers of welfare services.

## VIII.  WHY STRATEGIC PLANNING MAY NOT BE COST-EFFECTIVE IN THE PUBLIC SECTOR

In the case of many public organizations, the strategic planning exercise may not be cost-effective. Agencies may not benefit from getting involved in a strategic planning process, as an analytic or a learning process, as their counterparts in the private sector do. As a matter of fact, they may even experience a decline in productivity as a result of an attempt to develop a strategic plan because resources will be diverted from production to overhead. Such diversion can force the agency to serve fewer people for the amount of resources available to it, negatively affecting the input-to-output ratio of its production function.

As pointed out elsewhere (Halachmi, 1986, 1992), there are many reasons public agencies can develop strategic plans but may not be in a position to follow them. It should be noted in particular that the mere fact that an agency intends to start the process of strategic planning is enough to mobilize interest groups outside the agency to take a variety of actions to insure their interests. This is likely to make the reality the agency was dealing with in the immediate past very different from the one it will face while going through the strategic planning exercise or from the reality it will face well into the implementation phase. That is because interest groups must protect not only real benefits or desired results but a variety of symbols.

Manipulation of symbols is something most career managers in the public sector are not trained or expected to do. Yet if left to the alleged "experts," the political partners of such professional managers, objective analysis cannot be expected.

Where political operatives are too involved, the odds are not good that any strategic plan will succeed. In the private sector, however, the "symbols" that managers must consider, those that are commonly listed under the label "good will" when the value of the company is assessed, such as brand recognition and traditional character of its products or services, are much less complicated (although some are changing, as illustrated by the case of Disney). In addition, most of the elements that comprise the "good will" list in the private sector can be monetized, whereas the same is not true for most public entities. This difference between the two sectors allows private managers to conduct an objective analysis of the tradeoffs that may result from alternative courses of action. For example, a Disney manager can assess the tradeoffs between the cash revenues from an "R-rated" production of a movie and its possible negative influence on the company's "good will." In comparison, a police chief is not in a position to perform a simple assessment of the tradeoffs between productivity gains that may result when the talent pool of individuals with visible impairments such as mobility or vision is tapped and there are possible adverse effects on the image of the police department.

Yet these are not the only or the main reasons for the difference between the cost-effectiveness of strategic planning in the two sectors. The main reason is that public officials are less inclined to support strategic planning and analysis than their counterparts in the private sector, as indicated by the case of the GPRA. The need of Senator Ted Stevens (R., Alaska), Chairman of the Senate Appropriations Committee, to threaten agencies with penalties if they failed to meet the September 1997 deadline for developing the strategic plans and performance measurements under the GPRA (McAllister, 1997) suggests that agencies are not too eager to make these required long-term commitments.

There are other good reasons why there might be reluctance in the public sector to develop strategic plans. Newly elected officials are likely to assume the powers of their new office with a blueprint for action that may be unrelated to organizational strength or the historic demand for services or goods. Such blueprints, in the form of capital budgets, long-term contracts with various contractors, organizational structure, and personnel, can limit the strategic choices that may be considered by such an official. Thus, for example, a new Secretary of Agriculture may come in with a policy agenda for supporting the export of grains to serve the interests of farming corporations. This may be a shift from a strategy that saw the family farm as the target constituency of the department. To mobilize resources for the new department's priorities, past commitments may be broken and existing programs may be stopped, despite the associated sunk cost. The strategic plan of the department may be abandoned in favor of a new effort whose longevity may be limited, too, by the electoral cycle.

The blueprint for action that candidates use during a campaign might have been put together for the prospective officeholder in order to score points with specific groups. It may be strong on symbols and weak on substance. The actual contribution of the candidate to the development of the plan might be negligible, and the corresponding commitment to it may not be much higher. Following a successful campaign, candidates or their appointees assume office with a lot of fanfare but usually without the benefit of the important learning that is a byproduct of an analytical effort to develop a strategic plan. As a matter of fact, new officeholders in the public sector may not be fully familiar with all the subtle ideas, considerations, and values of the offices they assume. Thus there is likely to be little strategic analysis after the election, because the newly elected may not be able to do it, and those returning to office may assume they do not need it. As illustrated by our study of gubernatorial transitions in Tennessee (Rogers and Halachmi, 1988), the most radical change from one administration to another occurred when Governor Lamar Alexander succesded himself to serve a second term. This finding was a surprise, because the researchers expected to find a more radical change when the transition from one administration to another involved a change from one party to another or from one governor to another regardless of party affiliation.

It should also be noted that due to candidates' limited involvement in the strategic planning process, prior to their election, even if the plan is the result of a well-considered process, action and reaction to developing events during the campaign may lead to inconsistencies and an undermining of the plan. In the same vein, because candidates, before and after election, often act on the basis of impressions of the plan rather than on intimate familiarity with it, they can inadvertently undermine the strategic plans they or their appointees intend to carry out.

The mechanics of management in the public sector are such that one cannot assume the position of a manager without having some kind of blueprint for action. In the public sector one does not say, "I intend to learn all about it after settling into my new job." Public administrators, as candidates for election or appointment, are expected to demonstrate some knowledge and to take proactive positions. Indeed, election campaigns and confirmation hearings are geared to ascertain what a candidate for election or appointment to a policy-making position knows about the operations and the particulars of the post. Such candidates have strong incentives to articulate ideas in public, even without the benefit of first-hand learning on the job, because communicating (to a public that knows less than what they know) their ability to hit the ground running may determine their chances to get that post. For these reasons, an elected or appointed official may develop a plan of action that is right for obtaining a desired position but wrong for doing a good job.

In the case of many elected officials, the blueprint for action is etched in an incremental fashion on the campaign trail without thorough analysis of short- and long-term implications. A case in point is candidate George Bush's position during the presidential campaign in support of maternal leave and against new taxes, two positions he reversed as President. The case demonstrates how candidates often pay more attention to symbols and political values rather than to real-world managerial considerations. Bush's position illustrates the fact that during political campaigns, little effort is likely to be spent making sure that the rhetoric of the campaign does not call for operations or positions that are inconsistent with, mutually exclusive of, or contrary to the candidate's basic values. In June 1990, President Bush vetoed a bill calling for mandatory maternal leave. The idea behind the bill was consistent with the "Gentler America" and "Emphasis on Family" slogans of his campaign, but the bill was inconsistent with another position he took during the campaign, namely, that government should not dictate business practices. The President had to work hard to explain why in the face of this inconsistency he opted to favor business rights over women's rights. Bush's inconsistency on the maternity leave issue is not an isolated case. When interviewed on TV after losing the election, Bush claimed that it was the raising of taxes, after pledging on the campaign trail, "Read my lips no new taxes" that caused him the loss of a second term in the White House. In spite of this example, which suggests a real cost for a deviation from campaign promises, it seems that most candidates are not bothered by the possible inconsistencies of the positions they take during a campaign and the positions they end up taking if they win. Thus, for example, candidates taking a position against abortions seldom bother to ask their staff for the possible implications of such a position on the prospect of sustaining any one of their other positions, such as the opposition to increased government expenditures for education, housing, or health. Because the inconsistency between the two positions is not obvious, they reckon, most voters will not notice it.

After assuming office, an elected or appointed official may find that another plan for action was prepared for the agency under a previous administration. Such a plan may be the result of a premeditated effort by an outgoing administration to restrict the choices of the incoming officials. The plan may also result from efforts of career employees to reduce uncertainty. The primary purpose of the plan in this case may not be to optimize the process of attaining official goals. Using this pretext as a means for mobilizing support and complicating the introduction of change, the plan is developed to protect career employees. It is a way to make them less vulnerable to the short-lived wishes of political operators who do not stay on the job long enough to have a real stake in the welfare of the agency and its career employees. Such plans include long-term commitments that leave little room for maneuvers, changes, or new interpretation of priorities, goals, or the use of resources. At the federal level, this reality is manifested by the fact that the lion's share of the annual budget must be considered as given (Wildavsky, 1979).

For a candidate's staff to develop a plan for action when it is not certain that the candidate will get the opportunity to implement it, and for an agency to develop a plan before the new responsible official takes office are both inconsistent with some basic premises of strategic planning, specifically, with the expectation that the plan will result from the analysis of past record, present situations, and future demands coupled with the dominating values of top management (Katz and Kahn, 1978; Hodges and Anthony, 1984). In the public sector, the possible coexistence of more than one plan for action suggests the coexistence of different agendas: the (past and current) management agenda and the employees' agenda. The need to reconcile the differences between the plans may preempt any effort to treat productivity as a simple but desired goal. Instead, productivity issues may become means, a ploy, or a justification for actions for achieving some political ends other than productivity. By contrast, productivity in the private sector can be taken as the ultimate goal.

One reason for the difference between the two sectors when it comes to issues of productivity and strategizing is that the immediate past experience of a newly appointed executive, even when the executive is coming from another sector of the economy (as was the case of John Scully, who came to Apple Corp. from a soft drink

company), is likely to be accepted, by employees and associates, as valuable preparation for the job. In the public sector, any appointee with outside credentials is
regarded suspiciously, at least by agency insiders and their allies in other agencies.

The new administrator in the private sector may develop a blueprint for action
after assuming the job and having an opportunity to learn the intricate details of the
organization and its relevant environments. The private sector accepts the sunk cost
that results from doing away with prior plans as a legitimate cost of doing business.
Hence the strategic plan in the private sector is more likely to address the issues that
influence performance rather than the issues that may influence whether one is likely to
be elected or appointed to the desired position.

In the public sector, the appearance of deviation from the advertised platform is
discouraged by political advisers and party operatives. Because the election platform
has a symbolic value, it may deter innovations even after an elected official assumes an
office and finds that changes are overdue. In other words, the strategic analysis of the
environment or the agency may be constrained or it may be biased altogether by
symbolic values, that is sacred cows that cannot be touched. This, in turn, can deprive
any agency of the prospect of optimal performance and can create a strong disincentive to commission an indepth productivity study.

It should be noted that this prospect of a compromised strategic analysis is more
likely to happen in the case of elected officials, rather than appointed ones, due to the
need of the former to consider reelection. In the case of appointed officials, when long-
term retention of a position is usually a lesser consideration, the benefits of learning on
the job may result in significant changes of attitudes and, thus, in relaxing any constraints on strategic planning or analysis. A case in point is the U.S. Department of
Energy and the U.S. Department of Education, created during the Carter Administration. When campaigning for the 1980 Presidential election, candidate Ronald
Reagan promised to abolish both agencies, capitalizing on their unpopularity with
several interest groups. Indeed, in both cases, President Reagan's nominees for
secretary were confirmed by Congress with the understanding that they agreed with
the president's desire to abolish the two agencies. Immediately following the 1984
election, the Reagan administration developed a formal plan for reassigning various
responsibilities of the Department of Energy to other federal agencies. In both cases,
after taking office and getting a better insight, the secretaries changed course. Both
became advocates within the administration against abolishment, and both worked to
convert former opponents into vocal lobbyists supporting the agencies in dealings with
Congress.

Diverting resources from direct operations to planning is not popular among
elected or appointed officials. It contributes certain and immediate loss of support
from those who are negatively affected by the diversion, for example, service recipients
or the employees that are expected to continue doing the same with less. Such a
diversion cannot guarantee mobilization of the support of possible beneficiaries to
replace lost support, even in the long run. With increasing certainty about the economic and political cost and without decrease in the uncertainty about the benefits,
public administrators are likely to be very reluctant to invest in strategic analysis and
planning. The paradox is that only a thorough strategic analysis can yield an accurate
assessment of the actual loss of support and an estimate of possible gains from
pursuing optional courses of action.

Another disincentive to strategic analysis in public agencies has to do with the long time it takes to complete it. During all that time, the process exposes the public administrator and the agency to outside pressures and repeated attempts to influence it. Such exposure may interfere with the ability of the manager and other employees to carry out routine operations. This, in turn, may affect the productivity of individuals who get caught in the glare of media attention to controversy in connection with the strategic analysis process and the agency's performance in general. The effort to develop a strategic plan cannot guarantee a better state of affairs for the agency or its top management. As a matter of fact, it may even reduce the ability of the agency or its top administrators to cope with daily routines. For such reasons management, employees, or even service recipients may be content to support the status quo, which may not be optimal at the present and even wasteful in the future, but is free of threats and uncertainties to them.

## IX. PRODUCTIVITY AND STRATEGIC PLANNING IN THE PUBLIC SECTOR: SOME CONCLUDING REMARKS

As pointed out throughout this chapter, strategic planning in the public sector may not be a promising or a feasible proposition for every agency. However, public managers cannot afford to overlook the productivity implications of any decision they make just because of the many reasons that negate the ability of some public agencies to develop and successfully implement strategic planning.

Public agencies are constantly under surveillance by several groups. First there are reporters, who are hunting for a scoop that may earn them coveted accolades for public service and investigative reporting. Second are the auditors, who are pressed by tough legislators, elected or appointed officials, who are supposed to find anything that might usefully be targeted as possible waste, abuse, or inefficiency. Such findings allow the auditors' masters to communicate to their respective constituencies that they are watching out for the taxpayers' interests. Third are the lobbyists and representatives of various interest groups, including service recipients, good Samaritans (i.e., those who enlist themselves to defend or promote important causes because of a principle rather than due to expected benefit or cost), professional and trade associations of those representing them, and public watchdog groups. All this constant monitoring and snooping is meant to ensure that what is important to these interested parties, be it something of a symbolic value or something more tangible, remains a priority. Various interest groups outside and within each agency work hard to protect their interests as the pressure on the public sector grows to address an expanding number of issues with dwindling resources. For those monitoring an agency's performance, determining efficiency and effectiveness is derived by calculating how a given mode of operations is likely to affect important aspects of their own parochial interests.

Sunshine laws disallow policy deliberations behind closed doors, which means that any effort to develop a strategic plan in the public sector is likely to be scrutinized by several groups of the monitors listed above and by labor unions and the professional associations of the employees in any affected agency. Such scrutiny—including public hearings that must take place as part of the effort to develop a strategic plan, and lengthy discussions of the agency's mission, its mode of operation, its strengths, and weaknesses—is itself capable of changing the context of the agency's operation. In other words, an attempt to develop a strategic plan in the public sector can be disruptive enough to make any resulting plan either obsolete or infeasible, that is, dead on arrival.

Under laws such as the GPRA, public managers are expected to have strategic plans. The reason for having a strategic plan in the public sector is to advance an agency's productivity, as measured by reference to such matters as the efficient use of resources, responsiveness, service quality, effectiveness of programs, value for money, and competitiveness with and comparability to other providers. But how should public managers deal with the high odds that attempting to develop a strategic plan is likely to create the conditions that would undermine its implementation? Is it possible that working to enhance productivity by improving efficiency, effectiveness, service quality, value for money, responsiveness, and comparability to other providers (public and private, at home and abroad) may result in strategic gains? The attractiveness of such a possibility suggests that instead of pushing for strategic planning across the board, managers should be encouraged to seek greater productivity. The growing use of benchmarking and concepts such as reengineering indicates that managers recognize the prospect of strategic gains through enhanced productivity.

## REFERENCES

Adams, B., Sherman, B. (1978). Sunset implementation: A positive partnership to make government work. *Public Admin. Rev.* 38(1):78–81.

BLS. Bureau of Labor Statistics. (1998). *Measuring State and Local Government Labor Productivity: Examples from Eleven Services*. Washington, DC: U.S. Department of Labor, Bulletin, 2495.

Cobb, R. W., Elder, C. D. (1972). *Participation in American Politics: The Dynamics of Agenda Building*. Boston: Allyn & Bacon.

Denison, E. F. (1969). Some major issues in productivity analysis: An examination of estimates by Jorgenson & Griliches, Survey of Economic Issues. In *The Measurement of Productivity*. Washington, DC: Brookings Institute, pp.37–63. reprint no.244.

Dror, Y. (1968). *Public Policymaking Reexamined*. San Francisco: Chandler.

GAO ( July 11,1997). *Results Act: Observations on the Department of Justice's February 1997 Draft Strategic Plan*. GAO/GGD_97_153R.

Gore, A. (1993). *From Red Tape to Results: Creating Government That Works Better and Costs Less*. Washington, DC: Government Printing Office.

Halachmi, A. (1986, Winter). Strategic planning and management? Not necessarily. *Public Product. Rev.* 40:35–50.

Halachmi, A. (1992). Strategic management and productivity. In: Holzer, M., ed. *Public Productivity Handbook, (Ch. 28)*. New York: Marcel Dekker, pp.551–564.

Halachmi, A. (1995). Reengineering and public management. *Int. Rev. Admin. Sci.* 61(3):329–342.

Halachmi, A. (1996a). Measure of excellence. In: Hill, H., Klages, H., Loffler, E., eds., *Quality, Innovation and Measurement in the Public Sector*. Frankfurt: Peter Lang, pp.9–24.

Halachmi, A. (1996b). Promises and possible pitfalls on the way to SEA reporting. In: Halachmi, A., Bouckaert, G., eds., *Organizational Performance and Measurement in the Public Sector*. Westport, CT: Quorum, pp.77–100.

Halachmi, A. (1999). Performance and quality measurement in the public sector. In: Halachmi, A., ed., *Performance & Quality Measurement in Government*. Burke, VA: Chatelaine, pp.9–22.

Halachmi, A., Bovaird, T. (1997). Process reengineering in the public sector: Learning some private sector lessons. *Technovation* 17(5):227–235.

Halachmi, A., Holzer, M. (1986). Toward strategic perspectives on public productivity. In: Holzer, M., Halachmi, A., eds., *Strategic Issues in Public Sector Productivity*. San Francisco: Jossey-Bass, pp.5–14.

Hammer, M., Champy, J. (1993). *Reengineering the Corporation*. New York: HarperBusiness.

Hatry, H. P., Fisk, D. M. (1992). Measuring productivity in the public sector. In: Holzer, M., ed. *Public Productivity Handbook*. New York: Marcel Dekker, pp.139–160.

Hodges, B. J., Anthony, W. P. (1984). *Organization Theory*. 2nd ed. Boston: Allyn & Bacon.

Jorgenson, W. D., Griliches, Z. (1967). The explanation of productivity change. *Rev. Econ. Stud.* 34(3) In: The Measurement of Productivity. Washington, DC: Brookings Institute. reprint no. 244, pp. 3–64.

Katz, D., Kahn, R. L. (1978). *The Social Psychology of Organizations*. New York: Wiley.

Kingdon, J. W. (1984). *Agendas, Alternatives and Public Policy*. Boston: Little, Brown.

McAllister, B. (June 25,1997 ). Sen. Stevens threatens penalties for agencies low quality of performance-measuring plans disturbs Senate Appropriations Chairman. *Washington Post*, pp. A17.

Mintzberg, H. (1987). Five Ps for strategy. In: Mintzberg, H., Quinn, J. B., eds. *The Strategy Process: Concepts and Contexts (1992)*. Englewood Cliffs, NJ: Prentice-Hall, pp.12–19.

Mintzberg, H. (1994). *The Rise and Fall of Strategic Planning*. NY: Free Press.

Niskanen, W. A. (1971). *Bureaucracy and Representative Government*. Chicago: Aldine-Atherton.

Norman, D. A. (1999). The designing of everyday things. January 12. Available at http://www.sv.ntnu.no/psy/Bjarne.Fjeldsenden/svpsy342/Norman.html.

NUREG/CR_1250. (1980). Three Mile Island: A report to the commission and to the public. U.S. Nuclear Regulatory Commission. January.

Osborne, D., Gaebler, T. (1992). *Reinventing Government*. Reading, MA: Addison-Wesley.

Ouchi, W. G. (1982). *Theory Z*. New York: Avon.

Quinn, B. J., Mintzberg, H., James, R. M. (1988). *The Strategy Process: Concepts, Contexts, and Cases*. Englewoods Cliffs, NJ: Prentice-Hall.

Rawls, J. (1971). *A Theory of Justice*. Cambridge, MA: Harvard University Press.

Rogers, B., Halachmi, A. (1988). Gubernatorial transition. *Public Product. Rev.* 12(1):73–90.

Todorovic, J. (1999). The impact of human reliability on automobile quality. February 3. Available at http://www.cent.co.yu/jumv/radovi3/yu97002.htm.

van Bertalanffy, L. (1968). General system theory: A critical review. In: Buckley, W., ed. *Modern System Research for the Behavioral Scientist*. Chicago: Aldine.

Van Gigch, J. P. (1974). *Applied General System Theory*. New York: Harper and Row.

Wildavsky, A. (1979). *The Politics of the Budgetary Process*. Boston: Little, Brown.

Wilson, W. (1887). The study of administration. *Polit. Sci. Quart.* 2(1):197–222.

# 35

# Total Quality Management and Customer Focus

## Linking the Philosophy of TQM to Responsive Public Agencies

**SEOK-HWAN LEE**
*The Catholic University of Korea, Songsim Campus, South Korea*

**MARC HOLZER**
*Rutgers, The State University of New Jersey, Newark, New Jersey, U.S.A.*

## I. INTRODUCTION

Over the past two decades, adopting TQM (Total Quality Management) as a management philosophy in the public sector has been a source of major debate among scholars and practitioners. Objections notwithstanding, TQM, originally intended to change American workplaces in the private sector, has been adopted and implemented by numerous public agencies.

TQM is defined as "an enterprise lifestyle that emphasizes customer satisfaction, excellent service and rapid adjustment to address ever-changing customer needs" (McCloskey and Collett, 1993, cited in Flynn et al., 1995, p. 1325).

As such, TQM is a developing strategy for improving products, processes, and services on a continuing basis. From this perspective, customer focus, top management commitment, teamwork, continuous improvement, participate management, labor-management cooperation, and systematic analysis are key functions in developing a TQM environment (Shea and Howell, 1998; Motwani et al., 1996; Powell, 1995; Bowman and Hellein, 1998).

Given the difference between the public and private sectors, much has been discussed about what might prevent TQM from being adapted to the public sector

(Milakovich, 1992; Swiss, 1992; Rago, 1994, 1996). Furthermore, experience with TQM in the public sector has produced mixed results. Some agencies report success in adopting and implementing TQM, whereas other agencies believe TQM has not contributed to improving productivity. Perhaps this is partly attributable to the misunderstanding of TQM's management philosophy among managers and employees (White and Wolf, 1995).

TQM's primary emphasis is customer focus. If this focus were applied to the public sector, although the definition of customer is a matter of debate (Swiss, 1992; Dean and Evans, 1994), the implication would then be that we need to enhance the responsiveness of public agencies to the public.

In fact, it is ironic that many factors that are believed to hinder either responsiveness of public agencies or successful implementation of TQM are the ones that TQM originally intended to improve. Although TQM was originally invented to solve existing management problems, little has been discussed about the types of problems TQM can solve, particularly in terms of organizational responsiveness. From such a point of view, this chapter seeks to identify major assumptions of TQM and examine factors that are believed to hinder organizational responsiveness in the public sector. Assuming that top management support and leadership are a necessary first step in transformation of any organization, this chapter then discusses how TQM's philosophy helps solve those public sector problems relating to responsiveness to the public.

Understanding the underlying philosophy of TQM and identifying management problems enables public managers to correctly use TQM as a powerful management tool to solve various management problems.

## II.  ASSUMPTIONS OF TOTAL QUALITY MANAGEMENT

At the outset, W. Edward Deming (1986), a "father" of TQM, points out that it requires transformation of the American management style in business and is also applicable to governmental transformation.

The key elements of TQM are presented in various ways (Scherkenbach, 1987; Milakovich, 1992; Connor, 1997). Following Milakovich's (1992, pp. 584–586) summary this chapter describes Deming's 14 points as follows.

1. Create and publish to all employees a statement of the aims and purposes of the organization. Management must demonstrate constantly their commitment to this statement.
2. Learn the new philosophy, including top management and the entire organization.
3. Undertand the purpose of inspection, for improvement of processes and reduction of costs.
4. End the practice of awarding business on the basis of price tag alone.
5. Improve constantly and forever the system of production and service.
6. Institute moder methods of training.
7. Teach and institute leadership.
8. Drive out fear. Create trust. Create a climate for innovation.
9. Optimize toward the aims and purposes of the organization the efforts of teams, groups, and staff areas.

10. Eliminate exhortations for the workforce.
11. Eliminate numerical quotas for production. Instead, learn and institute methods for improvement. Eliminate Management By Objective (MBO).
12. Remove barriers which rob people of pride in workmanship.
13. Encourage education and self-improvement for everyone.
14. Take actions to accomplish the transformation.

Based on Deming's 14 points mentioned above, the following assumptions can be drawn.

## A. Customer Focus

The underlying assumption of TQM is a focus on the customer. It is assumed that the customer is the judge of quality, and productivity improvement, in principle, does not exist without customer satisfaction. Customers include both internal (employees) and external customers (citizens). Internal customers receive "any work output in the service or production process," and external customers purchase the product (McGowan and Wittmer, 1997).

Therefore customer satisfaction is the utmost priority of any organization. Both employee and citizen satisfactions are important elements with which to measure productivity and performance in any organization.

## B. Continuous Improvement

Another important assumption of TQM is found in the emphasis on continuous improvement. In fact, all productivity improvement programs require feedback from both employees and citizens on a regular basis. Continuous improvement includes: "(1) enhance value to the customer through new and improved products and services, (2) reduce errors, defects, and waste, (3) improve responsiveness and cycle-time performance, and (4) improve productivity and effectiveness in the use of all resources (McGowan and Wittmer, 1997, p. 313)."

As Swiss (1992, p. 358) points out, "Quality is not a static attribute; it is a constantly changing target because it represents a delighted customer."

It should also be noted that continuous improvement focuses on input and processes rather than on output (Swiss, 1992; Carr and Littman, 1990; Scholtes and Hacquebord, 1988). The assumption here is that focusing more on processes and input will eventually lead to productive outcomes, thereby achieving productivity improvement.

## C. Top Management Commitment and Leadership

In order for any organization to be successful in productivity improvement, top management commitment is always a necessary first step (Holzer and Callahan, 1998; Lee, 2000a). TQM will not work unless it is implemented through strong leadership. As do other productivity improvement strategies, TQM requires a long-term commitment from top management. Berman and West (1995) argue that many organizations are inclined to implement productivity improvement strategies such as TQM at "a token level rather than fully committing themselves to success." In this regard, Rago (1996, p. 234) points out that "agency vision and goals need to be clearly communicated throughout all levels of the agency and leadership needs to be actively involved in this effort."

Top management should also play a critical role in assessing and changing an organization's culture so that TQM initiatives can be fully supported by employees at all levels. It is essential to change bureaucratic organizational culture (hierarchical, power-oriented, and structured) to innovative (results-oriented, creative, and challenging) and supportive (collaborative, people-oriented, and trusting) cultures (Wallach, 1983). As White and Wolf (1995, p. 224) put it, "The culture of public sector organizations must be shifted away from blame and control to one of support for positive action."

This culture change cannot happen in the short run. It requires patience.

## D. Empowerment and Teamwork

The importance of teamwork and empowerment is based on the assumptions that no productivity improvement is the product of a single employee's effort, and no single action of the manager can earn the loyalty and full support of his or her people (Werther et al., 1986; Pollock 2001). Although definitions of empowerment abound, empowerment is a leadership approach in which management gives the authority to make decisions to lower-level employees, and assumes that employees will take ownership of their jobs as a function of that increased responsibility (Loretta and Polsky, 1991; Tenser, 1993; Holt et al., 2000).

In fact, empowered teams, such as autonomous task groups and self-managing groups, have received much attention from scholars and practitioners (Mohrman et al., 1995; Stewart and Manz, 1995; Hut and Mollenman, 1998). Because empowered teams are seen as the key to solving organizational problems, TQM suggests that employees collaboratively work as a tem to cope with existing management problems in an organization rather than asking external people for help. The reason for this is simple: employees are the people who really know what is going on in their organization, therefore no one can do a better job than employees in fixing existing management and work-related problems.

Teamwork can also be divided into three levels (McGowan and Wittmer, 1997; Dean and Evans, 1994). Vertical teamwork allows top management to give lower-level employees authority to make decisions that would meet customers' demands. In the meantime, horizontal teamwork makes it possible for different functional units or groups within an organization to cope with environmental demands immediately because, in a teamwork situation, it is much easier for the team to get cooperation from related agencies and departments. Finally, interorganizational teamwork includes developing teams of suppliers, customers, and other external groups. In the public sector, this form of teamwork could be useful in involving various interest groups, agency representatives, citizen representatives, subcontractors, and elected officials.

## III. ISSUES IN ORGANIZATIONAL RESPONSIVENESS

Responsiveness is a very critical value that public agencies must keep in a democratic society. Rourke (1984, p. 4) defines responsiveness as "the extent to which it promotes correspondence between the decisions of bureaucrats and the preferences of the community or the officeholders who are authorized to speak for the public." This responsiveness can be achieved in an "organizational arrangement under which a great deal of authority is delegated to lower levels of administration (p. 8)."

Obviously, responsiveness is directly related to decentralization. Decentralization, by placing government closer to the people, fosters greater responsiveness of policy makers to the will of the citizenry (Wolman, 1990; Sheldrake, 1992; Ashford, 1976; Yates, 1973). In this context, Kaufman (1987, p. 394) asserts that representativeness, politically neutral competency, and executive leadership should be regarded as important values in the public sector. In particular, as for representativeness, "there is a need to improve public representation within organizations because 'many unorganized interests' are excluded from formulation of decisions."

Because TQM is also a program of decentralization, it may help public agencies to enhance responsiveness in a turbulent environment. Below, barriers to responsiveness in the public sector are discussed and solutions based on TQM philosophy are suggested.

## IV. BARRIERS TO RESPONSIVENESS AND SOLUTIONS: LINKING TQM'S PHILOSOPHY

### A. Situation 1

#### 1. Problem 1: Interest Group Politics and Captive Bureaucracy

Sometimes public agencies are inclined to listen to political parties and organized interest groups rather than to what the public specifically expresses as its "wants." In relation to interest group politics, the concept of "captive agency" should be noted. Rourke (1984, p. 58) defines "captive agency" as follows.

> The agency may come to lean so heavily on the political support of an outside group that the group in time acquires veto power over many of the agency's major decisions. In extreme cases, the agency becomes in effect a "captive" organization, unable to move in any direction except those permitted it by the group upon which it is politically dependent.

Therefore a captive agency typically has difficulty in responding properly to the demands of the general public.

A case study by Lee (2001) shows how unbalanced participation led by organized interest groups makes it difficult for public agencies to reflect individual citizens' opinions. A common problem with citizen participation is that the majority of citizens remain silent, and organized interest groups actively participate in political life. In this situation, policy outcomes are likely to exist for organized interest groups, not for the majority of citizens.

Lee (2001) argues that this is not because the majority of citizens do not care about a specific policy issue, but because they do not have enough time and money, civic skills, and cooperative possibilities to participate in political life.

#### 2. TQM Solution 1: Establishing Interorganizational Teamwork and Training for External Customers

In most cases, a captive agency is a function of lack of institutional mechanisms for involving various citizen groups in the political process. As mentioned above, the concept of interorganizational teamwork can help solve this problem of unbalanced political participation. In other words, it may be possible to get various citizen groups, voluntary associations, and citizen representatives involved in major decision-making processes in a local community.

Furthermore, in order to enhance individual citizens' participation in political life, given that individual citizens do not participate simply because of lack of time and money, civic skills, and low levels of communication and cooperation possibilities, it may be necessary to employ online participation through the use of the Internet. To foster online participation, training for the majority of citizens is critical in the long term. It is the public sector's responsibility to provide local communities with appropriate training and information regarding online participation.

Washington State's online participation initiative explains how interorganizational teams composed of dozens of state agencies, boards, and commissions have contributed to a digital government that works to enhance citizen participation. An interorganizational team, called Access Washington, in the Department of Information Services, played a critical role in developing online participation tools. As the progress report (Washington State Governor's Office, 2000) states,

> The Access Washington state Internet portal was launched in 1998 to replace a static, billboard-style state website called *Homepage Washington* that averaged only 170,000 monthly visitors. Within one year, page views on *Access Washington* increased 488% to an average of one million per month, and the numbers keep climbing. Today's Access Washington turns government to face the people, organizing hundreds of government information programs and dozens of transactional services in citizen-centric navigation paths. *Access Washington* at access.wa.gov is the gateway to the digital government community: on-line storefronts and service centers filled with the government information and tools that citizens want, when they want them.

## B.  Situation 2

### 1.  Problem 2: Expertise and Information Distortion

It has been said that bureaucratic expertise is rooted both in the characteristics of public organizations and, increasingly, in the skills of their members. The operation of public agencies requires employment of an increasingly diverse and complex range of specialized people (Rourke, 1984).

Rourke (1984, p. 20) asserts that bureaucratic expertise influences the development of public policy through several primary channels:

> (1) the ability of bureaucrats to gather information and to give advice that often shapes the decisions of political officials; (2) the capacity of bureaucratic organizations to carry on the tasks that must be performed once policy goals are decided upon—the power of implementation; and (3) as a critical dimension of this power to implement policies, the discretion with which bureaucracies are commonly vested as they carry on the work of government.

However, it should also be noted that these three factors might result in such negative outcomes as information distortion in an organization. According to empirical research by O'Reilly (1980, p. 329), information distortion is defined as "the incorrect reproduction of objectively correct information and can result from either conscious or deliberate alteration or unconscious manipulation." He contends that unfavorable but important information is not delivered to higher-level decision makers, who may be dependent upon hierarchical communication flows. Downs (1967, p. 266) also contends that "each official tends to distort the information he passes upward in the hierarchy, exaggerating those data favorable to himself and minimizing those unfavorable to himself."

This intentional information distortion can make it difficult for a public organization to adapt itself to changes in its environment.

## 2.  TQM Solution 2: Utilizing Vertical Teamwork and Empowerment

As information distortion is likely to occur in a hierarchical structure where official communication is limited to the channel between superiors and subordinates, it is important to build multiple communication paths so that important information may be available to top management at any time. As Gortner and colleagues (1987, p. 203) put it,

> Information tends to be transmitted upward in the organization only if (1) its transmission will not have unpleasant consequences for the transmitter, or (2) the superior will hear of it anyway from other channels, and it is better to tell him first, or (3) it is information that the superior needs in his dealings with his own superiors, and he will be displeased if he is caught without it.

Using a vertical teamwork paradigm makes it possible for every employee to share important information without much trouble and to facilitate "information flows" within an organization. While making it possible for top-level management to have a chance to get critical information from lower-level management, a vertical team also allows lower-level employees to be empowered to make decisions that will satisfy citizens. A significant level of empowerment can preclude a possibility of information distortion in advance in that, for employees, empowerment is acceptance of full responsibility and risk for their actions. Given the full risk and responsibility they have to assume, empowered employees would not simply withhold unfavorable and important information. Rather, they will try to solve the problems with superiors and colleagues in a timel and cooperative manner.

## C.  Situation 3

### 1.  Problem 3: Specialized Structure and Parochialism

Administrative efficiency will increase as specialization increases (Simon, 1997). It seems that "a major problem in an effective organization is to specialize and subdivide activities in such a manner that the psychological forces of identification will contribute to, rather than hinder, correct decision making (Simon, 1997, p. 292)."

Golembiewski (1997) stresses that in order to grow, all organizations have to balance two basic tendencies: one is differentiation and the other is integration. In general, organizational structure are based on functional differentiation, and create cognitive and emotional differences between specialists and separate units. Therefore, to effectively link different functions to an organization's goal, it is also necessary to integrate and coordinate these separate and specialized functions.

In this regard, integration seems to be related to cooperation problems among departments in organizations. Golembiewski (1997, p. 107) also maintains that "the heightening of differentiation by the bureaucratic model wrongheadedly impedes the higher degree of required integration."

From such a point of view, it is to be noted that extreme functional specialization can lead to "parochialism" among agencies. Considering that functional specialization is directly related to the differentiation of function, it may be very difficult for public agencies to effectively respond to various demands of citizens in a timely manner. In addition, parochialism will simply delay delivery of public services to citizens.

## 2.  TQM Solution 3: Utilizing Horizontal Teamwork and Preventing Variation in the Product and Process

Although functional specialization is sometimes desirable for achieving efficiency and productivity in an organization in a turbulent environment, t may also be a barrier in delivering public services to citizens either in a timely manner or in an appropriate form.

As mentioned above, one of the elements that TQM emphasizes is elimination of barriers between departments. By using horizontal teams, it is possible to reduce conflicts and tensions between agencies and departments. In a horizontal team, members are able to develop mutual understanding and learn how to cooperate beyond the boundaries of the immediate unit.

Formation of these "cross-functional teams" must be encouraged at all levels in an organization. It will eventually reduce costs and times for producing and delivering services to citizens.

Sometimes producing high quality is a function of preventing variation in the product and process. Swiss (1992, p. 357) points out that "slippages in quality arise from too much variation in the product or service."

Utilizing multiunit teams also enables public agencies to fix process variation problems. The Department of Labor and Industries in Washington State is a good example. In July 2000, the department created a multiunit team called "Factory Assembled Structures (FAS) Process Improvement Team" to solve process problems:

> Labor and Industries approves plans for modular building construction. Manufacturers complained about the process, citing a low 30% acceptance rate for first time plans, poor communications and a lack of consistency and professionalism. In collaboration with manufacturers, the team improved communications, developed training and computerized processes. They raised approval rates and enhanced customer service without lowering standards or sacrificing public safety. The plan approval rate went from 30% to 72% for the following 19-month period, an increase of 140%. Training is provided on-site and on-line and issues get corrected over the phone, saving time and money for the manufacturers (Washington State, 2000).

## D.  Situation 4

### 1.  Problem 4: Attribution Error and Management Failure

Under some conditions, the development of stereotypic beliefs may have its foundation in cognitive, information-processing biases. In typical usage, "attribution refers to judgments about one's perceptions rather than causal perception" (Hamilton 1980,

p. 767). Attribution theory is concerned with the attempt of ordinary people to understand the cause and implications of events they witness. As Ross (1977, p. 183) put it, "fundamental attribution error is the tendency for attributers to underestimate the impact of situational factors and to overestimate the role of dispositional factors in controlling behavior."

Potential causal factors are thought of as internal to the actor (e.g., ability, effort, and intention) or external to the actor (e.g., task-related factors and luck). People search for the causal structure of events via reliance upon attributions to the environment (external attribution) or to something in the person involved in the event (internal attribution; Heider, 1958).

In reality, leaders of organizations are inclined to accept paradigms that attribute organizational success to their own actions and organizational failures to the actions of others or to external forces, but oppositional groups in an organization are likely to have the converse principle for attributing causality (Miller and Ross, 1975).

The same principle may apply to the relationship between supervisors and subordinates in terms of performance evaluations. As long as this kind of stereotypic belief dominates human beings' minds, productivity and performance improvement, whether it is at the individual or organizational level, is hard to achieve.

In this situation, people do not try to find out causes of policy or management failure, and would not admit that "it was our fault." This attribution makes it hard for public agencies to adapt themselves to a changing environment, thereby reducing responsiveness to the demands of customers.

## 2. TQM Solution 4: Admitting Variations in Employees' Performance and Eliminating Numerical Quotas

In fact, one of the underlying assumptions of TQM is that "it is the management, not the worker that is a problem in many cases."

As White and Wolf (1995, pp. 210–211) put it,

> Typically, when a manager sees a performance distribution in which one or some workers are low and others are high, the response is to evaluate the low workers as bad, the high workers as good, and then set out to make the bad workers like the good ones . . . . In contrast, the TQM manager simply considers that the workers at the good end of the distribution have been lucky and the ones at the bad end have been unlucky.

TQM assumes that any organization can have both good performers and poor performers. Becoming a good performer today does not mean being a good performer tomorrow. In the same way, nobody knows if a poor performer today will become an excellent performer tomorrow. As such, TQM managers do not blame employees for their low performance. Instead, they try to seek the reasons in the management process side. It should be noted that one of Deming's 14 points, "eliminating numerical quotas and standards" was recommended in this context. Where numerical standards and quotas are major performance indicators, the relationships between labor and management are likely to be adversarial. Managers try to attribute the cause of poor performance to employees, arguing that employees use official time for union activities, for example, and employees assert that poor performance is not their fault (Holzer and Lee, 1999). The following statement in the *Government Executive Magazine* (1999) by Bobby Harnage, President of American Federation of Government Employees, illustrates how each side may view causes differently.

> There is no such thing as one poor performer. That individual has a supervisor. If he or she is staying on the rolls, then we have two poor performers. Performance management rules, which were established by the Civil Service Reform Act, do not need to be changed. Instead, managers need to have the courage to deal with poor performance.

Harry Singletary, Jr., Secretary of the Florida Department of Corrections, points out that people are the key to successful TQM application. He states, "We, the members of the Florida Department of Corrections, believe in the worth of the individuals. Our most valuable asset is a well-trained, dedicated staff working as a team to meet and challenge" (Florida Department of Corrections, 1997).

Overall, when we value our employees, TQM will be more likely to take root. Within TQM the customer focus is paramount. Accepting some variation in employees' performance and eliminating numerical goals and quotas will help public agencies respond to the customers' demands in a more effective way.

## E.  Situation 5

### 1.  Problem 5: Organizational Entrapment and Trained Incapacity

Organizations often suffer from poor resource investments. Entrapment refers to "the tendency to persist in a failing course of action in order to justify the allocation of prior resources to that course of action (Brocker and Rubin, 1985, p. 242)." In many cases, organizational settings provide fertile ground for the growth of entrapment (Brocker and Rubin, 1985). "Trained incapacity" (Merton, 1987) may also impede an immediate response to customers' demands. Merton (1987, p. 109) asserts that "actions based upon training and skills which have been successfully applied in the past may result in inappropriate responses under changed conditions."

### 2.  TQM Solution 5: Driving Out Fear and Training on a Continuing Basis

One of the important elements of TQM is to "Drive out fear." This means that employees at all levels should be able to feel comfortable with suggesting creative ideas to their superiors and colleagues and with exhibiting innovative behaviors. Because managerial innovation often requires risk-taking behaviors, it is critical to have employees feel that a mistake in the process would be acceptable. In other words, creating an innovative culture of "it is okay if you make a mistake" becomes an important premise for productivity improvement.

As organizational entrapment is likely to occur in a situation in which failure will be attributed to the person who is in charge of a specific action, it is important that employees should be able to get out of a failing course of action as necessary. This is possible only if employees feel comfortable with suggesting and/or withdrawing creative ideas at any time. Therefore, the "Drive out fear" tenet ensures that the possibility of entrapment is prevented in advance.

The Florida Department of Corrections, which has been well known for successful implementation of TQM, places much emphasis on this tenet. As Harry Singletary, Jr., Secretary of the Department, states, "Thomas Edison once said: Genius is one percent inspiration and 99 percent perspiration. I am challenging each of you to perspire often and regularly. Go forth and sweat" (Florida Department of Corrections, 1997).

In addition, Pennsylvania State has recently paid special attention to employee innovation, assuming that front-line employees are key originators and installers of change. With the strong support of the governor, various innovation teams play an important role in changing state agencies. At the same time, many state agencies in Pennsylvania have developed new and unique ways to recognize for ideas change initiated by employees and individual or group creativity and innovation. As a result, numerous innovative ideas have been put forth by employees. One example is environmental site assessments in the Department of Transportation.

As the governor's office put it,

> The Pollution Prevention Division within PennDOT reexamined the process used to perform site investigations on underground fuel tanks. This involved obtaining soil samples by drilling into the ground around the tank and testing the samples for contaminants from possible leakage or spillage from the tanks. The testing and analysis of these sites was at the time being contracted to a private firm. The staff analysis showed that the testing and analysis could be accomplished more cost-effectively if they undertook the task themselves. Contracted testing was determined to cost $28,000 per site. PennDOT staff could perform the same investigation for $5,600 per site—saving $22,400 per site investigation. Consequently, the Pollution Prevention Division staff reaped a savings award of $26,000 (Pennsylvania State Governor's Office, 2001).

At the same time, it is crucial to support various training programs on a continuing basis to avoid "trained incapacity." Many agree that training is an integral part of managerial and organizational changes (Paddock, 1997; Hannah, 1995; Van Wart et al., 1993). In fact, despite the importance of management training, the training budget is likely to suffer in this era of cutback management (Paddock, 1997). Training is critical to improving employees' knowledge, skills, and abilities (KSAs) and reduces the likelihood of employee obsolescence in a changing environment (Klingner and Nalbandian, 1998).

Continuous training involves top-management support, ongoing program evaluation, stable financial support, and full support from participants. It is therefore, expected to reduce the possibility of trained incapacity in a changing environment.


## V. CONCLUDING REMARKS

### A. Importance of Learning: Continuous Improvement

TQMs customer focus assumes that every organization should be a learning one in a changing environment. As Argyris and Schon (1978) assert, learning is the key to organizational change. Many organizations suffer from learning disabilities that prevent them from identifying and responding to demands of customers. Learning disabilities also make it difficult for an organization to identify the factors potentially threatening to them (Senge, 1990).

As Argyris and Schon (1978, p. 19) argue, the function of organizational learning is based on an "error correction" process:

> Organizational learning occurs when individuals, acting from their images and maps, detect a match or mismatch of outcome to expectation which confirms or disconfirms

organizational theory in use. In the case of disconfirmation, Individuals move from error detection to error correction..."Error correction" is shorthand for a complex learning cycle.

This learning process enables organizations to capture the capacities of other organizations, such as technologies, procedures, and similar routines (Levitt and March, 1988). Therefore, to survive, an organization should be able to adapt itself to a changing environment. Through these learning processes, organizations can effectively respond to customers' demands in turbulent environments. In this regard, TQM's philosophy is critical in helping an organization effectively respond to the environment.

## B. Other Issues in the Public Sector

Many argue that short-term goals, frequent turnover of top-level managers, and an individualistic organizational culture may prevent TQM from being successfully implemented (Swiss, 1992; White and Wolf, 1995). However, there are many success stories documented in the public sector despite those concerns, and there are many areas in the public sector with which TQM is compatible. Most public service activities consist of routines, steps in processes. Furthermore, according to an empirical study examining managerial public employees' attitudes in New Jersey, Lee (2000b) found that of nineteen different productivity improvement strategies, public managerial employees reported "Total Quality Management" as the most preferred strategy for productivity improvement. In addition, "contracting out" (or privatization) as a strategy was ranked last by public managerial employees.

Considering that teamwork is receiving much more attention than ever before in American public administration, the high level of preference of group performance-driven strategies provides a bright future for productive workplaces in the United States. TQM is a management philosophy for transforming organizational cultures and structures to improve productivity. Transformed and changed organizations are customer-centered, cost-efficient, and globally competitive organizations. Correct understanding of the TQM philosophy will lead to responsive, customer-centered public agencies in a turbulent environment.

## REFERENCES

Argyris, C., Schon, D. (1978). *Organizational Learning: A Theory of Action Perspective*. Reading, MA: Addison-Wesley.

Ashford, D. E. (1976). *Democracy, Decentralization, and Decisions in Subnational Politics*. Beverly Hills, CA: Sage.

Berman, E., West, J. P. (1995). Municipal commitment to total quality management: A survey of recent progress. *Public Admin. Rev.* 55:57–66.

Bowman, J. S., Hellein, R. (1998). Total quality management in Florida: Implementation in state agencies. *Public Admin. Quart.* 22:114–129.

Brocker, J., Rubin, J. Z. (1985). *Entrapment in Escalating Conflicts: A Social Psychological Analysis*. New York: Springer-Verlag.

Carr, D., Littman, I. (1990). *Excellence in Government: Total Quality Management in the 1990s*. Arlington, VA: Coopers and Lybrand.

Connor, P. E. (1997). Total quality management: A selective commentary on its human dimensions, with special reference to its downsides. *Public Admin. Rev.* 57:501–509.

Dean, W. J. Jr., Evans, J. R. (1994). *Total Quality: Management, Organization, and Strategy.* Minneapolis: West.

Deming, W. E. (1986). *Out of the Crisis.* Cambridge, MA: MIT Center for Advanced Engineering Study.

Downs, A. (1967). *Inside Bureaucracy.* Boston: Little, Brown.

Florida Department of Corrections (1997). *Quality Drives the DC Train* (online). Available at http://www.dc.state.fl.us/pub/annual/9697/sec.html.

Flynn, B., Sakakibara, S., Schroeder, R. G. (1995). Relationship between JIT and TQM: Practices and performance. *Acad. Manage. J.* 38:1325–1360.

Golembiewski, R. (1997). Trends in the development of the organization sciences. In: Rabin, J., Hildreth, W. B., Miller, G., eds., *Handbook of Public Administration.* 2nd ed. New York: Marcel Dekker, pp. 103–116.

Gortner, H. F., Mahler, J., Nichoson, J. B. (1987). *Organization Theory: A Public Perspective.* Chicago: Dorsey Press.

*Government Executive Magazine* (1999). Officials debate the future of the civil service. January 12 (online). Available at http://www.govexec.com/dailyfed/0199/011299b2.htm.

Hamilton, V. L. (1980). Intuitive psychologist or intuitive lawyer? *J. Personality Social Psych.* 39:767–772.

Hannah, S. (1995). The correlates of innovation. *Public Product. Manage. Rev.* 19:216–228.

Heider, F. (1958). *The Psychology of Interpersonal Relations.* New York: Wiley.

Holt, G. D., Love, P., Nesan, L. J., Jawahar, L. (2000). Employee empowerment in construction: An implementation model for process improvement. *Team Perform. Manage.* 6:47–51.

Holzer, M., Callahan, K. (1998). *Government at work: Best Practices amd Model Programs.* Thousand Oaks, CA: Sage.

Holzer, M., Lee, S.-H. (1999). Labor-management tension and partnership: Where are we? What should we do? *Int. Rev. Public Admin.* 4:33–44.

Hut, J., Mollenman, E. (1998). Empowerment and team development. *Team Perform. Manage.* 4:53.

Kaufman, H. (1987). Administrative decentralization and political power. In: Shafritz, J. M. Hyde, A. C., eds., *Classics of Public Administration (1969).* 2nd ed. Chicago: Dorsey, pp. 389–404.

Klingner, D. E., Nalbandian, J. (1998). *Public Personnel Management: Context and Strategies.* 4th ed. Upper Saddle River, NJ: Prentice-Hall.

Lee, S.-H. (2000a). Understanding productivity improvement in a turbulent environment: A symposium introduction. *Public Product. Manage. Rev.* 23:423–427.

Lee, S.-H. (2000b). A multidimensional view of public sector employee commitment and willingness to support productivity improvement strategies: A comparative study of public employees at managerial level between the United Sates and South Korea. Unpublished dissertation, Rutgers University, Newark, NJ.

Lee, S.-H. (2001). Barriers to active citizen participation in the public sector: Lessons learned from South Korea. In: Rahim, M. A., Golembiewski, R. T., Mackenzie, K. D., eds., *Current Topics in Management.* Vol. 6. New York: JAI, pp. 309–330.

Levitt, B., March, J. G. (1988). Organizational learning. *Ann. Rev. Sociol.* 14:319–340.

Loretta, D., Polsky, W. (1991). Share the power. *Personnel J. September* 116.

McGowan, R. P., Wittmer, D. P. (1997). Five great issues in decision making. In: Rabin, J., Hildreth, W. B., Miller, G., eds, *Handbook of Public Administration.* 2nd ed. New York: Marcel Dekker, pp. 293–320.

Merton, R. K. (1987). Bureaucratic structure and personality (1940). In: Shafritz, J. M., Hyde, A. C., eds., *Classics of Public Administration.* 2nd ed. Chicago: Dorsey, pp. 107–116.

Milakovich, M. (1992). Total quality management for public service productivity improvement. In: Holzer, M., ed., *Public Productivity Handbook.* New York: Marcel Dekker, pp. 577–602.

Miller, D. T., Ross, M. (1975). Self-serving biases in the attribution of causality. *Psych. Bull.* 82:213–225.

Mohrman, S. A., Cohen, S. G., Mohrman, A. M. (1995). *Designing Team-Based Organizations.* San Francisco: Jossey-Bass.

Motwani, J., Sower, V., Brashier, L. (1996). Implementing TQM in the health care sector. *Health Care Manage. Rev.* 21:73–80.

O'Reilly, C. A. III. (1980). The intentional distortions of information in organizational communication: A laboratory and field investigation. In: Katz, D., et al., eds. *The Study of Organizations.* San Francisco: Jossey-Bass, pp. 328–344.

Paddock, S. (1997). Administrative benchmarks in management training. *Public Product. Manage. Rev.* 21:192–201.

Pennsylvania State Governor's Office (2001). Privatize, retain, innovate, modify, and eliminate (PRIME) (online). Available at http://www.prime.state.pa.us.

Pollock, T. (2001). For improved teamwork, keep them informed. *Automotive Des. Product.* 10:10.

Powell, T. (1995). Total quality management as competitive advantage: A review and empirical study. *Strategic Manage. J.* 16:15–37.

Rago, W. V. (1994). Adapting total quality management (TQM) to government: Another point of view. *Public Admin. Rev.* 54:61–64.

Rago, W. V. (1996). Struggles in transformation: A study in TQM, leadership and organizational culture in a government agency. *Public Admin. Rev.* 56:227–234.

Ross, L. D. (1977). Intuitive psychologist and his shortcomings: Distortions in the attribution process. *Adv. Exper. Social Psych.* 20:173–220.

Rourke, F. E. (1984). *Bureaucracy, Politics, and Public Policy.* 3rd ed.. Boston: Little, Brown.

Scherkenbach, W. W. (1987). *The Deming Route to Quality and Productivity: Road Maps and Roadblocks.* Rockville, MD: Mercury.

Scholtes, P. R., Hacquebord, H. (1988). Beginning the quality transformation. *Qual. Progress* 21:28–33.

Senge, P. M. (1990). *The Fifth Discipline.* New York: Doubleday.

Shea, C., Howell, J. (1998). Organizational antecedents to the successful implementation of total quality management. *J. Qual. Manage.* 3:3–24.

Sheldrake, J. (1992). *Modern Local Government.* Brookfield, VT: Dartmouth Publishing.

Simon, H. A. (1997). *Administrative Behavior: A Study of Decision Making Processes in Administrative Organizations.* 4th ed. New York: Free Press.

Stewart, G. L., Manz, C. C. (1995). Leadership for self-managing work teams: A typology an integrative model. *Hum. Rel.* 48:747–770.

Swiss, J. E. (1992). Adapting total quality management (TQM) to government. *Public Admin. Rev.* 52:356–362.

Tenser, R. K. (1993). Empowering high performing people to promote project quality. *J. Manage. Eng.* 12:321–328.

Van Wart, M., Cayer, N. J., Cook, S. J. (1993). *Handbook of Training and Education for the Public Sector.* San Francisco: Jossey-Bass.

Wallach, E. J. (1983). Individuals and organizations: The cultural match. *Train. Devel. J.* 37:29–36.

Washington State Governor's Office (2000). Governing for results: 2000 progress report (online). Available at http://www.governor.wa.gov/quality/reports/00annual/2000report.htm.

Werther, W. B., Ruch, W. A., McClure, L. (1986). *Productivity Through People.* New York: West.

White, O. F., Wolf, J. F. (1995). Deming's total quality management movement and the Baskin-Robbins problem: Part I: Is it time to go back to vanilla? *Admin. Soc.* 27:203–225.

Wolman, H. (1990). Decentralization: What it is and why we should care. In: Bennett, R. J., ed. *Decentralization, Local Government, and Markets.* New York: Oxford University Press, pp. 29–42.

Yates, D. (1973). *Neighborhood Democracy.* Lexington, MA: Heath.

# 36

# E-Government and Information Technology in the Public Sector

*Definitions, Distinctions,*
*and Organizational Capacity*

**JAMES MELITSKI**
*Marist College, Poughkeepsie, New York, and Rutgers,*
*The State University of New Jersey, Newark, New Jersey, U.S.A.*

## I. INTRODUCTION

Many now describe e-government and e-governance as a continuum that begins with information provision when organizations and public agencies publish static information to the Internet. As public organizations become more advanced, they are able to provide more dynamic, transactional services. Ideally, the continuum leads to organizational transformation, the transparency of public agencies, increased citizen participation in government, and facilitation of democratic processes.

Public organizations are beginning an "e-government journey" by publishing static information to the Internet and establishing an online presence in the hopes that they too will experience increases in efficiency, effectiveness, and organizational performance. As public agencies begin implementing e-government and e-governance initiatives, agencies believe that performance will improve and agencies will be better equipped to interact with citizens and provide services over the Internet. E-government and e-governance initiatives now enable citizens to access government documents, order publications, file taxes, reserve lodging, order vital records, and renew licenses and permits from any location, with an Internet connection. In addition, there are already signs that e-government is transforming organizations by breaking down organizational boundaries and providing greater access to information and enhancing communications.

However, public organizations need to proceed with caution as well as with optimism. E-government and e-governance initiatives, as do many technical innovations, have the potential to unintentionally distance citizens from government, leading to disenfranchisement. Public organizations also need to ensure that all citizens have access to the basic skills and infrastructure needed to participate in an increasingly technological society. As the digital divide takes a different shape in different locations, public policies will need to address issues of universal access and the educational needs of their citizens. In addition, as the Internet becomes a primary access point for millions of citizens to communicate with government, researchers and educators will need to consider issues such as the following.

How will e-government influence the performance of public organizations?
What are the organizational effects of e-government and information technology (IT)?
What are successful implementation strategies for e-government initiatives?
What skills do public employees need to maximize their performance in an information age?

These questions have important implications for researchers and practitioners in the field of public administration. There is already evidence to indicate that by automating service provision, e-government is increasing efficiency, effectiveness, and citizen satisfaction. However, more baseline data need to be collected to determine the longitudinal effects of e-government on public agencies. In addition, there is an ongoing academic debate regarding the structural effects of information technology on public and private organizations. For instance, researchers have debated for nearly forty years about whether technological innovations cause centralization or decentralization in organizations.

Many now claim that e-government, e-governance, and information technology empower individuals in organizations to move beyond the automation of paper-based transactions, resulting in a decentralization of organizational decision making. In addition, the potential exists for e-government to enhance basic democratic principles, such as citizen participation, and to fundamentally change how citizens and businesses interact with government. If this is the case, then there needs to be more e-government research conducted to maximize the advantages of the technology and prepare practitioners with management skills and strategies to improve performance in public organizations, increase citizen satisfaction, and increase citizen participation in government.

The focus of this chapter is on defining e-government and how the term has evolved in the public sector, differentiating e-government and information technology from previous technological innovations, and discussing how the private sector has addressed IT. Finally, a discussion of factors that contribute to an agency's capacity to conduct e-government and IT initiatives is addressed.

## II.  DEFINITIONS OF E-GOVERNMENT

The purpose of this section is to demonstrate that although the term e-government is relatively new, there seems to be a consensus regarding how the term is defined. Several definitions of e-government are discussed and then a concise definition of e-government is developed based on commonalities among the various definitions. Lastly, this section compares e-government to other information technologies and shows how research on information technologies is relevant to e-government.

According to Harris (2000), "E-government is not just about government web pages and e-mail. It is not just about service delivery over the Internet. It's not just about digital access to government information or electronic licensing and payment." Harris states that the challenge for e-government will be to incorporate "governance itself. . . [and] shift the way political and social power is organized and used."

In other words, the challenge for e-government will be to do the following (adapted from Harris, 2000).

> Provide citizens with access to government information.
> Deliver government services to citizens.
> Provide a portal for processing government information between citizens and businesses and government. (e.g., electronic licensing and permitting).
> Facilitate citizen participation in government, creating "digital citizens" in a "digital democracy."

The shift from service provision to citizen participation is a critical component of the Harris vision of e-government. Harris states that e-government will not have lived up to its fullest potential if it does not empower citizens and enable government to incorporate their views. He states that innovative efforts to put existing government services online are an important milestone, and worth noting, but that they are far from the whole journey.

A more concise definition of e-government can be found in the recent report *Benchmarking the eGovernment Revolution*, which states, "Electronic government, or e-government, is a birth of a new market and the advent of a new form of government—a form of government that is a powerful force in the Internet economy, bringing together citizens and business in a network of information knowledge and commerce" (Momentum Research Group, 2000). Two important aspects of this definition are that it limits e-government to the Internet (as opposed to broader technologies such as wireless communications and facsimile machines) and it emphasizes the interactive potential of e-government. In particular, the report claims that e-government initiatives are limited to those conducted over the Internet that link citizens to government (C2G), businesses to government (B2G), and government to government (G2G).

Yet another definition is contained in a report by Deloitte Research (2000) that defines e-government as "the use of technology to enhance access to and delivery of government services to benefit citizens, business partners and employers." Unlike other definitions, the Deloitte report focuses exclusively on the delivery of services and forgoes any aspirations of increasing citizen participation. Although the Deloitte definition cited above does not exclude non-Internet technologies, the rest of the report is consistent with other definitions in that it focuses on the use of the Internet to deliver government services.

Finally, the *Council for Excellence in Government* (2000) lists the following guiding e-principles for e-government.

1. Easy to use. Easy for all to utilize, and connecting federal, state, regional, local, tribal and international governments.
2. Available to everyone. Accessible to all—at home, at work, in schools, in libraries and in their communities.
3. Private and secure. High standards for privacy, security and authentication—generating trust—are required for e-government to serve the public, grow, and thrive.

4. Innovative and results-oriented. Emphasizing speed and advances in technology, while embracing continuous improvement.
5. Collaborative. Within a framework of government policy, standards and accountability, solutions are developed collectively and openly among public, private, nonprofit and research partners, based on their experience and expertise.
6. Cost-effective. Strategic investments and results that produce significant long term efficiencies and savings.
7. Transformational. Harnessing technology to transform government, rather than automating existing practices, through personal and organizational leadership.

The above principles are unique in several ways, but they are also consistent with the definitions offered earlier. Of particular importance is the call for e-government to be easy to use, available to everyone, and encouraging collaboration. These three principles suggest that e-government should also have a decentralizing effect on government organizations. Finally, by combining various aspects of multiple definitions with the seven principles outlined above, a single definition of e-government is articulated below.

E-government consists of Internet-driven innovations that improve citizen access to government information, access to government services, and ultimately equitable participation in government by decentralizing decision making, increasing citizen satisfaction, and enhancing productivity.

The above definition attempts to combine the citizen participation, organizational, and communicative potential of e-government with the e-commerce potential for productivity improvement. The term e-government is constantly evolving and, at the present time, it appears that e-government is, in fact, becoming associated with public sector adaptations of e-commerce that focus on transactional services. In contrast, the term e-government is emerging as a term used to describe the communicative and organizational properties of Internet-driven applications in the public sector. As e-government becomes more synonymous with e-commerce and business models, it will have several implications, a few of which are discussed in the next section on the "stages" approach to e-government.

## A.  The E-Government Model and the "Stages" Approach

As stated earlier, one of the issues with the term e-government today is its reliance on the business model of e-commerce. It is probably a natural leap; e-government is to the public sector as e-commerce is to the private sector. Certainly, the public sector should work to apply successful private sector management strategies where appropriate, but the e-commerce model relies heavily on a transactional exchange between e-commerce organizations and the consumer. However, the government–citizen relationship is more complex.

As stated earlier, the e-government hierarchy often starts with posting static information to the Internet, and ultimately leads to dynamic transactions between citizens and government designed to transform the organization of government. The hierarchy has been expressed in a variety of ways. For example, the Chief Information Officers (CIO) Council describes a fully implemented e-government in several stages (Balutis, 2001):

Phase 1: information dissemination;
Phase 2: forms only;

Phase 3: end-to-end electronic transactions where the initiative is transaction based e.g., e-payment of taxes);

Phase 4: transforming government.

Other conceptualizations may have a different number of stages or phases in their hierarchy, but the similarities are that they all begin with static information being posted to the Internet and move through "transactional" services that lead to some form of organizational transformation.

These hierarchies can be useful for managers seeking to adopt or implement new e-government initiatives, but there are several issues that need to be addressed when discussing the stages. First, the different phases of e-government implementation rely on the completion of the previous step or phase. However, some public organizations have attempted to skip several of the steps or leapfrog. Leapfrogging describes a process wherein public agencies skip or overlook aspects of implementation in favor of moving on to initiatives that are technologically more complex. Agencies benefit from leapfrogging by increasing the technological sophistication of certain programs and also by raising the profile of more advanced programs. The frenzy to Web-enable the public sector through leapfrogging is further encouraged by annual rankings whereby independent groups rank state and local Web sites by their ability to meet specific metrics related to their own version of the e-government continuum. Unfortunately, the process of leapfrogging leads agencies to ignore or skip steps that will aid them as they attempt to progress toward "organizational transformation."

The emphasis on greater technological sophistication and the rush to move agencies through the e-government stages toward higher levels of e-government places less importance on earlier necessary stages of the continuum. This can be problematic considering how and with whom most agencies typically begin the development of an agency's Web presence. Typically, technologically oriented information technology managers within government are the first champions of e-government. It is the IT managers who are most familiar with Internet-based technologies, and it is logical that they are the first to visualize its potential.

In most cases, the early champions of the Internet in the public sector attempted to re-create the organization, as they perceived it, on the Internet. However, re-creating the existing organizational structure, or an individual's interpretation of an organizational chart, does little to transform government and it does not help individuals unfamiliar with the organization navigate the site. The organizational transformation promised by e-government can only be realized if content is accurate, timely, citizen-centric, and designed specifically for the Internet.

However, instead of maintaining accurate and timely information online, the focus of many managers has been to move on to the next "stage" of implementation, and the result is a plethora of outdated and inconsistent information on many government Web sites. As public organizations seek to implement more complex e-government initiatives, they need to be aware of the importance of managing content and the dangers of moving ahead too quickly without adequately planning the maintenance at current service levels.

Defining e-government and mechanisms for implementation of Internet-based public sector initiatives is key if public managers are to maximize the potential of the Internet. Despite the fact that many private sector strategies for using the Internet are inappropriate, the overlap that exists between e-government and e-commerce is explored later in this chapter. However, before discussing the overlaps and opportunities between public and private sector Internet strategies, it is necessary to examine differences between the Internet and other innovative technologies.

## III.   HOW IS IT DIFFERENT FROM OTHER TECHNOLOGIES?

Exactly how do e-government, the Internet, and other information technologies differ from other technological innovations over time? Shoshana Zuboff (1988) examines information technology by comparing it to other innovative technologies throughout history, such as the cotton gin, steam engine, and so on. She defines information technology in the following terms.

> Information technology is a label that reflects the convergence of several streams of technical developments, including microelectronics, computer science, telecommunications, software engineering, and system analysis.
>
> [Information technology] is a technology that dramatically increases the ability to record, store, analyze and transmit information in ways that permit flexibility, accuracy, immediacy geographic independence and complexibility.
>
> Information technology has the unique capability to restructure operations that depend upon information for the purposes of transaction, record keeping, analysis, control or communication.

Her conclusion is that information technology has the potential to change organizations and society in ways not achievable by other types of technological innovations. She explains this by differentiating IT from other innovative technologies because of its ability to automate and "inform". She states that information technologies automate the physical operations of organizations in ways that many other nineteenth century machines do, "[by] replacing the human body with a technology that enables the same processes to be performed with more continuity and control" (Zuboff, 1988).

However, information technology is distinctly different from other industrial-age machines that are designed to spray-paint automobiles or perform routine clerical transactions. According to Zuboff, this distinction is due to IT's capabilities to "inform" or "simultaneously generate information about the underlying productive and administrative processes through which an organization accomplishes its work" (Zuboff, 1988). For example, Zuboff uses the example of scanner devices in supermarkets to illustrate how information technologies can change the way organizations use technology.

Zuboff explains that scanner devices automate the checkout process in supermarkets and therefore make the checkout process more productive and efficient. However, unlike other technological innovations, the checkout scanner simultaneously generates information or data that can be used for inventory control, warehousing, scheduling of deliveries, and market analysis. In addition, new technologies that track individual purchases can be used to generate individual customer profiles for marketing purposes.

Zuboff describes information technology's ability to move beyond automation (often unintentionally) toward informating as the duality of information technology. An important aspect of the duality is the hierarchical integration of technology. To understand the nature of information technology's duality, it is important to understand that the concept is not a dichotomy. In order for organizations to informate, they must first automate. An additional conclusion derived by Zuboff because of the duality of information technology is that information technology is not neutral or objective. According to Zuboff, managers must make a conscious decision whether to "automate" or "automate and informate."

## IV. PRIVATE SECTOR PERSPECTIVE ON IT AND PRODUCTIVITY

Although e-commerce is relevant to the public sector, we must first examine some of the broader questions being asked by private sector researchers and managers about the Internet and information technology. From a management science perspective the key questions about information technology and productivity are: Do computers pay off? Are computers cost-effective? Unfortunately, the questions have proven much easier to ask than answer. In management science literature, there is as much evidence to support the notion that IT increases productivity as there is against it. However, much of the management science research through the early 1990s focused on an apparent inability to show measurable productivity gains as a result of IT expenditures.

In fact, throughout the early 1990s much of the management science community had changed their key question about IT and productivity to: Why haven't computers measurably improved productivity? In 1993, Brynjolfsson summarized a growing body of research by stating, "The disappointment in IT [has] been chronicled in articles disclosing broad negative correlations with economy-wide productivity and information worker productivity. Econometric estimates have also indicated low IT capital productivity in a variety of manufacturing service industries."

Brynjolfsson specifically points to research conducted in 1991 by Roach that focuses on information workers in a variety of industries. Roach cites statistics showing significant increases in capital expenditures on IT for white-collar workers. At the same time, Roach cites information that shows an expansion in the number of service workers and a corresponding decrease in the number of blue-collar workers. Roach (1991) concludes, "We have in essence isolated America's productivity shortfall and shown it to be concentrated in the portion of the economy that is the largest employer of white-collar workers and the most heavily endowed with high-tech capital." In addition, Cron and Sobol's (1983) analysis of wholesalers found that IT seems to be associated with very high and very low performers. This led to conclusions that IT does little to effect productivity; rather, it reinforces existing management approaches.

However, Brynjolfsson disputes the conclusions of those who argue that IT decreases productivity. Specifically Brynjolfsson argues that much of the management literature that negatively correlates IT and productivity is flawed because it does not accurately measure productivity in nonmanufacturing corporations. This conclusion is especially relevant to managers in service industries and public sector managers.

Brynjolfsson and others are quick to point out research that shows productivity increases related to IT expenditures. Siegel and Griliches (1991) found a simple correlation between IT investment and a multifaceted approach to productivity during the 1980s. Osterman suggested in 1986 that relative productivity cannot be inferred by the number of information workers per unit of output. For example, a clerk with increased information technology capabilities who takes the place of two truckers increases the relative productivity of white-collar workers and of the corporation's productivity in general.

In 1990, Weill was able to calculate productivity by separate IT uses (e.g., email, sales support, data processing, etc.) and found that certain types of IT were more likely to be productive. Several studies (Parsons et al., 1990; Franke, 1987) support the argument that there is a lag in the return on investment of IT expenditures. According to Brynjolfsson (1993), they are "optimistic about the future potential of IT, citing the long time lags associated with previous technological transformations such as the conversion to steam power." In addition, Brynjolfsson and Hitt found a high return on investment (ROI) related to spending on information system labor and an ROI greater than 50% for spending on IT capital between 1987 and 1991. A recent study also supports the argument that "spending on IS staff and staff training is positively correlated with firm performance, even more so than computer capital" (Sircar et al., 2000).

In light of the research that finds positive correlations between IT spending and productivity, Brynjolfsson (1993) developed several explanations for the paradox of information technology: "1. Mismeasurement of outputs and inputs; 2. Lags due to learning and adjustment; 3. Redistribution and dissipation of profits; 4. Mismanagement of information technology." According to Brynjolfsson, the first two explanations point to shortcomings in research, and explanation three and four accept the researchers' conclusions that there are no productivity improvements related to IT. However, steps three and four take the extra step and explore potential reasons for the lack of productivity.

In a separate qualitative study, Brynjolfsson and Hitt (1995) survey 500 businesses that were identified by *InformationWeek* as "big spenders" on IT. The results suggest commonalities among successful corporations that aggressively spend on IT. According to the study, "Certain business strategies, organizational structures and information system tactics can play a role... But we...discover[ed] that the aggressive use of computers is associated with a coherent new strategy of customer focus and worker empowerment."

In addition, the study finds that successful companies were more likely to be in the midst of business process redesign (or reengineering, BPR). BPR is a process whereby organizations reorganize around customer-oriented processes, the heavy use of IT, and empowered workers. Also, the study concludes with several key lessons that are appropriate for both the public and private sectors regarding decentralized decision making. For example, the key lessons include, "Get closer to the customer, empower your workers, redesign business process to take advantage of IT, and create a partnership among the IS, line and management" (Brynjolfsson and Hitt, 1995).

## A.  E-Commerce and E-Government

A United Nations report on "Knowledge Societies" defines e-commerce as "the use of documents in electronic form rather than paper for carrying out functions of business or government (such as finance, logistics, procurement, and transportation) that require interchanges of information, obligations, or monetary value between organizations and individuals" (Mansell et al., 1998). As the above definition indicates, e-commerce is not just about business, but the aspects of it that deal directly with the private sector which have become "big business."

A 2000 survey conducted by The Center for Research in Electronic Commerce at the University of Texas at Austin reports that "the amount of business conducted directly on the Internet increased 127 percen from the first quarter of 1998 to the first quarter of 1999" (CREC, 2000). The study defines four separate layers to the Internet economy, and "Internet commerce" (or e-commerce) is the fourth level. Other levels in the Internet economy include the Internet infrastructure, Internet applications infrastructure, and Internet intermediary indicators. The study shows that very few businesses operate at all levels of the Internet economy and the research distinguishes between four levels of e-commerce. The report indicates that businesses rarely focus on all four levels, instead choosing one or two levels on which to focus. From a public sector perspective the question needs to be asked: at what level should local, state, and federal governments be involved?

If it is not appropriate for the public sector to address all aspects of the development of e-government, then one can assume that some aspects of e-government will be contracted out. Contracting out aspects of e-government affords managers more choices regarding methods of delivering e-government services to citizens. Outsourcing also has the potential of enabling government managers to deal more directly with aspects of e-government that are less subject to rapid change, as well as those that might involve initiatives not profitable to private sector organizations (e.g., ways of increasing citizen participation through e-government).

It should also be noted that e-government outsourcing could be a slippery slope that holds many potential pitfalls. Decreased accountability and the need to adapt systems designed for use in profit-driven, production-oriented, private sector organizations can often be more difficult, costly, and labor intensive than designing proprietary systems. As with any form of privatization, public managers should be very wary.

Tapscott (1999) suggests that e-commerce is causing businesses to reexamine their strategic focus to become more community-oriented and flexible. The study claims that "The market place is becoming smarter and more demanding. . . . Stovepipe bureaucracies, command-and-control management structures and stultifying decision making processes—whether found in large or small businesses—are guarantees of a shortened lifespan in the digital economy."

E-commerce benchmarks can also be adapted for use in the public sector. Examples include (Tamara, 2000):

Measuring the amount of time users spend on a Web site;
Measuring how often viewers of Web sites participate in a transaction on the Web site;
Calculating online transaction costs and comparing them to traditional transaction costs (e.g., telephone or mail order); and
Tracking the amount of service requests or user feedback received.

A report by Deloitte Research (2000) also suggests that as citizens grow accustomed to the instant options that e-commerce allows, they will expect the same from their government. The study states that unlike many government initiatives, the current shift toward e-government has been customer driven. As evidence of the customer-driven nature of e-government, the survey further states that respondents in all countries except the United Kingdom identified legislative mandates, political pressures, or the need to increase revenue as less than 15% of the primary factors driving e-government.

## V. PRODUCTIVITY AND INFORMATION TECHNOLOGY IN THE PUBLIC SECTOR

> The strategic use of IT by the City will help to create a dynamic climate of excitement and achievement that will help keep the city a magnet for talent, a hotbed of economic activity and growth, and a center for our nation's economy and culture. (City of New York, 1999)

Today it is evident that many managers throughout government are placing an emphasis on IT and its potential for improving productivity. As was stated earlier, an important component of this research will be to examine productivity improvements that result from the shift in e-government strategies between the electronic distribution of static information, and the provision of dynamic transactional services over the Internet. It is also worth restating that within the context of this chapter, e-government is viewed as a potential vehicle for facilitating public productivity improvement.

Using Holzer and Callahan's (1998) comprehensive public sector productivity improvement model, e-government can be seen as a tool to help managers integrate their internal capacities. Integrated internal capacities (e.g., managing for quality, developing human resources, adapting other technologies, building public and private secor partnerships, and measuring performance) lead to output (services) and outcomes (impacts). Legislatures, chief executives, the private sector, the media, and ultimately citizens, can interpret outcomes through both subjective and objective means. Holzer and Callahan (1998) suggest that feedback is then given to various actors in the public policy arena that will result in management decisions for midcourse corrections to improve productivity of current initiatives, future programs, and resource allocations.

In addition, other public sector productivity improvement strategies relevant to e-government echo those expressed by the private sector. Peters and Waterman's (1982) *In Search of Excellence* developed a set of suggestions for corporations that were not overlooked by public sector managers. Many of Peters and Waterman's suggestions, such as staying close to the customer, valuing autonomy and entrepreneurship, enhancing productivity through people, and encouraging a simple organizational structure and lean staff are very compatible with the principles of e-government described earlier.

Hale (1996) summarized strategies developed in many recent productivity improvement studies. Hale's strategies support teamwork and worker participation in management decisions, and suggest that public organizations should be flexible. The summary emphasizes principles such as customer orientation, employee empowerment, and the use of performance measurement. Rainey (1997) contends that the public sector has been at the forefront of adapting quality improvement techniques such as participative management, job redesign, Quality of Work Life (QWL), Quality Circles (QCs), and Total Quality Management (TQM).

Initiatives outlined in Osborne and Gaebler's (1993) book *Reinventing Government*, and the National Performance Review that followed, may not have been new, but they did highlight many strategies that are relevant to e-government. A recent

*Economist* article, "Survey Government and the Internet" (Symonds, 2000) gives Osborne and Gaebler a back-handed compliment by stating that "Reinventing government, a fashionable but premature idea a decade ago, is at last being made possible by the Internet." Although Symond's statement may be an exaggeration, several reinventing government strategies such as community-ownership, mission-driven, results-oriented, enterprising, and decentralized government seem to fit very nicely with the goals of e-government."

Alternatively, practical challenges to the adoption, application, and management of IT as they relate to reinventing government strategies do exist. Specifically, Scavo (2000) states that adoption at the local level will be hindered in some cases by the resources required by IT. In addition, "The reform efforts of the early 19th century had dual goals of democracy and efficiency. The experience has shown that the two are not always compatible... [and reinventing government strategies] may present a problem for managers concerned with efficiency" (Scavo, 2000).

## A. Y2K a Catalyst for Change

According to Dean (2000), an important factor that helped move government information systems and IT toward e-government initiatives was Y2K. Dean's article states that Y2K influenced government management of information technologies and information systems in several critical ways. First, Y2K gave government MIS managers a wake-up call and showed how dependent government agencies are on IT. It further showed the need for IT managers to be included in everything the government does. The article quotes John Koskinen, former chair of the President's Council on Y2K Conversion, as stating, "IT is a central part of how an organization operates. That was a basis for the passage of the Clinger–Cohen Act. That Act set out the need to make sure that IT decisions are made by an organization's senior management, not just the system administrators."

Governmental regulatory agencies that regularly dealt with IT issues were particularly hard pressed by Y2K. Dean (2000), states that "The Securities and Exchange Commission, the government body that regulates the securities industry, for instance was responsible not only for ensuring its own operation but also for guaranteeing that investment houses were ready for the year 2000." Government agencies also began realizing that because IT permeates all levels of an organization, it needs to be considered when key strategic decisions are made.

However, Y2K gave many government agencies the opportunity to reexamine their IT needs and the processes of upgrading and remediating old systems. Many agencies adopted new technologies that not only enhanced internal decision making, but also accessed modern Web-based applications on UNIX serves. As a result of Y2K, Dean (2000) states that agencies with geographically dispersed personnel, such as the Navy, began taking advantage of increased communications capability and global interconnectivity. The Navy's new program, the Navy Marine Corps Intranet program (N/MCI), is a prime example. Dean (2000) quotes a Navy MIS officer who states that "With N/MCI we will be taking advantage of a corporate intranet enabling e-business and knowledge management." By allowing agencies to reevaluate their IT needs and by forcing them to update their systems, Y2K facilitated the move toward greater information sharing, not just within government, but also acted as a catalyst for external information sharing and ultimately e-government.

## VI. SEVERAL FACTORS THAT INFLUENCE AN AGENCY'S ABILITY TO USE THE INTERNET AND IMPLEMENT E-GOVERNMENT APPLICATIONS

The next section addresses several factors that influence an agency's ability to effectively use the Internet as a tool for enhancing government services, including centralization, integration, content management, and knowledge management. These factors are by no means the only factors that influence an organization's IT capacity to implement Internet-based initiatives, but they represent internal activities that can be conducted by public sector agencies to improve their Internet, e-government, and information technology capabilities.

### A.   Centralization

Centralization is an interesting topic because it has been expressed many different ways by political and organizational theorists. First, centralization is discussed as it pertains to organizational structures and decision making, and then as it pertains to information technology and e-government. Depending on how far one wants to go backsearching, examples of centralization can be nearly always be found: Plato's "Philosopher King" is the epitome of an elite all-knowing leader sitting atop a centralized organization. Conversely, classical Greek democracy is an inherently decentralized model. In United States history, Alexander Hamilton called for increased centralization, when after the Revolutionary War, he advocated that the federal government assume the debts of war-torn states that had experienced economic distress.

The classic centralized model of an organization is described by Max Weber in *Bureaucracy*. Weber (1948) concludes that although highly centralized bureaucracy has its faults, it is also inevitable in large organizations. Advocates of rationalistic management also advocate centralization. For example, Herbert Simon (1945) recognizes the infeasibility of gathering all possible alternatives to a decision through his concept of "satisficing." Simon acknowledges that managers satisfice rather than make rational decisions, however, he still concludes that managers should aspire to make rational decisions gathering all possible alternatives before making a decision. In this way, employees at lower levels of organizations become conduits for feeding upper management decision-making alternatives. Once the employees at lower levels of the organization have filtered information to individuals at the top of the organizational hierarchy, upper management is able to use the information along with their expertise to make decisions that will benefit the entire organization.

Although rationalism is often synonymous with centralization, some rationalists recognize the value of decentralization. For example, Anthony Downs acknowledged a role for decentralized organizations, however, he advocated organizational centralization in mature agencies. According to Downs, "zealots" or "advocates" dominate public agencies or bureaus in their initial entrepreneurial stage. Zealots and advocates lead agencies from an initial struggle for autonomy to building political support for the agency that leads to legitimacy. These agencies tend to have decentralized decision-making structures enabling the zealots and advocates to champion innovative programs. Once the agency has achieved legitimacy, it experiences a rapid expansion, which leads to a hierarchical organizational structure and centralized decision making.

Ultimately, Downs claims that all agencies enter into a deceleration phase or rigidity cycle. In the deceleration phase, Downs claims that zealots and advocates either leave the agency or become "conservers." According to Downs (1988), "Conservers seek merely to retain the amount of power, income, and prestige they already have rather and maximize them." Downs' theory of organizational change implies that decentralization and centralization represent phases of organizational development, with mature organizations exhibiting centralization.

In contrast to Alexander Hamilton's centralized vision for the federal government, Thomas Jefferson felt that each state's debts should be its own responsibility. In addition, Jefferson's separation of power doctrine decentralized the federal government ensuring that power would not be unequally vested in a particular branch of the federal government. Later, other political theorists such as Tocqueville warned against the dangers of a powerful elite bureaucracy. According to Held (1996), "Tocqueville recommended a series of countervailing forces including the decentralization of aspects of government, strong independent associations and organization in political, social and economic life to stand between the individual and the state. . . to help form barriers to the exercises of excessive centralized power. Building on theories of Tocqueville and J.S. Mill, Robert Dahl's pluralism can be seen as a decentralized model of organizations where power is vested in the various interest groups and not centralized."

The calls for decentralization can also be seen in recent initiatives such as the reinventing government movement. For example, Osborne and Gaebler (1992) give the following reasons for advocating decentralized organizational structures.

1. Decentralized organizations are more flexible than centralized institutions; they can respond quickly to changing circumstances and customer needs.
2. Decentralized institutions are more effective than centralized organizations.
3. Decentralized institutions are far more innovative than centralized institutions.
4. Decentralized institutions generate higher morals, more commitment, and greater productivity.

Another perspective is that the answer lies not in either centralization or decentralization, but rather in some combination thereof. In a 2001 article, Frederickson explains the advantages and disadvantages of centralized and decentralized models of organizational change. The first is a centralized model he calls a "managed innovation" model, and he states that it typically involves the application of successful benchmarking techniques and best practices from other organizations. Fredrickson's second or decentralized model is referred to as a "sustaining innovation" model (derived from Paul C. Lights' "Sustaining innovation: Creating nonprofit and government organizations that innovate naturally"). Frederickson's sustaining innovation model is flexible, and works well with programs whose goals are "purposely ambiguous." Ultimately Frederickson favors the "sustaining innovation model" for its decentralized approach to innovation where individuals within organizations control innovation.

Other researchers, most notably Waldo (1948), state that for every argument in favor of centralization there is an equally powerful argument for decentralization. In *The Administrative State*, Waldo discusses what he deems dogmas of centralization and decentralization concluding skeptically that arguments for centralization or decentralization can be matched by equally plausible arguments to the contrary.

In addition, Peters and Waterman find value in both centralization and decentralization advocating a "loose–tight" style of leadership that incorporates aspects of both. Despite his skepticism toward theories of centralization and decentralization, ultimately Waldo (1948) also advocates a balanced approach. He states, "Centralization or decentralization is not something, then, to be argued about; a 'good' organization will be one which fits the pattern for all proper organization."

In other words, every organization is different, and sometimes a coordinated centralized approach is most appropriate, whereas in other cases it is best for managers to loosen the reins and allow individuals within the organization the freedom to be creative. The decentralized model can lead to fragmented programs that are difficult to coordinate, do not take advantage of economies of scale, and do not learn from other programs attempting similar initiatives. However, centralized organizations can become too rigid, thereby disenfranchising individuals and stifling innovation in the organization. In either case, it is often a delicate balancing act that must be dealt with on a case-by-case basis.

## B.  Impact of Information Technology on Organizational Centralization

There are many different perspectives regarding whether centralized or decentralized leadership is most appropriate in public organizations, however, another question needs to be asked: What impact does information technology have on organizational centralization or decentralization? This section examines whether information technology leads to centralization, decentralization, or whether recent advances in the Internet and information technology merely reinforce the status quo.

Early prognosticators, such as Leavitt and Whisler (1958), predicted that computers would increase centralization in organizations by automating routine decisions at lower levels of the organization, thereby pushing the majority of decision making higher up in organizational structures. In 1983, King also predicted that computers would lead to increased centralization in public organizations; however, the prediction was based on organizational tendencies to centralize computing operations due to economies of scale. According to Northrop et al., (1989), empirical studies show mixed results regarding the centralization of organization decisions and computers. They cite various empirical studies (Argyris, 1971; Mumford and Banks, 1967; Myers 1967; Leduc, 1979; Lippitt et al., 1980) that suggest computers have a centralizing effect on organizational decision making.

However, Northrop et al. also demonstrate that empirical studies (Blau and Schoenherr, 1971; Pfeffer, 1981; Withington, 1969) suggest that computers have had a decentralizing effect on organizational decision making. Although the literature on IT and centralization may be ambiguous, e-government's focus on external communications with citizens, rather then internal communication, could lead e-government to have a more centralizing effect on government structure.

Yet another point of view is expressed by Zuboff (1998). Zuboff explains that when organizations use information technology to merely automate and not informate, the technology has a centralizing effect. Centralizing organizations focused on automation use information technology "to defend and reproduce the legitimacy of managerial authority and channel potential innovation toward a conventional emphasis on automation. ... They use the technology as a fail-safe system to increase their certainty and control over both production and organizational functions."

Zuboff (1988) looks at organizations that use information technology for the purposes of automation from a historical perspective and concludes that the industrial age, with its focus on automation, had similar centralizing effects on assembly-line and mill workers. She cites information systems (e.g., decision support systems) that focus exclusively on providing upper-level managers with consolidated information to base their decisions on as modern examples of how information technology can cause centralized decision making and simultaneously alienate workers at lower levels of the organization.

In contrast, Zuboff claims that organizations can also use information technology to decentralize or informate. Zuboff (1988) states that decentralization is a choice that must be made by managers. In her terms, the decision to informate enables organizations to decentralize decisions and break down the distinctions between blue- and white-collar workers. The process of informating requires a management commitment to place more responsibility in the hands of workers for determining new ways to gather and analyze information that is generated due to normal organizational operations. According to Zuboff (1988), "Managerial work [in informating organizations] would thus be team oriented and interdisciplinary and would promote fluid movement of members across [the] domains of managerial activity."

Additionally, Zuboff (1988) claims that organizational leaders will recognize that the process of informating requires new skills and knowledge. "Organizations seeking to informate will direct their resources toward creating a workforce that can exercise critical judgment as it manages the surrounding machine systems. Work becomes more abstract as it depends upon understanding and manipulation of information." Consistent with Zuboff, Harris (2000) hypothesizes that e-government has the potential to reverse modern democratic tendencies, which can lead toward increased centralization. Harris states, "the centralization caused by the industrial revolution and dependence on mass production can be reversed by e-government."

Others have also seen the decentralizing capabilities of information technology. In his text *Organization Design and Theory*, Daft (2001) claims that information technology leads to these impacts on organization designs:

1. Smaller organizations,
2. Decentralized organization structures,
3. Improved internal and external coordination,
4. Additional professional staff and departments,
5. Greater employee participation.

Ultimately, Zuboff and Daft conclude that the utility of information technology is maximized when organizations choose to informate or decentralize; however they warn that decentralization is still an option many managers may take. Peled's (2001) "Two Tales of Online Government" demonstrates that in many cases managers do not choose to decentralize. Peled's analysis of centralization examines two different accounts of online government in Israel. Peled concludes centralization and decentralization lie in the eyes of the beholder/manager—in other words, he found that managers would choose centralization based on their style of management and their position in the organizational hierarchy.

Peled (2001) found that upper managers were more likely to favor centralization, whereas individuals at lower levels of the organizational hierarchy were more likely to favor decentralization. Peled's research tells a single story of how an e-government initiative was implemented from two perspectives. The first is from the point of view of an upper-level manager and the second point of view is that of a lower-level public manager. The first tale tells us, "that the existing power elite can manipulate glitzy new Internet-based technologies to expand (their) organizational empire. The second tale remind (s) us that knowledge diffuses power but that such diffusion can also lead to anarchy."

In sum, centralization seeks clarity and coordination while allowing organizations to take advantage of economies of scale and craft strategic enterprisewide visions. The grass roots or decentralized approach is characteristic of open and entrepreneurial organizations, many of which have led innovation in the information age. The decentralized approach allows organizations to empower individuals throughout the organization and facilitates innovation and creativity. Peled's "tales" demonstrate that each approach has distinct advantages, but ultimately a balanced approach is needed that takes into account the idiosyncrasies of each situation on a case-by-case basis.

## C.  Data Sharing and Integration

It is appropriate that the topic of integration follows a discussion of centralization and decentralization. In the strictest sense, integration is synonymous with centralization and, in fact, Waldo (1948) often refers to centralization as integration in *The Administrative State*. Although it is important to differentiate between systems integration and organizational centralization, it is also important to recognize that data managers have been struggling with many of the same issues as organizational theorists. For example, the field of information technology has spent a considerable amount of time debating Inmon's (1992) top-down enterprise vision versus Kimball's (1997) bottom-up project pragmatism. As with the organizational theorists, the solution is probably somewhere in the middle and the debate is probably best settled on a case-by-case basis.

The extent to which an agency integrates its computer systems may reflect its organizational approach to centralization, however, systems integration is still worth differentiating from organizational centralization. For the purposes of this chapter, systems integration, or simply integration, refers to a process where multiple computer systems are able to share data, and managers are able to analyze data from multiple databases. Integrated systems are needed if e-government is to reach its fullest potential. If e-government systems are to transform organizations making them more integrated, then the computer systems underlying e-government IT systems initiatives in the public sector must also be integrated.

## 1.  Legacy Systems

The importance of integration in public organizations has been highlighted recently by public managers responsible for "legacy systems." In sum, nonintegrated systems that vertically communicate information and perform analyses within an agency, but are unable to communicate across organizational boundaries with other computer systems, are often referred to as stove-pipes, silos, or legacy systems. Today legacy systems make up many computer applications used by government to perform routine administrative tasks such as writing checks and maintaining personnel records. In fact, a recent Deloitte Research survey revealed that 32% of governments found obsolete legacy systems to be more of an obstacle to implementation than project costs, staff expertise, administrative process, or legislative mandates.

Historically, when large organizations in the public or private sector have needed a new computer application, they gather their IT managers and programmers, perhaps bring in a consultant, and build the system from scratch. Building a system from the bottom up is often done for several reasons. However, most reasons for building custom systems stem from the lack of an off-the-shelf alternative, and because custom systems allow agencies to design applications that meet the exact system specifications, some of which are mandated by law. The flexibility inherent in custom-built applications is often necessary in government because the needs of the system may not be formulated by IT managers with an eye for what will be easiest to design. Rather, policy makers often dictate the system specifications. Instead of basing application-design decisions on technological strengths and limitations, policy makers frequently formulate design specifications through policy decisions based on the legislative history and compromises made during the policy-making process.

## D.   The Shift Toward Integrated Systems

Today the shift away from stovepipe or legacy systems toward integrated systems is fostered by several IT-related innovations. First, more and more agencies today are experimenting with off-the-shelf software that can perform the tasks needed with little or no customization. The second innovation that fosters data integration is the use of data warehouses and data marts in preexisting legacy or other customized systems. Off-the-shelf software solutions have emerged in several areas such as geographic information systems (GIS) and administrative applications known as enterprise resource planning (ERP) systems. As illustrated below, the public sector can benefit from private sector advances made in both GIS and ERP systems.

Just a few years ago, it was commonplace for several agencies within federal, state, and even city governments to have custom GIS systems that could not communicate with one another. Today, virtually any type of data can be standardized and made compatible with standard off-the-shelf GIS software such as ESRI's "ArcView" or "ArcInfo." This is particularly relevant for public agencies because so much of what they do is geospatially oriented. For example, agencies such as state departments of the environment can generate GIS maps using common data standards for environmental impact statements that can combine ecologically significant areas, local zoning regulations, public health data, proposed highway construction, and just about any other type of data another public agency collects that is relevant to the particular situation.

Enterprise resource planning systems represent another way of integrating systems using prepackaged software solutions. ERP systems such as SAP, PeopleSoft, and Oracle were initially developed for the private sector, but are now being implemented in the public sector to integrate outdated legacy systems. ERP systems typically can replace and integrate personnel, procurement, revenue, and accounts payable systems. Once these systems are integrated, reports can be run that combine data from a variety of sources. Integrated systems eliminate redundant data, thereby reducing data entry errors. In addition, there is less reliance on the one or two individuals or independent consultants that have maintained the system for years. Finally, ERP systems, much like off-the-shelf word processing programs, come with built-in help files and documentation to aid users.

Other advantages of ERP systems over custom software solutions are as follows (derived from www.erpfans.com.)

Modules are readymade and only need customization.

Documentation is part of the system.

The company takes care of maintenance instead of relying on individuals.

ERP systems are Electronic Data Interchange (EDI) compatible (fully integrated).

The package itself is designed as an enterprise package and so implementation and integration are not as difficult as when each agency or unit develops or purchases its own software option.

Updates on technology and processes are constant and assured, unlike custom software, which is more difficult to update on a regular basis.

There are disadvantages to ERP systems as well. For one, because they have been developed for the private sector they often require much customization. Also, system requirements that result from legislative mandates often prove very difficult to incorporate into ERP systems. The private sector also has identified disadvantages to using ERP systems. These include (from www.ecommerce-now.com):

The high price of the software, associated license fees, and annual charges that need to be adhered to;

There is a high cost of training involved with most ERP packages. Employee training and reeducation may be needed. In the transitional phase, this may cause a dip in morale;

Organizations that implement an ERP package need to ensure that all records are correct. An ERP system is only as honest as the data entered into it;

New ERP systems may require additional employees;

The current ERP packages may not be fully Web-enabled and may lack full Internet capabilities;

Presently, because ERP packages are unable to support e-commerce, businesses have to invest additional funds in e-commerce packages that need to run with the ERP packages; and

Businesses that have implemented ERP packages often criticize software designs regarding their lack of flexibility. Organizations investing in ERP systems need to do their homework to ensure that the package meets their business needs.

Even though many off-the shelf software solutions have been time-tested in the public sector, they often need to be modified or customized to work in the public sector. Unfortunately, the process of customization can decrease the functionality of a system and make it difficult if not impossible to upgrade. Oftentimes, if a product cannot be upgraded to a newer version it will not be supported by the manufacturer and this lack of technical support eliminates one of the main advantages of using such a system. Therefore, managers must be aware of the amount of customization needed before implementing an off-the-shelf solution.

If off-the shelf software requires an inordinate amount of customization, it is often in an agency's best interest to build its own integrated system. The main concern with building an integrated system is the potential to create a future legacy system. Public agencies that build integrated systems usually contract with a consultant for assistance and the systems are usually built on standard data management platforms such as Oracle, so that changes can be made and the system can be upgraded over time.

In cases where replacing a legacy system is not an option, public sector IT managers look to data warehouses and data marts, which systematically integrate key fields from nonintegrated databases. The data subset is placed in a separate data mart or warehouse, enabling managers to run integrated reports from nonintegrated systems. "Data mapping" the key data and common fields is the process that IT managers use to connect legacy systems to the data marts. The data mapping process not only enables data integration, but it is also useful if and when the legacy system is to be replaced. The mapping process can provide basic system architecture for replacing the legacy systems with a new integrated system. In addition, "middleware" solutions are now being used to place a Web-enabled front-end on many data marts and warehouses.

The debate between building the exact software needed at the risk of becoming beholden to consultants or a few individuals within a public organization and purchasing an integrated off-the-shelf solution that may not meet an organization's exact design specifications are issues that cannot be easily addressed. Managers should try to identify prepackaged software solutions to meet their needs, but they must recognize that not all software solutions for the private sector are applicable for public agencies. In many cases, the objectives of public agencies are such that no viable off-the-shelf software alternatives exist. In cases where managers need the flexibility of building a custom system, new systems should be built on platforms that will enable future integration.

## E.  Content Management

Before moving on to dynamic Web applications, public agencies must ensure that the information they provide on the Internet is timely, well written, designed for the Web, and meets standards for usability. Generally, this is referred to as managing the content of information on the Web, and its maintenance is critical for organizations seeking to increase their Web presence/sophistication presence. In developing an agency's Internet capacity, it is important to provide a mechanism for updating material regularly. There needs to be a link among online content, program managers, and the IT managers responsible for keeping servers online.

Public information officers also need to be trained in using the Internet as a communication medium. In addition, public information officers often are unable to make final changes to Internet content themselves, relying on IT managers to assist them. To ensure that online content can be updated and enhanced, the individuals charged with developing the online content need to have the skills and power to change it. By giving content managers complete control, they also become accountable for maintaining accurate and timely information on the Web sites of public agencies.

Online content managers need to recognize that online content is multidimensional and not just flat text. In addition, content managers must consider Web design issues. For example, the "transactional" service of online motor vehicle registration lends itself well to an e-commerce-based model of e-government. However, if the agency Web site is not organized in a manner that is intuitive to individuals unfamiliar with the organizational structure then they may not be able to find the registration site.

## F. Knowledge Management

If content managers need to be concerned with the content of public sector Internet sites, then knowledge managers must be concerned with the context of public sector Internet sites. Knowledge management refers "to the efforts to systematically find, organize and make available a company's intellectual capital and to foster a culture of continuous learning and knowledge sharing so that organizational activities build on what is already known" (Daft, 2001).

Before delving into methods of fostering the creation and management of knowledge, it is important to define knowledge. In short, knowledge is built on information, which is built on data. Data can be defined as "a set of discrete objective facts about events" (Davenport and Prusak, 2001). Information builds upon data by providing a context for the information. In their text *Working Knowledge*, Davenport and Prusak suggest, "thinking about information as data that makes a difference." When discussing knowledge, Davenport and Prusak (2001) state that knowledge is:

> A fluid mix of framed experience, values, contextual information, and expert insight that provides a framework for evaluating and incorporating new experiences and information. It originates and is applied in the minds of knowers. In organizations, it often becomes embedded not only in documents or repositories but also in organizational routines, processes, practices and norms.

Daft (2001) differentiates between knowledge and information by stating that "information is data that has been linked with other data and converted into a useful context for specific use. Knowledge goes a step further. It is a conclusion drawn from the information after it is linked to other information compared to what is already know." In addition, there are two types of knowledge, tacit and explicit (Daft, 2001).

> *Explicit knowledge* is formal systematic knowledge that can be codified, written down, and passed on to others in documents or general instruction.
> *Tacit knowledge* is based on personal experience, rules of thumb, intuition, and judgment. Tacit knowledge is often very difficult to put into words.

Next, two key questions facing managers today regarding knowledge management are addressed: how can knowledge creation and management be fostered in an organization and how can information technology be used as a tool to enhance this process. Today, many knowledge management systems have increasingly used new information technology innovations for implementation. Typically, knowledge management systems are making use of an organization's internal "intranets." In addition, knowledge management systems have evolved with the two different types of knowledge.

Explicit knowledge management systems seek to create an electronic repository for forms, documents, frequently asked questions, and electronic libraries. An example of such a system is the FAQ section of corporate Web sites. Often these Web sites contain volumes of technical information about a business's products. Many users often find that searching such systems yields too much information to be processed in a useful manner. For many organizations, the key has become providing explicit knowledge to users in an appropriate context so that they are able to use the knowledge stored in the system.

Unlike explicit knowledge management systems, tacit knowledge management systems attempt to create knowledge by providing a forum for interaction between individuals. By attempting to create virtual communities with interacting experts, tacit knowledge management systems become more than an archive of knowledge, but actually help to create knowledge. Most knowledge management systems started out as either explicit or tacit systems and are just now attempting to incorporate other approaches.

The history of knowledge management systems reveals that explicit systems were the first to evolve. These explicit knowledge management systems were sometimes developed under the guise of decision support systems, and they became archives for vast amounts of information. According to Junnarkar (2000), "It started with integration of information where the focus was on explicit or codified information. The next phase for knowledge management was to focus on interactivity between people, where the emphasis would be on capturing, sharing and enhancing context." As knowledge management systems have evolved, they have grown to encompass both explicit and tacit knowledge.

In addition, it is important to note that although many associate knowledge management with information technology, the technology is not entirely necessary. Davenport and Prusak (2001) compare new advances in information technology to television. When television was a new technology, many thought that it "would bind humanity into a global village and end world conflict." The compare such statements to the Internet stating that information technology is the medium not the message. In other words, new technologies—the Internet and intranets—are merely tools for facilitating the transformation of data and information into knowledge.

## VII. CONCLUSIONS

Centralization, integration, content management, and knowledge management all reflect an agency's capacity to create, implement, and maintain Internet-driven initiatives in the public sector. Although these factors are important, it is also important to note that they are not the only factors. This chapter has attempted to illustrate that Internet-driven innovations in the public sector such as e-government are in many ways different from previous technological innovations, but this is not to say that other organizational development techniques and best practices are not relevant. This clearly is not the case; initiatives such as strategic planning for information technology are essential if the public sector is to maximize its use of emerging information technologies. Planning activities such as business process reengineering are also critical as the public sector looks to create and implement new initiatives.

Finally, recent critics of how the Internet is being used in the public sector claim that public organizations are placing too much emphasis on building e-government systems using an e-commerce or business model. These criticisms state that the "dot.com plunge" that was experienced in the private sector should serve as a warning to managers attempting to Web-enable entire agencies. These criticisms often compare the public sector's current infatuation with the Internet and e-government to a "management fad" (Hyde, 2001, p. 31). The term "management fad" implies that the use of the Internet in the public sector will eventually fade and be surpassed by another administrative reform that will claim to increase the efficiency and effectiveness of public organizations.

The business model criticism is valid on another level. The early success of e-commerce strategies has led public sector agencies to adopt them in implementing e-government initiatives. Rather than focusing e-government initiatives on transaction-based, fee-for-service programs, public agencies will need to examine their business purpose. The e-commerce fee-for-service model may be appropriate for renewing drivers' licenses, selling fishing licenses, and purchasing environmental permits online, but these programs are not typical of most government programs. Instead, e-government strategies will need to analyze an agency's goals or business purpose and move forward with the implementation of e-government programs that best meet their needs.

By focusing on the basics of e-government, agencies will be more capable of matching their organizational needs with the most efficient and effective uses of the Internet. Integrated data sharing systems will enable public agencies to use the Internet as a medium to communicate and process information and knowledge from inside the organization, as well as to receive feedback from external sources. Finally, renewing the focus of information technology initiatives in the public sector on the entire process of implementing new initiatives will ensure that public organizations are able to maximize information technologies. They will move toward a fully realized vision that is effective, efficient, citizen-centered, and transformational and ultimately leads to organizational change.

## REFERENCES

Argyris. (1971). Management information systems: The challenge to rationality and emotionality. *Manage. Sci.* 17(6):275–292.

Avgerou. (2000). Information systems: What sort of science is it? *Omega Int. J. Manage. Sci.* 28:567–579.

Baker. (1994). *Comparative Public Management: Putting U.S. Public Policy and Implementation in Context*. Westport, CT: Prager.

Balutis. (Spring 2001). "E-government 2001, Part I: Understanding the Challenge and Evolving Strategies." *Public Manager*.

Banville, Landry. (1992). Can the field of MIS be disciplined. In: Galliers, ed. Information Research. Oxford: Blackwell.

Blau, Schoenherr. (1971). *The Structure of Organizations*. New York: Basic.

Bretschneider, S. (1986). Management information systems in public and private organizations: An empirical test. *Public Admin. Rev.* 50:536–544.

Brynjolfsson. (1993). The productivity paradox of information technology. *Commun. ACM*.

Brynjolfsson, Hitt. (1995). The productive keep producing—Successful companies support good business plans with the right information technologies. *Inf. Week*.

City of New York. (1999). *City of New York Information Technology Strategy*. Mayor, Rudolph Guiliani.

Council for Excellence in Government. (2000). Available at www.excelgov.org.

Cron, Sobol (1983). The relationship between computerization and performance. *J. Inf. Manage.* 6:171–181.

Daft, R. (2001). *Organization Theory and Design*. United States: South-Western, Thomson Learning.

Davenport, Prusak. (1998). *Working Knowledge*. Boston: Harvard Business School Press.

Dean. (2000). Y2K work changed course of IT. *Gov. Exec.* 8(32):96–103.

Deloitte Research. (2000). *At the Dawn of E-Government: The Citizen as Consumer*. Deloitte Consulting.

Dock, Wetherbe. (1988). *Computer Information Systems for Business*. St. Paul, MN: West.

Downs. (1967). *Inside Bureaucracy*. Boston: Little, Brown.

Franke. (1987). Technological revolution and productivity decline: computer introduction in the financial industry. *Tech. Forecast. Soc. Change* 31.

Gold. (1982). Managing for success: a comparison of the public and private sectors. *Public Admin. Rev.* 42:568–575.

Goles, Hirschheim. (2000). The paradigm is dead, the paradigm is dead... long live the paradigm: The legacy of Burrell and Morgan. *Omega: Int. J. Manage. Sci.* 28:249–268.

Hale. (1996). Achieving high performance in public organizations. In: Perry, ed. *Handbook of Public Administration*. 2nd ed. San Francisco.

Harris, B. (2000). E-government: Beyond service delivery. *Gov. Tech.* Available at http://egov.govtech.net/reports/power/power.phtml.

Held, D. (1996). *Models of Democracy*. Stanford, CA: Stanford University Press.

Holzer, Callahan. (1998). *Government at Work: Best Practices and Model Programs*. Thousand Oaks, CA: Sage.

Holzer, Gabrielian. (1998). Five great ideas in American public administration. In: Rabin, Hildreth, Bartley, Miller, eds. *Handbook of Public Administration*. New York: Marcel Dekker.

Hyde. (Spring, 2001). Management fad of the year 2000: E-gov. *Public Manage.*

Inmon, W. (1997). *Building the Data Warehouse*. Boston: QED Technical.

Junnarkar, B. (2000). Sharing and building context. In: Morey, Maybury, Thurisingham. eds. *Knowledge Management: Classic and Contemporary Works*. Cambridge, MA: MIT Press.

Kaplan. (1994). *The Conduct of Inquiry: Methodology for Behavior Science*. San Francisco: Chandler.

Kimball, R. (1997). The data warehouse toolkit: Practical techniques for building dimensional data-warehouses. *Inf. Syst. Manage.* 14(1):82–86.

King. (1983). Centralization vs. decentralization of computing: Organizational considerations and management options. *ACM Comput. Surv.* 16(4):81–104.

Kraemer, King. (1992). Computing and public organizations. Public administration in action: readings, profiles and cases. In: Denhardt, Hammond. eds. Pacific Grove, CA: Brooks/Cole.

Kuhn. (1996). *The Structure of Scientific Revolutions*. 3rd ed. Chicago: University of Chicago Press (original work published 1962).

Landry, Banville. (1992). A disciplined methodological pluralism for MIS research. *Account. Manage. Inf. Tech.* 2:77–97.

Leavitt, Whisler. (1988, November/December). Management in the 1980s. *Harvard Bus. Rev.* 36:41–48.

Ledue. (1982). Communicating through computers. *Telecomm. Policy* 17:226–227.

Lenard, Folescu. (2000, July). *Digital State Part III: Digital Democracy and Management/Administration*. Progress and Freedom Foundation and Center for Digital Government.

Lippitt, Miller, Lalamj. (1987). Patterns of use and correlates of adoption of an electronic mail system. Proceedings of the American Institute of Decision Sciences.

Mansell, Robin, When. (1998). *Knowledge Societies: Information Technology for Sustainable Development*. United Nations Commission on Science and Technologies for Development (UNCSTD). New York: Oxford (Published for and on behalf of the United Nations by Oxford University).

Meier, Stewart. (1987). Why are people saying all those nasty things about public administration, and what should be done about It? Or shoot low boys. They're riding shetland ponies. Proceedings of the American Political Science Association, Chicago.

Mumford, Banks. (1967). *The Computer and the Clerk*. London: Routledge and Kegan Paul.

Myers (1967). *The Impact of Computers on Management.* Cambridge, MA: MIT Press.

Northrop, Kraemer, King. (1989). What every public manager should know about computing. Managing public programs. In: Henry, Cleary, et al. eds. *Balancing Politics Administration and Public Needs.* San Francisco: Jossey-Bass.

Oleary, Williams. (1989). *Computers and Information Systems.* 2nd ed. Redwood City, CA: Benjamin/Cummings.

Osborne, Gaebler. (1993). *Reinventing Government.* New York: Penguin.

Osterman, P. (1986). The impact of computers on the employment of clerks and managers. *Indust. Labor Relations Rev.* 9:175–186.

Parsons, Gottlieb, Denny (1990). Productivity and computers in Canadian Banking. University of Toronto, Dept. of Economics, working paper #9012.

Peled, A. (2001). Centralization or diffusion? Two tales of online government. *Admin. Soc.* 32(6): 686–709.

Peters, Waterman. (1982). *In Search of Excellence: Lessons from America's Best-Run Companies.* New York: HarperCollins.

Pfeffer. (1981). *Power in Organizations.* Marshfield, MA: Pitman.

Rainey, H. (1997). *Understanding and Managing Public Organizations.* 2nd ed. San Francisco: Jossey-Bass.

Roach. (1991). S.S. services under siege: The restructuring imperative. *Harvard Bus.* 82–92.

Scavo, Shi. (2000). Public administration: The role of information technology in the reinventing government paradigm normative predicates and practical challenges. *Social Sci. Comput. Rev.* 18:2.

Siegel, D., Griliches, Z. (1991, April). *Purchased Services, Outsourcing, Computers and Productivity in Manufacturing.* National Bureau of Economic Research WP#3678.

Simon, H. (1945). *Administrative Behavior.* New York: Free Press.

Sircar, Turnbow, Bordoloi. (2000). Framework for assessing the relationship between information technology investments and firm performance. *J. Manage. Inf. Syst.*

Sprague. (1980). A framework for the development of decision support systems. *MIS Quart.* 4(4):1–25.

Swain, White. (1992). Information technology for productivity: Maybe, maybe not: An assessment. In: Holzer, Marc, ed. *Public Productivity Handbook.* New York: Marcel Dekker.

Swain, White, Hubbert, Elice. (1995). Issues in public management information systems. *Am. Rev. Public Admin.* 25:3.

Symonds, M. (2000, June). Survey government and the Internet. *The Economist.*

Tapscott. (1999). Governance in the digital economy. *Finan. Devel.* 4(36):34–37.

Waldo, D. (1948). *The Administrative State.* New York: Ronald.

Weber, M. (1922). Bureaucracy. In: Shafritz, Hyde, eds. *Classics of Public Administration.* New York: Harcourt Brace.

Weider. (2000, August 7). E-commerce benchmarking. *Computerworld.* 34:32.

Weill, P. (1990). *Do Computers Pay Off?* Washington, DC: ICT.

West, Darrel. (2000). Assessing e-government: The Internet, democracy, and service delivery by state and federal governments. Unpublished paper. Available at < http://www.inside politics.org/egovtreport00.html >. Providence, RI: Brown University.

Withington. (1969). *The Real Computer: Its Influences, Uses and Effects.* Reading, MA: Addison-Wesley.

Zuboff, S. (1988). *In the Age of the Smart Machine.* New York: Basic.

# 37

## Information Technology and Productivity

*Selected Issues and Considerations*

**ARIE HALACHMI**
*Tennessee State University, Nashville, Tennessee, U.S.A.,
and Zhongshan University, China*

## I. INTRODUCTION

Being aware of the high cost and the importance of information technology to effective government, the United States Congress and president enacted in 1996 the Information Technology Management Reform Act (ITMRA) and the Federal Acquisition Reform Act (FARA). These two acts together, known as the Clinger–Cohen Act (CCA), require the heads of federal agencies to link IT investments to agency accomplishments. The Clinger–Cohen Act also requires that agency heads establish a process to select, manage, and control their IT investments. The key IT management actions in the act require agency heads to do the following.

> Design and implement an IT management process for maximizing the value and assessing and managing the risks of IT acquisitions.
>
> Integrate the IT management process with the processes for making budget, financial, and program management decisions.
>
> Establish goals for improving the efficiency and effectiveness of agency operations and, as appropriate, the delivery of services to the public through the use of IT. Prepare an annual report, to be included in the executive agency's budget submission to Congress, on the progress toward achieving these goals.
>
> Ensure that performance measurements are prescribed for IT by or for the agency, and that they measure how well the IT supports agency programs.

Ensure that information security policies, procedures, and practices of the agency are adequate.

Appoint a chief information officer (CIO).

The passage of CCA highlights, among others, two important realities: the performance of government agencies cannot be separated from the issue of IT, and expenditures on IT by agencies are very high and the rate of return on the investment in IT is neither clear nor certain. Because there is currently no consensus among most writers about the functional relationship between IT and productivity, certain issues involved merit our examination.

According to Krohe (1993, p.55), "The magic machine that can do more work faster than ever so far has helped business do its work only a little. . . . Investment in IT had little, if any, effect on output or labor productivity." This claim is consistent with Brynjolfsson (1992), who asserts that "the relationship between information technology (IT) and productivity is widely discussed but little understood." Brynjolfsson points out that between 1970 and 1990 delivered computing power in the U.S. economy increased by more than two orders of magnitude, yet productivity, especially in the service sector, seems to have stagnated. Brynjolfsson goes on, however, to make some suggestions: first, poor returns on IT investments may be the result of faults in the way we measure productivity; and second, poor returns are the result of unresolved organizational issues, such as mismanagement. According to Uchitelle (1996), those who look to computers for economic miracles and insist on measuring their contributions only in dollars miss the less tangible improvement in quality that computers have made possible. Corcoran (1999), who asserts that new research shows that technology rarely saves businesses or money, offers a related position. In fact, Corcoran notes that innovations often come at considerable expense. These innovations do, however, allow for new opportunities that would otherwise be impossible. Thus, he concludes, "The truth is that government productivity statistics don't reflect the contributions that computers make. The numbers don't measure improvements in quality, innovation, flexibility or timeliness." According to a newsletter from the Federal Reserve Bank of San Francisco (Cornwell and Trehan, 2000), with the rapid growth in U.S. productivity in recent years, the debate over the contributions of IT to productivity growth has shifted. According to the newsletter, there is no dispute over the efficiency gains in the production of computers and related equipment. Instead the debate between skeptics and believers in the "new economy" centers on the benefits of using IT outside the production sector (i.e., within the service sector).

Being cognizant of the high level of expenditures on IT and the complexity and difficulty of assessing the justification and the return on investment in IT, the Office of Management and Budget (OMB) compiled many documents to assist agencies in managing IT. These include:

OMB circulars

A-11, Planning, budgeting, acquisition of capital assets, strategic plans, performance plans;
A-76, Performance of commercial activities (outsourcing);
A-94, Guidelines and discount rates for benefit–cost analysis of federal programs; and
A-130, Management of federal information resources.

Evaluating information technology investments of November 1995 (which is OMB's principal guidance on implementing ITMRA).
Memoranda

Funding information systems investments (October 1996) in which OMB establishes criteria for "evaluation of major information system investments/eight proposed for funding in the FY 98 President's budget."

The purpose of this chapter is to go beyond the issue of whether investment in IT is justified. There are several other issues public managers must consider in order to gain better understanding of the role of IT and its productivity consequences in government agencies, which are part of the service sector. The basic premise of this chapter is that government agencies have no choice in whether to use IT. As pointed out in earlier writings (Halachmi, 1994, 1995, 1996), regulatory agencies stand little chance of being able to carry out their mission without effective use of IT, because regulated entities use IT to avoid conforming to government regulations. Similarly, the public expects government service providers to use IT to facilitate access to information and services; lack of evident intensive use of IT is likely to be perceived as substandard service. Thus this chapter aims to highlight a few important points that may help managers to enhance productivity by counteracting possible dysfunctional outcomes of IT, while taking advantage of what it can offer for transforming labor into knowledgeable workers.

The chapter consists of certain major components: the first explores some of the ways in which IT influences the interface of government organizations with their environment; and the second touches briefly on the various ways in which IT modifies organizational behavior by changing the interface of individual employees with coworkers, their behavior as group members, and the formation and functioning of groups and their dealings with other groups. The chapter concludes by pointing out that organizations need to take a proactive stand to compensate for the absence of regular interpersonal interactions in order to retain employees' loyalty and commitment to the organization.

## II. HOW IT INFLUENCES THE INTERFACE OF THE ORGANIZATION WITH ITS ENVIRONMENT

### A. Changing the Pace of Work

One of the most noticeable changes resulting from the introduction of IT cnncerns time. To illustrate this change, I will share with you the following vignette. In the mid-1960s, when I was a government employee, I sent out a letter informing a particular business entity that it had incurred financial penalties, as the agency I worked for had not received by the stated due date certain requested information. I also warned the offending entity that additional penalties would likely be imposed if the requested information were not made available to the agency within a week. This letter was taken to the agency's mailroom at mid-morning. In the afternoon mail, however, I received the requested information. The agency's mailroom time stamp indicated that the information had come in by the due date, but was delayed en route to me by a delivery error within the agency. A quick dash down to the mailroom solved the problem. With the help of mailroom employees I was able to recover the threatening letter before it went out, saving myself and the agency from certain embarrassment. Given office practices today, chances are that such a communication to what seems to be a tardy entity would be generated by a computer without human intervention. Agency employees would not learn about any wrong action on the agency's part until a complaint had been filed against the agency, provoking the corresponding negative media coverage that is so common in such cases. To put such a potential incident in context, the reader should recall that many government agencies that embrace e-commerce as a template for e-government use such practices to improve efficiency and public confidence in prompt and correct action by government when the odds for human errors are reduced. The use of an IT interface with the respective publics they serve may help some agencies improve performance.

Such e-commerce practices cannot, however, help any organization with the timely interception of outgoing communication that was mistakenly generated due to an inhouse snafu. In short, such mistakes that are hard to preempt are undermining government efforts to increase efficiency—the reason for the transition to e-government (using e-commerce practices) in the first place. Considering this scenario, one may claim that in these e-government agencies virtual mail is not likely to be misdirected by an internal error such as that described above. However, the reality is that mail servers are down from time to time; due to this and other problems, incoming and outgoing email does get lost. However, when an email gets lost the sender and the recipients may not be aware of the problem until it is too late. Also, when email (or voice mail) reaches the correct electronic mailbox but the wrong organizational address, it is less likely to be forwarded to the correct unit or employee within the organization than a physical piece of mail, as happened in the case described above. The lack of a simple way to reverse or correct computer-generated administrative actions that trigger subsequent bad decisions and an additional wave of wrong actions should be recognized by every manager.

The discussion so far suggests some possible lessons that, although obvious, tend to be overlooked by many. The first lesson is that common sense, if not civic decency, suggests that a mechanism capable of a remedial action should be in place before any transition from an assembly-linelike string of manual administrative procedures to an IT-based virtual business process. Yet rarely do we find such precautions, as illustrated by occasional media stories concerning people who have been written off by computers as dead, while government employees are at a loss about an effective way to reverse the error. The second lesson is that with the greater efficiency that comes with the use of IT, damage to the agency is more likely to happen these days, and the ability to reverse a bad decision in a discreet manner is lost once the Enter key has been pressed. In other words, greater reliance on IT narrows the margin of error, but also reduces the window of opportunity to correct mistakes. The third lesson, which is illustrated by the vignette under discussion, is an aspect of the new reality at the workplace after the introduction of IT: the interface with the environment becomes much more sanative than before, and less tolerant of mistakes. This last lesson requires further elaboration, as it is related to a wider phenomenon.

Supervisors, coworkers, and service recipients now expect quick service turnaround and a more complete answer to any request for information. As I was writing this chapter during a federal holiday that falls on a Monday, I was interrupted several times by emails from one of my students. This industrious individual—a mid-career government employee—is enrolled in my Tuesday evening class and needed help with an assignment that was due the next day. The fact that the attempt to contact me took place on a holiday, which was the reason she was off work, was never factored into the student's decision to try to contact me again and again, even though she was well aware that I, too, was on holiday. The student expected to get an answer to her questions shortly after sending them, reflecting the same way she treats (and is treated by) her own clients. This propensity is not hers alone. We have all been conditioned by our interactions with IT to expect instant feedback received faster and faster as one generation of advanced central processing units (CPUs) is replaced by a speedier one. Kids who play video games grow accustomed to instant feedback and gratification. When they turn into adults, they expect to have the same experience. This may explain, in part, why they may prefer the Internet-based services over other options, and why they do not complain about performing tasks that used to be the domain of service providers not long ago. In the "instant" reality of today, books of many hundreds of pages are being reduced to a few hours of watching a videotape or television program. Fast-track sources such as CNN's *Headline News* or *USA Today* (a.k.a. "McPaper" in some circles) provide the common information diet of "road warriors," those who are often on the road as they travel to meetings or to serve clients. With the advent of wireless communication, even those who are not far from a real newspaper or TV news show resort to the time-saving, though more superficial, coverage of today's events by such sources as CNN or MSNBC.

Against this background, it is not surprising to expect frustration, and thus a perception of poor service, incompetence, or lack of responsiveness among those who fail to get the expected response within a very short time. Thus, even when response time is very reasonable in the eyes of the involved professionals, and even when, objectively, a faster response is not possible due to legal or other constraints, some service recipients perceive a lack of improvement in service quality. A sense of deterioration of service is very likely to evolve where service providers use, or are expected to use, IT. Such a feeling may explain, in part, the perception that investments in IT fail to generate the expected improvements. Unfortunately, little is done by public organizations to address this issue, that is, to explain to the public the inevitable gap between service expectations and organizational performance and, on the other hand, to study new options for reaching the same results that become available as IT improves. The latter is known as "business process reengineering" (BPR). The need for government agencies to address the gap between service expectations and performance is an important topic, but it is beyond the scope of this chapter.

## B.  24-7-365: Effects on Productivity

The earlier example of the persistent student who was consumed with her own needs while being oblivious to the rest of the world illustrates still another aspect of the new interface of offices and their environment. Known as "24-7-365" (twenty-four hours a day, seven days a week, every day of the year), this is the phenomenon of service recipients expecting seamless and full service around the clock. In the early days of the Internet, when access was available mostly through kiosks at public libraries, schools, and offices, the ability to conduct business with government agencies around the clock was limited to the computer-literate elite. At that time, most computers at home were standalone machines for games or schoolwork. Today, most homes are connected to the Internet through public and independent service providers (ISPs), and the dynamic of the interaction among government agencies and their clients is different from what it used to be. The Internet's graphic interface has created a new breed of cybershoppers who are computer savvy. According to the 2000 Census, over half the population—105 million households—had personal computers, and 42% of all households could log on to the Internet (New York Times, 2001). Americans who want to avoid the search for a parking place and conserve gasoline are taking their business with the government online. This, in turn, changes the entire nature and dynamic of the interface of government offices with their publics in terms of when and where services are provided. To be sure, a service such as the renewal of a driver's license in Tennessee can be done over the Internet around the clock, every day of the year, wherever Internet access is available.

What are the implications of widespread Internet accessibility for government productivity? To start with, the desire for greater transparency (openness) of government has been transformed from an abstract vague notion into a concrete expectation. It is anticipated that most government agencies will become more open to public review and participation by providing easy access around the clock to their annual work plans, performance and financial reports, the laws and regulations that govern their operations, minutes of meetings, and so on. Agency Web sites are expected to allow the public to comment on proposed changes in regulations or policies, apply for a given service (from the renewal of driver's licenses to applications for various kinds of permits), schedule appointments, make payments, or request additional information.

However, the agencies that are expected to provide such electronic-based services (which comprise a portion of what is known as e-government) are not exempt from making the very same services available through traditional channels. On first sight, more extensive use of IT-based services by agencies seems to be a sure way to improve productivity, but the reality, that is, the implications for the bottom line in terms of cost per dispensed unit of service, may be different. In theory, effectiveness (the ability to serve better) should increase as agencies take advantage of IT, and efficiency (the cost per unit of service rendered online) should also improve. Yet the reality, in many cases, is different. Expected savings are rarely realized, causing some administrators to question the justification of the ever-growing investments in IT.

There are only marginal, if any, savings on the cost of labor for delivering the service the old way. One reason is that agencies must be ready to deal with citizens who will not or cannot use the Internet to conduct business with the government. As noted by Corcoran (1999, p. 3), "Banks put out ATMs because they thought they'd save them money, save them tellers. But it turned out teller demand did not go down much." Second, any savings on the cost of labor may be more than offset by a new capital outlay and the cost of operating and maintaining the new IT systems. Because hardware and software must be updated or replaced at shorter and shorter intervals, the initial investment in IT is just that, the establishment of a recurring expenditure item in the annual budget. According to one source (Corcoran, 1999), introducing a new IT system helped the Washington Water Power Company cut eight jobs and realized a saving of $5,000,000. However, at a cost of $16.5 million, that writer concludes, "It would take 33 years to justify the cost of the system." Third, regular maintenance of IT requires the employment of highly paid IT specialists. As these are added to the workforce, the cost of labor (and thus the cost per unit of service) goes up and the status quo among the various pay scales within the organization is threatened. Fourth, if the IT-based service is successful, the need for additional investments in IT to meet the new cyberdemand for service may consume any alleged savings. Fifth, the ease and convenience of accessing the system may encourage some individuals to forgo the effort to find out what they need to do to complete a transaction with the agency, that is, to complete their part of the coproduction of the service, in favor of trying to get the "system" to do their part for them. As noted by Solomon (2001, p.6), "The Internet has been used for years as a way to keep pesky customers from calling and asking for information. . . . Web sites can also have the unfortunate effect of increased e-mail volume, since customers find it easy to fire off a missive to any address they see on a site—whether it is customer-service oriented e-mail or not."

Another change in the interface between agencies and citizens results from the fact that, at the present, the public expects to get easier access to information it did not use in the past. At the turn of the century, better-educated citizens and issues of governance and accountability resulted in demands for access to minutes of meetings and plans for future services, roads, or any proposed physical developments. During the 1990s, more of this information was expected by the public to be available online as taxpayers were asking their elected officials to follow the example set by government agencies in other jurisdictions. The same was true of school bus routes, information pertaining to schools closing or opening, school activities, highway construction, winter road conditions, agendas of elected and appointed bodies (such as legislatures, local councils, or zoning commissions), resolutions and ordinances, and so on.

These new uses of IT generated requests for additional resources to underwrite the cost of IT personnel, hardware, and software used to meet a demand to elevate the image, if not the virtue, of a given community as a civil society. These requests for additional and new resources, however, came at a time when governments did not experience a corresponding increase in revenues unless taxes were increased. The results in some cases involved reallocation of resources to meet the pressures of current demands, at the possible expense of building the capacity to meet future needs. A possible case in point is the inclination of some communities to opt for IT upgrades for their public libraries at the expense of purchasing hard copies of books or adding new reading areas. The jury is still out on the long-term community implications of the transformation of the civic institution known as "the public library" from a brick-and-mortar facility (where people interact with other people) into a cyberservice (where people use machines even when they may wish to interact with other people).

For students of public management in general and public productivity in particular, the experience with IT during the 1990s yielded some important lessons. First, it seems that IT can reduce the cost of production when it comes to manufacturing because it affects the cost of labor. However, when it comes to the production of services, IT may result in an overall cost increase per unit of service. Second, adding the price of new services to the cost of upgrading the quality of the service via IT still generates only a fraction of the cost that would have resulted from the use of manual labor to achieve the same improvements. This point was not lost on those criticizing the use of a simple productivity measurement to ascertain the benefits of investment in IT, such as Brynjolfsson (1992), Corcoran (1999), Cornwell and Trehan (2000), and Uchitelle (1996). Third, some of the full cost of new IT may be offset by better efficiencies of subprocesses, improvements in the quality of decision making due to better data (and thus better information!), and by the promotion of social values (such as civil society, Etzioni's (2001) notion of communitarism and governance) that contribute directly to quality of life. Fourth, the investment in IT is a recurring expense because hardware and software become obsolete at a growing pace. Fifth, the use of IT may not generate additional revenues or savings that can help underwrite the cost of keeping it relatively up to date, although public pressures to do so may increase.

As more government agencies list their activities, performance measurements, strategic plans, and other information on the Internet, the work of administrators who are looking for solutions to pressing problems becomes easier. The wealth of information on the Internet can provide administrators who are eager to improve productivity with ideas and contacts for exploring the applicability to their own situations of approaches and practices that proved successful elsewhere. Internet sources can, however, be problematic. First, the listing of information is just that— listing. The validity and reliability of data and information that is posted on the Internet cannot be assumed. With the help of clever editing and language use, the truths of minor success stories or minor failures may be misrepresented. A minor achievement or defeat may be presented as something else to allow agencies and their administrators to take credit for something they do not really deserve. An agency's Web page may be justified as a means for providing the public with information and for enhancing accountability. However, whether intended or not, it can also evolve into another medium for promoting the image of top administrators. Second, citizens who read the information about an agency's performance in another community might ask questions and anticipate the same level of service from their own government agencies. The problem with these unwarranted pressures for service, or criticism of agencies for lack of it, is that the listed information may be incorrect, or the conditions under which the other government or agency is working are very different from the ones under which the agency in question operates. Consider the frustration and anger of Hungarian students who participated in an exchange program with Dutch universities. Upon returning to Hungary they wanted to receive from the Hungarian government all the benefits the Dutch students were privy to, even though at the time (early 1990s) the Hungarian economy could not support it. In this example the students witnessed firsthand the differences between the relevant agencies in the two countries, however, one can see that the same impressions that may lead to misplaced expectations can be acquired by surfing the Internet and reading about the amenities offered to customers of a given agency in another locality. Elsewhere (Halachmi 1996, 1997; Keulen and Kuin 1996) I have discussed at length the dysfunctional aspect of what I call the "CNN Syndrome", watching a news story (that may be inaccurate) about other parts of the world and developing misplaced expectations about the performance of one's own government, or suspecting that one's own government is guilty of the same inefficiencies, ineffectiveness, or ethical problems of which other governments are being accused. Thus I do not dwell on this issue here. However, the reader should be aware that stories about gains in efficiencies and effectiveness due to innovative use of IT are attention-getters. The weekly and daily reports on IT developments in leading American newspapers such as *The New York Times* and *The Wall Street Journal*, and in magazines such as *Newsweek*, *Time*, and *U.S. News and World Report*, are a case in point.

One of the greatest contributions of IT to productivity is the standardization of service. Use of older technology involved many interpersonal contacts between service providers and service recipients. These interpersonal contacts were influenced (or were assumed to be influenced) by issues that concerned the service provider or the service recipients. Whether actual or assumed, any differences between the sociodemographic profiles of the provider and the recipient could have contributed to the quality of the service, whether requests were approved or denied. Those interacting with public employees earlier in the day could have gotten different service and had different experiences than those seeking the very same service at the end of the day, when employees were tired or more frustrated due to lack of resources and work overload. Elimination of the interpersonal interaction reduced, in some cases, service recipients' concerns about a possible negative bias against them due to any one of their socio-demographic and physical attributes such as wealth, education, age, gender, race, religion, ethic origin, height, weight, hair, attractiveness, or sexual preference.

As a result of using IT, decisions are more likely to be rendered on the basis of hard facts. When the fog and noise that result from the service provider's predisposition, past experiences, unconscious biases, and state of health and alertness are reduced, rules and regulations are likely to be applied more equally, thus allowing all citizens to be treated equally before the law. Indeed, when the Tennessee Department of Human Services (DHS) introduced its new interactive system for determining welfare eligibility, one consideration was to standardize service across the state (Halachmi, 2000). DHS wanted to ensure that an eligibility decision would be a function of the data in each case and not a function of whether the applicant lived in an urban or a rural area, or the training and qualifications of the employee on duty at the time of the application. DHS found that not only was the quality of decisions improved, but there were some additional benefits such as elimination of the inventories of various forms, fewer cases when the wrong forms were used, and reduction in the number of cases in which information was lost due to filing errors or mishandling of documents.

The productivity benefits of IT need to be considered along with their possible dysfunctional attributes. At this juncture, the reader should consider at least the following dysfunctions of IT.

The first dysfunction is that IT may prolong, complicate, and interfere with the delivery of services to which citizens are entitled. Such a dysfunction may result from the alienation, confusion, and mistrust of IT by those who are poorly educated or computer-illiterate. Many citizens who are seeking government services are not skilled in using IT and are intimidated or upset when they encounter a machine rather than a human being, even on the other end of a telephone line. As I pointed out earlier, agencies would have to keep personnel on hand to assist those incapable of using IT to interact with the government, or those who experience problems when attempting to do so. Problematic with the last group is that the frustration experienced during an attempt to connect electronically may influence the initial interaction with the agency following the failed attempt. Such adverse influences on clients' attitudes are even more likely to occur when service recipients are requested, upon contacting the agency for the first time, to use the electronic interface. Lack of goodwill and reluctance to cooperate or provide accurate information to the agency may slow the process of providing the service, while forcing the agency to waste resources to overcome those feelings.

A second dysfunction of IT is that for some citizens it is the instrument that denies them the human attention they crave. Some service recipients are looking for the opportunity to interact with other people as much as they are looking to secure a given government service. Many people visit government agencies not only in pursuit of specific services but also in search of attention or sympathy. The electronic interface that denies them the opportunity to meet that need may influence their perception of the quality of the service, or the method by which they prefer to secure it: online or through face-to-face interactions with agency employees. For those who crave attention and for those who have difficulty navigating through the electronic maze, interaction with government entities may become a frustration. A service recipient feeling that he or she is being treated as just another case results in the dehumanizing of the experience of dealing with the government and may be at a cost to the provider. For example, evoking such sentiments may not be conducive to or consistent with the goals of many social services.

A third dysfunction of IT is that the lack of an interpersonal interaction during the intake phase of a social service, or during many points of time as the service is being provided, may undermine the efficient use of agency resources. The well-trained employee of a government agency may see beyond the mere facts and deal with a given case in a better way, for example, by involving other elements of the agency or by mobilizing a more comprehensive response than the programmed answer that is adequate for an average case but not for the one under consideration. This human involvement, which calls for the use of tacit knowledge and experience, may save the agency resources by better targeting the solution to deal with the real problem rather than an apparent or nominal issue. A possible risk of virtual intake is that, on the basis of fact alone, an agency may authorize something that ends up depleting its resources in vain. A well-trained employee might be able to catch such aberrations better than a machine.

The fourth dysfunction of IT has to do with an important IT-related pathology, namely, the inability of organizations to evolve and to keep pace with the changes in technology. Due to this pathology agencies fail to change, reform, and reorganize for retaining or developing the necessary capacity to correct mistakes or compensate for inadequacies of the IT for addressing the concerns of citizens at the individual level. To be sure, although information systems are designed to deal with a whole class of residents they are not always geared to deal with the unique circumstances of individual citizens. Overriding information systems in order to correct mistakes or in order to comply with the spirit or the letter of the law in particular case can be very difficult and time consuming and thus very expensive to the involved citizen and agency. Addressing the prospect that with the advent of IT in government electronic red tape may intensify traditional bureaucracy Peled (2001) points out that because old systems are rarely retired government agencies have electronic mounds that slow operations (and add electronic red tape). This, in turn, fosters what Peled (2001) calls "infocrats," a new class of employees with their own vested interests of protecting the existing compatibility (or incompatibility) of old and new information systems. The resulting increase in the complexity of the bureaucratic process due to the use of incompatible IT systems, inconsistent definitions of common variables in databases that are used by various agencies (e.g., the different ways the Census Bureau and IRS define "household" and "family"), and the growing difficulty of correcting "bad" information across the board undermines productivity.

## III.  HOW IT INFLUENCES ORGANIZATIONAL BEHAVIOR

As IT changes the nature of the interface between organization and environment, it also changes the dynamic and nature of the interface among employees within the organization. These changes occur where the individual interacts with other individuals, individual employees interact with the group, and where the group interacts with other groups. Addressing all these changes in depth is beyond the scope of this chapter. Thus I say only few words on this important issue as it has the potential of having a profound effect on organizational productivity.

IT influences the frequency and depth of interpersonal interactions. Before the advent of IT, many organizational business processes were subroutines in a long assembly-linelike process. Under these circumstances an employee's work was greatly influenced by the work performed by the worker before him or her. Better coupling of the two steps in the process led to frequent contact in coordinating events and procedures, assuring smooth progress of the "assembly" process. Today, due to developments in IT, the assembly line is gone. The one-stop shop is the prevailing model and coordination among employees results from the use of expert software that ensures that what one employee is doing does not interfere with what other employees need to do. At best, comments in the electronic file and email replace the memorandum, telephone calls, and face-to-face meetings. Thus employees do not know each other as coworkers anymore. Warm and fuzzy camaraderie and friendship have been replaced by matter-of-fact comments from a template. This adverse development in the nature of interpersonal relations is even more likely to take place due to telecommuting at the second level of interactions: the individual and the group. As I have pointed out elsewhere (Halachmi, 1991), IT changes the social entity we call "work group" into a work-group—a temporary and artificial entity that comes into being when several people who work independently of each other are using a common network, database, and the like. These people may or may not know each other; they may not even be aware of the identity of other users of the "system." Without the sense of belonging to the same group, they are likely to pay little attention to each other and offer no support or help. Unlike the dynamics that were revealed by the Hawthorne studies (Sheldrake, 1997), such a temporary collection of individuals has no group norms, depriving the organization of one of the most potent modes of influencing individual behavior. Under these circumstances, it is no longer true that the sum of the members' contributions to the organization is greater than the arithmetic addition of the members' contributions. To be sure, telecommuting allows the organization to facilitate greater individual flexibility in the case of some members. Such members may be able to hold jobs while raising children, taking care of old parents, or avoiding the cost of expensive daily commute, rent, babysitting, and so on. The organization may also save on real estate expenses, heating and cooling, security, parking, and the like while allowing cities to reduce pollution, consumption of gasoline, and the need to widen access roads. However, the tradeoff for this is the loss of cross-fertilization, the commitment and loyalty to the organization that results from having the sense of belonging to a work group. For such employees, the reference group is likely to become the professional group, including everything that goes with it (e.g., when incongruity occurs between organizational and professional norms or interests, the latter would prevail, to the detriment of the organization).

IT changes employees' behavior in many other respects, but due to space limitations, only two other interrelated instances are mentioned here: IT as the cause of change in work habits and IT as the means for exposing job performance for what it is. Both of these changes have direct implications for productivity.

Because of new computer capabilities in the areas of word processing, database management, and spreadsheets, managers at all levels of organizations have a lesser need for support staff to type routine documents, conduct simple analyses, or create and study graphic presentations of data. The ease with which these tasks can be accomplished these days weakens claims that managers (senior middle-level managers in particular) should leave such activities to workers with lower salaries. Carrying out such tasks allows managers to avoid mistakes that often surface when a worker transcribes someone else's handwritten document or a dictation, and saves time managers used to spend proofreading before signing common documents. By the same token, first-hand impressions that result from the building of and experimenting with spreadsheets, analyses of data, or creation of graphic presentations, can provide managers (at the senior middle level, and the junior executive level when the complexity and amount of data are not too overwhelming) with greater insights than those they are likely to gain when they receive the finished product from an aide. An added bonus is that such managers can have better control of rumors and misinformation that result when the contents of draft memoranda, financial or data analyses, or modes are leaked.

The ability of managers to be self-sufficient in the creation of documents that involve the use of word processing, database management, spreadsheets, and graphic presentations (of data) can also influence how they are viewed by subordinates. Before the great advances in personal computers and networks, employees had limited access to data and could not discern which data were available to their superiors. Thus, if a senior manager made a decision that surprised one of his or her subordinates, the latter was forced to assume that the decision maker had additional data that made such a choice the right one. Today, when most employees have access to virtually all the data that are available to their superiors, a questionable choice may raise doubts concerning the management skills and talent of the decision maker. Thus IT changes the way managers must earn the respect of subordinates. Managers who lack very good computer skills for carrying out data analysis and spreadsheet and graphic presentations of data may undermine their analytical capacity and thus their careers. However, junior employees with outstanding skills in these areas can distinguish themselves quickly and travel on the fast track to senior positions, as such skills can compensate for inexperience.

## IV. WHAT CAN MANAGERS DO TO REAP THE PRODUCTIVITY BENEFITS OF IT?

It seems that the best way for managers to receive the benefits of IT without experiencing much of its possible dysfunctional implications is to take a proactive stand. Greater productivity is likely to result when the organization takes action to exploit new possibilities for accomplishing the agency's mission. IT allows organizations to offer easier and better access to information about the services they render. With proper use of IT, the interface between clients (customers) and service providers does not have to be time- or place-specific. Providers and recipients of services do not have to meet at a specific time in a specific place to "produce" the service. Even more important is the ability of IT to allow reengineering of the business process that is used to provide the service. Business process reengineering allows the retrieval and dissemination of information in ways that save both government employees and their clients precious time, making certain steps for verifying information or coordinating benefits with other agencies unnecessary. Thus, for example, when a person applies for welfare in Tennessee for the first time, verifying employment history, ages of children and legal custody, marital status, and so on is done by the retrieval of information from other states' databanks, which are in turn updated. Not having to search for support documents used to calculate eligibility for welfare benefits allows the Department of Human Services to conclude the intake interview by printing the claimant a check or making a direct deposit to a bank account.

Analysis of data reflecting the rate at which the public attempts to contact an agency (or its Web site), and the distribution of this contact according to time of day, time of year, and area of state, can provide managers with better ideas about trends and patterns of demands for service. By learning the history of such patterns, managers may be able to notice a developing change and be ready to address it. The use of maps with various overlays can help managers communicate with legislators and employees of other agencies where the centers for demands (or concentration of problems) are and see how these may have changed since an earlier period. In particular, analysis of patterns of demands for service may alert managers to services that used to be important but are becoming less important and to possible candidates for termination or outsourcing.

By the same token that managers must be proactive to harvest the benefits of IT, they need to be as active in taking steps to minimize the possible adverse effects of IT on the organization. As pointed out earlier, IT changes the interface of individual employees with peers and the group, along with the interactions among various groups at the workplace. As children grow up with "playstations," computer games, and the like, they are better adapted to deal with man–machine interaction than with person-to-person interaction. As primary and secondary schoolwork involve greater and greater use of IT, and as long-distance learning becomes more common for post-secondary education, lack of opportunities for learning how to socialize may take a toll. This alarming possibility is even more credible in the case of telecommuters. Because government services must retain their human nature, government employees must be able to empathize and relate to others as human beings. Employees must develop such capacity to satisfy the need for belonging, have a notion of self-identity, and be committed and loyal to the organization.

Some of the possible dysfunctions of IT can be addressed by any organization without much effort if the need for a remedy is recognized and the will to perform it exists. To preempt possible problems that result when employees have not developed social skills before beginning work or when they have missed opportunities to be socialized due to heavy use of IT and telecommuting, managers must develop a "social program." Organizations must create artificial opportunities for employees to meet with one another face-to-face even when such meetings are not necessary for accomplishing a specific task. Employees must have opportunities to compensate for the networking and camaraderie they miss through attending virtual meetings and limiting their direct interactions to email. By the same token, employees should have opportunities to meet some of the people who make up their agency's clientele or target population. They should develop firsthand impressions of who the agency deals with so that they are not dependent on a mental idea or abstract image of who they are.

Common budget requests from agencies include specific amounts for new IT, maintenance, or replacement of existing IT. However, agencies do not ask for any resources to underwrite the cost of counteracting the dysfunctions of IT. As we start the new millennium, it is time for managers to wake up and realize the need to address the human side of the enterprise by providing opportunities for employees to remedy the disappearing social fabric of the organization.

## REFERENCES

Brynjolfsson, E. (1992). *The productivity paradox of information technology: Review and assessment*. Available at http://ccs.mit.edu/papers/CCSWP130/ccswp130.html.

Corcoran, C. T. (1999). *We have computers. Why aren't we more productive*? Available at http://salon.com/tech/feature/1999/08/23/productivity.

Cornwell, C., Trehan, B. (2000). *Information technology and productivity*. Federal Reserve Bank of San Francisco economic letter no. 2000-34. November 10, pp. 1–4. Available at http://www.frbsf.org/econrsrch/wklyltr/2000/el2000-34.html.

Etzioni, A. (2001). *Next: The Road to the Good Society*. New York: Basic.

Halachmi, A. (1991). Productivity and information technology: Emerging issues and considerations. *Public Product. Manage. Rev.* XIV(4):327–350.

Halachmi, A. (1994). IRM: Perspectives, issues and implications. *Int. J. Public Admin.* 17(1): 209–252.

Halachmi, A. (1995). Preparing the public workforce for the twenty first century: The challenge. *Work Study* 44(2):8–13.

Halachmi, A. (1996). Enduring challenges of public sector productivity: A look at the issues of 1990's and beyond. *Indian J. Public Admin.* 42(4):642–664.

Halachmi, A. (1997). Government reforms and public productivity: Do we have all the answers? *Work Study* 46(7):233–245.

Halachmi, A. (2000). Information technology and performance measurement. *Nat. Product. Rev.* 19(3):87–92.

Keulen, M., Kuin, R. (1996). *En interview met Prof. dr. A. Halachmi. InterDisciplinar, Marrt 1996*. The Netherlands: University of Twente.

Krohe, J. Jr. (1993). The productivity pit. In: Schhellenberg, K., ed. (1996). Computers in Society. Gilford, CT: Dushkin, pp. 55–59.

New York Times (2001). *A census shows high Internet presence*. July 6. Available at http://www.nytimes.com/aponline/AP-Census-Computers.html.

O'Conner, K., Sabato, L. J. (2002). *Essentials of American Government*. New York: Longman.

Peled, A. (2001). Do computers cut red tape? *Am. Rev. Public Admin.* 31:414–435.

Sheldrake, J. (1997). *Management Theory: From Taylorism to Japanization*. Boston: Thomson.

Solomon, P. (2001). Computer service representative. *NetGov, supplement to Gov. Tech.* October, pp. 5–8.

Uchitelle, L. (1996). What has the computer done for us lately? *New York Times, December* 8: pp. 1–4.

# 38

# Productivity Improvement Resources

## In Print and on the Web

**MARC HOLZER**
*Rutgers, The State University of New Jersey, Newark, New Jersey, U.S.A.*

**SEOK-HWAN LEE**
*The Catholic University of Korea, Songsim Campus, South Korea*

## I. INTRODUCTION

Productivity improvement is comprehensive in scope and requires multiple approaches in which elements of improvement are effectively connected to each other. It is often difficult, however, for public sector scholars and practitioners to find appropriately helpful information to apply to specific organizational contexts.

Public sector productivity improvement resources are widely scattered in print or on the Web. It is useful, therefore, to build a database integrating all information relevant to productivity improvement in the public sector. This chapter provides some such recent information. Of course, it is important to keep updating these resources as new strategies and programs emerge. Although it is impossible to list all publications and reports due to limited space, this chapter introduces selected collections, including textbooks, handbooks, recent journal articles, government reports, professional assocation-related publications, and other comprehensive resources on the Web. These collections reflect approaches to management for productivity and performance, performance measurement and analysis, management of human resources, and technology issues. Some relevant resources in the private sector have also been included.

## II.   PRODUCTIVITY IMPROVEMENT RESOURCES IN PRINT AND ON THE WEB

### A.   Textbooks, Handbooks, and Encyclopedias

1.   Management for Productivity and Performance

Productivity improvement is a complicated concept. Understanding productivity improvement in the public sector requires a comprehensive approach. The publications below represent an array of important issues associated with public sector productivity in general.

Bass, M. D. (1985). *Leadership, Performance Beyond Expectations*. New York: Free Press. Available at < http://www.Simonsays.com > .

Berman, E. (1998). *Productivity in Public and Nonprofit Organizations*. Thousand Oaks, CA: SAGE. Available at < http://www.sagepub.com > .

Forsythe, D. W. (2001). *Quicker Better Cheaper: Managing Performance in American Government*. Albany, NY: Rockefeller Institute Press. Available at < http://www.sunypress.edu > .

Groccia, J. E., Miller, J. E., eds. (1998). *Enhancing Productivity: Administrative, Instructional, and Technological Strategies*. San Francisco: Jossey-Bass. Available at < http://www.josseybass.com > .

Halachmi, A., Holzer, M., eds. (1995). *Competent Government: Theory and Practices: The Best of Public Productivity and Management Review, 1985–1993*. Burke, VA: Chatelaine. Available at < http://www.chatpress.com > .

Holzer, M., ed. (1992). *Public Productivity Handbook*, New York: Marcel Dekker. Available at < http://www.dekker.com > .

Holzer, M., Callahan, K. (1998). *Government at Work: Best Practices and Model Programs*. Thousand Oaks, CA: SAGE. Available at < http://www.sagepub.com > .

Holzer, M., Gabrielian, V., eds. (1996). *Case Studies in Productive Public Management: From Public Productivity & Management Review*. Burke, VA: Chatelaine. Available at < http://www.chatpress.com > .

Holzer, M., Halachmi, A., eds. (1986). *Strategic Issues in Public Sector Productivity: The Best of Public Productivity Review, 1975–1985*. San Francisco: Jossey-Bass. Available at < http://www.josseybass.com > .

Osborne, D., Gaebler, T., (1992). *Reinventing Government: How the Entrepreneurial Spirit Is Transforming the Public Sector*. Reading, MA: Addison-Wesley. Available at < http://www.awl.com > .

Popovich, M., ed. (1998). *Creating High-Performance Government Organizations: A Practical Guide for Public Managers*. San Francisco: Jossey-Bass. Available at < http://www.josseybass.com > .

2.   Performance Measures and Analysis

Performance measures and evaluations are an important part of productivity improvement. Unless we measure output and outcomes of productivity improvement efforts, there is no way to track what public agencies have accomplished and what they will have to improve in the next iteration. Although some may argue that it is more difficult to measure the output and outcomes in the public sector than in the private sector—because public organizations' goals are ambiguous and complicated—extensive efforts among scholars and practitioners have been directed to just those concerns. Those efforts indicate that it is indeed possible to measure the performance and productivity of public organizations, if the measures are carefully designed and comprehensive in scope. The following publications are products of some of these endeavors.

Ammons, D. N. (1996). *Municipal Benchmarks: Assessing Local Performance and Establishing Community Standards.* Thousand Oaks, CA: Sage. Available at http://www.sagepub.com >.

Broom, C., Jackson, M., Vogelsang Coombs, V., Harris, J. (1998). *Performance Measurement: Concepts and Techniques.* Washington, DC: American Society for Public Administration. Available at < http://www. aspanet.org/store/publications. html >.

Epstein, P. (1992). *Measuring the performance of public service.* In: Holzer, M., ed. Public Productivity Handbook. New York: Marcel Dekker, pp. 161–194. Available at < http://www.dekker.com/index.jsp >.

Epstein, P. D. (1988). *Using Performance Measurement in Local Government: A Guide to Improving Decisions, Performance, and Accountability.* New York: National Civic League Press. Available at < http://www.ncl.org >.

Farquhar, C. R. (2000). *Goverments Get Focused on Results: Integrating Performance Measurement into Management Decision Making.* Ottawa, ON: Conference Board of Canada. Available at < http://www.conferenceboard.ca >.

Gianakis, G. (1996). Integrating performance measurement and budgeting. In: Halachmi A., Bouckaert G., eds. *Organizational Performance and Measurement in Public Sector. Toward Service, Effort and Accomplishment Reporting.* Westport, CT: Quorum. Available at < http://info.greenwood.com >.

Halachmi, A., ed. (1999). *Performance and Quality Measurement in Government.* Burke, VA: Chatelaine. Available at < http://www.chatpress.com >.

Halachmi, A., Bouckaert, G., eds. (1996). *Organizational Performance and Measurement in the Public Sector: Toward Service, Effort and Accomplishment Reporting.* Westport, CT: Quorum. Available at < http://www.info.greenwood.com >.

Hatry, H. (2000). *Performance Measurement: Getting Results.* Washington, DC: Urban Institute Press. Available at < http://www.urban.org/uipress/uip_titles. html >.

Hatry, H. P., Marcotte, J. E., Van Houten, T., Weiss, C. H. (1998). *Customer Surveys for Agency Managers: What Managers Need to Know.* Washington, DC: Urban Institute Press. Available at < http://www.urban.org/uipress/uip_titles.html >.

Hatry, P., Fisk, D. (1992). Measuring productivity in the public sector. In: Holzer, M., ed. *Public Productivity Handbook.* New York: Marcel Dekker, pp. 139–160. Available at < http://www.dekker.com/index.jsp >.

Holzer, M. (1992). Mastering public productivity improvement. In: Holzer, M., ed. *Public Productivity Handbook.* New York: Marcel Dekker. Available at < http://www.dekker.com/index.jsp >.

Holzer, M., Callahan, K. (1998). *Government at Work: Best Practices and Model Programs.* Thousand Oaks, CA: SAGE. Available at < http://www.sagepub. com >.

Newcomer, K., ed. (1997). *Using Performance Measurement to Improve Public and Nonprofit Programs. New Directions for Evaluation.* San Francisco: Jossey-Bass. Available at < http://www.josseybass.com >.

*Public Performance and Management Review (Formerly Public Productivity and Management Review)*. Available at < http://www.sagepub.co.uk > .

Wholey, J., Hatry, H., Newcomer, K., eds. (1994). *Handbook of Practical Program Evaluation*, San Francisco: Jossey-Bass. Available at < http://www.josseybass.com > .

## 3.  Managing Human Resources for Productivity

Productivity improvement requires a comprehensive approach, ranging from top management support to feedback and correction on budget management decisions; managing human resources is an essential element of such improvement. We cannot expect greater productivity from those who are disaffected and may be considering leaving their organizations. Productivity improvement is possible only when people at all levels in an organization are committed to the effort in a win–win manner. In the long run, it is the people in the organization who control the productivity of the organization.

The following publications pay special attention to the importance of human resource management for productivity.

Aaron, B., Najita, J. M., Stern, J. L., eds. (1989). *Public Sector Bargaining*. Washington, DC: Bureau of National Affairs, Inc. Available at < http://www.bna.com/ > .

Cappelli, P., ed. (1999). *Employment Practices and Business Strategy*. Oxford, UK: Oxford University Press. Available at < http://www.oup.co.uk > .

Carrel, M. R., Heavrin, C. (1991). *Collective Bargaining and Labor Relations: Cases, Practice, and Law*. 3rd ed. New York: Maxwell Macmillan. Available at < http://www.macmillan.com > .

Cascio, W. F. (1986). *Managing Human Resources: Productivity, Quality of Work Life, Profits*. New York: McGraw-Hill. Available at < http://mcgraw-hill.com > .

Champagne, P. J., McAfee, R. B. (1989). *Motivating Strategies for Performance and Productivity: A Guide to Human Resource Development*. New York: Quorum. Available at < http://info.greenwood.com > .

Coleman, C. J. (1990). *Managing Labor Relations in the Public Sector*. San Francisco: Jossey-Bass. Available at < http://www.josseybass.com > .

Cook, W. N. (1990). *Labor–Management Cooperation*. Kalamazoo, MI: W.E. Upjohn Institute for Employment Research. Available at < http://www.upjohninst.org/ > .

Csoka, L. S. (1995). *Performance Enhancement: Harnessing Potential for Productivity: A Research Report*. New York: Conference Board. Available at < http://www.conference-board.org > .

Duane, M. J. (1993). *The Grievance Process in Labor–Management Cooperation*. Westport, CT: Quorum. Available at < http://info.greenwood.com > .

Flamholtz, E. G., Das, T. K., eds. (1984). Human Resource Management and Productivity: State of the Art and Future Prospects. Los Angeles: University of California, Los Angeles.

Grindle, M. S., ed. (1997). *Getting Good Government: Capacity Building in the Public Sectors of Developing Countries*. Cambridge, MA: Harvard University Press. Available at < http://www.hbsp.harvard.edu > .

Holoviak, S. J., Sipkoff, S. S. (1987). *Managing Human Productivity: People Are Your Best Investment.* New York: Praeger. Available at < http://info.greenwood. com >.

Kershen, H., ed. (1983a). *Labor–Management Relations Among Government Employees.* Farmingdale, NY: Baywood. Available at < http://www.baywood.com >.

Kershen, H., ed. (1983b). *Collective Bargaining by Government Workers: The Public Employee.* Farmingdale, NY: Baywood. Available at < http://www.baywood. com >.

Levine, M., Hagburg, E. C., eds. (1979). *Labor Relations in the Public Sector: Readings, Cases, and Experimental Exercises.* Salt Lake, UT: Brighton.

Lewin, D., Feuille, P., Kochan, T. A., eds. (1981). *Public Sector Labor Relations: Analysis and Readings.* 2nd ed. Sun Lakes, AZ: Horton.

McKevitt, D. (1998). *Managing Core Public Services.* Malden, MA: Blackwell. Available at < http://www.blackwellpub.com >.

Saran, R., Sheldrake, J., eds. (1988). *Public Sector Bargaining in the 1980s.* Brookfield, VT: Avebury.

Volcker, P. A. (1990). *Leadership for America: Rebuilding the Public Service—The Report of the National Commission on the Public Service and the Task Force Reports to the National Commission on the Public Service.* Lexington, MA: Lexington.

Werther, W.B., Ruch, W.A., McClure, L. (1986). *Productivity Through People.* New York: West. Available at < http://www.westgroup.com >.

## 4. Technologies and Productivity

The use of new organizational technologies is increasingly important to the public and the private sectors. Information technology, for example, has recently received great attention. The general expectation is that many technologies will lead to productivity gains in an organization. Such technologies can enhance productivity only when organizational members are willing to accept a new, technologically rich, environment. New technologies, to be successfully adopted and utilized, require innovative and revitalized organizational cultures. The publications listed below reflect technology-1 oriented approaches to productivity improvement.

Banker, R. D., Kauffman, R. J., Mahmood, M. A. (1993). *Strategic Information Technology Management: Perspectives on Organizational Growth and Competitive Advantage.* Harrisburg, PA: Idea Group. Available at < http://www.idea-group.com >.

Keyes, J. (1995). *Solving the Productivity Paradox: TQM for Computer Professionals.* New York: McGraw-Hill. Available at < http://mcgraw-hill.com >.

Lehmann, E. J., ed. (1986). *Directory of Federal & State Business Assistance: A Guide for New and Growing Companies.* Springfield, VA: National Technical Information Service. Available at < http://www.ntis.gov >.

Lucas, H. C., Jr. (1999). *Information Technology and the Productivity Paradox: Assessing the Value of the Investment in IT.* New York: Oxford University Press. Available at < http://www.oup.co.uk >.

Murphy, J. W., Pardeck, J. T. (1986). *Technology and Human Productivity: Challenges for the Future.* Westport, CT: Quorum. Available at < http://info.greenwood. com >.

Pohjola, M., ed. (2001). *Information Technology, Productivity, and Economic Growth: International Evidence and Implications for Economic Development.* New York: Oxford University Press. Available at < http://www.oup.co.uk > .

Willcocks, L. P., Lester, S. (1999). *Beyond the IT Productivity Paradox.* New York: Wiley. Available at < http://www.wiley.com > .

## B. Recent Journal Articles and Partial List of Professional Journals with Particular Attention to Productivity and Performance Improvement

In addition to textbooks and handbooks, journal articles are important sources for productivity improvement. These articles provide readers with real solutions and policy suggestions based on either empirical studies or through literature reviews. These are monthly, bimonthly, or quarterly professional journals. Some have their own Web sites in which each journal's aim and focus are provided.

### 1. Recent Journal Articles in the Field of Productivity Improvement

Ammons, D. N. (2000). Benchmarking as a performance management tool: experiences among municipalities in North Carolina. *J. Public Budget. Account. Finan. Manage.* 12(1):106–124.

Ammons, D. N. (2002). Performance measurement and managerial thinking. *Public Perform. Manage. Rev.* 25(4):344.

Ammons, D. N., Condrey, S. E. (1991). Performance appraisal in local government: warranty conditions. *Public Product. Manage. Rev.* 14:253–266.

Ammons, D. N., Coe, C., Lombardo, M. (2001). Performance comparison projects in local government: participants' perspective. Public Admin. Rev. 61(1): 100–110. Available at < http://www.aspanet.org/publications/par/index2.html > .

Bajjaly, S. T. (1999). Managing emerging information systems in the public sector. *Public Product. Manage. Rev.* 23(1):40–47.

Balfour, D. L., Wechsler, B. (1991). Commitment, performance, and productivity in public organizations. *Public Product. Manage. Rev.* 14:355–368.

Balfour, D. L., Wechsler, B. (1996). Organizational commitment: Antecedents and outcomes in public organizations. *Public Product. Manage. Rev.,* 19:256–277.

Berman, E.M. (1997). Dealing with cynical citizens. *Public Admin. Rev.* 58(2): 105–112.

Berman, E. M. (1998). Productivity enhancement efforts in public and nonprofit organizations. *Public Product. Manage. Rev.* 22(2):207–219.

Berman, E. M. (1999). Using performance measurement in human resource management. *Rev. Public Person. Admin.* 19(2):5–12.

Berman, E. M. (2002). How useful is performance measurement. *Public Perform. Manage. Rev.* 25(4):348

Berman, E. M., Wang, X. H. (2000). Performance measurement in U.S. counties: capacity for reform. *Public Admin. Rev.* 60(5):409–420.

Berman, E. M., West, J. P. (1998). Productivity enhancement efforts in public and nonprofit organizations. *Public Product. Manage. Rev.* 22:207–219.

Bernstein, D. J. (1999). Comments on Perrin's effective use and misuse of performance measurement. *Am. J. Eval.* 20:85–93.

Bouckaert, G. (2002a). Performance measurement and management: the Achilles heel in administrative modernization. *Public Perform. Manage. Rev.* 25(4):359

Bouckaert, G. (2002b). Performance measurement: getting results. *Public Perform. Manage. Rev.* 25(4):329.

Boyne, G. A. (2002). Total quality management and performance: an evaluation of the evidence and lessons for research on public organizations. *Public Perform. Manage. Rev.* 26(2):111.

Brundney, J. L., Condrey, S. E. (1993), Pay for performance: explaining the differences in managerial motivation. *Public Product. Manage. Rev.* 17:129–144.

Bryson, J. M., Cunningham, G. L., Lokkesmoe, K. J. (2002). What to do when stakeholders matter: the case of problem formulation for the African American men project of Hennepin. *Public Admin. Rev.* 62(5):568–584.

Callahan, K. (2001). Results-oriented government: citizen involvement in performance measurement. Proceedings of the Winelands Conference, Stellenbosch, South Africa, September 12–15, 2001.

De Lancer Julnes, P., Holzer, M. (2001). Promoting the utilization of performance measures in public organizations: an empirical study of factors affecting adoption and implementation. *Public Admin. Rev.* 61:693–708.

Denhardt, R., Denhardt, J, V. (2000). The new public service: serving rather than steering. *Public Admin. Rev.* 60(4):549–559.

Epstein, J., Olsen, R. T. (1996). Managing for outcomes: lessons learned by state and local government. *Public Manager* 25:41–44.

Epstein, P., Wray, L., Marshall, M., Grifel, S. (2000). Engaging citizens in achieving results that matter: a model for effective 21st century governance. Proceedings of the ASPA CAP Symposium on Results-Oriented Government, February.

Fine, T. (1999). What is the difference between performance measurement and benchmarking? *PM Public Manage.* 81(1):24–25.

Fischer, R. J. (1994a). An overview of performance measurement. *Public Manage.* 77(9):s2–s8.

Fischer, R. J. (1994b). An overview of performance measurement. *Public Manage.* 76:2–8.

Foltin, C. (1999). State and local government performance: It's time to measure up! *Gov. Account. J.* 48(1):40–46.

Garsombke, H. P., Schrad, J. (1999). Performance measurement systems: results from a city and state survey. *Gov. Finan. Rev.*, 15:9–12.

Gooden, S. T. (2001). That old-time religion: efficiency, benchmarking, and productivity. *Public Admin. Rev.* 61(1):116–120.

Grifel, S. S. (1993). Performance measurement and budgeting decision making. *Public Product.Manage.Rev.* 16(4):403–407. Available at < http://www.sagepub.com >.

Grifel, S. S. (1994). Organizational culture: Its importance in performance measurement. *Public Manage.* 76:19–20.

Grizzle, G. A. (2002). Performance measurement and dysfunction: the dark side of quantifying work. *Public Perform. Manage. Rev.* 25(4):363.

Halachmi, A. (2002). Performance measurement, accountability, and improved performance. *Public Perform. Manage. Rev.* 25(4):370.

Hatry, H. (1999). *Performance Measurement: Getting Results.* Washington, DC: Urban Institute Press.

Hatry, H, P. (2002). Performance measurement: fashions and fallacies. *Public Perform. Manage. Rev.* 25(4):352.

Hendon, C. (1999). Performance budgeting in Florida—Half way there. *J. Public Budget. Account. Finan. Manage.* 11(4):670–679.

Hernandez, D. (2002). Local government performance measurement. *PM Public Manage.* 84(9):10–11.

Holzer, M., Halachmi, A. (1996). Measurement as a means of accountability. *Int. J. Public Admin.* 19(11&12):1921–1943. Available at < http://www.dekker.com/ servlet/product/productid/PAD/toc/ > .

Holzer, M., Lee, S-H. (1999). Labor–management tension and partnership: Where are we? What should we do? *Int. Rev. Public Admin.* 4:33–44.

Ittner, C. D. (2002). Determinants of performance measure choices in worker incentive plans. *J. Labor Econ.* 20(2):58–90.

Jones, D. S. (2001). Performance measurement and budgetary reform in the Singapore civil service. *J. Public Budget. Account. Finan. Manage.* 13(4):485–511.

Julnes, P. L. (2001). Does participation increase perceptions of usefulness? An evaluation of a participatory approach to the development of performance measures. *Public Perform. Manage. Rev.* 24(4):403–418.

Julnes, P. L., Holzer, M. (2001). Promoting the utilization of performance measures in public organizations: an empirical study of factors affecting adoption and implementation. *Public Admin. Rev.* 61(6):693–708.

Jurkiewicz, C. L., Massey, T. K. Jr., Brown, R. G. (1998). Motivation in public and private organizations: a comparative study. *Public Product. Manage. Rev.* 21: 230–250.

Kaczmarczyk, S. (2002). Measuring the performance of innovative workplaces. *J. Facilities Manage.* 1(2):163–176.

Kearney, R., Berman, E. (1999). *Public Sector Performance: Management, Motivation and Measurement*. New York: Westview.

Kelly, J. M. (2002a). A multiple-indicator approach to municipal service evaluation: correlating performance measurement and citizen satisfaction across jurisdictions. *Public Admin. Rev.* 62(5):610–621.

Kelly, J. M. (2002b). Why we should take performance measurement on faith (facts being hard to come by and not terribly important). *Public Perform. Manage. Rev.* 25(4):375

King, C. S., et al. (1998). The question of participation: toward authentic public participation in public administration. *Public Admin. Rev.* 58(3):317–327.

Kopcynski, M., Lombardo, M. (1999). Comparative performance measurement: insights and lessons learned from a consortium effort. *Public Admin. Rev.* 59(2):124–134.

Lee, S-H. (2000). Understanding productivity improvement in a turbulent environment: a symposium introduction. *Public Product. Manage. Rev.* 23:423–427.

Lemov, P. (1998). Measuring performance, making progress. *Governing* 11:54–58.

Likierman, A. (1993). Performance indicators: 20 early lessons from managerial use. *Public Money Manage.* 13:15–22.

Liou, K. T. (1995). Understanding employee commitment in the public organization: a study of the juvenile detention center. *Int. J. Public Admin.* 18:1269–1296.

Mani, B. G. (1996). Measuring productivity in federal agencies: does total quality management make a difference? *Am. Rev. Public Admin.* 26(1):19–39.

Marshall, M. (2000). 21st century community governance: better results by linking citizens, government, and performance measurement. Proceeding of the Annual Quality Congress. ASQC, 214–223.

Maters, M. F., Albright, R. R. (1998). How federal managers and union representatives view partnerships. *Public Manager. Fall* 33–36.

McAdam, R. (2000). Quality measurement frameworks in the public sector. *Total Qual. Manage.* 11(4–6):652–656.

McKevitt, D., Lawton, A. (1996). The manager, the citizen, the politician and performance measures. *Public Money Manage.* 16(3):49–54. Available at <http://www.blackwellpublishing.com/journal.asp?ref = 0954-0962>.

Melkers, J., Thomas, J. C. (1998). What do administrators think citizens think? Administrators predictions as an adjunct to citizen surveys. *Public Admin. Rev.* 58 (4):327–334.

Minzberg, H. (1996). Managing government, governing management. *Harvard Bus. Rev.* 74:75–83.

Nalbandian, J. (1999). Facilitating community, enabling democracy: new roles for local government managers. *Public Admin. Rev.* 59(3):187–197.

Newcomer, K. E., Wright, R. F. (1997). Effective use of performance measurement at the federal level. *PA Times* 20(1):2–4.

Nyhan, R. C. (1999). Comparative performance measurement. *Public Product. Manage. Rev.* 22(3):348–364.

Nyhan, R. C., Marlowe, H. A., Jr. (1995). Performance measurement in the public sector: challenges and opportunities. *Public Product. Manage. Rev.* 18(4):333–348.

Perrin, B. (1998). Effective use and misuse of performance measurement. *Am. J. Eval.* 19:367–379.

Pierce, J. C. (2002). Social capital and government performance: An analysis of 20 American cities. *Public Perform. Manage. Rev.* 25(4):381.

Poister, T. H., Streib, G. (1999). Performance measurement in municipal government: Assessing the state of the practice. *Public Admin. Rev.* 59:325–335.

Rivenbark, W. C. (2000a). Benchmarking and cost accounting: The North Carolina approach. *Public Perform. Manage. Rev.* 24(1):22–29.

Rivenbark, W. C. (2000b). Performance measurement: a local government response. *J. Public Budget. Account. Finan. Manage.* 12(1):74–86.

Rivenbark, W. C. (2000c). The role of capital cost in performance measurement and benchmarking. *J. Public Budget. Account. Finan. Manage.* 12(1):125–137.

Rivenbark, W. C. (2002). Auditing performance data in local government. *Public Perform. Manage. Rev.* 25(4):413.

Roberts, G. E. (1996). Performance appraisal participation, goal setting and feedback: the influence of supervisory style. *Rev. Public Person. Admin.* 16(4):29–60.

Romzek, B. (1990). Employee investment and commitment: the ties that bind. *Public Admin. Rev.* 50:374–382.

Sandra, T. (2002). The performance paradox in the public sector. *Public Perform. Manage. Rev.* 25(4):267.

Sheffield, S. R. (1999). Implementing Florida's performance and accountability act: a focus on program measurement and evaluation. *J. Public Budget. Account. Finan. Manage.* 11(4):649–669.

Smith, G., Huntsman, C. (1997). Reframing the metaphor of the citizen–government relationship. *Public Admin. Rev.* 57(3):309–318.

Streib, G. D. (1999). Assessing the validity, legitimacy, and functionality of performance measurement systems in municipal governments. *Am. Rev. Public Admin.*
29(2):107–123.

Sturdivant, J. (1997). The future of federal labor–management relations and partnership. *Public Manager, Summer*, 23–24.

Tang, S-Y, Robertson, P. J., Lane, C. E. (1996). Organizational types, commitment,
and managerial actions. *Public Product. Manage. Rev.* 19:289–312.

Tigue, P. (1994). Use of performance measures by GFOA members. *Gov. Perform.
Rev.* 10:42–45.

Vigoda, E. (2002). From responsiveness to collaboration: governance, citizens and the
next generation of public administration. *Public Admin. Rev.* 62(5):527–540.

Wang, X. H. (2002). Assessing performance measurement impact: a study of U.S. local
governments. *Public Perform. Manage. Rev.* 26(2):26.

Weeks, E. C. (2000). The practice of deliberative democracy: results from four large-
scale trials. *Public Admin. Rev.* 60(4):360–372.

West, J. P., Berman, E. M. (1997). Administrative creativity in local government.
*Public Product. Manage. Rev.* 20:446–457.

Wray, L., Hauer, J. (1997). Performance measurement to achieve quality of life. *PM
Public Manage.* 79(8):4–8.

## 2. Professional Journals Related to Productivity and Performance Improvement

*Academy of Management Journal.* Available at < http://aom.pace.edu/amjnew > .

*Academy of Management Review.* Available at < http://www.aom.pace.edu/amr > .

*Administrative Science Quarterly.* Available at < http://www.johnson.cornell. edu/
ASQ > .

*American Review of Public Administration.* Available at < http://www.umsl.edu/
divisions/graduate/mppa/arpa.htm > .

*Harvard Business Review.* Available at < http://www.hbsp.harvard.edu/products/
hbr/index.html > .

*Journal of Applied Behavioral Analysis.* Available at < http://www.envmed. rochester.
edu/wwwrap/behavior/jaba/jabahome.htm > .

*Journal of Applied Social Psychology.* Available at < http://www.bellpub.com/jasp > .

*Journal of Behavioral and Applied Management.* Available at < http://www. jbam.
org > .

*Journal of Management.* Available at < http://www.fsu.edu/~jom > .

*Journal of Organizational Behavior.* Available at < http://www.interscience.wiley.
com/jpages/0894–3796 > .

*Journal of Policy Analysis and Management.* Available at < http://qsilver.queensu.ca/
appam/services/jpam > .

*Journal of Public Administration Research and Theory.* Available at < http://www.
albany.edu/~jpart > .

*Organizational Behavior and Human Decision Processes.* Available at < http://www.
academicpress.com/obhdp > .

*Public Administration and Management.* Available at < http://www.pamij. com > .

*Public Administration Quarterly.* Available at < http://www.spaef.com/paq. html > .

*Public Administration Review.* Available at < http://www.aspanet.org/publications/
par/index2.html > .

*Public Budgeting and Finance.* Available at < http://www.aabpa.org/PBandF_ Journal.html > .

*Public Manager.* Available at < http://www.feiaa.org/Public%20Manager. htm > .

*Public Organization Review.* Available at < http://www.wkap.nl/prod/j/1566–7170 > .

*Public Performance and Management Review (formerly Public Productivity and Management Review).* Available at < http://www.sagepub.co.uk > ; < http://www. rutgers-newark.rutgers.edu/pubadmin/ncpp/ppmr.html > .

*State and Local Government Review.* Available at < http://www.cviog.uga.edu/ slgrevie/slgr.htm > .

## C. Government Reports and Other Professional Association-Related Publications

Publications by governmental and professional associations are also valuable sources. They often provide both the practitioner and the academician with problem-solving tools in the everyday world. Selected publications are as follows.

American Society for Public Administration. (2000). Performance Measurement: Concepts and techniques. Washington, DC: ASPA Center for Accountability and Performance. Available at < http://www.aspanet.org/cap/index.html > .

Ammons, D. N., ed. (1995). *Accountability for Performance: Measurement and Monitoring in Local Government.* Washington, DC: ICMA. Available at < http:// bookstore.icma.org > .

Benowitz, P. S., Schein, R. (1996). *Performance Measurement in Local Government. Municipal Yearbook.* Chicago: Government Finance Officers Association, pp. 19–23. Available at < http://www.gfoa.org > .

Bens, C. (1998). *Public Sector Performance Measurement: Successful Strategies and Tools.* Available at < http://www.municipalworld.com/bens.htm > .

Committee for Economic Development. (1976). *Improving Productivity in State and Local Government: A Statement by the Research and Policy Committee of the Committee for Economic Development.* New York: Committee for Economic Development. Available at < http://www.ced.org > .

Guajardo, S., McDonnell, R. (2000). *An Elected Officials Guide to Performance Measurement.* Chicago: Government Finance Officers Association. Available at < http://www.gfoa.org > .

Hatry, H. (2000). *Performance Measurement: Getting Results.* Washington, DC: Urban Institute Press. Available at < http://www.urban.org/uipress/uip_titles. html > .

Hatry, H., Marcotte, J. E., Van Houten, T., Weiss, C. (2000). *Customer Surveys for Agency Managers: What Managers Need to Know.* Washington, DC: Urban Institute Press. Available at < http://www.urban.org/uipress/uip_titles.html > .

International City/County Management Association and The Urban Institute (1995–2000). *Comparative Performance Measurement: FY 1995–1999 Data Reports.* Washington, DC: ICMA. Available at < http://bookstore.icma.org > .

International City/County Management Association. (2000). *Measurement for Results: Implementing Performance Measures in Local Government Training Package.* Washington, DC: ICMA. Available at < http://bookstore.icma. org > .

Kobayashi, M., Miller, T. (2000). *Citizen Surveys: How to Do Them, How to Use Them, What They Mean.* 2nd ed. Washington, DC: ICMA. Available at < http:// bookstore.icma.org > .

Leithe, J. L. (1997). *Implementing Performance Measurement in Government.* Chicago: Government Finance Officers Association. Available at < http://www. gfoa.org > .

McClure, C., Eppes, F., Sprehe, J., Eschenfelder, K. (2000). *Performance measures for federal agency websites.* Washington DC: Government Printing Office. Available at < http://fedbbs.access.gpo.gov/library/download/MEASURES/measures. doc > .

National Performance Review. (1993). *From Red Tape to Results: Creating a Government That Works Better and Costs Less.* Washington, DC: Government Printing Office. Available at < http://govinfo.library.unt.edu/npr/default.html > .

National Performance Review. (1997). *Serving the American Best Practice in Downsizing: A Benchmarking Study Report.* Washington, DC: Government Printing Office. Available at < http://govinfo.library.unt.edu/npr/default.html > .

United States General Accounting Office. (2000a). *Managing for Results: Emerging Benefits from Selected Agencies' Use of Performance Agreements.* Washington, DC: United States General Accounting Office. Available at < http://www.gao. gov/new. items/d01115.pdf > .

United States General Accounting Office. (2000b). *Managing for Results: Federal Managers' Views Show Need for Ensuring Top Leadership Skills.* Washington, DC: United States General Accounting Office. Available at < http://www.gao. gov/new. items/d01127.pdf > .

United States General Accounting Office. (2001a). *Managing for Results: Human Capital Management Discussions in Fiscal Year 2001 Performance Plans.* GAO-01-236. Washington, DC: United States General Accounting Office. Available at < http://www.gao.gov/new.items/d01236.pdf > .

United States General Accounting Office. (2001b). *Performance and Accountability: Challenges Facing the Department of Transportation.* GAO-01-443T. Washington, DC: United States General Accounting Office. Available at < http:// www.gao. gov/new.items/d01443t.pdf > .

United States General Accounting Office. (2001c). *Veterans' Employment and Training Service: Further Changes Needed to Strengthen Its Performance Measurement System. GAO-01-757T.* Washington, DC: United States General Accounting Office. Available at < http://www.gao.gov/new.items/d01757t.pdf > .

## D.　Other Comprehensive Resources on the Web

In our information-based society, countless governmental agencies and associations maintain Web sites. A brief introduction to each Web site is provided below.

## 1.　General Resources on Public Administration

*Research Resources in Public Administration and Public Affairs.*　< http://rutgers-newark.rutgers.edu/pubadmin/resource/index.htm > .

　　This Web site is developed and maintained by Rutgers University-Newark to provide detailed research resources in public administration and public affairs. Contents of this Web site are extensive. It comprehensively covers information on textbooks, encyclopedias and dictionaries, bibliographies, handbooks, cases and case studies, government documents, databases, writing aids, funding sources, directories of agencies and officials, career and job assistance, journals of public administration and public affairs, academic programs of public administration and public affairs, and publishers.

*Government Information Sharing Project.* < http://govinfo.kerr.orst.edu >.

This Web site provides a variety of statistical data including demographic, economic, and educational. It also provides links to government agencies and resources.

*FirstGOV.* < http://www.firstgov.gov >.

This is an initial gateway to various resources in government at both federal and state levels. In particular, this Web site addresses e-government, e-citizens, and e-business.

*Government Information and Data Resources.* < http://www.maxwell.syr.edu/ maxpages/students/paphd/sites1.htm >.

Maintained by the Maxwell School at Syracuse University, this Web site includes information regarding domestic and international governmental resources. It also provides statistical data on government at all levels.

*State and Local Government on the Net.* < http://www.piperinfo.com/state/index. cfm >.

This is a gateway to numerous state and local government Web sites, as well as to federal government and national organizations in the public sector.

*Public Administration Resources on the Web.* < http://web.syr.edu/~ ecoppola/ public.html >.

This Web site is a valuable source for access to government magazines, journals, newspapers, and professional associations and organizations in the public sector.

*Research Sources for Organizational Behavior.* < http://www.reference.unh.edu/ guides/orgbehavior.html >.

This Web site is especially helpful to those interested in behavioral research for individual performance and productivity. The site lists books, encyclopedias, and other references regarding organizational behavior.

*Human Resource Management Resources on the Internet.* < http://www.nbs. ntu.ac. uk/depts/hrm/hrm_link.htm >.

This is a comprehensive information source for human resource management for productivity. The information provided here includes organization management theories, recruitment strategies, and human resource manuals and handbooks online.

2. Productivity Improvement and Performance Measurement Resources with Help on Implementation Issues

*National Center for Public Productivity.* < http://www.rutgers-newark.rutgers. edu/ pubadmin/ncpp >.

The National Center for Public Productivity is a research and public service organization devoted to improving productivity in the public sector. Founded in 1975, the National Center is devoted to public sector productivity improvement. It provides numerous publications, conference information, and best practices regarding public sector productivity. The Citizen-Driven Government Performance portion of the site highlights case studies developed with funding from the Alfred P. Sloan Foundation, as well as curricular and bibliographic resources. The Performance Measurement Manuals section provides access to step-by-step productivity and performance improvement plans. The Exemplary State and Local Awards Program (EXSL) provides valuable public sector success stories which are helpful to both scholars and pratitioners. Through model programs and networking opportunities, the Center is devoted to bridging the gap between the theory and practice of productivity improvement.

*Public Sector Innovation Resources.* < http://www.ksg.harvard.edu/innovat/resource. htm > .

This site contains a variety of sources for information concerning public sector innovation. It provides links to public sector innovations including conference information, innovation award winners, innovation journals, and international programs on innovation in government sponsored by the Ford Foundation.

*Public Sector Continuous Improvement Site.* < *http://deming.ces.clemson.edu/pub/psci* > .

This site provides valuable tenets for improving performance and productivity in the public sector, with particular attention to Total Quality Management (TQM). It also provides reading list and online resources for continuous productivity improvement in the public sector. Specific improvement methods provided here include Deming's System of Profound Knowledge, Systems Thinking, Statistical Process Control, Customer Focus, Joy in Work, Learning Organizations, Process Improvement, Continual Improvement, and Innovation.

*Center for Human Resource Management.* < http://www.hrm.napawash. org > .

The Center for Human Resource Management is a valuable source for public sector managers seeking solutions in the real world. This Web site provides a source of practical expertise, best practices, and innovative solutions for improving the management of human resources. In particular, it contains a variety of publications and case studies relevant to human resource management, and extensive information regarding conferences and forums.

*The Center for Technology in Government (CTG).* < http://www.ctg.albany. edu > .

Maintained by the University at Albany/State University of New York, this Web site provides public managers and professionals with information technology research and demonstration resources for local, state, and federal government. CTG also has an award-winning program of partnerships, problem solving, and knowledge building to help public agencies test new ideas in a low-cost, low-risk environment. It contains numerous research reports and publications in the area of information technology in the public sector.

*Governing for Results: 2000 Progress Report.* < http://www.governor.wa.gov/quality/reports/00annual/2000report.htm > .

Maintained by the Washington State Governor's office, this Web site provides a progress report for making government work better in Washington State. In particular, it contains a number of success stories in quality improvements, and provides information regarding a digital government initiative.

*AFSCME Labor Links.* <http://www.afscme.org/otherlnk/weblnk09. htm>.

The American Federation of State, County, and Municipal Employees (AFSCME) is a comprehensive source for improving public sector performance and productivity by using public sector resources. It provides scholars and practitioners in the public sector with numerous links, such as labor–management cooperation projects, state and local government TQM programs, redesigning government, and privatization issues.

*Labor–Management Partnership: A Report to the President, December 2000.* <http://www.opm.gov/lmr/report/index.htm>.

The United States Office of Personnel Management (OPM) maintains this Web site. This report includes labor–management strategic planning, results and achievements, keys to success, barriers and struggles, and recommendations. This report is a comprehensive source for labor–management partnership at the federal government level. It provides numerous case studies and success stories in the field of labor–management cooperation.

*Project of Cornell Cooperative Extension.* <http://www.crp.cornell.edu/restructuring/main.asp>.

This Web site is designed and maintained by the Department of City and Regional Planning at Cornell University. The purpose of this Web site is to provide local governments and public sector employees with information on privatization, intermunicipal cooperation, and internal restructuring through labor–management cooperation. It contains numerous publications, reports, and case studies on privatization, labor–management partnership, and other employee management issues.

*Human Resources Learning Center.* <http://www.human-resources.org/associations. htm>.

This Web site contains a large collection of information on and links to a variety of human resource association, foundations, and societies from all over the world. It provides a brief description of each organization listed to help human resource professionals find the information they need. Sample organizations include the American Association of Retired Persons (AARP), American Productivity and Quality Center (APQC), American Society for Training and Development (ASTD), and American Association for Affirmative Action (AAAA).

*Working Together for Public Service. The U.S. Department of Labor (1996).* <http://www.dol.gov/asp/programs/history/reich/reports/worktogether/toc.htm>.

This is the first case study report conducted by the Task Force team in the U.S. Department of Labor. The Task Force's research includes five regional visits across the United States, seven Washington, DC hearings, and approximately 55 detailed responses to a Task Force survey. The report analyzes nearly 50 examples of cooperative approaches to successful labor–management relationships in government at all levels. The examples come from state, county, and city governments, schools, transit, and other special services.

*National Labor–Management Association (NLMA): Partnerships for Constructive Change.* < http://www.nlma.org > .

This Web site is especially helpful to those interested in linking labor–management partnerships to productivity improvement. The site contains labor–management resources on the Web, a directory of labor–management organizations, reports, and guides. In particular, it provides practitioners with a "Manual for Area and Industry Labor–Management Committees." Information on an annual national labor–management conference also contains a number of success stories documented in both the private and the public sectors.

*PRIME in Pennsylvania State.* < http://www.prime.state.pa.us > .

The governor's office in Pennsylvania State maintains this Web site. PRIME is the acronym of "Privatize, Retain, Innovate, Modify, and Eliminate," which is an initiative from former Governor Schweiker to produce positive change. PRIME is Pennsylvania's initiative to give state government a competitive edge. In particular, this Web site provides a number of best practices in management innovation for improving productivity.

*Quality Services Through Partnership in Ohio State.* < http://www.state.oh.us/quality > .

Based on the TQM philosophy, QStP in Ohio State is very well known for improving the quality of public services and productivity. Over $93 million has been saved through process improvement during the Taft administration. Annual reports and success stories provided here are valuable sources for public managers and scholars.

*IOWA Continuous Quality Improvement (ICQI).* < http://www.state.ia.us/iowanet/cqi/index.html > .

Since 1991, Iowa State Government has been committed to implementing Continuous Quality Improvement (CQI) programs to enhance productivity and performance on a continuing basis. General information training and assistance is offered to all interested departments, and intensive support is provided for process improvement teams. A downloadable IOWA Quality Results Report is available on this Web site.

*Government Accounting Standards Board's Web Site for Performance Measurement.* < http://www.seagov.org/index.html > .

This Web site provides information regarding the use and reporting of performance measures for government services. The information includes examples of the major categories of performance measures, and numerous links to Web sites with performance indicators, state and local government Web sites presenting or related to performance measures, federal and international government Web sites presenting or related to performance measures, and Web sites providing conceptual and background information on performance measurement. It also provides information on The Governmental Accounting Standards Board (GASB) Performance Measurement Project.

*Center for Accountability and Performance (CAP) Link from the American Society for Public Administration (ASPA) Web Site.* < http://www.aspanet.org/cap/index. html >.

It also provides workshops on performance measurement, budgeting, and
This center aims to improve the practice of public service by helping public administration professionals acquire the knowledge, technical skills, and resources necessary to successfully manage for results. CAP provides education, training, advocacy, technical assistance, resource sharing, and research to disseminate best practices in performance management.

It also provides workshops on performance measurement, budgeting, and contracting at ASPA's national and regional conferences. CAP trainers are available to speak or conduct workshops at ASPA chapter and section meetings. Publications and training materials are available to members and nonmembers of ASPA. CAP publishes PM CAPtions, its bimonthly electronic newsletter, and hosts regular brown bag lunches at George Washington University, where performance management issues are discussed by interested public managers and scholars.

*The Mayor's Management Report from New York City.* < http://www.nyc.gov/html/ ops/html/mmr.html >.

Mandated by the City Charter, the Mayor's Management Report (MMR) serves as a public report card about the way city services affect the lives of city residents. The MMR is released twice a year. The Preliminary MMR provides information about city service delivery during the first four months of the fiscal year. The Fiscal MMR covers the entire fiscal year. This report includes numerous online documents including the Fiscal 2002 Mayor's Management Report (MMR), Fiscal 2002 MMR Executive Summary, and Neighborhood statistics. It also contains MMR Archives in which Fiscal 1997 through Preliminary Fiscal 2002 MMRs are available.

*Budget Site for the City of Austin, Texas.* < http://www.ci.austin.tx.us/budget/ >.

The City of Austin fiscal year begins on October 1. In the Spring, the city begins the annual budget preparation process which includes opportunities for citizen participation and culminates with the adoption of a final budget in mid-September. Known as a leader in performance budgeting, the city's Web site provides a variety of information on managing for results with the Resource Guide for Business Planning, and the City of Austin Community Scorecard. In particular, it provides information on how the city is delivering services in four major categories: Public Safety; Youth, Family, and Neighborhood Vitality; Sustainable Community; and Affordability.

*San Diego's Site for Performance Measurement Reporting.* < http://www. sannet. gov/city-manager/service-efforts/ >.

This Web site concerns the service efforts and accomplishments in the City of San Diego. It provides information on 10 City of San Diego departments that provide major services to the public: City Attorney, Environmental Services, Fire and Life Safety Services, General Services, Library, Metropolitan Wastewater, Park and Recreation, Police, Transportation, and Water. Information provided in this annual document includes an overview of programs and services, major accomplishments/ service efforts, spending and staffing history, performance measures, comparison to other jurisdictions, and resident satisfaction ratings. It also provides performance measures for two additional departments: Development Services and Risk Management. Printed copies are available at City of San Diego public libraries.

## III. CONCLUSION: NEED FOR INTEGRATED DATABASE FOR RESEARCH AND PRACTICES

Researchers and practitioners who need to learn how to improve productivity in the public sector have a great deal of knowledge available through indexes, abstracts, online library catalogues, and so on. But searching is not easy. In this regard, Cherry (1992) presents steps for searching for productivity-relevant resources from a seemingly overwhelming cache of potentially useful knowledge. Although written prior to the advent of the Internet, the logic of this search strategy is still sound and includes: (1) knowing your resource collection, (2) learning to use the guide to the collection, (3) use of bibliographies in the search, (4) use of indexes and abstracts, (5) professional journals, (6) government publications, (7) handbooks and publications, and (8) other library services.

This chapter is a small effort that touches the tip of a bigger productivity improvement iceberg in the public sector. Continuing efforts to build a comprehensive database for public sector productivity improvement resources will lead to a great number of problem-solving tools for practitioners as well as to a high level of research productivity among scholars.

## REFERENCES

Cherry, V. R. (1992). Information search strategies. In: Holzer, M., ed., *Public Productivity Handbook*. New York: Marcel Dekker, pp. 667–682.

Holzer, M., Halachmi, A. (1988). *Public Sector Productivity: A Resource Guide*. New York: Garland.

Holzer, M., Kang, H.-S. (2000). Research resources in public administration and public affairs (online). Available at < http://rutgers-newark.rutgers.edu/pubadmin/resource/index.htm.

Lee, S.-H. (2000). Understanding productivity improvement in a turbulent environment: a symposium introduction. *Public Product. Manage. Rev.* 23:423–427.

# Index